*Less managing. More teaching. Greater learning.*

## Q: INSTRUCTORS...

Would you like your **students** to show up for class **more prepared**? *(Let's face it, class is much more fun if everyone is engaged and prepared...)*

Want an **easy way to assign** homework online and track student **progress**? *(Less time grading means more time teaching...)*

Want an **instant view** of student or class performance relative to learning objectives? *(No more wondering if students understand...)*

Need to **collect data and generate reports** required for administration or accreditation? *(Say goodbye to manually tracking student learning outcomes...)*

Want to **record and post your lectures** for students to view online?

## A: With McGraw-Hill's *Connect® Plus Accounting*,

### INSTRUCTORS GET:

- Simple **assignment management**, allowing you to spend more time teaching.
- **Auto-graded** assignments, quizzes, and tests.
- **Detailed Visual Reporting** where student and section results can be viewed and analyzed.
- Sophisticated **online testing** capability.
- A **filtering and reporting** function that allows you to easily assign and report on materials that are correlated to accreditation standards, learning outcomes, and Bloom's taxonomy.
- An easy-to-use **lecture capture** tool.
- The option to **upload course documents** for student access.

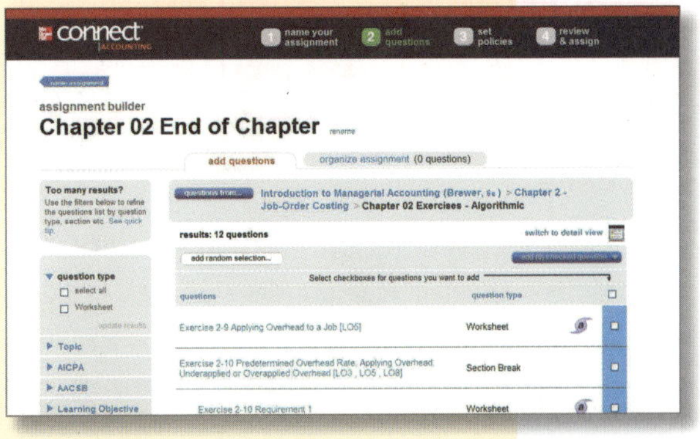

## Q: Want an online, **searchable version** of your textbook?

## Wish your textbook could be **available online** while you're doing your assignments?

## A: *Connect*® *Plus Accounting* eBook

If you choose to use *Connect*® *Plus Accounting*, you have an affordable and searchable online version of your book integrated with your other online tools.

### *Connect*® *Plus Accounting* eBook offers features like:

- Topic search
- Direct links from assignments
- Adjustable text size
- Jump to page number
- Print by section

## Q: Want to get more **value** from your textbook purchase?

## Think learning accounting should be a bit more **interesting**?

## A: Check out the STUDENT RESOURCES section under the *Connect*® Library tab.

Here you'll find a wealth of resources designed to help you achieve your goals in the course. You'll find things like **quizzes, PowerPoints, and Internet activities** to help you study. Every student has different needs, so explore the STUDENT RESOURCES to find the materials best suited to you.

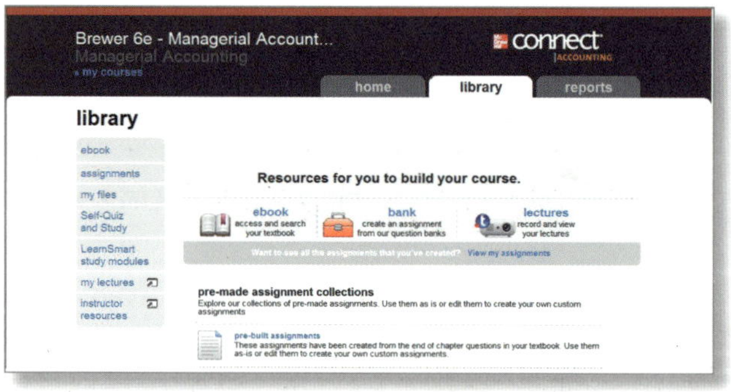

# introduction to MANAGERIAL ACCOUNTING

6TH EDITION

**Peter C. Brewer**
Professor, Miami University

**Ray H. Garrison**
Professor Emeritus, Brigham Young University

**Eric W. Noreen**
Professor Emeritus, University of Washington

McGraw-Hill Irwin

The McGraw-Hill Companies

McGraw-Hill Irwin

INTRODUCTION TO MANAGERIAL ACCOUNTING

Published by McGraw-Hill/Irwin, a business unit of The McGraw-Hill Companies, Inc., 1221 Avenue of the Americas, New York, NY, 10020. 

This book is printed on acid-free paper.

1 2 3 4 5 6 7 8 9 0 QDB/QDB 1 0 9 8 7 6 5 4 3 2

ISBN 978-0-07-802541-9
MHID 0-07-802541-9

Vice president and editor-in-chief: *Brent Gordon*
Publisher: *Tim Vertovec*
Sponsoring editor: *Donna Dillon*
Executive director of development: *Ann Torbert*
Development editor II: *Katie Jones*
Vice president and director of marketing: *Robin J. Zwettler*
Marketing director: *Brad Parkins*
Executive marketing manager: *Melissa S. Caughlin*
Vice president of editing, design, and production: *Sesha Bolisetty*
Lead project manager: *Pat Frederickson*
Buyer II: *Debra R. Sylvester*
Lead designer: *Matthew Baldwin*
Senior photo research coordinator: *Jeremy Cheshareck*
Lead media project manager: *Brian Nacik*
Media project manager: *Cathy L. Tepper*
Typeface: *10.5/12 Times Roman*
Compositor: *Laserwords Private Limited*
Printer: *Quad/Graphics*

**Library of Congress Cataloging-in-Publication Data**

Brewer, Peter C.
Introduction to managerial accounting / Peter C. Brewer, Ray H. Garrison, Eric W. Noreen. — 6th ed.
p. cm.
Includes index.
ISBN-13: 978-0-07-802541-9 (alk. paper)
ISBN-10: 0-07-802541-9 (alk. paper)
1. Managerial accounting. I. Garrison, Ray H. II. Noreen, Eric W. III. Title.
HF5657.4.F65 2013
658.15'11—dc23

2011047310

www.mhhe.com

# DEDICATION

*To our families and to our colleagues who use this book.*

—Peter C. Brewer, Ray H. Garrison, and Eric W. Noreen

# About the Authors

**Peter C. Brewer** is a professor in the Department of Accountancy at Miami University, Oxford, Ohio. He holds a BS degree in accounting from Penn State University, an MS degree in accounting from the University of Virginia, and a PhD from the University of Tennessee. He has published more than 35 articles in a variety of journals including: *Management Accounting Research*, the *Journal of Information Systems*, *Cost Management*, *Strategic Finance*, the *Journal of Accountancy*, *Issues in Accounting Education*, and the *Journal of Business Logistics*.

Professor Brewer is a member of the editorial board of the *Journal of Accounting Education* and has served on the editorial board of *Issues in Accounting Education*. His article "Putting Strategy into the Balanced Scorecard" won the 2003 International Federation of Accountants' Articles of Merit competition, and his articles "Using Six Sigma to Improve the Finance Function" and "Lean Accounting: What's It All About?" were awarded the Institute of Management Accountants' Lybrand Gold and Silver Medals in 2005 and 2006. He has received Miami University's Richard T. Farmer School of Business Teaching Excellence Award and has been recognized on two occasions by the Miami University Associated Student Government for "making a remarkable commitment to students and their educational development." He is a leading thinker in undergraduate management accounting curriculum innovation and is a frequent presenter at various professional and academic conferences.

Prior to joining the faculty at Miami University, Professor Brewer was employed as an auditor for Touche Ross in the firm's Philadelphia office. He also worked as an internal audit manager for the Board of Pensions of the Presbyterian Church (U.S.A.).

**Ray H. Garrison** is emeritus professor of accounting at Brigham Young University, Provo, Utah. He received his BS and MS degrees from Brigham Young University and his DBA degree from Indiana University.

As a certified public accountant, Professor Garrison has been involved in management consulting work with both national and regional accounting firms. He has published articles in *The Accounting Review*, *Management Accounting*, and other professional journals. Innovation in the classroom has earned Professor Garrison the Karl G. Maeser Distinguished Teaching Award from Brigham Young University.

**Eric W. Noreen** has held appointments at institutions in the United States, Europe, and Asia. He is emeritus professor of accounting at the University of Washington.

He received his BA degree from the University of Washington and MBA and PhD degrees from Stanford University. A Certified Management Accountant, he was awarded a Certificate of Distinguished Performance by the Institute of Certified Management Accountants.

Professor Noreen has served as associate editor of *The Accounting Review* and the *Journal of Accounting and Economics*. He has numerous articles in academic journals including: the *Journal of Accounting Research; The Accounting Review*; the *Journal of Accounting and Economics; Accounting Horizons; Accounting, Organizations and Society; Contemporary Accounting Research;* the *Journal of Management Accounting Research;* and the *Review of Accounting Studies*.

Professor Noreen has won a number of awards from students for his teaching.

# Pointing Students in the Right Direction

## "Why do I need to learn Managerial Accounting?"

Brewer's *Introduction to Managerial Accounting* has earned a reputation as the most accessible and readable book on the market. Its manageable chapters and clear presentation point students toward understanding just as the needle of a compass provides direction to travelers.

However, the book's authors also understand that everyone's destinations are different. Some students will become accountants, while others are destined for careers in management, marketing, or finance. Not only does the Brewer text teach students managerial accounting concepts in a clear and concise way, but it also asks students to consider how the concepts they're learning will apply to the real world situations they will eventually confront in their careers. This combination of conceptual understanding and the ability to apply that knowledge directs students toward success, whatever their final destination happens to be.



### Here's how your colleagues have described Brewer's *Introduction to Managerial Accounting*:

*"The **best introductory managerial accounting book** on the market. Plain and simple."*
—Paige Paulsen, Salt Lake Community College

*"It is an **excellent textbook**—very **clearly written,** good examples, good assignment material."*
—Arlene Strawn, Tallahassee Community College

*"It is the **best textbook for introductory managerial accounting to date.** It is concise, well-written and well-organized. With an abundance in real-world flavors, students will see the material as interesting and relevant."*
—Minwoo Lee, Western Kentucky University

*"This is a **well organized and written textbook.** It is easy to read and provides **excellent illustrations.** The coverage is clear and presented very well."*
—Gloria Stuart, Georgia Southern University

*"I think the content of this book is fantastic. The book is flexible and its contents are clear. It is **the best book I have utilized.**"*
—Ethan Kinory, CUNY Baruch

*"The **best resource to making your job in the classroom easier.** If students read the text and utilize the supplements, they are going to learn Managerial Accounting easier and faster than with any other text."*
—Tom Hrubec, Franklin University

*". . . **excellent depth and breadth of topic coverage** that will prepare the students for their advanced business and accounting classes. The textbook will also lay the foundation to ensure the students have the ability to successfully apply managerial accounting concepts in their full-time professional jobs!"*
—Michael Hammond, Missouri State University

*"I would describe this text as very well written and organized. Topics covered have been updated nicely to reflect most current business trends. I would say this book is **very student and professor friendly!**"*
—Matthew Muller, Adirondack Community College

*Introduction to Managerial Accounting*, 6th edition, by **BREWER/GARRISON/NOREEN** empowers your students by offering:

## CONCISE COVERAGE

Your students want a text that is concise and that presents material in a clear and readable manner. *Introduction to Managerial Accounting* keeps the material accessible while avoiding advanced topics related to cost accounting. Students' biggest concern is whether they can solve the end-of-chapter problems after reading the chapter. Market research indicates that Brewer/Garrison/Noreen helps students apply what they've learned better than any other managerial accounting text on the market. Additionally, the key supplements are written by the authors ensuring that students and instructors will work with clear, well-written supplements that employ consistent terminology.

## DECISION-MAKING FOCUS

All students who pass through your class need to know how accounting information is used to make business decisions, especially if they plan to be future managers. That's why Brewer, Garrison, and Noreen make decision making a pivotal component of *Introduction to Managerial Accounting.* In every chapter you'll find the following key features that are designed to teach your students how to use accounting information: Each chapter opens with a **Decision Feature** vignette that uses real-world examples to show how accounting information is used to make everyday business decisions; **Decision Point boxes** within the chapters help students to develop analytical, critical thinking, and problem-solving skills; and end-of-chapter **Building Your Skills** cases challenge students' decision-making skills.

## A CONTEMPORARY APPROACH TO LEARNING

Today's students rely on technology more than ever as a learning tool, and *Introduction to Managerial Accounting* offers the finest technology package of any text on the market. From study aids like narrated, animated Guided Examples to online grading and course management, our technology assets have one thing in common: they make your class time more productive, more stimulating, and more rewarding for you and your students. McGraw-Hill *Connect*® *Accounting* is an online assignment and assessment solution that connects students with the tools and resources they'll need to achieve success. *Connect*® *Plus Accounting* provides an online, media-rich, searchable version of the text in addition to access to *Connect*, giving students a convenient way to access everything they need to succeed in their course. The Online Learning Center and *Connect* library provide your students with a variety of multimedia aids to help them learn managerial accounting. iPod® content includes quizzes, audio and visual lecture presentations, and course-related videos—all of which can be downloaded to students' iPod or other portable MP3/MP4 players so they can study and review on the go. Students also can download an iPad® app for LearnSmart, an adaptive tool that helps students learn faster, study more efficiently, and retain more knowledge.

> *"The book's **number one feature is the real world examples** it incorporates in each chapter."*
>
> —Meghna Singhvi, Florida International University

# BREWER / GARRISON / NOREEN'S

**Introduction to Managerial Accounting** is full of pedagogy designed to make studying productive and hassle-free. On the following pages, you'll see the kind of engaging, helpful pedagogical features that have made Brewer one of the best-selling Managerial Accounting texts on the market.

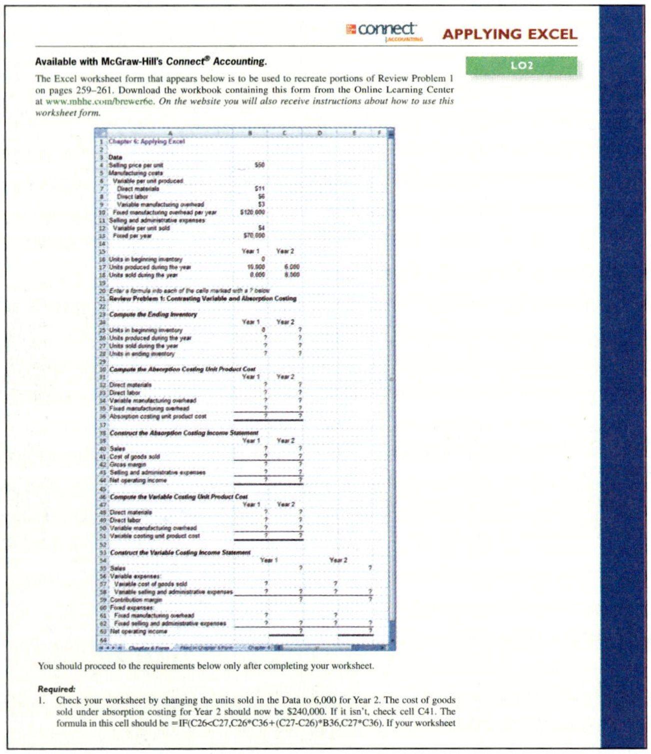

connect ACCOUNTING **APPLYING EXCEL**

**Available with McGraw-Hill's *Connect*® *Accounting*.**

LO2

The Excel worksheet form that appears below is to be used to recreate portions of Review Problem 1 on pages 259–261. Download the workbook containing this form from the Online Learning Center at www.mhhe.com/brewer6e. *On the website you will also receive instructions about how to use this worksheet form.*

You should proceed to the requirements below only after completing your worksheet.

***Required:***

1. Check your worksheet by changing the units sold in the Data to 6,000 for Year 2. The cost of goods sold under absorption costing for Year 2 should now be $240,000. If it isn't, check cell C41. The formula in this cell should be =IF(C26<C27,C26*C36+(C27-C26)*B36,C27*C36). If your worksheet

## APPLYING EXCEL

**NEW to the sixth edition of Brewer!**

This **NEW** and exciting end-of-chapter feature **links the power of Excel with managerial accounting concepts** by illustrating how Excel functionality can be used to better understand accounting data. Applying Excel goes beyond plugging numbers into a template by providing students with an opportunity to build their own Excel worksheets and formulas. Students are then asked "what if" questions in which they analyze not only **how** related pieces of accounting data affect each other but **why** they do. Applying Excel immediately precedes the Exercises in eleven of the thirteen chapters in the book and is also **integrated with McGraw-Hill *Connect*® *Accounting*,** allowing students to practice their skills online with algorithmically generated datasets and to watch animated, narrated tutorials on how to use formulas in Excel.

*"An excellent pedagogical feature that helps **further reinforce students' knowledge** of key concepts in the text book, while **strengthening students' Excel skills** that are so important in the work place. This will further enhance an already excellent text."*

—Marianne L. James, California State University, Los Angeles

*"**[Applying Excel is] an excellent way for students to programmatically develop spreadsheet skills** without having to be taught spreadsheet techniques by the instructor. A significant associated benefit is that students gain more exposure to the dynamics of accounting information by working with what-if scenarios."*

—Earl Godfrey, Gardner–Webb University

# POWERFUL *NEW PEDAGOGY*

## HELPFUL HINT

Helpful Hint boxes are found several times throughout each chapter and highlight a variety of common mistakes, key points, and "pulling it all together" insights for students.

> **HELPFUL HINT**
>
> A mixed cost expressed on a per unit basis decreases as the activity level increases. Do you know why? Although the variable portion of a mixed cost stays constant on a per unit basis as the activity level increases, the fixed portion of a mixed cost decreases on a per unit basis as the activity level increases. This occurs because the fixed cost is being spread across more units.

## THE FOUNDATIONAL 15

Each chapter now contains one Foundational 15 exercise that includes 15 "building-block" questions related to one concise set of data. These exercises can be used for in-class discussion or as homework assignments. They are found before the Exercises and are available in *Connect Accounting*.

connect ACCOUNTING **THE FOUNDATIONAL 15**

**Available with McGraw-Hill's *Connect® Accounting*.**

LO1, LO2, LO3, LO5, LO6, LO7

Martinez Company's relevant range of production is 7,500 units to 12,500 units. When it produces and sells 10,000 units, its unit costs are as follows:

| | Amount Per Unit |
|---|---|
| Direct materials | $6.00 |
| Direct labor | $3.50 |
| Variable manufacturing overhead | $1.50 |
| Fixed manufacturing overhead | $4.00 |
| Fixed selling expense | $3.00 |
| Fixed administrative expense | $2.00 |
| Sales commissions | $1.00 |
| Variable administrative expense | $0.50 |

***Required:***

1. For financial accounting purposes, what is the total amount of product costs incurred to make 10,000 units?
2. For financial accounting purposes, what is the total amount of period costs incurred to sell 10,000 units?
3. If 8,000 units are sold, what is the variable cost per unit sold?
4. If 12,500 units are sold, what is the variable cost per unit sold?
5. If 8,000 units are sold, what is the total amount of variable costs related to the units sold?
6. If 12,500 units are sold, what is the total amount of variable costs related to the units sold?
7. If 8,000 units are produced, what is the average fixed manufacturing cost per unit produced?
8. If 12,500 units are produced, what is the average fixed manufacturing cost per unit produced?
9. If 8,000 units are produced, what is the total amount of fixed manufacturing cost incurred to support this level of production?
10. If 12,500 units are produced, what is the total amount of fixed manufacturing cost incurred to support this level of production?
11. If 8,000 units are produced, what is the total amount of manufacturing overhead cost incurred to support this level of production? What is this total amount expressed on a per unit basis?

## TAKE TWO

Take Two is a new end-of-chapter feature that provides a set of alternate numbers for selected exercises. These alternate numbers can be plugged into the exercise, thereby providing instructors an option to work out the same exercise more than once during class and students an option for additional practice when completing their homework. The Take Two alternate solutions can be found in the instructor's solutions manual.

TAKE TWO

Estimated direct labor-hours = 50,000

## CHAPTER OUTLINE

Each chapter opens with an **outline** that provides direction to the student about the road they can expect to traverse throughout the chapter. The **A Look Back/A Look at This Chapter/A Look Ahead** feature reminds students what they have learned in previous chapters, what they can expect to learn in the current chapter, and how the topics will build on each other in chapters to come.

## DECISION FEATURE

The **Decision Feature** at the beginning of each chapter provides a real-world example for students, allowing them to see how the chapter's information and insights apply to the world outside the classroom. **Learning Objectives** alert students to what they should expect as they progress through the chapter.

**A LOOK BACK**

Chapter 1 defined many of the terms that are used to classify costs in business. We will use many of these terms in Chapter 2. Now would be a good time to check your understanding of those terms by referring to the glossary at the end of Chapter 1.

**A LOOK AT THIS CHAPTER**

Chapter 2 provides an in-depth look at a job-order costing system. We describe how direct material and direct labor costs are accumulated on jobs. Then we address manufacturing overhead, an indirect cost that must be allocated (or applied) to jobs. Finally, we take a more detailed look at the flow of costs through a company's accounting system using journal entries.

**A LOOK AHEAD**

Chapter 3 continues the discussion of the allocation of manufacturing overhead costs, showing how these costs can be more accurately assigned using activity-based costing. We cover process costing in Chapter 4.

2 Job-Order Costing

**CHAPTER OUTLINE**

**Job-Order Costing—An Overview**

**Job-Order Costing—An Example**

- Measuring Direct Materials Cost
- Job Cost Sheet
- Measuring Direct Labor Cost
- Computing Predetermined Overhead Rates
- Applying Manufacturing Overhead
- Manufacturing Overhead—A Closer Look
- The Need for a Predetermined Rate
- Choice of an Allocation Base for Overhead Cost
- Computation of Unit Costs

**Job-Order Costing—The Flow of Costs**

- The Purchase and Issue of Materials
- Labor Cost
- Manufacturing Overhead Costs
- Applying Manufacturing Overhead
- Nonmanufacturing Costs
- Cost of Goods Manufactured
- Cost of Goods Sold

**Schedules of Cost of Goods Manufactured and Cost of Goods Sold**

**Underapplied and Overapplied Overhead—A Closer Look**

- Computing Underapplied and Overapplied Overhead
- Disposition of Underapplied or Overapplied Overhead Balances
- A General Model of Product Cost Flows
- Multiple Predetermined Overhead Rates

**Job-Order Costing in Service Companies**

**DECISION FEATURE**

### Two Former College Students Succeeding as Entrepreneurs

When the University of Dayton athletic department needed 2,000 customized T-shirts to give away as part of a promotion for its first home basketball game of the year, it chose **University Tees** to provide the shirts. Numerous larger competitors could have been chosen, but University Tees won the order because of its fast customer response time, low price, and high quality.

University Tees is a small business that was started in February 2003 by two Miami University seniors—Joe Haddad and Nick Dadas (see the company's website at www.universitytees.com). The company creates the artwork for customized T-shirts and then relies on carefully chosen suppliers to manufacture the product. University Tees must provide a specific price quote for each potential customer order because each order is unique and the customer is always looking for the best deal.

Calculating the cost of a particular customer order is critically important to University Tees because the company needs to be sure that each price quote exceeds the cost associated with satisfying the order. The costs that University Tees factors into its bidding process include the cost of the T-shirts themselves, printing costs (which vary depending on the quantity of shirts produced and the number of colors printed per shirt), silk screen costs (which also vary depending on the number of colors included in a design), shipping costs, and the artwork needed to create a design. In addition to using cost information, the company also relies on knowledge of its competitors' pricing strategies when establishing price quotes.

Source: Conversation with Joe Haddad, cofounder of University Tees.

**LEARNING OBJECTIVES**

*After studying Chapter 2, you should be able to:*

**LO1** Compute a predetermined overhead rate.

**LO2** Apply overhead cost to jobs using a predetermined overhead rate.

**LO3** Compute the total cost and average cost per unit of a job.

**LO4** Understand the flow of costs in a job-order costing system and prepare appropriate journal entries to record costs.

**LO5** Use T-accounts to show the flow of costs in a job-order costing system.

**LO6** Prepare schedules of cost of goods manufactured and cost of goods sold and an income statement.

**LO7** Compute underapplied or overapplied overhead cost and prepare the journal entry to close the balance in Manufacturing Overhead to the appropriate accounts.

> *"I like . . . the 'A Look Back, A Look at This Chapter, A Look Ahead' and the Chapter Outline. I think **students will appreciate these tools.**"*
>
> —Cathy Larson, Middlesex Community College

*"The concept review questions and the problems allow students to check their knowledge as they go. Many textbooks provide the questions but not the answers so it is nice to have both. The In Business sections provide* ***useful anecdotes and clarifications*** *by providing students with* ***real world examples.****"*

—Nori Pearson, Washington State University

## IN BUSINESS BOXES

These helpful boxed features offer a glimpse into how real companies use the managerial accounting concepts discussed within the chapter. Every chapter contains these current examples.

**Royal Caribbean Cruises Launches *Oasis of the Seas*** IN BUSINESS

**Royal Caribbean Cruises** invested $1.4 billion to build the *Oasis of the Seas*, a cruise ship that carries 5,400 passengers and stands 20 stories above the sea. The vessel is a third larger than any other cruise ship and contains 21 pools, 24 restaurants, 13 retail shops, and 300-foot water slides. The company hopes the ship's extraordinary amenities will attract large numbers of customers willing to pay premium prices. However, the economic downturn has caused many customers to refrain from spending on lavish vacations.

Source: Mike Esterl, "Huge Cruise Ships Prepare for Launch but Face Uncertain Waters," *The Wall Street Journal*, December 4, 2009, pp. B1–B2.

*"I like the* ***In Business and Decision Point*** *features in the book that* ***bring the concepts down to a real world level.****"*

—Abbie Gail Parham, Georgia Southern University

The **DECISION POINT** feature fosters critical thinking and decision-making skills by providing real-world business scenarios that require the resolution of a business issue. The suggested solution is located at the end of the chapter.

**Treasurer, Class Reunion Committee** DECISION POINT

You've agreed to handle the financial arrangements for your high school reunion. You call the restaurant where the reunion will be held and jot down the most important information. The meal cost (including beverages) will be $30 per person plus a 15% gratuity. An additional $200 will be charged for a banquet room with a dance floor. A band has been hired for $500. One of the members of the reunion committee informs you that there is just enough money left in the class bank account to cover the printing and mailing costs. He mentions that at least one-half of the class of 400 will attend the reunion and wonders if he should add the 15% gratuity to the $30 per person meal cost when he drafts the invitation, which will indicate that a check must be returned with the reply card.

How should you respond? How much will you need to charge to cover the various costs? After making your decision, label your answer with the managerial accounting terms covered in this chapter. Finally, identify any issues that should be investigated further.

*"****The concept checks*** *for the chapters are great and very useful for the students to* ***stay focused*** *on the chapter when reading it. These are one of the* ***best features of this text.****"*

—Dawn Fischer, Texas Tech University

## CONCEPT CHECK

Concept Checks allow students to test their comprehension of topics and concepts covered at meaningful points throughout each chapter.

1. Which of the following statements is false? (You may select more than one answer.)
   a. Absorption costing assigns fixed and variable manufacturing overhead costs to products.
   b. Job-order costing systems are used when companies produce many different types of products.
   c. A normal costing system assigns overhead costs to products by multiplying the actual overhead rate by the actual amount of the allocation base.
   d. A unit product cost represents the additional cost that would be incurred if another unit were produced.

✓ CONCEPT CHECK

## UTILIZING THE ICONS

To reflect our service-based economy, the text is replete with examples from service-based businesses. A helpful icon distinguishes service-related examples in the text.

Ethics assignments and examples serve as a reminder that good conduct is vital in business. Icons call out content that relates to ethical behavior for students.

The writing icon denotes problems that require students to use critical thinking as well as writing skills to explain their decisions.

An Excel© icon alerts students that spreadsheet templates are available for use with select problems and cases.

The IFRS icon highlights content that may be affected by the impending change to IFRS and possible convergence between U.S. GAAP and IFRS.

TAKE TWO

This new marginal end-of-chapter icon indicates the Take Two alternate number set for select exercises.

## END-OF-CHAPTER MATERIAL

*Introduction to Managerial Acounting* has earned a reputation for the best end-of-chapter review and discussion material of any text on the market. Our problem and case material conforms to AICPA, AACSB, and Bloom's Taxonomy categories and makes a great starting point for class discussions and group projects. With review problems, discussion questions, Excel problems, the Foundational 15 set, exercises, problems, and cases, Brewer offers students practice material of varying complexity and depth. In order to provide even more practice opportunities, an **alternate problem set** is available on the text's website and in *Connect Accounting,* along with online quizzes and practice exams.

## AUTHOR-WRITTEN SUPPLEMENTS

Unlike other managerial accounting texts, Brewer, Garrison, and Noreen write all of the text's major supplements, ensuring a perfect fit between text and supplements. For more information on *Introduction to Managerial Accounting*'s supplements package see pages xx–xxii.

*"As Brewer, Garrison, and Noreen write most of the text's supplements, these materials really support the textbook material well. The* ***continuity/consistency between textbook and supporting materials*** *is not found with some other textbooks. All of the resources available with the Brewer book* ***help me to be a better teacher!"***

—Sheri Henson, Western Kentucky

# New to the 6th edition

Faculty feedback helps us continue to improve *Introduction to Managerial Accounting*. In response to reviewer suggestions we have implemented the following changes:

## Overall:

- **In Business** boxes updated throughout.
- ***Applying Excel*** problem added to Chapters 1–11.
- Added ***The Foundational 15*** questions to each chapter.
- Incorporated ***Helpful Hint*** boxes throughout.
- New ***Take Two*** marginal element in end-of-chapter exercises.

## Prologue

- The Prologue has been completely overhauled to help all business students better understand why managerial accounting is relevant to their future careers.

## Chapter 1

- This chapter has been extensively rewritten to include coverage of mixed costs and contribution format income statements. The redundant coverage of the schedule of cost of goods manufactured has been eliminated so that it is now only covered in Chapter 2. The comparison of financial and managerial accounting has been moved to the Prologue.

## Chapter 2

- This chapter has added a cost formula approach to computing predetermined overhead rates. It has deleted what were formerly learning objectives 1 and 2 while adding a new learning objective related to computing job costs. It has incorporated an exhibit formerly in Chapter 1 that provides a conceptual overview of manufacturing cost flows. It includes two new In Business boxes and some new EOC items as well.

## Chapter 3

- The learning objective related to activity-based cost flows for external financial reporting was deleted. Two new In Business boxes have been added to this chapter.

## Chapter 4

- Added a new In Business box.

## Chapter 5

- New In Business boxes.

## Chapter 6

- The variable costing appendix has been expanded to an entire chapter. The coverage of variable and absorption costing has also been extensively reorganized to improve the flow of discussion. The coverage of segmented income statements has been moved to this chapter.

## Chapter 7

- Added three new end-of-chapter exercises/problems. Added new In Business boxes.

## Chapter 8

- This chapter combines material from two chapters in the previous edition of the book. It discusses flexible budgets and their application in service businesses. It also explains how standards can be used to separate spending variances into quantity and price variances.

## Chapter 9

- This chapter has been reorganized, moving the segmented income statements to an earlier chapter and adding nonfinancial performance measures to the chapter. Many new In Business boxes have been written.

## Chapter 10

- The section dealing with elevating the constraint has been rewritten. A learning objective related to sell or process further decisions has been added to the chapter and several new In Business boxes have been created.

## Chapter 11

- A number of new In Business boxes have been added.

## Chapter 12

- This chapter has been completely overhauled to simplify the process of creating a statement of cash flows and to expand the discussion of how to interpret the statement of cash flows.

## Chapter 13

- Added new In Business boxes.

*"This book provides in depth coverage of basic managerial accounting concepts and procedures in a* ***clear and concise*** *manner in logically sequenced topics. It's designed to help students use accounting information and make a decision. It's* ***very easy to read.****"*

—Mehmet Kocakulah, University of Southern Indiana

*"An* ***excellent book*** *for an introductory Managerial Course* ***for all business students,*** *not just Accounting majors."*

—Tamara Phelan, Northern Illinois University

# A MARKET-LEADING BOOK DESERVES

## McGRAW-HILL CONNECT® ACCOUNTING

McGraw-Hill *Connect Accounting* is an online assignment and assessment solution that connects you with the tools and resources necessary to achieve success through faster learning, more efficient studying, and higher retention of knowledge.

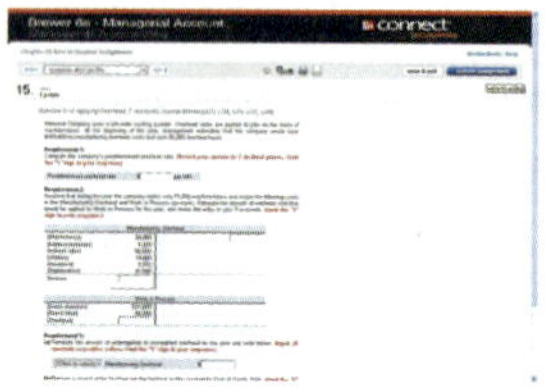

### Online Assignments

McGraw-Hill *Connect Accounting* helps students learn more efficiently by providing feedback and practice material when and where they need it. *Connect Accounting* grades homework automatically and students benefit from the immediate feedback that they receive, particularly on any questions they may have missed.

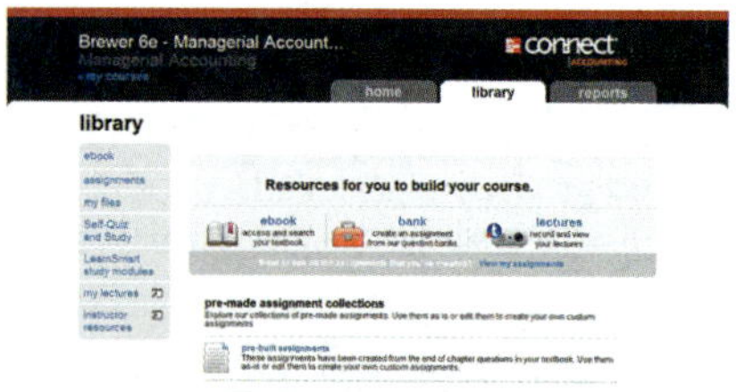


### Student Library

The *Connect Accounting* Student Library gives students access to additional resources such as recorded lectures, Self-Quiz and Study practice materials, an eBook, and more. With Self-Quiz and Study, for each chapter students can take a practice quiz and immediately see how well they performed. A study plan then recommends specific readings from the eBook, narrated slides, and practice exercises that will improve students' understanding and mastery of each learning objective.

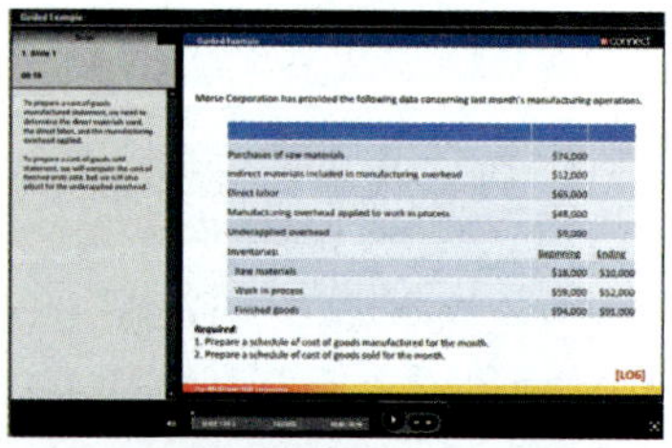

### Guided Examples

Guided Examples, embedded within *Connect Accounting* when enabled by the instructor, provide a narrated, animated, step-by-step walkthrough of select exercises similar to those assigned. These short presentations provide reinforcement when students need it most.

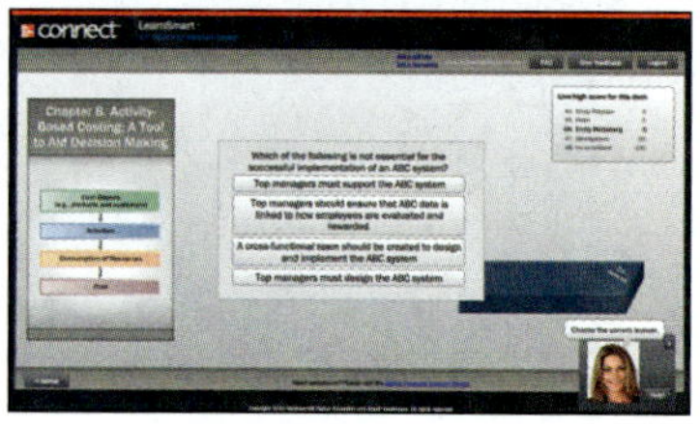

### LearnSmart

LearnSmart, an adaptive self-study technology that is housed within *Connect Accounting*, ensures your students are learning faster, studying more efficiently, and retaining more knowledge by pinpointing the concepts that each individual student does not understand and mapping out a personalized study plan for his or her success. Based on students' self-diagnoses of their proficiency, LearnSmart intelligently delivers a series of adaptive questions, providing students with a personalized one-on-one tutor experience. LearnSmart can be assigned within *Connect* together with quantitative end-of-chapter material to provide comprehensive and balanced homework for students.

### Interactive Presentations

Interactive Presentations, assignable by individual learning objective within *Connect Accounting*, teach the core concepts of the text in an animated, narrated, and interactive multimedia format, bringing the key concepts of the course to life—particularly helpful for online courses and for those audio and visual learners who struggle reading the textbook page by page.

> *"Student resources, such as an online learning center, provide a sample quiz and exam for each chapter. There are also* ***great instructor resources*** *in the online learning center."*
>
> —Abbie Gail Parham, Georgia Southern University

# MARKET-LEADING TECHNOLOGY

## LESS MANAGING. MORE TEACHING. GREATER LEARNING.

McGraw-Hill *Connect Accounting* offers a number of powerful tools and features to make managing assignments easier, so faculty can spend more time teaching. With *Connect Accounting,* students can engage with their coursework anytime, anywhere, making the learning process more accessible and efficient. Please see the previous page for a description of the student tools available within *Connect Accounting*.

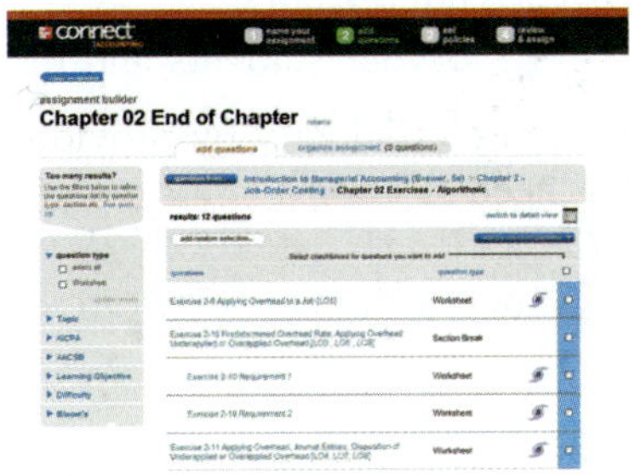


### McGraw-Hill *Connect® Accounting* for Instructors

**Simple Assignment Management and Smart Grading.** With McGraw-Hill's *Connect Accounting,* creating assignments is easier than ever, so you can spend more time teaching and less time managing. *Connect Accounting* enables you to:

- Create and deliver assignments and assessments easily with selectable end-of-chapter questions and test bank items.
- Go paperless with the eBook and online submission and grading of student assignments.
- Have assignments scored automatically, giving students immediate feedback on their work and comparisons with correct answers.
- Reinforce classroom concepts by assigning LearnSmart modules and Interactive Presentations.

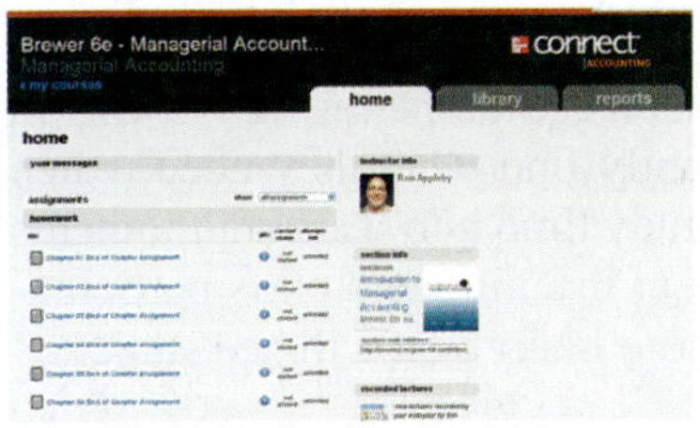


### Instructor Library

The *Connect Accounting* Instructor Library is your repository for additional resources to improve student engagement in and out of class. You can select and use any asset that enhances your lecture. The *Connect Accounting* Instructor Library includes access to:

- Solutions manual
- Test bank
- Instructor PowerPoint® slides
- Instructor's Resource Guide—includes Transparency Masters, Assignment Topic Grids and Lecture Notes that correspond with the Instructor PowerPoints
- Excel Template Solutions
- Applying Excel Solutions
- Sample Syllabus
- The eBook version of the text
- FIFO Supplement Chapter

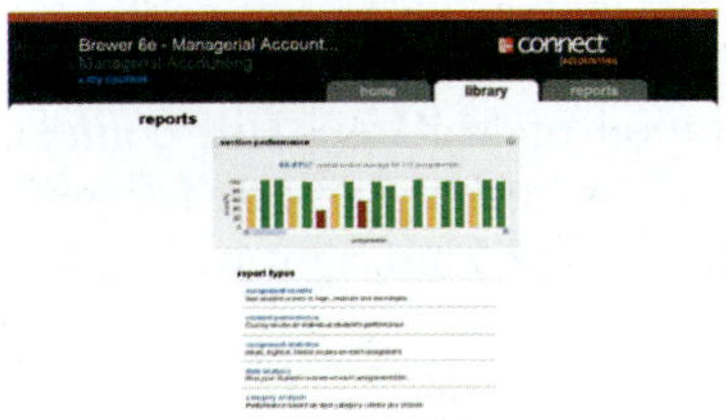


### Student Reports

McGraw-Hill *Connect Accounting* keeps instructors informed about how each student, section, and class is performing, allowing for more productive use of lecture and office hours. The reports tab enables you to:

- View scored work immediately and track individual or group performance with assignment and grade reports.
- Access an instant view of student or class performance relative to learning objectives.
- Collect data and generate reports required by many accreditation organizations, such as AACSB and AICPA.

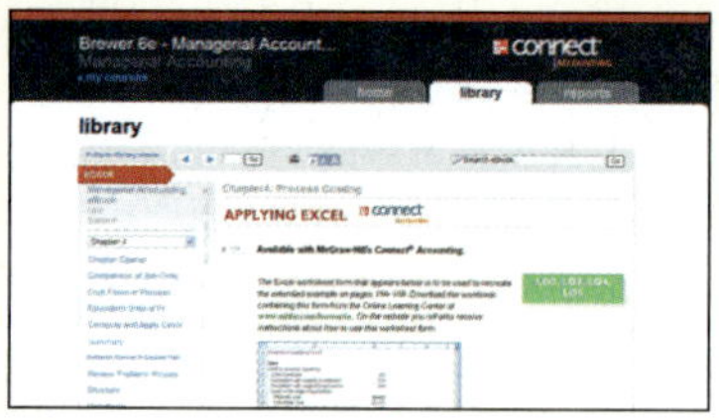


### McGraw-Hill *Connect*® *Plus Accounting*

McGraw-Hill reinvents the textbook learning experience for the modern student with *Connect Plus Accounting,* which provides a seamless integration of the eBook and *Connect Accounting. Connect Plus Accounting* provides all of the *Connect Accounting* features, as well as:

- An integrated eBook, allowing for anytime, anywhere access to the textbook.
- Dynamic links between the problems or questions you assign to your students and the location in the eBook where the concept related to that problem or question is covered.
- A powerful search function to pinpoint and connect key concepts in a snap.
- Highlighting, note-taking, and other media-rich capabilities.

For more information about *Connect Accounting*, go to www.mcgrawhillconnect.com, or contact your local McGraw-Hill sales representative.

## TEGRITY CAMPUS: LECTURES 24/7

Tegrity Campus, a new McGraw-Hill company, provides a service that makes class time available 24/7 by automatically capturing every lecture. With a simple one-click start-and-stop process, you capture all computer screens and corresponding audio in a format that is easily searchable, frame by frame. Students can replay any part of any class with easy-to-use browser-based viewing on a PC or Mac, an iPod, or other mobile device.

Educators know that the more students can see, hear, and experience class resources, the better they learn. In fact, studies prove it. Tegrity Campus's unique search feature helps students efficiently find what they need, when they need it, across an entire semester of class recordings. Help turn your students' study time into learning moments immediately supported by your lecture. With Tegrity Campus, you also increase intent listening and class participation by easing students' concerns about note-taking. Lecture Capture will make it more likely you will see students' faces, not the tops of their heads.

To learn more about Tegrity, watch a 2-minute Flash demo at http://tegritycampus.mhhe.com.

## ONLINE COURSE MANAGEMENT

McGraw-Hill Higher Education and Blackboard have teamed up. What does this mean for you?

Do More

1. Your life, simplified. Now you and your students can access McGraw-Hill *Connect*® and Create™ right from within your Blackboard course—all with one single sign-on. Say goodbye to the days of logging in to multiple applications.

2. **Deep integration of content and tools.** Not only do you get single sign-on with *Connect* and Create, you also get deep integration of McGraw-Hill content and content engines right in Blackboard. Whether you're choosing a book for your course or building *Connect* assignments, all the tools you need are right where you want them—inside of Blackboard.

3. **Seamless grade books.** Are you tired of keeping multiple grade books and manually synchronizing grades into Blackboard? We thought so. When a student completes an integrated *Connect* assignment, the grade for that assignment automatically (and instantly) feeds your Blackboard grade center.

4. **A solution for everyone.** Whether your institution is already using Blackboard or you just want to try Blackboard on your own, we have a solution for you. McGraw-Hill and Blackboard can now offer you easy access to industry leading technology and content, whether your campus hosts it, or we do. Be sure to ask your local McGraw-Hill representative for details.

eCollege℠

In addition to Blackboard integration, course cartridges for whatever online course management system you use (e.g., WebCT or eCollege) are available for Brewer 6e. Our cartridges are specifically designed to make it easy to navigate and access content online. They are easier than ever to install on the latest version of the course management system available today.

## McGRAW-HILL CUSTOMER EXPERIENCE

At McGraw-Hill, we understand that getting the most from new technology can be challenging. That's why our services don't stop after you purchase our book. You can e-mail our product specialists 24 hours a day, get product training online, or search our knowledge bank of Frequently Asked Questions on our support Website. For Customer experience, call 800-331-5094 or visit www.mhhe.com/support. One of our Technical Support Analysts will assist you in a timely fashion. You also can take advantage of the new "Contact Publisher" link within *Connect Accounting.*

McGraw Hill create

## McGRAW-HILL CREATE™

Your course evolves over time. Shouldn't your course material? Customize your own high-quality, well-designed, full-color textbook in print or eBook format in a few simple steps at http://create.mcgraw-hill.com. Search thousands of textbooks, articles, and cases to rearrange, add, and/or remove content to match better the way you teach your course. You even can add your own material, such as a syllabus or handout. Personalize your book's appearance by selecting the cover and adding your name, school, and course information. Order a *Create* book and you'll receive a complimentary print review copy in 3-5 business days or a complimentary electronic review copy (eComp) via email in about one hour.

# Instructor Supplements

## Assurance of Learning Ready

Many educational institutions today are focused on the notion of assurance of learning, an important element of some accreditation standards. *Introduction to Managerial Accounting,* 6e, is designed specifically to be support your assurance of learning initiatives with a simple, yet powerful, solution.

Each test bank question for *Introduction Managerial Accounting,* 6e maps to a specific chapter learning outcome/objective listed in the text. You can use our test bank software, EZ Test, and Connect to easily query for learning outcomes/objectives that directly relate to the learning objectives for your course. You can then use the reporting features of EZ Test and Connect to aggregate student results in similar fashion, making the collection and presentation of assurance of learning data simple and easy.

## AACSB Statement

The McGraw-Hill Companies, Inc., is a proud corporate member of AACSB International. Recognizing the importance and value of AACSB accreditation, we have sought to recognize the curricula guidelines detailed in AACSB standards for business accreditation by connecting selected questions in Brewer 6e, with the general knowledge and skill guidelines found in the AACSB standards. The statements contained in Brewer 6e are provided only as a guide for the users of this text. The AACSB leaves content coverage and assessment clearly within the realm and control of individual schools, the mission of the school, and the faculty. The AACSB does also charge schools with the obligation of doing assessment against their own content and learning goals. While Brewer 6e and its teaching package make no claim of any specific AACSB qualification or evaluation, we have labeled selected questions according to the six general knowledge and skills areas. The labels or tags within Brewer 6e are as indicated. There are, of course, many more within the test bank, the text, and the teaching package which might be used as a "standard" for your course. However, the labeled questions are suggested for your consideration.

## McGraw-Hill *Connect*® *Accounting*

McGraw-Hill *Connect Accounting* offers a number of powerful tools and features to make managing your classroom easier. *Connect Accounting* with Brewer 6e offers enhanced features and technology to help both you and your students make the most of your time inside and outside the classroom. See page xvi for more details.

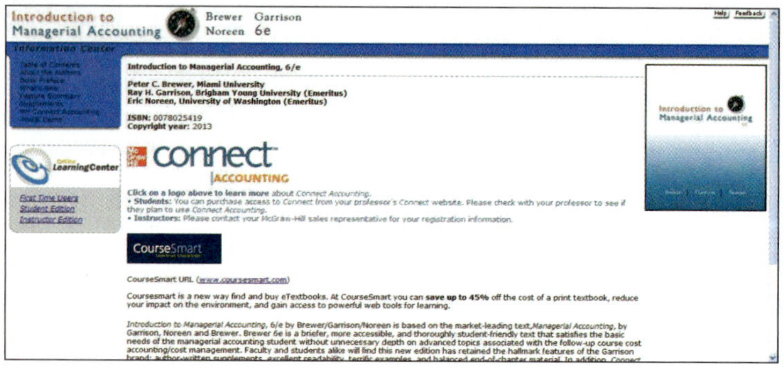


## Online Learning Center (www.mhhe.com/brewer6e)

The password protected instructor side of the book's Online Learning Center (OLC) houses all the instructor resources you need to administer your course, including:

- Solutions manual with suggested course outlines
- Test bank
- Instructor's Resource Guide—includes Transparency Masters, Assignment Topic Grids, and Lecture Notes
- Instructor PowerPoint slides
- Excel Template Solutions
- Applying Excel Solutions
- Sample Syllabus

If you choose to use *Connect Accounting* with Brewer, you will have access to these same resources via the Instructor Library.

## Instructor CD-ROM

MHID-0 0 7-742953-2
ISBN-13 978-0-07-742953-9

Allowing instructors to create a customized multimedia presentation, this all-in-one resource incorporates the Test bank, Instructor PowerPoint slides, Instructor's Resource Guide, and Solutions Manual.

## EZ Test Online

McGraw-Hill's EZ Test is a flexible electronic testing program. The program allows instructors to create tests from book-specific items. It accommodates a wide range of question types, plus instructors may add their own questions and sort questions by format. EZ Test can also scramble questions and answers for multiple versions of the same test.

### Instructor's Resource Guide

Available on the password-protected Instructor OLC and Instructor's Resource CD, and within the Connect Instructor Library.

This supplement contains the teaching transparency masters, PowerPoint slides, and extensive chapter-by-chapter lecture notes to help with classroom presentation. It contains useful suggestions for presenting key concepts and ideas.

This manual is coordinated with the PowerPoint slides, making lesson planning even easier.

### Solutions Manual

Available on the Instructor's CD, Instructor's OLC, and within the Connect Instructor Library.

This supplement contains completely worked-out solutions to all assignment material. In addition, the manual contains suggested course outlines and a listing of exercises, problems, and cases scaled according to difficulty and estimated time for completion. Solutions to the NEW Take Two and Applying Excel features are housed here and include the completed Excel forms.

# Student Supplements

## McGraw-Hill *Connect®* *Accounting*

McGraw-Hill *Connect Accounting* helps prepare you for your future by enabling faster learning, more efficient studying, and higher retention of knowledge. See page xvii for more details.

## CourseSmart

CourseSmart is a new way to find and buy eTextbooks. At CourseSmart you can save up to 55 percent off the cost of a print textbook, reduce your impact on the environment, and gain access to powerful Web tools for learning. CourseSmart has the largest selection of eTextbooks available anywhere, offering thousands of the most commonly adopted textbooks from a wide variety of higher education publishers. CourseSmart eTextbooks are available in one standard online reader with full text search, notes and highlighting, and e-mail tools for sharing notes between classmates.

## Online Learning Center

**www.mhhe.com/brewer6e**

The Online Learning Center (OLC) follows *Managerial Accounting* chapter by chapter, offering all kinds of supplementary help for you as you read.

The OLC includes the following resources to help you study more efficiently:

- NEW Applying Excel Forms
- Online Quizzes
- Practice Exams
- Internet Exercises
- Supplementary Chapters
- Alternate Problems
- Student PowerPoint slides
- Narrated PowerPoint lectures
- Excel Templates
- iPod Content

If your instructor chooses to use *Connect Accounting* in this course, you will have access to these same resources via the Student Library.

## Applying Excel

Forms available on the OLC and in the *Connect* Student Library.

This NEW and exciting feature has been added to Chapters 1-11 of the text. Applying Excel gives you the opportunity to build your own Excel worksheet using Excel formulas. You are then asked to answer "what if" questions, all of which illustrate the relationship among various pieces of accounting data. The Applying Excel feature links directly to the concepts introduced in the chapter, providing you with an invaluable opportunity to apply what you have learned utilizing an application you will use throughout your career.

## Workbook/Study Guide

MHID: 0-07-742955-9
ISBN-13: 978-0-07-742955-3

This printed study aid provides suggestions for studying chapter material, summarizes essential points in each chapter, and tests your knowledge using self-test questions and exercises.

## iPod Content

Available on the OLC and in the *Connect* Student Library.

Students can visit the Online Learning Center at www.mhhe.com/brewer6e to download our iPod content. For each chapter of the book they will be able to download narrated lecture presentations, managerial accounting videos, and even self-quizzes designed for use on various versions of iPods. It makes review and study time as easy as putting on earphones.

## Check Figures

Available with select problems in the end-of-chapter material, these provide key answers for selected problems and cases.

# Acknowledgments

## Sixth Edition Reviewers

Abbie Gail Parham, *Georgia Southern University*
Agatha E. Jeffers, *Montclair State University*
Aileen Ormiston, *Mesa Community College*
Allen Mcconnell, *University of Northern Colorado*
Amanda Farmer, *University of Georgia*
Amy Santos, *Manatee Community College*
Anita Hope, *Tarrant County College*
Anwar Salimi, *California State Polytechnic University-Pomona*
Arabian Morgan, *Orange Coast College*
Ariel Markelevich, *Bernard M. Baruch College*
Arlene Strawn, *Tallahassee Community College*
Barry S. Buchoff, *Towson University*
Bonnie K. Klamm, *North Dakota State University*
Britton A McKay, *Georgia Southern University*
Catherine Lumbattis, *Southern Illinois University-Carbondale*
Cathy Larson, *Middlesex Community College*
Cathy Lumbattis, *Southern Illinois University*
Chak-Tong Chau, *University of Houston*
Chiaho Chang, *Montclair State University*
Chuo-Hsuan Lee, *SUNY Plattsburgh*
Clark Wheatley, *FLorida International University-Miami*
Dan Law, *Gonzaga University*
Darlene Coarts, *University of Northern Iowa*
David G. Campbell, *Sierra Community College*
David Gorton, *Eastern Washington University*
Dean Steria, *SUNY Plattsburgh*
Debbie Beard, *Southeast Missouri State University*
Debra Cosgrove, *University Of Nebraska-Lincoln*
Debra Kerby, *Truman State University*
Dennis M. Lopez, *University of Texas-San Antonio*
Donna Viens, *Johnson & Wales University*
Earl Mitchell, *Santa Ana College*
Elizabeth M. Ammann, *Lindenwood University*
Emmanuel Emenyonu, *Southern Connecticut State University*
Ethan Kinory, *Baruch College, CUNY*
Frances Talavera, *California State University, San Marcos*
Frank Gersich, *Monmouth College*
Gayle Chaky, *Dutchess Community College*
Gene B. Elrod, *University of North Texas*
George Scott Pate, *Robeson Community College*
George Williams, *Bergen Community College*
Gloria Stuart, *Georgia Southern University*
Grant Pritchard, *Dominican University of California*
Harold T. Little Jr., *Western Kentucky University*
Heidi Hansel, *Kirkwood Community College*
Henry C. Smith, III, *Otterbein College*
Henry Schulman, *Grossmont College*
Jacci Rodgers, *Oklahoma City University*
Jacqueline Stoute, *Baruch College, CUNY*

Suggestions have been received from many of our colleagues throughout the world who have used the prior edition of *Introduction to Managerial Accounting*. This is vital feedback that we rely on in each edition. Each of those who have offered comments and suggestions has our thanks.

The efforts of many people are needed to develop and improve a text. Among these people are the reviewers and consultants who point out areas of concern, cite areas of strength, and make recommendations for change. We thank current and past reviewers who have provided feedback that was enormously helpful in preparing *Introduction to Managerial Accounting*.

James Weisel, *Georgia Gwinnett College*
Jane Stoneback, *Central Connecticut State University*
Jay Cohen, *Oakton Community College*
Jim Breyley, Jr., *University of New England*
Joan Hollister, *State University of New York–New Paltz*
Joan Van Hise, *Fairfield University*
Joseph Hagan, *East Carolina University*
Joseph M. Nicassio, *Westmoreland County Community College*
Joseph Weintrop, *Bernard M. Baruch College*
Judith Zander, *Grossmont College*
Julie Chenier, *Louisiana State University-Baton Rouge*
Kathleen Fitzpatrick, *University of Toledo-Scott Park*
Kathy Crusto-Way, *Tarrant County College*
Kristen Bigbee, *Texas Tech University*
Lansing Williams, *Washington College*
Laurie Hagberg, *Trident Technical College*
Leah Cabaniss, *Holyoke Community College*
Lee Nicholas, *University of Northern Iowa*
Leslie Vaughan, *University of Missouri-St. Louis*
Lianzan Xu, *William Paterson University of New Jersey*
Linda Batiste, *Baton Rouge Community College*
Lisa Gillespie, *Loyola University-Chicago*
Lorie Milam, *University of Northern Colorado*
Luther Ross, *Central Piedmont Community College*
Mark Cornman, *Youngstown State University*
Markus Ahrens, *St. Louis Community College—Meramec*
Martin L. Epstein, *Central New Mexico Community College*
Mary Zenner, *College of Lake County*
Matthew Muller, *Adirondack Community College*
Meghna Singhvi, *Florida International University*
Mehmet Kocakulah, *University of Southern Indiana*
Michael R. Hammond, *Missouri State University*
Michael Skaff, *College of the Sequoias*
Michael Stemkoski, *Utah Valley University Orem*
Minwoo Lee, *Western Kentucky University*
Nace Magner, *Western Kentucky University*
Nas Ahadiat, *Cal Poly Pomona*
Nori Pearson, *Washington State University*
Olen L. Greer, *Missouri State University*
Paige Paulsen, *Salt Lake Community College*
Pam Meyer, *University of Louisiana at Lafayette*
Patrick Stegman, *College of Lake County*
Peggy Dejong, *Kirkwood Community College*
Raj Kiani, *California State University, Northridge*
Raj Mashruwala, *University of Illinois-Chicago*
Randall Serrett, *University of Houston Downtown*
Rebecca Lohmann, *Southeast Missouri State University*
Rick Blumenfeld, *Sierra Community College*
Rick Roscher, *University of North Carolina-Wilmington*
Robert J. Angell, *North Carolina A&T State University*
Robert L. Hurt, *Cal Poly Pomona*
Robert S Ellison, *Texas State U–San Marcos*
Robyn Dawn Jarnagin, *Montana State University*
Ron Halsac, *Community College of Allegheny County*
Ronald Reed, *University of Northern Colorado*
Ronald Zhao, *Monmouth University*
Scott White, *Lindenwood University*
Sharon Walters, *Morehead State University*
Sheri L. Henson, *Western Kentucky University*
Stephen Benner, *Eastern Illinois University*
Steve Swirsky, *Florida A&M University*
Steven Ault, *Montana State University*
Steven LaFave, *Augsburg College*
Sueann Hely, *West Kentucky Community and Technical College*
Susan B Hughes, *University of Vermont*
Sushila Kedia, *University of Southern Indiana*
Suzanne Cercone, *Keystone College*
Suzanne Gradisher, *University Of Akron*
Tamara Phelan, *Northern Illinois University*
Terry Elliott, *Morehead State University*
Thomas Arcuri, *Florida Community College at Jacksonville*
Tom Hrubec, *Franklin University*
Tracie Nobles, *Austin Community College-Northridge*
Vasant Raval, *Creighton University–Omaha*
Weihong Xu, *State University of New York at Buffalo*
Youngwon Her, *University of Missouri–St. Louis*

## Previous Edition Reviewers

Natalie Allen, *Texas A&M University*
Rowland Atiase, *University of Texas at Austin*
Benjamin W. Bean, *Utah Valley State College*
Sarah Bee, *Seattle University*
Ramesh C. Bhatia, *Millersville University*
William J. Bradberry, *New River Community and Technical College*
Robert Burdette, *Salt Lake Community College*
Paul E. Dascher, *Stetson University*
Sandra Devona, *Northern Illinois University*
Jan Duffy, *Iowa State University*
Denise M. English, *Boise State University*
Diane Eure, *Texas State University*
Benjamin Foster, *University of Louisville*
Ananda Roop Ganguly, *Purdue University*
Annette Hebble, *University of St. Thomas*
Sueann Hely, *West Kentucky Community and Technical College*
Jay Holmen, *University of Wisconsin-Eau Claire*
Norma C. Holter, *Towson University*
Jai S. Kang, *San Francisco State University*
Roger P. Lewis, *Saint Cloud State University*
Dawn McKinley, *William Rainey Harper College*
Laurie B. McWhorter, *Mississippi State University*
Michael J. Meyer, *Ohio University*
Robert Milbrath, *University of Houston*
Valerie Milliron, *California State University, Chico*
Angela H. Sandberg, *Jacksonville State University*
Amy Santos, *Manatee Community College*
Diane Tanner, *University of North Florida*
Linda Tarrago, *Hillsborough Community College*
John M. Virchick, *Chapman University*
Joseph Weintrop, *Baruch College*
Clark Wheatley, *Florida International University*
Janice White, *Kalamazoo Valley Community College*
Jane G. Wiese, *Valencia Community College*
William Zahurak, *Community College of Allegheny County, Allegheny*
Omneya Abd-Elsalam, *Aston University*
L. M. Abney, *LaSalle University*
Sol Ahiarah, *SUNY College at Buffalo*
William Ambrose, *DeVry University*
Robert Appleton, *University of North Carolina-Wilmington*

Leonard Bacon, *California State University, Bakersfield*
Roderick Barclay, *Texas A&M University*
Larry Bitner, *Hood College*
Jay Blazer, *Milwaukee Area Technical College*
Nancy Bledsoe, *Millsaps College*
William Blouch, *Loyola College*
Eugene Blue, *Governor State University*
Linda Bolduc, *Mount Wachusett Community College*
Casey Bradley, *Troy State University*
Marley Brown, *Mt. Hood Community College*
Betty Jo Browning, *Bradley University*
Myra Bruegger, *Southeastern Community College*
Francis Bush, *Virginia Military Institute*
Rebecca Butler, *Gateway Community College*
June Calahan, *Redlands Community College*
John Callister, *Cornell University*
Annhenrie Campbell, *California State University, Stanislaus*
Elizabeth Cannata, *Stonehill College*
Dennis Caplan, *Iowa State University*
Kay Carnes, *Gonzaga University*
Siew Chan, *University of Massachusetts, Boston*
John Chandler, *University of Illinois-Champaign*
Lawrence Chin, *Golden Gate University*
Carolyn Clark, *St. Joseph's University*
Joanne Collins, *California State University-Los Angeles*
Judith Cook, *Grossmont College*
Charles Croxford, *Merced College*
Richard Cummings, *Benedictine College*
Jill Cunningham, *Santa Fe Community College*
Alan Czyzewski, *Indiana State University*
Betty David, *Francis Marion University*
Deborah Davis, *Hampton University*
G. DiLorenzo, *Gloucester County College*
Keith Dusenbery, *Johnson State College*
James Emig, *Villanova University*
Michael Farina, *Cerritos College*
John Farlin, *Ohio Dominican University*
Harriet Farney, *University of Hartford*
M. A. Fekrat, *Georgetown University*
W. L. Ferrara, *Stetson University*
Jerry Ferry, *University of North Alabama*
Joan Foster, *Collge Misericordia*
James Franklin, *Troy State University Montgomery*
Joseph Galante, *Millersville University of Pennsylvania*
David Gibson, *Hampden-Sydney College*
John Gill, *Jackson State University*
Jackson Gillespie, *University of Delaware*
Joe Goetz, *Louisiana State University*
Art Goldman, *University of Kentucky*
James Gravel, *Husson College*
Linda Hadley, *University of Dayton*
Dan Hary, *Southwestern Oklahoma State University*
Susan Hass, *Simmons College*
Robert Hayes, *Tennessee State University*
James Hendricks, *Northern Illinois University*
Nancy Thorley Hill, *DePaul University*
Kathy Ho, *Niagra University*
Mary Hollars, *Vincennes University*
Norma Holter, *Towson University*
Ronald Huntsman, *Texas Lutheran University*
Wayne Ingalls, *University of Maine College*
David Jacobson, *Salem State College*
Martha Janis, *University of Wisconsin-Waukesha*
Holly Johnston, *Boston University*
Sanford Kahn, *University of Cincinnati*
Marsha Kertz, *San Jose State University*
Michael Klimesh, *Gustav Adolphus University*
Greg Kordecki, *Clayton College and State University*
Michael Kulper, *Santa Barbara City College*
Christoper Kwak, *Ohlone College*
Steven LaFave, *Augsburg College*
Thomas Largay, *Thomas College*
Robert Larson, *Penn State University*
Chor Lau, *California State University, Los Angeles*
Angela Letourneau, *Winthrop University*
Barry Lewis, *Southwest Missouri State University*
Joan Litton, *Ferrum College*
G. D. Lorenzo, *Gloucester Community College*
Bob Mahan, *Milligan College*
Leland Mansuetti, *Sierra College*
Lisa Martin, *Western Michigan University*
Jayne Mass, *Towson University*
Laura Morgan, *University of New Hampshire*
Anthony Moses, *Saint Anselm College*
Daniel Mugavero, *Lake Superior State University*
Muroki Mwaura, *William Patterson University*
Presha Neidermeyer, *Union College*
Eizabeth Nolan, *Southwestern Oklahoma State University*
Michael O'Neill, *Seattle Central Community College*
George Otto, *Truman College*
Chei Paik, *George Washington University*
Eustace Phillip, *Emmanuel College*
Anthony Piltz, *Rocky Mountain College*
H. M. Pomroy, *Elizabethtown College*
Alan Porter, *Eastern New Mexico University*
Barbara Prince, *Cambridge Community College*
Ahmad Rahman, *La Roche College*
Joan Reicosky, *University of Minnesota-Morris*
Leonardo Rodriguez, *Florida International University*
Gary Ross, *College of the Southwest*
Martha Sampsell, *Elmhurst College*
John Savash-*Elmira College*
Roger Scherser, *Edison Community College*
Henry Schwarzbach, *University of Colorado*
Eldon Schafer, *University of Arizona*
Deborah Shafer, *Temple College*
Ola Smith, *Michigan State University*
John Snyder, *Florida Technical*
Soliman Soliman, *Tulane University*
Alice Steljes, *Illinois Valley Community College*
Joseph Ugras, *LaSalle University*
Edward Walker, *University of Texas-Pan American*
Frank Walker, *Lee College*
Robert Weprin, *Lourdes College*
Brent Wickham, *Owens Community College*
Geri Wink, *University of Texas at Tyler*
James Wolfson, *Wilson College*

We are grateful for the outstanding support from McGraw-Hill/Irwin. In particular, we would like to thank Tim Vertovec, Publisher; Donna Dillon, Sponsoring Editor; Katie Jones, Developmental Editor; Melissa Caughlin, Marketing Manager; Pat Frederickson, Lead Project Manager; Debra Sylvester, Lead Production Supervisor; Matt Baldwin, Lead Designer; Brian Nacik, Lead Media Project Manager; and Jeremy Cheshareck, Senior Photo Research Coordinator.

Thank you to our Digital Contributor, Margaret Shackell-Dowell (Cornell University), for her many contributions to *Connect Accounting*, including Guided Example content and Interactive Presentation review. Thanks also to Patti Lopez (Valencia College), for her efforts as lead subject matter expert on LearnSmart.

Finally, we would like to thank Helen Roybark and Beth Woods for working so hard to ensure an error-free sixth edition.

We are grateful to the Institute of Certified Management Accountants for permission to use questions and/or unofficial answers from past Certificate in Management Accounting (CMA) examinations. Likewise, we thank the American Institute of Certified Public Accountants, the Society of Management Accountants of Canada, and the Chartered Institute of Management Accountants (United Kingdom) for permission to use (or to adapt) selected problems from their examinations. These problems bear the notations CMA, CPA, SMA, and CIMA, respectively.

Peter C. Brewer
Ray H. Garrison
Eric W. Noreen

# BRIEF CONTENTS

# CONTENTS

## CHAPTER THREE
## Activity-Based Costing 116



## CHAPTER FOUR
## Process Costing 156

## CHAPTER FIVE
## Cost-Volume-Profit Relationships 186



## CHAPTER SIX
## Variable Costing and Segment Reporting: Tools for Management 236

## CHAPTER SEVEN
## Profit Planning 282



## CHAPTER EIGHT
## Flexible Budgets, Standard Costs, and Variance Analysis 334



## CHAPTER NINE
## Performance Measurement in Decentralized Organizations 398

## A LOOK AT THE PROLOGUE

The Prologue defines managerial accounting and explains why it is important to the future careers of all business students. It also discusses the role of ethics in business and corporate social responsibility.

## A LOOK AHEAD

Chapter 1 defines many of the cost terms that will be used throughout the textbook. It explains that in managerial accounting the term cost is used in many different ways depending on the immediate needs of management.

PROLOGUE

# Managerial Accounting: An Overview

## PROLOGUE OUTLINE

**What Is Managerial Accounting?**

- Planning
- Controlling
- Decision Making

**Why Does Managerial Accounting Matter to Your Career?**

- Business Majors
- Accounting Majors

**What Skills Do Managers Need to Succeed?**

- Strategic Management Skills
- Enterprise Risk Management Skills
- Process Management Skills
- Measurement Skills
- Leadership Skills

**The Importance of Ethics in Business**

- Code of Conduct for Management Accountants

**Corporate Social Responsibility**

This prologue explains why managerial accounting is important to the future careers of all business students. It begins by answering three questions: (1) What is managerial accounting? (2) Why does managerial accounting matter to your career? and (3) What skills do managers need to succeed? It concludes by discussing two topics important to all managers—the role of ethics in business and corporate social responsibility.

## WHAT IS MANAGERIAL ACCOUNTING?

Many students enrolled in this course will have recently completed an introductory *financial accounting* course. **Financial accounting** is concerned with reporting financial information to external parties, such as stockholders, creditors, and regulators. **Managerial accounting** is concerned with providing information to managers for use within the organization. Exhibit P–1 summarizes seven key differences between financial and managerial accounting. It recognizes that the fundamental difference between financial and managerial accounting is that financial accounting serves the needs of

**EXHIBIT P–1** Comparison of Financial and Managerial Accounting

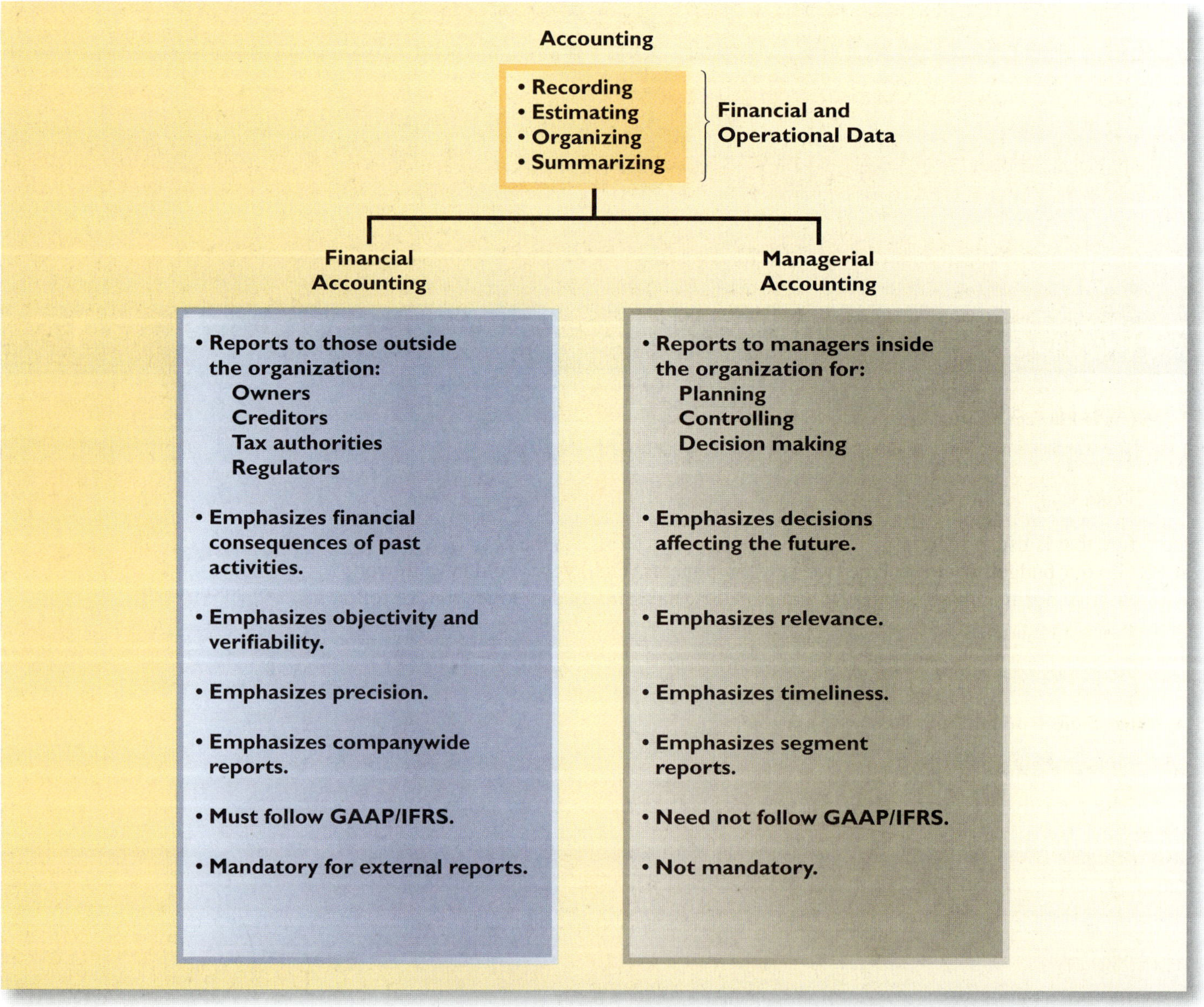

those *outside* the organization, whereas managerial accounting serves the needs of managers employed *inside* the organization. Because of this fundamental difference in users, financial accounting emphasizes the financial consequences of past activities, objectivity and verifiability, precision, and companywide performance, whereas managerial accounting emphasizes decisions affecting the future, relevance, timeliness, and *segment* performance. A **segment** is a part or activity of an organization about which managers would like cost, revenue, or profit data. Examples of business segments include product lines, customer groups (segmented by age, ethnicity, gender, volume of purchases, etc.), geographic territories, divisions, plants, and departments. Finally, financial accounting is mandatory for external reports and it needs to comply with rules, such as generally accepted accounting principles (GAAP) and international financial reporting standards (IFRS), whereas managerial accounting is not mandatory and it does not need to comply with externally imposed rules.

As mentioned in Exhibit P–1, managerial accounting helps managers perform three vital activities—*planning, controlling,* and *decision making.* **Planning** involves establishing goals and specifying how to achieve them. **Controlling** involves gathering feedback to ensure that the plan is being properly executed or modified as circumstances change. **Decision making** involves selecting a course of action from competing alternatives. Now let's take a closer look at these three pillars of managerial accounting.

## Planning

Assume that you work for **Procter & Gamble (P&G)** and that you are in charge of the company's campus recruiting for all undergraduate business majors. In this example, your planning process would begin by establishing a goal such as: our goal is to recruit the "best and brightest" college graduates. The next stage of the planning process would require specifying how to achieve this goal by answering numerous questions such as:

- How many students do we need to hire in total and from each major?
- What schools do we plan to include in our recruiting efforts?
- Which of our employees will be involved in each school's recruiting activities?
- When will we conduct our interviews?
- How will we compare students to one another to decide who will be extended job offers?
- What salary will we offer our new hires? Will the salaries differ by major?
- How much money can we spend on our recruiting efforts?

As you can see, there are many questions that need to be answered as part of the planning process. Plans are often accompanied by a *budget.* A **budget** is a detailed plan for the future that is usually expressed in formal quantitative terms. As the head of recruiting at P&G, your budget would include two key components. First, you would have to work with other senior managers inside the company to establish a budgeted amount of total salaries that can be offered to all new hires. Second, you would have to create a budget that quantifies how much you intend to spend on your campus recruiting activities.

## Controlling

Once you established and started implementing P&G's recruiting plan, you would transition to the control process. This process would involve gathering, evaluating, and responding to feedback to ensure that this year's recruiting process meets expectations. It would also include evaluating the feedback in search of ways to run a more effective recruiting campaign next year. The control process would involve answering questions such as:

- Did we succeed in hiring the planned number of students within each major and at each school?
- Did we lose too many exceptional candidates to competitors?

- Did each of our employees involved in the recruiting process perform satisfactorily?
- Is our method of comparing students to one another working?
- Did the on-campus and office interviews run smoothly?
- Did we stay within our budget in terms of total salary commitments to new hires?
- Did we stay within our budget regarding spending on recruiting activities?

As you can see, there are many questions that need to be answered as part of the control process. When answering these questions your goal would be to go beyond simple yes or no answers in search of the underlying reasons why performance exceeded or failed to meet expectations. Part of the control process includes preparing *performance reports.* A **performance report** compares budgeted data to actual data in an effort to identify and learn from excellent performance and to identify and eliminate sources of unsatisfactory performance. Performance reports can also be used as one of many inputs to help evaluate and reward employees.

Although this example focused on P&G's campus recruiting efforts, we could have described how planning enables **FedEx** to deliver packages across the globe overnight, or how it helped **Apple** develop and market the iPad. We could have discussed how the control process helps **Pfizer**, **Eli Lilly**, and **Abbott Laboratories** ensure that their pharmaceutical drugs are produced in conformance with rigorous quality standards, or how **Kroger** relies on the control process to keep its grocery shelves stocked. We also could have looked at planning and control failures such as **BP**'s massive oil spill in the Gulf of Mexico. In short, all managers (and that probably includes you someday) perform planning and controlling activities.

## Decision Making

Perhaps the most basic managerial skill is the ability to make intelligent, data-driven decisions. Broadly speaking, many of those decisions revolve around the following three questions. *What* should we be selling? *Who* should we be serving? *How* should we execute? Exhibit P–2 provides examples of decisions pertaining to each of these three categories.

The left-hand column of Exhibit P–2 suggests that every company must make decisions related to the products and services that it sells. For example, each year **Procter & Gamble** must decide how to allocate its marketing budget across 23 brands that each generates over $1 billion in sales as well as other brands that have promising growth potential. **Mattel** must decide what new toys to introduce to the market. **Southwest Airlines** must decide what ticket prices to establish for each of its thousands of flights per day. **General Motors** must decide whether to discontinue certain models of automobiles.

The middle column of Exhibit P–2 indicates that all companies must make decisions related to the customers that they serve. For example, **Sears** must decide how to allocate

**EXHIBIT P–2** Examples of Decisions

| What should we be selling? | Who should we be serving? | How should we execute? |
|---|---|---|
| What products and services should be the focus of our marketing efforts? | Who should be the focus of our marketing efforts? | How should we supply our parts and services? |
| What new products and services should we offer? | Who should we start serving? | How should we expand our capacity? |
| What prices should we charge for our products and services? | Who should pay price premiums or receive price discounts? | How should we reduce our capacity? |
| What products and services should we discontinue? | Who should we stop serving? | How should we improve our efficiency and effectiveness? |

its marketing budget between products that tend to appeal to male versus female customers. **FedEx** must decide whether to expand its services into new markets across the globe. **Hewlett-Packard** must decide what price discounts to offer corporate clients that purchase large volumes of its products. A bank must decide whether to discontinue customers that may be unprofitable.

The right-hand column of Exhibit P–2 shows that companies also make decisions related to how they execute. For example, **Boeing** must decide whether to rely on outside vendors such as **Goodrich**, **Saab**, and **Rolls-Royce** to manufacture many of the parts used to make its airplanes. **Cintas** must decide whether to expand its laundering and cleaning capacity in a given geographic region by adding square footage to an existing facility or by constructing an entirely new facility. In an economic downturn, a manufacturer might have to decide whether to eliminate one 8-hour shift at three plants or to close one plant. Finally, all companies have to decide among competing improvement opportunities. For example, a company may have to decide whether to implement a new software system, to upgrade a piece of equipment, or to provide extra training to its employees.

This portion of the chapter has explained that the three pillars of managerial accounting are planning, controlling, and decision making. This book helps prepare you to become an effective manager by explaining how to make intelligent data-driven decisions, how to create financial plans for the future, and how to continually make progress toward achieving goals by obtaining, evaluating, and responding to feedback.

## WHY DOES MANAGERIAL ACCOUNTING MATTER TO YOUR CAREER?

Many students feel anxious about choosing a major because they are unsure if it will provide a fulfilling career. To reduce these anxieties, we recommend deemphasizing what you cannot control about the future; instead focusing on what you can control right now. More specifically, concentrate on answering the following question: What can you do now to prepare for success in an unknown future career? The best answer is to learn skills that will make it easier for you to adapt to an uncertain future. You need to become adaptable!

Whether you end up working in the United States or abroad, for a large corporation, a small entrepreneurial company, a nonprofit organization, or a governmental entity, you'll need to know how to plan for the future, how to make progress toward achieving goals, and how to make intelligent decisions. In other words, managerial accounting skills are useful in just about any career, organization, and industry. If you commit energy to this course, you'll be making a smart investment in your future—even though you cannot clearly envision it. Next, we will elaborate on this point by explaining how managerial accounting relates to the future careers of business majors and accounting majors.

### Business Majors

Exhibit P–3 provides examples of how planning, controlling, and decision making affect three majors other than accounting—marketing, operations management, and human resource management.

The left-hand column of Exhibit P–3 describes some planning, controlling, and decision-making applications in the marketing profession. For example, marketing managers make planning decisions related to allocating advertising dollars across various communication mediums and to staffing new sales territories. From a control standpoint, they may closely track sales data to see if a budgeted price cut is generating an anticipated increase in unit sales, or they may study inventory levels during the holiday shopping season so that they can adjust prices as needed to optimize sales. Marketing managers also make many important decisions such as whether to bundle services together and sell them for one price or to

**EXHIBIT P–3** Relating Managerial Accounting to Three Business Majors

| | Marketing | Operations Management | Human Resource Management |
|---|---|---|---|
| Planning | How much should we budget for TV, print, and Internet advertising?<br>How many salespeople should we plan to hire to serve a new territory? | How many units should we plan to produce next period?<br>How much should we budget for next period's utility expense? | How much should we plan to spend for occupational safety training?<br>How much should we plan to spend on employee recruitment advertising? |
| Controlling | Is the budgeted price cut increasing unit sales as expected?<br>Are we accumulating too much inventory during the holiday shopping season? | Did we spend more or less than expected for the units we actually produced?<br>Are we achieving our goal of reducing the number of defective units produced? | Is our employee retention rate exceeding our goals?<br>Are we meeting our goal of completing timely performance appraisals? |
| Decision Making | Should we sell our services as one bundle or sell them separately?<br>Should we sell directly to customers or use a distributor? | Should we buy a new piece of equipment or upgrade our existing machine?<br>Should we redesign our manufacturing process to lower inventory levels? | Should we hire an on-site medical staff to lower our health care costs?<br>Should we hire temporary workers or full-time employees? |

sell each service separately. They may also decide whether to sell products directly to the customer or to sell to a distributor, who then sells to the end consumer.

The middle column of Exhibit P–3 states that operations managers have to plan how many units to produce to satisfy anticipated customer demand. They also need to budget for operating expenses such as utilities, supplies, and labor costs. In terms of control, they monitor actual spending relative to the budget, and closely watch operational measures such as the number of defects produced relative to the plan. Operations managers make numerous decisions, such as deciding whether to buy a new piece of equipment or upgrade an existing piece of equipment. They also decide whether to invest in redesigning a manufacturing process to reduce inventory levels.

The right-hand column of Exhibit P–3 explains how human resource managers make a variety of planning decisions, such as budgeting how much to spend on occupational safety training and employee recruitment advertising. They monitor feedback related to numerous management concerns, such as employee retention rates and the timely completion of employee performance appraisals. They also help make many important decisions such as whether to hire on-site medical staff in an effort to lower health care costs, and whether to hire temporary workers or full-time employees in an uncertain economy.

For brevity, Exhibit P–3 does not include all business majors, such as finance, supply chain management, management information systems, and economics. Can you explain how planning, controlling, and decision-making activities would relate to these majors?

## Accounting Majors

Many accounting graduates begin their careers working for public accounting firms that provide a variety of valuable services for their clients. Some of these graduates will build successful and fulfilling careers in the public accounting industry; however, most will leave public accounting at some point to work in other organizations. In fact, the **Institute of Management Accountants** (IMA) estimates that more than 80% of professional accountants in the United States work in nonpublic accounting environments (www.imanet.org/about_ima/our_mission.aspx).

The public accounting profession has a strong financial accounting orientation. Its most important function is to protect investors and other external parties by assuring them that companies are reporting historical financial results that comply with applicable accounting rules. Managerial accountants also have strong financial accounting skills. For example, they play an important role in helping their organizations design and maintain financial reporting systems that generate reliable financial disclosures. However, the primary role of managerial accountants is to partner with their co-workers within the organization to improve performance.

Given the 80% figure mentioned above, if you are an accounting major there is a very high likelihood that your future will involve working for a nonpublic accounting employer. Your employer will expect you to have strong financial accounting skills, but more importantly, it will expect you to help improve organizational performance by applying the planning, controlling, and decision-making skills that are the foundation of managerial accounting.

## A Networking Opportunity

IN BUSINESS

The **Institute of Management Accountants** (IMA) is a network of more than 60,000 accounting and finance professionals from over 120 countries. Every year the IMA hosts a student leadership conference that attracts 300 students from over 50 colleges and universities. Guest speakers at past conferences have discussed topics such as leadership, advice for a successful career, how to market yourself in a difficult economy, and excelling in today's multigenerational workforce. One student who attended the conference said, "I liked that I was able to interact with professionals who are in fields that could be potential career paths for me." For more information on this worthwhile networking opportunity, contact the IMA at the phone number and website shown below.

Source: Conversation with Jodi Ryan, the Institute of Management Accountants' Director of Alliances and Student/Academic Communities. (800) 638-4427 or visit its website at www.imanet.org.

**Professional Certification—A Smart Investment** If you plan to become an accounting major, the Certified Management Accountant (CMA) designation is a globally respected credential (sponsored by the IMA) that will increase your credibility, upward mobility, and compensation. Exhibit P–4 summarizes the topics covered in the two-part CMA exam. For brevity, we are not going to define all the terms included in this exhibit. Its purpose is simply to emphasize that the CMA exam focuses on the planning, controlling, and decision-making skills that are critically important to nonpublic accounting employers. The CMA's internal management orientation is a complement to the highly respected Certified Public Accountant (CPA) exam that focuses on rule-based compliance—assurance standards, financial accounting standards, business law, and the tax code. Information about becoming a CMA is available on the IMA's website (www.imanet.org) or by calling 1-800-638-4427.

**EXHIBIT P–4**
CMA Exam Content Specifications

| | |
|---|---|
| Part 1 | Financial Planning, Performance, and Control |
| | Planning, budgeting, and forecasting |
| | Performance management |
| | Cost management |
| | Internal controls |
| | Professional ethics |
| Part 2 | Financial Decision Making |
| | Financial statement analysis |
| | Corporate finance |
| | Decision analysis and risk management |
| | Investment decisions |
| | Professional ethics |

IN BUSINESS

## How's the Pay?

The Institute of Management Accountants has created the following table that allows individuals to estimate what their salary would be as a management accountant.

| | | | Your Calculation |
|---|---|---|---|
| Start with this base amount ........................ | | $75,469 | $75,469 |
| If you are top-level management ................ | ADD | $36,320 | |
| OR, if you are entry-level management ....... | SUBTRACT | $27,777 | |
| Number of years in the field _____ ............. | TIMES | $717 | |
| If you have an advanced degree................. | ADD | $11,028 | |
| If you hold the CMA .................................. | ADD | $12,971 | |
| OR, if you hold the CPA.............................. | ADD | $7,239 | _____ |
| Your estimated salary level ......................... | | | ===== |

For example, if you make it to top-level management in 10 years, have an advanced degree and a CMA, your estimated salary would be $142,958 [$75,469 + $36,320 + (10 × $717) + $11,028 + $12,971].

Source: Lee Schiffel, Kenneth A. Smith, and David L. Schroeder, "IMA 2010 Salary Survey," *Strategic Finance,* June 2011, pp. 26–46.

# WHAT SKILLS DO MANAGERS NEED TO SUCCEED?

Managers possess a variety of skills that enable them to do their jobs, including strategic management skills, enterprise risk management skills, process management skills, measurement skills, and leadership skills. We will discuss each of these skill sets in turn.

## Strategic Management Skills

Successful managers understand that the plans they set forth, the variables they seek to control, and the decisions they make are all influenced by their company's *strategy.* A **strategy** is a "game plan" that enables a company to attract customers by distinguishing itself from competitors. The focal point of a company's strategy should be its target customers. A company can only succeed if it creates a reason for customers to choose it over a competitor. These reasons, or what are more formally called *customer value propositions,* are the essence of strategy.

Customer value propositions tend to fall into three broad categories—*customer intimacy, operational excellence,* and *product leadership.* Companies that adopt a *customer intimacy* strategy are in essence saying to their customers, "You should choose us because we can customize our products and services to meet your individual needs better than our competitors." **Ritz-Carlton**, **Nordstrom**, and **Virtuoso** (a premium service travel agency) rely primarily on a customer intimacy value proposition for their success. Companies that pursue the second customer value proposition, called *operational excellence,* are saying to their target customers, "You should choose us because we deliver products and services faster, more conveniently, and at a lower price than our competitors." **Southwest Airlines**, **Walmart**, and **Google** are examples of companies that succeed first and foremost because of their operational excellence. Companies pursuing the third customer value proposition, called *product leadership,* are saying to their target customers, "You should choose us because we offer higher quality products than our competitors."

Apple, BMW, Cisco Systems, and W. L. Gore (the creator of GORE-TEX® fabrics) are examples of companies that succeed because of their product leadership. Although one company may offer its customers a combination of these three customer value propositions, one usually outweighs the other in terms of importance.[1]

## A Four-Year Waiting List at Vanilla Bicycles

IN BUSINESS

Sacha White started **Vanilla Bicycles** in Portland, Oregon, in 2001. After eight years in business, he had a four-year backlog of customer orders. He limits his annual production to 40–50 bikes per year that sell for an average of $7,000 each. He uses a silver alloy that costs 20 times as much as brass (which is the industry standard) to join titanium tubes together to form a bike frame. White spends three hours taking a buyer's measurements to determine the exact dimensions of the bike frame. He has resisted expanding production because it would undermine his strategy based on product leadership and customer intimacy. As White said, "If I ended up sacrificing what made Vanilla special just to make more bikes, that wouldn't be worth it to me."

Source: Christopher Steiner, "Heaven on Wheels," *Forbes*, April 13, 2009, p. 75.

## Enterprise Risk Management Skills

As a future manager, you need to understand that every business strategy, plan, and decision involves risks. **Enterprise risk management** is a process used by a company to identify those risks and develop responses to them that enable it to be reasonably assured of meeting its goals. The left-hand column of Exhibit P–5 provides 12 examples of business risks. This list is not exhaustive; rather, its purpose is to illustrate the diverse nature of business risks that companies face. Whether the risks relate to the weather, computer hackers, complying with the law, employee theft, or products harming customers, they all have one thing in common: If the risks are not managed effectively, they can threaten a company's ability to meet its goals.

Once a company identifies its risks, it can respond to them in various ways such as accepting, avoiding, or reducing the risk. Perhaps the most common risk management tactic is to reduce risks by implementing specific controls. The right-hand column of Exhibit P–5 provides an example of a control that could be implemented to help reduce each of the risks mentioned in the left-hand column of the exhibit. Although these types of controls cannot completely eliminate risks, companies understand that proactively managing risks is a superior alternative to reacting, perhaps too late, to unfortunate events.

## Managing the Risk of a Power Outage

IN BUSINESS

Between January and April of 2010, the United States had 35 major power outages. For business owners, these power outages can be costly. For example, a New York night club called the **Smoke Jazz and Supper Club** lost an estimated $1,500 in revenue when a power outage shut down its on-line reservation system for one night. George Pauli, the owner of **Great Embroidery LLC** in Mesa, Arizona, estimates that his company has an average of six power outages every year. Since Pauli's sewing machines cannot resume exactly where they leave off when abruptly shut down, each power outage costs him $120 in lost inventory. Pauli decided to buy $700 worth of batteries to keep his sewing machines running during power outages. The batteries paid for themselves in less than one year.

Source: Sarah E. Needleman, "Lights Out Means Lost Sales," *The Wall Street Journal*, July 22, 2010, p. B8.

[1]These three customer value propositions were defined by Michael Treacy and Fred Wiersema in "Customer Intimacy and Other Value Disciplines," *Harvard Business Review*, Volume 71 Issue 1, pp. 84–93.

**EXHIBIT P–5**
Identifying and Controlling Business Risks

| Examples of Business Risks | Examples of Controls to Reduce Business Risks |
|---|---|
| • Intellectual assets being stolen from computer files | • Create firewalls that prohibit computer hackers from corrupting or stealing intellectual property |
| • Products harming customers | • Develop a formal and rigorous new product testing program |
| • Losing market share due to the unforeseen actions of competitors | • Develop an approach for legally gathering information about competitors' plans and practices |
| • Poor weather conditions shutting down operations | • Develop contingency plans for overcoming weather-related disruptions |
| • A website malfunctioning | • Thoroughly test the website before going "live" on the Internet |
| • A supplier strike halting the flow of raw materials | • Establish a relationship with two companies capable of providing needed raw materials |
| • A poorly designed incentive compensation system causing employees to make bad decisions | • Create a balanced set of performance measures that motivates the desired behavior |
| • Financial statements inaccurately reporting the value of inventory | • Count the physical inventory on hand to make sure that it agrees with the accounting records |
| • An employee stealing assets | • Segregate duties so that the same employee does not have physical custody of an asset and the responsibility of accounting for it |
| • An employee accessing unauthorized information | • Create password-protected barriers that prohibit employees from obtaining information not needed to do their jobs |
| • Inaccurate budget estimates causing excessive or insufficient production | • Implement a rigorous budget review process |
| • Failing to comply with equal employment opportunity laws | • Create a report that tracks key metrics related to compliance with the laws |

## Process Management Skills

In addition to formulating strategies and controlling risks, managers need to continually improve the *business processes* that serve customers. A **business process** is a series of steps that are followed in order to carry out some task in a business. It is quite common for the linked set of steps comprising a business process to span departmental boundaries. The term *value chain* is often used to describe how an organization's functional departments interact with one another to form business processes. A **value chain,** as shown in Exhibit P–6, consists of the major business functions that add value to a company's products and services.

Managers frequently use two process management methods that are referred to throughout this book—*lean thinking,* or what is called *Lean Production* in the manufacturing sector, and the *Theory of Constraints.* We will briefly define these management methods now so that you recognize them in later chapters.

**EXHIBIT P–6** Business Functions Making Up the Value Chain

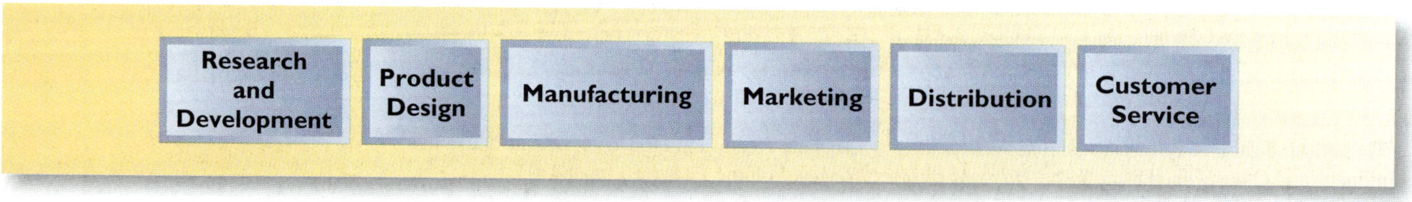

**Lean Production** **Lean Production** is a management approach that organizes resources such as people and machines around the flow of business processes and that only produces units in response to customer orders. It is often called *just-in-time* production (or *JIT*) because products are only manufactured in response to customer orders and they are completed just-in-time to be shipped to customers. Lean thinking differs from traditional manufacturing methods, which organize work departmentally and encourage those departments to maximize their output even if it exceeds customer demand and bloats inventories. Because lean thinking only allows production in response to customer orders, the number of units produced tends to equal the number of units sold, thereby resulting in minimal inventory. The lean approach also results in fewer defects, less wasted effort, and quicker customer response times than traditional production methods.

## Lean Supply Chain Management

IN BUSINESS

**Tesco**, a grocery retailer in Britain, used lean thinking to improve its replenishment process for cola products. Tesco and **Britvic** (its cola supplier) traced the cola delivery process from "the checkout counter of the grocery store through Tesco's regional distribution center (RDC), Britvic's RDC, the warehouse at the Britvic bottling plant, the filling lines for cola destined for Tesco, and the warehouse of Britvic's can supplier." Each step of the process revealed enormous waste. Tesco implemented numerous changes such as electronically linking its point-of-sale data from its grocery stores to its RDC. This change let customers pace the replenishment process and it helped increase store delivery frequency to every few hours around the clock. Britvic also began delivering cola to Tesco's RDC in wheeled dollies that could be rolled directly into delivery trucks and then to point-of-sale locations in grocery stores.

These changes reduced the total product "touches" from 150 to 50, thereby cutting labor costs. The elapsed time from the supplier's filling line to the customer's cola purchase dropped from 20 days to 5 days. The number of inventory stocking locations declined from five to two, and the supplier's distribution center was eliminated.

Source: Ghostwriter, "Teaching the Big Box New Tricks," *Fortune*, November 14, 2005, pp. 208B–208F.

**The Theory of Constraints (TOC)** A **constraint** is anything that prevents you from getting more of what you want. Every individual and every organization faces at least one constraint, so it is not difficult to find examples of constraints. You may not have enough time to study thoroughly for every subject *and* to go out with your friends on the weekend, so time is your constraint. **United Airlines** has only a limited number of loading gates available at its busy Chicago O'Hare hub, so its constraint is loading gates. **Vail Resorts** has only a limited amount of land to develop as homesites and commercial lots at its ski areas, so its constraint is land.

The **Theory of Constraints (TOC)** is based on the insight that effectively managing the constraint is a key to success. As an example, long waiting periods for surgery are a chronic problem in the **National Health Service (NHS)**, the government-funded provider of health care in the United Kingdom. The diagram in Exhibit P–7 illustrates a simplified version of the steps followed by a surgery patient. The number of patients who can be processed through each step in a day is indicated in the exhibit. For example, appointments for outpatient visits can be made for as many as 100 referrals from general practitioners in a day.

The constraint, or *bottleneck,* in the system is determined by the step that has the smallest capacity—in this case surgery. The total number of patients processed through the entire system cannot exceed 15 per day—the maximum number of patients who can be treated in surgery. No matter how hard managers, doctors, and nurses try to improve the processing rate elsewhere in the system, they will never succeed in driving down

**EXHIBIT P–7** Processing Surgery Patients at an NHS Facility (simplified)*

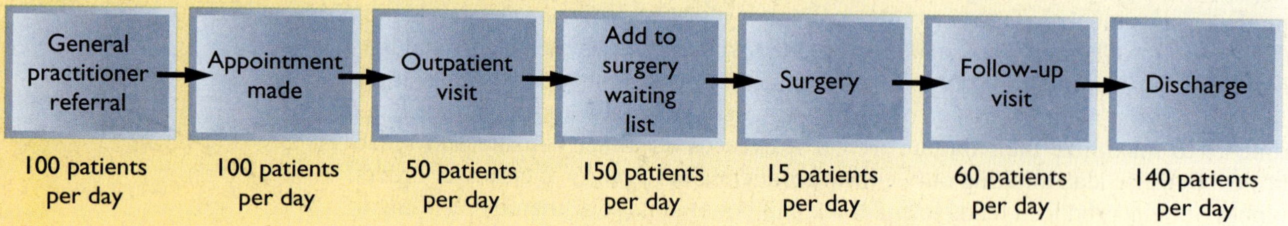


*This diagram originally appeared in the February 1999 issue of the U.K. magazine *Health Management*.

wait lists until the capacity of surgery is increased. In fact, improvements elsewhere in the system—particularly before the constraint—are likely to result in even longer waiting times and more frustrated patients and health care providers. Thus, to be effective, improvement efforts must be focused on the constraint. A business process, such as the process for serving surgery patients, is like a chain. If you want to increase the strength of a chain, what is the most effective way to do this? Should you concentrate your efforts on strengthening the strongest link, all the links, or the weakest link? Clearly, focusing your effort on the weakest link will bring the biggest benefit.

The procedure to follow to strengthen the chain is clear. First, identify the weakest link, which is the constraint. In the case of the NHS, the constraint is surgery. Second, do not place a greater strain on the system than the weakest link can handle—if you do, the chain will break. In the case of the NHS, more referrals than surgery can accommodate lead to unacceptably long waiting lists. Third, concentrate improvement efforts on strengthening the weakest link. In the case of the NHS, this means finding ways to increase the number of surgeries that can be performed in a day. Fourth, if the improvement efforts are successful, eventually the weakest link will improve to the point where it is no longer the weakest link. At that point, the new weakest link (i.e., the new constraint) must be identified, and improvement efforts must be shifted over to that link. This simple sequential process provides a powerful strategy for optimizing business processes.

## Measurement Skills

When you become a manager you'll need to complement your understanding of strategy, risks, and business processes, with data-driven analysis. If you cannot use measurement skills to provide competent, data-driven answers to challenging questions, then you'll struggle to persuade others to endorse your point-of-view.

The key to being an effective data analyst is to understand that the question you are trying to answer defines what you'll measure and how you'll analyze it. For example, if the question you wish to answer is what net income should my company report to its stockholders, then you'll be measuring and reporting historical financial data that must comply with applicable rules. If you are trying to determine how well your company is serving its customers, then you'll be measuring and analyzing mostly nonfinancial, process-oriented data. If you want to predict whether your company will need to borrow money next year, then your measurement efforts will focus on estimating future cash flows. You have to understand the question first before you can begin measuring and analyzing data.

The primary purpose of this course is to teach you measurement skills that managers use every day to answer the questions described in Exhibit P–8. Notice that this exhibit is organized by the chapters contained in this book. For example, Chapter 7 teaches you the measurement skills that managers use to answer the question: How should I create a financial plan for next year? Chapter 8 teaches you the measurement skills that managers use to answer the question: How well am I performing relative to my plan? Chapter 3

**EXHIBIT P–8**
Measurement Skills: A Manager's Perspective

| Chapter Number | The Key Question from a Manager's Perspective |
|---|---|
| Chapter 1 | What cost classifications do I use for different management purposes? |
| Chapters 2 & 4 | What is the value of our ending inventory and cost of goods sold for external reporting purposes? |
| Chapter 3 | How profitable is each of our products, services, and customers? |
| Chapter 5 | How will my profits change if I change my selling price, sales volume, or costs? |
| Chapter 6 | How should the income statement be presented? |
| Chapter 7 | How should I create a financial plan for next year? |
| Chapter 8 | How well am I performing relative to my plan? |
| Chapter 9 | What performance measures should we monitor to ensure that we achieve our strategic goals? |
| Chapter 10 | How do I quantify the profit impact of pursuing one course of action versus another? |
| Chapter 11 | How do I make long-term capital investment decisions? |
| Chapter 12 | What cash inflows and outflows explain the change in our cash balance? |
| Chapter 13 | How is our company performing through the eyes of our shareholders, short-term creditors, and long-term creditors? |

teaches you measurement skills related to product, service, and customer profitability. Exhibit P–8 emphasizes that every chapter in this book teaches you measurement and data analysis skills that you'll use throughout your career to plan, control, and make decisions.

## Leadership Skills

Leadership skills will be critical to your career development for the simple reason that organizations are managed by people, not data and spreadsheets. These people have their own personal interests, insecurities, beliefs, and data-supported conclusions that ensure unanimous support for a given course of action is the exception rather than the rule. Therefore, managers must possess strong leadership skills if they wish to channel their co-workers' efforts toward achieving organizational goals.

To become an effective leader, you'll need to develop six skills. First, you'll need to be technically competent within your area of expertise and knowledgeable of your company's operations outside your functional area of expertise. You cannot lead others (particularly those co-workers outside of your department) if they believe that you are technically incompetent or unfamiliar with how the company actually operates. Second, you must be a person of high integrity. This requires that you not only make ethically grounded decisions yourself, but also that your words and actions help build a culture of organizational integrity. We will have more to say about the importance of ethics shortly. Third, you need to understand how to effectively implement organizational change. People tend to prefer the status quo, so it is often difficult to implement any type of change in a company. To implement change, leaders need to define a vision for the future and be able to motivate and enable others to achieve the vision.

Fourth, leaders need strong communication skills. This includes compelling presentation skills and effective listening skills. They must be able to speak in operational terms and financial terms to communicate effectively with co-workers across the organization.

Fifth, leaders must be capable of motivating and mentoring other individuals. As your career evolves, if you cannot advance the skills of your subordinates, then you will not be promoted to jobs that have increasing numbers of people reporting to you. Finally, leaders need to effectively manage team-based decision processes. This requires motivating the team to objectively synthesize data, weigh alternatives, and build consensus around the chosen course of action.

## THE IMPORTANCE OF ETHICS IN BUSINESS

At the turn of this century, a series of major financial scandals involving **Enron**, **Tyco International**, **HealthSouth**, **Adelphia Communications**, **WorldCom**, **Global Crossing**, **Rite Aid**, and other companies raised deep concerns about ethics in business. The managers and companies involved in these scandals suffered mightily—from huge fines to jail terms and financial collapse. And the recognition that ethical behavior is absolutely essential for the functioning of our economy led to numerous regulatory changes. But why is ethical behavior so important? This is not a matter of just being "nice." Ethical behavior is the lubricant that keeps the economy running. Without that lubricant, the economy would operate much less efficiently—less would be available to consumers, quality would be lower, and prices would be higher. In other words, without fundamental trust in the integrity of businesses, the economy would operate much less efficiently. James Surowiecki summed up this point as follows:

> [F]lourishing economies require a healthy level of trust in the reliability and fairness of everyday transactions. If you assumed every potential deal was a rip-off or that the products you were buying were probably going to be lemons, then very little business would get done. More important, the costs of the transactions that did take place would be exorbitant because you'd have to do enormous work to investigate each deal and you'd have to rely on the threat of legal action to enforce every contract. For an economy to prosper, what's needed is not a Pollyannaish faith that everyone else has your best interests at heart—"caveat emptor" [buyer beware] remains an important truth—but a basic confidence in the promises and commitments that people make about their products and services.[2]

Thus, for the good of everyone—including profit-making companies—it is vitally important that business be conducted within an ethical framework that builds and sustains trust.

The Institute of Management Accountants (IMA) of the United States has adopted an ethical code called the *Statement of Ethical Professional Practice* that describes in some detail the ethical responsibilities of management accountants. Even though the standards were specifically developed for management accountants, they have much broader application.

### Code of Conduct for Management Accountants

The IMA's Statement of Ethical Professional Practice consists of two parts that are presented in full in Exhibit P–9. The first part provides general guidelines for ethical behavior. In a nutshell, a management accountant has ethical responsibilities in four broad areas: first, to maintain a high level of professional competence; second, to treat sensitive matters with confidentiality; third, to maintain personal integrity; and fourth, to disclose information in a credible fashion. The second part of the standards specifies what should be done if an individual finds evidence of ethical misconduct. We recommend that you stop at this point and read all of Exhibit P–9.

---

[2]James Surowiecki, "A Virtuous Cycle," *Forbes,* December 23, 2002, pp. 248–256. Reprinted by Permission of Forbes Magazine © 2006 Forbes Inc.

**EXHIBIT P–9** IMA Statement of Ethical Professional Practice

Members of IMA shall behave ethically. A commitment to ethical professional practice includes: overarching principles that express our values, and standards that guide our conduct.

**PRINCIPLES**

IMA's overarching ethical principles include: Honesty, Fairness, Objectivity, and Responsibility. Members shall act in accordance with these principles and shall encourage others within their organizations to adhere to them.

**STANDARDS**

A member's failure to comply with the following standards may result in disciplinary action.

**I. COMPETENCE**

Each member has a responsibility to:

1. Maintain an appropriate level of professional expertise by continually developing knowledge and skills.
2. Perform professional duties in accordance with relevant laws, regulations, and technical standards.
3. Provide decision support information and recommendations that are accurate, clear, concise, and timely.
4. Recognize and communicate professional limitations or other constraints that would preclude responsible judgment or successful performance of an activity.

**II. CONFIDENTIALITY**

Each member has a responsibility to:

1. Keep information confidential except when disclosure is authorized or legally required.
2. Inform all relevant parties regarding appropriate use of confidential information. Monitor subordinates' activities to ensure compliance.
3. Refrain from using confidential information for unethical or illegal advantage.

**III. INTEGRITY**

Each member has a responsibility to:

1. Mitigate actual conflicts of interest. Regularly communicate with business associates to avoid apparent conflicts of interest. Advise all parties of any potential conflicts.
2. Refrain from engaging in any conduct that would prejudice carrying out duties ethically.
3. Abstain from engaging in or supporting any activity that might discredit the profession.

**IV. CREDIBILITY**

Each member has a responsibility to:

1. Communicate information fairly and objectively.
2. Disclose all relevant information that could reasonably be expected to influence an intended user's understanding of the reports, analyses, or recommendations.
3. Disclose delays or deficiencies in information, timeliness, processing, or internal controls in conformance with organization policy and/or applicable law.

**RESOLUTION OF ETHICAL CONFLICT**

In applying the Standards of Ethical Professional Practice, you may encounter problems identifying unethical behavior or resolving an ethical conflict. When faced with ethical issues, you should follow your organization's established policies on the resolution of such conflict. If these policies do not resolve the ethical conflict, you should consider the following courses of action:

1. Discuss the issue with your immediate supervisor except when it appears that the supervisor is involved. In that case, present the issue to the next level. If you cannot achieve a satisfactory resolution, submit the issue to the next management level. If your immediate superior is the chief executive officer or equivalent, the acceptable reviewing authority may be a group such as the audit committee, executive committee, board of directors, board of trustees, or owners. Contact with levels above the immediate superior should be initiated only with your superior's knowledge, assuming he or she is not involved. Communication of such problems to authorities or individuals not employed or engaged by the organization is not considered appropriate, unless you believe there is a clear violation of the law.
2. Clarify relevant ethical issues by initiating a confidential discussion with an IMA Ethics Counselor or other impartial advisor to obtain a better understanding of possible courses of action.
3. Consult your own attorney as to legal obligations and rights concerning the ethical conflict.

The ethical standards provide sound, practical advice for management accountants and managers. Most of the rules in the ethical standards are motivated by a very practical consideration—if these rules were not generally followed in business, then the economy and all of us would suffer. Consider the following specific examples of the consequences of not abiding by the standards:

- Suppose employees could not be trusted with confidential information. Then top managers would be reluctant to distribute such information within the company and, as a result, decisions would be based on incomplete information and operations would deteriorate.
- Suppose employees accepted bribes from suppliers. Then contracts would tend to go to suppliers who pay the highest bribes rather than to the most competent suppliers. Would you like to fly in aircraft whose wings were made by the subcontractor who paid the highest bribe? Would you fly as often? What would happen to the airline industry if its safety record deteriorated due to shoddy workmanship on contracted parts and assemblies?
- Suppose the presidents of companies routinely lied in their annual reports and financial statements. If investors could not rely on the basic integrity of a company's financial statements, they would have little basis for making informed decisions. Suspecting the worst, rational investors would pay less for securities issued by companies and may not be willing to invest at all. As a consequence, companies would have less money for productive investments—leading to slower economic growth, fewer goods and services, and higher prices.

As these examples suggest, if ethical standards were not generally adhered to, everyone would suffer—businesses as well as consumers. Essentially, abandoning ethical standards would lead to a lower standard of living with lower-quality goods and services, less to choose from, and higher prices. In short, following ethical rules such as those in the Statement of Ethical Professional Practice is absolutely essential for the smooth functioning of an advanced market economy.

IN BUSINESS

## Toyota Encounters Major Problems

When **Toyota Motor Corporation** failed to meet its profit targets, the company set an aggressive goal of reducing the cost of its auto parts by 30%. The quality and safety of the company's automobiles eventually suffered mightily resulting in recalls, litigation, incentive campaigns, and marketing efforts that analysts estimate will cost the company more than $5 billion. The car maker's president, Akio Toyoda, blamed his company's massive quality lapses on an excessive focus on profits and market share. Similarly, Jim Press, Toyota's former top U.S. executive, said the problems were caused by "financially-oriented pirates who didn't have the character to maintain a customer-first focus."

Sources: Yoshio Takahashi, "Toyota Accelerates Its Cost-Cutting Efforts," *The Wall Street Journal*, December 23, 2009, p. B4; Norihiko Shirouzu, "Toyoda Rues Excessive Profit Focus," *The Wall Street Journal*, March 2, 2010, p. B3; and Mariko Sanchanta and Yoshio Takahashi, "Toyota's Recall May Top $5 Billion," *The Wall Street Journal*, March 10, 2010, p. B2.

## CORPORATE SOCIAL RESPONSIBILITY

Companies are responsible for producing financial results that satisfy stockholders. However, they also have a *corporate social responsibility* to serve other stakeholders—such as customers, employees, suppliers, communities, and environmental and human rights advocates—whose interests are tied to the company's performance. **Corporate**

**EXHIBIT P–10**
Examples of Corporate Social Responsibilities

Companies should provide customers with:
- Safe, high-quality products that are fairly priced.
- Competent, courteous, and rapid delivery of products and services.
- Full disclosure of product-related risks.
- Easy-to-use information systems for shopping and tracking orders.

Companies and their suppliers should provide employees with:
- Safe and humane working conditions.
- Nondiscriminatory treatment and the right to organize and file grievances.
- Fair compensation.
- Opportunities for training, promotion, and personal development.

Companies should provide suppliers with:
- Fair contract terms and prompt payments.
- Reasonable time to prepare orders.
- Hassle-free acceptance of timely and complete deliveries.
- Cooperative rather than unilateral actions.

Companies should provide communities with:
- Payment of fair taxes.
- Honest information about plans such as plant closings.
- Resources that support charities, schools, and civic activities.
- Reasonable access to media sources.

Companies should provide stockholders with:
- Competent management.
- Easy access to complete and accurate financial information.
- Full disclosure of enterprise risks.
- Honest answers to knowledgeable questions.

Companies should provide environmental and human rights advocates with:
- Greenhouse gas emissions data.
- Recycling and resource conservation data.
- Child labor transparency.
- Full disclosure of suppliers located in developing countries.

**social responsibility** (CSR) is a concept whereby organizations consider the needs of all stakeholders when making decisions. CSR extends beyond legal compliance to include voluntary actions that satisfy stakeholder expectations. Numerous companies, such as **Procter & Gamble**, **3M**, **Eli Lilly and Company**, **Starbucks**, **Microsoft**, **Genentech**, **Johnson & Johnson**, **Baxter International**, **Abbott Laboratories**, **KPMG**, **National City Bank**, **Deloitte**, **Southwest Airlines**, and **Caterpillar**, prominently describe their corporate social performance on their websites.

Exhibit P–10 presents examples of corporate social responsibilities that are of interest to six stakeholder groups. Many companies are paying increasing attention to these types of broadly defined responsibilities for four reasons. First, socially responsible investors control more than $2.3 trillion of investment capital. Companies that want access to this capital must excel in terms of their social performance. Second, a growing number of employees want to work for a company that recognizes and responds to its social responsibilities. If companies hope to recruit and retain these highly skilled employees, then they must offer fulfilling careers that serve the needs of broadly defined stakeholders. Third, many customers seek to purchase products and services from socially responsible companies. The Internet enables these customers to readily locate competing products, thereby making it even easier to avoid doing business with undesirable companies. Fourth, nongovernment organizations (NGOs) and activists are more capable than ever of tarnishing a company's reputation by publicizing its environmental or human rights missteps. The Internet has enabled these environmental and human rights advocacy groups to better organize their resources, spread negative information, and take coordinated actions against offending companies.[3]

[3]The insights from this paragraph and many of the examples in Exhibit P–10 were drawn from Terry Leap and Misty L. Loughry, "The Stakeholder-Friendly Firm," *Business Horizons,* March/April 2004, pp. 27–32; and Ronald W. Clement, "The Lessons from Stakeholder Theory for U.S. Business Leaders," *Business Horizons,* May/June 2005, pp. 255–264.

It is important to understand that a company's social performance can impact its financial performance. For example, if a company's poor social performance alienates customers, then its revenues and profits will suffer. This reality explains why companies use enterprise risk management, as previously described, to meet the needs of *all* stakeholders.

### IN BUSINESS — Skill-Based Volunteerism Grows in Popularity

**Ernst & Young**, a "Big 4" public accounting firm, paid one of its managers to spend 12 weeks in Buenos Aires providing free accounting services to a small publishing company. **UPS** paid one of its logistics supervisors to help coordinate the **Susan G. Komen Breast Cancer Foundation**'s annual Race for the Cure event. Why are these companies paying their employees to work for other organizations? A survey of 1,800 people ages 13–25 revealed that 79% intend to seek employment with companies that care about contributing to society—underscoring the value of skill-based volunteerism as an employee recruiting and retention tool. Furthermore, enabling employees to apply their skills in diverse business contexts makes them more effective when they return to their regular jobs.

Source: Sarah E. Needleman, "The Latest Office Perk: Getting Paid to Volunteer," *The Wall Street Journal*, April 29, 2008, pp. D1 and D5.

## SUMMARY

This Prologue defined managerial accounting, explained why it is relevant to business and accounting majors, and described various skills that managers need to do their jobs. It also discussed the importance of ethics in business and corporate social responsibility. The most important goal of this chapter was to help you understand that managerial accounting matters to your future career, regardless of your major. Accounting is the language of business and you'll need to speak this language to communicate effectively with and influence fellow managers.

## GLOSSARY

At the end of each chapter, a list of key terms for review is given, along with the definition of each term. (These terms are printed in boldface where they are defined in the chapter.) Carefully study each term to be sure you understand its meaning. The list for the Prologue follows.

**Budget** A detailed plan for the future that is usually expressed in formal quantitative terms. (p. 3)

**Business process** A series of steps that are followed in order to carry out some task in a business. (p. 10)

**Constraint** Anything that prevents you from getting more of what you want. (p. 11)

**Controlling** The process of gathering feedback to ensure that a plan is being properly executed or modified as circumstances change. (p. 3)

**Corporate social responsibility** A concept whereby organizations consider the needs of all stakeholders when making decisions. (p. 16)

**Decision making** Selecting a course of action from competing alternatives. (p. 3)

**Enterprise risk management** A process used by a company to identify its risks and develop responses to them that enable it to be reasonably assured of meeting its goals. (p. 9)

**Financial accounting** The phase of accounting that is concerned with reporting historical financial information to external parties, such as stockholders, creditors, and regulators. (p. 2)

**Lean Production** A management approach that organizes resources such as people and machines around the flow of business processes and that only produces units in response to customer orders. (p. 11)

**Managerial accounting** The phase of accounting that is concerned with providing information to managers for use within the organization. (p. 2)

**Performance report** A report that compares budgeted data to actual data to highlight instances of excellent and unsatisfactory performance. (p. 4)

**Planning** The process of establishing goals and specifying how to achieve them. (p. 3)

**Segment** A part or activity of an organization about which managers would like cost, revenue, or profit data. (p. 3)

**Strategy** A company's "game plan" for attracting customers by distinguishing itself from competitors. (p. 8)

**Theory of Constraints** A management approach that emphasizes the importance of managing constraints. (p. 11)

**Value chain** The major business functions that add value to a company's products and services, such as research and development, product design, manufacturing, marketing, distribution, and customer service. (p. 10)

## QUESTIONS

**P–1** How does managerial accounting differ from financial accounting?

**P–2** Pick any major television network and describe some planning and control activities that its managers would engage in.

**P–3** If you had to decide whether to continue making a component part or to begin buying the part from an overseas supplier, what quantitative and qualitative factors would influence your decision?

**P–4** Why do companies prepare budgets?

**P–5** Why is managerial accounting relevant to business majors and their future careers?

**P–6** Why is managerial accounting relevant to accounting majors and their future careers?

**P–7** Pick any large company and describe its strategy using the framework in the chapter.

**P–8** Why do management accountants need to understand their company's strategy?

**P–9** Pick any large company and describe three risks that it faces and how it responds to those risks.

**P–10** Provide three examples of how a company's risks can influence its planning, controlling, and decision-making activities.

**P–11** Pick any large company and explain three ways that it could segment its companywide performance.

**P–12** Locate the website of any company that publishes a corporate social responsibility report (also referred to as a sustainability report). Describe three nonfinancial performance measures included in the report. Why do you think the company publishes this report?

**P–13** Why do companies that implement Lean Production tend to have minimal inventories?

**P–14** Why are leadership skills important to managers?

**P–15** Why is ethics important to business?

## A LOOK BACK

The Prologue defined managerial accounting and explained why it is important to the careers of all business students. It also discussed the role of ethics in business and corporate social responsibility.

## A LOOK AT THIS CHAPTER

This chapter defines many of the cost terms that will be used throughout the book. It explains that in managerial accounting the term *cost* is used in many different ways depending on the needs of management.

## A LOOK AHEAD

Chapters 2, 3, and 4 describe costing systems that are used to compute product costs. Chapter 2 describes job-order costing. Chapter 3 describes activity-based costing, an elaboration of job-order costing. Chapter 4 covers process costing.

# 1 Managerial Accounting and Cost Concepts

## CHAPTER OUTLINE

## DECISION FEATURE

# Understanding Costs Aids the Growth of a Billion Dollar Company

In 1986, Women's World of Fitness went bankrupt despite having 14 locations and 50,000 members. The company's owner, Gary Heavin, says the fitness centers contained too many costly amenities such as swimming pools, tanning beds, cardio machines, kid's programs, juice bars, personal trainers, and aerobics classes. As costs escalated, he attempted to increase revenues by offering memberships to men, which alienated his female members. What did Heavin learn from his experience?

In 1992, Heavin founded a new brand of women's fitness centers called Curves. Rather than investing in every conceivable piece of fitness equipment and amenity, Heavin focused on simplicity. He created a simple fitness circuit that uses minimal equipment and is quick and easy for members to complete. Instead of operating almost 24 hours a day, he decided to close his gyms early. Even showers were deemed unnecessary. In short, Heavin eliminated numerous costs that did not provide benefits in the eyes of his customers. With dramatically lower costs, he has been able to maintain his "women only" approach while building a billion dollar company with nearly 10,000 locations worldwide.

Source: Alison Stein Wellner, "Gary Heavin Is on a Mission from God," *Inc.* magazine, October 2006, pp. 116–123.

## LEARNING OBJECTIVES

*After studying Chapter 1, you should be able to:*

**LO1** Identify and give examples of each of the three basic manufacturing cost categories.

**LO2** Distinguish between product costs and period costs and give examples of each.

**LO3** Understand cost behavior patterns including variable costs, fixed costs, and mixed costs.

**LO4** Analyze a mixed cost using a scattergraph plot and the high-low method.

**LO5** Prepare income statements for a merchandising company using the traditional and contribution formats.

**LO6** Understand the differences between direct and indirect costs.

**LO7** Understand cost classifications used in making decisions: differential costs, opportunity costs, and sunk costs.

**This chapter explains that in managerial accounting** the term *cost* is used in many different ways. The reason is that there are many types of costs, and these costs are classified differently according to the immediate needs of management. For example, managers may want cost data to prepare external financial reports, to prepare planning budgets, or to make decisions. Each different use of cost data demands a different classification and definition of costs. For example, the preparation of external financial reports requires the use of historical cost data, whereas decision making may require predictions about future costs. This notion of different costs for different purposes is a critically important aspect of managerial accounting.

## GENERAL COST CLASSIFICATIONS

We will start our discussion of cost concepts by focusing on manufacturing companies, because they are involved in most of the activities found in other types of organizations. Manufacturing companies such as **Texas Instruments**, **Ford**, and **DuPont** are involved in acquiring raw materials, producing finished goods, marketing, distributing, billing, and almost every other business activity. Therefore, an understanding of costs in a manufacturing company can be very helpful in understanding costs in other types of organizations.

### Manufacturing Costs

**LEARNING OBJECTIVE 1**

Identify and give examples of each of the three basic manufacturing cost categories.

Most manufacturing companies separate manufacturing costs into three broad categories: direct materials, direct labor, and manufacturing overhead. A discussion of each of these categories follows.

**Direct Materials** The materials that go into the final product are called **raw materials.** This term is somewhat misleading because it seems to imply unprocessed natural resources like wood pulp or iron ore. Actually, raw materials refer to any materials that are used in the final product; and the finished product of one company can become the raw materials of another company. For example, the plastics produced by **DuPont** are a raw material used by **Hewlett-Packard** in its personal computers.

Raw materials may include both *direct* and *indirect materials.* **Direct materials** are those materials that become an integral part of the finished product and whose costs can be conveniently traced to the finished product. This would include, for example, the seats that **Airbus** purchases from subcontractors to install in its commercial aircraft and the tiny electric motor **Panasonic** uses in its DVD players.

Sometimes it isn't worth the effort to trace the costs of relatively insignificant materials to end products. Such minor items would include the solder used to make electrical connections in a **Sony TV** or the glue used to assemble an **Ethan Allen** chair. Materials such as solder and glue are called **indirect materials** and are included as part of manufacturing overhead, which is discussed later in this section.

**Direct Labor** **Direct labor** consists of labor costs that can be easily (i.e., physically and conveniently) traced to individual units of product. Direct labor is sometimes called *touch labor* because direct labor workers typically touch the product while it is being made. Examples of direct labor include assembly-line workers at **Toyota**, carpenters at the home builder **KB Home**, and electricians who install equipment on aircraft at **Bombardier Learjet**.

Labor costs that cannot be physically traced to particular products, or that can be traced only at great cost and inconvenience, are termed **indirect labor.** Just like indirect materials, indirect labor is treated as part of manufacturing overhead. Indirect labor includes the labor costs of janitors, supervisors, materials handlers, and night security guards. Although the efforts of these workers are essential, it would be either impractical or impossible to accurately trace their costs to specific units of product. Hence, such labor costs are treated as indirect labor.

indirect cost

**Manufacturing Overhead** **Manufacturing overhead,** the third element of manufacturing cost, includes all manufacturing costs except direct materials and direct labor. Manufacturing overhead includes items such as indirect materials; indirect labor; maintenance and repairs on production equipment; and heat and light, property taxes, depreciation, and insurance on manufacturing facilities. A company also incurs costs for heat and light, property taxes, insurance, depreciation, and so forth, associated with its selling and administrative functions, but these costs are not included as part of manufacturing overhead. Only those costs associated with *operating the factory* are included in manufacturing overhead.

Various names are used for manufacturing overhead, such as *indirect manufacturing cost, factory overhead,* and *factory burden.* All of these terms are synonyms for *manufacturing overhead.*

## Nonmanufacturing Costs

Nonmanufacturing costs are often divided into two categories: (1) *selling costs* and (2) *administrative costs.* **Selling costs** include all costs that are incurred to secure customer orders and get the finished product to the customer. These costs are sometimes called *order-getting* and *order-filling costs.* Examples of selling costs include advertising, shipping, sales travel, sales commissions, sales salaries, and costs of finished goods warehouses.

**Administrative costs** include all costs associated with the *general management* of an organization rather than with manufacturing or selling. Examples of administrative costs include executive compensation, general accounting, secretarial, public relations, and similar costs involved in the overall, general administration of the organization *as a whole.*

Nonmanufacturing costs are also often called selling, general, and administrative (SG&A) costs or just selling and administrative costs.

# PRODUCT COSTS VERSUS PERIOD COSTS

**LEARNING OBJECTIVE 2**

Distinguish between product costs and period costs and give examples of each.

In addition to classifying costs as manufacturing or nonmanufacturing costs, there are other ways to look at costs. For instance, they can also be classified as either *product costs* or *period costs.* To understand the difference between product costs and period costs, we must first discuss the matching principle from financial accounting.

Generally, costs are recognized as expenses on the income statement in the period that benefits from the cost. For example, if a company pays for liability insurance in advance for two years, the entire amount is not considered an expense of the year in which the payment is made. Instead, one-half of the cost would be recognized as an expense each year. The reason is that both years—not just the first year—benefit from the insurance payment. The unexpensed portion of the insurance payment is carried on the balance sheet as an asset called prepaid insurance.

The *matching principle* is based on the *accrual* concept that *costs incurred to generate a particular revenue should be recognized as expenses in the same period that the revenue is recognized.* This means that if a cost is incurred to acquire or make something that will eventually be sold, then the cost should be recognized as an expense only when the sale takes place—that is, when the benefit occurs. Such costs are called *product costs.*

## Product Costs

For financial accounting purposes, **product costs** include all costs involved in acquiring or making a product. In the case of manufactured goods, these costs consist of direct materials, direct labor, and manufacturing overhead. Product costs "attach" to units of product as the goods are purchased or manufactured, and they remain attached as the goods go into inventory awaiting sale. Product costs are initially assigned to an inventory account on the balance sheet. When the goods are sold, the costs are released from inventory as expenses (typically called cost of goods sold) and matched against sales revenue. Because product costs are initially assigned to inventories, they are also known as **inventoriable costs.**

We want to emphasize that product costs are not necessarily treated as expenses in the period in which they are incurred. Rather, as explained above, they are treated as expenses in the period in which the related products *are sold.*

## Period Costs

**Period costs** are all the costs that are not product costs. *All selling and administrative expenses are treated as period costs.* For example, sales commissions, advertising, executive salaries, public relations, and the rental costs of administrative offices are all period costs. Period costs are not included as part of the cost of either purchased or manufactured goods; instead, period costs are expensed on the income statement in the period in which they are incurred using the usual rules of accrual accounting. Keep in mind that the period in which a cost is incurred is not necessarily the period in which cash changes hands. For example, as discussed earlier, the costs of liability insurance are spread across the periods that benefit from the insurance—regardless of the period in which the insurance premium is paid.

## Prime Cost and Conversion Cost

Two more cost categories are often used in discussions of manufacturing costs—*prime cost* and *conversion cost.* **Prime cost** is the sum of direct materials cost and direct labor cost. **Conversion cost** is the sum of direct labor cost and manufacturing overhead cost. The term *conversion cost* is used to describe direct labor and manufacturing overhead because these costs are incurred to convert materials into the finished product.

Exhibit 1–1 contains a summary of the cost terms that we have introduced so far.

IN BUSINESS

### The Challenges of Managing Charitable Organizations

Charitable organizations, such as **Harlem Children's Zone**, **Sports4Kids**, and **Citizen Schools**, are facing a difficult situation. Many donors—aware of stories involving charities that spent excessively on themselves while losing sight of their mission—have started prohibiting their charity of choice from using donated funds to pay for administrative costs. However, even the most efficient charitable organizations find it difficult to expand without making additions to their infrastructure. For example, Sports4Kids' nationwide expansion of its sports programs drove up administrative costs from 5.6% to 14.7% of its total budget. The organization claims that this cost increase was necessary to build a more experienced management team to oversee the dramatically increased scale of operations.

Many charitable organizations are starting to seek gifts explicitly to fund administrative expenses. Their argument is simple—they cannot do good deeds for other people without incurring such costs.

Source: Rachel Emma Silverman and Sally Beatty, "Save the Children (But Pay the Bills, Too)," *The Wall Street Journal*, December 26, 2006, pp. D1–D2.

**EXHIBIT 1–1** Summary of Cost Terms

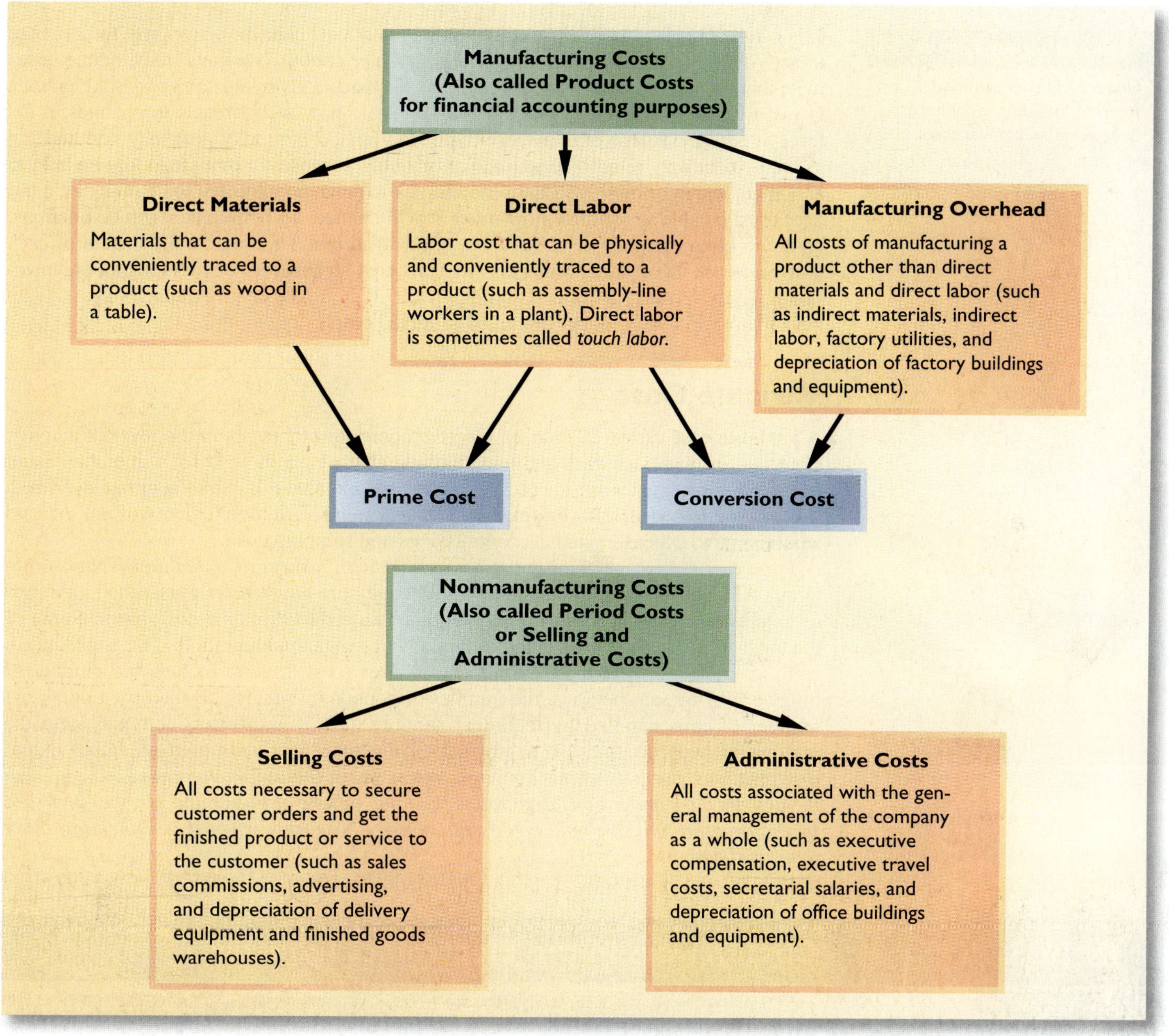


**CONCEPT CHECK**

1. Which of the following statements is true? (You may select more than one answer.)
   a. Product costs are expensed on the income statement in the period incurred.
   b. Direct labor is a manufacturing cost and a product cost.
   c. Conversion costs include direct materials and direct labor.
   d. Nonmanufacturing costs are treated as period costs.

# COST CLASSIFICATIONS FOR PREDICTING COST BEHAVIOR

**LEARNING OBJECTIVE 3**

Understand cost behavior patterns including variable costs, fixed costs, and mixed costs.

It is often necessary to predict how a certain cost will behave in response to a change in activity. For example, a manager at **Qwest**, a telephone company, may want to estimate the impact a 5 percent increase in long-distance calls by customers would have on Qwest's total electric bill. **Cost behavior** refers to how a cost reacts to changes in the level of activity. As the activity level rises and falls, a particular cost may rise and fall as well—or it may remain constant. For planning purposes, a manager must be able to anticipate which of these will happen; and if a cost can be expected to change, the manager must be able to estimate how much it will change. To help make such distinctions, costs are often categorized as *variable, fixed,* or *mixed.* The relative proportion of each type of cost in an organization is known as its **cost structure.** For example, an organization might have many fixed costs but few variable or mixed costs. Alternatively, it might have many variable costs but few fixed or mixed costs.

## Variable Cost

A **variable cost** varies, in total, in direct proportion to changes in the level of activity. Common examples of variable costs include cost of goods sold for a merchandising company, direct materials, direct labor, variable elements of manufacturing overhead, such as indirect materials, supplies, and power, and variable elements of selling and administrative expenses, such as commissions and shipping costs.[1]

For a cost to be variable, it must be variable *with respect to something.* That "something" is its *activity base.* An **activity base** is a measure of whatever causes the incurrence of a variable cost. An activity base is sometimes referred to as a *cost driver.* Some of the most common activity bases are direct labor-hours, machine-hours, units produced, and units sold. Other examples of activity bases (cost drivers) include the number of miles driven by salespersons, the number of pounds of laundry cleaned by a hotel, the number of calls handled by technical support staff at a software company, and the number of beds occupied in a hospital. *While there are many activity bases within organizations, throughout this textbook, unless stated otherwise, you should assume that the activity base under consideration is the total volume of goods and services provided by the organization. We will specify the activity base only when it is something other than total output.*

**IN BUSINESS**

### Cost Drivers In the Electronics Industry

**Accenture Ltd.** estimates that the U.S. electronics industry spends $13.8 billion annually to rebox, restock, and resell returned products. Conventional wisdom is that customers only return products when they are defective, but the data show that this explanation only accounts for 5% of customer returns. The biggest cost drivers that cause product returns are that customers often inadvertently buy the wrong products and that they cannot understand how to use the products that they have purchased. Television manufacturer **Vizio Inc.** has started including more information on its packaging to help customers avoid buying the wrong product. **Seagate Technologies** is replacing thick instruction manuals with simpler guides that make it easier for customers to begin using their products.

Source: Christopher Lawton, "The War on Returns," *The Wall Street Journal,* May 8, 2008, pp. D1 and D6.

[1] Direct labor costs often can be fixed instead of variable for a variety of reasons. For example, in some countries, such as France, Germany, and Japan, labor regulations and cultural norms may limit management's ability to adjust the labor force in response to changes in activity. In this textbook, always assume that direct labor is a variable cost unless you are explicitly told otherwise.

To provide an example of a variable cost, consider Nooksack Expeditions, a small company that provides daylong whitewater rafting excursions on rivers in the North Cascade Mountains. The company provides all of the necessary equipment and experienced guides, and it serves gourmet meals to its guests. The meals are purchased from a caterer for $30 a person for a daylong excursion. The behavior of this variable cost, on both a per unit and a total basis, is shown below:

| Number of Guests | Cost of Meals per Guest | Total Cost of Meals |
|---|---|---|
| 250........... | $30 | $7,500 |
| 500........... | $30 | $15,000 |
| 750........... | $30 | $22,500 |
| 1,000........... | $30 | $30,000 |

While total variable costs change as the activity level changes, it is important to note that a variable cost is constant if expressed on a *per unit* basis. For example, the per unit cost of the meals remains constant at $30 even though the total cost of the meals increases and decreases with activity. The graph on the left-hand side of Exhibit 1–2 illustrates that the total variable cost rises and falls as the activity level rises and falls. At an activity level of 250 guests, the total meal cost is $7,500. At an activity level of 1,000 guests, the total meal cost rises to $30,000.

## Fixed Cost

A **fixed cost** is a cost that remains constant, in total, regardless of changes in the level of activity. Examples of fixed costs include straight-line depreciation, insurance, property taxes, rent, supervisory salaries, administrative salaries, and advertising. Unlike variable costs, fixed costs are not affected by changes in activity. Consequently, as the activity level rises and falls, total fixed costs remain constant unless influenced by some outside force, such as a landlord increasing your monthly rental expense. To continue the Nooksack Expeditions example, assume the company rents a building for $500 per month to store

**EXHIBIT 1–2** Variable and Fixed Cost Behavior

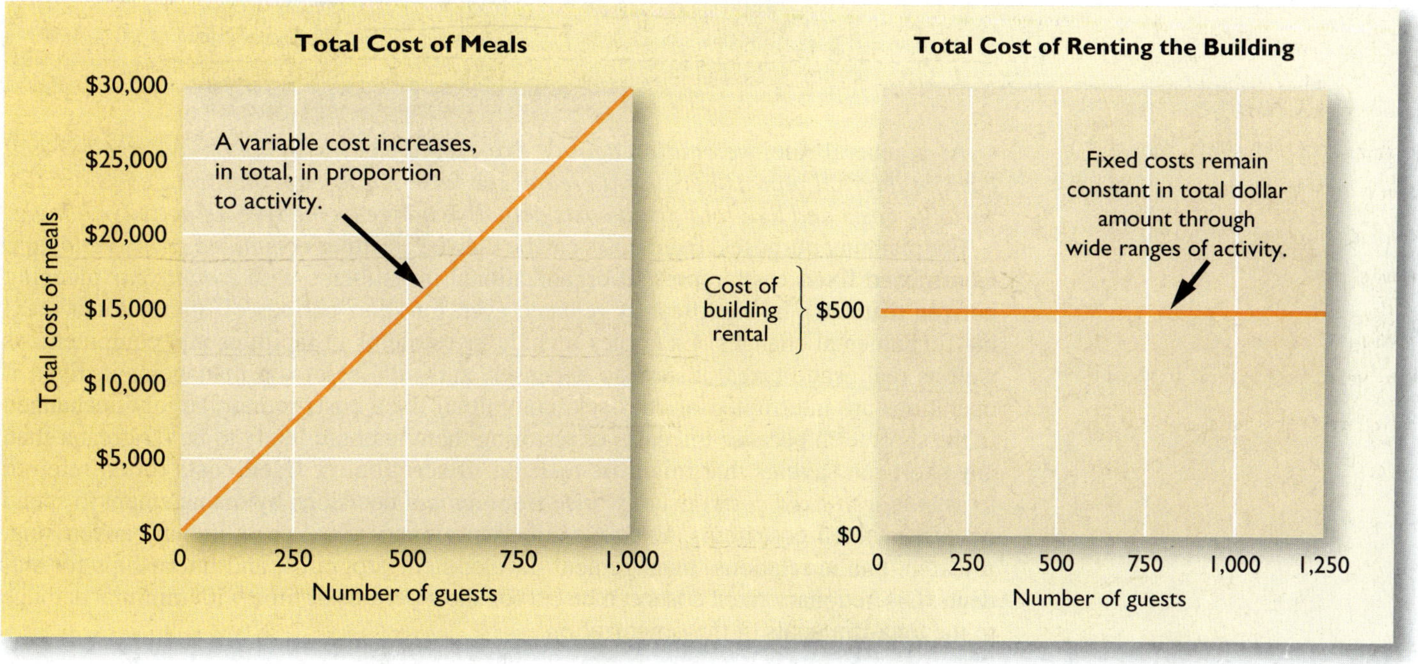

its equipment. The total amount of rent paid is the same regardless of the number of guests the company takes on its expeditions during any given month. The concept of a fixed cost is shown graphically on the right-hand side of Exhibit 1–2.

## IN BUSINESS

### Food Costs at a Luxury Hotel

The **Sporthotel Theresa** (http://www.theresa.at/), owned and operated by the Egger family, is a four-star hotel located in Zell im Zillertal, Austria. The hotel features access to hiking, skiing, biking, and other activities in the Ziller alps as well as its own fitness facility and spa.

Three full meals a day are included in the hotel room charge. Breakfast and lunch are served buffet-style while dinner is a more formal affair with as many as six courses. The chef, Stefan Egger, believes that food costs are roughly proportional to the number of guests staying at the hotel; that is, they are a variable cost. He must order food from suppliers two or three days in advance, but he adjusts his purchases to the number of guests who are currently staying at the hotel and their consumption patterns. In addition, guests make their selections from the dinner menu early in the day, which helps Stefan plan which foodstuffs will be required for dinner. Consequently, he is able to prepare just enough food so that all guests are satisfied and yet waste is held to a minimum.

Source: Conversation with Stefan Egger, chef at the Sporthotel Theresa.

Because total fixed costs remain constant for large variations in the level of activity, the average fixed cost *per unit* becomes progressively smaller as the level of activity increases. If Nooksack Expeditions has only 250 guests in a month, the $500 fixed rental cost would amount to an average of $2 per guest. If there are 1,000 guests, the fixed rental cost would average only 50 cents per guest. The table below illustrates this aspect of the behavior of fixed costs. Note that as the number of guests increase, the average fixed cost per guest drops.

| Monthly Rental Cost | Number of Guests | Average Cost per Guest |
|---|---|---|
| $500................. | 250 | $2.00 |
| $500................. | 500 | $1.00 |
| $500................. | 750 | $0.67 |
| $500................. | 1,000 | $0.50 |

As a general rule, *we caution against expressing fixed costs on an average per unit basis in internal reports because it creates the false impression that fixed costs are like variable costs and that total fixed costs actually change as the level of activity changes.*

For planning purposes, fixed costs can be viewed as either *committed* or *discretionary*. *****Committed fixed costs** represent organizational investments with a *multiyear* planning horizon that can't be significantly reduced even for short periods of time without making fundamental changes. Examples include investments in facilities and equipment, as well as real estate taxes, insurance expenses, and salaries of top management. Even if operations are interrupted or cut back, committed fixed costs remain largely unchanged in the short term because the costs of restoring them later are likely to be far greater than any short-run savings that might be realized. **Discretionary fixed costs** (often referred to as *managed fixed costs*) usually arise from *annual* decisions by management to spend on certain fixed cost items. Examples of discretionary fixed costs include advertising, research, public relations, management development programs, and internships for students. Discretionary fixed costs can be cut for short periods of time with minimal damage to the long-run goals of the organization.

Committed fixed cost.
long planning horizon (more than a yr.)
Once such cost have been incurred, the company is required to make future payments.

Discretionary
under a year. Cost arise from annual decisions of mgt. to spend specific fixed cost.

**HELPFUL HINT**

Students often assume that fixed costs expressed on a per unit basis behave like variable costs. This is not true! If the average fixed cost per unit is $5 at an activity level of 100 units, it means the total amount of the fixed cost is $500. If the activity level increases to 101 units it does not mean that fixed costs will increase by $5. The total fixed cost remains constant at $500 within the relevant range of activity.

## The Linearity Assumption and the Relevant Range

Management accountants ordinarily assume that costs are strictly linear; that is, the relation between cost on the one hand and activity on the other can be represented by a straight line. Economists point out that many costs are actually curvilinear; that is, the relation between cost and activity is a curve. Nevertheless, even if a cost is not strictly linear, it can be approximated within a narrow band of activity known as the *relevant range* by a straight line. The **relevant range** is the range of activity within which the assumption that cost behavior is strictly linear is reasonably valid. Outside of the relevant range, a fixed cost may no longer be strictly fixed or a variable cost may not be strictly variable. Managers should always keep in mind that assumptions made about cost behavior may be invalid if activity falls outside of the relevant range.

The concept of the relevant range is important in understanding fixed costs. For example, suppose the Mayo Clinic rents a machine for $20,000 per month that tests blood samples for the presence of leukemia cells. Furthermore, suppose that the capacity of the leukemia diagnostic machine is 3,000 tests per month. The assumption that the rent for the diagnostic machine is $20,000 per month is only valid within the relevant range of 0 to 3,000 tests per month. If the Mayo Clinic needed to test 5,000 blood samples per month, then it would need to rent another machine for an additional $20,000 per month. It would be difficult to rent half of a diagnostic machine; therefore, the step pattern depicted in Exhibit 1–3 is typical for such costs. This exhibit shows that the fixed rental expense is $20,000 for a relevant range of 0 to 3,000 tests. The fixed rental expense increases to $40,000 within the relevant range of 3,001 to 6,000 tests. The rental expense increases in discrete steps or increments of 3,000 tests, rather than increasing in a linear fashion per test.

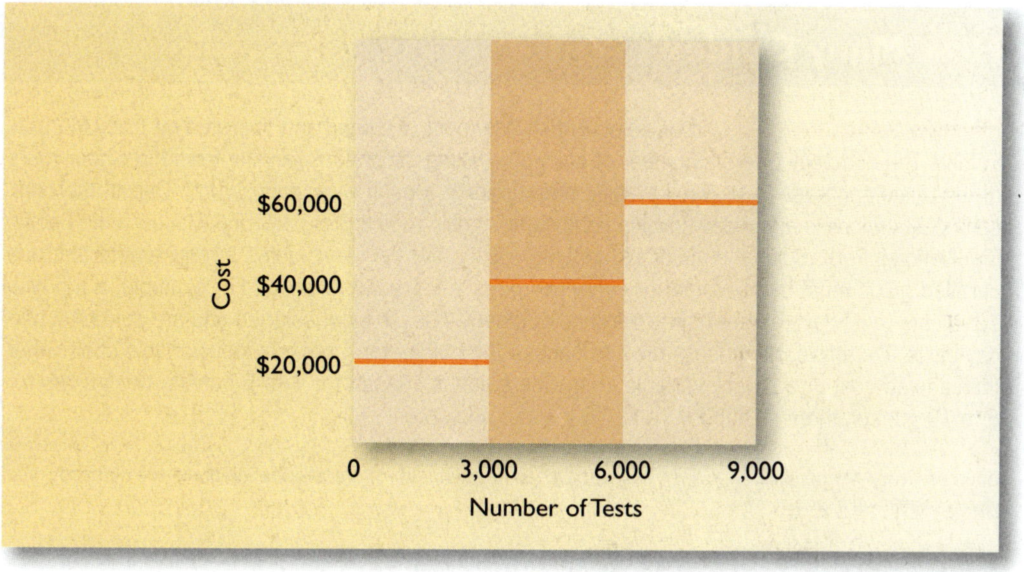


**EXHIBIT 1–3**
Fixed Costs and the Relevant Range

**EXHIBIT 1–4**
Summary of Variable and Fixed Cost Behavior

| | Behavior of the Cost (within the relevant range) | |
|---|---|---|
| **Cost** | **In Total** | **Per Unit** |
| Variable cost | Total variable cost increases and decreases in proportion to changes in the activity level. | Variable cost per unit remains constant. |
| Fixed cost | Total fixed cost is not affected by changes in the activity level within the relevant range. | Fixed cost per unit decreases as the activity level rises and increases as the activity level falls. |

This step-oriented cost behavior pattern can also be used to describe other costs, such as some labor costs. For example, salaried employee expenses can be characterized using a step pattern. Salaried employees are paid a fixed amount, such as $40,000 per year, for providing the capacity to work a prespecified amount of time, such as 40 hours per week for 50 weeks a year (= 2,000 hours per year). In this example, the total salaried employee expense is $40,000 within a relevant range of 0 to 2,000 hours of work. The total salaried employee expense increases to $80,000 (or two employees) if the organization's work requirements expand to a relevant range of 2,001 to 4,000 hours of work. Cost behavior patterns such as salaried employees are often called *step-variable costs*. Step-variable costs can often be adjusted quickly as conditions change. Furthermore, the width of the steps for step-variable costs is generally so narrow that these costs can be treated essentially as variable costs for most purposes. The width of the steps for fixed costs, on the other hand, is so wide that these costs should be treated as entirely fixed within the relevant range.

Exhibit 1–4 summarizes four key concepts related to variable and fixed costs. Study it carefully before reading further.

**CONCEPT CHECK**

2. Which of the following cost behavior assumptions is true? (You may select more than one answer.)
   a. Variable costs are constant if expressed on a per unit basis.
   b. Total variable costs increase as the level of activity increases.
   c. The average fixed cost per unit increases as the level of activity increases.
   d. Total fixed costs decrease as the level of activity decreases.

## IN BUSINESS

## How Many Guides?

**Majestic Ocean Kayaking**, of Ucluelet, British Columbia, is owned and operated by Tracy Morben-Eeftink. The company offers a number of guided kayaking excursions ranging from three-hour tours of the Ucluelet harbor to six-day kayaking and camping trips in Clayoquot Sound. One of the company's excursions is a four-day kayaking and camping trip to The Broken Group Islands in the Pacific Rim National Park. Special regulations apply to trips in the park—including a requirement that one certified guide must be assigned for every five guests or fraction thereof. For example, a trip with 12 guests must have at least three certified guides. Guides are not salaried and are paid on a per-day basis. Therefore, the cost to the company of the guides for a trip is a step-variable cost rather than a fixed cost or a strictly variable cost. One guide is needed for 1 to 5 guests, two guides for 6 to 10 guests, three guides for 11 to 15 guests, and so on.

Sources: Tracy Morben-Eeftink, owner, Majestic Ocean Kayaking. For more information about the company, see www.oceankayaking.com.

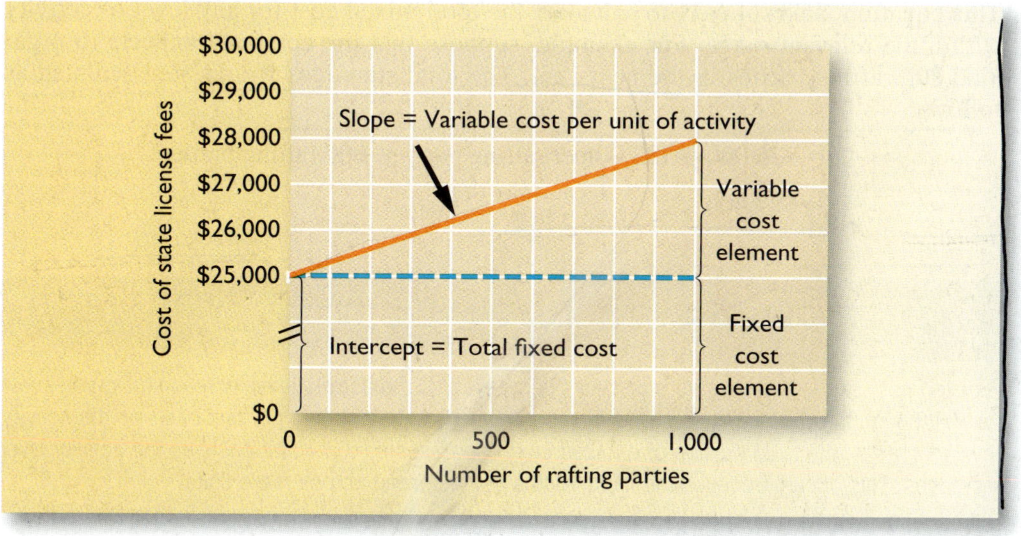


**EXHIBIT 1–5**
Mixed Cost Behavior

## Mixed Costs

A **mixed cost** contains both variable and fixed cost elements. Mixed costs are also known as semivariable costs. To continue the Nooksack Expeditions example, the company incurs a mixed cost called fees paid to the state. It includes a license fee of $25,000 per year plus $3 per rafting party paid to the state's Department of Natural Resources. If the company runs 1,000 rafting parties this year, then the total fees paid to the state would be $28,000, made up of $25,000 in fixed cost plus $3,000 in variable cost. Exhibit 1–5 depicts the behavior of this mixed cost.

Even if Nooksack fails to attract any customers, the company will still have to pay the license fee of $25,000. This is why the cost line in Exhibit 1–5 intersects the vertical cost axis at the $25,000 point. For each rafting party the company organizes, the total cost of the state fees will increase by $3. Therefore, the total cost line slopes upward as the variable cost of $3 per party is added to the fixed cost of $25,000 per year.

Because the mixed cost in Exhibit 1–5 is represented by a straight line, the following equation for a straight line can be used to express the relationship between a mixed cost and the level of activity:

$$Y = a + bX$$

In this equation,

$Y$ = The total mixed cost
$a$ = The total fixed cost (the vertical intercept of the line)
$b$ = The variable cost per unit of activity (the slope of the line)
$X$ = The level of activity

Because the variable cost per unit equals the slope of the straight line, the steeper the slope, the higher the variable cost per unit.

In the case of the state fees paid by Nooksack Expeditions, the equation is written as follows:

$$Y = \$25{,}000 + \$3.00X$$

- $Y$ ↑ Total mixed cost
- $25,000 ↑ Total fixed cost
- $3.00 ↑ Variable cost per unit of activity
- $X$ ↖ Activity level

This equation makes it easy to calculate the total mixed cost for any level of activity within the relevant range. For example, suppose that the company expects to organize 800 rafting parties in the next year. The total state fees would be calculated as follows:

$$Y = \$25{,}000 + (\$3.00 \text{ per rafting party} \times 800 \text{ rafting parties})$$
$$= \$27{,}400$$

HELPFUL HINT

A mixed cost expressed on a per unit basis decreases as the activity level increases. Do you know why? Although the variable portion of a mixed cost stays constant on a per unit basis as the activity level increases, the fixed portion of a mixed cost decreases on a per unit basis as the activity level increases. This occurs because the fixed cost is being spread across more units.

## THE ANALYSIS OF MIXED COSTS

Mixed costs are very common. For example, the overall cost of providing X-ray services to patients at the **Harvard Medical School Hospital** is a mixed cost. The costs of equipment depreciation and radiologists' and technicians' salaries are fixed, but the costs of X-ray film, power, and supplies are variable. At **Southwest Airlines**, maintenance costs are a mixed cost. The company incurs fixed costs for renting maintenance facilities and for keeping skilled mechanics on the payroll, but the costs of replacement parts, lubricating oils, tires, and so forth, are variable with respect to how often and how far the company's aircraft are flown.

The fixed portion of a mixed cost represents the minimum cost of having a service *ready and available* for use. The variable portion represents the cost incurred for *actual consumption* of the service, thus it varies in proportion to the amount of service actually consumed.

Managers can use a variety of methods to estimate the fixed and variable components of a mixed cost such as *account analysis,* the *engineering approach,* the *high-low method,* and *least-squares regression analysis.* In **account analysis,** an account is classified as either variable or fixed based on the analyst's prior knowledge of how the cost in the account behaves. For example, direct materials would be classified as variable and a building lease cost would be classified as fixed because of the nature of those costs. The **engineering approach** to cost analysis involves a detailed analysis of what cost behavior should be, based on an industrial engineer's evaluation of the production methods to be used, the materials specifications, labor requirements, equipment usage, production efficiency, power consumption, and so on.

The high-low and least-squares regression methods estimate the fixed and variable elements of a mixed cost by analyzing past records of cost and activity data. We will use an example from Brentline Hospital to illustrate the high-low method calculations and to compare the resulting high-low method cost estimates to those obtained using least-squares regression.

LEARNING OBJECTIVE 4

Analyze a mixed cost using a scattergraph plot and the high-low method.

### Diagnosing Cost Behavior with a Scattergraph Plot

Assume that Brentline Hospital is interested in predicting future monthly maintenance costs for budgeting purposes. The senior management team believes that maintenance cost is a mixed cost and that the variable portion of this cost is driven by the number of patient-days. Each day a patient is in the hospital counts as one patient-day.

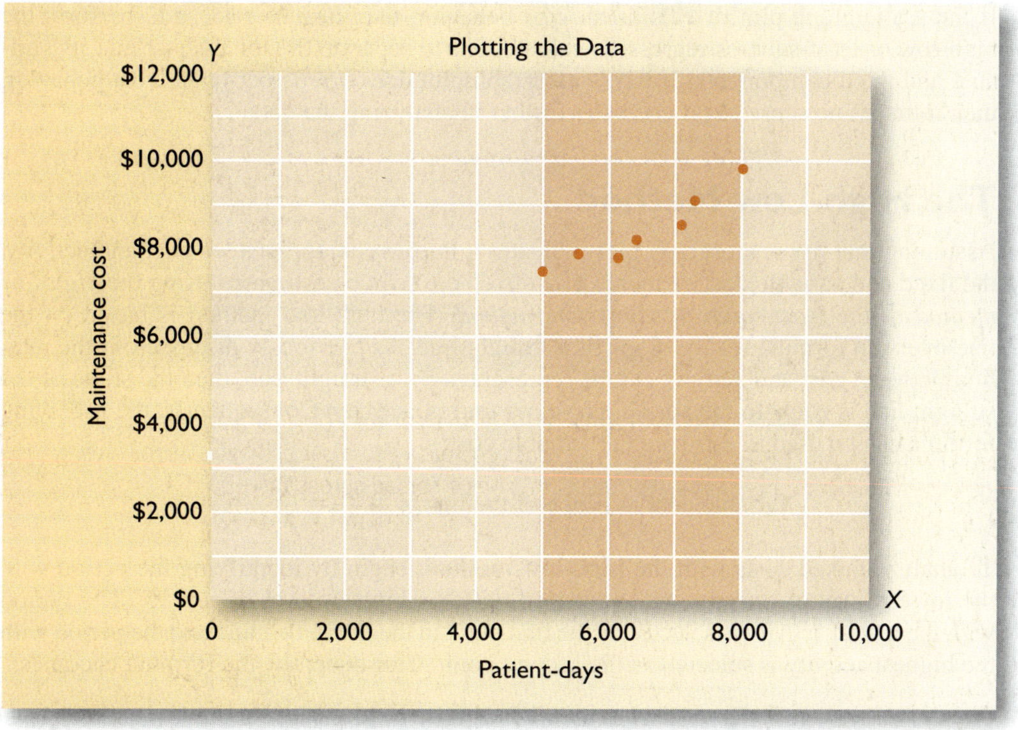


**EXHIBIT 1–6**
Scattergraph Method of Cost Analysis

The hospital's chief financial officer gathered the following data for the most recent seven-month period:

| Month | Activity Level: Patient-Days | Maintenance Cost Incurred |
|---|---|---|
| January............... | 5,600 | $7,900 |
| February............. | 7,100 | $8,500 |
| March.................. | 5,000 | $7,400 |
| April ................... | 6,500 | $8,200 |
| May..................... | 7,300 | $9,100 |
| June.................... | 8,000 | $9,800 |
| July ................... | 6,200 | $7,800 |

The first step in applying the high-low method or the least-squares regression method is to diagnose cost behavior with a scattergraph plot. The scattergraph plot of maintenance costs versus patient-days at Brentline Hospital is shown in Exhibit 1–6. Two things should be noted about this scattergraph:

1. The total maintenance cost, *Y*, is plotted on the vertical axis. Cost is known as the **dependent variable** because the amount of cost incurred during a period depends on the level of activity for the period. (That is, as the level of activity increases, total cost will also ordinarily increase.)
2. The activity, *X* (patient-days in this case), is plotted on the horizontal axis. Activity is known as the **independent variable** because it causes variations in the cost.

From the scattergraph plot, it is evident that maintenance costs do increase with the number of patient-days in an approximately *linear* fashion. In other words, the points lie more or less along a straight line that slopes upward and to the right. Cost behavior is considered **linear** whenever a straight line is a reasonable approximation for the relation between cost and activity.

Plotting the data on a scattergraph is an essential diagnostic step that should be performed before performing the high-low method or least-squares regression calculations.

If the scattergraph plot reveals linear cost behavior, then it makes sense to perform the high-low or least-squares regression calculations to separate the mixed cost into its variable and fixed components. If the scattergraph plot does not depict linear cost behavior, then it makes no sense to proceed any further in analyzing the data.

## The High-Low Method

Assuming that the scattergraph plot indicates a linear relation between cost and activity, the fixed and variable cost elements of a mixed cost can be estimated using the *high-low method* or the *least-squares regression method.* The high-low method is based on the rise-over-run formula for the slope of a straight line. As previously discussed, if the relation between cost and activity can be represented by a straight line, then the slope of the straight line is equal to the variable cost per unit of activity. Consequently, the following formula can be used to estimate the variable cost:

$$\text{Variable cost} = \text{Slope of the line} = \frac{\text{Rise}}{\text{Run}} = \frac{Y_2 - Y_1}{X_2 - X_1}$$

To analyze mixed costs with the **high-low method,** begin by identifying the period with the lowest level of activity and the period with the highest level of activity. The period with the lowest activity is selected as the first point in the above formula and the period with the highest activity is selected as the second point. Consequently, the formula becomes:

$$\text{Variable cost} = \frac{Y_2 - Y_1}{X_2 - X_1} = \frac{\text{Cost at the high activity level} - \text{Cost at the low activity level}}{\text{High activity level} - \text{Low activity level}}$$

or

$$\text{Variable cost} = \frac{\text{Change in cost}}{\text{Change in activity}}$$

Therefore, when the high-low method is used, the variable cost is estimated by dividing the difference in cost between the high and low levels of activity by the change in activity between those two points.

To return to the Brentline Hospital example, using the high-low method, we first identify the periods with the highest and lowest *activity*—in this case, June and March. We then use the activity and cost data from these two periods to estimate the variable cost component as follows:

| | Patient-Days | Maintenance Cost Incurred |
|---|---|---|
| High activity level (June) | 8,000 | $9,800 |
| Low activity level (March) | 5,000 | 7,400 |
| Change | 3,000 | $2,400 |

$$\text{Variable cost} = \frac{\text{Change in cost}}{\text{Change in activity}} = \frac{\$2{,}400}{3{,}000 \text{ patient-days}} = \$0.80 \text{ per patient-day}$$

Having determined that the variable maintenance cost is 80 cents per patient-day, we can now determine the amount of fixed cost. This is done by taking the total cost at *either* the high or the low activity level and deducting the variable cost element. In the computation below, total cost at the high activity level is used in computing the fixed cost element:

$$\begin{aligned}\text{Fixed cost element} &= \text{Total cost} - \text{Variable cost element}\\ &= \$9{,}800 - (\$0.80 \text{ per patient-day} \times 8{,}000 \text{ patient-days})\\ &= \$3{,}400\end{aligned}$$

**EXHIBIT 1–7**
High-Low Method of Cost Analysis

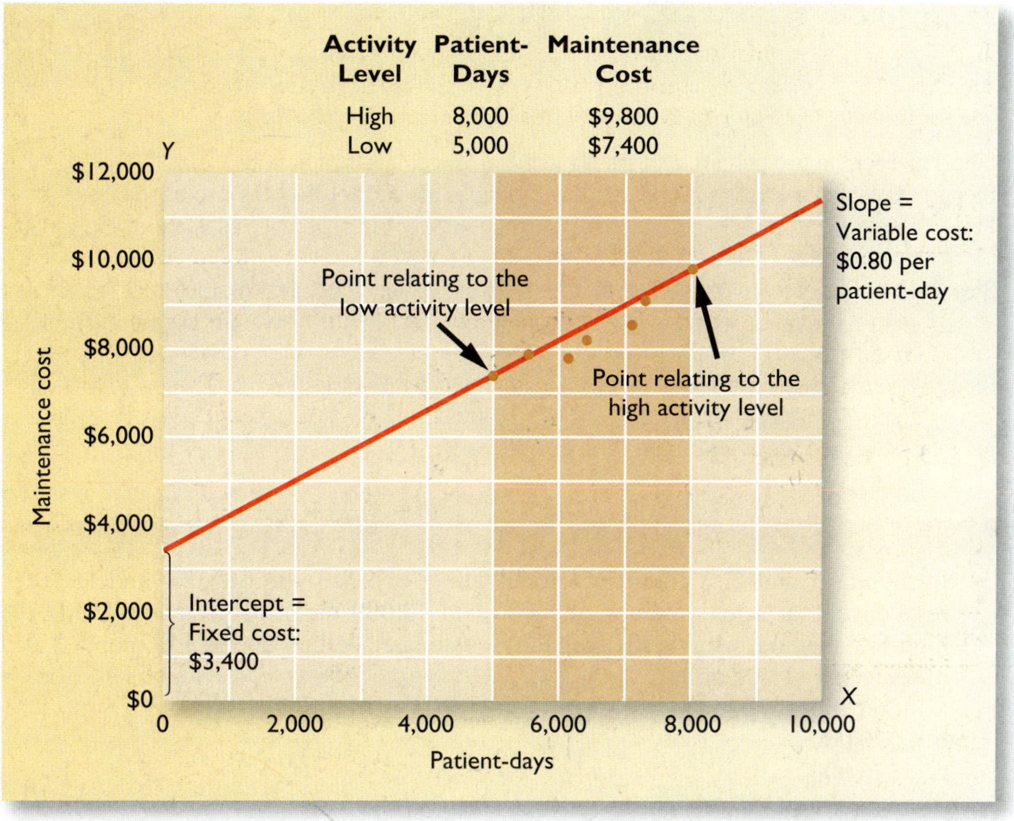


Both the variable and fixed cost elements have now been isolated. The cost of maintenance can be expressed as $3,400 per month plus 80 cents per patient-day or as:

$$Y = \$3{,}400 + \$0.80X$$

↑ Total maintenance cost (Y) ↑ Total patient-days (X)

The data used in this illustration are shown graphically in Exhibit 1–7. Notice that a straight line has been drawn through the points corresponding to the low and high levels of activity. In essence, that is what the high-low method does—it draws a straight line through those two points.

Sometimes the high and low levels of activity don't coincide with the high and low amounts of cost. For example, the period that has the highest level of activity may not have the highest amount of cost. Nevertheless, the costs at the highest and lowest levels of *activity* are always used to analyze a mixed cost under the high-low method. The reason is that the analyst would like to use data that reflect the greatest possible variation in activity.

The high-low method is very simple to apply, but it suffers from a major (and sometimes critical) defect—it utilizes only two data points. Generally, two data points are not enough to produce accurate results. Additionally, the periods with the highest and lowest activity tend to be unusual. A cost formula that is estimated solely using data from these unusual periods may misrepresent the true cost behavior during normal periods. Such a distortion is evident in Exhibit 1–7. The straight line should probably be shifted down somewhat so that it is closer to more of the data points. For these reasons, least-squares regression will generally be more accurate than the high-low method.

- Two data points not enough to produce accurate results
- Cost behavior can be misrepresented during unusual period as oppose to normal periods.

## HELPFUL HINT

Use the following five-step process to perform high-low method calculations:

Step 1: Select the two periods with the highest and lowest levels of activity.
Step 2: Compute the change in cost and the change in activity between the two periods.
Step 3: Divide the change in cost by the change in activity to derive your estimate of the variable cost per unit.
Step 4: Multiply the low (or high) level of activity by the variable cost per unit. Subtract this amount from the total cost at the low (or high) level of activity to derive the fixed portion of the mixed cost.
Step 5: Use the equation $Y = a + bx$ to estimate the total mixed cost for any level of activity within the relevant range.

## CONCEPT CHECK

3. In months 1 and 2, a company's total selling expense was $64,000 and $80,000, respectively, at sales volumes of 8,000 and 12,000 units, respectively. Using the high-low method, what is the company's estimated selling expense in month 3 if it plans to sell 11,000 units?
   a. $66,000
   b. $70,000
   c. $76,000
   d. $78,000

## The Least-Squares Regression Method

The **least-squares regression method,** unlike the high-low method, uses all of the data to separate a mixed cost into its fixed and variable components. A *regression line* of the form $Y = a + bX$ is fitted to the data, where $a$ represents the total fixed cost and $b$ represents the variable cost per unit of activity. The basic idea underlying the least-squares regression method is illustrated in Exhibit 1–8 using hypothetical data points.

**EXHIBIT 1–8**
The Concept of Least-Squares Regression

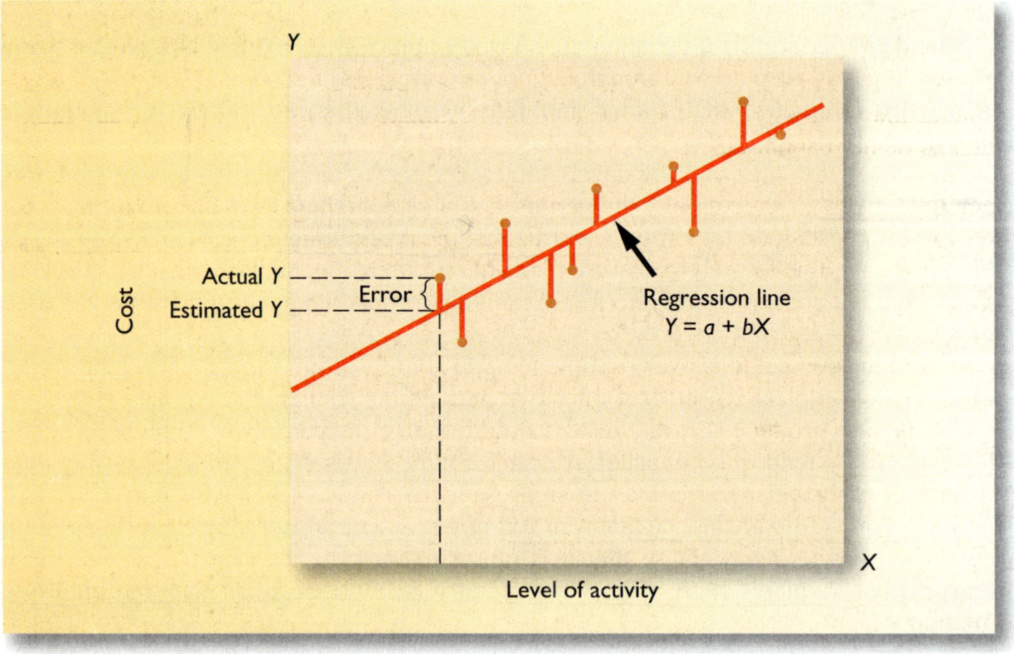

Notice from the exhibit that the deviations from the plotted points to the regression line are measured vertically on the graph. These vertical deviations are called the regression errors. There is nothing mysterious about the least-squares regression method. It simply computes the regression line that minimizes the sum of these squared errors. The formulas that accomplish this are fairly complex and involve numerous calculations, but the principle is simple.

= regression errors

Fortunately, computers are adept at carrying out the computations required by the least-squares regression formulas. The data—the observed values of $X$ and $Y$—are entered into the computer, and software does the rest. In the case of the Brentline Hospital maintenance cost data, a statistical software package on a personal computer can calculate the following least-squares regression estimates of the total fixed cost ($a$) and the variable cost per unit of activity ($b$):

$$a = \$3{,}431$$

$$b = \$0.759$$

Therefore, using the least-squares regression method, the fixed element of the maintenance cost is $3,431 per month and the variable portion is 75.9 cents per patient-day.

In terms of the linear equation $Y = a + bX$, the cost formula can be written as

$$Y = \$3{,}431 + \$0.759X$$

where activity ($X$) is expressed in patient-days.

Least-squares regression analysis generally provides more accurate cost estimates than the high-low method because, rather than relying on just two data points, it uses all of the data points to fit a line that minimizes the sum of the squared errors. The table below compares Brentline Hospital's cost estimates using the high-low method and the least-squares regression method:

| | High-Low Method | Least-Squares Regression Method |
|---|---|---|
| Variable cost estimate per patient-day............... | $0.800 | $0.759 |
| Fixed cost estimate per month.......................... | $3,400 | $3,431 |

When Brentline uses the least-squares regression method to create a straight line that minimizes the sum of the squared errors, it results in a $Y$-intercept that is $31 higher than the $Y$-intercept derived using the high-low method. It also decreases the slope of the straight line resulting in a lower variable cost estimate of $0.759 per patient-day rather than $0.80 per patient-day as derived using the high-low method.

## The Zipcar Comes to College Campuses

IN BUSINESS

**Zipcar** is a car sharing service based in Cambridge, Massachusetts. The company serves 13 cities and 120 university campuses. Members pay a $50 annual fee plus $7 an hour to rent a car. They can use their iPhones to rent a car, locate it in the nearest Zipcar parking lot, unlock it using an access code, and drive it off the lot. This mixed cost arrangement is attractive to customers who need a car infrequently and wish to avoid the large cash outlay that comes with buying or leasing a vehicle.

Source: Jefferson Graham, "An iPhone Gets Zipcar Drivers on Their Way," *USA Today*, September 30, 2009, p. 3B.

# TRADITIONAL AND CONTRIBUTION FORMAT INCOME STATEMENTS

**LEARNING OBJECTIVE 5**

Prepare income statements for a merchandising company using the traditional and contribution formats.

In this section of the chapter, we discuss how to prepare traditional and contribution format income statements for a merchandising company.[2] Merchandising companies do not manufacture the products that they sell to customers. For example, **Walmart** is a merchandising company because it buys finished products from manufacturers and then resells them to end consumers.

## The Traditional Format Income Statement

Traditional income statements are prepared primarily for external reporting purposes. The left-hand side of Exhibit 1–9 shows a traditional income statement format for merchandising companies. This type of income statement organizes costs into two categories—cost of goods sold and selling and administrative expenses. Sales minus cost of goods sold equals the *gross margin.* The gross margin minus selling and administrative expenses equals net operating income.

The cost of goods sold reports the *product costs* attached to the merchandise sold during the period. The selling and administrative expenses report all *period costs* that have been expensed as incurred. The cost of goods sold for a merchandising company can be computed directly by multiplying the number of units sold by their unit cost or indirectly using the equation below:

$$\text{Cost of goods sold} = \text{Beginning merchandise inventory} + \text{Purchases} - \text{Ending merchandise inventory}$$

For example, let's assume that the company depicted in Exhibit 1–9 purchased $3,000 of merchandise inventory during the period and had beginning and ending merchandise

**EXHIBIT 1–9** Comparing Traditional and Contribution Format Income Statements for Merchandising Companies (all numbers are given)

**Traditional Format**

| | | |
|---|---|---|
| Sales | | $12,000 |
| Cost of goods sold* | | 6,000 |
| Gross margin | | 6,000 |
| Selling and administrative expenses: | | |
| Selling | $3,100 | |
| Administrative | 1,900 | 5,000 |
| Net operating income | | $ 1,000 |

**Contribution Format**

| | | |
|---|---|---|
| Sales | | $12,000 |
| Variable expenses: | | |
| Cost of goods sold | $6,000 | |
| Variable selling | 600 | |
| Variable administrative | 400 | 7,000 |
| Contribution margin | | 5,000 |
| Fixed expenses: | | |
| Fixed selling | 2,500 | |
| Fixed administrative | 1,500 | 4,000 |
| Net operating income | | $ 1,000 |

*For a manufacturing company, the cost of goods sold would include some variable costs, such as direct materials, direct labor, and variable overhead, and some fixed costs, such as fixed manufacturing overhead. Income statement formats for manufacturing companies will be explored in greater detail in a subsequent chapter.

[2] Subsequent chapters discuss the cost classifications used on the financial statements of manufacturing companies.

inventory balances of $7,000 and $4,000, respectively. The equation above could be used to compute the cost of goods sold as follows:

$$\begin{aligned}\text{Cost of goods sold} &= \text{Beginning merchandise inventory} + \text{Purchases} - \text{Ending merchandise inventory}\\ &= \$7{,}000 + \$3{,}000 - \$4{,}000\\ &= \$6{,}000\end{aligned}$$

Although the traditional income statement is useful for external reporting purposes, it has serious limitations when used for internal purposes. It does not distinguish between fixed and variable costs. For example, under the heading "Selling and administrative expenses," both variable administrative costs ($400) and fixed administrative costs ($1,500) are lumped together ($1,900). Internally, managers need cost data organized by cost behavior to aid in planning, controlling, and decision making. The contribution format income statement has been developed in response to these needs.

## The Contribution Format Income Statement

The crucial distinction between fixed and variable costs is at the heart of the **contribution approach** to constructing income statements. The unique thing about the contribution approach is that it provides managers with an income statement that clearly distinguishes between fixed and variable costs and therefore aids planning, controlling, and decision making. The right-hand side of Exhibit 1–9 shows a contribution format income statement for merchandising companies.

The contribution approach separates costs into fixed and variable categories, first deducting variable expenses from sales to obtain the *contribution margin*. For a merchandising company, cost of goods sold is a variable cost that gets included in the "Variable expenses" portion of the contribution format income statement. The **contribution margin** is the amount remaining from sales revenues after variable expenses have been deducted. This amount *contributes* toward covering fixed expenses and then toward profits for the period.

The contribution format income statement is used as an internal planning and decision-making tool. Its emphasis on cost behavior aids cost-volume-profit analysis (such as we shall be doing in a subsequent chapter), management performance appraisals, and budgeting. Moreover, the contribution approach helps managers organize data pertinent to numerous decisions such as product-line analysis, pricing, use of scarce resources, and make or buy analysis. All of these topics are covered in later chapters.

# COST CLASSIFICATIONS FOR ASSIGNING COSTS TO COST OBJECTS

**LEARNING OBJECTIVE 6**

Understand the differences between direct and indirect costs.

Costs are assigned to cost objects for a variety of purposes including pricing, preparing profitability studies, and controlling spending. A **cost object** is anything for which cost data are desired—including products, customers, jobs, and organizational subunits. For purposes of assigning costs to cost objects, costs are classified as either *direct* or *indirect*.

## Direct Cost

A **direct cost** is a cost that can be easily and conveniently traced to a specified cost object. The concept of direct cost extends beyond just direct materials and direct labor. For example, if **Reebok** is assigning costs to its various regional and national sales offices, then the salary of the sales manager in its Tokyo office would be a direct cost of that office.

## Indirect Cost

An **indirect cost** is a cost that cannot be easily and conveniently traced to a specified cost object. For example, a **Campbell Soup** factory may produce dozens of varieties of canned soups. The factory manager's salary would be an indirect cost of a particular variety such as chicken noodle soup. The reason is that the factory manager's salary is incurred as a consequence of running the entire factory—it is not incurred to produce any one soup variety. *To be traced to a cost object such as a particular product, the cost must be caused by the cost object.* The factory manager's salary is called a *common cost* of producing the various products of the factory. A **common cost** is a cost that is incurred to support a number of cost objects but cannot be traced to them individually. A common cost is a type of indirect cost.

A particular cost may be direct or indirect, depending on the cost object. While the Campbell Soup factory manager's salary is an *indirect* cost of manufacturing chicken noodle soup, it is a *direct* cost of the manufacturing division. In the first case, the cost object is chicken noodle soup. In the second case, the cost object is the entire manufacturing division.

# COST CLASSIFICATIONS FOR DECISION MAKING

**LEARNING OBJECTIVE 7**

Understand cost classifications used in making decisions: differential costs, opportunity costs, and sunk costs.

Costs are an important feature of many business decisions. In making decisions, it is essential to have a firm grasp of the concepts *differential cost, opportunity cost,* and *sunk cost.*

## Differential Cost and Revenue

Decisions involve choosing between alternatives. In business decisions, each alternative will have costs and benefits that must be compared to the costs and benefits of the other available alternatives. A difference in costs between any two alternatives is known as a **differential cost.** A difference in revenues between any two alternatives is known as **differential revenue.**

A differential cost is also known as an **incremental cost,** although technically an incremental cost should refer only to an increase in cost from one alternative to another; decreases in cost should be referred to as *decremental costs.* Differential cost is a broader term, encompassing both cost increases (incremental costs) and cost decreases (decremental costs) between alternatives.

The accountant's differential cost concept can be compared to the economist's marginal cost concept. In speaking of changes in cost and revenue, the economist uses the terms *marginal cost* and *marginal revenue.* The revenue that can be obtained from selling one more unit of product is called marginal revenue, and the cost involved in producing one more unit of product is called marginal cost. The economist's marginal concept is basically the same as the accountant's differential concept applied to a single unit of output.

Differential costs can be either fixed or variable. To illustrate, assume that **Nature Way Cosmetics, Inc.**, is thinking about changing its marketing method from distribution through retailers to distribution by a network of neighborhood sales representatives. Present costs and revenues are compared to projected costs and revenues in the following table:

| | Retailer Distribution (present) | Sales Representatives (proposed) | Differential Costs and Revenues |
|---|---|---|---|
| Revenues (Variable) | $700,000 | $800,000 | $100,000 |
| Cost of goods sold (Variable) | 350,000 | 400,000 | 50,000 |
| Advertising (Fixed) | 80,000 | 45,000 | (35,000) |
| Commissions (Variable) | 0 | 40,000 | 40,000 |
| Warehouse depreciation (Fixed) | 50,000 | 80,000 | 30,000 |
| Other expenses (Fixed) | 60,000 | 60,000 | 0 |
| Total expenses | 540,000 | 625,000 | 85,000 |
| Net operating income | $160,000 | $175,000 | $ 15,000 |

According to the analysis on the previous page, the differential revenue is $100,000 and the differential costs total $85,000, leaving a positive differential net operating income of $15,000 under the proposed marketing plan.

The decision of whether Nature Way Cosmetics should stay with the present retail distribution or switch to sales representatives could be made on the basis of the net operating incomes of the two alternatives. The net operating income under the present distribution method is $160,000, whereas the net operating income with sales representatives is estimated to be $175,000. Therefore, using sales representatives is preferred because it would result in $15,000 higher net operating income. Note that we would have arrived at exactly the same conclusion by simply focusing on the differential revenues, differential costs, and differential net operating income, which also show a $15,000 advantage for sales representatives.

In general, only the differences between alternatives are relevant in decisions. Those items that are the same under all alternatives and that are not affected by the decision can be ignored. For example, in the Nature Way Cosmetics example, the "Other expenses" category, which is $60,000 under both alternatives, can be ignored because it has no effect on the decision. If it were removed from the calculations, the sales representatives would still be preferred by $15,000. This is an extremely important principle in management accounting that we will revisit in later chapters.

## Opportunity Cost

**Opportunity cost** is the potential benefit that is given up when one alternative is selected over another. To illustrate this important concept, consider the following examples:

**Example 1** Vicki has a part-time job that pays $200 per week while attending college. She would like to spend a week at the beach during spring break, and her employer has agreed to give her the time off, but without pay. The $200 in lost wages would be an opportunity cost of taking the week off to be at the beach.

**Example 2** Suppose that Neiman Marcus is considering investing a large sum of money in land that may be a site for a future store. Rather than invest the funds in land, the company could invest the funds in high-grade securities. The opportunity cost of buying the land is the investment income that could have been realized by purchasing the securities instead.

**Example 3** Steve is employed by a company that pays him a salary of $38,000 per year. He is thinking about leaving the company and returning to school. Because returning to school would require that he give up his $38,000 salary, the forgone salary would be an opportunity cost of seeking further education.

Opportunity costs are not usually found in accounting records, but they are costs that must be explicitly considered in every decision a manager makes. Virtually every alternative involves an opportunity cost.

### Your Decision to Attend Class

DECISION POINT

When you make the decision to attend class on a particular day, what are the opportunity costs that are inherent in that decision?

## Sunk Cost

A **sunk cost** is a cost *that has already been incurred* and that cannot be changed by any decision made now or in the future. Because sunk costs cannot be changed by any decision, they are not differential costs. And because only differential costs are relevant in a decision, sunk costs should always be ignored.

**EXHIBIT 1–10**
Summary of Cost Classifications

| Purpose of Cost Classification | Cost Classifications |
|---|---|
| Preparing external financial statements | • Product costs (inventoriable)<br>  • Direct materials<br>  • Direct labor<br>  • Manufacturing overhead<br>• Period costs (expensed)<br>  • Nonmanufacturing costs<br>    • Selling costs<br>    • Administrative costs |
| Predicting cost behavior in response to changes in activity | • Variable cost (proportional to activity)<br>• Fixed cost (constant in total)<br>• Mixed cost (has variable and fixed elements) |
| Assigning costs to cost objects (e.g., departments or products) | • Direct cost (can be easily traced)<br>• Indirect cost (cannot be easily traced) |
| Making decisions | • Differential cost (differs between alternatives)<br>• Sunk cost (past cost not affected by a decision)<br>• Opportunity cost (forgone benefit) |

To illustrate a sunk cost, assume that a company paid $50,000 several years ago for a special-purpose machine. The machine was used to make a product that is now obsolete and is no longer being sold. Even though in hindsight purchasing the machine may have been unwise, the $50,000 cost has already been incurred and cannot be undone. And it would be folly to continue making the obsolete product in a misguided attempt to "recover" the original cost of the machine. In short, the $50,000 originally paid for the machine is a sunk cost that should be ignored in current decisions.

Exhibit 1–10 summarizes the types of cost classifications that we discussed in this chapter. Refer to this exhibit to keep the big picture in mind, which is that *different costs for different purposes* is a critically important concept in management accounting. This chapter discussed four main cost classifications that managers can use for different purposes within organizations.

**CONCEPT CHECK**

4. Which of the following statements is true? (You may select more than one answer.)
   a. A common cost is one type of direct cost.
   b. A sunk cost is usually a differential cost.
   c. Opportunity costs are not usually recorded in the accounts of an organization.
   d. A particular cost may be direct or indirect depending on the cost object.

## SUMMARY

**LO1 Identify and give examples of each of the three basic manufacturing cost categories.**
Manufacturing costs consist of two categories of costs that can be conveniently and directly traced to units of product—direct materials and direct labor—and one category that cannot be conveniently traced to units of product—manufacturing overhead.

**LO2 Distinguish between product costs and period costs and give examples of each.**
For purposes of valuing inventories and determining expenses for the balance sheet and income statement, costs are classified as either product costs or period costs. Product costs are assigned to inventories and are considered assets until the products are sold. A product cost becomes an expense—cost of goods sold—only when the product is sold. In contrast, period costs are taken directly to the income statement as expenses in the period in which they are incurred.

In a merchandising company, product cost is whatever the company paid for its merchandise. For external financial reports in a manufacturing company, product costs consist of all manufacturing costs. In both kinds of companies, selling and administrative costs are considered to be period costs and are expensed as incurred.

**LO3 Understand cost behavior patterns including variable costs, fixed costs, and mixed costs.**
For purposes of predicting how costs will react to changes in activity, costs are classified into three categories—variable, fixed, and mixed. Variable costs, in total, are strictly proportional to activity. The variable cost per unit is constant. Fixed costs, in total, remain the same as the activity level changes within the relevant range. The average fixed cost per unit decreases as the activity level increases. Mixed costs consist of variable and fixed elements and can be expressed in equation form as $Y = a + bX$, where $X$ is the activity, $Y$ is the total cost, $a$ is the fixed cost element, and $b$ is the variable cost per unit of activity.

**LO4 Analyze a mixed cost using a scattergraph plot and the high-low method.**
A scattergraph plots activity on the horizontal, $X$, axis and total cost on the vertical, $Y$, axis. If the relation between cost and activity appears to be linear, then the variable and fixed components of a mixed cost can be estimated using the high-low method or least-squares regression method.

To use the high-low method, first identify the periods with the highest and lowest levels of activity. Second, estimate the variable cost element by dividing the change in total cost by the change in activity for these two periods. Third, estimate the fixed cost element by subtracting the total variable cost from the total cost at either the highest or lowest level of activity.

The high-low method relies on only two, often unusual, data points rather than all of the available data and therefore may provide misleading estimates of variable and fixed costs.

**LO5 Prepare income statements for a merchandising company using the traditional and contribution formats.**
The traditional income statement format is used primarily for external reporting purposes. It organizes costs using product and period cost classifications. The contribution format income statement aids decision making because it organizes costs using variable and fixed cost classifications. The contribution margin is the amount remaining from sales revenues after variable expenses have been deducted. This amount contributes toward covering fixed expenses and then toward profits for the period.

**LO6 Understand the differences between direct and indirect costs.**
A direct cost such as direct materials is a cost that can be easily and conveniently traced to a cost object. An indirect cost is a cost that cannot be easily and conveniently traced to a cost object. For example, the salary of the administrator of a hospital is an indirect cost of serving a particular patient.

**LO7 Understand cost classifications used in making decisions: differential costs, opportunity costs, and sunk costs.**
The concepts of differential cost and revenue, opportunity cost, and sunk cost are vitally important for purposes of making decisions. Differential costs and revenues refer to the costs and revenues that differ between alternatives. Opportunity cost is the benefit that is forgone when one alternative is selected over another. Sunk cost is a cost that occurred in the past and cannot be altered. Differential costs and opportunity costs are relevant in decisions and should be carefully considered. Sunk costs are always irrelevant in decisions and should be ignored.

The various cost classifications discussed in this chapter are different ways of looking at costs. A particular cost, such as the cost of cheese in a taco served at Taco Bell, can be a manufacturing cost, a product cost, a variable cost, a direct cost, and a differential cost—all at the same time.

Taco Bell essentially manufactures fast food. Therefore the cost of the cheese in a taco would be considered a manufacturing cost as well as a product cost. In addition, the cost of cheese would be considered variable with respect to the number of tacos served and would be a direct cost of serving tacos. Finally, the cost of the cheese in a taco would be considered a differential cost of the taco.

## GUIDANCE ANSWERS TO DECISION POINT

**Your Decision to Attend Class (p. 41)**

Every alternative involves an opportunity cost. Think about what you could be doing instead of attending class.

- You could have been working at a part-time job; you could quantify that cost by multiplying your pay rate by the time you spend preparing for and attending class.
- You could have spent the time studying for another class; the opportunity cost could be measured by the improvement in the grade that would result from spending more time on the other class.
- You could have slept in or taken a nap; depending on your level of sleep deprivation, this opportunity cost might be priceless.

## GUIDANCE ANSWERS TO CONCEPT CHECKS

1. **Choices b and d.** Product costs attach to units of production and are expensed on the income statement when the units are sold. Conversion costs do not include direct materials.
2. **Choices a and b.** The average fixed cost per unit decreases, rather than increases, as the level of activity increases. Total fixed costs do not change as the level of activity decreases (within the relevant range).
3. **Choice c.** The change in cost of $16,000 divided by the change in activity of 4,000 units provides an estimated variable cost of $4 per unit. Using the low-level of activity, $64,000 = $a$ + ($4 per unit)(8,000 units). Solving for $a$ provides an estimated fixed cost of $32,000. At an activity level of 11,000 units, $Y$ = $32,000 + ($4 per unit)(11,000 units). Solving for $Y$ provides an estimated selling expense of $76,000.
4. **Choices c and d.** A common cost is one type of indirect cost, rather than direct cost. A sunk cost is not a differential cost.

## REVIEW PROBLEM 1: COST TERMS

Many new cost terms have been introduced in this chapter. It will take you some time to learn what each term means and how to properly classify costs in an organization. Consider the following example: Chippen Corporation manufactures furniture, including tables. Selected costs are given below:

1. The tables are made of wood that costs $100 per table.
2. The tables are assembled by workers, at a wage cost of $40 per table.
3. Workers making the tables are supervised by a factory supervisor who is paid $38,000 per year.
4. Electrical costs are $2 per machine-hour. Four machine-hours are required to produce a table.
5. The depreciation on the machines used to make the tables totals $10,000 per year. The machines have no resale value and do not wear out through use.
6. The salary of the president of the company is $100,000 per year.
7. The company spends $250,000 per year to advertise its products.
8. Salespersons are paid a commission of $30 for each table sold.
9. Instead of producing the tables, the company could rent its factory space for $50,000 per year.

***Required:***

Classify these costs according to the various cost terms used in the chapter. *Carefully study the classification of each cost.* If you don't understand why a particular cost is classified the way it is, reread the section of the chapter discussing the particular cost term. The terms *variable cost* and *fixed cost* refer to how costs behave with respect to the number of tables produced in a year.

**Solution to Review Problem 1**

| | Variable Cost | Fixed Cost | Period (Selling and Administrative) Cost | Product Cost: Direct Materials | Product Cost: Direct Labor | Product Cost: Manufacturing Overhead | Sunk Cost | Opportunity Cost |
|---|---|---|---|---|---|---|---|---|
| 1. Wood used in a table ($100 per table) | X | | | X | | | | |
| 2. Labor cost to assemble a table ($40 per table) | X | | | | X | | | |
| 3. Salary of the factory supervisor ($38,000 per year) | | X | | | | X | | |
| 4. Cost of electricity to produce tables ($2 per machine-hour) | X | | | | | X | | |
| 5. Depreciation of machines used to produce tables ($10,000 per year) | | X | | | | X | X* | |
| 6. Salary of the company president ($100,000 per year) | | X | X | | | | | |
| 7. Advertising expense ($250,000 per year) | | X | X | | | | | |
| 8. Commissions paid to salespersons ($30 per table sold) | X | | X | | | | | |
| 9. Rental income forgone on factory space | | | | | | | | X† |

*This is a sunk cost because the outlay for the equipment was made in a previous period.

†This is an opportunity cost because it represents the potential benefit that is lost or sacrificed as a result of using the factory space to produce tables. Opportunity cost is a special category of cost that is not ordinarily recorded in an organization's accounting records. To avoid possible confusion with other costs, we will not attempt to classify this cost in any other way except as an opportunity cost.

## REVIEW PROBLEM 2: HIGH-LOW METHOD

The administrator of Azalea Hills Hospital would like a cost formula linking the administrative costs involved in admitting patients to the number of patients admitted during a month. The Admitting Department's costs and the number of patients admitted during the immediately preceding eight months are given in the following table:

| Month | Number of Patients Admitted | Admitting Department Costs |
|---|---|---|
| May | 1,800 | $14,700 |
| June | 1,900 | $15,200 |
| July | 1,700 | $13,700 |
| August | 1,600 | $14,000 |
| September | 1,500 | $14,300 |
| October | 1,300 | $13,100 |
| November | 1,100 | $12,800 |
| December | 1,500 | $14,600 |

***Required:***

1. Use the high-low method to estimate the fixed and variable components of admitting costs.
2. Express the fixed and variable components of admitting costs as a cost formula in the form $Y = a + bX$.

**Solution to Review Problem 2**

1. The first step in the high-low method is to identify the periods of the lowest and highest activity. Those periods are November (1,100 patients admitted) and June (1,900 patients admitted).

   The second step is to compute the variable cost per unit using those two data points:

| Month | Number of Patients Admitted | Admitting Department Costs |
|---|---|---|
| High activity level (June) | 1,900 | $15,200 |
| Low activity level (November) | 1,100 | 12,800 |
| Change | 800 | $ 2,400 |

$$\text{Variable cost} = \frac{\text{Change in cost}}{\text{Change in activity}} = \frac{\$2,400}{800 \text{ patients admitted}} = \$3 \text{ per patient admitted}$$

   The third step is to compute the fixed cost element by deducting the variable cost element from the total cost at either the high or low activity. In the computation below, the high point of activity is used:

$$\begin{aligned}\text{Fixed cost element} &= \text{Total cost} - \text{Variable cost element}\\ &= \$15,200 - (\$3 \text{ per patient admitted} \times 1,900 \text{ patients admitted})\\ &= \$9,500\end{aligned}$$

2. The cost formula is $Y = \$9,500 + \$3X$.

## GLOSSARY

**Account analysis** A method for analyzing cost behavior in which an account is classified as either variable or fixed based on the analyst's prior knowledge of how the cost in the account behaves. (p. 32)

**Activity base** A measure of whatever causes the incurrence of a variable cost. For example, the total cost of X-ray film in a hospital will increase as the number of X-rays taken increases. Therefore, the number of X-rays is the activity base that explains the total cost of X-ray film. (p. 26)

**Administrative costs** All executive, organizational, and clerical costs associated with the general management of an organization rather than with manufacturing or selling. (p. 23)

**Committed fixed costs** Investments in facilities, equipment, and basic organizational structure that can't be significantly reduced even for short periods of time without making fundamental changes. (p. 28)

**Common cost** A cost that is incurred to support a number of cost objects but that cannot be traced to them individually. For example, the wage cost of the pilot of a 747 airliner is a common cost of all of the passengers on the aircraft. Without the pilot, there would be no flight and no passengers. But no part of the pilot's wage is caused by any one passenger taking the flight. (p. 40)

**Contribution approach** An income statement format that organizes costs by their behavior. Costs are separated into variable and fixed categories rather than being separated into product and period costs for external reporting purposes. (p. 39)

**Contribution margin** The amount remaining from sales revenues after all variable expenses have been deducted. (p. 39)

**Conversion cost** Direct labor cost plus manufacturing overhead cost. (p. 24)

**Cost behavior** The way in which a cost reacts to changes in the level of activity. (p. 26)

**Cost object** Anything for which cost data are desired. Examples of cost objects are products, customers, jobs, and parts of the organization such as departments or divisions. (p. 39)

**Cost structure** The relative proportion of fixed, variable, and mixed costs in an organization. (p. 26)

**Dependent variable** A variable that responds to some causal factor; total cost is the dependent variable, as represented by the letter $Y$, in the equation $Y = a + bX$. (p. 33)

**Differential cost** A difference in cost between two alternatives. Also see *Incremental cost.* (p. 40)

**Differential revenue** The difference in revenue between two alternatives. (p. 40)

**Direct cost** A cost that can be easily and conveniently traced to a specified cost object. (p. 39)

**Direct labor** Factory labor costs that can be easily traced to individual units of product. Also called *touch labor.* (p. 22)

**Direct materials** Materials that become an integral part of a finished product and whose costs can be conveniently traced to it. (p. 22)
**Discretionary fixed costs** Those fixed costs that arise from annual decisions by management to spend on certain fixed cost items, such as advertising and research. (p. 28)
**Engineering approach** A detailed analysis of cost behavior based on an industrial engineer's evaluation of the inputs that are required to carry out a particular activity and of the prices of those inputs. (p. 32)
**Fixed cost** A cost that remains constant, in total, regardless of changes in the level of activity within the relevant range. If a fixed cost is expressed on a per unit basis, it varies inversely with the level of activity. (p. 27)
**High-low method** A method of separating a mixed cost into its fixed and variable elements by analyzing the change in cost between the high and low activity levels. (p. 34)
**Incremental cost** An increase in cost between two alternatives. Also see *Differential cost.* (p. 40)
**Independent variable** A variable that acts as a causal factor; activity is the independent variable, as represented by the letter $X$, in the equation $Y = a + bX$. (p. 33)
**Indirect cost** A cost that cannot be easily and conveniently traced to a specified cost object. (p. 40)
**Indirect labor** The labor costs of janitors, supervisors, materials handlers, and other factory workers that cannot be conveniently traced to particular products. (p. 22)
**Indirect materials** Small items of material such as glue and nails that may be an integral part of a finished product, but whose costs cannot be easily or conveniently traced to it. (p. 22)
**Inventoriable costs** Synonym for product costs. (p. 24)
**Least-squares regression method** A method of separating a mixed cost into its fixed and variable elements by fitting a regression line that minimizes the sum of the squared errors. (p. 36)
**Linear cost behavior** Cost behavior is said to be linear whenever a straight line is a reasonable approximation for the relation between cost and activity. (p. 33)
**Manufacturing overhead** All manufacturing costs except direct materials and direct labor. (p. 23)
**Mixed cost** A cost that contains both variable and fixed cost elements. (p. 31)
**Opportunity cost** The potential benefit that is given up when one alternative is selected over another. (p. 41)
**Period costs** Costs that are taken directly to the income statement as expenses in the period in which they are incurred or accrued. (p. 24)
**Prime cost** Direct materials cost plus direct labor cost. (p. 24)
**Product costs** All costs that are involved in acquiring or making a product. In the case of manufactured goods, these costs consist of direct materials, direct labor, and manufacturing overhead. Also see *Inventoriable costs.* (p. 23)
**Raw materials** Any materials that go into the final product. (p. 22)
**Relevant range** The range of activity within which assumptions about variable and fixed cost behavior are valid. (p. 29)
**Selling costs** All costs that are incurred to secure customer orders and get the finished product or service into the hands of the customer. (p. 23)
**Sunk cost** A cost that has already been incurred and that cannot be changed by any decision made now or in the future. (p. 41)
**Variable cost** A cost that varies, in total, in direct proportion to changes in the level of activity. A variable cost is constant per unit. (p. 26)

## QUESTIONS

**1–1** What are the three major elements of product costs in a manufacturing company?
**1–2** Define the following: (a) direct materials, (b) indirect materials, (c) direct labor, (d) indirect labor, and (e) manufacturing overhead.
**1–3** Explain the difference between a product cost and a period cost.
**1–4** Distinguish between (*a*) a variable cost, (*b*) a fixed cost, and (*c*) a mixed cost.
**1–5** What effect does an increase in volume have on—
*a.* Unit fixed costs?
*b.* Unit variable costs?
*c.* Total fixed costs?
*d.* Total variable costs?
**1–6** Define the following terms: (*a*) cost behavior and (*b*) relevant range.
**1–7** What is meant by an *activity base* when dealing with variable costs? Give several examples of activity bases.
**1–8** Managers often assume a strictly linear relationship between cost and volume. How can this practice be defended in light of the fact that many costs are curvilinear?
**1–9** Distinguish between discretionary fixed costs and committed fixed costs.
**1–10** Does the concept of the relevant range apply to fixed costs? Explain.
**1–11** What is the major disadvantage of the high-low method?

**1–12** Give the general formula for a mixed cost. Which term represents the variable cost? The fixed cost?
**1–13** What is meant by the term *least-squares regression?*
**1–14** What is the difference between a contribution format income statement and a traditional format income statement?
**1–15** What is the contribution margin?
**1–16** Define the following terms: differential cost, opportunity cost, and sunk cost.
**1–17** Only variable costs can be differential costs. Do you agree? Explain.

**Multiple-choice questions are provided on the text website at www.mhhe.com/brewer6e.**

## APPLYING EXCEL

connect ACCOUNTING

LO5

**Available with McGraw-Hill's *Connect*® *Accounting*.**

The Excel worksheet form that appears below is to be used to recreate Exhibit 1–9 on page 38. Download the workbook containing this form from the Online Learning Center at www.mhhe.com/brewer6e. *On the website you will also receive instructions about how to use this worksheet form.*

| | A | B | C | D |
|---|---|---|---|---|
| 1 | Chapter 1: Applying Excel | | | |
| 2 | | | | |
| 3 | **Data** | | | |
| 4 | Sales | $12,000 | | |
| 5 | Variable costs: | | | |
| 6 | Cost of goods sold | $6,000 | | |
| 7 | Variable selling | $600 | | |
| 8 | Variable administrative | $400 | | |
| 9 | Fixed costs: | | | |
| 10 | Fixed selling | $2,500 | | |
| 11 | Fixed administrative | $1,500 | | |
| 12 | | | | |
| 13 | *Enter a formula into each of the cells marked with a ? below* | | | |
| 14 | **Exhibit 1–9** | | | |
| 15 | | | | |
| 16 | **Traditional Format Income Statement** | | | |
| 17 | Sales | | ? | |
| 18 | Cost of goods sold | | ? | |
| 19 | Gross margin | | ? | |
| 20 | Selling and administrative expenses: | | | |
| 21 | Selling | ? | | |
| 22 | Administrative | ? | ? | |
| 23 | Net operating income | | ? | |
| 24 | | | | |
| 25 | **Contribution Format Income Statement** | | | |
| 26 | Sales | | ? | |
| 27 | Variable expenses: | | | |
| 28 | Cost of goods sold | ? | | |
| 29 | Variable selling | ? | | |
| 30 | Variable administration | ? | ? | |
| 31 | Contribution margin | | ? | |
| 32 | Fixed expenses: | | | |
| 33 | Fixed selling | ? | | |
| 34 | Fixed administrative | ? | ? | |
| 35 | Net operating income | | ? | |
| 36 | | | | |

Chapter 1 Form / Filled in Chapter 1 Fo

***Required:***

1. Check your worksheet by changing the variable selling cost in the Data area to $900, keeping all of the other data the same as in Exhibit 1–9. If your worksheet is operating properly, the net operating income under the traditional format income statement and under the contribution format income statement should now be $700 and the contribution margin should now be $4,700. If you do not get these answers, find the errors in your worksheet and correct them.

   How much is the gross margin? Did it change? Why or why not?
2. Suppose that sales are 10% higher as shown below:

| | |
|---|---|
| Sales | $13,200 |
| Variable costs: | |
| Cost of goods sold | $6,600 |
| Variable selling | $990 |
| Variable administrative | $440 |
| Fixed costs: | |
| Fixed selling | $2,500 |
| Fixed administrative | $1,500 |

Enter this new data into your worksheet. Make sure that you change all of the data that are different—not just the sales. Print or copy the income statements from your worksheet.

What happened to the variable costs and to the fixed costs when sales increased by 10%? Why? Did the contribution margin increase by 10%? Why or why not? Did the net operating income increase by 10%? Why or why not?

connect ACCOUNTING

## THE FOUNDATIONAL 15

**Available with McGraw-Hill's *Connect® Accounting.***

LO1, LO2, LO3, LO5, LO6, LO7

Martinez Company's relevant range of production is 7,500 units to 12,500 units. When it produces and sells 10,000 units, its unit costs are as follows:

| | Amount Per Unit |
|---|---|
| Direct materials | $6.00 |
| Direct labor | $3.50 |
| Variable manufacturing overhead | $1.50 |
| Fixed manufacturing overhead | $4.00 |
| Fixed selling expense | $3.00 |
| Fixed administrative expense | $2.00 |
| Sales commissions | $1.00 |
| Variable administrative expense | $0.50 |

***Required:***

1. For financial accounting purposes, what is the total amount of product costs incurred to make 10,000 units?
2. For financial accounting purposes, what is the total amount of period costs incurred to sell 10,000 units?
3. If 8,000 units are sold, what is the variable cost per unit sold?
4. If 12,500 units are sold, what is the variable cost per unit sold?
5. If 8,000 units are sold, what is the total amount of variable costs related to the units sold?
6. If 12,500 units are sold, what is the total amount of variable costs related to the units sold?
7. If 8,000 units are produced, what is the average fixed manufacturing cost per unit produced?
8. If 12,500 units are produced, what is the average fixed manufacturing cost per unit produced?
9. If 8,000 units are produced, what is the total amount of fixed manufacturing cost incurred to support this level of production?
10. If 12,500 units are produced, what is the total amount of fixed manufacturing cost incurred to support this level of production?
11. If 8,000 units are produced, what is the total amount of manufacturing overhead cost incurred to support this level of production? What is this total amount expressed on a per unit basis?

12. If 12,500 units are produced, what is the total amount of manufacturing overhead cost incurred to support this level of production? What is this total amount expressed on a per unit basis?
13. If the selling price is $22 per unit, what is the contribution margin per unit sold?
14. If 11,000 units are produced, what are the total amounts of direct and indirect manufacturing costs incurred to support this level of production?
15. What total incremental cost will Martinez incur if it increases production from 10,000 to 10,001 units?

## EXERCISES

**All applicable exercises are available with McGraw-Hill's *Connect® Accounting.***

### EXERCISE 1–1 Classifying Manufacturing Costs [LO1]

Your Boat, Inc., assembles custom sailboats from components supplied by various manufacturers. The company is very small and its assembly shop and retail sales store are housed in a Gig Harbor, Washington, boathouse. Below are listed some of the costs that are incurred at the company.

***Required:***

For each cost, indicate whether it would most likely be classified as direct labor, direct materials, manufacturing overhead, selling, or an administrative cost.

1. The wages of employees who build the sailboats.
2. The cost of advertising in the local newspapers.
3. The cost of an aluminum mast installed in a sailboat.
4. The wages of the assembly shop's supervisor.
5. Rent on the boathouse.
6. The wages of the company's bookkeeper.
7. Sales commissions paid to the company's salespeople.
8. Depreciation on power tools.

### EXERCISE 1–2 Classification of Costs as Product or Period Costs [LO2]

Suppose that you have been given a summer job at Fairwings Avionics, a company that manufactures sophisticated radar sets for commercial aircraft. The company, which is privately owned, has approached a bank for a loan to help finance its tremendous growth. The bank requires financial statements before approving such a loan.

***Required:***

Classify each cost listed below as either a product cost or a period cost for purposes of preparing the financial statements for the bank.

1. The cost of the memory chips used in a radar set.
2. Factory heating costs.
3. Factory equipment maintenance costs.
4. Training costs for new administrative employees.
5. The cost of the solder that is used in assembling the radar sets.
6. The travel costs of the company's salespersons.
7. Wages and salaries of factory security personnel.
8. The cost of air-conditioning executive offices.
9. Wages and salaries in the department that handles billing customers.
10. Depreciation on the equipment in the fitness room used by factory workers.
11. Telephone expenses incurred by factory management.
12. The costs of shipping completed radar sets to customers.
13. The wages of the workers who assemble the radar sets.
14. The president's salary.
15. Health insurance premiums for factory personnel.

### EXERCISE 1–3 Fixed and Variable Cost Behavior [LO3]

Koffee Express operates a number of espresso coffee stands in busy suburban malls. The fixed weekly expense of a coffee stand is $1,100 and the variable cost per cup of coffee served is $0.26.

***Required:***

1. Fill in the following table with your estimates of total costs and average cost per cup of coffee at the indicated levels of activity for a coffee stand. Round off the cost of a cup of coffee to the nearest tenth of a cent.

| | Cups of Coffee Served in a Week | | |
|---|---|---|---|
| | **1,800** | **1,900** | **2,000** |
| Fixed cost | ? | ? | ? |
| Variable cost | ? | ? | ? |
| Total cost | ? | ? | ? |
| Average cost per cup of coffee served | ? | ? | ? |

TAKE TWO

Fixed weekly expense = 1,000
Variable cost per cup = $0.30

2. Does the average cost per cup of coffee served increase, decrease, or remain the same as the number of cups of coffee served in a week increases? Explain.

**EXERCISE 1–4 High-Low Method [LO4]**

The Edelweiss Hotel in Vail, Colorado, has accumulated records of the total electrical costs of the hotel and the number of occupancy-days over the last year. An occupancy-day represents a room rented out for one day. The hotel's business is highly seasonal, with peaks occurring during the ski season and in the summer.

| Month | Occupancy-Days | Electrical Costs |
|---|---|---|
| January | 2,604 | $6,257 |
| February | 2,856 | $6,550 |
| March | 3,534 | $7,986 |
| April | 1,440 | $4,022 |
| May | 540 | $2,289 |
| June | 1,116 | $3,591 |
| July | 3,162 | $7,264 |
| August | 3,608 | $8,111 |
| September | 1,260 | $3,707 |
| October | 186 | $1,712 |
| November | 1,080 | $3,321 |
| December | 2,046 | $5,196 |

TAKE TWO

October occupancy-days = 580
October electrical cost = $2,315

***Required:***

1. Using the high-low method, estimate the fixed cost of electricity per month and the variable cost of electricity per occupancy-day. Round off the fixed cost to the nearest whole dollar and the variable cost to the nearest whole cent.
2. What other factors other than occupancy-days are likely to affect the variation in electrical costs from month to month?

**EXERCISE 1–5 Traditional and Contribution Format Income Statements [LO5]**

Redhawk, Inc., is a merchandiser that provided the following information:

| | |
|---|---|
| Number of units sold | 10,000 |
| Selling price per unit | $15 |
| Variable selling expense per unit | $2 |
| Variable administrative expense per unit | $1 |
| Total fixed selling expense | $20,000 |
| Total fixed administrative expense | $15,000 |
| Merchandise inventory, beginning balance | $12,000 |
| Merchandise inventory, ending balance | $22,000 |
| Merchandise purchases | $90,000 |

TAKE TWO

Number of units sold = 12,000
Merchandise purchases = $106,000

***Required:***

1. Prepare a traditional income statement.
2. Prepare a contribution format income statement.

**EXERCISE 1–6 Identifying Direct and Indirect Costs [LO6]**

The Empire Hotel is a four-star hotel located in downtown Seattle.

***Required:***

For each of the following costs incurred at the Empire Hotel, indicate whether it would most likely be a direct cost or an indirect cost of the specified cost object by placing an X in the appropriate column.

| Cost | Cost Object | Direct Cost | Indirect Cost |
|---|---|---|---|
| Ex. Room service beverages | A particular hotel guest | X | |
| 1. The salary of the head chef | The hotel's restaurant | | |
| 2. The salary of the head chef | A particular restaurant customer | | |
| 3. Room cleaning supplies | A particular hotel guest | | |
| 4. Flowers for the reception desk | A particular hotel guest | | |
| 5. The wages of the doorman | A particular hotel guest | | |
| 6. Room cleaning supplies | The housecleaning department | | |
| 7. Fire insurance on the hotel building | The hotel's gym | | |
| 8. Towels used in the gym | The hotel's gym | | |

**EXERCISE 1–7 Differential, Opportunity, and Sunk Costs [LO7]**

The Sorrento Hotel is a four-star hotel located in downtown Seattle. The hotel's operations vice president would like to replace the hotel's antiquated computer terminals at the registration desk with attractive state-of-the-art flat-panel displays. The new displays would take less space, would consume less power than the old computer terminals, and would provide additional security since they can only be viewed from a restrictive angle. The new computer displays would not require any new wiring. The hotel's chef believes the funds would be better spent on a new bulk freezer for the kitchen.

***Required:***

For each of the items below, indicate by placing an X in the appropriate column whether it should be considered a differential cost, an opportunity cost, or a sunk cost in the decision to replace the old computer terminals with new flat-panel displays. If none of the categories apply for a particular item, leave all columns blank.

| Item | Differential Cost | Opportunity Cost | Sunk Cost |
|---|---|---|---|
| Ex. Cost of electricity to run the terminals ................................ | X | | |
| 1. Cost of the new flat-panel displays .................................... | | | |
| 2. Cost of the old computer terminals .................................... | | | |
| 3. Rent on the space occupied by the registration desk...... | | | |
| 4. Wages of registration desk personnel ................................ | | | |
| 5. Benefits from a new freezer ................................................ | | | |
| 6. Costs of maintaining the old computer terminals............. | | | |
| 7. Cost of removing the old computer terminals ................... | | | |
| 8. Cost of existing registration desk wiring ............................ | | | |

**EXERCISE 1–8 Cost Behavior; Contribution Format Income Statement [LO3, LO5]**

Parker Company manufactures and sells a single product. A partially completed schedule of the company's total and per unit costs over a relevant range of 60,000 to 100,000 units produced and sold each year is given on the next page:

| | Units Produced and Sold | | |
|---|---|---|---|
| | 60,000 | 80,000 | 100,000 |
| Total costs: | | | |
| Variable costs .............. | $150,000 | ? | ? |
| Fixed costs .................. | 360,000 | ? | ? |
| Total costs ...................... | $510,000 | ? | ? |
| Cost per unit: | | | |
| Variable cost ................ | ? | ? | ? |
| Fixed cost .................... | ? | ? | ? |
| Total cost per unit ............ | ? | ? | ? |

***Required:***

1. Complete the schedule of the company's total and unit costs.
2. Assume that the company produces and sells 90,000 units during the year at the selling price of $7.50 per unit. Prepare a contribution format income statement for the year.

**EXERCISE 1–9 Cost Classification [LO1, LO2, LO3, LO7]**

Several years ago, Medex Company purchased a small building adjacent to its manufacturing plant in order to have room for expansion when needed. Since the company had no immediate need for the extra space, the building was rented out to another company for rental revenue of $40,000 per year. The renter's lease will expire next month, and rather than renewing the lease, Medex Company has decided to use the building itself to manufacture a new product.

Direct materials cost for the new product will total $40 per unit. It will be necessary to hire a supervisor to oversee production. Her salary will be $2,500 per month. Workers will be hired to manufacture the new product, with direct labor cost amounting to $18 per unit. Manufacturing operations will occupy all of the building space, so it will be necessary to rent space in a warehouse nearby in order to store finished units of product. The rental cost will be $1,000 per month. In addition, the company will need to rent equipment for use in producing the new product; the rental cost will be $3,000 per month. The company will continue to depreciate the building on a straight-line basis, as in past years. Depreciation on the building is $10,000 per year.

Advertising costs for the new product will total $50,000 per year. Costs of shipping the new product to customers will be $10 per unit. Electrical costs of operating machines will be $2 per unit.

To have funds to purchase materials, meet payrolls, and so forth, the company will have to liquidate some temporary investments. These investments are presently yielding a return of $6,000 per year.

***Required:***

Prepare an answer sheet with the following column headings:

| Name of the Cost | Variable Cost | Fixed Cost | Product Cost | | | Period (Selling and Administrative) Cost | Opportunity Cost | Sunk Cost |
|---|---|---|---|---|---|---|---|---|
| | | | Direct Materials | Direct Labor | Manufacturing Overhead | | | |

List the different costs associated with the new product decision down the extreme left column (under Name of the Cost). Then place an X under each heading that helps to describe the type of cost involved. There may be X's under several column headings for a single cost. (For example, a cost may be a fixed cost, a period cost, and a sunk cost; you would place an X under each of these column headings opposite the cost.)

**EXERCISE 1–10 High-Low Method; Scattergraph Analysis [LO4]**

Zerbel Company, a wholesaler of large, custom-built air-conditioning units for commercial buildings, has noticed considerable fluctuation in its shipping expense from month to month, as shown below:

| Month | Units Shipped | Total Shipping Expense |
|---|---|---|
| January................. | 4 | $2,200 |
| February............... | 7 | $3,100 |
| March.................... | 5 | $2,600 |
| April...................... | 2 | $1,500 |
| May....................... | 3 | $2,200 |
| June...................... | 6 | $3,000 |
| July........................ | 8 | $3,600 |

***Required:***

1. Prepare a scattergraph using the data given on the previous page. Plot cost on the vertical axis and activity on the horizontal axis. Is there an approximately linear relationship between shipping expense and the number of units shipped?
2. Using the high-low method, estimate the cost formula for shipping expense. Draw a straight line through the high and low data points shown in the scattergraph that you prepared in requirement 1. Make sure your line intersects the *Y* axis.
3. Comment on the accuracy of your high-low estimates assuming a least-squares regression analysis estimated the total fixed costs to be $1,010.71 per month and the variable cost to be $317.86 per unit. How would the straight line that you drew in requirement 2 differ from a straight line that minimizes the sum of the squared errors?
4. What factors, other than the number of units shipped, are likely to affect the company's shipping expense? Explain.

### EXERCISE 1–11 Traditional and Contribution Format Income Statements [LO5]

Haaki Shop, Inc., is a large retailer of surfboards. The company assembled the information shown below for the quarter ended May 31:

TAKE TWO

Total sales revenue = $840,000
Merchandise purchases = $335,000

| | Amount |
|---|---|
| Total sales revenue | $800,000 |
| Selling price per surfboard | $400 |
| Variable selling expense per surfboard | $50 |
| Variable administrative expense per surfboard | $20 |
| Total fixed selling expense | $150,000 |
| Total fixed administrative expense | $120,000 |
| Merchandise inventory, beginning balance | $80,000 |
| Merchandise inventory, ending balance | $100,000 |
| Merchandise purchases | $320,000 |

***Required:***

1. Prepare a traditional income statement for the quarter ended May 31.
2. Prepare a contribution format income statement for the quarter ended May 31.
3. What was the contribution toward fixed expenses and profits for each surfboard sold during the quarter? (State this figure in a single dollar amount per surfboard.)

### EXERCISE 1–12 Cost Behavior; High-Low Method [LO3, LO4]

TAKE TWO

Speedy Parcel Service operates a fleet of delivery trucks in a large metropolitan area. A careful study by the company's cost analyst has determined that if a truck is driven 120,000 miles during a year, the average operating cost is 11.6 cents per mile. If a truck is driven only 80,000 miles during a year, the average operating cost increases to 13.6 cents per mile.

Average operating cost = 10.0 cents per mile at 120,000 miles

***Required:***

1. Using the high-low method, estimate the variable and fixed cost elements of the annual cost of truck operation.
2. Express the variable and fixed costs in the form $Y = a + bX$.
3. If a truck were driven 100,000 miles during a year, what total cost would you expect to be incurred?

### EXERCISE 1–13 High-Low Method; Predicting Cost [LO3, LO4]

The number of X-rays taken and X-ray costs over the last nine months in Beverly Hospital are given below:

| Month | X-Rays Taken | X-Ray Costs |
|---|---|---|
| January | 6,250 | $28,000 |
| February | 7,000 | $29,000 |
| March | 5,000 | $23,000 |
| April | 4,250 | $20,000 |
| May | 4,500 | $22,000 |
| June | 3,000 | $17,000 |
| July | 3,750 | $18,000 |
| August | 5,500 | $24,000 |
| September | 5,750 | $26,000 |

***Required:***

1. Using the high-low method, estimate the cost formula for X-ray costs.
2. Using the cost formula you derived above, what X-ray costs would you expect to be incurred during a month in which 4,600 X-rays are taken?
3. Prepare a scattergraph using the data given above. Plot X-ray costs on the vertical axis and the number of X-rays taken on the horizontal axis. Draw a straight line through the two data points that correspond to the high and low levels of activity. Make sure your line intersects the *Y*-axis.
4. Comment on the accuracy of your high-low estimates assuming a least-squares regression analysis estimated the total fixed costs to be $6,529.41 per month and the variable cost to be $3.29 per X-ray taken. How would the straight line that you drew in requirement 3 differ from a straight line that minimizes the sum of the squared errors?
5. Using the least-squares regression estimates given in requirement 4, what X-ray costs would you expect to be incurred during a month in which 4,600 X-rays are taken?

**Alternate problem set is available on the text website and in *Connect® Accounting*.** connect ACCOUNTING

## PROBLEMS

**All applicable problems are available with McGraw-Hill's *Connect® Accounting*.**

**PROBLEM 1–14A Contribution Format versus Traditional Income Statement [LO5]**

House of Organs, Inc., purchases organs from a well-known manufacturer and sells them at the retail level. The organs sell, on the average, for $2,500 each. The average cost of an organ from the manufacturer is $1,500. The costs that the company incurs in a typical month are presented below:

excel

CHECK FIGURE
(2) Net operating income: $19,000

| Costs | Cost Formula |
|---|---|
| Selling: | |
| Advertising | $950 per month |
| Delivery of organs | $60 per organ sold |
| Sales salaries and commissions | $4,800 per month, plus 4% of sales |
| Utilities | $650 per month |
| Depreciation of sales facilities | $5,000 per month |
| Administrative: | |
| Executive salaries | $13,500 per month |
| Depreciation of office equipment | $900 per month |
| Clerical | $2,500 per month, plus $40 per organ sold |
| Insurance | $700 per month |

During November, the company sold and delivered 60 organs.

***Required:***

1. Prepare a traditional income statement for November.
2. Prepare a contribution format income statement for November. Show costs and revenues on both a total and a per unit basis down through contribution margin.
3. Refer to the income statement you prepared in (2) above. Why might it be misleading to show the fixed costs on a per unit basis?

**PROBLEM 1–15A Identifying Cost Behavior Patterns [LO3]**

A number of graphs displaying cost behavior patterns are shown on the next page. The vertical axis on each graph represents total cost and the horizontal axis represents the level of activity (volume).

***Required:***

1. For each of the following situations, identify the graph that illustrates the cost behavior pattern involved. Any graph may be used more than once.
   a. Electricity bill—a flat fixed charge, plus a variable cost after a certain number of kilowatt-hours are used.

b. City water bill, which is computed as follows:

| | |
|---|---|
| First 1,000,000 gallons or less ........ | $1,000 flat fee |
| Next 10,000 gallons ........................ | $0.003 per gallon used |
| Next 10,000 gallons ........................ | $0.006 per gallon used |
| Next 10,000 gallons ........................ | $0.009 per gallon used |
| Etc ................................................ | Etc. |

c. Depreciation of equipment, where the amount is computed by the straight-line method. When the depreciation rate was established, it was anticipated that the obsolescence factor would be greater than the wear and tear factor.

d. Rent on a factory building donated by the city, where the agreement calls for a fixed fee payment unless 200,000 labor-hours or more are worked, in which case no rent need be paid.

e. Cost of raw materials, where the cost starts at $7.50 per unit and then decreases by 5 cents per unit for each of the first 100 units purchased, after which it remains constant at $2.50 per unit.

f. Salaries of maintenance workers, where one maintenance worker is needed for every 1,000 hours of machine-hours or less (that is, 0 to 1,000 hours requires one maintenance worker, 1,001 to 2,000 hours requires two maintenance workers, etc.).

g. Cost of raw material used.

h. Rent on a factory building donated by the county, where the agreement calls for rent of $100,000 less $1 for each direct labor-hour worked in excess of 200,000 hours, but a minimum rental payment of $20,000 must be paid.

i. Use of a machine under a lease, where a minimum charge of $1,000 is paid for up to 400 hours of machine time. After 400 hours of machine time, an additional charge of $2 per hour is paid up to a maximum charge of $2,000 per period.

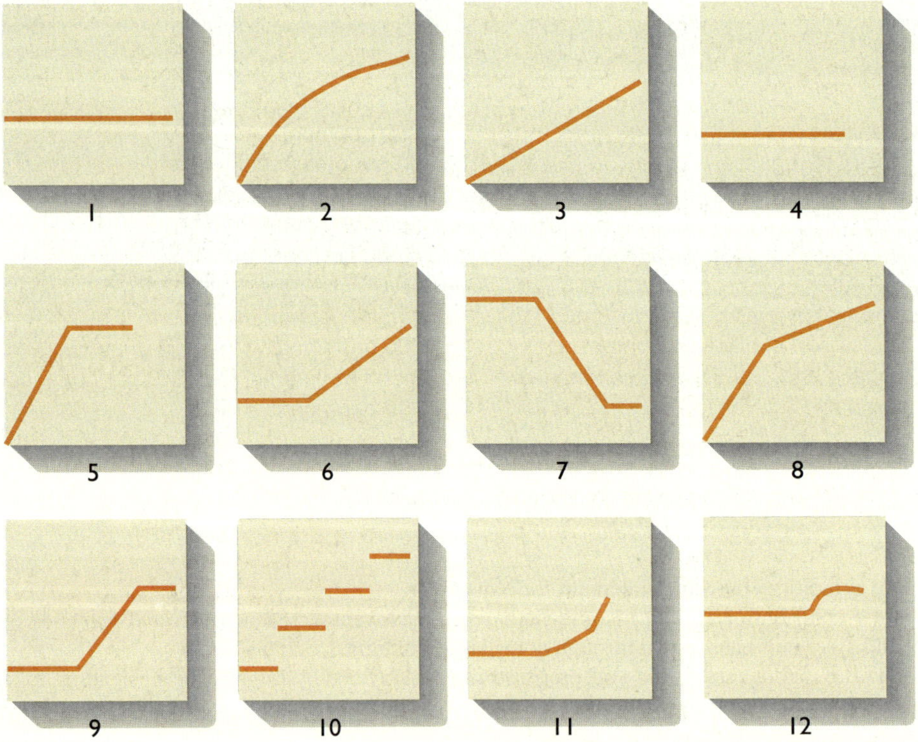


2. How would a knowledge of cost behavior patterns such as those above be of help to a manager in analyzing the cost structure of his or her company?

(CPA, adapted)

**PROBLEM 1–16A Variable and Fixed Costs; Subtleties of Direct and Indirect Costs [LO3, LO6]**
The Central Area Well-Baby Clinic provides a variety of health services to newborn babies and their parents. The clinic is organized into a number of departments, one of which is the Immunization Center. A number of costs of the clinic and the Immunization Center are listed on the following page.
**Example:** The cost of polio immunization tablets.

a. The salary of the head nurse in the Immunization Center.
b. Costs of incidental supplies consumed in the Immunization Center, such as paper towels.
c. The cost of lighting and heating the Immunization Center.
d. The cost of disposable syringes used in the Immunization Center.
e. The salary of the Central Area Well-Baby Clinic's Information Systems manager.
f. The costs of mailing letters soliciting donations to the Central Area Well-Baby Clinic.
g. The wages of nurses who work in the Immunization Center.
h. The cost of medical malpractice insurance for the Central Area Well-Baby Clinic.
i. Depreciation on the fixtures and equipment in the Immunization Center.

***Required:***
For each cost listed above, indicate whether it is a direct or indirect cost of the Immunization Center, whether it is a direct or indirect cost of immunizing particular patients, and whether it is variable or fixed with respect to the number of immunizations administered. Use the form shown below for your answer.

| | Direct or Indirect Cost of the Immunization Center | | Direct or Indirect Cost of Particular Patients | | Variable or Fixed with Respect to the Number of Immunizations Administered | |
|---|---|---|---|---|---|---|
| **Item Description** | **Direct** | **Indirect** | **Direct** | **Indirect** | **Variable** | **Fixed** |
| Example: The cost of polio immunization tablets.................... | X | | X | | X | |

**PROBLEM 1–17A High-Low Method; Predicting Cost [LO3, LO4]**

CHECK FIGURE
(3) Total cost: 283,500 pesos

Echeverria SA is an Argentinian manufacturing company whose total factory overhead costs fluctuate somewhat from year to year according to the number of machine-hours worked in its production facility. These costs (in Argentinian pesos) at high and low levels of activity over recent years are given below:

| | Level of Activity | |
|---|---|---|
| | **Low** | **High** |
| Machine-hours............................ | 60,000 | 80,000 |
| Total factory overhead costs........ | 274,000 pesos | 312,000 pesos |

The factory overhead costs above consist of indirect materials, rent, and maintenance. The company has analyzed these costs at the 60,000 machine-hours level of activity as follows:

| | |
|---|---|
| Indirect materials (variable) ................. | 90,000 pesos |
| Rent (fixed) ........................................ | 130,000 |
| Maintenance (mixed) .......................... | 54,000 |
| Total factory overhead costs ................. | 274,000 pesos |

For planning purposes, the company wants to break down the maintenance cost into its variable and fixed cost elements.

***Required:***
1. Estimate how much of the factory overhead cost of 312,000 pesos at the high level of activity consists of maintenance cost. (Hint: To do this, it may be helpful to first determine how much of the 312,000 pesos cost consists of indirect materials and rent. Think about the behavior of variable and fixed costs.)
2. Using the high-low method, estimate a cost formula for maintenance.
3. What *total* overhead costs would you expect the company to incur at an operating level of 65,000 machine-hours?

CHECK FIGURE
Shipping expenses:
(2) $Y = £20{,}000 + £8.00X$

**PROBLEM 1–18A Cost Behavior; High-Low Method; Contribution Format Income Statement [LO3, LO4, LO5]**

Frankel Ltd., a British merchandising company, is the exclusive distributor of a product that is gaining rapid market acceptance. The company's revenues and expenses (in British pounds) for the last three months are given below:

**Frankel Ltd.**
**Comparative Income Statements**
**For the Three Months Ended June 30**

| | April | May | June |
|---|---|---|---|
| Sales in units | 3,000 | 3,750 | 4,500 |
| Sales revenue | £420,000 | £525,000 | £630,000 |
| Cost of goods sold | 168,000 | 210,000 | 252,000 |
| Gross margin | 252,000 | 315,000 | 378,000 |
| Selling and administrative expenses: | | | |
| Shipping expense | 44,000 | 50,000 | 56,000 |
| Advertising expense | 70,000 | 70,000 | 70,000 |
| Salaries and commissions | 107,000 | 125,000 | 143,000 |
| Insurance expense | 9,000 | 9,000 | 9,000 |
| Depreciation expense | 42,000 | 42,000 | 42,000 |
| Total selling and administrative expenses | 272,000 | 296,000 | 320,000 |
| Net operating income (loss) | £ (20,000) | £ 19,000 | £ 58,000 |

(Note: Frankel Ltd.'s income statement has been recast in the functional format common in the United States. The British currency is the pound, denoted by £.)

***Required:***

1. Identify each of the company's expenses (including cost of goods sold) as either variable, fixed, or mixed.
2. Using the high-low method, separate each mixed expense into variable and fixed elements. State the cost formula for each mixed expense.
3. Redo the company's income statement at the 4,500-unit level of activity using the contribution format.

CHECK FIGURE
(1) $Y = \$800 + \$40X$

**PROBLEM 1–19A High-Low and Scattergraph Analysis [LO4]**

Sebolt Wire Company heats copper ingots to very high temperatures by placing the ingots in a large heat coil. The heated ingots are then run through a shaping machine that shapes the soft ingot into wire. Due to the long heat-up time, the coil is never turned off. When an ingot is placed in the coil, the temperature is raised to an even higher level, and then the coil is allowed to drop to the "waiting" temperature between ingots. Management needs to know the variable cost of power involved in heating an ingot and the fixed cost of power during "waiting" periods. The following data on ingots processed and power costs are available:

| Month | Number of Ingots | Power Cost |
|---|---|---|
| January | 110 | $5,500 |
| February | 90 | $4,500 |
| March | 80 | $4,400 |
| April | 100 | $5,000 |
| May | 130 | $6,000 |
| June | 120 | $5,600 |
| July | 70 | $4,000 |
| August | 60 | $3,200 |
| September | 50 | $3,400 |
| October | 40 | $2,400 |

***Required:***

1. Using the high-low method, estimate a cost formula for power cost. Express the formula in the form $Y = a + bX$.
2. Prepare a scattergraph by plotting ingots processed and power cost on a graph. Draw a straight line though the two data points that correspond to the high and low levels of activity. Make sure your line intersects the $Y$-axis.
3. Comment on the accuracy of your high-low estimates assuming a least-squares regression analysis estimated the total fixed costs to be $1,185.45 per month and the variable cost to be $37.82 per ingot. How would the straight line that you drew in requirement 2 differ from a straight line that minimizes the sum of the squared errors?

**PROBLEM 1–20A High-Low Method; Predicting Cost [LO3, LO4]**

Golden Company's total overhead cost at various levels of activity are presented below:

| Month | Machine-Hours | Total Overhead Cost |
|---|---|---|
| March | 50,000 | $194,000 |
| April | 40,000 | $170,200 |
| May | 60,000 | $217,800 |
| June | 70,000 | $241,600 |

CHECK FIGURE
(4) Total cost: $182,100

Assume that the overhead cost above consists of utilities, supervisory salaries, and maintenance. The breakdown of these costs at the 40,000 machine-hour level of activity is as follows:

| | |
|---|---|
| Utilities (variable) | $ 52,000 |
| Supervisory salaries (fixed) | 60,000 |
| Maintenance (mixed) | 58,200 |
| Total overhead cost | $170,200 |

The company wants to break down the maintenance cost into its variable and fixed cost elements.

***Required:***

1. Estimate how much of the $241,600 of overhead cost in June was maintenance cost. (Hint: To do this, it may be helpful to first determine how much of the $241,600 consisted of utilities and supervisory salaries. Think about the behavior of variable and fixed costs within the relevant range.)
2. Using the high-low method, estimate a cost formula for maintenance.
3. Express the company's total overhead cost in the form $Y = a + bX$.
4. What total overhead cost would you expect to be incurred at an activity level of 45,000 machine-hours?

**PROBLEM 1–21A Cost Classification [LO2, LO3, LO6]**

Listed below are costs found in various organizations.

1. Depreciation, executive jet.
2. Costs of shipping finished goods to customers.
3. Wood used in manufacturing furniture.
4. Sales manager's salary.
5. Electricity used in manufacturing furniture.
6. Secretary to the company president.
7. Aerosol attachment placed on a spray can produced by the company.
8. Billing costs.
9. Packing supplies for shipping products overseas.
10. Sand used in manufacturing concrete.
11. Supervisor's salary, factory.
12. Executive life insurance.
13. Sales commissions.
14. Fringe benefits, assembly-line workers.
15. Advertising costs.
16. Property taxes on finished goods warehouses.
17. Lubricants for production equipment.

CHECK FIGURE
Cost of shipping finished goods: variable, selling

***Required:***

Prepare an answer sheet with column headings as shown below. For each cost item, indicate whether it would be variable or fixed with respect to the number of units produced and sold; and then whether it would be a selling cost, an administrative cost, or a manufacturing cost. If it is a manufacturing cost, indicate whether it would typically be treated as a direct or indirect cost with respect to units of product. Three sample answers are provided for illustration.

| | | | | Manufacturing (Product) Cost | |
|---|---|---|---|---|---|
| **Cost Item** | **Variable or Fixed** | **Selling Cost** | **Administrative Cost** | **Direct** | **Indirect** |
| Direct labor | V | | | X | |
| Executive salaries | F | | X | | |
| Factory rent | F | | | | X |

**PROBLEM 1–22A High-Low Method; Contribution Format Income Statement [LO4, LO5]**

Alden Company has decided to use a contribution format income statement for internal planning purposes. The company has analyzed its expenses and has developed the following cost formulas:

CHECK FIGURE
(1) $Y = \$32{,}000 + \$8X$

| **Cost** | **Cost Formula** |
|---|---|
| Cost of goods sold | $20 per unit sold |
| Advertising expense | $170,000 per quarter |
| Sales commissions | 5% of sales |
| Administrative salaries | $80,000 per quarter |
| Shipping expense | ? |
| Depreciation expense | $50,000 per quarter |

Management has concluded that shipping expense is a mixed cost, containing both variable and fixed cost elements. Units sold and the related shipping expense over the last eight quarters are given below:

| **Quarter** | **Units Sold** | **Shipping Expense** |
|---|---|---|
| Year 1: | | |
| First | 16,000 | $160,000 |
| Second | 18,000 | $175,000 |
| Third | 23,000 | $217,000 |
| Fourth | 19,000 | $180,000 |
| Year 2: | | |
| First | 17,000 | $170,000 |
| Second | 20,000 | $185,000 |
| Third | 25,000 | $232,000 |
| Fourth | 22,000 | $208,000 |

Management would like a cost formula derived for shipping expense so that a budgeted contribution format income statement can be prepared for the next quarter.

***Required:***

1. Using the high-low method, estimate a cost formula for shipping expense.
2. In the first quarter of Year 3, the company plans to sell 21,000 units at a selling price of $50 per unit. Prepare a contribution format income statement for the quarter.

**PROBLEM 1–23A Cost Classification and Cost Behavior [LO2, LO3, LO6]**

Heritage Company manufactures a beautiful bookcase that enjoys widespread popularity. The company has a backlog of orders that is large enough to keep production going indefinitely at the plant's full capacity of 4,000 bookcases per year. Annual cost data at full capacity follow:

| | |
|---|---|
| Direct materials used (wood and glass) | $430,000 |
| Administrative office salaries | $110,000 |
| Factory supervision | $70,000 |
| Sales commissions | $60,000 |
| Depreciation, factory building | $105,000 |
| Depreciation, administrative office equipment | $2,000 |
| Indirect materials, factory | $18,000 |
| Factory labor (cutting and assembly) | $90,000 |
| Advertising | $100,000 |
| Insurance, factory | $6,000 |
| Administrative office supplies (billing) | $4,000 |
| Property taxes, factory | $20,000 |
| Utilities, factory | $45,000 |

CHECK FIGURE
(1) Total variable cost: $647,000

***Required:***

1. Prepare an answer sheet with the column headings shown below. Enter each cost item on your answer sheet, placing the dollar amount under the appropriate headings. As examples, this has been done already for the first two items in the list above. Note that each cost item is classified in two ways: first, as either variable or fixed with respect to the number of units produced and sold; and second, as either a selling and administrative cost or a product cost. (If the item is a product cost, it should also be classified as either direct or indirect as shown.)

| | Cost Behavior | | Selling or Administrative Cost | Product Cost | |
|---|---|---|---|---|---|
| **Cost Item** | **Variable** | **Fixed** | | **Direct** | **Indirect*** |
| Materials used | $430,000 | | | $430,000 | |
| Administrative office salaries | | $110,000 | $110,000 | | |

*To units of product.

2. Total the dollar amounts in each of the columns in (1) above. Compute the average product cost per bookcase.
3. Due to a recession, assume that production drops to only 2,000 bookcases per year. Would you expect the average product cost per bookcase to increase, decrease, or remain unchanged? Explain. No computations are necessary.
4. Refer to the original data. The president's next-door neighbor has considered making himself a bookcase and has priced the necessary materials at a building supply store. He has asked the president whether he could purchase a bookcase from the Heritage Company "at cost," and the president has agreed to let him do so.
   a. Would you expect any disagreement between the two men over the price the neighbor should pay? Explain. What price does the president probably have in mind? The neighbor?
   b. Because the company is operating at full capacity, what cost term used in the chapter might be justification for the president to charge the full, regular price to the neighbor and still be selling "at cost"? Explain.

# BUILDING YOUR SKILLS

## ANALYTICAL THINKING [LO4]

Mapleleaf Sweepers of Toronto manufactures replacement rotary sweeper brooms for the large sweeper trucks that clear leaves and snow from city streets. The business is seasonal, with the largest demand during and just preceding the fall and winter months. Because there are so many different kinds of sweeper brooms used by its customers, Mapleleaf Sweepers makes all of its brooms to order.

The company has been analyzing its overhead accounts to determine fixed and variable components for planning purposes. Following are data for the company's janitorial labor costs over the last nine months. (Cost data are in Canadian dollars.)

| | Number of Units Produced | Number of Janitorial Workdays | Janitorial Labor Cost |
|---|---|---|---|
| January | 115 | 21 | $3,840 |
| February | 109 | 19 | $3,648 |
| March | 102 | 23 | $4,128 |
| April | 76 | 20 | $3,456 |
| May | 69 | 23 | $4,320 |
| June | 108 | 22 | $4,032 |
| July | 77 | 16 | $2,784 |
| August | 71 | 14 | $2,688 |
| September | 127 | 21 | $3,840 |

The number of workdays varies from month to month due to the number of weekdays, holidays, days of vacation, and sick leave taken in the month. The number of units produced in a month varies depending on demand and the number of workdays in the month.

There are two janitors who each work an eight-hour shift each workday. They each can take up to 10 days of paid sick leave each year. Their wages on days they call in sick and their wages during paid vacations are charged to miscellaneous overhead rather than to the janitorial labor cost account.

***Required:***

1. Plot the janitorial labor cost and units produced on a scattergraph. (Place cost on the vertical axis and units produced on the horizontal axis.)
2. Plot the janitorial labor cost and number of workdays on a scattergraph. (Place cost on the vertical axis and the number of workdays on the horizontal axis.)
3. Which measure of activity—number of units produced or janitorial workdays—should be used as the activity base for explaining janitorial labor cost?

## ETHICS CHALLENGE [LO2]

The top management of General Electronics, Inc., is well known for "managing by the numbers." With an eye on the company's desired growth in overall net profit, the company's CEO (chief executive officer) sets target profits at the beginning of the year for each of the company's divisions. The CEO has stated her policy as follows: "I won't interfere with operations in the divisions. I am available for advice, but the division vice presidents are free to do anything they want so long as they hit the target profits for the year."

In November, Stan Richart, the vice president in charge of the Cellular Telephone Technologies Division, saw that making the current year's target profit for his division was going to be very difficult. Among other actions, he directed that discretionary expenditures be delayed until the beginning of the new year. On December 30, he was angered to discover that a warehouse clerk had ordered $350,000 of cellular telephone parts earlier in December even though the parts weren't really needed by the assembly department until January or February. Contrary to common accounting practice, the General Electronics, Inc., Accounting Policy Manual states that such parts are to be recorded as an expense when delivered. To avoid recording the expense, Mr. Richart asked that the order be canceled, but the purchasing department reported that the parts had already been delivered and the supplier would not accept returns. Because the bill had not yet been paid, Mr. Richart asked the accounting department to correct the clerk's mistake by delaying recognition of the delivery until the bill is paid in January.

***Required:***

1. Are Mr. Richart's actions ethical? Explain why they are or are not ethical.
2. Do the general management philosophy and accounting policies at General Electronics encourage or discourage ethical behavior? Explain.

### TEAMWORK IN ACTION [LO3]

Understanding the nature of fixed and variable costs is extremely important to managers. This knowledge is used in planning, making strategic and tactical decisions, evaluating performance, and controlling operations.

***Required:***

Form a team consisting of four persons. Each team member will be responsible for one of the following businesses:

a. Retail store that sells music CDs
b. Dental clinic
c. Fast-food restaurant
d. Auto repair shop

1. For each business, decide what single measure best reflects the overall level of activity in the business and give examples of costs that are fixed and variable with respect to small changes in the measure of activity you have chosen.
2. Explain the relationship between the level of activity in each business and each of the following: total fixed costs, fixed cost per unit of activity, total variable costs, variable cost per unit of activity, total costs, and average total cost per unit of activity.
3. Discuss and refine your answers to each of the above questions with your group. Which of the above businesses seems to have the highest ratio of variable to fixed costs? The lowest? Which of the businesses' profits would be most sensitive to changes in demand for its services? The least sensitive? Why?

### A LOOK BACK

Chapter 1 defined many of the terms that are used to classify costs in business. We will use many of these terms in Chapter 2. Now would be a good time to check your understanding of those terms by referring to the glossary at the end of Chapter 1.

### A LOOK AT THIS CHAPTER

Chapter 2 provides an in-depth look at a job-order costing system. We describe how direct material and direct labor costs are accumulated on jobs. Then we address manufacturing overhead, an indirect cost that must be allocated (or applied) to jobs. Finally, we take a more detailed look at the flow of costs through a company's accounting system using journal entries.

### A LOOK AHEAD

Chapter 3 continues the discussion of the allocation of manufacturing overhead costs, showing how these costs can be more accurately assigned using activity-based costing. We cover process costing in Chapter 4.

# 2 Job-Order Costing

## CHAPTER OUTLINE

## DECISION FEATURE

# Two Former College Students Succeeding as Entrepreneurs

When the University of Dayton athletic department needed 2,000 customized T-shirts to give away as part of a promotion for its first home basketball game of the year, it chose **University Tees** to provide the shirts. Numerous larger competitors could have been chosen, but University Tees won the order because of its fast customer response time, low price, and high quality.

University Tees is a small business that was started in February 2003 by two Miami University seniors—Joe Haddad and Nick Dadas (see the company's website at www.universitytees.com). The company creates the artwork for customized T-shirts and then relies on carefully chosen suppliers to manufacture the product. University Tees must provide a specific price quote for each potential customer order because each order is unique and the customer is always looking for the best deal.

Calculating the cost of a particular customer order is critically important to University Tees because the company needs to be sure that each price quote exceeds the cost associated with satisfying the order. The costs that University Tees factors into its bidding process include the cost of the T-shirts themselves, printing costs (which vary depending on the quantity of shirts produced and the number of colors printed per shirt), silk screen costs (which also vary depending on the number of colors included in a design), shipping costs, and the artwork needed to create a design. In addition to using cost information, the company also relies on knowledge of its competitors' pricing strategies when establishing price quotes.

Source: Conversation with Joe Haddad, cofounder of University Tees.

## LEARNING OBJECTIVES

*After studying Chapter 2, you should be able to:*

**LO1** Compute a predetermined overhead rate.

**LO2** Apply overhead cost to jobs using a predetermined overhead rate.

**LO3** Compute the total cost and average cost per unit of a job.

**LO4** Understand the flow of costs in a job-order costing system and prepare appropriate journal entries to record costs.

**LO5** Use T-accounts to show the flow of costs in a job-order costing system.

**LO6** Prepare schedules of cost of goods manufactured and cost of goods sold and an income statement.

**LO7** Compute underapplied or overapplied overhead cost and prepare the journal entry to close the balance in Manufacturing Overhead to the appropriate accounts.

**Understanding how products and services** are costed is vital to managers because the way in which these costs are determined can have a substantial impact on reported profits, as well as on key management decisions.

A managerial costing system should provide cost data to help managers plan, control, and make decisions. Nevertheless, external financial reporting and tax reporting requirements often heavily influence how costs are accumulated and summarized on managerial reports. This is true of product costing. In this chapter we use *absorption costing* to determine product costs. In **absorption costing,** all manufacturing costs, both fixed and variable, are assigned to units of product—units are said to *fully absorb manufacturing costs*. In later chapters we look at alternatives to absorption costing such as variable costing and activity-based costing.

Most countries—including the United States—require some form of absorption costing for both external financial reports and for tax reports. In addition, the vast majority of companies throughout the world also use absorption costing in their management reports. Because absorption costing is the most common approach to product costing throughout the world, we discuss it first and then discuss the alternatives in subsequent chapters.

## JOB-ORDER COSTING—AN OVERVIEW

Under absorption costing, product costs include all manufacturing costs. Some manufacturing costs, such as direct materials, can be directly traced to particular products. For example, the cost of the airbags installed in a **Toyota** Camry can be easily traced to that particular auto. But what about manufacturing costs like factory rent? Such costs do not change from month to month, whereas the number and variety of products made in the factory may vary dramatically from one month to the next. Because these costs remain unchanged from month to month regardless of what products are made, they are clearly not caused by—and can not be directly traced to—any particular product. Therefore, these types of costs are assigned to products and services by averaging across time and across products. The type of production process influences how this averaging is done.

**Job-order costing** is used in situations where many *different* products are produced each period. For example, a **Levi Strauss** clothing factory would typically make many different types of jeans for both men and women during a month. A particular order might consist of 1,000 boot-cut men's blue denim jeans, style number A312. This order of 1,000 jeans is called a *job*. In a job-order costing system, costs are traced and allocated to jobs and then the costs of the job are divided by the number of units in the job to arrive at an average cost per unit.

Other examples of situations where job-order costing would be used include large-scale construction projects managed by **Bechtel International**, commercial aircraft produced by **Boeing**, greeting cards designed and printed by **Hallmark**, and airline meals prepared by **LSG SkyChefs**. All of these examples are characterized by diverse outputs. Each Bechtel project is unique and different from every other—the company may be simultaneously constructing a dam in Zaire and a bridge in Indonesia. Likewise, each airline orders a different type of meal from LSG SkyChefs' catering service.

Job-order costing is also used extensively in service industries. For example, hospitals, law firms, movie studios, accounting firms, advertising agencies, and repair shops all use a variation of job-order costing to accumulate costs. Although the detailed example of job-order costing provided in the following section deals with a manufacturing company, the same basic concepts and procedures are used by many service organizations.

## Is This Really a Job?

IN BUSINESS

**VBT Bicycling Vacations** of Bristol, Vermont, offers deluxe bicycling vacations in the United States, Canada, Europe, and other locations throughout the world. For example, the company offers a 10-day tour of the Puglia region of Italy—the "heel of the boot." The tour price includes international airfare, 10 nights of lodging, most meals, use of a bicycle, and ground transportation as needed. Each tour is led by at least two local tour leaders, one of whom rides with the guests along the tour route. The other tour leader drives a "sag wagon" that carries extra water, snacks, and bicycle repair equipment and is available for a shuttle back to the hotel or up a hill. The sag wagon also transports guests' luggage from one hotel to another.

Each specific tour can be considered a job. For example, Giuliano Astore and Debora Trippetti, two natives of Puglia, led a VBT tour with 17 guests over 10 days in late April. At the end of the tour, Giuliano submitted a report, a sort of job cost sheet, to VBT headquarters. This report detailed the on the ground expenses incurred for this specific tour, including fuel and operating costs for the van, lodging costs for the guests, the costs of meals provided to guests, the costs of snacks, the cost of hiring additional ground transportation as needed, and the wages of the tour leaders. In addition to these costs, some costs are paid directly by VBT in Vermont to vendors. The total cost incurred for the tour is then compared to the total revenue collected from guests to determine the gross profit for the tour.

Sources: Giuliano Astore and Gregg Marston, President, VBT Bicycling Vacations. For more information about VBT, see www.vbt.com.

## JOB-ORDER COSTING—AN EXAMPLE

To introduce job-order costing, we will follow a specific job as it progresses through the manufacturing process. This job consists of two experimental couplings that Yost Precision Machining has agreed to produce for Loops Unlimited, a manufacturer of roller coasters. Couplings connect the cars on the roller coaster and are a critical component in the performance and safety of the ride. Before we begin our discussion, recall from the previous chapter that companies generally classify manufacturing costs into three broad categories: (1) direct materials, (2) direct labor, and (3) manufacturing overhead. As we study the operation of a job-order costing system, we will see how each of these three types of costs is recorded and accumulated.

**MANAGERIAL ACCOUNTING IN ACTION**
**The Issue**

Yost Precision Machining is a small company in Michigan that specializes in fabricating precision metal parts that are used in a variety of applications ranging from deep-sea exploration vehicles to the inertial triggers in automobile air bags. The company's top managers gather every morning at 8:00 A.M. in the company's conference room for the daily planning meeting. Attending the meeting this morning are: Jean Yost, the company's president; David Cheung, the marketing manager; Debbie Turner, the production manager; and Marc White, the company controller. The president opened the meeting:

YOST Precision Machining

***Jean:*** The production schedule indicates we'll be starting Job 2B47 today. Isn't that the special order for experimental couplings, David?

***David:*** That's right. That's the order from Loops Unlimited for two couplings for their new roller coaster ride for Magic Mountain.

***Debbie:*** Why only two couplings? Don't they need a coupling for every car?

***David:*** Yes. But this is a completely new roller coaster. The cars will go faster and will be subjected to more twists, turns, drops, and loops than on any other existing roller

**EXHIBIT 2–1**
Materials Requisition Form

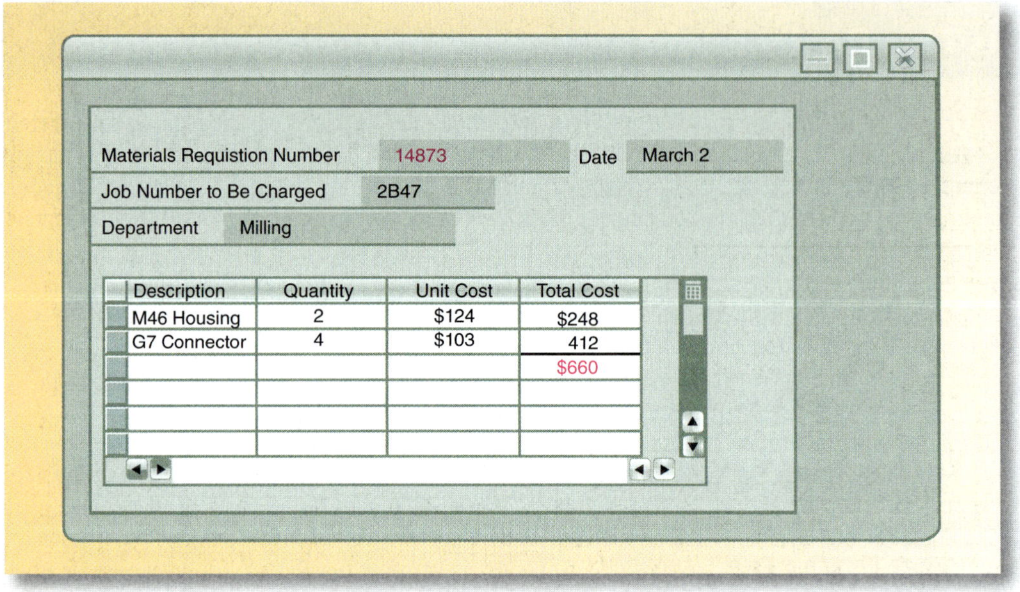

| | | | |
|---|---|---|---|
| Materials Requisition Number | 14873 | Date | March 2 |
| Job Number to Be Charged | 2B47 | | |
| Department | Milling | | |

| Description | Quantity | Unit Cost | Total Cost |
|---|---|---|---|
| M46 Housing | 2 | $124 | $248 |
| G7 Connector | 4 | $103 | 412 |
| | | | $660 |

coaster. To hold up under these stresses, Loops Unlimited's engineers completely redesigned the cars and couplings. They want us to make just two of these new couplings for testing purposes. If the design works, then we'll have the inside track on the order to supply couplings for the whole ride.

***Jean:*** We agreed to take on this initial order at our cost just to get our foot in the door. Marc, will there be any problem documenting our cost so we can get paid?

***Marc:*** No problem. The contract with Loops stipulates that they will pay us an amount equal to our cost of goods sold. With our job-order costing system, I can tell you the cost on the day the job is completed.

***Jean:*** Good. Is there anything else we should discuss about this job at this time? No? Well then let's move on to the next item of business.

## Measuring Direct Materials Cost

The blueprints submitted by Loops Unlimited indicate that each experimental coupling will require three parts that are classified as direct materials: two G7 Connectors and one M46 Housing. Each coupling requires two connectors and one housing, so to make two couplings, four connectors and two housings are required. This is a custom product that is being made for the first time, but if this were one of the company's standard products, it would have an established *bill of materials*. A **bill of materials** is a document that lists the type and quantity of each type of direct material needed to complete a unit of product.

When an agreement has been reached with the customer concerning the quantities, prices, and shipment date for the order, a *production order* is issued. The Production Department then prepares a *materials requisition form* similar to the form in Exhibit 2–1. The **materials requisition form** is a document that specifies the type and quantity of materials to be drawn from the storeroom and identifies the job that will be charged for the cost of the materials. The form is used to control the flow of materials into production and also for making entries in the accounting records.

requisition = a request for something (especially a formal written request)

The Yost Precision Machining materials requisition form in Exhibit 2–1 shows that the company's Milling Department has requisitioned two M46 Housings and four G7 Connectors for the Loops Unlimited job, which has been designated as Job 2B47.

## Job Cost Sheet

After a production order has been issued, the Accounting Department's job-order costing software system automatically generates a *job cost sheet* like the one presented in

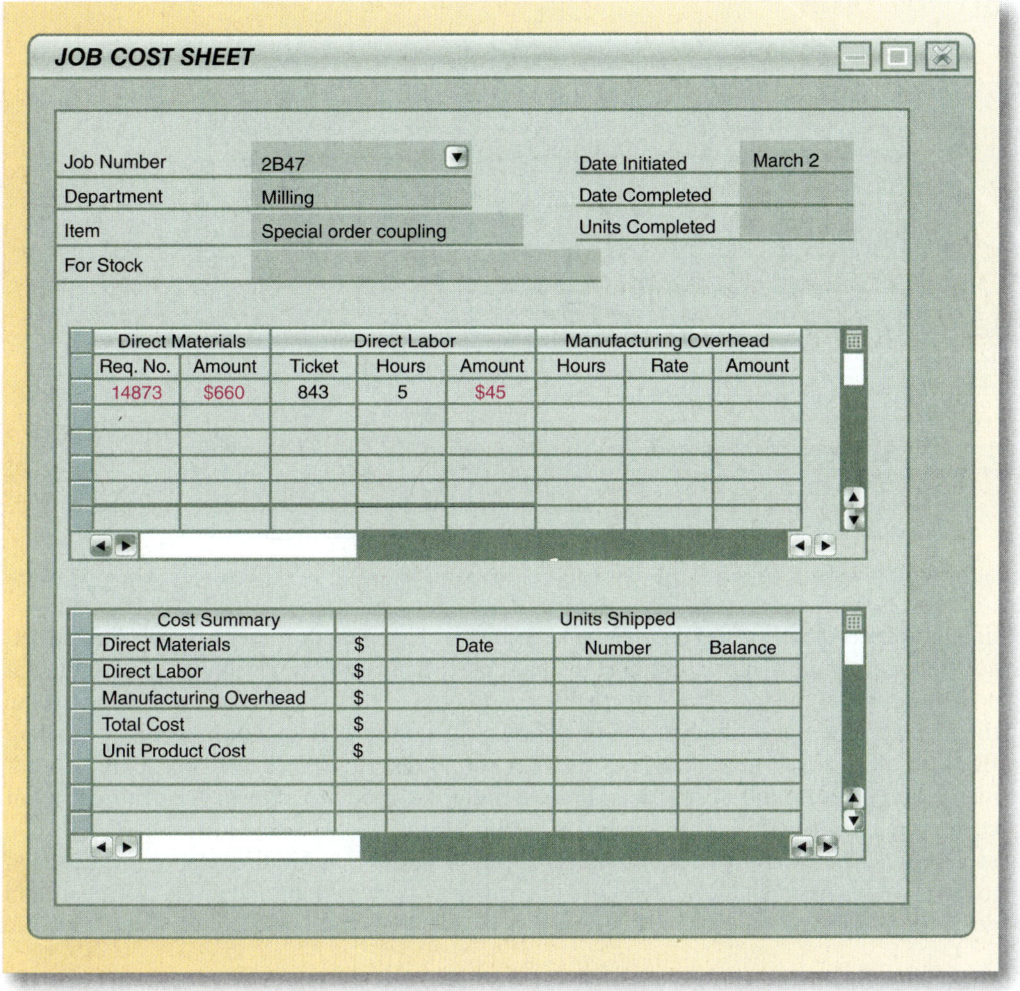

JOB COST SHEET

| | | | |
|---|---|---|---|
| Job Number | 2B47 | Date Initiated | March 2 |
| Department | Milling | Date Completed | |
| Item | Special order coupling | Units Completed | |
| For Stock | | | |

| Direct Materials | | Direct Labor | | | Manufacturing Overhead | | |
|---|---|---|---|---|---|---|---|
| Req. No. | Amount | Ticket | Hours | Amount | Hours | Rate | Amount |
| 14873 | $660 | 843 | 5 | $45 | | | |

| Cost Summary | | Units Shipped | | |
|---|---|---|---|---|
| Direct Materials | $ | Date | Number | Balance |
| Direct Labor | $ | | | |
| Manufacturing Overhead | $ | | | |
| Total Cost | $ | | | |
| Unit Product Cost | $ | | | |

**EXHIBIT 2–2**
Job Cost Sheet

Exhibit 2–2. A **job cost sheet** records the materials, labor, and manufacturing overhead costs charged to that job.

After direct materials are issued, the cost of these materials are automatically recorded on the job cost sheet. Note from Exhibit 2–2, for example, that the $660 cost for direct materials shown earlier on the materials requisition form has been charged to Job 2B47 on its job cost sheet. The requisition number 14873 from the materials requisition form appears on the job cost sheet to make it easier to identify the source document for the direct materials charge.

## Measuring Direct Labor Cost

Direct labor consists of labor charges that are easily traced to a particular job. Labor charges that cannot be easily traced directly to any job are treated as part of manufacturing overhead. As discussed in the previous chapter, this latter category of labor costs is called *indirect labor* and includes tasks such as maintenance, supervision, and cleanup.

Today many companies rely on computerized systems (rather than paper and pencil) to maintain employee *time tickets.* A completed **time ticket** is an hour-by-hour summary of the employee's activities throughout the day. One computerized approach to creating time tickets uses bar codes to capture data. Each employee and each job has a unique bar code. When beginning work on a job, the employee scans three bar codes using a handheld device much like the bar code readers at grocery store checkout stands. The first bar code indicates that a job is being started; the second is the unique bar code on the employee's identity badge; and the third is the unique bar code of the job itself. This information is fed automatically via an electronic network to a computer that notes the

**EXHIBIT 2–3** Employee Time Ticket

| | | | |
|---|---|---|---|
| Time Ticket No. | 843 | Date | March 3 |
| Employee | Mary Holden | Station | 4 |

| Started | Ended | Time Completed | Rate | Amount | Job Number |
|---|---|---|---|---|---|
| 7:00 | 12:00 | 5.0 | $9 | $45 | 2B47 |
| 12:30 | 2:30 | 2.0 | 9 | 18 | 2B50 |
| 2:30 | 3:30 | 1.0 | 9 | 9 | Maintenance |
| Totals | | 8.0 | | $72 | |

time and records all of the data. When the task is completed, the employee scans a bar code indicating the task is complete, the bar code on his or her identity badge, and the bar code attached to the job. This information is relayed to the computer that again notes the time, and a time ticket, such as the one shown in Exhibit 2–3, is automatically prepared. Because all of the source data is already in computer files, the labor costs can be automatically posted to job cost sheets. For example, Exhibit 2–3 shows $45 of direct labor cost related to Job 2B47. This amount is automatically posted to the job cost sheet shown in Exhibit 2–2. The time ticket in Exhibit 2–3 also shows $9 of indirect labor costs related to performing maintenance. This cost is treated as part of manufacturing overhead and does not get posted on a job cost sheet.

## IN BUSINESS — One-of-a-Kind Masterpiece

In a true job-order costing environment, every job is unique. For example, **Purdey** manufactures 80–90 shotguns per year with each gun being a specially commissioned one-of-a-kind masterpiece. The prices start at $110,000 because every detail is custom built, engraved, assembled, and polished by a skilled craftsman. The hand engraving can take months to complete and may add as much as $100,000 to the price. The guns are designed to shoot perfectly straight and their value increases over time even with heavy use. One Purdey gun collector said "when I shoot my Purdeys I feel like an orchestra conductor waving my baton."

Source: Eric Arnold, "Aim High," *Forbes*, December 28, 2009, p. 86.

## Computing Predetermined Overhead Rates

**LEARNING OBJECTIVE 1**
Compute a predetermined overhead rate.

Recall that product costs include manufacturing overhead as well as direct materials and direct labor. Therefore, manufacturing overhead also needs to be recorded on the job cost sheet. However, assigning manufacturing overhead to a specific job involves some difficulties. There are three reasons for this:

1. Manufacturing overhead is an *indirect cost*. This means that it is either impossible or difficult to trace these costs to a particular product or job.
2. Manufacturing overhead consists of many different items ranging from the grease used in machines to the annual salary of the production manager.

3. Because of the fixed costs in manufacturing overhead, total manufacturing overhead costs tend to remain relatively constant from one period to the next even though the number of units produced can fluctuate widely. Consequently, the average cost per unit will vary from one period to the next.

Given these problems, allocation is used to assign overhead costs to products. Allocation is accomplished by selecting an *allocation base* that is common to all of the company's products and services. An **allocation base** is a measure such as direct labor-hours (DLH) or machine-hours (MH) that is used to assign overhead costs to products and services. The most widely used allocation bases in manufacturing are direct labor-hours, direct labor cost, machine-hours, and (where a company has only a single product) units of product.

Manufacturing overhead is commonly assigned to products using *a predetermined overhead rate*. The **predetermined overhead rate** is computed by dividing the total estimated manufacturing overhead cost for the period by the estimated total amount of the allocation base as follows:

$$\text{Predetermined overhead rate} = \frac{\text{Estimated total manufacturing overhead cost}}{\text{Estimated total amount of the allocation base}}$$

The predetermined overhead rate is computed before the period begins using a four-step process. The first step is to estimate the total amount of the allocation base (the denominator) that will be required for next period's estimated level of production. The second step is to estimate the total fixed manufacturing overhead cost for the coming period and the variable manufacturing overhead cost per unit of the allocation base. The third step is to use the cost formula shown below to estimate the total manufacturing overhead cost (the numerator) for the coming period:

$$Y = a + bX$$

Where,

$Y$ = The estimated total manufacturing overhead cost
$a$ = The estimated total fixed manufacturing overhead cost
$b$ = The estimated variable manufacturing overhead cost per unit of the allocation base
$X$ = The estimated total amount of the allocation base

The fourth step is to compute the predetermined overhead rate. Notice, the estimated amount of the allocation base is determined before estimating the total manufacturing overhead cost. This needs to be done because total manufacturing overhead cost includes variable overhead costs that depend on the amount of the allocation base.

## Applying Manufacturing Overhead

**LEARNING OBJECTIVE 2**
Apply overhead cost to jobs using a predetermined overhead rate.

To repeat, the predetermined overhead rate is computed *before* the period begins. The predetermined overhead rate is then used to apply overhead cost to jobs throughout the period. The process of assigning overhead cost to jobs is called **overhead application.** The formula for determining the amount of overhead cost to apply to a particular job is:

$$\begin{matrix}\text{Overhead applied to} \\ \text{a particular job}\end{matrix} = \begin{matrix}\text{Predetermined} \\ \text{overhead rate}\end{matrix} \times \begin{matrix}\text{Amount of the allocation} \\ \text{base incurred by the job}\end{matrix}$$

For example, if the predetermined overhead rate is $8 per direct labor-hour, then $8 of overhead cost is *applied* to a job for each direct labor-hour incurred on the job. When the allocation base is direct labor-hours, the formula becomes:

$$\begin{matrix}\text{Overhead applied to} \\ \text{a particular job}\end{matrix} = \begin{matrix}\text{Predetermined} \\ \text{overhead rate}\end{matrix} \times \begin{matrix}\text{Actual direct labor-hours} \\ \text{charged to the job}\end{matrix}$$

## Manufacturing Overhead—A Closer Look

To illustrate the steps involved in computing and using a predetermined overhead rate, let's return to Yost Precision Machining and make the following assumptions. In step one, the company estimated that 40,000 direct labor-hours would be required to support the production planned for the year. In step two, it estimated $220,000 of total fixed manufacturing overhead cost for the coming year and $2.50 of variable manufacturing overhead cost per direct labor-hour. Given these assumptions, in step three the company used the cost formula shown below to estimate its total manufacturing overhead cost for the year:

$$Y = a + bX$$
$$Y = \$220{,}000 + (\$2.50 \text{ per direct labor-hour} \times 40{,}000 \text{ direct labor-hours})$$
$$Y = \$220{,}000 + \$100{,}000$$
$$Y = \$320{,}000$$

In step four, Yost Precision Machining computed its predetermined overhead rate for the year of $8 per direct labor-hour as shown below:

$$\text{Predetermined overhead rate} = \frac{\text{Estimated total manufacturing overhead cost}}{\text{Estimated total amount of the allocation base}}$$
$$= \frac{\$320{,}000}{40{,}000 \text{ direct labor-hours}}$$
$$= \$8 \text{ per direct labor-hour}$$

The job cost sheet in Exhibit 2–4 indicates that 27 direct labor-hours (i.e., DLHs) were charged to Job 2B47. Therefore, a total of $216 of manufacturing overhead cost would be applied to the job:

$$\begin{array}{c}\text{Overhead applied to}\\ \text{Job 2B47}\end{array} = \begin{array}{c}\text{Predetermined}\\ \text{overhead rate}\end{array} \times \begin{array}{c}\text{Actual direct labor-hours}\\ \text{charged to Job 2B47}\end{array}$$
$$= \$8 \text{ per DLH} \times 27 \text{ DLHs}$$
$$= \$216 \text{ of overhead applied to Job 2B47}$$

This amount of overhead has been entered on the job cost sheet in Exhibit 2–4. Note that this is *not* the actual amount of overhead caused by the job. Actual overhead costs are *not* assigned to jobs—if that could be done, the costs would be direct costs, not overhead. The overhead assigned to the job is simply a share of the total overhead that was estimated at the beginning of the year. A **normal cost system,** which we have been describing, applies overhead to jobs by multiplying a predetermined overhead rate by the actual amount of the allocation base incurred by the jobs.

### HELPFUL HINT

This chapter is based on the concept of normal costing. A normal cost system assigns actual direct materials and direct labor costs to jobs; however, it does *not* assign actual overhead costs to jobs. Instead, a predetermined overhead rate is used to apply overhead cost to jobs. The predetermined overhead rate is multiplied by the actual quantity of the allocation base consumed by a job to apply overhead cost to that job. Many companies use normal cost systems; however, companies can also use other types of cost systems, such as actual costing and standard costing, that will be discussed in later chapters.

## The Need for a Predetermined Rate

Instead of using a predetermined rate based on estimates, why not base the overhead rate on the *actual* total manufacturing overhead cost and the *actual* total amount of the allocation base incurred on a monthly, quarterly, or annual basis? If an actual rate is computed monthly

**EXHIBIT 2–4**
A Completed Job Cost Sheet

**JOB COST SHEET**

| | | | |
|---|---|---|---|
| Job Number | 2B47 | Date Initiated | March 2 |
| Department | Milling | Date Completed | March 8 |
| Item | Special order coupling | | |
| For Stock | | Units Completed | 2 |

| Direct Materials | | Direct Labor | | | Manufacturing Overhead | | |
|---|---|---|---|---|---|---|---|
| Req. No. | Amount | Ticket | Hours | Amount | Hours | Rate | Amount |
| 14873 | $ 660 | 843 | 5 | $ 45 | 27 | $8/DLH | $216 |
| 14875 | 506 | 846 | 8 | 60 | | | |
| 14912 | 238 | 850 | 4 | 21 | | | |
| | $1,404 | 851 | 10 | 54 | | | |
| | | | 27 | $180 | | | |

| Cost Summary | | Units Shipped | | |
|---|---|---|---|---|
| | | Date | Number | Balance |
| Direct Materials | $ 1,404 | March 8 | — | 2 |
| Direct Labor | $ 180 | | | |
| Manufacturing Overhead | $ 216 | | | |
| Total Product Cost | $ 1,800 | | | |
| Unit Product Cost | $ 900* | | | |

*$1,800 ÷ 2 units = $900 per unit.

or quarterly, seasonal factors in overhead costs or in the allocation base can produce fluctuations in the overhead rate. For example, the costs of heating and cooling a factory in Illinois will be highest in the winter and summer months and lowest in the spring and fall. If the overhead rate is recomputed at the end of each month or each quarter based on actual costs and activity, the overhead rate would go up in the winter and summer and down in the spring and fall. As a result, two identical jobs, one completed in the winter and one completed in the spring, would be assigned different manufacturing overhead costs. Many managers believe that such fluctuations in product costs serve no useful purpose. To avoid such fluctuations, actual overhead rates could be computed on an annual or less-frequent basis. However, if the overhead rate is computed annually based on the actual costs and activity for the year, the manufacturing overhead assigned to any particular job would not be known until the end of the year. For example, the cost of Job 2B47 at Yost Precision Machining would not be known until the end of the year, even though the job will be completed and shipped to the customer in March. For these reasons, most companies use predetermined overhead rates rather than actual overhead rates in their cost accounting systems.

## Choice of an Allocation Base for Overhead Cost

Ideally, the allocation base in the predetermined overhead rate should *drive* the overhead cost. A **cost driver** is a factor, such as machine-hours, beds occupied, computer time, or flight-hours, that causes overhead costs. If the base in the predetermined overhead rate does not "drive" overhead costs, product costs will be distorted. For example, if direct labor-hours is used to allocate overhead, but in reality overhead has little to do with direct labor-hours, then products with high direct labor-hour requirements will be overcosted.

Cost driver - factor that causes overhead costs

Most companies use direct labor-hours or direct labor cost as the allocation base for manufacturing overhead. In the past, direct labor accounted for up to 60% of the cost of many products, with overhead cost making up only a portion of the remainder. This situation has changed for two reasons. First, sophisticated automated equipment has taken over functions that used to be performed by direct labor workers. Because the costs of acquiring and maintaining such equipment are classified as overhead, this increases overhead while decreasing direct labor. Second, products are becoming more sophisticated and complex and are changed more frequently. This increases the need for highly skilled indirect workers such as engineers. As a result of these two trends, direct labor has decreased relative to overhead as a component of product costs.

In companies where direct labor and overhead costs have been moving in opposite directions, it would be difficult to argue that direct labor "drives" overhead costs. Accordingly, managers in some companies use *activity-based costing* principles to redesign their cost accounting systems. Activity-based costing is designed to more accurately reflect the demands that products, customers, and other cost objects make on overhead resources. The activity-based approach is discussed in more detail in Chapter 3.

Although direct labor may not be an appropriate allocation base in some industries, in others it continues to be a significant driver of manufacturing overhead. Indeed, most manufacturing companies in the United States continue to use direct labor as the primary or secondary allocation base for manufacturing overhead. The key point is that the allocation base used by the company should really drive, or cause, overhead costs, and direct labor is not always the most appropriate allocation base.

allocation base used by the company should really drive, or cause, overhead costs.

## IN BUSINESS

### Reducing Health-Damaging Behaviors

**Cianbro** is an industrial construction company headquartered in Pittsfield, Maine, whose goal is "To be the healthiest company in America." It introduced a corporate wellness program to attack employee behaviors that drive up health-care costs. The table below summarizes the number of employees in five health risk categories as of 2003 and 2005. The decreases in the number of employees in these high-risk categories are evidence that the wellness program was effective in helping employees make positive lifestyle changes. This should result in reduced health-care costs for the company.

| | Number of Employees | | |
|---|---|---|---|
| **Health Risk Category** | **January 2003** | **March 2005** | **Decrease** |
| Obesity | 432 | 353 | 79 |
| High cholesterol | 637 | 515 | 122 |
| Tobacco use | 384 | 274 | 110 |
| Inactivity | 354 | 254 | 100 |
| High blood pressure | 139 | 91 | 48 |

Source: Cianbro, WELCOA's *Absolute Advantage* Magazine, 2006.

## Computation of Unit Costs

**LEARNING OBJECTIVE 3**

Compute the total cost and average cost per unit of a job.

With the application of Yost Precision Machining's $216 of manufacturing overhead to the job cost sheet in Exhibit 2–4, the job cost sheet is complete except for two final steps. First, the totals for direct materials, direct labor, and manufacturing overhead are transferred to the Cost Summary section of the job cost sheet and added together to obtain the total cost for the job.[1] Then the total product cost ($1,800) is divided by the number of

[1] Notice, we are assuming that Job 2B47 required direct materials and direct labor beyond the charges shown in Exhibits 2–1 and 2–3.

units (2) to obtain the unit product cost ($900). This unit product cost information is used for valuing unsold units in ending inventory and for determining cost of goods sold. As indicated earlier, *this unit product cost is an average cost and should not be interpreted as the cost that would actually be incurred if another unit were produced.* The incremental cost of an additional unit is something less than the average unit cost of $900 because much of the actual overhead costs would not change if another unit were produced.

**MANAGERIAL ACCOUNTING IN ACTION**
**The Wrap-up**

In the 8:00 A.M. daily planning meeting on March 9, Jean Yost, the president of Yost Precision Machining, once again drew attention to Job 2B47, the experimental couplings:

***Jean:*** I see Job 2B47 is completed. Let's get those couplings shipped immediately to Loops Unlimited so they can get their testing program under way. Marc, how much are we going to bill Loops for those two units?

***Marc:*** Because we agreed to sell the experimental couplings at cost, we will be charging Loops Unlimited just $900 a unit.

***Jean:*** Fine. Let's hope the couplings work out and we make some money on the big order later.

YOST Precision Machining

**CONCEPT CHECK**

1. Which of the following statements is false? (You may select more than one answer.)
   a. Absorption costing assigns fixed and variable manufacturing overhead costs to products.
   b. Job-order costing systems are used when companies produce many different types of products.
   c. A normal costing system assigns overhead costs to products by multiplying the actual overhead rate by the actual amount of the allocation base.
   d. A unit product cost represents the additional cost that would be incurred if another unit were produced.
2. Assume that a company's total estimated fixed overhead cost for the coming year is $100,000 and its estimated variable overhead cost is $3.00 per direct labor-hour. If the company estimates that it will work 50,000 direct labor-hours in the coming year, what is its predetermined overhead rate per direct labor-hour?
   a. $2.00
   b. $3.00
   c. $4.00
   d. $5.00

**DECISION POINT**

## Treasurer, Class Reunion Committee

You've agreed to handle the financial arrangements for your high school reunion. You call the restaurant where the reunion will be held and jot down the most important information. The meal cost (including beverages) will be $30 per person plus a 15% gratuity. An additional $200 will be charged for a banquet room with a dance floor. A band has been hired for $500. One of the members of the reunion committee informs you that there is just enough money left in the class bank account to cover the printing and mailing costs. He mentions that at least one-half of the class of 400 will attend the reunion and wonders if he should add the 15% gratuity to the $30 per person meal cost when he drafts the invitation, which will indicate that a check must be returned with the reply card.

How should you respond? How much will you need to charge to cover the various costs? After making your decision, label your answer with the managerial accounting terms covered in this chapter. Finally, identify any issues that should be investigated further.

## JOB-ORDER COSTING—THE FLOW OF COSTS

**LEARNING OBJECTIVE 4**

Understand the flow of costs in a job-order costing system and prepare appropriate journal entries to record costs.

We are now ready to discuss the flow of costs through a job-order costing system. Exhibit 2–5 provides a conceptual overview of these cost flows. It highlights the fact that *product costs* flow through inventories on the balance sheet and then on to cost of goods sold in the income statement. More specifically, raw materials purchases are recorded in the *Raw Materials* inventory account. **Raw materials** include any materials that go into the final product. When raw materials are used in production, their costs are transferred to the *Work in Process* inventory account as direct materials.[2] **Work in process** consists of units of product that are only partially complete and will require further work before they are ready for sale to the customer. Notice that direct labor costs are added directly to Work in Process—they do not flow through Raw Materials inventory. Manufacturing overhead costs are applied to Work in Process by multiplying the predetermined overhead rate by the actual quantity of the allocation base consumed by each job.[3] When goods are completed, their costs are transferred from Work in Process to *Finished Goods*. **Finished goods** consist of completed units of product that have not yet been sold to customers. The amount transferred from Work in Process to Finished Goods is referred to as the *cost of goods manufactured*. The **cost of goods manufactured** includes the manufacturing costs associated with the goods that were finished during the period. As goods are sold, their costs are transferred from Finished Goods to Cost of Goods Sold. At this point, the various costs required to make the product are finally recorded as an expense. Until that point, these costs are in inventory accounts on the balance sheet. Period costs (or selling and administrative expenses) do not flow through inventories on the balance sheet. They are recorded as expenses on the income statement in the period incurred.

To illustrate the cost flows through a company's general ledger, we will consider a single month's activity at Ruger Corporation, a producer of gold and silver commemorative

**EXHIBIT 2–5** Cost Flows and Classifications in a Manufacturing Company

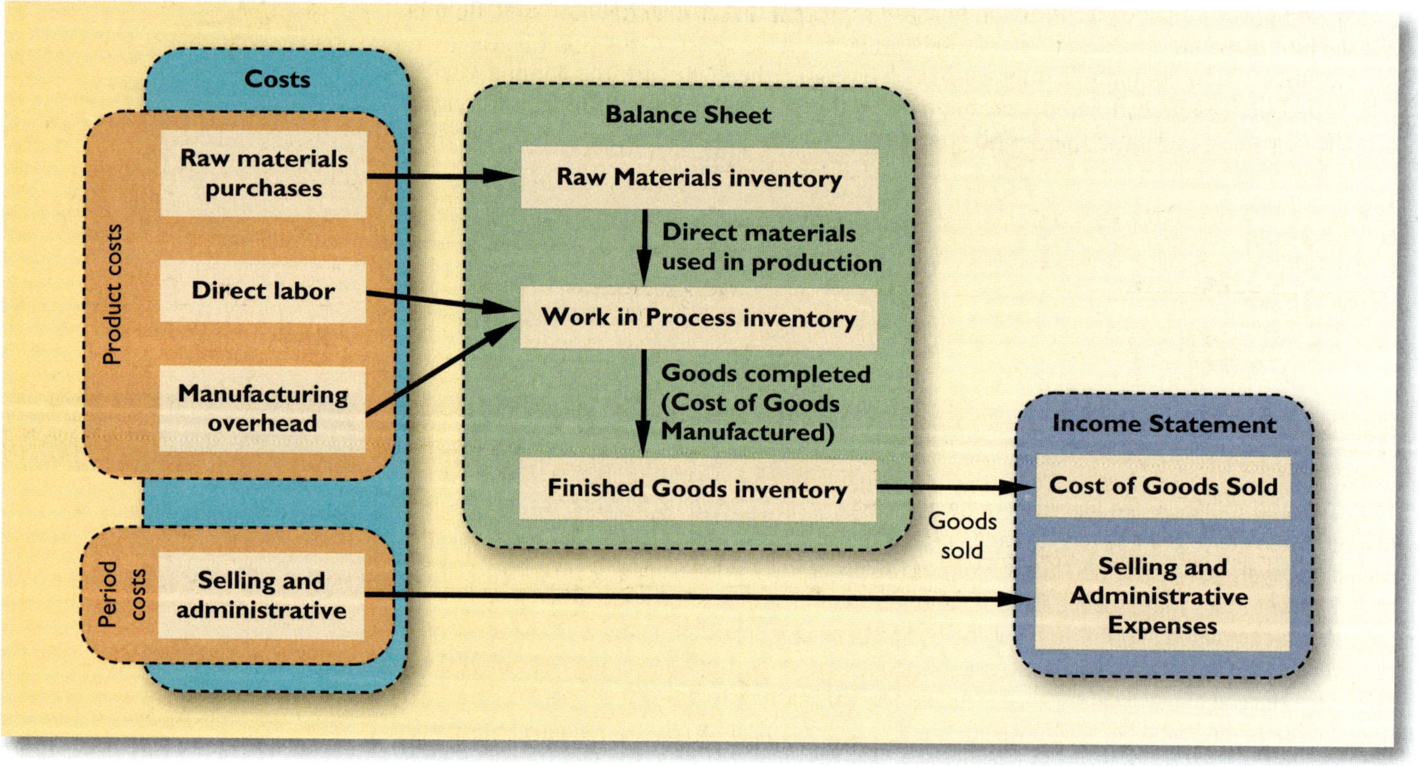


[2]Indirect material costs are accounted for as part of manufacturing overhead.

[3]For simplicity, Exhibit 2–5 assumes that Cost of Goods Sold does not need to be adjusted as discussed later in the chapter.

medallions. Ruger Corporation has two jobs in process during April, the first month of its fiscal year. Job A, a special minting of 1,000 gold medallions commemorating the invention of motion pictures, was started during March. By the end of March, $30,000 in manufacturing costs had been recorded for the job. Job B, an order for 10,000 silver medallions commemorating the fall of the Berlin Wall, was started in April.

## The Purchase and Issue of Materials

On April 1, Ruger Corporation had $7,000 in raw materials on hand. During the month, the company purchased on account an additional $60,000 in raw materials. The purchase is recorded in journal entry (1) below:

(1)

| | | |
|---|---|---|
| Raw Materials | 60,000 | |
| Accounts Payable | | 60,000 |

Remember that Raw Materials is an asset account. Thus, when raw materials are purchased, they are initially recorded as an asset—not as an expense.

**Issue of Direct and Indirect Materials** During April, $52,000 in raw materials were requisitioned from the storeroom for use in production. These raw materials included $50,000 of direct and $2,000 of indirect materials. Entry (2) records issuing the materials to the production departments.

(2)

| | | |
|---|---|---|
| Work in Process | 50,000 | |
| Manufacturing Overhead | 2,000 | |
| Raw Materials | | 52,000 |

The materials charged to Work in Process represent direct materials for specific jobs. These costs are also recorded on the appropriate job cost sheets. This point is illustrated in Exhibit 2–6, where $28,000 of the $50,000 in direct materials is charged to Job A's cost sheet and the remaining $22,000 is charged to Job B's cost sheet. (In this example, all data are presented in summary form and the job cost sheet is abbreviated.)

**EXHIBIT 2–6** Raw Materials Cost Flows

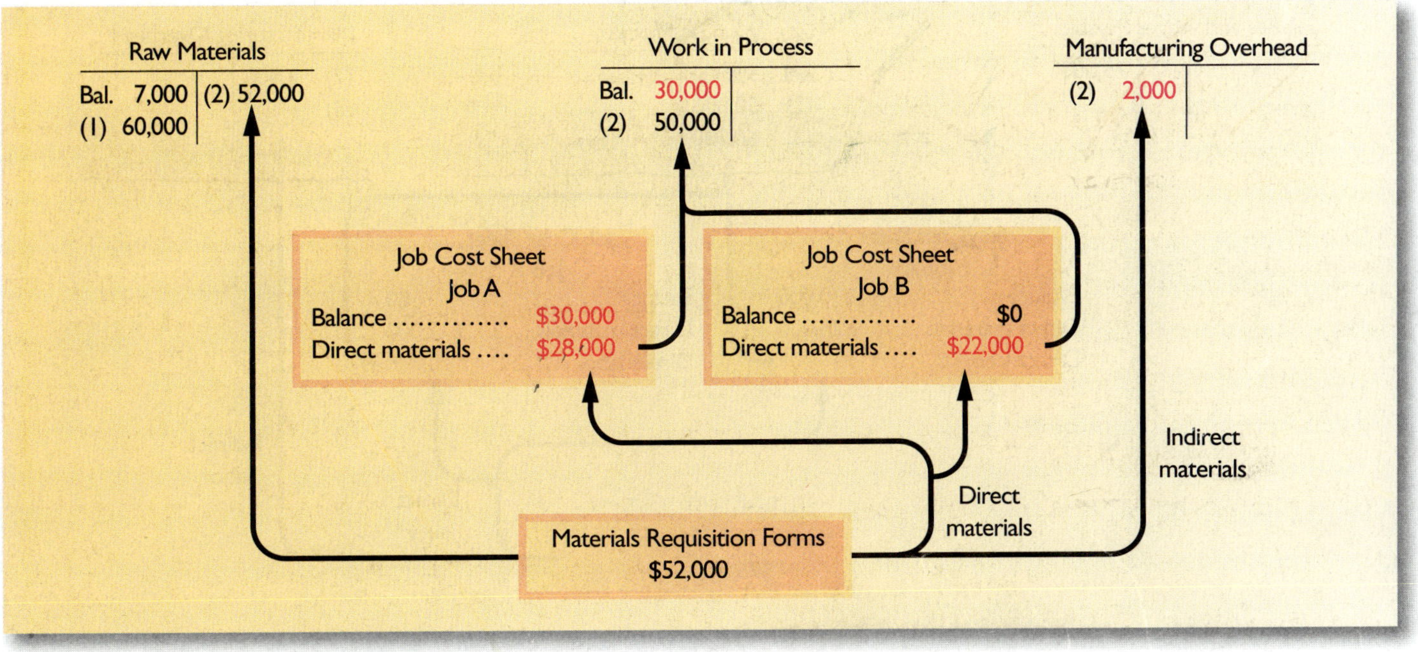

The $2,000 charged to Manufacturing Overhead in entry (2) represents indirect materials. Observe that the Manufacturing Overhead account is separate from the Work in Process account. The purpose of the Manufacturing Overhead account is to accumulate all manufacturing overhead costs as they are incurred during a period.

Before leaving Exhibit 2–6, we need to point out one additional thing. Notice from the exhibit that the job cost sheet for Job A contains a beginning balance of $30,000. We stated earlier that this balance represents the cost of work done during March that has been carried forward to April. Also note that the Work in Process account contains the same $30,000 balance. Thus, the Work in Process account summarizes all of the costs appearing on the job cost sheets of the jobs that are in process. Job A was the only job in process at the beginning of April, so the beginning balance in the Work in Process account equals Job A's beginning balance of $30,000.

## Labor Cost

In April, the employee time tickets included $60,000 recorded for direct labor and $15,000 for indirect labor. The following entry summarizes these costs:

(3)

| | | |
|---|---|---|
| Work in Process | 60,000 | |
| Manufacturing Overhead | 15,000 | |
| Salaries and Wages Payable | | 75,000 |

Only the direct labor cost of $60,000 is added to the Work in Process account. At the same time that direct labor costs are added to Work in Process, they are also added to the individual job cost sheets, as shown in Exhibit 2–7. During April, $40,000 of direct labor cost was charged to Job A and the remaining $20,000 was charged to Job B.

The labor costs charged to Manufacturing Overhead ($15,000) represent the indirect labor costs of the period, such as supervision, janitorial work, and maintenance.

## Manufacturing Overhead Costs

Recall that all manufacturing costs other than direct materials and direct labor are classified as manufacturing overhead costs. These costs are entered directly into the Manufacturing

**EXHIBIT 2–7** Labor Cost Flows

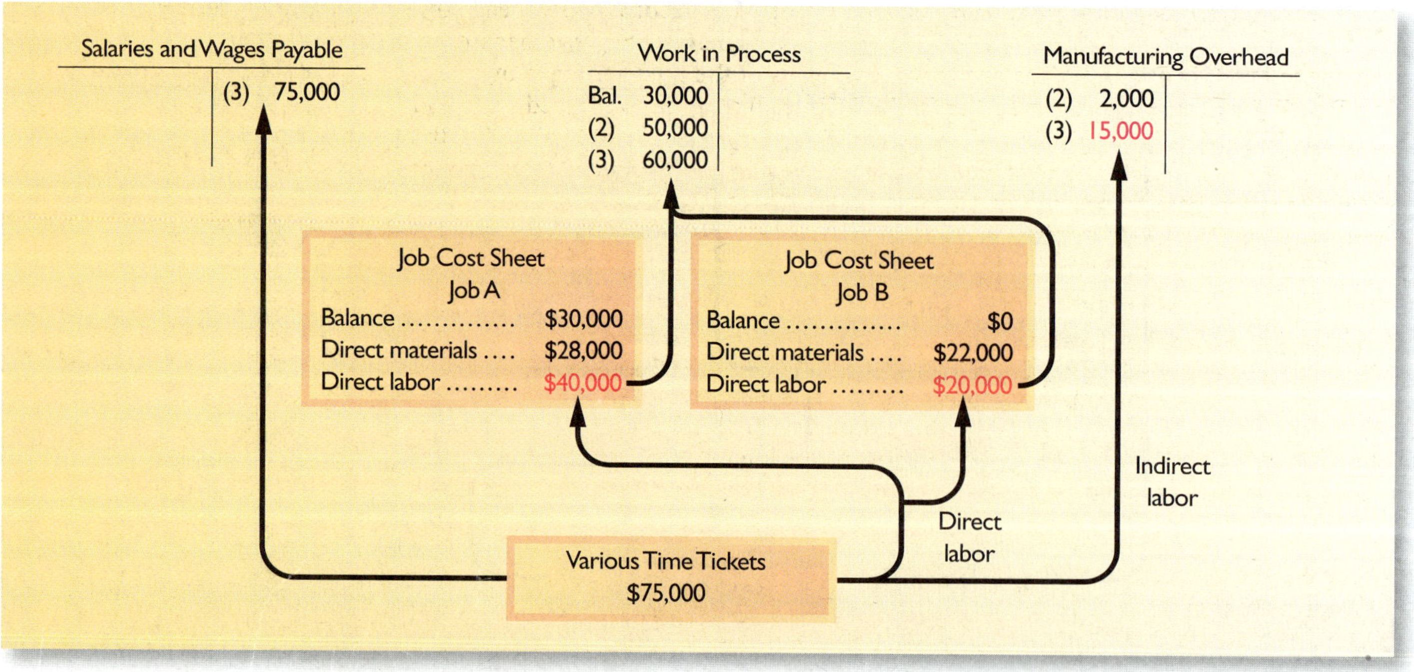

Overhead account as they are incurred. To illustrate, assume that Ruger Corporation incurred the following general factory costs during April:

| | |
|---|---|
| Utilities (heat, water, and power) | $21,000 |
| Rent on factory equipment | 16,000 |
| Miscellaneous factory overhead costs | 3,000 |
| Total | $40,000 |

The following entry records the incurrence of these costs:

(4)

| | | |
|---|---|---|
| Manufacturing Overhead | 40,000 | |
| Accounts Payable* | | 40,000 |

*Accounts such as Cash may also be credited

In addition, assume that during April, Ruger Corporation recognized $13,000 in accrued property taxes and that $7,000 in prepaid insurance expired on factory buildings and equipment. The following entry records these items:

(5)

| | | |
|---|---|---|
| Manufacturing Overhead | 20,000 | |
| Property Taxes Payable | | 13,000 |
| Prepaid Insurance | | 7,000 |

Finally, assume that the company recognized $18,000 in depreciation on factory equipment during April. The following entry records the accrual of this depreciation:

(6)

| | | |
|---|---|---|
| Manufacturing Overhead | 18,000 | |
| Accumulated Depreciation | | 18,000 |

In short, all actual manufacturing overhead costs are debited to the Manufacturing Overhead account as they are incurred.

## Applying Manufacturing Overhead

Because actual manufacturing costs are charged to the Manufacturing Overhead control account rather than to Work in Process, how are manufacturing overhead costs assigned to Work in Process? The answer is, by means of the predetermined overhead rate. Recall from our discussion earlier in the chapter that a predetermined overhead rate is established at the beginning of each year. The rate is calculated by dividing the estimated total manufacturing overhead cost for the year by the estimated total amount of the allocation base (measured in machine-hours, direct labor-hours, or some other base). The predetermined overhead rate is then used to apply overhead costs to jobs. For example, if machine-hours is the allocation base, overhead cost is applied to each job by multiplying the predetermined overhead rate by the number of machine-hours charged to the job.

To illustrate, assume that Ruger Corporation's predetermined overhead rate is $6 per machine-hour. Also assume that during April, 10,000 machine-hours were worked on Job A and 5,000 machine-hours were worked on Job B (a total of 15,000 machine-hours). Thus, $90,000 in overhead cost ($6 per machine-hour × 15,000 machine-hours = $90,000) would be applied to Work in Process. The following entry records the application of Manufacturing Overhead to Work in Process:

(7)

| | | |
|---|---|---|
| Work in Process | 90,000 | |
| Manufacturing Overhead | | 90,000 |

**EXHIBIT 2–8**
The Flow of Costs in Overhead Application

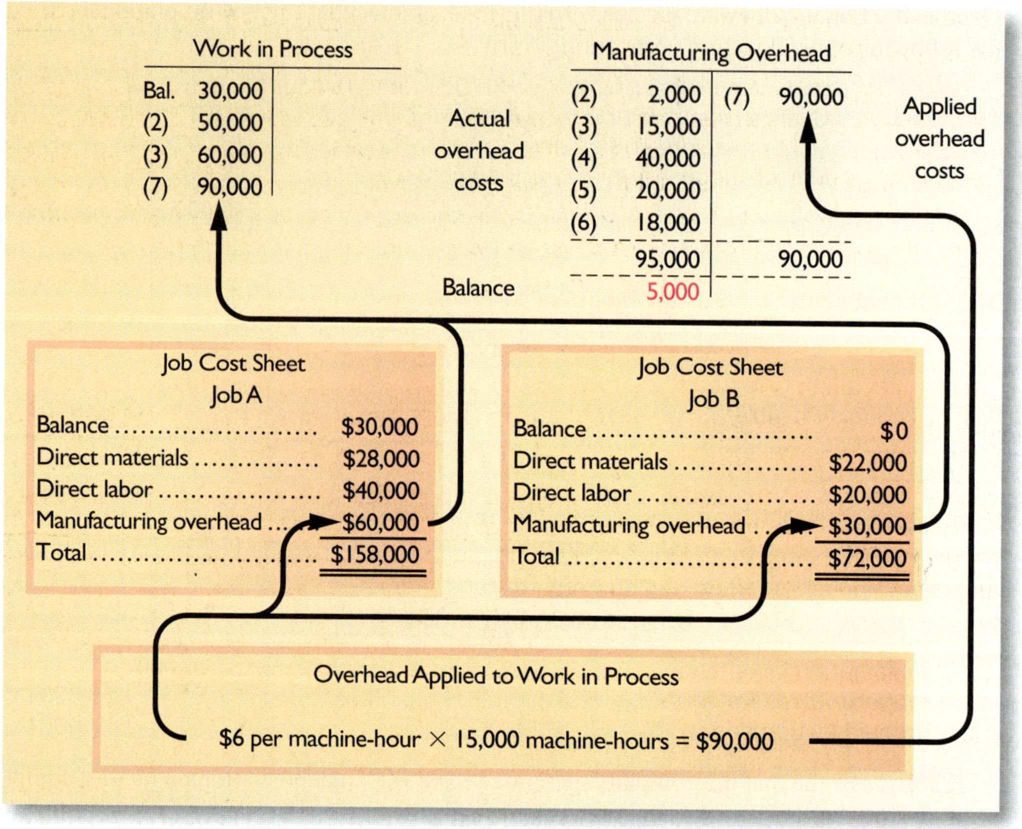


The flow of costs through the Manufacturing Overhead account is shown in Exhibit 2–8. The actual overhead costs on the debit side in the Manufacturing Overhead account in Exhibit 2–8 are the costs that were added to the account in entries (2)–(6). Observe that recording these actual overhead costs [entries (2)–(6)] and the application of overhead to Work in Process [entry (7)] represent two separate and entirely distinct processes.

**The Concept of a Clearing Account** The Manufacturing Overhead account operates as a clearing account. As we have noted, actual factory overhead costs are debited to the account as they are incurred throughout the year. When a job is completed (or at the end of an accounting period), overhead cost is applied to the job using the predetermined overhead rate, and Work in Process is debited and Manufacturing Overhead is credited. This sequence of events is illustrated below:

**Manufacturing Overhead**
**(a clearing account)**

| | |
|---|---|
| Actual overhead costs are charged to this account as they are incurred throughout the period. | Overhead is applied to Work in Process using the predetermined overhead rate. |

As we emphasized earlier, the predetermined overhead rate is based entirely on estimates of what the level of activity and overhead costs are *expected* to be, and it is established before the year begins. As a result, the overhead cost applied during a year will almost certainly turn out to be more or less than the actual overhead cost incurred. For example, notice from Exhibit 2–8 that Ruger Corporation's actual overhead costs for the period are $5,000 greater than the overhead cost that has been applied to Work in Process, resulting in a $5,000 debit balance in the Manufacturing

Overhead account. We will reserve discussion of what to do with this $5,000 balance until later in the chapter.

For the moment, we can conclude from Exhibit 2–8 that the cost of a completed job consists of the actual direct materials cost of the job, the actual direct labor cost of the job, and the manufacturing overhead cost *applied* to the job. Pay particular attention to the following subtle but important point: *Actual overhead costs are not charged to jobs; actual overhead costs do not appear on the job cost sheet nor do they appear in the Work in Process account. Only the applied overhead cost, based on the predetermined overhead rate, appears on the job cost sheet and in the Work in Process account.*

**HELPFUL HINT**

Actual manufacturing overhead costs are recorded as debits to the Manufacturing Overhead account. The amount of manufacturing overhead applied to all jobs using the predetermined overhead rate is recorded on the credit side of the Manufacturing Overhead account. The manufacturing overhead cost added to all job cost sheets during a period will equal the amount of the credits recorded in the Manufacturing Overhead account during that period.

## Nonmanufacturing Costs

In addition to manufacturing costs, companies also incur selling and administrative costs. These costs should be treated as period expenses and charged directly to the income statement. *Nonmanufacturing costs should not go into the Manufacturing Overhead account.* To illustrate the correct treatment of nonmanufacturing costs, assume that Ruger Corporation incurred $30,000 in selling and administrative salary costs during April. The following entry summarizes the accrual of those salaries:

(8)

| | | |
|---|---|---|
| Salaries Expense | 30,000 | |
| Salaries and Wages Payable | | 30,000 |

Assume that depreciation on office equipment during April was $7,000. The entry is as follows:

(9)

| | | |
|---|---|---|
| Depreciation Expense | 7,000 | |
| Accumulated Depreciation | | 7,000 |

Pay particular attention to the difference between this entry and entry (6) where we recorded depreciation on factory equipment. In journal entry (6), depreciation on factory equipment was debited to Manufacturing Overhead and is therefore a product cost. In journal entry (9) above, depreciation on office equipment is debited to Depreciation Expense. Depreciation on office equipment is a period expense rather than a product cost.

Finally, assume that advertising was $42,000 and that other selling and administrative expenses in April totaled $8,000. The following entry records these items:

(10)

| | | |
|---|---|---|
| Advertising Expense | 42,000 | |
| Other Selling and Administrative Expense | 8,000 | |
| Accounts Payable* | | 50,000 |

*Other accounts, such as Cash may be credited.

The amounts in entries (8) through (10) are recorded directly into expense accounts—they have no effect on product costs. The same will be true of any other selling and administrative expenses incurred during April, including sales commissions, depreciation on sales equipment, rent on office facilities, insurance on office facilities, and related costs.

## Cost of Goods Manufactured

When a job has been completed, the finished output is transferred from the production departments to the finished goods warehouse. By this time, the accounting department will have charged the job with direct materials and direct labor cost, and manufacturing overhead will have been applied using the predetermined overhead rate. A transfer of costs is made within the costing system that *parallels* the physical transfer of goods to the finished goods warehouse. The costs of the completed job are transferred out of the Work in Process account and into the Finished Goods account. The sum of all amounts transferred between these two accounts represents the cost of goods manufactured for the period.

In the case of Ruger Corporation, assume that Job A was completed during April. The following entry transfers the cost of Job A from Work in Process to Finished Goods:

(11)

| | | |
|---|---|---|
| Finished Goods | 158,000 | |
| Work in Process | | 158,000 |

The $158,000 represents the completed cost of Job A, as shown on the job cost sheet in Exhibit 2–8. Because Job A was the only job completed during April, the $158,000 also represents the cost of goods manufactured for the month.

Job B was not completed by the end of the month, so its cost will remain in the Work in Process account and carry over to the next month. If a balance sheet is prepared at the end of April, the cost accumulated thus far on Job B will appear as the asset "Work in Process inventory."

## Cost of Goods Sold

As finished goods are shipped to customers, their accumulated costs are transferred from the Finished Goods account to the Cost of Goods Sold account. If an entire job is shipped at one time, then the entire cost appearing on the job cost sheet is transferred to the Cost of Goods Sold account. In most cases, however, only a portion of the units involved in a particular job will be immediately sold. In these situations, the unit product cost must be used to determine how much product cost should be removed from Finished Goods and charged to Cost of Goods Sold.

For Ruger Corporation, we will assume 750 of the 1,000 gold medallions in Job A were shipped to customers by the end of the month for total sales revenue of $225,000. Because 1,000 units were produced and the total cost of the job from the job cost sheet was $158,000, the unit product cost was $158. The following journal entries would record the sale (all sales were on account):

(12)

| | | |
|---|---|---|
| Accounts Receivable | 225,000 | |
| Sales | | 225,000 |

(13)

| | | |
|---|---|---|
| Cost of Goods Sold | 118,500 | |
| Finished Goods | | 118,500 |
| (750 units × $158 per unit = $118,500) | | |

Entry (13) completes the flow of costs through the job-order costing system. To pull the entire Ruger Corporation example together, journal entries (1) through (13) are summarized in Exhibit 2–9. The flow of costs through the accounts is presented in T-account form in Exhibit 2–10.

**LEARNING OBJECTIVE 5**

Use T-accounts to show the flow of costs in a job-order costing system.

**EXHIBIT 2–9**
Summary of Journal Entries—Ruger Corporation

| | | |
|---|---|---|
| (1) | | |
| Raw Materials | 60,000 | |
| Accounts Payable | | 60,000 |
| (2) | | |
| Work in Process | 50,000 | |
| Manufacturing Overhead | 2,000 | |
| Raw Materials | | 52,000 |
| (3) | | |
| Work in Process | 60,000 | |
| Manufacturing Overhead | 15,000 | |
| Salaries and Wages Payable | | 75,000 |
| (4) | | |
| Manufacturing Overhead | 40,000 | |
| Accounts Payable | | 40,000 |
| (5) | | |
| Manufacturing Overhead | 20,000 | |
| Property Taxes Payable | | 13,000 |
| Prepaid Insurance | | 7,000 |
| (6) | | |
| Manufacturing Overhead | 18,000 | |
| Accumulated Depreciation | | 18,000 |
| (7) | | |
| Work in Process | 90,000 | |
| Manufacturing Overhead | | 90,000 |
| (8) | | |
| Salaries Expense | 30,000 | |
| Salaries and Wages Payable | | 30,000 |
| (9) | | |
| Depreciation Expense | 7,000 | |
| Accumulated Depreciation | | 7,000 |
| (10) | | |
| Advertising Expense | 42,000 | |
| Other Selling and Administrative Expense | 8,000 | |
| Accounts Payable | | 50,000 |
| (11) | | |
| Finished Goods | 158,000 | |
| Work in Process | | 158,000 |
| (12) | | |
| Accounts Receivable | 225,000 | |
| Sales | | 225,000 |
| (13) | | |
| Cost of Goods Sold | 118,500 | |
| Finished Goods | | 118,500 |

**EXHIBIT 2–10** Summary of Cost Flows—Ruger Corporation

**Accounts Receivable**

| | | | |
|---|---|---|---|
| Bal. | XX | | |
| (12) | 225,000 | | |

**Prepaid Insurance**

| | | | |
|---|---|---|---|
| Bal. | XX | | |
| | | (5) | 7,000 |

**Raw Materials**

| | | | |
|---|---|---|---|
| Bal. | 7,000 | (2) | 52,000 |
| (1) | 60,000 | | |
| Bal. | 15,000 | | |

**Work in Process**

| | | | |
|---|---|---|---|
| Bal. | 30,000 | (11) | 158,000 |
| (2) | 50,000 | | |
| (3) | 60,000 | | |
| (7) | 90,000 | | |
| Bal. | 72,000 | | |

**Finished Goods**

| | | | |
|---|---|---|---|
| Bal. | 10,000 | (13) | 118,500 |
| (11) | 158,000 | | |
| Bal. | 49,500 | | |

**Accumulated Depreciation**

| | | | |
|---|---|---|---|
| | | Bal. | XX |
| | | (6) | 18,000 |
| | | (9) | 7,000 |

**Manufacturing Overhead**

| | | | |
|---|---|---|---|
| (2) | 2,000 | (7) | 90,000 |
| (3) | 15,000 | | |
| (4) | 40,000 | | |
| (5) | 20,000 | | |
| (6) | 18,000 | | |
| | 95,000 | | 90,000 |
| Bal. | 5,000 | | |

**Accounts Payable**

| | | | |
|---|---|---|---|
| | | Bal. | XX |
| | | (1) | 60,000 |
| | | (4) | 40,000 |
| | | (10) | 50,000 |

**Salaries and Wages Payable**

| | | | |
|---|---|---|---|
| | | Bal. | XX |
| | | (3) | 75,000 |
| | | (8) | 30,000 |

**Property Taxes Payable**

| | | | |
|---|---|---|---|
| | | Bal. | XX |
| | | (5) | 13,000 |

**Sales**

| | | | |
|---|---|---|---|
| | | (12) | 225,000 |

**Cost of Goods Sold**

| | | | |
|---|---|---|---|
| (13) | 118,500 | | |

**Salaries Expense**

| | | | |
|---|---|---|---|
| (8) | 30,000 | | |

**Depreciation Expense**

| | | | |
|---|---|---|---|
| (9) | 7,000 | | |

**Advertising Expense**

| | | | |
|---|---|---|---|
| (10) | 42,000 | | |

**Other Selling and Administrative Expense**

| | | | |
|---|---|---|---|
| (10) | 8,000 | | |

Explanation of entries:

(1) Raw materials purchased.
(2) Direct and indirect materials issued into production.
(3) Direct and indirect factory labor cost incurred.
(4) Utilities and other factory costs incurred.
(5) Property taxes and insurance incurred on the factory.
(6) Depreciation recorded on factory assets.
(7) Overhead cost applied to Work in Process.
(8) Administrative salaries expense incurred.
(9) Depreciation recorded on office equipment.
(10) Advertising and other selling and administrative expense incurred.
(11) Cost of goods manufactured transferred to finished goods.
(12) Sale of Job A recorded.
(13) Cost of goods sold recorded for Job A.

## SCHEDULES OF COST OF GOODS MANUFACTURED AND COST OF GOODS SOLD

**LEARNING OBJECTIVE 6**

Prepare schedules of cost of goods manufactured and cost of goods sold and an income statement.

This section uses the Ruger Corporation example to explain how to prepare schedules of cost of goods manufactured and cost of goods sold as well as an income statement. The **schedule of cost of goods manufactured** contains three elements of product costs—direct materials, direct labor, and manufacturing overhead—and it summarizes the portions of those costs that remain in ending Work in Process inventory and that are transferred out of Work in Process into Finished Goods. The **schedule of cost of goods sold** also contains three elements of product costs—direct materials, direct labor, and manufacturing overhead—and it summarizes the portions of those costs that remain in ending Finished Goods inventory and that are transferred out of Finished Goods into Cost of Goods Sold.

Exhibit 2–11 presents Ruger Corporation's schedules of cost of goods manufactured and cost of goods sold. We want to draw your attention to three key aspects of the schedule of cost of goods manufactured. First, three amounts are always added together—direct materials used in production ($50,000), direct labor ($60,000), and manufacturing overhead applied to work in process ($90,000)—to yield the total manufacturing costs ($200,000). Notice, the direct materials used in production ($50,000) is included in total manufacturing costs instead of raw material purchases ($60,000). The direct materials used in production will usually differ from the amount of raw material purchases when the raw materials inventory balance changes or indirect materials are withdrawn from raw materials inventory. Second, the amount of manufacturing overhead applied to Work in Process ($90,000) is computed by multiplying the predetermined overhead rate by the actual amount of the allocation base recorded on all jobs. *The actual manufacturing overhead costs incurred*

**EXHIBIT 2–11**
Schedules of Cost of Goods Manufactured and Cost of Goods Sold

| | | |
|---|---|---|
| ***Cost of Goods Manufactured*** | | |
| Direct materials: | | |
| Raw materials inventory, beginning | $ 7,000 | |
| Add: Purchases of raw materials | 60,000 | |
| Total raw materials available | 67,000 | |
| Deduct: Raw materials inventory, ending | 15,000 | |
| Raw materials used in production | 52,000 | |
| Deduct: Indirect materials included in manufacturing overhead | 2,000 | $ 50,000 |
| Direct labor | | 60,000 |
| Manufacturing overhead applied to work in process | | 90,000 |
| Total manufacturing costs | | 200,000 |
| Add: Beginning work in process inventory | | 30,000 |
| | | 230,000 |
| Deduct: Ending work in process inventory | | 72,000 |
| Cost of goods manufactured | | $158,000 |
| ***Cost of Goods Sold*** | | |
| Finished goods inventory, beginning | | $ 10,000 |
| Add: Cost of goods manufactured | | 158,000 |
| Cost of goods available for sale | | 168,000 |
| Deduct: Finished goods inventory, ending | | 49,500 |
| Unadjusted cost of goods sold | | 118,500 |
| Add: Underapplied overhead | | 5,000 |
| Adjusted cost of goods sold | | $123,500 |

*Note that the underapplied overhead is added to cost of goods sold. If overhead were overapplied, it would be deducted from cost of goods sold.

**EXHIBIT 2–12**
Income Statement

| Ruger Corporation<br>Income Statement<br>For the Month Ending April 30 | | |
|---|---|---|
| Sales | | $225,000 |
| Cost of goods sold ($118,500 + $5,000) | | 123,500 |
| Gross margin | | 101,500 |
| Selling and administrative expenses: | | |
| Salaries expense | $30,000 | |
| Depreciation expense | 7,000 | |
| Advertising expense | 42,000 | |
| Other expense | 8,000 | 87,000 |
| Net operating income | | $ 14,500 |

*during the period are not added to the Work in Process account.* Third, total manufacturing costs ($200,000) plus beginning Work in Process inventory ($30,000) minus ending Work in Process inventory ($72,000) equals the cost of goods manufactured ($158,000). The cost of goods manufactured represents the cost of the goods completed during the period and transferred from Work in Process to Finished Goods.

The schedule of cost of goods sold shown in Exhibit 2–11 relies on the following equation to compute the unadjusted cost of goods sold:

$$\text{Unadjusted cost of goods sold} = \text{Beginning finished goods inventory} + \text{Cost of goods manufactured} - \text{Ending finished goods inventory}$$

The beginning finished goods inventory ($10,000) plus the cost of goods manufactured ($158,000) equals the cost of goods available for sale ($168,000). The cost of goods available for sale ($168,000) minus the ending finished goods inventory ($49,500) equals the unadjusted cost of goods sold ($118,500). Finally, the unadjusted cost of goods sold ($118,500) plus the underapplied overhead ($5,000) equals adjusted cost of goods sold ($123,500). The next section of the chapter takes a closer look at why cost of goods sold needs to be adjusted for the amount of underapplied or overapplied overhead

Exhibit 2–12 presents Ruger Corporation's income statement for April. Observe that the cost of goods sold on this statement is carried over from Exhibit 2–11. The selling and administrative expenses (which total $87,000) did not flow through the schedules of cost of goods manufactured and cost of goods sold. Journal entries 8–10 (page 83) show that these items were immediately debited to expense accounts rather than being debited to inventory accounts.

## UNDERAPPLIED AND OVERAPPLIED OVERHEAD—A CLOSER LOOK

**LEARNING OBJECTIVE 7**

Compute underapplied or overapplied overhead cost and prepare the journal entry to close the balance in Manufacturing Overhead to the appropriate accounts.

This section explains how to compute underapplied and overapplied overhead and how to dispose of any balance remaining in the Manufacturing Overhead account at the end of a period.

### Computing Underapplied and Overapplied Overhead

Because the predetermined overhead rate is established before the period begins and is based entirely on estimated data, the overhead cost applied to Work in Process will generally differ from the amount of overhead cost actually incurred. In the case of Ruger Corporation, for example, the predetermined overhead rate of $6 per hour was used to apply $90,000 of overhead cost to Work in Process, whereas actual overhead costs for April proved to be $95,000 (see Exhibit 2–8). The difference between the overhead cost applied to Work in Process and the actual overhead costs of a period is called either **underapplied** or **overapplied overhead.** For Ruger Corporation, overhead was underapplied by $5,000 because the applied cost ($90,000) was $5,000 less than the actual cost ($95,000). If the situation had been reversed and the company had applied $95,000 in overhead cost to Work in Process while incurring actual overhead costs of only $90,000, then the overhead would have been overapplied.

What is the cause of underapplied or overapplied overhead? Basically, the method of applying overhead to jobs using a predetermined overhead rate assumes that actual overhead costs will be proportional to the actual amount of the allocation base incurred during the period. If, for example, the predetermined overhead rate is $6 per machine-hour, then it is assumed that actual overhead costs incurred will be $6 for every machine-hour that is actually worked. There are at least two reasons why this may not be true. First, much of the overhead often consists of fixed costs that do not change as the number of machine-hours incurred goes up or down. Second, spending on overhead items may or may not be under control. If individuals who are responsible for overhead costs do a good job, those costs should be less than were expected at the beginning of the period. If they do a poor job, those costs will be more than expected.

To illustrate these concepts, suppose that two companies—Turbo Crafters and Black & Howell—have prepared the following estimated data for the coming year:

| | Turbo Crafters | Black & Howell |
|---|---|---|
| Allocation base | Machine-hours | Direct materials cost |
| Estimated manufacturing overhead cost (a) | $300,000 | $120,000 |
| Estimated total amount of the allocation base (b) | 75,000 machine-hours | $80,000 direct materials cost |
| Predetermined overhead rate (a) ÷ (b) | $4 per machine-hour | 150% of direct materials cost |

Note that when the allocation base is dollars (such as direct materials cost in the case of Black & Howell) the predetermined overhead rate is expressed as a percentage of the allocation base. When dollars are divided by dollars, the result is a percentage.

Now assume that because of unexpected changes in overhead spending and in demand for the companies' products, the *actual* overhead cost and the actual activity recorded during the year in each company are as follows:

| | Turbo Crafters | Black & Howell |
|---|---|---|
| Actual manufacturing overhead cost | $290,000 | $130,000 |
| Actual total amount of the allocation base | 68,000 machine-hours | $90,000 direct materials cost |

For each company, note that the actual data for both cost and the allocation base differ from the estimates used in computing the predetermined overhead rate. This results in underapplied and overapplied overhead as follows:

| | Turbo Crafters | Black & Howell |
|---|---|---|
| Actual manufacturing overhead cost | $290,000 | $130,000 |
| Manufacturing overhead cost applied to Work in Process during the year: | | |
| Predetermined overhead rate (a) | $4 per machine-hour | 150% of direct materials cost |
| Actual total amount of the allocation base (b) | 68,000 machine-hours | $90,000 direct materials cost |
| Manufacturing overhead applied (a) × (b) | $272,000 | $135,000 |
| Underapplied (overapplied) manufacturing overhead | $18,000 | $(5,000) |

**EXHIBIT 2–13**
Summary of Overhead Concepts

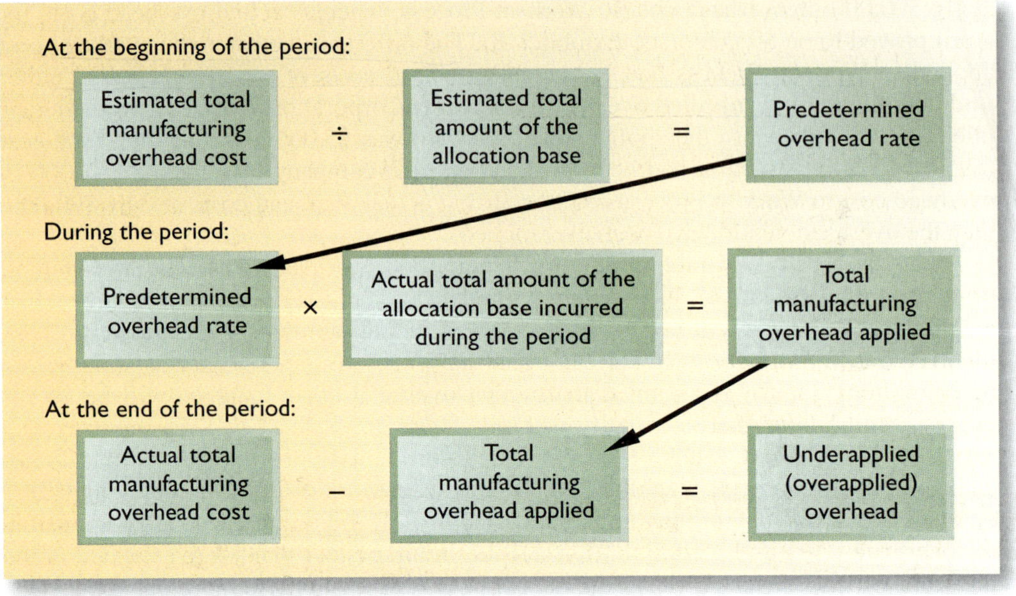


For Turbo Crafters, the amount of overhead cost applied to Work in Process ($272,000) is less than the actual overhead cost for the year ($290,000). Therefore, overhead is underapplied.

For Black & Howell, the amount of overhead cost applied to Work in Process ($135,000) is greater than the actual overhead cost for the year ($130,000), so overhead is overapplied.

A summary of these concepts is presented in Exhibit 2–13.

## Disposition of Underapplied or Overapplied Overhead Balances

If we return to the Ruger Corporation example and look at the Manufacturing Overhead T-account in Exhibit 2–10, you will see that there is a debit balance of $5,000. Remember that debit entries to the account represent actual overhead costs incurred, whereas credit entries represent overhead costs applied to jobs. In this case, the actual overhead costs incurred exceeded the overhead costs applied to jobs by $5,000—hence the debit balance of $5,000. This may sound familiar. We just discussed in the previous section the fact that the overhead costs incurred ($95,000) exceeded the overhead costs applied ($90,000), and that the difference is called underapplied overhead. These are just two ways of looking at the same thing. If there is a *debit* balance in the Manufacturing Overhead account of X dollars, then the overhead is *underapplied* by X dollars. On the other hand, if there is a *credit* balance in the Manufacturing Overhead account of Y dollars, then the overhead is *overapplied* by Y dollars.

What happens to any underapplied or overapplied balance remaining in the Manufacturing Overhead account at the end of a period? The simplest method is to close out the balance to Cost of Goods Sold. More complicated methods are sometimes used, but they are beyond the scope of this book. To illustrate the simplest method, recall that Ruger Corporation had underapplied overhead of $5,000. The entry to close this underapplied overhead to Cost of Goods Sold would be:

(14)

| | | |
|---|---|---|
| Cost of Goods Sold ............................................................ | 5,000 | |
| Manufacturing Overhead.................................................... | | 5,000 |

Note that because the Manufacturing Overhead account has a debit balance, Manufacturing Overhead must be credited to close out the account. This has the effect of increasing Cost of Goods Sold for April to $123,500:

| | |
|---|---|
| Unadjusted cost of goods sold [from entry (13)] | $118,500 |
| Add underapplied overhead [from entry (14)] | 5,000 |
| Adjusted cost of goods sold | $123,500 |

After this adjustment has been made, Ruger Corporation's income statement for April will appear as shown earlier in Exhibit 2–12.

Note that this adjustment makes sense. The unadjusted cost of goods sold is based on the amount of manufacturing overhead applied to jobs, not the manufacturing overhead costs actually incurred. Because overhead was underapplied, not enough cost was applied to jobs. Hence, the cost of goods sold was understated. Adding the underapplied overhead to the cost of goods sold corrects this understatement.

**CONCEPT CHECK**

3. Which of the following statements is true? (You may select more than one answer.)
   a. The Manufacturing Overhead account is debited when manufacturing overhead is applied to Work in Process. F.
   b. Job cost sheets accumulate the actual overhead costs incurred to complete a job.
   c. When products are transferred from work in process to finished goods it results in a debit to Finished Goods and a credit to Work in Process. T.
   d. Selling expenses are applied to production using a predetermined overhead rate that is computed at the beginning of the period. F.
4. The predetermined overhead rate is $50 per machine-hour, underapplied overhead is $5,000, and the actual amount of machine-hours is 2,000. What is the actual amount of total manufacturing overhead incurred during the period?
   a. $105,000
   b. $95,000
   c. $150,000
   d. $110,000

## A General Model of Product Cost Flows

Exhibit 2–14 presents a T-account model of the flow of costs in a product costing system. This model can be very helpful in understanding how production costs flow through a costing system and finally end up as Cost of Goods Sold on the income statement.

## Multiple Predetermined Overhead Rates

Our discussion in this chapter has assumed that there is a single predetermined overhead rate for an entire factory called a **plantwide overhead rate.** This is a fairly common practice—particularly in smaller companies. But in larger companies, *multiple predetermined overhead rates* are often used. In a **multiple predetermined overhead rate** system each production department may have its own predetermined overhead rate. Such a system, while more complex, is more accurate because it can reflect differences across departments in how overhead costs are incurred. For example, in departments that are relatively labor intensive overhead might be allocated based on direct labor-hours and in departments that are relatively machine intensive overhead might be allocated based on machine-hours. When multiple predetermined overhead rates are used, overhead is applied in each department according to its own overhead rate as jobs proceed through the department.

**EXHIBIT 2–14** A General Model of Cost Flows

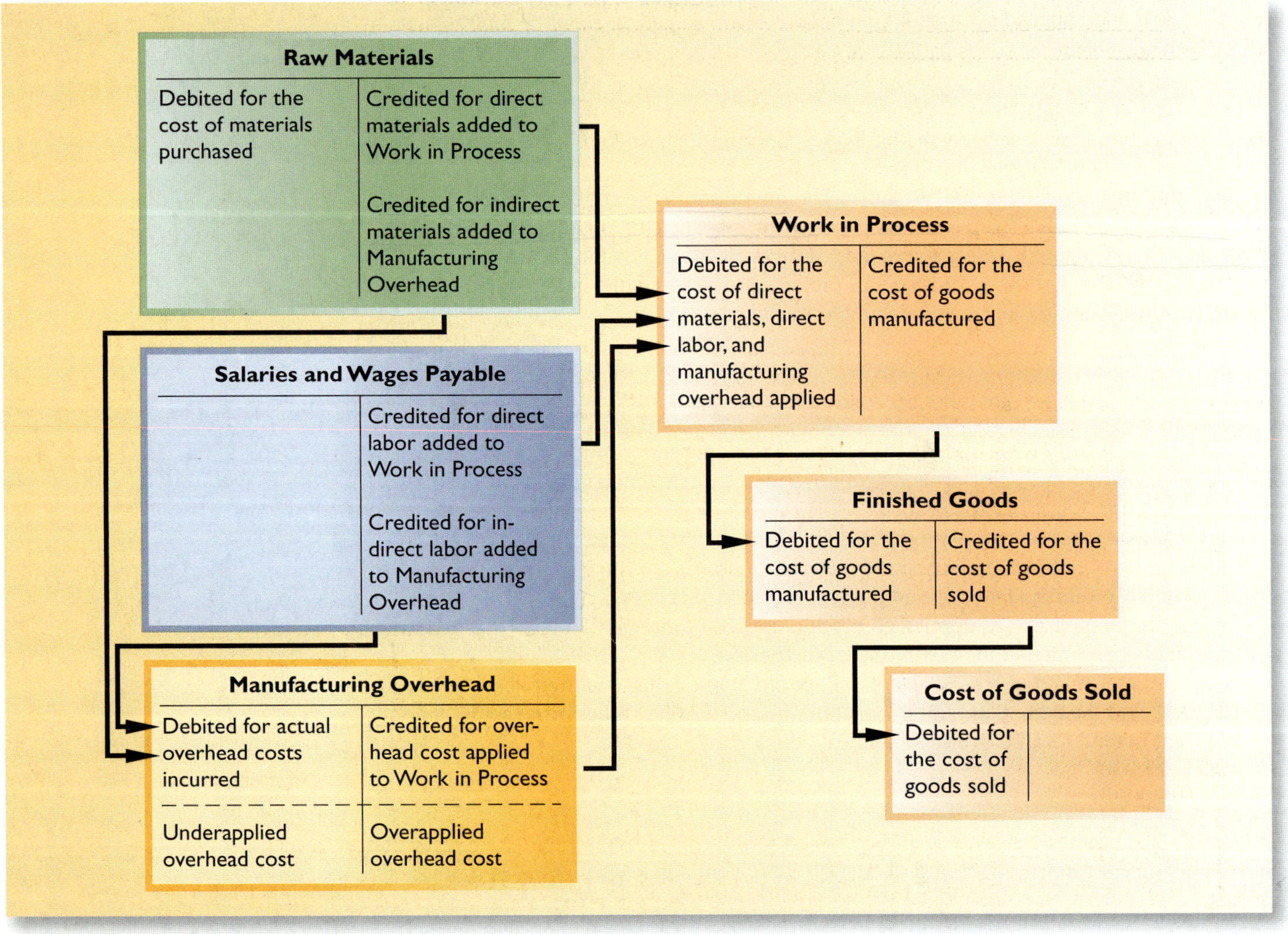


## HELPFUL HINT

Students struggle to understand two key points with respect to underapplied or overapplied overhead. First, underapplied or overapplied overhead is *not* computed for each job. It is computed for the company as a whole (if a plantwide overhead rate is used) or for each department (if departmental overhead rates are used). Second, students often fail to grasp the chronology of events in a normal costing system. Predetermined overhead rates are computed at the *beginning* of the period. Overhead is applied to jobs *throughout* the period. Underapplied or overapplied overhead is computed at the *end* of the period.

## JOB-ORDER COSTING IN SERVICE COMPANIES

Job-order costing is used in service organizations such as law firms, movie studios, hospitals, and repair shops, as well as in manufacturing companies. In a law firm, for example, each client is a "job," and the costs of that job are accumulated day by day on a job cost sheet as the client's case is handled by the firm. Legal forms and similar inputs represent the direct materials for the job; the time expended by attorneys is like direct labor; and the costs of secretaries and legal aids, rent, depreciation, and so forth, represent the overhead.

In a movie studio such as **Columbia Pictures**, each film produced by the studio is a "job," and the costs of direct materials (costumes, props, film, etc.) and direct labor (actors, directors, and extras) are charged to each film's job cost sheet. A share of the studio's overhead costs, such as utilities, depreciation of equipment, wages of maintenance workers, and so forth, is also charged to each film.

In sum, job-order costing is a versatile and widely used costing method that may be encountered in virtually any organization that provides diverse products or services.

## Managing Job Costs In a Service Business

IN BUSINESS

**IBM** has created a software program called Professional Marketplace to match IBM employees with client needs. "Using Marketplace, IBM consultants working for customers can search through 100 job classifications and 10,000 skills, figuring out who inside IBM is available, where they are located and roughly how much it costs the company to use them." Thus far, the results have been encouraging. IBM has reduced its reliance on outside contractors by up to 7% and its consultants spend more of their time in billable work. Furthermore, IBM's senior consultants can search across the globe for available employees with particular niche skills with the click of a mouse instead of having to rely on numerous time-consuming phone calls and emails.

Source: Charles Forelle, "IBM Tool Deploys Employees Efficiently," *The Wall Street Journal*, July 14, 2005, p. B3.

## SUMMARY

### LO1 Compute a predetermined overhead rate.

Manufacturing overhead costs are assigned to jobs using a predetermined overhead rate. The rate is determined at the beginning of the period so that jobs can be costed throughout the period rather than waiting until the end of the period. The predetermined overhead rate is determined by dividing the estimated total manufacturing overhead cost for the period by the estimated total amount of the allocation base for the period.

### LO2 Apply overhead cost to jobs using a predetermined overhead rate.

Overhead is applied to jobs by multiplying the predetermined overhead rate by the actual amount of the allocation base used by the job.

### LO3 Compute the total cost and average cost per unit of a job.

The total cost of a job includes the actual direct materials and direct labor costs assigned to the job plus the applied overhead. The average cost per unit of a job is computed by dividing the total cost of a job by the number of units included in the job. Importantly, the average cost per unit does not represent the additional cost that would be incurred if another unit were produced.

### LO4 Understand the flow of costs in a job-order costing system and prepare appropriate journal entries to record costs.

Direct materials costs are debited to Work in Process when they are released for use in production. Direct labor costs are debited to Work in Process as incurred. Actual manufacturing overhead costs are debited to the Manufacturing Overhead account as incurred. Manufacturing overhead costs are applied to Work in Process using the predetermined overhead rate. The journal entry that accomplishes this is a debit to Work in Process and a credit to Manufacturing Overhead.

### LO5 Use T-accounts to show the flow of costs in a job-order costing system.

See Exhibits 2–10 and 2–14 for summaries of the cost flows through the T-accounts.

**LO6 Prepare schedules of cost of goods manufactured and cost of goods sold and an income statement.**
See Exhibits 2–11 and 2–12 for an example of these schedules and an income statement.

**LO7 Compute underapplied or overapplied overhead cost and prepare the journal entry to close the balance in Manufacturing Overhead to the appropriate accounts.**
The difference between the actual overhead cost incurred during a period and the amount of overhead cost applied to production is referred to as underapplied or overapplied overhead. Underapplied or overapplied overhead is closed out to Cost of Goods Sold. When overhead is underapplied, the balance in the Manufacturing Overhead account is debited to Cost of Goods Sold. This has the effect of increasing the Cost of Goods Sold and occurs because costs assigned to products have been understated. When overhead is overapplied, the balance in the Manufacturing Overhead account is credited to Cost of Goods Sold. This has the effect of decreasing the Cost of Goods Sold and occurs because costs assigned to products have been overstated.

## GUIDANCE ANSWER TO DECISION POINT

**Treasurer, Class Reunion Committee** (p. 75)
You should charge $38.00 per person to cover the costs calculated as follows:

| | | |
|---|---|---|
| Meal cost | $30.00 | Direct material cost |
| Gratuity ($30 × 0.15) | 4.50 | Direct labor cost |
| Room charge ($200 ÷ 200 expected attendees) | 1.00 | Overhead cost |
| Band cost ($500 ÷ 200 expected attendees) | 2.50 | Overhead cost |
| Total cost | $38.00 | |

If exactly 200 classmates attend the reunion, the $7,600 of receipts (200 × $38) will cover the expenditures of $7,600 [meal cost of $6,000 (or 200 × $30) plus gratuity cost of $900 (or $6,000 × 0.15) plus the $200 room charge plus the $500 band cost]. Unfortunately, if less than 200 attend, the Reunion Committee will come up short in an amount equal to the difference between the 200 estimated attendees and the actual number of attendees times $3.50 (the total per person overhead charge). As such, you should talk to the members of the Reunion Committee to ensure that (1) the estimate is as reasonable as possible, and (2) there is a plan to deal with any shortage. On the other hand, if more than 200 attend, the Reunion Committee will collect more money than it needs to disburse. The amount would be equal to the difference between the actual number of attendees and the 200 estimated attendees times $3.50.

## GUIDANCE ANSWERS TO CONCEPT CHECKS

1. **Choices c and d.** A predetermined overhead rate rather than an actual overhead rate is used in a normal costing system. A unit product cost does not represent an incremental cost.
2. **Choice d.** At an activity level of 50,000 direct labor-hours, $Y$ = $100,000 + ($3 per direct labor-hour) (50,000 direct labor-hours). Solving for $Y$ provides an estimated total manufacturing overhead cost of $250,000. The total manufacturing overhead ($250,000) divided by the total estimated direct labor-hours (50,000) equals the predetermined overhead rate of $5 per direct labor-hour.
3. **Choice c.** The Manufacturing Overhead account is credited when manufacturing overhead is applied to Work in Process. Job cost sheets do not accumulate actual overhead costs. They accumulate the amount of the overhead that has been applied to jobs using the predetermined overhead rate. Selling expenses are period costs. They are not applied to production.
4. **Choice a.** The amount of overhead applied to production is 2,000 hours multiplied by the $50 predetermined rate, or $100,000. If overhead is underapplied by $5,000, the actual amount of overhead is $100,000 + $5,000, or $105,000.

## REVIEW PROBLEM: JOB-ORDER COSTING

Hogle Corporation is a manufacturer that uses job-order costing. On January 1, the beginning of its fiscal year, the company's inventory balances were as follows:

| | |
|---|---|
| Raw materials | $20,000 |
| Work in process | $15,000 |
| Finished goods | $30,000 |

The company applies overhead cost to jobs on the basis of machine-hours worked. For the current year, the company's predetermined overhead rate was based on a cost formula that estimated $450,000 of total manufacturing overhead for an estimated activity level of 75,000 machine-hours. The following transactions were recorded for the year:

a. Raw materials were purchased on account, $410,000.
b. Raw materials were requisitioned for use in production, $380,000 ($360,000 direct materials and $20,000 indirect materials).
c. The following costs were accrued for employee services: direct labor, $75,000; indirect labor, $110,000; sales commissions, $90,000; and administrative salaries, $200,000.
d. Sales travel costs were $17,000.
e. Utility costs in the factory were $43,000.
f. Advertising costs were $180,000.
g. Depreciation was recorded for the year, $350,000 (80% relates to factory operations, and 20% relates to selling and administrative activities).
h. Insurance expired during the year, $10,000 (70% relates to factory operations, and the remaining 30% relates to selling and administrative activities).
i. Manufacturing overhead was applied to production. Due to greater than expected demand for its products, the company worked 80,000 machine-hours on all jobs during the year.
j. Goods costing $900,000 to manufacture according to their job cost sheets were completed during the year.
k. Goods were sold on account to customers during the year for a total of $1,500,000. The goods cost $870,000 to manufacture according to their job cost sheets.

***Required:***

1. Prepare journal entries to record the preceding transactions.
2. Post the entries in (1) above to T-accounts (don't forget to enter the beginning balances in the inventory accounts).
3. Is Manufacturing Overhead underapplied or overapplied for the year? Prepare a journal entry to close any balance in the Manufacturing Overhead account to Cost of Goods Sold.
4. Prepare an income statement for the year.

**Solution to Review Problem**

1.

| | | | |
|---|---|---|---|
| a. | Raw Materials | 410,000 | |
| | Accounts Payable | | 410,000 |
| b. | Work in Process | 360,000 | |
| | Manufacturing Overhead | 20,000 | |
| | Raw Materials | | 380,000 |
| c. | Work in Process | 75,000 | |
| | Manufacturing Overhead | 110,000 | |
| | Sales Commissions Expense | 90,000 | |
| | Administrative Salaries Expense | 200,000 | |
| | Salaries and Wages Payable | | 475,000 |
| d. | Sales Travel Expense | 17,000 | |
| | Accounts Payable | | 17,000 |
| e. | Manufacturing Overhead | 43,000 | |
| | Accounts Payable | | 43,000 |
| f. | Advertising Expense | 180,000 | |
| | Accounts Payable | | 180,000 |
| g. | Manufacturing Overhead | 280,000 | |
| | Depreciation Expense | 70,000 | |
| | Accumulated Depreciation | | 350,000 |

| | | Debit | Credit |
|---|---|---|---|
| h. | Manufacturing Overhead | 7,000 | |
| | Insurance Expense | 3,000 | |
| | Prepaid Insurance | | 10,000 |

i. The predetermined overhead rate for the year is computed as follows:

$$\text{Predetermined overhead rate} = \frac{\text{Estimated total manufacturing overhead cost}}{\text{Estimated total amount of the allocation base}}$$

$$= \frac{\$450{,}000}{75{,}000 \text{ machine-hours}}$$

$$= \$6 \text{ per machine-hour}$$

Based on the 80,000 machine-hours actually worked during the year, the company applied $480,000 in overhead cost to production: $6 per machine-hour × 80,000 machine-hours = $480,000. The following entry records this application of overhead cost:

| | | Debit | Credit |
|---|---|---|---|
| | Work in Process | 480,000 | |
| | Manufacturing Overhead | | 480,000 |
| j. | Finished Goods | 900,000 | |
| | Work in Process | | 900,000 |
| k. | Accounts Receivable | 1,500,000 | |
| | Sales | | 1,500,000 |
| | Cost of Goods Sold | 870,000 | |
| | Finished Goods | | 870,000 |

2.

**Accounts Receivable**

| | Debit | | Credit |
|---|---|---|---|
| (k) | 1,500,000 | | |

**Prepaid Insurance**

| | Debit | | Credit |
|---|---|---|---|
| | | (h) | 10,000 |

**Raw Materials**

| | Debit | | Credit |
|---|---|---|---|
| Bal. | 20,000 | (b) | 380,000 |
| (a) | 410,000 | | |
| Bal. | 50,000 | | |

**Work in Process**

| | Debit | | Credit |
|---|---|---|---|
| Bal. | 15,000 | (j) | 900,000 |
| (b) | 360,000 | | |
| (c) | 75,000 | | |
| (i) | 480,000 | | |
| Bal. | 30,000 | | |

**Finished Goods**

| | Debit | | Credit |
|---|---|---|---|
| Bal. | 30,000 | (k) | 870,000 |
| (j) | 900,000 | | |
| Bal. | 60,000 | | |

**Manufacturing Overhead**

| | Debit | | Credit |
|---|---|---|---|
| (b) | 20,000 | (i) | 480,000 |
| (c) | 110,000 | | |
| (e) | 43,000 | | |
| (g) | 280,000 | | |
| (h) | 7,000 | | |
| | 460,000 | | 480,000 |
| | | Bal. | 20,000 |

**Accumulated Depreciation**

| | Debit | | Credit |
|---|---|---|---|
| | | (g) | 350,000 |

**Accounts Payable**

| | Debit | | Credit |
|---|---|---|---|
| | | (a) | 410,000 |
| | | (d) | 17,000 |
| | | (e) | 43,000 |
| | | (f) | 180,000 |

**Salaries and Wages Payable**

| | Debit | | Credit |
|---|---|---|---|
| | | (c) | 475,000 |

**Sales**

| | Debit | | Credit |
|---|---|---|---|
| | | (k) | 1,500,000 |

**Cost of Goods Sold**

| | Debit | | Credit |
|---|---|---|---|
| (k) | 870,000 | | |

**Sales Commissions Expense**

| | Debit | | Credit |
|---|---|---|---|
| (c) | 90,000 | | |

**Administrative Salaries Expense**

| | Debit | | Credit |
|---|---|---|---|
| (c) | 200,000 | | |

**Sales Travel Expense**

| | Debit | | Credit |
|---|---|---|---|
| (d) | 17,000 | | |

**Advertising Expense**

| | Debit | | Credit |
|---|---|---|---|
| (f) | 180,000 | | |

**Depreciation Expense**

| | Debit | | Credit |
|---|---|---|---|
| (g) | 70,000 | | |

**Insurance Expense**

| | Debit | | Credit |
|---|---|---|---|
| (h) | 3,000 | | |

3. Manufacturing overhead is overapplied for the year. The entry to close it out to Cost of Goods Sold is as follows:

| | | |
|---|---|---|
| Manufacturing Overhead | 20,000 | |
| Cost of Goods Sold | | 20,000 |

4.

**Hogle Corporation**
**Income Statement**
**For the Year Ended December 31**

| | | |
|---|---|---|
| Sales | | $1,500,000 |
| Cost of goods sold ($870,000 – $20,000) | | 850,000 |
| Gross margin | | 650,000 |
| Selling and administrative expenses: | | |
| Sales commissions expense | $ 90,000 | |
| Administrative salaries expense | 200,000 | |
| Sales travel expense | 17,000 | |
| Advertising expense | 180,000 | |
| Depreciation expense | 70,000 | |
| Insurance expense | 3,000 | 560,000 |
| Net operating income | | $ 90,000 |

## GLOSSARY

**Absorption costing** A costing method that includes all manufacturing costs—direct materials, direct labor, and both variable and fixed manufacturing overhead—in the cost of a product. (p. 66)

**Allocation base** A measure of activity such as direct labor-hours or machine-hours that is used to assign costs to cost objects. (p. 71)

**Bill of materials** A document that shows the quantity of each type of direct material required to make a product. (p. 68)

**Cost driver** A factor, such as machine-hours, beds occupied, computer time, or flight-hours, that causes overhead costs. (p. 73)

**Cost of goods manufactured** The manufacturing costs associated with the goods that were finished during the period. (p. 76)

**Finished goods** Units of product that have been completed but not yet sold to customers. (p. 76)

**Job cost sheet** A form that records the materials, labor, and manufacturing overhead costs charged to a job. (p. 69)

**Job-order costing** A costing system used in situations where many different products, jobs, or services are produced each period. (p. 66)

**Materials requisition form** A document that specifies the type and quantity of materials to be drawn from the storeroom and that identifies the job that will be charged for the cost of those materials. (p. 68)

**Multiple predetermined overhead rates** A costing system with multiple overhead cost pools and a different predetermined overhead rate for each cost pool, rather than a single predetermined overhead rate for the entire company. Each production department may be treated as a separate overhead cost pool. (p. 89)

**Normal cost system** A costing system in which overhead costs are applied to a job by multiplying a predetermined overhead rate by the actual amount of the allocation base incurred by the job. (p. 72)

**Overapplied overhead** A credit balance in the Manufacturing Overhead account that occurs when the amount of overhead cost applied to Work in Process exceeds the amount of overhead cost actually incurred during a period. (p. 87)

**Overhead application** The process of charging manufacturing overhead cost to job cost sheets and to the Work in Process account. (p. 71)

**Plantwide overhead rate** A single predetermined overhead rate that is used throughout a plant. (p. 89)

**Predetermined overhead rate** A rate used to charge manufacturing overhead cost to jobs that is established in advance for each period. It is computed by dividing the estimated total manufacturing overhead cost for the period by the estimated total amount of the allocation base for the period. (p. 71)

**Raw materials** Any materials that go into the final product. (p. 76)

**Schedule of cost of goods manufactured** A schedule that contains three elements of product costs—direct materials, direct labor, and manufacturing overhead—and that summarizes the portions of those costs that remain in ending Work in Process inventory and that are transferred out of Work in Process into Finished Goods. (p. 85)

**Schedule of cost of goods sold** A schedule that contains three elements of product costs—direct materials, direct labor, and manufacturing overhead—and that summarizes the portions of those costs that remain in ending Finished Goods inventory and that are transferred out of Finished Goods into Cost of Goods Sold. (p. 85)

**Time ticket** A document that is used to record the amount of time an employee spends on various activities. (p. 69)

**Underapplied overhead** A debit balance in the Manufacturing Overhead account that occurs when the amount of overhead cost actually incurred exceeds the amount of overhead cost applied to Work in Process during a period. (p. 87)

**Work in process** Units of product that are only partially complete and will require further work before they are ready for sale to the customer. (p. 76)

## QUESTIONS

**2–1** Why aren't actual manufacturing overhead costs traced to jobs just as direct materials and direct labor costs are traced to jobs?

**2–2** Explain the four-step process used to compute a predetermined overhead rate.

**2–3** What is the purpose of the job cost sheet in a job-order costing system?

**2–4** Explain why some production costs must be assigned to products through an allocation process.

**2–5** Why do companies use predetermined overhead rates rather than actual manufacturing overhead costs to apply overhead to jobs?

**2–6** What factors should be considered in selecting a base to be used in computing the predetermined overhead rate?

**2–7** If a company fully allocates all of its overhead costs to jobs, does this guarantee that a profit will be earned for the period?

**2–8** What account is credited when overhead cost is applied to Work in Process? Would you expect the amount applied for a period to equal the actual overhead costs of the period? Why or why not?

**2–9** What is underapplied overhead? Overapplied overhead? What disposition is made of these amounts at the end of the period?

**2–10** Provide two reasons why overhead might be underapplied in a given year.

**2–11** What adjustment is made for underapplied overhead on the schedule of cost of goods sold? What adjustment is made for overapplied overhead?

**2–12** What is a plantwide overhead rate? Why are multiple overhead rates, rather than a plantwide overhead rate, used in some companies?

**2–13** What happens to overhead rates based on direct labor when automated equipment replaces direct labor?

**Multiple-choice questions are provided on the text website at www.mhhe.com/brewer6e.**

## APPLYING EXCEL

LO1, LO4, LO7

**Available with McGraw-Hill's *Connect*® *Accounting*.**

The Excel worksheet form that appears on the following page is to be used to recreate part of the example on page 87. Download the workbook containing this form from the Online Learning Center at www.mhhe.com/brewer6e. *On the website you will also receive instructions about how to use this worksheet form.*

| | A | B | C | D |
|---|---|---|---|---|
| 1 | **Chapter 2: Applying Excel** | | | |
| 2 | | | | |
| 3 | **Data** | | | |
| 4 | Allocation base | Machine-hours | | |
| 5 | Estimated manufacturing overhead cost | $300,000 | | |
| 6 | Estimated total amount of the allocation base | 75,000 | machine-hours | |
| 7 | Actual manufacturing overhead cost | $290,000 | | |
| 8 | Actual total amount of the allocation base | 68,000 | machine-hours | |
| 9 | | | | |
| 10 | *Enter a formula into each of the cells marked with a ? below* | | | |
| 11 | | | | |
| 12 | **Computation of the predetermined overhead rate** | | | |
| 13 | Estimated manufacturing overhead cost | ? | | |
| 14 | Estimated total amount of the allocation base | ? | machine-hours | |
| 15 | Predetermined overhead rate | ? | per machine-hour | |
| 16 | | | | |
| 17 | **Computation of underapplied or overapplied manufacturing overhead** | | | |
| 18 | Actual manufacturing overhead cost | ? | | |
| 19 | Manufacturing overhead cost applied to Work in Process during the year: | | | |
| 20 | Predetermined overhead rate | ? | per machine-hour | |
| 21 | Actual total amount of the allocation base | ? | machine-hours | |
| 22 | Manufacturing overhead applied | ? | | |
| 23 | Underapplied (overapplied) manufacturing overhead | ? | | |
| 24 | | | | |
| 25 | | | | |
| 26 | | | | |
| 27 | | | | |
| 28 | | | | |
| 29 | | | | |
| 30 | | | | |
| 31 | | | | |

Chapter 2 Form / Filled in Chapter 2 Form / Chapter 2 Formulas / Chapter 2 Requirement 1 / Chapter 2 Rec

You should proceed to the requirements below only after completing your worksheet.

***Required:***

1. Check your worksheet by changing the estimated total amount of the allocation base in the Data area to 60,000 machine-hours, keeping all of the other data the same as in the original example. If your worksheet is operating properly, the predetermined overhead rate should now be $5.00 per machine-hour. If you do not get this answer, find the errors in your worksheet and correct them.

   How much is the underapplied (overapplied) manufacturing overhead? Did it change? Why or why not?
2. Determine the underapplied (overapplied) manufacturing overhead for a different company with the following data:

| | |
|---|---|
| Allocation base | Machine-hours |
| Estimated manufacturing overhead cost | $100,000 |
| Estimated total amount of the allocation base | 50,000 machine-hours |
| Actual manufacturing overhead cost | $90,000 |
| Actual total amount of the allocation base | 40,000 machine-hours |

3. What happens to the underapplied (overapplied) manufacturing overhead from part (2) if the estimated total amount of the allocation base is changed to 40,000 machine-hours and everything else remains the same? Why is the amount of underapplied (overapplied) manufacturing overhead different from part (2)?

4. Change the estimated total amount of the allocation base back to 50,000 machine-hours so that the data look exactly like they did in part (2). Now change the actual manufacturing overhead cost to $100,000. What is the underapplied (overapplied) manufacturing overhead now? Why is the amount of underapplied (overapplied) manufacturing overhead different from part (2)?

## THE FOUNDATIONAL 15

**Available with McGraw-Hill's *Connect*® *Accounting*.**

LO1, LO2, LO3, LO4, LO5, LO6, LO7

Sweeten Company had no jobs in progress at the beginning of March and no beginning inventories. It started only two jobs during March—Job P and Job Q. Job P was completed and sold by the end of the March and Job Q was incomplete at the end of the March. The company uses a plantwide predetermined overhead rate based on direct labor-hours. The following additional information is available for the company as a whole and for Jobs P and Q (all data and questions relate to the month of March):

| | |
|---|---|
| Estimated total fixed manufacturing overhead | $10,000 |
| Estimated variable manufacturing overhead per direct labor-hour | $1.00 |
| Estimated total direct labor-hours to be worked | $2,000 |
| Total actual manufacturing overhead costs incurred | $12,500 |

| | Job P | Job Q |
|---|---|---|
| Direct materials | $13,000 | $8,000 |
| Direct labor cost | $21,000 | $7,500 |
| Actual direct labor-hours worked | 1,400 | 500 |

***Required:***

1. What is the company's predetermined overhead rate?
2. How much manufacturing overhead was applied to Job P and Job Q?
3. What is the direct labor hourly wage rate?
4. If Job P included 20 units, what is its unit product cost? What is the total amount of manufacturing cost assigned to Job Q as of the end of March (including applied overhead)?
5. Assume the ending raw materials inventory is $1,000 and the company does not use any indirect materials. Prepare the journal entries to record raw materials purchases and the issuance of direct materials for use in production.
6. Assume that the company does not use any indirect labor. Prepare the journal entry to record the direct labor costs added to production.
7. Prepare the journal entry to apply manufacturing overhead to production.
8. Assume the ending raw materials inventory is $1,000 and the company does not use any indirect materials. Prepare a schedule of cost of goods manufactured.
9. Prepare the journal entry to transfer costs from Work in Process to Finished Goods.
10. Prepare a completed Work in Process T-account including the beginning and ending balances and all debits and credits posted to the account.
11. Prepare a schedule of cost of goods sold. (Stop after computing the unadjusted cost of goods sold.)
12. Prepare the journal entry to transfer costs from Finished Goods to Cost of Goods Sold.
13. What is the amount of underapplied or overapplied overhead?
14. Prepare the journal entry to close the amount of underapplied or overapplied overhead to Cost of Goods Sold.
15. Assume that Job P includes 20 units that each sell for $3,000 and that the company's selling and administrative expenses in March were $14,000. Prepare an absorption costing income statement for March.

## EXERCISES

**All applicable exercises are available with McGraw-Hill's *Connect*® *Accounting*.**

TAKE TWO

Estimated direct labor-hours = 50,000

**EXERCISE 2–1 Compute the Predetermined Overhead Rate [LO1]**

Logan Products computes its predetermined overhead rate annually on the basis of direct labor-hours. At the beginning of the year, it estimated that 40,000 direct labor-hours would be required for the period's estimated level of production. The company also estimated $466,000 of fixed manufacturing overhead expenses for the coming period and variable manufacturing overhead of $3.00 per direct labor-hour. Logan's actual manufacturing overhead for the year was $713,400 and its actual total direct labor was 41,000 hours.

***Required:***
Compute the company's predetermined overhead rate for the year.

### EXERCISE 2–2 Apply Overhead [LO2]

Westan Corporation uses a predetermined overhead rate of $23.10 per direct labor-hour. This predetermined rate was based on a cost formula that estimated $277,200 of total manufacturing overhead for an estimated activity level of 12,000 direct labor-hours.

The company incurred actual total manufacturing overhead costs of $266,000 and 12,600 total direct labor-hours during the period.

TAKE TWO

Actual total manufacturing overhead costs = $270,000

***Required:***
Determine the amount of manufacturing overhead that would have been applied to all jobs during the period.

### EXERCISE 2–3 Computing Job Costs [LO3]

Weaver Company's predetermined overhead rate is $18.00 per direct labor-hour and its direct labor wage rate is $12.00 per hour. The following information pertains to Job A-200:

TAKE TWO

Predetermined overhead rate = $24 per DLH

| | |
|---|---|
| Direct materials | $200 |
| Direct labor | $120 |

***Required:***
1. What is the total manufacturing cost assigned to Job A-200?
2. If Job A-200 consists of 50 units, what is the average cost assigned to each unit included in the job?

### EXERCISE 2–4 Prepare Journal Entries [LO4]

Kirkaid Company had the following transactions for the just completed month.

a. $86,000 in raw materials were purchased on account.
b. $84,000 in raw materials were requisitioned for use in production. Of this amount, $72,000 was for direct materials and the remainder was for indirect materials.
c. Total labor wages of $108,000 were incurred. Of this amount, $105,000 was for direct labor and the remainder was for indirect labor.
d. Additional manufacturing overhead costs of $197,000 were incurred.

***Required:***
Record the above transactions in journal entries.

### EXERCISE 2–5 Prepare T-Accounts [LO5, LO7]

Granger Products had the following transactions for the just completed month. The company had no beginning inventories.

a. $75,000 in raw materials were purchased for cash.
b. $73,000 in raw materials were requisitioned for use in production. Of this amount, $67,000 was for direct materials and the remainder was for indirect materials.
c. Total labor wages of $152,000 were incurred and paid. Of this amount, $134,000 was for direct labor and the remainder was for indirect labor.
d. Additional manufacturing overhead costs of $126,000 were incurred and paid.
e. Manufacturing overhead costs of $178,000 were applied to jobs using the company's predetermined overhead rate.
f. All of the jobs in progress at the end of the month were completed and shipped to customers.
g. Any underapplied or overapplied overhead for the period was closed out to Cost of Goods Sold.

***Required:***
1. Post the above transactions to T-accounts.
2. Determine the cost of goods sold for the period.

### EXERCISE 2–6 Schedules of Cost of Goods Manufactured and Cost of Goods Sold [LO6]

TAKE TWO

Ending raw material inventory = $25,000; Ending work in process inventory = $43,000

Parmitan Corporation has provided the following data concerning last month's manufacturing operations.

| | |
|---|---|
| Purchases of raw materials | $53,000 |
| Indirect materials included in manufacturing overhead | $8,000 |
| Direct labor | $62,000 |
| Manufacturing overhead applied to work in process | $41,000 |
| Underapplied overhead | $8,000 |

| Inventories: | Beginning of Year | Ending of Year |
|---|---|---|
| Raw materials | $24,000 | $6,000 |
| Work in process | $41,000 | $38,000 |
| Finished goods | $86,000 | $93,000 |

***Required:***

1. Prepare a schedule of cost of goods manufactured for the month.
2. Prepare a schedule of cost of goods sold for the month.

### EXERCISE 2–7 Underapplied and Overapplied Overhead [LO7]

TAKE TWO

Actual total manufacturing overhead costs = $178,000

Cretin Enterprises uses a predetermined overhead rate of $21.40 per direct labor-hour. This predetermined rate was based on a cost formula that estimated $171,200 of total manufacturing overhead for an estimated activity level of 8,000 direct labor-hours.

The company incurred actual total manufacturing overhead costs of $172,500 and 8,250 total direct labor-hours during the period.

***Required:***

1. Determine the amount of underapplied or overapplied manufacturing overhead for the period.
2. Assuming that the entire amount of the underapplied or overapplied overhead is closed out to Cost of Goods Sold, what would be the effect of the underapplied or overapplied overhead on the company's gross margin for the period?

### EXERCISE 2–8 Schedules of Cost of Goods Manufactured and Cost of Goods Sold; Income Statement [LO6]

TAKE TWO

Ending raw material inventory = $8,000; Ending work in process inventory = $16,000

The following data from the just completed year are taken from the accounting records of Eccles Company:

| | |
|---|---|
| Sales | $643,000 |
| Direct labor cost | $90,000 |
| Raw material purchases | $132,000 |
| Selling expenses | $100,000 |
| Administrative expenses | $43,000 |
| Manufacturing overhead applied to work in process | $210,000 |
| Actual manufacturing overhead costs | $220,000 |

| Inventories: | Beginning of Year | End of Year |
|---|---|---|
| Raw materials | $8,000 | $10,000 |
| Work in process | $5,000 | $20,000 |
| Finished goods | $70,000 | $25,000 |

***Required:***

1. Prepare a schedule of cost of goods manufactured. Assume all raw materials used in production were direct materials.
2. Prepare a schedule of cost of goods sold.
3. Prepare an income statement.

**EXERCISE 2–9 Apply Overhead to a Job [LO2]**

Winston Company applies overhead cost to jobs on the basis of direct labor cost. Job X, which was started and completed during the current period, shows charges of $18,000 for direct materials, $10,000 for direct labor, and $15,000 for overhead on its job cost sheet. Job Q, which is still in process at year-end, shows charges of $20,000 for direct materials, and $8,000 for direct labor.

TAKE TWO

Direct labor charges for Job X = $5,000

***Required:***

Should any overhead cost be added to Job Q at year-end? If so, how much? Explain.

**EXERCISE 2–10 Applying Overhead; Computing Unit Product Cost [LO2, LO3]**

A company assigns overhead cost to completed jobs on the basis of 120% of direct labor cost. The job cost sheet for Job 413 shows that $12,000 in direct materials has been used on the job and that $8,000 in direct labor cost has been incurred. A total of 200 units were produced in Job 413.

TAKE TWO

Direct labor charges for Job 413 = $10,000

***Required:***

What is the total manufacturing cost assigned to Job 413? What is the unit product cost for Job 413?

**EXERCISE 2–11 Journal Entries and T-Accounts [LO2, LO4, LO5]**

Foley Company uses a job-order costing system. The following data relate to the month of October, the first month of the company's fiscal year:

a. Raw materials purchased on account, $210,000.
b. Raw materials issued to production, $190,000 (80% direct and 20% indirect).
c. Direct labor cost incurred, $49,000; and indirect labor cost incurred, $21,000.
d. Depreciation recorded on factory equipment, $105,000.
e. Other manufacturing overhead costs incurred during October, $130,000 (credit Accounts Payable).
f. The company applies manufacturing overhead cost to production on the basis of $4 per machine-hour. A total of 75,000 machine-hours were recorded for October.
g. Production orders costing $510,000 according to their job cost sheets were completed during October and transferred to Finished Goods.
h. Production orders that had cost $450,000 to complete according to their job cost sheets were shipped to customers during the month. These goods were sold on account at 50% above cost.

***Required:***

1. Prepare journal entries to record the information given above.
2. Prepare T-accounts for Manufacturing Overhead and Work in Process. Post the relevant information above to each account. Compute the ending balance in each account, assuming that Work in Process has a beginning balance of $35,000.

**EXERCISE 2–12 Computing Predetermined Overhead Rates and Job Costs [LO1, LO2, LO3, LO7]**

Kody Corporation uses a job-order costing system with a plantwide overhead rate based on machine-hours. At the beginning of the year, the company made the following estimates:

TAKE TWO

Machine-hours required to support estimated production = 120,000

| | |
|---|---|
| Machine-hours required to support estimated production .................. | 150,000 |
| Fixed manufacturing overhead cost .................................................. | $750,000 |
| Variable manufacturing overhead cost per machine-hour .................. | $4.00 |

***Required:***

1. Compute the predetermined overhead rate.
2. During the year Job 500 was started and completed. The following information was available with respect to this job:

| | |
|---|---|
| Direct materials requisitioned ............................ | $350 |
| Direct labor cost ................................................ | $230 |
| Machine-hours used ........................................ | 30 |

   Compute the total manufacturing cost assigned to Job 500.
3. During the year the company worked a total of 147,000 machine-hours on all jobs and incurred actual manufacturing overhead costs of $1,325,000. What is the amount of underapplied or overapplied overhead for the year? If this amount were closed out entirely to Cost of Goods Sold, would the journal entry increase or decrease net operating income?

### EXERCISE 2–13 Applying Overhead; Cost of Goods Manufactured [LO2, LO6, LO7]

The following cost data relate to the manufacturing activities of Black Company during the just completed year:

Purchases of raw materials = $35,000

| | |
|---|---|
| Manufacturing overhead costs: | |
| Property taxes, factory | $ 3,000 |
| Utilities, factory | 5,000 |
| Indirect labor | 10,000 |
| Depreciation, factory | 24,000 |
| Insurance, factory | 6,000 |
| Total actual manufacturing overhead costs | $48,000 |
| Other costs incurred: | |
| Purchases of raw materials | $32,000 |
| Direct labor cost | $40,000 |
| Inventories: | |
| Raw materials, beginning | $8,000 |
| Raw materials, ending | $7,000 |
| Work in process, beginning | $6,000 |
| Work in process, ending | $7,500 |

The company uses a predetermined overhead rate to apply overhead cost to jobs. The rate for the year was $5 per machine-hour; a total of 10,000 machine-hours was recorded for the year. All raw materials ultimately become direct materials—none are classified as indirect materials.

***Required:***

1. Compute the amount of underapplied or overapplied overhead cost for the year.
2. Prepare a schedule of cost of goods manufactured for the year.

### EXERCISE 2–14 Varying Predetermined Overhead Rates [LO1, LO2, LO3]

Javadi Company makes a single product that is subject to wide seasonal variations in demand. The company uses a job-order costing system and computes predetermined overhead rates on a quarterly basis using the number of units to be produced as the allocation base. Its estimated costs, by quarter, for the coming year are given below:

| | Quarter | | | |
|---|---|---|---|---|
| | First | Second | Third | Fourth |
| Direct materials | $240,000 | $120,000 | $ 60,000 | $180,000 |
| Direct labor | 96,000 | 48,000 | 24,000 | 72,000 |
| Manufacturing overhead | 228,000 | 204,000 | 192,000 | ? |
| Total manufacturing costs (a) | $564,000 | $372,000 | $276,000 | $ ? |
| Number of units to be produced (b) | 80,000 | 40,000 | 20,000 | 60,000 |
| Estimated unit product cost (a) ÷ (b) | $7.05 | $9.30 | $13.80 | ? |

Management finds the variation in quarterly unit product costs to be confusing and difficult to work with. It has been suggested that the problem lies with manufacturing overhead because it is the largest element of total manufacturing cost. Accordingly, you have been asked to find a more appropriate way of assigning manufacturing overhead cost to units of product.

***Required:***

1. Using the high-low method, estimate the fixed manufacturing overhead cost per quarter and the variable manufacturing overhead cost per unit. Create a cost formula to estimate the total manufacturing overhead cost for the fourth quarter. Compute the total manufacturing cost and unit product cost for the fourth quarter.
2. What is causing the estimated unit product cost to fluctuate from one quarter to the next?
3. How would you recommend stabilizing the company's unit product cost? Support your answer with computations that adapt the cost formula you created in requirement 1.

**EXERCISE 2–15 Departmental Overhead Rates [LO1, LO2, LO3]**

Diewold Company has two departments, Milling and Assembly. The company uses a job-order costing system and computes a predetermined overhead rate in each department. The Milling Department bases its rate on machine-hours, and the Assembly Department bases its rate on direct labor-hours. At the beginning of the year, the company made the following estimates:

| | Department | |
|---|---|---|
| | Milling | Assembly |
| Direct labor-hours | 8,000 | 80,000 |
| Machine-hours | 60,000 | 3,000 |
| Total fixed manufacturing overhead cost | $390,000 | $500,000 |
| Variable manufacturing overhead per machine-hour | $2.00 | — |
| Variable manufacturing overhead per direct labor-hour | — | $3.75 |

***Required:***

1. Compute the predetermined overhead rate in each department.
2. Assume that the overhead rates you computed in (1) above are in effect. The job cost sheet for Job 407, which was started and completed during the year, showed the following:

| | Department | |
|---|---|---|
| | Milling | Assembly |
| Direct labor-hours | 5 | 20 |
| Machine-hours | 90 | 4 |
| Materials requisitioned | $800 | $370 |
| Direct labor cost | $45 | $160 |

   Compute the total manufacturing cost assigned to Job 407.
3. Would you expect substantially different amounts of overhead cost to be charged to some jobs if the company used a plantwide overhead rate based on direct labor-hours instead of using departmental rates? Explain. No computations are necessary.

**EXERCISE 2–16 Applying Overhead; Journal Entries; Disposition of Underapplied or Overapplied Overhead [LO4, LO5, LO7]**

The following information is taken from the accounts of FasGrow Company. The entries in the T-accounts are summaries of the transactions that affected those accounts during the year.

**Manufacturing Overhead**

| | | | |
|---|---|---|---|
| (a) | 380,000 | (b) | 410,000 |
| | | Bal. | 30,000 |

**Work in Process**

| | | | |
|---|---|---|---|
| Bal. | 105,000 | (c) | 760,000 |
| | 210,000 | | |
| | 115,000 | | |
| (b) | 410,000 | | |
| Bal. | 80,000 | | |

**Finished Goods**

| | | | |
|---|---|---|---|
| Bal. | 160,000 | (d) | 820,000 |
| (c) | 760,000 | | |
| Bal. | 100,000 | | |

**Cost of Goods Sold**

| | | | |
|---|---|---|---|
| (d) | 820,000 | | |

***Required:***

1. Identify the reasons for entries (a) through (d).
2. Assume that the company closes any balance in the Manufacturing Overhead account directly to Cost of Goods Sold. Prepare the necessary journal entry.

**EXERCISE 2–17 Applying Overhead; T-Accounts; Journal Entries [LO1, LO2, LO4, LO5, LO7]**

Medusa Products uses a job-order costing system. Overhead costs are applied to jobs on the basis of machine-hours. At the beginning of the year, management estimated that 85,000 machine-hours would be required for the period's estimated level of production. The company also estimated $106,250 of fixed manufacturing overhead expenses for the coming period and variable manufacturing overhead of $0.75 per machine-hour.

TAKE TWO

Estimated variable manufacturing overhead per machine-hour = $0.80

***Required:***

1. Compute the company's predetermined overhead rate.
2. Assume that during the year the company actually works only 80,000 machine-hours and incurs the following costs in the Manufacturing Overhead and Work in Process accounts:

**Manufacturing Overhead**

| | | |
|---|---|---|
| (Utilities) | 14,000 | ? |
| (Insurance) | 9,000 | |
| (Maintenance) | 33,000 | |
| (Indirect materials) | 7,000 | |
| (Indirect labor) | 65,000 | |
| (Depreciation) | 40,000 | |

**Work in Process**

| | | |
|---|---|---|
| (Direct materials) | 530,000 | |
| (Direct labor) | 85,000 | |
| (Overhead) | ? | |

Copy the data in the T-accounts above onto your answer sheet. Compute the amount of overhead cost that would be applied to Work in Process for the year, and make the entry in your T-accounts.

3. Compute the amount of underapplied or overapplied overhead for the year, and show the balance in your Manufacturing Overhead T-account. Prepare a journal entry to close out the balance in this account to Cost of Goods Sold.
4. Explain why the manufacturing overhead was underapplied or overapplied for the year.

**EXERCISE 2–18 Plantwide and Departmental Overhead Rates; Job Costs [LO1, LO2, LO3]**

Smithson Company uses a job-order costing system and has two manufacturing departments—Molding and Fabrication. The company provided the following estimates at the beginning of the year:

| | Molding | Fabrication | Total |
|---|---|---|---|
| Machine-hours | 20,000 | 30,000 | 50,000 |
| Fixed manufacturing overhead costs | $800,000 | $300,000 | $1,100,000 |
| Variable manufacturing overhead per machine-hour | $5.00 | $5.00 | |

During the year, the company had no beginning or ending inventories and it started, completed, and sold only two jobs—Job D-75 and Job C-100. It provided the following information related to those two jobs:

| Job D-75: | Molding | Fabrication | Total |
|---|---|---|---|
| Direct materials cost | $375,000 | $325,000 | $700,000 |
| Direct labor cost | $200,000 | $160,000 | $360,000 |
| Machine-hours | 15,000 | 5,000 | 20,000 |

| Job C-100: | Molding | Fabrication | Total |
|---|---|---|---|
| Direct materials cost | $300,000 | $250,000 | $550,000 |
| Direct labor cost | $175,000 | $225,000 | $400,000 |
| Machine-hours | 5,000 | 25,000 | 30,000 |

Smithson had no overapplied or underapplied manufacturing overhead during the year.

***Required:***

1. Assume Smithson uses a plantwide overhead rate based on machine-hours.
   a. Compute the predetermined plantwide overhead rate.
   b. Compute the total manufacturing costs assigned to Job D-75 and Job C-100.
   c. If Smithson establishes bid prices that are 150% of total manufacturing costs, what bid price would it have established for Job D-75 and Job C-100?
   d. What is Smithson's cost of goods sold for the year?
2. Assume Smithson uses departmental overhead rates based on machine-hours.
   a. Compute the predetermined departmental overhead rates.
   b. Compute the total manufacturing costs assigned to Job D-75 and Job C-100.
   c. If Smithson establishes bid prices that are 150% of total manufacturing costs, what bid price would it have established for Job D-75 and Job C-100?
   d. What is Smithson's cost of goods sold for the year?
3. What managerial insights are revealed by the computations that you performed in this problem? (Hint: Do the cost of goods sold amounts that you computed in requirements 1 and 2 differ from one another? Do the bid prices that you computed in requirements 1 and 2 differ from one another? Why?)

**EXERCISE 2–19 Applying Overhead; Journal Entries; T-Accounts [LO1, LO2, LO3, LO4, LO5]**

Custom Metal Works produces castings and other metal parts to customer specifications. The company uses a job-order costing system and applies overhead costs to jobs on the basis of machine-hours. At the beginning of the year, the company used a cost formula to estimate that it would incur $4,320,000 in manufacturing overhead cost at an activity level of 576,000 machine-hours.

The company had no work in process at the beginning of the year. The company spent the entire month of January working on one large order—Job 382, which was an order for 8,000 machined parts. Cost data for January follow:

a. Raw materials purchased on account, $315,000.
b. Raw materials requisitioned for production, $270,000 (80% direct and 20% indirect).
c. Labor cost incurred in the factory, $190,000, of which $80,000 was direct labor and $110,000 was indirect labor.
d. Depreciation recorded on factory equipment, $63,000.
e. Other manufacturing overhead costs incurred, $85,000 (credit Accounts Payable).
f. Manufacturing overhead cost was applied to production on the basis of 40,000 machine-hours actually worked during January.
g. The completed job was moved into the finished goods warehouse on January 31 to await delivery to the customer. (In computing the dollar amount for this entry, remember that the cost of a completed job consists of direct materials, direct labor, and *applied* overhead.)

***Required:***

1. Prepare journal entries to record items (a) through (f) above. Ignore item (g) for the moment.
2. Prepare T-accounts for Manufacturing Overhead and Work in Process. Post the relevant items from your journal entries to these T-accounts.
3. Prepare a journal entry for item (g) above.
4. Compute the unit product cost that will appear on the job cost sheet for Job 382.

**EXERCISE 2–20 Applying Overhead in a Service Company [LO1, LO2, LO3]**

Pearson Architectural Design began operations on January 2. The following activity was recorded in the company's Work in Process account for the first month of operations:

**Work in Process**

| | | | |
|---|---|---|---|
| Costs of subcontracted work | 90,000 | To completed projects | 570,000 |
| Direct staff costs | 200,000 | | |
| Studio overhead | 320,000 | | |

Pearson Architectural Design is a service firm, so the names of the accounts it uses are different from the names used in manufacturing companies. Costs of Subcontracted Work is comparable to Direct Materials; Direct Staff Costs is the same as Direct Labor; Studio Overhead is the same as Manufacturing Overhead; and Completed Projects is the same as Finished Goods. Apart from the difference in terms, the accounting methods used by the company are identical to the methods used by manufacturing companies.

Pearson Architectural Design uses a job-order costing system and applies studio overhead to Work in Process on the basis of direct staff costs. At the end of January, only one job was still in process. This job (the Krimmer Corporation Headquarters project) had been charged with $13,500 in direct staff costs.

***Required:***

1. Compute the predetermined overhead rate that was in use during January.
2. Complete the following job cost sheet for the partially completed Krimmer Corporation Headquarters project.

| Job Cost Sheet<br>Krimmer Corporation Headquarters Project<br>As of January 31 | |
|---|---|
| Costs of subcontracted work .................... | $ ? |
| Direct staff costs ...................................... | ? |
| Studio overhead ...................................... | ? |
| Total cost to January 31 ........................... | $ ? |

## PROBLEMS

connect ACCOUNTING

Alternate problem set is available on the text website and in *Connect® Accounting.*

**All applicable problems are available with McGraw-Hill's *Connect® Accounting.***

CHECK FIGURE
(2) Underapplied: $270,000

**PROBLEM 2–21A Predetermined Overhead Rate; Disposition of Underapplied or Overapplied Overhead [LO1, LO7]**

Savallas Company is highly automated and uses computers to control manufacturing operations. The company uses a job-order costing system and applies manufacturing overhead cost to products on the basis of computer-hours. The following estimates were used in preparing the predetermined overhead rate at the beginning of the year:

| | |
|---|---|
| Computer-hours ............................................ | 85,000 |
| Fixed manufacturing overhead cost ........................ | $1,275,000 |
| Variable manufacturing overhead per computer-hour ........ | $3.00 |

During the year, a severe economic recession resulted in cutting back production and a buildup of inventory in the company's warehouse. The company's cost records revealed the following actual cost and operating data for the year:

| | |
|---|---|
| Computer-hours .............................. | 60,000 |
| Manufacturing overhead cost .............. | $1,350,000 |
| Inventories at year-end: | |
| Raw materials ............................. | $400,000 |
| Work in process ........................... | $160,000 |
| Finished goods ............................ | $1,040,000 |
| Cost of goods sold .......................... | $2,800,000 |

***Required:***

1. Compute the company's predetermined overhead rate for the year.
2. Compute the underapplied or overapplied overhead for the year.
3. Assume the company closes any underapplied or overapplied overhead directly to Cost of Goods Sold. Prepare the appropriate journal entry. Will this entry increase or decrease net operating income?

**PROBLEM 2–22A Schedules of Cost of Goods Manufactured and Cost of Goods Sold; Income Statement [LO6]**

CHECK FIGURE
Direct labor: $65,000

Valenko Company provided the following account balances for the year ended December 31 (all raw materials are used in production as direct materials):

| | |
|---|---|
| Selling expenses | $215,000 |
| Purchases of raw materials | $260,000 |
| Direct labor | ? |
| Administrative expenses | $160,000 |
| Manufacturing overhead applied to work in process | $340,000 |
| Total actual manufacturing overhead costs | $350,000 |

Inventory balances at the beginning and end of the year were as follows:

| | Beginning of Year | End of Year |
|---|---|---|
| Raw materials | $50,000 | $40,000 |
| Work in process | ? | $33,000 |
| Finished goods | $30,000 | ? |

The total manufacturing costs for the year were $675,000; the cost of goods available for sale totaled $720,000; the unadjusted cost of goods sold totaled $665,000; and the net operating income was $35,000. The company's overapplied or underapplied overhead is closed entirely to cost of goods sold.

***Required:***

Prepare schedules of cost of goods manufactured and cost of goods sold and an income statement. (Hint: Prepare the income statement and schedule of cost of goods sold first followed by the schedule of cost of goods manufactured.)

CHECK FIGURE
(4) Cost of Goods manufactured: $810,000
(7) overapplied: $15,000

**PROBLEM 2–23A T-Account Analysis of Cost Flows [LO1, LO5, LO6, LO7]**

Selected T-accounts for Rolm Company are given below for the just completed year:

**Raw Materials**

| | | | |
|---|---|---|---|
| Bal. 1/1 | 30,000 | Credits | ? |
| Debits | 420,000 | | |
| Bal. 12/31 | 60,000 | | |

**Manufacturing Overhead**

| | | | |
|---|---|---|---|
| Debits | 385,000 | Credits | ? |

**Work in Process**

| | | | |
|---|---|---|---|
| Bal. 1/1 | 70,000 | Credits | 810,000 |
| Direct materials | 320,000 | | |
| Direct labor | 110,000 | | |
| Overhead | 400,000 | | |
| Bal. 12/31 | ? | | |

**Factory Wages Payable**

| | | | |
|---|---|---|---|
| Debits | 179,000 | Bal. 1/1 | 10,000 |
| | | Credits | 175,000 |
| | | Bal. 12/31 | 6,000 |

**Finished Goods**

| | | | |
|---|---|---|---|
| Bal. 1/1 | 40,000 | Credits | ? |
| Debits | ? | | |
| Bal. 12/31 | 130,000 | | |

**Cost of Goods Sold**

| | | | |
|---|---|---|---|
| Debits | ? | | |

***Required:***

1. What was the cost of raw materials put into production during the year?
2. How much of the materials in (1) above consisted of indirect materials?
3. How much of the factory labor cost for the year consisted of indirect labor?
4. What was the cost of goods manufactured for the year?
5. What was the cost of goods sold for the year (before considering underapplied or overapplied overhead)?
6. If overhead is applied to production on the basis of direct materials cost, what predetermined rate was in effect during the year?
7. Was manufacturing overhead underapplied or overapplied? By how much?
8. Compute the ending balance in the Work in Process inventory account. Assume that this balance consists entirely of goods started during the year. If $32,000 of this balance is direct materials cost, how much of it is direct labor cost? Manufacturing overhead cost?

eXcel

**PROBLEM 2–24A Schedule of Cost of Goods Manufactured; Overhead Analysis [LO1, LO2, LO3, LO6, LO7]**

CHECK FIGURE
(2) Cost of Goods manufactured: $342,000
(5) Direct materials: $20,000

The Pacific Manufacturing Company operates a job-order costing system and applies overhead cost to jobs on the basis of direct labor cost. Its predetermined overhead rate was based on a cost formula that estimated $126,000 of manufacturing overhead for an estimated allocation base of $84,000 direct labor dollars. The company has provided the following data for the year:

| | |
|---|---|
| Purchase of raw materials (all direct) | $133,000 |
| Direct labor cost | $80,000 |
| Actual manufacturing overhead costs: | |
| Insurance, factory | $7,000 |
| Depreciation of equipment | $18,000 |
| Indirect labor | $42,000 |
| Property taxes | $9,000 |
| Maintenance | $11,000 |
| Rent, building | $36,000 |

| | Beginning | Ending |
|---|---|---|
| Inventories: | | |
| Raw materials | $21,000 | $16,000 |
| Work in process | $44,000 | $40,000 |
| Finished goods | $68,000 | $60,000 |

***Required:***

1. a. Compute the predetermined overhead rate for the year.
   b. Compute the amount of underapplied or overapplied overhead for the year.
2. Prepare a schedule of cost of goods manufactured for the year. Assume all raw materials are used in production as direct materials.
3. Compute the unadjusted cost of goods sold for the year. (Do not include any underapplied or overapplied overhead in your cost of goods sold figure.)
4. Job 137 was started and completed during the year. What price would have been charged to the customer if the job required $3,200 in materials and $4,200 in direct labor cost, and the company priced its jobs at 40% above the job's cost according to the accounting system?
5. Direct labor made up $8,000 of the $40,000 ending Work in Process inventory balance. Supply the information missing below:

| | |
|---|---|
| Direct materials | $ ? |
| Direct labor | 8,000 |
| Manufacturing overhead | ? |
| Work in process inventory | $40,000 |

eXcel

**PROBLEM 2–25A Journal Entries; T-Accounts; Financial Statements [LO1, LO2, LO3, LO4, LO5, LO6, LO7]**

Southworth Company uses a job-order costing system and applies manufacturing overhead cost to jobs on the basis of the cost of direct materials used in production. Its predetermined overhead rate was based on a cost formula that estimated $248,000 of manufacturing overhead for an estimated allocation base of

$155,000 direct material dollars. The following transactions took place during the year (all purchases and services were acquired on account):

a. Raw materials purchased, $142,000.
b. Raw materials requisitioned for use in production (all direct materials), $150,000.
c. Utility bills incurred in the factory, $21,000.
d. Costs for salaries and wages were incurred as follows:

CHECK FIGURE
(3) Cost of Goods manufactured; $590,000
(6) $48.16 per unit

| | |
|---|---|
| Direct labor | $216,000 |
| Indirect labor | $90,000 |
| Selling and administrative salaries | $145,000 |

e. Maintenance costs incurred in the factory, $15,000.
f. Advertising costs incurred, $130,000.
g. Depreciation recorded for the year, $50,000 (90% relates to factory assets, and the remainder relates to selling and administrative assets).
h. Rental cost incurred on buildings, $90,000 (80% of the space is occupied by the factory, and 20% is occupied by sales and administration).
i. Miscellaneous selling and administrative costs incurred, $17,000.
j. Manufacturing overhead cost was applied to jobs, $ ? .
k. Cost of goods manufactured for the year, $590,000.
l. Sales for the year (all on account) totaled $1,000,000. These goods cost $600,000 according to their job cost sheets.

The balances in the inventory accounts at the beginning of the year were as follows:

| | |
|---|---|
| Raw Materials | $18,000 |
| Work in Process | $24,000 |
| Finished Goods | $35,000 |

***Required:***

1. Prepare journal entries to record the above data.
2. Post your entries to T-accounts. (Don't forget to enter the opening inventory balances above.) Determine the ending balances in the inventory accounts and in the Manufacturing Overhead account.
3. Prepare a schedule of cost of goods manufactured.
4. Prepare a journal entry to close any balance in the Manufacturing Overhead account to Cost of Goods Sold. Prepare a schedule of cost of goods sold.
5. Prepare an income statement for the year.
6. Job 218 was one of the many jobs started and completed during the year. The job required $3,600 in direct materials and 400 hours of direct labor time at a rate of $11 per hour. If the job contained 500 units and the company billed at 75% above the unit product cost on the job cost sheet, what price per unit would have been charged to the customer?

**PROBLEM 2–26A Multiple Departments; Applying Overhead [LO1, LO2, LO3, LO7]**

eXcel

WoodGrain Technology makes home office furniture from fine hardwoods. The company uses a job-order costing system and predetermined overhead rates to apply manufacturing overhead cost to jobs. The predetermined overhead rate in the Preparation Department is based on machine-hours, and the rate in the Fabrication Department is based on direct labor-hours. At the beginning of the year, the company's management made the following estimates for the year:

CHECK FIGURE
(2) Total overhead: $3,692
(3) $300.88 per unit

| | Department | |
|---|---|---|
| | Preparation | Fabrication |
| Machine-hours | 80,000 | 21,000 |
| Direct labor-hours | 35,000 | 50,000 |
| Direct materials cost | $190,000 | $400,000 |
| Direct labor cost | $280,000 | $530,000 |
| Fixed manufacturing overhead cost | $256,000 | $520,000 |
| Variable manufacturing overhead per machine-hour | $2.00 | — |
| Variable manufacturing overhead per direct labor-hour | — | $4.00 |

Job 127 was started on April 1 and completed on May 12. The company's cost records show the following information concerning the job:

| | Department | |
|---|---|---|
| | Preparation | Fabrication |
| Machine-hours | 350 | 70 |
| Direct labor-hours | 80 | 130 |
| Direct materials cost | $940 | $1,200 |
| Direct labor cost | $710 | $980 |

***Required:***

1. Compute the predetermined overhead rate used during the year in the Preparation Department. Compute the rate used in the Fabrication Department.
2. Compute the total overhead cost applied to Job 127.
3. What would be the total cost recorded for Job 127? If the job contained 25 units, what would be the unit product cost?
4. At the end of the year, the records of WoodGrain Technology revealed the following *actual* cost and operating data for all jobs worked on during the year:

| | Department | |
|---|---|---|
| | Preparation | Fabrication |
| Machine-hours | 73,000 | 24,000 |
| Direct labor-hours | 30,000 | 54,000 |
| Direct materials cost | $165,000 | $420,000 |
| Manufacturing overhead cost | $390,000 | $740,000 |

What was the amount of underapplied or overapplied overhead in each department at the end of the year?

CHECK FIGURE
(3) Underapplied: £13,000
(4) Net operating income: £82,000

**PROBLEM 2–27A A Comprehensive Problem [LO1, LO2, LO4, LO5, LO6, LO7]**

Sovereign Millwork, Ltd., produces reproductions of antique residential moldings at a plant located in Manchester, England. Because there are hundreds of products, some of which are made only to order, the company uses a job-order costing system. On July 1, the start of the company's fiscal year, inventory account balances were as follows:

| | |
|---|---|
| Raw Materials | £10,000 |
| Work in Process | £4,000 |
| Finished Goods | £8,000 |

The company applies overhead cost to jobs on the basis of machine-hours. Its predetermined overhead rate for the fiscal year starting July 1 was based on a cost formula that estimated £99,000 of manufacturing overhead for an estimated activity level of 45,000 machine-hours. During the year, the following transactions were completed:

a. Raw materials purchased on account, £160,000.
b. Raw materials requisitioned for use in production, £140,000 (materials costing £120,000 were chargeable directly to jobs; the remaining materials were indirect).
c. Costs for employee services were incurred as follows:

| | |
|---|---|
| Direct labor | £90,000 |
| Indirect labor | £60,000 |
| Sales commissions | £20,000 |
| Administrative salaries | £50,000 |

d. Prepaid insurance expired during the year, £18,000 (£13,000 of this amount related to factory operations, and the remainder related to selling and administrative activities).
e. Utility costs incurred in the factory, £10,000.

f. Advertising costs incurred, £15,000.
g. Depreciation recorded on equipment, £25,000. (£20,000 of this amount was on equipment used in factory operations; the remaining £5,000 was on equipment used in selling and administrative activities.)
h. Manufacturing overhead cost was applied to jobs, £?. (The company recorded 50,000 machine-hours of operating time during the year.)
i. Goods that had cost £310,000 to manufacture according to their job cost sheets were completed.
j. Sales (all on account) to customers during the year totaled £498,000. These goods had cost £308,000 to manufacture according to their job cost sheets.

***Required:***
1. Prepare journal entries to record the transactions for the year.
2. Prepare T-accounts for inventories, Manufacturing Overhead, and Cost of Goods Sold. Post relevant data from your journal entries to these T-accounts (don't forget to enter the opening balances in your inventory accounts). Compute an ending balance in each account.
3. Is Manufacturing Overhead underapplied or overapplied for the year? Prepare a journal entry to close any balance in the Manufacturing Overhead account to Cost of Goods Sold.
4. Prepare an income statement for the year. (Do not prepare a schedule of cost of goods manufactured; all of the information needed for the income statement is available in the journal entries and T-accounts you have prepared.)

**PROBLEM 2–28A Cost Flows; T-Accounts; Income Statement [LO1, LO2, LO5, LO6, LO7]**

CHECK FIGURE
(3) Overapplied: $3,000
(4) Net operating income: $32,200

Fantastic Props, Inc., designs and fabricates movie props such as mock-ups of star-fighters and cybernetic robots. The company's balance sheet as of January 1, the beginning of the current year, appears below:

**Fantastic Props, Inc.**
**Balance Sheet**
**January 1**

| | | |
|---|---|---|
| **Assets** | | |
| Current assets: | | |
| Cash | | $ 15,000 |
| Accounts receivable | | 40,000 |
| Inventories: | | |
| Raw materials | $ 25,000 | |
| Work in process | 30,000 | |
| Finished goods (props awaiting shipment) | 45,000 | 100,000 |
| Prepaid insurance | | 5,000 |
| Total current assets | | 160,000 |
| Buildings and equipment | 500,000 | |
| Less accumulated depreciation | 210,000 | 290,000 |
| Total assets | | $450,000 |
| **Liabilities and Stockholders' Equity** | | |
| Accounts payable | | $ 75,000 |
| Common stock | $250,000 | |
| Retained earnings | 125,000 | 375,000 |
| Total liabilities and stockholders' equity | | $450,000 |

Because each prop is a unique design and may require anything from a few hours to a month or more to complete, Fantastic Props uses a job-order costing system. Overhead in the fabrication shop is charged to props on the basis of direct labor cost. The company's predetermined overhead rate for the year is based on a cost formula that estimated $80,000 in manufacturing overhead for an estimated allocation base of $100,000 direct labor dollars. The following transactions were recorded during the year:
a. Raw materials, such as wood, paints, and metal sheeting, were purchased on account, $80,000.
b. Raw materials were issued to production, $90,000; $5,000 of this amount was for indirect materials.
c. Payroll costs incurred and paid: direct labor, $120,000; indirect labor, $30,000; and selling and administrative salaries, $75,000.
d. Fabrication shop utilities costs incurred, $12,000.

e. Depreciation recorded for the year, $30,000 ($5,000 on selling and administrative assets; $25,000 on fabrication shop assets).
f. Prepaid insurance expired, $4,800 ($4,000 related to fabrication shop operations, and $800 related to selling and administrative activities).
g. Shipping expenses incurred, $40,000.
h. Other manufacturing overhead costs incurred, $17,000 (credit Accounts Payable).
i. Manufacturing overhead was applied to production. Overhead is applied on the basis of direct labor cost.
j. Movie props that cost $310,000 to produce according to their job cost sheets were completed.
k. Sales for the year totaled $450,000 and were all on account. The total cost to produce these movie props was $300,000 according to their job cost sheets.
l. Collections on account from customers, $445,000.
m. Payments on account to suppliers, $150,000.

***Required:***

1. Prepare a T-account for each account on the company's balance sheet, and enter the beginning balances.
2. Make entries directly into the T-accounts for transactions (a) through (m). Create new T-accounts as needed. Determine an ending balance for each T-account.
3. Was manufacturing overhead underapplied or overapplied for the year? Prepare a journal entry to close any balance in the Manufacturing Overhead account to Cost of Goods Sold.
4. Prepare an income statement for the year. (Do not prepare a schedule of cost of goods manufactured; all of the information needed for the income statement is available in the T-accounts.)

# BUILDING YOUR SKILLS

### CASE [LO1, LO2, LO3, LO7]

CHECK FIGURE
(2) Overhead applied: $21,750

"Don't tell me we've lost another bid!" exclaimed Sandy Kovallas, president of Lenko Products, Inc. "I'm afraid so," replied Doug Martin, the operations vice president. "One of our competitors underbid us by about $10,000 on the Hastings job." "I just can't figure it out," said Kovallas. "It seems we're either too high to get the job or too low to make any money on half the jobs we bid anymore. What's happened?"

Lenko Products manufactures specialized goods to customers' specifications and operates a job-order costing system. Manufacturing overhead cost is applied to jobs on the basis of direct labor cost. The following estimates were made at the beginning of the year:

| | Department | | | |
|---|---|---|---|---|
| | Cutting | Machining | Assembly | Total Plant |
| Direct labor ............................ | $300,000 | $200,000 | $400,000 | $900,000 |
| Manufacturing overhead .......... | $540,000 | $800,000 | $100,000 | $1,440,000 |

Jobs require varying amounts of work in the three departments. The Hastings job, for example, would have required manufacturing costs in the three departments as follows:

| | Department | | | |
|---|---|---|---|---|
| | Cutting | Machining | Assembly | Total Plant |
| Direct materials ........................ | $12,000 | $900 | $5,600 | $18,500 |
| Direct labor ............................ | $6,500 | $1,700 | $13,000 | $21,200 |
| Manufacturing overhead .......... | ? | ? | ? | ? |

The company uses a plantwide overhead rate to apply manufacturing overhead cost to jobs.

***Required:***

1. Assuming the use of a plantwide overhead rate:
   a. Compute the rate for the current year.
   b. Determine the amount of manufacturing overhead cost that would have been applied to the Hastings job.

2. Suppose that instead of using a plantwide overhead rate, the company had used a separate predetermined overhead rate in each department. Under these conditions:
   a. Compute the rate for each department for the current year.
   b. Determine the amount of manufacturing overhead cost that would have been applied to the Hastings job.
3. Explain the difference between the manufacturing overhead that would have been applied to the Hastings job using the plantwide rate in question 1(b) and using the departmental rates in question 2(b).
4. Assume that it is customary in the industry to bid jobs at 150% of total manufacturing cost (direct materials, direct labor, and applied overhead). What was the company's bid price on the Hastings job? What would the bid price have been if departmental overhead rates had been used to apply overhead cost?
5. At the end of the year, the company assembled the following *actual* cost data relating to all jobs worked on during the year:

| | Department | | | |
|---|---|---|---|---|
| | **Cutting** | **Machining** | **Assembly** | **Total Plant** |
| Direct materials | $760,000 | $90,000 | $410,000 | $1,260,000 |
| Direct labor | $320,000 | $210,000 | $340,000 | $870,000 |
| Manufacturing overhead | $560,000 | $830,000 | $92,000 | $1,482,000 |

Compute the underapplied or overapplied overhead for the year (a) assuming that a plantwide overhead rate is used, and (b) assuming that departmental overhead rates are used.

## ETHICS CHALLENGE [LO1, LO2, LO7]

Cristin Madsen has recently been transferred to the Appliances Division of Solequin Corporation. Shortly after taking over her new position as divisional controller, she was asked to develop the division's predetermined overhead rate for the upcoming year. The accuracy of the rate is important because it is used throughout the year and any overapplied or underapplied overhead is closed out to Cost of Goods Sold at the end of the year. Solequin Corporation uses direct labor-hours in all of its divisions as the allocation base for manufacturing overhead.

To compute the predetermined overhead rate, Cristin divided her estimate of the total manufacturing overhead for the coming year by the production manager's estimate of the total direct labor-hours for the coming year. She took her computations to the division's general manager for approval but was quite surprised when he suggested a modification in the base. Her conversation with the general manager of the Appliances Division, Lance Jusic, went like this:

***Madsen:*** Here are my calculations for next year's predetermined overhead rate. If you approve, we can enter the rate into the computer on January 1 and be up and running in the job-order costing system right away this year.

***Jusic:*** Thanks for coming up with the calculations so quickly, and they look just fine. There is, however, one slight modification I would like to see. Your estimate of the total direct labor-hours for the year is 110,000 hours. How about cutting that to about 105,000 hours?

***Madsen:*** I don't know if I can do that. The production manager says she will need about 110,000 direct labor-hours to meet the sales projections for next year. Besides, there are going to be over 108,000 direct labor-hours during the current year and sales are projected to be higher next year.

***Jusic:*** Cristin, I know all of that. I would still like to reduce the direct labor-hours in the base to something like 105,000 hours. You probably don't know that I had an agreement with your predecessor as divisional controller to shave 5% or so off the estimated direct labor-hours every year. That way, we kept a reserve that usually resulted in a big boost to net operating income at the end of the fiscal year in December. We called it our Christmas bonus. Corporate headquarters always seemed as pleased as punch that we could pull off such a miracle at the end of the year. This system has worked well for many years, and I don't want to change it now.

***Required:***

1. Explain how shaving 5% off the estimated direct labor-hours in the base for the predetermined overhead rate usually results in a big boost in net operating income at the end of the fiscal year.
2. Should Cristin Madsen go along with the general manager's request to reduce the direct labor-hours in the predetermined overhead rate computation to 105,000 direct labor-hours?

CHECK FIGURE
(3) WIP inventory: $5,300

**TEAMWORK IN ACTION [LO1, LO2 LO4, LO5, LO7]**

After a dispute concerning wages, Orville Arson tossed an incendiary device into the Sparkle Company's record vault. Within moments, only a few charred fragments were readable from the company's factory ledger, as shown below:

**Raw Materials**

| | |
|---|---|
| Balance 4/1 12,000 | |

**Manufacturing Overhead**

| | |
|---|---|
| Actual costs for April 14,800 | |

**Work in Process**

| | |
|---|---|
| Balance 4/1 4,500 | |

**Accounts Payable**

| | |
|---|---|
| | Balance 4/30 8,000 |

**Finished Goods**

| | |
|---|---|
| Balance 4/30 16,000 | |

**Cost of Goods Sold**

| | |
|---|---|
| | |

Sifting through ashes and interviewing selected employees has turned up the following additional information:

a. The controller remembers clearly that the predetermined overhead rate was based on an estimated 60,000 direct labor-hours to be worked over the year and an estimated $180,000 in manufacturing overhead costs.

b. The production superintendent's cost sheets showed only one job in process on April 30. Materials of $2,600 had been added to the job, and 300 direct labor-hours had been expended at $6 per hour.

c. The accounts payable are for raw material purchases only, according to the accounts payable clerk. He clearly remembers that the balance in the account was $6,000 on April 1. An analysis of canceled checks (kept in the treasurer's office) shows that payments of $40,000 were made to suppliers during April. (All materials used during April were direct materials.)

d. A charred piece of the payroll ledger shows that 5,200 direct labor-hours were recorded for the month. The personnel department has verified that there were no variations in pay rates among employees.

e. Records maintained in the finished goods warehouse indicate that the finished goods inventory totaled $11,000 on April 1.

f. From another charred piece in the vault, you are able to discern that the cost of goods manufactured for April was $89,000.

***Required:***

1. Assign one of the following sets of accounts to each member of the team:
   a. Raw Materials and Accounts Payable.
   b. Work in Process and Manufacturing Overhead.
   c. Finished Goods and Cost of Goods Sold.

   Determine the types of transactions that would be posted to each account and present a summary to the other team members. When agreement is reached, the team should work together to complete steps 2 through 4.
2. Determine the company's predetermined overhead rate and the total manufacturing overhead applied for the month.
3. Determine the April 30 balance in the company's Work in Process account.
4. Prepare the company's T-accounts for the month. (It is easiest to complete the T-accounts in the following order: Accounts Payable, Work in Process, Raw Materials, Manufacturing Overhead, Finished Goods, Cost of Goods Sold.)

## COMMUNICATING IN PRACTICE [LO1, LO2]

Look in the yellow pages or contact your local chamber of commerce or local chapter of the Institute of Management Accountants to find the names of manufacturing companies in your area. Call or make an appointment to meet with the controller or chief financial officer of one of these companies.

***Required:***

Ask the following questions and write a brief memorandum to your instructor that addresses what you found out.

1. What are the company's main products?
2. Does the company use job-order costing or some other method of determining product costs?
3. How is overhead applied to products? What is the overhead rate? What is the basis of allocation? Is more than one overhead rate used?
4. Has the company recently changed its cost system or is it considering changing its cost system? If so, why? What changes were made or what changes are being considered?.

## A LOOK BACK

Chapter 2 provided an overview of job-order costing. Direct materials and direct labor costs are traced directly to jobs. Manufacturing overhead is applied to jobs using a predetermined overhead rate.

## A LOOK AT THIS CHAPTER

In Chapter 3, we continue the discussion of allocation of overhead in job-order costing. Activity-based costing is a technique that uses a number of allocation bases to assign overhead costs to products.

## A LOOK AHEAD

After comparing job-order and process costing systems, we go into the details of a process costing system in Chapter 4.

# 3 Activity-Based Costing

## CHAPTER OUTLINE

DECISION FEATURE

## Managing Product Complexity

Managers often understand that increasing the variety of raw material inputs used in their products increases costs. For example, **General Mills** studied its 50 varieties of Hamburger Helper and concluded that it could lower costs by discontinuing half of them without alienating customers. **Seagate** studied seven varieties of its computer hard drives and found that only 2% of their parts could be shared by more than one hard drive. The engineers fixed the problem by redesigning the hard drives so that they used more common component parts. Instead of using 61 types of screws to make the hard drives, the engineers reduced the number of screws needed to 19. Eventually all Seagate products were designed so that 75% of their component parts were shared with other product lines.

Activity-based costing systems quantify the increase in costs, such as procurement costs, material handling costs, and assembly costs that are caused by inefficient product designs and other factors.

Sources: Mina Kimes, "Cereal Cost Cutters," *Fortune,* November 10, 2008, p. 24; Erika Brown, "Drive Fast, Drive Hard," *Forbes,* January 9, 2006, pp. 92–96.

## LEARNING OBJECTIVES

*After studying Chapter 3, you should be able to:*

**LO1** Understand the basic approach in activity-based costing and how it differs from conventional costing.

**LO2** Compute activity rates for an activity-based costing system.

**LO3** Compute product costs using activity-based costing.

**LO4** Contrast the product costs computed under activity-based costing and conventional costing methods.

**As discussed in earlier chapters,** direct materials and direct labor costs can be directly traced to products. Overhead costs, on the other hand, cannot be easily traced to products. Some other means must be found for assigning them to products for financial reporting and other purposes. In the previous chapter, overhead costs were assigned to products using a plantwide predetermined overhead rate. This method is simpler than the methods of assigning overhead costs to products described in this chapter, but this simplicity has a cost. A plantwide predetermined overhead rate spreads overhead costs uniformly over products in proportion to whatever allocation base is used—most commonly, direct labor-hours. This procedure results in high overhead costs for products with a high direct labor-hour content and low overhead costs for products with a low direct labor-hour content. However, the real causes of overhead may have little to do with direct labor-hours and as a consequence, product costs may be distorted. Activity-based costing attempts to correct these distortions by more accurately assigning overhead costs to products.

## ASSIGNING OVERHEAD COSTS TO PRODUCTS

**LEARNING OBJECTIVE 1**

Understand the basic approach in activity-based costing and how it differs from conventional costing.

Companies use three common approaches to assign overhead costs to products. The simplest method is to use a plantwide overhead rate. A slightly more refined approach is to use departmental overhead rates. The most complex method is activity-based costing, which is the most accurate of the three approaches to overhead cost assignment.

### Plantwide Overhead Rate

The preceding chapter assumed that a single overhead rate, called a *plantwide overhead rate,* was used throughout an entire factory. This simple approach to overhead assignment can result in distorted unit product costs, as we shall see below.

When cost systems were developed in the 1800s, cost and activity data had to be collected by hand and all calculations were done with paper and pen. Consequently, the emphasis was on simplicity. Companies often established a single overhead cost pool for an entire facility or department as described in Chapter 2. Direct labor was the obvious choice as an allocation base for overhead costs. Direct labor-hours were already being recorded for purposes of determining wages. In the labor-intensive production processes of that time, direct labor was a large component of product costs—larger than it is today. Moreover, managers believed direct labor and overhead costs were highly correlated. (Two variables, such as direct labor and overhead costs, are highly correlated if they tend to move together.) And finally, most companies produced a very limited variety of similar products, so in fact there was probably little difference in the overhead costs attributable to different products. Under these conditions, it was not cost-effective to use a more elaborate costing system.

Conditions have changed. Many companies now sell a large variety of products that consume significantly different amounts of overhead resources. Consequently, a costing system that assigns essentially the same overhead cost to every product may no longer be adequate. Additionally, factors other than direct labor often drive overhead costs.

On an economywide basis, direct labor and overhead costs have been moving in opposite directions for a long time. As a percentage of total cost, direct labor has been declining, whereas overhead has been increasing. Many tasks previously done by hand are now done with largely automated equipment—a component of overhead. Furthermore, product diversity has increased. Companies are introducing new products and services at an ever-accelerating rate. Managing and sustaining this product diversity requires many more overhead resources such as production schedulers and product design engineers, and many of these overhead resources have no obvious connection with direct labor. Finally, computers, bar code readers, and other technology have dramatically reduced the costs of collecting and processing data—making more complex (and accurate) costing systems such as activity-based costing much less expensive to build and maintain.

Nevertheless, direct labor remains a viable base for applying overhead to products in some companies—particularly for external reports. Direct labor is an appropriate allocation base for overhead when overhead costs and direct labor are highly correlated. And indeed, most companies throughout the world continue to base overhead allocations on direct labor or machine-hours. However, if factorywide overhead costs do not move in tandem with factorywide direct labor or machine-hours, product costs will be distorted.

## Departmental Overhead Rates

Rather than use a plantwide overhead rate, many companies use departmental overhead rates with a different predetermined overhead rate in each production department. The nature of the work performed in a department will determine the department's allocation base. For example, overhead costs in a machining department may be allocated on the basis of machine-hours. In contrast, the overhead costs in an assembly department may be allocated on the basis of direct labor-hours.

Unfortunately, even departmental overhead rates will not correctly assign overhead costs in situations where a company has a range of products and complex overhead costs. The reason is that the departmental approach usually relies on a single measure of activity as the base for allocating overhead cost to products. For example, if the machining department's overhead is applied to products on the basis of machine-hours, it is assumed that the department's overhead costs are caused by, and are directly proportional to, machine-hours. However, the department's overhead costs are probably more complex than this and are caused by a variety of factors, including the range of products processed in the department, the number of batch setups that are required, the complexity of the products, and so on. A more sophisticated method like *activity-based costing* is required to adequately account for these diverse factors.

### HELPFUL HINT

Conventional cost systems that use plantwide or departmental overhead rates suffer from an important limitation. They tend to inaccurately assign too much overhead to high-volume products and too little overhead to low-volume products. This distortion occurs because conventional cost systems rely exclusively on allocation bases, such as direct labor-hours and machine-hours, that are highly correlated with (or move in tandem with) the volume of production. Make a point of noticing a recurring theme throughout this chapter—activity-based costing systems usually reveal that low-volume (high-volume) products cost more than (less than) reported by conventional cost systems.

## Activity-Based Costing (ABC)

**Activity-based costing (ABC)** is a technique that attempts to assign overhead costs more accurately to products than the simpler methods discussed thus far. The basic idea underlying the activity-based costing approach is illustrated in Exhibit 3–1. A customer order triggers a number of activities. For example, if **Nordstrom** orders a line of women's skirts from **Calvin Klein**, a production order is generated, patterns are created, materials are ordered, textiles are cut to pattern and then sewn, and the finished products are packed for shipping. These activities consume resources. For example, ordering the appropriate materials consumes clerical time—a resource the company must pay for. In activity-based costing, an attempt is made to trace these costs directly to the products that cause them.

Rather than a single allocation base such as direct labor-hours or machine-hours, in activity-based costing a company uses a number of allocation bases for assigning costs to products. Each allocation base in an activity-based costing system represents a major

**EXHIBIT 3–1**
The Activity-Based Costing Model

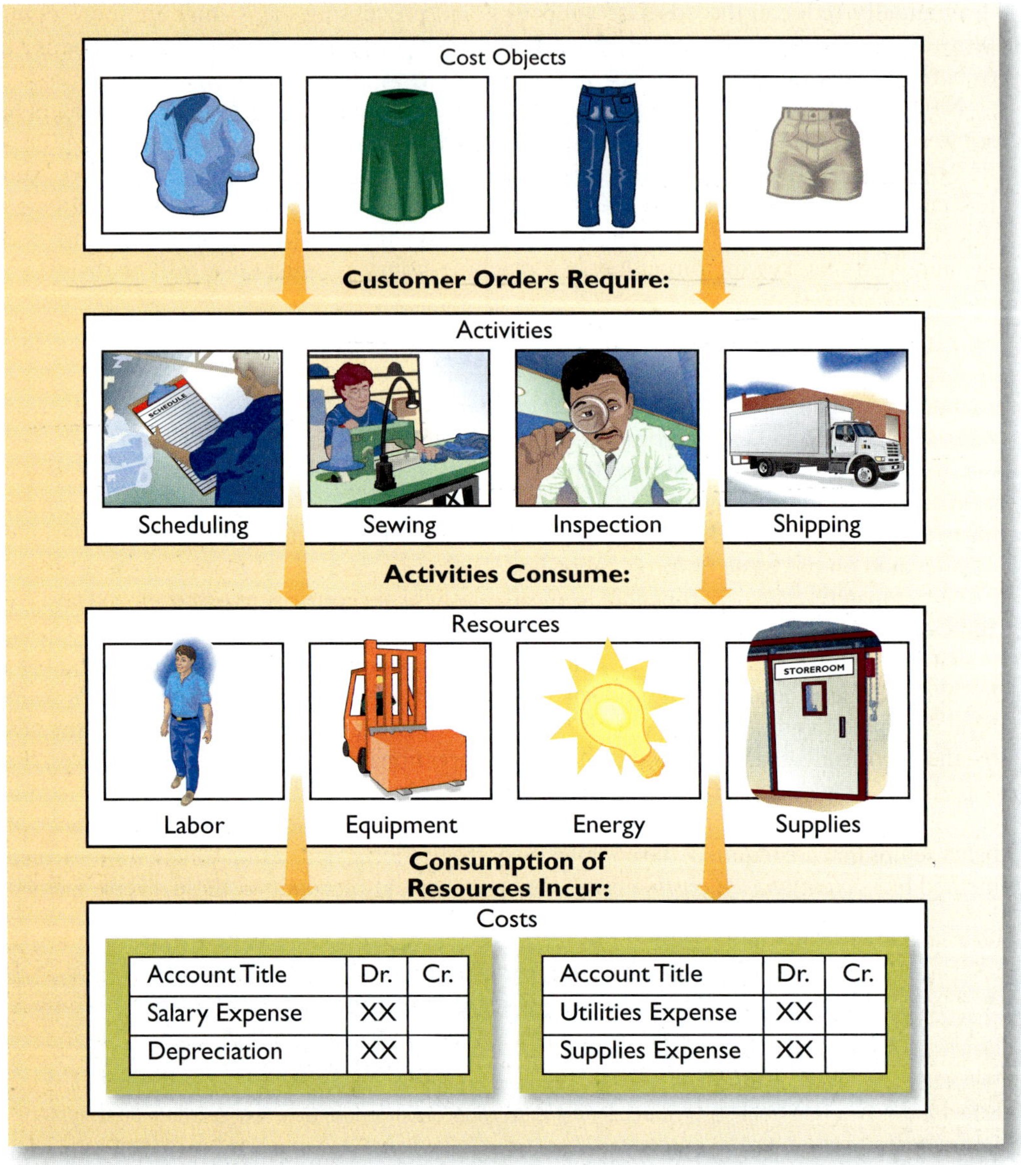


*activity* that causes overhead costs. An **activity** in activity-based costing is an event that causes the consumption of overhead resources. Examples of activities in various organizations include the following:

- Setting up machines.
- Admitting patients to a hospital.
- Scheduling production.
- Performing blood tests at a clinic.
- Billing customers.
- Maintaining equipment.
- Ordering materials or supplies.
- Stocking shelves at a store.
- Meeting with clients at a law firm.
- Preparing shipments.
- Inspecting materials for defects.
- Opening an account at a bank.

Activity-based costing focuses on these activities. Each major activity has its own overhead cost pool (also known as an *activity cost pool*), its own *activity measure,* and its own overhead rate (also known as an *activity rate*). An **activity cost pool** is a "cost bucket" in which costs related to a particular activity measure are accumulated. The **activity measure** expresses how much of the activity is carried out and it is used as the allocation base for assigning overhead costs to products and services. For example, *the number of patients admitted* is a natural choice of an activity measure for the activity *admitting patients to the hospital.* An **activity rate** is an overhead rate in an activity-based costing system. Each activity has its own activity rate that is used to assign overhead costs to cost objects.

For example, the activity *setting up machines to process a batch* would have its own activity cost pool. Products are ordinarily processed in batches. And because each product has its own machine settings, machines must be set up when changing over from a batch of one product to another. If the total cost in this activity cost pool is $150,000 and the total expected activity is 1,000 machine setups, the activity rate for this activity would be $150 per machine setup ($150,000 ÷ 1,000 machine setups = $150 per machine setup). Each product that requires a machine setup would be charged $150. Note that this charge does not depend on how many units are produced after the machine is set up. A small batch requiring a machine setup would be charged $150—just the same as a large batch.

Taking each activity in isolation, this system works exactly like the job-order costing system described in the last chapter. An activity rate is computed for each activity and then these rates are used to assign costs to jobs and products based on the amount of activity consumed by the job or product.

## DESIGNING AN ACTIVITY-BASED COSTING SYSTEM

The most important decisions in designing an activity-based costing system concern what activities will be included in the system and how the activities will be measured. In most companies, hundreds or even thousands of different activities cause overhead costs. These activities range from taking a telephone order to training new employees. Setting up and maintaining a complex costing system that includes all of these activities would be prohibitively expensive. The challenge in designing an activity-based costing system is to identify a reasonably small number of activities that explain the bulk of the variation in overhead costs. This is usually done by interviewing a broad range of managers in the organization to find out what activities they think are important and that consume most of the resources they manage. This often results in a long list of potential activities that could be included in the activity-based costing system. This list is refined and pruned in consultation with top managers. Related activities are frequently combined to reduce the amount of detail and record-keeping cost. For example, several actions may be involved in handling and moving raw materials, but these may be combined into a single activity titled *material handling.* The end result of this stage of the design process is an *activity dictionary* that defines each of the activities that will be included in the activity-based costing system and how the activities will be measured.

Some of the activities commonly found in activity-based costing systems in manufacturing companies are listed in Exhibit 3–2. In the exhibit, activities have been grouped into a four-level hierarchy: *unit-level activities, batch-level activities, product-level activities,* and *facility-level activities.* This cost hierarchy is useful in understanding the difference between activity-based costing and conventional approaches. It also serves as a guide when simplifying an activity-based costing system. In general, activities and costs should be combined in the activity-based costing system only if they fall within the same level in the cost hierarchy.

**EXHIBIT 3–2** Examples of Activities and Activity Measures in Manufacturing Companies

| Level | Activities | Activity Measures |
|---|---|---|
| *Unit-level* | Processing units on machines<br>Processing units by hand<br>Consuming factory supplies | Machine-hours<br>Direct labor-hours<br>Units produced |
| *Batch-level* | Processing purchase orders<br>Processing production orders<br>Setting up equipment<br>Handling material | Purchase orders processed<br>Production orders processed<br>Number of setups; setup hours<br>Pounds of material handled; number of times material moved |
| *Product-level* | Testing new products<br>Administering parts inventories<br>Designing products | Hours of testing time<br>Number of part types<br>Hours of design time |
| *Facility-level* | General factory administration<br>Plant building and grounds | Direct labor-hours*<br>Direct labor-hours* |

*Facility-level costs cannot be traced on a cause-and-effect basis to individual products. Nevertheless, companies that choose to use activity-based absorption costing will allocate these costs to products using some arbitrary allocation base such as direct labor-hours.

IN BUSINESS

## Gastronomic Cost Drivers at the Club Med—Bora Bora

The Club Med—Bora Bora of Tahiti is a resort owned and operated by the French company **Club Med**. Most guests buy all-inclusive packages that include lodging, participation in the resort's many activities, a full range of beverages, and sumptuous buffet meals. The resort's guests come from around the world including Asia, North America, South America, and Europe. The international nature of the club's guests poses challenges for the kitchen staff—for example, Japanese breakfasts feature miso soup, stewed vegetables in soy sauce, and rice porridge whereas Germans are accustomed to cold cuts, cheese, and bread for breakfast. Moreover, the number of guests varies widely from 300 in the high season to 20 in the low season. The chefs in the kitchen must ensure that food in the correct quantities and variety are available to please the club's varied clientele. To make this possible, a report is prepared each day that lists how many Japanese guests, German guests, French guests, Polish guests, U.S. guests, and so forth, are currently registered. This information helps the chefs prepare the appropriate quantities of specialized foods. In essence, costs in the kitchen are driven not by the number of guests alone, but by how many guests are Japanese, how many German, how many French, and so on. The costs are driven by multiple drivers.

Source: Conversation with Dominique Tredano, Chef de Village (i.e., general manager), Club Med—Bora Bora. For information about Club Med, see www.clubmed.com.

## Hierarchy of Activities

**Unit-level activities** are performed each time a unit is produced. The costs of unit-level activities should be proportional to the number of units produced. For example, providing power to run processing equipment is a unit-level activity because power tends to be consumed in proportion to the number of units produced.

**Batch-level activities** consist of tasks that are performed each time a batch is processed, such as processing purchase orders, setting up equipment, packing shipments to customers, and handling material. Costs at the batch level depend on *the number of*

*batches processed* rather than on the number of units produced. For example, the cost of processing a purchase order is the same no matter how many units of an item are ordered.

**Product-level activities** (sometimes called *product-sustaining activities*) relate to specific products and typically must be carried out regardless of how many batches or units of the product are manufactured. Product-level activities include maintaining inventories of parts for a product, issuing engineering change notices to modify a product to meet a customer's specifications, and developing special test routines when a product is first placed into production.

**Facility-level activities** (also called *organization-sustaining activities*) are activities that are carried out regardless of which products are produced, how many batches are run, or how many units are made. Facility-level costs include items such as factory management salaries, insurance, property taxes, and building depreciation. These costs cannot be traced on a cause-and-effect basis to individual products. Therefore, companies that choose to implement an activity-based absorption costing system will be required to arbitrarily allocate facility-level cost to products. As we will see later in the book, these types of arbitrary allocations can lead to bad decisions.

## HELPFUL HINT

Students often struggle to grasp the meaning of unit-level, batch-level, and product-level activities. Imagine a professor who teaches one section of managerial accounting that includes 35 students and one section of financial accounting that includes 25 students. In this example, the two courses represent two separate products. The activity "preparing a syllabus" would be product-level activity because it needs to be performed once for each course regardless of the number of class meetings during the semester or the number of enrolled students per class. The activity "preparing a lesson plan" would be a batch-level activity because it needs to be performed once for each class session regardless of the number of enrolled students in each class. The activity "grading exams" would be a unit-level activity because it needs to be performed once for each student enrolled in each class.

## Dining in the Canyon

IN BUSINESS

**Western River Expeditions** (www.westernriver.com) runs river rafting trips on the Colorado, Green, and Salmon rivers. One of its most popular trips is a six-day trip down the Grand Canyon, which features famous rapids such as Crystal and Lava Falls as well as the awesome scenery accessible only from the bottom of the Grand Canyon. The company runs trips of one or two rafts, each of which carries two guides and up to 18 guests. The company provides all meals on the trip, which are prepared by the guides.

In terms of the hierarchy of activities, a guest can be considered as a unit and a raft as a batch. In that context, the wages paid to the guides are a batch-level cost because each raft requires two guides regardless of the number of guests in the raft. Each guest is given a mug to use during the trip and to take home at the end of the trip as a souvenir. The cost of the mug is a unit-level cost because the number of mugs given away is strictly proportional to the number of guests on a trip.

What about the costs of food served to guests and guides—is this a unit-level cost, a batch-level cost, a product-level cost, or an organization-sustaining cost? At first glance, it might be thought that food costs are a unit-level cost—the greater the number of guests, the higher the food costs. However, that is not quite correct. Standard menus have been created for each day of the trip. For example, the first night's menu might consist of shrimp cocktail, steak, cornbread, salad, and cheesecake. The day before a trip begins, all of the food needed for the trip is taken from the central warehouse and packed in modular containers. It isn't practical to finely adjust the amount of food for the actual number of guests planned to be on a trip—most of the food comes prepackaged in large lots. For example, the shrimp cocktail menu may call for two large bags of frozen shrimp per raft and that many bags will be packed regardless of how many guests are expected on the raft. Consequently, the costs of food are not a unit-level cost that varies with the number of guests actually on a trip. Instead, the costs of food are a batch-level cost.

Source: Conversations with Western River Expeditions personnel.

## An Example of an Activity-Based Costing System Design

The complexity of an activity-based costing system will differ from company to company. In some companies, the activity-based costing system will be simple with only one or two activity cost pools at the unit, batch, and product levels. For other companies, the activity-based costing system will be much more complex.

Under activity-based costing, the manufacturing overhead costs at the top of Exhibit 3–3 are allocated to products via a two-stage process. In the first stage, overhead costs are assigned to the activity cost pools. In the second stage, the costs in the activity cost pools are allocated to products using activity rates and activity measures. For example, in the first-stage cost assignment, various manufacturing overhead costs are assigned to the production-order activity cost pool. These costs could include the salaries of engineers who modify products for individual orders, the costs of scheduling and monitoring orders, and other costs that are incurred as a consequence of the number of different orders received and processed by the company. We will not go into the details of how these first-stage cost assignments are made. In all of the examples and assignments in this book, the first-stage cost assignments have already been completed. Once the amount of cost in the production-order activity cost pool is known, the activity rate for the cost pool is computed by dividing the total cost in the production-order activity cost pool by the anticipated number of orders for the upcoming year. For example, the total cost in the production-order activity cost pool might be $450,000 and the company might expect to process a total of 1,200 orders. In that case, the activity rate would be $375 per order. Each order would be charged $375 for production-order costs. This is no different from the way overhead was assigned to products in Chapter 2 except that the number of orders is the allocation base rather than direct labor-hours.

**EXHIBIT 3–3** Graphic Example of Activity-Based Costing

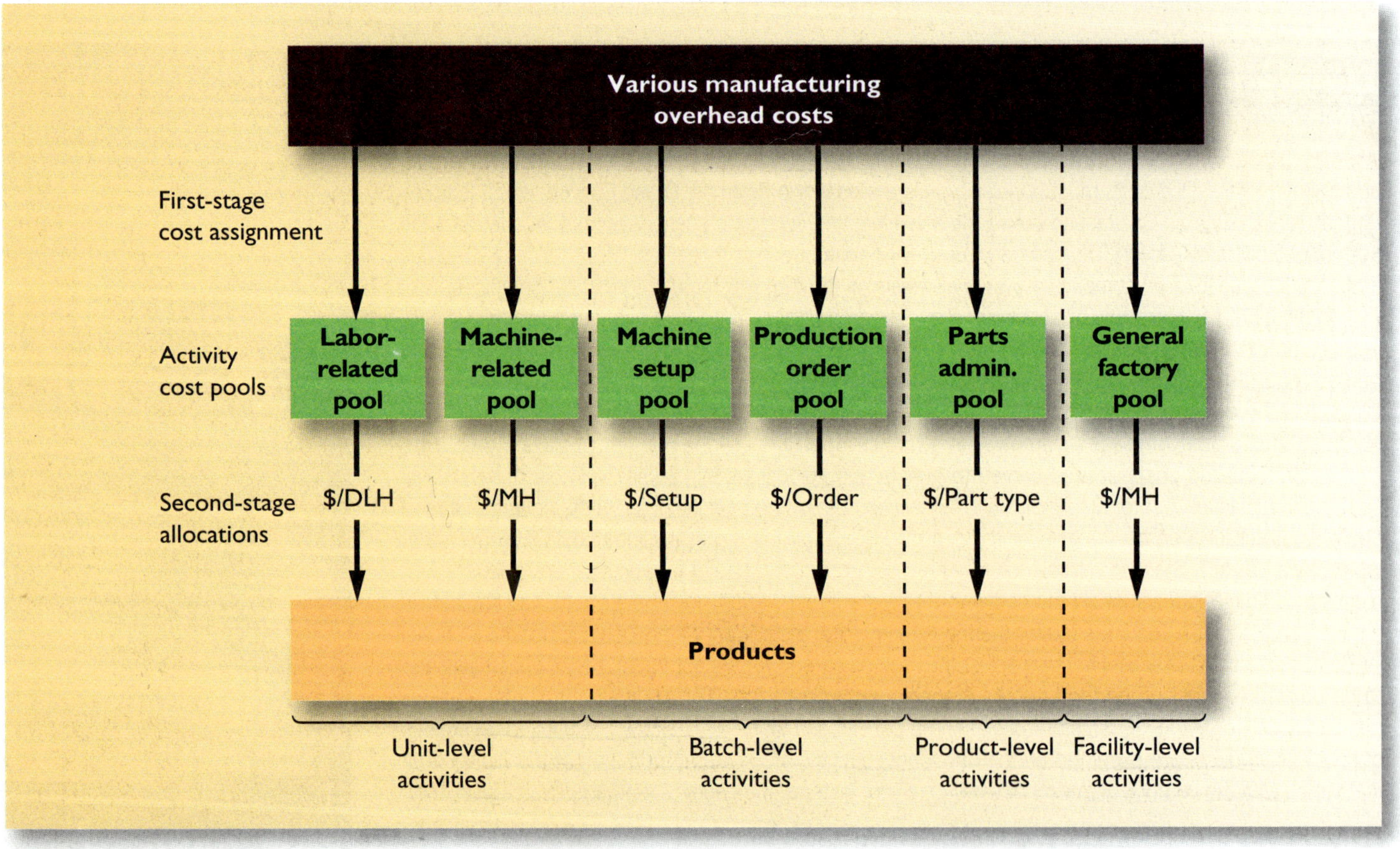

1. Which of the following statements is false? (You may select more than one answer.)
   a. In recent years, most companies have experienced increasing manufacturing overhead costs in relation to direct labor costs. F.
   b. Activity-based costing systems may use direct labor-hours and/or machine-hours to assign unit-level costs to products. T
   c. Facility-level costs are not caused by particular products. T.
   d. Product-level costs are larger for high-volume products than for low-volume products. F

CONCEPT CHECK

## USING ACTIVITY-BASED COSTING

Different products place different demands on resources. This is not recognized by conventional costing systems, which assume that overhead resources are consumed in direct proportion to direct labor-hours or machine-hours. The following example illustrates the distortions in product costs that can result from using a traditional costing system.

Comtek Sound, Inc., makes two products, a CD player (called a CD unit) and a DVD player (called a DVD unit), that are both sold to automobile manufacturers for installation in new vehicles. Recently, the company has been losing bids to supply CD players because competitors have been bidding less than Comtek Sound has been willing to bid. At the same time, Comtek Sound has been winning every bid it has submitted for its DVD player, which management regards as a secondary product. The marketing manager has been complaining that at the prices Comtek Sound is willing to bid, competitors are taking the company's high-volume CD business and leaving Comtek Sound with just the low-volume DVD business. However, the prices competitors quote on the CD players are below Comtek Sound's manufacturing cost for these units—at least according to Comtek Sound's conventional accounting system that applies manufacturing overhead to products based on direct labor-hours. Production managers suspected that the conventional costing system might be distorting the relative costs of the CD player and the DVD player—the DVD player takes more overhead resources to make than the CD player and yet their manufacturing overhead costs are identical under the conventional costing system. With the enthusiastic cooperation of the company's accounting department, a cross-functional team was formed to develop an activity-based costing system to more accurately assign overhead costs to the two products.

### Comtek Sound, Inc.'s Basic Data

The ABC team gathered basic information relating to the company's two products. A summary of some of this information follows. For the current year, the company's budget provides for selling 50,000 DVD units and 200,000 CD units. Both products require two direct labor-hours to complete. Therefore, the company plans to work 500,000 direct labor-hours (DLHs) during the current year, computed as follows:

| | |
|---|---|
| DVD units: 50,000 units × 2 DLHs per unit | 100,000 |
| CD units: 200,000 units × 2 DLHs per unit | 400,000 |
| Total direct labor-hours | 500,000 |

Costs for direct materials and direct labor for one unit of each product are given below:

| | DVD Units | CD Units |
|---|---|---|
| Direct materials | $90 | $50 |
| Direct labor (at $10 per DLH) | $20 | $20 |

The company's estimated manufacturing overhead costs for the current year total \$10,000,000. The ABC team discovered that although the same amount of direct labor time is required for each product, the more complex DVD units require more machine time, more machine setups, and more testing than the CD units. Also, the team found that it is necessary to manufacture the DVD units in smaller batches; consequently, they require more production orders than the CD units.

The company has always used direct labor-hours as the base for assigning overhead costs to its products.

With these data in hand, the ABC team was prepared to begin the design of the new activity-based costing system. But first, they wanted to compute the cost of each product using the company's existing cost system.

**HELPFUL HINT**

As you continue to read through the Comtek Sound, Inc., example, keep the following "big picture" insight in mind. The company's existing cost system and the ABC system will both assign a total of \$10 million in manufacturing overhead costs to the two products. In other words, the total amount of the "pie" being assigned to CD and DVD players will be the same in both cost systems. However, the two cost systems will assign different portions of the pie to each product. The existing cost system will assign \$8,000,000 (= 200,000 units × \$40 per unit) of manufacturing overhead cost to the high-volume CD players and \$2,000,000 (= 50,000 units × \$40 per unit) of overhead cost to the low-volume DVD players. The ABC system will correct this inaccuracy by assigning \$5,110,000 of overhead to CD players and \$4,890,000 of overhead to DVD players. Again, both cost systems will be assigning a total \$10 million in manufacturing overhead to the CD and DVD players. They will simply apportion the pie differently.

## Direct Labor-Hours as a Base

Under the company's existing costing system, the predetermined overhead rate would be \$20 per direct labor-hour, computed as follows:

$$\text{Predetermined overhead rate} = \frac{\text{Estimated total manufacturing overhead}}{\text{Estimated total amount of the allocation base}}$$

$$= \frac{\$10{,}000{,}000}{500{,}000 \text{ DLHs}} = \$20 \text{ per DLH}$$

Using this rate, the ABC team computed the unit product costs as given below:

| | DVD Units | CD Units |
|---|---|---|
| Direct materials | \$ 90 | \$ 50 |
| Direct labor | 20 | 20 |
| Manufacturing overhead (2 DLHs × \$20 per DLH) | 40 | 40 |
| Unit product cost | \$150 | \$110 |

The problem with this costing approach is that it relies entirely on direct labor-hours to assign overhead cost to products and does not consider the impact of other factors—such as setups and testing—on the overhead costs of the company. Even though these other factors suggest that the two products place different demands on overhead resources, under the company's conventional costing system, the two products are assigned the same overhead cost per unit because they require equal amounts of direct labor time.

While this method of computing costs is fast and simple, it is accurate only in those situations where other factors affecting overhead costs are not significant. These other factors *are* significant in the case of Comtek Sound, Inc.

## Computing Activity Rates

**LEARNING OBJECTIVE 2**

Compute activity rates for an activity-based costing system.

The ABC team then analyzed Comtek Sound, Inc.'s operations and identified six major activities to include in the new activity-based costing system. Cost and other data relating to the activities are presented in Exhibit 3–4. That exhibit shows the amount of overhead cost for each activity cost pool, along with the expected amount of activity for the current year. The machine setups activity cost pool, for example, was assigned $1,600,000 in overhead cost. The company expects to complete 4,000 setups during the year, of which 3,000 will be for DVD units and 1,000 will be for CD units. Data for other activities are also shown in the exhibit.

The ABC team then computed an activity rate for each activity. (See the middle panel in Exhibit 3–4.) The activity rate of $400 per machine setup, for example, was computed

**EXHIBIT 3–4** Comtek Sound's Activity-Based Costing System

**Basic Data**

| Activities and Activity Measures | Estimated Overhead Cost | Expected Activity: DVD Units | Expected Activity: CD Units | Expected Activity: Total |
|---|---|---|---|---|
| Labor-related (direct labor-hours) | $ 800,000 | 100,000 | 400,000 | 500,000 |
| Machine-related (machine-hours) | 2,100,000 | 300,000 | 700,000 | 1,000,000 |
| Machine setups (setups) | 1,600,000 | 3,000 | 1,000 | 4,000 |
| Production orders (orders) | 3,150,000 | 800 | 400 | 1,200 |
| Parts administration (part types) | 350,000 | 400 | 300 | 700 |
| General factory (machine-hours) | 2,000,000 | 300,000 | 700,000 | 1,000,000 |
| | $10,000,000 | | | |

**Computation of Activity Rates**

| Activities | (a) Estimated Overhead Cost | (b) Total Expected Activity | (a) ÷ (b) Activity Rate |
|---|---|---|---|
| Labor-related | $800,000 | 500,000 DLHs | $1.60 per DLH |
| Machine-related | $2,100,000 | 1,000,000 MHs | $2.10 per MH |
| Machine setups | $1,600,000 | 4,000 setups | $400.00 per setup |
| Production orders | $3,150,000 | 1,200 orders | $2,625.00 per order |
| Parts administration | $350,000 | 700 part types | $500.00 per part type |
| General factory | $2,000,000 | 1,000,000 MHs | $2.00 per MH |

**Computation of the Overhead Cost per Unit of Product**

| Activities and Activity Rates | DVD Units: Expected Activity | DVD Units: Amount | CD Units: Expected Activity | CD Units: Amount |
|---|---|---|---|---|
| Labor-related, at $1.60 per DLH | 100,000 | $ 160,000 | 400,000 | $ 640,000 |
| Machine-related, at $2.10 per MH | 300,000 | 630,000 | 700,000 | 1,470,000 |
| Machine setups, at $400 per setup | 3,000 | 1,200,000 | 1,000 | 400,000 |
| Production orders, at $2,625 per order | 800 | 2,100,000 | 400 | 1,050,000 |
| Parts administration, at $500 per part type | 400 | 200,000 | 300 | 150,000 |
| General factory, at $2.00 per MH | 300,000 | 600,000 | 700,000 | 1,400,000 |
| Total overhead costs assigned (a) | | $4,890,000 | | $5,110,000 |
| Number of units produced (b) | | 50,000 | | 200,000 |
| Overhead cost per unit (a) ÷ (b) | | $97.80 | | $25.55 |

by dividing the total estimated overhead cost in the activity cost pool, $1,600,000, by the expected amount of activity, 4,000 setups. This process was repeated for each of the other activities in the activity-based costing system.

HELPFUL HINT

Students often make the mistake of trying to compute an activity rate for each product. This is incorrect because you should compute only one activity rate for each activity cost pool. The activity rate is then multiplied by the amount of the activity measure used by each product to assign overhead costs to that product.

## Computing Product Costs

LEARNING OBJECTIVE 3

Compute product costs using activity-based costing.

Once the activity rates were calculated, it was easy to compute the overhead cost that would be allocated to each product. (See the bottom panel of Exhibit 3–4.) For example, the amount of machine setup cost allocated to DVD units was determined by multiplying the activity rate of $400 per setup by the 3,000 expected setups for DVD units during the year. This yielded a total of $1,200,000 in machine setup costs to be assigned to the DVD units.

Note from the exhibit that the use of an activity approach has resulted in $97.80 in overhead cost being assigned to each DVD unit and $25.55 to each CD unit. The ABC team then used these amounts to determine unit product costs under activity-based costing, as presented in Exhibit 3–5. For comparison, the exhibit also shows the unit product costs derived earlier when direct labor-hours were used as the base for assigning overhead costs to the products.

The ABC team members summarized their findings as follows in the team's report:

> In the past, the company has been charging $40.00 in overhead cost to a unit of either product, whereas it should have been charging $97.80 in overhead cost to each DVD unit and only $25.55 to each CD unit. Thus, unit costs have been badly distorted as a result of using direct labor-hours as the allocation base. The company may even have been suffering a loss on the DVD units without knowing it because the cost of these units has been so vastly understated. Through activity-based costing, we have been able to more accurately assign overhead costs to each product.
>
> Although in the past we thought our competitors were pricing below their cost on the CD units, it turns out that we were overcharging for these units because our costs were overstated. Similarly, we always used to believe that our competitors were overpricing the DVD units, but now we realize that our prices have been way too low because the cost of our DVD units was being understated. It turns out that we, not our competitors, had everything backwards.

**EXHIBIT 3–5**
Comparison of Unit Product Costs

| | Activity-Based Costing | | Direct-Labor-Based Costing | |
|---|---|---|---|---|
| | DVD Units | CD Units | DVD Units | CD Units |
| Direct materials | $ 90.00 | $ 50.00 | $ 90.00 | $ 50.00 |
| Direct labor | 20.00 | 20.00 | 20.00 | 20.00 |
| Manufacturing overhead | 97.80 | 25.55 | 40.00 | 40.00 |
| Unit product cost | $207.80 | $ 95.55 | $150.00 | $110.00 |

The pattern of cost distortion shown by the ABC team's findings is quite common. Such distortion can happen in any company that relies on direct labor-hours or machine-hours in assigning overhead cost to products and ignores other significant causes of overhead costs.

## How Much Does it Cost to Handle a Piece of Luggage?

IN BUSINESS

It costs an airline about $15 to carry a piece of checked luggage from one destination another. The activity "transporting luggage" consists of numerous subactivities such as tagging bags, sorting them, placing them on carts, transporting bags planeside, loading them into the airplane, and delivering them to carousels and connecting flights.

A variety of employees invest a portion of their labor hours "transporting luggage" including ground personnel, check-in agents, service clerks, baggage service managers, and maintenance workers. In total, labor costs comprise $9 per bag. Airlines also spend millions of dollars on baggage equipment, sorting systems, carts, tractors, and conveyors, as well as rental costs related to bag rooms, carousels, and offices. They also pay to deliver misplaced bags to customers' homes and to compensate customers for lost bags that are never found. These expenses add up to about $4 per bag. The final expense related to transporting luggage is fuel costs, which average about $2 per bag.

Many major airlines are now charging fees for checked luggage. In fact, United Airlines expects to collect $275 million annually for its first and second bag fees.

Source: Scott McCartney, "What It Costs an Airline to Fly Your Luggage," *The Wall Street Journal*, November 25, 2008, pp. D1 and D8.

## Shifting of Overhead Cost

**LEARNING OBJECTIVE 4**

Contrast the product costs computed under activity-based costing and conventional costing methods.

When a company implements activity-based costing, overhead cost often shifts from high-volume products to low-volume products, with a higher unit product cost resulting for the low-volume products. We saw this happen in the example above, where the product cost of the low-volume DVD units increased from $150.00 to $207.80 per unit. This increase in cost resulted from batch-level and product-level costs, which shifted from the high-volume product to the low-volume product. For example, consider the cost of issuing production orders, which is a batch level activity. As shown in Exhibit 3–4, the average cost to Comtek Sound to issue a single production order is $2,625. This cost is assigned to a production order regardless of how many units are processed in that order. The key here is to realize that fewer DVD units (the low-volume product) are processed per production order than CD units:

| | DVD Units | CD Units |
|---|---|---|
| Number of units produced per year (a) | 50,000 | 200,000 |
| Number of production orders issued per year (b) | 800 | 400 |
| Average number of units processed per production order (a) ÷ (b) | 62.5 | 500 |

Spreading the $2,625 cost to issue a production order over the number of units processed per order results in the following average cost per unit:

| | DVD Units | CD Units |
|---|---|---|
| Cost to issue a production order (a) | $2,625 | $2,625 |
| Average number of units processed per production order (see above) (b) | 62.5 | 500 |
| Average production order cost per unit (a) ÷ (b) | $42.00 | $5.25 |

Thus, the production order cost for a DVD unit (the low-volume product) is $42, which is *eight times* the $5.25 cost for a CD unit.

Product-level costs—such as parts administration—have a similar impact. In a conventional costing system, these costs are spread more or less uniformly across all units that are produced. In an activity-based costing system, these costs are assigned more accurately to products. Because product-level costs are fixed with respect to the number of units processed, the average cost per unit of an activity such as parts administration will be higher for low-volume products than for high-volume products.

IN BUSINESS

## Comparing Activity-Based and Traditional Product Costs

**Airco Heating and Air Conditioning (Airco)**, located in Van Buren, Arkansas, implemented an ABC system to better understand the profitability of its products. The ABC system assigned $4,458,605 of overhead costs to eight activities as follows:

| Activity Cost Pool | Total Cost | Total Activity | Activity Rate |
|---|---|---|---|
| Machines | $ 435,425 | 73,872 machine-hours | $5.89 |
| Data record maintenance | 132,597 | 14 products administered | $9,471.21 |
| Material handling | 1,560,027 | 16,872 products | $92.46 |
| Product changeover | 723,338 | 72 setup hours | $10,046.36 |
| Scheduling | 24,877 | 2,788 production runs | $8.92 |
| Raw material receiving | 877,107 | 2,859 receipts | $306.79 |
| Product shipment | 561,014 | 13,784,015 miles | $0.04 |
| Customer service | 144,220 | 2,533 customer contacts | $56.94 |
| Total | $4,458,605 | | |

Airco's managers were surprised that 55% [($1,560,027 + $877,107) ÷ $4,458,605] of its overhead resources were consumed by material handling and receiving activities. They responded by reducing the raw material and part transport distances within the facility. In addition, they compared the traditional and ABC product margin percentages (computed by dividing each product's margin by the sales of the product) for the company's seven product lines of air conditioners as summarized below:

| | Product | | | | | | |
|---|---|---|---|---|---|---|---|
| | 5-ton | 6-ton | 7.5-ton | 10-ton | 12.5-ton | 15-ton | 20-ton |
| Traditional product margin %.... | −20% | 4% | 40% | −4% | 20% | 42% | 70% |
| ABC product margin %............ | −15% | −8% | 50% | 1% | −6% | 40% | 69% |

In response to the ABC data, Airco decided to explore the possibility of raising prices on 5-ton, 6-ton, and 12.5-ton air conditioners while at the same time seeking to reduce overhead consumption by these products.

Source: Copyright 2004 from "An Application of Activity-Based Costing in the Air Conditioner Manufacturing Industry," *The Engineering Economist*, Volume 49, Issue 3, 2004, pp. 221–236, by Heather Nachtmann and Mohammad Hani Al-Rifai. Reproduced by permission of Taylor & Francis Group, LLC., http://www.taylorandfrancis.com.

## TARGETING PROCESS IMPROVEMENTS

Activity-based costing can be used to identify activities that would benefit from process improvements. When used in this way, activity-based costing is often called *activity-based management.* Basically, **activity-based management** involves focusing on activities to eliminate waste, decrease processing time, and reduce defects. Activity-based management is used in organizations as diverse as manufacturing companies, hospitals, and the U.S. Marine Corps.

The first step in any improvement program is to decide what to improve. The Theory of Constraints approach discussed in the Prologue is a powerful tool for targeting the area in an organization whose improvement will yield the greatest benefit. Activity-based management provides another approach. The activity rates computed in activity-based costing can provide valuable clues concerning where there is waste and opportunity for improvement. For example, looking at the activity rates in Exhibit 3–4, Comtek's managers may conclude that $2,625 to process a production order is far too expensive for an activity that adds no value to the product. As a consequence, they may target production-order processing for a process improvement project.

*Benchmarking* is another way to leverage the information in activity rates. **Benchmarking** is a systematic approach to identifying the activities with the greatest room for improvement. It is based on comparing the performance in an organization with the performance of other, similar organizations known for their outstanding performance. If a particular part of the organization performs far below the world-class standard, managers will target that area for improvement.

### Process Improvements Help Nurses

IN BUSINESS

**Providence Portland Medical Center (PPMC)** used ABC to improve one of the most expensive and error-prone processes within its nursing units—ordering, distributing, and administering medications to patients. To the surprise of everyone involved, the ABC data showed that "medication-related activities made up 43% of the nursing unit's total operating costs." The ABC team members knew that one of the root causes of this time-consuming process was the illegibility of physician orders that are faxed to the pharmacy. Replacing the standard fax machine with a much better $5,000 machine virtually eliminated unreadable orders and decreased follow-up telephone calls by more than 90%—saving the hospital $500,000 per year. In total, the ABC team generated improvement ideas that offered $1 million of net savings in redeployable resources. "This amount translates to additional time that nurses and pharmacists can spend on direct patient care."

Source: "How ABC Analysis Will Save PPMC Over $1 Million a Year," *Financial Analysis, Planning & Reporting,* November 2003, pp. 6–10.

## EVALUATION OF ACTIVITY-BASED COSTING

Activity-based costing improves the accuracy of product costs, helps managers to understand the nature of overhead costs, and helps target areas for improvement through benchmarking and other techniques. These benefits are discussed in this section.

### The Benefits of Activity-Based Costing

Activity-based costing improves the accuracy of product costs in three ways. First, activity-based costing usually increases the number of cost pools used to accumulate overhead costs. Rather than accumulating all overhead costs in a single, plantwide pool, or accumulating them in departmental pools, the company accumulates costs for each major activity. Second, the activity cost pools are more homogeneous than departmental cost pools. In principle, all of the costs in an activity cost pool pertain to a single activity. In contrast, departmental cost pools contain the costs of many different activities carried out in the department. Third, activity-based costing uses a variety of activity measures to assign overhead costs to products, some of which are correlated with volume and some of which are not. This differs from conventional approaches that rely exclusively on direct labor-hours or other measures of volume such as machine-hours to assign overhead costs to products.

Because conventional costing systems typically apply overhead costs to products using direct labor-hours, it may appear to managers that overhead costs are caused by direct labor-hours. Activity-based costing makes it clear that batch setups, engineering change orders, and other activities cause overhead costs rather than just direct labor. Managers thus have a better understanding of the causes of overhead costs, which should lead to better decisions and better cost control.

Finally, activity-based costing highlights the activities that could benefit most from process improvement initiatives. Thus, activity-based costing can be used as a part of programs to improve operations.

IN BUSINESS

## Is Activity-Based Costing Still Being Used?

Researchers surveyed 348 managers to determine which costing methods their companies use. The table below shows the percentage of respondents whose companies use the various costing methods to assign departmental costs to cost objects such as products.

| | Departments | | | | | | |
|---|---|---|---|---|---|---|---|
| Costing Method | Research and Development | Product and Process Design | Production | Sales and Marketing | Distribution | Customer Service | Shared Services |
| Activity-based | 13.0% | 14.7% | 18.3% | 17.3% | 17.2% | 21.8% | 23.0% |
| Standard[1] | 17.6% | 20.7% | 42.0% | 18.1% | 28.4% | 18.5% | 23.0% |
| Normal[2] | 4.6% | 8.6% | 9.9% | 7.9% | 6.0% | 8.1% | 5.6% |
| Actual[3] | 23.1% | 25.0% | 23.7% | 23.6% | 26.7% | 16.9% | 15.9% |
| Other | 1.9% | 0.9% | 0.0% | 0.8% | 0.9% | 1.6% | 2.4% |
| Not allocated | 39.8% | 30.2% | 6.1% | 32.3% | 20.7% | 33.1% | 30.2% |

[1]Standard costing is used for the variance computations in Chapter 8.
[2]Normal costing is used for the job-order costing computations in Chapter 2.
[3]Actual costing is used to create the absorption and variable costing income statements in Chapter 6.

The results show that 18.3% of respondents use ABC to allocate production costs to cost objects and 42% use standard costing for the same purpose. ABC is used by at least 13% of respondents within all functional departments across the value chain. Many companies do not allocate nonproduction costs to cost objects.

Source: William O. Stratton, Denis Desroches, Raef Lawson, and Toby Hatch, "Activity-Based Costing: Is It Still Relevant?" *Management Accounting Quarterly,* Spring 2009, pp. 31–40.

## Limitations of Activity-Based Costing

Any discussion of activity-based costing is incomplete without some cautionary warnings. First, the cost of implementing and maintaining an activity-based costing system may outweigh the benefits. Second, it would be naïve to assume that product costs provided even by an activity-based costing system are always relevant when making decisions. These limitations are discussed below.

**The Cost of Implementing Activity-Based Costing** Implementing ABC is a major project that requires substantial resources. First, the cost system must be designed—preferably by a cross-functional team. This requires taking valued employees away from other tasks for a major project. In addition, the data used in the activity-based costing system must be collected and verified. In some cases, this requires collecting data that has never been collected before. In short, implementing and maintaining an activity-based costing system can present a formidable challenge, and management may decide that the costs are too great to justify the expected benefits. Nevertheless, it should be kept in mind that the costs of collecting and processing data have dropped dramatically over the last several decades due to bar coding and other technologies, and these costs can be expected to continue to fall.

When are the benefits of activity-based costing most likely to be worth the cost? Companies that have some of the following characteristics are most likely to benefit from activity-based costing:

1. Products differ substantially in volume, batch size, and in the activities they require.
2. Conditions have changed substantially since the existing cost system was established.
3. Overhead costs are high and increasing and no one seems to understand why.
4. Management does not trust the existing cost system and ignores cost data from the system when making decisions.

**Limitations of the ABC Model** The activity-based costing model relies on a number of critical assumptions.[1] Perhaps the most important of these assumptions is that the cost in each activity cost pool is strictly proportional to its activity measure. What little evidence we have on this issue suggests that overhead costs are less than proportional to activity.[2] Economists call this increasing returns to scale—as activity increases, the average cost drops. As a practical matter, this means that product costs computed by a traditional or activity-based costing system will be overstated for the purposes of making decisions. The product costs generated by activity-based costing are almost certainly more accurate than those generated by a conventional costing system, but they should nevertheless be viewed with caution. Managers should be particularly alert to product costs that contain allocations of facility-level costs. As we shall see later in the book, product costs that include facility-level or organization-sustaining costs can easily lead managers astray.

**Modifying the ABC Model** The discussion in this chapter has assumed that companies use an absorption costing approach when they design an activity-based costing system. If the product costs are to be used by managers for internal decisions, some modifications should be made to the absorption approach. For example, for decision-making purposes, the distinction between manufacturing costs on the one hand and selling and administrative expenses on the other hand is unimportant. Managers need to know what costs a product causes, and it doesn't matter whether the costs are manufacturing costs or selling and administrative expenses. Consequently, for decision-making purposes, some selling and administrative expenses should be assigned to products as well as manufacturing costs. Moreover, as mentioned above, facility-level and organization-sustaining costs should be removed from product costs when making decisions. Nevertheless, the

---

[1]Eric Noreen, "Conditions under Which Activity-Based Cost Systems Provide Relevant Costs," *Journal of Management Accounting Research,* Fall 1991, pp. 159–168.

[2]Eric Noreen and Naomi Soderstrom, "The Accuracy of Proportional Cost Models: Evidence from Hospital Service Departments," *Review of Accounting Studies* 2, 1997; and Eric Noreen and Naomi Soderstrom, "Are Overhead Costs Proportional to Activity? Evidence from Hospital Service Departments," *Journal of Accounting and Economics*, January 1994, pp. 253–278.

## DECISION POINT **Bakery Owner**

You are the owner of a bakery that makes a complete line of specialty breads, pastries, cakes, and pies for the retail and wholesale markets. A summer intern has just completed an activity-based costing study that concluded, among other things, that one of your largest recurring jobs is losing money. A local luxury hotel orders the same assortment of desserts every week for its Sunday brunch buffet for a fixed price of $975 per week. The hotel is quite happy with the quality of the desserts the bakery has been providing, but it would seek bids from other local bakeries if the price were increased.

The activity-based costing study conducted by the intern revealed that the cost to the bakery of providing these desserts is $1,034 per week, resulting in an apparent loss of $59 per week or over $3,000 per year. Scrutinizing the intern's report, you find that the weekly cost of $1,034 includes facility-level costs of $329. These facility-level costs include portions of the rent on the bakery's building, your salary, depreciation on the office personal computer, and so on. The facility-level costs were arbitrarily allocated to the Sunday brunch job on the basis of direct labor-hours.

Should you demand an increase in price from the luxury hotel for the Sunday brunch desserts to at least $1,034? If an increase is not forthcoming, should you withdraw from the agreement and discontinue providing the desserts?

techniques covered in this chapter provide a good basis for understanding the mechanics of activity-based costing. For a more complete coverage of the use of activity-based costing in decisions, see more advanced texts.[3]

## Activity-Based Costing and Service Industries

Although initially developed as a tool for manufacturing companies, activity-based costing is also being used in service industries. Successful implementation of an activity-based costing system depends on identifying the key activities that generate costs and tracking how many of those activities are performed for each service the organization provides. Activity-based costing has been implemented in a wide variety of service industries including railroads, hospitals, banks, and data services companies.

**CONCEPT CHECK**

2. Which of the following statements is false? (You may select more than one answer.)
   a. Activity-based costing systems usually shift costs from low-volume products to high-volume products. F.
   b. Benchmarking can be used to identify activities with the greatest potential for improvement. T.
   c. Activity-based costing is most valuable to companies that manufacture products that are similar in terms of their volume of production, batch size, and complexity. F.
   d. Activity-based costing systems are based on the assumption that the costs included in each activity cost pool are strictly proportional to the cost pool's activity measure. F. pg. 133

[3]See, for example, Chapter 7 and its Appendix 7A in Ray Garrison, Eric Noreen, and Peter Brewer, *Managerial Accounting,* 14th edition, McGraw-Hill/Irwin © 2012.

## SUMMARY

**LO1 Understand the basic approach in activity-based costing and how it differs from conventional costing.**
Activity-based costing was developed to more accurately assign overhead costs to products. Activity-based costing differs from conventional costing as described in Chapter 2 in two major ways. First, in activity-based costing, each major activity that consumes overhead resources has its own cost pool and its own activity rate, whereas in Chapter 2 there was only a single overhead cost pool and a single predetermined overhead rate. Second, the allocation bases (or activity measures) in activity-based costing are diverse. They may include machine setups, purchase orders, engineering change orders, and so on, in addition to direct labor-hours or machine-hours.

**LO2 Compute activity rates for an activity-based costing system.**
Each activity in an activity-based costing system has its own cost pool and its own activity measure. The activity rate for a particular activity is computed by dividing the total cost in the activity's cost pool by the total amount of activity.

**LO3 Compute product costs using activity-based costing.**
Product costs in activity-based costing, as in conventional costing systems, consist of direct materials, direct labor, and overhead. In the case of an activity-based costing system, each activity has its own activity rate. The activities required by a product are multiplied by their respective activity rates to determine the amount of overhead that is assigned to the product.

**LO4 Contrast the product costs computed under activity-based costing and conventional costing methods.**
Under conventional costing methods, overhead costs are applied to products using some measure of volume such as direct labor-hours or machine-hours. This results in most of the overhead cost being applied to high-volume products. In contrast, under activity-based costing, some overhead costs are assigned on the basis of batch-level or product-level activities. This change in allocation bases shifts overhead costs from high-volume products to low-volume products. Accordingly, product costs for high-volume products are commonly lower under activity-based costing than under conventional costing methods, and product costs for low-volume products are higher.

## GUIDANCE ANSWER TO DECISION POINT

**Bakery Owner (p. 134)**
The bakery really isn't losing money on the weekly order of desserts from the luxury hotel. By definition, facility-level costs are not affected by individual products and jobs—these costs would continue unchanged even if the weekly order were dropped. Recalling the discussion in Chapter 1 concerning decision making, only those costs and benefits that differ between alternatives in a decision are relevant. Because the facility-level costs would be the same whether the dessert order is kept or dropped, they are not relevant in this decision and should be ignored. Hence, the real cost of the job is $705 ($1,034 − $329), which reveals that the job actually yields a weekly profit of $270 ($975 − $705) rather than a loss.

No, the bakery owner should not press for a price increase—particularly if that would result in the hotel seeking bids from competitors. And no, the bakery owner certainly should not withdraw from the agreement to provide the desserts.

## GUIDANCE ANSWERS TO CONCEPT CHECKS

1. **Choice d.** Product-level costs are unrelated to the amount of a product that is made.
2. **Choices a and c.** Activity-based costing systems usually shift costs from high-volume products to low-volume products. Activity-based costing is most valuable for companies with highly diverse products rather than with similar products.

## REVIEW PROBLEM: ACTIVITY-BASED COSTING

Aerodec, Inc., manufactures and sells two types of wooden deck chairs: Deluxe and Tourist. Annual sales in units, direct labor-hours (DLHs) per unit, and total direct labor-hours per year are provided below:

| | |
|---|---|
| Deluxe deck chair: 2,000 units × 5 DLHs per unit | 10,000 |
| Tourist deck chair: 10,000 units × 4 DLHs per unit | 40,000 |
| Total direct labor-hours | 50,000 |

Costs for direct materials and direct labor for one unit of each product are given below:

| | Deluxe | Tourist |
|---|---|---|
| Direct materials | $25 | $17 |
| Direct labor (at $12 per DLH) | $60 | $48 |

Manufacturing overhead costs total $800,000 each year. The breakdown of these costs among the company's six activity cost pools is given below. The activity measures are shown in parentheses.

| Activities and Activity Measures | Estimated Overhead Cost | Expected Activity | | |
|---|---|---|---|---|
| | | Deluxe | Tourist | Total |
| Labor-related (direct labor-hours) | $ 80,000 | 10,000 | 40,000 | 50,000 |
| Machine setups (number of setups) | 150,000 | 3,000 | 2,000 | 5,000 |
| Parts administration (number of parts) | 160,000 | 50 | 30 | 80 |
| Production orders (number of orders) | 70,000 | 100 | 300 | 400 |
| Material receipts (number of receipts) | 90,000 | 150 | 600 | 750 |
| General factory (machine-hours) | 250,000 | 12,000 | 28,000 | 40,000 |
| | $800,000 | | | |

***Required:***

1. Classify each of Aerodec's activities as either a unit-level, batch-level, product-level, or facility-level activity.
2. Assume that the company applies overhead cost to products on the basis of direct labor-hours.
   a. Compute the predetermined overhead rate.
   b. Determine the unit product cost of each product, using the predetermined overhead rate computed in (2)(a) above.
3. Assume that the company uses activity-based costing to compute overhead rates.
   a. Compute the activity rate for each of the six activities listed above.
   b. Using the rates developed in (3)(a) above, determine the amount of overhead cost that would be assigned to a unit of each product.
   c. Determine the unit product cost of each product and compare this cost to the cost computed in (2)(b) above.

### Solution to Review Problem

1.

| Activity Cost Pool | Type of Activity |
|---|---|
| Labor-related | Unit-level |
| Machine setups | Batch-level |
| Parts administration | Product-level |
| Production orders | Batch-level |
| Material receipts | Batch-level |
| General factory | Facility-level |

2. a.

$$\text{Predetermined overhead rate} = \frac{\text{Estimated total manufacturing overhead}}{\text{Estimated total amount of the allocation base}}$$

$$= \frac{\$800{,}000}{50{,}000 \text{ DLHs}} = \$16 \text{ per DLH}$$

b.

| | Deluxe | Tourist |
|---|---|---|
| Direct materials | $ 25 | $ 17 |
| Direct labor | 60 | 48 |
| Manufacturing overhead applied: | | |
| Deluxe: 5 DLHs × $16 per DLH | 80 | |
| Tourist: 4 DLHs × $16 per DLH | | 64 |
| Unit product cost | $165 | $129 |

3. a.

| Activities | (a) Estimated Overhead Cost | (b) Total Expected Activity | (a) ÷ (b) Activity Rate |
|---|---|---|---|
| Labor-related | $80,000 | 50,000 DLHs | $1.60 per DLH |
| Machine setups | $150,000 | 5,000 setups | $30.00 per setup |
| Parts administration | $160,000 | 80 parts | $2,000.00 per part |
| Production orders | $70,000 | 400 orders | $175.00 per order |
| Material receipts | $90,000 | 750 receipts | $120.00 per receipt |
| General factory | $250,000 | 40,000 MHs | $6.25 per MH |

b.

| | Deluxe | | Tourist | |
|---|---|---|---|---|
| Activities and Activity Rates | Expected Activity | Amount | Expected Activity | Amount |
| Labor-related, at $1.60 per DLH | 10,000 | $ 16,000 | 40,000 | $ 64,000 |
| Machine setups, at $30 per setup | 3,000 | 90,000 | 2,000 | 60,000 |
| Parts administration, at $2,000 per part | 50 | 100,000 | 30 | 60,000 |
| Production orders, at $175 per order | 100 | 17,500 | 300 | 52,500 |
| Material receipts, at $120 per receipt | 150 | 18,000 | 600 | 72,000 |
| General factory, at $6.25 per MH | 12,000 | 75,000 | 28,000 | 175,000 |
| Total overhead cost assigned (a) | | $316,500 | | $483,500 |
| Number of units produced (b) | | 2,000 | | 10,000 |
| Overhead cost per unit, (a) ÷ (b) | | $158.25 | | $48.35 |

c.

| | Deluxe | Tourist |
|---|---|---|
| Direct materials | $ 25.00 | $ 17.00 |
| Direct labor | 60.00 | 48.00 |
| Manufacturing overhead (see above) | 158.25 | 48.35 |
| Unit product cost | $243.25 | $113.35 |

Under activity-based costing, the unit product cost of the Deluxe deck chair is much greater than the cost computed in (2)(b), and the unit product cost of the Tourist deck chair is much less. Using volume (direct labor-hours) in (2)(b) to apply overhead cost to products results in too little overhead cost being applied to the Deluxe deck chair (the low-volume product) and too much overhead cost being applied to the Tourist deck chair (the high-volume product).

## GLOSSARY

**Activity** An event that causes the consumption of overhead resources. (p. 120)

**Activity-based costing (ABC)** A two-stage costing method in which overhead costs are assigned to products on the basis of the activities they require. (p. 119)

**Activity-based management** A management approach that focuses on managing activities as a way of eliminating waste and reducing delays and defects. (p. 131)

**Activity cost pool** A "bucket" in which costs are accumulated that relate to a single activity measure in an activity-based costing system. (p. 121)

**Activity measure** An allocation base in an activity-based costing system; ideally, a measure of whatever causes the costs in an activity cost pool. (p. 121)

**Activity rate** An overhead rate in activity-based costing. Each activity cost pool has its own activity rate which is used to assign overhead to products and services. (p. 121)

**Batch-level activities** Activities that are performed each time a batch of goods is handled or processed, regardless of how many units are in a batch. The amount of resources consumed depends on the number of batches run rather than on the number of units in the batch. (p. 122)

**Benchmarking** A systematic approach to identifying the activities with the greatest room for improvement. It is based on comparing the performance in an organization with the performance of other, similar organizations known for their outstanding performance. (p. 131)

**Facility-level activities** Activities that are carried out regardless of which products are produced, how many batches are run, or how many units are made. (p. 123)

**Product-level activities** Activities that relate to specific products that must be carried out regardless of how many units are produced and sold or batches run. (p. 123)

**Unit-level activities** Activities that arise as a result of the total volume of goods and services that are produced, and that are performed each time a unit is produced. (p. 122)

## QUESTIONS

**3–1** What are the three common approaches for assigning overhead costs to products?

**3–2** Why does activity-based costing appeal to some companies?

**3–3** Why do departmental overhead rates sometimes result in inaccurate product costs?

**3–4** What are the four hierarchical levels of activity discussed in the chapter?

**3–5** Why is activity-based costing described as a "two-stage" costing method?

**3–6** Why do overhead costs often shift from high-volume products to low-volume products when a company switches from a conventional costing method to activity-based costing?

**3–7** What are the three major ways in which activity-based costing improves the accuracy of product costs?

**3–8** What are the major limitations of activity-based costing?

**Multiple-choice questions are provided on the text website at www.mhhe.com/brewer6e.**

## APPLYING EXCEL

connect ACCOUNTING

LO1, LO2, LO3 LO4

**Available with McGraw-Hill's *Connect®* *Accounting*.**

A form for using Excel to recreate the Review Problem on pages 136–138 appears on the following page. Download the workbook containing this form from the Online Learning Center at www.mhhe.com/brewer6e. *On the website you will also receive instructions about how to use this worksheet form.*

| | A | B | C | D | E | F | G |
|---|---|---|---|---|---|---|---|
| 1 | Chapter 3: Applying Excel | | | | | | |
| 2 | | | | | | | |
| 3 | *Enter a formula into each of the cells marked with a ? below* | | | | | | |
| 4 | **Review Problem: Activity-Based Costing** | | | | | | |
| 5 | | | | | | | |
| 6 | **Data** | | | | | | |
| 7 | | *Deluxe* | *Tourist* | | | | |
| 8 | Annual sales in units | 2,000 | 10,000 | | | | |
| 9 | Direct materials per unit | $25 | $17 | | | | |
| 10 | Direct labor-hours per unit | 5 | 4 | | | | |
| 11 | | | | | | | |
| 12 | Direct labor rate | $12 | per DLH | | | | |
| 13 | | | | | | | |
| 14 | | *Estimated* | | | | | |
| 15 | | *Overhead* | | *Expected Activity* | | | |
| 16 | *Activities and Activity Measures* | *Cost* | *Deluxe* | *Tourist* | *Total* | | |
| 17 | Labor-related (direct labor-hours) | $ 80,000 | ? | ? | ? | | |
| 18 | Machine setups (setups) | 150,000 | 3,000 | 2,000 | ? | | |
| 19 | Production orders (orders) | 70,000 | 100 | 300 | ? | | |
| 20 | General factory (machine-hours) | 250,000 | 12,000 | 28,000 | ? | | |
| 21 | | ? | | | | | |
| 22 | | | | | | | |
| 23 | ***Compute the predetermined overhead rate*** | | | | | | |
| 24 | Estimated total manufacturing overhead (a) | | ? | | | | |
| 25 | Estimated total amount of the allocation base (b) | | ? | DLHs | | | |
| 26 | Predetermined overhead rate (a) ÷ (b) | | ? | per DLH | | | |
| 27 | | | | | | | |
| 28 | ***Compute the manufacturing overhead applied*** | *Deluxe* | | *Tourist* | | | |
| 29 | Direct labor-hours per unit (a) | ? | DLHs | ? | DLHs | | |
| 30 | Predetermined overhead rate (b) | ? | per DLH | ? | per DLH | | |
| 31 | Manufacturing overhead applied per unit (a) × (b) | ? | | ? | | | |
| 32 | | | | | | | |
| 33 | ***Compute traditional unit product costs*** | *Deluxe* | *Tourist* | | | | |
| 34 | Direct materials | ? | ? | | | | |
| 35 | Direct labor | ? | ? | | | | |
| 36 | Manufacturing overhead applied | ? | ? | | | | |
| 37 | Traditonal unit product cost | ? | ? | | | | |
| 38 | | | | | | | |
| 39 | ***Compute activity rates*** | *Estimated* | | | | | |
| 40 | | *Overhead* | | | | | |
| 41 | *Activities* | *Cost* | *Total Expected Activity* | | | *Activity Rate* | |
| 42 | Labor-related | ? | ? | DLHs | ? | per DLH | |
| 43 | Machine setups | ? | ? | setups | ? | per setup | |
| 44 | Production orders | ? | ? | orders | ? | per order | |
| 45 | General factory | ? | ? | MHs | ? | per MH | |
| 46 | | | | | | | |
| 47 | ***Compute the ABC overhead cost per unit*** | | *Deluxe* | | *Tourist* | | |
| 48 | | *Activity* | *Expected* | | *Expected* | | |
| 49 | *Activities* | *Rate* | *Activity* | *Amount* | *Activity* | *Amount* | |
| 50 | Labor-related | ? | ? | ? | ? | ? | |
| 51 | Machine setups | ? | ? | ? | ? | ? | |
| 52 | Production orders | ? | ? | ? | ? | ? | |
| 53 | General factory | ? | ? | ? | ? | ? | |
| 54 | Total overhead cost assigned (a) | | | ? | | ? | |
| 55 | Number of units produced (b) | | | ? | | ? | |
| 56 | ABC overhead cost per unit (a) ÷ (b) | | | ? | | ? | |
| 57 | | | | | | | |
| 58 | ***Compute the ABC unit product costs*** | *Deluxe* | *Tourist* | | | | |
| 59 | Direct materials | ? | ? | | | | |
| 60 | Direct labor | ? | ? | | | | |
| 61 | ABC overhead cost per unit (see above) | ? | ? | | | | |
| 62 | ABC unit product cost | ? | ? | | | | |
| 63 | | | | | | | |

**Chapter 3 Form** / Chapter 3 Master / Filled in Chapter 3 Form

You should proceed to the requirements below only after completing your worksheet.

***Required:***

1. Check your worksheet by reducing the direct labor-hours per unit to 2 for the Deluxe model in cell B10. The Data area of the worksheet should look like this:

**Data**

| | Deluxe | Tourist |
|---|---|---|
| Annual sales in units............... | 2,000 | 10,000 |
| Direct materials per unit.......... | $25 | $17 |
| Direct labor-hours per unit ...... | 2 | 4 |
| Direct labor rate ...................... | $12 per DLH | |

| Activities and Activity Measures | Estimated Overhead Cost | Expected Activity | | |
|---|---|---|---|---|
| | | Deluxe | Tourist | Total |
| Labor-related (direct labor-hours) ..... | $ 80,000 | 4,000 | 40,000 | 44,000 |
| Machine setups (setups)................. | 150,000 | 3,000 | 2,000 | 5,000 |
| Production orders (orders)............... | 70,000 | 100 | 300 | 400 |
| General factory (machine-hours)...... | 250,000 | 12,000 | 28,000 | 40,000 |
| | $550,000 | | | |

The Deluxe model's unit product cost under traditional costing should now be $74.00 and the ABC unit product cost should be $143.89. If you do not get these results, find the errors in your worksheet and correct them.

a. What happened to the predetermined overhead rate when the direct labor-hour requirement for the Deluxe model dropped from 5 hours to 2 hours? Explain.

b. Compare the unit product costs for the *Tourist* model before and after changing the direct labor-hour requirements for the *Deluxe* model. The traditional unit product cost of the Tourist model increased from $109 to $115 when the direct labor-hour requirement for the Deluxe model changed from 5 to 2 hours per unit. In contrast, the ABC unit product cost of the Tourist model increased from $100.15 to $101.20. Which costing method do you trust more for making decisions? Explain.

2. Change the direct labor-hour requirement for the Deluxe model back to 5 hours in cell B10. Assume that the production orders change so that the Deluxe model will have 300 orders in cell C19 and the Tourist model will have 100 orders in cell D19. The Data area should now look like this:

**Data**

| | Deluxe | Tourist |
|---|---|---|
| Annual sales in units................ | 2,000 | 10,000 |
| Direct materials per unit........... | $25 | $17 |
| Direct labor-hours per unit ....... | 5 | 4 |
| Direct labor rate ....................... | $12 per DLH | |

| Activities and Activity Measures | Estimated Overhead Cost | Expected Activity | | |
|---|---|---|---|---|
| | | Deluxe | Tourist | Total |
| Labor-related (direct labor-hours) ........ | $ 80,000 | 10,000 | 40,000 | 50,000 |
| Machine setups (setups).................... | 150,000 | 3,000 | 2,000 | 5,000 |
| Production orders (orders).................. | 70,000 | 300 | 100 | 400 |
| General factory (machine-hours)......... | 250,000 | 12,000 | 28,000 | 40,000 |
| | $550,000 | | | |

a. What effect does this change have on the traditional unit product costs? Explain.
b. What effect does this change have on the ABC unit product costs? Explain.
c. Which method, the traditional direct labor-based costing system or the ABC costing system, apparently provides more accurate costs? Explain.

3. Change the data in red so that the Data area looks like this:

**Data**

| | Deluxe | Tourist |
|---|---|---|
| Annual sales in units.............. | 1,000 | 9,000 |
| Direct materials per unit.......... | $20 | $20 |
| Direct labor-hours per unit ...... | 1 | 1 |
| Direct labor rate ...................... | $10 per DLH | |

| | | Expected Activity | | |
|---|---|---|---|---|
| Activities and Activity Measures | Estimated Overhead Cost | Deluxe | Tourist | Total |
| Labor-related (direct labor-hours) ...... | $ 33,000 | 1,000 | 9,000 | 10,000 |
| Machine setups (setups).................. | 120,000 | 20 | 80 | 100 |
| Production orders (orders)................ | 70,000 | 15 | 35 | 50 |
| General factory (machine-hours)....... | 150,000 | 10,000 | 10,000 | 20,000 |
| | $373,000 | | | |

a. Are the traditional unit product costs for the two products the same or different? Explain.
b. Are the ABC unit product costs for the two products the same or different? Explain.
c. Which method, the traditional direct labor-based costing system or the ABC costing system, apparently provides more accurate costs? Explain.

## THE FOUNDATIONAL 15

connect ACCOUNTING

**Available with McGraw-Hill's *Connect® Accounting.***

LO1, LO2, LO3 LO4

Hickory Company manufactures two products—14,000 units of Product Y and 6,000 units of Product Z. The company uses a plantwide overhead rate based on direct labor-hours. It is considering implementing an activity-based costing (ABC) system that allocates all of its manufacturing overhead to four cost pools. The following additional information is available for the company as a whole and for Products Y and Z:

| Activity Cost Pool | Activity Measure | Estimated Overhead Cost | Expected Activity |
|---|---|---|---|
| Machining............................. | Machine-hours | $200,000 | 10,000 MHs |
| Machine setups..................... | Number of setups | $100,000 | 200 setups |
| Production design.................. | Number of products | $84,000 | 2 products |
| General factory...................... | Direct labor-hours | $300,000 | 12,000 DLHs |

| Activity Measure | Product Y | Product Z |
|---|---|---|
| Machining.............................. | 7,000 | 3,000 |
| Number of setups.................. | 50 | 150 |
| Number of products............... | 1 | 1 |
| Direct labor-hours.................. | 8,000 | 4,000 |

1. What is the company's plantwide overhead rate?
2. Using the plantwide overhead rate, how much manufacturing overhead cost is allocated to Product Y? How much is allocated to Product Z?

3. What is the activity rate for the Machining activity cost pool?
4. What is the activity rate for the Machine Setups activity cost pool?
5. What is the activity rate for the Product Design activity cost pool?
6. What is the activity rate for the General Factory activity cost pool?
7. Which of the four activities is a batch-level activity? Why?
8. Which of the four activities is a product-level activity? Why?
9. Using the ABC system, how much total manufacturing overhead cost would be assigned to Product Y?
10. Using the ABC system, how much total manufacturing overhead cost would be assigned to Product Z?
11. Using the plantwide overhead rate, what percentage of the total overhead cost is allocated to Product Y? What percentage is allocated to Product Z?
12. Using the ABC system, what percentage of the Machining costs is assigned to Product Y? What percentage is assigned to Product Z? Are these percentages similar to those obtained in question 11? Why?
13. Using the ABC system, what percentage of Machine Setups cost is assigned to Product Y? What percentage is assigned to Product Z? Are these percentages similar to those obtained in question 11? Why?
14. Using the ABC system, what percentage of the Product Design cost is assigned to Product Y? What percentage is assigned to Product Z? Are these percentages similar to those obtained in question 11? Why?
15. Using the ABC system, what percentage of the General Factory cost is assigned to Product Y? What percentage is assigned to Product Z? Are these percentages similar to those obtained in question 11? Why?

## EXERCISES

connect ACCOUNTING

**All applicable exercises are available with McGraw-Hill's *Connect® Accounting*.**

### EXERCISE 3–1 ABC Cost Hierarchy [LO1]

The following activities occur at Greenwich Corporation, a company that manufactures a variety of products:

a. Various individuals manage the parts inventories.
b. A clerk in the factory issues purchase orders for a job.
c. The personnel department trains new production workers.
d. The factory's general manager meets with other department heads to coordinate plans.
e. Direct labor workers assemble products.
f. Engineers design new products.
g. The materials storekeeper issues raw materials to be used in jobs.
h. The maintenance department performs periodic preventive maintenance on general-use equipment.

***Required:***

Classify each of the activities above as either a unit-level, batch-level, product-level, or facility-level activity.

TAKE TWO

### EXERCISE 3–2 Compute Activity Rates [LO2]

Rustafson Corporation is a diversified manufacturer of consumer goods. The company's activity-based costing system has the following seven activity cost pools:

Estimated direct labor-hours = 10,000

| Activity Cost Pool | Estimated Overhead Cost | Expected Activity |
|---|---|---|
| Labor-related ............... | $52,000 | 8,000 direct labor-hours |
| Machine-related .......... | $15,000 | 20,000 machine-hours |
| Machine setups ........... | $42,000 | 1,000 setups |
| Production orders......... | $18,000 | 500 orders |
| Product testing ............ | $48,000 | 2,000 tests |
| Packaging .................... | $75,000 | 5,000 packages |
| General factory ........... | $108,800 | 8,000 direct labor-hours |

***Required:***

1. Compute the activity rate for each activity cost pool.
2. Compute the company's predetermined overhead rate, assuming that the company uses a single plantwide predetermined overhead rate based on direct labor-hours.

**EXERCISE 3–3 Compute ABC Product Costs [LO3]**

Larner Corporation is a diversified manufacturer of industrial goods. The company's activity-based costing system contains the following six activity cost pools and activity rates:

| Activity Cost Pool | Activity Rates |
|---|---|
| Labor-related | $7.00 per direct labor-hour |
| Machine-related | $3.00 per machine-hour |
| Machine setups | $40.00 per setup |
| Production orders | $160.00 per order |
| Shipments | $120.00 per shipment |
| General factory | $4.00 per direct labor-hour |

Number of units of J78 produced = 3,000

Cost and activity data have been supplied for the following products:

| | J78 | B52 |
|---|---|---|
| Direct materials cost per unit | $6.50 | $31.00 |
| Direct labor cost per unit | $3.75 | $6.00 |
| Number of units produced per year | 4,000 | 100 |

| | Total Expected Activity | |
|---|---|---|
| | J78 | B52 |
| Direct labour-hours | 1,000 | 40 |
| Machine-hours | 3,200 | 30 |
| Machine setups | 5 | 1 |
| Production orders | 5 | 1 |
| Shipments | 10 | 1 |

***Required:***

Compute the unit product cost of each product listed above.

**EXERCISE 3–4 Contrast ABC and Conventional Product Costs [LO4]**

Pacifica Industrial Products Corporation makes two products, Product H and Product L. Product H is expected to sell 40,000 units next year and Product L is expected to sell 8,000 units. A unit of either product requires 0.4 direct labor-hours.

The company's total manufacturing overhead for the year is expected to be $1,632,000.

***Required:***

1. The company currently applies manufacturing overhead to products using direct labor-hours as the allocation base. If this method is followed, how much overhead cost would be applied to each product? Compute both the overhead cost per unit and the total amount of overhead cost that would be applied to each product. (In other words, how much overhead cost is applied to a unit of Product H? Product L? How much overhead cost is applied in total to all the units of Product H? Product L?)
2. Management is considering an activity-based costing system and would like to know what impact this change might have on product costs. For purposes of discussion, it has been suggested that all of the manufacturing overhead be treated as a product-level cost. The total manufacturing overhead would be divided in half between the two products, with $816,000 assigned to Product H and $816,000 assigned to Product L.

   If this suggestion is followed, how much overhead cost per unit would be assigned to each product?
3. Explain the impact on unit product costs of the switch in costing systems.

Direct labor-hours per unit of either product = 0.5 hours

### EXERCISE 3–5 Assigning Overhead to Products in ABC [LO2, LO3]

Sultan Company uses an activity-based costing system.

At the beginning of the year, the company made the following estimates of cost and activity for its five activity cost pools:

| Activity Cost Pool | Activity Measure | Expected Overhead Cost | Expected Activity |
|---|---|---|---|
| Labor-related | Direct labor-hours | $156,000 | 26,000 DLHs |
| Purchase orders | Number of orders | $11,000 | 220 orders |
| Parts management | Number of part types | $80,000 | 100 part types |
| Board etching | Number of boards | $90,000 | 2,000 boards |
| General factory | Machine-hours | $180,000 | 20,000 MHs |

***Required:***

1. Compute the activity rate for each of the activity cost pools.
2. The expected activity for the year was distributed among the company's four products as follows:

| | Expected Activity | | | |
|---|---|---|---|---|
| Activity Cost Pool | Product A | Product B | Product C | Product D |
| Labor-related (DLHs) | 6,000 | 11,000 | 4,000 | 5,000 |
| Purchase orders (orders) | 60 | 30 | 40 | 90 |
| Parts management (part types) | 30 | 15 | 40 | 15 |
| Board etching (boards) | 500 | 900 | 600 | 0 |
| General factory (MHs) | 3,000 | 8,000 | 3,000 | 6,000 |

Using the ABC data, determine the total amount of overhead cost assigned to each product.

### EXERCISE 3–6 Cost Hierarchy and Activity Measures [LO1]

Various activities at Companhia de Textils, S.A., a manufacturing company located in Brazil, are listed below. The company makes a variety of products in its plant outside São Paulo.

a. Preventive maintenance is performed on general-purpose production equipment.
b. Products are assembled by hand.
c. A security guard patrols the company grounds after normal working hours.
d. Purchase orders are issued for materials to be used in production.
e. Modifications are made to product designs.
f. New employees are hired by the personnel office.
g. Machine settings are changed between batches of different products.
h. Parts inventories are maintained in the storeroom. (Each product requires its own unique parts.)
i. Insurance costs are incurred on the company's facilities.

***Required:***

1. Classify each of the activities as either a unit-level, batch-level, product-level, or facility-level activity.
2. Where possible, name one or more activity measures that could be used to assign costs generated by the activity to products or customers.

### EXERCISE 3–7 Contrast ABC and Conventional Product Costs [LO2, LO3, LO4]

Kunkel Company makes two products and uses a conventional costing system in which a single plantwide predetermined overhead rate is computed based on direct labor-hours. Data for the two products for the upcoming year follow:

TAKE TWO

Number of units of Wurcon = 48,000

| | Mercon | Wurcon |
|---|---|---|
| Direct materials cost per unit | $10.00 | $8.00 |
| Direct labor cost per unit | $3.00 | $3.75 |
| Direct labor-hours per unit | 0.20 | 0.25 |
| Number of units produced | 10,000 | 40,000 |

These products are customized to some degree for specific customers.

***Required:***

1. The company's manufacturing overhead costs for the year are expected to be $336,000. Using the company's conventional costing system, compute the unit product costs for the two products.
2. Management is considering an activity-based costing system in which half of the overhead would continue to be allocated on the basis of direct labor-hours and half would be allocated on the basis of engineering design time. This time is expected to be distributed as follows during the upcoming year:

| | Mercon | Wurcon | Total |
|---|---|---|---|
| Engineering design time (in hours) .......... | 4,000 | 4,000 | 8,000 |

   Compute the unit product costs for the two products using the proposed ABC system.
3. Explain why the product costs differ between the two systems.

**EXERCISE 3–8 Computing ABC Product Costs [LO2, LO3]**

Performance Products Corporation makes two products, titanium Rims and Posts. Data regarding the two products follow:

| | Direct Labor-Hours per Unit | Annual Production |
|---|---|---|
| Rims .............................. | 0.40 | 20,000 units |
| Posts .............................. | 0.20 | 80,000 units |

Additional information about the company follows:

a. Rims require $17 in direct materials per unit, and Posts require $10.
b. The direct labor wage rate is $16 per hour.
c. Rims are more complex to manufacture than Posts and they require special equipment.
d. The ABC system has the following activity cost pools:

| | | | Estimated Activity | | |
|---|---|---|---|---|---|
| Activity Cost Pool | Activity Measure | Estimated Overhead Cost | Rims | Posts | Total |
| Machine setups ...................................... | Number of setups | $21,000 | 100 | 80 | 180 |
| Special processing ................................. | Machine-hours | $180,000 | 4,000 | 0 | 4,000 |
| General factory ...................................... | Direct labor-hours | $288,000 | 8,000 | 16,000 | 24,000 |

***Required:***

1. Compute the activity rate for each activity cost pool.
2. Determine the unit product cost of each product according to the ABC system.

**EXERCISE 3–9 Compute and Use Activity Rates to Determine the Costs of Serving Customers [LO2, LO3]**

TAKE TWO

Total number of deliveries = 4,000

Med Max buys surgical supplies from a variety of manufacturers and then resells and delivers these supplies to dozens of hospitals. In the face of declining profits, Med Max decided to implement an activity-based costing system to improve its understanding of the costs incurred to serve each hospital. The company broke its selling and administrative expenses into four activities as shown below:

| Activity Cost Pool | Activity Measure | Total Cost | Total Activity |
|---|---|---|---|
| Customer deliveries ............................................ | Number of deliveries | $ 400,000 | 5,000 deliveries |
| Manual order processing....................................... | Number of manual orders | 300,000 | 4,000 orders |
| Electronic order processing.................................. | Number of electronic orders | 200,000 | 12,500 orders |
| Line item picking ................................................ | Number of line items picked | 500,000 | 400,000 line items |
| Total selling and administrative expenses .............. | | $1,400,000 | |

Med Max gathered the data below for two of the many hospitals that it serves—City General and County General:

| Activity Measure | Activity: City General | Activity: County General |
|---|---|---|
| Number of deliveries | 10 | 20 |
| Number of manual orders | 0 | 40 |
| Number of electronic orders | 10 | 0 |
| Number of line items picked | 100 | 260 |

***Required:***

1. Compute the activity rate for each activity cost pool.
2. Compute the total activity costs that would be assigned to City General and County General.
3. Describe the purchasing behaviors that are likely to increase Med Max's cost to serve its customers.

**EXERCISE 3–10 Contrasting ABC and Conventional Product Costs [LO2, LO3, LO4]**

Rocky Mountain Corporation makes two types of hiking boots—Xactive and Pathbreaker. Data concerning these two product lines appear below:

| | Xactive | Pathbreaker |
|---|---|---|
| Direct materials per unit | $64.80 | $51.00 |
| Direct labor cost per unit | $18.20 | $13.00 |
| Direct labor-hours per unit | 1.4 DLHs | 1.0 DLHs |
| Estimated annual production and sales | 25,000 units | 75,000 units |

The company has a conventional costing system in which manufacturing overhead is applied to units based on direct labor-hours. Data concerning manufacturing overhead and direct labor-hours for the upcoming year appear below:

| | |
|---|---|
| Estimated total manufacturing overhead | $2,200,000 |
| Estimated total direct labor-hours | 110,000 DLHs |

***Required:***

1. Compute the predetermined overhead rate based on direct labor-hours. Using this rate and other data from the problem, determine the unit product cost of each product.
2. The company is considering replacing its conventional costing system with an activity-based costing system that would assign its manufacturing overhead to the following four activity cost pools:

| Activities and Activity Measures | Estimated Overhead Cost | Expected Activity: Xactive | Expected Activity: Pathbreaker | Expected Activity: Total |
|---|---|---|---|---|
| Supporting direct labor (direct labor-hours) | $ 797,500 | 35,000 | 75,000 | 110,000 |
| Batch setups (setups) | 680,000 | 250 | 150 | 400 |
| Product sustaining (number of products) | 650,000 | 1 | 1 | 2 |
| General factory (machine-hours) | 72,500 | 2,500 | 7,500 | 10,000 |
| Total manufacturing overhead cost | $2,200,000 | | | |

   Determine the activity rate for each of the four activity cost pools.
3. Using the activity rates and other data from the problem, determine the unit product cost of each product.
4. Explain why the conventional and activity-based cost assignments differ.

**EXERCISE 3–11 Contrasting Activity-Based Costing and Conventional Product Costing [LO2, LO3, LO4]**

Rusties Company recently implemented an activity-based costing system. At the beginning of the year, management made the following estimates of cost and activity in the company's five activity cost pools:

| Activity Cost Pool | Activity Measure | Expected Overhead Cost | Expected Activity |
|---|---|---|---|
| Labor-related | Direct labor-hours | $18,000 | 2,000 DLHs |
| Purchase orders | Number of orders | $1,050 | 525 orders |
| Product testing | Number of tests | $3,500 | 350 tests |
| Template etching | Number of templates | $700 | 28 templates |
| General factory | Machine-hours | $50,000 | 10,000 MHs |

***Required:***

1. Compute the activity rate for each of the activity cost pools.
2. The expected activity for the year was distributed among the company's four products as follows:

| Activity Cost Pool | Expected Activity | | | |
|---|---|---|---|---|
| | Product A | Product B | Product C | Product D |
| Labor-related (DLHs) | 500 | 100 | 700 | 700 |
| Purchase orders (orders) | 80 | 105 | 180 | 160 |
| Product testing (tests) | 200 | 60 | 0 | 90 |
| Template etching (templates) | 0 | 14 | 10 | 4 |
| General factory (MHs) | 3,400 | 2,200 | 1,800 | 2,600 |

   Using the ABC data, determine the total amount of overhead cost assigned to each product.
3. Assume that prior to implementing ABC, Rusties used a conventional cost system that applied all manufacturing overhead to products based on direct labor-hours. Explain how the conventional overhead cost assignments would differ from the activity-based cost assignments with respect to Product B.

Alternate problem set is available on the text website and in *Connect*® *Accounting*.

## PROBLEMS

**All applicable problems are available with McGraw-Hill's *Connect*® *Accounting*.**

**PROBLEM 3–12A Contrasting ABC and Conventional Product Costs [LO2, LO3, LO4]**

Precision Manufacturing Inc. (PMI) makes two types of industrial component parts—the EX300 and the TX500. It annually produces 60,000 units of EX300 and 12,500 units of TX500. The company's conventional cost system allocates manufacturing overhead to products using a plantwide overhead rate and direct labor dollars as the allocation base. Additional information relating to the company's two product lines is shown below:

CHECK FIGURE
(2) Unit product cost for EX300: $12.13

| | EX300 | TX500 | Total |
|---|---|---|---|
| Direct materials | $366,325 | $162,550 | $528,875 |
| Direct labor | $120,000 | $42,500 | 162,500 |

The company is considering implementing an activity-based costing system that distributes all of its manufacturing overhead to four activities as shown below:

| Activity Cost Pool ( and Activity Measure) | Manufacturing Overhead | Activity | | |
|---|---|---|---|---|
| | | EX300 | TX500 | Total |
| Machining (machine-hours) | $198,250 | 90,000 | 62,500 | 152,500 |
| Setups (setup hours) | 150,000 | 75 | 300 | 375 |
| Product-level (number of products) | 100,250 | 1 | 1 | 2 |
| General factory (direct labor dollars) | 60,125 | $120,000 | $42,500 | $162,500 |
| Total manufacturing overhead cost | $508,625 | | | |

***Required:***

1. Compute the plantwide overhead rate that would be used in the company's conventional cost system. Using the plantwide rate, compute the unit product cost for each product.
2. Compute the activity rate for each activity cost pool. Using the activity rates, compute the unit product cost for each product.
3. Why do the conventional and activity-based cost assignments differ from one another?

**PROBLEM 3–13A ABC Cost Hierarchy [LO1]**

Mitchell Corporation manufactures a variety of products in a single facility. Consultants hired by the company to do an activity-based costing analysis have identified the following activities carried out in the company on a routine basis:

a. Milling machines are used to make components for products.
b. A percentage of all completed goods are inspected on a random basis.
c. Production orders are issued for jobs.
d. The company's grounds crew maintains planted areas surrounding the factory.
e. Employees are trained in general procedures.
f. The human resources department screens and hires new employees.
g. Purchase orders are issued for materials required in production.
h. Material is received on the receiving dock and moved to the production area.
i. The plant controller prepares periodic accounting reports.
j. The engineering department makes modifications in the designs of products.
k. Machines are set up between batches of different products.
i. The maintenance crew does routine periodic maintenance on general-purpose equipment.

***Required:***

1. Classify each of the above activities as a unit-level, batch-level, product-level, or facility-level activity.
2. For each of the above activities, suggest an activity measure that could be used to allocate its costs to products.

CHECK FIGURE
(3b) $8.65 per diner

**PROBLEM 3–14A Compute and Use Activity Rates to Determine the Costs of Serving Customers [LO2, LO3, LO4]**

Gino's Restaurant is a popular restaurant in Boston, Massachusetts. The owner of the restaurant has been trying to better understand costs at the restaurant and has hired a student intern to conduct an activity-based costing study. The intern, in consultation with the owner, identified the following major activities:

| Activity Cost Pool | Activity Measure |
|---|---|
| Serving a party of diners | Number of parties served |
| Serving a diner | Number of diners served |
| Serving drinks | Number of drinks ordered |

A group of diners who ask to sit at the same table is counted as a party. Some costs, such as the costs of cleaning linen, are the same whether one person is at a table or the table is full. Other costs, such as washing dishes, depend on the number of diners served.

Data concerning these activities are shown below.

| | Serving a Party | Serving a Diner | Serving Drinks | Total |
|---|---|---|---|---|
| Total cost | $32,800 | $211,200 | $69,600 | $313,600 |
| Total activity | 8,000 parties | 32,000 diners | 58,000 drinks | |

Prior to the activity-based costing study, the owner knew very little about the costs of the restaurant. She knew that the total cost for the month was $313,600 and that 32,000 diners had been served. Therefore, the average cost per diner was $9.80 ($313,600 ÷ 32,000 diners = $9.80 per diner).

***Required:***

1. Compute the activity rates for each of the three activities.
2. According to the activity-based costing system, what is the total cost of serving each of the following parties of diners?

a. A party of four diners who order three drinks in total.
b. A party of two diners who do not order any drinks.
c. A lone diner who orders two drinks.

3. Convert the total costs you computed in part (1) above to costs per diner. In other words, what is the average cost per diner for serving each of the following parties?
a. A party of four diners who order three drinks in total.
b. A party of two diners who do not order any drinks.
c. A lone diner who orders two drinks.
4. Why do the costs per diner for the three different parties differ from each other and from the overall average cost of $9.80 per diner?

**PROBLEM 3–15A Contrasting ABC and Conventional Product Costs [LO2, LO3, LO4]**

CHECK FIGURE
(3b) Rigid: $131.70 per unit

Marine, Inc., manufactures a product that is available in both a flexible and a rigid model. The company has made the rigid model for years; the flexible model was introduced several years ago to tap a new segment of the market. Since introduction of the flexible model, the company's profits have steadily declined, and management has become concerned about the accuracy of its costing system. Sales of the flexible model have been increasing rapidly.

Overhead is applied to products on the basis of direct labor-hours. At the beginning of the current year, management estimated that $600,000 in overhead costs would be incurred and the company would produce and sell 1,000 units of the flexible model and 10,000 units of the regular model. The flexible model requires 2.0 hours of direct labor time per unit, and the regular model requires 1.0 hours. Direct materials and labor costs per unit are given below:

| | Flexible | Rigid |
|---|---|---|
| Direct materials cost per unit................ | $110.00 | $80.00 |
| Direct labor cost per unit ...................... | $30.00 | $15.00 |

***Required:***

1. Compute the predetermined overhead rate using direct labor-hours as the basis for allocating overhead costs to products. Compute the unit product cost for one unit of each model.
2. An intern suggested that the company use activity-based costing to cost its products. A team was formed to investigate this idea. It came back with the recommendation that four activity cost pools be used. These cost pools and their associated activities are listed as follows:

| Activity Cost Pool and Activity Measure | Estimated Overhead Cost | Expected Activity | | |
|---|---|---|---|---|
| | | Flexible | Rigid | Total |
| Purchase orders (number of orders)............... | $ 20,000 | 100 | 300 | 400 |
| Rework requests (number of requests) .......... | 10,000 | 60 | 140 | 200 |
| Product testing (number of tests).................... | 210,000 | 900 | 1,200 | 2,100 |
| Machine related (machine-hours)................... | 360,000 | 1,500 | 2,500 | 4,000 |
| | $600,000 | | | |

Compute the activity rate for each of the activity cost pools.

3. Using activity-based costing, do the following:
a. Determine the total amount of overhead that would be assigned to each model for the year.
b. Compute the unit product cost for one unit of each model.
4. Can you identify a possible explanation for the company's declining profits? If so, what is it?

**PROBLEM 3–16A Contrasting ABC and Conventional Product Costs [LO2, LO3, LO4]**

CHECK FIGURE
(3a) LEC 40 overhead cost: $5.06

For many years, Thomson Company manufactured a single product called LEC 40. Then three years ago, the company automated a portion of its plant and at the same time introduced a second product called LEC 90 that has become increasingly popular. The LEC 90 is a more complex product, requiring 0.80 hours of direct labor time per unit to manufacture and extensive machining in the automated portion of the plant. The LEC 40 requires only 0.40 hours of direct labor time per unit and only a small amount of machining. Manufacturing overhead costs are currently assigned to products on the basis of direct labor-hours.

Despite the growing popularity of the company's new LEC 90, profits have been declining steadily. Management is beginning to believe that there may be a problem with the company's costing system. Direct material and direct labor costs per unit are as follows:

| | LEC 40 | LEC 90 |
|---|---|---|
| Direct materials ........ | $30.00 | $50.00 |
| Direct labor (0.40 hours and 0.80 hours @ $15.00 per hour)........ | $6.00 | $12.00 |

Management estimates that the company will incur $912,000 in manufacturing overhead costs during the current year and 60,000 units of the LEC 40 and 20,000 units of the LEC 90 will be produced and sold.

***Required:***

1. Compute the predetermined manufacturing overhead rate assuming that the company continues to apply manufacturing overhead cost on the basis of direct labor-hours. Using this rate and other data from the problem, determine the unit product cost of each product.
2. Management is considering using activity-based costing to assign manufacturing overhead cost to products. The activity-based costing system would have the following four activity cost pools:

| Activity Cost Pool | Activity Measure | Estimated Overhead Cost |
|---|---|---|
| Maintaining parts inventory ........ | Number of part types | $225,000 |
| Processing purchase orders ........ | Number of purchase orders | $182,000 |
| Quality control ........ | Number of tests run | $45,000 |
| Machine-related ........ | Machine-hours | $460,000 |
| | | $912,000 |

| | Expected Activity | | |
|---|---|---|---|
| Activity Measure | LEC 40 | LEC 90 | Total |
| Number of part types ........ | 600 | 900 | 1,500 |
| Number of purchase orders ........ | 2,000 | 800 | 2,800 |
| Number of tests run ........ | 500 | 1,750 | 2,250 |
| Machine-hours ........ | 1,600 | 8,400 | 10,000 |

   Determine the activity rate for each of the four activity cost pools.
3. Using the activity rates you computed in part (2) above, do the following:
   a. Determine the total amount of manufacturing overhead cost that would be assigned to each product using the activity-based costing system. After these totals have been computed, determine the amount of manufacturing overhead cost per unit of each product.
   b. Compute the unit product cost of each product.
4. From the data you have developed in parts (1) through (3) above, identify factors that may account for the company's declining profits.

CHECK FIGURE
(2b) N 800 XL unit product cost: $404.00

**PROBLEM 3–17A Contrast Activity-Based Costing and Conventional Product Costs [LO2, LO3, LO4]**
Puget World, Inc., manufactures two models of television sets, the N 800 XL model and the N 500 model. Data regarding the two products follow:

| | Direct Labor-Hours per Unit | Annual Production | Total Direct Labor-Hours |
|---|---|---|---|
| Model N 800 XL ........ | 3.0 | 3,000 units | 9,000 |
| Model N 500 ........ | 1.0 | 12,000 units | 12,000 |
| | | | 21,000 |

Additional information about the company follows:

a. Model N 800 XL requires $75 in direct materials per unit, and Model N 500 requires $25.
b. The direct labor wage rate is $18 per hour.
c. The company has always used direct labor-hours as the base for applying manufacturing overhead cost to products.
d. Model N 800 XL is more complex to manufacture than Model N 500 and requires the use of special equipment. Consequently, the company is considering the use of activity-based costing to assign manufacturing overhead cost to products. Three activity cost pools have been identified as follows:

| Activity Cost Pool | Activity Measure | Estimated Overhead Cost |
|---|---|---|
| Machine setups | Number of setups | $ 360,000 |
| Special processing | Machine-hours | 165,000 |
| General factory | Direct labor-hours | 1,260,000 |
| | | $1,785,000 |

| | Expected Activity | | |
|---|---|---|---|
| Activity Measure | Model N 800 XL | Model N 500 | Total |
| Number of setups | 100 | 200 | 300 |
| Machine-hours | 16,500 | 0 | 16,500 |
| Direct labor-hours | 9,000 | 12,000 | 21,000 |

***Required:***

1. Assume that the company continues to use direct labor-hours as the base for applying overhead cost to products.
   a. Compute the predetermined overhead rate.
   b. Compute the unit product cost of each model.
2. Assume that the company decides to use activity-based costing to assign manufacturing overhead cost to products.
   a. Compute the activity rate for each activity cost pool and determine the amount of overhead cost that would be assigned to each model using the activity-based costing system.
   b. Compute the unit product cost of each model.
3. Explain why manufacturing overhead cost shifts from Model N 500 to Model N 800 XL under activity-based costing.

### PROBLEM 3–18A Contrasting Activity-Based Costing and Conventional Product Costing [LO2, LO3, LO4]

CHECK FIGURE
(2) Total overhead cost for Product D: $85,020

Adria Company recently implemented an activity-based costing system. At the beginning of the year, management made the following estimates of cost and activity in the company's five activity cost pools:

| Activity Cost Pool | Activity Measure | Expected Overhead Cost | Expected Activity |
|---|---|---|---|
| Labor-related | Direct labor-hours | $35,000 | 7,000 DLHs |
| Purchase orders | Number of orders | $4,000 | 2,000 orders |
| Material receipts | Number of receipts | $10,450 | 950 receipts |
| Relay assembly | Number of relays | $7,000 | 1,000 relays |
| General factory | Machine-hours | $240,000 | 40,000 MHs |

***Required:***

1. Compute the activity rate for each of the activity cost pools.
2. The expected activity for the year was distributed among the company's four products as follows:

| | Expected Activity | | | |
|---|---|---|---|---|
| **Activity Cost Pool** | **Product A** | **Product B** | **Product C** | **Product D** |
| Labor-related (DLHs) | 2,400 | 500 | 3,500 | 600 |
| Production orders (orders) | 100 | 350 | 800 | 750 |
| Materials receipts (receipts) | 400 | 208 | 342 | 0 |
| Relay assembly (relays) | 170 | 170 | 300 | 360 |
| General factory (MHs) | 12,000 | 7,000 | 8,000 | 13,000 |

Using the ABC data, determine the total amount of overhead cost assigned to each product.

3. Assume that prior to implementing ABC, Adria used a conventional cost system that applied all manufacturing overhead to products based on machine-hours. Explain how the conventional cost assignments would differ from the activity-based cost assignments with respect to Product C.

## BUILDING YOUR SKILLS

### COMMUNICATING IN PRACTICE [LO1]

You often provide advice to Maria Graham, a client who is interested in diversifying her company. Maria is considering the purchase of a small manufacturing company that assembles and packages its many products by hand. She plans to automate the factory and her projections indicate that the company will once again be profitable within two to three years. During her review of the company's records, she discovered that the company currently uses direct labor-hours to allocate overhead to its products. Because of its simplicity, Maria hopes that this approach can continue to be used.

***Required:***

Write a memorandum to Maria that addresses whether or not direct labor should continue to be used as an allocation base for overhead.

### TEAMWORK IN ACTION [LO1]

Your team should visit and closely observe the operations at a fast-food restaurant.

***Required:***

Identify activities and costs at the restaurant that fall into each of the following categories:

a. Unit-level activities and costs.
b. Customer-level activities and costs. (This is like a batch-level activity at a manufacturing company.)
c. Product-level activities and costs.
d. Facility-level activities and costs.

### ETHICS CHALLENGE [LO1]

You and your friends go to a restaurant as a group. At the end of the meal, the issue arises of how the bill for the group should be shared. One alternative is to figure out the cost of what each individual consumed and divide up the bill accordingly. Another alternative is to split the bill equally among the individuals.

***Required:***

Which system for dividing the bill is more equitable? Which system is easier to use? How does this issue relate to the material covered in this chapter?

CHECK FIGURE
(2c) Mona Loa unit product cost: $4.83

### CASE [LO2, LO3, LO4]

Coffee Bean, Inc. (CBI), is a processor and distributor of a variety of blends of coffee. The company buys coffee beans from around the world and roasts, blends, and packages them for resale. CBI offers a large variety of different coffees that it sells to gourmet shops in one-pound bags. The major cost of the coffee is raw materials. However, the company's predominantly automated roasting, blending, and packing processes require a substantial amount of manufacturing overhead. The company uses relatively little direct labor. Some of CBI's coffees are very popular and sell in large volumes, while a few of the newer blends sell in very low volumes.

For the coming year, CBI's budget includes estimated manufacturing overhead cost of $3,000,000. CBI assigns manufacturing overhead to products on the basis of direct labor-hours. The expected direct labor cost totals $600,000, which represents 50,000 hours of direct labor time.

The expected costs for direct materials and direct labor for one-pound bags of two of the company's coffee products appear below.

| | Mona Loa | Malaysian |
|---|---|---|
| Direct materials | $4.20 | $3.20 |
| Direct labor (0.025 hours per bag) | $0.30 | $0.30 |

CBI's controller believes that the company's traditional costing system may be providing misleading cost information. To determine whether or not this is correct, the controller has prepared an analysis of the year's expected manufacturing overhead costs, as shown in the following table:

| Activity Cost Pool | Activity Measure | Expected Activity for the Year | Expected Cost for the Year |
|---|---|---|---|
| Purchasing | Purchase orders | 1,710 orders | $ 513,000 |
| Material handling | Number of setups | 1,800 setups | 720,000 |
| Quality control | Number of batches | 600 batches | 144,000 |
| Roasting | Roasting hours | 96,100 roasting hours | 961,000 |
| Blending | Blending hours | 33,500 blending hours | 402,000 |
| Packaging | Packaging hours | 26,000 packaging hours | 260,000 |
| Total manufacturing overhead cost | | | $3,000,000 |

Data regarding the expected production of Mona Loa and Malaysian coffee are presented below. There will be no raw materials inventory for either of these coffees at the beginning of the year.

| | Mona Loa | Malaysian |
|---|---|---|
| Expected sales | 100,000 pounds | 2,000 pounds |
| Batch size | 10,000 pounds | 500 pounds |
| Setups | 3 per batch | 3 per batch |
| Purchase order size | 20,000 pounds | 500 pounds |
| Roasting time per 100 pounds | 1.0 roasting hours | 1.0 roasting hours |
| Blending time per 100 pounds | 0.5 blending hours | 0.5 blending hours |
| Packaging time per 100 pounds | 0.1 packaging hours | 0.1 packaging hours |

***Required:***

1. Using direct labor-hours as the base for assigning manufacturing overhead cost to products, do the following:
   a. Determine the predetermined overhead rate that will be used during the year.
   b. Determine the unit product cost of one pound of the Mona Loa coffee and one pound of the Malaysian coffee.
2. Using activity-based costing as the basis for assigning manufacturing overhead cost to products, do the following:
   a. Determine the total amount of manufacturing overhead cost assigned to the Mona Loa coffee and to the Malaysian coffee for the year.
   b. Using the data developed in part (2a) above, compute the amount of manufacturing overhead cost per pound of the Mona Loa coffee and the Malaysian coffee. Round all computations to the nearest whole cent.
   c. Determine the unit product cost of one pound of the Mona Loa coffee and one pound of the Malaysian coffee.
3. Write a brief memo to the president of CBI explaining what you have found in parts (1) and (2) above and discussing the implications to the company of using direct labor as the base for assigning manufacturing overhead cost to products.

(CMA, adapted)

CHECK FIGURE
(2) Standard briefcase unit product cost: $20.48

**ANALYTICAL THINKING* [LO2, LO3, LO4)**

"Two dollars of gross margin per briefcase? That's ridiculous!" roared Roy Thurmond, president of FirstLine Cases, Inc. "Why do we go on producing those standard briefcases when we're able to make over $11 per unit on our specialty items? Maybe it's time to get out of the standard line and focus the whole plant on specialty work."

Mr. Thurmond was referring to a summary of unit costs and revenues that he had just received from the company's accounting department:

| | Standard Briefcases | Specialty Briefcases |
|---|---|---|
| Selling price per unit | $26.25 | $42.50 |
| Unit product cost | 24.25 | 31.40 |
| Gross margin per unit | $ 2.00 | $11.10 |

FirstLine Cases produces briefcases from leather, fabric, and synthetic materials in a single plant. The basic product is a standard briefcase that is made from leather lined with fabric. The standard briefcase is a high-quality item and has sold well for many years.

Last year, the company decided to expand its product line and produce specialty briefcases for special orders. These briefcases differ from the standard in that they vary in size, they contain the finest leather and synthetic materials, and they are imprinted with the buyer's name. To reduce labor costs on the specialty briefcases, automated machines do most of the cutting and stitching. These machines are used to a much lesser degree in the production of standard briefcases.

"I agree that the specialty business is looking better and better," replied Beth Mersey, the company's marketing manager. "And there seems to be plenty of demand out there, particularly because the competition hasn't been able to touch our price. Did you know that Velsun Company, our biggest competitor, charges over $50 a unit for its specialty items? Now that's what I call gouging the customer!"

A breakdown of the manufacturing cost for each of FirstLine Cases' products is given below:

| | Standard Briefcases | Specialty Briefcases |
|---|---|---|
| Units produced each month | 10,000 | 2,500 |
| Direct materials: | | |
| Leather | $ 8.00 | $12.00 |
| Fabric | 2.00 | 1.00 |
| Synthetic | 0 | 7.00 |
| Total materials | 10.00 | 20.00 |
| Direct labor (0.5 DLH and 0.40 DLH @ $12.00 per DLH) | 6.00 | 4.80 |
| Manufacturing overhead (0.5 DLH and 0.4 DLH @ $16.50 per DLH) | 8.25 | 6.60 |
| Total cost per unit | $24.25 | $31.40 |

Manufacturing overhead is applied to products on the basis of direct labor-hours. The rate of $16.50 per hour was determined by dividing the total manufacturing overhead cost for a month by the direct labor-hours:

$$\text{Predetermined overhead rate} = \frac{\text{Manufacturing overhead}}{\text{Direct labor-hours}} = \frac{\$99{,}000}{6{,}000\text{ DLHs}} = \$16.50\text{ per DLH}$$

*Adapted from Harold P. Roth and Imogene Posey, "Management Accounting Case Study: Carry All Company," *Management Accounting Campus Report,* Institute of Management Accountants, Fall 1991, p. 9. Used by permission from the IMA, Montvale, NJ, USA, www.imanet.org.

The following additional information is available about the company and its products:

a. Standard briefcases are produced in batches of 1,000 units, and specialty briefcases are produced in batches of 100 units. Thus, the company does 10 setups for the standard items each month and 25 setups for the specialty items. A setup for the standard items requires one hour, whereas a setup for the specialty items requires two hours.

b. All briefcases are inspected to ensure that quality standards are met. Each month a total of 200 hours is spent inspecting the standard briefcases and 400 hours is spent inspecting the specialty briefcases.

c. A standard briefcase requires 0.5 hours of machine time, and a specialty briefcase requires 1.2 hours of machine time.

d. The company is considering the use of activity-based costing as an alternative to its traditional costing system for computing unit product costs. The activity-based costing system has already been designed and costs have been allocated to the activity cost pools. The activity cost pools and activity measures are detailed below:

| Activity Cost Pool | Activity Measure | Estimated Overhead Cost |
|---|---|---|
| Purchasing | Number of orders | $15,000 |
| Material handling | Number of receipts | 16,000 |
| Production orders and setups | Setup-hours | 6,000 |
| Inspection | Inspection-hours | 18,000 |
| Frame assembly | Assembly-hours | 12,000 |
| Machine-related | Machine-hours | 32,000 |
| | | $99,000 |

| | Expected Activity | | |
|---|---|---|---|
| Activity Measure | Standard Briefcases | Specialty Briefcases | Total |
| Number of orders: | | | |
| Leather | 50 | 10 | 60 |
| Fabric | 70 | 20 | 90 |
| Synthetic material | 0 | 150 | 150 |
| Number of receipts: | | | |
| Leather | 70 | 10 | 80 |
| Fabric | 85 | 20 | 105 |
| Synthetic material | 0 | 215 | 215 |
| Setup-hours | ? | ? | ? |
| Inspection-hours | 200 | 400 | 600 |
| Assembly-hours | 700 | 800 | 1,500 |
| Machine-hours | ? | ? | ? |

***Required:***

1. Using activity-based costing, determine the amount of manufacturing overhead cost that would be assigned to each standard briefcase and each specialty briefcase.
2. Using the data computed in part (1) above and other data from the case as needed, determine the unit product cost of each product line from the perspective of the activity-based costing system.
3. Within the limitations of the data that have been provided, evaluate the president's concern about the profitability of the two product lines. Would you recommend that the company shift its resources entirely to the production of specialty briefcases? Explain.
4. Beth Mersey stated that "the competition hasn't been able to touch our price on specialty business." Why do you suppose the competition hasn't been able to touch FirstLine Cases' price?

## A LOOK BACK

We described a basic job-order costing system in Chapter 2 that used a single plantwide overhead rate. Then, in Chapter 3, we looked at activity-based costing, a more sophisticated technique that uses a variety of allocation bases to assign overhead costs to products.

## A LOOK AT THIS CHAPTER

Chapter 4 covers process costing, which is an important alternative to job-order costing. In process costing, departmental costs are applied uniformly to the products processed through the department during the period.

## A LOOK AHEAD

Chapter 5 describes the basics of cost-volume-profit analysis, a tool that helps managers understand the interrelationships among cost, volume, and profit.

# 4 Process Costing

## CHAPTER OUTLINE



## SUPPLEMENT: PROCESS COSTING USING THE FIFO METHOD (available on the Web at www.mhhe.com/brewer6e)

## DECISION FEATURE

# Costing the "Quicker-Picker-Upper"

If you have ever spilled milk, there is a good chance that you used Bounty paper towels to clean up the mess. **Procter & Gamble (P&G)** manufactures Bounty in two main processing departments—Paper Making and Paper Converting. In the Paper Making Department, wood pulp is converted into paper and then spooled into 2,000-pound rolls that are inventoried and retrieved as needed to supply the paper converting process. In the Paper Converting Department, two 2,000-pound rolls of paper are simultaneously unwound into a machine that creates a two-ply paper towel that is decorated, perforated, and embossed to create texture. The large sheets of paper towels that emerge from this process are wrapped around a cylinder-shaped cardboard core measuring eight feet in length. Once enough sheets wrap around the core, the eight-foot roll is cut into individual rolls of Bounty that are sent down a conveyor to be wrapped, packed, and shipped.

In this type of manufacturing environment, costs cannot be readily traced to individual rolls of Bounty; however, given the homogeneous nature of the product, the total costs incurred in the Paper Making Department can be spread uniformly across its output of 2,000-pound rolls of paper. Similarly, the total costs incurred to produce a particular style of Bounty in the Paper Converting Department (including the cost of the 2,000-pound rolls that are transferred in from the Paper Making Department) can be spread uniformly across the number of cases produced of that style.

P&G uses a similar costing approach for many of its products such as Tide, Crest toothpaste, and Dawn dishwashing liquid.

Source: Conversation with Brad Bays, retired financial executive from Procter & Gamble.

## LEARNING OBJECTIVES

*After studying Chapter 4, you should be able to:*

**LO1** Record the flow of materials, labor, and overhead through a process costing system.

**LO2** Compute the equivalent units of production using the weighted-average method.

**LO3** Compute the cost per equivalent unit using the weighted-average method.

**LO4** Assign costs to units using the weighted-average method.

**LO5** Prepare a cost reconciliation report.

Job-order costing and process costing are two common methods for determining unit product costs. Job-order costing is used when many different jobs or products are worked on each period. Examples of industries that use job-order costing include furniture manufacturing, special-order printing, shipbuilding, and many types of service organizations.

By contrast, **process costing** is used most commonly in industries that convert raw materials into homogeneous (i.e., uniform) products, such as bricks, soda, or paper, on a continuous basis. Examples of companies that would use process costing include **Reynolds Aluminum** (aluminum ingots), **Scott Paper** (toilet paper), **General Mills** (flour), **Exxon** (gasoline and lubricating oils), **Coppertone** (sunscreens), and **Kellogg's** (breakfast cereals). In addition, process costing is sometimes used in companies with assembly operations. A form of process costing may also be used in utilities that produce gas, water, and electricity.

Our purpose in this chapter is to explain how product costing works in a process costing system.

## COMPARISON OF JOB-ORDER AND PROCESS COSTING

In some ways process costing is very similar to job-order costing, and in some ways it is very different. In this section, we focus on these similarities and differences to provide a foundation for the detailed discussion of process costing that follows.

### Similarities between Job-Order and Process Costing

Much of what you learned in Chapter 2 about costing and cost flows applies equally well to process costing in this chapter. We are not throwing out all that we have learned about costing and starting from "scratch" with a whole new system. The similarities between job-order and process costing can be summarized as follows:

1. Both systems have the same basic purposes—to assign material, labor, and manufacturing overhead costs to products and to provide a mechanism for computing unit product costs.
2. Both systems use the same basic manufacturing accounts, including Manufacturing Overhead, Raw Materials, Work in Process, and Finished Goods.
3. The flow of costs through the manufacturing accounts is basically the same in both systems.

As can be seen from this comparison, much of the knowledge that you have already acquired about costing is applicable to a process costing system. Our task now is to refine and extend your knowledge to process costing.

### Differences between Job-Order and Process Costing

There are three differences between job-order and process costing. First, process costing is used when a company produces a continuous flow of units that are indistinguishable from one another. Job-order costing is used when a company produces many different jobs that have unique production requirements. Second, under process costing, it makes no sense to try to identify materials, labor, and overhead costs with a particular customer order (as we did with job-order costing) because each order is just one of many that are filled from a continuous flow of virtually identical units from the production line. Accordingly, process costing accumulates costs by department (rather than by order) and assigns these costs uniformly to all units that pass through the department during a period. Job cost sheets (which we used for job-order costing) are not used to accumulate costs. Third, process costing systems compute unit costs by department. This differs from

| Job-Order Costing | Process Costing |
|---|---|
| 1. Many different jobs are worked on during each period, with each job having different production requirements. | 1. A single product is produced either on a continuous basis or for long periods of time. All units of product are identical. |
| 2. Costs are accumulated by individual job. | 2. Costs are accumulated by department. |
| 3. Unit costs are computed *by job* on the job cost sheet. | 3. Unit costs are computed *by department.* |

**EXHIBIT 4–1**
Differences between Job-Order and Process Costing

job-order costing where unit costs are computed by job on the job cost sheet. Exhibit 4–1 summarizes the differences just described.

## COST FLOWS IN PROCESS COSTING

Before going through a detailed example of process costing, it will be helpful to see how, in a general way, manufacturing costs flow through a process costing system.

### Processing Departments

A **processing department** is an organizational unit where work is performed on a product and where materials, labor, or overhead costs are added to the product. For example, a **Nalley's** potato chip factory might have three processing departments—one for preparing potatoes, one for cooking, and one for inspecting and packaging. A brick factory might have two processing departments—one for mixing and molding clay into brick form and one for firing the molded brick. Some products and services may go through a number of processing departments, while others may go through only one or two. Regardless of the number of processing departments, they all have two essential features. First, the activity in the processing department is performed uniformly on all of the units passing through it. Second, the output of the processing department is homogeneous; in other words, all of the units produced are identical.

Products in a process costing environment, such as bricks or potato chips, typically flow in sequence from one department to another as in Exhibit 4–2.

**EXHIBIT 4–2** Sequential Processing Departments

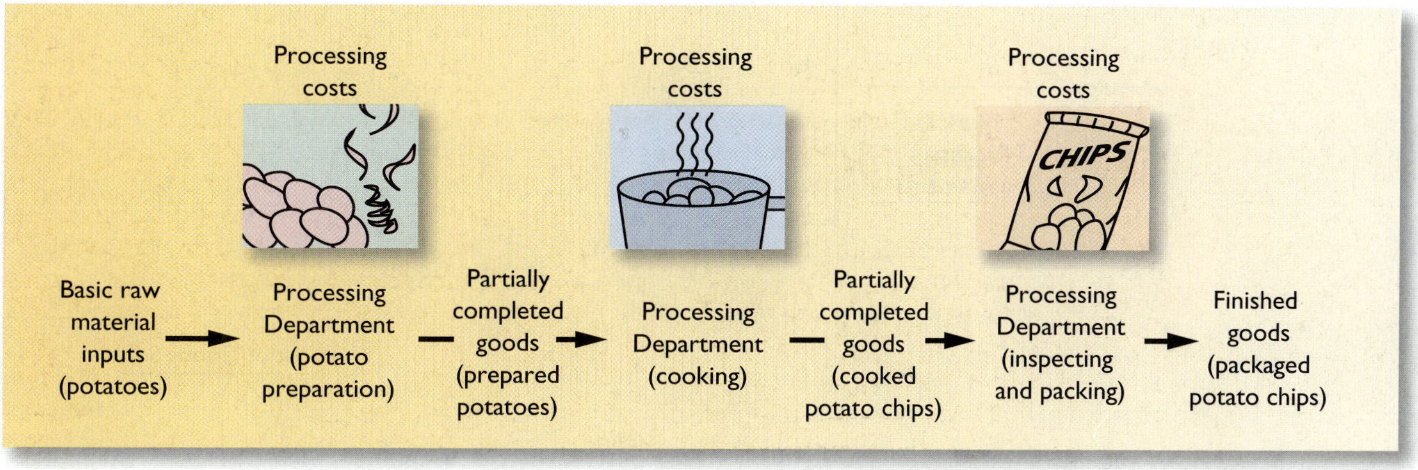

IN BUSINESS

## Monks Make a Living Selling Beer

The Trappist monks of St. Sixtus monastery in Belgium have been brewing beer since 1839. Customers must make an appointment with the monastery to buy a maximum of two 24-bottle cases per month. The scarce and highly prized beer sells for more than $15 per 11-ounce bottle.

The monk's brewing ingredients include water, malt, hops, sugar, and yeast. The sequential steps of the beer-making process include grinding and crushing the malt grain, brewing by adding water to the crushed malt, filtering to separate a liquid called wort from undissolved grain particles, boiling to sterilize the wort (including adding sugar to increase the density of the wort), fermentation by adding yeast to convert sugar into alcohol and carbon dioxide, storage where the beer is aged for at least three weeks, and bottling where more sugar and yeast are added to enable two weeks of additional fermentation in the bottle.

Unlike growth-oriented for-profit companies, the monastery has not expanded its production capacity since 1946, seeking instead to sell just enough beer to sustain the monks' modest lifestyle.

Source: John W. Miller, "Trappist Command: Thou Shalt Not Buy Too Much of Our Beer," *The Wall Street Journal*, November 29, 2007, pp. A1 and A14.

## The Flow of Materials, Labor, and Overhead Costs

Cost accumulation is simpler in a process costing system than in a job-order costing system. In a process costing system, instead of having to trace costs to hundreds of different jobs, costs are traced to only a few processing departments.

A T-account model of materials, labor, and overhead cost flows in a process costing system is shown in Exhibit 4–3. Several key points should be noted from this exhibit. First, note that a separate Work in Process account is maintained for *each processing*

**EXHIBIT 4–3** T-Account Model of Process Costing Flows

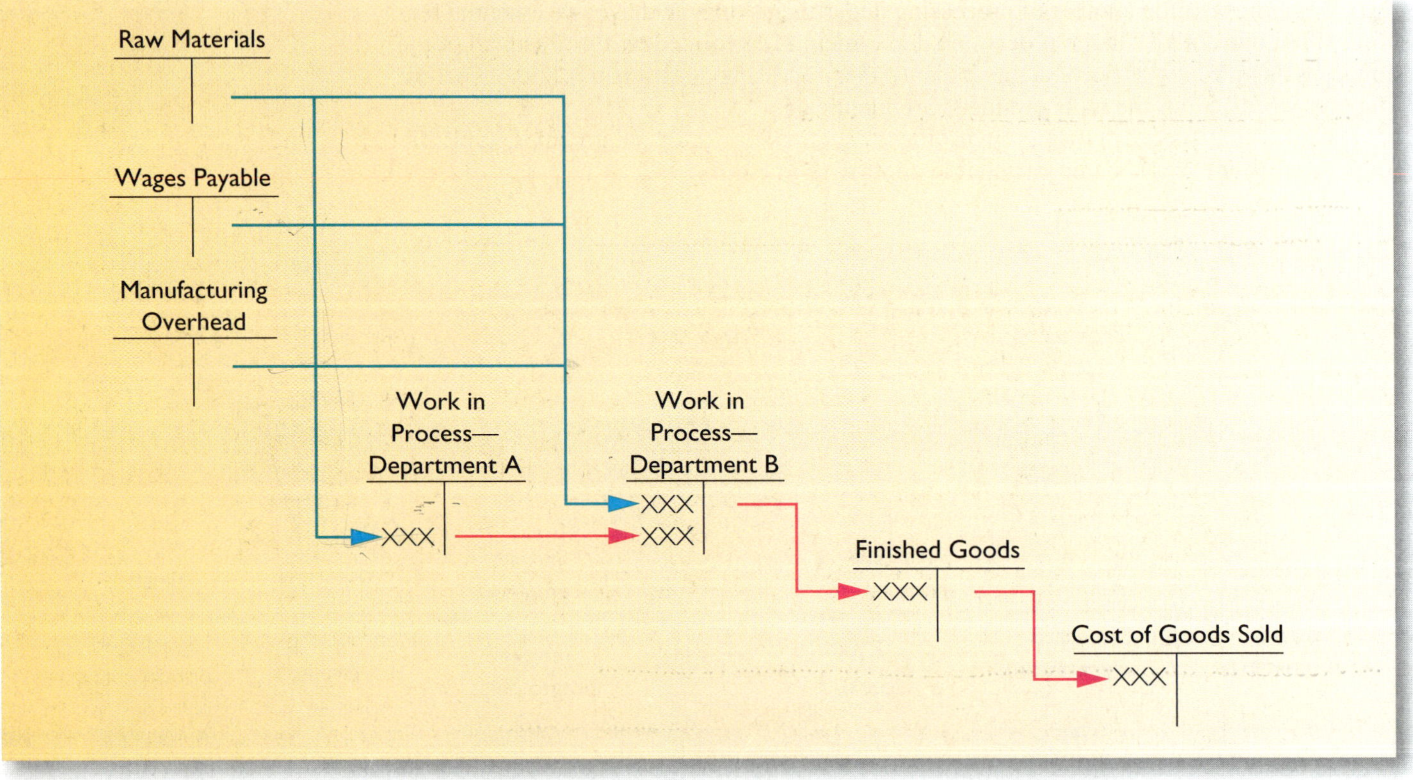

*department.* In contrast, in a job-order costing system the entire company may have only one Work in Process account. Second, note that the completed production of the first processing department (Department A in the exhibit) is transferred to the Work in Process account of the second processing department (Department B). After further work in Department B, the completed units are then transferred to Finished Goods. (In Exhibit 4–3, we show only two processing departments, but a company can have many processing departments.)

Finally, note that materials, labor, and overhead costs can be added in *any* processing department—not just the first. Costs in Department B's Work in Process account consist of the materials, labor, and overhead costs incurred in Department B plus the costs attached to partially completed units transferred in from Department A (called transferred-in costs).

## Materials, Labor, and Overhead Cost Entries

**LEARNING OBJECTIVE 1**

Record the flow of materials, labor, and overhead through a process costing system.

To complete our discussion of cost flows in a process costing system, in this section we show journal entries relating to materials, labor, and overhead costs at Megan's Classic Cream Soda, a company that has two processing departments—Formulating and Bottling. In the Formulating Department, ingredients are checked for quality and then mixed and injected with carbon dioxide to create bulk cream soda. In the Bottling Department, bottles are checked for defects, filled with cream soda, capped, visually inspected again for defects, and then packed for shipping.

**Materials Costs** As in job-order costing, materials are drawn from the storeroom using a materials requisition form. Materials can be added in any processing department, although it is not unusual for materials to be added only in the first processing department, with subsequent departments adding only labor and overhead costs.

At Megan's Classic Cream Soda, some materials (i.e., water, flavors, sugar, and carbon dioxide) are added in the Formulating Department and some materials (i.e., bottles, caps, and packing materials) are added in the Bottling Department. The journal entry to record the materials used in the first processing department, the Formulating Department, is as follows:

| | | |
|---|---|---|
| Work in Process—Formulating | XXX | |
| Raw Materials | | XXX |

The journal entry to record the materials used in the second processing department, the Bottling Department, is as follows:

| | | |
|---|---|---|
| Work in Process—Bottling | XXX | |
| Raw Materials | | XXX |

**Labor Costs** In process costing, labor costs are traced to departments—not to individual jobs. The following journal entry records the labor costs in the Formulating Department at Megan's Classic Cream Soda:

| | | |
|---|---|---|
| Work in Process—Formulating | XXX | |
| Salaries and Wages Payable | | XXX |

A similar entry would be made to record labor costs in the Bottling Department.

**Overhead Costs** In process costing, as in job-order costing, predetermined overhead rates are usually used. Manufacturing overhead cost is applied according to the amount of the allocation base that is incurred in the department. The following journal entry records the overhead cost applied in the Formulating Department:

| | | |
|---|---|---|
| Work in Process—Formulating | XXX | |
| Manufacturing Overhead | | XXX |

A similar entry would be made to apply manufacturing overhead costs in the Bottling Department.

**Completing the Cost Flows** Once processing has been completed in a department, the units are transferred to the next department for further processing, as illustrated in the T-accounts in Exhibit 4–3. The following journal entry transfers the cost of partially completed units from the Formulating Department to the Bottling Department:

| | | |
|---|---|---|
| Work in Process—Bottling | XXX | |
| Work in Process—Formulating | | XXX |

After processing has been completed in the Bottling Department, the costs of the completed units are transferred to the Finished Goods inventory account:

| | | |
|---|---|---|
| Finished Goods | XXX | |
| Work in Process—Bottling | | XXX |

Finally, when a customer's order is filled and units are sold, the cost of the units is transferred to Cost of Goods Sold:

| | | |
|---|---|---|
| Cost of Goods Sold | XXX | |
| Finished Goods | | XXX |

To summarize, the cost flows between accounts are basically the same in a process costing system as they are in a job-order costing system. The only difference at this point is that in a process costing system each department has a separate Work in Process account.

IN BUSINESS

## The Difference between Labor Rates and Labor Cost

The emergence of China as a global competitor has increased the need for managers to understand the difference between labor rates and labor cost. Labor rates reflect the amount paid to employees per hour or month. Labor costs measure the employee compensation paid per unit of output. For example, **Tenneco** has plants in Shanghai, China, and Litchfield, Michigan, that both manufacture exhaust systems for automobiles. The monthly labor rate per employee at the Shanghai plant ranges from $210–$250, whereas the same figure for the Litchfield plant ranges from $1,880–$4,064. A naïve interpretation of these labor rates would be to automatically assume that the Shanghai plant is the lower labor cost facility. A wiser comparison of the two plants' labor costs would account for the fact that the Litchfield plant produced 1.4 million exhaust systems in 2005 compared to 400,000 units at the Shanghai plant, while having only 20% more employees than the Shanghai plant.

Source: Alex Taylor III, "A Tale of Two Factories," *Fortune,* September 18, 2006, pp. 118–126.

We now turn our attention to Double Diamond Skis, a company that manufactures a high-performance deep-powder ski, and that uses process costing to determine its unit product costs. The company's production process is illustrated in Exhibit 4–4. Skis go through a sequence of five processing departments, starting with the Shaping and Milling Department and ending with the Finishing and Pairing Department. The basic idea in process costing is to add together all of the costs incurred in a department during a period and then to spread those costs uniformly across the units processed in that department during that period. As we shall see, applying this simple idea involves a few complications.

**EXHIBIT 4–4** The Production Process at Double Diamond Skis*

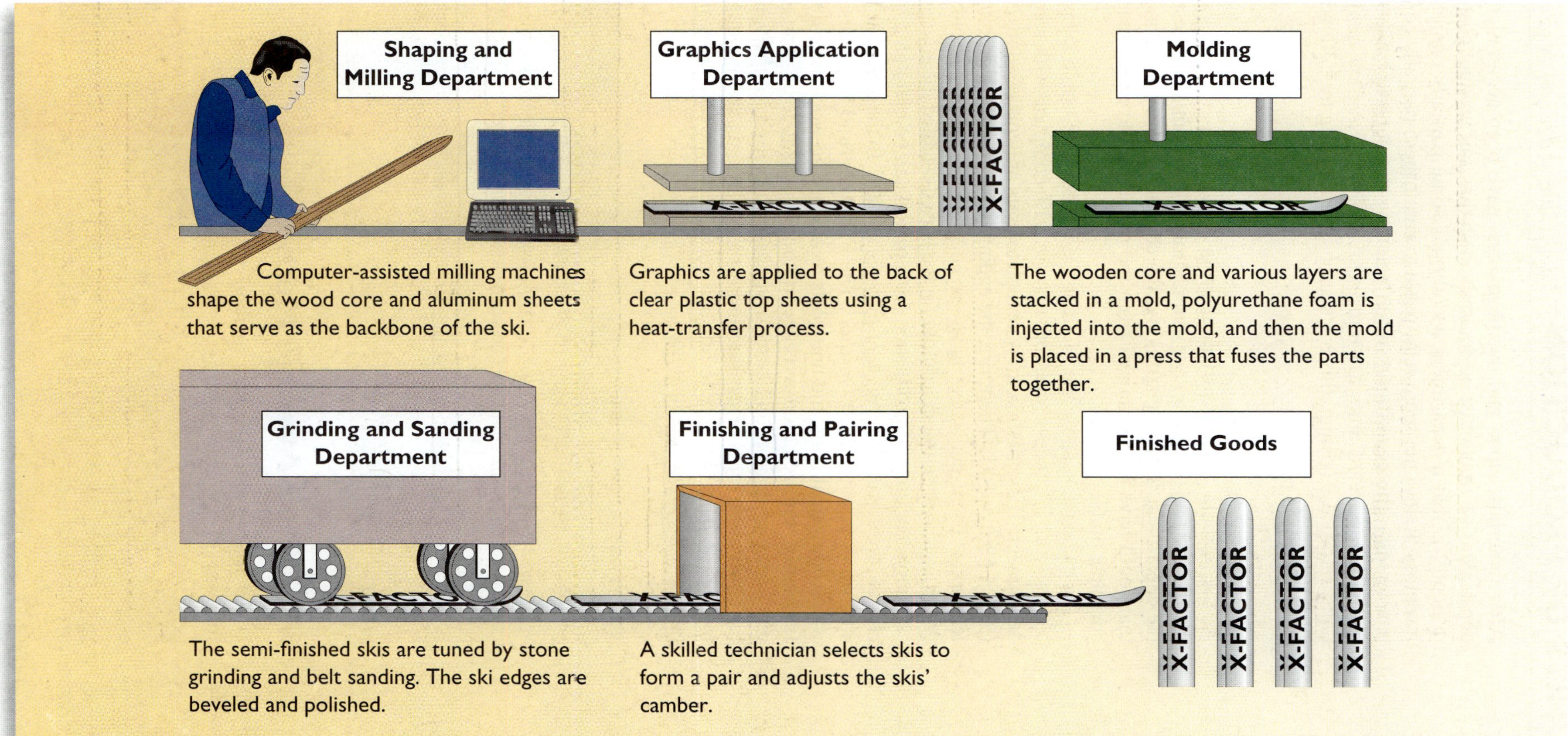


*Adapted from Bill Gout, Jesse James Doquilo, and Studio M D, "Capped Crusaders," *Skiing,* October 1993, pp. 138–144.

# EQUIVALENT UNITS OF PRODUCTION

After materials, labor, and overhead costs have been accumulated in a department, the department's output must be determined so that unit product costs can be computed. The difficulty is that a department usually has some partially completed units in its ending inventory. It does not seem reasonable to count these partially completed units as equivalent to fully completed units when counting the department's output. Therefore, these partially completed units are translated into an *equivalent* number of fully completed units. In process costing, this translation is done using the following formula:

Equivalent units = Number of partially completed units × Percentage completion

As the formula states, **equivalent units** is the product of the number of partially completed units and the percentage completion of those units with respect to the processing in the department. Roughly speaking, the equivalent units is the number of complete units that could have been obtained from the materials and effort that went into the partially complete units.

For example, suppose the Molding Department at Double Diamond has 500 units in its ending work in process inventory that are 60% complete with respect to processing in the department. These 500 partially complete units are equivalent to 300 fully complete units (500 × 60% = 300). Therefore, the ending work in process inventory contains 300 equivalent units. These equivalent units are added to any units completed during the period to determine the department's output for the period—called the *equivalent units of production.*

Equivalent units of production for a period can be computed in different ways. In this chapter, we discuss the *weighted-average method.* In the available Supplement on the website, we discuss the *FIFO method.* The **FIFO method** of process costing is a method in which equivalent units and unit costs relate only to work done during the current period. In contrast, the **weighted-average method** blends together units and costs from the current period with units and costs from the prior period. In the weighted-average method, the **equivalent units of production** for a department are the number of units transferred to the next department (or to finished goods) plus the equivalent units in the department's ending work in process inventory.

## HELPFUL HINT

You need to perform separate equivalent units of production calculations for each manufacturing cost category, such as materials and conversion. When using the weighted-average method to compute equivalent units of production for a cost category you should ignore the completion percentage for the units in beginning inventory. The units transferred to the next department plus the units in ending work in process inventory multiplied by their percentage completion equals the equivalent units of production.

## Weighted-Average Method

**LEARNING OBJECTIVE 2**

Compute the equivalent units of production using the weighted-average method.

Under the weighted-average method, a department's equivalent units are computed as follows:

WEIGHTED-AVERAGE METHOD
(a separate calculation is made for each cost category in each processing department)

Equivalent units of production = Units transferred to the next department or to finished goods + Equivalent units in ending work in process inventory

Note that the computation of the equivalent units of production involves adding the number of units transferred out of the department to the equivalent units in the department's ending inventory. There is no need to compute the equivalent units for the units transferred out of the department—they are 100% complete with respect to the work done in that department or they would not be transferred out. In other words, each unit transferred out of the department is counted as one equivalent unit.

Consider the Shaping and Milling Department at Double Diamond. This department uses computerized milling machines to precisely shape the wooden core and metal sheets that will be used to form the backbone of the ski. (See Exhibit 4–4 for an overview of the production process at Double Diamond.) The activity shown below took place in the department in May:

| | | Percent Complete | |
|---|---|---|---|
| **Shaping and Milling Department** | **Units** | **Materials** | **Conversion** |
| Beginning work in process | 200 | 55% | 30% |
| Units started into production during May | 5,000 | | |
| Units completed during May and transferred to the next department | 4,800 | 100%* | 100%* |
| Ending work in process | 400 | 40% | 25% |

*We always assume that units transferred out of a department are 100% complete with respect to the processing done in that department.

Note the use of the term *conversion* in the table shown above. **Conversion cost**, as defined in an earlier chapter, is direct labor cost plus manufacturing overhead cost. In process costing, conversion cost is often treated as a single element of product cost.

Note that the beginning work in process inventory was 55% complete with respect to materials costs and 30% complete with respect to conversion costs. This means that 55% of the materials costs required to complete the units in the department had already been incurred. Likewise, 30% of the conversion costs required to complete the units had already been incurred.

Two equivalent unit figures must be computed—one for materials and one for conversion. These computations are shown in Exhibit 4–5.

**EXHIBIT 4–5**
Equivalent Units of Production: Weighted-Average Method

| **Shaping and Milling Department** | **Materials** | **Conversion** |
|---|---|---|
| Units transferred to the next department | 4,800 | 4,800 |
| Ending work in process: | | |
| Materials: 400 units × 40% complete | 160 | |
| Conversion: 400 units × 25% complete | | 100 |
| Equivalent units of production | 4,960 | 4,900 |

Note that the computations in Exhibit 4–5 ignore the fact that the units in the beginning work in process inventory were partially complete. For example, the 200 units in beginning inventory were already 30% complete with respect to conversion costs. Nevertheless, the weighted-average method is concerned only with the 4,900 equivalent units that are in ending inventories and in units transferred to the next department; it is not concerned with the fact that the beginning inventory was already partially complete. In other words, the 4,900 equivalent units computed using the weighted-average method include work that was accomplished in prior periods. This is a key point concerning the weighted-average method and it is easy to overlook.

**EXHIBIT 4–6**
Visual Perspective of Equivalent Units of Production

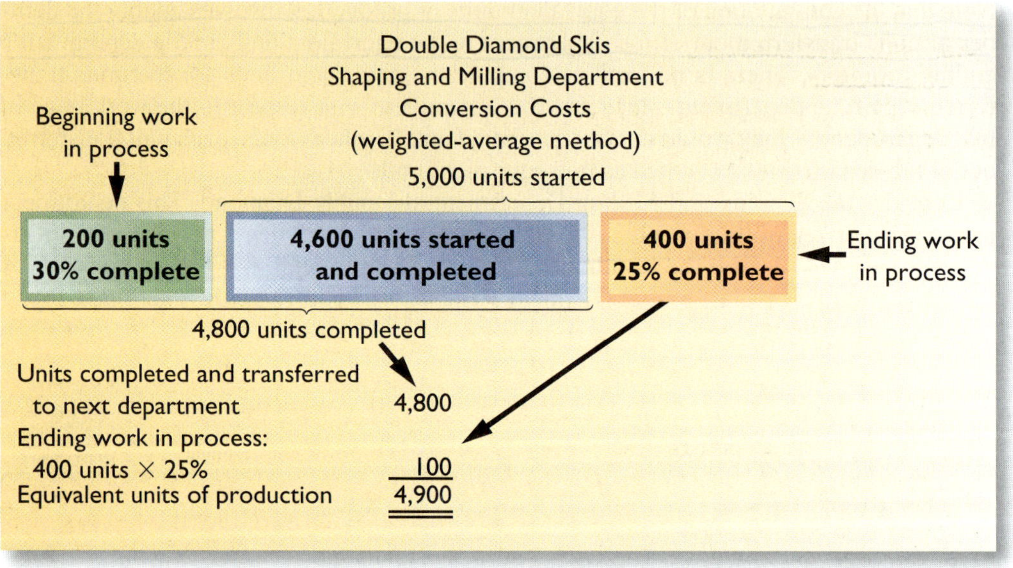


Exhibit 4–6 provides another way of looking at the computation of equivalent units of production. This exhibit depicts the equivalent units computation for conversion costs. Study it carefully before going on.

**DECISION POINT**

### Writing Term Papers

Assume your professors assigned four separate five-page papers that were all due on the same day. You turned in two complete papers and two incomplete papers—one of which was two pages long and the other was three pages long. Assuming that each page requires the same time and effort, how many complete papers could you have turned in with the same expenditure of time and effort?

## COMPUTE AND APPLY COSTS

**LEARNING OBJECTIVE 3**

Compute the cost per equivalent unit using the weighted-average method.

In the last section we computed the equivalent units of production for materials and for conversion at Double Diamond Skis. In this section we will compute the cost per equivalent unit for materials and for conversion. We will then use these costs to value ending work in process and finished goods inventories. Exhibit 4–7 displays all of the data concerning May's operations in the Shaping and Milling Department that we will need to complete these tasks.

### Cost per Equivalent Unit—Weighted-Average Method

In the weighted-average method, the cost per equivalent unit is computed as follows:

WEIGHTED-AVERAGE METHOD
(a separate calculation is made for each cost category in each processing department)

$$\text{Cost per equivalent unit} = \frac{\text{Cost of beginning work in process inventory} + \text{Cost added during the period}}{\text{Equivalent units of production}}$$

**EXHIBIT 4–7**
Shaping and Milling Department Data for May Operations

| | |
|---|---|
| Work in process, beginning: | |
| Units in process | 200 |
| Completion with respect to materials | 55% |
| Completion with respect to conversion | 30% |
| Costs in the beginning inventory: | |
| Materials cost | $ 9,600 |
| Conversion cost | 5,575 |
| Total cost in the beginning inventory | $15,175 |
| Units started into production during the period | 5,000 |
| Units completed and transferred out | 4,800 |
| Costs added to production during the period: | |
| Materials cost | $368,600 |
| Conversion cost | 350,900 |
| Total cost added in the department | $719,500 |
| Work in process, ending: | |
| Units in process | 400 |
| Completion with respect to materials | 40% |
| Completion with respect to conversion | 25% |

Note that the numerator is the sum of the cost of beginning work in process inventory and of the cost added during the period. Thus, the weighted-average method blends together costs from the prior and current periods. That is why it is called the weighted-average method; it averages together units and costs from both the prior and current periods.

The costs per equivalent unit for materials and for conversion are computed below for the Shaping and Milling Department for May:

| Shaping and Milling Department<br>Costs per Equivalent Unit | Materials | Conversion |
|---|---|---|
| Cost of beginning work in process inventory | $ 9,600 | $ 5,575 |
| Costs added during the period | 368,600 | 350,900 |
| Total cost (a) | $378,200 | $356,475 |
| Equivalent units of production (see Exhibit 4–5) (b) | 4,960 | 4,900 |
| Cost per equivalent unit (a) ÷ (b) | $76.25 | $72.75 |

## Applying Costs—Weighted-Average Method

**LEARNING OBJECTIVE 4**
Assign costs to units using the weighted-average method.

The costs per equivalent unit are used to value units in ending inventory and units that are transferred to the next department. For example, each unit transferred out of Double Diamond's Shaping and Milling Department to the Graphics Application Department, as depicted in Exhibit 4–4, will carry with it a cost of $149.00 ($76.25 for materials cost and $72.75 for conversion cost). Because 4,800 units were transferred out in May to the next department, the total cost assigned to those units would be $715,200 (= 4,800 units × $149.00 per unit).

A complete accounting of the costs of both ending work in process inventory and the units transferred out appears below:

**Shaping and Milling Department**
**Costs of Ending Work in Process Inventory and the Units Transferred Out**

| | Materials | Conversion | Total |
|---|---|---|---|
| Ending work in process inventory: | | | |
| Equivalent units of production (materials: 400 units × 40% complete; conversion: 400 units × 25% complete) (a) ....................... | 160 | 100 | |
| Cost per equivalent unit (see above) (b).............. | $76.25 | $72.75 | |
| Cost of ending work in process inventory (a) × (b) | $12,200 | $7,275 | $19,475 |
| Units completed and transferred out: | | | |
| Units transferred to the next department (a)......... | 4,800 | 4,800 | |
| Cost per equivalent unit (see above) (b) ............. | $76.25 | $72.75 | |
| Cost of units transferred out (a) × (b) ................. | $366,000 | $349,200 | $715,200 |

In each case, the equivalent units are multiplied by the cost per equivalent unit to determine the cost assigned to the units. This is done for each cost category—in this case, materials and conversion. The equivalent units for the units completed and transferred out are simply the number of units transferred to the next department because they would not have been transferred unless they were complete.

## Cost Reconciliation Report

**LEARNING OBJECTIVE 5**

Prepare a cost reconciliation report.

The costs assigned to ending work in process inventory and to the units transferred out reconcile with the costs we started with in Exhibit 4–7 as shown below:

**Shaping and Milling Department**
**Cost Reconciliation**

| | |
|---|---|
| Costs to be accounted for: | |
| Cost of beginning work in process inventory (Exhibit 4–7)...................... | $ 15,175 |
| Costs added to production during the period (Exhibit 4–7) ................... | 719,500 |
| Total cost to be accounted for.............................................................. | $734,675 |
| Costs accounted for as follows: | |
| Cost of ending work in process inventory (see above)........................... | $ 19,475 |
| Cost of units transferred out (see above)................................................ | 715,200 |
| Total cost accounted for.......................................................................... | $734,675 |

The $715,200 cost of the units transferred to the next department, Graphics Application, will be accounted for in that department as "costs transferred in." It will be treated in the process costing system as just another category of costs like materials or conversion costs. The only difference is that the costs transferred in will always be 100% complete with respect to the work done in the Graphics Applications Department. Costs are passed on from one department to the next in this fashion, until they reach the last processing department, Finishing and Pairing. When the products are completed in this last department, their costs are transferred to finished goods.

## HELPFUL HINT

To help you understand the logic of a cost reconciliation report, imagine that you have a non-interest bearing checking account with a balance on March 1 of $200. Also, assume that during March you earned paychecks totaling $1,000. On March 31, you would have $1,200 to be accounted for. Each of these $1,200 dollars must be accounted for at the end of the month in one of two ways. Either it remains in your checking account as of March 31 or it has been transferred out during the month (perhaps to your landlord, to the supermarket, or to your savings account). The ending balance in your checking account plus the total amount of cash transferred out during the month must equal $1,200.

The same concepts apply to the cost reconciliation report in this chapter. The cost of beginning work in process inventory plus the costs added to production during the period equals the total cost to be accounted for. The cost of ending work in process inventory plus the cost of units transferred out equals the total cost accounted for. The total cost to be accounted for must always equal the total cost accounted for.

## CONCEPT CHECK

1. Beginning work in process includes 400 units that are 20% complete with respect to conversion and 30% complete with respect to materials. Ending work in process includes 200 units that are 40% complete with respect to conversion and 50% complete with respect to materials. If 2,000 units were started during the period, what are the equivalent units of production for the period according to the weighted-average method?
   a. Conversion equivalent units = 2,280 units; Material equivalent units = 2,100 units
   b. Conversion equivalent units = 1,980 units; Material equivalent units = 2,080 units
   c. Conversion equivalent units = 2,480 units; Material equivalent units = 1,980 units
   d. Conversion equivalent units = 2,280 units; Material equivalent units = 2,300 units
2. Assume the same facts as above in Concept Check 1. Also, assume that $9,900 of material costs and $14,880 of conversion costs were in the beginning inventory and $180,080 of materials and $409,200 of conversion costs were added to production during the period. What is the total cost per equivalent unit using the weighted-average method?
   a. $268.60
   b. $267.85
   c. $280.00
   d. $265.00

## SUMMARY

**LO1 Record the flow of materials, labor, and overhead through a process costing system.**

The journal entries to record the flow of costs in process costing are basically the same as in job-order costing. Direct materials costs are debited to Work in Process when the materials are released for use in production. Direct labor costs are debited to Work in Process as incurred. Manufacturing overhead costs are applied to Work in Process by debiting Work in Process. Costs are accumulated by department in process costing and by job in job-order costing.

**LO2 Compute the equivalent units of production using the weighted-average method.**
To compute unit costs for a department, the department's output in terms of equivalent units must be determined. In the weighted-average method, the equivalent units for a period are the sum of the units transferred out of the department during the period and the equivalent units in ending work in process inventory at the end of the period.

**LO3 Compute the cost per equivalent unit using the weighted-average method.**
The cost per equivalent unit for a particular cost category in a department is computed by dividing the sum of the cost of beginning work in process inventory and the cost added during the period by the equivalent units of production for the period.

**LO4 Assign costs to units using the weighted-average method.**
The cost per equivalent unit is used to value units in ending inventory and units transferred to the next department. The cost assigned to ending inventory is determined by multiplying the cost per equivalent unit by the equivalent units in ending inventory. The cost assigned to the units transferred to the next department is determined by multiplying the cost per equivalent unit by the number of units transferred.

**LO5 Prepare a cost reconciliation report.**
The costs to be accounted for consist of beginning work in process inventory plus the cost added to work in process. These costs must equal the cost of ending work in process inventory plus the cost of the units transferred out.

## GUIDANCE ANSWER TO DECISION POINT

**Writing Term Papers (p. 166)**
Each complete paper is five pages long and, by assumption, each page requires the same time and effort to write. Therefore, the time and effort that went into writing one incomplete two-page paper and one incomplete three-page paper could have been used to write one complete five-page paper. Added to the two complete papers that were turned in, this would have resulted in three complete papers.

## GUIDANCE ANSWERS TO CONCEPT CHECKS

1. **Choice d.** Material equivalent units are 2,200 units completed and transferred to the next department plus 100 equivalent units in ending work in process inventory (200 units × 50%). Conversion equivalent units are 2,200 units completed and transferred to the next department plus 80 equivalent units in ending work in process inventory (200 units × 40%).
2. **Choice a.** ($189,980 ÷ 2,300 equivalent units) + ($424,080 ÷ 2,280 equivalent units) = $268.60.

## REVIEW PROBLEM: PROCESS COST FLOWS AND COSTING UNITS

Luxguard Home Paint Company produces exterior latex paint, which it sells in one-gallon containers. The company has two processing departments—Base Fab and Finishing. White paint, which is used as a base for all the company's paints, is mixed from raw ingredients in the Base Fab Department. Pigments are then added to the basic white paint, the pigmented paint is squirted under pressure into one-gallon containers, and the containers are labeled and packed for shipping in the Finishing Department. Information relating to the company's operations for April follows:

a. Issued raw materials for use in production: Base Fab Department, $851,000; and Finishing Department, $629,000.
b. Incurred direct labor costs: Base Fab Department, $330,000; and Finishing Department, $270,000.

c. Applied manufacturing overhead cost: Base Fab Department, $665,000; and Finishing Department, $405,000.
d. Transferred basic white paint from the Base Fab Department to the Finishing Department, $1,850,000.
e. Transferred paint that had been prepared for shipping from the Finishing Department to Finished Goods, $3,200,000.

***Required:***

1. Prepare journal entries to record items (a) through (e) above.
2. Post the journal entries from (1) above to T-accounts. The balance in the Base Fab Department's Work in Process account on April 1 was $150,000; the balance in the Finishing Department's Work in Process account was $70,000. After posting entries to the T-accounts, find the ending balance in each department's Work in Process account.
3. Determine the cost of ending work in process inventories and of units transferred out of the Base Fab Department in April. The following additional information is available regarding production in the Base Fab Department during April:

| | |
|---|---|
| **Production data:** | |
| Units (gallons) in process, April 1: materials 100% complete; labor and overhead 60% complete | 30,000 |
| Units (gallons) started into production during April | 420,000 |
| Units (gallons) completed and transferred to the Finishing Department | 370,000 |
| Units (gallons) in process, April 30: materials 50% complete; labor and overhead 25% complete | 80,000 |
| **Cost data:** | |
| Work in process inventory, April 1: | |
| Materials | $ 92,000 |
| Labor | 21,000 |
| Overhead | 37,000 |
| Total cost of work in process | $150,000 |
| Cost added during April: | |
| Materials | $ 851,000 |
| Labor | 330,000 |
| Overhead | 665,000 |
| Total cost added during April | $1,846,000 |

4. Prepare a cost reconciliation report for April.

**Solution to Review Problem**

| | | | | |
|---|---|---|---|---|
| 1. | a. | Work in Process—Base Fab Department | 851,000 | |
| | | Work in Process—Finishing Department | 629,000 | |
| | | Raw Materials | | 1,480,000 |
| | b. | Work in Process—Base Fab Department | 330,000 | |
| | | Work in Process—Finishing Department | 270,000 | |
| | | Salaries and Wages Payable | | 600,000 |
| | c. | Work in Process—Base Fab Department | 665,000 | |
| | | Work in Process—Finishing Department | 405,000 | |
| | | Manufacturing Overhead | | 1,070,000 |
| | d. | Work in Process—Finishing Department | 1,850,000 | |
| | | Work in Process—Base Fab Department | | 1,850,000 |
| | e. | Finished Goods | 3,200,000 | |
| | | Work in Process—Finishing Department | | 3,200,000 |

2.

**Raw Materials**

| | | | |
|---|---|---|---|
| Bal. | XXX | (a) | 1,480,000 |

**Salaries and Wages Payable**

| | | | |
|---|---|---|---|
| | | (b) | 600,000 |

**Work in Process—Base Fab Department**

| | | | |
|---|---|---|---|
| Bal. | 150,000 | (d) | 1,850,000 |
| (a) | 851,000 | | |
| (b) | 330,000 | | |
| (c) | 665,000 | | |
| Bal. | 146,000 | | |

**Manufacturing Overhead**

| | | | |
|---|---|---|---|
| (Various actual costs) | | (c) | 1,070,000 |

**Work in Process—Finishing Department**

| | | | |
|---|---|---|---|
| Bal. | 70,000 | (e) | 3,200,000 |
| (a) | 629,000 | | |
| (b) | 270,000 | | |
| (c) | 405,000 | | |
| (d) | 1,850,000 | | |
| Bal. | 24,000 | | |

**Finished Goods**

| | | | |
|---|---|---|---|
| Bal. | XXX | | |
| (e) | 3,200,000 | | |

3. First, we must compute the equivalent units of production for each cost category:

**Base Fab Department**
**Equivalent Units of Production**

| | Materials | Labor | Overhead |
|---|---|---|---|
| Units transferred to the next department | 370,000 | 370,000 | 370,000 |
| Ending work in process inventory (materials: 80,000 units × 50% complete; labor: 80,000 units × 25% complete; overhead: 80,000 units × 25% complete) | 40,000 | 20,000 | 20,000 |
| Equivalent units of production | 410,000 | 390,000 | 390,000 |

Then we must compute the cost per equivalent unit for each cost category:

**Base Fab Department**
**Costs per Equivalent Unit**

| | Materials | Labor | Overhead |
|---|---|---|---|
| Costs: | | | |
| Cost of beginning work in process inventory | $ 92,000 | $ 21,000 | $ 37,000 |
| Costs added during the period | 851,000 | 330,000 | 665,000 |
| Total cost (a) | $943,000 | $351,000 | $702,000 |
| Equivalent units of production (b) | 410,000 | 390,000 | 390,000 |
| Cost per equivalent unit (a) ÷ (b) | $2.30 | $0.90 | $1.80 |

The costs per equivalent unit can then be applied to the units in ending work in process inventory and the units transferred out as follows:

| Base Fab Department<br>Costs of Ending Work in Process Inventory and the Units Transferred Out | Materials | Labor | Overhead | Total |
|---|---|---|---|---|
| *Ending work in process inventory:* | | | | |
| Equivalent units of production | 40,000 | 20,000 | 20,000 | |
| Cost per equivalent unit | $2.30 | $0.90 | $1.80 | |
| Cost of ending work in process inventory | $92,000 | $18,000 | $36,000 | $146,000 |
| *Units completed and transferred out:* | | | | |
| Units transferred to the next department | 370,000 | 370,000 | 370,000 | |
| Cost per equivalent unit | $2.30 | $0.90 | $1.80 | |
| Cost of units completed and transferred out | $851,000 | $333,000 | $666,000 | $1,850,000 |

4.

| Base Fab Department<br>Cost Reconciliation | |
|---|---|
| *Costs to be accounted for:* | |
| Cost of beginning work in process inventory | $ 150,000 |
| Costs added to production during the period | 1,846,000 |
| Total cost to be accounted for | $1,996,000 |
| *Costs accounted for as follows:* | |
| Cost of ending work in process inventory | $ 146,000 |
| Cost of units transferred out | 1,850,000 |
| Total cost accounted for | $1,996,000 |

## GLOSSARY

**Conversion cost** Direct labor cost plus manufacturing overhead cost. (p. 165)

**Equivalent units** The product of the number of partially completed units and their percentage of completion with respect to a particular cost. Equivalent units are the number of complete whole units that could be obtained from the materials and effort contained in partially completed units. (p. 164)

**Equivalent units of production (weighted-average method)** The units transferred to the next department (or to finished goods) during the period plus the equivalent units in the department's ending work in process inventory. (p. 164)

**FIFO method** A process costing method in which equivalent units and unit costs relate only to work done during the current period. (p. 164)

**Process costing** A costing method used when essentially homogeneous products are produced on a continuous basis. (p. 158)

**Processing department** An organizational unit where work is performed on a product and where materials, labor, or overhead costs are added to the product. (p. 159)

**Weighted-average method** A process costing method that blends together units and costs from both the current and prior periods. (p. 164)

## QUESTIONS

**4–1** Under what conditions would it be appropriate to use a process costing system?

**4–2** In what ways are job-order and process costing similar?

**4–3** Why is cost accumulation simpler in a process costing system than it is in a job-order costing system?

**4–4** How many Work in Process accounts are maintained in a company that uses process costing?

4–5 Assume that a company has two processing departments—Mixing followed by Firing. Prepare a journal entry to show a transfer of work in process from the Mixing Department to the Firing Department.

4–6 Assume that a company has two processing departments—Mixing followed by Firing. Explain what costs might be added to the Firing Department's Work in Process account during a period.

4–7 What is meant by the term *equivalent units of production* when the weighted-average method is used?

4–8 Watkins Trophies, Inc., produces thousands of medallions made of bronze, silver, and gold. The medallions are identical except for the materials used in their manufacture. What costing system would you advise the company to use?

**Multiple-choice questions are provided on the text website at www.mhhe.com/brewer6e.**

## APPLYING EXCEL

LO2, LO3, LO4, LO5

**Available with McGraw-Hill's *Connect® Accounting.***

The Excel worksheet form that appears below is to be used to recreate the extended example on pages 166–168. Download the workbook containing this form from the Online Learning Center at www.mhhe.com/brewer6e. *On the website you will also receive instructions about how to use this worksheet form.*

| | A | B | C | D | E |
|---|---|---|---|---|---|
| 1 | Chapter 4: Applying Excel | | | | |
| 2 | | | | | |
| 3 | **Data** | | | | |
| 4 | Work in process, beginning: | | | | |
| 5 | Units in process | 200 | | | |
| 6 | Completion with respect to materials | 55% | | | |
| 7 | Completion with respect to conversion | 30% | | | |
| 8 | Costs in the beginning inventory: | | | | |
| 9 | Materials cost | $9,600 | | | |
| 10 | Conversion cost | $5,575 | | | |
| 11 | Units started into production during the period | 5,000 | | | |
| 12 | Costs added to production during the period: | | | | |
| 13 | Materials cost | $368,600 | | | |
| 14 | Conversion cost | $350,900 | | | |
| 15 | Work in process, ending: | | | | |
| 16 | Units in process | 400 | | | |
| 17 | Completion with respect to materials | 40% | | | |
| 18 | Completion with respect to conversion | 25% | | | |
| 19 | | | | | |
| 20 | *Enter a formula into each of the cells marked with a ? below* | | | | |
| 21 | | | | | |
| 22 | **Weighted = average method:** | | | | |
| 23 | | | | | |
| 24 | ***Equivalent Units of Production*** | | | | |
| 25 | | Materials | Conversion | | |
| 26 | Units transferred to the next department | ? | ? | | |
| 27 | Ending work in process: | | | | |
| 28 | Materials | ? | | | |
| 29 | Conversion | | ? | | |
| 30 | Equivalent units of production | ? | ? | | |
| 31 | | | | | |
| 32 | ***Costs per Equivalent Unit*** | | | | |
| 33 | | Materials | Conversion | | |
| 34 | Cost of beginning work in process inventory | ? | ? | | |
| 35 | Costs added during the period | ? | ? | | |
| 36 | Total cost | ? | ? | | |
| 37 | Equivalent units of production | ? | ? | | |
| 38 | Cost per equivalent unit | ? | ? | | |
| 39 | | | | | |
| 40 | ***Costs of Ending Work in Process Inventory and the Units Transferred Out*** | | | | |
| 41 | | Materials | Conversion | Total | |
| 42 | Ending work in process inventory: | | | | |
| 43 | Equivalent units of production | ? | ? | | |
| 44 | Cost per equivalent unit | ? | ? | | |
| 45 | Cost of ending work in process inventory | ? | ? | ? | |
| 46 | | | | | |
| 47 | Units completed and transferred out: | | | | |
| 48 | Units transferred to the next department | ? | ? | | |
| 49 | Cost per equivalent unit | ? | ? | | |
| 50 | Cost of units transferred out | ? | ? | ? | |
| 51 | | | | | |
| 52 | ***Cost Reconciliation*** | | | | |
| 53 | Costs to be accounted for: | | | | |
| 54 | Cost of beginning work in process inventory | ? | | | |
| 55 | Costs added to production during the period | ? | | | |
| 56 | Total cost to be accounted for | ? | | | |
| 57 | Costs to be accounted for as follows: | | | | |
| 58 | Cost of ending work in process inventory | ? | | | |
| 59 | Cost of units transferred out | ? | | | |
| 60 | Total cost accounted for | ? | | | |
| 61 | | | | | |

You should proceed to the requirements below only after completing your worksheet.

***Required:***

1. Check your worksheet by changing the beginning work in process inventory to 100 units, the units started into production during the period to 2,500 units, and the units in ending work in process inventory to 200 units, keeping all of the other data the same as in the original example. If your worksheet is operating properly, the cost per equivalent unit for materials should now be $152.50 and the cost per equivalent unit for conversion should be $145.50. If you do not get these answers, find the errors in your worksheet and correct them.

   How much is the total cost of the units transferred out? Did it change? Why or why not?
2. Enter the following data from a different company into your worksheet:

| | |
|---|---|
| Work in process, beginning: | |
| Units in process | 200 |
| Completion with respect to materials | 100% |
| Completion with respect to conversion | 20% |
| Costs in the beginning inventory: | |
| Materials cost | $2,000 |
| Conversion cost | $800 |
| Units started into production during the period | 1,800 |
| Costs added to production during the period: | |
| Materials cost | $18,400 |
| Conversion cost | $38,765 |
| Work in process, ending: | |
| Units in process | 100 |
| Completion with respect to materials | 100% |
| Completion with respect to conversion | 30% |

   What is the cost of the units transferred out?
3. What happens to the cost of the units transferred out in part (2) above if the percentage completion with respect to conversion for the beginning inventory is changed from 20% to 40% and everything else remains the same? What happens to the cost per equivalent unit for conversion? Explain.

connect ACCOUNTING

## THE FOUNDATIONAL 15

**Available with McGraw-Hill's *Connect*® *Accounting*.**

LO1, LO2, LO3, LO4, LO5

Clopack Company manufactures one product that goes through one processing department called Mixing. All raw materials are introduced at the start of work in the Mixing Department. The company uses the weighted-average method to account for units and costs. Its Work in Process T-account for the Mixing Department for June follows (all forthcoming questions pertain to June):

**Work in Process—Mixing Department**

| | | | |
|---|---|---|---|
| June 1 balance | 28,000 | Completed and transferred to Finished Goods | ? |
| Materials | 120,000 | | |
| Direct labor | 79,500 | | |
| Overhead | 97,000 | | |
| June 30 balance | ? | | |

The June 1 work in process inventory consisted of 5,000 pounds with $16,000 in materials cost and $12,000 in conversion cost. The June 1 work in process inventory was 100% complete with respect to materials and 50% complete with respect to conversion. During June 37,500 pounds were started into production. The June 30 work in process inventory consisted of 8,000 pounds that were 100% complete with respect to materials and 40% complete with respect to conversion.

1. Prepare the journal entries to record the raw materials used in production and the direct labor cost incurred.
2. Prepare the journal entry to record the overhead cost applied to production.

3. How many units were completed and transferred to finished goods during the period?
4. Compute the equivalent units of production for materials.
5. Compute the equivalent units of production for conversion.
6. What is the amount of the cost of beginning work in process inventory plus the cost added during the period for materials?
7. What is the amount of the cost of beginning work in process inventory plus the cost added during the period for conversion?
8. What is the cost per equivalent unit for materials?
9. What is the cost per equivalent unit for conversion?
10. What is the cost of ending work in process for materials?
11. What is the cost of ending work in process for conversion?
12. What is the cost of materials transferred to finished goods?
13. What is the amount of conversion cost transferred to finished goods?
14. Prepare the journal entry to record the transfer of costs from Work in Process to Finished Goods.
15. What is the total cost to be accounted for? What is the total cost accounted for?

## EXERCISES

connect ACCOUNTING

**All applicable exercises are available with McGraw-Hill's *Connect® Accounting.***

### EXERCISE 4–1 Process Costing Journal Entries [LO1]

Arizona Brick Corporation produces bricks in two processing departments—Molding and Firing. Information relating to the company's operations in March follows:

a. Raw materials were issued for use in production: Molding Department, $28,000; and Firing Department, $5,000.
b. Direct labor costs were incurred: Molding Department, $18,000; and Firing Department, $5,000.
c. Manufacturing overhead was applied: Molding Department, $24,000; and Firing Department, $37,000.
d. Unfired, molded bricks were transferred from the Molding Department to the Firing Department. According to the company's process costing system, the cost of the unfired, molded bricks was $67,000.
e. Finished bricks were transferred from the Firing Department to the finished goods warehouse. According to the company's process costing system, the cost of the finished bricks was $108,000.
f. Finished bricks were sold to customers. According to the company's process costing system, the cost of the finished bricks sold was $106,000.

***Required:***

Prepare journal entries to record items (a) through (f) above.

### EXERCISE 4–2 Computation of Equivalent Units—Weighted-Average Method [LO2]

TAKE TWO

Lindex Company uses a process costing system. The following data are available for one department for October:

Work in process, October 1: materials 20% complete

| | | Percent Completed | |
|---|---|---|---|
| | Units | Materials | Conversion |
| Work in process, October 1 ........................... | 50,000 | 90% | 60% |
| Work in process, October 31 ......................... | 30,000 | 70% | 50% |

The department started 390,000 units into production during the month and transferred 410,000 completed units to the next department.

***Required:***

Compute the equivalent units of production for October, assuming that the company uses the weighted-average method of accounting for units and costs.

**EXERCISE 4–3 Cost Per Equivalent Unit—Weighted-Average Method [LO3]**

Billinstaff Industries uses the weighted-average method in its process costing system. Data for the Assembly Department for May appear below:

| | Materials | Labor | Overhead |
|---|---|---|---|
| Work in process, May 1 ........................ | $14,550 | $23,620 | $118,100 |
| Cost added during May ........................ | $88,350 | $14,330 | $71,650 |
| Equivalent units of production................ | 1,200 | 1,100 | 1,100 |

TAKE TWO

Cost added during May, labor: $16,530

***Required:***
1. Compute the cost per equivalent unit for materials, for labor, and for overhead.
2. Compute the total cost per equivalent whole unit.

**EXERCISE 4–4 Applying Costs to Units—Weighted-Average Method [LO4]**

Data concerning a recent period's activity in the Prep Department, the first processing department in a company that uses process costing, appear below:

| | Materials | Conversion |
|---|---|---|
| Equivalent units of production in ending work in process............. | 300 | 100 |
| Cost per equivalent unit............................................................. | $31.56 | $9.32 |

TAKE TWO

Cost per equivalent unit, conversion: $10.00

A total of 1,300 units were completed and transferred to the next processing department during the period.

***Required:***

Compute the cost of the units transferred to the next department during the period and the cost of ending work in process inventory.

**EXERCISE 4–5 Cost Reconciliation Report—Weighted-Average Method [LO5]**

Lech-Zurs Bakerie Corporation uses a process costing system. The Baking Department is one of the processing departments in its apple strudel manufacturing facility. In July in the Baking Department, the cost of beginning work in process inventory was $4,830, the cost of ending work in process inventory was $1,120, and the cost added to production was $25,650.

TAKE TWO

Cost of ending work in process inventory: $1,300

***Required:***

Prepare a cost reconciliation report for the Baking Department for July.

**EXERCISE 4–6 Equivalent Units and Cost per Equivalent Unit—Weighted-Average Method [LO2, LO3]**

Kalox, Inc., manufactures an antacid product that passes through two departments. Data for May for the first department follow:

| | Gallons | Materials | Labor | Overhead |
|---|---|---|---|---|
| Work in process, May 1.......... | 80,000 | $68,600 | $30,000 | $48,000 |
| Gallons started in process...... | 760,000 | | | |
| Gallons transferred out............ | 790,000 | | | |
| Work in process, May 31........ | 50,000 | | | |
| Cost added during May.......... | | $907,200 | $370,000 | $592,000 |

TAKE TWO

Work in process, May 1: 70,000 gallons; gallons transferred out: 780,000

The beginning work in process inventory was 80% complete with respect to materials and 75% complete with respect to labor and overhead. The ending work in process inventory was 60% complete with respect to materials and 20% complete with respect to labor and overhead.

***Required:***

Assume that the company uses the weighted-average method of accounting for units and costs.
1. Compute the equivalent units for May's activity for the first department.
2. Determine the costs per equivalent unit for May.

**EXERCISE 4–7 Comprehensive Exercise; Second Production Department—Weighted-Average Method [LO2, LO3, LO4, LO5]**

Papyrutech Corporation produces fine papers in three production departments—Pulping, Drying, and Finishing. In the Pulping Department, raw materials such as wood fiber and rag cotton are mechanically and chemically treated to separate their fibers. The result is a thick slurry of fibers. In the Drying Department, the wet fibers transferred from the Pulping Department are laid down on porous webs, pressed to remove excess liquid, and dried in ovens. In the Finishing Department, the dried paper is coated, cut, and spooled onto reels. The company uses the weighted-average method in its process costing system. Data for October for the Drying Department follow:

| | | Percent Completed | |
|---|---|---|---|
| | Units | Pulping | Conversion |
| Work in process inventory, October 1 | 4,000 | 100% | 60% |
| Work in process inventory, October 31 | 6,000 | 100% | 75% |
| Pulping cost in work in process inventory, October 1 | | | $1,500 |
| Conversion cost in work in process inventory, October 1 | | | $400 |
| Units transferred to the next production department | | | 146,000 |
| Pulping cost added during October | | | $59,300 |
| Conversion cost added during October | | | $22,100 |

No materials are added in the Drying Department. Pulping cost represents the costs of the wet fibers transferred in from the Pulping Department. Wet fiber is processed in the Drying Department in batches; each unit in the above table is a batch, and one batch of wet fibers produces a set amount of dried paper that is passed on to the Finishing Department.

***Required:***

1. Determine the equivalent units for October for pulping and conversion.
2. Compute the costs per equivalent unit for October for pulping and conversion.
3. Determine the total cost of ending work in process inventory and the total cost of units transferred to the Finishing Department in October.
4. Prepare a cost reconciliation report for the Drying Department for October.

**EXERCISE 4–8 Process Costing Journal Entries [LO1]**

Schneider Brot is a bread-baking company located in Aachen, Germany, near the Dutch border. The company uses a process costing system for its single product—a popular pumpernickel bread. Schneider Brot has two processing departments—Mixing and Baking. The T-accounts below show the flow of costs through the two departments in April (all amounts are in the currency euros):

**Work in Process—Mixing**

| | | | |
|---|---|---|---|
| Balance 4/1 | 10,000 | Transferred out | 760,000 |
| Direct materials | 330,000 | | |
| Direct labor | 260,000 | | |
| Overhead | 190,000 | | |

**Work in Process—Baking**

| | | | |
|---|---|---|---|
| Balance 4/1 | 20,000 | Transferred out | 980,000 |
| Transferred in | 760,000 | | |
| Direct labor | 120,000 | | |
| Overhead | 90,000 | | |

***Required:***

Prepare journal entries showing the flow of costs through the two processing departments during April.

**EXERCISE 4–9 Cost Assignment; Cost Reconciliation—Weighted-Average Method [LO2, LO4, LO5]**

Kenton Industrial Corporation uses the weighted-average method in its process costing system. During April, the Baker Assembly Department completed its processing of 18,000 units and transferred them to the next department. The cost of beginning inventory and the costs added during April amounted to $855,000 in total. The ending inventory in April consisted of 1,500 units, which were 90% complete with respect to materials and 40% complete with respect to labor and overhead. The costs per equivalent unit for the month were as follows:

| | Materials | Labor | Overhead |
|---|---|---|---|
| Cost per equivalent unit | $24.00 | $7.00 | $14.00 |

TAKE TWO

Cost per equivalent unit of materials: $23.00; Total cost to be accounted for: $835,650

***Required:***

1. Compute the equivalent units of materials, labor, and overhead in the ending inventory for the month.
2. Compute the cost of ending inventory and of the units transferred to the next department for April.
3. Prepare a cost reconciliation for April. (Note: You will not be able to break the cost to be accounted for into the cost of beginning inventory and costs added during the month.)

**EXERCISE 4–10 Equivalent Units—Weighted-Average Method [LO2]**

Societe Clemeau, a company located in Lyons, France, manufactures cement for the construction industry. Data relating to the kilograms of cement processed through the Mixing Department, the first department in the production process, are provided below for May:

| | | Percent Completed | |
|---|---|---|---|
| | Kilograms of Cement | Materials | Conversion |
| Work in process, May 1 | 80,000 | 80% | 20% |
| Work in process, May 31 | 50,000 | 40% | 10% |
| Started into production during May | 300,000 | | |

TAKE TWO

Started into production during May: 270,000

***Required:***

1. Compute the number of kilograms of cement completed and transferred out of the Mixing Department during May.
2. Compute the equivalent units of production for materials and for conversion for May.

**EXERCISE 4–11 Equivalent Units and Cost per Equivalent Unit—Weighted-Average Method [LO2, LO3, LO4]**

Solex Company produces a high-quality insulation material that passes through two production processes. Data for June for the first process follow:

| | Units | Completion with Respect to Materials | Completion with Respect to Conversion |
|---|---|---|---|
| Work in process inventory, June 1 | 60,000 | 75% | 40% |
| Work in process inventory, June 30 | 40,000 | 50% | 25% |
| Materials cost in work in process inventory, June 1 | | $56,600 | |
| Conversion cost in work in process inventory, June 1 | | $14,900 | |
| Units started into production | | 280,000 | |
| Units transferred to the next process | | 300,000 | |
| Materials cost added during June | | $385,000 | |
| Conversion cost added during June | | $214,500 | |

***Required:***

1. Assume that the company uses the weighted-average method of accounting for units and costs. Determine the equivalent units for June for the first process.
2. Compute the costs per equivalent unit for June for the first process.
3. Determine the total cost of ending work in process inventory and the total cost of units transferred to the next process in June.

TAKE TWO

**EXERCISE 4–12 Equivalent Units—Weighted-Average Method [LO2]**

Gulf Fisheries, Inc., processes tuna for various distributors. Two departments are involved—Cleaning and Packing. Data relating to pounds of tuna processed in the Cleaning Department during May are given below:

Work in process, May 1: 40,000 pounds of tuna

| | Pounds of Tuna | Percent Completed: Materials | Percent Completed: Labor and Overhead |
|---|---|---|---|
| Work in process, May 1 .............. | 30,000 | 100% | 55% |
| Work in process, May 31 ............ | 20,000 | 100% | 90% |

A total of 480,000 pounds of tuna were started into processing during May. All materials are added at the beginning of processing in the Cleaning Department.

***Required:***

Compute the equivalent units for May for both materials and labor and overhead assuming that the company uses the weighted-average method of accounting for units.

## PROBLEMS

connect ACCOUNTING

Alternate problem set is available on the text website and in *Connect® Accounting.*

CHECK FIGURE
(1) Conversion: 390,000 equivalent units;
(3) Ending work in process: $45,000.

**All applicable problems are available with McGraw-Hill's *Connect® Accounting*.**

**PROBLEM 4–13A Comprehensive Problem Weighted-Average Method [LO2, LO3, LO4, LO5]**

The PVC Company manufactures a high-quality plastic pipe that goes through three processing stages prior to completion.

Information on work in the first department, Cooking, is given below for May:

| | |
|---|---|
| Production data: | |
| Pounds in process, May 1: materials 100% complete; conversion 90% complete ....................................... | 70,000 |
| Pounds started into production during May................................. | 350,000 |
| Pounds completed and transferred to the next department .......... | ? |
| Pounds in process, May 31: materials 75% complete; conversion 25% complete ....................................................... | 40,000 |
| Cost data: | |
| Work in process inventory, May 1: | |
| Materials cost ........................................................................... | $86,000 |
| Conversion cost........................................................................... | $36,000 |
| Cost added during May: | |
| Materials cost ........................................................................... | $447,000 |
| Conversion cost........................................................................... | $198,000 |

The company uses the weighted-average method.

***Required:***
1. Compute the equivalent units of production.
2. Compute the costs per equivalent unit for the month.
3. Determine the cost of ending work in process inventory and of the units transferred out to the next department.
4. Prepare a cost reconciliation report for the month.

**PROBLEM 4–14A Comprehensive Problem—Weighted-Average Method [LO2, LO3, LO4, LO5]**

CHECK FIGURE
(3) Ending work in process: $63,200

Honeybutter, Inc., manufactures a product that goes through two departments prior to completion—the Mixing Department followed by the Packaging Department. The following information is available about work in the first department, the Mixing Department, during June.

| | | Percent Completed | |
|---|---|---|---|
| | Units | Materials | Conversion |
| Work in process, beginning | 70,000 | 70% | 40% |
| Started into production | 460,000 | | |
| Completed and transferred out | 450,000 | | |
| Work in process, ending | 80,000 | 75% | 25% |
| Work in process, beginning | | $36,550 | $13,500 |
| Cost added during June | | $391,850 | $287,300 |

***Required:***
Assume that the company uses the weighted-average method.
1. Determine the equivalent units for June for the Mixing Department.
2. Compute the costs per equivalent unit for June for the Mixing Department.
3. Determine the total cost of ending work in process inventory and the total cost of units transferred to the Packaging Department.
4. Prepare a cost reconciliation report for the Mixing Department for June.

**PROBLEM 4–15A Analysis of Work in Process T-account—Weighted-Average Method [LO1, LO2, LO3, LO4]**

eXcel

CHECK FIGURE
(3) Cost of units completed and transferred out: $567,000

Brady Products manufactures a silicone paste wax that goes through three processing departments—Cracking, Blending, and Packing. All raw materials are introduced at the start of work in the Cracking Department. The Work in Process T-account for the Cracking Department for a recent month is given below:

**Work in Process—Cracking Department**

| | | | |
|---|---|---|---|
| Inventory, May 1 | 63,700 | Completed and transferred | |
| Materials | 397,600 | to the Blending Department | ? |
| Conversion | 187,600 | | |
| Inventory, May 31 | ? | | |

The May 1 work in process inventory consisted of 35,000 pounds with $43,400 in materials cost and $20,300 in conversion cost. The May 1 work in process inventory was 100% complete with respect to materials and 80% complete with respect to conversion. During May, 280,000 pounds were started into production. The May 31 inventory consisted of 45,000 pounds that were 100% complete with respect to materials and 60% complete with respect to conversion. The company uses the weighted-average method to account for units and costs.

***Required:***
1. Determine the equivalent units of production for May.
2. Determine the costs per equivalent unit for May.
3. Determine the cost of the units completed and transferred to the Blending Department during May.

CHECK FIGURE
(2) Manufacturing overhead: $7,000 debit balance

**PROBLEM 4–16A Cost Flows [LO1]**

Nature's Way, Inc., keeps one of its production facilities busy making a perfume called Essence de la Vache. The perfume goes through two processing departments: Blending and Bottling.

The following incomplete Work in Process account is provided for the Blending Department for March:

**Work in Process—Blending**

| | | | |
|---|---|---|---|
| March 1 balance | 32,800 | Completed and transferred to Bottling (760,000 ounces) | ? |
| Materials | 147,600 | | |
| Direct labor | 73,200 | | |
| Overhead | 481,000 | | |
| March 31 balance | ? | | |

The $32,800 beginning inventory in the Blending Department consisted of the following elements: materials, $8,000; direct labor, $4,000; and overhead applied, $20,800.

Costs incurred during March in the Bottling Department were: materials used, $45,000; direct labor, $17,000; and overhead cost applied to production, $108,000.

***Required:***

1. Prepare journal entries to record the costs incurred in both the Blending Department and Bottling Department during March. Key your entries to items (a) through (g) below:
   a. Raw materials were issued for use in production.
   b. Direct labor costs were incurred.
   c. Manufacturing overhead costs for the entire factory were incurred, $596,000. (Credit Accounts Payable and use a single Manufacturing Overhead control account for the entire factory.)
   d. Manufacturing overhead was applied to production using a predetermined overhead rate.
   e. Units that were complete with respect to processing in the Blending Department were transferred to the Bottling Department, $722,000.
   f. Units that were complete with respect to processing in the Bottling Department were transferred to Finished Goods, $920,000.
   g. Completed units were sold on account for $1,400,000. The cost of goods sold was $890,000.
2. Post the journal entries from (1) above to T-accounts. The following account balances existed at the beginning of March. (The beginning balance in the Blending Department's Work in Process account is given above.)

| | |
|---|---|
| Raw Materials | $198,600 |
| Work in Process—Bottling Department | $49,000 |
| Finished Goods | $20,000 |

After posting the entries to the T-accounts, find the ending balances in the inventory accounts and the Manufacturing Overhead account.

CHECK FIGURE
(3) Ending work in process: $1,710

**PROBLEM 4–17A Comprehensive Problem; Second Production Department—Weighted-Average Method [LO2, LO3, LO4, LO5]**

Bohemian Links Inc. produces sausages in three production departments—Mixing, Casing and Curing, and Packaging. In the Mixing Department, meats are prepared and ground and then mixed with spices. The spiced meat mixture is then transferred to the Casing and Curing Department, where the mixture is force-fed into casings and then hung and cured in climate-controlled smoking chambers. In the Packaging Department, the cured sausages are sorted, packed, and labeled. The company uses the weighted-average method in its process costing system. Data for April for the Casing and Curing Department follow:

| | | Percent Completed | | |
|---|---|---|---|---|
| | Units | Mixing | Materials | Conversion |
| Work in process inventory, April 1 | 1 | 100% | 60% | 50% |
| Work in process inventory, April 30 | 1 | 100% | 20% | 10% |

| | Mixing | Materials | Conversion |
|---|---|---|---|
| Work in process inventory, April 1 | $1,640 | $26 | $105 |
| Cost added during April | $94,740 | $8,402 | $61,197 |

Mixing cost represents the costs of the spiced meat mixture transferred in from the Mixing Department. The spiced meat mixture is processed in the Casing and Curing Department in batches; each unit in the above table is a batch, and one batch of spiced meat mixture produces a set amount of sausages that are passed on to the Packaging Department. During April, 60 batches (i.e., units) were completed and transferred to the Packaging Department.

***Required:***

1. Determine the equivalent units for April for mixing, materials, and conversion.
2. Compute the costs per equivalent unit for April for mixing, materials, and conversion.
3. Determine the total cost of ending work in process inventory and the total cost of units transferred to the Packaging Department in April.
4. Prepare a cost reconciliation report for the Casing and Curing Department for April.

**PROBLEM 4–18A Interpreting a Report—Weighted-Average Method [LO2, LO3, LO4]**

CHECK FIGURE
(2) Conversion: 32,000 equivalent units

Bell Computers, Ltd., located in Liverpool, England, assembles a standardized personal computer from parts it purchases from various suppliers. The production process consists of several steps, starting with assembly of the "mother" circuit board, which contains the central processing unit. This assembly takes place in the CPU Assembly Department. The company recently hired a new accountant who prepared the following report for the department for May using the weighted-average method:

| | |
|---|---|
| Units to be accounted for: | |
| Work in process, May 1: materials 90% complete; conversion 80% complete | 5,000 |
| Started into production | 29,000 |
| Total units | 34,000 |
| Units accounted for as follows: | |
| Transferred to next department | 30,000 |
| Work in process, May 31: materials 75% complete; conversion 50% complete | 4,000 |
| Total units | 34,000 |

| Cost Reconciliation | |
|---|---|
| Cost to be accounted for: | |
| Work in process, May 1 | £ 13,400 |
| Cost added in the department | 87,800 |
| Total cost to be accounted for | £101,200 |
| Cost accounted for as follows: | |
| Work in process, May 31 | £ 8,200 |
| Transferred to next department | 93,000 |
| Total cost accounted for | £101,200 |

The company's management would like some additional information about May's operation in the CPU Assembly Department. (The currency in England is the pound, which is denoted by the symbol £.)

***Required:***

1. How many units were started and completed during May?
2. What were the equivalent units for May for materials and conversion costs?

3. What were the costs per equivalent unit for May? The following additional data are available concerning the department's costs:

| | Materials | Conversion | Total |
|---|---|---|---|
| Work in process, May 1 | £9,000 | £4,400 | £13,400 |
| Costs added during May | £57,000 | £30,800 | £87,800 |

4. Verify the accountant's ending work in process inventory figure (£8,200) given in the report.
5. The new manager of the CPU Assembly Department was asked to estimate the incremental cost of processing an additional 1,000 units through the department. He took the unit cost for an equivalent whole unit you computed in (3) above and multiplied this figure by 1,000. Will this method yield a valid estimate of incremental cost? Explain.

## BUILDING YOUR SKILLS

CHECK FIGURE
(1) Materials: $0.31 per equivalent unit; Ending work in process: $6,400

### ANALYTICAL THINKING [LO2, LO3, LO4]

Durall Company manufactures a plastic gasket that is used in automobile engines. The gaskets go through three processing departments: Mixing, Forming, and Stamping. The company's accountant (who is very inexperienced) has prepared a summary of production and costs for the Forming Department for October as follows:

| | |
|---|---|
| Forming Department costs: | |
| Work in process inventory, October 1, 8,000 units: materials 100% complete; conversion 7/8 complete | $ 22,420* |
| Costs transferred in from the Mixing Department | 81,480 |
| Material added during October (added when processing is 50% complete in the Forming Department) | 27,600 |
| Conversion costs added during October | 96,900 |
| Total departmental costs | $228,400 |
| Forming Department costs assigned to: | |
| Units completed and transferred to the Stamping Department, 100,000 units at $2.284 each | $228,400 |
| Work in process inventory, October 31, 5,000 units: conversion 2/5 complete | — |
| Total departmental costs assigned | $228,400 |

*Consists of cost transferred in, $8,820; materials cost, $3,400; and conversion costs, $10,200.

After mulling over the data above, Durall's president commented, "I can't understand what's happening here. Despite a concentrated effort at cost reduction, our unit cost actually went up in the Forming Department last month. With that kind of performance, year-end bonuses are out of the question for the people in that department."

The company uses the weighted-average method in its process costing.

***Required:***

1. Prepare a report for the Forming Department for October showing how much cost should have been assigned to the units completed and transferred to the Stamping Department and to the ending work in process inventory.
2. Explain to the president why the unit cost appearing on the report prepared by the accountant is so high.

## ETHICS CHALLENGE [LO2, LO3, LO4]

Thad Kostowski and Carol Lee are production managers in the Appliances Division of Mesger Corporation, which has several dozen plants scattered in locations throughout the world. Carol manages the plant located in Kansas City, Missouri, while Thad manages the plant in Roseville, Oregon. Production managers are paid a salary and get an additional bonus equal to 10% of their base salary if the entire division meets or exceeds its target profits for the year. The bonus is determined in March after the company's annual report has been prepared and issued to stockholders.

Late in February, Carol received a phone call from Thad that went like this:

***Thad:*** How's it going, Carol?

***Carol:*** Fine, Thad. How's it going with you?

***Thad:*** Great! I just got the preliminary profit figures for the division for last year and we are within $62,500 of making the year's target profits. All we have to do is to pull a few strings, and we'll be over the top!

***Carol:*** What do you mean?

***Thad:*** Well, one thing that would be easy to change is your estimate of the percentage completion of your ending work in process inventories.

***Carol:*** I don't know if I should do that, Thad. Those percentage completion numbers are supplied by Jean Jackson, my lead supervisor. I have always trusted her to provide us with good estimates. Besides, I have already sent the percentage completion figures to the corporate headquarters.

***Thad:*** You can always tell them there was a mistake. Think about it, Carol. All of us managers are doing as much as we can to pull this bonus out of the hat. You may not want the bonus check, but the rest of us sure could use it.

The final processing department in Carol's production facility began the year with no work in process inventories. During the year, 270,000 units were transferred in from the prior processing department and 250,000 units were completed and sold. Costs transferred in from the prior department totaled $49,221,000. No materials are added in the final processing department. A total of $16,320,000 of conversion cost was incurred in the final processing department during the year.

***Required:***

1. Jean Jackson estimated that the units in ending inventory in the final processing department were 25% complete with respect to the conversion costs of the final processing department. If this estimate of the percentage completion is used, what would be the cost of goods sold for the year?
2. Does Thad Kostowski want the estimated percentage completion to be increased or decreased? Explain why.
3. What percentage completion figure would result in increasing the reported net operating income by $62,500 over the net operating income that would be reported if the 25% figure were used?
4. Do you think Carol Lee should go along with the request to alter estimates of the percentage completion? Why or why not?

### A LOOK BACK

We provided overviews of the systems that are used to accumulate product costs in Chapters 2 (job-order costing), 3 (activity-based costing), and 4 (process costing).

### A LOOK AT THIS CHAPTER

Chapter 5 describes the basics of cost-volume-profit analysis, an essential tool for decision making. Cost-volume-profit analysis helps managers understand the interrelationships among cost, volume, and profit.

### A LOOK AHEAD

Chapter 6 contrasts variable costing and absorption costing income statements for manufacturers and it explains how the contribution format can be used to measure the profitability of business segments.

# 5 Cost-Volume-Profit Relationships

## CHAPTER OUTLINE

## DECISION FEATURE

# Moreno Turns Around the Los Angeles Angels

When Arturo Moreno bought Major League Baseball's **Los Angeles Angels** in 2003, the team was drawing 2.3 million fans and losing $5.5 million per year. Moreno immediately cut prices to attract more fans and increase profits. In his first spring training game, he reduced the price of selected tickets from $12 to $6. By increasing attendance, Moreno understood that he would sell more food and souvenirs. He dropped the price of draft beer by $2 and cut the price of baseball caps from $20 to $7.

The Angels now consistently draw about 3.4 million fans per year. This growth in attendance helped double stadium sponsorship revenue to $26 million, and it motivated the Fox Sports Network to pay the Angels $500 million to broadcast all of its games for the next ten years. Since Moreno bought the Angels, annual revenues have jumped from $127 million to $212 million, and the team's operating loss of $5.5 million has been transformed to a profit of $10.3 million.

Source: Matthew Craft, "Moreno's Math," *Forbes,* May 11, 2009, pp. 84–87.

## LEARNING OBJECTIVES

*After studying Chapter 5, you should be able to:*

**LO1** Explain how changes in activity affect contribution margin and net operating income.

**LO2** Prepare and interpret a cost-volume-profit (CVP) graph and a profit graph.

**LO3** Use the contribution margin ratio (CM ratio) to compute changes in contribution margin and net operating income resulting from changes in sales volume.

**LO4** Show the effects on net operating income of changes in variable costs, fixed costs, selling price, and volume.

**LO5** Determine the level of sales needed to achieve a desired target profit.

**LO6** Determine the break-even point.

**LO7** Compute the margin of safety and explain its significance.

**LO8** Compute the degree of operating leverage at a particular level of sales and explain how it can be used to predict changes in net operating income.

**LO9** Compute the break-even point for a multiproduct company and explain the effects of shifts in the sales mix on contribution margin and the break-even point.

**Cost-volume-profit (CVP) analysis is** a powerful tool that helps managers understand the relationships among cost, volume, and profit. CVP analysis focuses on how profits are affected by the following five factors:

1. Selling prices.
2. Sales volume.
3. Unit variable costs.
4. Total fixed costs.
5. Mix of products sold.

Because CVP analysis helps managers understand how profits are affected by these key factors, it is a vital tool in many business decisions. These decisions include what products and services to offer, what prices to charge, what marketing strategy to use, and what cost structure to implement. To help understand the role of CVP analysis in business decisions, consider the case of Acoustic Concepts, Inc., a company founded by Prem Narayan.

**MANAGERIAL ACCOUNTING IN ACTION**
**The Issue**

Prem, who was a graduate student in engineering at the time, started Acoustic Concepts to market a radical new speaker he had designed for automobile sound systems. The speaker, called the Sonic Blaster, uses an advanced microprocessor and proprietary software to boost amplification to awesome levels. Prem contracted with a Taiwanese electronics manufacturer to produce the speaker. With seed money provided by his family, Prem placed an order with the manufacturer and ran advertisements in auto magazines.

The Sonic Blaster was an almost immediate success, and sales grew to the point that Prem moved the company's headquarters out of his apartment and into rented quarters in a nearby industrial park. He also hired a receptionist, an accountant, a sales manager, and a small sales staff to sell the speakers to retail stores. The accountant, Bob Luchinni, had worked for several small companies where he had acted as a business advisor as well as accountant and bookkeeper. The following discussion occurred soon after Bob was hired:

***Prem:*** Bob, I've got a lot of questions about the company's finances that I hope you can help answer.

***Bob:*** We're in great shape. The loan from your family will be paid off within a few months.

***Prem:*** I know, but I am worried about the risks I've taken on by expanding operations. What would happen if a competitor entered the market and our sales slipped? How far could sales drop without putting us into the red? Another question I've been trying to resolve is how much our sales would have to increase to justify the big marketing campaign the sales staff is pushing for.

***Bob:*** Marketing always wants more money for advertising.

***Prem:*** And they are always pushing me to drop the selling price on the speaker. I agree with them that a lower price will boost our volume, but I'm not sure the increased volume will offset the loss in revenue from the lower price.

***Bob:*** It sounds like these questions are all related in some way to the relationships among our selling prices, our costs, and our volume. I shouldn't have a problem coming up with some answers.

***Prem:*** Can we meet again in a couple of days to see what you have come up with?

***Bob:*** Sounds good. By then I'll have some preliminary answers for you as well as a model you can use for answering similar questions in the future.

## THE BASICS OF COST-VOLUME-PROFIT (CVP) ANALYSIS

Bob Luchinni's preparation for his forthcoming meeting with Prem begins with the contribution income statement. The contribution income statement emphasizes the behavior of costs and therefore is extremely helpful to managers in judging the impact on profits of changes in selling price, cost, or volume. Bob will base his analysis on the following contribution income statement he prepared last month:

**Acoustic Concepts, Inc.**
**Contribution Income Statement**
**For the Month of June**

| | Total | Per Unit |
|---|---|---|
| Sales (400 speakers) | $100,000 | $250 |
| Variable expenses | 60,000 | 150 |
| Contribution margin | 40,000 | $100 |
| Fixed expenses | 35,000 | |
| Net operating income | $ 5,000 | |

Notice that sales, variable expenses, and contribution margin are expressed on a per unit basis as well as in total on this contribution income statement. The per unit figures will be very helpful to Bob in some of his calculations. Note that this contribution income statement has been prepared for management's use inside the company and would not ordinarily be made available to those outside the company.

**HELPFUL HINT**

Students often struggle to derive the selling price per unit and the variable expense per unit when they are not explicitly stated in a problem. Therefore, remember that the total sales and total variable expenses can each be divided by the quantity of units sold to derive the selling price per unit and the variable expense per unit.

## Contribution Margin

**LEARNING OBJECTIVE 1**

Explain how changes in activity affect contribution margin and net operating income.

Contribution margin is the amount remaining from sales revenue after variable expenses have been deducted. Thus, it is the amount available to cover fixed expenses and then to provide profits for the period. Notice the sequence here—contribution margin is used *first* to cover the fixed expenses, and then whatever remains goes toward profits. If the contribution margin is not sufficient to cover the fixed expenses, then a loss occurs for the period. To illustrate with an extreme example, assume that Acoustic Concepts sells only one speaker during a particular month. The company's income statement would appear as follows:

**Contribution Income Statement**
**Sales of 1 Speaker**

| | Total | Per Unit |
|---|---|---|
| Sales (1 speaker) | $ 250 | $250 |
| Variable expenses | 150 | 150 |
| Contribution margin | 100 | $100 |
| Fixed expenses | 35,000 | |
| Net operating loss | $(34,900) | |

For each additional speaker the company sells during the month, $100 more in contribution margin becomes available to help cover the fixed expenses. If a second speaker is sold, for example, then the total contribution margin will increase by $100 (to a total of $200) and the company's loss will decrease by $100, to $34,800:

| Contribution Income Statement<br>Sales of 2 Speakers | Total | Per Unit |
|---|---|---|
| Sales (2 speakers) | $ 500 | $250 |
| Variable expenses | 300 | 150 |
| Contribution margin | 200 | $100 |
| Fixed expenses | 35,000 | |
| Net operating loss | $(34,800) | |

If enough speakers can be sold to generate $35,000 in contribution margin, then all of the fixed expenses will be covered and the company will *break even* for the month—that is, it will show neither profit nor loss but just cover all of its costs. To reach the break-even point, the company will have to sell 350 speakers in a month because each speaker sold yields $100 in contribution margin:

| Contribution Income Statement<br>Sales of 350 Speakers | Total | Per Unit |
|---|---|---|
| Sales (350 speakers) | $87,500 | $250 |
| Variable expenses | 52,500 | 150 |
| Contribution margin | 35,000 | $100 |
| Fixed expenses | 35,000 | |
| Net operating income | $ 0 | |

Computation of the break-even point is discussed in detail later in the chapter; for the moment, note that the **break-even point** is the level of sales at which profit is zero.

*Once the break-even point has been reached, net operating income will increase by the amount of the unit contribution margin for each additional unit sold.* For example, if 351 speakers are sold in a month, then the net operating income for the month will be $100 because the company will have sold 1 speaker more than the number needed to break even:

| Contribution Income Statement<br>Sales of 351 Speakers | Total | Per Unit |
|---|---|---|
| Sales (351 speakers) | $87,750 | $250 |
| Variable expenses | 52,650 | 150 |
| Contribution margin | 35,100 | $100 |
| Fixed expenses | 35,000 | |
| Net operating income | $ 100 | |

If 352 speakers are sold (2 speakers above the break-even point), the net operating income for the month will be $200. If 353 speakers are sold (3 speakers above the break-even point), the net operating income for the month will be $300, and so forth. To estimate the profit at any sales volume above the break-even point, simply multiply the number of units sold in excess of the break-even point by the unit contribution margin. The result represents the anticipated profits for the period. Or, to estimate the effect of a planned increase in sales on profits, simply multiply the increase in units sold by the unit contribution margin. The result will be the expected increase in profits. To illustrate, if Acoustic Concepts is currently selling 400 speakers per month and plans to increase sales to 425 speakers per month, the anticipated impact on profits can be computed as follows:

| | |
|---|---|
| Increased number of speakers to be sold .............. | 25 |
| Contribution margin per speaker .......................... | × $100 |
| Increase in net operating income .......................... | $2,500 |

These calculations can be verified as follows:

| | Sales Volume | | | |
|---|---|---|---|---|
| | 400 Speakers | 425 Speakers | Difference (25 Speakers) | Per Unit |
| Sales (@ $250 per speaker) .......... | $100,000 | $106,250 | $6,250 | $250 |
| Variable expenses | | | | |
| (@ $150 per speaker)................ | 60,000 | 63,750 | 3,750 | 150 |
| Contribution margin ....................... | 40,000 | 42,500 | 2,500 | $100 |
| Fixed expenses.............................. | 35,000 | 35,000 | 0 | |
| Net operating income...................... | $ 5,000 | $ 7,500 | $2,500 | |

To summarize, if sales are zero, the company's loss would equal its fixed expenses. Each unit that is sold reduces the loss by the amount of the unit contribution margin. Once the break-even point has been reached, each additional unit sold increases the company's profit by the amount of the unit contribution margin.

## CVP Relationships in Equation Form

The contribution format income statement can be expressed in equation form as follows:

Profit = (Sales  Variable expenses)  Fixed expenses

For brevity, we use the term *profit* to stand for net operating income in equations.

When a company has only a *single* product, as at Acoustic Concepts, we can further refine the equation as follows:

$$\text{Sales} = \text{Selling price per unit} \times \text{Quantity sold} = P \times Q$$

$$\text{Variable expenses} = \text{Variable expenses per unit} \times \text{Quantity sold} = V \times Q$$

$$\text{Profit} = (P \times Q - V \times Q) - \text{Fixed expenses}$$

We can do all of the calculations of the previous section using this simple equation. For example, on page 190 we computed the net operating income (profit) at sales of 351 speakers as $100. We can arrive at the same conclusion using the above equation as follows:

$$\text{Profit} = (P \times Q - V \times Q) - \text{Fixed expenses}$$

$$\begin{aligned}\text{Profit} &= (\$250 \times 351 - \$150 \times 351) - \$35{,}000\\ &= (\$250 - \$150) \times 351 - \$35{,}000\\ &= (\$100) \times 351 - \$35{,}000\\ &= \$35{,}100 - \$35{,}000 = \$100\end{aligned}$$

It is often useful to express the simple profit equation in terms of the unit contribution margin (Unit CM) as follows:

$$\text{Unit CM} = \text{Selling price per unit} - \text{Variable expenses per unit} = P - V$$

$$\text{Profit} = (P \times Q - V \times Q) - \text{Fixed expenses}$$

$$\text{Profit} = (P - V) \times Q - \text{Fixed expenses}$$

$$\text{Profit} = \text{Unit CM} \times Q - \text{Fixed expenses}$$

We could also have used this equation to determine the profit at sales of 351 speakers as follows:

$$\begin{aligned}\text{Profit} &= \text{Unit CM} \times Q - \text{Fixed expenses}\\ &= \$100 \times 351 - \$35{,}000\\ &= \$35{,}100 - \$35{,}000 = \$100\end{aligned}$$

For those who are comfortable with algebra, the quickest and easiest approach to solving the problems in this chapter may be to use the simple profit equation in one of its forms.

## CVP Relationships in Graphic Form

**LEARNING OBJECTIVE 2**

Prepare and interpret a cost-volume-profit (CVP) graph and a profit graph.

The relationships among revenue, cost, profit, and volume are illustrated on a **cost-volume-profit (CVP) graph.** A CVP graph highlights CVP relationships over wide ranges of activity. To help explain his analysis to Prem Narayan, Bob Luchinni prepared a CVP graph for Acoustic Concepts.

**Preparing the CVP Graph** In a CVP graph (sometimes called a *break-even chart*), unit volume is represented on the horizontal (*X*) axis and dollars on the vertical (*Y*) axis. Preparing a CVP graph involves three steps as depicted in Exhibit 5–1:

1. Draw a line parallel to the volume axis to represent total fixed expense. For Acoustic Concepts, total fixed expenses are $35,000.
2. Choose some volume of unit sales and plot the point representing total expense (fixed and variable) at the sales volume you have selected. In Exhibit 5–1, Bob Luchinni chose a volume of 600 speakers. Total expense at that sales volume is:

| | |
|---|---|
| Fixed expense | $ 35,000 |
| Variable expense (600 speakers × $150 per speaker) | 90,000 |
| Total expense | $125,000 |

   After the point has been plotted, draw a line through it back to the point where the fixed expense line intersects the dollars axis.
3. Again choose some sales volume and plot the point representing total sales dollars at the activity level you have selected. In Exhibit 5–1, Bob Luchinni again chose a volume of 600 speakers. Sales at that sales volume total $150,000 (600 speakers × $250 per speaker). Draw a line through this point back to the origin.

The interpretation of the completed CVP graph is given in Exhibit 5–2. The anticipated profit or loss at any given level of sales is measured by the vertical distance between the total revenue line (sales) and the total expense line (variable expense plus fixed expense).

The break-even point is where the total revenue and total expense lines cross. The break-even point of 350 speakers in Exhibit 5–2 agrees with the break-even point computed earlier.

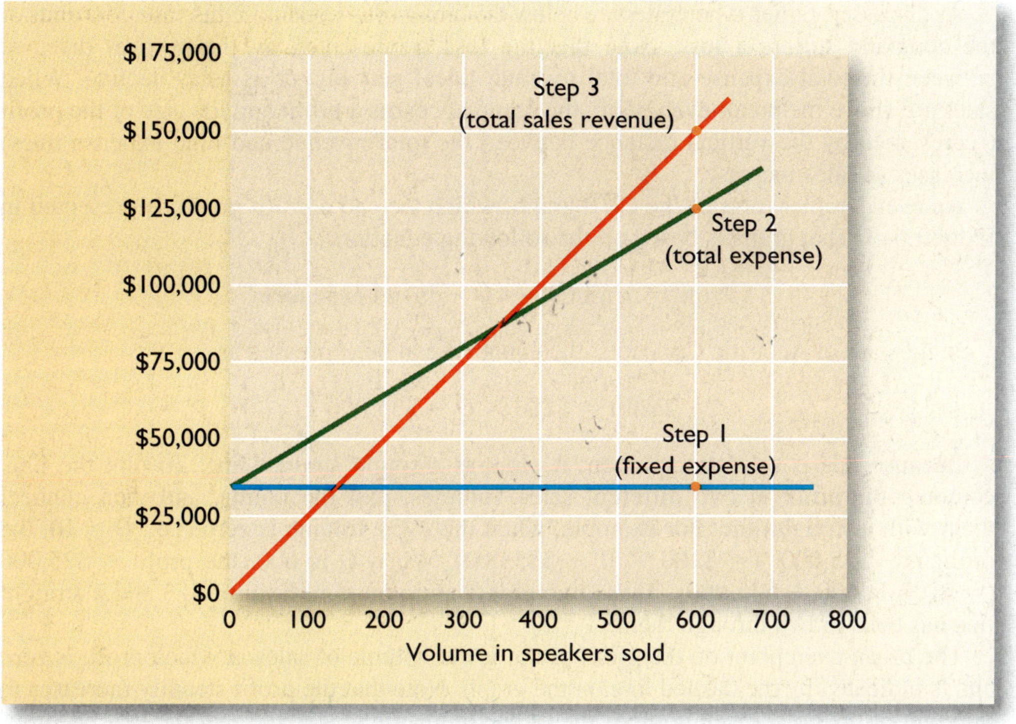


**EXHIBIT 5–1**
Preparing the CVP Graph

**EXHIBIT 5–2** The Completed CVP Graph

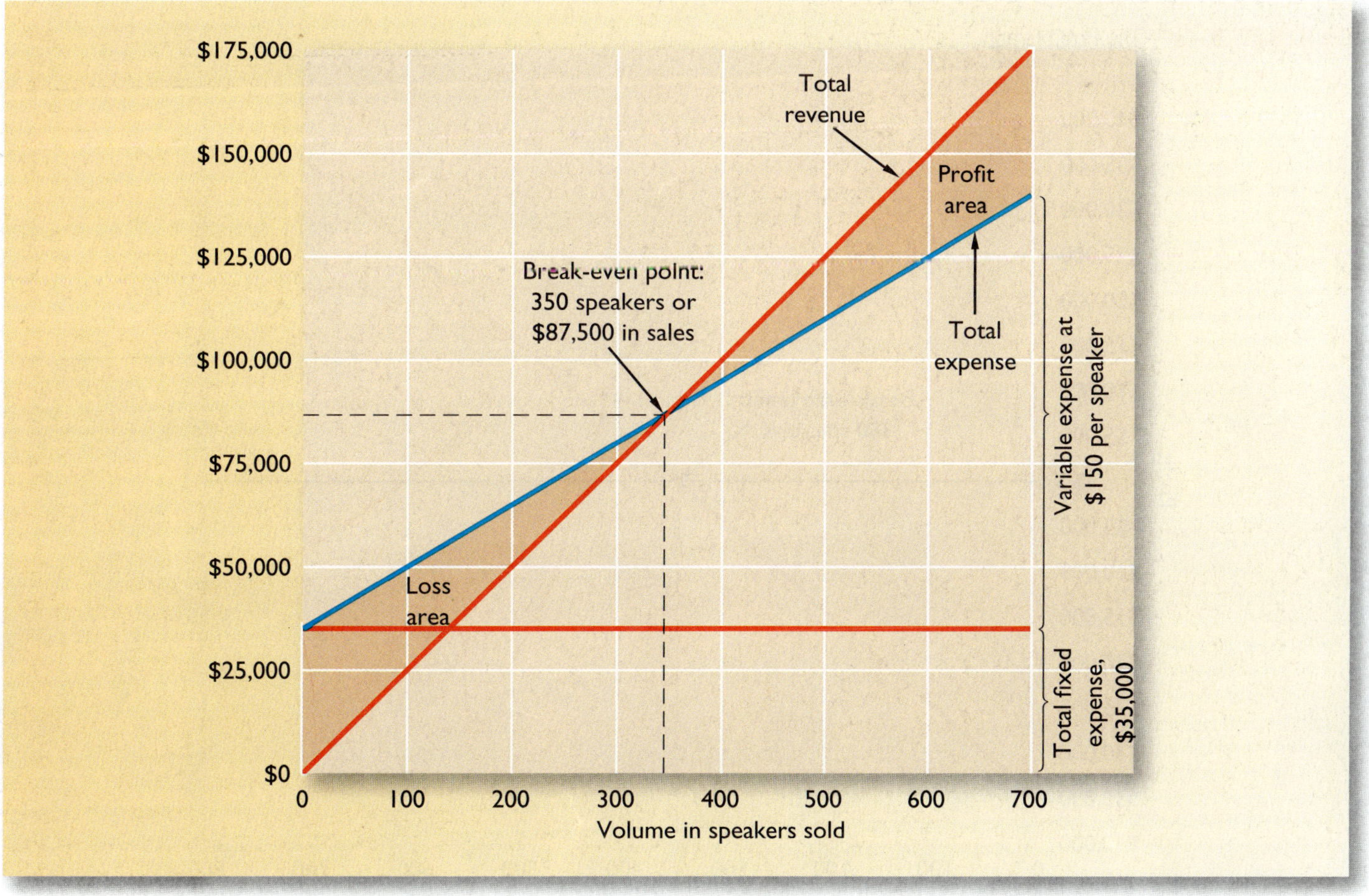

As discussed earlier, when sales are below the break-even point—in this case, 350 units—the company suffers a loss. Note that the loss (represented by the vertical distance between the total expense and total revenue lines) gets bigger as sales decline. When sales are above the break-even point, the company earns a profit and the size of the profit (represented by the vertical distance between the total revenue and total expense lines) increases as sales increase.

An even simpler form of the CVP graph, which we call a profit graph, is presented in Exhibit 5–3. That graph is based on the following equation:

$$\text{Profit} = \text{Unit CM} \times Q - \text{Fixed expenses}$$

In the case of Acoustic Concepts, the equation can be expressed as:

$$\text{Profit} = \$100 \times Q - \$35{,}000$$

Because this is a linear equation, it plots as a single straight line. To plot the line, compute the profit at two different sales volumes, plot the points, and then connect them with a straight line. For example, when the sales volume is zero (i.e., $Q = 0$), the profit is $-\$35{,}000$ $(= \$100 \times 0 - \$35{,}000)$. When $Q$ is 600, the profit is \$25,000 $(= \$100 \times 600 - \$35{,}000)$. These two points are plotted in Exhibit 5–3 and a straight line has been drawn through them.

The break-even point on the profit graph is the volume of sales at which profit is zero and is indicated by the dashed line on the graph. Note that the profit steadily increases to the right of the break-even point as the sales volume increases and that the loss becomes steadily worse to the left of the break-even point as the sales volume decreases.

**EXHIBIT 5–3** The Profit Graph

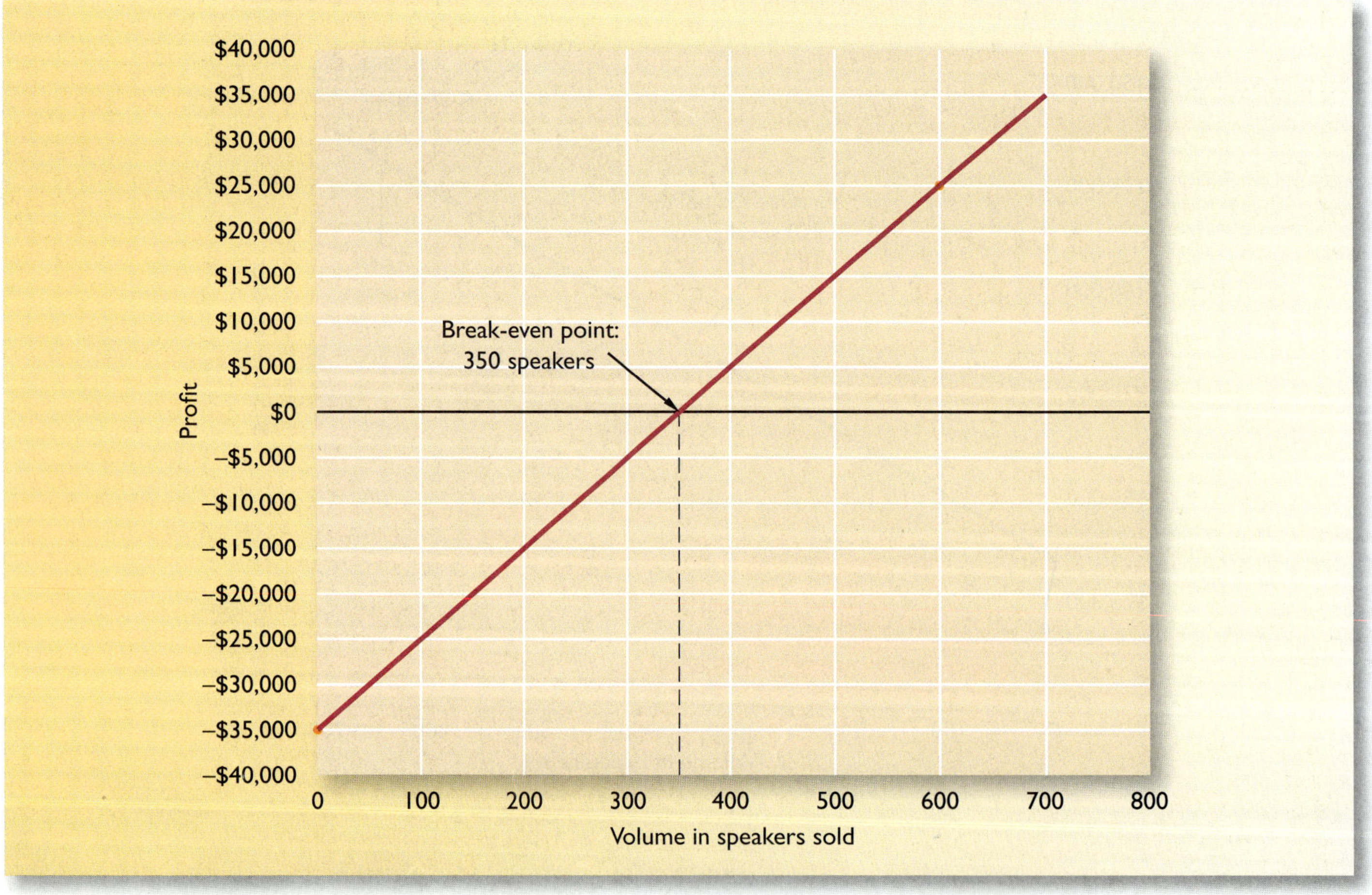

## Contribution Margin Ratio (CM Ratio)

**LEARNING OBJECTIVE 3**

Use the contribution margin ratio (CM ratio) to compute changes in contribution margin and net operating income resulting from changes in sales volume.

In the previous section, we explored how cost-volume-profit relationships can be visualized. In this section, we show how the *contribution margin ratio* can be used in cost-volume-profit calculations. As the first step, we have added a column to Acoustic Concepts' contribution format income statement in which sales revenues, variable expenses, and contribution margin are expressed as a percentage of sales:

| | Total | Per Unit | Percent of Sales |
|---|---|---|---|
| Sales (400 speakers) | $100,000 | $250 | 100% |
| Variable expenses | 60,000 | 150 | 60% |
| Contribution margin | 40,000 | $100 | 40% |
| Fixed expenses | 35,000 | | |
| Net operating income | $ 5,000 | | |

The contribution margin as a percentage of sales is referred to as the **contribution margin ratio (CM ratio).** This ratio is computed as follows:

$$\text{CM ratio} = \frac{\text{Contribution margin}}{\text{Sales}}$$

For Acoustic Concepts, the computations are:

$$\text{CM ratio} = \frac{\text{Total contribution margin}}{\text{Total sales}} = \frac{\$40{,}000}{\$100{,}000} = 40\%$$

In a company such as Acoustic Concepts that has only one product, the CM ratio can also be computed on a per unit basis as follows:

$$\text{CM ratio} = \frac{\text{Unit contribution margin}}{\text{Unit selling price}} = \frac{\$100}{\$250} = 40\%$$

The CM ratio shows how the contribution margin will be affected by a change in total sales. Acoustic Concepts' CM ratio of 40% means that for each dollar increase in sales, total contribution margin will increase by 40 cents ($1 sales × CM ratio of 40%). Net operating income will also increase by 40 cents, assuming that fixed costs are not affected by the increase in sales. Generally, the effect of a change in sales on the contribution margin is expressed in equation form as:

$$\text{Change in contribution margin} = \text{CM ratio} \times \text{Change in sales}$$

As this illustration suggests, *the impact on net operating income of any given dollar change in total sales can be computed by applying the CM ratio to the dollar change.* For example, if Acoustic Concepts plans a $30,000 increase in sales during the coming month, the contribution margin should increase by $12,000 ($30,000 increase in sales × CM ratio of 40%). As we noted above, net operating income will also increase by $12,000 if fixed costs do not change. This is verified by the following table:

| | Sales Volume | | | Percent of Sales |
|---|---|---|---|---|
| | Present | Expected | Increase | |
| Sales | $100,000 | $130,000 | $30,000 | 100% |
| Variable expenses | 60,000 | 78,000* | 18,000 | 60% |
| Contribution margin | 40,000 | 52,000 | 12,000 | 40% |
| Fixed expenses | 35,000 | 35,000 | 0 | |
| Net operating income | $ 5,000 | $ 17,000 | $12,000 | |

*$130,000 expected sales ÷ $250 per unit = 520 units. 520 units × $150 per unit = $78,000.

The relation between profit and the CM ratio can also be expressed using the following equation:

$$\text{Profit} = \text{CM ratio} \times \text{Sales} - \text{Fixed expenses}^{1}$$

For example, at sales of $130,000, the profit is expected to be $17,000 as shown below:

$$\begin{aligned}\text{Profit} &= \text{CM ratio} \times \text{Sales} - \text{Fixed expenses}\\ &= 0.40 \times \$130{,}000 - \$35{,}000\\ &= \$52{,}000 - \$35{,}000 = \$17{,}000\end{aligned}$$

Again, if you are comfortable with algebra, this approach will often be quicker and easier than constructing contribution format income statements.

The CM ratio is particularly valuable in situations where the dollar sales of one product must be traded off against the dollar sales of another product. In this situation, products that yield the greatest amount of contribution margin per dollar of sales should be emphasized.

**CONCEPT CHECK**

1. The contribution margin ratio always increases when (you may select more than one answer):
   a. Sales increase.
   b. Fixed costs decrease.
   c. Total variable costs decrease.
   d. Variable costs as a percent of sales decrease.

## Some Applications of CVP Concepts

**LEARNING OBJECTIVE 4**

Show the effects on net operating income of changes in variable costs, fixed costs, selling price, and volume.

Bob Luchinni, the accountant at Acoustic Concepts, wanted to demonstrate to the company's president Prem Narayan how the concepts developed on the preceding pages can be used in planning and decision making. Bob gathered the following basic data:

| | Per Unit | Percent of Sales |
|---|---|---|
| Selling price | $250 | 100% |
| Variable expenses | 150 | 60% |
| Contribution margin | $100 | 40% |

Recall that fixed expenses are $35,000 per month. Bob Luchinni will use these data to show the effects of changes in variable costs, fixed costs, sales price, and sales volume on the company's profitability in a variety of situations.

Before proceeding further, however, we need to introduce another concept—the *variable expense ratio.* The **variable expense ratio** is the ratio of variable expenses to sales. It can be computed by dividing the total variable expenses by the total sales, or in a single product analysis, it can be computed by dividing the variable expenses per unit by the unit selling price. In the case of Acoustic Concepts, the variable expense ratio is 0.60;

---

[1]This equation can be derived using the basic profit equation and the definition of the CM ratio as follows:

$$\text{Profit} = (\text{Sales} - \text{Variable expenses}) - \text{Fixed expenses}$$

$$\text{Profit} = \text{Contribution margin} - \text{Fixed expenses}$$

$$\text{Profit} = \frac{\text{Contribution margin}}{\text{Sales}} \times \text{Sales} - \text{Fixed expenses}$$

$$\text{Profit} = \text{CM ratio} \times \text{Sales} - \text{Fixed expenses}$$

that is, variable expense is 60% of sales. Expressed as an equation, the definition of the variable expense ratio is:

$$\text{Variable expense ratio} = \frac{\text{Variable expenses}}{\text{Sales}}$$

This leads to a useful equation that relates the CM ratio to the variable expense ratio as follows:

$$\text{CM ratio} = \frac{\text{Contribution margin}}{\text{Sales}}$$

$$\text{CM ratio} = \frac{\text{Sales} - \text{Variable expenses}}{\text{Sales}}$$

$$\text{CM ratio} = 1 - \text{Variable expense ratio}$$

## HELPFUL HINT

The picture below may improve your understanding of Learning Objective 4. It highlights the four variables that impact net operating income—the number of units sold (also called sales volume), the selling price per unit, the variable expense per unit, and total fixed expenses. Once you input the proper amounts for each of these variables in the tan boxes shown below, follow four steps to compute the new net operating income. First, multiply the number of units sold by the selling price per unit to derive total sales. The second step is to multiply the number of units sold by the variable expense per unit to derive total variable expenses. The third step is to subtract the total variable expenses from total sales to derive the contribution margin. The fourth step is to subtract total fixed expenses from the contribution margin to derive the new net operating income.

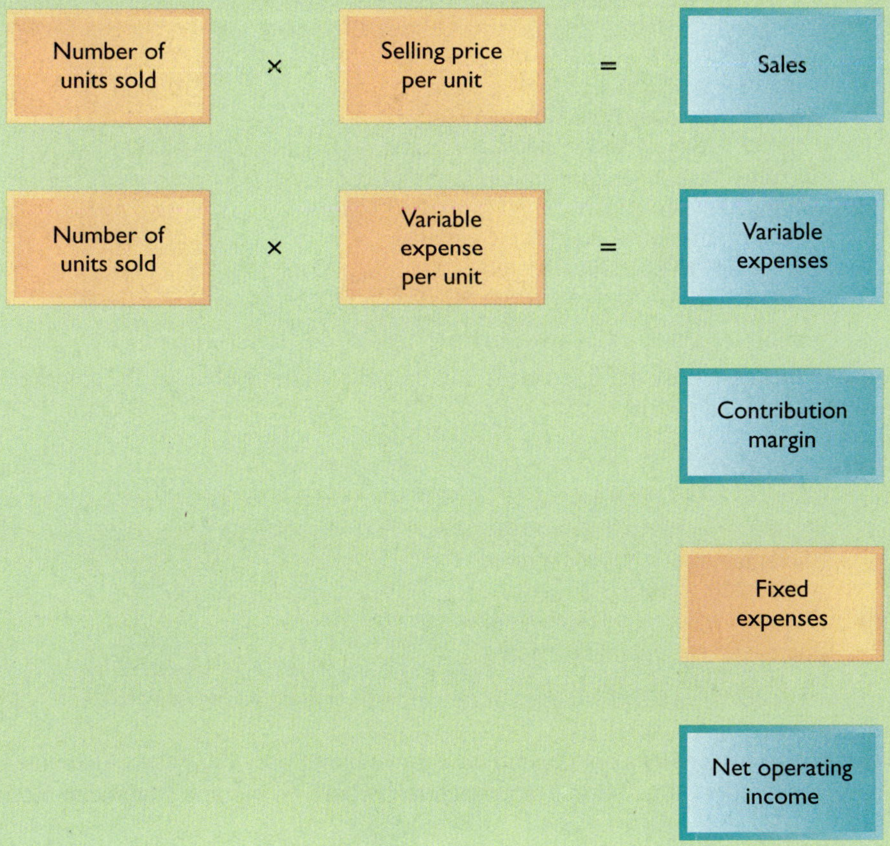

**Change in Fixed Cost and Sales Volume** Acoustic Concepts is currently selling 400 speakers per month at $250 per speaker for total monthly sales of $100,000. The sales manager feels that a $10,000 increase in the monthly advertising budget would increase monthly sales by $30,000 to a total of 520 units. Should the advertising budget be increased? The table below shows the financial impact of the proposed change in the monthly advertising budget.

| | Current Sales | Sales with Additional Advertising Budget | Difference | Percent of Sales |
|---|---|---|---|---|
| Sales | $100,000 | $130,000 | $30,000 | 100% |
| Variable expenses | 60,000 | 78,000* | 18,000 | 60% |
| Contribution margin | 40,000 | 52,000 | 12,000 | 40% |
| Fixed expenses | 35,000 | 45,000† | 10,000 | |
| Net operating income | $ 5,000 | $ 7,000 | $ 2,000 | |

*520 units × $150 per unit = $78,000.
†$35,000 + additional $10,000 monthly advertising budget = $45,000.

Assuming no other factors need to be considered, the increase in the advertising budget should be approved because it would increase net operating income by $2,000. There are two shorter ways to arrive at this solution. The first alternative solution follows:

## Alternative Solution 1

| | |
|---|---|
| Expected total contribution margin: | |
| $130,000 × 40% CM ratio | $52,000 |
| Present total contribution margin: | |
| $100,000 × 40% CM ratio | 40,000 |
| Incremental contribution margin | 12,000 |
| Change in fixed expenses: | |
| Less incremental advertising expense | 10,000 |
| Increased net operating income | $ 2,000 |

Because in this case only the fixed costs and the sales volume change, the solution can also be quickly derived as follows:

## Alternative Solution 2

| | |
|---|---|
| Incremental contribution margin: | |
| $30,000 × 40% CM ratio | $12,000 |
| Less incremental advertising expense | 10,000 |
| Increased net operating income | $ 2,000 |

Notice that this approach does not depend on knowledge of previous sales. Also note that it is unnecessary under either shorter approach to prepare an income statement. Both of the alternative solutions involve **incremental analysis**—they consider only the revenue, cost, and volume that will change if the new program is implemented. Although in each case a new income statement could have been prepared, the incremental approach is simpler and more direct and focuses attention on the specific changes that would occur as a result of the decision.

**Change in Variable Costs and Sales Volume** Refer to the original data. Recall that Acoustic Concepts is currently selling 400 speakers per month. Prem is considering the use of higher-quality components, which would increase variable costs (and thereby reduce the contribution margin) by $10 per speaker. However, the sales manager predicts that using higher-quality components would increase sales to 480 speakers per month. Should the higher-quality components be used?

The $10 increase in variable costs would decrease the unit contribution margin by $10—from $100 down to $90.

### Solution

| | |
|---|---|
| Expected total contribution margin with higher-quality components: | |
| 480 speakers × $90 per speaker | $43,200 |
| Present total contribution margin: | |
| 400 speakers × $100 per speaker | 40,000 |
| Increase in total contribution margin | $ 3,200 |

According to this analysis, the higher-quality components should be used. Because fixed costs would not change, the $3,200 increase in contribution margin shown above should result in a $3,200 increase in net operating income.

**Change in Fixed Cost, Selling Price, and Sales Volume** Refer to the original data and recall again that Acoustic Concepts is currently selling 400 speakers per month. To increase sales, the sales manager would like to cut the selling price by $20 per speaker and increase the advertising budget by $15,000 per month. The sales manager believes that if these two steps are taken, unit sales will increase by 50% to 600 speakers per month. Should the changes be made?

A decrease in the selling price of $20 per speaker would decrease the unit contribution margin by $20 down to $80.

### Solution

| | |
|---|---|
| Expected total contribution margin with lower selling price: | |
| 600 speakers × $80 per speaker | $48,000 |
| Present total contribution margin: | |
| 400 speakers × $100 per speaker | 40,000 |
| Incremental contribution margin | 8,000 |
| Change in fixed expenses: | |
| Less incremental advertising expense | 15,000 |
| Reduction in net operating income | $ (7,000) |

According to this analysis, the changes should not be made. The $7,000 reduction in net operating income that is shown above can be verified by preparing comparative income statements as shown on the next page.

| | Present 400 Speakers per Month | | Expected 600 Speakers per Month | | |
|---|---|---|---|---|---|
| | Total | Per Unit | Total | Per Unit | Difference |
| Sales | $100,000 | $250 | $138,000 | $230 | $38,000 |
| Variable expenses | 60,000 | 150 | 90,000 | 150 | 30,000 |
| Contribution margin | 40,000 | $100 | 48,000 | $ 80 | 8,000 |
| Fixed expenses | 35,000 | | 50,000* | | 15,000 |
| Net operating income (loss) | $ 5,000 | | $ (2,000) | | $ (7,000) |

*35,000 + Additional monthly advertising budget of $15,000 = $50,000.

**Change in Variable Cost, Fixed Cost, and Sales Volume** Refer to Acoustic Concepts' original data. As before, the company is currently selling 400 speakers per month. The sales manager would like to pay salespersons a sales commission of $15 per speaker sold, rather than the flat salaries that now total $6,000 per month. The sales manager is confident that the change would increase monthly sales by 15% to 460 speakers per month. Should the change be made?

**Solution** Changing the sales staff's compensation from salaries to commissions would affect both fixed and variable expenses. Fixed expenses would decrease by $6,000, from $35,000 to $29,000. Variable expenses per unit would increase by $15, from $150 to $165, and the unit contribution margin would decrease from $100 to $85.

| | |
|---|---|
| Expected total contribution margin with sales staff on commissions: | |
| 460 speakers × $85 per speaker | $39,100 |
| Present total contribution margin: | |
| 400 speakers × $100 per speaker | 40,000 |
| Decrease in total contribution margin | (900) |
| Change in fixed expenses: | |
| Add salaries avoided if a commission is paid | 6,000 |
| Increase in net operating income | $ 5,100 |

According to this analysis, the changes should be made. Again, the same answer can be obtained by preparing comparative income statements:

| | Present 400 Speakers per Month | | Expected 460 Speakers per Month | | |
|---|---|---|---|---|---|
| | Total | Per Unit | Total | Per Unit | Difference |
| Sales | $100,000 | $250 | $115,000 | $250 | $15,000 |
| Variable expenses | 60,000 | 150 | 75,900 | 165 | 15,900 |
| Contribution margin | 40,000 | $100 | 39,100 | $ 85 | 900 |
| Fixed expenses | 35,000 | | 29,000 | | (6,000)* |
| Net operating income | $ 5,000 | | $ 10,100 | | $ 5,100 |

*Note: A *reduction* in fixed expenses has the effect of *increasing* net operating income.

**Change in Selling Price** Refer to the original data where Acoustic Concepts is currently selling 400 speakers per month. The company has an opportunity to make a bulk sale of 150 speakers to a wholesaler if an acceptable price can be negotiated. This sale would not disturb the company's regular sales and would not affect the company's total fixed expenses. What price per speaker should be quoted to the wholesaler if Acoustic Concepts is seeking a profit of $3,000 on the bulk sale?

**Solution**

| | |
|---|---|
| Variable cost per speaker ................ | $150 |
| Desired profit per speaker: | |
| $3,000 ÷ 150 speakers ................ | 20 |
| Quoted price per speaker ................. | $170 |

Notice that fixed expenses are not included in the computation. This is because fixed expenses are not affected by the bulk sale, so all of the additional contribution margin increases the company's profits.

## Managing Risk in the Book Publishing Industry

IN BUSINESS

**Greenleaf Book Group** is a book publishing company in Austin, Texas, that attracts authors who are willing to pay publishing costs and forgo up-front advances in exchange for a larger royalty rate on each book sold. For example, assume a typical publisher prints 10,000 copies of a new book that it sells for $12.50 per unit. The publisher pays the author an advance of $20,000 to write the book and then incurs $60,000 of expenses to market, print, and edit the book. The publisher also pays the author a 20% royalty (or $2.50 per unit) on each book sold above 8,000 units. In this scenario, the publisher must sell 6,400 books to break even (= $80,000 in fixed costs ÷ $12.50 per unit). If all 10,000 copies are sold, the author earns $25,000 (= $20,000 advance + 2,000 copies × $2.50) and the publisher earns $40,000 (= $125,000 − $60,000 − $20,000 − $5,000).

Greenleaf alters the financial arrangement described above by requiring the author to assume the risk of poor sales. It pays the author a 70% royalty on all units sold (or $8.75 per unit), but the author forgoes the $20,000 advance and pays Greenleaf $60,000 to market, print, and edit the book. If the book flops, the author fails to recover her production costs. If all 10,000 units are sold, the author earns $27,500 (= $10,000 units × $8.75 − $60,000) and Greenleaf earns $37,500 (= 10,000 units × ($12.50 − $8.75)).

Source: Christopher Steiner, "Book It," *Forbes*, September 7, 2009, p. 58.

## TARGET PROFIT AND BREAK-EVEN ANALYSIS

Target profit analysis and break-even analysis are used to answer questions such as how much would we have to sell to make a profit of $10,000 per month or how much would we have to sell to avoid incurring a loss?

### Target Profit Analysis

*Target profit analysis* is one of the key uses of CVP analysis. In **target profit analysis,** we estimate what sales volume is needed to achieve a specific target profit. For example, suppose that Prem Narayan of Acoustic Concepts would like to know what sales would have to be achieved to attain a target profit of $40,000 per month. To answer this question, we can proceed using the equation method or the formula method.

**LEARNING OBJECTIVE 5**

Determine the level of sales needed to achieve a desired target profit.

**The Equation Method** We can use a basic profit equation to find the sales volume required to attain a target profit. In the case of Acoustic Concepts, the company has only one product so we can use the contribution margin form of the equation. Remembering that the target profit is \$40,000, the unit contribution margin is \$100, and the fixed expense is \$35,000, we can solve as follows:

$$\begin{aligned}\text{Profit} &= \text{Unit CM} \times Q - \text{Fixed expense}\\ \$40{,}000 &= \$100 \times Q - \$35{,}000\\ \$100 \times Q &= \$40{,}000 + \$35{,}000\\ Q &= (\$40{,}000 + \$35{,}000) \div \$100\\ Q &= 750\end{aligned}$$

Thus, the target profit can be achieved by selling 750 speakers per month.

**The Formula Method** The formula method is a short-cut version of the equation method. Note that in the next to the last line of the above solution, the sum of the target profit of \$40,000 and the fixed expense of \$35,000 is divided by the unit contribution margin of \$100. In general, in a single-product situation, we can compute the sales volume required to attain a specific target profit using the following formula:

$$\text{Unit sales to attain the target profit} = \frac{\text{Target profit} + \text{Fixed expenses}^{2}}{\text{Unit CM}}$$

In the case of Acoustic Concepts, the formula yields the following answer:

$$\begin{aligned}\text{Unit sales to attain the target profit} &= \frac{\text{Target profit} + \text{Fixed expenses}}{\text{Unit CM}}\\ &= \frac{\$40{,}000 + \$35{,}000}{\$100}\\ &= 750\end{aligned}$$

Note that this is the same answer we got when we used the equation method—and it always will be. The formula method simply skips a few steps in the equation method.

**Target Profit Analysis in Terms of Sales Dollars** Instead of unit sales, we may want to know what dollar sales are needed to attain the target profit. We can get this answer using several methods. First, we could solve for the unit sales to attain the target profit using the equation method or the formula method and then multiply the result by the selling price. In the case of Acoustic Concepts, the required sales volume using this approach would be computed as 750 speakers × \$250 per speaker or \$187,500 in total sales.

We can also solve for the required sales volume to attain the target profit of \$40,000 at Acoustic Concepts using the basic equation stated in terms of the contribution margin ratio:

$$\begin{aligned}\text{Profit} &= \text{CM ratio} \times \text{Sales} - \text{Fixed expenses}\\ \$40{,}000 &= 0.40 \times \text{Sales} - \$35{,}000\\ 0.40 \times \text{Sales} &= \$40{,}000 + \$35{,}000\\ \text{Sales} &= (\$40{,}000 + \$35{,}000) \div 0.40\\ \text{Sales} &= \$187{,}500\end{aligned}$$

[2]This equation can be derived as follows:

$$\begin{aligned}\text{Profit} &= \text{Unit CM} \times Q - \text{Fixed expenses}\\ \text{Target profit} &= \text{Unit CM} \times Q - \text{Fixed expenses}\\ \text{Unit CM} \times Q &= \text{Target profit} + \text{Fixed expenses}\\ Q &= (\text{Target profit} + \text{Fixed expenses}) \div \text{Unit CM}\end{aligned}$$

Note that in the next to the last line of the previous solution, the sum of the target profit of $40,000 and the fixed expense of $35,000 is divided by the contribution margin ratio of 0.40. In general, we can compute dollar sales to attain a target profit as follows:

$$\text{Dollar sales to attain a target profit} = \frac{\text{Target profit} + \text{Fixed expenses}^3}{\text{CM ratio}}$$

At Acoustic Concepts, the formula yields the following answer:

$$\text{Dollar sales to attain a target profit} = \frac{\text{Target profit} + \text{Fixed expenses}}{\text{CM ratio}}$$

$$= \frac{\$40{,}000 + \$35{,}000}{0.40}$$

$$= \$187{,}500$$

Again, you get exactly the same answer whether you use the equation method or the formula method.

In companies with multiple products, sales volume is more conveniently expressed in terms of total sales dollars than in terms of unit sales. The contribution margin ratio approach to target profit analysis is particularly useful for such companies.

## Break-Even Analysis

**LEARNING OBJECTIVE 6**
Determine the break-even point.

Earlier in the chapter we defined the break-even point as the level of sales at which the company's profit is zero. What we call *break-even analysis* is really just a special case of target profit analysis in which the target profit is zero. We can use either the equation method or the formula method to solve for the break-even point, but for brevity we will illustrate just the formula method. The equation method works exactly like it did in target profit analysis. The only difference is that the target profit is zero in break-even analysis.

**Break-Even in Unit Sales** In a single product situation, recall that the formula for the unit sales to attain a specific target profit is:

$$\text{Unit sales to attain the target profit} = \frac{\text{Target profit} + \text{Fixed expenses}}{\text{Unit CM}}$$

To compute the unit sales to break even, all we have to do is to set the target profit to zero in the above equation as follows:

$$\text{Unit sales to break even} = \frac{\$0 + \text{Fixed expenses}}{\text{Unit CM}}$$

$$\text{Unit sales to break even} = \frac{\text{Fixed expenses}}{\text{Unit CM}}$$

In the case of Acoustic Concepts, the break-even point can be computed as follows:

$$\text{Unit sales to break even} = \frac{\text{Fixed expenses}}{\text{Unit CM}}$$

$$= \frac{\$35{,}000}{\$100}$$

$$= 350$$

[3]This equation can be derived as follows:

$$\text{Profit} = \text{CM ratio} \times \text{Sales} - \text{Fixed expenses}$$

$$\text{Target profit} = \text{CM ratio} \times \text{Sales} - \text{Fixed expenses}$$

$$\text{CM ratio} \times \text{Sales} = \text{Target profit} + \text{Fixed expenses}$$

$$\text{Sales} = (\text{Target profit} + \text{Fixed expenses}) \div \text{CM ratio}$$

Thus, as we determined earlier in the chapter, Acoustic Concepts breaks even at sales of 350 speakers per month.

**CONCEPT CHECK**

2. Assume the selling price per unit is \$30, the contribution margin ratio is 40%, and the total fixed cost is \$60,000. What is the break-even point in unit sales?
   a. 2,000
   b. 3,000
   c. 4,000
   d. 5,000

**Break-Even in Sales Dollars** We can find the break-even point in sales dollars using several methods. First, we could solve for the break-even point in unit sales using the equation method or the formula method and then multiply the result by the selling price. In the case of Acoustic Concepts, the break-even point in sales dollars using this approach would be computed as 350 speakers × \$250 per speaker or \$87,500 in total sales.

We can also solve for the break-even point in sales dollars at Acoustic Concepts using the basic profit equation stated in terms of the contribution margin ratio or we can use the formula for the target profit. Again, for brevity, we will use the formula.

$$\text{Dollar sales to attain a target profit} = \frac{\text{Target profit} + \text{Fixed expenses}}{\text{CM ratio}}$$

$$\text{Dollar sales to break even} = \frac{\$0 + \text{Fixed expenses}}{\text{CM ratio}}$$

$$\text{Dollar sales to break even} = \frac{\text{Fixed expenses}}{\text{CM ratio}}$$

The break-even point at Acoustic Concepts would be computed as follows:

$$\begin{aligned}\text{Dollar sales to break even} &= \frac{\text{Fixed expenses}}{\text{CM ratio}}\\ &= \frac{\$35{,}000}{0.40}\\ &= \$87{,}500\end{aligned}$$

## IN BUSINESS — Cost Overruns Increase the Break-Even Point

When **Airbus** launched the A380 555-seat jetliner in 2000, the company said it would need to sell 250 units to break even on the project. By 2006, Airbus was admitting that more than \$3 billion of cost overruns had raised the project's break-even point to 420 airplanes. Although Airbus has less than 170 orders for the A380, the company remains optimistic that it will sell 751 units over the next 20 years. Given that Airbus rival **Boeing** predicts the total market size for all airplanes with more than 400 seats will not exceed 990 units, it remains unclear if Airbus will ever break even on its investment in the A380 aircraft.

Source: Daniel Michaels, "Embattled Airbus Lifts Sales Target for A380 to Profit," *The Wall Street Journal*, October 20, 2006, p. A6.

## The Margin of Safety

**LEARNING OBJECTIVE 7**

Compute the margin of safety and explain its significance.

The **margin of safety** is the excess of budgeted or actual sales dollars over the break-even volume of sales dollars. It is the amount by which sales can drop before losses are incurred. The higher the margin of safety, the lower the risk of not breaking even and incurring a loss. The formula for the margin of safety is:

$$\text{Margin of safety in dollars} = \text{Total budgeted (or actual) sales} - \text{Break-even sales}$$

The margin of safety can also be expressed in percentage form by dividing the margin of safety in dollars by total dollar sales:

$$\text{Margin of safety percentage} = \frac{\text{Margin of safety in dollars}}{\text{Total budgeted (or actual) sales in dollars}}$$

The calculation of the margin of safety for Acoustic Concepts is:

| | |
|---|---|
| Sales (at the current volume of 400 speakers) (a) | $100,000 |
| Break-even sales (at 350 speakers) | 87,500 |
| Margin of safety in dollars (b) | $ 12,500 |
| Margin of safety percentage, (b) ÷ (a) | 12.5% |

This margin of safety means that at the current level of sales and with the company's current prices and cost structure, a reduction in sales of $12,500, or 12.5%, would result in just breaking even.

In a single-product company like Acoustic Concepts, the margin of safety can also be expressed in terms of the number of units sold by dividing the margin of safety in dollars by the selling price per unit. In this case, the margin of safety is 50 speakers ($12,500 ÷ $250 per speaker = 50 speakers).

**MANAGERIAL ACCOUNTING IN ACTION**
**The Wrap-up**

Prem Narayan and Bob Luchinni met to discuss the results of Bob's analysis.

***Prem:*** Bob, everything you have shown me is pretty clear. I can see what impact the sales manager's suggestions would have on our profits. Some of those suggestions are quite good and others are not so good. I am concerned that our margin of safety is only 50 speakers. What can we do to increase this number?

***Bob:*** Well, we have to increase total sales or decrease the break-even point or both.

***Prem:*** And to decrease the break-even point, we have to either decrease our fixed expenses or increase our unit contribution margin?

***Bob:*** Exactly.

***Prem:*** And to increase our unit contribution margin, we must either increase our selling price or decrease the variable cost per unit?

***Bob:*** Correct.

***Prem:*** So what do you suggest?

***Bob:*** Well, the analysis doesn't tell us which of these to do, but it does indicate we have a potential problem here.

***Prem:*** If you don't have any immediate suggestions, I would like to call a general meeting next week to discuss ways we can work on increasing the margin of safety. I think everyone will be concerned about how vulnerable we are to even small downturns in sales.

DECISION POINT

## Loan Officer

Steve Becker owns **Blue Ridge Brewery**, a microbrewery in Arden, North Carolina. He charges distributors $100 per case for his premium beer. The distributors tack on 25% when selling to retailers who in turn add a 30% markup before selling the beer to consumers. In the most recent year, Blue Ridge's revenue was $8 million and its net operating income was $700,000. Becker reports that the costs of making one case of his premium beer are $32 for raw ingredients, $20 for labor, $4 for bottling and packaging, and $12 for utilities.

Assume that Becker has approached your bank for a loan. As the loan officer, you should consider a variety of factors, including the company's margin of safety. Assuming that other information about the company is favorable, would you consider Blue Ridge's margin of safety to be comfortable enough to extend a loan?

CONCEPT CHECK ✓

3. Assume a company produces one product that sells for $55, has a variable cost per unit of $35, and has fixed costs of $100,000. How many units must the company sell to earn a target profit of $50,000?
   a. 7,500 units
   b. 10,000 units
   c. 12,500 units
   d. 15,000 units
4. Given the same facts as in question 3 above, if the company exactly meets its target profit, what will be its margin of safety in sales dollars?
   a. $110,000
   b. $127,500
   c. $137,500
   d. $150,000

## CVP CONSIDERATIONS IN CHOOSING A COST STRUCTURE

Cost structure refers to the relative proportion of fixed and variable costs in an organization. Managers often have some latitude in trading off between these two types of costs. For example, fixed investments in automated equipment can reduce variable labor costs. In this section, we discuss the choice of a cost structure. We also introduce the concept of *operating leverage.*

### Cost Structure and Profit Stability

Which cost structure is better—high variable costs and low fixed costs, or the opposite? No single answer to this question is possible; each approach has its advantages. To show what we mean, refer to the contribution format income statements given on the following page for two blueberry farms. Bogside Farm depends on migrant workers to pick its berries by hand, whereas Sterling Farm has invested in expensive berry-picking machines. Consequently, Bogside Farm has higher variable costs, but Sterling Farm has higher fixed costs:

| | Bogside Farm | | Sterling Farm | |
|---|---|---|---|---|
| | Amount | Percent | Amount | Percent |
| Sales | $100,000 | 100% | $100,000 | 100% |
| Variable expenses | 60,000 | 60% | 30,000 | 30% |
| Contribution margin | 40,000 | 40% | 70,000 | 70% |
| Fixed expenses | 30,000 | | 60,000 | |
| Net operating income | $ 10,000 | | $ 10,000 | |

Which farm has the better cost structure? The answer depends on many factors, including the long-run trend in sales, year-to-year fluctuations in the level of sales, and the attitude of the owners toward risk. If sales are expected to exceed $100,000 in the future, then Sterling Farm probably has the better cost structure. The reason is that its CM ratio is higher, and its profits will therefore increase more rapidly as sales increase. To illustrate, assume that each farm experiences a 10% increase in sales without any increase in fixed costs. The new income statements would be as follows:

| | Bogside Farm | | Sterling Farm | |
|---|---|---|---|---|
| | Amount | Percent | Amount | Percent |
| Sales | $110,000 | 100% | $110,000 | 100% |
| Variable expenses | 66,000 | 60% | 33,000 | 30% |
| Contribution margin | 44,000 | 40% | 77,000 | 70% |
| Fixed expenses | 30,000 | | 60,000 | |
| Net operating income | $ 14,000 | | $ 17,000 | |

Sterling Farm has experienced a greater increase in net operating income due to its higher CM ratio even though the increase in sales was the same for both farms.

What if sales drop below $100,000? What are the farms' break-even points? What are their margins of safety? The computations needed to answer these questions are shown below using the formula method:

| | Bogside Farm | Sterling Farm |
|---|---|---|
| Fixed expenses | $ 30,000 | $ 60,000 |
| Contribution margin ratio | ÷ 0.40 | ÷ 0.70 |
| Dollar sales to break even | $ 75,000 | $ 85,714 |
| Total current sales (a) | $100,000 | $100,000 |
| Break-even sales | 75,000 | 85,714 |
| Margin of safety in sales dollars (b) | $ 25,000 | $ 14,286 |
| Margin of safety percentage (b) ÷ (a) | 25.0% | 14.3% |

Bogside Farm's margin of safety is greater and its contribution margin ratio is lower than Sterling Farm. Therefore, Bogside Farm is less vulnerable to downturns than Sterling Farm. Due to its lower contribution margin ratio, Bogside Farm will not lose contribution margin as rapidly as Sterling Farm when sales decline. Thus, Bogside Farm's profit will be less volatile. We saw earlier that this is a drawback when sales increase, but it provides more protection when sales drop. And because its break-even point is lower, Bogside Farm can suffer a larger sales decline before losses emerge.

To summarize, without knowing the future, it is not obvious which cost structure is better. Both have advantages and disadvantages. Sterling Farm, with its higher fixed costs and lower variable costs, will experience wider swings in net operating income as sales fluctuate, with greater profits in good years and greater losses in bad years. Bogside Farm, with its lower fixed costs and higher variable costs, will enjoy greater profit stability and will be more protected from losses during bad years, but at the cost of lower net operating income in good years.

## Operating Leverage

**LEARNING OBJECTIVE 8**

Compute the degree of operating leverage at a particular level of sales and explain how it can be used to predict changes in net operating income.

A lever is a tool for multiplying force. Using a lever, a massive object can be moved with only a modest amount of force. In business, *operating leverage* serves a similar purpose. **Operating leverage** is a measure of how sensitive net operating income is to a given percentage change in dollar sales. Operating leverage acts as a multiplier. If operating leverage is high, a small percentage increase in sales can produce a much larger percentage increase in net operating income.

Operating leverage can be illustrated by returning to the data for the two blueberry farms. We previously showed that a 10% increase in sales (from \$100,000 to \$110,000 in each farm) results in a 70% increase in the net operating income of Sterling Farm (from \$10,000 to \$17,000) and only a 40% increase in the net operating income of Bogside Farm (from \$10,000 to \$14,000). Thus, for a 10% increase in sales, Sterling Farm experiences a much greater percentage increase in profits than does Bogside Farm. Therefore, Sterling Farm has greater operating leverage than Bogside Farm.

The **degree of operating leverage** at a given level of sales is computed by the following formula:

+ NO

$$\text{Degree of operating leverage} = \frac{\text{Contribution margin}}{\text{Net operating income}}$$

*The degree of operating leverage is a measure, at a given level of sales, of how a percentage change in sales volume will affect profits.* To illustrate, the degree of operating leverage for the two farms at \$100,000 sales would be computed as follows:

$$\text{Bogside Farm: } \frac{\$40{,}000}{\$10{,}000} = 4$$

$$\text{Sterling Farm: } \frac{\$70{,}000}{\$10{,}000} = 7$$

Because the degree of operating leverage for Bogside Farm is 4, the farm's net operating income grows four times as fast as its sales. In contrast, Sterling Farm's net operating income grows seven times as fast as its sales. Thus, if sales increase by 10%, then we can expect the net operating income of Bogside Farm to increase by four times this amount, or by 40%, and the net operating income of Sterling Farm to increase by seven times this amount, or by 70%. In general, this relation between the percentage change in sales and the percentage change in net operating income is given by the following formula:

$$\begin{array}{c}\text{Percentage change in} \\ \text{net operating income}\end{array} = \begin{array}{c}\text{Degree of} \\ \text{operating leverage}\end{array} \times \begin{array}{c}\text{Percentage} \\ \text{change in sales}\end{array}$$

Bogside Farm: Percentage change in net operating income = 4 × 10% = 40%

Sterling Farm: Percentage change in net operating income = 7 × 10% = 70%

What is responsible for the higher operating leverage at Sterling Farm? The only difference between the two farms is their cost structure. If two companies have the same total revenue and same total expense but different cost structures, then the company with the higher proportion of fixed costs in its cost structure will have higher operating leverage. Referring back to the original example on page 207, when both farms have sales of $100,000 and total expenses of $90,000, one-third of Bogside Farm's costs are fixed but two-thirds of Sterling Farm's costs are fixed. As a consequence, Sterling's degree of operating leverage is higher than Bogside's.

The degree of operating leverage is not a constant; it is greatest at sales levels near the break-even point and decreases as sales and profits rise. The following table shows the degree of operating leverage for Bogside Farm at various sales levels. (Data used earlier for Bogside Farm are shown in color.)

| | | | | | |
|---|---|---|---|---|---|
| Sales | $75,000 | $80,000 | $100,000 | $150,000 | $225,000 |
| Variable expenses | 45,000 | 48,000 | 60,000 | 90,000 | 135,000 |
| Contribution margin (a) | 30,000 | 32,000 | 40,000 | 60,000 | 90,000 |
| Fixed expenses | 30,000 | 30,000 | 30,000 | 30,000 | 30,000 |
| Net operating income (b) | $ 0 | $ 2,000 | $ 10,000 | $ 30,000 | $ 60,000 |
| Degree of operating leverage, (a) ÷ (b) | ∞ | 16 | 4 | 2 | 1.5 |

Thus, a 10% increase in sales would increase profits by only 15% (10% × 1.5) if sales were previously $225,000, as compared to the 40% increase we computed earlier at the $100,000 sales level. The degree of operating leverage will continue to decrease the farther the company moves from its break-even point. At the break-even point, the degree of operating leverage is infinitely large ($30,000 contribution margin ÷ $0 net operating income = ∞).

## The Dangers of a High Degree of Operating Leverage

IN BUSINESS

In recent years, computer chip manufacturers have poured more than $75 billion into constructing new manufacturing facilities to meet the growing demand for digital devices such as iPhones and Blackberrys. Because 70% of the costs of running these facilities are fixed, a sharp drop in customer demand forces these companies to choose between two undesirable options. They can slash production levels and absorb large amounts of unused capacity costs, or they can continue producing large volumes of output in spite of shrinking demand, thereby flooding the market with excess supply and lowering prices. Either choice distresses investors who tend to shy away from computer chip makers in economic downturns.

Source: Bruce Einhorn, "Chipmakers on the Edge," *BusinessWeek*, January 5, 2009, pp. 30–31.

The degree of operating leverage can be used to quickly estimate what impact various percentage changes in sales will have on profits, without the necessity of preparing detailed income statements. As shown by our examples, the effects of operating leverage can be dramatic. If a company is near its break-even point, then even small percentage increases in sales can yield large percentage increases in profits. *This explains why management will often work very hard for only a small increase in sales volume.* If the degree of operating leverage is 5, then a 6% increase in sales would translate into a 30% increase in profits.

# STRUCTURING SALES COMMISSIONS

Companies usually compensate salespeople by paying them a commission based on sales, a salary, or a combination of the two. Commissions based on sales dollars can lead to lower profits. To illustrate, consider Pipeline Unlimited, a producer of surfing equipment. Salespersons sell the company's products to retail sporting goods stores throughout North America and the Pacific Basin. Data for two of the company's surfboards, the XR7 and Turbo models, appear below:

| | Model | |
|---|---|---|
| | XR7 | Turbo |
| Selling price | $695 | $749 |
| Variable expenses | 344 | 410 |
| Contribution margin | $351 | $339 |

Which model will salespeople push hardest if they are paid a commission of 10% of sales revenue? The answer is the Turbo because it has the higher selling price and hence the larger commission. On the other hand, from the standpoint of the company, profits will be greater if salespeople steer customers toward the XR7 model because it has the higher contribution margin.

To eliminate such conflicts, commissions can be based on contribution margin rather than on selling price. If this is done, the salespersons will want to sell the mix of products that maximizes contribution margin. Providing that fixed costs are not affected by the sales mix, maximizing the contribution margin will also maximize the company's profit.[4] In effect, by maximizing their own compensation, salespersons will also maximize the company's profit.

# SALES MIX

**LEARNING OBJECTIVE 9**

Compute the break-even point for a multiproduct company and explain the effects of shifts in the sales mix on contribution margin and the break-even point.

Before concluding our discussion of CVP concepts, we need to consider the impact of changes in *sales mix* on a company's profit.

## The Definition of Sales Mix

The term **sales mix** refers to the relative proportions in which a company's products are sold. The idea is to achieve the combination, or mix, that will yield the greatest profits. Most companies have many products, and often these products are not equally profitable. Hence, profits will depend to some extent on the company's sales mix. Profits will be greater if high-margin rather than low-margin items make up a relatively large proportion of total sales.

Changes in the sales mix can cause perplexing variations in a company's profits. A shift in the sales mix from high-margin items to low-margin items can cause total profits to decrease even though total sales may increase. Conversely, a shift in the sales mix from low-margin items to high-margin items can cause the reverse effect—total profits may increase even though total sales decrease. It is one thing to achieve a particular sales volume; it is quite another to sell the most profitable mix of products.

[4]This also assumes the company has no production constraint. If it does, the sales commissions should be modified.

## Walmart Attempts to Shift its Sales Mix

IN BUSINESS

Almost 130 million customers shop at **Walmart's** 3,200 U.S. stores each week. However, less than half of them shop the whole store—choosing to buy only low-margin basics while skipping higher-margin departments such as apparel. In an effort to shift its sales mix toward higher-margin merchandise, Walmart has reduced spending on advertising and plowed the money into remodeling the clothing departments within its stores. The company hopes this remodeling effort will entice its customers to add clothing to their shopping lists while bypassing the apparel offerings of competitors such as **Kohl's** and **Target**.

Source: Robert Berner, "Fashion Emergency at Walmart," *BusinessWeek*, July 31, 2006, p. 67.

## Sales Mix and Break-Even Analysis

If a company sells more than one product, break-even analysis is more complex than discussed to this point. The reason is that different products will have different selling prices, different costs, and different contribution margins. Consequently, the break-even point depends on the mix in which the various products are sold. To illustrate, consider Virtual Journeys Unlimited, a small company that imports DVDs from France. At present, the company sells two DVDs: the Le Louvre DVD, a tour of the famous art museum in Paris; and the Le Vin DVD, which features the wines and wine-growing regions of France. The company's September sales, expenses, and break-even point are shown in Exhibit 5–4.

As shown in the exhibit, the break-even point is $60,000 in sales, which was computed by dividing the company's fixed expenses of $27,000 by its overall CM ratio of 45%. However, this is the break-even only if the company's sales mix does not change. Currently, the Le Louvre DVD is responsible for 20% and the Le Vin DVD for 80% of the company's dollar sales. Assuming this sales mix does not change, if total sales are $60,000, the sales of the Le Louvre DVD would be $12,000 (20% of $60,000) and the sales of the Le Vin DVD would be $48,000 (80% of $60,000). As shown in Exhibit 5–4, at these levels of sales, the company would indeed break even. But $60,000 in sales represents the break-even point for the company only if the sales mix does not change. *If the sales mix changes, then the break-even point will also usually change.* This is illustrated by the results for October in which the sales mix shifted away from the more profitable Le Vin DVD (which has a 50% CM ratio) toward the less profitable Le Louvre CD (which has a 25% CM ratio). These results appear in Exhibit 5–5.

Although sales have remained unchanged at $100,000, the sales mix is exactly the reverse of what it was in Exhibit 5–4, with the bulk of the sales now coming from the less profitable Le Louvre DVD. Notice that this shift in the sales mix has caused both the overall CM ratio and total profits to drop sharply from the prior month even though total sales are the same. The overall CM ratio has dropped from 45% in September to only 30% in October, and net operating income has dropped from $18,000 to only $3,000. In addition, with the drop in the overall CM ratio, the company's break-even point is no longer $60,000 in sales. Because the company is now realizing less average contribution margin per dollar of sales, it takes more sales to cover the same amount of fixed costs. Thus, the break-even point has increased from $60,000 to $90,000 in sales per year.

In preparing a break-even analysis, an assumption must be made concerning the sales mix. Usually the assumption is that it will not change. However, if the sales mix is expected to change, then this must be explicitly considered in any CVP computations.

**EXHIBIT 5–4** Multiproduct Break-Even Analysis

**Virtual Journeys Unlimited**
**Contribution Income Statement**
**For the Month of September**

| | Le Louvre DVD | | Le Vin DVD | | Total | |
|---|---|---|---|---|---|---|
| | **Amount** | **Percent** | **Amount** | **Percent** | **Amount** | **Percent** |
| Sales | $20,000 | 100% | $80,000 | 100% | $100,000 | 100% |
| Variable expenses | 15,000 | 75% | 40,000 | 50% | 55,000 | 55% |
| Contribution margin | $ 5,000 | 25% | $40,000 | 50% | 45,000 | 45% |
| Fixed expenses | | | | | 27,000 | |
| Net operating income | | | | | $ 18,000 | |

Computation of the break-even point:

$$\frac{\text{Fixed expenses}}{\text{Overall CM ratio}} = \frac{\$27{,}000}{0.45} = \$60{,}000$$

Verification of the break-even point:

| | Le Louvre DVD | Le Vin DVD | Total |
|---|---|---|---|
| Current dollar sales | $20,000 | $80,000 | $100,000 |
| Percentage of total dollar sales | 20% | 80% | 100% |
| Sales at the break-even point | $12,000 | $48,000 | $60,000 |

| | Le Louvre DVD | | Le Vin DVD | | Total | |
|---|---|---|---|---|---|---|
| | **Amount** | **Percent** | **Amount** | **Percent** | **Amount** | **Percent** |
| Sales | $12,000 | 100% | $48,000 | 100% | $60,000 | 100% |
| Variable expenses | 9,000 | 75% | 24,000 | 50% | 33,000 | 55% |
| Contribution margin | $ 3,000 | 25% | $24,000 | 50% | 27,000 | 45% |
| Fixed expenses | | | | | 27,000 | |
| Net operating income | | | | | $ 0 | |

**EXHIBIT 5–5** Multiproduct Break-Even Analysis: A Shift in Sales Mix (see Exhibit 5–4)

**Virtual Journeys Unlimited**
**Contribution Income Statement**
**For the Month of October**

| | Le Louvre DVD | | Le Vin DVD | | Total | |
|---|---|---|---|---|---|---|
| | **Amount** | **Percent** | **Amount** | **Percent** | **Amount** | **Percent** |
| Sales | $80,000 | 100% | $20,000 | 100% | $100,000 | 100% |
| Variable expenses | 60,000 | 75% | 10,000 | 50% | 70,000 | 70% |
| Contribution margin | $20,000 | 25% | $10,000 | 50% | 30,000 | 30% |
| Fixed expenses | | | | | 27,000 | |
| Net operating income | | | | | $ 3,000 | |

Computation of the break-even point:

$$\frac{\text{Fixed expenses}}{\text{Overall CM ratio}} = \frac{\$27{,}000}{0.30} = \$90{,}000$$

## ASSUMPTIONS OF CVP ANALYSIS

A number of assumptions commonly underlie CVP analysis:

1. Selling price is constant. The price of a product or service will not change as volume changes.
2. Costs are linear and can be accurately divided into variable and fixed elements. The variable element is constant per unit, and the fixed element is constant in total over the entire relevant range.
3. In multiproduct companies, the sales mix is constant.
4. In manufacturing companies, inventories do not change. The number of units produced equals the number of units sold.

While these assumptions may be violated in practice, the results of CVP analysis are often "good enough" to be quite useful. Perhaps the greatest danger lies in relying on simple CVP analysis when a manager is contemplating a large change in volume that lies outside of the relevant range. For example, a manager might contemplate increasing the level of sales far beyond what the company has ever experienced before. However, even in these situations the model can be adjusted as we have done in this chapter to take into account anticipated changes in selling prices, fixed costs, and the sales mix that would otherwise violate the assumptions mentioned above. For example, in a decision that would affect fixed costs, the change in fixed costs can be explicitly taken into account as illustrated earlier in the chapter in the Acoustic Concepts example on pages 198–200.

## SUMMARY

**LO1 Explain how changes in activity affect contribution margin and net operating income.**
The unit contribution margin, which is the difference between a unit's selling price and its variable cost, indicates how net operating income will change as the result of selling one more or one less unit. For example, if a product's unit contribution margin is $10, then selling one more unit will add $10 to the company's profit.

**LO2 Prepare and interpret a cost-volume-profit (CVP) graph and a profit graph.**
A cost-volume-profit graph displays sales revenues and expenses as a function of unit sales. The break-even point on the graph is the point at which the total sales revenue and total expense lines intersect. A profit graph displays profit as a function of unit sales. The break-even point on the profit graph is the point at which profit is zero.

**LO3 Use the contribution margin ratio (CM ratio) to compute changes in contribution margin and net operating income resulting from changes in sales volume.**
The contribution margin ratio is computed by dividing the unit contribution margin by the unit selling price, or by dividing the total contribution margin by the total sales.

The contribution margin shows how much a dollar increase in sales affects the total contribution margin and net operating income. For example, if a product has a 40% contribution margin ratio, then a $100 increase in sales should result in a $40 increase in contribution margin and in net operating income.

**LO4 Show the effects on net operating income of changes in variable costs, fixed costs, selling price, and volume.**
Contribution margin concepts can be used to estimate the effects of changes in various parameters such as variable costs, fixed costs, selling prices, and volume on net operating income.

**LO5 Determine the level of sales needed to achieve a desired target profit.**
The level of sales needed to achieve a desired target profit can be computed using several methods. The answer can be derived using the fundamental profit equation and simple algebra or formulas can be used. In either approach, the unit sales required to attain a desired target profit

is ultimately determined by summing the desired target profit and the fixed expenses and then dividing the result by the unit contribution margin.

**LO6 Determine the break-even point.**

The break-even point is the level of sales at which profit is zero. This is just a special case of solving for the level of sales needed to achieve a desired target profit—in this special case the target profit is zero.

**LO7 Compute the margin of safety and explain its significance.**

The margin of safety is the difference between the total budgeted (or actual) sales dollars of a period and the break-even sales dollars. It expresses how much cushion there is in the current level of sales above the break-even point.

**LO8 Compute the degree of operating leverage at a particular level of sales and explain how it can be used to predict changes in net operating income.**

The degree of operating leverage is computed by dividing the total contribution margin by net operating income. The degree of operating leverage can be used to determine the impact a given percentage change in sales would have on net operating income. For example, if a company's degree of operating leverage is 2.5, then a 10% increase in sales from the current level of sales should result in a 25% increase in net operating income.

**LO9 Compute the break-even point for a multiproduct company and explain the effects of shifts in the sales mix on contribution margin and the break-even point.**

The break-even point for a multiproduct company can be computed by dividing the company's total fixed expenses by the overall contribution margin ratio.

This method for computing the break-even point assumes that the sales mix is constant. If the sales mix shifts toward products with a lower contribution margin ratio, then more total sales are required to attain any given level of profits.

## GUIDANCE ANSWER TO DECISION POINT

**Loan Officer (p. 206)**

To determine the company's margin of safety, you need to determine its break-even point. Start by estimating the company's variable expense ratio:

$$\text{Variable cost per unit} \div \text{Selling price per unit} = \text{Variable expense ratio}$$

$$\$68 \div \$100 = 68\%$$

Then, estimate the company's variable expenses:

$$\text{Sales} \times \text{Variable expense ratio} = \text{Estimated amount of variable expenses}$$

$$\$8{,}000{,}000 \times 0.68 = \$5{,}440{,}000$$

Next, estimate the company's current level of fixed expenses as follows:

$$\text{Sales} = \text{Variable expenses} + \text{Fixed expenses} + \text{Profits}$$

$$\$8{,}000{,}000 = \$5{,}440{,}000 + X + \$700{,}000$$

$$X = \$8{,}000{,}000 - \$5{,}440{,}000 - \$700{,}000$$

$$X = \$1{,}860{,}000$$

Use the equation approach to estimate the company's break-even point:

$$\text{Sales} = \text{Variable expenses} + \text{Fixed expenses} + \text{Profits}$$

$$X = 0.68X + \$1{,}860{,}000 + \$0$$

$$0.32X = \$1{,}860{,}000$$

$$X = \$5{,}812{,}500$$

Finally, compute the company's margin of safety:

$$\begin{aligned}\text{Margin of safety} &= (\text{Sales} - \text{Break-even sales}) \div \text{Sales}\\ &= (\$8{,}000{,}000 - \$5{,}812{,}500) \div \$8{,}000{,}000\\ &= 27.3\%\end{aligned}$$

The margin of safety appears to be adequate, so if the other information about the company is favorable, a loan would seem to be justified.

## GUIDANCE ANSWERS TO CONCEPT CHECKS

1. **Choice d.** The contribution margin ratio equals 1.0 − Variable costs as a percent of sales.
2. **Choice d.** The contribution margin per unit is $12 (40% of $30). Therefore, the break-even point in units sold = $60,000 ÷ $12 = 5,000.
3. **Choice a.** ($100,000 + $50,000) ÷ $20 contribution margin per unit = 7,500 units.
4. **Choice c.** 7,500 units is 2,500 units above the break-even point. Therefore, the margin of safety is 2,500 units × $55 per unit = $137,500.

## REVIEW PROBLEM: CVP RELATIONSHIPS

Voltar Company manufactures and sells a specialized cordless telephone for high electromagnetic radiation environments. The company's contribution format income statement for the most recent year is given below:

| | Total | Per Unit | Percent of Sales |
|---|---|---|---|
| Sales (20,000 units) | $1,200,000 | $60 | 100% |
| Variable expenses | 900,000 | 45 | ? % |
| Contribution margin | 300,000 | $15 | ? % |
| Fixed expenses | 240,000 | | |
| Net operating income | $ 60,000 | | |

Management is anxious to increase the company's profit and has asked for an analysis of a number of items.

***Required:***

1. Compute the company's CM ratio and variable expense ratio.
2. Compute the company's break-even point in both units and sales dollars. Use the equation method.
3. Assume that sales increase by $400,000 next year. If cost behavior patterns remain unchanged, by how much will the company's net operating income increase? Use the CM ratio to compute your answer.
4. Refer to the original data. Assume that next year management wants the company to earn a profit of at least $90,000. How many units will have to be sold to meet this target profit?
5. Refer to the original data. Compute the company's margin of safety in both dollar and percentage form.
6. a. Compute the company's degree of operating leverage at the present level of sales.
   b. Assume that through a more intense effort by the sales staff, the company's sales increase by 8% next year. By what percentage would you expect net operating income to increase? Use the degree of operating leverage to obtain your answer.
   c. Verify your answer to (*b*) by preparing a new contribution format income statement showing an 8% increase in sales.
7. In an effort to increase sales and profits, management is considering the use of a higher-quality speaker. The higher-quality speaker would increase variable costs by $3 per unit, but management could eliminate one quality inspector who is paid a salary of $30,000 per year. The sales manager estimates that the higher-quality speaker would increase annual sales by at least 20%.

a. Assuming that changes are made as described above, prepare a projected contribution format income statement for next year. Show data on a total, per unit, and percentage basis.
b. Compute the company's new break-even point in both units and dollars of sales. Use the formula method.
c. Would you recommend that the changes be made?

**Solution to Review Problem**

1.

$$\text{CM ratio} = \frac{\text{Unit contribution margin}}{\text{Unit selling price}} = \frac{\$15}{\$60} = 25\%$$

$$\text{Variable expense ratio} = \frac{\text{Variable expense}}{\text{Selling price}} = \frac{\$45}{\$60} = 75\%$$

2.

$$\begin{aligned} \text{Profit} &= \text{Unit CM} \times Q - \text{Fixed expenses} \\ \$0 &= (\$60 - \$45) \times Q - \$240{,}000 \\ \$15Q &= \$240{,}000 \\ Q &= \$240{,}000 \div \$15 \\ Q &= 16{,}000 \text{ units; or at \$60 per unit, \$960,000} \end{aligned}$$

3.

| | |
|---|---|
| Increase in sales | $400,000 |
| Multiply by the CM ratio | × 25% |
| Expected increase in contribution margin | $100,000 |

Because the fixed expenses are not expected to change, net operating income will increase by the entire $100,000 increase in contribution margin computed above.

4. Equation method:

$$\begin{aligned} \text{Profit} &= \text{Unit CM} \times Q - \text{Fixed expenses} \\ \$90{,}000 &= (\$60 - \$45) \times Q - \$240{,}000 \\ \$15Q &= \$90{,}000 + \$240{,}000 \\ Q &= \$330{,}000 \div \$15 \\ Q &= 22{,}000 \text{ units} \end{aligned}$$

Formula method:

$$\frac{\text{Unit sales to attain}}{\text{the target profit}} = \frac{\text{Target profit} + \text{Fixed expenses}}{\text{Contribution margin per unit}} = \frac{\$90{,}000 + \$240{,}000}{\$15 \text{ per unit}} = 22{,}000 \text{ units}$$

5.

$$\begin{aligned} \text{Margin of safety in dollars} &= \text{Total sales} - \text{Break-even sales} \\ &= \$1{,}200{,}000 - \$960{,}000 = \$240{,}000 \end{aligned}$$

$$\text{Margin of safety percentage} = \frac{\text{Margin of safety in dollars}}{\text{Total sales}} = \frac{\$240{,}000}{\$1{,}200{,}000} = 20\%$$

6. a. $$\text{Degree of operating leverage} = \frac{\text{Contribution margin}}{\text{Net operating income}} = \frac{\$300{,}000}{\$60{,}000} = 5$$

b.

| | |
|---|---|
| Expected increase in sales | 8% |
| Degree of operating leverage | × 5 |
| Expected increase in net operating income | 40% |

c. If sales increase by 8%, then 21,600 units (20,000 × 1.08 = 21,600) will be sold next year. The new contribution format income statement would be as follows:

| | Total | Per Unit | Percent of Sales |
|---|---|---|---|
| Sales (21,600 units) | $1,296,000 | $60 | 100% |
| Variable expenses | 972,000 | 45 | 75% |
| Contribution margin | 324,000 | $15 | 25% |
| Fixed expenses | 240,000 | | |
| Net operating income | $ 84,000 | | |

Thus, the $84,000 expected net operating income for next year represents a 40% increase over the $60,000 net operating income earned during the current year:

$$\frac{\$84,000 - \$60,000}{\$60,000} = \frac{\$24,000}{\$60,000} = 40\% \text{ increase}$$

Note from the income statement above that the increase in sales from 20,000 to 21,600 units has increased *both* total sales and total variable expenses.

7. a. A 20% increase in sales would result in 24,000 units being sold next year: 20,000 units × 1.20 = 24,000 units.

| | Total | Per Unit | Percent of Sales |
|---|---|---|---|
| Sales (24,000 units) | $1,440,000 | $60 | 100% |
| Variable expenses | 1,152,000 | 48* | 80% |
| Contribution margin | 288,000 | $12 | 20% |
| Fixed expenses | 210,000† | | |
| Net operating income | $ 78,000 | | |

*$45 + $3 = $48; $48 ÷ $60 = 80%.
†$240,000 − $30,000 = $210,000.

Note that the change in per unit variable expenses results in a change in both the per unit contribution margin and the CM ratio.

b.

$$\text{Unit sales to break even} = \frac{\text{Fixed expenses}}{\text{Unit contribution margin}}$$

$$= \frac{\$210,000}{\$12 \text{ per unit}} = 17,500 \text{ units}$$

$$\text{Dollar sales to break even} = \frac{\text{Fixed expenses}}{\text{CM ratio}}$$

$$= \frac{\$210,000}{0.20} = \$1,050,000$$

c. Yes, based on these data the changes should be made. The changes increase the company's net operating income from the present $60,000 to $78,000 per year. Although the changes also result in a higher break-even point (17,500 units as compared to the present 16,000 units), the company's margin of safety actually becomes greater than before:

$$\text{Margin of safety in dollars} = \text{Total sales} - \text{Break-even sales}$$

$$= \$1,440,000 - \$1,050,000 = \$390,000$$

As shown in (5) on the prior page, the company's present margin of safety is only $240,000. Thus, several benefits will result from the proposed changes.

# GLOSSARY

**Break-even point** The level of sales at which profit is zero. (p. 190)

**Contribution margin ratio (CM ratio)** A ratio computed by dividing contribution margin by dollar sales. (p. 195)

**Cost-volume-profit (CVP) graph** A graphical representation of the relationships between an organization's revenues, costs, and profits on the one hand and its sales volume on the other hand. (p. 192)

**Degree of operating leverage** A measure, at a given level of sales, of how a percentage change in sales will affect profits. The degree of operating leverage is computed by dividing contribution margin by net operating income. (p. 208)

**Incremental analysis** An analytical approach that focuses only on those costs and revenues that change as a result of a decision. (p. 199)

**Margin of safety** The excess of budgeted (or actual) dollar sales over the break-even dollar sales. (p. 205)

**Operating leverage** A measure of how sensitive net operating income is to a given percentage change in dollar sales. (p. 208)

**Sales mix** The relative proportions in which a company's products are sold. Sales mix is computed by expressing the sales of each product as a percentage of total sales. (p. 210)

**Target profit analysis** Estimating what sales volume is needed to achieve a specific target profit. (p. 201)

**Variable expense ratio** A ratio computed by dividing variable expenses by dollar sales. (p. 196)

# QUESTIONS

**5–1** What is meant by a product's contribution margin ratio? How is this ratio useful in planning business operations?

**5–2** Often the most direct route to a business decision is an incremental analysis. What is meant by an *incremental analysis?*

**5–3** In all respects, Company A and Company B are identical except that Company A's costs are mostly variable, whereas Company B's costs are mostly fixed. When sales increase, which company will tend to realize the greatest increase in profits? Explain.

**5–4** What is meant by the term *operating leverage?*

**5–5** What is meant by the term *break-even point?*

**5–6** In response to a request from your immediate supervisor, you have prepared a CVP graph portraying the cost and revenue characteristics of your company's product and operations. Explain how the lines on the graph and the break-even point would change if (*a*) the selling price per unit decreased, (*b*) fixed cost increased throughout the entire range of activity portrayed on the graph, and (*c*) variable cost per unit increased.

**5–7** What is meant by the margin of safety?

**5–8** What is meant by the term *sales mix?* What assumption is usually made concerning sales mix in CVP analysis?

**5–9** Explain how a shift in the sales mix could result in both a higher break-even point and a lower net income.

**Multiple-choice questions are provided on the text website at www.mhhe.com/brewer6e.**

# APPLYING EXCEL

**LO6, LO7, LO8**

**Available with McGraw-Hill's *Connect® Accounting*.**

The Excel worksheet form that appears on the next page is to be used to recreate portions of the Review Problem on pages 215–217. Download the workbook containing this form from the Online Learning Center at www.mhhe.com/brewer6e. *On the website you will also receive instructions about how to use this worksheet form.*

| | A | B | C | D |
|---|---|---|---|---|
| 1 | Chapter 5: Applying Excel | | | |
| 2 | | | | |
| 3 | **Data** | | | |
| 4 | Unit sales | 20,000 | units | |
| 5 | Selling price per unit | $60 | per unit | |
| 6 | Variable expenses per unit | $45 | per unit | |
| 7 | Fixed expenses | $240,000 | | |
| 8 | | | | |
| 9 | *Enter a formula into each of the cells marked with a ? below* | | | |
| 10 | **Review Problem: CVP Relationships** | | | |
| 11 | | | | |
| 12 | ***Compute the CM ratio and variable expense ratio*** | | | |
| 13 | Selling price per unit | ? | per unit | |
| 14 | Variable expenses per unit | ? | per unit | |
| 15 | Contribution margin per unit | ? | per unit | |
| 16 | | | | |
| 17 | CM ratio | ? | | |
| 18 | Variable expense ratio | ? | | |
| 19 | | | | |
| 20 | ***Compute the break-even*** | | | |
| 21 | Break-even in unit sales | ? | units | |
| 22 | Break-even in dollar sales | ? | | |
| 23 | | | | |
| 24 | ***Compute the margin of safety*** | | | |
| 25 | Margin of safety in dollars | ? | | |
| 26 | Margin of safety percentage | ? | | |
| 27 | | | | |
| 28 | ***Compute the degree of operating leverage*** | | | |
| 29 | Sales | ? | | |
| 30 | Variable expenses | ? | | |
| 31 | Contribution margin | ? | | |
| 32 | Fixed expenses | ? | | |
| 33 | Net operating income | ? | | |
| 34 | | | | |
| 35 | Degree of operating leverage | ? | | |
| 36 | | | | |

Chapter 5 Form | Filled in Chapter 5 Form

You should proceed to the requirements below only after completing your worksheet.

***Required:***

1. Check your worksheet by changing the fixed expenses to $270,000. If your worksheet is operating properly, the degree of operating leverage should be 10. If you do not get this answer, find the errors in your worksheet and correct them. How much is the margin of safety percentage? Did it change? Why or why not?
2. Enter the following data from a different company into your worksheet:

| | |
|---|---|
| Unit sales | 10,000 units |
| Selling price per unit | $120 per unit |
| Variable expenses per unit | $72 per unit |
| Fixed expenses | $420,000 |

   What is the margin of safety percentage? What is the degree of operating leverage?
3. Using the degree of operating leverage and without changing anything in your worksheet, calculate the percentage change in net operating income if unit sales increase by 15%.
4. Confirm the calculations you made in part (3) above by increasing the unit sales in your worksheet by 15%. What is the new net operating income and by what percentage did it increase?

5. Thad Morgan, a motorcycle enthusiast, has been exploring the possibility of relaunching the Western Hombre brand of cycle that was popular in the 1930s. The retro-look cycle would be sold for $10,000 and at that price, Thad estimates 600 units would be sold each year. The variable cost to produce and sell the cycles would be $7,500 per unit. The annual fixed cost would be $1,200,000.
   a. What would be the break-even unit sales, the margin of safety in dollars, and the degree of operating leverage?
   b. Thad is worried about the selling price. Rumors are circulating that other retro brands of cycles may be revived. If so, the selling price for the Western Hombre would have to be reduced to $9,000 to compete effectively. In that event, Thad would also reduce fixed expenses by $300,000 by reducing advertising expenses, but he still hopes to sell 600 units per year. Do you think this is a good plan? Explain. Also, explain the degree of operating leverage that appears on your worksheet.

## THE FOUNDATIONAL 15

**Available with McGraw-Hill's *Connect® Accounting.***

LO1, LO3, LO4
LO5, LO6, LO7, LO8

Oslo Company prepared the following contribution format income statement based on a sales volume of 1,000 units (the relevant range of production is 500 units to 1,500 units):

| | |
|---|---|
| Sales | $20,000 |
| Variable expenses | 12,000 |
| Contribution margin | 8,000 |
| Fixed expenses | 6,000 |
| Net operating income | $ 2,000 |

***Required:***

(Answer each question independently and always refer to the original data unless instructed otherwise.)

1. What is the contribution margin per unit?
2. What is the contribution margin ratio?
3. What is the variable expense ratio?
4. If sales increase to 1,001 units, what would be the increase in net operating income?
5. If sales decline to 900 units, what would be the net operating income?
6. If the selling price increases by $2 per unit and the sales volume decreases by 100 units, what would be the net operating income?
7. If the variable cost per unit increases by $1, spending on advertising increases by $1,500, and unit sales increase by 250 units, what would be the net operating income?
8. What is the break-even point in unit sales?
9. What is the break-even point in sales dollars?
10. How many units must be sold to achieve a target profit of $5,000?
11. What is the margin of safety in dollars? What is the margin of safety percentage?
12. What is the degree of operating leverage?
13. Using the degree of operating leverage, what is the estimated percent increase in net operating income of a 5% increase in sales?
14. Assume that the amounts of the company's total variable expenses and total fixed expenses were reversed. In other words, assume that the total variable expenses are $6,000 and the total fixed expenses are $12,000. Under this scenario and assuming that total sales remain the same, what is the degree of operating leverage?
15. Using the degree of operating leverage that you computed in the previous question, what is the estimated percent increase in net operating income of a 5% increase in sales?

## EXERCISES

**All applicable exercises are available with McGraw-Hill's *Connect® Accounting.***

**EXERCISE 5–1 Preparing a Contribution Format Income Statement [LO1]**

Wheeler Corporation's most recent income statement follows:

| | Total | Per Unit |
|---|---|---|
| Sales (8,000 units) | $208,000 | $26.00 |
| Variable expenses | 144,000 | 18.00 |
| Contribution margin | 64,000 | $ 8.00 |
| Fixed expenses | 56,000 | |
| Net operating income | $ 8,000 | |

***Required:***

Prepare a new contribution format income statement under each of the following conditions (consider each case independently):

1. The sales volume increases by 50 units.
2. The sales volume declines by 50 units.
3. The sales volume is 7,000 units.

### EXERCISE 5–2 Prepare a Cost-Volume-Profit (CVP) Graph [LO2]

Katara Enterprises distributes a single product whose selling price is $36 and whose variable expense is $24 per unit. The company's monthly fixed expense is $12,000.

***Required:***

1. Prepare a cost-volume-profit graph for the company up to a sales level of 2,000 units.
2. Estimate the company's break-even point in unit sales using your cost-volume-profit graph.

### EXERCISE 5–3 Prepare a Profit Graph [LO2]

Capricio Enterprises distributes a single product whose selling price is $19 and whose variable expense is $15 per unit. The company's fixed expense is $12,000 per month.

***Required:***

1. Prepare a profit graph for the company up to a sales level of 4,000 units.
2. Estimate the company's break-even point in unit sales using your profit graph.

### EXERCISE 5–4 Computing and Using the CM Ratio [LO3]

Last month when Harrison Creations, Inc., sold 40,000 units, total sales were $300,000, total variable expenses were $240,000, and fixed expenses were $45,000.

Total variable expenses = $210,000

***Required:***

1. What is the company's contribution margin (CM) ratio?
2. Estimate the change in the company's net operating income if it were to increase its total sales by $1,500.

### EXERCISE 5–5 Changes in Variable Costs, Fixed Costs, Selling Price, and Sales Volume [LO4]

Data for Herron Corporation are shown below:

Selling price = $100; Variable expenses per unit = $40

| | Per Unit | Percent of Sales |
|---|---|---|
| Selling price | $75 | 100% |
| Variable expenses | 45 | 60% |
| Contribution margin | $30 | 40% |

Fixed expenses are $75,000 per month and the company is selling 3,000 units per month.

***Required:***

1. The marketing manager believes that an $8,000 increase in the monthly advertising budget would increase monthly sales by $15,000. Should the advertising budget be increased?
2. Refer to the original data. Management is considering using higher-quality components that would increase the variable cost by $3 per unit. The marketing manager believes that the higher-quality product would increase sales by 15% per month. Should the higher-quality components be used?

Selling price = $160

**EXERCISE 5–6 Compute the Level of Sales Required to Attain a Target Profit [LO5]**
Liman Corporation has a single product whose selling price is $140 and whose variable expense is $60 per unit. The company's monthly fixed expense is $40,000.

***Required:***
1. Using the equation method, solve for the unit sales that are required to earn a target profit of $6,000.
2. Using the formula method, solve for the unit sales that are required to earn a target profit of $8,000.

Monthly fixed expense = $6,000

**EXERCISE 5–7 Compute the Break-Even Point [LO6]**
Maxson Products distributes a single product, a woven basket whose selling price is $8 and whose variable cost is $6 per unit. The company's monthly fixed expense is $5,500.

***Required:***
1. Solve for the company's break-even point in unit sales using the equation method.
2. Solve for the company's break-even point in sales dollars using the equation method and the CM ratio.
3. Solve for the company's break-even point in unit sales using the formula method.
4. Solve for the company's break-even point in sales dollars using formula method and the CM ratio.

Unit sales = 900 units per month

**EXERCISE 5–8 Compute the Margin of Safety [LO7]**
Mohan Corporation is a distributor of a sun umbrella used at resort hotels. Data concerning next month's budget appear below:

| | |
|---|---|
| Selling price | $25 per unit |
| Variable expenses | $15 per unit |
| Fixed expenses | $8,500 per month |
| Unit sales | 1,000 units per month |

***Required:***
1. Compute the company's margin of safety.
2. Compute the company's margin of safety as a percentage of its sales.

Sales = $240,000; Variable expenses = $168,000

**EXERCISE 5–9 Compute and Use the Degree of Operating Leverage [LO8]**
Eneliko Company installs home theater systems. The company's most recent monthly contribution format income statement appears below:

| | Amount | Percent of Sales |
|---|---|---|
| Sales | $120,000 | 100% |
| Variable expenses | 84,000 | 70% |
| Contribution margin | 36,000 | 30% |
| Fixed expenses | 24,000 | |
| Net operating income | $ 12,000 | |

***Required:***
1. Compute the company's degree of operating leverage.
2. Using the degree of operating leverage, estimate the impact on net operating income of a 10% increase in sales.
3. Verify your estimate from part (2) above by constructing a new contribution format income statement for the company assuming a 10% increase in sales.

Runway sales = $100,000; Runway variable expenses = $10,000

**EXERCISE 5–10 Compute the Break-Even Point for a Multiproduct Company [LO9]**
Lucky Products markets two computer games: Predator and Runway. A contribution format income statement for a recent month for the two games appears below:

| | Predator | Runway | Total |
|---|---|---|---|
| Sales | $100,000 | $50,000 | $150,000 |
| Variable expenses | 25,000 | 5,000 | 30,000 |
| Contribution margin | $ 75,000 | $45,000 | 120,000 |
| Fixed expenses | | | 90,000 |
| Net operating income | | | $ 30,000 |

***Required:***
1. Compute the overall contribution margin (CM) ratio for the company.
2. Compute the overall break-even point for the company in sales dollars.
3. Verify the overall break-even point for the company by constructing a contribution format income statement showing the appropriate levels of sales for the two products.

**EXERCISE 5–11 Break-Even Analysis; Target Profit; Margin of Safety; CM Ratio [LO1, LO3, LO5, LO6, LO7]**

Pringle Company distributes a single product. The company's sales and expenses for a recent month follow:

| | Total | Per Unit |
|---|---|---|
| Sales | $600,000 | $40 |
| Variable expenses | 420,000 | 28 |
| Contribution margin | 180,000 | $12 |
| Fixed expenses | 150,000 | |
| Net operating income | $ 30,000 | |

***Required:***
1. What is the monthly break-even point in units sold and in sales dollars?
2. Without resorting to computations, what is the total contribution margin at the break-even point?
3. How many units would have to be sold each month to earn a target profit of $18,000? Use the formula method. Verify your answer by preparing a contribution format income statement at the target level of sales.
4. Refer to the original data. Compute the company's margin of safety in both dollar and percentage terms.
5. What is the company's CM ratio? If monthly sales increase by $80,000 and there is no change in fixed expenses, by how much would you expect monthly net operating income to increase?

**EXERCISE 5–12 Break-Even and Target Profit Analysis [LO4, LO5, LO6]**

Reveen Products sells camping equipment. One of the company's products, a camp lantern, sells for $90 per unit. Variable expenses are $63 per lantern, and fixed expenses associated with the lantern total $135,000 per month.

Variable expenses = $45 per lantern

***Required:***
1. Compute the company's break-even point in number of lanterns and in total sales dollars.
2. If the variable expenses per lantern increase as a percentage of the selling price, will it result in a higher or a lower break-even point? Why? (Assume that the fixed expenses remain unchanged.)
3. At present, the company is selling 8,000 lanterns per month. The sales manager is convinced that a 10% reduction in the selling price will result in a 25% increase in the number of lanterns sold each month. Prepare two contribution format income statements, one under present operating conditions, and one as operations would appear after the proposed changes. Show both total and per unit data on your statements.
4. Refer to the data in (3) above. How many lanterns would have to be sold at the new selling price to yield a minimum net operating income of $72,000 per month?

**EXERCISE 5–13 Break-Even Analysis and CVP Graphing [LO2, LO4, LO6]**

Chi Omega Sorority is planning its annual Riverboat Extravaganza. The Extravaganza committee has assembled the following expected costs for the event:

| | |
|---|---|
| Dinner (per person) | $7 |
| Favors and program (per person) | $3 |
| Band | $1,500 |
| Tickets and advertising | $700 |
| Riverboat rental | $4,800 |
| Floorshow and strolling entertainers | $1,000 |

The committee members would like to charge $30 per person for the evening's activities.

***Required:***

1. Compute the break-even point for the Extravaganza (in terms of the number of persons that must attend).
2. Assume that only 250 persons attended the Extravaganza last year. If the same number attend this year, what price per ticket must be charged to break even?
3. Refer to the original data ($30 ticket price per person). Prepare a CVP graph for the Extravaganza from zero tickets up to 600 tickets sold.

### EXERCISE 5–14 Multiproduct Break-Even Analysis [LO9]

Okabee Enterprises is the distributor for two products, Model A100 and Model B900. Monthly sales and the contribution margin ratios for the two products follow:

| | Product | | |
|---|---|---|---|
| | Model A100 | Model B900 | Total |
| Sales | $700,000 | $300,000 | $1,000,000 |
| Contribution margin ratio | 60% | 70% | ? |

The company's fixed expenses total $598,500 per month.

***Required:***

1. Prepare a contribution format income statement for the company as a whole.
2. Compute the break-even point for the company based on the current sales mix.
3. If sales increase by $50,000 per month, by how much would you expect net operating income to increase? What are your assumptions?

### EXERCISE 5–15 Operating Leverage [LO4, LO8]

Superior Door Company sells prehung doors to home builders. The doors are sold for $60 each. Variable costs are $42 per door, and fixed costs total $450,000 per year. The company is currently selling 30,000 doors per year.

Fixed costs = $486,000

***Required:***

1. Prepare a contribution format income statement for the company at the present level of sales and compute the degree of operating leverage.
2. Management is confident that the company can sell 37,500 doors next year (an increase of 7,500 doors, or 25%, over current sales). Compute the following:
   a. The expected percentage increase in net operating income for next year
   b. The expected net operating income for next year. (Do not prepare an income statement; use the degree of operating leverage to compute your answer.)

### EXERCISE 5–16 Break-Even and Target Profit Analysis [LO3, LO4, LO5, LO6]

Super Sales Company is the exclusive distributor for a revolutionary bookbag. The product sells for $60 per unit and has a CM ratio of 40%. The company's fixed expenses are $360,000 per year. The company plans to sell 17,000 bookbags this year.

***Required:***

1. What are the variable expenses per unit?
2. Using the equation method:
   a. What is the break-even point in units and in sales dollars?
   b. What sales level in units and in sales dollars is required to earn an annual profit of $90,000?
   c. Assume that through negotiation with the manufacturer the Super Sales Company is able to reduce its variable expenses by $3 per unit. What is the company's new break-even point in units and in sales dollars?
3. Repeat (2) above using the formula method.

**EXERCISE 5–17 Using a Contribution Format Income Statement [LO1, LO4]**

Porter Company's most recent contribution format income statement is shown below:

| | Total | Per Unit |
|---|---|---|
| Sales (30,000 units) | $150,000 | $5 |
| Variable expenses | 90,000 | 3 |
| Contribution margin | 60,000 | $2 |
| Fixed expenses | 50,000 | |
| Net operating income | $ 10,000 | |

***Required:***

Prepare a new contribution format income statement under each of the following conditions (consider each case independently):

1. The number of units sold increases by 15%.
2. The selling price decreases by 50 cents per unit, and the number of units sold increases by 20%.
3. The selling price increases by 50 cents per unit, fixed expenses increase by $10,000, and the number of units sold decreases by 5%.
4. Variable expenses increase by 20 cents per unit, the selling price increases by 12%, and the number of units sold decreases by 10%.

**EXERCISE 5–18 Missing Data; Basic CVP Concepts [LO1, LO9]**

Fill in the missing amounts in each of the eight case situations below. Each case is independent of the others. (Hint: One way to find the missing amounts would be to prepare a contribution format income statement for each case, enter the known data, and then compute the missing items.)

a. Assume that only one product is being sold in each of the four following case situations:

| Case | Units Sold | Sales | Variable Expenses | Contribution Margin per Unit | Fixed Expenses | Net Operating Income (Loss) |
|---|---|---|---|---|---|---|
| 1 | 9,000 | $270,000 | $162,000 | ? | $90,000 | ? |
| 2 | ? | $350,000 | ? | $15 | $170,000 | $ 40,000 |
| 3 | 20,000 | ? | $280,000 | $6 | ? | $ 35,000 |
| 4 | 5,000 | $160,000 | ? | ? | $82,000 | $(12,000) |

b. Assume that more than one product is being sold in each of the four following case situations:

| Case | Sales | Variable Expenses | Average Contribution Margin (Percent) | Fixed Expenses | Net Operating Income (Loss) |
|---|---|---|---|---|---|
| 1 | $450,000 | ? | 40% | ? | $65,000 |
| 2 | $200,000 | $130,000 | ? | $60,000 | ? |
| 3 | ? | ? | 80% | $470,000 | $90,000 |
| 4 | $300,000 | $90,000 | ? | ? | $(15,000) |

## PROBLEMS

connect ACCOUNTING

Alternate problem set is available on the text website and in Connect® Accounting.

**All applicable problems are available with McGraw-Hill's *Connect®* *Accounting*.**

CHECK FIGURE
(1) Break even: 20,000 shirts; (3) $15,000 loss

**PROBLEM 5–19A Basic CVP Analysis; Graphing [LO1, LO2, LO4, LO6]**

Shirts Unlimited operates a chain of shirt stores that carry many styles of shirts that are all sold at the same price. To encourage sales personnel to be aggressive in their sales efforts, the company pays a substantial sales commission on each shirt sold. Sales personnel also receive a small base salary.

The following worksheet contains cost and revenue data for Store 36. These data are typical of the company's many outlets:

| | Per Shift |
|---|---|
| Selling price | $ 40.00 |
| Variable expenses: | |
| Invoice cost | $ 18.00 |
| Sales commission | 7.00 |
| Total variable expenses | $ 25.00 |
| | **Annual** |
| Fixed expenses: | |
| Rent | $ 80,000 |
| Advertising | 150,000 |
| Salaries | 70,000 |
| Total fixed expenses | $300,000 |

The company has asked you, as a member of its planning group, to assist in some basic analysis of its stores and company policies.

***Required:***

1. Calculate the annual break-even point in dollar sales and in unit sales for Store 36.
2. Prepare a CVP graph showing cost and revenue data for Store 36 from zero shirts up to 30,000 shirts sold each year. Clearly indicate the break-even point on the graph.
3. If 19,000 shirts are sold in a year, what would be Store 36's net operating income or loss?
4. The company is considering paying the store manager of Store 36 an incentive commission of $3 per shirt (in addition to the salespersons' commissions). If this change is made, what will be the new break-even point in dollar sales and in unit sales?
5. Refer to the original data. As an alternative to (4) above, the company is considering paying the store manager a $3 commission on each shirt sold in excess of the break-even point. If this change is made, what will be the store's net operating income or loss if 23,500 shirts are sold in a year?
6. Refer to the original data. The company is considering eliminating sales commissions entirely in its stores and increasing fixed salaries by $107,000 annually.
   a. If this change is made, what will be the new break-even point in dollar sales and in unit sales in Store 36?
   b. Would you recommend that the change be made? Explain.

eXcel

CHECK FIGURE
(1) Break even: 15,000 units; (4) 17,500 units

**PROBLEM 5–20A Basics of CVP Analysis; Cost Structure [LO1, LO3, LO4, LO5, LO6]**

Memofax, Inc., produces memory enhancement kits for fax machines. Sales have been very erratic, with some months showing a profit and some months showing a loss. The company's contribution format income statement for the most recent month is given below:

| | |
|---|---|
| Sales (13,500 units at $20 per unit) | $270,000 |
| Variable expenses | 189,000 |
| Contribution margin | 81,000 |
| Fixed expenses | 90,000 |
| Net operating loss | $ (9,000) |

***Required:***

1. Compute the company's CM ratio and its break-even point in both units and dollars.
2. The sales manager feels that an $8,000 increase in the monthly advertising budget, combined with an intensified effort by the sales staff, will result in a $70,000 increase in monthly sales. If the sales manager is right, what will be the effect on the company's monthly net operating income or loss? (Use the incremental approach in preparing your answer.)
3. Refer to the original data. The president is convinced that a 10% reduction in the selling price, combined with an increase of $35,000 in the monthly advertising budget, will double unit sales. What will the new contribution format income statement look like if these changes are adopted?
4. Refer to the original data. The company's advertising agency thinks that a new package would help sales. The new package being proposed would increase packaging costs by $0.60 per unit. Assuming no other changes, how many units would have to be sold each month to earn a profit of $4,500?
5. Refer to the original data. By automating, the company could slash its variable expenses in half. However, fixed costs would increase by $118,000 per month.
   a. Compute the new CM ratio and the new break-even point in both units and dollars.
   b. Assume that the company expects to sell 20,000 units next month. Prepare two contribution format income statements, one assuming that operations are not automated and one assuming that they are.
   c. Would you recommend that the company automate its operations? Explain.

**PROBLEM 5–21A Basic CVP Analysis [LO1, LO3, LO4, LO6, LO8]**

eXcel

Stratford Company distributes a lightweight lawn chair that sells for $15 per unit. Variable expenses are $6 per unit, and fixed expenses total $180,000 annually.

CHECK FIGURE
(2) Break even $300,000

***Required:***

Answer the following independent questions:

1. What is the product's CM ratio?
2. Use the CM ratio to determine the break-even point in sales dollars.
3. The company estimates that sales will increase by $45,000 during the coming year due to increased demand. By how much should net operating income increase?
4. Assume that the operating results for last year were as follows:

| | |
|---|---|
| Sales | $360,000 |
| Variable expenses | 144,000 |
| Contribution margin | 216,000 |
| Fixed expenses | 180,000 |
| Net operating income | $ 36,000 |

   a. Compute the degree of operating leverage at the current level of sales.
   b. The president expects sales to increase by 15% next year. By how much should net operating income increase?
5. Refer to the original data. Assume that the company sold 28,000 units last year. The sales manager is convinced that a 10% reduction in the selling price, combined with a $70,000 increase in advertising expenditures, would increase annual unit sales by 50%. Prepare two contribution format income statements, one showing the results of last year's operations and one showing what the results of operations would be if these changes were made. Would you recommend that the company do as the sales manager suggests?
6. Refer to the original data. Assume again that the company sold 28,000 units last year. The president feels that it would be unwise to change the selling price. Instead, he wants to increase the sales commission by $2 per unit. He thinks that this move, combined with some increase in advertising, would double annual unit sales. By how much could advertising be increased with profits remaining unchanged? Do not prepare an income statement; use the incremental analysis approach.

**PROBLEM 5–22A Sales Mix; Multiproduct Break-Even Analysis [LO9]**
Marlin Company, a wholesale distributor, has been operating for only a few months. The company sells three products—sinks, mirrors, and vanities. Budgeted sales by product and in total for the coming month are shown below:

| | Product | | | | | | | |
|---|---|---|---|---|---|---|---|---|
| | Sinks | | Mirrors | | Vanities | | Total | |
| Percentage of total sales | 48% | | 20% | | 32% | | 100% | |
| Sales | $240,000 | 100% | $100,000 | 100% | $160,000 | 100% | $500,000 | 100% |
| Variable expenses | 72,000 | 30% | 80,000 | 80% | 88,000 | 55% | 240,000 | 48% |
| Contribution margin | $168,000 | 70% | $ 20,000 | 20% | $ 72,000 | 45% | 260,000 | 52% |
| Fixed expenses | | | | | | | 223,600 | |
| Net operating income | | | | | | | $ 36,400 | |

CHECK FIGURE
(1) $8,600 loss

$$\text{Dollar sales to break-even} = \frac{\text{Fixed expenses}}{\text{CM ratio}} = \frac{\$223{,}600}{0.52} = \$430{,}000$$

As shown by these data, net operating income is budgeted at $36,400 for the month, and break-even sales at $430,000.

Assume that actual sales for the month total $500,000 as planned. Actual sales by product are: sinks, $160,000; mirrors, $200,000; and vanities, $140,000.

***Required:***
1. Prepare a contribution format income statement for the month based on actual sales data. Present the income statement in the format shown above.
2. Compute the break-even point in sales dollars for the month, based on your actual data.
3. Considering the fact that the company met its $500,000 sales budget for the month, the president is shocked at the results shown on your income statement in (1) above. Prepare a brief memo for the president explaining why both the operating results and the break-even point in sales dollars are different from what was budgeted.

**PROBLEM 5–23A Sales Mix; Break-Even Analysis; Margin of Safety [LO7, LO9]**
Puleva Milenario SA, a company located in Toledo, Spain, manufactures and sells two models of luxuriously finished cutlery—Alvaro and Bazan. Present revenue, cost, and unit sales data for the two products appear below. All currency amounts are stated in terms of euros, which are indicated by the symbol €.

CHECK FIGURE
(1b) Margin if safety: €80

| | Alvaro | Bazan |
|---|---|---|
| Selling price per unit | €4.00 | €6.00 |
| Variable expenses per unit | €2.40 | €1.20 |
| Number of units sold monthly | 200 units | 80 units |

Fixed expenses are €660 per month.

***Required:***
1. Assuming the sales mix above, do the following:
   a. Prepare a contribution format income statement showing both euro and percent columns for each product and for the company as a whole.
   b. Compute the break-even point in euros for the company as a whole and the margin of safety in both euros and percent of sales.
2. The company has developed another product, Cano, that the company plans to sell for €8 each. At this price, the company expects to sell 40 units per month of the product. The variable expense would be €6 per unit. The company's fixed expenses would not change.

a. Prepare another contribution format income statement, including sales of Cano (sales of the other two products would not change).
b. Compute the company's new break-even point in euros for the company as a whole and the new margin of safety in both euros and percent of sales.

3. The president of the company was puzzled by your analysis. He did not understand why the break-even point has gone up even though there has been no increase in fixed expenses and the addition of the new product has increased the total contribution margin. Explain to the president what has happened.

**PROBLEM 5–24A Sales Mix; Multiproduct Break-Even Analysis [LO9]**

CHECK FIGURE
(1) April net operating income: $62,000

Topper Sports, Inc., produces high-quality sports equipment. The company's Racket Division manufactures three tennis rackets—the Standard, the Deluxe, and the Pro—that are widely used in amateur play. Selected information on the rackets is given below:

| | Standard | Deluxe | Pro |
|---|---|---|---|
| Selling price per racket | $40.00 | $60.00 | $90.00 |
| Variable expenses per racket: | | | |
| Production | $22.00 | $27.00 | $31.50 |
| Selling (5% of selling price) | $2.00 | $3.00 | $4.50 |

All sales are made through the company's own retail outlets. The Racket Division has the following fixed costs:

| | Per Month |
|---|---|
| Fixed production costs | $120,000 |
| Advertising expense | 100,000 |
| Administrative salaries | 50,000 |
| Total | $270,000 |

Sales, in units, over the past two months have been as follows:

| | Standard | Deluxe | Pro | Total |
|---|---|---|---|---|
| April | 2,000 | 1,000 | 5,000 | 8,000 |
| May | 8,000 | 1,000 | 3,000 | 12,000 |

***Required:***

1. Prepare contribution format income statements for April and May. Use the following headings:

| | Standard | | Deluxe | | Pro | | Total | |
|---|---|---|---|---|---|---|---|---|
| | Amount | Percent | Amount | Percent | Amount | Percent | Amount | Percent |
| Sales | | | | | | | | |
| Etc. | | | | | | | | |

Place the fixed expenses only in the Total column. Do not show percentages for the fixed expenses.

2. Upon seeing the income statements in (1) above, the president stated, "I can't believe this! We sold 50% more rackets in May than in April, yet profits went down. It's obvious that costs are out of control in that division." What other explanation can you give for the drop in net operating income?
3. Compute the Racket Division's break-even point in dollar sales for April.
4. Without doing any calculations, explain whether the break-even point would be higher or lower with May's sales mix than with April's sales mix.
5. Assume that sales of the Standard racket increase by $20,000. What would be the effect on net operating income? What would be the effect if Pro racket sales increased by $20,000? Do not prepare income statements; use the incremental analysis approach in determining your answer.

CHECK FIGURE
(2) Break even: 28,000 units

**PROBLEM 5–25A Break-Even Analysis; Pricing [LO1, LO4, LO6]**

Detmer Holdings AG of Zurich, Switzerland, has just introduced a new fashion watch for which the company is trying to find an optimal selling price. Marketing studies suggest that the company can increase sales by 5,000 units for each SFr2 per unit reduction in the selling price. (SFr2 denotes 2 Swiss francs.) The company's present selling price is SFr90 per unit, and variable expenses are SFr60 per unit. Fixed expenses are SFr840,000 per year. The present annual sales volume (at the SFr90 selling price) is 25,000 units.

***Required:***

1. What is the present yearly net operating income or loss?
2. What is the present break-even point in units and in Swiss franc sales?
3. Assuming that the marketing studies are correct, what is the *maximum* profit that the company can earn yearly? At how many units and at what selling price per unit would the company generate this profit?
4. What would be the break-even point in units and in Swiss franc sales using the selling price you determined in (3) above (i.e., the selling price at the level of maximum profits)? Why is this break-even point different from the break-even point you computed in (2) above?

CHECK FIGURE
(2c) Present margin of safety: $160,000

**PROBLEM 5–26A Changes in Cost Structure; Break-Even Analysis; Operating Leverage; Margin of Safety [LO4, LO6, LO7, LO8]**

Frieden Company's contribution format income statement for the most recent month is given below:

| | |
|---|---|
| Sales (40,000 units) | $800,000 |
| Variable expenses | 560,000 |
| Contribution margin | 240,000 |
| Fixed expenses | 192,000 |
| Net operating income | $ 48,000 |

The industry in which Frieden Company operates is quite sensitive to cyclical movements in the economy. Thus, profits vary considerably from year to year according to general economic conditions. The company has a large amount of unused capacity and is studying ways of improving profits.

***Required:***

1. New equipment has come on the market that would allow Frieden Company to automate a portion of its operations. Variable expenses would be reduced by $6 per unit. However, fixed expenses would increase to a total of $432,000 each month. Prepare two contribution format income statements, one showing present operations and one showing how operations would appear if the new equipment is purchased. Show an Amount column, a Per Unit column, and a Percent column on each statement. Do not show percentages for the fixed expenses.
2. Refer to the income statements in (1) above. For both present operations and the proposed new operations, compute (*a*) the degree of operating leverage, (*b*) the break-even point in dollars, and (*c*) the margin of safety in both dollar and percentage terms.
3. Refer again to the data in (1) above. As a manager, what factor would be paramount in your mind in deciding whether to purchase the new equipment? (Assume that ample funds are available to make the purchase.)
4. Refer to the original data. Rather than purchase new equipment, the marketing manager argues that the company's marketing strategy should be changed. Instead of paying sales commissions, which are included in variable expenses, the marketing manager suggests that salespersons be paid fixed salaries and that the company invest heavily in advertising. The marketing manager claims that this new approach would increase unit sales by 50% without any change in selling price; the company's new monthly fixed expenses would be $240,000; and its net operating income would increase by 25%. Compute the break-even point in dollar sales for the company under the new marketing strategy. Do you agree with the marketing manager's proposal?

**PROBLEM 5–27A Interpretive Questions on the CVP Graph [LO2, LO6]**

A CVP graph, as illustrated on the next page, is a useful technique for showing relationships among an organization's costs, volume, and profits.

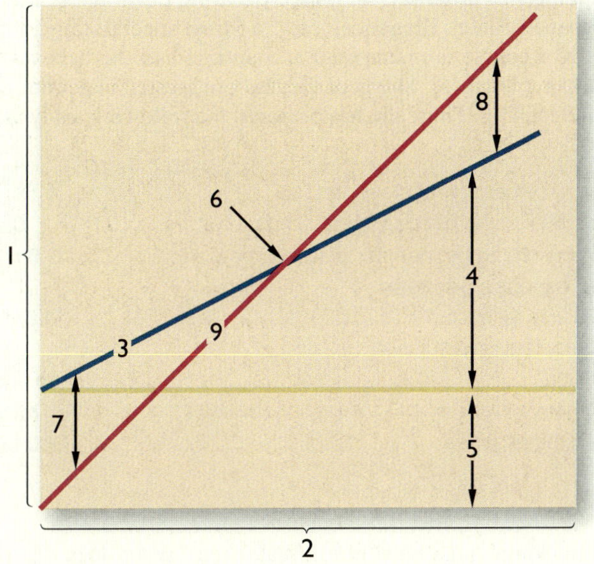


***Required:***

1. Identify the numbered components in the CVP graph.
2. State the effect of each of the following actions on line 3, line 9, and the break-even point. For line 3 and line 9, state whether the action will cause the line to:

   Remain unchanged.
   Shift upward.
   Shift downward.
   Have a steeper slope (i.e., rotate upward).
   Have a flatter slope (i.e., rotate downward).
   Shift upward *and* have a steeper slope.
   Shift upward *and* have a flatter slope.
   Shift downward *and* have a steeper slope.
   Shift downward *and* have a flatter slope.

   In the case of the break-even point, state whether the action will cause the break-even point to:

   Remain unchanged.
   Increase.
   Decrease.
   Probably change, but the direction is uncertain.

   Treat each case independently.

   x. *Example.* Fixed costs are increased by $20,000 each period.
   *Answer* (see choices above): Line 3: Shift upward.
   Line 9: Remain unchanged.
   Break-even point: Increase.

   a. The unit selling price is decreased from $30 to $27.
   b. The per unit variable costs are increased from $12 to $15.
   c. The total fixed costs are reduced by $40,000.
   d. Five thousand fewer units are sold during the period than were budgeted.
   e. Due to purchasing a robot to perform a task that was previously done by workers, fixed costs are increased by $25,000 per period, and variable costs are reduced by $8 per unit.
   f. As a result of a decrease in the cost of materials, both unit variable costs and the selling price are decreased by $3.
   g. Advertising costs are increased by $50,000 per period, resulting in a 10% increase in the number of units sold.
   h. Due to paying salespersons a commission rather than a flat salary, fixed costs are reduced by $21,000 per period, and unit variable costs are increased by $6.

**PROBLEM 5–28A Graphing; Incremental Analysis; Operating Leverage [LO2, LO4, LO5, LO6, LO8]**
Teri Hall has recently opened Sheer Elegance, Inc., a store specializing in fashionable stockings. Ms. Hall has just completed a course in managerial accounting, and she believes that she can apply certain aspects of the course to her business. She is particularly interested in adopting the cost-volume-profit (CVP) approach to decision making. Thus, she has prepared the following analysis:

CHECK FIGURE
(1) Break even: $100,000;
(3) 57,500 pairs

| | |
|---|---|
| Sales price per pair of stockings | $2.00 |
| Variable expense per pair of stockings | 0.80 |
| Contribution margin per pair of stockings | $1.20 |
| Fixed expense per year: | |
| Building rental | $12,000 |
| Equipment depreciation | 3,000 |
| Selling | 30,000 |
| Administrative | 15,000 |
| Total fixed expense | $60,000 |

***Required:***

1. How many pairs of stockings must be sold to break even? What does this represent in total dollar sales?
2. Prepare a CVP graph or a profit graph for the store from zero pairs up to 70,000 pairs of stockings sold each year. Indicate the break-even point on the graph.
3. How many pairs of stockings must be sold to earn a $9,000 target profit for the first year?
4. Ms. Hall now has one full-time and one part-time salesperson working in the store. It will cost her an additional $8,000 per year to convert the part-time position to a full-time position. Ms. Hall believes that the change would bring in an additional $20,000 in sales each year. Should she convert the position? Use the incremental approach. (Do not prepare an income statement.)
5. Refer to the original data. Actual operating results for the first year are as follows:

| | |
|---|---|
| Sales | $125,000 |
| Variable expenses | 50,000 |
| Contribution margin | 75,000 |
| Fixed expenses | 60,000 |
| Net operating income | $ 15,000 |

a. What is the store's degree of operating leverage?
b. Ms. Hall is confident that with some effort she can increase sales by 20% next year. What would be the expected percentage increase in net operating income? Use the degree of operating leverage to compute your answer.

**PROBLEM 5–29A Various CVP Questions: Break-Even Point; Cost Structure; Target Sales [LO1, LO3, LO4, LO5, LO6, LO8]**
Tyrene Products manufactures recreational equipment. One of the company's products, a skateboard, sells for $37.50. The skateboards are manufactured in an antiquated plant that relies heavily on direct labor workers. Thus, variable costs are high, totaling $22.50 per skateboard of which 60% is direct labor cost.

CHECK FIGURE
(2) Break even: 40,000 skateboards; (6a) 43,000 skateboards

Over the past year the company sold 40,000 skateboards, with the following operating results:

| | |
|---|---|
| Sales (40,000 skateboards) | $1,500,000 |
| Variable expenses | 900,000 |
| Contribution margin | 600,000 |
| Fixed expenses | 480,000 |
| Net operating income | $ 120,000 |

Management is anxious to maintain and perhaps even improve its present level of income from the skateboards.

***Required:***

1. Compute (*a*) the CM ratio and the break-even point in skateboards, and (*b*) the degree of operating leverage at last year's level of sales.
2. Due to an increase in labor rates, the company estimates that variable costs will increase by $3 per skateboard next year. If this change takes place and the selling price per skateboard remains constant at $37.50, what will be the new CM ratio and the new break-even point in skateboards?
3. Refer to the data in (2) above. If the expected change in variable costs takes place, how many skateboards will have to be sold next year to earn the same net operating income, $120,000, as last year?
4. Refer again to the data in (2) above. The president has decided that the company may have to raise the selling price of its skateboards. If Tyrene Products wants to maintain *the same CM ratio as last year,* what selling price per skateboard must it charge next year to cover the increased labor costs?
5. Refer to the original data. The company is considering the construction of a new, automated plant. The new plant would slash variable costs by 40%, but it would cause fixed costs to increase by 90%. If the new plant is built, what would be the company's new CM ratio and new break-even point in skateboards?
6. Refer to the data in (5) above.
   a. If the new plant is built, how many skateboards will have to be sold next year to earn the same net operating income, $120,000, as last year?
   b. Assume that the new plant is constructed and that next year the company manufactures and sells 40,000 skateboards (the same number as sold last year). Prepare a contribution format income statement, and compute the degree of operating leverage.
   c. If you were a member of top management, would you have been in favor of constructing the new plant? Explain.

**PROBLEM 5–30A Break-Even and Target Profit Analysis [LO5, LO6]**

The Marbury Stein Shop sells steins from all parts of the world. The owner of the shop, Clint Marbury, is thinking of expanding his operations by hiring college students, on a commission basis, to sell steins at the local college. The steins will bear the school emblem.

These steins must be ordered from the manufacturer three months in advance, and because of the unique emblem of each college, they cannot be returned. The steins would cost Marbury $15 each with a minimum order of 200 steins. Any additional steins would have to be ordered in increments of 50.

CHECK FIGURE
(1) $24,000 total sales

Because Marbury's plan would not require any additional facilities, the only costs associated with the project would be the cost of the steins and the cost of sales commissions. The selling price of the steins would be $30 each. Marbury would pay the students a commission of $6 for each stein sold.

***Required:***

1. To make the project worthwhile in terms of his own time, Marbury would require a $7,200 profit for the first six months of the venture. What level of sales in units and dollars would be required to attain this target net operating income? Show all computations.
2. Assume that the venture is undertaken and an order is placed for 200 steins. What would be Marbury's break-even point in units and in sales dollars? Show computations, and explain the reasoning behind your answer.

**PROBLEM 5–31A Changes in Fixed and Variable Costs; Break-Even and Target Profit Analysis [LO4, LO5, LO6]**

CHECK FIGURE
(1) Break even: 50,000 units

Novelties, Inc., produces and sells highly faddish products directed toward the preteen market. A new product has come onto the market that the company is anxious to produce and sell. Enough capacity exists in the company's plant to produce 30,000 units each month. Variable expenses to manufacture and sell one unit would be $1.60, and fixed expenses would total $40,000 per month.

The Marketing Department predicts that demand for the product will exceed the 30,000 units that the company is able to produce. Additional production capacity can be rented from another company at a fixed expense of $2,000 per month. Variable expenses in the rented facility would total $1.75 per unit, due to somewhat less efficient operations than in the main plant. The product would sell for $2.50 per unit.

***Required:***

1. Compute the monthly break-even point for the new product in units and in total dollar sales.
2. How many units must be sold each month to make a monthly profit of $9,000?
3. If the sales manager receives a bonus of 15 cents for each unit sold in excess of the break-even point, how many units must be sold each month to earn a return of 25% on the monthly investment in fixed expenses?

# BUILDING YOUR SKILLS

CHECK FIGURE
(2c) Break even:
$26,875,000

## CASE [LO4, LO5, LO6]

Marston Corporation manufactures disposable thermometers that are sold to hospitals through a network of independent sales agents located in the United States and Canada. These sales agents sell a variety of products to hospitals in addition to Marston's disposable thermometer. The sales agents are currently paid an 18% commission on sales, and this commission rate was used when Marston's management prepared the following budgeted absorption income statement for the upcoming year.

| Marston Corporation<br>Budgeted Income Statement | | |
|---|---|---|
| Sales | | $30,000,000 |
| Cost of goods sold: | | |
| Variable | $17,400,000 | |
| Fixed | 2,800,000 | 20,200,000 |
| Gross margin | | 9,800,000 |
| Selling and administrative expenses: | | |
| Commissions | 5,400,000 | |
| Fixed advertising expense | 800,000 | |
| Fixed administrative expense | 3,200,000 | 9,400,000 |
| Net operating income | | $ 400,000 |

Since the completion of the above statement, Marston's management has learned that the independent sales agents are demanding an increase in the commission rate to 20% of sales for the upcoming year. This would be the third increase in commissions demanded by the independent sales agents in five years. As a result, Marston's management has decided to investigate the possibility of hiring its own sales staff to replace the independent sales agents.

Marston's controller estimates that the company will have to hire eight salespeople to cover the current market area, and the total annual payroll cost of these employees will be about $700,000, including fringe benefits. The salespeople will also be paid commissions of 10% of sales. Travel and entertainment expenses are expected to total about $400,000 for the year. The company will also have to hire a sales manager and support staff whose salaries and fringe benefits will come to $200,000 per year. To make up for the promotions that the independent sales agents had been running on behalf of Marston, management believes that the company's budget for fixed advertising expenses should be increased by $500,000.

***Required:***

1. Assuming sales of $30,000,000, construct a budgeted contribution format income statement for the upcoming year for each of the following alternatives:
   a. The independent sales agents' commission rate remains unchanged at 18%.
   b. The independent sales agents' commission rate increases to 20%.
   c. The company employs its own sales force.
2. Calculate Marston Corporation's break-even point in sales dollars for the upcoming year assuming the following:
   a. The independent sales agents' commission rate remains unchanged at 18%.
   b. The independent sales agents' commission rate increases to 20%.
   c. The company employs its own sales force.
3. Refer to your answer to (1)(b) above. If the company employs its own sales force, what volume of sales would be necessary to generate the net operating income the company would realize if sales are $30,000,000 and the company continues to sell through agents (at a 20% commission rate)?
4. Determine the volume of sales at which net operating income would be equal regardless of whether Marston Corporation sells through agents (at a 20% commission rate) or employs its own sales force.
5. Prepare a graph on which you plot the profits for both of the following alternatives.
   a. The independent sales agents' commission rate increases to 20%.
   b. The company employs its own sales force.
   
   On the graph, use total sales revenue as the measure of activity.
6. Write a memo to the president of Marston Corporation in which you make a recommendation as to whether the company should continue to use independent sales agents (at a 20% commission rate) or employ its own sales force. Fully explain the reasons for your recommendation in the memo.

(CMA, adapted)

## ANALYTICAL THINKING [LO6, LO9]

CHECK FIGURE
(1) $700,100 (rounded)

Jasmine Park encountered her boss, Rick Gompers, at the pop machine in the lobby. Rick is the vice president of marketing at Down South Lures Corporation. Jasmine was puzzled by some calculations she had been doing, so she asked him:

***Jasmine:*** "Rick, I'm not sure how to go about answering the questions that came up at the meeting with the president yesterday."

***Rick:*** "What's the problem?"

***Jasmine:*** "The president wanted to know the break even for each of the company's products, but I am having trouble figuring them out."

***Rick:*** "I'm sure you can handle it, Jasmine. And, by the way, I need your analysis on my desk tomorrow morning at 8:00 A.M. sharp so I can look at it before the follow-up meeting at 9:00."

Down South Lures makes three fishing lures in its manufacturing facility in Alabama. Data concerning these products appear below.

| | Frog | Minnow | Worm |
|---|---|---|---|
| Normal annual sales volume .................... | 100,000 | 200,000 | 300,000 |
| Unit selling price....................................... | $2.00 | $1.40 | $0.80 |
| Variable cost per unit................................ | $1.20 | $0.80 | $0.50 |

Total fixed expenses for the entire company are $282,000 per year. All three products are sold in highly competitive markets, so the company is unable to raise its prices without losing unacceptable numbers of customers. The company has no work in process or finished goods inventories due to an extremely effective lean manufacturing system.

***Required:***

1. What is the company's overall break-even point in total sales dollars?
2. Of the total fixed costs of $282,000, $18,000 could be avoided if the Frog lure product were dropped, $96,000 if the Minnow lure product were dropped, and $60,000 if the Worm lure product were dropped. The remaining fixed expenses of $108,000 consist of common fixed costs such as administrative salaries and rent on the factory building that could be avoided only by going out of business entirely.
   a. What is the break-even point in units for each product?
   b. If the company sells exactly the break-even quantity of each product, what will be the overall profit of the company? Explain this result.

## TEAMWORK IN ACTION [LO1, LO4]

Revenue from major intercollegiate sports is an important source of funds for many colleges. Most of the costs of putting on a football or basketball game may be fixed and may increase very little as the size of the crowd increases. Thus, the revenue from every extra ticket sold may be almost pure profit.

Choose a sport played at your college or university, such as football or basketball, that generates significant revenue. Talk with the business manager of your college's sports programs before answering the following questions:

***Required:***

1. What is the maximum seating capacity of the stadium or arena in which the sport is played? During the past year, what was the average attendance at the games? On average, what percentage of the stadium or arena capacity was filled?
2. The number of seats sold often depends on the opponent. The attendance for a game with a traditional rival (e.g., Nebraska vs. Colorado, University of Washington vs. Washington State, or Texas vs. Texas A&M) is usually substantially above the average. Also, games against conference foes may draw larger crowds than other games. As a consequence, the number of tickets sold for a game is somewhat predictable. What implications does this have for the nature of the costs of putting on a game? Are most of the costs really fixed with respect to the number of tickets sold?
3. Estimate the variable cost per ticket sold.
4. Estimate the total additional revenue that would be generated in an average game if all of the tickets were sold at their normal prices. Estimate how much profit is lost because these tickets are not sold.
5. Estimate the ancillary revenue (parking and concessions) per ticket sold. Estimate how much profit is lost in an average game from these sources of revenue as a consequence of not having a sold-out game.
6. Estimate how much additional profit would be generated for your college if every game were sold out for the entire season.

## A LOOK BACK

Chapter 5 explained how to compute a break-even point and how to determine the sales needed to achieve a desired profit. We also described how to compute and use the margin of safety and operating leverage.

## A LOOK AT THIS CHAPTER

This chapter explains how to use the contribution format to create variable costing income statements for manufacturers and segmented income statements. It also contrasts variable costing income statements and absorption income statements.

## A LOOK AHEAD

Chapter 7 describes the budgeting process.

# 6 Variable Costing and Segment Reporting: Tools for Management

## CHAPTER OUTLINE

DECISION FEATURE

# IBM's $2.5 Billion Investment in Technology

When it comes to state-of-the-art in automation, **IBM**'s $2.5 billion semiconductor manufacturing facility in East Fishkill, New York, is tough to beat. The plant uses wireless networks, 600 miles of cable, and more than 420 servers to equip itself with what IBM claims is more computing power than NASA uses to launch a space shuttle.

Each batch of 25 wafers (one wafer can be processed into 1,000 computer chips) travels through the East Fishkill plant's manufacturing process without ever being touched by human hands. A computer system "looks at orders and schedules production runs . . . adjusts schedules to allow for planned maintenance and . . . feeds vast reams of production data into enterprise-wide management and financial-reporting systems." The plant can literally run itself as was the case a few years ago when a snowstorm hit and everyone went home while the automated system continued to manufacture computer chips until it ran out of work.

In a manufacturing environment such as this, labor costs are insignificant and fixed overhead costs are huge. There is a strong temptation to build inventories and increase profits without increasing sales. How can this be done you ask? It would seem logical that producing more units would have no impact on profits unless the units were sold, right? Wrong! As we will discover in this chapter, absorption costing—the most widely used method of determining product costs—can artificially increase profits by increasing the quantity of units produced.

Source: Ghostwriter, "Big Blue's $2.5 Billion Sales Tool," *Fortune*, September 19, 2005, pp. 316F–316J.

## LEARNING OBJECTIVES

*After studying Chapter 6, you should be able to:*

**LO1** Explain how variable costing differs from absorption costing and compute unit product costs under each method.

**LO2** Prepare income statements using both variable and absorption costing.

**LO3** Reconcile variable costing and absorption costing net operating incomes and explain why the two amounts differ.

**LO4** Prepare a segmented income statement that differentiates traceable fixed costs from common fixed costs and use it to make decisions.

**This chapter describes two applications** of the contribution format income statements that were introduced in Chapters 1 and 5. First, it explains how manufacturing companies can prepare *variable costing* income statements, which rely on the contribution format, for internal decision making purposes. The variable costing approach will be contrasted with *absorption costing* income statements, which were discussed in Chapter 2 and are generally used for external reports. Ordinarily, variable costing and absorption costing produce different net operating income figures, and the difference can be quite large. In addition to showing how these two methods differ, we will describe the advantages of variable costing for internal reporting purposes and we will show how management decisions can be affected by the costing method chosen.

Second, the chapter explains how the contribution format can be used to prepare segmented income statements. In addition to companywide income statements, managers need to measure the profitability of individual *segments* of their organizations. A **segment** is a part or activity of an organization about which managers would like cost, revenue, or profit data. This chapter explains how to create contribution format income statements that report profit data for business segments, such as divisions, individual stores, geographic regions, customers, and product lines.

## OVERVIEW OF VARIABLE AND ABSORPTION COSTING

**LEARNING OBJECTIVE 1**

Explain how variable costing differs from absorption costing and compute unit product costs under each method.

As you begin to read about variable and absorption costing income statements in the coming pages, focus your attention on three key concepts. First, both income statement formats include product costs and period costs, although they define these cost classifications differently. Second, variable costing income statements are grounded in the contribution format. They categorize expenses based on cost behavior—variable costs are reported separately from fixed costs. Absorption costing income statements ignore variable and fixed cost distinctions. Third, as mentioned in the paragraph above, variable and absorption costing net operating income figures often differ from one another. The reason for these differences always relates to the fact the variable costing and absorption costing income statements account for fixed manufacturing overhead differently. *Pay very close attention to the two different ways that variable costing and absorption costing account for fixed manufacturing overhead.*

### Variable Costing

Under **variable costing,** only those manufacturing costs that vary with output are treated as product costs. This would usually include direct materials, direct labor, and the variable portion of manufacturing overhead. Fixed manufacturing overhead is not treated as a product cost under this method. Rather, fixed manufacturing overhead is treated as a period cost and, like selling and administrative expenses, it is expensed in its entirety each period. Consequently, the cost of a unit of product in inventory or in cost of goods sold under the variable costing method does not contain any fixed manufacturing overhead cost. Variable costing is sometimes referred to as *direct costing* or *marginal costing.*

### Absorption Costing

As discussed in Chapter 2, **absorption costing** treats *all* manufacturing costs as product costs, regardless of whether they are variable or fixed. The cost of a unit of product under the absorption costing method consists of direct materials, direct labor, and *both* variable and fixed manufacturing overhead. Thus, absorption costing allocates a portion of fixed manufacturing overhead cost to each unit of product, along with the variable manufacturing costs. Because absorption costing includes all manufacturing costs in product costs, it is frequently referred to as the *full cost* method.

## Selling and Administrative Expenses

Selling and administrative expenses are never treated as product costs, regardless of the costing method. Thus, under absorption and variable costing, variable and fixed selling and administrative expenses are always treated as period costs and are expensed as incurred.

**Summary of Differences** The essential difference between variable costing and absorption costing, as illustrated in Exhibit 6–1, is how each method accounts for fixed manufacturing overhead costs—all other costs are treated the same under the two methods. In absorption costing, fixed manufacturing overhead costs are included as part of the costs of work in process inventories. When units are completed, these costs are transferred to finished goods and only when the units are sold do these costs flow through to the income statement as part of cost of goods sold. In variable costing, fixed manufacturing overhead costs are considered to be period costs—just like selling and administrative costs—and are taken immediately to the income statement as period expenses.

**EXHIBIT 6–1** Variable Costing versus Absorption Costing

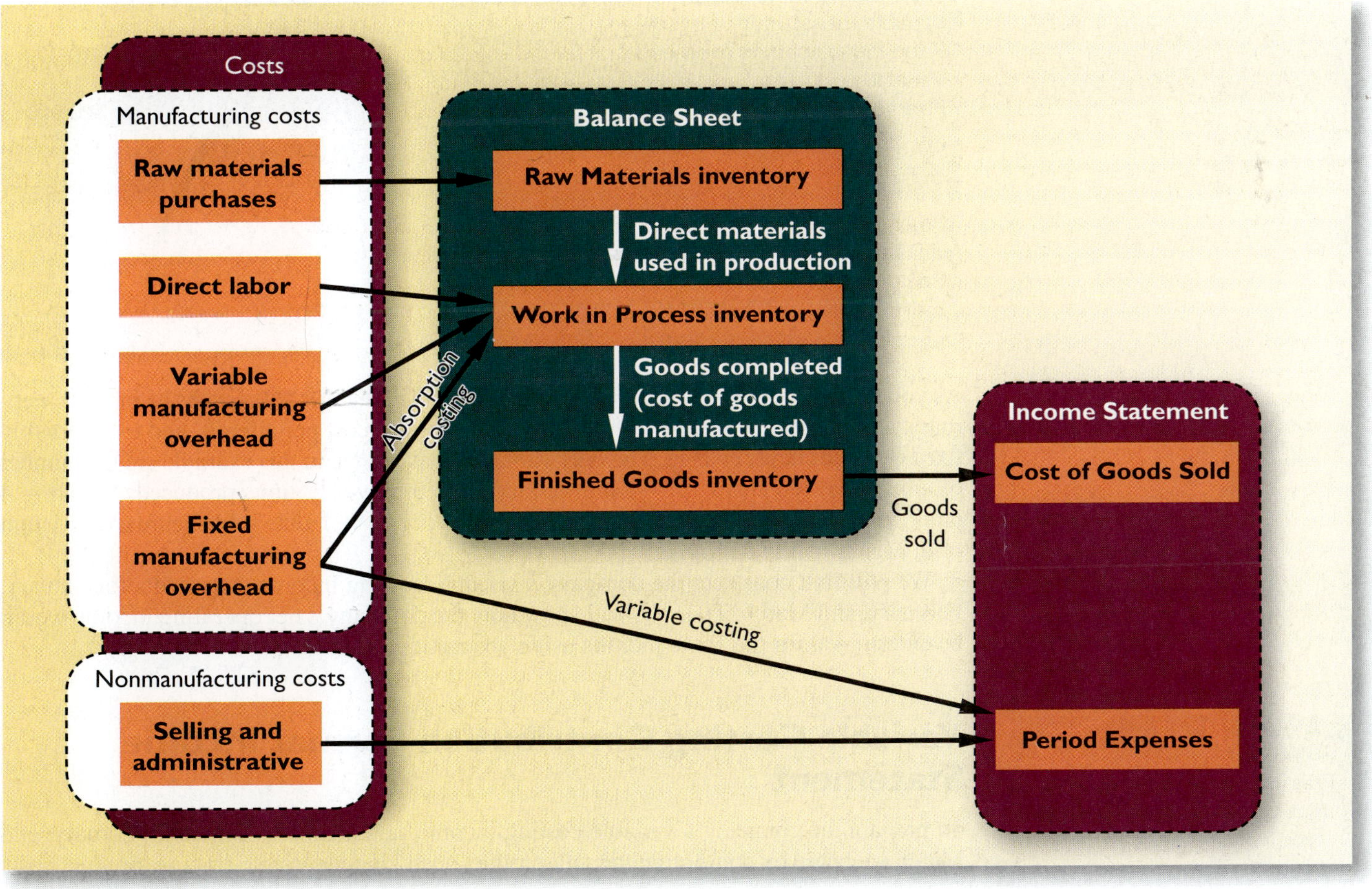

## HELPFUL HINT

In this chapter all differences in net operating income between variable costing and absorption costing will be caused by the accounting for fixed manufacturing overhead. Variable costing treats fixed manufacturing overhead as a period cost. This means that the entire amount of fixed manufacturing overhead incurred each period is recorded as an expense on the income statement within that period. Fixed manufacturing overhead is not attached to units of production. Absorption costing treats fixed manufacturing overhead as a product cost. This means that the entire amount of fixed manufacturing overhead incurred each period is attached to the units produced during that period. The fixed manufacturing overhead attached to units of production is recorded as an expense on the income statement only when the units are sold.

# VARIABLE AND ABSORPTION COSTING—AN EXAMPLE

To illustrate the difference between variable costing and absorption costing, consider Weber Light Aircraft, a company that produces light recreational aircraft. Data concerning the company's operations appear below:

| | Per Aircraft | Per Month |
|---|---|---|
| Selling price | $100,000 | |
| Direct materials | $19,000 | |
| Direct labor | $5,000 | |
| Variable manufacturing overhead | $1,000 | |
| Fixed manufacturing overhead | | $70,000 |
| Variable selling and administrative expenses | $10,000 | |
| Fixed selling and administrative expenses | | $20,000 |

| | January | February | March |
|---|---|---|---|
| Beginning inventory | 0 | 0 | 1 |
| Units produced | 1 | 2 | 4 |
| Units sold | 1 | 1 | 5 |
| Ending inventory | 0 | 1 | 0 |

As you review the data above, it is important to realize that for the months of January, February, and March, the selling price per aircraft, variable cost per aircraft, and total monthly fixed expenses never change. The only variables that change in this example are the number of units produced (January = 1 unit produced; February = 2 units produced; March = 4 units produced) and the number of units sold (January = 1 unit sold; February = 1 unit sold; March = 5 units sold).

We will first construct the company's variable costing income statements for January, February, and March. Then we will show how the company's net operating income would be determined for the same months using absorption costing.

**LEARNING OBJECTIVE 2**

Prepare income statements using both variable and absorption costing.

## Variable Costing Contribution Format Income Statement

To prepare the company's variable costing income statements for January, February, and March we begin by computing the unit product cost. Under variable costing, product costs consist solely of variable production costs. At Weber Light Aircraft, the variable production cost per unit is $25,000, determined as follows:

| Variable Costing Unit Product Cost | |
|---|---|
| Direct materials | $19,000 |
| Direct labor | 5,000 |
| Variable manufacturing overhead | 1,000 |
| Variable costing unit product cost | $25,000 |

Since each month's variable production cost is $25,000 per aircraft, the variable costing cost of goods sold for all three months can be easily computed as follows:

| Variable Costing Cost of Goods Sold | January | February | March |
|---|---|---|---|
| Variable production cost (a) | $25,000 | $25,000 | $25,000 |
| Units sold (b) | 1 | 1 | 5 |
| Variable cost of goods sold (a) × (b) | $25,000 | $25,000 | $125,000 |

And the company's total selling and administrative expense would be derived as follows:

| Selling and Administrative Expenses | January | February | March |
|---|---|---|---|
| Variable selling and administrative expense (@ $10,000 per unit sold) | $10,000 | $10,000 | $50,000 |
| Fixed selling and administrative expense | 20,000 | 20,000 | 20,000 |
| Total selling and administrative expense | $30,000 | $30,000 | $70,000 |

Putting it all together, the variable costing income statements would appear as shown in Exhibit 6–2. Notice, the contribution format has been used in these income statements. Also, the monthly fixed manufacturing overhead costs ($70,000) have been recorded as a period expense in the month incurred.

**EXHIBIT 6–2**
Variable Costing Income Statements

| Variable Costing Contribution Format Income Statements | January | February | March |
|---|---|---|---|
| Sales | $100,000 | $100,000 | $500,000 |
| Variable expenses: | | | |
| Variable cost of goods sold | 25,000 | 25,000 | 125,000 |
| Variable selling and administrative expense | 10,000 | 10,000 | 50,000 |
| Total variable expenses | 35,000 | 35,000 | 175,000 |
| Contribution margin | 65,000 | 65,000 | 325,000 |
| Fixed expenses: | | | |
| Fixed manufacturing overhead | 70,000 | 70,000 | 70,000 |
| Fixed selling and administrative expense | 20,000 | 20,000 | 20,000 |
| Total fixed expenses | 90,000 | 90,000 | 90,000 |
| Net operating income (loss) | $ (25,000) | $ (25,000) | $235,000 |

A simple method for understanding how Weber Light Aircraft computed its variable costing net operating income figures is to focus on the contribution margin per aircraft sold, which is computed as follows:

| Contribution Margin per Aircraft Sold | | |
|---|---|---|
| Selling price per aircraft | | $100,000 |
| Variable production cost per aircraft | $25,000 | |
| Variable selling and administrative expense per aircraft | 10,000 | 35,000 |
| Contribution margin per aircraft | | $ 65,000 |

*The variable costing net operating income for each period can always be computed by multiplying the number of units sold by the contribution margin per unit and then subtracting total fixed costs.* For Weber Light Aircraft these computations would appear as follows:

| | January | February | March |
|---|---|---|---|
| Number of aircraft sold | 1 | 1 | 5 |
| Contribution margin per aircraft | × $65,000 | × $65,000 | × $65,000 |
| Total contribution margin | $65,000 | $65,000 | $325,000 |
| Total fixed expenses | 90,000 | 90,000 | 90,000 |
| Net operating income (loss) | $(25,000) | $(25,000) | $235,000 |

Notice, January and February have the same net operating loss. This occurs because one aircraft was sold in each month and, as previously mentioned, the selling price per aircraft, variable cost per aircraft, and total monthly fixed expenses remain constant.

**HELPFUL HINT**

When students prepare variable costing income statements they often mistakenly assume that variable selling and administrative expense is a product cost. The confusion arises because variable selling and administrative expense *is* included in the calculation of contribution margin; however, it *is not* a product cost. Variable selling and administrative expense is always a period cost and the total amount of this expense included in the income statement is always derived by multiplying the variable selling and administrative expense per unit by the number of units sold—not the number of units produced.

## Absorption Costing Income Statement

As we begin the absorption costing portion of the example, remember that the only reason absorption costing income differs from variable costing is that the methods account for fixed manufacturing overhead differently. Under absorption costing, fixed manufacturing overhead is included in product costs. In variable costing, fixed manufacturing overhead is not included in product costs and instead is treated as a period expense just like selling and administrative expenses.

The first step in preparing Weber's absorption costing income statements for January, February, and March is to determine the company's unit product costs for each month as follows[1]:

[1]For simplicity, we assume in this section that an actual costing system is used in which actual costs are spread over the units produced during the period. If a predetermined overhead rate were used, the analysis would be similar, but more complex.

| Absorption Costing Unit Product Cost | January | February | March |
|---|---|---|---|
| Direct materials | $19,000 | $19,000 | $19,000 |
| Direct labor | 5,000 | 5,000 | 5,000 |
| Variable manufacturing overhead | 1,000 | 1,000 | 1,000 |
| Fixed manufacturing overhead ($70,000 ÷ 1 unit produced in January; $70,000 ÷ 2 units produced in February; $70,000 ÷ 4 units produced in March) | 70,000 | 35,000 | 17,500 |
| Absorption costing unit product cost | $95,000 | $60,000 | $42,500 |

**HELPFUL HINT**

Compute the unit product cost for each period mentioned in a problem before attempting to create the income statements. To compute absorption costing unit product costs, always take the fixed manufacturing overhead incurred in each period and divide it by the number of units *produced* during that period. Do not use the number of units sold to calculate unit product costs. The number of units sold is used to calculate the cost of goods sold for an income statement; however, the number of units produced is used to compute unit product costs.

Notice that in each month, Weber's fixed manufacturing overhead cost of $70,000 is divided by the number of units produced to determine the fixed manufacturing overhead cost per unit.

Given these unit product costs, the company's absorption costing net operating income in each month would be determined as shown in Exhibit 6–3.

The sales for all three months in Exhibit 6–3 are the same as the sales shown in the variable costing income statements. The January cost of goods sold consists of one unit produced during January at a cost of $95,000 according to the absorption costing system. The February cost of goods sold consists of one unit produced during February at a cost of $60,000 according to the absorption costing system. The March cost of goods sold ($230,000) consists of one unit produced during February at an absorption cost of $60,000 plus four units produced in March with a total absorption cost of $170,000 (= 4 units produced × $42,500 per unit). The selling and administrative expenses equal the amounts reported in the variable costing income statements; however they are reported as one amount rather than being separated into variable and fixed components.

Note that even though sales were exactly the same in January and February and the cost structure did not change, net operating income was $35,000 higher in February than in January under absorption costing. This occurs because one aircraft produced in

**EXHIBIT 6–3**
Absorption Costing Income Statements

| Absorption Costing Income Statements | January | February | March |
|---|---|---|---|
| Sales | $100,000 | $100,000 | $500,000 |
| Cost of goods sold ($95,000 × 1 unit; $60,000 × 1 unit; $60,000 × 1 unit + $42,500 × 4 units) | 95,000 | 60,000 | 230,000 |
| Gross margin | 5,000 | 40,000 | 270,000 |
| Selling and administrative expenses | 30,000 | 30,000 | 70,000 |
| Net operating income (loss) | $ (25,000) | $ 10,000 | $200,000 |

February is not sold until March. This aircraft has $35,000 of fixed manufacturing overhead attached to it that was incurred in February, but will not be recorded as part of cost of goods sold until March.

Contrasting the variable costing and absorption costing income statements in Exhibits 6–2 and 6–3, note that net operating income is the same in January under variable costing and absorption costing, but differs in the other two months. We will discuss this in some depth shortly. Also note that the format of the variable costing income statement differs from the absorption costing income statement. An absorption costing income statement categorizes costs by function—manufacturing versus selling and administrative. All of the manufacturing costs flow through the absorption costing cost of goods sold and all of the selling and administrative costs are listed separately as period expenses. In contrast, in the contribution approach, costs are categorized according to how they behave. All of the variable expenses are listed together and all of the fixed expenses are listed together. The variable expenses category includes manufacturing costs (i.e., variable cost of goods sold) as well as selling and administrative expenses. The fixed expenses category also includes both manufacturing costs and selling and administrative expenses.

**HELPFUL HINT**

Be careful computing the cost of goods sold under absorption costing when the units that have been sold were produced in *more than one period.* For example, if a company produces 8,000 units and sells 10,000 units in year 2, it is wrong to compute the cost of goods sold for year 2 by multiplying 10,000 units by the unit product cost for units produced in year 2. Logically speaking, it is impossible for this solution to be correct because only 8,000 units were produced in year 2. Assuming there is no ending inventory at the end of year 2, the correct cost of goods sold figure would include 8,000 units multiplied by the unit product cost for units produced in year 2 plus 2,000 units multiplied by the unit product cost for units produced in year 1.

## RECONCILIATION OF VARIABLE COSTING WITH ABSORPTION COSTING INCOME

**LEARNING OBJECTIVE 3**

Reconcile variable costing and absorption costing net operating incomes and explain why the two amounts differ.

As noted earlier, variable costing and absorption costing net operating incomes may not be the same. In the case of Weber Light Aircraft, the net operating incomes are the same in January, but differ in the other two months. These differences occur because under absorption costing some fixed manufacturing overhead is capitalized in inventories (i.e., included in product costs) rather than currently expensed on the income statement. If inventories increase during a period, under absorption costing some of the fixed manufacturing overhead of the current period will be *deferred* in ending inventories. For example, in February two aircraft were produced and each carried with it $35,000 (= $70,000 ÷ 2 aircraft produced) in fixed manufacturing overhead. Since only one aircraft was sold, $35,000 of this fixed manufacturing overhead was on February's absorption costing income statement as part of cost of goods sold, but $35,000 would have been on the balance sheet as part of finished goods inventories. In contrast, under variable costing *all* of the $70,000 of fixed manufacturing overhead appeared on the February income statement as a period expense. Consequently, net operating income was higher under absorption costing than under variable costing by $35,000 in February. This was reversed in March when four units were produced, but five were sold. In March, under absorption costing $105,000 of fixed manufacturing overhead was included in cost of goods sold ($35,000 for the unit produced in February and sold in March plus $17,500 for each of the four units produced and sold in March), but only $70,000 was recognized as a period expense under variable costing. Hence, the net operating income in March was $35,000 lower under absorption costing than under variable costing.

Important to Know *

In general, when the units produced exceed unit sales and hence inventories increase, net operating income is higher under absorption costing than under variable costing. This occurs because some of the fixed manufacturing overhead of the period is *deferred* in inventories under absorption costing. In contrast, when unit sales exceed the units produced and hence inventories decrease, net operating income is lower under absorption costing than under variable costing. This occurs because some of the fixed manufacturing overhead of previous periods is *released* from inventories under absorption costing. When the units produced and unit sales are equal, no change in inventories occurs and absorption costing and variable costing net operating incomes are the same.[2]

Variable costing and absorption costing net operating incomes can be reconciled by determining how much fixed manufacturing overhead was deferred in, or released from, inventories during the period:

**Fixed Manufacturing Overhead Deferred in, or Released from, Inventories under Absorption Costing**

| | January | February | March |
|---|---|---|---|
| Fixed manufacturing overhead in beginning inventories | $0 | $ 0 | $ 35,000 |
| Fixed manufacturing overhead in ending inventories | 0 | 35,000 | 0 |
| Fixed manufacturing overhead deferred in (released from) inventories | $0 | $35,000 | $(35,000) |

The reconciliation would then be reported as shown in Exhibit 6–4:

**EXHIBIT 6–4**
Reconciliation of Variable Costing and Absorption Costing Net Operating Incomes

**Reconciliation of Variable Costing and Absorption Costing Net Operating Incomes**

| | January | February | March |
|---|---|---|---|
| Variable costing net operating income (loss) | $(25,000) | $(25,000) | $235,000 |
| Add (deduct) fixed manufacturing overhead deferred in (released from) inventory under absorption costing | 0 | 35,000 | (35,000) |
| Absorption costing net operating income (loss) | $(25,000) | $ 10,000 | $200,000 |

Again note that the difference between variable costing net operating income and absorption costing net operating income is entirely due to the amount of fixed manufacturing overhead that is deferred in, or released from, inventories during the period under absorption costing. Changes in inventories affect absorption costing net operating income—they do not affect variable costing net operating income, providing that variable manufacturing costs per unit are stable.

The reasons for differences between variable and absorption costing net operating incomes are summarized in Exhibit 6–5. When the units produced equal the units sold, as in January for Weber Light Aircraft, absorption costing net operating income will equal variable costing net operating income. This occurs because when production equals sales, all of the fixed manufacturing overhead incurred in the current period flows through to the income statement under both methods. For companies that use Lean Production, the number of units produced tends to equal the number of units sold. This occurs because goods are produced in response to customer orders, thereby eliminating finished goods inventories and reducing work in process inventory to almost nothing. So, when a company uses Lean Production differences in variable costing and absorption costing net operating income will largely disappear.

When the units produced exceed the units sold, absorption costing net operating income will exceed variable costing net operating income. This occurs because inventories have increased;

[2]These general statements about the relation between variable costing and absorption costing net operating income assume LIFO is used to value inventories. Even when LIFO is not used, the general statements tend to be correct. Although U.S. GAAP allows LIFO and FIFO inventory flow assumptions, International Financial Reporting Standards do not allow a LIFO inventory flow assumption.

**EXHIBIT 6–5** Comparative Income Effects—Absorption and Variable Costing

| Relation between Production and Sales for the Period | Effect on Inventories | Relation between Absorption and Variable Costing Net Operating Incomes |
|---|---|---|
| Units produced = Units sold | No change in inventories | Absorption costing net operating income = Variable costing net operating income |
| Units produced > Units sold | Inventories increase | Absorption costing net operating income > Variable costing net operating income* |
| Units produced < Units sold | Inventories decrease | Absorption costing net operating income < Variable costing net operating income† |

*Net operating income is higher under absorption costing because fixed manufacturing overhead cost is *deferred* in inventory under absorption costing as inventories increase.
†Net operating income is lower under absorption costing because fixed manufacturing overhead cost is *released* from inventory under absorption costing as inventories decrease.

therefore, under absorption costing some of the fixed manufacturing overhead incurred in the current period is deferred in ending inventories on the balance sheet, whereas under variable costing all of the fixed manufacturing overhead incurred in the current period flows through to the income statement. In contrast, when the units produced are less than the units sold, absorption costing net operating income will be less than variable costing net operating income. This occurs because inventories have decreased; therefore, under absorption costing fixed manufacturing overhead that had been deferred in inventories during a prior period flows through to the current period's income statement together with all of the fixed manufacturing overhead incurred during the current period. Under variable costing, just the fixed manufacturing overhead of the current period flows through to the income statement.

## IN BUSINESS — Lean Manufacturing Shrinks Inventories

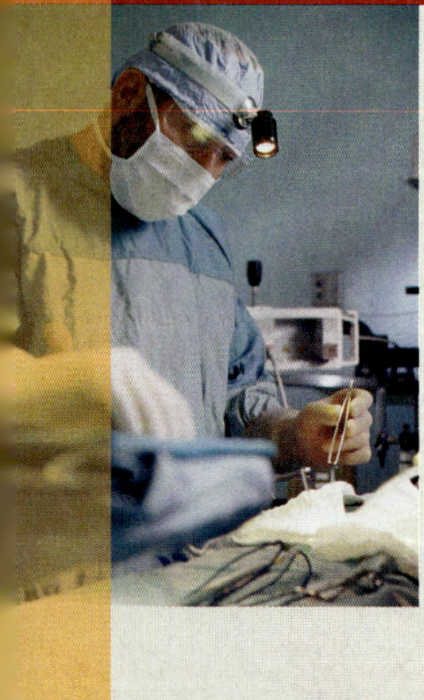

**Conmed**, a surgical device maker in Utica, New York, switched to lean manufacturing by replacing its assembly lines with U-shaped production cells. It also started producing only enough units to satisfy customer demand rather than producing as many units as possible and storing them in warehouses. The company calculated that its customers use one of its disposable surgical devices every 90 seconds, so that is precisely how often it produces a new unit. Its assembly area for fluid-injection devices used to occupy 3,300 square feet of space and contained $93,000 worth of parts. Now the company produces its fluid-injection devices in 660 square feet of space while maintaining only $6,000 of parts inventory.

When Conmed adopted lean manufacturing, it substantially reduced its finished goods inventories. What impact do you think this initial reduction in inventories may have had on net operating income? Why?

Source: Pete Engardio, "Lean and Mean Gets Extreme," *BusinessWeek*, March 23 and 30, 2009, pp. 60–62.

**CONCEPT CHECK**

In its first year of operations, Kelley Company produced 10,000 units and sold 7,000 units. Its direct materials, direct labor, variable manufacturing overhead, and variable selling and administrative unit costs were $12, $8, $2, and $1, respectively. Its total fixed manufacturing overhead for the year was $50,000.

1. What is the amount of cost of goods sold under variable costing?
   a. $220,000.
   b. $161,000.
   c. $154,000.
   d. $230,000.
2. What is the amount of cost of goods sold under absorption costing?
   a. $189,000.
   b. $196,000.
   c. $179,000.
   d. $186,000.
3. When comparing Kelley's absorption costing net operating income to its variable costing net operating income, which of the following will be true?
   a. Its absorption costing net operating income will be $35,000 lower than its variable costing net operating income.
   b. Its absorption costing net operating income will be $35,000 higher than its variable costing net operating income.
   c. Its absorption costing net operating income will be $15,000 lower than its variable costing net operating income.
   d. Its absorption costing net operating income will be $15,000 higher than its variable costing net operating income.

# ADVANTAGES OF VARIABLE COSTING AND THE CONTRIBUTION APPROACH

Variable costing, together with the contribution approach, offers appealing advantages for internal reports. This section discusses four of those advantages.

## Enabling CVP Analysis

CVP analysis requires that we break costs down into their fixed and variable components. Because variable costing income statements categorize costs as fixed and variable, it is much easier to use this income statement format to perform CVP analysis than attempting to use the absorption costing format, which mixes together fixed and variable costs.

Moreover, absorption costing net operating income may or may not agree with the results of CVP analysis. For example, let's suppose that you are interested in computing the sales that would be necessary to generate a target profit of $235,000 at Weber Light Aircraft. A CVP analysis based on the January variable costing income statement from Exhibit 6–2 would proceed as follows:

| | |
|---|---|
| Sales (a) | $100,000 |
| Contribution margin (b) | $65,000 |
| Contribution margin ratio (b) ÷ (a) | 65% |
| Total fixed expenses | $90,000 |

Note to self highlight pgs. 202-204

$$\text{Dollar sales to attain target profit} = \frac{\text{Target profit} + \text{Fixed expenses}}{\text{CM ratio}}$$

$$= \frac{\$235{,}000 + \$90{,}000}{0.65} = \$500{,}000$$

Thus, a CVP analysis based on the January variable costing income statement predicts that the net operating income would be $235,000 when sales are $500,000. And indeed, the net operating income under variable costing *is* $235,000 when the sales are $500,000 in March. However, the net operating income under absorption costing is *not* $235,000 in March, even though the sales are $500,000. Why is this? The reason is that under absorption costing, net operating income can be distorted by changes in inventories. In March, inventories decreased, so some of the fixed manufacturing overhead that had been deferred in February's ending inventories was released to the March income statement, resulting in a net operating income that is $35,000 lower than the $235,000 predicted by CVP analysis. If inventories had increased in March, the opposite would have occurred—the absorption costing net operating income would have been higher than the $235,000 predicted by CVP analysis.

## Explaining Changes in Net Operating Income

The variable costing income statements in Exhibit 6–2 are clear and easy to understand. All other things the same, when sales go up, net operating income goes up. When sales go down, net operating income goes down. When sales are constant, net operating income is constant. The number of units produced does not affect net operating income.

Absorption costing income statements can be confusing and are easily misinterpreted. Look again at the absorption costing income statements in Exhibit 6–3; a manager might wonder why net operating income went up from January to February even though sales were exactly the same. Was it a result of lower selling costs, more efficient operations, or was it some other factor? In fact, it was simply because the number of units produced exceeded the number of units sold in February and so some of the fixed manufacturing overhead costs were deferred in inventories in that month. These costs have not gone away—they will eventually flow through to the income statement in a later period when inventories go down. There is no way to tell this from the absorption costing income statements.

To avoid mistakes when absorption costing is used, readers of financial statements should be alert to changes in inventory levels. Under absorption costing, if inventories increase, fixed manufacturing overhead costs are deferred in inventories, which in turn increases net operating income. If inventories decrease, fixed manufacturing overhead costs are released from inventories, which in turn decreases net operating income. Thus, when absorption costing is used, fluctuations in net operating income can be due to changes in inventories rather than to changes in sales.

## Supporting Decision Making

The variable costing method correctly identifies the additional variable costs that will be incurred to make one more unit. It also emphasizes the impact of fixed costs on profits. The total amount of fixed manufacturing costs appears explicitly on the income statement, highlighting that the whole amount of fixed manufacturing costs must be covered for the company to be truly profitable. In the Weber Light Aircraft example, the variable costing income statements correctly report that the cost of producing another unit is $25,000 and they explicitly recognize that $70,000 of fixed manufactured overhead must be covered to earn a profit.

Under absorption costing, fixed manufacturing overhead costs appear to be variable with respect to the number of units sold, but they are not. For example, in January, the absorption unit product cost at Weber Light Aircraft is $95,000, but the variable portion of this cost is only $25,000. The fixed overhead costs of $70,000 are commingled with variable production costs, thereby obscuring the impact of fixed overhead costs on profits. Because absorption unit product costs are stated on a per unit basis, managers may mistakenly believe that if another unit is produced, it will cost the company $95,000. But of course it would not. The cost of producing another unit would be only $25,000.

Misinterpreting absorption unit product costs as variable can lead to many problems, including inappropriate pricing decisions and decisions to drop products that are in fact profitable.

## Adapting to the Theory of Constraints

The Theory of Constraints (TOC), which was introduced in the Prologue, suggests that the key to improving a company's profits is managing its constraints. For reasons that will be discussed in a later chapter, this requires careful identification of each product's variable costs. Consequently, companies involved in TOC use a form of variable costing.

Variable costing income statements require one adjustment to support the TOC approach. Direct labor costs need to be removed from variable production costs and reported as part of the fixed manufacturing costs that are entirely expensed in the period incurred. The TOC treats direct labor costs as a fixed cost for three reasons. First, even though direct labor workers may be paid on an hourly basis, many companies have a commitment—sometimes enforced by labor contracts or by law—to guarantee workers a minimum number of paid hours. Second, direct labor is not usually the constraint; therefore, there is no reason to increase it. Hiring more direct labor workers would increase costs without increasing the output of saleable products and services. Third, TOC emphasizes continuous improvement to maintain competitiveness. Without committed and enthusiastic employees, sustained continuous improvement is virtually impossible. Because layoffs often have devastating effects on employee morale, managers involved in TOC are extremely reluctant to lay off employees.

For these reasons, most managers in TOC companies regard direct labor as a committed-fixed cost rather than a variable cost. Hence, in the modified form of variable costing used in TOC companies, direct labor is not usually classified as a product cost.

### The Pricing Decision

DECISION POINT

Each year Webb Company produces and sells 20,000 units of its only product. The selling price for this product is $100 per unit and its direct materials, direct labor, and variable manufacturing overhead costs per unit are $25, $15, and $10, respectively. Webb's annual fixed manufacturing overhead expenses and fixed selling and administrative expenses are $400,000 and $150,000, respectively. It does not have any variable selling and administrative expenses.

The company's marketing manager believes a 10% price increase would lead to a 20% decline in the number of units sold. He claims that if the level of production stays at 20,000 units his price hike will increase gross margins and net operating income by $40,000. Would you support the price increase? Do you think it will increase profits?

# SEGMENTED INCOME STATEMENTS AND THE CONTRIBUTION APPROACH

**LEARNING OBJECTIVE 4**

Prepare a segmented income statement that differentiates traceable fixed costs from common fixed costs and use it to make decisions.

In the remainder of the chapter, we'll learn how to use the contribution approach to construct income statements for business segments. These segmented income statements are useful for analyzing the profitability of segments, making decisions, and measuring the performance of segment managers.

## Traceable and Common Fixed Costs and the Segment Margin

You need to understand three new terms to prepare segmented income statements using the contribution approach—*traceable fixed cost, common fixed cost,* and *segment margin.*

A **traceable fixed cost** of a segment is a fixed cost that is incurred because of the existence of the segment—if the segment had never existed, the fixed cost would not have been incurred; and if the segment were eliminated, the fixed cost would disappear. Examples of traceable fixed costs include the following:

- The salary of the Fritos product manager at **PepsiCo** is a *traceable* fixed cost of the Fritos business segment of PepsiCo.
- The maintenance cost for the building in which Boeing 747s are assembled is a *traceable* fixed cost of the 747 business segment of **Boeing**.
- The liability insurance at **Disney World** is a *traceable* fixed cost of the Disney World business segment of the **Disney Corporation**.

A **common fixed cost** is a fixed cost that supports the operations of more than one segment, but is not traceable in whole or in part to any one segment. Even if a segment were entirely eliminated, there would be no change in a true common fixed cost. For example:

- The salary of the CEO of **General Motors** is a *common* fixed cost of the various divisions of General Motors.
- The cost of heating a **Safeway** or **Kroger** grocery store is a *common* fixed cost of the store's various departments—groceries, produce, bakery, meat, etc.
- The cost of the receptionist's salary at an office shared by a number of doctors is a *common* fixed cost of the doctors. The cost is traceable to the office, but not to individual doctors.

To prepare a segmented income statement, variable expenses are deducted from sales to yield the contribution margin for the segment. The contribution margin tells us what happens to profits as volume changes—holding a segment's capacity and fixed costs constant. The contribution margin is especially useful in decisions involving temporary uses of capacity such as special orders. These types of decisions often involve only variable costs and revenues—the two components of contribution margin.

The **segment margin** is obtained by deducting the traceable fixed costs of a segment from the segment's contribution margin. It represents the margin available after a segment has covered all of its own costs. *The segment margin is the best gauge of the long-run profitability of a segment* because it includes only those costs that are caused by the segment. If a segment can't cover its own costs, then that segment probably should be dropped (unless it has important side effects on other segments). Notice, common fixed costs are not allocated to segments.

From a decision-making point of view, the segment margin is most useful in major decisions that affect capacity such as dropping a segment. By contrast, as we noted earlier, the contribution margin is most useful in decisions involving short-run changes in volume, such as pricing special orders that involve temporary use of existing capacity.

## IN BUSINESS — Has The Internet Killed Catalogs?

**Smith & Hawken**, an outdoor-accessories retailer, has experienced growing Internet sales and declining catalog sales. These trends seem consistent with conventional wisdom, which suggests that the Internet will make catalogs obsolete. Yet, Smith & Hawken, like many retailers with growing Internet sales, has no plans to discontinue its catalogs. In fact, the total number of catalogs mailed in the United States by all companies has jumped from 16.6 billion in 2002 to 19.2 billion in 2005. Why?

Catalog shoppers and Internet shoppers are not independent customer segments. Catalog shoppers frequently choose to complete their sales transactions online rather than placing telephone orders. This explains why catalogs remain a compelling marketing medium even though catalog sales are declining for many companies. If retailers separately analyze catalog sales and Internet sales, they may discontinue the catalogs segment while overlooking the adverse impact of this decision on Internet segment margins.

Source: Louise Lee, "Catalogs, Catalogs, Everywhere," *BusinessWeek*, December 4, 2006, pp. 32–34.

## Identifying Traceable Fixed Costs

The distinction between traceable and common fixed costs is crucial in segment reporting because traceable fixed costs are charged to segments and common fixed costs are not. In an actual situation, it is sometimes hard to determine whether a cost should be classified as traceable or common.

The general guideline is to treat as traceable costs *only those costs that would disappear over time if the segment itself disappeared.* For example, if one division within a company were sold or discontinued, it would no longer be necessary to pay that division manager's salary. Therefore the division manager's salary would be classified as a traceable fixed cost of the division. On the other hand, the president of the company undoubtedly would continue to be paid even if one of many divisions was dropped. In fact, he or she might even be paid more if dropping the division was a good idea. Therefore, the president's salary is common to the company's divisions and should not be charged to them.

When assigning costs to segments, the key point is to resist the temptation to allocate costs (such as depreciation of corporate facilities) that are clearly common and that will continue regardless of whether the segment exists or not. *Any allocation of common costs to segments reduces the value of the segment margin as a measure of long-run segment profitability and segment performance.*

## Traceable Costs Can Become Common Costs

Fixed costs that are traceable to one segment may be a common cost of another segment. For example, **United Airlines** might want a segmented income statement that shows the segment margin for a particular flight from Chicago to Paris further broken down into first-class, business-class, and economy-class segment margins. The airline must pay a substantial landing fee at Charles DeGaulle airport in Paris. This fixed landing fee is a traceable cost of the flight, but it is a common cost of the first-class, business-class, and economy-class segments. Even if the first-class cabin is empty, the entire landing fee must be paid. So the landing fee is not a traceable cost of the first-class cabin. But on the other hand, paying the fee is necessary in order to have any first-class, business-class, or economy-class passengers. So the landing fee is a common cost of these three classes.

# SEGMENTED INCOME STATEMENTS—AN EXAMPLE

ProphetMax, Inc., is a rapidly growing computer software company. Exhibit 6–6 shows its variable costing income statement for the most recent month. As the company has grown, its senior managers have asked for segmented income statements that could be used to make decisions and evaluate managerial performance. ProphetMax's controller responded by creating examples of contribution format income statements segmented by the company's divisions, product lines, and sales channels. She created Exhibit 6–7 to explain that ProphetMax's profits can be segmented into its two divisions—the Business Products Division and the Consumer Products Division. The Consumer Products Division's profits can be further segmented into the Clip Art and Computer Games product lines. Finally, the Computer Games product line's profits (within the Consumer Products Division) can be segmented into the Online and Retail Stores sales channels.

### Computing Segment Margins Helps An Entrepreneur — IN BUSINESS

In 2001, **Victoria Pappas Collection**, a small company specializing in women's sportswear, reported a net loss of $280,000 on sales of $1 million. When the company's founder, Vickie Giannukos, segmented her company's income statement into the six markets that she was serving, the results were revealing. The Dallas and Atlanta markets generated $825,000 of sales and incurred $90,000 of

## IN BUSINESS

(continued)

traceable fixed costs. The other four markets combined produced $175,000 of sales and also incurred $90,000 of traceable fixed costs. Given the average contribution margin ratio of 38%, the Dallas and Atlanta markets earned a segment margin of $223,500 [($825,000 × 38%) − $90,000] while the other four markets combined incurred a loss of $23,500 [($175,000 × 38%) − $90,000].

Vicky had made a common mistake—she chased every possible dollar of sales without knowing if her efforts were profitable. Based on her segmented income statements, she discontinued operations in three cities and hired a new sales representative in Los Angeles. She decided to focus on growing sales in Dallas and Atlanta while deferring expansion into new markets until it could be done profitably.

Source: Norm Brodsky, "The Thin Red Line," *Inc.* Magazine, January 2004, pp. 49–52.

**EXHIBIT 6–6**
ProphetMax, Inc. Variable Costing Income Statement

**ProphetMax, Inc.**
**Variable Costing Income Statement**

| | |
|---|---|
| Sales | $500,000 |
| Variable expenses: | |
| Variable cost of goods sold | 180,000 |
| Other variable expenses | 50,000 |
| Total variable expenses | 230,000 |
| Contribution margin | 270,000 |
| Fixed expenses | 255,000 |
| Net operating income | $ 15,000 |

**EXHIBIT 6–7**
ProphetMax, Inc.: Examples of Business Segments

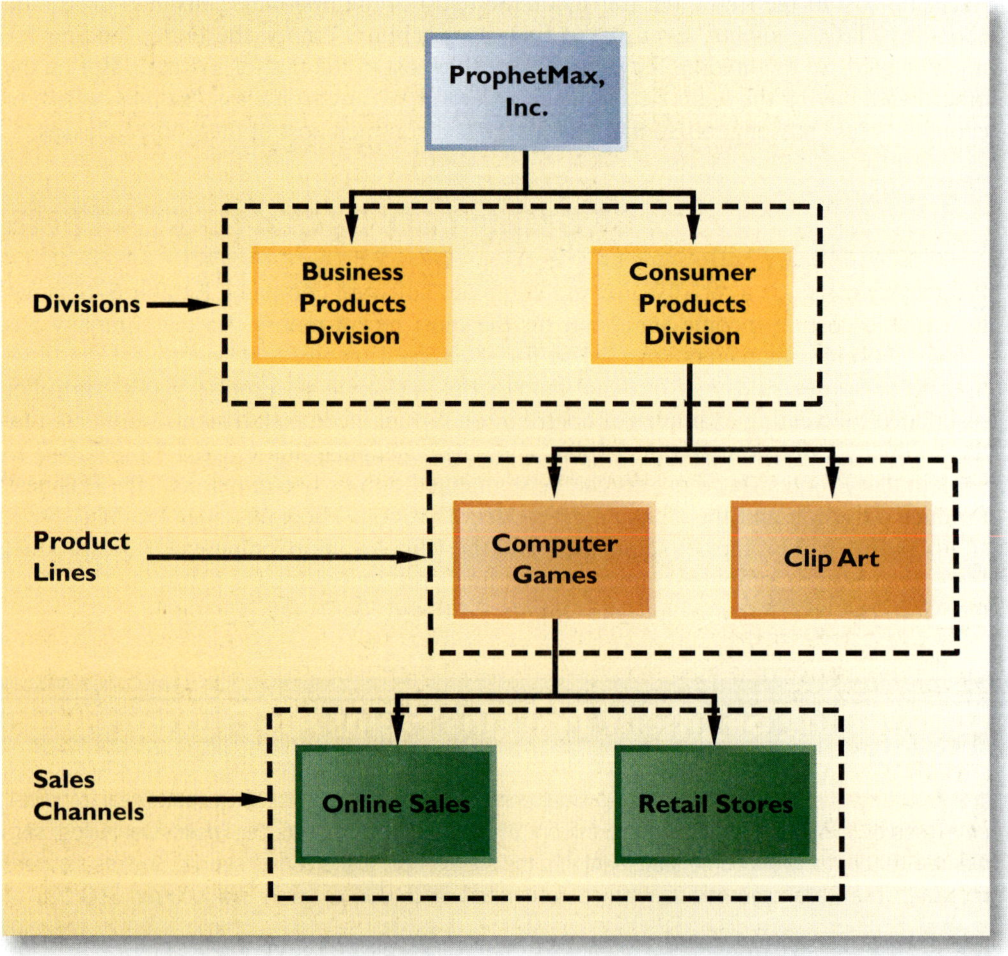

## Levels of Segmented Income Statements

Exhibit 6–8, on the next page, contains the controller's segmented income statements for the segments depicted in Exhibit 6–7. The contribution format income statement for the entire company appears at the very top of the exhibit under the column labeled Total Company. Notice, the net operating income shown in this column ($15,000) is the same as the net operating income shown in Exhibit 6–6. Immediately to the right of the Total Company column are two columns—one for each of the two divisions. We can see that the Business Products Division's traceable fixed expenses are $90,000 and the Consumer Products Division's are $80,000. These $170,000 of traceable fixed expenses (as shown in the Total Company column) plus the $85,000 of common fixed expenses not traceable to individual divisions equals ProphetMax's total fixed expenses ($255,000) as shown in Exhibit 6–6. We can also see that the Business Products Division's segment margin is $60,000 and the Consumer Products Division's is $40,000. These segment margins show the company's divisional managers how much each of their divisions is contributing to the company's profits.

The middle portion of Exhibit 6–8 further segments the Consumer Products Division into its two product lines, Clip Art and Computer Games. The dual nature of some fixed costs can be seen in this portion of the exhibit. Notice, in the top portion of Exhibit 6–8 when segments are defined as divisions, the Consumer Products Division has $80,000 in traceable fixed expenses. However, when we drill down to the product lines (in the middle portion of the exhibit), only $70,000 of the $80,000 cost that was traceable to the Consumer Products Division is traceable to the product lines. The other $10,000 becomes a common fixed cost of the two product lines of the Consumer Products Division.

Why would $10,000 of traceable fixed costs become a common fixed cost when the division is divided into product lines? The $10,000 is the monthly depreciation expense on a machine that is used to encase products in tamper-proof packages for the consumer market. The depreciation expense is a traceable cost of the Consumer Products Division as a whole, but it is a common cost of the division's two product lines. Even if one of the product lines were discontinued entirely, the machine would still be used to wrap the remaining products. Therefore, none of the depreciation expense can really be traced to individual products.

The $70,000 traceable fixed cost of the product lines consists of the costs of product specific advertising. A total of $30,000 was spent on advertising clip art and $40,000 was spent on advertising computer games. Clearly, these costs can be traced to the individual product lines.

## Segmented Income Statements and Decision Making

The bottom portion of Exhibit 6–8 can be used to illustrate how segmented income statements support decision making. It further segments the Computer Games product line into its two sales channels, Online Sales and Retail Stores. The Online Sales segment has a segment margin of $48,000 and the Retail Stores segment has a segment margin of $(3,000). Let's assume that ProphetMax wants to know the profit impact of discontinuing the sale of computer games through its Retail Stores sales channel. The company believes that online sales of its computer games will increase 10% if it discontinues the Retail Stores sales channel. It also believes that the Business Products Division and Clip Art product line will be unaffected by this decision. How would you compute the profit impact of this decision?

The first step is to calculate the profit impact of the Retail Stores sales channel disappearing. If this sales channel disappears, we assume its sales, variable expenses, and traceable fixed expenses would all disappear. The quickest way to summarize these financial impacts is to focus on the Retail Stores' segment margin. In other words, if the Retail Stores sales channel disappears, then its segment margin of a loss of $3,000 would also disappear. This would increase ProphetMax's net operating income by $3,000. The second step is to calculate the profit impact of increasing online sales of computer games by 10%. To perform this calculation, we assume that the Online Sales total traceable fixed expenses ($15,000) remain constant and its contribution margin ratio remains constant at 63% (= $63,000 ÷ $100,000). If online sales increase $10,000 (= $100,000 × 10%), then the Online Sales segment's

**EXHIBIT 6–8**
ProphetMax, Inc.—Segmented Income Statements in the Contribution Format

**Segments Defined as Divisions**

| | Total Company | Divisions: Business Products Division | Divisions: Consumer Products Division |
|---|---|---|---|
| Sales | $500,000 | $300,000 | $200,000 |
| Variable expenses: | | | |
| Variable cost of goods sold | 180,000 | 120,000 | 60,000 |
| Other variable expenses | 50,000 | 30,000 | 20,000 |
| Total variable expenses | 230,000 | 150,000 | 80,000 |
| Contribution margin | 270,000 | 150,000 | 120,000 |
| Traceable fixed expenses | 170,000 | 90,000 | 80,000 |
| Divisional segment margin | 100,000 | $ 60,000 | $ 40,000 |
| Common fixed expenses not traceable to individual divisions | 85,000 | | |
| Net operating income | $ 15,000 | | |

**Segments Defined as Product Lines of the Consumer Products Division**

| | Consumer Products Division | Product Line: Clip Art | Product Line: Computer Games |
|---|---|---|---|
| Sales | $200,000 | $75,000 | $125,000 |
| Variable expenses: | | | |
| Variable cost of goods sold | 60,000 | 20,000 | 40,000 |
| Other variable expenses | 20,000 | 5,000 | 15,000 |
| Total variable expenses | 80,000 | 25,000 | 55,000 |
| Contribution margin | 120,000 | 50,000 | 70,000 |
| Traceable fixed expenses | 70,000 | 30,000 | 40,000 |
| Product-line segment margin | 50,000 | $20,000 | $ 30,000 |
| Common fixed expenses not traceable to individual product lines | 10,000 | | |
| Divisional segment margin | $ 40,000 | | |

**Segments Defined as Sales Channels for One Product Line, Computer Games, of the Consumer Products Division**

| | Computer Games | Sales Channels: Online Sales | Sales Channels: Retail Stores |
|---|---|---|---|
| Sales | $125,000 | $100,000 | $25,000 |
| Variable expenses: | | | |
| Variable cost of goods sold | 40,000 | 32,000 | 8,000 |
| Other variable expenses | 15,000 | 5,000 | 10,000 |
| Total variable expenses | 55,000 | 37,000 | 18,000 |
| Contribution margin | 70,000 | 63,000 | 7,000 |
| Traceable fixed expenses | 25,000 | 15,000 | 10,000 |
| Sales-channel segment margin | 45,000 | $ 48,000 | $ (3,000) |
| Common fixed expenses not traceable to individual sales channels | 15,000 | | |
| Product-line segment margin | $ 30,000 | | |

contribution margin will increase by $6,300 (= $10,000 × 63%). The overall profit impact of discontinuing the Retail Stores sales channel can be summarized as follows:

| | |
|---|---|
| Avoidance of the retail segment's loss | $3,000 |
| Online Sales additional contribution margin | 6,300 |
| Increase in ProphetMax's net operating income | $9,300 |

## SEGMENTED INCOME STATEMENTS—COMMON MISTAKES

All of the costs attributable to a segment—and only those costs—should be assigned to the segment. Unfortunately, companies often make mistakes when assigning costs to segments. They omit some costs, inappropriately assign traceable fixed costs, and arbitrarily allocate common fixed costs.

### Omission of Costs

The costs assigned to a segment should include all costs attributable to that segment from the company's entire value chain. All of these functions, from research and development, through product design, manufacturing, marketing, distribution, and customer service, are required to bring a product or service to the customer and generate revenues.

However, only manufacturing costs are included in product costs under absorption costing, which is widely regarded as required for external financial reporting. To avoid having to maintain two costing systems and to provide consistency between internal and external reports, many companies also use absorption costing for their internal reports such as segmented income statements. As a result, such companies omit from their profitability analysis part or all of the "upstream" costs in the value chain, which consist of research and development and product design, and the "downstream" costs, which consist of marketing, distribution, and customer service. Yet these nonmanufacturing costs are just as essential in determining product profitability as are the manufacturing costs. These upstream and downstream costs, which are usually included in selling and administrative expenses on absorption costing income statements, can represent half or more of the total costs of an organization. If either the upstream or downstream costs are omitted in profitability analysis, then the product is undercosted and management may unwittingly develop and maintain products that in the long run result in losses.

### Inappropriate Methods for Assigning Traceable Costs among Segments

In addition to omitting costs, many companies do not correctly handle traceable fixed expenses on segmented income statements. First, they do not trace fixed expenses to segments even when it is feasible to do so. Second, they use inappropriate allocation bases to allocate traceable fixed expenses to segments.

**Failure to Trace Costs Directly** Costs that can be traced directly to a specific segment should be charged directly to that segment and should not be allocated to other segments. For example, the rent for a branch office of an insurance company should be charged directly to the branch office rather than included in a companywide overhead pool and then spread throughout the company.

**Inappropriate Allocation Base** Some companies use arbitrary allocation bases to allocate costs to segments. For example, some companies allocate selling and administrative expenses on the basis of sales revenues. Thus, if a segment generates 20% of total company sales, it would be allocated 20% of the company's selling and administrative expenses as its "fair share." This same basic procedure is followed if cost of goods sold or some other measure is used as the allocation base.

Costs should be allocated to segments for internal decision-making purposes only when the allocation base actually drives the cost being allocated (or is very highly correlated with the real cost driver). For example, sales should be used to allocate selling and administrative expenses only if a 10% increase in sales will result in a 10% increase in selling and administrative expenses. To the extent that selling and administrative expenses are not driven by sales volume, these expenses will be improperly allocated—with a disproportionately high percentage of the selling and administrative expenses assigned to the segments with the largest sales.

### Arbitrarily Dividing Common Costs among Segments

The third business practice that leads to distorted segment costs is the practice of assigning nontraceable costs to segments. For example, some companies allocate the common costs of the corporate headquarters building to products on segment reports. However, in a multiproduct company, no single product is likely to be responsible for any significant amount of this cost. Even if a product were eliminated entirely, there would usually be no significant effect on any of the costs of the corporate headquarters building. In short, there is no cause-and-effect relation between the cost of the corporate headquarters building and the existence of any one product. As a consequence, any allocation of the cost of the corporate headquarters building to the products must be arbitrary.

Common costs like the costs of the corporate headquarters building are necessary, of course, to have a functioning organization. The practice of arbitrarily allocating common costs to segments is often justified on the grounds that "someone" has to "cover the common costs." While it is undeniably true that a company must cover its common costs to earn a profit, arbitrarily allocating common costs to segments does not ensure that this will happen. In fact, adding a share of common costs to the real costs of a segment may make an otherwise profitable segment appear to be unprofitable. If a manager eliminates the apparently unprofitable segment, the real traceable costs of the segment will be saved, but its revenues will be lost. And what happens to the common fixed costs that were allocated to the segment? They don't disappear; they are reallocated to the remaining segments of the company. That makes all of the remaining segments appear to be less profitable—possibly resulting in dropping other segments. The net effect will be to reduce the overall profits of the company and make it even more difficult to "cover the common costs."

Additionally, common fixed costs are not manageable by the manager to whom they are arbitrarily allocated; they are the responsibility of higher-level managers. When common fixed costs are allocated to managers, they are held responsible for those costs even though they cannot control them.

## INCOME STATEMENTS—AN EXTERNAL REPORTING PERSPECTIVE

### Companywide Income Statements

Practically speaking, absorption costing is required for external reports according to U.S. generally accepted accounting principles (GAAP).[3] Furthermore, International Financial Reporting Standards (IFRS) explicitly require companies to use absorption costing. Probably because of the cost and possible confusion of maintaining two separate costing

[3]The Financial Accounting Standards Board (FASB) has created a single source of authoritative nongovernmental U.S. generally accepted accounting principles (GAAP) called the FASB Accounting Standards Codification (FASB codification). Although the FASB codification does not explicitly disallow variable costing, it does explicitly prohibit companies from excluding all manufacturing overhead costs from product costs. It also provides an in-depth discussion of fixed overhead allocation to products, thereby implying that absorption costing is required for external reports. Although some companies expense significant elements of fixed manufacturing costs on their external reports, practically speaking, U.S. GAAP requires absorption costing for external reports.

systems—one for external reporting and one for internal reporting—most companies use absorption costing for their external and internal reports.

With all of the advantages of the contribution approach, you may wonder why the absorption approach is used at all. While the answer is partly due to adhering to tradition, absorption costing is also attractive to many accountants and managers because they believe it better matches costs with revenues. Advocates of absorption costing argue that *all* manufacturing costs must be assigned to products in order to properly match the costs of producing units of product with their revenues when they are sold. The fixed costs of depreciation, taxes, insurance, supervisory salaries, and so on, are just as essential to manufacturing products as are the variable costs.

Advocates of variable costing argue that fixed manufacturing costs are not really the costs of any particular unit of product. These costs are incurred to have the *capacity* to make products during a particular period and will be incurred even if nothing is made during the period. Moreover, whether a unit is made or not, the fixed manufacturing costs will be exactly the same. Therefore, variable costing advocates argue that fixed manufacturing costs are not part of the costs of producing a particular unit of product, and thus, the matching principle dictates that fixed manufacturing costs should be charged to the current period.

## Segmented Financial Information

U.S. GAAP and IFRS require that publicly traded companies include segmented financial and other data in their annual reports and that the segmented reports prepared for external users *must use the same methods and definitions that the companies use in internal segmented reports that are prepared to aid in making operating decisions.* This is a very unusual stipulation because companies are not ordinarily required to report the same data to external users that are used for internal decision-making purposes. This requirement creates incentives for publicly traded companies to avoid using the contribution format for internal segmented reports. Segmented contribution format income statements contain vital information that companies are often very reluctant to release to the public (and hence competitors). In addition, this requirement creates problems in reconciling internal and external reports.

### 3M Reports Segmented Profitability to Shareholders

IN BUSINESS

In 2009, **3M Company** reported segmented profitability to its shareholders by product lines and geographic areas. A portion of the company's segmented information is summarized below (all numbers are in millions):

| | Net Sales | Net Operating Income |
|---|---|---|
| *Product Lines:* | | |
| Industrial and transportation | $7,116 | $1,238 |
| Health care | $4,294 | $1,350 |
| Consumer and office | $3,471 | $748 |
| Safety, security, and protection services | $3,180 | $745 |
| Display and graphics | $3,132 | $590 |
| Electro and communications | $2,276 | $322 |
| *Geographic Areas:* | | |
| United States | $8,509 | $1,640 |
| Asia Pacific | $6,120 | $1,528 |
| Europe, Middle East and Africa | $5,972 | $1,003 |
| Latin America and Canada | $2,516 | $631 |

3M's annual report does not report the gross margins or contribution margins for its business segments. Why do you think this is the case?

Source: 3M Company, 2009 Annual Report.

## SUMMARY

**LO1 Explain how variable costing differs from absorption costing and compute unit product costs under each method.**

Variable and absorption costing are alternative methods of determining unit product costs. Under variable costing, only variable manufacturing costs (direct materials, direct labor, and variable manufacturing overhead) are treated as product costs. Fixed manufacturing overhead is treated as a period cost and it is expensed on the income statement as incurred. By contrast, absorption costing treats fixed manufacturing overhead as a product cost, along with direct materials, direct labor, and variable overhead.

**LO2 Prepare income statements using both variable and absorption costing.**

The unit product costs under the two methods are different and so the cost of goods sold are different on the income statement. Additionally, fixed manufacturing overhead is expensed on the income statement under variable costing, but is included in unit product costs under absorption costing. Under both costing methods, selling and administrative expenses are treated as period costs and are expensed on the income statement as incurred.

**LO3 Reconcile variable costing and absorption costing net operating incomes and explain why the two amounts differ.**

Because absorption costing treats fixed manufacturing overhead as a product cost, a portion of fixed manufacturing overhead is assigned to each unit as it is produced. If units of product are unsold at the end of a period, then the fixed manufacturing overhead cost attached to those units is carried with them into the inventory account and deferred to a future period. When these units are later sold, the fixed manufacturing overhead cost attached to them is released from the inventory account and charged against income as part of cost of goods sold. Thus, under absorption costing, it is possible to defer a portion of the fixed manufacturing overhead cost from one period to a future period through the inventory account.

**LO4 Prepare a segmented income statement that differentiates traceable fixed costs from common fixed costs and use it to make decisions.**

Segmented income statements provide information for evaluating the profitability and performance of divisions, product lines, sales territories, and other segments of a company. Under the contribution approach covered in this chapter, variable costs and fixed costs are clearly distinguished from each other and only those costs that are traceable to a segment are assigned to the segment. A cost is considered traceable to a segment only if the cost is caused by the segment and could be avoided by eliminating the segment. Fixed common costs are not allocated to segments. The segment margin consists of revenues, less variable expenses, less traceable fixed expenses of the segment.

## GUIDANCE ANSWER TO DECISION POINT

**The Pricing Decision (p. 249)**

Under absorption costing, the fixed manufacturing overhead cost per unit is $20 ($400,000 ÷ 20,000 units). The absorption costing unit product cost is $70 ($25 + $15 + $10 + $20) and the gross margin per unit is $30 ($100 − $70). The variable costing unit product cost is $50 ($25 + $15 + $10) and the contribution margin per unit is $50 ($100 − $50). When the company produces and sells 20,000 units at a price of $100, it earns a total gross margin of $600,000 (20,000 units × $30) and a total contribution margin of $1,000,000 (20,000 units × $50).

A 10% price increase would raise the selling price to $110 per unit, whereas a 20% decline in unit sales would drop the sales volume to 16,000 units. In this scenario, the total gross margin earned is $640,000 (16,000 units × $40), which is $40,000 higher than the gross margin from the original scenario. This explains why the marketing manager thinks the price increase is a good idea. However, if the price increase is implemented the total contribution margin earned would become $960,000 (16,000 units × $60), which is $40,000 lower than the contribution margin from the original scenario. The price increase will lower profits by $40,000.

## GUIDANCE ANSWERS TO CONCEPT CHECKS

1. **Choice c.** The variable costing unit product cost is $22 ($12 + $8 + $2). The cost of goods sold is $154,000 (7,000 units sold × $22 per unit). The variable selling and administrative expense is a period cost, not a product cost.
2. **Choice a.** The absorption costing fixed manufacturing overhead cost per unit is $5 ($50,000 ÷ 10,000 units). The absorption costing unit product cost is $27 ($12 + $8 + $2 + 5). The cost of goods sold is $189,000 (7,000 units sold × $27 per unit).
3. **Choice d.** Absorption costing income is $15,000 higher because it defers $15,000 (3,000 units × $5 per unit) of fixed manufacturing overhead in inventory, whereas variable costing expenses the entire $50,000 of fixed manufacturing overhead during the current period.

## REVIEW PROBLEM 1: CONTRASTING VARIABLE AND ABSORPTION COSTING

Dexter Corporation produces and sells a single product, a wooden hand loom for weaving small items such as scarves. Selected cost and operating data relating to the product for two years are given below:

| | |
|---|---|
| Selling price per unit | $50 |
| Manufacturing costs: | |
| Variable per unit produced: | |
| Direct materials | $11 |
| Direct labor | $6 |
| Variable manufacturing overhead | $3 |
| Fixed manufacturing overhead per year | $120,000 |
| Selling and administrative expenses: | |
| Variable per unit sold | $4 |
| Fixed per year | $70,000 |

| | Year 1 | Year 2 |
|---|---|---|
| Units in beginning inventory | 0 | 2,000 |
| Units produced during the year | 10,000 | 6,000 |
| Units sold during the year | 8,000 | 8,000 |
| Units in ending inventory | 2,000 | 0 |

***Required:***

1. Assume the company uses absorption costing.
   a. Compute the unit product cost in each year.
   b. Prepare an income statement for each year.
2. Assume the company uses variable costing.
   a. Compute the unit product cost in each year.
   b. Prepare an income statement for each year.
3. Reconcile the variable costing and absorption costing net operating incomes.

**Solution to Review Problem 1**

1. a. Under absorption costing, all manufacturing costs, variable and fixed, are included in unit product costs:

| | Year 1 | Year 2 |
|---|---|---|
| Direct materials | $11 | $11 |
| Direct labor | 6 | 6 |
| Variable manufacturing overhead | 3 | 3 |
| Fixed manufacturing overhead | | |
| ($120,000 ÷ 10,000 units) | 12 | |
| ($120,000 ÷ 6,000 units) | | 20 |
| Absorption costing unit product cost | $32 | $40 |

b. The absorption costing income statements follow:

| | Year 1 | Year 2 |
|---|---|---|
| Sales (8,000 units × $50 per unit) | $400,000 | $400,000 |
| Cost of goods sold (8,000 units × $32 per unit); (2,000 units × $32 per unit) + (6,000 units × $40 per unit) | 256,000 | 304,000 |
| Gross margin | 144,000 | 96,000 |
| Selling and administrative expenses (8,000 units × $4 per unit + $70,000) | 102,000 | 102,000 |
| Net operating income (loss) | $ 42,000 | $ (6,000) |

2. a. Under variable costing, only the variable manufacturing costs are included in unit product costs:

| | Year 1 | Year 2 |
|---|---|---|
| Direct materials | $11 | $11 |
| Direct labor | 6 | 6 |
| Variable manufacturing overhead | 3 | 3 |
| Variable costing unit product cost | $20 | $20 |

b. The variable costing income statements follow:

| | Year 1 | | Year 2 | |
|---|---|---|---|---|
| Sales (8,000 units × $50 per unit) | | $400,000 | | $400,000 |
| Variable expenses: | | | | |
| Variable cost of goods sold (8,000 units × $20 per unit) | $160,000 | | $160,000 | |
| Variable selling and administrative expenses (8,000 units × $4 per unit) | 32,000 | 192,000 | 32,000 | 192,000 |
| Contribution margin | | 208,000 | | 208,000 |
| Fixed expenses: | | | | |
| Fixed manufacturing overhead | 120,000 | | 120,000 | |
| Fixed selling and administrative expenses | 70,000 | 190,000 | 70,000 | 190,000 |
| Net operating income | | $ 18,000 | | $ 18,000 |

3. The reconciliation of the variable and absorption costing net operating incomes follows:

| | Year 1 | Year 2 |
|---|---|---|
| Variable costing net operating income | $18,000 | $ 18,000 |
| Add fixed manufacturing overhead costs deferred in inventory under absorption costing (2,000 units × $12 per unit) | 24,000 | |
| Deduct fixed manufacturing overhead costs released from inventory under absorption costing (2,000 units × $12 per unit) | | (24,000) |
| Absorption costing net operating income (loss) | $42,000 | $ (6,000) |

## REVIEW PROBLEM 2: SEGMENTED INCOME STATEMENTS

The business staff of the law firm Frampton, Davis & Smythe has constructed the following report which breaks down the firm's overall results for last month into two business segments—family law and commercial law:

| | Total | Family Law | Commercial Law |
|---|---|---|---|
| Revenues from clients | $1,000,000 | $400,000 | $600,000 |
| Variable expenses | 220,000 | 100,000 | 120,000 |
| Contribution margin | 780,000 | 300,000 | 480,000 |
| Traceable fixed expenses | 670,000 | 280,000 | 390,000 |
| Segment margin | 110,000 | 20,000 | 90,000 |
| Common fixed expenses | 60,000 | 24,000 | 36,000 |
| Net operating income (loss) | $ 50,000 | $ (4,000) | $ 54,000 |

However, this report is not quite correct. The common fixed expenses such as the managing partner's salary, general administrative expenses, and general firm advertising have been allocated to the two segments based on revenues from clients.

***Required:***

1. Redo the segment report, eliminating the allocation of common fixed expenses. Would the firm be better off financially if the family law segment were dropped? (Note: Many of the firm's commercial law clients also use the firm for their family law requirements such as drawing up wills.)
2. The firm's advertising agency has proposed an ad campaign targeted at boosting the revenues of the family law segment. The ad campaign would cost $20,000, and the advertising agency claims that it would increase family law revenues by $100,000. The managing partner of Frampton, Davis & Smythe believes this increase in business could be accommodated without any increase in fixed expenses. Estimate the effect this ad campaign would have on the family law segment margin and on the firm's overall net operating income.

**Solution to Review Problem 2**

1. The corrected segmented income statement appears below:

| | Total | Family Law | Commercial Law |
|---|---|---|---|
| Revenues from clients | $1,000,000 | $400,000 | $600,000 |
| Variable expenses | 220,000 | 100,000 | 120,000 |
| Contribution margin | 780,000 | 300,000 | 480,000 |
| Traceable fixed expenses | 670,000 | 280,000 | 390,000 |
| Segment margin | 110,000 | $ 20,000 | $ 90,000 |
| Common fixed expenses | 60,000 | | |
| Net operating income | $ 50,000 | | |

No, the firm would not be financially better off if the family law practice were dropped. The family law segment is covering all of its own costs and is contributing $20,000 per month to covering the common fixed expenses of the firm. While the segment margin for family law is much lower than for commercial law, it is still profitable. Moreover, family law may be a service that the firm must provide to its commercial clients in order to remain competitive.

2. The ad campaign can be estimated to increase the family law segment margin by $55,000 as follows:

| | |
|---|---|
| Increased revenues from clients | $100,000 |
| Family law contribution margin ratio ($300,000 ÷ $400,000) | × 75% |
| Incremental contribution margin | $ 75,000 |
| Less cost of the ad campaign | 20,000 |
| Increased segment margin | $ 55,000 |

Because there would be no increase in fixed expenses (including common fixed expenses), the increase in overall net operating income is also $55,000.

## GLOSSARY

**Absorption costing** A costing method that includes all manufacturing costs—direct materials, direct labor, and both variable and fixed manufacturing overhead—in unit product costs. (p. 238)

**Common fixed cost** A fixed cost that supports more than one business segment, but is not traceable in whole or in part to any one of the business segments. (p. 250)

**Segment** Any part or activity of an organization about which managers seek cost, revenue, or profit data. (p. 238)

**Segment margin** A segment's contribution margin less its traceable fixed costs. It represents the margin available after a segment has covered all of its own traceable costs. (p. 250)

**Traceable fixed cost** A fixed cost that is incurred because of the existence of a particular business segment and that would be eliminated if the segment were eliminated. (p. 250)

**Variable costing** A costing method that includes only variable manufacturing costs—direct materials, direct labor, and variable manufacturing overhead—in unit product costs. (p. 238)

## QUESTIONS

**6–1** What is the basic difference between absorption costing and variable costing?

**6–2** Are selling and administrative expenses treated as product costs or as period costs under variable costing?

**6–3** Explain how fixed manufacturing overhead costs are shifted from one period to another under absorption costing.

**6–4** What are the arguments in favor of treating fixed manufacturing overhead costs as product costs?

**6–5** What are the arguments in favor of treating fixed manufacturing overhead costs as period costs?

**6–6** If the units produced and unit sales are equal, which method would you expect to show the higher net operating income, variable costing or absorption costing? Why?

**6–7** If the units produced exceed unit sales, which method would you expect to show the higher net operating income, variable costing or absorption costing? Why?

**6–8** If fixed manufacturing overhead costs are released from inventory under absorption costing, what does this tell you about the level of production in relation to the level of sales?

**6–9** Under absorption costing, how is it possible to increase net operating income without increasing sales?

**6–10** How does Lean Production reduce or eliminate the difference in reported net operating income between absorption and variable costing?

**6–11** What is a segment of an organization? Give several examples of segments.

**6–12** What costs are assigned to a segment under the contribution approach?

**6–13** Distinguish between a traceable cost and a common cost. Give several examples of each.

**6–14** Explain how the segment margin differs from the contribution margin.

**6–15** Why aren't common costs allocated to segments under the contribution approach?

**6–16** How is it possible for a cost that is traceable to a segment to become a common cost if the segment is divided into further segments?

**Multiple-choice questions are provided on the text website at www.mhhe.com/brewer6e.**

connect ACCOUNTING

## APPLYING EXCEL

LO2

**Available with McGraw-Hill's *Connect® Accounting*.**

The Excel worksheet form that appears below is to be used to recreate portions of Review Problem 1 on pages 259–261. Download the workbook containing this form from the Online Learning Center at www.mhhe.com/brewer6e. *On the website you will also receive instructions about how to use this worksheet form.*

| | A | B | C | D | E | F |
|---|---|---|---|---|---|---|
| 1 | Chapter 6: Applying Excel | | | | | |
| 2 | | | | | | |
| 3 | **Data** | | | | | |
| 4 | Selling price per unit | $50 | | | | |
| 5 | Manufacturing costs: | | | | | |
| 6 | Variable per unit produced: | | | | | |
| 7 | Direct materials | $11 | | | | |
| 8 | Direct labor | $6 | | | | |
| 9 | Variable manufacturing overhead | $3 | | | | |
| 10 | Fixed manufacturing overhead per year | $120,000 | | | | |
| 11 | Selling and administrative expenses: | | | | | |
| 12 | Variable per unit sold | $4 | | | | |
| 13 | Fixed per year | $70,000 | | | | |
| 14 | | | | | | |
| 15 | | Year 1 | Year 2 | | | |
| 16 | Units in beginning inventory | 0 | | | | |
| 17 | Units produced during the year | 10,000 | 6,000 | | | |
| 18 | Units sold during the year | 8,000 | 8,000 | | | |
| 19 | | | | | | |
| 20 | *Enter a formula into each of the cells marked with a ? below* | | | | | |
| 21 | **Review Problem 1: Contrasting Variable and Absorption Costing** | | | | | |
| 22 | | | | | | |
| 23 | ***Compute the Ending Inventory*** | | | | | |
| 24 | | Year 1 | Year 2 | | | |
| 25 | Units in beginning inventory | 0 | ? | | | |
| 26 | Units produced during the year | ? | ? | | | |
| 27 | Units sold during the year | ? | ? | | | |
| 28 | Units in ending inventory | ? | ? | | | |
| 29 | | | | | | |
| 30 | ***Compute the Absorption Costing Unit Product Cost*** | | | | | |
| 31 | | Year 1 | Year 2 | | | |
| 32 | Direct materials | ? | ? | | | |
| 33 | Direct labor | ? | ? | | | |
| 34 | Variable manufacturing overhead | ? | ? | | | |
| 35 | Fixed manufacturing overhead | ? | ? | | | |
| 36 | Absorption costing unit product cost | ? | ? | | | |
| 37 | | | | | | |
| 38 | ***Construct the Absorption Costing Income Statement*** | | | | | |
| 39 | | Year 1 | Year 2 | | | |
| 40 | Sales | ? | ? | | | |
| 41 | Cost of goods sold | ? | ? | | | |
| 42 | Gross margin | ? | ? | | | |
| 43 | Selling and administrative expenses | ? | ? | | | |
| 44 | Net operating income | ? | ? | | | |
| 45 | | | | | | |
| 46 | ***Compute the Variable Costing Unit Product Cost*** | | | | | |
| 47 | | Year 1 | Year 2 | | | |
| 48 | Direct materials | ? | ? | | | |
| 49 | Direct labor | ? | ? | | | |
| 50 | Variable manufacturing overhead | ? | ? | | | |
| 51 | Variable costing unit product cost | ? | ? | | | |
| 52 | | | | | | |
| 53 | ***Construct the Variable Costing Income Statement*** | | | | | |
| 54 | | Year 1 | | Year 2 | | |
| 55 | Sales | | ? | | ? | |
| 56 | Variable expenses: | | | | | |
| 57 | Variable cost of goods sold | ? | | ? | | |
| 58 | Variable selling and administrative expenses | ? | ? | ? | ? | |
| 59 | Contribution margin | | ? | | ? | |
| 60 | Fixed expenses: | | | | | |
| 61 | Fixed manufacturing overhead | ? | | ? | | |
| 62 | Fixed selling and administrative expenses | ? | ? | ? | ? | |
| 63 | Net operating income | | ? | | ? | |
| 64 | | | | | | |

Chapter 6 Form / Filled in Chapter 6 Form / Chapter 6

You should proceed to the requirements below only after completing your worksheet.

***Required:***

1. Check your worksheet by changing the units sold in the Data to 6,000 for Year 2. The cost of goods sold under absorption costing for Year 2 should now be $240,000. If it isn't, check cell C41. The formula in this cell should be =IF(C26<C27,C26*C36+(C27-C26)*B36,C27*C36). If your worksheet

is operating properly, the net operating income under both absorption costing and variable costing should be $(34,000) for Year 2. That is, the loss in Year 2 is $34,000 under both systems. If you do not get these answers, find the errors in your worksheet and correct them.

Why is the absorption costing net operating income now equal to the variable costing net operating income in Year 2?

2. Enter the following data from a different company into your worksheet:

| Data | | |
|---|---|---|
| Selling price per unit | $75 | |
| Manufacturing costs: | | |
| Variable per unit produced: | | |
| Direct materials | $12 | |
| Direct labor | $5 | |
| Variable manufacturing overhead | $7 | |
| Fixed manufacturing overhead per year | $150,000 | |
| Selling and administrative expenses: | | |
| Variable per unit sold | $1 | |
| Fixed per year | $60,000 | |
| | **Year 1** | **Year 2** |
| Units in beginning inventory | 0 | |
| Units produced during the year | 15,000 | 10,000 |
| Units sold during the year | 12,000 | 12,000 |

Is the net operating income under variable costing different in Year 1 and Year 2? Why or why not? Explain the relation between the net operating income under absorption costing and variable costing in Year 1. Explain the relation between the net operating income under absorption costing and variable costing in Year 2.

3. At the end of Year 1, the company's board of directors set a target for Year 2 of net operating income of $500,000 under absorption costing. If this target is met, a hefty bonus would be paid to the CEO of the company. Keeping everything else the same from part (2) above, change the units produced in Year 2 to 50,000 units. Would this change result in a bonus being paid to the CEO? Do you think this change would be in the best interests of the company? What is likely to happen in Year 3 to the absorption costing net operating income if sales remain constant at 12,000 units per year?

## THE FOUNDATIONAL 15

**Available with McGraw-Hill's *Connect® Accounting.***

LO1, LO2, LO3 LO4

Diego Company manufactures one product that is sold for $80 per unit in two geographic regions—the East and West regions. The following information pertains to the company's first year of operations in which it produced 40,000 units and sold 35,000 units.

| | |
|---|---|
| Variable costs per unit: | |
| Manufacturing: | |
| Direct materials | $24 |
| Direct labor | $14 |
| Variable manufacturing overhead | $2 |
| Variable selling and administrative | $4 |
| Fixed costs per year: | |
| Fixed manufacturing overhead | $800,000 |
| Fixed selling and administrative expenses | $496,000 |

The company sold 25,000 units in the East region and 10,000 units in the West region. It determined that $250,000 of its fixed selling and administrative expenses is traceable to the West region, $150,000 is traceable to the East region, and the remaining $96,000 is a common fixed cost. The company will continue to incur the total amount of its fixed manufacturing overhead costs as long as it continues to produce any amount of its only product.

***Required:***

Answer each question independently based on the original data unless instructed otherwise. You do not need to prepare a segmented income statement until question 13.

1. What is the unit product cost under variable costing?
2. What is the unit product cost under absorption costing?
3. What is the company's total contribution margin under variable costing?
4. What is the company's net operating income under variable costing?
5. What is the company's total gross margin under absorption costing?
6. What is the company's net operating income under absorption costing?
7. What is the amount of the difference between the variable costing and absorption costing net operating incomes? What is the cause of this difference?
8. What is the company's break-even point in unit sales? Is it above or below the actual sales volume? Compare the break-even sales volume to your answer for question 6 and comment.
9. If the sales volumes in the East and West regions had been reversed, what would be the company's overall break-even point in unit sales?
10. What would have been the company's variable costing net operating income if it had produced and sold 35,000 units? You do not need to perform any calculations to answer this question.
11. What would have been the company's absorption costing net operating income if it had produced and sold 35,000 units? You do not need to perform any calculations to answer this question.
12. If the company produces 5,000 fewer units than it sells in its second year of operations, will absorption costing net operating income be higher or lower than variable costing net operating income in Year 2? Why? No calculations are necessary.
13. Prepare a contribution format segmented income statement that includes a Total column and columns for the East and West regions.
14. Diego is considering eliminating the West region because an internally generated report suggests the region's total *gross margin* in the first year of operations was $50,000 less than its traceable fixed selling and administrative expenses. Diego believes that if it drops the West region, the East region's sales will grow by 5% in Year 2. Using the contribution approach for analyzing segment profitability and assuming all else remains constant in Year 2, what would be the profit impact of dropping the West region in Year 2?
15. Assume the West region invests $30,000 in a new advertising campaign in Year 2 that increases its unit sales by 20%. If all else remains constant, what would be the profit impact of pursuing the advertising campaign?

## EXERCISES

**All applicable exercises are available with McGraw-Hill's *Connect®* Accounting.**

**EXERCISE 6–1 Variable and Absorption Costing Unit Product Costs [LO1]**

Shastri Bicycle of Mumbai, India, produces an inexpensive, yet rugged, bicycle for use on the city's crowded streets that it sells for 500 rupees. (Indian currency is denominated in rupees, denoted by R.) Selected data for the company's operations last year follow:

Units sold = 9,000

| | |
|---|---|
| Units in beginning inventory | 0 |
| Units produced | 10,000 |
| Units sold | 8,000 |
| Units in ending inventory | 2,000 |
| Variable costs per unit: | |
| Direct materials | R120 |
| Direct labor | R140 |
| Variable manufacturing overhead | R50 |
| Variable selling and administrative | R20 |
| Fixed costs: | |
| Fixed manufacturing overhead | R600,000 |
| Fixed selling and administrative | R400,000 |

***Required:***

1. Assume that the company uses absorption costing. Compute the unit product cost for one bicycle.
2. Assume that the company uses variable costing. Compute the unit product cost for one bicycle.

**EXERCISE 6–2 Variable Costing Income Statement; Explanation of Difference in Net Operating Income [LO2]**

Refer to the data in Exercise 6–1 for Shastri Bicycle. The absorption costing income statement prepared by the company's accountant for last year appears below:

| | |
|---|---|
| Sales | R4,000,000 |
| Cost of goods sold | 2,960,000 |
| Gross margin | 1,040,000 |
| Selling and administrative expense | 560,000 |
| Net operating income | R 480,000 |

***Required:***

1. Determine how much of the ending inventory consists of fixed manufacturing overhead cost deferred in inventory to the next period.
2. Prepare an income statement for the year using variable costing. Explain the difference in net operating income between the two costing methods.

**EXERCISE 6–3 Reconciliation of Absorption and Variable Costing Net Operating Incomes [LO3]**

High Tension Transformers, Inc., manufactures heavy-duty transformers for electrical switching stations. The company uses variable costing for internal management reports and absorption costing for external reports to shareholders, creditors, and the government. The company has provided the following data:

Year 1 ending inventory = 140 units

| | Year 1 | Year 2 | Year 3 |
|---|---|---|---|
| Inventories: | | | |
| Beginning (units) | 180 | 150 | 160 |
| Ending (units) | 150 | 160 | 200 |
| Variable costing net operating income | $292,400 | $269,200 | $251,800 |

The company's fixed manufacturing overhead per unit was constant at $450 for all three years.

***Required:***

1. Determine each year's absorption costing net operating income. Present your answer in the form of a reconciliation report.
2. In Year 4, the company's variable costing net operating income was $240,200 and its absorption costing net operating income was $267,200. Did inventories increase or decrease during Year 4? How much fixed manufacturing overhead cost was deferred or released from inventory during Year 4?

**EXERCISE 6–4 Basic Segmented Income Statement [LO4]**

Caltec, Inc., produces and sells recordable CD and DVD packs. Revenue and cost information relating to the products follow:

Unit sales = 18,000 CD packs and 37,500 DVD packs

| | Product | |
|---|---|---|
| | CD | DVD |
| Selling price per pack | $8.00 | $25.00 |
| Variable expenses per pack | $3.20 | $17.50 |
| Traceable fixed expenses per year | $138,000 | $45,000 |

Common fixed expenses in the company total $105,000 annually. Last year the company produced and sold 37,500 CD packs and 18,000 DVD packs.

***Required:***

Prepare a contribution format income statement for the year segmented by product lines.

### EXERCISE 6–5 Deducing Changes in Inventories [LO3]

Ferguson Products Inc., a manufacturer, reported $130 million in sales and a loss of $25 million in its absorption costing income statement provided to shareholders. According to a CVP analysis prepared for management, the company's break-even point is $120 million in sales.

***Required:***

Assuming that the CVP analysis is correct, is it likely that the company's inventory level increased, decreased, or remained unchanged during the year? Explain.

TAKE TWO

Sales = $110 million; absorption income = $10 million

### EXERCISE 6–6 Inferring Costing Method; Unit Product Cost [LO1]

Amcor, Inc., incurs the following costs to produce and sell a single product.

| | |
|---|---|
| Variable costs per unit: | |
| Direct materials | $10 |
| Direct labor | $5 |
| Variable manufacturing overhead | $2 |
| Variable selling and administrative expenses | $4 |
| Fixed costs per year: | |
| Fixed manufacturing overhead | $90,000 |
| Fixed selling and administrative expenses | $300,000 |

TAKE TWO

Fixed manufacturing overhead = $120,000

During the last year, 30,000 units were produced and 25,000 units were sold. The Finished Goods inventory account at the end of the year shows a balance of $85,000 for the 5,000 unsold units.

***Required:***

1. Is the company using absorption costing or variable costing to cost units in the Finished Goods inventory account? Show computations to support your answer.
2. Assume that the company wishes to prepare financial statements for the year to issue to its stockholders.
   a. Is the $85,000 figure for Finished Goods inventory the correct amount to use on these statements for external reporting purposes? Explain.
   b. At what dollar amount *should* the 5,000 units be carried in inventory for external reporting purposes?

### EXERCISE 6–7 Variable and Absorption Costing Unit Product Costs and Income Statements [LO1, LO2]

Maxwell Company manufactures and sells a single product. The following costs were incurred during the company's first year of operations:

| | |
|---|---|
| Variable costs per unit: | |
| Manufacturing: | |
| Direct materials | $18 |
| Direct labor | $7 |
| Variable manufacturing overhead | $2 |
| Variable selling and administrative | $2 |
| Fixed costs per year: | |
| Fixed manufacturing overhead | $200,000 |
| Fixed selling and administrative expenses | $110,000 |

During the year, the company produced 20,000 units and sold 16,000 units. The selling price of the company's product is $50 per unit.

***Required:***

1. Assume that the company uses absorption costing:
   a. Compute the unit product cost.
   b. Prepare an income statement for the year.
2. Assume that the company uses variable costing:
   a. Compute the unit product cost.
   b. Prepare an income statement for the year.

3. The company's controller believes that the company should have set last year's selling price at $51 instead of $50 per unit. She estimates the company could have sold 15,000 units at a price of $51 per unit, thereby increasing the company's gross margin by $2,000 and its net operating income by $4,000. Assuming the controller's estimates are accurate, do you think the price increase would have been a good idea?

**EXERCISE 6–8 Segmented Income Statement [LO4]**

Michaels Company segments its income statement into its East and West Divisions. The company's overall sales, contribution margin ratio, and net operating income are $600,000, 50%, and $50,000, respectively. The West Division's contribution margin and contribution margin ratio are $150,000 and 75%, respectively. The East Division's segment margin is $70,000. The company has $60,000 of common fixed costs that cannot be traced to either division.

***Required:***

Prepare an income statement for Michaels Company that uses the contribution format and is segmented by divisions. In addition, for the company as a whole and for each segment, show each item on the segmented income statements as a percent of sales.

TAKE TWO

**EXERCISE 6–9 Variable Costing Unit Product Cost and Income Statement; Break-Even [LO1, LO2]**

CompuDesk, Inc., makes an oak desk specially designed for personal computers. The desk sells for $200. Data for last year's operations follow:

Fixed manufacturing overhead = $250,000

| | |
|---|---|
| Units in beginning inventory | 0 |
| Units produced | 10,000 |
| Units sold | 9,000 |
| Units in ending inventory | 1,000 |
| Variable costs per unit: | |
| Direct materials | $ 60 |
| Direct labor | 30 |
| Variable manufacturing overhead | 10 |
| Variable selling and administrative | 20 |
| Total variable cost per unit | $120 |
| Fixed costs: | |
| Fixed manufacturing overhead | $300,000 |
| Fixed selling and administrative | 450,000 |
| Total fixed costs | $750,000 |

***Required:***

1. Assume that the company uses variable costing. Compute the unit product cost for one computer desk.
2. Assume that the company uses variable costing. Prepare a contribution format income statement for the year.
3. What is the company's break-even point in terms of units sold?

TAKE TWO

**EXERCISE 6–10 Absorption Costing Unit Product Cost and Income Statement [LO1, LO2]**

Refer to the data in Exercise 6–9 for CompuDesk. Assume in this exercise that the company uses absorption costing.

See Exercise 6-9

***Required:***

1. Compute the unit product cost for one computer desk.
2. Prepare an income statement.

**EXERCISE 6–11 Segmented Income Statement [LO4]**

Bovine Company, a wholesale distributor of DVDs, has been experiencing losses for some time, as shown by its most recent monthly contribution format income statement below:

| | |
|---|---|
| Sales | $1,500,000 |
| Variable expenses | 588,000 |
| Contribution margin | 912,000 |
| Fixed expenses | 945,000 |
| Net operating loss | $ (33,000) |

In an effort to isolate the problem, the president has asked for an income statement segmented by geographic market. Accordingly, the Accounting Department has developed the following data:

| | Geographic Market | | |
|---|---|---|---|
| | South | Central | North |
| Sales | $400,000 | $600,000 | $500,000 |
| Variable expenses as a percentage of sales | 52% | 30% | 40% |
| Traceable fixed expenses | $240,000 | $330,000 | $200,000 |

TAKE TWO

Variable expense percentage for Central = 75%

***Required:***

1. Prepare a contribution format income statement segmented by geographic market, as desired by the president.
2. The company's sales manager believes that sales in the Central geographic market could be increased by 15% if monthly advertising were increased by $25,000. Would you recommend the increased advertising? Show computations to support your answer.

**EXERCISE 6–12 Variable and Absorption Costing Unit Product Costs and Income Statements [LO1, LO2, LO3]**

Fletcher Company manufactures and sells one product. The following information pertains to each of the company's first two years of operations:

| | |
|---|---|
| Variable costs per unit: | |
| Manufacturing: | |
| Direct materials | $20 |
| Direct labor | $12 |
| Variable manufacturing overhead | $4 |
| Variable selling and administrative | $3 |
| Fixed costs per year: | |
| Fixed manufacturing overhead | $200,000 |
| Fixed selling and administrative expenses | $80,000 |

TAKE TWO

Fixed manufacturing overhead = $400,000

During its first year of operations, Fletcher produced 50,000 units and sold 40,000 units. During its second year of operations, it produced 40,000 units and sold 50,000 units. The selling price of the company's product is $50 per unit.

***Required:***

1. Assume the company uses variable costing:
   a. Compute the unit product cost for year 1 and year 2.
   b. Prepare an income statement for year 1 and year 2.
2. Assume the company uses absorption costing:
   a. Compute the unit product cost for year 1 and year 2.
   b. Prepare an income statement for year 1 and year 2.
3. Explain the difference between variable costing and absorption costing net operating income in year 1. Also, explain why the two net operating incomes differ in year 2.

**EXERCISE 6–13 Variable Costing Income Statement; Reconciliation [LO2, LO3]**

Morey Company has just completed its first year of operations. The company's absorption costing income statement for the year appears below:

| Morey Company<br>Income Statement | |
|---|---|
| Sales (40,000 units × $33.75 per unit) | $1,350,000 |
| Cost of goods sold (40,000 units × $21 per unit) | 840,000 |
| Gross margin | 510,000 |
| Selling and administrative expenses | 420,000 |
| Net operating income | $ 90,000 |

The company's selling and administrative expenses consist of $300,000 per year in fixed expenses and $3 per unit sold in variable expenses. The company's $21 per unit product cost shown on the previous page is computed as follows:

| | |
|---|---|
| Direct materials | $10 |
| Direct labor | 4 |
| Variable manufacturing overhead | 2 |
| Fixed manufacturing overhead ($250,000 ÷ 50,000 units) | 5 |
| Absorption costing unit product cost | $21 |

***Required:***

1. Redo the company's income statement in the contribution format using variable costing.
2. Reconcile any difference between the net operating income on your variable costing income statement and the net operating income on the absorption costing income statement.

**EXERCISE 6–14 Working with a Segmented Income Statement [LO4]**

Marple Associates is a consulting firm that specializes in information systems for construction and landscaping companies. The firm has two offices—one in Houston and one in Dallas. The firm classifies the direct costs of consulting jobs as variable costs. A segmented contribution format income statement for the company's most recent year is given below:

| | | | Office | | | |
|---|---|---|---|---|---|---|
| | Total Company | | Houston | | Dallas | |
| Sales | $750,000 | 100.0% | $150,000 | 100% | $600,000 | 100% |
| Variable expenses | 405,000 | 54.0 | 45,000 | 30 | 360,000 | 60 |
| Contribution margin | 345,000 | 46.0 | 105,000 | 70 | 240,000 | 40 |
| Traceable fixed expenses | 168,000 | 22.4 | 78,000 | 52 | 90,000 | 15 |
| Office segment margin | 177,000 | 23.6 | $ 27,000 | 18% | $150,000 | 25% |
| Common fixed expenses not traceable to offices | 120,000 | 16.0 | | | | |
| Net operating income | $ 57,000 | 7.6% | | | | |

***Required:***

1. By how much would the company's net operating income increase if Dallas increased its sales by $75,000 per year? Assume no change in cost behavior patterns.
2. Refer to the original data. Assume that sales in Houston increase by $50,000 next year and that sales in Dallas remain unchanged. Assume no change in fixed costs.
   a. Prepare a new segmented income statement for the company using the above format. Show both amounts and percentages.
   b. Observe from the income statement you have prepared that the CM ratio for Houston has remained unchanged at 70% (the same as in the above data) but that the segment margin ratio has changed. How do you explain the change in the segment margin ratio?

**EXERCISE 6–15 Working with a Segmented Income Statement [LO4]**

Refer to the data in Exercise 6–14. Assume that Dallas' sales by major market are as follows:

| | | | Market | | | |
|---|---|---|---|---|---|---|
| | Dallas | | Construction Clients | | Landscaping Clients | |
| Sales | $600,000 | 100% | $400,000 | 100% | $200,000 | 100% |
| Variable expenses | 360,000 | 60 | 260,000 | 65 | 100,000 | 50 |
| Contribution margin | 240,000 | 40 | 140,000 | 35 | 100,000 | 50 |
| Traceable fixed expenses | 72,000 | 12 | 20,000 | 5 | 52,000 | 26 |
| Market segment margin | 168,000 | 28 | $120,000 | 30% | $ 48,000 | 24% |
| Common fixed expenses not traceable to markets | 18,000 | 3 | | | | |
| Office segment margin | $150,000 | 25% | | | | |

The company would like to initiate an intensive advertising campaign in one of the two markets during the next month. The campaign would cost $8,000. Marketing studies indicate that such a campaign would increase sales in the construction market by $70,000 or increase sales in the landscaping market by $60,000.

***Required:***

1. In which of the markets would you recommend that the company focus its advertising campaign? Show computations to support your answer.
2. In Exercise 6–14, Dallas shows $90,000 in traceable fixed expenses. What happened to the $90,000 in this exercise?

Alternate problem set is available on the text website and in *Connect® Accounting.*

## PROBLEMS

### All applicable problems are available with McGraw-Hill's *Connect® Accounting*.

**PROBLEM 6–16A Variable and Absorption Costing Unit Product Costs and Income Statements; Explanation of Difference in Net Operating Income [LO1, LO2, LO3]**

CHECK FIGURE
(1b) Net operating income: $70,000; (2b) Net operating loss: $10,000

Brock Company produces and sells an industrial product. The company has just opened a new plant to manufacture the product, and the following cost and revenue data have been provided for the first month of the plant's operation:

| | |
|---|---|
| Beginning inventory | 0 |
| Units produced | 40,000 |
| Units sold | 35,000 |
| Selling price per unit | $60 |
| Selling and administrative expenses: | |
| Variable per unit | $2 |
| Fixed (total) | $560,000 |
| Manufacturing costs | |
| Direct materials cost per unit | $15 |
| Direct labor cost per unit | $7 |
| Variable manufacturing overhead cost per unit | $2 |
| Fixed manufacturing overhead cost (total) | $640,000 |

***Required:***

1. Assume that the company uses absorption costing.
   a. Determine the unit product cost.
   b. Prepare an income statement for the month.
2. Assume that the company uses variable costing.
   a. Determine the unit product cost.
   b. Prepare a contribution format income statement for the month.
3. Explain the reason for any difference in the ending inventory balances under the two costing methods and the impact of this difference on reported net operating income.

**PROBLEM 6–17A Variable and Absorption Costing Unit Product Costs and Income Statements [LO1, LO2]**

CHECK FIGURE
(3b) Year 3 net operating income: $(60,000)

Nickelson Company manufactures and sells one product. The following information pertains to each of the company's first three years of operations:

| | |
|---|---|
| Variable costs per unit: | |
| Manufacturing: | |
| Direct materials | $25 |
| Direct labor | $16 |
| Variable manufacturing overhead | $5 |
| Variable selling and administrative | $2 |
| Fixed costs per year: | |
| Fixed manufacturing overhead | $300,000 |
| Fixed selling and administrative expenses | $180,000 |

During its first year of operations Nickelson produced 60,000 units and sold 60,000 units. During its second year of operations it produced 75,000 units and sold 50,000 units. In its third year, Nickelson produced 40,000 units and sold 65,000 units. The selling price of the company's product is $56 per unit.

***Required:***

1. Compute the company's break-even point in units sold.
2. Assume the company uses variable costing:
   a. Compute the unit product cost for year 1, year 2, and year 3.
   b. Prepare an income statement for year 1, year 2, and year 3.
3. Assume the company uses absorption costing:
   a. Compute the unit product cost for year 1, year 2, and year 3.
   b. Prepare an income statement for year 1, year 2, and year 3.
4. Compare the net operating income figures that you computed in requirements 2 and 3 to the break-even point that you computed in requirement 1. Which net operating income figures seem counterintuitive? Why?

eXcel

CHECK FIGURE
(1) Year 2 net operating income: $210,000

**PROBLEM 6–18A Variable Costing Income Statement; Reconciliation [LO2, LO3]**

During Denton Company's first two years of operations, the company reported absorption costing net operating income as follows:

| | Year 1 | Year 2 |
|---|---|---|
| Sales (@ $50 per unit) | $1,000,000 | $1,500,000 |
| Cost of goods sold (@ $34 per unit) | 680,000 | 1,020,000 |
| Gross margin | 320,000 | 480,000 |
| Selling and administrative expenses* | 310,000 | 340,000 |
| Net operating income | $ 10,000 | $ 140,000 |

*$3 per unit variable; $250,000 fixed each year.

The company's $34 unit product cost is computed as follows:

| | |
|---|---|
| Direct materials | $ 8 |
| Direct labor | 10 |
| Variable manufacturing overhead | 2 |
| Fixed manufacturing overhead ($350,000 ÷ 25,000 units) | 14 |
| Absorption costing unit product cost | $34 |

Production and cost data for the two years are given below:

| | Year 1 | Year 2 |
|---|---|---|
| Units produced | 25,000 | 25,000 |
| Units sold | 20,000 | 30,000 |

***Required:***

1. Prepare a variable costing contribution format income statement for each year.
2. Reconcile the absorption costing and variable costing net operating income figures for each year.

**PROBLEM 6–19A Comprehensive Problem with Labor Fixed [LO1, LO2, LO3]**

CHECK FIGURE
(2) Net operating income: $40,000

Advance Products, Inc., has just organized a new division to manufacture and sell specially designed tables using select hardwoods for personal computers. The division's monthly costs are shown in the schedule below:

| | |
|---|---|
| Manufacturing costs: | |
| Variable costs per unit: | |
| Direct materials | $86 |
| Variable manufacturing overhead | $4 |
| Fixed manufacturing overhead costs (total) | $240,000 |
| Selling and administrative costs: | |
| Variable | 15% of sales |
| Fixed (total) | $160,000 |

Advance Products regards all of its workers as full-time employees and the company has a long-standing no-layoff policy. Furthermore, production is highly automated. Accordingly, the company includes its labor costs in its fixed manufacturing overhead. The tables sell for $250 each.

During the first month of operations, the following activity was recorded:

| | |
|---|---|
| Units produced | 4,000 |
| Units sold | 3,200 |

***Required:***

1. Compute the unit product cost under:
   a. Absorption costing.
   b. Variable costing.
2. Prepare an income statement for the month using absorption costing.
3. Prepare a contribution format income statement for the month using variable costing.
4. Assume that the company must obtain additional financing. As a member of top management, which of the statements that you have prepared in (2) and (3) above would you prefer to take with you to negotiate with the bank? Why?
5. Reconcile the absorption costing and variable costing net operating incomes in (2) and (3) above.

**PROBLEM 6–20A Prepare and Reconcile Variable Costing Statements [LO1, LO2, LO3]**

CHECK FIGURE
(2) June net operating income: $90,000

Linden Company manufactures and sells a single product. Cost data for the product follow:

| | |
|---|---|
| Variable costs per unit: | |
| Direct materials | $ 6 |
| Direct labor | 12 |
| Variable factory overhead | 4 |
| Variable selling and administrative | 3 |
| Total variable costs per unit | $25 |
| Fixed costs per month: | |
| Fixed manufacturing overhead | $240,000 |
| Fixed selling and administrative | 180,000 |
| Total fixed cost per month | $420,000 |

The product sells for $40 per unit. Production and sales data for May and June, the first two months of operations, are as follows:

| | Units Produced | Units Sold |
|---|---|---|
| May | 30,000 | 26,000 |
| June | 30,000 | 34,000 |

Income statements prepared by the accounting department, using absorption costing, are presented below:

| | May | June |
|---|---|---|
| Sales | $1,040,000 | $1,360,000 |
| Cost of goods sold | 780,000 | 1,020,000 |
| Gross margin | 260,000 | 340,000 |
| Selling and administrative expenses | 258,000 | 282,000 |
| Net operating income | $ 2,000 | $ 58,000 |

***Required:***

1. Determine the unit product cost under:
   a. Absorption costing.
   b. Variable costing.
2. Prepare contribution format variable costing income statements for May and June.
3. Reconcile the variable costing and absorption costing net operating incomes.
4. The company's Accounting Department has determined the break-even point to be 28,000 units per month, computed as follows:

$$\frac{\text{Fixed cost per month}}{\text{Unit contribution margin}} = \frac{\$420{,}000}{\$15 \text{ per unit}} = 28{,}000 \text{ units}$$

Upon receiving this figure, the president commented, "There's something peculiar here. The controller says that the break-even point is 28,000 units per month. Yet we sold only 26,000 units in May, and the income statement we received showed a $2,000 profit. Which figure do we believe?" Prepare a brief explanation of what happened on the May income statement.

**PROBLEM 6–21A Absorption and Variable Costing; Production Constant, Sales Fluctuate [LO1, LO2, LO3]**

CHECK FIGURE
(1b) Net operating income: $10,000; (3a) Net operating income: $40,000

Sandi Scott obtained a patent on a small electronic device and organized Scott Products, Inc., to produce and sell the device. During the first month of operations, the device was very well received on the market, so Ms. Scott looked forward to a healthy profit. For this reason, she was surprised to see a loss for the month on her income statement. This statement was prepared by her accounting service, which takes great pride in providing its clients with timely financial data. The statement follows:

**Scott Products, Inc.**
**Income Statement**

| | | |
|---|---|---|
| Sales (40,000 units) | | $200,000 |
| Variable expenses: | | |
| Variable cost of goods sold | $80,000 | |
| Variable selling and administrative expenses | 30,000 | 110,000 |
| Contribution margin | | 90,000 |
| Fixed expenses: | | |
| Fixed manufacturing overhead | 75,000 | |
| Fixed selling and administrative expenses | 20,000 | 95,000 |
| Net operating loss | | $ (5,000) |

Ms. Scott is discouraged over the loss shown for the month, particularly because she had planned to use the statement to encourage investors to purchase stock in the new company. A friend, who is a CPA, insists that the company should be using absorption costing rather than variable costing. He argues that if absorption costing had been used, the company would probably have reported a profit for the month.

Selected cost data relating to the product and to the first month of operations follow:

| | |
|---|---|
| Units produced | 50,000 |
| Units sold | 40,000 |
| Variable costs per unit: | |
| Direct materials | $1.00 |
| Direct labor | $0.80 |
| Variable manufacturing overhead | $0.20 |
| Variable selling and administrative expenses | $0.75 |

***Required:***

1. Complete the following:
   a. Compute the unit product cost under absorption costing.
   b. Redo the company's income statement for the month using absorption costing.
   c. Reconcile the variable and absorption costing net operating income (loss) figures.
2. Was the CPA correct in suggesting that the company really earned a "profit" for the month? Explain.
3. During the second month of operations, the company again produced 50,000 units but sold 60,000 units. (Assume no change in total fixed costs.)
   a. Prepare a contribution format income statement for the month using variable costing.
   b. Prepare an income statement for the month using absorption costing.
   c. Reconcile the variable costing and absorption costing net operating incomes.

**PROBLEM 6–22A Restructuring a Segmented Income Statement [LO4]**

CHECK FIGURE
(3) Middle Europe segment margin: €184,000

Brabant NV of the Netherlands is a wholesale distributor of Dutch cheeses that it sells throughout the European Community. Unfortunately, the company's profits have been declining, which has caused considerable concern. To help understand the condition of the company, the managing director of the company has requested that the monthly income statement be segmented by sales territory. Accordingly, the company's accounting department has prepared the following statement for March, the most recent month. (The Dutch currency is the euro which is designated by €.)

| | Sales Territory | | |
|---|---|---|---|
| | Southern Europe | Middle Europe | Northern Europe |
| Sales | €300,000 | €800,000 | € 700,000 |
| Territorial expenses (traceable): | | | |
| Cost of goods sold | 93,000 | 240,000 | 315,000 |
| Salaries | 54,000 | 56,000 | 112,000 |
| Insurance | 9,000 | 16,000 | 14,000 |
| Advertising | 105,000 | 240,000 | 245,000 |
| Depreciation | 21,000 | 32,000 | 28,000 |
| Shipping | 15,000 | 32,000 | 42,000 |
| Total territorial expenses | 297,000 | 616,000 | 756,000 |
| Territorial income (loss) before corporate expenses | 3,000 | 184,000 | (56,000) |
| Corporate expenses: | | | |
| Advertising (general) | 15,000 | 40,000 | 35,000 |
| General administrative | 20,000 | 20,000 | 20,000 |
| Total corporate expenses | 35,000 | 60,000 | 55,000 |
| Net operating income (loss) | € (32,000) | €124,000 | €(111,000) |

Cost of goods sold and shipping expenses are both variable; other costs are all fixed. Brabant NV purchases cheeses at auction and from farmers' cooperatives, and it distributes them in the three territories listed above. Each of the three sales territories has its own manager and sales staff. The cheeses vary widely in profitability; some have a high margin and some have a low margin. (Certain cheeses, after having been aged for long periods, are the most expensive and carry the highest margins.)

***Required:***

1. List any disadvantages or weaknesses that you see to the statement format illustrated above.
2. Explain the basis that is apparently being used to allocate the corporate expenses to the territories. Do you agree with these allocations? Explain.
3. Prepare a new segmented contribution format income statement for March. Show a Total column as well as data for each territory. In addition, for the company as a whole and for each sales territory, show each item on the segmented income statement as a percent of sales.
4. Analyze the statement that you prepared in (3) above. What points that might help to improve the company's performance would you bring to management's attention?

eXcel

CHECK FIGURE
(1) Year 3 net operating income: $30,000

**PROBLEM 6–23A Prepare and Interpret Statements; Changes in Both Sales and Production; Lean Production [LO1, LO2, LO3]**

Memotec, Inc., manufactures and sells a unique electronic part. Operating results for the first three years of activity were as follows (absorption costing basis):

| | Year 1 | Year 2 | Year 3 |
|---|---|---|---|
| Sales | $1,000,000 | $800,000 | $1,000,000 |
| Cost of goods sold | 800,000 | 560,000 | 850,000 |
| Gross margin | 200,000 | 240,000 | 150,000 |
| Selling and administrative expenses | 170,000 | 150,000 | 170,000 |
| Net operating income (loss) | $ 30,000 | $ 90,000 | $ (20,000) |

Sales dropped by 20% during Year 2 due to the entry of several foreign competitors into the market. Memotec had expected sales to remain constant at 50,000 units for the year; production was set at 60,000 units in order to build a buffer of protection against unexpected spurts in demand. By the start of Year 3, management could see that spurts in demand were unlikely and that the inventory was excessive. To work off the excessive inventories, Memotec cut back production during Year 3, as shown below:

| | Year 1 | Year 2 | Year 3 |
|---|---|---|---|
| Production in units | 50,000 | 60,000 | 40,000 |
| Sales in units | 50,000 | 40,000 | 50,000 |

Additional information about the company follows:

a. The company's plant is highly automated. Variable manufacturing costs (direct materials, direct labor, and variable manufacturing overhead) total only $4 per unit, and fixed manufacturing overhead costs total $600,000 per year.
b. Fixed manufacturing overhead costs are applied to units of product on the basis of each year's production. That is, a new fixed overhead rate is computed each year.
c. Variable selling and administrative expenses are $2 per unit sold. Fixed selling and administrative expenses total $70,000 per year.
d. The company uses a FIFO inventory flow assumption.

Memotec's management can't understand why profits tripled during Year 2 when sales dropped by 20%, and why a loss was incurred during Year 3 when sales recovered to previous levels.

***Required:***

1. Prepare a contribution format variable costing income statement for each year.
2. Refer to the absorption costing income statements above.
   a. Compute the unit product cost in each year under absorption costing. (Show how much of this cost is variable and how much is fixed.)
   b. Reconcile the variable costing and absorption costing net operating incomes for each year.
3. Refer again to the absorption costing income statements. Explain why net operating income was higher in Year 2 than it was in Year 1 under the absorption approach, in light of the fact that fewer units were sold in Year 2 than in Year 1.
4. Refer again to the absorption costing income statements. Explain why the company suffered a loss in Year 3 but reported a profit in Year 1, although the same number of units was sold in each year.
5. a. Explain how operations would have differed in Year 2 and Year 3 if the company had been using Lean Production with the result that ending inventory was zero.
   b. If Lean Production had been in use during Year 2 and Year 3, and the predetermined overhead rate is based on 50,000 units per year, what would the company's net operating income (or loss) have been in each year under absorption costing? Explain the reason for any differences between these income figures and the figures reported by the company in the statements above.

CHECK FIGURE
(1) Flour segment margin: $42,000

**PROBLEM 6–24A Segmented Income Statements [LO4]**

Vega Foods, Inc., has recently purchased a small mill that it intends to operate as one of its subsidiaries. The newly acquired mill has three products that it offers for sale—wheat cereal, pancake mix, and flour. Each product sells for $10 per package. Materials, labor, and other variable production costs are $3.00 per bag of wheat cereal, $4.20 per bag of pancake mix, and $1.80 per bag of flour. Sales commissions are 10% of sales for any product. All other costs are fixed.

The mill's income statement for the most recent month is given below:

| | | Product Line | | |
|---|---|---|---|---|
| | Total Company | Wheat Cereal | Pancake Mix | Flour |
| Sales | $600,000 | $200,000 | $300,000 | $100,000 |
| Expenses: | | | | |
| Materials, labor, and other | 204,000 | 60,000 | 126,000 | 18,000 |
| Sales commissions | 60,000 | 20,000 | 30,000 | 10,000 |
| Advertising | 123,000 | 48,000 | 60,000 | 15,000 |
| Salaries | 66,000 | 34,000 | 21,000 | 11,000 |
| Equipment depreciation | 30,000 | 10,000 | 15,000 | 5,000 |
| Warehouse rent | 12,000 | 4,000 | 6,000 | 2,000 |
| General administration | 90,000 | 30,000 | 30,000 | 30,000 |
| Total expenses | 585,000 | 206,000 | 288,000 | 91,000 |
| Net operating income (loss) | $ 15,000 | $ (6,000) | $ 12,000 | $ 9,000 |

The following additional information is available about the company:

a. The same equipment is used to mill and package all three products. In the above income statement, equipment depreciation has been allocated on the basis of sales dollars. An analysis of equipment usage indicates that it is used 40% of the time to make wheat cereal, 50% of the time to make pancake mix, and 10% of the time to make flour.

b. All three products are stored in the same warehouse. In the above income statement, the warehouse rent has been allocated on the basis of sales dollars. The warehouse contains 24,000 square feet of space, of which 8,000 square feet are used for wheat cereal, 14,000 square feet are used for pancake mix, and 2,000 square feet are used for flour. The warehouse space costs the company $0.50 per square foot per month to rent.

c. The general administration costs relate to the administration of the company as a whole. In the above income statement, these costs have been divided equally among the three product lines.

d. All other costs are traceable to the product lines.

Vega Foods' management is anxious to improve the mill's 2.5% margin on sales.

***Required:***

1. Prepare a new contribution format segmented income statement for the month. Adjust the allocation of equipment depreciation and warehouse rent as indicated by the additional information provided.
2. After seeing the income statement in the main body of the problem, management has decided to eliminate the wheat cereal because it is not returning a profit, and to focus all available resources on promoting the pancake mix.
   a. Based on the statement you have prepared, do you agree with the decision to eliminate the wheat cereal? Explain.
   b. Based on the statement you have prepared, do you agree with the decision to focus all available resources on promoting the pancake mix? Assume that an ample market is available for all three products. (Hint: compute the contribution margin ratio for each product.)

# BUILDING YOUR SKILLS

## ANALYTICAL THINKING [LO4]

CHECK FIGURE
(1) Central segment margin: $32,000

The most recent monthly contribution format income statement for Reston Company is given below:

**Reston Company**
**Income Statement**
**For the Month Ended May 31**

| | | |
|---|---|---|
| Sales | $900,000 | 100.0% |
| Variable expenses | 408,000 | 45.3 |
| Contribution margin | 492,000 | 54.7 |
| Fixed expenses | 465,000 | 51.7 |
| Net operating income | $ 27,000 | 3.0% |

Management is disappointed with the company's performance and is wondering what can be done to improve profits. By examining sales and cost records, you have determined the following:

a. The company is divided into two sales territories—Central and Eastern. The Central Territory recorded $400,000 in sales and $208,000 in variable expenses during May. The remaining sales and variable expenses were recorded in the Eastern Territory. Fixed expenses of $160,000 and $130,000 are traceable to the Central and Eastern Territories, respectively. The rest of the fixed expenses are common to the two territories.

b. The company is the exclusive distributor for two products—Awls and Pows. Sales of Awls and Pows totaled $100,000 and $300,000, respectively, in the Central Territory during May. Variable expenses are 25% of the selling price for Awls and 61% for Pows. Cost records show that $60,000 of the Central Territory's fixed expenses are traceable to Awls and $54,000 to Pows, with the remainder common to the two products.

***Required:***

1. Prepare contribution format segmented income statements, first showing the total company broken down between sales territories and then showing the Central Territory broken down by product line. In addition, for the company as a whole and for each segment, show each item on the segmented income statements as a percent of sales.
2. Look at the statement you have prepared showing the total company segmented by sales territory. What points revealed by this statement should be brought to management's attention?
3. Look at the statement you have prepared showing the Central Territory segmented by product lines. What points revealed by this statement should be brought to management's attention?

## ETHICS CHALLENGE [LO2]

Aristotle Constantinos, the manager of DuraProducts' Australian Division, is trying to set the production schedule for the last quarter of the year. The Australian Division had planned to sell 100,000 units during the year, but current projections indicate sales will be only 78,000 units in total. By September 30 the following activity had been reported:

| | Units |
|---|---|
| Inventory, January 1 | 0 |
| Production | 72,000 |
| Sales | 60,000 |
| Inventory, September 30 | 12,000 |

Demand has been soft, and the sales forecast for the last quarter is only 18,000 units.

The division can rent warehouse space to store up to 30,000 units. The division should maintain a minimum inventory level of at least 1,500 units. Mr. Constantinos is aware that production must be at least 6,000 units per quarter in order to retain a nucleus of key employees. Maximum production capacity is 45,000 units per quarter.

Due to the nature of the division's operations, fixed manufacturing overhead is a major element of product cost.

***Required:***

1. Assume that the division is using variable costing. How many units should be scheduled for production during the last quarter of the year? (The basic formula for computing the required production for a period in a company is: Expected sales + Desired ending inventory − Beginning inventory = Required production.) Show computations and explain your answer. Will the number of units scheduled for production affect the division's reported profit for the year? Explain.
2. Assume that the division is using absorption costing and that the divisional manager is given an annual bonus based on the division's net operating income. If Mr. Constantinos wants to maximize his division's net operating income for the year, how many units should be scheduled for production during the last quarter? [See the formula in (1) above.] Explain.
3. Identify the ethical issues involved in the decision Mr. Constantinos must make about the level of production for the last quarter of the year.

**CASE [LO4]**

CHECK FIGURE
(1) Journal segment margin: $95,000

The American Association of Acupuncturists is a professional association for acupuncturists that has 10,000 members. The association operates from a central headquarters but has local chapters throughout North America. The association's monthly journal, *American Acupuncture,* features recent developments in the field. The association also publishes special reports and books, and it sponsors courses that qualify members for the continuing professional education credit required by state certification boards. The association's statement of revenues and expenses for the current year is presented below:

**American Association of Acupuncturists**
**Statement of Revenues and Expenses**
**For the Year Ended December 31**

| | |
|---|---|
| Revenues | $970,000 |
| Expenses: | |
| Salaries | 440,000 |
| Occupancy costs | 120,000 |
| Distributions to local chapters | 210,000 |
| Printing | 82,000 |
| Mailing | 24,000 |
| Continuing education instructors' fees | 60,000 |
| General and administrative | 27,000 |
| Total expenses | 963,000 |
| Excess of revenues over expenses | $ 7,000 |

The board of directors of the association has requested that you construct a segmented income statement that shows the financial contribution of each of the association's four major programs— membership service, journal, books and reports, and continuing education. The following data have been gathered to aid you:

a. Membership dues are $60 per year, of which $15 covers a one-year subscription to the association's journal. The other $45 pays for general membership services.
b. One-year subscriptions to *American Acupuncture* are sold to nonmembers and libraries at $20 per subscription. A total of 1,000 of these subscriptions were sold last year. In addition to subscriptions, the journal generated $50,000 in advertising revenues. The costs per journal subscription, for members as well as nonmembers, were $4 for printing and $1 for mailing.
c. A variety of technical reports and professional books were sold for a total of $70,000 during the year. Printing costs for these materials totaled $25,000, and mailing costs totaled $8,000.
d. The association offers a number of continuing education courses. The courses generated revenues of $230,000 last year.
e. Salary costs and space occupied by each program and the central staff are as follows:

| | Salaries | Space Occupied (square feet) |
|---|---|---|
| Membership services | $170,000 | 3,000 |
| Journal | 60,000 | 1,000 |
| Books and reports | 40,000 | 1,000 |
| Continuing education | 50,000 | 2,000 |
| Central staff | 120,000 | 3,000 |
| Total | $440,000 | 10,000 |

f. The $120,000 in occupancy costs incurred last year includes $20,000 in rental cost for a portion of the warehouse used by the Membership Services program for storage purposes. The association has a flexible rental agreement that allows it to pay rent only on the warehouse space it uses.

g. Printing costs other than for journal subscriptions are for books and reports related to Continuing Education.

h. Distributions to local chapters are for general membership services.

i. General and administrative expenses include costs relating to overall administration of the association as a whole. The association's central staff does some mailing of materials for general administrative purposes.

j. The expenses that can be traced or assigned to the central staff, as well as any other expenses that are not traceable to the programs, will be treated as common costs. It is not necessary to distinguish between variable and fixed costs.

***Required:***

1. Prepare a contribution format segmented income statement for the American Association of Acupuncturists for last year. This statement should show the segment margin for each program as well as results for the association as a whole.
2. Give arguments for and against allocating all costs of the association to the four programs.

(CMA, adapted)

### A LOOK BACK

Chapter 6 explained how the contribution format can be used to create variable costing income statements for manufacturers and segmented income statements that distinguish between traceable fixed costs and common fixed costs. It also contrasted variable costing with the absorption format.

### A LOOK AT THIS CHAPTER

After discussing why organizations prepare budgets and the process they use to create a budget, Chapter 7 overviews each of the parts of a master budget including the cash budget, the budgeted income statement, and the budgeted balance sheet.

### A LOOK AHEAD

In Chapter 8, we turn our attention from the planning process to management control, focusing on the use of flexible budgets and variance analysis.

# 7 Profit Planning

## CHAPTER OUTLINE

**The Basic Framework of Budgeting**

- Advantages of Budgeting
- Responsibility Accounting
- Choosing a Budget Period
- The Self-Imposed Budget
- Human Factors in Budgeting
- The Master Budget: An Overview

**Preparing the Master Budget**

- The Sales Budget
- The Production Budget
- Inventory Purchases—Merchandising Company
- The Direct Materials Budget
- The Direct Labor Budget
- The Manufacturing Overhead Budget
- The Ending Finished Goods Inventory Budget
- The Selling and Administrative Expense Budget
- The Cash Budget
- The Budgeted Income Statement
- The Budgeted Balance Sheet

## DECISION FEATURE

# Planning for a Crisis—Civil War Preservation Trust

The **Civil War Preservation Trust** (CWPT) is a private, nonprofit organization with 70,000 members that works to preserve the nation's remaining Civil War battlefields—many of which are threatened by commercial development such as shopping centers, houses, industrial parks, and casinos. To forestall development, the CWPT typically purchases the land or development rights to the land. The CWPT has saved over 25,000 acres from development, including, for example, 698 acres of battlefield at Gettysburg.

CWPT's management team was particularly concerned about the budget proposal for 2009, which was to be presented to the board of directors in the fall of 2008. The CWPT is wholly supported by contributions from its members and many of those members had been adversely affected by the ongoing financial crisis that followed the collapse of the subprime mortgage market. Consequently, the funds that would be available for operations in 2009 were particularly difficult to predict. Accordingly, the budget for 2009 contained three variations based on progressively pessimistic economic assumptions. The more pessimistic budgets were called contingent budgets. As 2008 progressed and member contributions declined somewhat from previous levels, CWPT switched to the first contingent budget. This contingent budget required a number of actions to reduce costs including a hiring freeze and a salary freeze, but maintained an aggressive program of protecting battlefield acreage through purchases of land and development rights. Fortunately, the CWPT did not have to switch to the most pessimistic budget—which would have involved layoffs and other extraordinary cost-saving measures.

Instead of reacting in a panic mode to unfavorable developments, CWPT used the budgeting process to carefully plan in advance for a number of possible contingencies.

Sources: Communications with James Lighthizer, president, and David Duncan, director of membership and development, Civil War Preservation Trust; and the CWPT website, civilwar.org.

## LEARNING OBJECTIVES

*After studying Chapter 7, you should be able to:*

**LO1** Understand why organizations budget and the processes they use to create budgets.

**LO2** Prepare a sales budget, including a schedule of expected cash collections.

**LO3** Prepare a production budget.

**LO4** Prepare a direct materials budget, including a schedule of expected cash disbursements for purchases of materials.

**LO5** Prepare a direct labor budget.

**LO6** Prepare a manufacturing overhead budget.

**LO7** Prepare a selling and administrative expense budget.

**LO8** Prepare a cash budget.

**LO9** Prepare a budgeted income statement.

**LO10** Prepare a budgeted balance sheet.

**In this chapter, we focus on the steps** taken by businesses to achieve their planned levels of profits—a process called *profit planning*. Profit planning is accomplished by preparing a number of budgets that together form an integrated business plan known as the *master budget*. The master budget is an essential management tool that communicates management's plans throughout the organization, allocates resources, and coordinates activities.

## THE BASIC FRAMEWORK OF BUDGETING

**LEARNING OBJECTIVE 1**

Understand why organizations budget and the processes they use to create budgets.

A **budget** is a detailed plan for the future that is usually expressed in formal quantitative terms. Individuals sometimes create household budgets that balance their income and expenditures for food, clothing, housing, and so on while providing for some savings. Once the budget is established, actual spending is compared to the budget to make surc the plan is being followed. Companies use budgets in a similar way, although the amount of work and underlying details far exceed a personal budget.

Budgets are used for two distinct purposes—*planning* and *control*. **Planning** involves developing goals and preparing various budgets to achieve those goals. **Control** involves gathering feedback to ensure that the plan is being properly executed or modified as circumstances change. To be effective, a good budgeting system must provide for both planning and control. Good planning without effective control is a waste of time and effort.

### Advantages of Budgeting

Organizations realize many benefits from budgeting including:

1. Budgets *communicate* management's plans throughout the organization.
2. Budgets force managers to *think about* and *plan* for the future. In the absence of the necessity to prepare a budget, many managers would spend all of their time dealing with day-to-day emergencies.
3. The budgeting process provides a means of *allocating resources* to those parts of the organization where they can be used most effectively.
4. The budgeting process can uncover potential *bottlenecks* before they occur.
5. Budgets *coordinate* the activities of the entire organization by *integrating* the plans of its various parts. Budgeting helps to ensure that everyone in the organization is pulling in the same direction.
6. Budgets define goals and objectives that can serve as *benchmarks* for evaluating subsequent performance.

**IN BUSINESS**

### Executing Strategy With Budgets

Robert DeMartini, the CEO of **New Balance**, set a goal of tripling his company's revenues to $3 billion in four years. He tripled the company's annual advertising budget and doubled its consumer research budget in an effort to attract more young customers. These decisions represented a strategic shift for New Balance, which usually spends less than $20 million per year in advertising compared to competitors such as **Nike** and **Adidas**, which annually invest $184 million and $80 million, respectively.

One reason companies prepare budgets is to allocate resources across departments in a manner that supports strategic priorities. DeMartini used the budget to send a clear signal that his marketing department was expected to play a huge role in achieving the company's revenue growth targets. As time progresses, he will compare the company's actual revenue growth from young consumers to the marketing department's expenditures to see if his strategy is working or requires adjustment.

Source: Stephanie Kang, "New Balance Steps up Marketing Drive," *The Wall Street Journal*, March 21, 2008, p. B3.

## Responsibility Accounting

Most of what we say in this chapter and in the next three chapters is concerned with *responsibility accounting*. The basic idea underlying **responsibility accounting** is that a manager should be held responsible for those items—and *only* those items—that the manager can actually control to a significant extent. Each line item (i.e., revenue or cost) in the budget is the responsibility of a manager who is held responsible for subsequent deviations between budgeted goals and actual results. In effect, responsibility accounting *personalizes* accounting information by holding individuals responsible for revenues and costs. This concept is central to any effective profit planning and control system. Someone must be held responsible for each cost or else no one will be responsible and the cost will inevitably grow out of control.

What happens if actual results do not measure up to the budgeted goals? The manager is not necessarily penalized. However, the manager should take the initiative to correct any unfavorable discrepancies, should understand the source of significant favorable or unfavorable discrepancies, and should be prepared to explain the reasons for discrepancies to higher management. The point of an effective responsibility accounting system is to make sure that nothing "falls through the cracks," that the organization reacts quickly and appropriately to deviations from its plans, and that the organization learns from the feedback it gets by comparing budgeted goals to actual results. The point is *not* to penalize individuals for missing targets.

### New York City Mayor Benefits From Budgets

IN BUSINESS

Michael Bloomberg, the mayor of **New York City**, makes annual budget presentations to his fellow elected officials, the city council, and the media. Historically, the city's mayors had delegated these types of presentations to one of their budget directors; however, Bloomberg believes that by investing his time in explaining the factors influencing the city's economy, his constituents will gain a better understanding of his fiscal priorities. This, in turn, helps improve his negotiations with the city council and his relationships with various advocacy groups. The mayor also makes his entire budget available online so that New Yorkers can scrutinize budgeting details, such as the cost of running specific government agencies.

Source: Tom Lowry, "The CEO Mayor," *BusinessWeek*, June 25, 2007, pp. 58–64.

## Choosing a Budget Period

Operating budgets ordinarily cover a one-year period corresponding to the company's fiscal year. Many companies divide their budget year into four quarters. The first quarter is then subdivided into months, and monthly budgets are developed. The last three quarters may be carried in the budget as quarterly totals only. As the year progresses, the figures for the second quarter are broken down into monthly amounts, then the third-quarter figures are broken down, and so forth. This approach has the advantage of requiring periodic review and reappraisal of budget data throughout the year.

*Continuous* or *perpetual budgets* are sometimes used. A **continuous** or **perpetual budget** is a 12-month budget that rolls forward one month (or quarter) as the current month (or quarter) is completed. In other words, one month (or quarter) is added to the end of the budget as each month (or quarter) comes to a close. This approach keeps managers focused at least one year ahead so that they do not become too narrowly focused on short-term results.

In this chapter, we will look at one-year operating budgets. However, using basically the same techniques, operating budgets can be prepared for periods that extend over many years. It may be difficult to accurately forecast sales and other data much beyond a year, but even rough estimates can be invaluable in uncovering potential problems and opportunities that would otherwise be overlooked.

## The Self-Imposed Budget

The success of a budget program is largely determined by the way a budget is developed. Oftentimes, the budget is imposed from above, with little participation by lower-level managers. However, in the most successful budget programs, managers actively participate in preparing their own budgets. Imposing expectations from above and then penalizing employees who do not meet those expectations will generate resentment rather than cooperation and commitment. In fact, many managers believe that being empowered to create their own *self-imposed budgets* is the most effective method of budget preparation. A **self-imposed budget** or **participative budget,** as illustrated in Exhibit 7–1, is a budget that is prepared with the full cooperation and participation of managers at all levels.

Self-imposed budgets have a number of advantages:

1. Individuals at all levels of the organization are recognized as members of the team whose views and judgments are valued by top management.
2. Budget estimates prepared by front-line managers are often more accurate and reliable than estimates prepared by top managers who have less intimate knowledge of markets and day-to-day operations.
3. Motivation is generally higher when individuals participate in setting their own goals than when the goals are imposed from above. Self-imposed budgets create commitment.

**EXHIBIT 7–1** The Initial Flow of Budget Data in a Participative Budgeting System

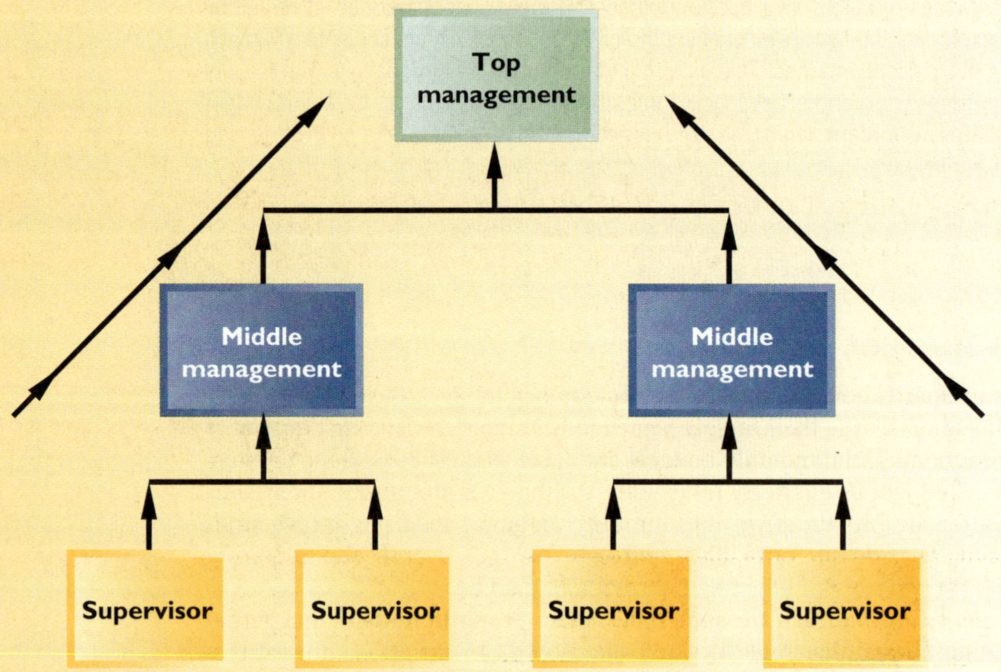


The initial flow of budget data in a participative budgeting system is from lower levels of responsibility to higher levels of responsibility. Each person with responsibility for cost control will prepare his or her own budget estimates and submit them to the next higher level of management. These estimates are reviewed and consolidated as they move upward in the organization.

4. A manager who is not able to meet a budget that has been imposed from above can always say that the budget was unrealistic and impossible to meet. With a self-imposed budget, this claim cannot be made.

One important limitation of self-imposed budgeting is that lower-level managers may allow too much *budgetary slack.* Since the manager who creates the budget will be held accountable for actual results that deviate from the budget, the manager will have a natural tendency to submit a budget that is easy to attain (i.e., the manager will build slack into the budget). For this reason, budgets prepared by lower-level managers should be scrutinized by higher levels of management. Questionable items should be discussed and modified as appropriate. Without such a review, self-imposed budgets may be too slack, resulting in suboptimal performance.

As these comments suggest, all levels in the organization should work together to produce the budget. Lower-level managers are more familiar with day-to-day operations than top managers. Top managers should have a more strategic perspective than lower-level managers. Each level of responsibility in an organization should contribute its unique knowledge and perspective in a cooperative effort to develop an integrated budget. Nevertheless, a self-imposed approach to setting budgets works best when all managers understand the organization's strategy. Otherwise, the budgets proposed by the lower-level managers will lack coherent direction. In a later chapter, we discuss in greater detail how a company can go about formulating its strategy and communicating it throughout the organization.

Unfortunately, most companies do not follow the budgeting process we have described. Typically, top managers initiate the budgeting process by issuing profit targets. Lower-level managers are directed to prepare budgets that meet those targets. The difficulty is that the targets set by top managers may be unrealistically high or may allow too much slack. If the targets are too high and employees know they are unrealistic, motivation will suffer. If the targets allow too much slack, waste will occur. Unfortunately, top managers are often not in a position to know whether the targets are appropriate. Admittedly, a self-imposed budgeting system may lack sufficient strategic direction and lower-level managers may be tempted to build slack into their budgets. Nevertheless, because of the motivational advantages of self-imposed budgets, top managers should be cautious about imposing inflexible targets from above.

## Human Factors in Budgeting

The success of a budget program also depends on the degree to which top management accepts the budget program as a vital part of the company's activities and the way in which top management uses budgeted data.

If a budget program is to be successful, it must have the complete acceptance and support of the persons who occupy key management positions. If lower or middle managers sense that top management is lukewarm about budgeting, or if they sense that top management simply tolerates budgeting as a necessary evil, then their own attitudes will reflect a similar lack of enthusiasm. Budgeting is hard work, and if top management is not enthusiastic about and committed to the budget program, then it is unlikely that anyone else in the organization will be either.

In administering the budget program, it is particularly important that top management not use the budget to pressure or blame employees. Using budgets in such negative ways will breed hostility, tension, and mistrust rather than cooperation and productivity. Unfortunately, the budget is too often used as a pressure device and excessive emphasis is placed on "meeting the budget" under all circumstances. Rather than being used as a weapon, the budget should be used as a positive instrument to assist in establishing goals, measuring operating results, and isolating areas that need attention.

The human aspects of budgeting are extremely important. The remainder of the chapter deals with technical aspects of budgeting, but do not lose sight of the human aspects. The purpose of the budget is to motivate people and to coordinate their efforts. This purpose is undermined if managers become preoccupied with the technical aspects or if the budget is used in a rigid and inflexible manner to control people.

How challenging should budget targets be? Some experts argue that budget targets should be very challenging and should require managers to stretch to meet goals. Even the most capable managers may have to scramble to meet such a "stretch budget" and they may not always succeed. In practice, most companies set their budget targets at a "highly achievable" level. A highly achievable budget may be challenging, but it can almost always be met by competent managers exerting reasonable effort.

Bonuses based on meeting and exceeding budgets are often a key element of management compensation. Typically, no bonus is paid unless the budget is met. The bonus often increases when the budget target is exceeded, but the bonus is usually capped out at some level. For obvious reasons, managers who have such a bonus plan or whose performance is evaluated based on meeting budget targets usually prefer to be evaluated based on highly achievable budgets rather than on stretch budgets. Moreover, highly achievable budgets may help build a manager's confidence and generate greater commitment to the budget. And finally, highly achievable budgets may result in less undesirable behavior at the end of budgetary periods by managers who are intent on earning their bonuses.

## The Master Budget: An Overview

The **master budget** consists of a number of separate but interdependent budgets that formally lay out the company's sales, production, and financial goals. The master budget culminates in a cash budget, a budgeted income statement, and a budgeted balance sheet. Exhibit 7–2 provides an overview of the various parts of the master budget and how they are related.

**EXHIBIT 7–2**
The Master Budget Interrelationships

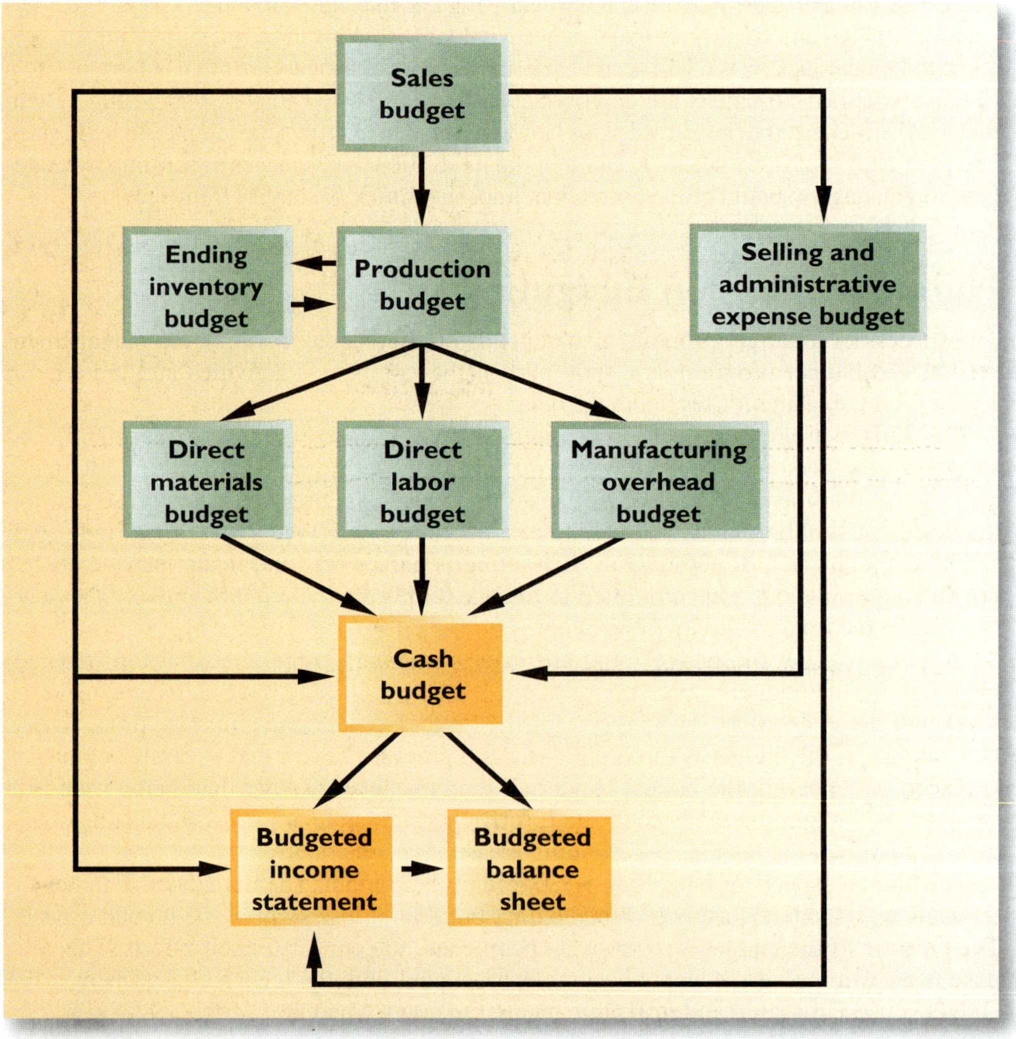

The first step in the budgeting process is the preparation of the **sales budget,** which is a detailed schedule showing the expected sales for the budget period. An accurate sales budget is the key to the entire budgeting process. As illustrated in Exhibit 7–2, all other parts of the master budget depend on the sales budget. If the sales budget is inaccurate, the rest of the budget will be inaccurate. The sales budget is based on the company's sales forecast, which may require the use of sophisticated mathematical models and statistical tools. We will not go into the details of how sales forecasts are made. This is a subject that is most appropriately covered in marketing courses.

The sales budget helps determine how many units need to be produced. Thus, the production budget is prepared after the sales budget. The production budget in turn is used to determine the budgets for manufacturing costs including the direct materials budget, the direct labor budget, and the manufacturing overhead budget. These budgets are then combined with data from the sales budget and the selling and administrative expense budget to determine the *cash budget.* A **cash budget** is a detailed plan showing how cash resources will be acquired and used. Observe from Exhibit 7–2 that all of the operating budgets have an impact on the cash budget. After the cash budget is prepared, the budgeted income statement and then the budgeted balance sheet can be prepared.

## PREPARING THE MASTER BUDGET

**MANAGERIAL ACCOUNTING IN ACTION**
**The Issue**

Tom Wills is the majority stockholder and chief executive officer of Hampton Freeze, Inc., a company he started in 2011. The company makes premium popsicles using only natural ingredients and featuring exotic flavors such as tangy tangerine and minty mango. The company's business is highly seasonal, with most of the sales occurring in spring and summer.

In 2012, the company's second year of operations, a major cash crunch in the first and second quarters almost forced the company into bankruptcy. In spite of this cash crunch, 2012 turned out to be a very successful year in terms of both cash flow and net income. Partly as a result of that harrowing experience, Tom decided toward the end of 2012 to hire a professional financial manager. Tom interviewed several promising candidates for the job and settled on Larry Giano, who had considerable experience in the packaged foods industry. In the job interview, Tom questioned Larry about the steps he would take to prevent a recurrence of the 2012 cash crunch:

***Tom:*** As I mentioned earlier, we are going to end 2012 with a very nice profit. What you may not know is that we had some very big financial problems this year.

***Larry:*** Let me guess. You ran out of cash sometime in the first or second quarter.

***Tom:*** How did you know?

***Larry:*** Most of your sales are in the second and third quarter, right?

***Tom:*** Sure, everyone wants to buy popsicles in the spring and summer, but nobody wants them when the weather turns cold.

***Larry:*** So you don't have many sales in the first quarter?

***Tom:*** Right.

***Larry:*** And in the second quarter, which is the spring, you are producing like crazy to fill orders?

***Tom:*** Sure.

***Larry:*** Do your customers, the grocery stores, pay you the day you make your deliveries?

***Tom:*** Are you kidding? Of course not.

***Larry:*** So in the first quarter, you don't have many sales. In the second quarter, you are producing like crazy, which eats up cash, but you aren't paid by your customers until long after you have paid your employees and suppliers. No wonder you had a cash problem. I see this pattern all the time in food processing because of the seasonality of the business.

***Tom:*** So what can we do about it?

***Larry:*** The first step is to predict the magnitude of the problem before it occurs. If we can predict early in the year what the cash shortfall is going to be, we can go to the bank and arrange for credit before we really need it. Bankers tend to be leery of panicky people who show up begging for emergency loans. They are much more likely to make the loan if you look like you are in control of the situation.

***Tom:*** How can we predict the cash shortfall?

***Larry:*** You can put together a cash budget. While you're at it, you might as well do a master budget. You'll find it is well worth the effort.

***Tom:*** I don't like budgets. They are too confining. My wife budgets everything at home, and I can't spend what I want.

***Larry:*** Can I ask a personal question?

***Tom:*** What?

***Larry:*** Where did you get the money to start this business?

***Tom:*** Mainly from our family's savings. I get your point. We wouldn't have had the money to start the business if my wife hadn't been forcing us to save every month.

***Larry:*** Exactly. I suggest you use the same discipline in your business. It is even more important here because you can't expect your employees to spend your money as carefully as you would.

With the full backing of Tom Wills, Larry Giano set out to create a master budget for the company for the year 2013. In his planning for the budgeting process, Larry drew up the following list of documents that would be a part of the master budget:

1. A sales budget, including a schedule of expected cash collections.
2. A production budget (a merchandise purchases budget would be used in a merchandising company).
3. A direct materials budget, including a schedule of expected cash disbursements for purchases of materials.
4. A direct labor budget.
5. A manufacturing overhead budget.
6. An ending finished goods inventory budget.
7. A selling and administrative expense budget.
8. A cash budget.
9. A budgeted income statement.
10. A budgeted balance sheet.

Larry felt it was important to have everyone's cooperation in the budgeting process, so he asked Tom to call a companywide meeting to explain the budgeting process. At the meeting there was initially some grumbling, but Tom was able to convince nearly everyone of the necessity for planning and getting better control over spending. It helped that the cash crisis earlier in the year was still fresh in everyone's minds. As much as some people disliked the idea of budgets, they liked their jobs more.

In the months that followed, Larry worked closely with all of the managers involved in the master budget, gathering data from them and making sure that they understood and fully supported the parts of the master budget that would affect them. In subsequent years, Larry hoped to turn the whole budgeting process over to the managers and to take a more advisory role.

The interdependent documents that Larry Giano prepared for Hampton Freeze are Schedules 1 through 10 of the company's master budget. In this section, we will study these schedules.

**HELPFUL HINT**

The 10 schedules that we are about to explain can often be overwhelming to students. To help you see the "big picture," keep in mind that Hampton Freeze's master budget is designed to help it estimate the answers to 10 questions for each quarter and the entire year:

1. How much sales revenue will we earn?
2. How much cash will we collect from customers?
3. How much raw material will we need to purchase?
4. How much manufacturing cost (including direct materials, direct labor, and manufacturing overhead) will we need to add to production?
5. How much cash will we pay to our suppliers and our direct laborers, and how much will we pay for manufacturing overhead resources?
6. What is the total cost that will be transferred from finished goods inventory to cost of goods sold?
7. How much selling and administrative expense will we incur and how much cash will we pay related to those expenses?
8. How much cash will we pay for equipment purchases?
9. How much will we pay in cash dividends?
10. How much money will we borrow from or repay to lenders including interest?

Estimating the answers to these 10 questions enables Hampton Freeze to prepare a budgeted balance sheet and income statement and to proactively manage its cash flows.

## The Sales Budget

**LEARNING OBJECTIVE 2**

Prepare a sales budget, including a schedule of expected cash collections.

The sales budget is the starting point in preparing the master budget. As shown earlier in Exhibit 7–2, all other items in the master budget, including production, purchases, inventories, and expenses, depend on it.

The sales budget is constructed by multiplying budgeted unit sales by the selling price. Schedule 1 contains the quarterly sales budget for Hampton Freeze for the year 2013. Notice from the schedule that the company plans to sell 100,000 cases of popsicles during the year, with sales peaking in the third quarter.

A schedule of expected cash collections, such as the one that appears in the bottom portion of Schedule 1, is prepared after the sales budget. This schedule will be needed later to prepare the cash budget. Cash collections consist of collections on credit sales made to customers in prior periods plus collections on sales made in the current budget period. At Hampton Freeze, all sales are on credit; furthermore, experience has shown that 70% of sales are collected in the quarter in which the sale is made and the remaining 30% are collected in the following quarter. For example, 70% of the first quarter sales of $200,000 (or $140,000) is collected during the first quarter and 30% (or $60,000) is collected during the second quarter.

## The Importance of Sales Risk Management

**IN BUSINESS**

David Flynn founded **Amistad Media Group** in 1994 to help companies market themselves to growing Hispanic communities in places such as Nebraska, Kansas, and North Carolina. While Amistad's sales steadily grew to a peak of $49 million in 2003, its customer base had not grown much in nine years. In fact, just two companies generated the bulk of Amistad's sales—**Novamex** and the **U.S. Army**. When the U.S. Army dropped Amistad as a supplier in 2005, the company's sales plummeted and it was bankrupt by 2006.

Amistad's demise highlights the importance of evaluating a company's sales forecast not only in terms of dollars, but also in terms of the number of customers served. Small companies in particular should seek to diversify their customer base, thereby reducing the risk that losing one or two customers will put them out of business.

Source: Patrick Cliff, "Adios to a Pioneering Hispanic Marketing Firm," *Inc.* Magazine, May, 2006, p. 34.

## SCHEDULE 1

Homework 7 #1

Be sure to understand the red arrows

**Hampton Freeze, Inc.**
**Sales Budget**
**For the Year Ended December 31, 2013**

| | Quarter 1 | Quarter 2 | Quarter 3 | Quarter 4 | Year |
|---|---|---|---|---|---|
| Budgeted sales in cases | 10,000 | 30,000 | 40,000 | 20,000 | 100,000 |
| Selling price per case | $ 20.00 | $ 20.00 | $ 20.00 | $ 20.00 | $ 20.00 |
| Total sales | $200,000 | $600,000 | $800,000 | $400,000 | $2,000,000 |
| | | | | | |
| Percentage of sales collected in the period of the sale | | | 70% | | |
| Percentage of sales collected in the period after the sale | | | 30% | | |
| | 70% | 30% | | | |

**Schedule of Expected Cash Collections**

| | Quarter 1 | Quarter 2 | Quarter 3 | Quarter 4 | Year |
|---|---|---|---|---|---|
| Accounts receivable, beginning balance[1] | $ 90,000 | | | | $ 90,000 |
| First-quarter sales[2] | 140,000 | $ 60,000 | | | 200,000 |
| Second-quarter sales[3] | | 420,000 | $180,000 | | 600,000 |
| Third-quarter sales[4] | | | 560,000 | $240,000 | 800,000 |
| Fourth-quarter sales[5] | - | - | - | 280,000 | 280,000 |
| Total cash collections[6] | $230,000 | $480,000 | $740,000 | $520,000 | $1,970,000 |

Schedule 1 | Schedule 2 | Schedule 3 | Schedule 4 | Schedule 5 | Schedule 6 | Sched

[1]Cash collections from last year's fourth-quarter sales. See the beginning-of-year balance sheet on page 306.
[2]\$200,000 × 70%; \$200,000 × 30%.
[3]\$600,000 × 70%; \$600,000 × 30%.
[4]\$800,000 × 70%; \$800,000 × 30%.
[5]\$400,000 × 70%.
[6]Uncollected fourth-quarter sales (\$120,000) appear as accounts receivable on the company's end-of-year budgeted balance sheet (see Schedule 10 on page 307).

## CONCEPT CHECK ✓

1. March, April, and May sales are \$100,000, \$120,000, and \$125,000, respectively. A total of 80% of all sales are credit sales and 20% are cash sales. A total of 60% of credit sales are collected in the month of the sale and 40% are collected in the next month. There are no bad debt expenses. What is the amount of cash collections for April?
   a. \$89,600
   b. \$111,600
   c. \$113,600
   d. \$132,600
2. Referring to the facts in question 1 above, what is the accounts receivable balance at the end of May?
   a. \$40,000
   b. \$50,000
   c. \$72,000
   d. \$80,000

## The Production Budget

LEARNING OBJECTIVE 3

Prepare a production budget.

The production budget is prepared after the sales budget. The **production budget** lists the number of units that must be produced to satisfy sales needs and to provide for the desired ending inventory. Production needs can be determined as follows:

| | |
|---|---|
| Budgeted unit sales | XXXX |
| Add desired ending inventory of finished goods | XXXX |
| Total needs | XXXX |
| Less beginning inventory of finished goods | XXXX |
| Required production | XXXX |

Note that production requirements are influenced by the desired level of the ending inventory. Inventories should be carefully planned. Excessive inventories tie up funds and create storage problems. Insufficient inventories can lead to lost sales or last-minute, high-cost production efforts. At Hampton Freeze, management believes that an ending inventory equal to 20% of the next quarter's sales strikes the appropriate balance.

Schedule 2 contains the production budget for Hampton Freeze. The first row in the production budget contains the budgeted sales, which have been taken directly from the sales budget (Schedule 1). The total needs for the first quarter are determined by adding together the budgeted sales of 10,000 cases for the quarter and the desired ending inventory of 6,000 cases. As discussed above, the ending inventory is intended to provide some cushion in the event that problems develop in production or sales increase unexpectedly. Because the budgeted sales for the second quarter are 30,000 cases and management would like the ending inventory in each quarter to equal 20% of the following quarter's sales, the desired ending inventory for the first quarter is 6,000 cases (20% of 30,000 cases). Consequently, the total needs for the first quarter are 16,000 cases. However, because the company already has 2,000 cases in beginning inventory, only 14,000 cases need to be produced in the first quarter.

### SCHEDULE 2

**Hampton Freeze, Inc.**
**Production Budget**
**For the Year Ended December 31, 2013**
**(in cases)**

| | Quarter 1 | Quarter 2 | Quarter 3 | Quarter 4 | Year |
|---|---|---|---|---|---|
| Budgeted sales (Schedule 1) | 10,000 | 30,000 | 40,000 | 20,000 | 100,000 |
| Add desired ending inventory of finished goods* | 6,000 | 8,000 | 4,000 | 3,000 | 3,000 |
| Total needs | 16,000 | 38,000 | 44,000 | 23,000 | 103,000 |
| Less beginning inventory of finished goods† | 2,000 | 6,000 | 8,000 | 4,000 | 2,000 |
| Required production | 14,000 | 32,000 | 36,000 | 19,000 | 101,000 |

(20% arrows link each quarter's ending inventory to the next quarter's sales; Assumed: 3,000)

Schedule 1 | Schedule 2 | Schedule 3 | Schedule 4 | Schedule 5 | Schedule 6

*Twenty percent of the next quarter's sales. The ending inventory of 3,000 cases is assumed.
†The beginning inventory in each quarter is the same as the prior quarter's ending inventory.

Pay particular attention to the Year column to the right of the production budget in Schedule 2. In some cases (e.g., budgeted sales, total needs, and required production), the amount listed for the year is the sum of the quarterly amounts for the item. In other cases (e.g., desired ending inventory of finished goods and beginning inventory of finished goods), the amount listed for the year is not simply the sum of the quarterly amounts. From the standpoint of the entire year, the beginning finished goods inventory is the same as the beginning finished goods inventory for the first quarter—it is *not* the sum of the beginning finished goods inventories for all quarters. Similarly, from the standpoint of the entire year, the ending finished goods inventory is the same as the ending finished goods inventory for the fourth quarter—it is *not* the sum of the ending finished goods inventories for all four quarters. It is important to pay attention to such distinctions in all of the schedules that follow.

## Inventory Purchases—Merchandising Company

Hampton Freeze prepares a production budget because it is a *manufacturing* company. If it were a *merchandising* company, instead it would prepare a **merchandise purchases budget** showing the amount of goods to be purchased from suppliers during the period.

The format of the merchandise purchases budget is shown below:

| | |
|---|---|
| Budgeted cost of goods sold | XXXXX |
| Add desired ending merchandise inventory | XXXXX |
| Total needs | XXXXX |
| Less beginning merchandise inventory | XXXXX |
| Required purchases | XXXXX |

A merchandising company would prepare a merchandise purchases budget such as the one above for each item carried in stock. The merchandise purchases budget can be expressed in dollars (as shown above) or in units. The top line of a merchandise purchases budget based on units would say Budgeted unit sales instead of Budgeted cost of goods sold.

**CONCEPT CHECK**

3. If a company has a beginning merchandise inventory of $50,000, a desired ending merchandise inventory of $30,000, and a budgeted cost of goods sold of $300,000, what is the amount of required inventory purchases?
   a. $320,000
   b. $280,000
   c. $380,000
   d. $300,000
4. Budgeted unit sales for March, April, and May are 75,000, 80,000, and 90,000 units. Management desires to maintain an ending inventory equal to 30% of the next month's unit sales. How many units should be produced in April?
   a. 80,000 units
   b. 83,000 units
   c. 77,000 units
   d. 85,000 units

**LEARNING OBJECTIVE 4**

Prepare a direct materials budget, including a schedule of expected cash disbursements for purchases of materials.

## The Direct Materials Budget

*A direct materials budget* is prepared after the production requirements have been computed. The **direct materials budget** details the raw materials that must be purchased to fulfill the production budget and to provide for adequate inventories. The required purchases of raw materials are computed as follows:

| | |
|---|---|
| Required production in units of finished goods | XXXXX |
| Times raw materials required per unit of finished goods | XXXXX |
| Raw materials needed to meet the production schedule | XXXXX |
| Add desired ending raw materials inventory | XXXXX |
| Total raw material needs | XXXXX |
| Less beginning raw materials inventory | XXXXX |
| Raw materials to be purchased | XXXXX |
| Times unit cost of raw materials | XXXXX |
| Cost of raw materials to be purchased | XXXXX |

Schedule 3 contains the direct materials budget for Hampton Freeze. The only raw material included in that budget is high fructose sugar, which is the major ingredient in popsicles other than water. The remaining raw materials are relatively insignificant and are included in variable manufacturing overhead. As with finished goods, management would like to maintain some inventories of raw materials to act as a cushion. In this case, management would like to maintain ending inventories of sugar equal to 10% of the following quarter's production needs.

The first line in the direct materials budget contains the required production for each quarter, which is taken directly from the production budget (Schedule 2). Looking at the first quarter, because the production schedule calls for production of 14,000 cases of popsicles and each case requires 15 pounds of sugar, the total production needs are 210,000 pounds of sugar (14,000 cases × 15 pounds per case). In addition, management wants to have ending inventories of 48,000 pounds of sugar, which is 10% of the following quarter's needs of 480,000 pounds. Consequently, the total needs are 258,000 pounds (210,000 pounds for the current quarter's production plus 48,000 pounds for the desired ending inventory). However, because the company already has 21,000 pounds in beginning inventory, only 237,000 pounds of sugar (258,000 pounds − 21,000 pounds) will need to be purchased. Finally, the cost of the raw materials purchases is determined by multiplying the amount of raw material to be purchased by its unit cost. In this case, because 237,000 pounds of sugar need to be purchased during the first quarter and sugar costs $0.20 per pound, the total cost will be $47,400 (237,000 pounds × $0.20 per pound).

As with the production budget, the amounts listed under the Year column are not always the sum of the quarterly amounts. The desired ending raw materials inventory for the year is the same as the desired ending raw materials inventory for the fourth quarter. Likewise, the beginning raw materials inventory for the year is the same as the beginning raw materials inventory for the first quarter.

The direct materials budget (or the merchandise purchases budget for a merchandising company) is usually accompanied by a schedule of expected cash disbursements for raw materials (or merchandise purchases). This schedule is needed to prepare the overall cash budget. Disbursements for raw materials (or merchandise purchases) consist of payments for purchases on account in prior periods plus any payments for purchases in the current budget period. Schedule 3 contains such a schedule of cash disbursements for Hampton Freeze.

Ordinarily, companies do not immediately pay their suppliers. At Hampton Freeze, the policy is to pay for 50% of purchases in the quarter in which the purchase is made and 50% in the following quarter, so while the company intends to purchase $47,400 worth of sugar in the first quarter, the company will only pay for half, $23,700, in the first quarter and the other half will be paid in the second quarter. The company will also pay $25,800 in the first quarter for sugar that was purchased on account in the previous quarter, but not yet paid for. This is the beginning balance in the accounts payable. Therefore, the total cash disbursements for sugar in the first quarter are $49,500—the $25,800 payment for sugar acquired in the previous quarter plus the $23,700 payment for sugar acquired during the first quarter.

## SCHEDULE 3

| | A | B | C | D | E | F |
|---|---|---|---|---|---|---|
| 3 | **Hampton Freeze, Inc.** | | | | | |
| 4 | **Direct Materials Budget** | | | | | |
| 5 | **For the Year Ended December 31, 2013** | | | | | |
| 6 | | | | | | Assumed |
| 7 | | *Quarter* | | | | |
| 8 | | *1* | *2* | *3* | *4* | *Year* |
| 9 | Required production in cases (Schedule 2) | 14,000 | 32,000 | 36,000 | 19,000 | 101,000 |
| 10 | Raw materials needed per case (pounds) | 15 | 15 | 15 | 15 | 15 |
| 11 | Raw materials needed to meet production | 210,000 | 480,000 | 540,000 | 285,000 | 1,515,000 |
| 12 | Add desired ending raw materials inventory[1] | 48,000 | 10% 54,000 | 10% 28,500 | 10% 22,500 | 22,500 |
| 13 | Total raw material needs | 258,000 | 534,000 | 568,500 | 307,500 | 1,537,500 |
| 14 | Less beginning raw materials inventory | 21,000 | 48,000 | 54,000 | 28,500 | 21,000 |
| 15 | Raw materials to be purchased | 237,000 | 486,000 | 514,500 | 279,000 | 1,516,500 |
| 16 | Cost of raw materials per pound | $ 0.20 | $ 0.20 | $ 0.20 | $ 0.20 | $ 0.20 |
| 17 | Cost of raw materials to be purchased | $ 47,400 | $ 97,200 | $ 102,900 | $ 55,800 | $ 303,300 |
| 18 | | | | | | |
| 19 | Percentage of purchases paid for in the period of the purchase | | | 50% | | |
| 20 | Percentage of purchases paid for in the period after purchase | | | 50% | | |
| 21 | | 50% | 50% | | | |
| 22 | **Schedule of Expected Cash Disbursements for Materials** | | | | | |
| 23 | | | | | | |
| 24 | Accounts payable, beginning balance[2] | $ 25,800 | | | | $ 25,800 |
| 25 | First-quarter purchases[3] | 23,700 | $ 23,700 | | | 47,400 |
| 26 | Second-quarter purchases[4] | | 48,600 | $ 48,600 | | 97,200 |
| 27 | Third-quarter purchases[5] | | | 51,450 | $ 51,450 | 102,900 |
| 28 | Fourth-quarter purchases[6] | - | - | - | 27,900 | 27,900 |
| 29 | Total cash disbursements for materials | $ 49,500 | $ 72,300 | $ 100,050 | $ 79,350 | $ 301,200 |
| 30 | | | | | | |
| 31 | | | | | | |

Schedule 1 | Schedule 2 | **Schedule 3** | Schedule 4 | Schedule 5

[1]Ten percent of the next quarter's production needs. For example, the second-quarter production needs are 480,000 pounds. Therefore, the desired ending inventory for the first quarter would be 10% × 480,000 pounds = 48,000 pounds. The ending inventory of 22,500 pounds for the fourth quarter is assumed.

[2]Cash payments for last year's fourth-quarter material purchases. See the beginning-of-year balance sheet on page 306.

[3]$47,400 × 50%; $47,400 × 50%.

[4]$97,200 × 50%; $97,200 × 50%.

[5]$102,900 × 50%; $102,900 × 50%.

[6]$55,800 × 50%. Unpaid fourth-quarter purchases ($27,900) appear as accounts payable on the company's end-of-year budgeted balance sheet (see Schedule 10 on page 307).

### HELPFUL HINT

The direct materials budget includes three different units of measure. It begins by defining the number of *units of finished goods* that need to be produced each period. It then defines the *quantity of raw material inputs* (measured in terms such as pounds or ounces) that need to be purchased to support production. It concludes by translating the quantity of raw materials to be purchased into the *cost of raw materials* to be purchased.

## The Direct Labor Budget

LEARNING OBJECTIVE 5

Prepare a direct labor budget.

The **direct labor budget** shows the direct labor-hours required to satisfy the production budget. By knowing in advance how much labor time will be needed throughout the budget year, the company can develop plans to adjust the labor force as the situation requires. Companies that neglect to budget run the risk of facing labor shortages or having to hire and lay off workers at awkward times. Erratic labor policies lead to insecurity, low morale, and inefficiency.

The direct labor budget for Hampton Freeze is shown in Schedule 4. The first line in the direct labor budget consists of the required production for each quarter, which is taken directly from the production budget (Schedule 2). The direct labor requirement for each quarter is computed by multiplying the number of units to be produced in that quarter by the number of direct labor-hours required to make a unit. For example, 14,000 cases are to be produced in the first quarter and each case requires 0.40 direct labor-hours, so a total of 5,600 direct labor-hours (14,000 cases × 0.40 direct labor-hours per case) will be required in the first quarter. The direct labor requirements can then be translated into budgeted direct labor costs. How this is done will depend on the company's labor policy. In Schedule 4, Hampton Freeze has assumed that the direct labor force will be adjusted as the work requirements change from quarter to quarter. In that case, the direct labor cost is computed by simply multiplying the direct labor-hour requirements by the direct labor rate per hour. For example, the direct labor cost in the first quarter is $84,000 (5,600 direct labor-hours × $15 per direct labor-hour).

However, many companies have employment policies or contracts that prevent them from laying off and rehiring workers as needed. Suppose, for example, that Hampton Freeze has 25 workers who are classified as direct labor, but each of them is guaranteed at least 480 hours of pay each quarter at a rate of $15 per hour. In that case, the minimum direct labor cost for a quarter would be as follows:

25 workers × 480 hours per worker × $15 per hour = $180,000

Note that in this case the direct labor costs for the first and fourth quarters would have to be increased to $180,000.

### SCHEDULE 4

**Hampton Freeze, Inc.**
**Direct Labor Budget**
**For the Year Ended December 31, 2013**

| | Quarter 1 | Quarter 2 | Quarter 3 | Quarter 4 | Year |
|---|---|---|---|---|---|
| Required production in cases (Schedule 2) | 14,000 | 32,000 | 36,000 | 19,000 | 101,000 |
| Direct labor-hours per case | 0.40 | 0.40 | 0.40 | 0.40 | 0.40 |
| Total direct labor-hours needed | 5,600 | 12,800 | 14,400 | 7,600 | 40,400 |
| Direct labor cost per hour | $ 15.00 | $ 15.00 | $ 15.00 | $ 15.00 | $ 15.00 |
| Total direct labor cost* | $ 84,000 | $ 192,000 | $ 216,000 | $ 114,000 | $ 606,000 |

Schedule 1 | Schedule 2 | Schedule 3 | Schedule 4 | Schedule 5

*This schedule assumes that the direct labor workforce will be fully adjusted to the total direct labor-hours needed each quarter.

IN BUSINESS

## Managing Labor Costs in a Difficult Economy

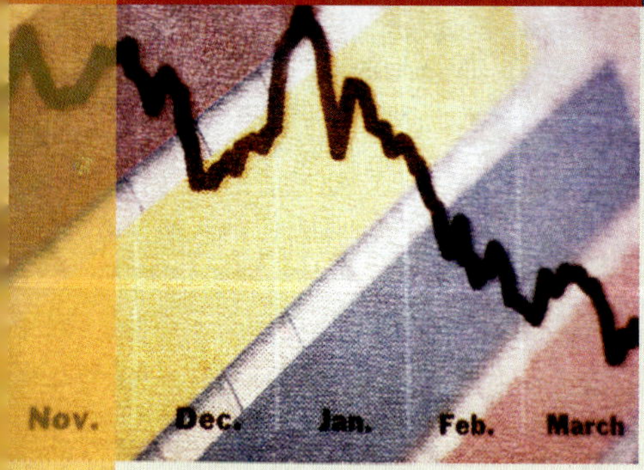


When the economy sours, many companies choose to lay off employees. While this tactic lowers costs in the short run, it also lowers the morale and productivity of retained employees, sacrifices the institutional knowledge possessed by terminated employees, and increases future recruiting and training costs. **Hypertherm Inc**. has not fired a permanent employee since its founding in 1968, instead responding to economic hardship by eliminating overtime, cutting temporary staff, delaying capital investments, shifting cross-trained employees to new job responsibilities, and implementing a four-day work week. Hypertherm's employees regularly share their process improvement ideas with the company because they know if they eliminate non–value-added portions of their job responsibilities the company will redeploy them rather than eliminate non–value-added labor costs by firing them.

Source: Cari Tuna, "Some Firms Cut Costs Without Resorting to Layoffs," *The Wall Street Journal,* December 15, 2008, p. B4.

# The Manufacturing Overhead Budget

**LEARNING OBJECTIVE 6**

Prepare a manufacturing overhead budget.

The **manufacturing overhead budget** lists all costs of production other than direct materials and direct labor. Schedule 5 shows the manufacturing overhead budget for Hampton Freeze. At Hampton Freeze, manufacturing overhead is separated into variable and fixed components. The variable component is $4 per direct labor-hour and the fixed component is $60,600 per quarter. Because the variable component of manufacturing overhead depends on direct labor, the first line in the manufacturing overhead budget consists of the budgeted direct labor-hours from the direct labor budget (Schedule 4). The budgeted direct labor-hours in each quarter are multiplied by the variable rate to determine the variable component of manufacturing overhead. For example, the variable manufacturing overhead for the first quarter is $22,400 (5,600 direct labor-hours × $4.00 per direct labor-hour). This is added to the fixed manufacturing overhead for the quarter to determine the total manufacturing overhead for the quarter of $83,000 ($22,400 + $60,600).

A few words about fixed costs and the budgeting process are in order. In most cases, fixed costs are the costs of supplying capacity to make products, process purchase orders, handle customer calls, and so on. The amount of capacity that will be required depends on the expected level of activity for the period. If the expected level of activity is greater than the company's current capacity, then fixed costs may have to be increased. Or, if the expected level is appreciably below the company's current capacity, then it may be desirable to decrease fixed costs if possible. However, once the level of the fixed costs has been determined in the budget, the costs really are fixed. The time to adjust fixed costs is during the budgeting process. An activity-based costing system can help to determine the appropriate level of fixed costs at budget time by answering questions like, "How many clerks will we need to process the anticipated number of purchase orders next year?" For simplicity, in all of the budgeting examples in this book assume that the appropriate levels of fixed costs have already been determined.

The last line of Schedule 5 for Hampton Freeze shows the budgeted cash disbursements for manufacturing overhead. Because some of the overhead costs are not cash outflows, the total budgeted manufacturing overhead costs must be adjusted to determine the cash disbursements for manufacturing overhead. At Hampton Freeze, the only significant noncash manufacturing overhead cost is depreciation, which is $15,000 per quarter. These noncash depreciation charges are deducted from the total budgeted manufacturing overhead to determine the expected cash disbursements. Hampton Freeze pays all overhead costs involving cash disbursements in the quarter incurred. Note that the company's predetermined overhead rate for the year is $10 per direct labor-hour, which is determined by dividing the total budgeted manufacturing overhead for the year by the total budgeted direct labor-hours for the year.

## SCHEDULE 5

| | | | | | |
|---|---|---|---|---|---|
| **Hampton Freeze, Inc.** | | | | | |
| **Manufacturing Overhead Budget** | | | | | |
| **For the Year Ended December 31, 2013** | | | | | |
| | *Quarter* | | | | |
| | *1* | *2* | *3* | *4* | *Year* |
| Budgeted direct labor-hours (Schedule 4) | 5,600 | 12,800 | 14,400 | 7,600 | 40,400 |
| Variable manufacturing overhead rate | $ 4.00 | $ 4.00 | $ 4.00 | $ 4.00 | $ 4.00 |
| Variable manufacturing overhead | $ 22,400 | $ 51,200 | $ 57,600 | $ 30,400 | $ 161,600 |
| Fixed manufacturing overhead | 60,600 | 60,600 | 60,600 | 60,600 | 242,400 |
| Total manufacturing overhead | 83,000 | 111,800 | 118,200 | 91,000 | 404,000 |
| Less depreciation | 15,000 | 15,000 | 15,000 | 15,000 | 60,000 |
| Cash disbursements for manufacturing overhead | $ 68,000 | $ 96,800 | $ 103,200 | $ 76,000 | $ 344,000 |
| | | | | | |
| Total manufacturing overhead (a) | | | | | $ 404,000 |
| Budgeted direct labor-hours (b) | | | | | 40,400 |
| Predetermined overhead rate for the year (a)÷(b) | | | | | $ 10.00 |

Schedule 2 | Schedule 3 | Schedule 4 | **Schedule 5** | Schedule 6

## The Ending Finished Goods Inventory Budget

After completing Schedules 1–5, Larry Giano had all of the data he needed to compute unit product costs. This computation was needed for two reasons: first, to determine cost of goods sold on the budgeted income statement; and second, to value ending inventories. The cost of unsold units is computed on the **ending finished goods inventory budget.**

## SCHEDULE 6

| | | | | | |
|---|---|---|---|---|---|
| **Hampton Freeze, Inc.** | | | | | |
| **Ending Finished Goods Inventory Budget** | | | | | |
| **(absorption costing basis)** | | | | | |
| **For the Year Ended December 31, 2013** | | | | | |
| *Item* | *Quantity* | | *Cost* | | *Total* |
| Production cost per case: | | | | | |
| Direct materials | 15.00 | pounds | $ 0.20 | per pound | $ 3.00 |
| Direct labor | 0.40 | hours | $ 15.00 | per hour | 6.00 |
| Manufacturing overhead | 0.40 | hours | $ 10.00 | per hour | 4.00 |
| Unit product cost | | | | | $ 13.00 |
| | | | | | |
| Budgeted finished goods inventory: | | | | | |
| Ending finished goods inventory in cases (Schedule 2) | | | | | 3,000 |
| Unit product cost (see above) | | | | | $ 13.00 |
| Ending finished goods inventory in dollars | | | | | $ 39,000 |

Schedule 3 | Schedule 4 | Schedule 5 | **Schedule 6** | Sche

Larry Giano considered using variable costing to prepare Hampton Freeze's budget statements, but he decided to use absorption costing instead because the bank would very likely require absorption costing. He also knew that it would be easy to convert the absorption costing financial statements to a variable costing basis later. At this point, the primary concern was to determine what financing, if any, would be required in 2013 and then to arrange for that financing from the bank.

The unit product cost computations are shown in Schedule 6. For Hampton Freeze, the absorption costing unit product cost is $13 per case of popsicles—consisting of $3 of direct materials, $6 of direct labor, and $4 of manufacturing overhead. The manufacturing overhead is applied to units of product at the rate of $10 per direct labor-hour. The budgeted carrying cost of the ending inventory is $39,000.

## The Selling and Administrative Expense Budget

**LEARNING OBJECTIVE 7**

Prepare a selling and administrative expense budget.

The **selling and administrative expense budget** lists the budgeted expenses for areas other than manufacturing. In large organizations, this budget would be a compilation of many smaller, individual budgets submitted by department heads and other persons responsible for selling and administrative expenses. For example, the marketing manager would submit a budget detailing the advertising expenses for each budget period.

Schedule 7 contains the selling and administrative expense budget for Hampton Freeze. Like the manufacturing overhead budget, the selling and administrative expense budget is divided into variable and fixed cost components. In the case of Hampton Freeze, the variable selling and administrative expense is $1.80 per case. Consequently, budgeted sales in cases for each quarter are entered at the top of the schedule. These data are taken from the sales budget (Schedule 1). The budgeted variable selling and administrative expenses are determined by multiplying the budgeted cases sold by the variable selling and administrative expense per case. For example, the budgeted variable selling and administrative expense for the first quarter is $18,000 (10,000 cases × $1.80 per case). The fixed selling and administrative expenses (all given data) are then added to the variable selling and administrative expenses to arrive at the total budgeted selling and administrative expenses. Finally, to determine the cash disbursements for selling and administrative items, the total budgeted selling and administrative expense is adjusted by subtracting any noncash selling and administrative expenses (in this case, just depreciation).[1]

**DECISION POINT**

### Budget Analyst

You have been hired as a budget analyst by a regional chain of Italian restaurants with attached bars. Management has had difficulty in the past predicting some of its costs; the assumption has always been that all operating costs are variable with respect to gross restaurant sales. What would you suggest doing to improve the accuracy of the budget forecasts?

[1]Other adjustments might need to be made for differences between cash flows on the one hand and revenues and expenses on the other hand. For example, if property taxes are paid twice a year in installments of $8,000 each, the expense for property tax would have to be "backed out" of the total budgeted selling and administrative expenses and the cash installment payments added to the appropriate quarters to determine the cash disbursements. Similar adjustments might also need to be made in the manufacturing overhead budget. We generally ignore these complications in this chapter.

**SCHEDULE 7**

| | A | B | C | D | E | F |
|---|---|---|---|---|---|---|
| 1 | **Hampton Freeze, Inc.** | | | | | |
| 2 | **Selling and Administrative Expense Budget** | | | | | |
| 3 | **For the Year Ended December 31, 2013** | | | | | |
| 4 | | | | | | |
| 5 | | *Quarter* | | | | |
| 6 | | *1* | *2* | *3* | *4* | *Year* |
| 7 | Budgeted sales in cases (Schedule 1) | 10,000 | 30,000 | 40,000 | 20,000 | 100,000 |
| 8 | Variable selling and administrative expense per case | $ 1.80 | $ 1.80 | $ 1.80 | $ 1.80 | $ 1.80 |
| 9 | Variable selling and administrative expense | $ 18,000 | $ 54,000 | $ 72,000 | $ 36,000 | $180,000 |
| 10 | Fixed selling and administrative expenses: | | | | | |
| 11 | Advertising | 20,000 | 20,000 | 20,000 | 20,000 | 80,000 |
| 12 | Executive salaries | 55,000 | 55,000 | 55,000 | 55,000 | 220,000 |
| 13 | Insurance | 10,000 | 10,000 | 10,000 | 10,000 | 40,000 |
| 14 | Property taxes | 4,000 | 4,000 | 4,000 | 4,000 | 16,000 |
| 15 | Depreciation | 10,000 | 10,000 | 10,000 | 10,000 | 40,000 |
| 16 | Total fixed selling and administrative expenses | 99,000 | 99,000 | 99,000 | 99,000 | 396,000 |
| 17 | Total selling and administrative expenses | 117,000 | 153,000 | 171,000 | 135,000 | 576,000 |
| 18 | Less depreciation | 10,000 | 10,000 | 10,000 | 10,000 | 40,000 |
| 19 | Cash disbursements for selling and administrative expenses | $107,000 | $143,000 | $161,000 | $125,000 | $536,000 |
| 20 | | | | | | |

Schedule 6 | **Schedule 7** | Schedule 8 | Schedule 9 | Schedule 10

## The Cash Budget

**LEARNING OBJECTIVE 8**

Prepare a cash budget.

As illustrated in Exhibit 7–2, the cash budget combines much of the data developed in the preceding steps. It is a good idea to review Exhibit 7–2 to get the big picture firmly in your mind before moving on.

The cash budget is composed of four major sections:

1. The receipts section.
2. The disbursements section.
3. The cash excess or deficiency section.
4. The financing section.

The receipts section lists all of the cash inflows, except from financing, expected during the budget period. Generally, the major source of receipts is from sales.

### Mismatched Cash Flows—Climbing the Hills and Valleys

**IN BUSINESS**

The Washington Trails Association (WTA) is a private, nonprofit organization primarily concerned with protecting and maintaining hiking trails in the state of Washington. Some 2,000 WTA volunteer workers donate more than 80,000 hours per year maintaining trails in rugged landscapes on federal, state, and private lands. The organization is supported by membership dues, voluntary contributions, grants, and some contract work for government.

The organization's income and expenses are erratic—although somewhat predictable—over the course of the year as shown in the chart on the following page. Expenses tend to be highest in the spring and summer when most of the trail maintenance work is done. However, income spikes in December well after the expenses have been incurred. With cash outflows running ahead of cash

## IN BUSINESS

(continued)

inflows for much of the year, it is very important for the WTA to carefully plan its cash budget and to maintain adequate cash reserves to be able to pay its bills.

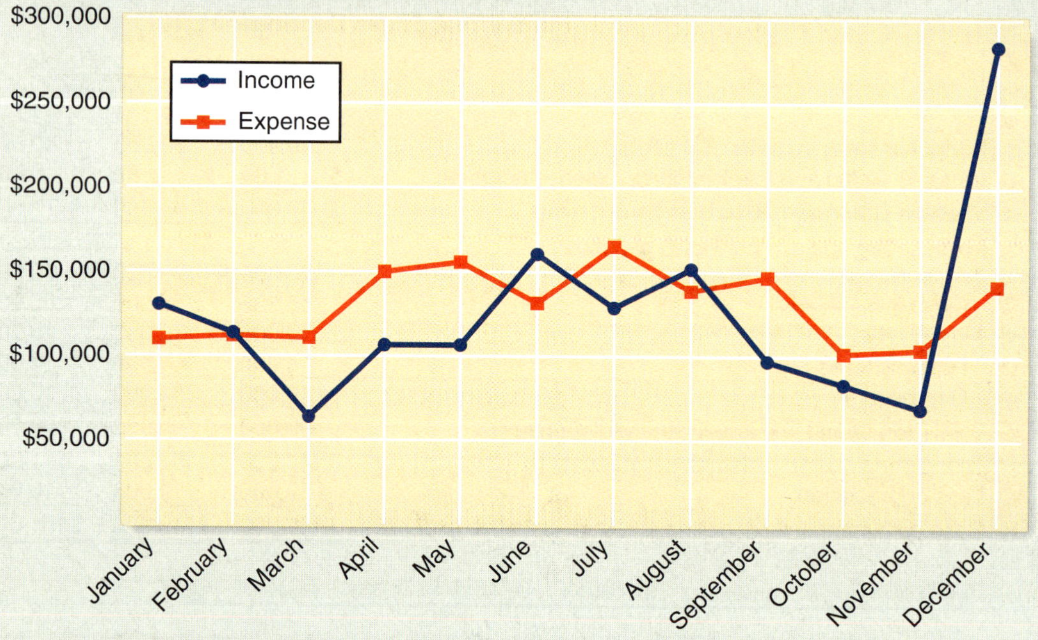


Note: Total income and total expense are approximately equal over the course of the year.

Sources: Conversation with Elizabeth Lunney, President of the Washington Trails Association; WTA documents; and the WTA website www.wta.org.

The disbursements section summarizes all cash payments that are planned for the budget period. These payments include raw materials purchases, direct labor payments, manufacturing overhead costs, and so on, as contained in their respective budgets. In addition, other cash disbursements such as equipment purchases and dividends are listed.

The cash excess or deficiency section is computed as follows:

| | |
|---|---|
| Cash balance, beginning | XXXX |
| Add receipts | XXXX |
| Total cash available | XXXX |
| Less disbursements | XXXX |
| Excess (deficiency) of cash available over disbursements | XXXX |

If a cash deficiency exists during any budget period, the company will need to borrow funds. If there is a cash excess during any budget period, funds borrowed in previous periods can be repaid or the excess funds can be invested.

The financing section details the borrowings and repayments projected to take place during the budget period. It also lists interest payments that will be due on money borrowed.[2]

[2]The format for the statement of cash flows, which is discussed in a later chapter, may also be used for the cash budget.

## SCHEDULE 8

| | | | | | | |
|---|---|---|---|---|---|---|
| **Hampton Freeze, Inc.** | | | | | | |
| **Cash Budget** | | | | | | |
| **For the Year Ended December 31, 2013** | | | | | | |
| | | *Quarter* | | | | |
| | *Schedule* | 1 | 2 | 3 | 4 | *Year* |
| Cash balance, beginning | | $ 42,500 | $ 36,000 | $ 33,900 | $ 165,650 | $ 42,500 |
| Add receipts: | | | | | | |
| Collections from customers | 1 | 230,000 | 480,000 | 740,000 | 520,000 | 1,970,000 |
| Total cash available | | 272,500 | 516,000 | 773,900 | 685,650 | 2,012,500 |
| Less disbursements: | | | | | | |
| Direct materials | 3 | 49,500 | 72,300 | 100,050 | 79,350 | 301,200 |
| Direct labor | 4 | 84,000 | 192,000 | 216,000 | 114,000 | 606,000 |
| Manufacturing overhead | 5 | 68,000 | 96,800 | 103,200 | 76,000 | 344,000 |
| Selling and administrative | 7 | 107,000 | 143,000 | 161,000 | 125,000 | 536,000 |
| Equipment purchases | | 50,000 | 40,000 | 20,000 | 20,000 | 130,000 |
| Dividends | | 8,000 | 8,000 | 8,000 | 8,000 | 32,000 |
| Total disbursements | | 366,500 | 552,100 | 608,250 | 422,350 | 1,949,200 |
| Excess (deficiency) of cash available over disbursements | | (94,000) | (36,100) | 165,650 | 263,300 | 63,300 |
| Financing: | | | | | | |
| Borrowings (at the beginnings of quarters) | | 130,000 | 70,000 | - | - | 200,000 |
| Repayments (at end of the year) | | - | - | - | (200,000) | (200,000) |
| Interest | | - | - | - | (21,900) | (21,900) |
| Total financing | | 130,000 | 70,000 | - | (221,900) | (21,900) |
| Cash balance, ending | | $ 36,000 | $ 33,900 | $ 165,650 | $ 41,400 | $ 41,400 |

Schedule 6 | Schedule 7 | **Schedule 8** | Schedule 9 | Schedule 10

The cash balances at both the beginning and end of the year may be adequate even though a serious cash deficit occurs at some point during the year. Consequently, the cash budget should be broken down into time periods that are short enough to capture major fluctuations in cash balances. While a monthly cash budget is most common, some organizations budget cash on a weekly or even daily basis. Larry Giano has prepared a quarterly cash budget for Hampton Freeze that can be further refined as necessary. This budget appears in Schedule 8. The cash budget builds on the earlier schedules and on additional data that are provided below:

- The beginning cash balance is $42,500 (see the beginning-of-year balance sheet on page 306).
- Management plans to spend $130,000 during the year on equipment purchases: $50,000 in the first quarter; $40,000 in the second quarter; $20,000 in the third quarter; and $20,000 in the fourth quarter.
- The board of directors has approved cash dividends of $8,000 per quarter.
- Management would like to have a cash balance of at least $30,000 at the beginning of each quarter for contingencies.
- Hampton Freeze has an agreement with a local bank that allows the company to borrow in increments of $10,000 at the beginning of each quarter, up to a total loan balance of $250,000. The interest rate on these loans is 1% per month, and for simplicity, we will assume that interest is not compounded. The company would, as far as it is able, repay the loan plus accumulated interest at the end of the year.

The cash budget is prepared one quarter at a time, starting with the first quarter. Larry began the cash budget by entering the beginning balance of cash for the first quarter of $42,500—a number that is given on the previous page. Receipts—in this case, just the $230,000 in cash collections from customers—are added to the beginning balance to arrive at the total cash available of $272,500. Because the total disbursements are $366,500 and the total cash available is only $272,500, there is a shortfall of $94,000. Because management would like to have a beginning cash balance of at least $30,000 for the second quarter, the company will need to borrow at least $124,000.

| Required Borrowings at the Beginning of the First Quarter | |
|---|---|
| Desired ending cash balance | $ 30,000 |
| Plus deficiency of cash available over disbursements | 94,000 |
| Minimum required borrowings | $124,000 |

Recall that the bank requires that loans be made in increments of $10,000. Because Hampton Freeze needs to borrow at least $124,000, it will have to borrow $130,000.

The second quarter of the cash budget is handled similarly. Note that the ending cash balance for the first quarter is brought forward as the beginning cash balance for the second quarter. Also note that additional borrowing is required in the second quarter because of the continued cash shortfall.

| Required Borrowings at the Beginning of the Second Quarter | |
|---|---|
| Desired ending cash balance | $30,000 |
| Plus deficiency of cash available over disbursements | 36,100 |
| Minimum required borrowings | $66,100 |

Again, recall that the bank requires that loans be made in increments of $10,000. Because Hampton Freeze needs to borrow at least $66,100 at the beginning of the second quarter, the company will have to borrow $70,000 from the bank.

In the third quarter, the cash flow situation improves dramatically and the excess of cash available over disbursements is $165,650. Therefore, the company will end the quarter with ample cash and no further borrowing is necessary.

At the end of the fourth quarter, the loan and accumulated interest must be repaid. The accumulated interest can be computed as follows:

| | |
|---|---|
| Interest on $130,000 borrowed at the beginning of the first quarter: | |
| $130,000 × 0.01 per month × 12 months* | $15,600 |
| Interest on $70,000 borrowed at the beginning of the second quarter: | |
| $70,000 × 0.01 per month × 9 months* | 6,300 |
| Total interest accrued to the end of the fourth quarter | $21,900 |

*Simple, rather than compounded, interest is assumed for simplicity.

Note that the loan repayment of $200,000 ($130,000 + $70,000) appears in the financing section for the fourth quarter along with the interest payment of $21,900 computed above.

As with the production and raw materials budgets, the amounts under the Year column in the cash budget are not always the sum of the amounts for the four quarters. In particular, the beginning cash balance for the year is the same as the beginning cash balance for the first quarter and the ending cash balance for the year is the same as the ending cash balance for the fourth quarter. Also note the beginning cash balance in any quarter is the same as the ending cash balance for the previous quarter.

HELPFUL HINT

Students often incorrectly calculate the interest payments in the cash budget. To reduce your chances of making mistakes, remember that we always assume that money is borrowed on the first day of the period and that principal and interest payments are made on the last day of the period. This explains why Hampton Freeze will pay 12 months of interest on the $130,000 it plans to borrow on the first day of Quarter 1 (January 1, 2013) and repay on the last day of Quarter 4 (December 31, 2013). It also explains why Hampton Freeze will pay nine months of interest on the $70,000 it plans to borrow on the first day of Quarter 2 (April 1, 2013) and repay on the last day of Quarter 4 (December 31, 2013).

## New Inspections Pinch Cash Flows

IN BUSINESS

**Herald Metal and Plastic Works** is a Chinese toy manufacturer that produces Star Wars action figures and G.I. Joes for **Hasbro Inc**. in the United States. The company used to ship its toys to America immediately after they rolled off the production line. However, this changed when American consumers discovered that some Chinese companies were using poisonous lead-based paint in their manufacturing processes. The Chinese government now requires toy manufacturers to store finished goods in warehouses for anywhere from three weeks to two months until its inspectors certify them for export.

Herald Metal and Plastic Works borrows money from lenders to buy raw materials and pay laborers to make its toys. The company is struggling to repay its loans because the government's inspection process delays cash receipts from customers.

Source: Chi-Chu Tschang, "Bottlenecks in Toyland," *BusinessWeek*, October 15, 2007, p. 52.

## The Budgeted Income Statement

**LEARNING OBJECTIVE 9**

Prepare a budgeted income statement.

A budgeted income statement can be prepared from the data developed in Schedules 1–8. *The budgeted income statement is one of the key schedules in the budget process.* It shows the company's planned profit and serves as a benchmark against which subsequent company performance can be measured.

Schedule 9 contains the budgeted income statement for Hampton Freeze.

**SCHEDULE 9**

| | A | B | C |
|---|---|---|---|
| 1 | **Hampton Freeze, Inc.** | | |
| 2 | **Budgeted Income Statement** | | |
| 3 | **For the Year Ended December 31, 2013** | | |
| 4 | | | |
| 5 | | *Schedules* | |
| 6 | Sales | 1 | $ 2,000,000 |
| 7 | Cost of goods sold* | 1,6 | 1,300,000 |
| 8 | Gross margin | | 700,000 |
| 9 | Selling and administrative expenses | 7 | 576,000 |
| 10 | Net operating Income | | 124,000 |
| 11 | Interest expense | 8 | 21,900 |
| 12 | Net Income | | $ 102,100 |
| 13 | | | |

Schedule 6 / Schedule 7 / Schedule 8

*100,000 cases sold × $13 per case = $1,300,000.

## The Budgeted Balance Sheet

LEARNING OBJECTIVE 10

Prepare a budgeted balance sheet.

The budgeted balance sheet is developed using data from the balance sheet from the beginning of the budget period and data contained in the various schedules. Hampton Freeze's budgeted balance sheet is presented in Schedule 10. Some of the data on the budgeted balance sheet have been taken from the company's previous end-of-year balance sheet for 2012 which appears below:

**Hampton Freeze, Inc.**
**Balance Sheet**
**December 31, 2012**

| | | |
|---|---|---|
| **Assets** | | |
| Current assets: | | |
| Cash | $ 42,500 | |
| Accounts receivable | 90,000 | |
| Raw materials inventory (21,000 pounds) | 4,200 | |
| Finished goods inventory (2,000 cases) | 26,000 | |
| Total current assets | | $162,700 |
| Plant and equipment: | | |
| Land | 80,000 | |
| Buildings and equipment | 700,000 | |
| Accumulated depreciation | (292,000) | |
| Plant and equipment, net | | 488,000 |
| Total assets | | $650,700 |
| **Liabilities and Stockholders' Equity** | | |
| Current liabilities: | | |
| Accounts payable (raw materials) | | $ 25,800 |
| Stockholders' equity: | | |
| Common stock, no par | $175,000 | |
| Retained earnings | 449,900 | |
| Total stockholders' equity | | 624,900 |
| Total liabilities and stockholders' equity | | $650,700 |

After completing the master budget, Larry Giano took the documents to Tom Wills, chief executive officer of Hampton Freeze, for his review.

**MANAGERIAL ACCOUNTING IN ACTION**
**The Wrap-up**

***Larry:*** Here's the budget. Overall, the net income is excellent, and the net cash flow for the entire year is positive.

***Tom:*** Yes, but I see on this cash budget that we have the same problem with negative cash flows in the first and second quarters that we had last year.

***Larry:*** That's true. I don't see any way around that problem. However, there is no doubt in my mind that if you take this budget to the bank today, they'll approve an open line of credit that will allow you to borrow enough money to make it through the first two quarters without any problem.

***Tom:*** Are you sure? They didn't seem very happy to see me last year when I came in for an emergency loan.

***Larry:*** Did you repay the loan on time?

***Tom:*** Sure.

***Larry:*** I don't see any problem. You won't be asking for an emergency loan this time. The bank will have plenty of warning. And with this budget, you have a solid plan that shows when and how you are going to pay off the loan. Trust me, they'll go for it.

## SCHEDULE 10

| | A | B | C | D | E |
|---|---|---|---|---|---|
| 1 | **Hampton Freeze, Inc.** | | | | |
| 2 | **Budgeted Balance Sheet** | | | Not on | |
| 3 | **December 31, 2013** | | | Exam | |
| 4 | | | | | |
| 5 | *Assets* | | | | |
| 6 | Current assets: | | | | |
| 7 | Cash | $ 41,400 | (a) | | |
| 8 | Accounts receivable | 120,000 | (b) | | |
| 9 | Raw materials inventory | 4,500 | (c) | | |
| 10 | Finished goods inventory | 39,000 | (d) | | |
| 11 | Total current assets | | | $ 204,900 | |
| 12 | Plant and equipment: | | | | |
| 13 | Land | 80,000 | (e) | | |
| 14 | Buildings and equipment | 830,000 | (f) | | |
| 15 | Accumulated depreciation | (392,000) | (g) | | |
| 16 | Plant and equipment, net | | | 518,000 | |
| 17 | Total assets | | | $ 722,900 | |
| 18 | | | | | |
| 19 | *Liabilities and Stockholders' Equity* | | | | |
| 20 | Current liabilities: | | | | |
| 21 | Accounts payable (raw materials) | | | $ 27,900 | (h) |
| 22 | Stockholders' equity: | | | | |
| 23 | Common stock, no par | $ 175,000 | (i) | | |
| 24 | Retained earnings | 520,000 | (j) | | |
| 25 | Total stockholders' equity | | | 695,000 | |
| 26 | Total liabilities and stockholders' equity | | | $ 722,900 | |
| 27 | | | | | |

Schedule 9 | **Schedule 10**

Explanation of December 31, 2013, balance sheet figures:

(a) The ending cash balance, as projected by the cash budget in Schedule 8.

(b) Thirty percent of fourth-quarter sales, from Schedule 1 ($400,000 × 30% = $120,000).

(c) From Schedule 3, the ending raw materials inventory will be 22,500 pounds. This material costs $0.20 per pound. Therefore, the ending inventory in dollars will be 22,500 pounds × $0.20 per pound = $4,500.

(d) From Schedule 6.

(e) From the December 31, 2012, balance sheet (no change).

(f) The December 31, 2012, balance sheet indicated a balance of $700,000. During 2013, $130,000 of additional equipment will be purchased (see Schedule 8), bringing the December 31, 2013, balance to $830,000.

(g) The December 31, 2012, balance sheet indicated a balance of $292,000. During 2013, $100,000 of depreciation will be taken ($60,000 on Schedule 5 and $40,000 on Schedule 7), bringing the December 31, 2013, balance to $392,000.

(h) One-half of the fourth-quarter raw materials purchases, from Schedule 3.

(i) From the December 31, 2012, balance sheet (no change).

(j)

| | |
|---|---|
| December 31, 2012, balance | $449,900 |
| Add net income, from Schedule 9 | 102,100 |
| | 552,000 |
| Deduct dividends paid, from Schedule 8 | 32,000 |
| December 31, 2013, balance | $520,000 |

**HELPFUL HINT**

One of the most important equations that you should learn while studying accounting is shown in item (j) of Schedule 10. The beginning balance in Retained Earnings plus net income minus dividends equals the ending balance in Retained Earnings. This equation highlights how the income statement and the balance sheet connect to one another. The net income from the income statement plugs into Retained Earnings on the balance sheet. This concept, which is formally referred to as articulated financial statements, is something that all business students must understand.

## SUMMARY

**LO1 Understand why organizations budget and the processes they use to create budgets.**

Organizations budget for a variety of reasons, including to communicate management's plans throughout the organization, to force managers to think about and plan for the future, to allocate resources within the organization, to identify bottlenecks before they occur, to coordinate activities, and to provide benchmarks for evaluating subsequent performance.

Budgets should be developed with the full participation of all managers who will be subject to budgetary controls.

**LO2 Prepare a sales budget, including a schedule of expected cash collections.**

The sales budget forms the foundation for the master budget. It provides details concerning the anticipated unit and dollar sales.

The schedule of expected cash collections is based on the sales budget, the expected breakdown between cash and credit sales, and the expected pattern of collections on credit sales.

**LO3 Prepare a production budget.**

The production budget details how many units must be produced each budget period to satisfy expected sales and to provide for adequate levels of finished goods inventories.

**LO4 Prepare a direct materials budget, including a schedule of expected cash disbursements for purchases of materials.**

The direct materials budget shows the materials that must be purchased each budget period to meet anticipated production requirements and to provide for adequate levels of materials inventories.

Cash disbursements for purchases of materials will depend on the amount of materials purchased in each budget period and the company's policies concerning payments to suppliers for materials bought on credit.

**LO5 Prepare a direct labor budget.**

The direct labor budget shows the direct labor-hours that are required to meet the production schedule as detailed in the production budget. The direct labor-hour requirements are used to determine the direct labor cost in each budget period.

**LO6 Prepare a manufacturing overhead budget.**

Manufacturing overhead consists of both variable and fixed manufacturing overhead. The variable manufacturing overhead depends on the number of units produced from the production budget. The variable and fixed manufacturing overhead costs are combined to determine the total manufacturing overhead. Any noncash manufacturing overhead such as depreciation is deducted from the total manufacturing overhead to determine the cash disbursements for manufacturing overhead.

**LO7 Prepare a selling and administrative expense budget.**

Like manufacturing overhead, selling and administrative expenses consist of both variable and fixed expenses. The variable expenses depend on the number of units sold or some other measure of activity. The variable and fixed expenses are combined to determine the total selling and administrative expense. Any noncash selling and administrative expenses such as depreciation are deducted from the total to determine the cash disbursements for selling and administrative expenses.

### LO8 Prepare a cash budget.

The cash budget is a critical piece of the master budget. It permits managers to anticipate and plan for cash shortfalls.

The cash budget is organized into a receipts section, a disbursements section, a cash excess or deficiency section, and a financing section. The cash budget draws on information taken from nearly all of the other budgets and schedules including the schedule of cash collections, the schedule of cash disbursements for purchases of materials, the direct labor budget, the manufacturing overhead budget, and the selling and administrative expense budget.

### LO9 Prepare a budgeted income statement.

The budgeted income statement is constructed using data from the sales budget, the ending finished goods inventory budget, the manufacturing overhead budget, the selling and administrative budget, and the cash budget.

### LO10 Prepare a budgeted balance sheet.

The budgeted balance sheet is constructed using data from virtually all other parts of the master budget.

## GUIDANCE ANSWER TO DECISION POINT

**Budget Analyst (p. 300)**

Not all costs are variable with respect to gross restaurant sales. For example, assuming no change in the number of restaurant sites, rental costs are probably fixed. To more accurately forecast costs for the budget, costs should be separated into variable and fixed components. Furthermore, more appropriate activity measures should be selected for the variable costs. For example, gross restaurant sales may be divided into food sales and bar sales—each of which could serve as an activity measure for some costs. In addition, some costs (such as the costs of free dinner rolls) may be variable with respect to the number of diners rather than with respect to food or bar sales. Other activity measures may permit even more accurate cost predictions.

## GUIDANCE ANSWERS TO CONCEPT CHECKS

1. **Choice c.** Cash collections for April are calculated as follows: ($100,000 × 80% × 40%) + ($120,000 × 20%) + ($120,000 × 80% × 60%) = $113,600.
2. **Choice a.** The May 31 accounts receivable balance is $125,000 × 80% × 40% = $40,000.
3. **Choice b.** Required inventory purchases are calculated as follows: Cost of goods sold of $300,000 + Ending inventory of $30,000 − Beginning inventory of $50,000 = $280,000.
4. **Choice b.** 80,000 units sold in April + 27,000 units of desired ending inventory − 24,000 units of beginning inventory = 83,000 units.

## REVIEW PROBLEM: BUDGET SCHEDULES

Mynor Corporation manufactures and sells a seasonal product that has peak sales in the third quarter. The following information concerns operations for Year 2—the coming year—and for the first two quarters of Year 3:

a. The company's single product sells for $8 per unit. Budgeted sales in units for the next six quarters are as follows (all sales are on credit):

| | Year 2 Quarter | | | | Year 3 Quarter | |
|---|---|---|---|---|---|---|
| | 1 | 2 | 3 | 4 | 1 | 2 |
| Budgeted unit sales.......... | 40,000 | 60,000 | 100,000 | 50,000 | 70,000 | 80,000 |

b. Sales are collected in the following pattern: 75% in the quarter the sales are made, and the remaining 25% in the following quarter. On January 1, Year 2, the company's balance sheet showed $65,000 in accounts receivable, all of which will be collected in the first quarter of the year. Bad debts are negligible and can be ignored.
c. The company desires an ending finished goods inventory at the end of each quarter equal to 30% of the budgeted unit sales for the next quarter. On December 31, Year 1, the company had 12,000 units on hand.
d. Five pounds of raw materials are required to complete one unit of product. The company requires ending raw materials inventory at the end of each quarter equal to 10% of the following quarter's production needs. On December 31, Year 1, the company had 23,000 pounds of raw materials on hand.
e. The raw material costs $0.80 per pound. Raw material purchases are paid for in the following pattern: 60% paid in the quarter the purchases are made, and the remaining 40% paid in the following quarter. On January 1, Year 2, the company's balance sheet showed $81,500 in accounts payable for raw material purchases, all of which will be paid for in the first quarter of the year.

***Required:***

Prepare the following budgets and schedules for the year, showing both quarterly and total figures:
1. A sales budget and a schedule of expected cash collections.
2. A production budget.
3. A direct materials budget and a schedule of expected cash payments for purchases of materials.

**Solution to Review Problem**

1. The sales budget is prepared as follows:

| | Year 2 Quarter | | | | |
|---|---|---|---|---|---|
| | 1 | 2 | 3 | 4 | Year |
| Budgeted unit sales | 40,000 | 60,000 | 100,000 | 50,000 | 250,000 |
| Selling price per unit | × $8 | × $8 | × $8 | × $8 | × $8 |
| Total sales | $320,000 | $480,000 | $800,000 | $400,000 | $2,000,000 |

Based on the budgeted sales above, the schedule of expected cash collections is prepared as follows:

| | Year 2 Quarter | | | | |
|---|---|---|---|---|---|
| | 1 | 2 | 3 | 4 | Year |
| Accounts receivable, beginning balance | $ 65,000 | | | | $ 65,000 |
| First-quarter sales ($320,000 × 75%, 25%) | 240,000 | $ 80,000 | | | 320,000 |
| Second-quarter sales ($480,000 × 75%, 25%) | | 360,000 | $120,000 | | 480,000 |
| Third-quarter sales ($800,000 × 75%, 25%) | | | 600,000 | $200,000 | 800,000 |
| Fourth-quarter sales ($400,000 × 75%) | | | | 300,000 | 300,000 |
| Total cash collections | $305,000 | $440,000 | $720,000 | $500,000 | $1,965,000 |

2. Based on the sales budget in units, the production budget is prepared as follows:

| | Year 2 Quarter | | | | | Year 3 Quarter | |
|---|---|---|---|---|---|---|---|
| | 1 | 2 | 3 | 4 | Year 2 | 1 | 2 |
| Budgeted unit sales | 40,000 | 60,000 | 100,000 | 50,000 | 250,000 | 70,000 | 80,000 |
| Add desired ending finished goods inventory* | 18,000 | 30,000 | 15,000 | 21,000† | 21,000 | 24,000 | |
| Total needs | 58,000 | 90,000 | 115,000 | 71,000 | 271,000 | 94,000 | |
| Less beginning finished goods inventory | 12,000 | 18,000 | 30,000 | 15,000 | 12,000 | 21,000 | |
| Required production | 46,000 | 72,000 | 85,000 | 56,000 | 259,000 | 73,000 | |

*30% of the following quarter's budgeted sales in units.
†30% of the budgeted Year 3 first-quarter sales.

3. Based on the production budget, raw materials will need to be purchased during the year as follows:

| | Year 2 Quarter | | | | | Year 3 Quarter |
|---|---|---|---|---|---|---|
| | 1 | 2 | 3 | 4 | Year 2 | 1 |
| Required production (units) | 46,000 | 72,000 | 85,000 | 56,000 | 259,000 | 73,000 |
| Raw materials needed per unit (pounds) | × 5 | × 5 | × 5 | × 5 | × 5 | × 5 |
| Production needs (pounds) | 230,000 | 360,000 | 425,000 | 280,000 | 1,295,000 | 365,000 |
| Add desired ending inventory of raw materials (pounds)* | 36,000 | 42,500 | 28,000 | 36,500† | 36,500 | |
| Total needs (pounds) | 266,000 | 402,500 | 453,000 | 316,500 | 1,331,500 | |
| Less beginning inventory of raw materials (pounds) | 23,000 | 36,000 | 42,500 | 28,000 | 23,000 | |
| Raw materials to be purchased (pounds) | 243,000 | 366,500 | 410,500 | 288,500 | 1,308,500 | |
| Cost of raw materials per pound | × $0.80 | × $0.80 | × $0.80 | × $0.80 | × $0.80 | |
| Cost of raw materials to be purchased | $194,400 | $293,200 | $328,400 | $230,800 | $1,046,800 | |

*10% of the following quarter's production needs in pounds.
†10% of the Year 3 first-quarter production needs in pounds.

Based on the raw material purchases above, expected cash payments are computed as follows:

| | Year 2 Quarter | | | | |
|---|---|---|---|---|---|
| | 1 | 2 | 3 | 4 | Year 2 |
| Accounts payable, beginning balance | $ 81,500 | | | | $ 81,500 |
| First-quarter purchases ($194,400 × 60%, 40%) | 116,640 | $ 77,760 | | | 194,400 |
| Second-quarter purchases ($293,200 × 60%, 40%) | | 175,920 | $117,280 | | 293,200 |
| Third-quarter purchases ($328,400 × 60%, 40%) | | | 197,040 | $131,360 | 328,400 |
| Fourth-quarter purchases ($230,800 × 60%) | | | | 138,480 | 138,480 |
| Total cash disbursements | $198,140 | $253,680 | $314,320 | $269,840 | $1,035,980 |

## GLOSSARY

**Budget** A quantitative plan for acquiring and using resources over a specified time period. (p. 284)

**Cash budget** A detailed plan showing how cash resources will be acquired and used over a specific time period. (p. 289)

**Continuous budget** A 12-month budget that rolls forward one month as the current month is completed. (p. 285)

**Control** Those steps taken by management to increase the likelihood that all parts of the organization are working together to achieve the goals set down at the planning stage. (p. 284)

**Direct labor budget** A detailed plan that shows the direct labor-hours required to fulfill the production budget. (p. 297)

**Direct materials budget** A detailed plan showing the amount of raw materials that must be purchased to fulfill the production budget and to provide for adequate inventories. (p. 294)

**Ending finished goods inventory budget** A budget showing the dollar amount of unsold finished goods inventory that will appear on the ending balance sheet. (p. 299)

**Manufacturing overhead budget** A detailed plan showing the production costs, other than direct materials and direct labor, that will be incurred over a specified time period. (p. 298)

**Master budget** A number of separate but interdependent budgets that formally lay out the company's sales, production, and financial goals and that culminates in a cash budget, budgeted income statement, and budgeted balance sheet. (p. 288)

**Merchandise purchases budget** A detailed plan used by a merchandising company that shows the amount of goods that must be purchased from suppliers during the period. (p. 294)

**Participative budget** See *Self-imposed budget.* (p. 286)

**Perpetual budget** See *Continuous budget.* (p. 285)

**Planning** Developing goals and preparing budgets to achieve those goals. (p. 284)

**Production budget** A detailed plan showing the number of units that must be produced during a period in order to satisfy both sales and inventory needs. (p. 293)

**Responsibility accounting** A system of accountability in which managers are held responsible for those items of revenue and cost—and only those items—over which they can exert significant control. The managers are held responsible for differences between budgeted and actual results. (p. 285)

**Sales budget** A detailed schedule showing expected sales expressed in both dollars and units. (p. 289)

**Self-imposed budget** A method of preparing budgets in which managers prepare their own budgets. These budgets are then reviewed by higher-level managers, and any issues are resolved by mutual agreement. (p. 286)

**Selling and administrative expense budget** A detailed schedule of planned expenses that will be incurred in areas other than manufacturing during a budget period. (p. 300)

## QUESTIONS

**7–1** What is a budget? What is budgetary control?

**7–2** Discuss some of the major benefits to be gained from budgeting.

**7–3** What is meant by the term *responsibility accounting?*

**7–4** What is a master budget? Briefly describe its contents.

**7–5** Why is the sales forecast the starting point in budgeting?

**7–6** "As a practical matter, planning and control mean exactly the same thing." Do you agree? Explain.

**7–7** Describe the flow of budget data in an organization. Who are the participants in the budgeting process, and how do they participate?

**7–8** What is a self-imposed budget? What are the major advantages of self-imposed budgets? What caution must be exercised in their use?

**7–9** How can budgeting assist a company in planning its workforce staffing levels?

**7–10** "The principal purpose of the cash budget is to see how much cash the company will have in the bank at the end of the year." Do you agree? Explain.

**Multiple-choice questions are provided on the text website at www.mhhe.com/brewer6e.**

## APPLYING EXCEL connect ACCOUNTING

LO2, LO3, LO4

**Available with McGraw-Hill's *Connect® Accounting.***

The Excel worksheet form that appears on the next page is to be used to recreate the Review Problem on pages 309–311. Download the workbook containing this form from the Online Learning Center at www.mhhe.com/brewer6e. *On the website you will also receive instructions about how to use this worksheet form.*

| | A | B | C | D | E | F | G | H | I |
|---|---|---|---|---|---|---|---|---|---|
| 1 | Chapter 7: Applying Excel | | | | | | | | |
| 2 | | | | | | | | | |
| 3 | **Data** | | *Year 2 Quarter* | | | *Year 3 Quarter* | | | |
| 4 | | *1* | *2* | *3* | *4* | *1* | *2* | | |
| 5 | Budgeted unit sales | 40,000 | 60,000 | 100,000 | 50,000 | 70,000 | 80,000 | | |
| 6 | | | | | | | | | |
| 7 | • Selling price per unit | $8 | per unit | | | | | | |
| 8 | • Accounts receivable, beginning balance | $65,000 | | | | | | | |
| 9 | • Sales collected in the quarter sales are made | 75% | | | | | | | |
| 10 | • Sales collected in the quarter after sales are made | 25% | | | | | | | |
| 11 | • Desired ending finished goods inventory is | 30% | of the budgeted unit sales of the next quarter | | | | | | |
| 12 | • Finished goods inventory, beginning | 12,000 | units | | | | | | |
| 13 | • Raw materials required to produce one unit | 5 | pounds | | | | | | |
| 14 | • Desired ending inventory of raw materials is | 10% | of the next quarter's production needs | | | | | | |
| 15 | • Raw materials inventory, beginning | 23,000 | pounds | | | | | | |
| 16 | • Raw material costs | $0.80 | per pound | | | | | | |
| 17 | • Raw materials purchases are paid | 60% | in the quarter the purchases are made | | | | | | |
| 18 | and | 40% | in the quarter following purchase | | | | | | |
| 19 | • Accounts payable for raw materials, beginning balance | $81,500 | | | | | | | |
| 20 | | | | | | | | | |
| 21 | *Enter a formula into each of the cells marked with a ? below* | | | | | | | | |
| 22 | **Review Problem: Budget Schedules** | | | | | | | | |
| 23 | | | | | | | | | |
| 24 | ***Construct the sales budget*** | | *Year 2 Quarter* | | | *Year 3 Quarter* | | | |
| 25 | | *1* | *2* | *3* | *4* | *1* | *2* | | |
| 26 | Budgeted unit sales | ? | ? | ? | ? | ? | ? | | |
| 27 | Selling price per unit | ? | ? | ? | ? | ? | ? | | |
| 28 | Total sales | ? | ? | ? | ? | ? | ? | | |
| 29 | | | | | | | | | |
| 30 | ***Construct the schedule of expected cash collections*** | | *Year 2 Quarter* | | | | | | |
| 31 | | *1* | *2* | *3* | *4* | *Year* | | | |
| 32 | Accounts receivable, beginning balance | ? | | | | ? | | | |
| 33 | First-quarter sales | ? | ? | | | ? | | | |
| 34 | Second-quarter sales | | ? | ? | | ? | | | |
| 35 | Third-quarter sales | | | ? | ? | ? | | | |
| 36 | Fourth-quarter sales | | | | ? | ? | | | |
| 37 | Total cash collections | ? | ? | ? | ? | ? | | | |
| 38 | | | | | | | | | |
| 39 | ***Construct the production budget*** | | *Year 2 Quarter* | | | | *Year 3 Quarter* | | |
| 40 | | *1* | *2* | *3* | *4* | *Year* | *1* | *2* | |
| 41 | Budgeted unit sales | ? | ? | ? | ? | ? | ? | ? | |
| 42 | Add desired finished goods inventory | ? | ? | ? | ? | ? | ? | | |
| 43 | Total needs | ? | ? | ? | ? | ? | ? | | |
| 44 | Less beginning inventory | ? | ? | ? | ? | ? | ? | | |
| 45 | Required production | ? | ? | ? | ? | ? | ? | | |
| 46 | | | | | | | | | |
| 47 | ***Construct the raw materials purchases budget*** | | *Year 2 Quarter* | | | | *Year 3 Quarter* | | |
| 48 | | *1* | *2* | *3* | *4* | *Year* | *1* | | |
| 49 | Required production (units) | ? | ? | ? | ? | ? | ? | | |
| 50 | Raw materials required to produce one unit | ? | ? | ? | ? | ? | ? | | |
| 51 | Production needs (pounds) | ? | ? | ? | ? | ? | ? | | |
| 52 | Add desired ending inventory of raw materials (pounds) | ? | ? | ? | ? | ? | | | |
| 53 | Total needs (pounds) | ? | ? | ? | ? | ? | | | |
| 54 | Less beginning inventory of raw materials (pounds) | ? | ? | ? | ? | ? | | | |
| 55 | Raw materials to be purchased | ? | ? | ? | ? | ? | | | |
| 56 | Cost of raw materials per pound | ? | ? | ? | ? | ? | | | |
| 57 | Cost of raw materials to be purchased | ? | ? | ? | ? | ? | | | |
| 58 | | | | | | | | | |
| 59 | ***Construct the schedule of expected cash payments*** | | *Year 2 Quarter* | | | | | | |
| 60 | | *1* | *2* | *3* | *4* | *Year* | | | |
| 61 | Accounts payable, beginning balance | ? | | | | ? | | | |
| 62 | First-quarter purchases | ? | ? | | | ? | | | |
| 63 | Second-quarter purchases | | ? | ? | | ? | | | |
| 64 | Third-quarter purchases | | | ? | ? | ? | | | |
| 65 | Fourth-quarter purchases | | | | ? | ? | | | |
| 66 | Total cash disbursements | ? | ? | ? | ? | ? | | | |
| 67 | | | | | | | | | |

Chapter 7 Form / Filled in Chapter 7 Form / Chapter 7 Formulas / Chapter 7 Requirement

You should proceed to the requirements below only after completing your worksheet.

***Required:***

1. Check your worksheet by changing the budgeted unit sales in Quarter 2 of Year 2 in cell C5 to 75,000 units. The total expected cash collections for the year should now be $2,085,000. If you do not get this answer, find the errors in your worksheet and correct them. Have the total cash disbursements for the year changed? Why or why not?
2. The company has just hired a new marketing manager who insists that unit sales can be dramatically increased by dropping the selling price from $8 to $7. The marketing manager would like to use the following projections in the budget:

| | Year 2 Quarter | | | | Year 3 Quarter | |
|---|---|---|---|---|---|---|
| **Data** | **1** | **2** | **3** | **4** | **1** | **2** |
| Budgeted unit sales .......... | 50,000 | 70,000 | 120,000 | 80,000 | 90,000 | 100,000 |
| Selling price per unit ......... | $7 | | | | | |

a. What are the total expected cash collections for the year under this revised budget?
b. What is the total required production for the year under this revised budget?
c. What is the total cost of raw materials to be purchased for the year under this revised budget?
d. What are the total expected cash disbursements for raw materials for the year under this revised budget?
e. After seeing this revised budget, the production manager cautioned that due to the current production constraint, a complex milling machine, the plant can produce no more than 90,000 units in any one quarter. Is this a potential problem? If so, what can be done about it?

## THE FOUNDATIONAL 15

connect ACCOUNTING

**Available with McGraw-Hill's *Connect® Accounting*.**

LO2, LO3, LO4, LO5, LO7, LO9, LO10

Morganton Company makes one product and it provided the following information to help prepare the master budget for its first four months of operations:

a. The budgeted selling price per unit is $70. Budgeted unit sales for June, July, August, and September are 8,400, 10,000, 12,000, and 13,000 units, respectively. All sales are on credit.
b. Forty-percent of credit sales are collected in the month of the sale and 60% in the following month.
c. The ending finished goods inventory equals 20% of the following month's unit sales.
d. The ending raw materials inventory equals 10% of the following month's raw materials production needs. Each unit of finished goods requires 5 pounds of raw materials. The raw materials cost $2.00 per pound.
e. Thirty-percent of raw materials purchases are paid for in the month of purchase and 70% in the following month.
f. The direct labor wage rate is $15 per hour. Each unit of finished goods requires two direct labor-hours.
g. The variable selling and administrative expense per unit sold is $1.80. The fixed selling and administrative expense per month is $60,000.

***Required:***

1. What are the budgeted sales for July?
2. What are the expected cash collections for July?
3. What is the accounts receivable balance at the end of July?
4. According to the production budget, how many units should be produced in July?
5. If 61,000 pounds of raw materials are needed to meet production in August, how many pounds of raw materials should be purchased in July?
6. What is the estimated cost of raw materials purchases for July?
7. If the cost of raw materials purchases in June is $88,880, what are the estimated cash disbursements for raw materials purchases in July?
8. What is the estimated accounts payable balance at the end of July?
9. What is the estimated raw materials inventory balance at the end of July?
10. What is the total estimated direct labor cost for July assuming the direct labor workforce is adjusted to match the hours required to produce the forecasted number of units produced?
11. If the company always uses an estimated predetermined plantwide overhead rate of $10 per direct labor-hour, what is the estimated unit product cost?
12. What is the estimated finished goods inventory balance at the end of July?
13. What is the estimated cost of goods sold and gross margin for July?
14. What is the estimated total selling and administrative expense for July?
15. What is the estimated net operating income for July?

## EXERCISES

connect ACCOUNTING

**All applicable exercises are available with McGraw-Hill's *Connect® Accounting*.**

**EXERCISE 7–1 Schedule of Expected Cash Collections [LO2]**

Midwest Products is a wholesale distributor of leaf rakes. Thus, peak sales occur in August of each year as shown in the company's sales budget for the third quarter, given below:

| | July | August | September | Total |
|---|---|---|---|---|
| Budgeted sales (all on account) ........ | $600,000 | $900,000 | $500,000 | $2,000,000 |

From past experience, the company has learned that 20% of a month's sales are collected in the month of sale, another 70% are collected in the month following sale, and the remaining 10% are collected in the second month following sale. Bad debts are negligible and can be ignored. May sales totaled $430,000, and June sales totaled $540,000.

TAKE TWO

Budgeted sales in July = $700,000

***Required:***

1. Prepare a schedule of expected cash collections from sales, by month and in total, for the third quarter.
2. Assume that the company will prepare a budgeted balance sheet as of September 30. Compute the accounts receivable as of that date.

**EXERCISE 7–2 Production Budget [LO3]**

Crystal Telecom has budgeted the sales of its innovative mobile phone over the next four months as follows:

TAKE TWO

Ending finished goods inventory = 20% of next month's sales

| | Sales in Units |
|---|---|
| July | 30,000 |
| August | 45,000 |
| September | 60,000 |
| October | 50,000 |

The company is now in the process of preparing a production budget for the third quarter. Past experience has shown that end-of-month finished goods inventories must equal 10% of the next month's sales.

***Required:***

Prepare a production budget for the third quarter showing the number of units to be produced each month and for the quarter in total.

**EXERCISE 7–3 Direct Materials Budget [LO4]**

Micro Products, Inc., has developed a very powerful electronic calculator. Each calculator requires three small "chips" that cost $2 each and are purchased from an overseas supplier. Micro Products has prepared a production budget for the calculator by quarters for Year 2 and for the first quarter of Year 3, as shown below:

TAKE TWO

Each calculator requires four small chips

| | Year 2 | | | | Year 3 |
|---|---|---|---|---|---|
| | First | Second | Third | Fourth | First |
| Budgeted production, in calculators | 60,000 | 90,000 | 150,000 | 100,000 | 80,000 |

The chip used in production of the calculator is sometimes hard to get, so it is necessary to carry large inventories as a precaution against stockouts. For this reason, the inventory of chips at the end of a quarter must equal 20% of the following quarter's production needs.

***Required:***

Prepare a direct materials budget for chips, by quarter and in total, for Year 2. At the bottom of your budget, show the dollar amount of purchases for each quarter and for the year in total.

**EXERCISE 7–4 Direct Labor Budget [LO5]**

The production manager of Junnen Corporation has submitted the following forecast of units to be produced for each quarter of the upcoming fiscal year:

TAKE TWO

Each unit requires 0.3 direct labor-hours

| | 1st Quarter | 2nd Quarter | 3rd Quarter | 4th Quarter |
|---|---|---|---|---|
| Units to be produced | 5,000 | 4,400 | 4,500 | 4,900 |

Each unit requires 0.40 direct labor-hours and direct labor-hour workers are paid $11 per hour.

***Required:***

1. Construct the company's direct labor budget for the upcoming fiscal year, assuming that the direct labor workforce is adjusted each quarter to match the number of hours required to produce the forecasted number of units produced.

2. Construct the company's direct labor budget for the upcoming fiscal year, assuming that the direct labor workforce is *not* adjusted each quarter. Instead, assume that the company's direct labor workforce consists of permanent employees who are guaranteed to be paid for at least 1,800 hours of work each quarter. If the number of required direct labor-hours is less than this number, the workers are paid for 1,800 hours anyway. Any hours worked in excess of 1,800 hours in a quarter are paid at the rate of 1.5 times the normal hourly rate for direct labor.

TAKE TWO

**EXERCISE 7–5 Manufacturing Overhead Budget [LO6]**
The direct labor budget of Krispin Corporation for the upcoming fiscal year includes the following budgeted direct labor-hours:

Variable overhead rate = $2.00 per direct labor-hour

| | 1st Quarter | 2nd Quarter | 3rd Quarter | 4th Quarter |
|---|---|---|---|---|
| Budgeted direct labor-hours ........ | 5,000 | 4,800 | 5,200 | 5,400 |

The company's variable manufacturing overhead rate is $1.75 per direct labor-hour and the company's fixed manufacturing overhead is $35,000 per quarter. The only noncash item included in fixed manufacturing overhead is depreciation, which is $15,000 per quarter.

***Required:***
1. Construct the company's manufacturing overhead budget for the upcoming fiscal year.
2. Compute the company's manufacturing overhead rate (including both variable and fixed manufacturing overhead) for the upcoming fiscal year. Round off to the nearest whole cent.

**EXERCISE 7–6 Selling and Administrative Expense Budget [LO7]**
The budgeted unit sales of Haerve Company for the upcoming fiscal year are provided below:

| | 1st Quarter | 2nd Quarter | 3rd Quarter | 4th Quarter |
|---|---|---|---|---|
| Budgeted unit sales ................... | 12,000 | 14,000 | 11,000 | 10,000 |

The company's variable selling and administrative expenses per unit are $2.75. Fixed selling and administrative expenses include advertising expenses of $12,000 per quarter, executive salaries of $40,000 per quarter, and depreciation of $16,000 per quarter. In addition, the company will make insurance payments of $6,000 in the 2nd Quarter and $6,000 in the 4th Quarter. Finally, property taxes of $6,000 will be paid in the 3rd Quarter.

***Required:***
Prepare the company's selling and administrative expense budget for the upcoming fiscal year.

TAKE TWO

**EXERCISE 7–7 Cash Budget [LO8]**
Forest Outfitters is a retailer that is preparing its budget for the upcoming fiscal year. Management has prepared the following summary of its budgeted cash flows:

| | 1st Quarter | 2nd Quarter | 3rd Quarter | 4th Quarter |
|---|---|---|---|---|
| Total cash receipts ........................ | $340,000 | $670,000 | $410,000 | $470,000 |
| Total cash disbursements .............. | $530,000 | $450,000 | $430,000 | $480,000 |

Minimum cash balance = $35,000

The company's beginning cash balance for the upcoming fiscal year will be $50,000. The company requires a minimum cash balance of $30,000 and may borrow any amount needed from a local bank at a quarterly interest rate of 3%. The company may borrow any amount at the beginning of any quarter and may repay its loans, or any part of its loans, at the end of any quarter. Interest payments are due on any principal at the time it is repaid.

***Required:***
Prepare the company's cash budget for the upcoming fiscal year.

**EXERCISE 7–8 Budgeted Income Statement [LO9]**

Seattle Cat is the wholesale distributor of a small recreational catamaran sailboat. Management has prepared the following summary data to use in its annual budgeting process:

| | |
|---|---|
| Budgeted unit sales | 380 |
| Selling price per unit | $1,850 |
| Cost per unit | $1,425 |
| Variable selling and administrative expenses (per unit) | $85 |
| Fixed selling and administrative expenses (per year) | $105,000 |
| Interest expense for the year | $11,000 |

TAKE TWO

Budgeted unit sales = 400

***Required:***

Prepare the company's budgeted income statement using an absorption income statement format as shown in Schedule 9.

**EXERCISE 7–9 Budgeted Balance Sheet [LO10]**

The management of Academic Copy, a photocopying center located on University Avenue, has compiled the following data to use in preparing its budgeted balance sheet for next year:

| | Ending Balances |
|---|---|
| Cash | ? |
| Accounts receivable | $6,500 |
| Supplies inventory | $2,100 |
| Equipment | $28,000 |
| Accumulated depreciation | $9,000 |
| Accounts payable | $1,900 |
| Common stock | $4,000 |
| Retained earnings | ? |

TAKE TWO

Net income = $10,000

The beginning balance of retained earnings was $21,000, net income is budgeted to be $8,600, and dividends are budgeted to be $3,500.

***Required:***

Prepare the company's budgeted balance sheet.

**EXERCISE 7–10 Sales and Production Budgets [LO2, LO3]**

The marketing department of Graber Corporation has submitted the following sales forecast for the upcoming fiscal year:

TAKE TWO

Selling price per unit = $25.00; Budgeted unit sales in 2nd Quarter = 16,000

| | 1st Quarter | 2nd Quarter | 3rd Quarter | 4th Quarter |
|---|---|---|---|---|
| Budgeted unit sales | 16,000 | 15,000 | 14,000 | 15,000 |

The selling price of the company's product is $22.00 per unit. Management expects to collect 75% of sales in the quarter in which the sales are made, 20% in the following quarter, and 5% of sales are expected to be uncollectible. The beginning balance of accounts receivable, all of which is expected to be collected in the first quarter, is $66,000.

The company expects to start the first quarter with 3,200 units in finished goods inventory. Management desires an ending finished goods inventory in each quarter equal to 20% of the next quarter's budgeted sales. The desired ending finished goods inventory for the fourth quarter is 3,400 units.

***Required:***

1. Prepare the company's sales budget and schedule of expected cash collections.
2. Prepare the company's production budget for the upcoming fiscal year.

## EXERCISE 7–11 Direct Materials and Direct Labor Budgets [LO4, LO5]

Units to be produced in 2nd Quarter = 7,500 units

The production department of Priston Company has submitted the following forecast of units to be produced by quarter for the upcoming fiscal year:

| | 1st Quarter | 2nd Quarter | 3rd Quarter | 4th Quarter |
|---|---|---|---|---|
| Units to be produced ............ | 6,000 | 7,000 | 8,000 | 5,000 |

In addition, the beginning raw materials inventory for the 1st Quarter is budgeted to be 3,600 pounds and the beginning accounts payable for the 1st Quarter is budgeted to be $11,775.

Each unit requires three pounds of raw material that costs $2.50 per pound. Management desires to end each quarter with a raw materials inventory equal to 20% of the following quarter's production needs. The desired ending inventory for the 4th Quarter is 3,700 pounds. Management plans to pay for 70% of raw material purchases in the quarter acquired and 30% in the following quarter. Each unit requires 0.50 direct labor-hours and direct labor-hour workers are paid $12 per hour.

***Required:***

1. Prepare the company's direct materials budget and schedule of expected cash disbursements for purchases of materials for the upcoming fiscal year.
2. Prepare the company's direct labor budget for the upcoming fiscal year, assuming that the direct labor workforce is adjusted each quarter to match the number of hours required to produce the forecasted number of units produced.

## EXERCISE 7–12 Direct Labor and Manufacturing Overhead Budgets [LO5, LO6]

Each unit requires 1.00 direct labor-hours

The Production Department of Harveton Corporation has submitted the following forecast of units to be produced by quarter for the upcoming fiscal year:

| | 1st Quarter | 2nd Quarter | 3rd Quarter | 4th Quarter |
|---|---|---|---|---|
| Units to be produced ................. | 16,000 | 15,000 | 14,000 | 15,000 |

Each unit requires 0.80 direct labor-hours and direct labor-hour workers are paid $11.50 per hour.

In addition, the variable manufacturing overhead rate is $2.50 per direct labor-hour. The fixed manufacturing overhead is $90,000 per quarter. The only noncash element of manufacturing overhead is depreciation, which is $34,000 per quarter.

***Required:***

1. Prepare the company's direct labor budget for the upcoming fiscal year, assuming that the direct labor workforce is adjusted each quarter to match the number of hours required to produce the forecasted number of units produced.
2. Prepare the company's manufacturing overhead budget.

## EXERCISE 7–13 Production and Direct Materials Budgets [LO3, LO4]

Tonga Toys manufactures and distributes a number of products to retailers. One of these products, Playclay, requires three pounds of material A135 in the manufacture of each unit. The company is now planning raw materials needs for the third quarter—July, August, and September. Peak sales of Playclay occur in the third quarter of each year. To keep production and shipments moving smoothly, the company has the following inventory requirements:

a. The finished goods inventory on hand at the end of each month must be equal to 5,000 units plus 30% of the next month's sales. The finished goods inventory on June 30 is budgeted to be 17,000 units.

b. The raw materials inventory on hand at the end of each month must be equal to one-half of the following month's production needs for raw materials. The raw materials inventory on June 30 for material A135 is budgeted to be 64,500 pounds.

c. The company maintains no work in process inventories.

A sales budget for Playclay for the last six months of the year follows:

| | Budgeted Sales in Units |
|---|---|
| July | 40,000 |
| August | 50,000 |
| September | 70,000 |
| October | 35,000 |
| November | 20,000 |
| December | 10,000 |

***Required:***

1. Prepare a production budget for Playclay for the months July, August, September, and October.
2. Examine the production budget that you prepared. Why will the company produce more units than it sells in July and August and less units than it sells in September and October?
3. Prepare a direct materials budget showing the quantity of material A135 to be purchased for July, August, and September and for the quarter in total.

**EXERCISE 7–14 Schedules of Expected Cash Collections and Disbursements; Income Statement; Balance Sheet [LO2, LO4, LO9, LO10]**

Estimated sales for September = $240,000

Colerain Corporation is a merchandising company that is preparing a profit plan for the third quarter of the calendar year. The company's balance sheet as of June 30 is shown below:

| Colerain Corporation<br>Balance Sheet<br>June 30 | |
|---|---|
| **Assets** | |
| Cash | $ 80,000 |
| Accounts receivable | 126,000 |
| Inventory | 52,000 |
| Plant and equipment, net of depreciation | 200,000 |
| Total assets | $458,000 |
| **Liabilities and Stockholders' Equity** | |
| Accounts payable | $ 61,100 |
| Common stock | 300,000 |
| Retained earnings | 96,900 |
| Total liabilities and stockholders' equity | $458,000 |

Colerain's managers have made the following additional assumptions and estimates:

1. Estimated sales for July, August, September, and October will be $200,000, $220,000, $210,000, and $230,000, respectively.
2. All sales are on credit and all credit sales are collected. Each month's credit sales are collected 30% in the month of sale and 70% in the month following the sale. All of the accounts receivable at June 30 will be collected in July.
3. Each month's ending inventory must equal 40% of the cost of next month's sales. The cost of goods sold is 65% of sales. The company pays for 50% of its merchandise purchases in the month of the purchase and the remaining 50% in the month following the purchase. All of the accounts payable at June 30 will be paid in July.
4. Monthly selling and administrative expenses are always $65,000. Each month $5,000 of this total amount is depreciation expense and the remaining $60,000 relates to expenses that are paid in the month they are incurred.
5. The company does not plan to borrow money or pay or declare dividends during the quarter ended September 30. The company does not plan to issue any common stock or repurchase its own stock during the quarter ended September 30.

***Required:***

1. Prepare a schedule of expected cash collections for July, August, and September. Also compute total cash collections for the quarter ended September 30th.
2. a. Prepare a merchandise purchases budget for July, August, and September. Also compute total merchandise purchases for the quarter ended September 30th.
   b. Prepare a schedule of expected cash disbursements for merchandise purchases for July, August, and September. Also compute total cash disbursements for merchandise purchases for the quarter ended September 30th.
3. Prepare an income statement for the quarter ended September 30th. Use the absorption format shown in Schedule 9.
4. Prepare a balance sheet as of September 30th.

**EXERCISE 7–15 Cash Budget Analysis [LO8]**

A cash budget, by quarters, is shown below for a retail company (000 omitted). The company requires a minimum cash balance of $5,000 to start each quarter.

| | Quarter | | | | |
|---|---|---|---|---|---|
| | 1 | 2 | 3 | 4 | Year |
| Cash balance, beginning | $ 9 | $ ? | $ ? | $ ? | $ ? |
| Add collections from customers | ? | ? | 125 | ? | 391 |
| Total cash available | 85 | ? | ? | ? | ? |
| Less disbursements: | | | | | |
| Purchases of inventory | 40 | 58 | ? | 32 | ? |
| Operating expenses | ? | 42 | 54 | ? | 180 |
| Equipment purchases | 10 | 8 | 8 | ? | 36 |
| Dividends | 2 | 2 | 2 | 2 | ? |
| Total disbursements | ? | 110 | ? | ? | ? |
| Excess (deficiency) of cash available over disbursements | (3) | ? | 30 | ? | ? |
| Financing: | | | | | |
| Borrowings | ? | 20 | — | — | ? |
| Repayments (including interest)* | — | — | (?) | (7) | (?) |
| Total financing | ? | ? | ? | ? | ? |
| Cash balance, ending | $ ? | $ ? | $ ? | $ ? | $ ? |

*Interest will total $4,000 for the year.

***Required:***

Fill in the missing amounts in the table above.

## PROBLEMS

connect ACCOUNTING Alternate problem set is available on the text website and in *Connect*® *Accounting*.

**All applicable problems are available with McGraw-Hill's *Connect*® *Accounting*.**

**PROBLEM 7–16A Schedules of Expected Cash Collections and Disbursements [LO2, LO4, LO8]**

CHECK FIGURE
(3) Ending cash balance: $5,000

Calgon Products, a distributor of organic beverages, needs a cash budget for September. The following information is available:

a. The cash balance at the beginning of September is $9,000.
b. Actual sales for July and August and expected sales for September are as follows:

| | July | August | September |
|---|---|---|---|
| Cash sales | $ 6,500 | $ 5,250 | $ 7,400 |
| Sales on account | 20,000 | 30,000 | 40,000 |
| Total sales | $26,500 | $35,250 | $47,400 |

Sales on account are collected over a three-month period as follows: 10% collected in the month of sale, 70% collected in the month following sale, and 18% collected in the second month following sale. The remaining 2% is uncollectible.

c. Purchases of inventory will total $25,000 for September. Twenty percent of a month's inventory purchases are paid for during the month of purchase. The accounts payable remaining from August's inventory purchases total $16,000, all of which will be paid in September.
d. Selling and administrative expenses are budgeted at $13,000 for September. Of this amount, $4,000 is for depreciation.
e. Equipment costing $18,000 will be purchased for cash during September, and dividends totaling $3,000 will be paid during the month.
f. The company maintains a minimum cash balance of $5,000. An open line of credit is available from the company's bank to bolster the cash balance as needed.

***Required:***

1. Prepare a schedule of expected cash collections for September.
2. Prepare a schedule of expected cash disbursements for inventory purchases for September.
3. Prepare a cash budget for September. Indicate in the financing section any borrowing that will be needed during September. Assume that any interest will not be paid until the following month.

**PROBLEM 7–17A Cash Budget with Supporting Schedules [LO2, LO4, LO8]**

CHECK FIGURE
(1) August collections: $47,760;
(3) July ending cash balance: $8,410

Janus Products, Inc., is a merchandising company that sells binders, paper, and other school supplies. The company is planning its cash needs for the third quarter. In the past, Janus Products has had to borrow money during the third quarter to support peak sales of back-to-school materials, which occur during August. The following information has been assembled to assist in preparing a cash budget for the quarter:

a. Budgeted monthly absorption costing income statements for July–October are as follows:

| | July | August | September | October |
|---|---|---|---|---|
| Sales | $40,000 | $70,000 | $50,000 | $45,000 |
| Cost of goods sold | 24,000 | 42,000 | 30,000 | 27,000 |
| Gross margin | 16,000 | 28,000 | 20,000 | 18,000 |
| Selling and administrative expenses: | | | | |
| Selling expense | 7,200 | 11,700 | 8,500 | 7,300 |
| Administrative expense* | 5,600 | 7,200 | 6,100 | 5,900 |
| Total selling and administratire expenses | 12,800 | 18,900 | 14,600 | 13,200 |
| Net operating income | $ 3,200 | $ 9,100 | $ 5,400 | $ 4,800 |

*Includes $2,000 depreciation each month.

b. Sales are 20% for cash and 80% on credit.
c. Credit sales are collected over a three-month period with 10% collected in the month of sale, 70% in the month following sale, and 20% in the second month following sale. May sales totaled $30,000, and June sales totaled $36,000.
d. Inventory purchases are paid for within 15 days. Therefore, 50% of a month's inventory purchases are paid for in the month of purchase. The remaining 50% is paid in the following month. Accounts payable for inventory purchases at June 30 total $11,700.
e. The company maintains its ending inventory levels at 75% of the cost of the merchandise to be sold in the following month. The merchandise inventory at June 30 is $18,000.
f. Land costing $4,500 will be purchased in July.
g. Dividends of $1,000 will be declared and paid in September.
h. The cash balance on June 30 is $8,000; the company must maintain a cash balance of at least this amount at the end of each month.
i. The company has an agreement with a local bank that allows it to borrow in increments of $1,000 at the beginning of each month, up to a total loan balance of $40,000. The interest rate on these loans is 1% per month, and for simplicity, we will assume that interest is not compounded. The company would, as far as it is able, repay the loan plus accumulated interest at the end of the quarter.

***Required:***

1. Prepare a schedule of expected cash collections for July, August, and September and for the quarter in total.

2. Prepare the following for merchandise inventory:
   a. A merchandise purchases budget for July, August, and September.
   b. A schedule of expected cash disbursements for merchandise purchases for July, August, and September and for the quarter in total.
3. Prepare a cash budget for July, August, and September and for the quarter in total.

**PROBLEM 7–18A Cash Budget with Supporting Schedules; Changing Assumptions [LO2, LO4, LO8]**

CHECK FIGURE
(1) August collections: $52,960; (3) July ending cash balance: $13,710

Refer to the data for Janus Products, Inc., in Problem 7–17. The company's president is interested in knowing how reducing inventory levels and collecting accounts receivable sooner will impact the cash budget. He revises the cash collection and ending inventory assumptions as follows:

1. Sales continue to be 20% for cash and 80% on credit. However, credit sales from July, August, and September are collected over a three-month period with 25% collected in the month of sale, 60% collected in the month following sale, and 15% in the second month following sale. Credit sales from May and June are collected during the third quarter using the collection percentages specified in Problem 7–17.
2. The company maintains its ending inventory levels for July, August, and September at 25% of the cost of merchandise to be sold in the following month. The merchandise inventory at June 30 remains $18,000 and accounts payable for inventory purchases at June 30 remains $11,700.

All other information from Problem 7–17 that is not referred to above remains the same.

***Required:***

1. Using the president's new assumptions in (1) above, prepare a schedule of expected cash collections for July, August, and September and for the quarter in total.
2. Using the president's new assumptions in (2) above, prepare the following for merchandise inventory:
   a. A merchandise purchases budget for July, August, and September.
   b. A schedule of expected cash disbursements for merchandise purchases for July, August, and September and for the quarter in total.
3. Using the president's new assumptions, prepare a cash budget for July, August, September, and for the quarter in total.
4. Prepare a brief memorandum for the president explaining how his revised assumptions affect the cash budget.

**PROBLEM 7–19A Integration of Sales, Production, and Direct Materials Budgets [LO2, LO3, LO4]**

CHECK FIGURE
(1) August collections: $290,000; (3) August payments: $31,740

Crydon, Inc., manufactures an advanced swim fin for scuba divers. Management is now preparing detailed budgets for the third quarter, July through September, and has assembled the following information to assist in preparing the budget:

a. The Marketing Department has estimated sales as follows for the remainder of the year (in pairs of swim fins):
   The selling price of the swim fins is $50 per pair.

| | | | |
|---|---|---|---|
| July | 6,000 | October | 4,000 |
| August | 7,000 | November | 3,000 |
| September | 5,000 | December | 3,000 |

b. All sales are on account. Based on past experience, sales are expected to be collected in the following pattern:

   40% in the month of sale
   50% in the month following sale
   10% uncollectible

   The beginning accounts receivable balance (excluding uncollectible amounts) on July 1 will be $130,000.
c. The company maintains finished goods inventories equal to 10% of the following month's sales. The inventory of finished goods on July 1 will be 600 pairs.
d. Each pair of swim fins requires 2 pounds of geico compound. To prevent shortages, the company would like the inventory of geico compound on hand at the end of each month to be equal to 20% of the following month's production needs. The inventory of geico compound on hand on July 1 will be 2,440 pounds.

e. Geico compound costs $2.50 per pound. Crydon pays for 60% of its purchases in the month of purchase; the remainder is paid for in the following month. The accounts payable balance for geico compound purchases will be $11,400 on July 1.

***Required:***

1. Prepare a sales budget, by month and in total, for the third quarter. (Show your budget in both pairs of swim fins and dollars.) Also prepare a schedule of expected cash collections, by month and in total, for the third quarter.
2. Prepare a production budget for each of the months July through October.
3. Prepare a direct materials budget for geico compound, by month and in total, for the third quarter. Also prepare a schedule of expected cash disbursements for geico compound, by month and in total, for the third quarter.

**PROBLEM 7–20A Cash Budget; Income Statement; Balance Sheet [LO2, LO4, LO8, LO9, LO10]**

eXcel

CHECK FIGURE
(1) Ending cash balance: $7,500

The balance sheet of Phototec, Inc., a distributor of photographic supplies, as of May 31 is given below:

**Phototec, Inc.**
**Balance Sheet**
**May 31**

| | |
|---|---|
| **Assets** | |
| Cash | $ 8,000 |
| Accounts receivable | 72,000 |
| Inventory | 30,000 |
| Buildings and equipment, net of depreciation | 500,000 |
| Total assets | $610,000 |
| **Liabilities and Stockholders' Equity** | |
| Accounts payable | $ 90,000 |
| Note payable | 15,000 |
| Capital stock | 420,000 |
| Retained earnings | 85,000 |
| Total liabilities and stockholders' equity | $610,000 |

The company is in the process of preparing a budget for June and has assembled the following data:

a. Sales are budgeted at $250,000 for June. Of these sales, $60,000 will be for cash; the remainder will be credit sales. One-half of a month's credit sales are collected in the month the sales are made, and the remainder is collected the following month. All of the May 31 accounts receivable will be collected in June.
b. Purchases of inventory are expected to total $200,000 during June. These purchases will all be on account. Forty percent of all inventory purchases are paid for in the month of purchase; the remainder are paid in the following month. All of the May 31 accounts payable to suppliers will be paid during June.
c. The June 30 inventory balance is budgeted at $40,000.
d. Selling and administrative expenses for June are budgeted at $51,000, exclusive of depreciation. These expenses will be paid in cash. Depreciation is budgeted at $2,000 for the month.
e. The note payable on the May 31 balance sheet will be paid during June. The company's interest expense for June (on all borrowing) will be $500, which will be paid in cash.
f. New warehouse equipment costing $9,000 will be purchased for cash during June.
g. During June, the company will borrow $18,000 from its bank by giving a new note payable to the bank for that amount. The new note will be due in one year.

***Required:***

1. Prepare a cash budget for June. Support your budget with a schedule of expected cash collections from sales and a schedule of expected cash disbursements for inventory purchases.
2. Prepare a budgeted income statement for June. Use the absorption costing income statement format as shown in Schedule 9.
3. Prepare a budgeted balance sheet as of June 30.

CHECK FIGURE
(1) July: $290,700;
(2) July 31 cash balance: $28,700

**PROBLEM 7–21A Schedule of Expected Cash Collections; Cash Budget [LO2, LO8]**

Natural Care Corp., a distributor of natural cosmetics, is ready to begin its third quarter, in which peak sales occur. The company has requested a $60,000, 90-day loan from its bank to help meet cash requirements during the quarter. Because Natural Care has experienced difficulty in paying off its loans in the past, the bank's loan officer has asked the company to prepare a cash budget for the quarter. In response to this request, the following data have been assembled:

a. On July 1, the beginning of the third quarter, the company will have a cash balance of $43,000.
b. Actual sales for the last two months and budgeted sales for the third quarter follow (all sales are on account):

| | |
|---|---|
| May (actual) | $360,000 |
| June (actual) | $280,000 |
| July (budgeted) | $350,000 |
| August (budgeted) | $420,000 |
| September (budgeted) | $360,000 |

Past experience shows that 25% of a month's sales are collected in the month of sale, 70% in the month following sale, and 2% in the second month following sale. The remainder is uncollectible.

c. Budgeted merchandise purchases and budgeted expenses for the third quarter are given below:

| | July | August | September |
|---|---|---|---|
| Merchandise purchases | $170,000 | $155,000 | $165,000 |
| Salaries and wages | $70,000 | $70,000 | $65,000 |
| Advertising | $80,000 | $90,000 | $100,000 |
| Rent payments | $30,000 | $30,000 | $30,000 |
| Depreciation | $40,000 | $40,000 | $40,000 |

Merchandise purchases are paid in full during the month following purchase. Accounts payable for merchandise purchases on June 30, which will be paid during July, total $160,000.

d. Equipment costing $25,000 will be purchased for cash during July.
e. In preparing the cash budget, assume that the $60,000 loan will be made in July and repaid in September. Interest on the loan will total $2,000.

***Required:***

1. Prepare a schedule of expected cash collections for July, August, and September and for the quarter in total.
2. Prepare a cash budget, by month and in total, for the third quarter.
3. If the company needs a minimum cash balance of $20,000 to start each month, can the loan be repaid as planned? Explain.

CHECK FIGURE
(1) May: $217,200; (2) May ending cash balance: $20,200

**PROBLEM 7–22A Schedule of Expected Cash Collections; Cash Budget [LO2, LO8]**

Jodi Horton, president of the retailer Crestline Products, has just approached the company's bank with a request for a $30,000, 90-day loan. The purpose of the loan is to assist the company in acquiring inventories in support of peak April sales. Because the company has had some difficulty in paying off its loans in the past, the loan officer has asked for a cash budget to help determine whether the loan should be made. The following data are available for the months April–June, during which the loan will be used:

a. On April 1, the start of the loan period, the cash balance will be $26,000. Accounts receivable on April 1 will total $151,500, of which $141,000 will be collected during April and $7,200 will be collected during May. The remainder will be uncollectible.
b. Past experience shows that 20% of a month's sales are collected in the month of sale, 75% in the month following sale, and 4% in the second month following sale. The other 1% represents bad debts that are never collected. Budgeted sales and expenses for the three-month period follow:

| | April | May | June |
|---|---|---|---|
| Sales (all on account) | $200,000 | $300,000 | $250,000 |
| Merchandise purchases | $120,000 | $180,000 | $150,000 |
| Payroll | $9,000 | $9,000 | $8,000 |
| Lease payments | $15,000 | $15,000 | $15,000 |
| Advertising | $70,000 | $80,000 | $60,000 |
| Equipment purchases | $8,000 | — | — |
| Depreciation | $10,000 | $10,000 | $10,000 |

c. Merchandise purchases are paid in full during the month following purchase. Accounts payable for merchandise purchases on March 31, which will be paid during April, total $108,000.
d. In preparing the cash budget, assume that the $30,000 loan will be made in April and repaid in June. Interest on the loan will total $1,200.

***Required:***
1. Prepare a schedule of expected cash collections for April, May, and June and for the three months in total.
2. Prepare a cash budget, by month and in total, for the three-month period.
3. If the company needs a minimum cash balance of $20,000 to start each month, can the loan be repaid as planned? Explain.

**PROBLEM 7–23A Cash Budget with Supporting Schedules [LO2, LO4, LO7, LO8]**

eXcel

CHECK FIGURE
(1a) Third quarter cash collections: $523,000;
(3) Third quarter ending cash balance: $18,500

The president of Univax, Inc., has just approached the company's bank seeking short-term financing for the coming year, Year 2. Univax is a distributor of commercial vacuum cleaners. The bank has stated that the loan request must be accompanied by a detailed cash budget that shows the quarters in which financing will be needed, as well as the amounts that will be needed and the quarters in which repayments can be made.

To provide this information for the bank, the president has directed that the following data be gathered from which a cash budget can be prepared:

a. Budgeted sales and merchandise purchases for Year 2, as well as actual sales and purchases for the last quarter of Year 1, are as follows:

| | Sales | Merchandise Purchases |
|---|---|---|
| Year 1: | | |
| Fourth quarter actual .................... | $300,000 | $180,000 |
| Year 2: | | |
| First quarter estimated .................. | $400,000 | $260,000 |
| Second quarter estimated............. | $500,000 | $310,000 |
| Third quarter estimated ................ | $600,000 | $370,000 |
| Fourth quarter estimated............... | $480,000 | $240,000 |

b. The company typically collects 33% of a quarter's sales before the quarter ends and another 65% in the following quarter. The remainder is uncollectible. This pattern of collections is now being experienced in the actual data for the Year 1 fourth quarter.
c. Some 20% of a quarter's merchandise purchases are paid for within the quarter. The remainder is paid in the following quarter.
d. Selling and administrative expenses for Year 2 are budgeted at $90,000 per quarter plus 12% of sales. Of the fixed amount, $20,000 each quarter is depreciation.
e. The company will pay $10,000 in cash dividends each quarter.
f. Land purchases will be made as follows during the year: $80,000 in the second quarter and $48,500 in the third quarter.
g. The Cash account contained $20,000 at the end of Year 1. The company must maintain a minimum cash balance of at least $18,000.
h. The company has an agreement with a local bank that allows the company to borrow in increments of $10,000 at the beginning of each quarter, up to a total loan balance of $100,000. The interest rate on these loans is 1% per month, and for simplicity, we will assume that interest is not compounded. The company would, as far as it is able, repay the loan plus accumulated interest at the end of the year.
i. At present, the company has no loans outstanding.

***Required:***
1. Prepare the following, by quarter and in total, for Year 2:
   a. A schedule of expected cash collections on sales.
   b. A schedule of expected cash disbursements for merchandise purchases.
2. Compute the expected cash disbursements for selling and administrative expenses, by quarter and in total, for Year 2.
3. Prepare a cash budget by quarter and in total for Year 2.

**PROBLEM 7–24A Behavioral Aspects of Budgeting [LO1]**

Five years ago, Jack Cadence left his position at a large company to start Advanced Technologies Co. (ATC), a software design company. ATC's first product was a unique software package that seamlessly integrates networked PCs. Robust sales of this initial product permitted the company to begin development of other software products and to hire additional personnel. The staff at ATC quickly grew from three people working out of Cadence's basement to over 70 individuals working in leased spaces at an industrial park. Continued growth led Cadence to hire seasoned marketing, distribution, and production managers and an experienced accountant, Bill Cross.

Recently, Cadence decided that the company had become too large to run on an informal basis and that a formalized planning and control program centered around a budget was necessary. Cadence asked the accountant, Bill Cross, to work with him in developing the initial budget for ATC.

Cadence forecasted sales revenues based on his projections for both the market growth for the initial software and successful completion of new products. Cross used this data to construct the master budget for the company, which he then broke down into departmental budgets. Cadence and Cross met a number of times over a three-week period to hammer out the details of the budgets.

When Cadence and Cross were satisfied with their work, the various departmental budgets were distributed to the department managers with a cover letter explaining ATC's new budgeting system. The letter requested everyone's assistance in working together to achieve the budget objectives.

Several of the department managers were displeased with how the budgeting process was undertaken. In discussing the situation among themselves, they felt that some of the budget projections were overly optimistic and not realistically attainable.

***Required:***

1. How does the budgeting process Cadence and Cross used at ATC differ from recommended practice?
2. What are the behavioral implications of the way Cadence and Cross went about preparing the master budget?

(CMA, adapted)

**PROBLEM 7–25A Completing a Master Budget [LO2, LO4, LO7, LO8, LO9, LO10]**

The following data relate to the operations of Picanuy Corporation, a wholesale distributor of consumer goods:

CHECK FIGURE
(2) March purchases: $55,300; (5) Net income: $7,690

| | |
|---|---|
| Current assets as of December 31: | |
| Cash | $6,000 |
| Accounts receivable | $36,000 |
| Inventory | $9,800 |
| Buildings and equipment, net | $110,885 |
| Accounts payable | $32,550 |
| Capital stock | $100,000 |
| Retained earnings | $30,135 |

a. The gross margin is 30% of sales. (In other words, cost of goods sold is 70% of sales.)
b. Actual and budgeted sales data are as follows:

| | |
|---|---|
| December (actual) | $60,000 |
| January | $70,000 |
| February | $80,000 |
| March | $85,000 |
| April | $55,000 |

c. Sales are 40% for cash and 60% on credit. Credit sales are collected in the month following sale. The accounts receivable at December 31 are the result of December credit sales.
d. Each month's ending inventory should equal 20% of the following month's budgeted cost of goods sold.
e. One-quarter of a month's inventory purchases is paid for in the month of purchase; the other three-quarters is paid for in the following month. The accounts payable at December 31 are the result of December purchases of inventory.
f. Monthly expenses are as follows: commissions, $12,000; rent, $1,800; other expenses (excluding depreciation), 8% of sales. Assume that these expenses are paid monthly. Depreciation is $2,400 for the quarter and includes depreciation on new assets acquired during the quarter.
g. Equipment will be acquired for cash: $3,000 in January and $8,000 in February.

h. Management would like to maintain a minimum cash balance of $5,000 at the end of each month. The company has an agreement with a local bank that allows the company to borrow in increments of $1,000 at the beginning of each month, up to a total loan balance of $50,000. The interest rate on these loans is 1% per month, and for simplicity, we will assume that interest is not compounded. The company would, as far as it is able, repay the loan plus accumulated interest at the end of the quarter.

***Required:***

Using the data above:

1. Complete the following schedule:

**Schedule of Expected Cash Collections**

| | January | February | March | Quarter |
|---|---|---|---|---|
| Cash sales | $28,000 | | | |
| Credit sales | 36,000 | | | |
| Total collections | $64,000 | | | |

2. Complete the following:

**Merchandise Purchases Budget**

| | January | February | March | Quarter |
|---|---|---|---|---|
| Budgeted cost of goods sold | $49,000* | | | |
| Add desired ending inventory | 11,200† | | | |
| Total needs | 60,200 | | | |
| Less beginning inventory | 9,800 | | | |
| Required purchases | $50,400 | | | |

*$70,000 sales × 70% = $49,000.
†$80,000 × 70% × 20% = $11,200.

**Schedule of Expected Cash Disbursements—Merchandise Purchases**

| | January | February | March | Quarter |
|---|---|---|---|---|
| December purchases | $32,550* | | | $32,550 |
| January purchases | 12,600 | $37,800 | | 50,400 |
| February purchases | | | | |
| March purchases | | | | |
| Total disbursements | $45,150 | | | |

*Beginning balance of the accounts payable.

3. Complete the following schedule:

**Schedule of Expected Cash Disbursements—Selling and Administrative Expenses**

| | January | February | March | Quarter |
|---|---|---|---|---|
| Commissions | $12,000 | | | |
| Rent | 1,800 | | | |
| Other expenses | 5,600 | | | |
| Total disbursements | $19,400 | | | |

4. Complete the following cash budget:

| Cash Budget | January | February | March | Quarter |
|---|---|---|---|---|
| Cash balance, beginning | $ 6,000 | | | |
| Add cash collections | 64,000 | | | |
| Total cash available | 70,000 | | | |
| Less cash disbursements: | | | | |
| For inventory | 45,150 | | | |
| For operating expenses | 19,400 | | | |
| For equipment | 3,000 | | | |
| Total cash disbursements | 67,550 | | | |
| Excess (deficiency) of cash | 2,450 | | | |
| Financing | | | | |
| Etc. | | | | |

5. Prepare an absorption costing income statement, similar to the one shown in Schedule 9 in the chapter, for the quarter ended March 31.
6. Prepare a balance sheet as of March 31.

**PROBLEM 7–26A Completing a Master Budget [LO2, LO4, LO7, LO8, LO9, LO10]**

CHECK FIGURE
(2a) May purchases: $51,900; (5) Net income: $26,700

Nordic Company, a merchandising company, prepares its master budget on a quarterly basis. The following data have been assembled to assist in preparation of the master budget for the second quarter.

a. As of March 31 (the end of the prior quarter), the company's balance sheet showed the following account balances:

| | | |
|---|---|---|
| Cash | $ 9,000 | |
| Accounts receivable | 48,000 | |
| Inventory | 12,600 | |
| Buildings and equipment (net) | 214,100 | |
| Accounts payable | | $ 18,300 |
| Common stock | | 190,000 |
| Retained earnings | | 75,400 |
| | $283,700 | $283,700 |

b. Actual sales for March and budgeted sales for April–July are as follows:

| | |
|---|---|
| March (actual) | $60,000 |
| April | $70,000 |
| May | $85,000 |
| June | $90,000 |
| July | $50,000 |

c. Sales are 20% for cash and 80% on credit. All payments on credit sales are collected in the month following the sale. The accounts receivable at March 31 are a result of March credit sales.
d. The company's gross margin percentage is 40% of sales. (In other words, cost of goods sold is 60% of sales.)
e. Monthly selling and administrative expenses are budgeted as follows: salaries and wages, $7,500 per month; shipping, 6% of sales; advertising, $6,000 per month; other expenses, 4% of sales. Depreciation, including depreciation on new assets acquired during the quarter, will be $6,000 for the quarter.
f. Each month's ending inventory should equal 30% of the following month's cost of goods sold.
g. Half of a month's inventory purchases are paid for in the month of purchase and half in the following month.

h. Equipment purchases during the quarter will be as follows: April, $11,500; and May, $3,000.
i. Dividends totaling $3,500 will be declared and paid in June.
j. Management wants to maintain a minimum cash balance of $8,000. The company has an agreement with a local bank that allows the company to borrow in increments of $1,000 at the beginning of each month, up to a total loan balance of $20,000. The interest rate on these loans is 1% per month, and for simplicity, we will assume that interest is not compounded. The company would, as far as it is able, repay the loan plus accumulated interest at the end of the quarter.

***Required:***

Using the data above, complete the following statements and schedules for the second quarter:

1. Schedule of expected cash collections:

| | April | May | June | Total |
|---|---|---|---|---|
| Cash sales | $14,000 | | | |
| Credit sales | 48,000 | | | |
| Total collections | $62,000 | | | |

2. a. Merchandise purchases budget:

| | April | May | June | Total |
|---|---|---|---|---|
| Budgeted cost of goods sold | $42,000* | $51,000 | | |
| Add desired ending inventory | 15,300† | | | |
| Total needs | 57,300 | | | |
| Less beginning inventory | 12,600 | | | |
| Required purchases | $44,700 | | | |

*$70,000 sales × 60% = $42,000.
†$51,000 × 30% = $15,300.

b. Schedule of expected cash disbursements for merchandise purchases:

| | April | May | June | Total |
|---|---|---|---|---|
| For March purchases | $18,300 | | | $18,300 |
| For April purchases | 22,350 | $22,350 | | 44,700 |
| For May purchases | | | | |
| For June purchases | | | | |
| Total cash disbursements for purchases | $40,650 | | | |

3. Schedule of expected cash disbursements for selling and administrative expenses:

| | April | May | June | Total |
|---|---|---|---|---|
| Salaries and wages | $ 7,500 | | | |
| Shipping | 4,200 | | | |
| Advertising | 6,000 | | | |
| Other expenses | 2,800 | | | |
| Total cash disbursements for selling and administrative expenses | $20,500 | | | |

4. Cash budget:

| | April | May | June | Total |
|---|---|---|---|---|
| Cash balance, beginning | $ 9,000 | | | |
| Add cash collections | 62,000 | | | |
| Total cash available | 71,000 | | | |
| Less cash disbursements: | | | | |
| For inventory purchases | 40,650 | | | |
| For selling and administrative expenses | 20,500 | | | |
| For equipment purchases | 11,500 | | | |
| For dividends | — | | | |
| Total cash disbursements | 72,650 | | | |
| Excess (deficiency) of cash | (1,650) | | | |
| Financing | | | | |
| Etc. | | | | |

5. Prepare an absorption costing income statement for the quarter ending June 30 as shown in Schedule 9 in the chapter.
6. Prepare a balance sheet as of June 30.

## BUILDING YOUR SKILLS

### ANALYTICAL THINKING [LO1]

Tom Emory and Jim Morris strolled back to their plant from the administrative offices of Ferguson & Son Manufacturing Company. Tom is manager of the machine shop in the company's factory; Jim is manager of the equipment maintenance department.

The men had just attended the monthly performance evaluation meeting for plant department heads. These meetings had been held on the third Tuesday of each month since Robert Ferguson, Jr., the president's son, had become plant manager a year earlier.

As they were walking, Tom Emory spoke: "Boy, I hate those meetings! I never know whether my department's accounting reports will show good or bad performance. I'm beginning to expect the worst. If the accountants say I saved the company a dollar, I'm called 'Sir,' but if I spend even a little too much—boy, do I get in trouble. I don't know if I can hold on until I retire."

Tom had just been given the worst evaluation he had ever received in his long career with Ferguson & Son. He was the most respected of the experienced machinists in the company. He had been with Ferguson & Son for many years and was promoted to supervisor of the machine shop when the company expanded and moved to its present location. The president (Robert Ferguson, Sr.) had often stated that the company's success was due to the high-quality work of machinists like Tom. As supervisor, Tom stressed the importance of craftsmanship and told his workers that he wanted no sloppy work coming from his department.

When Robert Ferguson, Jr., became the plant manager, he directed that monthly performance comparisons be made between actual and budgeted costs for each department. The departmental budgets were intended to encourage the supervisors to reduce inefficiencies and to seek cost reduction opportunities. The company controller was instructed to have his staff "tighten" the budget slightly whenever a department attained its budget in a given month; this was done to reinforce the plant manager's desire to reduce costs. The young plant manager often stressed the importance of continued progress toward attaining the budget; he also made it known that he kept a file of these performance reports for future reference when he succeeded his father.

Tom Emory's conversation with Jim Morris continued as follows:

***Emory:*** I really don't understand. We've worked so hard to meet the budget, and the minute we do so they tighten it on us. We can't work any faster and still maintain quality. I think my men are ready to quit trying. Besides, those reports don't tell the whole story. We always seem to be interrupting the big jobs for all those small rush orders. All that setup and machine adjustment time is killing us. And quite frankly, Jim, you were no help. When our hydraulic press broke down last month, your people were nowhere to be found. We had to take it apart ourselves and got stuck with all that idle time.

***Morris:*** I'm sorry about that, Tom, but you know my department has had trouble making budget, too. We were running well behind at the time of that problem, and if we'd spent a day on that old machine, we would never have made it up. Instead we made the scheduled inspections of the forklift trucks because we knew we could do those in less than the budgeted time.

***Emory:*** Well, Jim, at least you have some options. I'm locked into what the scheduling department assigns to me and you know they're being harassed by sales for those special orders. Incidentally, why didn't your report show all the supplies you guys wasted last month when you were working in Bill's department?

***Morris:*** We're not out of the woods on that deal yet. We charged the maximum we could to other work and haven't even reported some of it yet.

***Emory:*** Well, I'm glad you have a way of avoiding the pressure. The accountants seem to know everything that's happening in my department, sometimes even before I do. I thought all that budget and accounting stuff was supposed to help, but it just gets me into trouble. It's all a big pain. I'm trying to put out quality work; they're trying to save pennies.

***Required:***
1. Identify the problems that exist in Ferguson & Son Manufacturing Company's budgetary control system and explain how the problems are likely to reduce the effectiveness of the system.
2. Explain how Ferguson & Son Manufacturing Company's budgetary control system could be revised to improve its effectiveness.

(CMA, adapted)

## CASE [LO2, LO4, LO8, LO9, LO10]

eXcel

CHECK FIGURE
(2) June ending cash balance: $10,730;
(3) Net income: $151,880

You have just been hired as a management trainee by Cravat Sales Company, a nationwide distributor of a designer's silk ties. The company has an exclusive franchise on the distribution of the ties, and sales have grown so rapidly over the last few years that it has become necessary to add new members to the management team. You have been given responsibility for all planning and budgeting. Your first assignment is to prepare a master budget for the next three months, starting April 1. You are anxious to make a favorable impression on the president and have assembled the information below.

The company desires a minimum ending cash balance each month of $10,000. The ties are sold to retailers for $8 each. Recent and forecasted sales in units are as follows:

| | | | |
|---|---|---|---|
| January (actual) | 20,000 | June | 60,000 |
| February (actual) | 24,000 | July | 40,000 |
| March (actual) | 28,000 | August | 36,000 |
| April | 35,000 | September | 32,000 |
| May | 45,000 | | |

The large buildup in sales before and during June is due to Father's Day. Ending inventories are supposed to equal 90% of the next month's sales in units. The ties cost the company $5 each.

Purchases are paid for as follows: 50% in the month of purchase and the remaining 50% in the following month. All sales are on credit, with no discount, and payable within 15 days. The company has found, however, that only 25% of a month's sales are collected by month-end. An additional 50% is collected in the following month, and the remaining 25% is collected in the second month following sale. Bad debts have been negligible.

The company's monthly selling and administrative expenses are given below:

| | |
|---|---|
| Variable: | |
| Sales commissions | $1 per tie |
| Fixed: | |
| Wages and salaries | $22,000 |
| Utilities | $14,000 |
| Insurance | $1,200 |
| Depreciation | $1,500 |
| Miscellaneous | $3,000 |

All selling and administrative expenses are paid during the month, in cash, with the exception of depreciation and insurance expired. Land will be purchased during May for $25,000 cash. The company declares dividends of $12,000 each quarter, payable in the first month of the following quarter. The company's balance sheet at March 31 is given below:

| | |
|---|---|
| **Assets** | |
| Cash | $ 14,000 |
| Accounts receivable ($48,000 February sales; $168,000 March sales) | 216,000 |
| Inventory (31,500 units) | 157,500 |
| Prepaid insurance | 14,400 |
| Fixed assets, net of depreciation | 172,700 |
| Total assets | $574,600 |
| **Liabilities and Stockholders' Equity** | |
| Accounts payable | $ 85,750 |
| Dividends payable | 12,000 |
| Common stock | 300,000 |
| Retained earnings | 176,850 |
| Total liabilities and stockholders' equity | $574,600 |

The company has an agreement with a bank that allows it to borrow in increments of $1,000 at the beginning of each month, up to a total loan balance of $140,000. The interest rate on these loans is 1% per month, and for simplicity, we will assume that interest is not compounded. At the end of the quarter, the company would pay the bank all of the accumulated interest on the loan and as much of the loan as possible (in increments of $1,000), while still retaining at least $10,000 in cash.

***Required:***

Prepare a master budget for the three-month period ending June 30. Include the following detailed budgets:

1. a. A sales budget by month and in total.
   b. A schedule of expected cash collections from sales, by month and in total.
   c. A merchandise purchases budget in units and in dollars. Show the budget by month and in total.
   d. A schedule of expected cash disbursements for merchandise purchases, by month and in total.
2. A cash budget. Show the budget by month and in total.
3. A budgeted income statement for the three-month period ending June 30. Use the contribution approach.
4. A budgeted balance sheet as of June 30.

## ETHICS CHALLENGE [LO1]

Granger Stokes, managing partner of the venture capital firm of Halston and Stokes, was dissatisfied with the top management of PrimeDrive, a manufacturer of computer disk drives. Halston and Stokes had invested $20 million in PrimeDrive, and the return on their investment had been below expectations for several years. In a tense meeting of the board of directors of PrimeDrive, Stokes exercised his firm's rights as the major equity investor in PrimeDrive and fired PrimeDrive's chief executive officer (CEO). He then quickly moved to have the board of directors of PrimeDrive appoint himself as the new CEO.

Stokes prided himself on his hard-driving management style. At the first management meeting, he asked two of the managers to stand and fired them on the spot, just to show everyone who was in control of the company. At the budget review meeting that followed, he ripped up the departmental budgets that had been submitted for his review and yelled at the managers for their "wimpy, do nothing targets." He then ordered everyone to submit new budgets calling for at least a 40% increase in sales volume and announced that he would not accept excuses for results that fell below budget.

Keri Kalani, an accountant working for the production manager at PrimeDrive, discovered toward the end of the year that her boss had not been scrapping defective disk drives that had been returned by customers. Instead, he had been shipping them in new cartons to other customers to avoid booking losses. Quality control had deteriorated during the year as a result of the push for increased volume, and returns of defective disk drives were running as high as 15% of the new drives shipped. When she confronted her boss with her discovery, he told her to mind her own business. And then, to justify his actions, he said, "All of us managers are finding ways to hit Stokes's targets."

***Required:***

1. Is Granger Stokes using budgets as a planning and control tool?
2. What are the behavioral consequences of the way budgets are being used at PrimeDrive?
3. What, if anything, do you think Keri Kalani should do?

### COMMUNICATING IN PRACTICE [LO1]

In recent years, public universities have experienced major budget cuts due to reduced funding from their state governments. These budget cuts usually occur at the most inopportune time—during the school year when contractual commitments with faculty and staff had been signed, programs had been planned, and students were enrolled and taking classes.

***Required:***

1. Should the administration be "fair" to all affected and institute across-the-board cuts whenever the state announces a reduction in funding?
2. If not across-the-board cutbacks in programs, then would you recommend more focused reductions, and if so, what priorities would you establish for bringing spending in line with revenues?
3. Since these usually are not one-time-only cutbacks, how would you manage continuous, long-term reductions in budgets extending over a period of years?
4. Should the decision-making process be top-down (centralized with top administrators) or bottom-up (participative)? Why?
5. How should issues such as protect-your-turf mentality, resistance to change, and consensus building be dealt with?

### A LOOK BACK

In Chapter 7, we discussed the budgeting process and each of the schedules in the master budget.

### A LOOK AT THIS CHAPTER

Chapter 8 begins our discussion of management control and performance measures. We explain how to prepare flexible budgets and how to compare them to actual results for the purposes of computing revenue and spending variances. We also describe how standards are used to isolate the effects of various factors on actual results. In particular, we compute material, labor, and overhead variances.

### A LOOK AHEAD

In Chapter 9, we continue the discussion of management control and performance measures by focusing on how decentralized organizations are managed.

# 8 Flexible Budgets, Standard Costs, and Variance Analysis

## CHAPTER OUTLINE

**The Variance Analysis Cycle**

**Flexible Budgets**

- Characteristics of a Flexible Budget
- Deficiencies of the Static Planning Budget
- How a Flexible Budget Works

**Flexible Budget Variances**

- Revenue Variances
- Spending Variances

**Flexible Budgets with Multiple Cost Drivers**

**Standard Costs—Setting the Stage**

- Setting Direct Materials Standards
- Setting Direct Labor Standards
- Setting Variable Manufacturing Overhead Standards
- Using Standards in Flexible Budgets

**A General Model for Standard Cost Variance Analysis**

**Using Standard Costs—Direct Materials Variances**

- The Materials Quantity Variance
- The Materials Price Variance

**Using Standard Costs—Direct Labor Variances**

- The Labor Efficiency Variance
- The Labor Rate Variance

**Using Standard Costs—Variable Manufacturing Overhead Variances**

- The Variable Manufacturing Overhead Efficiency and Rate Variances

**An Important Subtlety in the Materials Variances**

## DECISION FEATURE

# Managing Materials and Labor

**Schneider Electric**'s Oxford, Ohio, plant manufactures *busways* that transport electricity from its point of entry into a building to remote locations throughout the building. The plant's managers pay close attention to direct material costs because they are more than half of the plant's total manufacturing costs. To help control scrap rates for direct materials such as copper, steel, and aluminum, the accounting department prepares direct materials quantity variances. These variances compare the standard quantity of direct materials that should have been used to make a product (according to computations by the plant's engineers) to the amount of direct materials that were actually used. Keeping a close eye on these differences helps to identify and deal with the causes of excessive scrap, such as an inadequately trained machine operator, poor quality raw material inputs, or a malfunctioning machine.

Because direct labor is also a significant component of the plant's total manufacturing costs, the management team daily monitors the direct labor efficiency variance. This variance compares the standard amount of labor time allowed to make a product to the actual amount of labor time used. When idle workers cause an unfavorable labor efficiency variance, managers temporarily move workers from departments with slack to departments with a backlog of work to be done.

Source: Author's conversation with Doug Taylor, plant controller, Schneider Electric's Oxford, Ohio, plant.

## LEARNING OBJECTIVES

*After studying Chapter 8, you should be able to:*

**LO1** Prepare a flexible budget.

**LO2** Prepare a report showing revenue and spending variances.

**LO3** Prepare a flexible budget with more than one cost driver.

**LO4** Compute the direct materials quantity and price variances and explain their significance.

**LO5** Compute the direct labor efficiency and rate variances and explain their significance.

**LO6** Compute the variable manufacturing overhead efficiency and rate variances and explain their significance.

**LO7** (Appendix 8A) Compute and interpret the fixed overhead volume and budget variances.

**LO8** (Appendix 8B) Prepare journal entries to record standard costs and variances.

In the last chapter we explored how budgets are developed before a period begins. In this chapter we explain how budgets can be adjusted to help guide actual operations and influence the performance evaluation process. For example, an organization's actual spending will rarely equal its budgeted spending as determined at the beginning of the period. The reason is that the actual level of activity (such as unit sales) will rarely be the same as the budgeted activity; therefore, many actual costs and revenues will naturally differ from what was budgeted. Should a manager be penalized for spending 10% more than budgeted for a variable cost like direct materials if unit sales are 10% higher than budgeted? Of course not. After studying this chapter, you'll know how to adjust a budget to enable meaningful comparisons to actual results.

## THE VARIANCE ANALYSIS CYCLE

Companies use the *variance analysis cycle,* as illustrated in Exhibit 8–1, to compare budgets to actual results for the purposes of solving problems and evaluating performance. The cycle begins with the preparation of performance reports in the accounting department. These reports highlight variances, which are the differences between the actual results and what should have occurred according to the budget. The variances raise questions. Why did this variance occur? Why is this variance larger than it was last period? The significant variances are investigated to discover their root causes and corrective actions are taken. Then, next period's operations are carried out and the cycle begins again with the preparation of a new performance report for the latest period. The emphasis should be on highlighting problems, finding their root causes, and then taking corrective action, rather than seeking to assign blame.

Managers frequently use the concept of *management by exception* in conjunction with the variance analysis cycle. **Management by exception** is a management system that compares actual results to a budget so that significant deviations can be flagged as exceptions and investigated further. This approach enables managers to focus on the most important variances while bypassing trivial discrepancies between the budget and actual results. For example, a variance of $5 is probably not big enough to warrant attention, whereas a variance of $5,000 might be worth tracking down. Another clue is the size of the variance relative to the amount of spending. A variance that is only 0.1% of spending on an item is probably caused by random factors. On the other hand, a variance of 10% of spending is much more likely to be a signal that something is wrong.

Next, we explain how service organizations use flexible budgets to analyze variances followed by a discussion of how companies can use standard costs for those same purposes.

**EXHIBIT 8–1**
The Variance Analysis Cycle

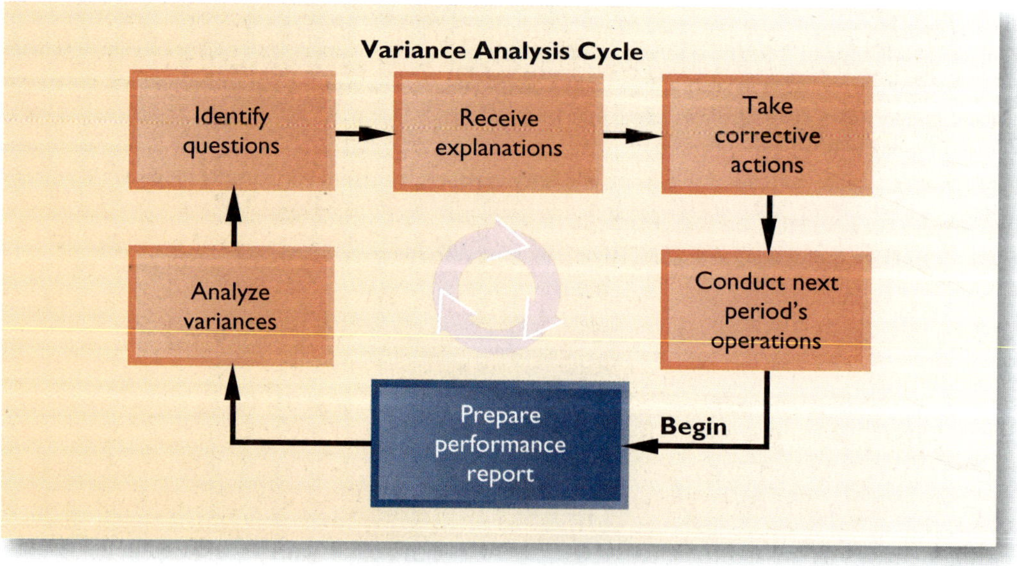

# FLEXIBLE BUDGETS

## Characteristics of a Flexible Budget

LEARNING OBJECTIVE 1

Prepare a flexible budget.

The budgets that we explored in the last chapter were *planning budgets.* A **planning budget** is prepared before the period begins and is valid for only the planned level of activity. A static planning budget is suitable for planning but is inappropriate for evaluating how well costs are controlled. If the actual level of activity differs from what was planned, it would be misleading to compare actual costs to the static, unchanged planning budget. If activity is higher than expected, variable costs should be higher than expected; and if activity is lower than expected, variable costs should be lower than expected.

*Flexible budgets* take into account how changes in activity affect costs. A **flexible budget** is an estimate of what revenues and costs should have been, given the actual level of activity for the period. When a flexible budget is used in performance evaluation, actual costs are compared to what the costs *should have been for the actual level of activity during the period* rather than to the static planning budget. This is a very important distinction. If adjustments for the level of activity are not made, it is very difficult to interpret discrepancies between budgeted and actual costs.

## Deficiencies of the Static Planning Budget

To illustrate the difference between a static planning budget and a flexible budget, consider Rick's Hairstyling, an upscale hairstyling salon located in Beverly Hills that is owned and managed by Rick Manzi. At the end of February, Rick prepared the March budget that appears in Exhibit 8–2. Rick believes that the number of customers served in a month (also known as the number of client-visits) is the best way to measure the overall level of activity in his salon. A customer who comes into the salon and has his or her hair styled is counted as one client-visit.

Note that the term *revenue* is used in the planning budget rather than *sales.* We use the term revenue throughout the chapter because some organizations have sources of revenue other than sales. For example, donations, as well as sales, are counted as revenue in non-profit organizations.

Rick has identified eight major categories of costs—wages and salaries, hairstyling supplies, client gratuities, electricity, rent, liability insurance, employee health insurance, and miscellaneous. Client gratuities consist of flowers, candies, and glasses of champagne that Rick gives to his customers while they are in the salon. He has also estimated a cost

**EXHIBIT 8–2**
Planning Budget

**Rick's Hairstyling**
**Planning Budget**
**For the Month Ended March 31**

| | |
|---|---|
| *Budgeted* client-visits (*q*) | 1,000 |
| Revenue ($180.00*q*) | $180,000 |
| Expenses: | |
| Wages and salaries ($65,000 + $37.00*q*) | 102,000 |
| Hairstyling supplies ($1.50*q*) | 1,500 |
| Client gratuities ($4.10*q*) | 4,100 |
| Electricity ($1,500 + $0.10*q*) | 1,600 |
| Rent ($28,500) | 28,500 |
| Liability insurance ($2,800) | 2,800 |
| Employee health insurance ($21,300) | 21,300 |
| Miscellaneous ($1,200 + $0.20*q*) | 1,400 |
| Total expense | 163,200 |
| Net operating income | $ 16,800 |

**EXHIBIT 8–3**
Actual Results—Income Statement

| Rick's Hairstyling<br>Income Statement<br>For the Month Ended March 31 | |
|---|---|
| *Actual* client-visits | 1,100 |
| Revenue | $194,200 |
| Expenses: | |
| Wages and salaries | 106,900 |
| Hairstyling supplies | 1,620 |
| Client gratuities | 6,870 |
| Electricity | 1,550 |
| Rent | 28,500 |
| Liability insurance | 2,800 |
| Employee health insurance | 22,600 |
| Miscellaneous | 2,130 |
| Total expense | 172,970 |
| Net operating income | $ 21,230 |

formula for each cost. For example, the cost formula for electricity is $1,500 + $0.10*q*, where *q* equals the number of client-visits. In other words, electricity is a mixed cost with a $1,500 fixed element and a $0.10 per client-visit variable element. Once the budgeted level of activity was set at 1,000 client-visits, Rick computed the budgeted amount for each line item in the budget. For example, using the cost formula, the budgeted cost for electricity was set at $1,600 (= $1,500 + $0.10 × 1,000).

At the end of March, Rick found that his actual profit was $21,230 as shown in the income statement in Exhibit 8–3. It is important to realize that the actual results are *not* determined by plugging the actual number of client-visits into the revenue and cost formulas. The formulas are simply estimates of what the revenues and costs should be for a given level of activity. What actually happens usually differs from what is supposed to happen.

Referring back to Exhibit 8–2, the budgeted net operating income was $16,800, so the actual profit was substantially higher than planned at the beginning of the month. This was, of course, good news, but Rick wanted to know more. Business was up by 10%—the salon had 1,100 client-visits instead of the budgeted 1,000 client-visits. Could this alone explain the higher net income? The answer is no. An increase in net operating income of 10% would have resulted in net operating income of only $18,480 (= 1.1 × $16,800), not the $21,230 actually earned during the month. What is responsible for this better outcome? Higher prices? Lower costs? Something else? Whatever the cause, Rick would like to know the answer and then hopefully repeat the same performance next month.

In an attempt to analyze what happened in March, Rick prepared the report comparing actual to budgeted costs that appears in Exhibit 8–4. Note that most of the variances in this report are labeled unfavorable (U) rather than favorable (F) even though net operating income was actually higher than expected. For example, wages and salaries show an unfavorable variance of $4,900 because the budget called for wages and salaries of $102,000, whereas the actual wages and salaries expense was $106,900. The problem with the report, as Rick immediately realized, is that it compares revenues and costs at one level of activity (1,000 client-visits) to revenues and costs at a different level of activity (1,100 client-visits). This is like comparing apples to oranges. Because Rick had 100 more client-visits than expected, some of his costs should be higher than budgeted. From Rick's standpoint, the increase in activity was good; however, it appears to be having a negative impact on most of the costs in the report. Rick knew that something would have to be done to make the report more meaningful, but he was unsure of what to do. So he contacted his accountant, Victoria Kho, and asked her to analyze his salon's performance using the data in Exhibits 8–2 and 8–3.

**EXHIBIT 8–4**
Comparison of Static Planning Budget to Actual Results

**Rick's Hairstyling**
**Comparison of Planning Budget to Actual Results**
**For the Month Ended March 31**

| | Planning Budget | Actual Results | Variances |
|---|---|---|---|
| Client-visits | 1,000 | 1,100 | |
| Revenue | $180,000 | $194,200 | $14,200 F |
| Expenses: | | | |
| Wages and salaries | 102,000 | 106,900 | 4,900 U |
| Hairstyling supplies | 1,500 | 1,620 | 120 U |
| Client gratuities | 4,100 | 6,870 | 2,770 U |
| Electricity | 1,600 | 1,550 | 50 F |
| Rent | 28,500 | 28,500 | 0 |
| Liability insurance | 2,800 | 2,800 | 0 |
| Employee health insurance | 21,300 | 22,600 | 1,300 U |
| Miscellaneous | 1,400 | 2,130 | 730 U |
| Total expense | 163,200 | 172,970 | 9,770 U |
| Net operating income | $ 16,800 | $ 21,230 | $ 4,430 F |

## How a Flexible Budget Works

Victoria responded to Rick's request by preparing the flexible budget shown in Exhibit 8–5. Her flexible budget shows what the *revenues and costs should have been given the actual level of activity* in March. She calculated the expenses in her flexible budget by using Rick's cost formulas from Exhibit 8–2 to estimate what each expense should have been for 1,100 client-visits—the actual level of activity. For example, using the cost formula $1,500 + $0.10*q*, the cost of electricity in March *should have been* $1,610 (= $1,500 + $0.10 × 1,100). Note that the amounts of rent ($28,500), liability insurance ($2,800), and employee health insurance ($21,300) in Victoria's flexible budget equal the corresponding amounts included in Rick's planning budget. This occurs because fixed costs are not affected by the activity level.

We can see from the flexible budget that the net operating income in March *should have been* $30,510, but recall from Exhibit 8–3 that the net operating income was actually only $21,230. The results are not as good as we thought. Why? We will answer that question shortly.

**EXHIBIT 8–5**
Flexible Budget Based on Actual Activity

**Rick's Hairstyling**
**Flexible Budget**
**For the Month Ended March 31**

| | |
|---|---|
| *Actual* client-visits (*q*) | 1,100 |
| Revenue ($180.00*q*) | $198,000 |
| Expenses: | |
| Wages and salaries ($65,000 + $37.00*q*) | 105,700 |
| Hairstyling supplies ($1.50*q*) | 1,650 |
| Client gratuities ($4.10*q*) | 4,510 |
| Electricity ($1,500 + $0.10*q*) | 1,610 |
| Rent ($28,500) | 28,500 |
| Liability insurance ($2,800) | 2,800 |
| Employee health insurance ($21,300) | 21,300 |
| Miscellaneous ($1,200 + $0.20*q*) | 1,420 |
| Total expense | 167,490 |
| Net operating income | $ 30,510 |

To summarize to this point, Rick had budgeted for a profit of $16,800. The actual profit was quite a bit higher—$21,230. However, Victoria's analysis shows that given the actual number of client-visits in March, the profit should have been even higher—$30,510. What are the causes of these discrepancies? Rick would certainly like to build on the positive factors, while working to reduce the negative factors. But what are they?

## FLEXIBLE BUDGET VARIANCES

**LEARNING OBJECTIVE 2**

Prepare a report showing revenue and spending variances.

Recall that the flexible budget based on the actual level of activity in Exhibit 8–5 shows what *should have happened given the actual level of activity.* Therefore, Victoria's next step was to compare the flexible budget to actual results—in essence comparing what should have happened to what actually happened. This is done in Exhibit 8–6.

### Revenue Variances

Focusing first on revenue, the flexible budget indicates that, given the actual level of activity, revenue should have been $198,000. However, actual revenue totaled $194,200. Consequently, revenue was $3,800 less than it should have been, given the actual number of client-visits for the month. This discrepancy is labeled as a $3,800 U (unfavorable) variance and is called a *revenue variance.* A **revenue variance** is the difference between what the total revenue should have been, given the actual level of activity for the period, and the actual total revenue. If actual revenue exceeds what the revenue should have been, the variance is labeled favorable. If actual revenue is less than what the revenue should have been, the variance is labeled unfavorable. Why would actual revenue be less than or more than it should have been, given the actual level of activity? Basically, the revenue variance is favorable if the average selling price is greater than expected; it is unfavorable if the average selling price is less than expected. This could happen for a variety of reasons including a change in selling price, a different mix of products sold, a change in the amount of discounts given, poor accounting controls, and so on.

**EXHIBIT 8–6**
Revenue and Spending Variances from Comparing the Flexible Budget to the Actual Results

**Rick's Hairstyling**
**Revenue and Spending Variances**
**For the Month Ended March 31**

| | Flexible Budget | Actual Results | Revenue and Spending Variances |
|---|---|---|---|
| Client-visits | 1,100 | 1,100 | |
| Revenue ($180.00*q*) | $198,000 | $194,200 | $3,800 U |
| Expenses: | | | |
| Wages and salaries ($65,000 + $37.00*q*) | 105,700 | 106,900 | 1,200 U |
| Hairstyling supplies ($1.50*q*) | 1,650 | 1,620 | 30 F |
| Client gratuities ($4.10*q*) | 4,510 | 6,870 | 2,360 U |
| Electricity ($1,500 + $0.10*q*) | 1,610 | 1,550 | 60 F |
| Rent ($28,500) | 28,500 | 28,500 | 0 |
| Liability insurance ($2,800) | 2,800 | 2,800 | 0 |
| Employee health insurance ($21,300) | 21,300 | 22,600 | 1,300 U |
| Miscellaneous ($1,200 + $0.20*q*) | 1,420 | 2,130 | 710 U |
| Total expense | 167,490 | 172,970 | 5,480 U |
| Net operating income | $ 30,510 | $ 21,230 | $9,280 U |

## Spending Variances

Focusing next on costs, the flexible budget indicates that electricity costs should have been $1,610 for the 1,100 client-visits in March. However, the actual electricity cost was $1,550. Because the cost was $60 less than we would have expected for the actual level of activity during the period, it is labeled as a favorable variance, $60 F. This is an example of a *spending variance*. A **spending variance** is the difference between how much a cost should have been, given the actual level of activity, and the actual amount of the cost. If the actual cost is greater than what the cost should have been, the variance is labeled as unfavorable. If the actual cost is less than what the cost should have been, the variance is labeled as favorable. Why would a cost have a favorable or unfavorable variance? There are many possible explanations including paying a higher price for inputs than should have been paid, using too many inputs for the actual level of activity, a change in technology, and so on. We will explore these types of explanations in greater detail when we begin discussing standard costs.

Note from Exhibit 8–6 that the overall net operating income variance is $9,280 U (unfavorable). This means that given the actual level of activity for the period, the net operating income was $9,280 lower than it should have been. There are a number of reasons for this. The most prominent is the unfavorable revenue variance of $3,800. Next in line is the $2,360 U (unfavorable) variance for client gratuities. Looking at this in another way, client gratuities were more than 50% larger than they should have been according to the flexible budget. This is a variance that Rick would almost certainly want to investigate further. He may find that this unfavorable variance is not necessarily a bad thing. It is possible, for example, that more lavish use of gratuities led to the 10% increase in client-visits.

Exhibit 8–6 also includes a $1,300 U (unfavorable) variance related to employee health insurance, thereby highlighting how a fixed cost can have a spending variance. While fixed costs do not depend on the level of activity, the actual amount of a fixed cost can differ from the estimated amount included in a flexible budget. For example, perhaps Rick's employee health insurance premiums unexpectedly increased by $1,300 during March.

In conclusion, the revenue and spending variances in Exhibit 8–6 will help Rick better understand why his actual net operating income differs from what should have happened given the actual level of activity.

### Owner of Micro-Brewery

DECISION POINT

Hops is an essential ingredient in beer. The brewery's budget for the current month, which was based on the production of 800 barrels of beer, allowed for an expense of $960 for hops. The actual production for the month was 850 barrels of beer and the actual cost of the hops used to produce that beer was $1,020. Hops is a variable cost. Do you think the expense for hops for the month was too high?

## FLEXIBLE BUDGETS WITH MULTIPLE COST DRIVERS

**LEARNING OBJECTIVE 3**

Prepare a flexible budget with more than one cost driver.

At Rick's Hairstyling, we have thus far assumed that there is only one cost driver—the number of client-visits. However, in the activity-based costing chapter, we found that more than one cost driver might be needed to adequately explain all of the costs in an organization. For example, some of the costs at Rick's Hairstyling probably depend more on the number of hours that the salon is open for business than the number of client-visits. Specifically, most of Rick's employees are paid salaries, but some are paid on an hourly basis. None of the employees is paid on the basis of the number of customers actually served. Consequently, the cost formula for wages and salaries would be more accurate if

**EXHIBIT 8–7**
Flexible Budget Based on More than One Cost Driver

| Rick's Hairstyling<br>Flexible Budget<br>For the Month Ended March 31 | |
|---|---|
| *Actual* client-visits ($q_1$) | 1,100 |
| *Actual* hours of operation ($q_2$) | 185 |
| Revenue ($180.00$q_1$) | $198,000 |
| Expenses: | |
| Wages and salaries ($65,000 + $220$q_2$) | 105,700 |
| Hairstyling supplies ($1.50$q_1$) | 1,650 |
| Client gratuities ($4.10$q_1$) | 4,510 |
| Electricity ($390 + $0.10$q_1$ + $6.00$q_2$) | 1,610 |
| Rent ($28,500) | 28,500 |
| Liability insurance ($2,800) | 2,800 |
| Employee health insurance ($21,300) | 21,300 |
| Miscellaneous ($1,200 + $0.20$q_1$) | 1,420 |
| Total expense | 167,490 |
| Net operating income | $ 30,510 |

it were stated in terms of the hours of operation rather than the number of client-visits. The cost of electricity is even more complex. Some of the cost is fixed—the heat must be kept at some minimum level even at night when the salon is closed. Some of the cost depends on the number of client-visits—the power consumed by hair dryers depends on the number of customers served. Some of the cost depends on the number of hours the salon is open—the costs of lighting the salon and heating it to a comfortable temperature. Consequently, the cost formula for electricity would be more accurate if it were stated in terms of both the number of client-visits and the hours of operation rather than just in terms of the number of client-visits.

Exhibit 8–7 shows a flexible budget in which these changes have been made. In that flexible budget, two cost drivers are listed—client-visits and hours of operation—where $q_1$ refers to client-visits and $q_2$ refers to hours of operation. For example, wages and salaries depend on the hours of operation and its cost formula is $65,000 + $220$q_2$. Because the salon actually operated 185 hours, the flexible budget amount for wages and salaries is $105,700 (= $65,000 + $220 × 185). The electricity cost depends on both client-visits and the hours of operation and its cost formula is $390 + $0.10$q_1$ + $6.00$q_2$. Because the actual number of client-visits was 1,100 and the salon actually operated for 185 hours, the flexible budget amount for electricity is $1,610 (= $390 + $0.10 × 1,100 + $6.00 × 185).

This revised flexible budget based on both client-visits and hours of operation can be used exactly like we used the earlier flexible budget based on just client-visits to compute revenue and spending variances as in Exhibit 8–6. The difference is that because the cost formulas based on more than one cost driver are more accurate than the cost formulas based on just one cost driver, the variances will also be more accurate.

Beyond using more than one cost driver to improve its budgeting and performance analysis process, a company can also decompose its spending variances into two parts—a part that measures how well resources were used and a part that measures how well the acquisition prices of those resources were controlled. For example, at Rick's Hairstyling, an unfavorable spending variance for hairstyling supplies could be due to using too many supplies or paying too much for the supplies, or some combination of the two. *The remainder of the chapter explains how standard cost systems can be used to decompose spending variances into these two parts.* Shortly, we'll transition from our example involving Rick's Hairstyling to an example involving a manufacturing company called The Colonial Pewter Company. Because standard cost systems are frequently used in manufacturing companies, we are shifting our focus accordingly.

**CONCEPT CHECK**

1. A five-star hotel buys bouquets of flowers to decorate its common areas and guest rooms. Its flexible budget for flowers is $325 per day of operations plus $7.20 per room-day. (A room day is a room rented for one day; a room is decorated with flowers only if it is occupied.) If this month the hotel operated for 30 days and it had 7,680 room-days, what would be the flexible budget amount for flowers for the month?
   a. $55,296
   b. $65,046
   c. $9,750
   d. $332.20
2. Refer to the data in the above question. If the actual spending on flowers for the month was $61,978 and the hotel originally budgeted for 30 operating days and 7,500 room-days, what was the spending variance for the month?
   a. $3,068 Favorable
   b. $3,068 Unfavorable
   c. $1,772 Favorable
   d. $1,772 Unfavorable

## STANDARD COSTS—SETTING THE STAGE

A *standard* is a benchmark for measuring performance. Standards are found everywhere. Your doctor evaluates your weight using standards for individuals of your age, height, and gender. The food we eat in restaurants is prepared using standardized recipes. The buildings we live in conform to standards set in building codes. Standards are also widely used in managerial accounting where they relate to the *quantity* and *cost* (or acquisition price) of inputs used in manufacturing goods or providing services.

Quantity and price standards are set for each major input such as raw materials and labor time.[1] *Quantity standards* specify how much of an input should be used to make a product or provide a service. *Price standards* specify how much should be paid for each unit of the input. Actual quantities and actual costs of inputs are compared to these standards. If either the quantity or the cost of inputs departs significantly from the standards, managers investigate the discrepancy to find the cause of the problem and eliminate it.

Next we'll demonstrate how a company can establish quantity and price standards and use them to calculate variances and manage operations.

**MANAGERIAL ACCOUNTING IN ACTION**
**The Issue**

Colonial Pewter Company

The Colonial Pewter Company makes only one product—an elaborate reproduction of an eighteenth century pewter bookend. The bookend is made largely by hand, using traditional metalworking tools. Consequently, the manufacturing process is labor intensive and requires a high level of skill.

Colonial Pewter has recently expanded its workforce to take advantage of unexpected demand for the bookends as gifts. The company started with a small cadre of experienced pewter workers but has had to hire less experienced workers as a result of the expansion. The president of the company, J. D. Wriston, has called a meeting to discuss production problems. Attending the meeting are Tom Kuchel, the production manager; Janet Warner, the purchasing manager; and Terry Sherman, the corporate controller.

***J. D.:*** I've got a feeling that we aren't getting the production we should out of our new people.

***Tom:*** Give us a chance. Some of the new people have been with the company for less than a month.

[1]Throughout the chapter, we assume that "tight but attainable" practical standards are used rather than ideal standards that can only be attained by the most skilled and efficient employees working at peak effort 100% of the time.

***Janet:*** Let me add that production seems to be wasting an awful lot of material—particularly pewter. That stuff is very expensive.

***Tom:*** What about the shipment of defective pewter that you bought—the one with the iron contamination? That caused us major problems.

***Janet:*** How was I to know it was off-grade? Besides, it was a great deal.

***J. D.:*** Calm down everybody. Let's get the facts before we start attacking each other.

***Tom:*** I agree. The more facts the better.

***J. D.:*** Okay, Terry, it's your turn. Facts are the controller's department.

***Terry:*** I'm afraid I can't provide the answers off the top of my head, but if you give me about a week I can set up a system that can routinely answer questions relating to worker productivity, material waste, and input prices.

***J. D.:*** Let's mark it on our calendars.

## Setting Direct Materials Standards

Terry Sherman's first task was to prepare price and quantity standards for the company's only significant raw material, pewter ingots. The **standard price per unit** for direct materials should reflect the final, delivered cost of the materials. After consulting with purchasing manager Janet Warner, Terry set the standard price of pewter at $4.00 per pound.

The **standard quantity per unit** for direct materials should reflect the amount of material required for each unit of finished product as well as an allowance for waste.[2] After consulting with the production manager, Tom Kuchel, Terry set the quantity standard for pewter at 3.0 pounds per pair of bookends.

Once Terry established the price and quantity standards he computed the standard cost of material per unit of the finished product as follows:

3.0 pounds per unit × $4.00 per pound = $12.00 per unit

## Setting Direct Labor Standards

Direct labor price and quantity standards are usually expressed in terms of a labor rate and labor-hours. The **standard rate per hour** for direct labor should include hourly wages, employment taxes, and fringe benefits. Using wage records and in consultation with the production manager, Terry Sherman determined the standard rate per direct labor-hour to be $22.00. This standard rate reflects the expected "mix" of workers, even though the actual wage rates may vary somewhat from individual to individual due to differing skills or seniority.

The standard direct labor time required to complete a unit of product (called the **standard hours per unit**) is perhaps the single most difficult standard to determine. One approach is for an industrial engineer to do a time and motion study, actually clocking the time required for each task. The standard time should include allowances for breaks, personal needs of employees, cleanup, and machine downtime.

After consulting with the production manager, Terry set the standard for direct labor time at 0.50 direct labor-hours per pair of bookends.[3]

[2]Although allowances for waste, spoilage, and rejects are often built into standards, this practice is often criticized because it contradicts the zero defects goal that underlies many process improvement programs. If various allowances are built into the standard cost, they should be periodically reviewed and reduced over time to reflect improved processes, better training, and better equipment.

[3]Labor quantity standards assume that the production process is labor-paced—if labor works faster, output will go up. However, output in many companies is determined by the processing speed of machines, not by labor efficiency.

Once Terry established the rate and time standards, he computed the standard direct labor cost per unit of product as follows:

0.50 direct labor-hours per unit × \$22.00 per direct labor-hour = \$11.00 per unit

## Setting Variable Manufacturing Overhead Standards

As with direct labor, the price and quantity standards for variable manufacturing overhead are usually expressed in terms of rate and hours. The rate represents *the variable portion of the predetermined overhead rate* discussed in the job-order costing chapter; the hours relate to the activity base that is used to apply overhead to units of product (usually machine-hours or direct labor-hours). At Colonial Pewter, the variable portion of the predetermined overhead rate is \$6.00 per direct labor-hour. Therefore, Terry computed the standard variable manufacturing overhead cost per unit as follows:

0.50 direct labor-hours per unit × \$6.00 per direct labor-hour = \$3.00 per unit

This \$3.00 per unit cost for variable manufacturing overhead appears along with direct materials (\$12 per unit) and direct labor (\$11 per unit) on the *standard cost card* in Exhibit 8–8. A **standard cost card** shows the standard quantities and costs of the inputs required to produce a unit of a specific product. Observe that the **standard cost per unit** for variable manufacturing overhead is computed the same way as for direct materials or direct labor—the standard quantity allowed per unit of the output is multiplied by the standard price. In this case, the standard quantity is expressed as 0.5 direct labor-hours per unit and the standard price (or rate) is expressed as \$6.00 per direct labor-hour.

**EXHIBIT 8–8**
Standard Cost Card—Variable Manufacturing Costs

| Inputs | (1) Standard Quantity or Hours | (2) Standard Price or Rate | Standard Cost (1) × (2) |
|---|---|---|---|
| Direct materials | 3.0 pounds | \$4.00 per pound | \$12.00 |
| Direct labor | 0.50 hours | \$22.00 per hour | 11.00 |
| Variable manufacturing overhead | 0.50 hours | \$6.00 per hour | 3.00 |
| Total standard cost per unit | | | \$26.00 |

## Using Standards in Flexible Budgets

During June Colonial Pewter recorded the following actual results:

| | |
|---|---|
| Actual output in June | 2,000 units |
| Actual direct materials cost in June* | \$24,700 |
| Actual direct labor cost in June | \$22,680 |
| Actual variable manufacturing overhead cost in June | \$7,140 |

*There were no beginning or ending inventories of raw materials in June; all materials purchased were used.

Using the above actual results and the standard cost data from Exhibit 8–8, Colonial Pewter computed the spending variances shown in Exhibit 8–9. The flexible budget and

**EXHIBIT 8–9**
Spending Variances for Manufacturing Costs

**Colonial Pewter**
**Spending Variances**
**For the Month Ended June 30**

| | Flexible Budget | Spending Variances | Actual Results |
|---|---|---|---|
| Bookends produced ($q$) | 2,000 | | 2,000 |
| Direct materials ($12.00$q$) | $24,000 | $700 U | $24,700 |
| Direct labor ($11.00$q$) | $22,000 | $680 U | $22,680 |
| Variable manufacturing overhead ($3.00$q$) | $6,000 | $1,140 U | $7,140 |

actual results columns in Exhibit 8–9 are each based on the actual output of 2,000 bookends. The standard costs of $12.00 per unit for materials, $11.00 per unit for direct labor, and $3.00 per unit for variable manufacturing overhead are each multiplied by the actual output of 2,000 bookends to compute the amounts in the flexible budget column. For example, the standard direct labor cost per unit of $11.00 multiplied by 2,000 bookends equals the direct labor flexible budget of $22,000. The spending variances shown in the exhibit represent the differences between the actual results and the amounts contained in the flexible budget.

While the information in Exhibit 8–9 is useful, it would be even more useful if the spending variances could be broken down into their price-related and quantity-related components. For example, the direct materials spending variance in the report is $700 unfavorable. This means that, given the actual level of production for the period, direct materials costs were too high by $700—at least according to the standard costs. Was this due to higher than expected prices for materials? Or was it due to too much material being used? The standard cost variances we will be discussing in the rest of the chapter are designed to answer these questions.

## A GENERAL MODEL FOR STANDARD COST VARIANCE ANALYSIS

Standard cost variance analysis decomposes spending variances from the flexible budget into two elements—one due to the amount of the input that is used and the other due to the price paid for the input. A **quantity variance** is the difference between how much of an input was actually used and how much should have been used and is stated in dollar terms using the standard price of the input. A **price variance** is the difference between the actual price of an input and its standard price, multiplied by the actual amount of the input purchased.

Why are standards separated into two categories—quantity and price? Quantity variances and price variances usually have different causes. In addition, different managers are usually responsible for buying and for using inputs. For example, in the case of a raw material, a purchasing manager is responsible for its price and the production manager is responsible for the amount of the raw material actually used to make products. Therefore, it is important to clearly distinguish between deviations from price standards (the responsibility of the purchasing manager) and deviations from quantity standards (the responsibility of the production manager).

Exhibit 8–10 presents a general model that can be used to decompose the spending variance for a variable cost into a *quantity variance* and a *price variance.* Column (1) in this exhibit corresponds with the Flexible Budget column in Exhibit 8–9. Column (3) corresponds with the Actual Results column in Exhibit 8–9. Column (2) has been inserted into Exhibit 8–10 to enable separating the spending variance into a quantity variance and a price variance.

Three things should be noted from Exhibit 8–10. First, a quantity variance and a price variance can be computed for each of the three variable cost elements—direct materials, direct labor, and variable manufacturing overhead—even though the variances have

**EXHIBIT 8–10** A General Model for Standard Cost Variance Analysis—Variable Manufacturing Costs

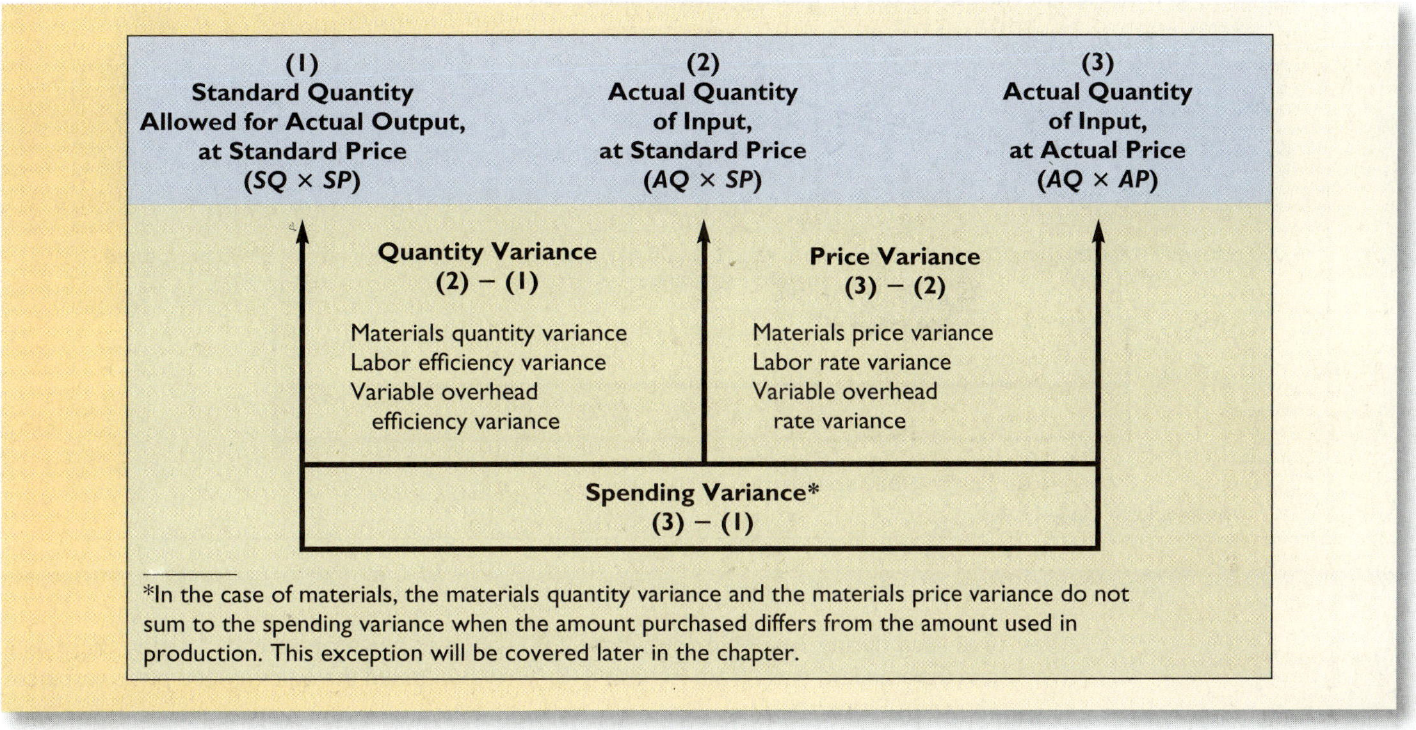


different names. For example, a price variance is called a *materials price variance* in the case of direct materials but a *labor rate variance* in the case of direct labor and a *variable overhead rate variance* in the case of variable manufacturing overhead.

Second, the quantity and price variances—regardless of what they are called—are computed in exactly the same way regardless of whether one is dealing with direct materials, direct labor, or variable manufacturing overhead.

Third, the input is the actual quantity of direct materials or direct labor purchased; the output is the amount of finished goods produced during the period. As shown in column 1 of Exhibit 8–10, he **standard quantity allowed for actual output** (also called the **standard hours allowed for actual output** when dealing with direct labor and variable overhead) means the amount of an input *that should have been used* to produce the actual output of the period. This could be more or less than the actual amount of the input, depending on the efficiency or inefficiency of operations. The standard quantity allowed is computed by multiplying the actual output in units by the standard input allowed per unit of output.

With this general model as the foundation, we will now calculate Colonial Pewter's quantity and price variances.

## USING STANDARD COSTS—DIRECT MATERIALS VARIANCES

**LEARNING OBJECTIVE 4**

Compute the direct materials quantity and price variances and explain their significance.

After determining Colonial Pewter Company's standard costs for direct materials, direct labor, and variable manufacturing overhead, Terry Sherman's next step was to compute the company's variances for June. As discussed in the preceding section, variances are computed by comparing standard costs to actual costs. Terry referred to the standard cost card in Exhibit 8–8 that shows the standard cost of direct materials was computed as follows:

$$3.0 \text{ pounds per unit} \times \$4.00 \text{ per pound} = \$12.00 \text{ per unit}$$

Colonial Pewter's records for June showed that 6,500 pounds of pewter were purchased at a cost of $3.80 per pound, for a total cost of $24,700. All of the material purchased

**EXHIBIT 8–11** Standard Cost Variance Analysis—Direct Materials
(Note: The quantity of materials purchased equals the quantity used in production.)

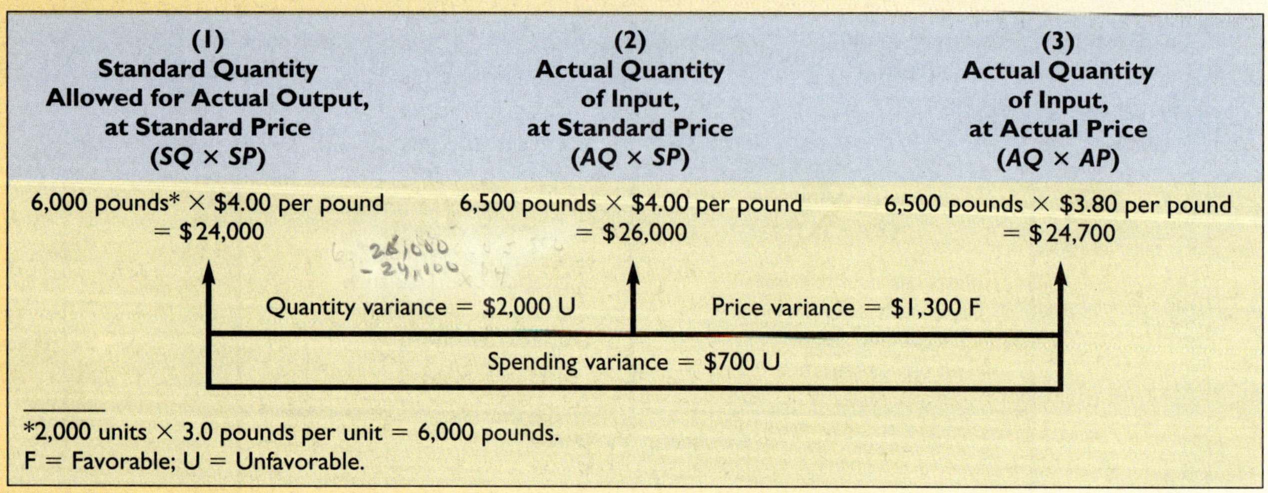


was used during June to manufacture 2,000 pairs of pewter bookends.[4] Using these data and the standard costs from Exhibit 8–8, Terry computed the quantity and price variances shown in Exhibit 8–11.

The variances in Exhibit 8–11 are based on three different total costs—$24,000, $26,000, and $24,700. The first, $24,000, refers to how much should have been spent on pewter to produce the actual output of 2,000 bookends. The standards call for 3 pounds of pewter per pair of bookends. Because 2,000 bookends were produced, 6,000 pounds of pewter should have been used. This is referred to as the *standard quantity allowed for the actual output.* If this 6,000 pounds of pewter had been purchased at the standard price of $4.00 per pound, the company would have spent $24,000. This is the amount that appears in the company's flexible budget for the month.

The third total cost figure, $24,700, is the actual amount paid for the actual amount of pewter purchased. The difference between the $24,700 actually spent and the amount that should have been spent, $24,000, is the spending variance for the month of $700. This variance is unfavorable (denoted by U) because the amount that was actually spent exceeded the amount that should have been spent. Note that this spending variance agrees with the direct materials spending variance in Exhibit 8–9.

The second total cost figure, $26,000, is the key that allows us to decompose the spending variance into two distinct elements—one due to quantity and one due to price. It represents how much the company should have spent if it had purchased the actual amount of input, 6,500 pounds, at the standard price of $4.00 a pound rather than the actual price of $3.80 a pound.

## The Materials Quantity Variance

Using the $26,000 total cost figure in column (2), we can make two comparisons—one with the total cost of $24,000 in column (1) and one with the total cost of $24,700 in column (3). The difference between the $26,000 in column (2) and the $24,000 in column (1) is the *materials quantity variance* of $2,000, which is labeled as unfavorable (denoted by U).

[4]Throughout this section, we assume zero beginning and ending inventories of materials and that all materials purchased during a period are used during that period. The more general case in which there are beginning and ending inventories of materials and materials are not necessarily used during the period in which they are purchased is considered later in the chapter.

The **materials quantity variance** measures the difference between the actual quantity of materials used in production and the standard quantity allowed for the actual output, multiplied by the standard price per unit of materials. It is labeled as unfavorable (favorable) when the quantity of materials used in production is greater than (less than) the quantity that should have been used according to the standard.

To understand this quantity variance, note that the actual amount of pewter used in production was 6,500 pounds. However, the standard amount of pewter allowed for the actual output is 6,000 pounds. Therefore, too much pewter was used to produce the actual output—by a total of 500 pounds. To express this in dollar terms, the 500 pounds is multiplied by the standard price of $4.00 per pound to yield the quantity variance of $2,000. Why is the standard price of the pewter, rather than the actual price, used in this calculation? The production manager is ordinarily responsible for the quantity variance. If the actual price were used in the calculation of the quantity variance, the production manager's performance would be unfairly influenced by the efficiency or inefficiency of the purchasing manager.

Excessive materials usage can result from many factors, including faulty machines, inferior materials quality, untrained workers, and poor supervision. Generally speaking, it is the responsibility of the production department to see that material usage is kept in line with standards. There may be times, however, when the *purchasing* department is responsible for an unfavorable materials quantity variance. For example, if the purchasing department buys inferior materials at a lower price, the materials may be unsuitable for use and may result in excessive waste. Thus, purchasing rather than production would be responsible for the quantity variance.

## The Materials Price Variance

The difference between the $24,700 in column (3) and the $26,000 in column (2) is the *materials price variance* of $1,300, which is labeled as favorable (denoted by F). A **materials price variance** measures the difference between the actual price per unit of an input and its standard price, multiplied by the actual quantity purchased.

To understand the price variance, note that the $3.80 per pound price paid for the pewter is $0.20 less than the $4.00 per pound standard price allowed for the pewter. Because 6,500 pounds were purchased, the total amount of the variance is $1,300 (= $0.20 per pound × 6,500 pounds). This variance is labeled favorable (F) because the actual purchase price was less than the standard purchase price. A price variance is labeled unfavorable (U) if the actual purchase price exceeds the standard purchase price.

### Direct Material Purchases: A Risk Management Perspective

IN BUSINESS

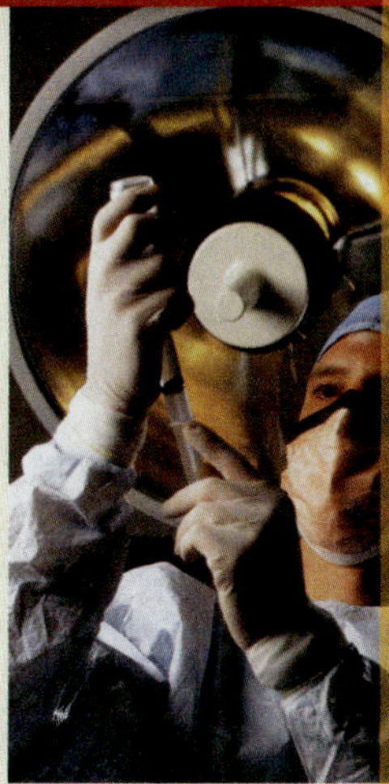

**Shenzhen Hepalink** manufactures heparin, a blood-thinning medication that is injected directly into the bloodstream of some surgical patients. The company relies on suppliers to extract its raw material, called crude heparin, from the intestines of slaughtered pigs. The harvesting of crude heparin is susceptible to contamination if the process is improperly managed and monitored. For example, **Baxter International** recently recalled tainted heparin that some people believe caused illnesses, allergic reactions, and deaths in some patients in the United States and Germany.

Shenzhen Hepalink strives to reduce contamination risks by buying crude heparin only from Chinese government-regulated slaughterhouses instead of rural unregulated slaughterhouses. The company also maintains quality assurance laboratories on each supplier's premises to ensure compliance with applicable rules. These safeguards increase Shenzhen Hepalink's raw materials cost, but they also reduce the risk of contaminated heparin eventually being injected into a patient's bloodstream.

Source: Gordon Fairclough, "How a Heparin Maker in China Tackles Risks," *The Wall Street Journal,* March 10, 2009, pp. B1 and B5.

Generally speaking, the purchasing manager has control over the price paid for goods and is therefore responsible for the materials price variance. Many factors influence the prices paid for goods including how many units are ordered, how the order is delivered, whether the order is a rush order, and the quality of materials purchased. If any of these factors deviates from what was assumed when the standards were set, a price variance can result. For example, purchasing second-grade materials rather than top-grade materials may result in a favorable price variance because the lower-grade materials may be less costly. However, the lower-grade materials may create production problems. It also bears emphasizing that someone other than the purchasing manager could be responsible for a materials price variance. For example, due to production problems beyond the purchasing manager's control, the purchasing manager may have to use express delivery. In these cases, the production manager should be held responsible for the resulting price variances.

## HELPFUL HINT

The Colonial Pewter Company's materials quantity and price variances can also be computed using the equations shown below where:

$AQ$ = Actual quantity of pounds purchased and used in production
$SQ$ = Standard quantity of pounds allowed for the actual output
$AP$ = Actual price per unit of the input
$SP$ = Standard price per unit of the input

*Materials Quantity Variance:*

Materials quantity variance = $(AQ \times SP) - (SQ \times SP)$
Materials quantity variance = $(AQ - SQ)SP$
Materials quantity variance = (6,500 pounds − 6,000 pounds) × \$4.00 per pound
Materials quantity variance = \$2,000 U

The materials quantity variance is unfavorable because the company used 500 more pounds than it should have to make 2,000 bookends.

*Materials Price Variance:*

Materials price variance = $(AQ \times AP) - (AQ \times SP)$
Materials price variance = $AQ(AP - SP)$
Materials price variance = 6,500 pounds (\$3.80 per pound − \$4.00 per pound)
Materials price variance = \$1,300 F

The materials price variance is favorable because the actual price paid per pound was \$0.20 less than the standard price per pound.

## CONCEPT CHECK

3. The standard and actual prices per pound of raw material are \$4.00 and \$4.50, respectively. A total of 10,500 pounds of raw material was purchased and then used to produce 5,000 units. The quantity standard allows two pounds of the raw material per unit produced. What is the materials quantity variance?
   a. \$5,000 unfavorable
   b. \$5,000 favorable
   c. \$2,000 favorable
   d. \$2,000 unfavorable
4. Referring to the facts in question 1 above, what is the material price variance?
   a. \$5,250 favorable
   b. \$5,250 unfavorable
   c. \$5,000 unfavorable
   d. \$5,000 favorable

## USING STANDARD COSTS—DIRECT LABOR VARIANCES

**LEARNING OBJECTIVE 5**

Compute the direct labor efficiency and rate variances and explain their significance.

Terry Sherman's next step in determining Colonial Pewter's variances for June was to compute the direct labor variances for the month. Recall from Exhibit 8–8 that the standard direct labor cost per unit of product is \$11, computed as follows:

0.50 hours per unit × \$22.00 per hour = \$11.00 per unit

During June, the company paid its direct labor workers \$22,680, including payroll taxes and fringe benefits, for 1,050 hours of work. This was an average of \$21.60 per hour. Using these data and the standard costs from Exhibit 8–8, Terry computed the direct labor efficiency and rate variances that appear in Exhibit 8–12.

Notice that the column headings in Exhibit 8–12 are the same as those used in the prior two exhibits, except that in Exhibit 8–12 the terms *hours* and *rate* are used in place of the terms *quantity* and *price.*

### The Labor Efficiency Variance

Using the \$23,100 total cost figure in column (2), we can make two comparisons—one with the total cost of \$22,000 in column (1) and one with the total cost of \$22,680 in column (3). The difference between the \$23,100 in column (2) and the \$22,000 in column (1) is the *labor efficiency variance* of \$1,100 U. The **labor efficiency variance** measures the difference between the actual hours taken to complete a task and the standard hours allowed for the actual output, multiplied by the standard hourly rate.

To understand Colonial Pewter's efficiency variance, note that the actual amount of hours used in production was 1,050 hours. However, the standard amount of hours allowed for the actual output is 1,000 hours. Therefore, the company used 50 more hours for the actual output than the standards allow. To express this in dollar terms, the 50 hours are multiplied by the standard rate of \$22.00 per hour to yield the efficiency variance of \$1,100 U.

Possible causes of an unfavorable labor efficiency variance include poorly trained or motivated workers; poor quality materials, requiring more labor time; faulty equipment, causing breakdowns and work interruptions; poor supervision of workers; and inaccurate standards. The managers in charge of production would usually be responsible for control of the labor efficiency variance. However, the purchasing manager could be held responsible if the purchase of poor-quality materials resulted in excessive labor processing time.

**EXHIBIT 8–12** Standard Cost Variance Analysis—Direct Labor

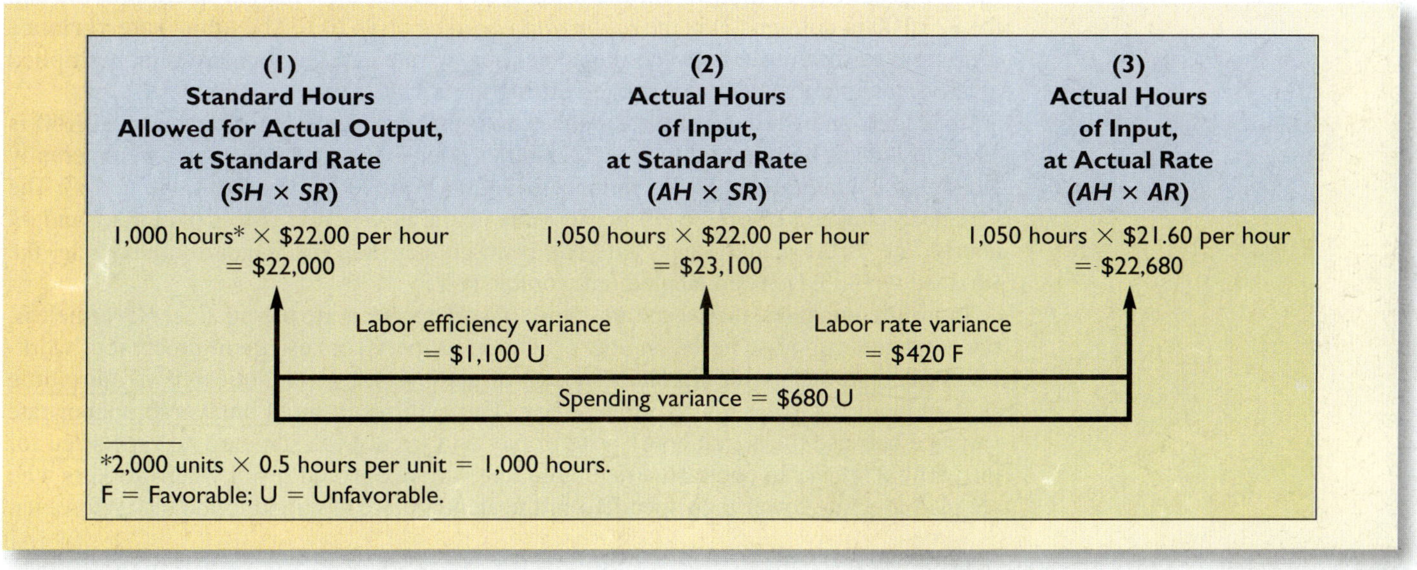

Another important cause of an unfavorable labor efficiency variance may be insufficient demand for the company's products. Managers in some companies argue that it is difficult, and perhaps unwise, to constantly adjust the workforce in response to changes in the amount of work that needs to be done. In such companies, the direct labor workforce is essentially fixed in the short run. If demand is insufficient to keep everyone busy, workers are not laid off and an unfavorable labor efficiency variance will often be recorded.

If customer orders are insufficient to keep the workers busy, the work center manager has two options—either accept an unfavorable labor efficiency variance or build inventory. A central lesson of Lean Production is that building inventory with no immediate prospect of sale is a bad idea. Excessive inventory—particularly work in process inventory—leads to high defect rates, obsolete goods, and inefficient operations. As a consequence, when the workforce is basically fixed in the short term, managers must be cautious about how labor efficiency variances are used. Some experts advocate eliminating labor efficiency variances in such situations—at least for the purposes of motivating and controlling workers on the shop floor.

IN BUSINESS

## Cashiers Face The Stopwatch

**Operations Workforce Optimization** (OWO) writes software that uses engineered labor standards to determine how long it should take a cashier to check out a customer. The software measures an employee's productivity by continuously comparing actual customer checkout times to pre-established labor efficiency standards. For example, the cashiers at **Meijer**, a regional retailer located in the Midwest, may be demoted or terminated if they do not meet or exceed labor efficiency standards for at least 95% of customers served. In addition to Meijer, OWO has attracted other clients such as **Gap**, **Limited Brands**, **Office Depot**, **Nike**, and **Toys "R" Us**, based on claims that its software can reduce labor costs by 5–15%. The software has also attracted the attention of the **United Food and Commercial Workers Union**, which represents 27,000 Meijer employees. The union has filed a grievance against Meijer related to its cashier monitoring system.

Source: Vanessa O'Connell, "Stores Count Seconds to Cut Labor Costs," *The Wall Street Journal,* November 17, 2008, pp. A1–A15.

## The Labor Rate Variance

Referring back to Exhibit 8–12, the difference between the $22,680 in column (3) and the $23,100 in column (2) is the *labor rate variance* of $420 F. The **labor rate variance** measures the difference between the actual hourly rate and the standard rate, multiplied by the actual number of hours worked during the period

To understand the labor rate variance, note that the actual hourly rate of $21.60 is $0.40 less than the standard rate of $22.00 per hour. Because 1,050 hours were actually worked, the total amount of the variance is $420 (= $0.40 per hour × 1,050 hours). The variance is labeled favorable (F) because the actual hourly rate is less than the standard hourly rate. If the actual hourly rate had been greater than the standard hourly rate, the variance would have been labeled unfavorable (U).

In most companies, the wage rates paid to workers are quite predictable. Nevertheless, rate variances can arise based on how production supervisors use their direct labor workers. Skilled workers with high hourly rates of pay may be given duties that require little skill and call for lower hourly rates of pay. This will result in an unfavorable labor rate variance because the actual hourly rate of pay will exceed the standard rate specified for the particular task. In contrast, a favorable rate variance would result when workers who are paid at a rate lower than specified in the standard are assigned to the task. However, the lower-paid workers may not be as efficient. Finally, overtime work at premium rates will result in an unfavorable rate variance if the overtime premium is charged to the direct labor account.

### HELPFUL HINT

The Colonial Pewter Company's direct labor efficiency and rate variances can also be computed using the equations shown below where:

$AH$ = Actual quantity of hours used in production
$SH$ = Standard quantity of hours allowed for the actual output
$AR$ = Actual rate per direct labor hour
$SR$ = Standard rate per direct labor hour

*Labor Efficiency Variance:*

Labor efficiency variance = $(AH \times SR) - (SH \times SR)$
Labor efficiency variance = $(AH - SH)SR$
Labor efficiency variance = (1,050 hours − 1,000 hours) × \$22.00 per hour
Labor efficiency variance = \$1,100 U

The labor efficiency variance is unfavorable because the company used 50 more hours than it should have to make 2,000 bookends.

*Labor Rate Variance:*

Labor rate variance = $(AH \times AR) - (AH \times SR)$
Labor rate variance = $AH(AR - SR)$
Labor rate variance = 1,050 hours (\$21.60 per hour − \$22.00 per hour)
Labor rate variance = \$420 F

The labor rate variance is favorable because the actual hourly rate of \$21.60 is \$0.40 less than the standard hourly rate of \$22.00.

## USING STANDARD COSTS—VARIABLE MANUFACTURING OVERHEAD VARIANCES

**LEARNING OBJECTIVE 6**

Compute the variable manufacturing overhead efficiency and rate variances and explain their significance.

The final step in Terry Sherman's analysis of Colonial Pewter's variances for June was to compute the variable manufacturing overhead variances. The variable portion of manufacturing overhead can be analyzed using the same basic formulas that we used to analyze direct materials and direct labor. Recall from Exhibit 8–8 that the standard variable manufacturing overhead is \$3.00 per unit of product, computed as follows:

0.5 hours per unit × \$6.00 per hour = \$3.00 per unit

Colonial Pewter's cost records showed that the total actual variable manufacturing overhead cost for June was \$7,140. Recall from the earlier discussion of the direct labor variances that 1,050 hours of direct labor time were recorded during the month and that the company produced 2,000 pairs of bookends. Terry's analysis of this overhead data appears in Exhibit 8–13.

Notice the similarities between Exhibits 8–12 and 8–13. These similarities arise from the fact that direct labor-hours are being used as the base for allocating overhead cost to units of product; thus, the same hourly figures appear in Exhibit 8–13 for variable manufacturing overhead as in Exhibit 8–12 for direct labor. The main difference between the two exhibits is in the standard hourly rate being used, which in this company is much lower for variable manufacturing overhead than for direct labor.

**EXHIBIT 8–13** Standard Cost Variance Analysis—Variable Manufacturing Overhead

| (1) Standard Hours Allowed for Actual Output, at Standard Rate (*SH* × *SR*) | (2) Actual Hours of Input, at Standard Rate (*AH* × *SR*) | (3) Actual Hours of Input, at Actual Rate (*AH* × *AR*) |
|---|---|---|
| 1,000 hours* × \$6.00 per hour = \$6,000 | 1,050 hours × \$6.00 per hour = \$6,300 | 1,050 hours × \$6.80 per hour† = \$7,140 |

Variable overhead efficiency variance = \$300 U

Variable overhead rate variance = \$840 U

Spending Variance = \$1,140 U

*2,000 units × 0.5 hours per unit = 1,000 hours.
†\$7,140 ÷ 1,050 hours = \$6.80 per hour.
F = Favorable; U = Unfavorable.

## The Variable Manufacturing Overhead Efficiency and Rate Variances

Using the \$6,300 total cost figure in column (2) of Exhibit 8–13, we can make two comparisons—one with the total cost of \$6,000 in column (1) and one with the total cost of \$7,140 in column (3). The difference between the \$6,300 in column (2) and the \$6,000 in column (1) is the *variable overhead efficiency variance* of \$300 U. The **variable overhead efficiency variance** measures the difference between the actual level of activity and the standard activity allowed, multiplied by the variable part of the predetermined overhead rate.

To understand Colonial Pewter's efficiency variance, note that the actual amount of hours used in production was 1,050 hours. However, the standard amount of hours allowed for the actual output is 1,000 hours. Therefore, the company used 50 more hours for the actual output than the standards allow. To express this in dollar terms, the 50 hours are multiplied by the variable part of the predetermined overhead rate of \$6.00 per hour to yield the variable overhead efficiency variance of \$300 U.

The difference between the \$7,140 in column (3) and the \$6,300 in column (2) is the *variable overhead rate variance* of \$840 U. The **variable overhead rate variance** measures the difference between the actual variable overhead cost incurred during a period and the standard cost that should have been incurred based on the actual activity of the period.

The interpretation of the variable overhead variances is not as clear as the direct materials and direct labor variances. In particular, the variable overhead efficiency variance is exactly the same as the direct labor efficiency variance except for one detail—the rate that is used to translate the variance into dollars. In both cases, the variance is the difference between the actual hours worked and the standard hours allowed for the actual output. In the case of the direct labor efficiency variance, this difference is multiplied by the direct labor rate. In the case of the variable overhead efficiency variance, this difference is multiplied by the variable overhead rate. So when direct labor is used as the base for overhead, whenever the direct labor efficiency variance is favorable, the variable overhead efficiency variance will be favorable. And whenever the direct labor efficiency variance is unfavorable, the variable overhead efficiency variance will be unfavorable. Indeed, the variable overhead efficiency variance really doesn't tell us anything about how efficiently overhead resources were used. It depends solely on how efficiently direct labor was used.

## HELPFUL HINT

The Colonial Pewter Company's variable overhead efficiency and rate variances can also be computed using the equations shown below where:

*AH* = Actual quantity of hours used in production
*SH* = Standard quantity of hours allowed for the actual output
*AR* = Actual rate per direct labor hour
*SR* = Standard rate per direct labor hour

*Variable Overhead Efficiency Variance:*
Variable overhead efficiency variance = $(AH \times SR) - (SH \times SR)$
Variable overhead efficiency variance = $(AH - SH)SR$
Variable overhead efficiency variance = (1,050 hours − 1,000 hours) × \$6.00 per hour
Variable overhead efficiency variance = \$300 U

The variable overhead efficiency variance is unfavorable because the company used 50 more hours than it should have to make 2,000 bookends.

*Variable Overhead Rate Variance:*
Variable overhead rate variance = $(AH \times AR) - (AH \times SR)$
Variable overhead rate variance = \$7,140 − (1,050 hours × \$6.00 per hour)
Variable overhead rate variance = \$840 U

**MANAGERIAL ACCOUNTING IN ACTION**
**The Wrap-up**

# Colonial Pewter Company

In preparation for the scheduled meeting to discuss his analysis of Colonial Pewter's standard costs and variances, Terry distributed Exhibits 8–8 through 8–13 to the management group of Colonial Pewter. This included J. D. Wriston, the president of the company; Tom Kuchel, the production manager; and Janet Warner, the purchasing manager. J. D. Wriston opened the meeting with the following question:

***J. D.:*** Terry, I think I understand the report you distributed, but just to make sure, would you mind summarizing the highlights of what you found?

***Terry:*** As you can see, the biggest problems are the unfavorable materials quantity variance of \$2,000 and the unfavorable labor efficiency variance of \$1,100.

***J. D.:*** Tom, you're the production boss. What do you think is causing the unfavorable labor efficiency variance?

***Tom:*** It has to be the new production workers. Our experienced workers shouldn't have much problem meeting the standard of half an hour per unit. We all knew that there would be some inefficiency for a while as we brought new people on board. My plan for overcoming the problem is to pair up each of the new guys with one of our old-timers and have them work together for a while. It would slow down our older guys a bit, but I'll bet the unfavorable variance disappears and our new workers would learn a lot.

***J. D.:*** Sounds good. Now, what about that \$2,000 unfavorable materials quantity variance?

***Terry:*** Tom, are the new workers generating a lot of scrap?

***Tom:*** Yeah, I guess so.

***J. D.:*** I think that could be part of the problem. Can you do anything about it?

***Tom:*** I can watch the scrap closely for a few days to see where it's being generated. If it is the new workers, I can have the old-timers work with them on the problem when I team them up.

***J. D.:*** Janet, the favorable materials price variance of \$1,300 isn't helping us if it is contributing to the unfavorable materials quantity and labor efficiency variances. Let's make sure that our raw material purchases conform to our quality standards.

***Janet:*** Fair enough.

***J. D.:*** Good. Let's reconvene in a few weeks to see what has happened. Hopefully, we can get those unfavorable variances under control.

## AN IMPORTANT SUBTLETY IN THE MATERIALS VARIANCES

Most companies use the *quantity of materials purchased* to compute the materials price variance and the *quantity of materials used* in production to compute the materials quantity variance. There are two reasons for this practice. First, delaying the computation of the price variance until the materials are used in production would result in less timely variance reports. Second, computing the price variance when materials are purchased allows materials to be carried in the inventory accounts at their standard costs. This greatly simplifies bookkeeping (see Appendix 8B at the end of the chapter for an explanation of how the bookkeeping works in a standard costing system).[5]

When we computed materials quantity and price variances for Colonial Pewter in Exhibit 8–11, we assumed that 6,500 pounds of materials were purchased *and* used in production. However, it is very common for a company's quantity of materials purchased to differ from its quantity used in production. When this happens, the materials quantity variance is computed using the *quantity of materials used* in production, whereas the materials price variance is computed using the *quantity of materials purchased.*

To illustrate, assume that during June Colonial Pewter purchased 7,000 pounds of materials at $3.80 per pound instead of 6,500 pounds as assumed earlier in the chapter. Also assume that the company continued to use 6,500 pounds of materials in production and that the standard price remained at $4.00 per pound.

Given these assumptions, Exhibit 8–14 shows how to compute the materials quantity variance of $2,000 U and the materials price variance of $1,400 F. Note that the compu-

**EXHIBIT 8–14** Standard Cost Variance Analysis—Direct Materials
(Note: The quantity of materials purchased does not equal the quantity used in production.)

| (1) Standard Quantity Allowed for Actual Output, at Standard Price (SQ × SP) | (2) Actual Quantity of Input, at Standard Price (AQ × SP) | (3) Actual Quantity of Input, at Actual Price (AQ × AP) |
|---|---|---|
| 6,000 pounds* × $4.00 per pound = $24,000 | 6,500 Pounds × $4.00 per pound = $26,000 | 7,000 pounds × $3.80 per pound = $26,600 |

Quantity variance = $2,000 U

7,000 pounds × $4.00 per pound = $28,000

Price variance = $1,400 F

In this case, the quantity variance and the price variance do not sum to the spending variance because the price variance is based on the quantity purchased whereas the quantity variance is based on the quantity used in production, and the two numbers differ.

*2,000 units × 3.0 pounds per unit = 6,000 pounds.
F = Favorable; U = Unfavorable.

---

[5]Standard cost systems are typically used as part of a company's financial reporting system. Therefore, standard cost variance reports are often prepared on a monthly basis as part of the financial closing process. As a consequence, the reports may be produced too infrequently to enable real-time operational improvements. To combat this problem, some companies are now reporting variances and other key operating data daily or even more frequently.

tation of the quantity variance is based on the actual input used whereas the computation of the price variance is based on the amount of the input purchased. Column (2) of Exhibit 8–14 contains two different total costs for this reason. When the quantity variance is computed, the total cost used from column (2) is $26,000—which is the cost of the actual input *used,* evaluated at the standard price. When the price variance is computed, the total cost used from column (2) is $28,000—which is the cost of the input *purchased,* evaluated at the standard price.

Exhibit 8–14 shows that the price variance is computed on the entire amount of material purchased (7,000 pounds), whereas the quantity variance is computed only on the amount of materials used in production during the month (6,500 pounds). What about the other 500 pounds of material that were purchased during the period, but that have not yet been used? When those materials are used in future periods, a quantity variance will be computed. However, a price variance will not be computed when the materials are finally used because the price variance was computed when the materials were purchased.

Finally, because the quantity variance is based on the amount used whereas the price variance is based on the amount purchased, the two variances do not generally sum to the spending variance from the flexible budget, which is wholly based on the amount used.

We would like to emphasize that *Exhibit 8–14 can always be used to compute the direct materials variances. However, Exhibit 8–11 can only be used in the special case when the quantity of materials purchased equals the quantity of materials used!*

## HELPFUL HINT

When Colonial Pewter purchases 7,000 pounds of materials and uses 6,500 pounds in production, the materials quantity and price variances can be computed using the equations shown below:

*Materials Quantity Variance:*

*AQ* = Actual quantity of pounds *used in production*
*SQ* = Standard quantity of pounds allowed for the actual output
*SP* = Standard price per unit of the input

Materials quantity variance = $(AQ \times SP) - (SQ \times SP)$
Materials quantity variance = $(AQ - SQ)SP$
Materials quantity variance = (6,500 pounds − 6,000 pounds) × $4.00 per pound
Materials quantity variance = $2,000 U

*Materials Price Variance:*

*AQ* = Actual quantity of pounds *purchased*
*AP* = Actual price per unit of the input
*SP* = Standard price per unit of the input

Materials price variance = $(AQ \times AP) - (AQ \times SP)$
Materials price variance = $AQ(AP - SP)$
Materials price variance = 7,000 pounds ($3.80 per pound − $4.00 per pound)
Materials price variance = $1,400 F

# SUMMARY

**LO1 Prepare a flexible budget.**
A flexible budget is a budget that is adjusted to the actual level of activity. It is the best estimate of what revenues and costs should have been, given the actual level of activity during the period. The flexible budget can be compared to the budget from the beginning of the period or to the actual results.

**LO2 Prepare a report showing revenue and spending variances.**
When the flexible budget is compared to actual results, revenue and spending variances are the result. A favorable revenue variance indicates that revenue was larger than should have been expected, given the actual level of activity. An unfavorable revenue variance indicates that revenue was less than it should have been, given the actual level of activity. A favorable spending variance indicates that the cost was less than expected, given the actual level of activity. An unfavorable spending variance indicates that the cost was greater than expected, given the actual level of activity.

**LO3 Prepare a flexible budget with more than one cost driver.**
A cost may depend on more than one cost driver. If so, the flexible budget for that cost should be stated in terms of all of the cost drivers.

**LO4 Compute the direct materials quantity and price variances and explain their significance.**
The materials quantity variance is the difference between the amount of materials actually used and the amount that should have been used to produce the actual good output of the period, multiplied by the standard price per unit of the input. An unfavorable materials quantity variance occurs when the amount of materials actually used exceeds the amount that should have been used according to the materials quantity standard. A favorable variance occurs when the amount of materials actually used is less than the amount that should have been used according to the standard.

The materials price variance is the difference between the actual price paid for materials and the standard price, multiplied by the quantity purchased. An unfavorable variance occurs whenever the actual price exceeds the standard price. A favorable variance occurs when the actual price is less than the standard price for the input.

**LO5 Compute the direct labor efficiency and rate variances and explain their significance.**
The labor efficiency variance is the difference between the hours actually worked and the hours that should have been used to produce the actual good output of the period, multiplied by the standard wage rate. An unfavorable labor efficiency variance occurs when the hours actually worked exceed the hours allowed for the actual output. A favorable variance occurs when the hours actually worked are less than hours allowed for the actual output.

The direct labor rate variance is the difference between the actual wage rate paid and the standard wage rate, multiplied by the hours worked. An unfavorable variance occurs whenever the actual wage rate exceeds the standard wage rate. A favorable variance occurs when the actual wage rate is less than the standard wage rate.

**LO6 Compute the variable manufacturing overhead efficiency and rate variances and explain their significance.**
The variable manufacturing overhead efficiency variance is the difference between the hours actually worked and the hours that should have been used to produce the actual good output of the period, multiplied by the standard variable manufacturing overhead rate. The variable manufacturing overhead rate variance is the difference between the actual variable manufacturing overhead cost incurred and the actual hours worked multiplied by the standard variable manufacturing overhead rate.

## GUIDANCE ANSWER TO DECISION POINT

**Owner of Micro-Brewery (p. 341)**

The cost of hops is a purely variable cost. Since the cost for producing 800 barrels of beer is \$960, the cost of hops in one barrel of beer is \$1.20 (= \$960 ÷ 800 barrels). Therefore, if 850 barrels of beer are produced, the cost of the hops should be \$1.20 per barrel times 850 barrels, or \$1,020. Since that is how much was actually spent, there is no indication that too much or too little was spent on hops.

## GUIDANCE ANSWERS TO CONCEPT CHECKS

1. **Choice b.** The cost for flowers according to the flexible budget is \$65,046 (= \$325 per operating day × 30 operating days + \$7.20 per room-day × 7,680 room-days).
2. **Choice a.** The spending variance is \$3,068 favorable (= \$65,046 − \$61,978).
3. **Choice d.** The materials quantity variance is (10,500 pounds used − 10,000 pounds allowed) × \$4.00 per pound = \$2,000 unfavorable.
4. **Choice b.** The materials price variance is (\$4.50 actual price per pound − \$4.00 standard price per pound) × 10,500 pounds purchased = \$5,250 unfavorable.

## REVIEW PROBLEM 1: VARIANCE ANALYSIS USING A FLEXIBLE BUDGET

Harrald's Fish House is a family-owned restaurant that specializes in Scandinavian-style seafood. Data concerning the restaurant's monthly revenues and costs appear below ($q$ refers to the number of meals served):

| | Formula |
|---|---|
| Revenue | \$16.50$q$ |
| Cost of ingredients | \$6.25$q$ |
| Wages and salaries | \$10,400 |
| Utilities | \$800 + \$0.20$q$ |
| Rent | \$2,200 |
| Miscellaneous | \$600 + \$0.80$q$ |

***Required:***

1. Prepare the restaurant's planning budget for April assuming that 1,800 meals are served.
2. Assume that 1,700 meals were actually served in April. Prepare a flexible budget for this level of activity.
3. The actual results for April appear below. Compute the revenue and spending variances for the restaurant for April.

| | |
|---|---|
| Revenue | \$27,920 |
| Cost of ingredients | \$11,110 |
| Wages and salaries | \$10,130 |
| Utilities | \$1,080 |
| Rent | \$2,200 |
| Miscellaneous | \$2,240 |

**Solution to Review Problem**

1. The planning budget for April appears below:

| Harrald's Fish House<br>Planning Budget<br>For the Month Ended April 30 | |
|---|---|
| *Budgeted* meals served ($q$) | 1,800 |
| Revenue ($16.50$q$) | $29,700 |
| Expenses: | |
| Cost of ingredients ($6.25$q$) | 11,250 |
| Wages and salaries ($10,400) | 10,400 |
| Utilities ($800 + $0.20$q$) | 1,160 |
| Rent ($2,200) | 2,200 |
| Miscellaneous ($600 + $0.80$q$) | 2,040 |
| Total expense | 27,050 |
| Net operating income | $ 2,650 |

2. The flexible budget for April appears below:

| Harrald's Fish House<br>Flexible Budget<br>For the Month Ended April 30 | |
|---|---|
| *Actual* meals served ($q$) | 1,700 |
| Revenue ($16.50$q$) | $28,050 |
| Expenses: | |
| Cost of ingredients ($6.25$q$) | 10,625 |
| Wages and salaries ($10,400) | 10,400 |
| Utilities ($800 + $0.20$q$) | 1,140 |
| Rent ($2,200) | 2,200 |
| Miscellaneous ($600 + $0.80$q$) | 1,960 |
| Total expense | 26,325 |
| Net operating income | $ 1,725 |

3. The revenue and spending variances for April appear below:

**Harrald's Fish House**
**Revenue and Spending Variances**
**For the Month Ended April 30**

| | (1) Flexible Budget | Revenue and Spending Variances (2) – (1) | (2) Actual Results |
|---|---|---|---|
| Meals served | 1,700 | | 1,700 |
| Revenue ($16.50$q$) | $28,050 | $130 U | $27,920 |
| Expenses: | | | |
| Cost of ingredients ($6.25$q$) | 10,625 | 485 U | 11,110 |
| Wages and salaries ($10,400) | 10,400 | 270 F | 10,130 |
| Utilities ($800 + $0.20$q$) | 1,140 | 60 F | 1,080 |
| Rent ($2,200) | 2,200 | 0 | 2,200 |
| Miscellaneous ($600 + $0.80$q$) | 1,960 | 280 U | 2,240 |
| Total expense | 26,325 | 435 U | 26,760 |
| Net operating income | $ 1,725 | $565 U | $ 1,160 |

# REVIEW PROBLEM 2: STANDARD COSTS

Xavier Company produces a single product. Variable manufacturing overhead is applied to products on the basis of direct labor-hours. The standard costs for one unit of product are as follows:

| | |
|---|---|
| Direct material: 6 ounces at $0.50 per ounce | $ 3.00 |
| Direct labor: 0.6 hours at $30.00 per hour | 18.00 |
| Variable manufacturing overhead: 0.6 hours at $10.00 per hour | 6.00 |
| Total standard variable cost per unit | $27.00 |

During June, 2,000 units were produced. The costs associated with June's operations were as follows:

| | |
|---|---|
| Material purchased: 18,000 ounces at $0.60 per ounce | $10,800 |
| Material used in production: 14,000 ounces | — |
| Direct labor: 1,100 hours at $30.50 per hour | $33,550 |
| Variable manufacturing overhead costs incurred | $12,980 |

***Required:***
Compute the direct materials, direct labor, and variable manufacturing overhead variances.

**Solution to Review Problem**

### Direct Materials Variances

| Standard Quantity Allowed for Actual Output, at Standard Price (*SQ* × *SP*) | Actual Quantity of Input, at Standard Price (*AQ* × *SP*) | Actual Quantity of Input, at Actual Price (*AQ* × *AP*) |
|---|---|---|
| 12,000 ounces* × $0.50 per ounce = $6,000 | 14,000 ounces × $0.50 per ounce = $7,000 | 18,000 ounces × $0.60 per pound = $10,800 |

Quantity variance = $1,000 U

18,000 ounces × $0.50 per ounce = $9,000

Price variance = $1,800 U

*2,000 units × 6 ounces per unit = 12,000 ounces.

Using formulas, the same variances would be computed as follows:

$$\text{Materials quantity variance} = (AQ - SQ)SP$$

$$(14{,}000 \text{ ounces} - 12{,}000 \text{ ounces})\ \$0.50 \text{ per ounce} = \$1{,}000\ \text{U}$$

$$\text{Materials price variance} = AQ(AP - SP)$$

$$18{,}000 \text{ ounces } (\$0.60 \text{ per ounce} - \$0.50 \text{ per ounce}) = \$1{,}800\ \text{U}$$

### Direct Labor Variances

| Standard Hours Allowed for Actual Output, at Standard Rate (*SH* × *SR*) | Actual Hours of Input, at Standard Rate (*AH* × *SR*) | Actual Hours of Input, at Actual Rate (*AH* × *AR*) |
|---|---|---|
| 1,200 hours* × $30.00 per hour = $36,000 | 1,100 hours × $30.00 per hour = $33,000 | 1,100 hours × $30.50 per hour = $33,550 |

Labor efficiency variance = $3,000 F

Labor rate variance = $550 U

Spending variance = $2,450 F

*2,000 units × 0.6 hours per unit = 1,200 hours.
F = Favorable; U = Unfavorable.

Using formulas, the same variances can be computed as follows:

Labor efficiency variance = $(AH - SH)SR$

= (1,100 hours − 1,200 hours) × $30.00 per hour

= $3,000 F

Labor rate variance = $AH(AR - SR)$

= 1,100 hours × ($30.50 per hour − $30.00 per hour)

= $550 U

### Variable Manufacturing Overhead Variances

| Standard Hours Allowed for Actual Output, at Standard Rate (*SH* × *SR*) | Actual Hours of Input, at Standard Rate (*AH* × *SR*) | Actual Hours of Input, at Actual Rate (*AH* × *AR*) |
|---|---|---|
| 1,200 hours* × $10.00 per hour = $12,000 | 1,100 hours × $10.00 per hour = $11,000 | 1,100 hours × $11.80 per hour† = $12,980 |

Variable overhead effciency variance = $1,000 F

Variable overhead rate variance = $1,980 U

Spending variance = $980 U

*2,000 units × 0.6 hours per unit = 1,200 hours.
†$12,980 ÷ 1,100 hours = $11.80 per hour.
F = Favorable; U = Unfavorable.

Using formulas, the same variances can be computed as follows:

Variable overhead efficiency variance = $(AH - SH)SR$

= (1,100 hours − 1,200 hours) × $10.00 per hour

= $1,000 F

Variable overhead rate variance = $(AH \times AR) - (AH \times SR)$

= $12,980 − (1,100 hours × $10.00 per hour)

= $1,980 U

## GLOSSARY

**Flexible budget** A report showing estimates of what revenues and costs should have been, given the actual level of activity for the period. (p. 337)

**Labor efficiency variance** The difference between the actual hours taken to complete a task and the standard hours allowed for the actual output, multiplied by the standard hourly labor rate. (p. 351)

**Labor rate variance** The difference between the actual hourly labor rate and the standard rate, multiplied by the number of hours worked during the period. (p. 352)

**Management by exception** A management system in which actual results are compared to a budget. Significant deviations from the budget are flagged as exceptions and investigated further. (p. 336)

**Materials price variance** The difference between the actual unit price paid for an item and the standard price, multiplied by the quantity purchased. (p. 349)

**Materials quantity variance** The difference between the actual quantity of materials used in production and the standard quantity allowed for the actual output, multiplied by the standard price per unit of materials. (p. 349)

**Planning budget** A budget created at the beginning of the budgeting period that is valid only for the planned level of activity. (p. 337)

**Price variance** A variance that is computed by taking the difference between the actual price and the standard price and multiplying the result by the actual quantity of the input. (p. 346)

**Quantity variance** A variance that is computed by taking the difference between the actual quantity of the input used and the amount of the input that should have been used for the actual level of output and multiplying the result by the standard price of the input. (p. 346)

**Revenue variance** The difference between how much the revenue should have been, given the actual level of activity, and the actual revenue for the period. A favorable (unfavorable) revenue variance occurs because the revenue is higher (lower) than expected, given the actual level of activity for the period. (p. 340)

**Spending variance** The difference between how much a cost should have been, given the actual level of activity, and the actual amount of the cost. A favorable (unfavorable) spending variance occurs because the cost is lower (higher) than expected, given the actual level of activity for the period. (p. 341)

**Standard cost card** A detailed listing of the standard amounts of inputs and their costs that are required to produce one unit of a specific product. (p. 345)

**Standard cost per unit** The standard quantity allowed of an input per unit of a specific product, multiplied by the standard price of the input. (p. 345)

**Standard hours allowed for actual output** The time that should have been taken to complete the period's output. It is computed by multiplying the actual number of units produced by the standard hours per unit. (p. 347)

**Standard hours per unit** The amount of direct labor time that should be required to complete a single unit of product, including allowances for breaks, machine downtime, cleanup, rejects, and other normal inefficiencies. (p. 344)

**Standard price per unit** The price that should be paid for an input. (p. 344)

**Standard quantity allowed for actual output** The amount of an input that should have been used to complete the period's actual output. It is computed by multiplying the actual number of units produced by the standard quantity per unit. (p. 347)

**Standard quantity per unit** The amount of an input that should be required to complete a single unit of product, including allowances for normal waste, spoilage, rejects, and other normal inefficiencies. (p. 344)

**Standard rate per hour** The labor rate that should be incurred per hour of labor time, including employment taxes and fringe benefits. (p. 344)

**Variable overhead efficiency variance** The difference between the actual level of activity (direct labor-hours, machine-hours, or some other base) and the standard activity allowed, multiplied by the variable part of the predetermined overhead rate. (p. 354)

**Variable overhead rate variance** The difference between the actual variable overhead cost incurred during a period and the standard cost that should have been incurred based on the actual activity of the period. (p. 354)

## QUESTIONS

**8–1** What is a static planning budget?

**8–2** What is a flexible budget and how does it differ from a static planning budget?

**8–3** What are some of the possible reasons that actual results may differ from what had been budgeted at the beginning of a period?

**8–4** Why is it difficult to interpret a difference between how much expense was budgeted at the beginning of the period and how much was actually spent?

**8–5** What is a revenue variance and what does it mean?

**8–6** What is a spending variance and what does it mean?

**8–7** What does a flexible budget enable that a simple comparison of the planning budget to actual results does not do?

**8–8** How does a flexible budget based on two cost drivers differ from a flexible budget based on a single cost driver?

**8–9** What is a quantity standard? What is a price standard?

**8–10** Why are separate price and quantity variances computed?

**8–11** Who is generally responsible for the materials price variance? The materials quantity variance? The labor efficiency variance?

**8–12** The materials price variance can be computed at what two different points in time? Which point is better? Why?

**8–13** If the materials price variance is favorable but the materials quantity variance is unfavorable, what might this indicate?

**8–14** "Our workers are all under labor contracts; therefore, our labor rate variance is bound to be zero." Discuss.

**8–15** What effect, if any, would you expect poor-quality materials to have on direct labor variances?

**8–16** If variable manufacturing overhead is applied to production on the basis of direct labor-hours and the direct labor efficiency variance is unfavorable, will the variable overhead efficiency variance be favorable or unfavorable, or could it be either? Explain.

**8–17** Why can undue emphasis on labor efficiency variances lead to excess work in process inventories?

**Multiple-choice questions are provided on the text website at www.mhhe.com/brewer6e.**

## APPLYING EXCEL connect ACCOUNTING

**LO4, LO5, LO6**

### Available with McGraw-Hill's *Connect® Accounting*.

The Excel worksheet form that appears below is to be used to recreate the main example in the text on pages 345–355. Download the workbook containing this form from the Online Learning Center at www.mhhe.com/brewer6e. *On the website you will also receive instructions about how to use this worksheet form.*

| | A | B | C | D | E | F | G |
|---|---|---|---|---|---|---|---|
| 1 | Chapter 8: Applying Excel | | | | | | |
| 2 | | | | | | | |
| 3 | **Data** | | | | | | |
| 4 | ***Exhibit 8-8: Standard Cost Card*** | | | | | | |
| 5 | *Inputs* | *Standard Quantity* | | *Standard Price* | | | |
| 6 | Direct materials | 3.0 | pounds | $4.00 | per pound | | |
| 7 | Direct labor | 0.50 | hours | $22.00 | per hour | | |
| 8 | Variable manufacturing overhead | 0.50 | hours | $6.00 | per hour | | |
| 9 | | | | | | | |
| 10 | Actual results: | | | | | | |
| 11 | Actual output | 2,000 | units | | | | |
| 12 | Actual variable manufacturing overhead cost | $7,140 | | | | | |
| 13 | | *Actual Quantity* | | *Actual price* | | | |
| 14 | Actual direct materials cost | 6,500 | pounds | $3.80 | per pound | | |
| 15 | Actual direct labor cost | 1,050 | hours | $21.60 | per hour | | |
| 16 | | | | | | | |
| 17 | *Enter a formula into each of the cells marked with a ? below* | | | | | | |
| 18 | **Main Example: Chapter 8** | | | | | | |
| 19 | | | | | | | |
| 20 | ***Exhibit 8-11: Standard Cost Variance Analysis–Direct Materials*** | | | | | | |
| 21 | Standard Quantity Allowed for the Actual Output, at Standard Price | ? | pounds × | ? | per pound = | ? | |
| 22 | Actual Quantity of Input, at Standard Price | ? | pounds × | ? | per pound = | ? | |
| 23 | Actual Quantity of Input, at Actual Price | ? | pounds × | ? | per pound = | ? | |
| 24 | Direct materials variances: | | | | | | |
| 25 | Materials quantity variance | ? | | | | | |
| 26 | Materials price variance | ? | | | | | |
| 27 | Materials spending variance | ? | | | | | |
| 28 | | | | | | | |
| 29 | ***Exhibit 8-12: Standard Cost Variance Analysis–Direct Labor*** | | | | | | |
| 30 | Standard Hours Allowed for the Actual Output, at Standard Rate | ? | hours × | ? | per hour = | ? | |
| 31 | Actual Hours of Input, at Standard Rate | ? | hours × | ? | per hour = | ? | |
| 32 | Actual Hours of Input, at Actual Rate | ? | hours × | ? | per hour = | ? | |
| 33 | Direct labor variances: | | | | | | |
| 34 | Labor efficiency variance | ? | | | | | |
| 35 | Labor rate variance | ? | | | | | |
| 36 | Labor spending variance | ? | | | | | |
| 37 | | | | | | | |
| 38 | ***Exhibit 8-13: Standard Cost Variance Analysis–Variable Manufacturing Overhead*** | | | | | | |
| 39 | Standard Hours Allowed for the Actual Output, at Standard Rate | ? | hours × | ? | per hour = | ? | |
| 40 | Actual Hours of Input, at Standard Rate | ? | hours × | ? | per hour = | ? | |
| 41 | Actual Hours of Input, at Actual Rate | ? | hours × | ? | per hour = | ? | |
| 42 | Variable overhead variances: | | | | | | |
| 43 | Variable overhead efficiency variance | ? | | | | | |
| 44 | Variable overhead rate variance | ? | | | | | |
| 45 | Variable overhead spending variance | ? | | | | | |
| 46 | | | | | | | |

Chapter 8 Form / Filled in Chapter 8 Form / Chapter 8 Formulas / Chap

You should proceed to the requirements below only after completing your worksheet.

***Required:***

1. Check your worksheet by changing the direct materials standard quantity in cell B6 to 2.9 pounds, the direct labor quantity standard quantity in cell B7 to 0.6 hours, and the variable manufacturing overhead in cell B8 to 0.6 hours. The materials spending variance should now be $1,500 U, the labor spending variance should now be $3,720 F, and the variable overhead spending variance should now be $60 F. If you do not get these answers, find the errors in your worksheet and correct them.
   a. What is the materials quantity variance? Explain this variance.
   b. What is the labor rate variance? Explain this variance.
2. Revise the data in your worksheet to reflect the results for the subsequent period:

| **Data**<br>**Exhibit 8–8: Standard Cost Card** | | |
|---|---|---|
| **Inputs** | **Standard Quantity** | **Standard Price** |
| Direct materials | 3.0 pounds | $4.00 per pound |
| Direct labor | 0.50 hours | $22.00 per hour |
| Variable manufacturing overhead | 0.50 hours | $6.00 per hour |
| Actual results: | | |
| Actual output | 2,100 units | |
| Actual variable manufacturing overhead cost | $5,100 | |
| | **Actual Quantity** | **Actual Price** |
| Actual direct materials cost | 6,350 pounds | $4.10 per pound |
| Actual direct labor cost | 1,020 hours | $22.10 per hour |

   a. What is the materials quantity variance? What is the materials price variance?
   b. What is the labor efficiency variance? What is the labor rate variance?
   c. What is the variable overhead efficiency variance? What is the variable overhead rate variance?

## connect ACCOUNTING THE FOUNDATIONAL 15

**Available with McGraw-Hill's *Connect*® *Accounting.***

LO1, LO2, LO4, LO5, LO6

Preble Company manufactures one product. Its variable manufacturing overhead is applied to production based on direct labor-hours and its standard cost card per unit is as follows:

| | |
|---|---|
| Direct material: 5 pounds at $8.00 per pound | $40.00 |
| Direct labor: 2 hours at $14 per hour | 28.00 |
| Variable overhead: 2 hours at $5 per hour | 10.00 |
| Total standard variable cost per unit | $78.00 |

The company also established the following cost formulas for its selling expenses:

| | Fixed Cost per Month | Variable Cost per Unit Sold |
|---|---|---|
| Advertising | $200,000 | |
| Sales salaries and commissions | $100,000 | $12.00 |
| Shipping expenses | | $3.00 |

The planning budget for March was based on producing and selling 25,000 units. However, during March the company actually produced and sold 30,000 units and incurred the following costs:

a. Purchased 160,000 pounds of raw materials at a cost of $7.50 per pound. All of this material was used in production.
b. Direct-laborers worked 55,000 hours at a rate of $15.00 per hour.

c. Total variable manufacturing overhead for the month was $280,500.
d. Total advertising, sales salaries and commissions, and shipping expenses were $210,000, $455,000, and $115,000, respectively.

***Required:***

1. What raw materials cost would be included in the company's flexible budget for March?
2. What is the materials quantity variance for March?
3. What is the materials price variance for March?
4. If Preble had purchased 170,000 pounds of materials at $7.50 per pound and used 160,000 pounds in production, what would be the materials quantity variance for March?
5. If Preble had purchased 170,000 pounds of materials at $7.50 per pound and used 160,000 pounds in production, what would be the materials price variance for March?
6. What direct labor cost would be included in the company's flexible budget for March?
7. What is the direct labor efficiency variance for March?
8. What is the direct labor rate variance for March?
9. What variable manufacturing overhead cost would be included in the company's flexible budget for March?
10. What is the variable overhead efficiency variance for March?
11. What is the variable overhead rate variance for March?
12. What amounts of advertising, sales salaries and commissions, and shipping expenses would be included in the company's flexible budget for March?
13. What is the spending variance related to advertising?
14. What is the spending variance related to sales salaries and commissions?
15. What is the spending variance related to shipping expenses?

## EXERCISES

**All applicable exercises are available with McGraw-Hill's *Connect® Accounting.***

TAKE TWO

### EXERCISE 8–1 Prepare a Flexible Budget [LO1]

Gator Divers is a company that provides diving services such as underwater ship repairs to clients in the Tampa Bay area. The company's planning budget for March appears below:

Actual diving-hours = 180

| Gator Divers<br>Planning Budget<br>For the Month Ended March 31 | |
|---|---|
| Budgeted diving-hours (*q*) | 200 |
| Revenue ($380.00*q*) | $76,000 |
| Expenses: | |
| Wages and salaries ($12,000 + $130.00*q*) | 38,000 |
| Supplies ($5.00*q*) | 1,000 |
| Equipment rental ($2,500 + $26.00*q*) | 7,700 |
| Insurance ($4,200) | 4,200 |
| Miscellaneous ($540 + $1.50*q*) | 840 |
| Total expense | 51,740 |
| Net operating income | $24,260 |

***Required:***

During March, the company's activity was actually 190 diving-hours. Prepare a flexible budget for that level of activity.

**EXERCISE 8–2 Prepare a Report Showing Revenue and Spending Variances [LO2]**

Olympia Bivalve farms and sells oysters in the Pacific Northwest. The company harvested and sold 7,000 pounds of oysters in July. The company's flexible budget for July appears below:

TAKE TWO

Actual revenue = $30,000

| Olympia Bivalve<br>Flexible Budget<br>For the Month Ended July 31 | |
|---|---|
| Actual pounds ($q$) | 7,000 |
| Revenue ($4.20$q$) | $29,400 |
| Expenses: | |
| Packing supplies ($0.40$q$) | 2,800 |
| Oyster bed maintenance ($3,600) | 3,600 |
| Wages and salaries ($2,540 + $0.50$q$) | 6,040 |
| Shipping ($0.75$q$) | 5,250 |
| Utilities ($1,260) | 1,260 |
| Other ($510 + $0.05$q$) | 860 |
| Total expense | 19,810 |
| Net operating income | $ 9,590 |

The actual results for July appear below:

| Olympia Bivalve<br>Income Statement<br>For the Month Ended July 31 | |
|---|---|
| Actual pounds | 7,000 |
| Revenue | $28,600 |
| Expenses: | |
| Packing supplies | 2,970 |
| Oyster bed maintenance | 3,460 |
| Wages and salaries | 6,450 |
| Shipping | 4,980 |
| Utilities | 1,070 |
| Other | 1,480 |
| Total expense | 20,410 |
| Net operating income | $ 8,190 |

***Required:***

Prepare a report showing the company's revenue and spending variances for July.

**EXERCISE 8–3 Prepare a Flexible Budget with More Than One Cost Driver [LO3]**

Icicle Bay Tours operates day tours of coastal glaciers in Alaska on its tour boat the Emerald Glacier. Management has identified two cost drivers—the number of cruises and the number of passengers—that it uses in its budgeting and performance reports. The company publishes a schedule of day cruises that it may supplement with special sailings if there is sufficient demand. Up to 80 passengers can be accommodated on the tour boat. Data concerning the company's cost formulas appear below:

TAKE TWO

Budgeted passengers = 3,400

| | Fixed Cost per Month | Cost per Cruise | Cost per Passenger |
|---|---|---|---|
| Vessel operating costs | $6,800 | $475.00 | $3.50 |
| Advertising | $2,700 | | |
| Administrative costs | $5,800 | $36.00 | $1.80 |
| Insurance | $3,600 | | |

For example, vessel operating costs should be $6,800 per month plus $475.00 per cruise plus $3.50 per passenger. The company's sales should average $28.00 per passenger. The company's planning budget for August is based on 58 cruises and 3,200 passengers.

***Required:***
Prepare the company's planning budget for August.

**EXERCISE 8–4 Material Variances [LO4]**

Standard board feet per unit = 3.0

Harmon Household Products, Inc., manufactures a number of consumer items for general household use. One of these products, a chopping board, requires an expensive hardwood. During a recent month, the company manufactured 4,000 chopping boards using 11,000 board feet of hardwood. The hardwood cost the company $18,700.

The company's standards for one chopping board are 2.5 board feet of hardwood, at a cost of $1.80 per board foot.

***Required:***
1. According to the standards, what cost for wood should have been incurred to make 4,000 chopping blocks? How much greater or less is this than the cost that was incurred?
2. Break down the difference computed in (1) above into a materials quantity variance and a materials price variance.

**EXERCISE 8–5 Direct Labor Variances [LO5]**

AirMeals, Inc., prepares in-flight meals for a number of major airlines. One of the company's products is stuffed cannelloni with roasted pepper sauce, fresh baby corn, and spring salad. During the most recent week, the company prepared 6,000 of these meals using 1,150 direct labor-hours. The company paid these direct labor workers a total of $11,500 for this work, or $10 per hour.

According to the standard cost card for this meal, it should require 0.20 direct labor-hours at a cost of $9.50 per hour.

Standard direct labor cost per hour = $10.00

***Required:***
1. According to the standards, what direct labor cost should have been incurred to prepare 6,000 meals? How much does this differ from the actual direct labor cost?
2. Break down the difference computed in (1) above into a labor efficiency variance and a labor rate variance.

**EXERCISE 8–6 Variable Overhead Variances [LO6]**

Order Up, Inc., provides order fulfillment services for dot.com merchants. The company maintains warehouses that stock items carried by its dot.com clients. When a client receives an order from a customer, the order is forwarded to Order Up, which pulls the item from storage, packs it, and ships it to the customer. The company uses a predetermined variable overhead rate based on direct labor-hours.

In the most recent month, 140,000 items were shipped to customers using 5,800 direct labor-hours. The company incurred a total of $15,950 in variable overhead costs.

According to the company's standards, 0.04 direct labor-hours are required to fulfill an order for one item and the variable overhead rate is $2.80 per direct labor-hour.

***Required:***
1. According to the standards, what variable overhead cost should have been incurred to fill the orders for the 140,000 items? How much does this differ from the actual variable overhead cost?
2. Break down the difference computed in (1) above into a variable overhead efficiency variance and a variable overhead rate variance.

**EXERCISE 8–7 Planning Budget [LO1]**

Auto Lavage is a Canadian company that owns and operates a large automatic carwash facility near Quebec. The following table provides data concerning the company's costs:

Planning budget = 8,200 cars washed

| | Fixed Cost per Month | Cost per Car Washed |
|---|---|---|
| Cleaning supplies | | $0.70 |
| Electricity | $1,400 | $0.10 |
| Maintenance | | $0.30 |
| Wages and salaries | $4,700 | $0.40 |
| Depreciation | $8,300 | |
| Rent | $2,100 | |
| Administrative expenses | $1,800 | $0.05 |

For example, electricity costs are $1,400 per month plus $0.10 per car washed. The company expects to wash 8,000 cars in October and to collect an average of $5.90 per car washed.

***Required:***

Prepare the company's planning budget for October.

**EXERCISE 8–8 Flexible Budget [LO1]**

Refer to the data for Auto Lavage in Exercise 8–7. The company actually washed 8,100 cars in October.

***Required:***

Prepare the company's flexible budget for October.

**EXERCISE 8–9 Prepare a Report Showing Revenue and Spending Variances [LO2]**

Refer to the data for Auto Lavage in Exercises 8–7 and 8–8. The actual operating results for October appear below:

| Auto Lavage<br>Income Statement<br>For the Month Ended October 31 | |
|---|---|
| Actual cars washed | 8,100 |
| Revenue | $49,300 |
| Expenses: | |
| Cleaning supplies | 6,100 |
| Electricity | 2,170 |
| Maintenance | 2,640 |
| Wages and salaries | 8,260 |
| Depreciation | 8,300 |
| Rent | 2,300 |
| Administrative expenses | 2,100 |
| Total expense | 31,870 |
| Net operating income | $17,430 |

***Required:***

Prepare a report showing revenue and spending variances.

**EXERCISE 8–10 Labor and Variable Manufacturing Overhead Variances [LO5, LO6]**

Hollowell Audio, Inc., manufactures military specification compact discs. The company uses standards to control its costs. The labor standards that have been set for one disc are as follows:

| Standard Hours | Standard Rate per Hour | Standard Cost |
|---|---|---|
| 6 minutes | $24.00 | $2.40 |

Standard hours = 9 minutes

During July, 2,125 hours of direct labor time were required to make 20,000 discs. The direct labor cost totaled $49,300 for the month.

***Required:***

1. According to the standards, what direct labor cost should have been incurred to make the 20,000 discs? By how much does this differ from the cost that was incurred?
2. Break down the difference in cost from (1) above into a labor efficiency variance and a labor rate variance.
3. The budgeted variable manufacturing overhead rate is $16.00 per direct labor-hour. During July, the company incurred $39,100 in variable manufacturing overhead cost. Compute the variable overhead efficiency and rate variances for the month.

**EXERCISE 8–11 Working Backwards from Labor Variances [LO5]**

The Worldwide Credit Card, Inc., uses standards to control the labor time involved in opening mail from card holders and recording the enclosed remittances. Incoming mail is gathered into batches, and a standard time is set for opening and recording each batch. The labor standards relating to one batch are as follows:

| | Standard Hours | Standard Rate | Standard Cost |
|---|---|---|---|
| Per batch ............ | 1.25 | $12.00 | $15.00 |

The record showing the time spent last week in opening batches of mail has been misplaced. However, the batch supervisor recalls that 168 batches were received and opened during the week, and the controller recalls the following variance data relating to these batches:

| | |
|---|---|
| Total labor spending variance .............. | $330 U |
| Labor rate variance ............................. | $150 F |

***Required:***

1. Determine the number of actual labor-hours spent opening batches during the week.
2. Determine the actual hourly rate paid to employees for opening batches last week.

(Hint: A useful way to proceed would be to work from known to unknown data either by using the variance formulas or by using the columnar format shown in Exhibit 8–12.)

**EXERCISE 8–12 Working with More Than One Cost Driver [LO2, LO3]**

The Toque Cooking Academy runs short cooking courses at its small campus. Management has identified two cost drivers that it uses in its budgeting and performance reports—the number of courses and the total number of students. For example, the school might run four courses in a month and have a total of 60 students enrolled in those four courses. Data concerning the company's cost formulas appear below:

| | Fixed Cost per Month | Cost per Course | Cost per Student |
|---|---|---|---|
| Instructor wages ........................ | | $2,980 | |
| Classroom supplies ................... | | | $310 |
| Utilities ...................................... | $1,230 | $85 | |
| Campus rent ............................. | $5,100 | | |
| Insurance .................................. | $2,340 | | |
| Administrative expenses ........... | $3,940 | $46 | $7 |

For example, administrative expenses should be $3,940 per month plus $46 per course plus $7 per student. The company's sales should average $850 per student.

The actual operating results for October appear below:

| | Actual |
|---|---|
| Revenue ................................ | $48,100 |
| Instructor wages ..................... | $11,200 |
| Classroom supplies ................. | $18,450 |
| Utilities .................................. | $1,980 |
| Campus rent ........................... | $5,100 |
| Insurance ................................ | $2,480 |
| Administrative expenses .......... | $3,970 |

***Required:***

1. The Toque Cooking Academy expects to run four courses with a total of 60 students in October. Prepare the company's planning budget for this level of activity.
2. The school actually ran four courses with a total of 58 students in October. Prepare the company's flexible budget for this level of activity.
3. Calculate revenue and spending variances for October.

### EXERCISE 8–13 Material and Labor Variances [LO4, LO5]

TAKE TWO

Standard price per ounce = $3.00

Sonne Company produces a perfume called Whim. The direct materials and direct labor standards for one bottle of Whim are given below:

| | Standard Quantity or Hours | Standard Price or Rate | Standard Cost |
|---|---|---|---|
| Direct materials.................. | 7.2 ounces | $2.50 per ounce | $18.00 |
| Direct labor ........................ | 0.4 hours | $10.00 per hour | $4.00 |

During the most recent month, the following activity was recorded:

a. Twenty thousand ounces of material were purchased at a cost of $2.40 per ounce.
b. All of the material was used to produce 2,500 bottles of Whim.
c. Nine hundred hours of direct labor time were recorded at a total labor cost of $10,800.

***Required:***

1. Compute the direct materials quantity and price variances for the month.
2. Compute the direct labor efficiency and rate variances for the month.

### EXERCISE 8–14 Material Variances [LO4]

TAKE TWO

See Exercise 8–13

Refer to the data in Exercise 8–13. Assume that instead of producing 2,500 bottles of Whim during the month, the company produced only 2,000 bottles using 16,000 ounces of material. (The rest of the material purchased remained in raw materials inventory.)

***Required:***

Compute the direct materials quantity and price variances for the month.

### EXERCISE 8–15 Flexible Budgets and Revenue and Spending Variances [LO1, LO2]

TAKE TWO

Budgeted revenue per liter = $14.50

Gelato Supremo is a popular neighborhood gelato shop. The company has provided the following data concerning its operations:

| | Fixed Element per Month | Variable Element per Liter | Actual Total for July |
|---|---|---|---|
| Revenue ........................... | | $13.50 | $69,420 |
| Raw materials.................... | | $5.10 | $26,890 |
| Wages .............................. | $4,800 | $1.20 | $11,200 |
| Utilities............................. | $1,860 | $0.15 | $2,470 |
| Rent.................................. | $3,150 | | $3,150 |
| Insurance.......................... | $1,890 | | $1,890 |
| Miscellaneous.................... | $540 | $0.15 | $1,390 |

While gelato is sold by the cone or cup, the shop measures its activity in terms of the total number of liters of gelato sold. For example, wages should be $4,800 plus $1.20 per liter of gelato sold, and the actual wages for July were $11,200. Gelato Supremo expected to sell 5,000 liters in July, but actually sold 4,900 liters.

***Required:***

Prepare a report showing Gelato Supremo revenue and spending variances for July.

**EXERCISE 8–16 Flexible Budget Performance Report in a Cost Center [LO1, LO2]**

Triway Packaging Corporation manufactures and sells a wide variety of packaging products. Performance reports are prepared monthly for each department. The planning budget and flexible budget for the Production Department are based on the following formulas, where $q$ is the number of direct labor-hours worked in a month:

| | |
|---|---|
| Direct labor | $16.30$q$ |
| Indirect labor | $4,300 + $1.80$q$ |
| Utilities | $5,600 + $0.70$q$ |
| Supplies | $1,400 + $0.30$q$ |
| Equipment depreciation | $18,600 + $2.80$q$ |
| Factory rent | $8,300 |
| Property taxes | $2,800 |
| Factory administration | $13,400 + $0.90$q$ |

The actual costs incurred in November in the Production Department are listed below:

| | Actual Cost Incurred in November |
|---|---|
| Direct labor | $63,520 |
| Indirect labor | $10,680 |
| Utilities | $8,790 |
| Supplies | $2,810 |
| Equipment depreciation | $29,240 |
| Factory rent | $8,700 |
| Property taxes | $2,800 |
| Factory administration | $16,230 |

***Required:***

1. The company had budgeted for an activity level of 4,000 labor-hours in November. Prepare the Production Department's planning budget for the month.
2. The company actually worked 3,800 labor-hours in November. Prepare the Production Department's flexible budget for the month.
3. Calculate the spending variances for all expense items.

**EXERCISE 8–17 Material and Labor Variances [LO4, LO5]**

Topper Toys has developed a new toy called the Brainbuster. The company has a standard cost system to help control costs and has established the following standards for the Brainbuster toy:

| |
|---|
| Direct materials: 8 diodes per toy at $0.30 per diode |
| Direct labor: 0.6 hours per toy at $14.00 per hour |

TAKE TWO

Standard direct labor-hours per toy = 0.75 hours

During August, the company produced 5,000 Brainbuster toys. Production data on the toy for August follow:

| |
|---|
| Direct materials: 70,000 diodes were purchased at a cost of $0.28 per diode. 20,000 of these diodes were still in inventory at the end of the month. |
| Direct labor: 3,200 direct labor-hours were worked at a cost of $48,000. |

***Required:***

1. Compute the following variances for August:
   a. Direct materials quantity and price variances.
   b. Direct labor efficiency and rate variances.
2. Prepare a brief explanation of the possible causes of each variance.

Alternate problem set is available on the text website and in *Connect® Accounting.*

connect ACCOUNTING

## PROBLEMS

**All applicable problems are available with McGraw-Hill's *Connect® Accounting*.**

**PROBLEM 8–18A Comprehensive Variance Analysis [LO4, LO5, LO6]**

CHECK FIGURE
(1a) Materials quantity variance: 500 F;
(1b) Labor rate variance: $1,080 F

Portland Company's Ironton Plant produces precast ingots for industrial use. Carlos Santiago, who was recently appointed general manager of the Ironton Plant, has just been handed the plant's contribution format income statement for October. The statement is shown below:

| | Budgeted | Actual |
|---|---|---|
| Sales (5,000 ingots) | $250,000 | $250,000 |
| Variable expenses: | | |
| Variable cost of goods sold* | 80,000 | 96,390 |
| Variable selling expenses | 20,000 | 20,000 |
| Total variable expenses | 100,000 | 116,390 |
| Contribution margin | 150,000 | 133,610 |
| Fixed expenses: | | |
| Manufacturing overhead | 60,000 | 60,000 |
| Selling and administrative | 75,000 | 75,000 |
| Total fixed expenses | 135,000 | 135,000 |
| Net operating income (loss) | $ 15,000 | $ (1,390) |

*Contains direct materials, direct labor, and variable manufacturing overhead.

Mr. Santiago was shocked to see the loss for the month, particularly because sales were exactly as budgeted. He stated, "I sure hope the plant has a standard cost system in operation. If it doesn't, I won't have the slightest idea of where to start looking for the problem."

The plant does use a standard cost system, with the following standard variable cost per ingot:

| | Standard Quantity or Hours | Standard Price or Rate | Standard Cost |
|---|---|---|---|
| Direct materials | 4.0 pounds | $2.50 per pound | $10.00 |
| Direct labor | 0.6 hours | $9.00 per hour | 5.40 |
| Variable manufacturing overhead | 0.3 hours* | $2.00 per hour | 0.60 |
| Total standard variable cost | | | $16.00 |

*Based on machine-hours.

During October the plant produced 5,000 ingots and incurred the following costs:

a. Purchased 25,000 pounds of materials at a cost of $2.95 per pound. There were no raw materials in inventory at the beginning of the month.
b. Used 19,800 pounds of materials in production. (Finished goods and work in process inventories are insignificant and can be ignored.)
c. Worked 3,600 direct labor-hours at a cost of $8.70 per hour.
d. Incurred total variable manufacturing overhead costs of $4,320 for the month. A total of 1,800 machine-hours was recorded.

***Required:***

1. Compute the following variances for October:
   a. Direct materials quantity and price variances.
   b. Direct labor efficiency and rate variances.
   c. Variable overhead efficiency and rate variances.

2. Summarize the variances that you computed in requirement 1 by showing the net overall favorable or unfavorable variance for October. If the company closed all variances to cost of goods sold, what impact did the net overall favorable or unfavorable variance have on the company's income statement?
3. Pick out the two most significant variances that you computed in requirement 1. Explain to Mr. Santiago possible causes of these variances.

CHECK FIGURE
(1) Flexible budget total cost: $17,670

**PROBLEM 8–19A More Than One Cost Driver [LO2, LO3]**

Verona Pizza is a small neighborhood pizzeria that has a small area for in-store dining as well offering takeout and free home delivery services. The pizzeria's owner has determined that the shop has two major cost drivers—the number of pizzas sold and the number of deliveries made. Data concerning the pizzeria's costs appear below:

| | Fixed Cost per Month | Cost per Pizza | Cost per Delivery |
|---|---|---|---|
| Pizza ingredients | | $4.20 | |
| Kitchen staff | $5,870 | | |
| Utilities | $590 | $0.10 | |
| Delivery person | | | $2.90 |
| Delivery vehicle | $610 | | $1.30 |
| Equipment depreciation | $384 | | |
| Rent | $1,790 | | |
| Miscellaneous | $710 | $0.05 | |

In October, the pizzeria budgeted for 1,500 pizzas at an average selling price of $13.00 per pizza and for 200 deliveries.

Data concerning the pizzeria's operations in October appear below:

| | Actual Results |
|---|---|
| Pizzas | 1,600 |
| Deliveries | 180 |
| Revenue | $21,340 |
| Pizza ingredients | $6,850 |
| Kitchen staff | $5,810 |
| Utilities | $875 |
| Delivery person | $522 |
| Delivery vehicle | $982 |
| Equipment depreciation | $384 |
| Rent | $1,790 |
| Miscellaneous | $778 |

***Required:***

1. Compute the revenue and spending variances for the pizzeria for October.
2. Explain the revenue and spending variances.

**PROBLEM 8–20A Basic Variance Analysis; the Impact of Variances on Unit Costs [LO4, LO5, LO6]**

Landers Company manufactures a number of products. The standards relating to one of these products are shown below, along with actual cost data for May.

| | Standard Cost per Unit | | Actual Cost per Unit |
|---|---|---|---|
| Direct materials: | | | |
| Standard: 1.80 feet at $3.00 per foot | $5.40 | | |
| Actual: 1.75 feet at $3.20 per foot | | | $5.60 |
| Direct labor: | | | |
| Standard: 0.90 hours at $18.00 per hour | 16.20 | | |
| Actual: 0.95 hours at $17.40 per hour | | | 16.53 |
| Variable overhead: | | | |
| Standard: 0.90 hours at $5.00 per hour | 4.50 | | |
| Actual: 0.95 hours at $4.60 per hour | | | 4.37 |
| Total cost per unit | $26.10 | | $26.50 |
| Excess of actual cost over standard cost per unit | | $0.40 | |

CHECK FIGURE
(1b) Labor rate variance: $6,840 F; (1c) Variable overhead efficiency variance: $3,000 U

The production superintendent was pleased when he saw this report and commented: "This $0.40 excess cost is well within the 2 percent limit management has set for acceptable variances. It's obvious that there's not much to worry about with this product."

Actual production for the month was 12,000 units. Variable overhead cost is assigned to products on the basis of direct labor-hours. There were no beginning or ending inventories of materials.

***Required:***

1. Compute the following variances for May:
   a. Materials quantity and price variances.
   b. Labor efficiency and rate variances.
   c. Variable overhead efficiency and rate variances.
2. How much of the $0.40 excess unit cost is traceable to each of the variances computed in (1) above.
3. How much of the $0.40 excess unit cost is traceable to apparent inefficient use of labor time?
4. Do you agree that the excess unit cost is not of concern?

**PROBLEM 8–21A Multiple Products, Materials, and Processes [LO4, LO5]**

Monte Rosa Corporation produces two products, Alpha8s and Zeta9s, which pass through two operations, Sintering and Finishing. Each of the products uses two raw materials, X342 and Y561. The company uses a standard cost system, with the following standards for each product (on a per unit basis):

CHECK FIGURE
(2) Materials quantity variance—material Y561: $1,400 U

| | Raw Material | | Standard Labor Time | |
|---|---|---|---|---|
| Product | X342 | Y561 | Sintering | Finishing |
| Alpha8 | 1.8 kilos | 2.0 liters | 0.20 hours | 0.80 hours |
| Zeta9 | 3.0 kilos | 4.5 liters | 0.35 hours | 0.90 hours |

Information relating to materials purchased and materials used in production during May follows:

| Material | Purchases | Purchase Cost | Standard Price | Used in Production |
|---|---|---|---|---|
| X342 | 14,000 kilos | $51,800 | $3.50 per kilo | 8,500 kilos |
| Y561 | 15,000 liters | $19,500 | $1.40 per liter | 13,000 liters |

The following additional information is available:

a. The company recognizes price variances when materials are purchased.
b. The standard labor rate is $20.00 per hour in Sintering and $19.00 per hour in Finishing.

c. During May, 1,200 direct labor-hours were worked in Sintering at a total labor cost of $27,000, and 2,850 direct labor-hours were worked in Finishing at a total labor cost of $59,850.
d. Production during May was 1,500 Alpha8s and 2,000 Zeta9s.

***Required:***

1. Prepare a standard cost card for each product, showing the standard cost of direct materials and direct labor.
2. Compute the materials quantity and price variances for each material.
3. Compute the direct labor efficiency and rate variances for each operation.

CHECK FIGURE
(1) Materials price variance: $1,600 F; (2a) Labor efficiency variance: $5,400 U

**PROBLEM 8–22A Variance Analysis in a Hospital [LO4, LO5, LO6]**

"What's going on in that lab?" asked Derek Warren, chief administrator for Cottonwood Hospital, as he studied the prior month's reports. "Every month the lab teeters between a profit and a loss. Are we going to have to increase our lab fees again?"

"We can't," replied Lois Ankers, the controller. "We're getting *lots* of complaints about the last increase, particularly from the insurance companies and governmental health units. They're now paying only about 80% of what we bill. I'm beginning to think the problem is on the cost side."

To determine if lab costs are in line with other hospitals, Mr. Warren has asked you to evaluate the costs for the past month. Ms. Ankers has provided you with the following information:

a. Two basic types of tests are performed in the lab—smears and blood tests. During the past month, 2,700 smears and 900 blood tests were performed in the lab.
b. Small glass plates are used in both types of tests. During the past month, the hospital purchased 16,000 plates at a cost of $38,400. This cost is net of a 4% purchase discount. A total of 2,000 of these plates were unused at the end of the month; no plates were on hand at the beginning of the month.
c. During the past month, 1,800 hours of labor time were used in performing smears and blood tests. The cost of this labor time was $18,450.
d. The lab's variable overhead cost last month totaled $11,700.

Cottonwood Hospital has never used standard costs. By searching industry literature, however, you have determined the following nationwide averages for hospital labs:

***Plates:*** Three plates are required per lab test. These plates cost $2.50 each and are disposed of after the test is completed.

***Labor:*** Each smear should require 0.3 hours to complete, and each blood test should require 0.6 hours to complete. The average cost of this lab time is $12 per hour.

***Overhead:*** Overhead cost is based on direct labor-hours. The average rate of variable overhead is $6 per hour.

***Required:***

1. Compute the materials quantity variance for the plates used last month and compute the materials price variance for the plates purchased last month.
2. For labor cost in the lab:
   a. Compute a labor efficiency variance and a labor rate variance.
   b. In most hospitals, three-fourths of the workers in the lab are certified technicians and one-fourth are assistants. In an effort to reduce costs, Cottonwood Hospital employs only one-half certified technicians and one-half assistants. Would you recommend that this policy be continued? Explain.
3. Compute the variable overhead efficiency and rate variances. Is there any relation between the variable overhead efficiency variance and the labor efficiency variance? Explain.

CHECK FIGURE
(2) Overall spending variance: $5,300 U

**PROBLEM 8–23A Flexible Budgets and Spending Variances [LO1, LO2]**

You have just been hired by SecuriDoor Corporation, the manufacturer of a revolutionary new garage door opening device. The president has asked that you review the company's costing system and "do what you can to help us get better control of our manufacturing overhead costs." You find that the company has never used a flexible budget, and you suggest that preparing such a budget would be an excellent first step in overhead planning and control.

After much effort and analysis, you determined the following cost formulas and gathered the following actual cost data for April:

| | Cost Formula | Actual Cost in April |
|---|---|---|
| Utilities | $16,500 plus $0.15 per machine-hour | $21,300 |
| Maintenance | $38,600 plus $1.80 per machine-hour | $68,400 |
| Supplies | $0.50 per machine-hour | $9,800 |
| Indirect labor | $94,300 plus $1.20 per machine-hour | $119,200 |
| Depreciation | $68,000 | $69,700 |

During April, the company worked 18,000 machine-hours and produced 12,000 units. The company had originally planned to work 20,000 machine-hours during April.

***Required:***

1. Prepare a flexible budget for April.
2. Prepare a report showing the spending variances for April. Explain what these variances mean.

**PROBLEM 8–24A Comprehensive Variance Analysis [LO4, LO5, LO6]**

eXcel

CHECK FIGURE
(1) Materials price variance: $3,000 F; (3) Variable overhead rate variance: $1,520 U

Helix Company produces several products in its factory, including a karate robe. The company uses a standard cost system to assist in the control of costs. According to the standards that have been set for the robes, the factory should work 780 direct labor-hours each month and produce 1,950 robes. The standard costs associated with this level of production are as follows:

| | Total | Per Unit of Product |
|---|---|---|
| Direct materials | $35,490 | $18.20 |
| Direct labor | $7,020 | 3.60 |
| Variable manufacturing overhead (based on direct labor-hours) | $2,340 | 1.20 |
| | | $23.00 |

During April, the factory worked only 760 direct labor-hours and produced 2,000 robes. The following actual costs were recorded during the month:

| | Total | Per Unit of Product |
|---|---|---|
| Direct materials (6,000 yards) | $36,000 | $18.00 |
| Direct labor | $7,600 | 3.80 |
| Variable manufacturing overhead | $3,800 | 1.90 |
| | | $23.70 |

At standard, each robe should require 2.8 yards of material. All of the materials purchased during the month were used in production.

***Required:***

Compute the following variances for April:

1. The materials quantity and price variances.
2. The labor efficiency and rate variances.
3. The variable manufacturing overhead efficiency and rate variances.

**PROBLEM 8–25A Materials and Labor Variances; Computations from Incomplete Data [LO4, LO5]**

CHECK FIGURE
(1a) Standard price: $3.00 per pound; (2b) Labor rate variance: $1,500 U

Topaz Company makes one product and has set the following standards for materials and labor:

| | Direct Materials | Direct Labor |
|---|---|---|
| Standard quantity or hours per unit | ? pounds | 2.5 hours |
| Standard price or rate | ? per pound | $9.00 per hour |
| Standard cost per unit | ? | $22.50 |

During the past month, the company purchased 6,000 pounds of direct materials at a cost of $16,500. All of this material was used in the production of 1,400 units of product. Direct labor cost totaled $28,500 for the month. The following variances have been computed:

| | |
|---|---|
| Materials quantity variance | $1,200 U |
| Total materials spending variance | $300 F |
| Labor efficiency variance | $4,500 F |

***Required:***

1. For direct materials:
   a. Compute the standard price per pound for materials.
   b. Compute the standard quantity allowed for materials for the month's production.
   c. Compute the standard quantity of materials allowed per unit of product.
2. For direct labor:
   a. Compute the actual direct labor cost per hour for the month.
   b. Compute the labor rate variance.

(Hint: In completing the problem, it may be helpful to move from known to unknown data either by using the variance formulas or by using the columnar format shown in Exhibits 8–11 and 8–12.)

## BUILDING YOUR SKILLS

### ETHICS CHALLENGE [LO2]

Lance Prating is the controller of the Colorado Springs manufacturing facility of Prudhom Enterprises, Inc. The annual cost control report is one of the many reports that must be filed with corporate headquarters and is due at corporate headquarters shortly after the beginning of the New Year. Prating does not like putting work off to the last minute, so just before Christmas he prepared a preliminary draft of the cost control report. Some adjustments would later be required for transactions that occur between Christmas and New Year's Day. A copy of the preliminary draft report, which Prating completed on December 21, follows:

**Colorado Springs Manufacturing Facility**
**Cost Control Report**
**December 21 Preliminary Draft**

| | Flexible Budget | Actual Results | Spending Variances |
|---|---|---|---|
| Labor-hours | 9,000 | 9,000 | |
| Direct labor | $162,000 | $164,600 | $2,600 U |
| Power | 2,700 | 2,950 | 250 U |
| Supplies | 28,800 | 29,700 | 900 U |
| Equipment depreciation | 226,500 | 228,300 | 1,800 U |
| Supervisory salaries | 189,000 | 187,300 | 1,700 F |
| Insurance | 23,000 | 23,000 | 0 |
| Industrial engineering | 160,000 | 154,000 | 6,000 F |
| Factory building lease | 46,000 | 46,000 | 0 |
| Total expense | $838,000 | $835,850 | $2,150 F |

Tab Kapp, the general manager at the Colorado Springs facility, asked to see a copy of the preliminary draft report. Prating carried a copy of the report to Kapp's office where the following discussion took place:

***Kapp:*** Wow! Almost all of the variances on the report are unfavorable. The only favorable variances are for supervisory salaries and industrial engineering. How did we have an unfavorable variance for depreciation?

***Prating:*** Do you remember that milling machine that broke down because the wrong lubricant was used by the machine operator?

***Kapp:*** Yes.

***Prating:*** We couldn't fix it. We had to scrap the machine and buy a new one.

***Kapp:*** This report doesn't look good. I was raked over the coals last year when we had just a few unfavorable variances.

***Prating:*** I'm afraid the final report is going to look even worse.

***Kapp:*** Oh?

***Prating:*** The line item for industrial engineering on the report is for work we hired Sanchez Engineering to do for us. The original contract was for $160,000, but we asked them to do some additional work that was not in the contract. We have to reimburse Sanchez Engineering for the costs of that additional work. The $154,000 in actual costs that appears on the preliminary draft report reflects only their billings up through

December 21. The last bill they had sent us was on November 28, and they completed the project just last week. Yesterday I got a call from Mary Jurney over at Sanchez and she said they would be sending us a final bill for the project before the end of the year. The total bill, including the reimbursements for the additional work, is going to be . . .

***Kapp:*** I am not sure I want to hear this.

***Prating:*** $176,000.

***Kapp:*** Ouch!

***Prating:*** The additional work added $16,000 to the cost of the project.

***Kapp:*** I can't turn in a report with an overall unfavorable variance! They'll kill me at corporate headquarters. Call up Mary at Sanchez and ask her not to send the bill until after the first of the year. We have to have that $6,000 favorable variance for industrial engineering on the report.

***Required:***
What should Lance Prating do? Explain.

## ANALYTICAL THINKING [LO4, LO5, LO6]

eXcel

CHECK FIGURE
(1) Standard cost: $11,400;
(5) Labor rate variance: $450 U

Vitalite, Inc., produces a number of products, including a body-wrap kit. Standard variable costs relating to a single kit are given below:

| | Standard Quantity or Hours | Standard Price or Rate | Standard Cost |
|---|---|---|---|
| Direct materials | ? | $6 per yard | $ ? |
| Direct labor | ? | ? | ? |
| Variable manufacturing overhead | ? | $2 per direct labor-hour | ? |
| Total standard cost per kit | | | $42 |

During August, 500 kits were manufactured and sold. Selected information relating to the month's production is given below:

| | Materials Used | Direct Labor | Variable Manufacturing Overhead |
|---|---|---|---|
| Total standard cost* | ? | $8,000 | $1,600 |
| Actual costs incurred | $10,000 | ? | $1,620 |
| Materials price variance | ? | | |
| Materials quantity variance | $600 U | | |
| Labor rate variance | | ? | |
| Labor efficiency variance | | ? | |
| Variable overhead rate variance | | | ? |
| Variable overhead efficiency variance | | | ? |

*For the month's production.

The following additional information is available for August's production of kits:

| | |
|---|---|
| Actual direct labor-hours | 900 |
| Difference between standard and actual cost per kit produced during August | $0.14 U |

***Required:***
1. What was the total standard cost of the materials used during August?
2. How many yards of material are required at standard per kit?
3. What was the materials price variance for August if there were no beginning or ending inventories of materials?

4. What is the standard direct labor rate per hour?
5. What was the labor efficiency variance for August? The labor rate variance?
6. What was the variable overhead efficiency variance for August? The variable overhead rate variance?
7. Complete the standard cost card for one kit shown at the beginning of the problem.

CHECK FIGURE
(2) Flexible budget total cost: $340,112

**CASE [LO1, LO2, LO3]**

The Munchkin Theater is a nonprofit organization devoted to staging plays for children. The theater has a very small full-time professional administrative staff. Through a special arrangement with the actors' union, actors and directors rehearse without pay and are paid only for actual performances.

The costs from the current year's planning budget appear below. The Munchkin Theater had tentatively planned to put on five different productions with a total of 60 performances. For example, one of the productions was *Peter Rabbit,* which had five performances.

**The Munchkin Theater**
**Costs from the Planning Budget**
**For the Year Ended December 31**

| | |
|---|---|
| Budgeted number of productions | 5 |
| Budgeted number of performances | 60 |
| Actors' and directors' wages | $144,000 |
| Stagehands' wages | 27,000 |
| Ticket booth personnel and ushers' wages | 10,800 |
| Scenery, costumes, and props | 43,000 |
| Theater hall rent | 45,000 |
| Printed programs | 10,500 |
| Publicity | 13,000 |
| Administrative expenses | 43,200 |
| Total | $336,500 |

Some of the costs vary with the number of productions, some with the number of performances, and some are fixed and depend on neither the number of productions nor the number of performances. The costs of scenery, costumes, props, and publicity vary with the number of productions. It doesn't make any difference how many times *Peter Rabbit* is performed, the cost of the scenery is the same. Likewise, the cost of publicizing a play with posters and radio commercials is the same whether there are 10, 20, or 30 performances of the play. On the other hand, the wages of the actors, directors, stagehands, ticket booth personnel, and ushers vary with the number of performances. The greater the number of performances, the higher the wage costs will be. Similarly, the costs of renting the hall and printing the programs will vary with the number of performances. Administrative expenses are more difficult to pin down, but the best estimate is that approximately 75% of the budgeted costs are fixed, 15% depend on the number of productions staged, and the remaining 10% depend on the number of performances.

After the beginning of the year, the board of directors of the theater authorized changing the theater's program to four productions and a total of 64 performances. Actual costs were higher than the costs from the planning budget. (Grants from donors and ticket sales were also correspondingly higher, but are not shown here.) Data concerning the actual costs appear below:

**The Munchkin Theater**
**Actual Costs**
**For the Year Ended December 31**

| | |
|---|---|
| Actual number of productions | 4 |
| Actual number of performances | 64 |
| Actors' and directors' wages | $148,000 |
| Stagehands' wages | 28,600 |
| Ticket booth personnel and ushers' wages | 12,300 |
| Scenery, costumes, and props | 39,300 |
| Theater hall rent | 49,600 |
| Printed programs | 10,950 |
| Publicity | 12,000 |
| Administrative expenses | 41,650 |
| Total | $342,400 |

***Required:***

1. Prepare a flexible budget for The Munchkin Theater based on the actual activity of the year.
2. Prepare a report that summarizes the spending variances for all expense items.
3. If you were on the board of directors of the theater, would you be pleased with how well costs were controlled during the year? Why or why not?
4. The cost formulas provide figures for the average cost per production and average cost per performance. How accurate do you think these figures would be for predicting the cost of a new production or of an additional performance of a particular production?

# APPENDIX 8A: PREDETERMINED OVERHEAD RATES AND OVERHEAD ANALYSIS IN A STANDARD COSTING SYSTEM

LEARNING OBJECTIVE 7

Compute and interpret the fixed overhead volume and budget variances.

In this appendix, we will investigate how the predetermined overhead rates that we discussed in the job-order costing chapter can be used in a standard costing system. Throughout this appendix, we assume that an absorption costing system is used in which *all* manufacturing costs—both fixed and variable—are included in product costs.

## Predetermined Overhead Rates

The data in Exhibit 8A–1 pertain to MicroDrive Corporation, a company that produces miniature electric motors. Note that the company budgeted for 50,000 machine-hours based on production of 25,000 motors. At this level of activity, the budgeted variable manufacturing overhead was $75,000 and the budgeted fixed manufacturing overhead was $300,000.

Recall from the job-order costing chapter that the following formula is used to set the predetermined overhead rate at the beginning of the period:

$$\text{Predetermined overhead rate} = \frac{\text{Estimated total manufacturing overhead cost}}{\text{Estimated total amount of the allocation base}}$$

The estimated total amount of the allocation base in the formula for the predetermined overhead rate is called the **denominator activity**.

As discussed in the job-order costing chapter, once the predetermined overhead rate has been determined, it remains unchanged throughout the period, even if the actual level

**EXHIBIT 8A–1**
MicroDrive Corporation Data

| | |
|---|---|
| Budgeted production | 25,000 motors |
| Standard machine-hours per motor | 2 machine-hours per motor |
| Budgeted machine-hours (2 machine-hours per motor × 25,000 motors) | 50,000 machine-hours |
| Actual production | 20,000 motors |
| Standard machine-hours allowed for the actual production (2 machine-hours per motor × 20,000 motors) | 40,000 machine-hours |
| Actual machine-hours | 42,000 machine-hours |
| Budgeted variable manufacturing overhead | $75,000 |
| Budgeted fixed manufacturing overhead | $300,000 |
| Total budgeted manufacturing overhead | $375,000 |
| Actual variable manufacturing overhead | $71,000 |
| Actual fixed manufacturing overhead | $308,000 |
| Total actual manufacturing overhead | $379,000 |

of activity differs from what was estimated. Consequently, the amount of overhead applied to each unit of product is the same regardless of when it is produced during the period.

MicroDrive Corporation uses budgeted machine-hours as its denominator activity in the predetermined overhead rate. Consequently, the company's predetermined overhead rate would be computed as follows:

$$\text{Predetermined overhead rate} = \frac{\$375{,}000}{50{,}000 \text{ MHs}} = \$7.50 \text{ per MH}$$

This predetermined overhead rate can be broken down into its variable and fixed components as follows:

$$\text{Variable component of the predetermined overhead rate} = \frac{\$75{,}000}{50{,}000 \text{ MHs}} = \$1.50 \text{ per MH}$$

$$\text{Fixed component of the predetermined overhead rate} = \frac{\$300{,}000}{50{,}000 \text{ MHs}} = \$6.00 \text{ per MH}$$

For every standard machine-hour recorded, work in process is charged with $7.50 of manufacturing overhead, of which $1.50 represents variable manufacturing overhead and $6.00 represents fixed manufacturing overhead. In total, MicroDrive Corporation would apply $300,000 of overhead to work in process as shown below:

$$\begin{aligned}\text{Overhead applied} &= \text{Predetermined overhead rate} \times \text{Standard hours allowed for the actual output}\\ &= \$7.50 \text{ per machine-hour} \times 40{,}000 \text{ machine-hours}\\ &= \$300{,}000\end{aligned}$$

## Overhead Application in a Standard Cost System

To understand fixed overhead variances, we first have to understand how overhead is applied to work in process in a standard cost system. Recall that in the job-order costing chapter we applied overhead to work in process on the basis of the actual level of activity. This procedure was correct because at the time we were dealing with a normal cost system.[1] However, we are now dealing with a standard cost system. In such a system, overhead is applied to work in process on the basis of the *standard hours allowed for the actual output of the period* rather than on the basis of the actual number of hours worked. Exhibit 8A–2 illustrates this point. In a standard cost system, every unit of a particular product is charged with the same amount of overhead cost, regardless of how much time the unit actually requires for processing.

**EXHIBIT 8A–2**
Applied Overhead Costs: Normal Cost System versus Standard Cost System

| Normal Cost System | | Standard Cost System | |
|---|---|---|---|
| Manufacturing Overhead | | Manufacturing Overhead | |
| Actual overhead costs incurred. | Applied overhead costs: Actual hours × Predetermined overhead rate. | Actual overhead costs incurred. | Applied overhead costs: Standard hours allowed for actual output × Predetermined overhead rate. |
| Underapplied or overapplied overhead | | Underapplied or overapplied overhead | |

[1]Normal cost systems are discussed on page 72 in the job-order costing chapter.

**EXHIBIT 8A–3** Fixed Overhead Variances

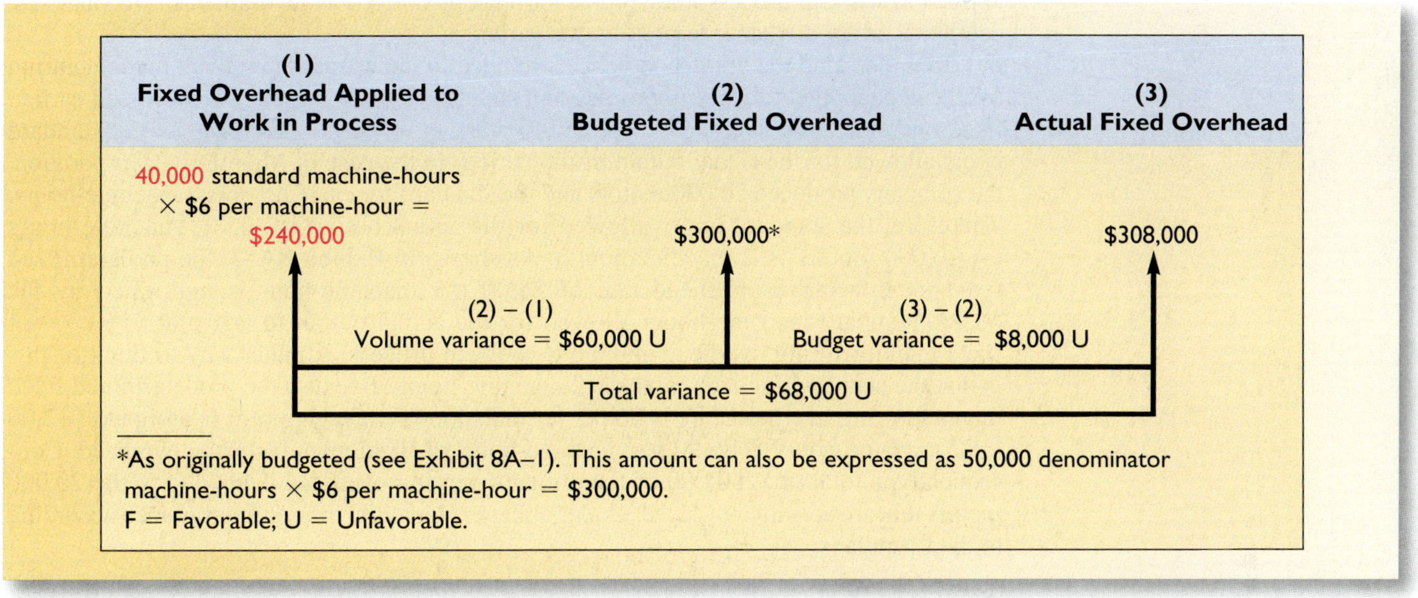


## Budget Variance

Two fixed manufacturing overhead variances are computed in a standard costing system—a *budget variance* and a *volume variance.* These variances are computed in Exhibit 8A–3. The **budget variance** is simply the difference between the actual fixed manufacturing overhead and the budgeted fixed manufacturing overhead for the period. The formula is:

$$\text{Budget variance} = \text{Actual fixed overhead} - \text{Budgeted fixed overhead}$$

If the actual fixed overhead cost exceeds the budgeted fixed overhead cost, the budget variance is labeled unfavorable. If the actual fixed overhead cost is less than the budgeted fixed overhead cost, the budget variance is labeled favorable.

Applying the formula to the MicroDrive Corporation data, the budget variance is computed as follows:

$$\text{Budget variance} = \$308{,}000 - \$300{,}000 = \$8{,}000 \text{ U}$$

According to the budget, the fixed manufacturing overhead should have been $300,000, but it was actually $308,000. Because the actual cost exceeds the budget by $8,000, the variance is labeled as unfavorable; however, this label does not automatically signal ineffective managerial performance. For example, this variance may be the result of waste and inefficiency, or it may be due to an unforeseen yet prudent investment in fixed overhead resources that improves product quality or manufacturing cycle efficiency.

## Volume Variance

The **volume variance** is defined by the following formula:

$$\text{Volume variance} = \begin{array}{c}\text{Budgeted fixed}\\ \text{overhead}\end{array} - \begin{array}{c}\text{Fixed overhead applied}\\ \text{to work in process}\end{array}$$

When the budgeted fixed manufacturing overhead exceeds the fixed manufacturing overhead applied to work in process, the volume variance is labeled as unfavorable. When the budgeted fixed manufacturing overhead is less than the fixed manufacturing overhead applied to work in process, the volume variance is labeled as favorable. As we shall see, caution is advised when interpreting this variance.

To understand the volume variance, we need to understand how fixed manufacturing overhead is applied to work in process in a standard costing system. As discussed earlier, fixed manufacturing overhead is applied to work in process on the basis of the standard hours allowed for the actual output of the period. In the case of MicroDrive Corporation, the company produced 20,000 motors and the standard for each motor is 2 machine-hours. Therefore, the standard hours allowed for the actual output is 40,000 machine-hours (= 20,000 motors × 2 machine-hours). As shown in Exhibit 8A–3, the predetermined fixed manufacturing overhead rate of $6.00 per machine-hour is multiplied by the 40,000 standard machine-hours allowed for the actual output to arrive at $240,000 of fixed manufacturing overhead applied to work in process. Another way to think of this is that the standard for each motor is 2 machine-hours. Because the predetermined fixed manufacturing overhead rate is $6.00 per machine-hour, each motor is assigned $12.00 (= 2 machine-hours × $6.00 per machine-hour) of fixed manufacturing overhead. Consequently, a total of $240,000 of fixed manufacturing overhead is applied to the 20,000 motors that are actually produced. Under either explanation, the volume variance according to the formula is:

$$\text{Volume variance} = \$300{,}000 - \$240{,}000 = \$60{,}000\text{ U}$$

The key to interpreting the volume variance is to understand that it depends on the difference between the hours used in the denominator to compute the predetermined overhead rate and the standard hours allowed for the actual output of the period. While it is not obvious, the volume variance can also be computed using the following formula:

$$\begin{matrix}\text{Volume}\\\text{variance}\end{matrix} = \begin{matrix}\text{Fixed component of the}\\\text{predetermined overhead rate}\end{matrix} \times \left(\begin{matrix}\text{Denominator}\\\text{hours}\end{matrix} - \begin{matrix}\text{Standard hours allowed}\\\text{for the actual output}\end{matrix}\right)$$

In the case of MicroDrive Corporation, the volume variance can be computed using this formula as follows:

$$\begin{aligned}\text{Volume variance} &= \frac{\$6.00\text{ per}}{\text{machine-hour}} \times \left(\begin{matrix}50{,}000\\\text{machine-hours}\end{matrix} - \begin{matrix}40{,}000\\\text{machine-hours}\end{matrix}\right)\\ &= \$6.00\text{ per machine-hour} \times (10{,}000\text{ machine-hours})\\ &= \$60{,}000\text{ U}\end{aligned}$$

Note that this agrees with the volume variance computed using the earlier formula.

Focusing on this new formula, if the denominator hours exceed the standard hours allowed for the actual output, the volume variance is unfavorable. If the denominator hours are less than the standard hours allowed for the actual output, the volume variance is favorable. Stated differently, the volume variance is unfavorable if the actual level of activity is less than expected. The volume variance is favorable if the actual level of activity is greater than expected. It is important to note that the volume variance does not measure overspending or underspending. A company should incur the same dollar amount of fixed overhead cost regardless of whether the period's activity was above or below the planned (denominator) level.

The volume variance is often viewed as a measure of the utilization of facilities. If the standard hours allowed for the actual output are greater than (less than) the denominator hours, it signals efficient (inefficient) usage of facilities. However, other measures of utilization—such as the percentage of capacity utilized—are easier to compute and understand. Perhaps a better interpretation of the volume variance is that it is the error that occurs when the level of activity is incorrectly estimated and the costing system assumes fixed costs behave as if they are variable. This interpretation may be clearer in the next section that graphically analyzes the fixed manufacturing overhead variances.

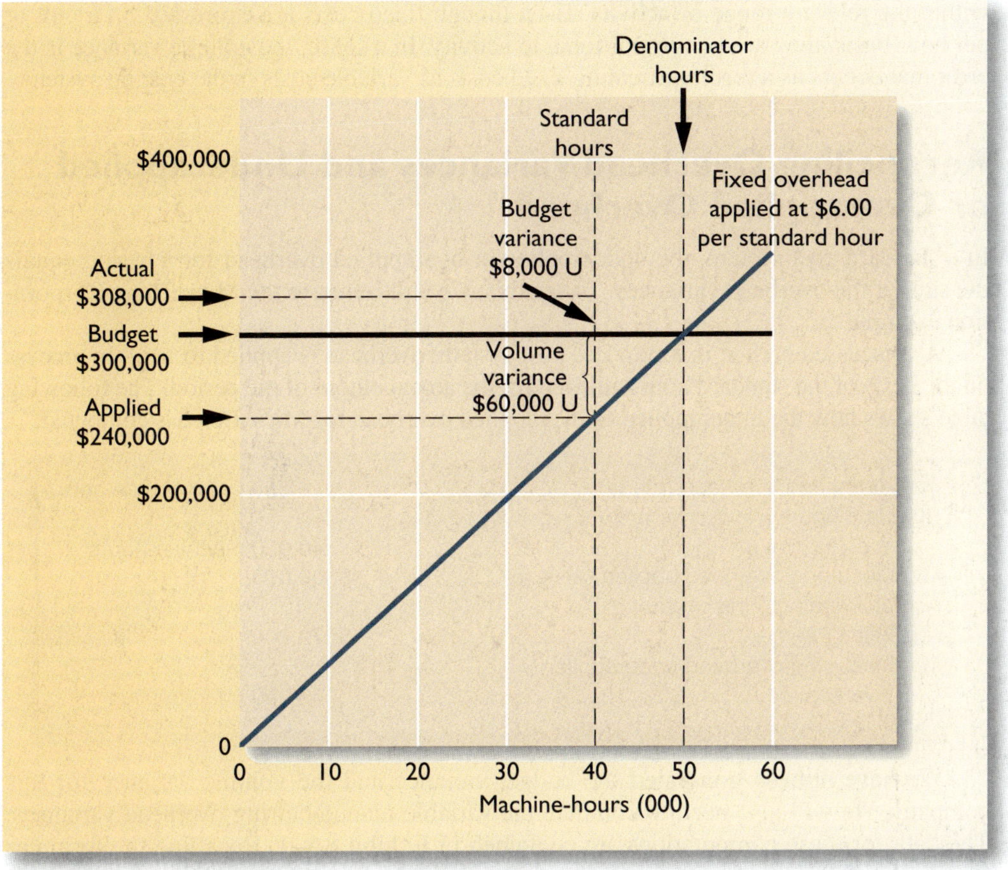


**EXHIBIT 8A–4**
Graphic Analysis of Fixed Overhead Variances

## Graphic Analysis of Fixed Overhead Variances

Exhibit 8A–4 shows a graphic analysis that offers insights into the fixed overhead budget and volume variances. As shown in the graph, fixed overhead cost is applied to work in process at the predetermined rate of $6.00 for each standard hour of activity. (The applied-cost line is the upward-sloping line on the graph.) Because a denominator level of 50,000 machine-hours was used in computing the $6.00 rate, the applied-cost line crosses the budget-cost line at exactly 50,000 machine-hours. If the denominator hours and the standard hours allowed for the actual output are the same, there is no volume variance. It is only when the standard hours differ from the denominator hours that a volume variance arises.

In MicroDrive's case, the standard hours allowed for the actual output (40,000 hours) are less than the denominator hours (50,000 hours). The result is an unfavorable volume variance because less cost was applied to production than was originally budgeted. If the situation had been reversed and the standard hours allowed for the actual output had exceeded the denominator hours, then the volume variance on the graph would have been favorable.

## Cautions in Fixed Overhead Analysis

A volume variance for fixed overhead arises because when applying the costs to work in process, we act *as if* the fixed costs are variable. The graph in Exhibit 8A–4 illustrates this point. Notice from the graph that fixed overhead costs are applied to work in process at a rate of $6 per hour *as if* they are variable. Treating these costs as if they are variable is necessary for product costing purposes, but some real dangers lurk here. Managers can easily be misled into thinking that fixed costs are *in fact* variable.

Keep clearly in mind that fixed overhead costs come in large chunks. Expressing fixed costs on a unit or per hour basis, though necessary for product costing for external reports, is artificial. Increases or decreases in activity in fact have no effect on total fixed costs within the relevant range of activity. Even though fixed costs are expressed on a unit or per hour basis, they are *not* proportional to activity. In a sense, the volume variance is the error that occurs as a result of treating fixed costs as variable costs in the costing system.

## Reconciling Overhead Variances and Underapplied or Overapplied Overhead

In a standard cost system, the underapplied or overapplied overhead for a period equals the sum of the overhead variances. To see this, we will return to the MicroDrive Corporation example.

As discussed earlier, in a standard cost system, overhead is applied to work in process on the basis of the standard hours allowed for the actual output of the period. The following table shows how the underapplied or overapplied overhead for MicroDrive is computed:

| | |
|---|---|
| Predetermined overhead rate (a) | $7.50 per machine-hour |
| Standard hours allowed for the actual output [Exhibit 8A–1] (b) | 40,000 machine-hours |
| Manufacturing overhead applied (a) × (b) | $300,000 |
| Actual manufacturing overhead [Exhibit 8A–1] | $379,000 |
| Manufacturing overhead underapplied or overapplied | $79,000 underapplied |

We have already computed the budget variance and the volume variance for this company. We will also need to compute the variable manufacturing overhead variances. The data for these computations are contained in Exhibit 8A–1. Recalling the formulas for the variable manufacturing overhead variances from earlier in this chapter, we can compute the variable overhead efficiency and rate variances as follows:

$$\text{Variable overhead efficiency variance} = (AH - SH)SR$$

$$= \left(\begin{matrix}42{,}000\\ \text{machine-hours}\end{matrix} - \begin{matrix}40{,}000\\ \text{machine-hours}\end{matrix}\right) \times \begin{matrix}\$1.50\text{ per}\\ \text{machine-hour}\end{matrix}$$

$$= \$3{,}000\text{ U}$$

$$\text{Variable overhead rate variance} = (AH \times AR) - (AH \times SR)$$

$$= (\$71{,}000) - \left(\begin{matrix}42{,}000\\ \text{machine-hours}\end{matrix} \times \begin{matrix}\$1.50\text{ per}\\ \text{machine-hour}\end{matrix}\right)$$

$$= \$71{,}000 - \$63{,}000 = \$8{,}000\text{ U}$$

We can now compute the sum of all of the overhead variances as follows:

| | |
|---|---|
| Variable overhead efficiency variance | $ 3,000 U |
| Variable overhead rate variance | 8,000 U |
| Fixed overhead volume variance | 60,000 U |
| Fixed overhead budget variance | 8,000 U |
| Total of the overhead variances | $79,000 U |

Note that the total of the overhead variances is $79,000, which equals the underapplied overhead of $79,000. In general, if the overhead is underapplied, the total of the standard cost overhead variances is unfavorable. If the overhead is overapplied, the total of the standard cost overhead variances is favorable.

## APPENDIX 8A GLOSSARY

**Budget variance** The difference between the actual fixed overhead costs and the budgeted fixed overhead costs for the period. (p. 383)

**Denominator activity** The level of activity used to compute the predetermined overhead rate. (p. 381)

**Volume variance** The variance that arises whenever the standard hours allowed for the actual output of a period are different from the denominator activity level that was used to compute the predetermined overhead rate. It is computed by multiplying the fixed component of the predetermined overhead rate by the difference between the denominator hours and the standard hours allowed for the actual output. (p. 383)

## APPENDIX 8A EXERCISES AND PROBLEMS

**All applicable exercises and problems are available with McGraw-Hill's *Connect® Accounting*.**

### EXERCISE 8A–1 Applying Overhead in a Standard Costing System [LO7]

Mosbach Corporation has a standard cost system in which it applies overhead to products based on the standard direct labor-hours allowed for the actual output of the period. Data concerning the most recent year are as follows:

| | |
|---|---|
| Variable overhead cost per direct labor-hour | $3.50 |
| Total fixed overhead cost per year | $600,000 |
| Budgeted standard direct labor-hours (denominator level of activity) | 80,000 |
| Actual direct labor-hours | 84,000 |
| Standard direct labor-hours allowed for the actual output | 82,000 |

***Required:***

1. Compute the predetermined overhead rate for the year.
2. Determine the amount of overhead that would be applied to the output of the period.

### EXERCISE 8A–2 Fixed Overhead Variances [LO7]

Lusive Corporation has a standard cost system in which it applies overhead to products based on the standard direct labor-hours allowed for the actual output of the period. Data concerning the most recent year appear below:

| | |
|---|---|
| Total budgeted fixed overhead cost for the year | $400,000 |
| Actual fixed overhead cost for the year | $394,000 |
| Budgeted standard direct labor-hours (denominator level of activity) | 50,000 |
| Actual direct labor-hours | 51,000 |
| Standard direct labor-hours allowed for the actual output | 48,000 |

***Required:***

1. Compute the fixed portion of the predetermined overhead rate for the year.
2. Compute the fixed overhead budget and volume variances.

### EXERCISE 8A–3 Fixed Overhead Variances [LO7]

Selected operating information on three different companies for a recent period is given below:

| | Company | | |
|---|---|---|---|
| | X | Y | Z |
| Full-capacity direct labor-hours | 20,000 | 9,000 | 10,000 |
| Budgeted direct labor-hours* | 19,000 | 8,500 | 8,000 |
| Actual direct labor-hours | 19,500 | 8,000 | 9,000 |
| Standard direct labor-hours allowed for actual output | 18,500 | 8,250 | 9,500 |

*Denominator activity for computing the predetermined overhead rate.

***Required:***

For each company, state whether the volume variance would be favorable or unfavorable and explain why.

**EXERCISE 8A–4 Relations Among Fixed Overhead Variances [LO7]**

Selected information relating to the fixed overhead costs of Westwood Company for the most recent year is given below:

| | |
|---|---|
| Activity: | |
| Number of units produced | 9,500 |
| Standard machine-hours allowed per unit | 2 |
| Denominator activity (machine-hours) | 20,000 |
| Costs: | |
| Actual fixed overhead costs incurred | $79,000 |
| Budget variance | $1,000 F |

Overhead cost is applied to products on the basis of standard machine-hours.

***Required:***

1. What was the fixed portion of the predetermined overhead rate?
2. What were the standard machine-hours allowed for the period's production?
3. What was the volume variance?

**EXERCISE 8A–5 Predetermined Overhead Rates [LO7]**

Operating at a normal level of 24,000 direct labor-hours per year, Trone Company produces 8,000 units of product. The direct labor wage rate is $12.60 per hour. Two pounds of raw materials go into each unit of product at a cost of $4.20 per pound. Variable manufacturing overhead should be $1.60 per standard direct labor-hour. Fixed manufacturing overhead should be $84,000 per year.

***Required:***

1. Using 24,000 direct labor-hours as the denominator activity, compute the predetermined overhead rate and break it down into fixed and variable elements.
2. Complete the standard cost card below for one unit of product:

| | |
|---|---|
| Direct materials, 2 pounds at $4.20 per pound | $8.40 |
| Direct labor, ? | ? |
| Variable manufacturing overhead, ? | ? |
| Fixed manufacturing overhead, ? | ? |
| Total standard cost per unit | $ ? |

**EXERCISE 8A–6 Predetermined Overhead Rate; Overhead Variances [LO6, LO7]**

Weller Company's variable manufacturing overhead should be $1.05 per standard machine-hour and its fixed manufacturing overhead should be $24,800 per month. The following information is available for a recent month:

a. The denominator activity of 8,000 machine-hours was chosen to compute the predetermined overhead rate.
b. At the 8,000 standard machine-hours level of activity, the company should produce 3,200 units of product.
c. The company's actual operating results were as follows:

| | |
|---|---|
| Number of units produced | 3,500 |
| Actual machine-hours | 8,500 |
| Actual variable manufacturing overhead cost | $9,860 |
| Actual fixed manufacturing overhead cost | $25,100 |

***Required:***

1. Compute the predetermined overhead rate and break it down into variable and fixed cost elements.
2. What were the standard hours allowed for the year's actual output?
3. Compute the variable overhead efficiency and rate variances and the fixed overhead budget and volume variances.

**EXERCISE 8A–7 Using Fixed Overhead Variances [LO7]**

The standard cost card for the single product manufactured by Prince Company is given below:

| Standard Cost Card—Per Unit | |
|---|---|
| Direct materials, 3.5 feet at $4.00 per foot | $14.00 |
| Direct labor, 0.8 direct labor-hours at $18.00 per direct labor-hour | 14.40 |
| Variable overhead, 0.8 direct labor-hours at $2.50 per direct labor-hour | 2.00 |
| Fixed overhead, 0.8 direct labor-hours at $6.00 per direct labor-hour | 4.80 |
| Total standard cost per unit | $35.20 |

Last year, the company produced 10,000 units of product and worked 8,200 actual direct labor-hours. Manufacturing overhead cost is applied to production on the basis of direct labor-hours. Selected data relating to the company's fixed manufacturing overhead cost for the year are shown below:

| Fixed Overhead Applied to Work in Process | Budgeted Fixed Overhead | Actual Fixed Overhead |
|---|---|---|
| ? hours × $6 per hour = $ ? | ? | $45,600 |

Volume variance = $3,000 F

Budget variance = $?

*Required:*

1. What were the standard hours allowed for the year's production?
2. What was the amount of budgeted fixed overhead cost for the year?
3. What was the budget variance for the year?
4. What denominator activity level did the company use in setting the predetermined overhead rate for the year?

**PROBLEM 8A–8A Comprehensive Standard Cost Variances [LO4, LO5, LO6, LO7]**

CHECK FIGURE
(3a) Variable overhead rate variance: $3,250 U;
(3b) Budget variance: $2,000 F

"It certainly is nice to see that small variance on the income statement after all the trouble we've had lately in controlling manufacturing costs," said Linda White, vice president of Molina Company. "The $12,250 overall manufacturing variance reported last period is well below the 3% limit we have set for variances. We need to congratulate everybody on a job well done."

The company produces and sells a single product. The standard cost card for the product follows:

| Standard Cost Card—Per Unit | |
|---|---|
| Direct materials, 4 yards at $3.50 per yard | $14.00 |
| Direct labor, 1.5 direct labor-hours at $12.00 per direct labor-hour | 18.00 |
| Variable overhead, 1.5 direct labor-hours at $2.00 per direct labor-hour | 3.00 |
| Fixed overhead, 1.5 direct-labor hours at $6.00 per direct labor-hour | 9.00 |
| Standard cost per unit | $44.00 |

The following additional information is available for the year just completed:

a. The company manufactured 20,000 units of product during the year.
b. A total of 78,000 yards of material was purchased during the year at a cost of $3.75 per yard. All of this material was used to manufacture the 20,000 units. There were no beginning or ending inventories for the year.
c. The company worked 32,500 direct labor-hours during the year at a cost of $11.80 per hour.

d. Overhead cost is applied to products on the basis of standard direct labor-hours. Data relating to manufacturing overhead costs follow:

| | |
|---|---|
| Denominator activity level (direct labor-hours) | 25,000 |
| Budgeted fixed overhead costs | $150,000 |
| Actual fixed overhead costs | $148,000 |
| Actual variable overhead costs | $68,250 |

***Required:***

1. Compute the direct materials quantity and price variances for the year.
2. Compute the direct labor efficiency and rate variances for the year.
3. For manufacturing overhead, compute the following:
   a. The variable overhead efficiency and rate variances for the year.
   b. The fixed overhead budget and volume variances for the year.
4. Total the variances you have computed, and compare the net amount with the $12,250 mentioned by the vice president. Do you agree that everyone should be congratulated for a job well done? Explain.

CHECK FIGURE
(4a) 46,250 standard hours;
(4c) Volume variance: $50,000 F

**PROBLEM 8A–9A Selection of a Denominator; Overhead Analysis; Standard Cost Card [LO6, LO7]**

Scott Company's variable manufacturing overhead should be $2.50 per standard direct labor-hour and fixed manufacturing overhead should be $320,000 per year.

The company produces a single product that requires 2.5 direct labor-hours to complete. The direct labor wage rate is $20 per hour. Three yards of raw material are required for each unit of product, at a cost of $5 per yard.

Demand for the company's product differs widely from year to year. Expected activity for this year is 50,000 direct labor-hours; normal activity is 40,000 direct labor-hours per year.

***Required:***

1. Assume that the company chooses 40,000 direct labor-hours as the denominator level of activity. Compute the predetermined overhead rate, breaking it down into fixed and variable cost components.
2. Assume that the company chooses 50,000 direct labor-hours as the denominator level of activity. Repeat the computations in (1) above.
3. Complete two standard cost cards as outlined below.

| Denominator Activity: 40,000 DLHs | |
|---|---|
| Direct materials, 3 yards at $5 per yard | $15.00 |
| Direct labor, ? | ? |
| Variable manufacturing overhead, ? | ? |
| Fixed manufacturing overhead, ? | ? |
| Total standard cost per unit | $ ? |

| Denominator Activity: 50,000 DLHs | |
|---|---|
| Direct materials, 3 yards at $5 per yard | $15.00 |
| Direct labor, ? | ? |
| Variable manufacturing overhead, ? | ? |
| Fixed manufacturing overhead, ? | ? |
| Total standard cost per unit | $ ? |

4. Assume that 48,000 actual hours are worked during the year, and that 18,500 units are produced. Actual manufacturing overhead costs for the year are as follows:

| | |
|---|---|
| Variable manufacturing overhead cost | $124,800 |
| Fixed manufacturing overhead cost | 321,700 |
| Total manufacturing overhead cost | $446,500 |

a. Compute the standard hours allowed for the year's actual output.
b. Compute the missing items from the Manufacturing Overhead account below. Assume that the company uses 40,000 direct labor-hours (normal activity) as the denominator activity figure in computing overhead rates, as you have used in requirement 1.

**Manufacturing Overhead**

| | | |
|---|---|---|
| Actual costs | 446,500 | ? |
| | ? | ? |

c. Analyze your underapplied or overapplied overhead balance in terms of variable overhead efficiency and rate variances and fixed overhead budget and volume variances.

5. Looking at the variances that you have computed, what appears to be the major disadvantage of using normal activity rather than expected actual activity as a denominator in computing the predetermined overhead rate? What advantages can you see to offset this disadvantage?

**PROBLEM 8A–10A Applying Overhead; Overhead Variances [LO6, LO7]**

CHECK FIGURE
(2) Overhead applied: £92,000; (3) Volume variance: £8,000 U

Highland Shortbread, Ltd., of Aberdeen, Scotland, produces a single product and uses a standard cost system to help control costs. Manufacturing overhead is applied to production on the basis of standard machine-hours. According to the company's flexible budget, the following overhead costs should be incurred at an activity level of 18,000 machine-hours (the denominator activity level chosen for the year):

| | |
|---|---|
| Variable manufacturing overhead cost ...... | £ 31,500 |
| Fixed manufacturing overhead cost........... | 72,000 |
| Total manufacturing overhead cost............ | £103,500 |

During the year, the following operating results were recorded:

| | |
|---|---|
| Actual machine-hours worked ........................................ | 15,000 |
| Standard machine-hours allowed .................................. | 16,000 |
| Actual variable manufacturing overhead cost incurred.... | £26,500 |
| Actual fixed manufacturing overhead cost incurred......... | £70,000 |

At the end of the year, the company's Manufacturing Overhead account contained the following data:

**Manufacturing Overhead**

| | | | |
|---|---|---|---|
| Actual costs | 96,500 | Applied costs | 92,000 |
| | 4,500 | | |

Management would like to determine the cause of the £4,500 underapplied overhead.

***Required:***

1. Compute the predetermined overhead rate for the year. Break it down into variable and fixed cost elements.
2. Show how the £92,000 "Applied costs" figure in the Manufacturing Overhead account was computed.
3. Analyze the £4,500 underapplied overhead figure in terms of the variable overhead efficiency and rate variances and the fixed overhead budget and volume variances.
4. Explain the meaning of each variance that you computed in (3) above.

**PROBLEM 8A–11A Applying Overhead; Overhead Variances [LO6, LO7]**

CHECK FIGURE
(3a) 33,000 standard DLH; (4) Budget variance: $1,000 U

Wymont Company produces a single product that requires a large amount of labor time. Overhead cost is applied on the basis of standard direct labor-hours. Variable manufacturing overhead should be $2.00 per standard direct labor-hour and fixed manufacturing overhead should be $180,000 per year.

The company's product requires 4 feet of direct material that has a standard cost of $3.00 per foot. The product requires 1.5 hours of direct labor time. The standard labor rate is $12.00 per hour.

During the year, the company had planned to operate at a denominator activity level of 30,000 direct labor-hours and to produce 20,000 units of product. Actual activity and costs for the year were as follows:

| | |
|---|---|
| Number of units produced | 22,000 |
| Actual direct labor-hours worked | 35,000 |
| Actual variable manufacturing overhead cost incurred | \$63,000 |
| Actual fixed manufacturing overhead cost incurred | \$181,000 |

***Required:***

1. Compute the predetermined overhead rate for the year. Break the rate down into variable and fixed components.
2. Prepare a standard cost card for the company's product; show the details for all manufacturing costs on your standard cost card.
3. a. Compute the standard direct labor-hours allowed for the year's production.
   b. Complete the following Manufacturing Overhead T-account for the year:

**Manufacturing Overhead**

| | |
|---|---|
| ? | ? |
| ? | ? |

4. Determine the reason for the underapplied or overapplied overhead from (3) above by computing the variable overhead efficiency and rate variances and the fixed overhead budget and volume variances.
5. Suppose the company had chosen 36,000 direct labor-hours as the denominator activity rather than 30,000 hours. State which, if any, of the variances computed in (4) above would have changed, and explain how the variance(s) would have changed. No computations are necessary.

eXcel

CHECK FIGURE
(2) Materials price variance: \$3,000 F. (3) Volume variance: \$4,200 F

**PROBLEM 8A–12A Comprehensive Standard Cost Variances [LO4, LO5, LO6, LO7]**

Dresser Company uses a standard cost system and sets predetermined overhead rates on the basis of direct labor-hours. The following data are taken from the company's budget for the current year:

| | |
|---|---|
| Denominator activity (direct labor-hours) | 9,000 |
| Variable manufacturing overhead cost at 9,000 direct labor-hours | \$34,200 |
| Fixed manufacturing overhead cost | \$63,000 |

The standard cost card for the company's only product is given below:

| | |
|---|---|
| Direct materials, 4 pounds at \$2.60 per pound | \$10.40 |
| Direct labor, 2 direct labor-hours at \$9.00 per direct labor-hour | 18.00 |
| Overhead, 120% of direct labor cost | 21.60 |
| Standard cost per unit | \$50.00 |

During the year, the company produced 4,800 units of product and incurred the following costs:

| | |
|---|---|
| Materials purchased, 30,000 pounds at \$2.50 per pound | \$75,000 |
| Materials used in production (in pounds) | 20,000 |
| Direct labor cost incurred, 10,000 direct labor-hours at \$8.60 per direct labor-hour | \$86,000 |
| Variable manufacturing overhead cost incurred | \$35,900 |
| Fixed manufacturing overhead cost incurred | \$64,800 |

***Required:***

1. Redo the standard cost card in a clearer, more usable format by detailing the variable and fixed overhead cost elements.
2. Prepare an analysis of the variances for materials and labor for the year.
3. Prepare an analysis of the variances for variable and fixed overhead for the year.
4. What effect, if any, does the choice of a denominator activity level have on standard unit costs? Is the volume variance a controllable variance from a spending point of view? Explain.

# APPENDIX 8B: JOURNAL ENTRIES TO RECORD VARIANCES

LEARNING OBJECTIVE 8

Prepare journal entries to record standard costs and variances.

Although standard costs and variances can be computed and used by management without being formally entered into the accounting records, many organizations prefer to make formal journal entries. Formal entry tends to give variances a greater emphasis than informal, off-the-record computations. This emphasis signals management's desire to keep costs within the limits that have been set. In addition, formal use of standard costs simplifies the bookkeeping process enormously. Inventories and cost of goods sold can be valued at their standard costs—eliminating the need to keep track of the actual cost of each unit.

## Direct Materials Variances

To illustrate the journal entries needed to record standard cost variances, we will return to the data contained in Review Problem 2 at the end of the chapter. The entry to record the purchase of direct materials would be as follows:

| | | |
|---|---|---|
| Raw Materials (18,000 ounces at $0.50 per ounce) | 9,000 | |
| Materials Price Variance (18,000 ounces at $0.10 per ounce U) | 1,800 | |
| Accounts Payable (18,000 ounces at $0.60 per ounce) | | 10,800 |

Notice that the price variance is recognized when purchases are made, rather than when materials are actually used in production and that the materials are carried in the inventory account at standard cost. As direct materials are later drawn from inventory and used in production, the quantity variance is isolated as follows:

| | | |
|---|---|---|
| Work in Process (12,000 ounces at $0.50 per ounce) | 6,000 | |
| Materials Quantity Variance (2,000 ounces U at $0.50 per ounce) | 1,000 | |
| Raw Materials (14,000 ounces at $0.50 per ounce) | | 7,000 |

Thus, direct materials are added to the Work in Process account at the standard cost of the materials that should have been used to produce the actual output.

Notice that both the price variance and the quantity variance above are unfavorable and are debit entries. If either of these variances had been favorable, it would have appeared as a credit entry.

## Direct Labor Variances

Referring again to the cost data in Review Problem 2 at the end of the chapter, the journal entry to record the incurrence of direct labor cost would be:

| | | |
|---|---|---|
| Work in Process (1,200 hours at $30.00 per hour) | 36,000 | |
| Labor Rate Variance (1,100 hours at $0.50 U) | 550 | |
| Labor Efficiency Variance (100 hours F at $30.00 per hour) | | 3,000 |
| Wages Payable (1,100 hours at $30.50 per hour) | | 33,550 |

Thus, as with direct materials, direct labor costs enter into the Work in Process account at standard, both in terms of the rate and in terms of the hours allowed for the actual production of the period. Note that the unfavorable labor rate variance is a debit entry whereas the favorable labor efficiency variance is a credit entry.

## Cost Flows in a Standard Cost System

The flow of costs through the company's accounts are illustrated in Exhibit 8B–1. Note that entries into the various inventory accounts are made at standard cost—not actual cost. The differences between actual and standard costs are entered into special accounts that accumulate the various standard cost variances. Ordinarily, these

**EXHIBIT 8B–1** Cost Flows in a Standard Cost System*

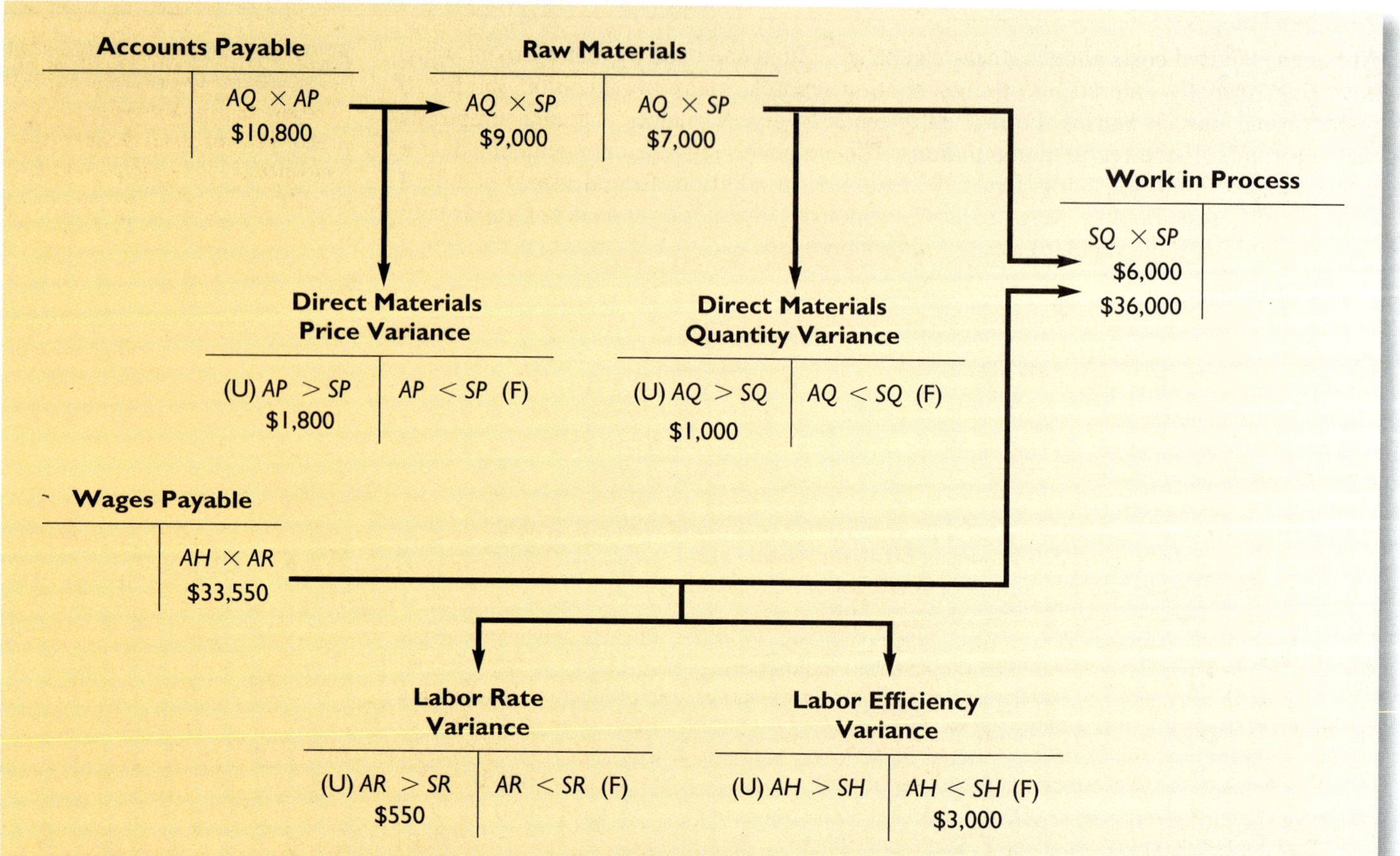


*The authors would like to thank Professor Rick French for suggesting this exhibit.

standard cost variance accounts are closed out to Cost of Goods Sold at the end of the period. Unfavorable variances increase Cost of Goods Sold, while favorable variances decrease Cost of Goods Sold.

## APPENDIX 8B: EXERCISES AND PROBLEMS

**All applicable exercises and problems are available with McGraw-Hill's *Connect*® *Accounting*.**

**EXERCISE 8B–1 Recording Variances in the General Ledger [LO8]**

Kinkel Corporation makes a product with the following standard costs for direct material and direct labor:

| | |
|---|---|
| Direct material: 1.50 meters at $5.40 per meter ............... | $8.10 |
| Direct labor: 0.25 hours at $14.00 per hour ..................... | $3.50 |

During the most recent month, 8,000 units were produced. The costs associated with the month's production of this product were as follows:

| | |
|---|---|
| Material purchased: 15,000 meters at $5.60 per meter .... | $84,000 |
| Material used in production: 11,900 meters..................... | — |
| Direct labor: 1,950 hours at $14.20 per hour .................... | $27,690 |

The standard cost variances for direct material and direct labor are:

| | |
|---|---|
| Materials quantity variance: 100 meters at $5.40 per meter F........ | $540 F |
| Materials price variance: 15,000 meters at $0.20 per meter U....... | $3,000 U |
| Labor efficiency variance: 50 hours at $14.00 per hour F............... | $700 F |
| Labor rate variance: 1,950 hours at $0.20 per hour U..................... | $390 U |

***Required:***

1. Prepare the journal entry to record the purchase of materials on account for the month.
2. Prepare the journal entry to record the use of materials for the month.
3. Prepare the journal entry to record the incurrence of direct labor cost for the month.

**EXERCISE 8B–2 Material and Labor Variances; Journal Entries [LO4, LO5, LO8]**

Aspen Products, Inc., began production of a new product on April 1. The company uses a standard cost system and has established the following standards for one unit of the new product:

| | Standard Quantity or Hours | Standard Price or Rate | Standard Cost |
|---|---|---|---|
| Direct materials......... | 3.5 feet | $6.00 per foot | $21.00 |
| Direct labor............... | 0.4 hours | $10.00 per hour | $4.00 |

During April, the following activity was recorded regarding the new product:

a. Purchased 7,000 feet of material at a cost of $5.75 per foot.
b. Used 6,000 feet of material to produce 1,500 units of the new product.
c. Worked 725 direct labor-hours on the new product at a cost of $8,120.

***Required:***

1. For direct materials:
   a. Compute the direct materials quantity and price variances.
   b. Prepare journal entries to record the purchase of materials and the use of materials in production.
2. For direct labor:
   a. Compute the direct labor efficiency and rate variances.
   b. Prepare journal entries to record the incurrence of direct labor cost for the month.
3. Post the entries you have prepared to the T-accounts below:

**Raw Materials**

| | | |
|---|---|---|
| | ? | ? |
| Bal. | ? | |

**Accounts Payable**

| | |
|---|---|
| | 40,250 |

**Materials Price Variance**

| | |
|---|---|
| | |

**Wages Payable**

| | |
|---|---|
| | 8,120 |

**Materials Quantity Variance**

| | |
|---|---|
| | |

**Labor Rate Variance**

| | |
|---|---|
| | |

**Work in Process**

| | |
|---|---|
| Materials used ? | |
| Labor cost ? | |

**Labor Efficiency Variance**

| | |
|---|---|
| | |

eXcel

CHECK FIGURE
(1a) Materials price variance: $3,000 F;
(2a) Labor rate variance: $1,300 F

**PROBLEM 8B–3A Comprehensive Variance Analysis with Incomplete Data; Journal Entries [LO4, LO5, LO6, LO8]**

Topline Surf Boards manufactures a single product. The standard cost of one unit of this product is as follows:

| | |
|---|---|
| Direct materials: 6 feet at $1.00 per foot | $ 6.00 |
| Direct labor: 1 hour at $4.50 per hour | 4.50 |
| Variable manufacturing overhead: 1 hour at $3.00 per hour | 3.00 |
| Total standard variable cost per unit | $13.50 |

During October, 6,000 units were produced. Selected data relating to the month's production follow:

| | |
|---|---|
| Material purchased: 60,000 feet at $0.95 per foot | $57,000 |
| Material used in production: 38,000 feet | — |
| Direct labor: ? hours at $ ? per hour | $27,950 |
| Variable manufacturing overhead cost incurred | $20,475 |
| Variable manufacturing overhead efficiency variance | $1,500 U |

There was no beginning inventory of raw materials. The variable manufacturing overhead rate is based on direct labor-hours.

***Required:***

1. For direct materials:
   a. Compute the quantity and price variances for October.
   b. Prepare journal entries to record activity for October.
2. For direct labor:
   a. Compute the efficiency and rate variances for October.
   b. Prepare a journal entry to record labor activity for October.
3. For variable manufacturing overhead:
   a. Compute the spending variance for October, and verify the efficiency variance given above.
   b. If manufacturing overhead is applied to production on the basis of direct labor-hours, is it possible to have a favorable direct labor efficiency variance and an unfavorable variable overhead efficiency variance? Explain.
4. State possible causes of each variance that you have computed.

CHECK FIGURE
(1a) Materials price variance: $5,280 F;
(2a) Labor efficiency variance: $4,320 F

**PROBLEM 8B–4A Comprehensive Variance Analysis; Journal Entries [LO4, LO5, LO6, LO8]**

Vermont Mills, Inc., is a large producer of men's and women's clothing. The company uses standard costs for all of its products. The standard costs and actual costs for a recent period are given below for one of the company's product lines (per unit of product):

| | Standard Cost | Actual Cost |
|---|---|---|
| Direct materials: | | |
| Standard: 4.0 yards at $3.60 per yard | $14.40 | |
| Actual: 4.4 yards at $3.35 per yard | | $14.74 |
| Direct labor: | | |
| Standard: 1.6 hours at $4.50 per hour | 7.20 | |
| Actual: 1.4 hours at $4.85 per hour | | 6.79 |
| Variable manufacturing overhead: | | |
| Standard: 1.6 hours at $1.80 per hour | 2.88 | |
| Actual: 1.4 hours at $2.15 per hour | | 3.01 |
| Total cost per unit | $24.48 | $24.54 |

During this period, the company produced 4,800 units of product. A comparison of standard and actual costs for the period on a total cost basis is given below:

| | |
|---|---|
| Actual costs: 4,800 units at $24.54 ............... | $117,792 |
| Standard costs: 4,800 units at $24.48 ........... | 117,504 |
| Difference in cost—unfavorable ..................... | $ 288 |

There was no inventory of materials on hand to start the period. During the period, 21,120 yards of materials were purchased and used in production.

***Required:***

1. For direct materials:
   a. Compute the quantity and price variances for the period.
   b. Prepare journal entries to record all activity relating to direct materials for the period.
2. For direct labor:
   a. Compute the efficiency and rate variances.
   b. Prepare a journal entry to record the incurrence of direct labor cost for the period.
3. Compute the variable manufacturing overhead efficiency and rate variances.
4. On seeing the $288 total cost variance, the company's president stated, "This variance of $288 is only 0.2% of the $117,504 standard cost for the period. It's obvious that our costs are well under control." Do you agree? Explain.
5. State possible causes of each variance that you have computed.

### A LOOK BACK

In Chapter 8, we looked at flexible budgets and spending variances. Standards were used to isolate the effects of various factors on actual results. In particular, we computed material, labor, and overhead variances.

### A LOOK AT THIS CHAPTER

In Chapter 9, we continue our coverage of performance measurement. Return on investment and residual income measures are used to motivate managers and monitor progress. The balanced scorecard is an integrated set of performance measures that are derived from and support the organization's strategy.

### A LOOK AHEAD

In Chapter 10, we concentrate on the identification of differential costs and benefits to aid decision making.

# 9 Performance Measurement in Decentralized Organizations

## CHAPTER OUTLINE

**Decentralization in Organizations**

- Advantages and Disadvantages of Decentralization

**Responsibility Accounting**

- Cost, Profit, and Investment Centers

**Evaluating Investment Center Performance—Return on Investment**

- The Return on Investment (ROI) Formula
- Net Operating Income and Operating Assets Defined
- Understanding ROI
- Criticisms of ROI

**Residual Income**

- Motivation and Residual Income
- Divisional Comparison and Residual Income

**Operating Performance Measures**

- Delivery Cycle Time
- Throughput (Manufacturing Cycle) Time
- Manufacturing Cycle Efficiency (MCE)

**Balanced Scorecard**

- Common Characteristics of Balanced Scorecards
- A Company's Strategy and the Balanced Scorecard
- Tying Compensation to the Balanced Scorecard
- Advantages of Timely and Graphic Feedback

## DECISION FEATURE

# Sony Attempts to Rebound

In the past, **Sony** has delighted customers with its Walkman, the Trinitron TV, the PlayStation, and the CD. However, in the digital media era Sony has lost ground to many better-managed competitors such as Microsoft, Apple, Sharp, and Nokia. Sony is attempting to rebound by discontinuing unprofitable segments such as Aibo, a line of robotic pets; Qualia, a line of boutique electronics; 1,220 cosmetic salons; and 18 Maxim de Paris restaurants. In addition, the company has closed nine plants, sold $705 million worth of assets, and eliminated 5,700 jobs.

The next step for Sony is to improve communications across its remaining business units. For example, at one point Sony had three business units unknowingly competing against one another by developing their own digital music players. Sony's challenge is to encourage decentralized decision making to spur product innovation, while centralizing control of communications across the company so that engineers do not create competing or incompatible products.

Source: Marc Gunther, "The Welshman, the Walkman, and the Salarymen," *Fortune,* June 12, 2006, pp. 70–83.

## LEARNING OBJECTIVES

*After studying Chapter 9, you should be able to:*

**LO1** Compute return on investment (ROI) and show how changes in sales, expenses, and assets affect ROI.

**LO2** Compute residual income and understand its strengths and weaknesses.

**LO3** Compute delivery cycle time, throughput time, and manufacturing cycle efficiency (MCE).

**LO4** Understand how to construct and use a balanced scorecard.

**Except in very small organizations, top managers must** delegate some decisions. For example, the CEO of the Hyatt Hotel chain cannot be expected to decide whether a particular hotel guest at the Hyatt Hotel on Maui should be allowed to check out later than the normal checkout time. Instead, employees at Maui are authorized to make this decision. As in this example, managers in large organizations have to delegate some decisions to those who are at lower levels in the organization.

## DECENTRALIZATION IN ORGANIZATIONS

In a **decentralized organization,** decision-making authority is spread throughout the organization rather than being confined to a few top executives. As noted above, out of necessity all large organizations are decentralized to some extent. Organizations do differ, however, in the extent to which they are decentralized. In strongly centralized organizations, decision-making authority is reluctantly delegated to lower-level managers who have little freedom to make decisions. In strongly decentralized organizations, even the lowest-level managers are empowered to make as many decisions as possible. Most organizations fall somewhere between these two extremes.

### Advantages and Disadvantages of Decentralization

The major advantages of decentralization include:

1. By delegating day-to-day problem solving to lower-level managers, top management can concentrate on bigger issues such as overall strategy.
2. Empowering lower-level managers to make decisions puts the decision-making authority in the hands of those who tend to have the most detailed and up-to-date information about day-to-day operations.
3. By eliminating layers of decision making and approvals, organizations can respond more quickly to customers and to changes in the operating environment.
4. Granting decision-making authority helps train lower-level managers for higher-level positions.
5. Empowering lower-level managers to make decisions can increase their motivation and job satisfaction.

The major disadvantages of decentralization include:

1. Lower-level managers may make decisions without fully understanding the big picture.
2. If lower-level managers make their own decisions independently of each other, coordination may be lacking.
3. Lower-level managers may have objectives that clash with the objectives of the entire organization.[1] For example, a manager may be more interested in increasing the size of his or her department, leading to more power and prestige, than in increasing the department's effectiveness.

[1]Similar problems exist with top-level managers as well. The shareholders of the company delegate their decision-making authority to the top managers. Unfortunately, top managers may abuse that trust by rewarding themselves and their friends too generously, spending too much company money on palatial offices, and so on. The issue of how to ensure that top managers act in the best interests of the company's owners continues to challenge experts. To a large extent, the owners rely on performance evaluation using return on investment and residual income measures as discussed later in the chapter, and on bonuses and stock options. The stock market is also an important disciplining mechanism. If top managers squander the company's resources, the price of the company's stock will almost surely fall—possibly resulting in a loss of prestige, bonuses, and a job. And, of course, particularly outrageous self-dealing may land a CEO in court, as historical events have demonstrated.

4. Spreading innovative ideas may be difficult in a decentralized organization. Someone in one part of the organization may have a terrific idea that would benefit other parts of the organization, but without strong central direction the idea may not be shared with, and adopted by, other parts of the organization.

# RESPONSIBILITY ACCOUNTING

Decentralized organizations need *responsibility accounting systems* that link lower-level managers' decision-making authority with accountability for the outcomes of those decisions. The term **responsibility center** is used for any part of an organization whose manager has control over and is accountable for cost, profit, or investments. The three primary types of responsibility centers are *cost centers, profit centers,* and *investment centers.*

## Cost, Profit, and Investment Centers

**Cost Center** The manager of a **cost center** has control over costs, but not over revenue or the use of investment funds. Service departments such as accounting, finance, general administration, legal, and personnel are usually classified as cost centers. In addition, manufacturing facilities are often considered to be cost centers. The managers of cost centers are expected to minimize costs while providing the level of products and services demanded by other parts of the organization. For example, the manager of a manufacturing facility would be evaluated at least in part by comparing actual costs to how much costs should have been for the actual level of output during the period. Standard cost variances and flexible budget variances, such as those discussed in the previous chapter, are often used to evaluate cost center performance.

**Profit Center** The manager of a **profit center** has control over both costs and revenue, but not over the use of investment funds. For example, the manager in charge of a **Six Flags** amusement park would be responsible for both the revenues and costs, and hence the profits, of the amusement park, but may not have control over major investments in the park. Profit center managers are often evaluated by comparing actual profit to targeted or budgeted profit.

**Investment Center** The manager of an **investment center** has control over cost, revenue, and investments in operating assets. For example, **General Motors**' vice president of manufacturing in North America would have a great deal of discretion over investments in manufacturing—such as investing in equipment to produce more fuel-efficient engines. Once General Motors' top-level managers and board of directors approve the vice president's investment proposals, he is held responsible for making them pay off. As discussed in the next section, investment center managers are often evaluated using return on investment (ROI) or residual income measures.

**CONCEPT CHECK**

1. Managers in which of the following responsibility centers are held responsible for profits? (You may select more than one answer.)
   a. Revenue centers
   b. Cost centers
   c. Profit centers
   d. Investment centers

# EVALUATING INVESTMENT CENTER PERFORMANCE—RETURN ON INVESTMENT

**LEARNING OBJECTIVE 1**

Compute return on investment (ROI) and show how changes in sales, expenses, and assets affect ROI.

An investment center is responsible for earning an adequate return on investment. The following two sections present two methods for evaluating this aspect of an investment center's performance. The first method, covered in this section, is called *return on investment (ROI).* The second method, covered in the next section, is called *residual income.*

## The Return on Investment (ROI) Formula

**Return on investment (ROI)** is defined as net operating income divided by average operating assets:

$$\text{ROI} = \frac{\text{Net operating income}}{\text{Average operating assets}}$$

The higher a business segment's return on investment (ROI), the greater the profit earned per dollar invested in the segment's operating assets.

## Net Operating Income and Operating Assets Defined

Note that *net operating income,* rather than net income, is used in the ROI formula. **Net operating income** is income before interest and taxes and is sometimes referred to as EBIT (earnings before interest and taxes). Net operating income is used in the formula because the base (i.e., denominator) consists of *operating assets.* To be consistent, we use net operating income in the numerator.

**Operating assets** include cash, accounts receivable, inventory, plant and equipment, and all other assets held for operating purposes. Examples of assets that are not included in operating assets (i.e., examples of nonoperating assets) include land held for future use, an investment in another company, or a building rented to someone else. These assets are not held for operating purposes and therefore are excluded from operating assets. The operating assets base used in the formula is typically computed as the average of the operating assets between the beginning and the end of the year.

Most companies use the net book value (i.e., acquisition cost less accumulated depreciation) of depreciable assets to calculate average operating assets. This approach has drawbacks. An asset's net book value decreases over time as the accumulated depreciation increases. This decreases the denominator in the ROI calculation, thus increasing ROI. Consequently, ROI mechanically increases over time. Moreover, replacing old depreciated equipment with new equipment increases the book value of depreciable assets and decreases ROI. Hence, using net book value in the calculation of average operating assets results in a predictable pattern of increasing ROI over time as accumulated depreciation grows and discourages replacing old equipment with new, updated equipment. An alternative to using net book value is the gross cost of the asset, which ignores accumulated depreciation. Gross cost stays constant over time because depreciation is ignored; therefore, ROI does not grow automatically over time, and replacing a fully depreciated asset with a comparably priced new asset will not adversely affect ROI.

Nevertheless, most companies use the net book value approach to computing average operating assets because it is consistent with their financial reporting practices of recording the net book value of assets on the balance sheet and including depreciation as an operating expense on the income statement. In this text, we will use the net book value approach unless a specific exercise or problem directs otherwise.

## Understanding ROI

The equation for ROI, net operating income divided by average operating assets, does not provide much help to managers interested in taking actions to improve their ROI. It only offers two levers for improving performance—net operating income and average operating assets. Fortunately, ROI can also be expressed in terms of **margin** and **turnover** as follows:

$$\text{ROI} = \text{Margin} \times \text{Turnover}$$

where

$$\text{Margin} = \frac{\text{Net operating income}}{\text{Sales}}$$

and

$$\text{Turnover} = \frac{\text{Sales}}{\text{Average operating assets}}$$

Note that the sales terms in the margin and turnover formulas cancel out when they are multiplied together, yielding the original formula for ROI stated in terms of net operating income and average operating assets. So either formula for ROI will give the same answer. However, the margin and turnover formulation provides some additional insights.

Margin and turnover are important concepts in understanding how a manager can affect ROI. All other things the same, margin is ordinarily improved by increasing selling prices, reducing operating expenses, or increasing unit sales. Increasing selling prices and reducing operating expenses both increase net operating income and therefore margin. Increasing unit sales also ordinarily increases the margin because of operating leverage. As discussed in a previous chapter, because of operating leverage, a given percentage increase in unit sales usually leads to an even larger percentage increase in net operating income. Therefore, an increase in unit sales ordinarily has the effect of increasing margin. Some managers tend to focus too much on margin and ignore turnover. However, turnover incorporates a crucial area of a manager's responsibility—the investment in operating assets. Excessive funds tied up in operating assets (e.g., cash, accounts receivable, inventories, plant and equipment, and other assets) depress turnover and lower ROI. In fact, excessive operating assets can be just as much of a drag on ROI as excessive operating expenses, which depress margin.

Many actions involve combinations of changes in sales, expenses, and operating assets. For example, a manager may make an investment in (i.e., increase) operating assets to reduce operating expenses or increase sales. Whether the net effect is favorable or not is judged in terms of its overall impact on ROI.

**HELPFUL HINT**

To better understand the concepts of margin and turnover, link them to actual companies. For example, the local jewelry store in your hometown relies more on margin than turnover to generate a satisfactory return on investment (ROI). It completes a small number of transactions each day, so to be profitable it needs to earn a high margin per transaction. Conversely, Walmart relies more on turnover than margin to generate its ROI. Walmart completes an enormous number of transactions each day so, even though each transaction earns a very small margin, the company's extraordinary turnover creates a favorable ROI.

For example, suppose that the Montvale Burger Grill expects the following operating results next month:

| | |
|---|---|
| Sales | $100,000 |
| Operating expenses | $90,000 |
| Net operating income | $10,000 |
| Average operating assets | $50,000 |

The expected return on investment (ROI) for the month is computed as follows:

$$\text{ROI} = \frac{\text{Net operating income}}{\text{Sales}} \times \frac{\text{Sales}}{\text{Average operating assets}}$$
$$= \frac{\$10{,}000}{\$100{,}000} \times \frac{\$100{,}000}{\$50{,}000}$$
$$= 10\% \times 2 = 20\%$$

Suppose that the manager of the Montvale Burger Grill is considering investing $2,000 in a state-of-the-art soft-serve ice cream machine that can dispense a number of different flavors. This new machine would boost sales by $4,000, but would require additional operating expenses of $1,000. Thus, net operating income would increase by $3,000, to $13,000. The new ROI would be:

$$\text{ROI} = \frac{\text{Net operating income}}{\text{Sales}} \times \frac{\text{Sales}}{\text{Average operating assets}}$$
$$= \frac{\$13{,}000}{\$104{,}000} \times \frac{\$104{,}000}{\$52{,}000}$$
$$= 12.5\% \times 2 = 25\% \text{ (as compared to 20\% originally)}$$

In this particular example, the investment increases ROI, but that will not always happen.

**E.I. du Pont de Nemours and Company** (better known as DuPont) pioneered the use of ROI and recognized the importance of looking at both margin and turnover in assessing a manager's performance. ROI is now widely used as the key measure of investment center performance. ROI reflects in a single figure many aspects of the manager's responsibilities. It can be compared to the returns of other investment centers in the organization, the returns of other companies in the industry, and to the past returns of the investment center itself. DuPont also developed the diagram that appears in Exhibit 9–1. This exhibit helps managers understand how they can improve ROI.

## IN BUSINESS — Microsoft Manages In An Economic Downturn

**Microsoft** responded to tough economic times by lowering its prices, thereby accepting lower margins per unit sold in exchange for higher turnover. For example, Microsoft lowered the price of its Office software from $150 to $100 (after promotional discounts) and realized a 415% increase in unit sales. In China, the company combated huge piracy problems by dropping the price of Office to $29, resulting in an 800% increase in sales. Microsoft established a selling price of $200 for its Windows 7 PC operating system, which was $40 less than the price the company charged for its predecessor Vista PC operating system.

Source: Peter Burrows, "Microsoft's Aggressive New Pricing Strategy," *BusinessWeek*, July 27, 2009, p. 51.

**EXHIBIT 9–1** Elements of Return on Investment (ROI)

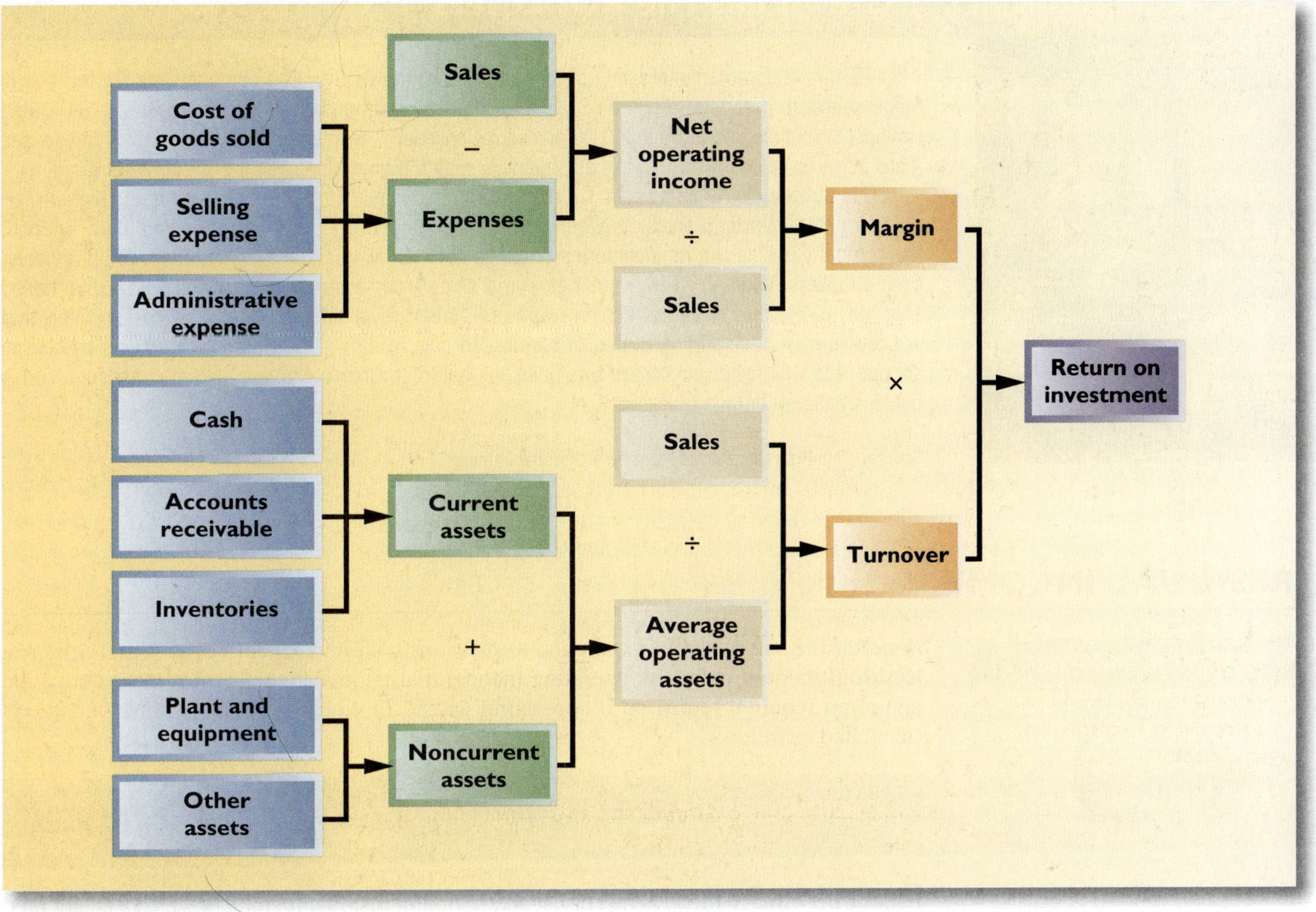


## Criticisms of ROI

Although ROI is widely used in evaluating performance, it is subject to the following criticisms:

1. Just telling managers to increase ROI may not be enough. Managers may not know how to increase ROI; they may increase ROI in a way that is inconsistent with the company's strategy; or they may take actions that increase ROI in the short run but harm the company in the long run (such as cutting back on research and development). This is why ROI is best used as part of a balanced scorecard, as discussed later in this chapter. A balanced scorecard can provide concrete guidance to managers, making it more likely that their actions are consistent with the company's strategy and reducing the likelihood that they will boost short-run performance at the expense of long-term performance.
2. A manager who takes over a business segment typically inherits many committed costs over which the manager has no control. These committed costs may be relevant in assessing the performance of the business segment as an investment but they make it difficult to fairly assess the performance of the manager.
3. As discussed in the next section, a manager who is evaluated based on ROI may reject investment opportunities that are profitable for the whole company but would have a negative impact on the manager's performance evaluation.

## IN BUSINESS — J. Crew Pulls The ROI Levers

**J. Crew** has adopted an interesting strategy for improving its ROI. The company has started selling "super-premium products—such as $1,500 cashmere coats and $1,500 beaded tunics—in limited editions, sometimes no more than 100 pieces nationwide." The intentional creation of scarcity causes many items to sell out within weeks as shoppers snatch them up before they are gone for good.

This strategy is helping boost J. Crew's ROI in two ways. First, the company earns higher margins on premium-priced products where customer demand dramatically exceeds supply. Second, the company is slashing its inventories because such small quantities of each item are purchased from suppliers. While J. Crew sacrifices some sales from customers who would have purchased sold out items, the overall effect on profits has been favorable. "Tighter inventories mean that J. Crew is no longer putting reams of clothes on sale, a move that kills profit margins and trains shoppers to wait for discounts. At one point . . . half of J. Crew's clothing sold at a discount. Today only a small percentage of it does."

Source: Julia Boorstin, "Mickey Drexler's Second Coming," *Fortune*, May 2, 2005, pp. 101–104.

# RESIDUAL INCOME

**LEARNING OBJECTIVE 2**

Compute residual income and understand its strengths and weaknesses.

*Residual income* is another approach to measuring an investment center's performance. **Residual income** is the net operating income that an investment center earns above the minimum required return on its operating assets. In equation form, residual income is calculated as follows:

$$\text{Residual income} = \text{Net operating income} - \left(\text{Average operating assets} \times \text{Minimum required rate of return}\right)$$

**Economic Value Added (EVA®)** is an adaptation of residual income that has been adopted by many companies.[2] Under EVA, companies often modify their accounting principles in various ways. For example, funds used for research and development are often treated as investments rather than as expenses.[3] These complications are best dealt with in a more advanced course; in this text we will not draw any distinction between residual income and EVA.

When residual income or EVA is used to measure performance, the objective is to maximize the total amount of residual income or EVA, not to maximize ROI. This is an important distinction. If the objective were to maximize ROI, then every company should divest all of its products except the single product with the highest ROI.

A wide variety of organizations have embraced some version of residual income or EVA, including **Bausch & Lomb**, **Best Buy**, **Boise Cascade**, **Coca-Cola**, **Dun and Bradstreet**, **Eli Lilly**, **Federated Mogul**, **Georgia-Pacific**, **Guidant Corporation**, **Hershey Foods**, **Husky Injection Molding**, **J.C. Penney**, **Kansas City Power & Light**, **Olin**, **Quaker Oats**, **Silicon Valley Bank**, **Sprint**, **Toys R Us**, **Tupperware**, and the **United States Postal Service**. In addition, financial institutions such as **Credit Suisse**

[2]The basic idea underlying residual income and economic value added has been around for over 100 years. In recent years, economic value added has been popularized and trademarked by the consulting firm Stern, Stewart & Co.

[3]Over 100 different adjustments could be made for deferred taxes, LIFO reserves, provisions for future liabilities, mergers and acquisitions, gains or losses due to changes in accounting rules, operating leases, and other accounts, but most companies make only a few. For further details, see John O'Hanlon and Ken Peasnell, "Wall Street's Contribution to Management Accounting: the Stern Stewart EVA® Financial Management System," *Management Accounting Research* 9, 1998, pp. 421–444.

**First Boston** now use EVA—and its allied concept, market value added—to evaluate potential investments in other companies.

For purposes of illustration, consider the following data for an investment center—the Ketchikan Division of Alaskan Marine Services Corporation.

| **Alaskan Marine Services Corporation**<br>**Ketchikan Division**<br>**Basic Data for Performance Evaluation** | |
|---|---|
| Average operating assets | $100,000 |
| Net operating income | $20,000 |
| Minimum required rate of return | 15% |

Alaskan Marine Services Corporation has long had a policy of using ROI to evaluate its investment center managers, but it is considering switching to residual income. The controller of the company, who is in favor of the change to residual income, has provided the following table that shows how the performance of the division would be evaluated under each of the two methods:

**Alaskan Marine Services Corporation**
**Ketchikan Division**

| | Alternative Performance Measures | |
|---|---|---|
| | **ROI** | **Residual Income** |
| Average operating assets (a) | $100,000 | $100,000 |
| Net operating income (b) | $20,000 | $20,000 |
| ROI, (b) ÷ (a) | 20% | |
| Minimum required return (15% × $100,000) | | 15,000 |
| Residual income | | $ 5,000 |

The reasoning underlying the residual income calculation is straightforward. The company is able to earn a rate of return of at least 15% on its investments. Because the company has invested $100,000 in the Ketchikan Division in the form of operating assets, the company should be able to earn at least $15,000 (15% × $100,000) on this investment. Because the Ketchikan Division's net operating income is $20,000, the residual income above and beyond the minimum required return is $5,000. If residual income is adopted as the performance measure to replace ROI, the manager of the Ketchikan Division would be evaluated based on the growth in residual income from year to year.

## Motivation and Residual Income

One of the primary reasons why the controller of Alaskan Marine Services Corporation would like to switch from ROI to residual income relates to how managers view new investments under the two performance measurement methods. The residual income approach encourages managers to make investments that are profitable for the entire company but that would be rejected by managers who are evaluated using the ROI formula.

To illustrate this problem with ROI, suppose that the manager of the Ketchikan Division is considering purchasing a computerized diagnostic machine to aid in servicing marine diesel engines. The machine would cost $25,000 and is expected to generate additional operating income of $4,500 a year. From the standpoint of the company, this would be a good investment because it promises a rate of return of 18% ($4,500 ÷ $25,000), which exceeds the company's minimum required rate of return of 15%.

If the manager of the Ketchikan Division is evaluated based on residual income, she would be in favor of the investment in the diagnostic machine as shown below:

**Alaskan Marine Services Corporation**
**Ketchikan Division**
**Performance Evaluated Using Residual Income**

| | Present | New Project | Overall |
|---|---|---|---|
| Average operating assets | $100,000 | $25,000 | $125,000 |
| Net operating income | $20,000 | $4,500 | $24,500 |
| Minimum required return | 15,000 | 3,750* | 18,750 |
| Residual income | $ 5,000 | $ 750 | $ 5,750 |

*$25,000 × 15% = $3,750.

Because the project would increase the residual income of the Ketchikan Division by $750, the manager would choose to invest in the new diagnostic machine.

Now suppose that the manager of the Ketchikan Division is evaluated based on ROI. The effect of the diagnostic machine on the division's ROI is computed below:

**Alaskan Marine Services Corporation**
**Ketchikan Division**
**Performance Evaluated Using ROI**

| | Present | New Project | Overall |
|---|---|---|---|
| Average operating assets (a) | $100,000 | $25,000 | $125,000 |
| Net operating income (b) | $20,000 | $4,500 | $24,500 |
| ROI, (b) ÷ (a) | 20% | 18% | 19.6% |

The new project reduces the division's ROI from 20% to 19.6%. This happens because the 18% rate of return on the new diagnostic machine, while above the company's 15% minimum required rate of return, is below the division's current ROI of 20%. Therefore, the new diagnostic machine would decrease the division's ROI even though it would be a good investment from the standpoint of the company as a whole. If the manager of the division is evaluated based on ROI, she will be reluctant to even propose such an investment.

Generally, a manager who is evaluated based on ROI will reject any project whose rate of return is below the division's current ROI even if the rate of return on the project is above the company's minimum required rate of return. In contrast, managers who are evaluated using residual income will pursue any project whose rate of return is above the minimum required rate of return because it will increase their residual income. Because it is in the best interests of the company as a whole to accept any project whose rate of return is above the minimum required rate of return, managers who are evaluated based on residual income will tend to make better decisions concerning investment projects than managers who are evaluated based on ROI.

## HELPFUL HINT

When managers are evaluated and rewarded based on return on investment (ROI) it can create situations where managers make decisions that are not in the company's best interest. For example, assume that the company establishes a minimum required return of 15%, thereby implying that the company wants its managers to pursue investment opportunities that can earn a return equal to or greater than 15%. However, let's also assume that the manager has historically earned an ROI of 20% and that her bonus is based on her ability to meet or exceed this 20% threshold.

## HELPFUL HINT

(continued)

In this situation, the manager and the company will both want to bypass investment opportunities with an ROI less than 15%. They will both want to pursue investment opportunities with an ROI greater than 20%. The problem arises with investment opportunities that earn greater than 15% but less than 20%. The company will want the manager to pursue these opportunities, whereas the manager will want to bypass them because they will reduce her historical ROI and lower her chances of earning a bonus. This problem can be resolved by using residual income to evaluate managerial performance because it would reward the manager for pursuing all investments that exceed the minimum required return of 15%.

## Divisional Comparison and Residual Income

The residual income approach has one major disadvantage. It can't be used to compare the performance of divisions of different sizes. Larger divisions often have more residual income than smaller divisions, not necessarily because they are better managed but simply because they are bigger.

As an example, consider the following residual income computations for the Wholesale Division and the Retail Division of Sisal Marketing Corporation:

| | Wholesale Division | Retail Division |
|---|---|---|
| Average operating assets (a) | $1,000,000 | $250,000 |
| Net operating income | $120,000 | $40,000 |
| Minimum required return: 10% × (a) | 100,000 | 25,000 |
| Residual income | $ 20,000 | $15,000 |

Observe that the Wholesale Division has slightly more residual income than the Retail Division, but that the Wholesale Division has $1,000,000 in operating assets as compared to only $250,000 in operating assets for the Retail Division. Thus, the Wholesale Division's greater residual income is probably due to its larger size rather than the quality of its management. In fact, it appears that the smaller division may be better managed because it has been able to generate nearly as much residual income with only one-fourth as much in operating assets. When comparing investment centers, it is probably better to focus on the percentage change in residual income from year to year rather than on the absolute amount of the residual income.

## CONCEPT CHECK

2. Last year sales were $300,000, net operating income was $75,000, and average operating assets were $500,000. If sales next year remain the same as last year and expenses and average operating assets are reduced by 5%, what will be the return on investment next year?
   a. 12.2%
   b. 18.2%
   c. 20.2%
   d. 25.2%
3. Referring to the facts in question 2 above, if the minimum required rate of return is 12%, what will be the residual income next year?
   a. $26,250
   b. $27,250
   c. $28,250
   d. $29,250

## DECISION POINT Shoe Store Manager

You are the manager of a shoe store in a busy shopping mall. The store is part of a national chain that evaluates its store managers on the basis of return on investment (ROI). As the manager of the store, you have control over costs, pricing, and the inventory you carry. The ROI of your store was 17.21% last year and is projected to be 17.00% this year unless some action is taken. The projected ROI has been computed as follows:

| | |
|---|---|
| Average operating assets (a) | $2,000,000 |
| Net operating income (b) | $340,000 |
| ROI, (b) ÷ (a) | 17.00% |

Your bonus this year will depend on improving your ROI performance over last year. The minimum required rate of return on investment for the national chain is 15%.

You are considering two alternatives for improving this year's ROI:

a. Cut inventories (and average operating assets) by $500,000. This will unfortunately result in a reduction in sales, with a negative impact on net operating income of $79,000.
b. Add a new product line that would increase average operating assets by $200,000, but would increase net operating income by $33,000.

Which alternative would result in your earning a bonus for the year? Which alternative is in the best interests of the national chain?

# OPERATING PERFORMANCE MEASURES

**LEARNING OBJECTIVE 3**

Compute delivery cycle time, throughput time, and manufacturing cycle efficiency (MCE).

In addition to financial performance measures, organizations use many nonfinancial performance measures. While financial measures pick up the *results* of what people in the organization do, they do not measure what *drives* organizational performance. For example, activity and revenue variances pick up the results of efforts aimed at increasing sales, but they do not measure the actions that actually drive sales such as improving quality, exposing more potential customers to the product, filling customer orders on time, and so on. Consequently, many organizations use a variety of nonfinancial performance measures in addition to financial measures. In this section we will discuss three examples of such measures that are critical to success in many organizations—delivery cycle time, throughput time, and manufacturing cycle efficiency (MCE). Note that while these examples focus on manufacturers, very similar measures can be used by any service organization that experiences a delay between receiving a customer request and responding to that request.

## Delivery Cycle Time

The amount of time from when a customer order is received to when the completed order is shipped is called **delivery cycle time.** This time is an important concern to many customers, who would like the delivery cycle time to be as short as possible. Cutting the delivery cycle time may give a company a key competitive advantage—and may be necessary for survival.

## Throughput (Manufacturing Cycle) Time

The amount of time required to turn raw materials into completed products is called **throughput time,** or *manufacturing cycle time.* The relation between the delivery cycle time and the throughput (manufacturing cycle) time is illustrated in Exhibit 9–2.

**EXHIBIT 9–2** Delivery Cycle Time and Throughput (Manufacturing Cycle) Time

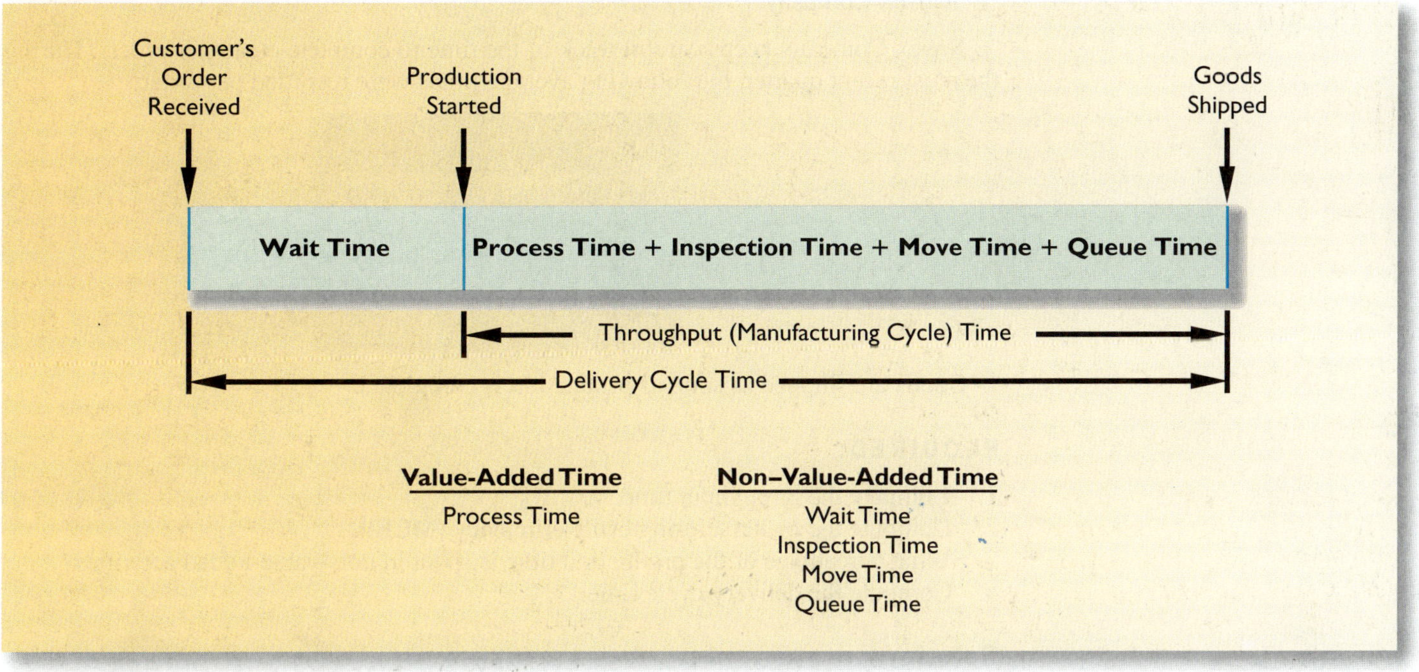


As shown in Exhibit 9–2, the throughput time, or manufacturing cycle time, is made up of process time, inspection time, move time, and queue time. *Process time* is the amount of time work is actually done on the product. *Inspection time* is the amount of time spent ensuring that the product is not defective. *Move time* is the time required to move materials or partially completed products from workstation to workstation. *Queue time* is the amount of time a product spends waiting to be worked on, to be moved, to be inspected, or to be shipped.

As shown at the bottom of Exhibit 9–2, only one of these four activities adds value to the product—process time. The other three activities—inspecting, moving, and queuing—add no value and should be eliminated as much as possible.

## Manufacturing Cycle Efficiency (MCE)

Through concerted efforts to eliminate the *non–value-added* activities of inspecting, moving, and queuing, some companies have reduced their throughput time to only a fraction of previous levels. In turn, this has helped to reduce the delivery cycle time from months to only weeks or hours. Throughput time, which is a key measure in delivery performance, can be put into better perspective by computing the **manufacturing cycle efficiency (MCE).** The MCE is computed by relating the value-added time to the throughput time. The formula is:

$$\text{MCE} = \frac{\text{Value-added time (Process time)}}{\text{Throughput (manufacturing cycle) time}}$$

Any non-value-added time results in an MCE of less than 1. An MCE of 0.5, for example, would mean that half of the total production time consists of inspection, moving, and similar non–value-added activities. In many manufacturing companies, the MCE is less than 0.1 (10%), which means that 90% of the time a unit is in process is spent on activities that do not add value to the product. Monitoring the MCE helps companies to reduce non–value-added activities and thus get products into the hands of customers more quickly and at a lower cost.

MC ☆

**Example** To provide an example of these measures, consider the following data for Novex Company:

Novex Company keeps careful track of the time to complete customer orders. During the most recent quarter, the following average times were recorded per order:

| | Days |
|---|---|
| Wait time | 17.0 |
| Inspection time | 0.4 |
| Process time | 2.0 |
| Move time | 0.6 |
| Queue time | 5.0 |

Goods are shipped as soon as production is completed.

**REQUIRED:**

1. Compute the throughput time.
2. Compute the manufacturing cycle efficiency (MCE).
3. What percentage of the production time is spent in non–value-added activities?
4. Compute the delivery cycle time.

## Solution

1. Throughput time = Process time + Inspection time + Move time + Queue time
   = 2.0 days + 0.4 days + 0.6 days + 5.0 days
   = 8.0 days

## IN BUSINESS — Lean Operating Performance Measures

**Watlow Electric Manufacturing Company** implemented *lean accounting* to support its lean manufacturing methods. The company stopped providing standard cost variance reports to operating managers because the information was generated too late (at the end of each month) and it could not be understood by frontline employees. Instead, the company began reporting daily and hourly process-oriented measures that helped frontline workers improve performance.

Examples of lean operating performance measures are shown in the table below:

| Measure | Description of Measure |
|---|---|
| On-time delivery percentage | Measures the percentage of orders that customers would define as being delivered on time. |
| Day-by-the-hour | Measures the quantity of production on an hourly basis to ensure that it is synchronized with customer demand. |
| First time through percentage | Measures the percentage of completed units that are free of defects. |
| Number of accidents and injuries | Measures the number of accidents and injuries on the manufacturing floor. |
| 5S audit | Measures the cell workers' ability to keep their work area organized and clean. |

Note: 5S stands for Sort, Straighten, Shine, Standardize, and Sustain

Sources: Jan Brosnahan, "Unleash the Power of Lean Accounting," *Journal of Accountancy,* July 2008, pp. 60–66; and Brian Maskell and Frances Kennedy, "Why Do We Need Lean Accounting and How Does It Work?" *Journal of Corporate Accounting and Finance,* March/April 2007, pp. 59–73.

2. Only process time represents value-added time; therefore, MCE would be computed as follows:

$$\text{MCE} = \frac{\text{Value-added time}}{\text{Throughput time}} = \frac{2.0 \text{ days}}{8.0 \text{ days}}$$
$$= 0.25$$

Thus, once put into production, a typical order is actually being worked on only 25% of the time.

3. Because the MCE is 25%, 75% (100% − 25%) of total production time is spent in non–value-added activities.
4. Delivery cycle time = Wait time + Throughput time
= 17.0 days + 8.0 days
= 25.0 days

# BALANCED SCORECARD

**LEARNING OBJECTIVE 4**
Understand how to construct and use a balanced scorecard.

Financial measures, such as ROI and residual income, and operating measures, such as those discussed in the previous section, may be included in a *balanced scorecard.* A **balanced scorecard** consists of an integrated set of performance measures that are derived from and support a company's strategy. A strategy is essentially a theory about how to achieve the organization's goals. For example, **Southwest Airlines**' strategy is to offer an *operational excellence* customer value proposition that has three key components—low ticket prices, convenience, and reliability. The company operates only one type of aircraft, the Boeing 737, to reduce maintenance and training costs and simplify scheduling. It further reduces costs by not offering meals, seat assignments, or baggage transfers and by booking a large portion of its passenger revenue over the Internet. Southwest also uses point-to-point flights rather than the hub-and-spoke approach of its larger competitors, thereby providing customers convenient, nonstop service to their final destination. Because Southwest serves many less-congested airports such as Chicago Midway, Burbank, Manchester, Oakland, and Providence, it offers quicker passenger check-ins and reliable departures, while maintaining high asset utilization (i.e., the company's average gate turnaround time of 25 minutes enables it to function with fewer planes and gates). Overall, the company's strategy has worked. At a time when Southwest Airlines' larger competitors are struggling, it continues to earn substantial profits.

Under the balanced scorecard approach, top management translates its strategy into performance measures that employees can understand and influence. For example, the amount of time passengers have to wait in line to have their baggage checked might be a performance measure for the supervisor in charge of the Southwest Airlines check-in counter at the Burbank airport. This performance measure is easily understood by the supervisor, and can be improved by the supervisor's actions.

## Common Characteristics of Balanced Scorecards

Know definition

Performance measures used in balanced scorecards tend to fall into the four groups illustrated in Exhibit 9–3: financial, customer, internal business processes, and learning and growth. Internal business processes are what the company does in an attempt to satisfy customers. For example, in a manufacturing company, assembling a product is an internal business process. In an airline, handling baggage is an internal business process. The idea underlying these groupings (as indicated by the vertical arrows in Exhibit 9–3) is that learning is necessary to improve internal business processes; improving business processes is necessary to improve customer satisfaction; and improving customer satisfaction is necessary to improve financial results.

**EXHIBIT 9–3** From Strategy to Performance Measures: The Balanced Scorecard

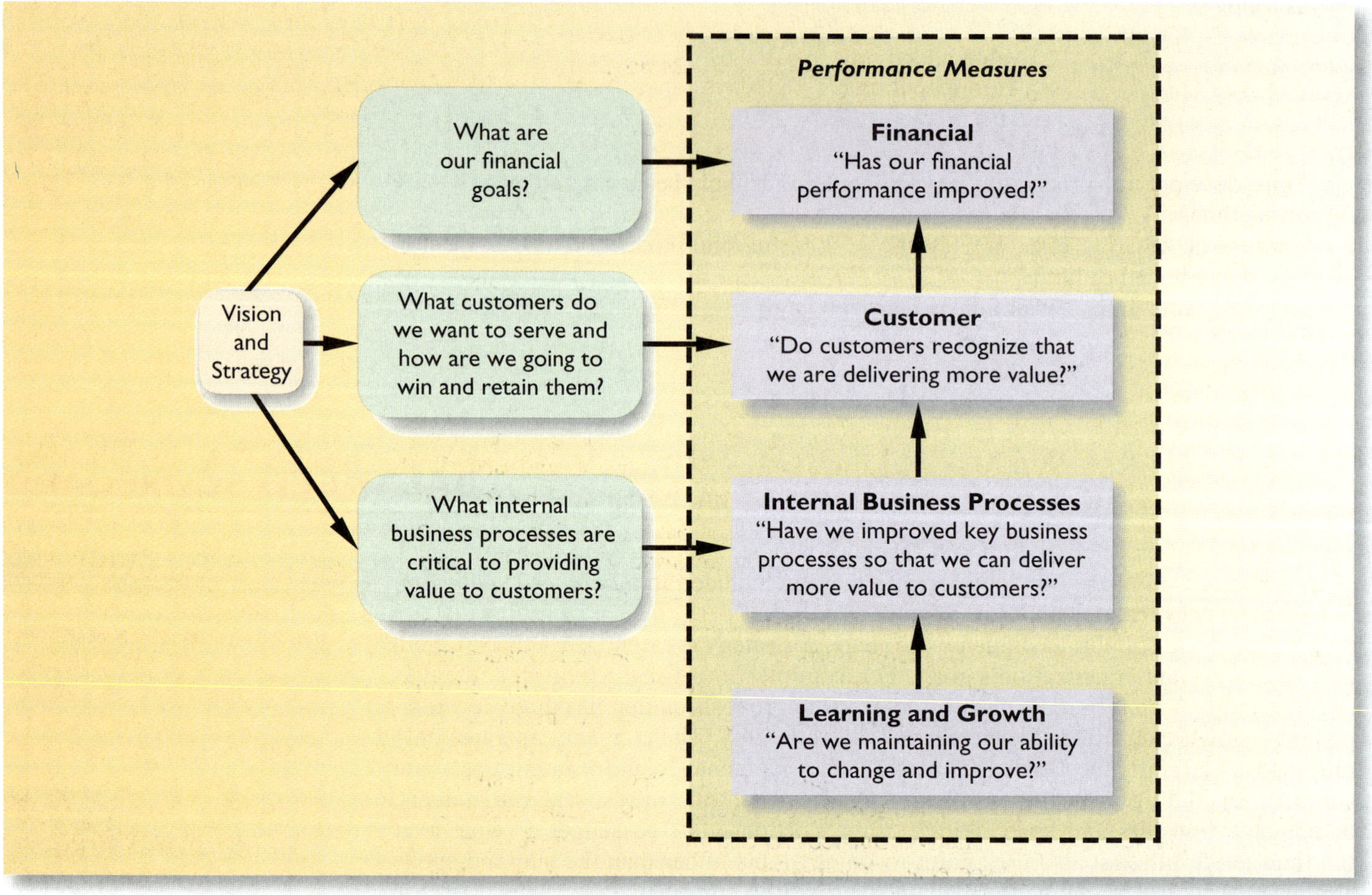


Note that the emphasis in Exhibit 9–3 is on *improvement*—not on just attaining some specific objective such as profits of $10 million. In the balanced scorecard approach, continual improvement is encouraged. If an organization does not continually improve, it will eventually lose out to competitors that do.

## IN BUSINESS — Why Do Companies Fail to Execute their Strategies?

Robert Paladino served as the vice president and global leader of the Telecommunications and Utility Practice for the **Balanced Scorecard Collaborative**—a consulting organization that works with companies to implement balanced scorecards. He offers four reasons why nine out of ten organizations fail to execute their business strategies.

First, only 5% of a company's workforce understands their organization's strategy. Paladino commented "if employees don't understand the strategic objectives, then they could be focused on closing the wrong performance gaps." Second, 85% of management teams spend less than one hour per month discussing strategy. Managers cannot effectively implement strategies if they do not spend enough time talking about them. Third, 60% of organizations do not link their budgets to strategy. The inevitable result is that companies pursue "financial strategies that differ from or, worse, may be in conflict with their business and customer quality strategies." Finally, only 25% of managers have their incentives linked to strategy. Thus, most managers are working to maximize their compensation by improving strategically misguided metrics.

Paladino says the balanced scorecard overcomes these four barriers because it helps employees focus their actions on executing organizational strategies.

Source: Robert E. Paladino, "Balanced Forecasts Drive Value," *Strategic Finance*, January 2005, pp. 37–42.

Financial performance measures appear at the top of Exhibit 9–3. Ultimately, most companies exist to provide financial rewards to owners. There are exceptions. Some companies—for example, **The Body Shop**—may have loftier goals such as providing environmentally friendly products to consumers. However, even nonprofit organizations must generate enough financial resources to stay in operation.

However, for several reasons, financial performance measures are not sufficient in themselves—they should be integrated with nonfinancial measures in a well-designed balanced scorecard. First, financial measures are lag indicators that report on the results of past actions. In contrast, nonfinancial measures of key success drivers such as customer satisfaction are leading indicators of future financial performance. Second, top managers are ordinarily responsible for the financial performance measures—not lower-level managers. The supervisor in charge of checking in passengers can be held responsible for how long passengers have to wait in line. However, this supervisor cannot reasonably be held responsible for the entire company's profit. That is the responsibility of the airline's top managers.

Exhibit 9–4 lists some examples of performance measures that can be found on the balanced scorecards of companies. However, few companies, if any, would use all of these performance measures, and almost all companies would add other performance measures. Managers should carefully select performance measures for their own company's balanced scorecard, keeping the following points in mind. First and foremost, the performance measures should be consistent with, and follow from, the company's strategy. If the performance measures are not consistent with the company's strategy, people will find themselves working at cross-purposes. Second, the performance measures should be understandable and controllable to a significant extent by those being evaluated. Third, the scorecard should not have too many performance measures. This can lead to a lack of focus and confusion.

While the entire organization will have an overall balanced scorecard, each responsible individual will have his or her own personal scorecard as well. This scorecard should consist of items the individual can personally influence that relate directly to the performance measures on the overall balanced scorecard. The performance measures on this personal scorecard should not be overly influenced by actions taken by others in the company or by events that are outside of the individual's control. And, focusing on the performance measure should not lead an individual to take actions that are counter to the organization's objectives.

With those broad principles in mind, we will now take a look at how a company's strategy affects its balanced scorecard.

## Measuring Customer Loyalty

IN BUSINESS

**Bain & Company** consultant Fred Reichheld recommends measuring customer loyalty with one question—"On a scale of 0 to 10, how likely is it that you would recommend us to your friends and colleagues?" Customers who choose a score of 9 or 10 are labeled promoters. Those who choose a score of 0 to 6 are categorized as detractors, while those who select 7 or 8 are deemed passively satisfied. The net promoter score measures the difference between the percentages of customers who are promoters and detractors. Reichheld's research suggests that changes in a company's net promoter score correlate with (or move in tandem with) changes in its sales.

**General Electric**'s Healthcare Division used net promoter scores to determine 20% of its managers' bonuses. The metric was eventually rolled out to all General Electric divisions. Other adopters of the net promoter score include **American Express**, consulting firm **BearingPoint**, and software maker **Intuit**.

Source: Jean McGregor, "Would You Recommend Us?" *BusinessWeek,* January 30, 2006, p. 94.

**EXHIBIT 9–4**
Examples of Performance Measures for Balanced Scorecards

| Customer Perspective | |
|---|---|
| **Performance Measure** | **Desired Change** |
| Customer satisfaction as measured by survey results | + |
| Number of customer complaints | − |
| Market share | + |
| Product returns as a percentage of sales | − |
| Percentage of customers retained from last period | + |
| Number of new customers | + |

| Internal Business Processes Perspective | |
|---|---|
| **Performance Measure** | **Desired Change** |
| Percentage of sales from new products | + |
| Time to introduce new products to market | − |
| Percentage of customer calls answered within 20 seconds | + |
| On-time deliveries as a percentage of all deliveries | + |
| Work in process inventory as a percentage of sales | − |
| Unfavorable standard cost variances | − |
| Defect-free units as a percentage of completed units | + |
| Delivery cycle time | − |
| Throughput time | − |
| Manufacturing cycle efficiency | + |
| Quality costs | − |
| Setup time | − |
| Time from call by customer to repair of product | − |
| Percent of customer complaints settled on first contact | + |
| Time to settle a customer claim | − |

| Learning and Growth Perspective | |
|---|---|
| **Performance Measure** | **Desired Change** |
| Suggestions per employee | + |
| Employee turnover | − |
| Hours of in-house training per employee | + |

## A Company's Strategy and the Balanced Scorecard

Returning to the performance measures in Exhibit 9–3, each company must decide which customers to target and what internal business processes are crucial to attracting and retaining those customers. Different companies, having different strategies, will target different customers with different kinds of products and services. Take the automobile industry as an example. **BMW** stresses engineering and handling; **Volvo**, safety; **Jaguar**, luxury detailing; and **Honda**, reliability. Because of these differences in emphasis, a one-size-fits-all approach to performance measurement won't work even within this one industry. Performance measures must be tailored to the specific strategy of each company.

Suppose, for example, that Jaguar's strategy is to offer distinctive, richly finished luxury automobiles to wealthy individuals who prize handcrafted, individualized products.

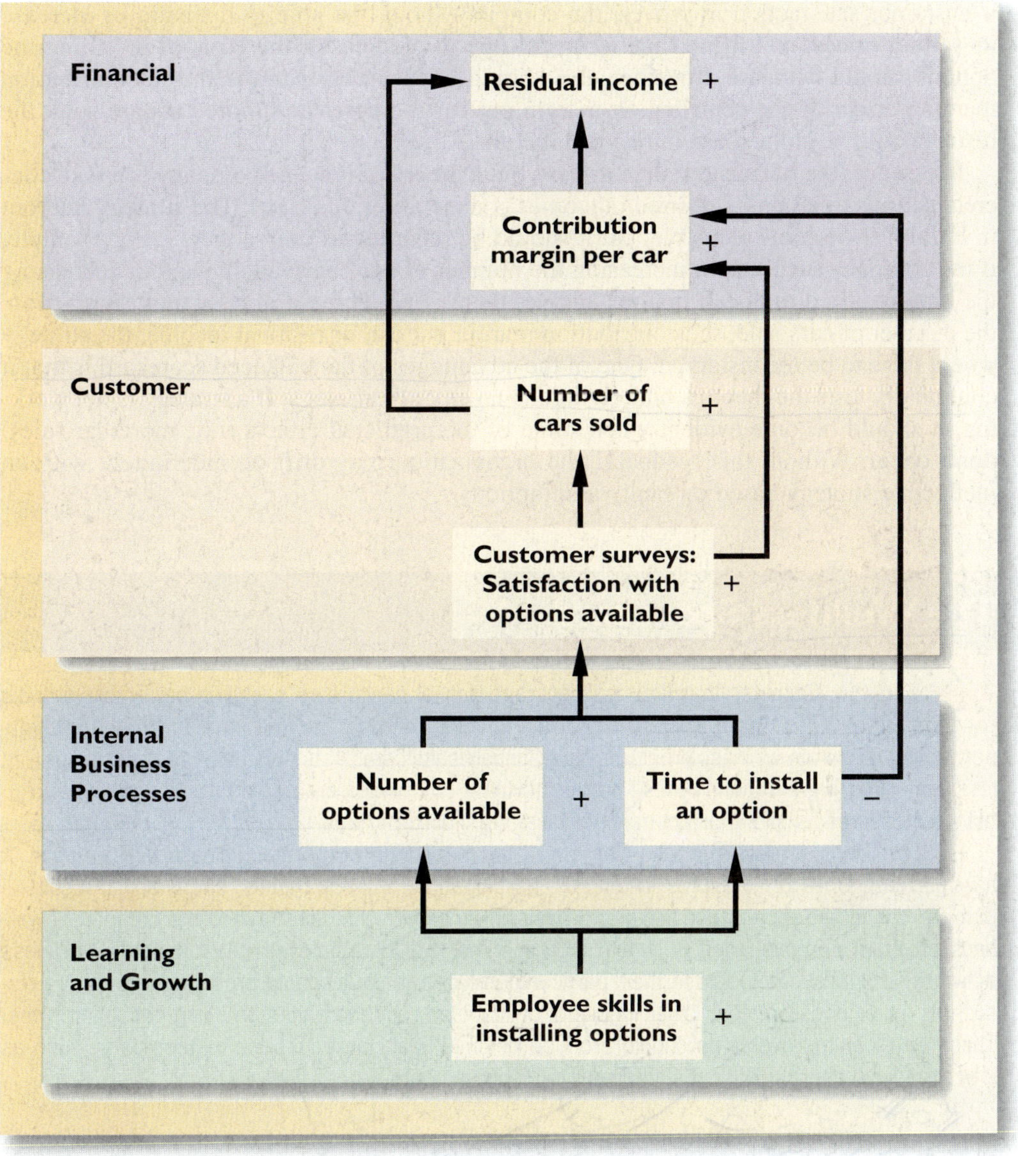


**EXHIBIT 9–5**
A Possible Strategy at Jaguar and the Balanced Scorecard

To deliver this customer intimacy value proposition to its wealthy target customers, Jaguar might create such a large number of options for details, such as leather seats, interior and exterior color combinations, and wooden dashboards, that each car becomes virtually one of a kind. For example, instead of just offering tan or blue leather seats in standard cowhide, the company may offer customers the choice of an almost infinite palette of colors in any of a number of different exotic leathers. For such a system to work effectively, Jaguar would have to be able to deliver a completely customized car within a reasonable amount of time—and without incurring more cost for this customization than the customer is willing to pay. Exhibit 9–5 suggests how Jaguar might reflect this strategy in its balanced scorecard.

If the balanced scorecard is correctly constructed, the performance measures should be linked together on a cause-and-effect basis. Each link can then be read as a hypothesis in the form "If we improve this performance measure, then this other performance measure should also improve." Starting from the bottom of Exhibit 9–5, we can read the links between performance measures as follows. If employees acquire the skills to install new options more effectively, then the company can offer more options and the options can be installed in less time. If more options are available and they are installed in less time, then customer surveys should show greater satisfaction with the range of options available. If customer satisfaction improves, then the number of cars sold should increase. In addition, if customer satisfaction improves, the company should be able to maintain or increase its selling prices, and if the time to install options decreases, the costs of installing the options should decrease. Together, this should result in an increase in the contribution margin per car. If the contribution margin per car increases and more cars are sold, the result should be an increase in residual income.

In essence, the balanced scorecard lays out a theory of how the company can take concrete actions to attain its desired outcomes (financial, in this case). The strategy laid out in Exhibit 9–5 seems plausible, but it should be regarded as only a theory. For example, if the company succeeds in increasing the number of options available and in decreasing the time required to install options and yet there is no increase in customer satisfaction, the number of cars sold, the contribution margin per car, or residual income, the strategy would have to be reconsidered. One of the advantages of the balanced scorecard is that it continually tests the theories underlying management's strategy. If a strategy is not working, it should become evident when some of the predicted effects (i.e., more car sales) don't occur. Without this feedback, the organization may drift on indefinitely with an ineffective strategy based on faulty assumptions.

IN BUSINESS

### The Wellness Scorecard

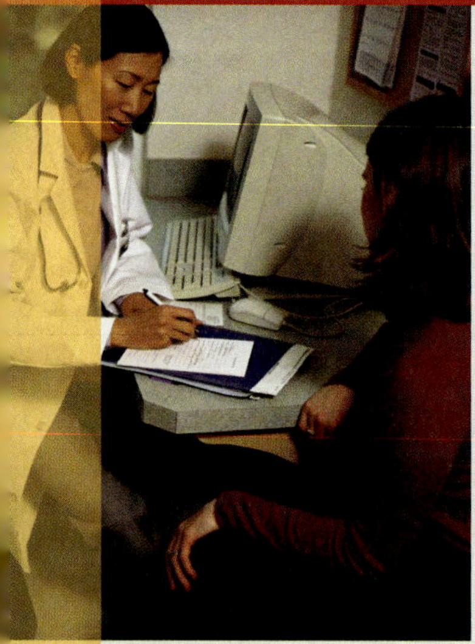

**Towers Watson** estimates that America's average annual health care spending per employee now exceeds $10,000, up from $5,386 in 2002. However, companies that have implemented high-performing corporate wellness programs have annual health care costs that are $1,800 per employee less than other organizations. These high-performing companies create and track wellness performance measures as an important part of managing their programs.

The wellness scorecard is one framework for measuring corporate wellness performance. It has four categories of measures—attitudes, participation, physical results, and financial results—that are connected on a cause-and-effect basis. If employee attitudes toward the company's wellness program improve, then it should increase the rate of employee participation in wellness activities. If employees increase their participation rates, then it should produce physical results, such as lower obesity rates, lower incidents of diabetes, and increased smoking cessation rates. These physical improvements should produce positive financial results for the company, such as lower medical, pharmaceutical, and disability disbursements.

Sources: Towers Perrin, "2010 Health Care Cost Survey," www.towerswatson.com; and Peter C. Brewer, Angela Gallo, and Melanie R. Smith, "Getting Fit with Corporate Wellness Programs," *Strategic Finance*, May 2010, pp. 27–33.

The balanced scorecard has been embraced by a wide variety of organizations including **Bank of Tokyo-Mitsubishi UFJ**, **Brigham & Women's Hospital**, **KeyCorp**, **Chilectra**, **China Resources Microelectronics**, **Delta Dental of Kansas**, **Gerdau Acominas**, **Korea East-West Power**, **Luxfer Gas Cylinders**, **Marriott Vacation Club International**, **Metro de Madrid**, **National Federation of Coffee Growers of Colombia**, **Sprint Nextel**, **Best Buy**, **Ingersoll Rand**, **Serono**, **Tennessee Valley Authority**, **Royal Canadian Mounted Police**, **Crown Castle International**, **Ricoh Corporation**, **Mobistar**, **Hilton Hotels**, and the **United States Postal Service**. It has been estimated that about half of all Fortune 1000 companies have implemented a balanced scorecard.

## Tying Compensation to the Balanced Scorecard

Incentive compensation for employees, such as bonuses, can, and probably should, be tied to balanced scorecard performance measures. However, this should be done only after the organization has been successfully managed with the scorecard for some time—perhaps a year or more. Managers must be confident that the performance measures are reliable, sensible, understood by those who are being evaluated, and not easily manipulated. As Robert Kaplan and David Norton, the originators of the balanced scorecard concept point out, "compensation is such a powerful lever that you have to be pretty confident that you have the right measures and have good data for the measures before making the link."[4]

## Sustainability and the Balanced Scorecard

IN BUSINESS

The **Sustainable Investment Research Analyst Network (SIRAN)** studied changes in the sustainability reporting practices of the Standard & Poor's (S&P) 100 companies from 2005 to 2007. Eighty-six of the S&P 100 companies had corporate sustainability websites as of 2007, an increase of 48% since 2005. Forty-nine of the S&P 100 companies published sustainability reports in 2007, up 26% from 2005.

Graham Hubbard, a professor at the University of Adelaide, recommends incorporating sustainability reporting into the balanced scorecard by adding two categories of measures related to social performance and environmental performance. Social performance measures focus on a company's philanthropic investments, community service, and employee safety and satisfaction. Environmental measures focus on a company's energy and water use per unit of output and its waste generation and disposal performance.

Sources: Ghostwriter, "Rise in Sustainability Reporting by S&P 100 Companies," *Business and the Environment with ISO14000 Updates*, October 2008, pp. 5–6; and Graham Hubbard, "Measuring Organizational Performance: Beyond the Triple Bottom Line," *Business Strategy and the Environment*, March 2009, pp. 177–191.

## Advantages of Timely and Graphic Feedback

Whatever performance measures are used, they should be reported on a frequent and timely basis. For example, data about defects should be reported to the responsible managers at least once a day so that action can be quickly taken if an unusual number of defects occurs. In the most advanced companies, any defect is reported *immediately,* and its cause is tracked down before any more defects occur. Another common characteristic of the performance measures under the balanced scorecard approach is that managers focus on *trends* in the performance measures over time. The emphasis is on progress and *improvement* rather than on meeting any specific standard.

[4]Lori Calabro, "On Balance: A CFO Interview," *CFO,* February 2001, pp. 73–78.

## SUMMARY

### LO1 Compute return on investment (ROI) and show how changes in sales, expenses, and assets affect ROI.

Return on investment (ROI) is defined as net operating income divided by average operating assets. Alternatively, it can be defined as the product of margin and turnover, where margin is net operating income divided by sales and turnover is sales divided by average operating assets.

The relations among sales, expenses, assets, and ROI are complex. The effect of a change in any one variable on the others will depend on the specific circumstances. Nevertheless, an increase in sales often leads to an increase in ROI via the effect of sales on net operating income. If the organization has significant fixed costs, then a given percentage increase in sales is likely to have an even larger percentage effect on net operating income.

**LO2 Compute residual income and understand its strengths and weaknesses.**
Residual income is the difference between net operating income and the minimum required return on average operating assets. The minimum required return on average operating assets is computed by applying the minimum rate of return to the average operating assets.

A major advantage of residual income over ROI is that it encourages investment in projects whose rates of return are above the minimum required rate of return for the entire organization, but below the segment's current ROI.

**LO3 Compute delivery cycle time, throughput time, and manufacturing cycle efficiency (MCE).**
In addition to financial measures, companies use operating performance measures to assess their performance. The delivery cycle time is the amount of time from when a customer order is received to when the completed order is shipped. The amount of time required to turn raw materials into completed products is called throughput time. The manufacturing cycle efficiency (MCE) measures the value-added time divided by the throughput time. Any non-value-added time results in an MCE of less than 1.

**LO4 Understand how to construct and use a balanced scorecard.**
A balanced scorecard is an integrated system of performance measures designed to support an organization's strategy. The various measures in a balanced scorecard should be linked on a plausible cause-and-effect basis from the very lowest level up through the organization's ultimate objectives. The balanced scorecard is essentially a theory about how specific actions taken by various people in the organization will further the organization's objectives. The theory should be viewed as tentative and subject to change if the actions do not in fact result in improvements in the organization's financial and other goals. If the theory changes, then the performance measures on the balanced scorecard should also change. The balanced scorecard is a dynamic measurement system that evolves as an organization learns more about what works and what doesn't work and refines its strategy accordingly.

## GUIDANCE ANSWER TO DECISION POINT

**Shoe Store Manager (p. 410)**
The effects of the two alternatives on your store's ROI for the year can be computed as follows:

| | Present | Alternative (a) | Overall |
|---|---|---|---|
| Average operating assets (a) | $2,000,000 | $(500,000) | $1,500,000 |
| Net operating income (b) | $340,000 | $(79,000) | $261,000 |
| ROI, (b) ÷ (a) | 17.00% | 15.80% | 17.40% |

| | Present | Alternative (b) | Overall |
|---|---|---|---|
| Average operating assets (a) | $2,000,000 | $200,000 | $2,200,000 |
| Net operating income (b) | $340,000 | $33,000 | $373,000 |
| ROI, (b) ÷ (a) | 17.00% | 16.50% | 16.95% |

Alternative (a) would increase your store's ROI to 17.40%—beating last year's ROI and hence earning you a bonus. Alternative (b) would actually decrease your store's ROI and would result in no bonus for the year. So to earn the bonus, you would select Alternative (a). However, this alternative is not in the best interests of the national chain since the ROI of the lost sales is 15.8%, which exceeds the national chain's minimum required rate of return of 15%. Rather, it would be in the national chain's interests to adopt Alternative (b)—the addition of a new product line. The ROI on these sales would be 16.5%, which exceeds the minimum required rate of return of 15%.

## GUIDANCE ANSWERS TO CONCEPT CHECKS

1. **Choices c and d.** Both profit and investment center managers are held responsible for profits. In addition, an investment center manager is held responsible for earning an adequate return on investment or residual income.
2. **Choice b.** The net operating income would be $300,000 − ($225,000 × 95%) = $86,250. The return on investment would be ($86,250 ÷ ($500,000 × 95%) = 18.2%.
3. **Choice d.** The residual income would be $86,250 − ($475,000 × 12%) = $29,250.

## REVIEW PROBLEM: RETURN ON INVESTMENT (ROI) AND RESIDUAL INCOME

The Magnetic Imaging Division of Medical Diagnostics, Inc., has reported the following results for last year's operations:

| | |
|---|---|
| Sales | $25 million |
| Net operating income | $3 million |
| Average operating assets | $10 million |

***Required:***

1. Compute the Magnetic Imaging Division's margin, turnover, and ROI.
2. Top management of Medical Diagnostics, Inc., has set a minimum required rate of return on average operating assets of 25%. What is the Magnetic Imaging Division's residual income for the year?

**Solution to Review Problem**

1. The required calculations follow:

$$\text{Margin} = \frac{\text{Net operating income}}{\text{Sales}}$$

$$= \frac{\$3{,}000{,}000}{\$25{,}000{,}000}$$

$$= 12\%$$

$$\text{Turnover} = \frac{\text{Sales}}{\text{Average operating assets}}$$

$$= \frac{\$25{,}000{,}000}{\$10{,}000{,}000}$$

$$= 2.5$$

$$\text{ROI} = \text{Margin} \times \text{Turnover}$$

$$= 12\% \times 2.5$$

$$= 30\%$$

2. The Magnetic Imaging Division's residual income is computed as follows:

| | |
|---|---|
| Average operating assets | $10,000,000 |
| Net operating income | $3,000,000 |
| Minimum required return (25% × $10,000,000) | 2,500,000 |
| Residual income | $ 500,000 |

## GLOSSARY

**Balanced scorecard** An integrated set of performance measures that are derived from and support the organization's strategy. (p. 413)

**Cost center** A business segment whose manager has control over cost but has no control over revenue or investments in operating assets. (p. 401)

**Decentralized organization** An organization in which decision-making authority is not confined to a few top executives but rather is spread throughout the organization. (p. 400)

**Delivery cycle time** The elapsed time from receipt of a customer order to when the completed goods are shipped to the customer. (p. 410)

**Economic Value Added (EVA)** A concept similar to residual income in which a variety of adjustments may be made to GAAP financial statements for performance evaluation purposes. (p. 406)

**Investment center** A business segment whose manager has control over cost, revenue, and investments in operating assets. (p. 401)

**Manufacturing cycle efficiency (MCE)** Process (value-added) time as a percentage of throughput time. (p. 411)

**Margin** Net operating income divided by sales. (p. 403)

**Net operating income** Income before interest and income taxes have been deducted. (p. 402)

**Operating assets** Cash, accounts receivable, inventory, plant and equipment, and all other assets held for operating purposes. (p. 402)

**Profit center** A business segment whose manager has control over cost and revenue but has no control over investments in operating assets. (p. 401)

**Residual income** The net operating income that an investment center earns above the minimum required return on its operating assets. (p. 406)

**Responsibility center** Any business segment whose manager has control over costs, revenues, or investments in operating assets. (p. 401)

**Return on investment (ROI)** Net operating income divided by average operating assets. It also equals margin multiplied by turnover. (p. 402)

**Throughput time** The amount of time required to turn raw materials into completed products. (p. 410)

**Turnover** Sales divided by average operating assets. (p. 403)

## QUESTIONS

**9–1** What is meant by the term *decentralization?*

**9–2** What benefits result from decentralization?

**9–3** Distinguish between a cost center, a profit center, and an investment center.

**9–4** What is meant by the terms *margin* and *turnover* in ROI calculations?

**9–5** What is meant by residual income?

**9–6** In what way can the use of ROI as a performance measure for investment centers lead to bad decisions? How does the residual income approach overcome this problem?

**9–7** What is the difference between delivery cycle time and throughput time? What four elements make up throughput time? What elements of throughput time are value-added and what elements are non–value-added?

**9–8** What does a manufacturing cycle efficiency (MCE) of less than 1 mean? How would you interpret an MCE of 0.40?

**9–9** Why do the measures used in a balanced scorecard differ from company to company?

**9–10** Why does the balanced scorecard include financial performance measures as well as measures of how well internal business processes are doing?

**Multiple-choice questions are provided on the text website at www.mhhe.com/brewer6e.**

## APPLYING EXCEL

connect ACCOUNTING

**LO1, LO2**

**Available with McGraw-Hill's *Connect*® *Accounting*.**

The Excel worksheet form that appears on the next page is to be used to recreate the Review Problem in the text on page 421. Download the workbook containing this form from the Online Learning Center at www.mhhe.com/brewer6e. *On the website you will also receive instructions about how to use this worksheet form.*

| | A | B | C | D |
|---|---|---|---|---|
| 1 | Chapter 9: Applying Excel | | | |
| 2 | | | | |
| 3 | **Data** | | | |
| 4 | Sales | $25,000,000 | | |
| 5 | Net operating income | $3,000,000 | | |
| 6 | Average operating assets | $10,000,000 | | |
| 7 | Minimum required rate of return | 25% | | |
| 8 | | | | |
| 9 | *Enter a formula into each of the cells marked with a ? below* | | | |
| 10 | **Review Problem: Return on Investment (ROI) and Residual Income** | | | |
| 11 | | | | |
| 12 | ***Compute the ROI*** | | | |
| 13 | Margin | ? | | |
| 14 | Turnover | ? | | |
| 15 | ROI | ? | | |
| 16 | | | | |
| 17 | ***Compute the residual income*** | | | |
| 18 | Average operating assets | ? | | |
| 19 | Net operating income | ? | | |
| 20 | Minimum required return | ? | | |
| 21 | Residual income | ? | | |
| 22 | | | | |

Chapter 9 Form / Filled in Chapter 9 Form

You should proceed to the requirements below only after completing your worksheet.

***Required:***

1. Check your worksheet by changing the average operating assets in cell B6 to $8,000,000. The ROI should now be 38% and the residual income should now be $1,000,000. If you do not get these answers, find the errors in your worksheet and correct them.

   Explain why the ROI and the residual income both increase when the average operating assets decrease.
2. Revise the data in your worksheet as follows:

| **Data** | |
|---|---|
| Sales | $1,200 |
| Net operating income | $72 |
| Average operating assets | $500 |
| Minimum required rate of return | 15% |

   a. What is the ROI?
   b. What is the residual income?
   c. Explain the relationship between the ROI and the residual income?

connect ACCOUNTING

## THE FOUNDATIONAL 15

LO1, LO2

**Available with McGraw-Hill's *Connect® Accounting.***

Westerville Company reported the following results from last year's operations:

| | |
|---|---|
| Sales | $1,000,000 |
| Variable expenses | 300,000 |
| Contribution margin | 700,000 |
| Fixed expenses | 500,000 |
| Net operating income | $ 200,000 |
| Average operating assets | $625,000 |

This year the company has a $120,000 investment opportunity with the following cost and revenue characteristics:

| | |
|---|---|
| Sales | $200,000 |
| Contribution margin ratio | 60% of sales |
| Fixed expenses | $90,000 |

The company's minimum required rate of return is 15%.

***Required:***

1. What is last year's margin?
2. What is last year's turnover?
3. What is last year's return on investment (ROI)?
4. What is the margin related to this year's investment opportunity?
5. What is the turnover related to this year's investment opportunity?
6. What is the ROI related to this year's investment opportunity?
7. If the company pursues the investment opportunity and otherwise performs the same as last year, what margin will it earn this year?
8. If the company pursues the investment opportunity and otherwise performs the same as last year, what turnover will it earn this year?
9. If the company pursues the investment opportunity and otherwise performs the same as last year, what ROI will it earn this year?
10. If Westerville's Chief Executive Officer will earn a bonus only if her ROI from this year exceeds her ROI from last year, would she pursue the investment opportunity? Would the owners of the company want her to pursue the investment opportunity?
11. What is last year's residual income?
12. What is the residual income of this year's investment opportunity?
13. If the company pursues the investment opportunity and otherwise performs the same as last year, what residual income will it earn this year?
14. If Westerville's Chief Executive Officer will earn a bonus only if her residual income from this year exceeds her residual income from last year, would she pursue the investment opportunity?
15. Assume that the contribution margin ratio of the investment opportunity was 50% instead of 60%. If Westerville's Chief Executive Officer will earn a bonus only if her residual income from this year exceeds her residual income from last year, would she pursue the investment opportunity? Would the owners of the company want her to pursue the investment opportunity?

## EXERCISES

connect ACCOUNTING

**All applicable exercises are available with McGraw-Hill's *Connect® Accounting.***

### EXERCISE 9–1 Compute the Return on Investment (ROI) [LO1]

Tundra Services Company, a division of a major oil company, provides various services to the operators of the North Slope oil field in Alaska. Data concerning the most recent year appear below:

| | |
|---|---|
| Sales | $18,000,000 |
| Net operating income | $5,400,000 |
| Average operating assets | $36,000,000 |

Sales = $21,600,000

***Required:***

1. Compute the margin for Tundra Services Company.
2. Compute the turnover for Tundra Services Company.
3. Compute the return on investment (ROI) for Tundra Services Company.

### EXERCISE 9–2 Residual Income [LO2]

Midlands Design Ltd. of Manchester, England, is a company specializing in providing design services to residential developers. Last year the company had net operating income of £400,000 on sales of £2,000,000. The company's average operating assets for the year were £2,200,000 and its minimum required rate of return was 16%. (The currency in the United Kingdom is the pound, denoted by £.)

Minimum required rate of return = 15%

***Required:***
Compute the company's residual income for the year.

**EXERCISE 9–3 Measures of Internal Business Process Performance [LO3]**

TAKE TWO

Process time = 4.8 days

Lipex, Ltd., of Birmingham, England, is interested in cutting the amount of time between when a customer places an order and when the order is completed. For the first quarter of the year, the following data were reported:

| | |
|---|---|
| Inspection time .................................... | 0.5 days |
| Process time ........................................ | 2.8 days |
| Wait time.............................................. | 16.0 days |
| Queue time .......................................... | 4.0 days |
| Move time ............................................ | 0.7 days |

***Required:***
1. Compute the throughput time.
2. Compute the manufacturing cycle efficiency (MCE) for the quarter.
3. What percentage of the throughput time was spent in non–value-added activities?
4. Compute the delivery cycle time.
5. If by using Lean Production all queue time can be eliminated in production, what will be the new MCE?

**EXERCISE 9–4 Creating a Balanced Scorecard [LO4]**

Mason Paper Company (MPC) manufactures commodity grade papers for use in computer printers and photocopiers. MPC has reported net operating losses for the last two years due to intense price pressure from much larger competitors. The MPC management team—including Kristen Townsend (CEO), Mike Martinez (vice president of Manufacturing), Tom Andrews (vice president of Marketing), and Wendy Chen (CFO)—is contemplating a change in strategy to save the company from impending bankruptcy. Excerpts from a recent management team meeting are shown below:

***Townsend:*** As we all know, the commodity paper manufacturing business is all about economies of scale. The largest competitors with the lowest cost per unit win. The limited capacity of our older machines prohibits us from competing in the high-volume commodity paper grades. Furthermore, expanding our capacity by acquiring a new paper-making machine is out of the question given the extraordinarily high price tag. Therefore, I propose that we abandon cost reduction as a strategic goal and instead pursue manufacturing flexibility as the key to our future success.

***Chen:*** Manufacturing flexibility? What does that mean?

***Martinez:*** It means we have to abandon our "crank out as many tons of paper as possible" mentality. Instead, we need to pursue the low-volume business opportunities that exist in the nonstandard, specialized paper grades. To succeed in this regard, we'll need to improve our flexibility in three ways. First, we must improve our ability to switch between paper grades. Right now, we require an average of four hours to change over to another paper grade. Timely customer deliveries are a function of changeover performance. Second, we need to expand the range of paper grades that we can manufacture. Currently, we can only manufacture three paper grades. Our customers must perceive that we are a "one-stop shop" that can meet all of their paper grade needs. Third, we will need to improve our yields (e.g., tons of acceptable output relative to total tons processed) in the nonstandard paper grades. Our percentage of waste within these grades will be unacceptably high unless we do something to improve our processes. Our variable costs will go through the roof if we cannot increase our yields!

***Chen:*** Wait just a minute! These changes are going to destroy our equipment utilization numbers!

***Andrews:*** You're right Wendy; however, equipment utilization is not the name of the game when it comes to competing in terms of flexibility. Our customers don't care about our equipment utilization. Instead, as Mike just alluded to, they want just-in-time delivery of smaller quantities of a full range of paper grades. If we can shrink the elapsed time from order placement to order delivery and expand our product offerings, it will increase sales from current customers and bring in new customers. Furthermore, we will be able to charge a premium price because of the limited competition within this niche from our cost-focused larger competitors. Our contribution margin per ton should drastically improve!

***Martinez:*** Of course, executing the change in strategy will not be easy. We'll need to make a substantial investment in training because ultimately it is our people who create our flexible manufacturing capabilities.

***Chen:*** If we adopt this new strategy, it is definitely going to impact how we measure performance. We'll need to create measures that motivate our employees to make decisions that support our flexibility goals.

***Townsend:*** Wendy, you hit the nail right on the head. For our next meeting, could you pull together some potential measures that support our new strategy?

***Required:***

1. Contrast MPC's previous manufacturing strategy with its new manufacturing strategy.
2. Generally speaking, why would a company that changes its strategic goals need to change its performance measurement system as well? What are some examples of measures that would have been appropriate for MPC prior to its change in strategy? Why would those measures fail to support MPC's new strategy?
3. Construct a balanced scorecard that would support MPC's new manufacturing strategy. Use arrows to show the causal links between the performance measures and show whether the performance measure should increase or decrease over time. Feel free to create measures that may not be specifically mentioned in the chapter, but nonetheless make sense given the strategic goals of the company.
4. What hypotheses are built into MPC's balanced scorecard? Which of these hypotheses do you believe are most questionable and why?

### EXERCISE 9–5 Cost-Volume-Profit Analysis and Return on Investment (ROI) [LO1]

Images.com is a small Internet retailer of high-quality posters. The company has $800,000 in operating assets and fixed expenses of $160,000 per year. With this level of operating assets and fixed expenses, the company can support sales of up to $5 million per year. The company's contribution margin ratio is 10%, which means that an additional dollar of sales results in additional contribution margin, and net operating income, of 10 cents.

***Required:***

Contribution margin ratio = 12%

1. Complete the following table showing the relationship between sales and return on investment (ROI):

| Sales | Net Operating Income | Average Operating Assets | ROI |
|---|---|---|---|
| $4,500,000 | $290,000 | $800,000 | ? |
| $4,600,000 | ? | $800,000 | ? |
| $4,700,000 | ? | $800,000 | ? |
| $4,800,000 | ? | $800,000 | ? |
| $4,900,000 | ? | $800,000 | ? |
| $5,000,000 | ? | $800,000 | ? |

2. What happens to the company's return on investment (ROI) as sales increase? Explain.

### EXERCISE 9–6 Effects of Changes in Sales, Expenses, and Assets on ROI [LO1]

BusServ.com Corporation provides business-to-business services on the Internet. Data concerning the most recent year appear below:

| | |
|---|---|
| Sales | $8,000,000 |
| Net operating income | $800,000 |
| Average operating assets | $3,200,000 |

Net operating income = $960,000

***Required:***

Consider each question below independently. Carry out all computations to two decimal places.

1. Compute the company's return on investment (ROI).
2. The entrepreneur who founded the company is convinced that sales will increase next year by 150% and that net operating income will increase by 400%, with no increase in average operating assets. What would be the company's ROI?
3. The Chief Financial Officer of the company believes a more realistic scenario would be a $2 million increase in sales, requiring an $800,000 increase in average operating assets, with a resulting $250,000 increase in net operating income. What would be the company's ROI in this scenario?

**EXERCISE 9–7 Contrasting Return on Investment (ROI) and Residual Income [LO1, LO2]**

Rains Nickless Ltd. of Australia has two divisions that operate in Perth and Darwin. Selected data on the two divisions follow:

| | Division | |
|---|---|---|
| | Perth | Darwin |
| Sales | $9,000,000 | $20,000,000 |
| Net operating income | $630,000 | $1,800,000 |
| Average operating assets | $3,000,000 | $10,000,000 |

TAKE TWO

Perth net operating income = $660,000

***Required:***

1. Compute the return on investment (ROI) for each division.
2. Assume that the company evaluates performance using residual income and that the minimum required rate of return for any division is 16%. Compute the residual income for each division.
3. Is the Darwin Division's greater residual income an indication that it is better managed? Explain.

**EXERCISE 9–8 Return on Investment (ROI) and Residual Income Relations [LO1, LO2]**

A family friend has asked your help in analyzing the operations of three anonymous companies operating in the same service sector industry. Supply the missing data in the table below:

| | Company | | |
|---|---|---|---|
| | A | B | C |
| Sales | $400,000 | $750,000 | $600,000 |
| Net operating income | $ ? | $ 45,000 | $ ? |
| Average operating assets | $160,000 | ? | $150,000 |
| Return on investment (ROI) | 20% | 18% | ? |
| Minimum required rate of return: | | | |
| Percentage | 15% | ? | 12% |
| Dollar amount | $ ? | $ 50,000 | $ ? |
| Residual income | $ ? | $ ? | $ 6,000 |

**EXERCISE 9–9 Evaluating New Investments Using Return on Investment (ROI) and Residual Income [LO1, LO2]**

Selected sales and operating data for three divisions of three different companies are given below:

| | Division A | Division B | Division C |
|---|---|---|---|
| Sales | $6,000,000 | $10,000,000 | $8,000,000 |
| Average operating assets | $1,500,000 | $5,000,000 | $2,000,000 |
| Net operating income | $300,000 | $900,000 | $180,000 |
| Minimum required rate of return | 15% | 18% | 12% |

TAKE TWO

Minimum required rate of return for all divisions = 20%

***Required:***

1. Compute the return on investment (ROI) for each division, using the formula stated in terms of margin and turnover.
2. Compute the residual income for each division.
3. Assume that each division is presented with an investment opportunity that would yield a rate of return of 17%.
   a. If performance is being measured by ROI, which division or divisions will probably accept the opportunity? Reject? Why?
   b. If performance is being measured by residual income, which division or divisions will probably accept the opportunity? Reject? Why?

## EXERCISE 9–10 Computing and Interpreting Return on Investment (ROI) [LO1]

Selected operating data on the two divisions of York Company are given below:

Western Division net operating income = $140,000

| | Division | |
|---|---|---|
| | Eastern | Western |
| Sales | $1,000,000 | $1,750,000 |
| Average operating assets | $500,000 | $500,000 |
| Net operating income | $90,000 | $105,000 |
| Property, plant, and equipment | $250,000 | $200,000 |

***Required:***

1. Compute the rate of return for each division using the return on investment (ROI) formula stated in terms of margin and turnover.
2. Which divisional manager seems to be doing the better job? Why?

## EXERCISE 9–11 Creating a Balanced Scorecard [LO4]

Ariel Tax Services prepares tax returns for individual and corporate clients. As the company has gradually expanded to 10 offices, the founder, Max Jacobs, has begun to feel as though he is losing control of operations. In response to this concern, he has decided to implement a performance measurement system that will help control current operations and facilitate his plans of expanding to 20 offices.

Jacobs describes the keys to the success of his business as follows:

> "Our only real asset is our people. We must keep our employees highly motivated and we must hire the 'cream of the crop.' Interestingly, employee morale and recruiting success are both driven by the same two factors—compensation and career advancement. In other words, providing superior compensation relative to the industry average coupled with fast-track career advancement opportunities keeps morale high and makes us a very attractive place to work. It drives a high rate of job offer acceptances relative to job offers tendered."

> "Hiring highly qualified people and keeping them energized ensures operational success, which in our business is a function of productivity, efficiency, and effectiveness. Productivity boils down to employees being billable rather than idle. Efficiency relates to the time required to complete a tax return. Finally, effectiveness is critical to our business in the sense that we cannot tolerate errors. Completing a tax return quickly is meaningless if the return contains errors."

> "Our growth depends on acquiring new customers through word-of-mouth from satisfied repeat customers. We believe that our customers come back year after year because they value error-free, timely, and courteous tax return preparation. Common courtesy is an important aspect of our business! We call it service quality, and it all ties back to employee morale in the sense that happy employees treat their clients with care and concern."

> "While sales growth is obviously important to our future plans, growth without a corresponding increase in profitability is useless. Therefore, we understand that increasing our profit margin is a function of cost-efficiency as well as sales growth. Given that payroll is our biggest expense, we must maintain an optimal balance between staffing levels and the revenue being generated. As I alluded to earlier, the key to maintaining this balance is employee productivity. If we can achieve cost-efficient sales growth, we should eventually have 20 profitable offices!"

***Required:***

1. Create a balanced scorecard for Ariel Tax Services. Link your scorecard measures using the framework from Exhibit 9–5. Indicate whether each measure is expected to increase or decrease. Feel free to create measures that may not be specifically mentioned in the chapter, but make sense given the strategic goals of the company.
2. What hypotheses are built into the balanced scorecard for Ariel Tax Services? Which of these hypotheses do you believe are most questionable and why?
3. Discuss the potential advantages and disadvantages of implementing an internal business process measure called *total dollar amount of tax refunds generated.* Would you recommend using this measure in Ariel's balanced scorecard?
4. Would it be beneficial to attempt to measure each office's individual performance with respect to the scorecard measures that you created? Why or why not?

**EXERCISE 9–12 Effects of Changes in Profits and Assets on Return on Investment (ROI) [LO1]**

The Abs Shoppe is a regional chain of health clubs. The managers of the clubs, who have authority to make investments as needed, are evaluated based largely on return on investment (ROI). The Abs Shoppe reported the following results for the past year:

| | |
|---|---|
| Sales | $800,000 |
| Net operating income | $16,000 |
| Average operating assets | $100,000 |

TAKE TWO

Average operating assets = $200,000

***Required:***

The following questions are to be considered independently. Carry out all computations to two decimal places.

1. Compute the club's return on investment (ROI).
2. Assume that the manager of the club is able to increase sales by $80,000 and that as a result net operating income increases by $6,000. Further assume that this is possible without any increase in operating assets. What would be the club's return on investment (ROI)?
3. Assume that the manager of the club is able to reduce expenses by $3,200 without any change in sales or operating assets. What would be the club's return on investment (ROI)?
4. Assume that the manager of the club is able to reduce operating assets by $20,000 without any change in sales or net operating income. What would be the club's return on investment (ROI)?

**EXERCISE 9–13 Return on Investment (ROI) Relations [LO1]**

Provide the missing data in the following table:

| | Division | | |
|---|---|---|---|
| | Fab | Consulting | IT |
| Sales | $800,000 | $ ? | $ ? |
| Net operating income | $ 72,000 | $ ? | $40,000 |
| Average operating assets | $ ? | $130,000 | $ ? |
| Margin | ? | 4% | 8% |
| Turnover | ? | 5 | ? |
| Return on investment (ROI) | 18% | ? | 20% |

Alternate problem set is available on the text website and in *Connect*® *Accounting*.

## PROBLEMS

**All applicable problems are available with McGraw-Hill's *Connect*® *Accounting*.**

**PROBLEM 9–14A Return on Investment (ROI) and Residual Income [LO1, LO2]**

"I know headquarters wants us to add that new product line," said Fred Halloway, manager of Kirsi Products' East Division. "But I want to see the numbers before I make a move. Our division's return on investment (ROI) has led the company for three years, and I don't want any letdown."

Kirsi Products is a decentralized wholesaler with four autonomous divisions. The divisions are evaluated on the basis of ROI, with year-end bonuses given to divisional managers who have the highest ROI. Operating results for the company's East Division for last year are given below:

CHECK FIGURE
(1) Total ROI: 28%

| | |
|---|---|
| Sales | $21,000,000 |
| Variable expenses | 13,400,000 |
| Contribution margin | 7,600,000 |
| Fixed expenses | 5,920,000 |
| Net operating income | $ 1,680,000 |
| Divisional operating assets | $ 5,250,000 |

The company had an overall ROI of 18% last year (considering all divisions). The company's East Division has an opportunity to add a new product line that would require an investment of $3,000,000. The cost and revenue characteristics of the new product line per year would be as follows:

| | |
|---|---|
| Sales | $9,000,000 |
| Variable expenses | 65% of sales |
| Fixed expenses | $2,520,000 |

***Required:***

1. Compute the East Division's ROI for last year; also compute the ROI as it would appear if the company performed the same as last year and added the new product line.
2. If you were in Fred Halloway's position, would you accept or reject the new product line? Explain.
3. Why do you suppose headquarters is anxious for the East Division to add the new product line?
4. Suppose that the company's minimum required rate of return on operating assets is 15% and that performance is evaluated using residual income.
   a. Compute the East Division's residual income for last year; also compute the residual income as it would appear if the company performed the same as last year and added the new product line.
   b. Under these circumstances, if you were in Fred Halloway's position would you accept or reject the new product line? Explain.

**PROBLEM 9–15A Comparison of Performance Using Return on Investment (ROI) [LO1]**

Comparative data on three companies in the same service industry are given below:

CHECK FIGURE
(2) Company A margin: 14%

| | Company | | |
|---|---|---|---|
| | A | B | C |
| Sales | $4,000,000 | $1,500,000 | $ ? |
| Net operating income | $ 560,000 | $ 210,000 | $ ? |
| Average operating assets | $2,000,000 | ? | $3,000,000 |
| Margin | ? | ? | 3.5% |
| Turnover | ? | ? | 2 |
| Return on investment (ROI) | ? | 7% | ? |

***Required:***

1. What advantages are there to breaking down the ROI computation into two separate elements, margin and turnover?
2. Fill in the missing information above, and comment on the relative performance of the three companies in as much detail as the data permit. Make *specific recommendations* about how to improve the ROI.

(Adapted from National Association of Accountants, *Research Report No. 35,* p. 34)

**PROBLEM 9–16A Measures of Internal Business Process Performance [LO3]**

MacIntyre Fabrications, Ltd., of Aberdeen, Scotland, has recently begun a continuous improvement campaign in conjunction with a move toward Lean Production. Management has developed new performance measures as part of this campaign. The following operating data have been gathered over the last four months:

CHECK FIGURE
(1a) MCE month 1: 11.1%;
(3a) MCE month 5: 33.3%

| | Month | | | |
|---|---|---|---|---|
| | 1 | 2 | 3 | 4 |
| Throughput time | ? | ? | ? | ? |
| Manufacturing cycle efficiency | ? | ? | ? | ? |
| Delivery cycle time | ? | ? | ? | ? |
| Percentage of on-time deliveries | 72% | 73% | 78% | 85% |
| Total sales (units) | 10,540 | 10,570 | 10,550 | 10,490 |

Management would like to know the company's throughput time, manufacturing cycle efficiency, and delivery cycle time. The data to compute these measures have been gathered and appear below:

| | Month | | | |
|---|---|---|---|---|
| | 1 | 2 | 3 | 4 |
| Move time per unit, in days.................. | 0.5 | 0.5 | 0.4 | 0.5 |
| Process time per unit, in days.............. | 0.6 | 0.5 | 0.5 | 0.4 |
| Wait time per order before start of production, in days........................... | 9.6 | 8.7 | 5.3 | 4.7 |
| Queue time per unit, in days................ | 3.6 | 3.6 | 2.6 | 1.7 |
| Inspection time per unit, in days.......... | 0.7 | 0.7 | 0.4 | 0.3 |

***Required:***

1. For each month, compute the following:
   a. The throughput time.
   b. The manufacturing cycle efficiency (MCE).
   c. The delivery cycle time.
2. Using the performance measures given in the problem and those you computed in (1) above, identify whether the trend over the four months is generally favorable, generally unfavorable, or mixed. What areas apparently require improvement and how might they be improved?
3. Refer to the move time, process time, and so forth, given for month 4.
   a. Assume that in month 5 the move time, process time, and so forth, are the same as for month 4, except that through the implementation of Lean Production, the company is able to completely eliminate the queue time during production. Compute the new throughput time and MCE.
   b. Assume that in month 6 the move time, process time, and so forth, are the same as for month 4, except that the company is able to completely eliminate both the queue time during production and the inspection time. Compute the new throughput time and MCE.

**PROBLEM 9–17A Building a Balanced Scorecard [LO4]**

Deer Creek ski resort was for many years a small, family-owned resort serving day skiers from nearby towns. Deer Creek was recently acquired by Mountain Associates, a major ski resort operator with destination resorts in several western states. The new owners have plans to upgrade the resort into a destination resort for vacationers staying for a week or more. As part of this plan, the new owners would like to make major improvements in the Lynx Lair Lodge, the resort's on-the-hill fast-food restaurant. The menu at the Lodge is very limited—hamburgers, hot dogs, chili, tuna fish sandwiches, french fries, and packaged snacks. The previous owners of the resort had felt no urgency to upgrade the food service at the Lodge because there is little competition. If skiers want lunch on the mountain, the only alternatives are the Lynx Lair Lodge or a brown bag lunch brought from home.

As part of the deal when acquiring Deer Creek, Mountain Associates agreed to retain all of the current employees of the resort. The manager of the Lodge, while hardworking and enthusiastic, has very little experience in the restaurant business. The manager is responsible for selecting the menu, finding and training employees, and overseeing daily operations. The kitchen staff prepares food and washes dishes. The dining room staff takes orders, serves as cashiers, and cleans the dining room area.

Shortly after taking over Deer Creek, management of Mountain Associates held a day-long meeting with all of the employees of the Lynx Lair Lodge to discuss the future of the ski resort and management's plans for the Lodge. At the end of this meeting, top management and Lodge employees created a balanced scorecard for the Lodge that would help guide operations for the coming ski season. Almost everyone who participated in the meeting seemed to be enthusiastic about the scorecard and management's plans for the Lodge.

The following performance measures were included on the balanced scorecard for the Lynx Lair Lodge:

- Customer satisfaction with service, as measured by customer surveys.
- Total Lynx Lair Lodge profit.
- Dining area cleanliness, as rated by a representative from Mountain Associates management.
- Average time to prepare an order.
- Customer satisfaction with menu choices, as measured by surveys.
- Average time to take an order.
- Percentage of kitchen staff completing institutional cooking course at the local community college.

- Sales.
- Percentage of dining room staff completing hospitality course at the local community college.
- Number of menu items.

Mountain Associates will pay for the costs of staff attending courses at the local community college.

***Required:***

1. Using the above performance measures, construct a balanced scorecard for the Lynx Lair Lodge. Use Exhibit 9–5 as a guide. Use arrows to show causal links and indicate with a + or − whether the performance measure should increase or decrease.
2. What hypotheses are built into the balanced scorecard for the Lynx Lair Lodge? Which of these hypotheses do you believe are most questionable? Why?
3. How will management know if one of the hypotheses underlying the balanced scorecard is false?

excel

**PROBLEM 9–18A Return on Investment (ROI) and Residual Income [LO1, LO2]**

Financial data for Bridger, Inc., for last year are as follows:

CHECK FIGURE
(1) ROI: 33%

**Bridger, Inc.**
**Balance Sheet**

| | Beginning Balance | Ending Balance |
|---|---|---|
| **Assets** | | |
| Cash | $ 125,000 | $ 130,000 |
| Accounts receivable | 340,000 | 480,000 |
| Inventory | 570,000 | 490,000 |
| Plant and equipment, net | 845,000 | 820,000 |
| Investment in Brier Company | 400,000 | 430,000 |
| Land (undeveloped) | 250,000 | 250,000 |
| Total assets | $2,530,000 | $2,600,000 |
| **Liabilities and Stockholders' Equity** | | |
| Accounts payable | $ 380,000 | $ 340,000 |
| Long-term debt | 1,000,000 | 1,000,000 |
| Stockholders' equity | 1,150,000 | 1,260,000 |
| Total liabilities and stockholders' equity | $2,530,000 | $2,600,000 |

**Bridger, Inc.**
**Income Statement**

| | | |
|---|---|---|
| Sales | | $4,180,000 |
| Operating expenses | | 3,553,000 |
| Net operating income | | 627,000 |
| Interest and taxes: | | |
| Interest expense | $120,000 | |
| Tax expense | 200,000 | 320,000 |
| Net income | | $ 307,000 |

The company paid dividends of $197,000 last year. The "Investment in Brier Company" on the balance sheet represents an investment in the stock of another company.

***Required:***

1. Compute the company's margin, turnover, and return on investment (ROI) for last year.
2. The board of directors of Bridger, Inc., has set a minimum required return of 20%. What was the company's residual income last year?

**PROBLEM 9–19A Perverse Effects of Some Performance Measures [LO4]**

There is often more than one way to improve a performance measure. Unfortunately, some of the actions taken by managers to make their performance look better may actually harm the organization. For example, suppose the marketing department is held responsible only for increasing the performance measure "total revenues." Increases in total revenues may be achieved by working harder and smarter, but they can also usually be achieved by simply cutting prices. The increase in volume from cutting prices almost always results in greater total revenues; however, it does not always lead to greater total profits. Those who design performance measurement systems need to keep in mind that managers who are under pressure to perform may take actions to improve performance measures that have negative consequences elsewhere.

***Required:***

For each of the following situations, describe actions that managers might take to show improvement in the performance measure but which do not actually lead to improvement in the organization's overall performance.

1. Concerned with the slow rate at which new products are brought to market, top management of a consumer electronics company introduces a new performance measure—speed-to-market. The research and development department is given responsibility for this performance measure, which measures the average amount of time a product is in development before it is released to the market for sale.
2. The CEO of a telephone company has been under public pressure from city officials to fix the large number of public pay phones that do not work. The company's repair people complain that the problem is vandalism and damage caused by theft of coins from coin boxes—particularly in high-crime areas in the city. The CEO says she wants the problem solved and has pledged to city officials that there will be substantial improvement by the end of the year. To ensure that this is done, she makes the managers in charge of installing and maintaining pay phones responsible for increasing the percentage of public pay phones that are fully functional.
3. A manufacturing company has been plagued by the chronic failure to ship orders to customers by the promised date. To solve this problem, the production manager has been given the responsibility of increasing the percentage of orders shipped on time. When a customer calls in an order, the production manager and the customer agree to a delivery date. If the order is not completed by that date, it is counted as a late shipment.
4. Concerned with the productivity of employees, the board of directors of a large multinational corporation has dictated that the manager of each subsidiary will be held responsible for increasing the revenue per employee of his or her subsidiary.

**PROBLEM 9–20A Return on Investment (ROI) Analysis [LO1]**

The contribution format income statement for Westex, Inc., for its most recent period is given below:

CHECK FIGURE
(3) ROI: 20%; (6) ROI. 25%

| | Total | Unit |
|---|---|---|
| Sales | $1,000,000 | $50.00 |
| Variable expenses | 600,000 | 30.00 |
| Contribution margin | 400,000 | 20.00 |
| Fixed expenses | 320,000 | 16.00 |
| Net operating income | 80,000 | 4.00 |
| Income taxes @40% | 32,000 | 1.60 |
| Net income | $ 48,000 | $ 2.40 |

The company had average operating assets of $500,000 during the period.

***Required:***

1. Compute the company's return on investment (ROI) for the period using the ROI formula stated in terms of margin and turnover.

For each of the following questions, indicate whether the margin and turnover will increase, decrease, or remain unchanged as a result of the events described, and then compute the new ROI figure. Consider each question separately, starting in each case from the original ROI computed in (1) above.

2. The company achieves a cost savings of $10,000 per period by using less costly materials.

3. Using Lean Production, the company is able to reduce the average level of inventory by $100,000. (The released funds are used to pay off bank loans.)
4. Sales are increased by $100,000; operating assets remain unchanged.
5. The company issues bonds and uses the proceeds to purchase $125,000 in machinery and equipment at the beginning of the period. Interest on the bonds is $15,000 per period. Sales remain unchanged. The new, more efficient equipment reduces production costs by $5,000 per period.
6. The company invests $180,000 of cash (received on accounts receivable) in a plot of land that is to be held for possible future use as a plant site.
7. Obsolete inventory carried on the books at a cost of $20,000 is scrapped and written off as a loss.

**PROBLEM 9–21A Creating Balanced Scorecards that Support Different Strategies [LO4]**
The Midwest Consulting Group (MCG) helps companies build balanced scorecards. As part of its marketing efforts, MCG conducts an annual balanced scorecard workshop for prospective clients. As MCG's newest employee, your boss has asked you to participate in this year's workshop by explaining to attendees how a company's strategy determines the measures that are appropriate for its balanced scorecard. Your boss has provided you with the excerpts below from the annual reports of two current MCG clients. She has asked you to use these excerpts in your portion of the workshop.

Excerpt from Applied Pharmaceuticals' annual report:

> The keys to our business are consistent and timely new product introductions and manufacturing process integrity. The new product introduction side of the equation is a function of research and development (R&D) yield (e.g., the number of marketable drug compounds created relative to the total number of potential compounds pursued). We seek to optimize our R&D yield and first-to-market capability by investing in state-of-the-art technology, hiring the highest possible percentage of the "best and the brightest" engineers that we pursue, and providing world-class training to those engineers. Manufacturing process integrity is all about establishing world-class quality specifications and then relentlessly engaging in prevention and appraisal activities to minimize defect rates. Our customers must have an awareness of, and respect for, our brand image of being "first to market and first in quality." If we deliver on this pledge to our customers, then our financial goal of increasing our return on stockholders' equity should take care of itself.

Excerpt from Destination Resorts International's annual report:

> Our business succeeds or fails based on the quality of the service that our front-line employees provide to customers. Therefore, it is imperative that we strive to maintain high employee morale and minimize employee turnover. In addition, it is critical that we train our employees to use technology to create one seamless worldwide experience for our repeat customers. Once an employee enters a customer preference (e.g., provide two extra pillows in the room, deliver fresh brewed coffee to the room at 8:00 A.M., etc.) into our database, our worldwide workforce strives to ensure that a customer will never need to repeat it at any of our destination resorts. If we properly train and retain a motivated workforce, we should see continuous improvement in our percentage of error-free repeat customer check-ins, the time taken to resolve customer complaints, and our independently assessed room cleanliness. This in turn should drive improvement in our customer retention, which is the key to meeting our revenue growth goals.

***Required:***
1. Based on the excerpts above, compare and contrast the strategies of Applied Pharmaceuticals and Destination Resorts International.
2. Select balanced scorecard measures for each company and link the scorecard measures using the framework from Exhibit 9–5. Use arrows to show the causal links between the performance measures and show whether the performance measure should increase or decrease over time. Feel free to create measures that may not be specifically mentioned in the chapter, but nonetheless make sense given the strategic goals of each company.
3. What hypotheses are built into each balanced scorecard? Why do the hypotheses differ between the two companies?

**PROBLEM 9–22A Internal Business Process Performance Measures [LO3]**

CHECK FIGURE
(1) MCE month 1: 7.8%;
(3a) MCE month 5: 21.4%

Exeter Corporation has recently begun a continuous improvement campaign. As a consequence, there have been many changes in operating procedures. Progress has been slow, particularly in trying to develop new performance measures for the factory.

Management has been gathering the following data over the past four months:

| | Month | | | |
|---|---|---|---|---|
| | 1 | 2 | 3 | 4 |
| Quality control measures: | | | | |
| Customer complaints as a percentage of units sold .... | 1.4% | 1.3% | 1.1% | 1.0% |
| Warranty claims as a percentage of units sold............ | 2.3% | 2.1% | 2.0% | 1.8% |
| Defects as a percentage of units produced ................ | 4.0% | 4.2% | 3.7% | 3.4% |
| Material control measures: | | | | |
| Scrap as a percentage of total cost .......................... | 3.2% | 2.9% | 3.0% | 2.7% |
| Machine performance measures: | | | | |
| Percentage of machine availability ............................ | 80% | 82% | 81% | 79% |
| Use as a percentage of availability ............................ | 75% | 73% | 71% | 70% |
| Average setup time (hours) ....................................... | 2.7 | 2.5 | 2.5 | 2.6 |
| Delivery performance measures: | | | | |
| Throughput time ....................................................... | ? | ? | ? | ? |
| Manufacturing cycle efficiency .................................. | ? | ? | ? | ? |
| Delivery cycle time ................................................... | ? | ? | ? | ? |
| Percentage of on-time deliveries ............................... | 84% | 87% | 91% | 95% |

The president has attended conferences at which the importance of throughput time, manufacturing cycle efficiency, and delivery cycle time were stressed, but no one at the company is sure how they are computed. The data to compute these measures have been gathered and appear below:

| | Month | | | |
|---|---|---|---|---|
| | 1 | 2 | 3 | 4 |
| Wait time per order before start of production, in days .... | 16.7 | 15.2 | 12.3 | 9.6 |
| Inspection time per unit, in days ...................................... | 0.1 | 0.3 | 0.6 | 0.8 |
| Process time per unit, in days ......................................... | 0.6 | 0.6 | 0.6 | 0.6 |
| Queue time per unit, in days ........................................... | 5.6 | 5.7 | 5.6 | 5.7 |
| Move time per unit, in days ............................................. | 1.4 | 1.3 | 1.3 | 1.4 |

***Required:***

1. For each month, compute the following operating performance measures:
   a. Throughput time.
   b. Manufacturing cycle efficiency (MCE).
   c. Delivery cycle time.
2. Using the performance measures given in the problem and those you computed in (1) above, do the following:
   a. Identify areas where the company seems to be improving.
   b. Identify areas where the company seems to be deteriorating or stagnating.
   c. Explain why you think some specific areas are improving while others are not.
3. Refer to the move time, process time, and so forth, given above for month 4.
   a. Assume that in month 5 the move time, process time, and so forth, are the same as for month 4, except that through the implementation of Lean Production, the company is able to completely eliminate the queue time during production. Compute the new throughput time and MCE.
   b. Assume that in month 6 the move time, process time, and so forth, are the same as for month 4, except that the company is able to completely eliminate both the queue time during production and the inspection time. Compute the new throughput time and MCE.

# BUILDING YOUR SKILLS

## COMMUNICATING IN PRACTICE [LO2, LO3]

How do the performance measurement and compensation systems of service companies compare with those of manufacturers? Ask the manager of your local McDonald's, Wendy's, Burger King, or other fast-food chain if he or she could spend some time discussing the performance measures that the company uses to evaluate store managers and how the performance measures tie in with their compensation.

***Required:***

After asking the following questions, write a brief memorandum to your instructor that summarizes what you discovered during your interview with the manager of the franchise.

1. What are the national chain's goals, that is, the broad, long-range plans of the company (e.g., to increase market share)?
2. What performance measures are used to help motivate the store managers and monitor progress toward achieving the corporation's goals?
3. Are the performance measures consistent with the store manager's compensation plan?

## CASE [LO4]

Weierman Department Store is located in the downtown area of a medium-sized city in the American Midwest. While the store had been profitable for many years, it is facing increasing competition from large national chains that have set up stores in the city's suburbs. Recently, the downtown area has been undergoing revitalization, and the owners of Weierman Department Store are somewhat optimistic that profitability can be restored.

In an attempt to accelerate the return to profitability, the management of Weierman Department Store is in the process of designing a balanced scorecard for the company. Management believes the company should focus on two key problems. First, customers are taking longer and longer to pay the bills they incur on the department store's charge card, and they have far more bad debts than are normal for the industry. If this problem were solved, the company would have more cash to make much needed renovations. Investigation has revealed that much of the problem with late payments and unpaid bills is apparently due to disputed bills that are the result of incorrect charges on the customer bills. These incorrect charges usually occur because salesclerks enter data incorrectly on the charge account slip. Second, the company has been incurring large losses on unsold seasonal apparel. Such items are ordinarily resold at a loss to discount stores that specialize in such distress items.

The meeting in which the balanced scorecard approach was discussed was disorganized and ineffectively led—possibly because no one other than one of the vice presidents had read anything about how to create a balanced scorecard. Nevertheless, a number of potential performance measures were suggested by various managers. These potential performance measures are:

**Performance measures suggested by various managers:**

- Total sales revenue.
- Percentage of salesclerks trained to correctly enter data on charge account slips.
- Customer satisfaction with accuracy of charge account bills from monthly customer survey.
- Sales per employee.
- Travel expenses for buyers for trips to fashion shows.
- Average age of accounts receivables.
- Courtesy shown by junior staff members to senior staff members based on surveys of senior staff.
- Unsold inventory at the end of the season as a percentage of total cost of sales.
- Sales per square foot of floor space.
- Percentage of suppliers making just-in-time deliveries.
- Quality of food in the staff cafeteria based on staff surveys.
- Written-off accounts receivables (bad debts) as a percentage of sales.
- Percentage of charge account bills containing errors.
- Percentage of employees who have attended the city's cultural diversity workshop.
- Total profit.
- Profit per employee.

***Required:***

1. As someone with more knowledge of the balanced scorecard than almost anyone else in the company, you have been asked to build an integrated balanced scorecard. In your scorecard, use only performance measures that are mentioned on the previous page. You do not have to use all of the performance measures suggested by the managers, but you should build a balanced scorecard that reveals a strategy for dealing with the problems with accounts receivable and with unsold merchandise. Construct the balanced scorecard following the format used in Exhibit 9–5. Do not be particularly concerned with whether a specific performance measure falls within the learning and growth, internal business process, customer, or financial perspective. However, clearly show the causal links between the performance measures with arrows and whether the performance measures should show increases or decreases.
2. Assume that the company adopts your balanced scorecard. After operating for a year, there are improvements in some performance measures but not in others. What should management do next?
3. a. Suppose that customers express greater satisfaction with the accuracy of their charge account bills, but the performance measures for the average age of accounts receivable and for bad debts do not improve. Explain why this might happen.
   b. Suppose that the performance measures for the average age of accounts receivable, bad debts, and unsold inventory improve, but total profits do not. Explain why this might happen. Assume in your answer that the explanation lies within the company.

### A LOOK BACK

We concluded our coverage of performance measures in Chapter 9 by focusing on decentralized organizations. Return on investment (ROI) and residual income are used to motivate the managers of investment centers and to monitor the performance of these centers.

### A LOOK AT THIS CHAPTER

We continue our coverage of decision making in Chapter 10 by focusing on the use of differential analysis when analyzing alternatives. In general, only those costs and benefits that differ between alternatives are relevant in a decision. This basic idea is applied in a wide variety of situations in this chapter.

### A LOOK AHEAD

Common approaches to making major investment decisions, which can have significant long-term implications for any organization, are discussed in Chapter 11.

# 10 Differential Analysis: The Key to Decision Making

## CHAPTER OUTLINE

## DECISION FEATURE

# Massaging the Numbers

Building and expanding convention centers appears to be an obsession with politicians. Indeed, in 44 cities across the United States, billions of dollars are being spent to build or expand convention centers—adding more than 7 million square feet of convention space to the 64 million square feet that already exists. Given that trade show attendance across the country has been steadily declining, how do politicians justify these enormous investments? Politicians frequently rely on consultants who produce studies that purport to show the convention center will have a favorable economic impact on the area.

These economic impact studies are bogus in two respects. First, a large portion of the so-called favorable economic impact that is cited by consultants would be realized by a city even if it did not invest in a new or expanded convention center. For example, Portland, Oregon, voters overwhelmingly opposed spending $82 million to expand their city's convention center. Nonetheless, local politicians proceeded with the project. After completing the expansion, more than 70% of the people spending money at trade shows in Portland were from the Portland area. How much of the money spent by these locals would have been spent in Portland anyway if the convention center had not been expanded? We don't know, but in all likelihood much of this money would have been spent anyway at the zoo, the art museum, the theater, local restaurants, and so on. This portion of the "favorable" economic impact cited by consultants and used by politicians to justify expanding convention centers should be ignored because of its irrelevance. Second, since the supply of convention centers throughout the United States substantially exceeds demand, convention centers must offer substantial economic incentives, such as waiving rental fees, to attract trade shows. The cost of these concessions, although often excluded from consultants' projections, further erodes the genuine economic viability of building or expanding a convention center.

Source: Victoria Murphy, "The Answer Is Always Yes," *Forbes,* February, 28, 2005, pp. 82–84.

## LEARNING OBJECTIVES

*After studying Chapter 10, you should be able to:*

**LO1** Identify relevant and irrelevant costs and benefits in a decision.

**LO2** Prepare an analysis showing whether a product line or other business segment should be added or dropped.

**LO3** Prepare a make or buy analysis.

**LO4** Prepare an analysis showing whether a special order should be accepted.

**LO5** Determine the most profitable use of a constrained resource.

**LO6** Determine the value of obtaining more of the constrained resource.

**LO7** Prepare an analysis showing whether joint products should be sold at the split-off point or processed further.

**Managers must decide what products to sell,** whether to make or buy component parts, what prices to charge, what channels of distribution to use, whether to accept special orders at special prices, and so forth. Making such decisions is often a difficult task that is complicated by numerous alternatives and massive amounts of data, only some of which may be relevant.

Every decision involves choosing from among at least two alternatives. In making a decision, the costs and benefits of one alternative must be compared to the costs and benefits of other alternatives. The key to making such comparisons is *differential analysis*—focusing on the costs and benefits that *differ* between the alternatives. Costs that differ between alternatives are called **relevant costs.** Benefits that differ between alternatives are called **relevant benefits.** Distinguishing between relevant and irrelevant costs and benefits is critical for two reasons. First, irrelevant data can be ignored—saving decision makers tremendous amounts of time and effort. Second, bad decisions can easily result from erroneously including irrelevant costs and benefits when analyzing alternatives. To be successful in decision making, managers must be able to tell the difference between relevant and irrelevant data and must be able to correctly use the relevant data in analyzing alternatives. The purpose of this chapter is to develop these skills by illustrating their use in a wide range of decision-making situations. These decision-making skills are as important in your personal life as they are to managers. After completing your study of this chapter, you should be able to think more clearly about decisions in many facets of your life.

Sunk costs = irrelevant costs

## COST CONCEPTS FOR DECISION MAKING

### Identifying Relevant Costs and Benefits

**LEARNING OBJECTIVE 1**

Identify relevant and irrelevant costs and benefits in a decision.

Only those costs and benefits that differ in total between alternatives are relevant in a decision. If the total amount of a cost will be the same regardless of the alternative selected, then the decision has no effect on the cost, so the cost can be ignored. For example, if you are trying to decide whether to go to a movie or rent a DVD for the evening, the rent on your apartment is irrelevant. Whether you go to a movie or rent a DVD, the rent on your apartment will be exactly the same and is therefore irrelevant to the decision. On the other hand, the cost of the movie ticket and the cost of renting the DVD would be relevant in the decision because they are *avoidable costs.*

An **avoidable cost** is a cost that can be eliminated by choosing one alternative over another. By choosing the alternative of going to the movie, the cost of renting the DVD can be avoided. By choosing the alternative of renting the DVD, the cost of the movie ticket can be avoided. Therefore, the cost of the movie ticket and the cost of renting the DVD are both avoidable costs. On the other hand, the rent on your apartment is not an avoidable cost of either alternative. You would continue to rent your apartment under either alternative. Avoidable costs are relevant costs. Unavoidable costs are irrelevant costs.

To refine the notion of relevant costs a little further, two broad categories of costs are never relevant in decisions—sunk costs and future costs that do not differ between the alternatives. As we learned in an earlier chapter, a **sunk cost** is a cost that has already been incurred and cannot be avoided regardless of what a manager decides to do. For example, suppose a used car dealer purchased a five-year-old Toyota Camry for $12,000. The amount paid for the Camry is a sunk cost because it has already been incurred and the transaction cannot be undone. Even though it is perhaps counterintuitive, the amount the dealership paid for the Camry is irrelevant in making decisions such as how much to sell the car for. Sunk costs are always the same no matter what alternatives are being considered; therefore, they are irrelevant and should be ignored when making decisions.

Future costs that do not differ between alternatives should also be ignored. Continuing with the example discussed earlier, suppose you plan to order a pizza after you go to the movie theater or you rent a DVD. If you are going to buy the same pizza regardless of your choice of entertainment, the cost of the pizza is irrelevant to the choice of whether you go to the movie theater or rent a DVD. Notice, the cost of the pizza is not a sunk cost because it has not yet been incurred. Nonetheless, the cost of the pizza is irrelevant to the entertainment decision because it is a future cost that does not differ between the alternatives.

To summarize, only those costs and benefits that differ between alternatives are relevant in a decision. Relevant costs are often called *avoidable costs.* The key to successful decision making is to focus on just these relevant costs and benefits and to ignore everything else—including the sunk costs and future costs and benefits that do not differ between the alternatives.

## The Relevant Cost of Executive Perks

IN BUSINESS

The **Securities and Exchange Commission** is concerned about CEOs who use company-owned airplanes for personal travel. For example, consider a CEO who uses his employers' Gulfstream V luxury airplane to transport his family on a 2,000 mile roundtrip vacation from New York City to Orlando, Florida. The standard practice among companies with personal travel reimbursement policies would be to charge their CEO $1,500 for this flight based on a per-mile reimbursement rate established by the **Internal Revenue Service** (the IRS rates are meant to approximate the per-mile cost of a first-class ticket on a commercial airline). However, critics argue that using IRS reimbursement rates grossly understates the flight costs that are borne by shareholders. Some of these critics claim that the $11,000 incremental cost of the flight, including fuel, landing fees, and crew hotel charges, should be reimbursed by the CEO. Still others argue that even basing reimbursements on incremental costs understates the true cost of a flight because fixed costs such as the cost of the airplane, crew salaries, and insurance should be included. These costs are relevant because the excessive amount of personal travel by corporate executives essentially requires their companies to purchase, insure, and staff additional airplanes. This latter group of critics argues that the relevant cost of the trip from New York City to Orlando is $43,000—the market price that would have to be paid to charter a comparable size airplane for this flight. What is the relevant cost of this flight? Should shareholders expect their CEO to reimburse $0 (as is the practice at some companies), $1,500, $11,000, or $43,000? Or, should all companies disallow personal use of corporate assets?

Source: Mark Maremont, "Amid Crackdown, the Jet Perk Suddenly Looks a Lot Pricier," *The Wall Street Journal,* May 25, 2005, pp. A1 and A8.

## Different Costs for Different Purposes

We need to recognize a fundamental concept from the outset of our discussion—costs that are relevant in one decision situation are not necessarily relevant in another. This means that *managers need different costs for different purposes.* For one purpose, a particular group of costs may be relevant; for another purpose, an entirely different group of costs may be relevant. Thus, *each* decision situation must be carefully analyzed to isolate the relevant costs. Otherwise, irrelevant data may cloud the situation and lead to a bad decision.

The concept of "different costs for different purposes" is basic to managerial accounting; we shall frequently see its application in the pages that follow.

## An Example of Identifying Relevant Costs and Benefits

Cynthia is currently a student in an MBA program in Boston and would like to visit a friend in New York City over the weekend. She is trying to decide whether to drive or take the train. Because she is on a tight budget, she wants to carefully consider the costs of the two alternatives. If one alternative is far less expensive than the other, that may be decisive in her choice. By car, the distance between her apartment in Boston and her friend's apartment in New York City is 230 miles. Cynthia has compiled the following list of items to consider:

**Automobile Costs**

| | Item | Annual Cost of Fixed Items | Cost per Mile (based on 10,000 miles per year) |
|---|---|---|---|
| (a) | Annual straight-line depreciation on car [($24,000 original cost − $10,000 estimated resale value in 5 years)/5 years] | $2,800 | $0.280 |
| (b) | Cost of gasoline ($3.30 per gallon ÷ 33 miles per gallon) | | 0.100 |
| (c) | Annual cost of auto insurance and license | $1,380 | 0.138 |
| (d) | Maintenance and repairs | | 0.065 |
| (e) | Parking fees at school ($45 per month × 8 months) | $360 | 0.036 |
| (f) | Total average cost per mile | | $0.619 |

**Additional Data**

| | Item | |
|---|---|---|
| (g) | Reduction in the resale value of car due solely to wear and tear | $0.026 per mile |
| (h) | Cost of round-trip train ticket from Boston to New York City | $104 |
| (i) | Benefit of relaxing and being able to study during the train ride rather than having to drive | ? |
| (j) | Cost of putting the dog in a kennel while gone | $40 |
| (k) | Benefit of having a car available in New York City | ? |
| (l) | Hassle of parking the car in New York City | ? |
| (m) | Cost of parking the car in New York City | $25 per day |

Which costs and benefits are relevant in this decision? Remember, only those costs and benefits that differ between alternatives are relevant. Everything else is irrelevant and can be ignored.

Start at the top of the list with item (a): the original cost of the car is a sunk cost. This cost has already been incurred and therefore can never differ between alternatives. Consequently, it is irrelevant and should be ignored. The same is true of the accounting depreciation of $2,800 per year, which simply spreads the sunk cost across five years.

Item (b), the cost of gasoline consumed by driving to New York City, is a relevant cost. If Cynthia takes the train, this cost would not be incurred. Hence, the cost differs between alternatives and is therefore relevant.

Item (c), the annual cost of auto insurance and license, is not relevant. Whether Cynthia takes the train or drives on this particular trip, her annual auto insurance premium and her auto license fee will remain the same.[1]

Item (d), the cost of maintenance and repairs, is relevant. While maintenance and repair costs have a large random component, over the long run they should be more or less

[1]If Cynthia has an accident while driving to New York City or back, this might affect her insurance premium when the policy is renewed. The increase in the insurance premium would be a relevant cost of this particular trip, but the normal amount of the insurance premium is not relevant in any case.

proportional to the number of miles the car is driven. Thus, the average cost of $0.065 per mile is a reasonable estimate to use.

Item (e), the monthly fee that Cynthia pays to park at her school during the academic year is not relevant. Regardless of which alternative she selects—driving or taking the train—she will still need to pay for parking at school.

Item (f) is the total average cost of $0.619 per mile. As discussed above, some elements of this total are relevant, but some are not relevant. Because it contains some irrelevant costs, it would be incorrect to estimate the cost of driving to New York City and back by simply multiplying the $0.619 by 460 miles (230 miles each way × 2). This erroneous approach would yield a cost of driving of $284.74. Unfortunately, such mistakes are often made in both personal life and in business. Because the total cost is stated on a per-mile basis, people are easily misled. Often people think that if the cost is stated as $0.619 per mile, the cost of driving 100 miles is $61.90. But it is not. Many of the costs included in the $0.619 cost per mile are sunk and/or fixed and will not increase if the car is driven another 100 miles. The $0.619 is an average cost, not an incremental cost. Beware of such unitized costs (i.e., costs stated in terms of a dollar amount per unit, per mile, per direct labor-hour, per machine-hour, and so on)—they are often misleading.

Item (g), the decline in the resale value of the car that occurs as a consequence of driving more miles, is relevant in the decision. Because she uses the car, its resale value declines, which is a real cost of using the car that should be taken into account. Cynthia estimated this cost by accessing the *Kelly Blue Book* website at www.kbb.com. The reduction in resale value of an asset through use or over time is often called *real* or *economic depreciation*. This is different from accounting depreciation, which attempts to match the sunk cost of an asset with the periods that benefit from that cost.

Item (h), the $104 cost of a round-trip ticket on the train, is relevant in this decision. If she drives, she would not have to buy the ticket.

Item (i) is relevant to the decision, even if it is difficult to put a dollar value on relaxing and being able to study while on the train. It is relevant because it is a benefit that is available under one alternative but not under the other.

Item (j), the cost of putting Cynthia's dog in the kennel while she is gone, is irrelevant in this decision. Whether she takes the train or drives to New York City, she will still need to put her dog in a kennel.

Like item (i), items (k) and (l) are relevant to the decision even if it is difficult to measure their dollar impacts.

Item (m), the cost of parking in New York City, is relevant to the decision.

Bringing together all of the relevant data, Cynthia would estimate the relevant costs of driving and taking the train as follows:

| | |
|---|---|
| **Relevant financial cost of driving to New York City:** | |
| Gasoline (460 miles × $0.100 per mile) | $ 46.00 |
| Maintenance and repairs (460 miles × $0.065 per mile) | 29.90 |
| Reduction in the resale value of car due solely to wear and tear (460 miles × $0.026 per mile) | 11.96 |
| Cost of parking the car in New York City (2 days × $25 per day) | 50.00 |
| Total | $137.86 |
| **Relevant financial cost of taking the train to New York City:** | |
| Cost of round-trip train ticket from Boston to New York City | $104.00 |

What should Cynthia do? From a purely financial standpoint, it would be cheaper by $33.86 ($137.86 − $104.00) to take the train than to drive. Cynthia has to decide if the convenience of having a car in New York City outweighs the additional cost and the disadvantages of being unable to relax and study on the train and the hassle of finding parking in the city.

In this example, we focused on identifying the relevant costs and benefits— everything else was ignored. In the next example, we include all of the costs and benefits—relevant or not. Nonetheless, we'll still get the correct answer because the irrelevant costs and benefits will cancel out when we compare the alternatives.

**IN BUSINESS**

### Dell Stumbles Due to Poor Customer Services

**Dell Inc.** decided to cut customer service costs by shifting most of its call centers overseas and staffing them with temporary workers who were rewarded for minimizing the length of customer calls. The unintended consequences of Dell's choices were predictable—the number of angry repeat callers skyrocketed and the company's customer satisfaction and "likely to repurchase" survey scores plummeted.

Fearful that unhappy customers would take their business elsewhere, Dell spent $150 million to hire thousands of full-time call center employees in North America. The company also began rewarding these employees based on how well they solved callers' problems. These changes paid off as Dell began receiving two million fewer customer service calls per quarter. Customer satisfaction and "likely to repurchase" scores rose substantially.

Dell's experience highlights the danger of overemphasizing cost cutting while overlooking the revenues that may be lost due to customer dissatisfaction.

Source: David Kirkpatrick, "Dell in the Penalty Box," *Fortune*, September 18, 2006, pp. 70–78.

## Reconciling the Total and Differential Approaches

Oak Harbor Woodworks is considering a new labor-saving machine that rents for $3,000 per year. The machine will be used on the company's butcher block production line. Data concerning the company's annual sales and costs of butcher blocks with and without the new machine are shown below:

| | Current Situation | Situation with the New Machine |
|---|---|---|
| Units produced and sold | 5,000 | 5,000 |
| Selling price per unit | $40 | $40 |
| Direct materials cost per unit | $14 | $14 |
| Direct labor cost per unit | $8 | $5 |
| Variable overhead cost per unit | $2 | $2 |
| Fixed costs, other | $62,000 | $62,000 |
| Fixed costs, rental of new machine | — | $3,000 |

Given the data above, the net operating income for the product under the two alternatives can be computed as shown in Exhibit 10–1.

Note that the net operating income is $12,000 higher with the new machine, so that is the better alternative. Note also that the $12,000 advantage for the new machine can be obtained in two different ways. It is the difference between the $30,000 net operating income with the new machine and the $18,000 net operating income for the current situation. It is also the sum of the differential costs and benefits as shown in the last column of Exhibit 10–1. A positive number in the Differential Costs and Benefits column indicates that the difference between the alternatives favors the new machine; a negative number indicates that the difference favors the current situation. A zero in that column simply means that the total amount for the item is exactly the same for both alternatives. Thus,

**EXHIBIT 10–1**
Total and Differential Costs

| | Current Situation | Situation with New Machine | Differential Costs and Benefits |
|---|---|---|---|
| Sales (5,000 units × $40 per unit) | $200,000 | $200,000 | $ 0 |
| Variable expenses: | | | |
| Direct materials (5,000 units × $14 per unit) | 70,000 | 70,000 | 0 |
| Direct labor (5,000 units × $8 per unit; 5,000 units × $5 per unit) | 40,000 | 25,000 | 15,000 |
| Variable overhead (5,000 units × $2 per unit) | 10,000 | 10,000 | 0 |
| Total variable expenses | 120,000 | 105,000 | |
| Contribution margin | 80,000 | 95,000 | |
| Fixed expenses: | | | |
| Other | 62,000 | 62,000 | 0 |
| Rental of new machine | 0 | 3,000 | (3,000) |
| Total fixed expenses | 62,000 | 65,000 | |
| Net operating income | $ 18,000 | $ 30,000 | $12,000 |

because the difference in the net operating incomes equals the sum of the differences for the individual items, any cost or benefit that is the same for both alternatives will have no impact on which alternative is preferred. This is the reason that costs and benefits that do not differ between alternatives are irrelevant and can be ignored. If we properly account for them, they will cancel out when we compare the alternatives.

We could have arrived at the same solution much more quickly by completely ignoring the irrelevant costs and benefits.

- The selling price per unit and the number of units sold do not differ between the alternatives. Therefore, the total sales revenues are exactly the same for the two alternatives as shown in Exhibit 10–1. Because the sales revenues are exactly the same, they have no effect on the difference in net operating income between the two alternatives. That is shown in the last column in Exhibit 10–1, which shows a $0 differential benefit.
- The direct materials cost per unit, the variable overhead cost per unit, and the number of units produced and sold do not differ between the alternatives. Consequently, the total direct materials cost and the total variable overhead cost are the same for the two alternatives and can be ignored.
- The "other" fixed expenses do not differ between the alternatives, so they can be ignored as well.

Indeed, the only costs that do differ between the alternatives are direct labor costs and the fixed rental cost of the new machine. Hence, the two alternatives can be compared based only on these relevant costs:

| Net Advantage of Renting the New Machine | |
|---|---|
| Decrease in direct labor costs (5,000 units at a cost savings of $3 per unit) | $15,000 |
| Increase in fixed expenses | (3,000) |
| Net annual cost savings from renting the new machine | $12,000 |

If we focus on just the relevant costs and benefits, we get exactly the same answer as when we listed all of the costs and benefits—including those that do not differ between the alternatives and, hence, are irrelevant. We get the same answer because the only costs and benefits that matter in the final comparison of the net operating incomes are those that differ between the two alternatives and, hence, are not zero in the last column of Exhibit 10–1. Those two relevant costs are both included in the analysis at the bottom of the previous page that quantifies the net advantage of renting the new machine.

## Why Isolate Relevant Costs?

In the preceding example, we used two different approaches to analyze the alternatives. First, we considered all costs, both those that were relevant and those that were not; and second, we considered only the relevant costs. We obtained the same answer under both approaches. It would be natural to ask, "Why bother to isolate relevant costs when total costs will do the job just as well?" Isolating relevant costs is desirable for at least two reasons.

First, only rarely will enough information be available to prepare a detailed income statement for both alternatives. Assume, for example, that you are called on to make a decision relating to a portion of a single business process in a multidepartmental, multiproduct company. Under these circumstances, it would be virtually impossible to prepare an income statement of any type. You would have to rely on your ability to recognize which costs are relevant and which are not in order to assemble the data necessary to make a decision.

Second, mingling irrelevant costs with relevant costs may cause confusion and distract attention from the information that is really critical. Furthermore, the danger always exists that an irrelevant piece of data may be used improperly, resulting in an incorrect decision. The best approach is to ignore irrelevant data and base the decision entirely on relevant data.

Relevant cost analysis, combined with the contribution approach to the income statement, provides a powerful tool for making decisions. We will investigate various uses of this tool in the remaining sections of this chapter.

Understand what cost are relevant

**CONCEPT CHECK**

1. Which of the following statements is false? (You may select more than one answer.)
   a. Under some circumstances, a sunk cost may be a relevant cost.
   b. Future costs that do not differ between alternatives are irrelevant.
   c. The same cost may be relevant or irrelevant depending on the decision context.
   d. Only variable costs are relevant costs. Fixed costs cannot be relevant costs.
2. Assume that in October you bought a $450 nonrefundable airline ticket to Telluride, Colorado, for a 5-day/4-night winter ski vacation. You now have an opportunity to buy an airline ticket for a 5-day/4-night winter ski vacation in Stowe, Vermont, for $400 that includes a free ski lift ticket. The price of your lift ticket for the Telluride vacation would be $300. The price of a hotel room in Telluride is $180 per night. The price of a hotel room in Stowe is $150 per night. Which of the following costs is not relevant in a decision of whether to proceed with the planned trip to Telluride or to change to a trip to Stowe?
   a. The $450 airline ticket to Telluride.
   b. The $400 airline ticket to Stowe.
   c. The $300 lift ticket for the Telluride vacation.
   d. The $180 per night hotel room in Telluride.
3. Based on the facts in question 2 above, does a differential cost analysis favor Telluride or Stowe, and by how much?
   a. Stowe by $470.
   b. Stowe by $20.
   c. Telluride by $70.
   d. Telluride by $20.

# ADDING AND DROPPING PRODUCT LINES AND OTHER SEGMENTS

LEARNING OBJECTIVE 2

Prepare an analysis showing whether a product line or other business segment should be added or dropped.

Decisions relating to whether product lines or other segments of a company should be dropped and new ones added are among the most difficult that a manager has to make. In such decisions, many qualitative and quantitative factors must be considered. Ultimately, however, any final decision to drop a business segment or to add a new one hinges primarily on the impact the decision will have on net operating income. To assess this impact, costs must be carefully analyzed.

## An Illustration of Cost Analysis

Exhibit 10–2 provides sales and cost information for the preceding month for the Discount Drug Company and its three major product lines—drugs, cosmetics, and housewares. A quick review of this exhibit suggests that dropping the housewares segment would increase the company's overall net operating income by $8,000. However, this would be a flawed conclusion because the data in Exhibit 10–2 do not distinguish between fixed expenses that can be avoided if a product line is dropped and common fixed expenses that cannot be avoided by dropping any particular product line.

In this scenario, the two alternatives under consideration are keeping the housewares product line and dropping the housewares product line. Therefore, only those costs that differ between these two alternatives (i.e., that can be avoided by dropping the housewares product line) are relevant. In deciding whether to drop housewares, it is crucial to identify which costs can be avoided, and hence are relevant to the decision, and which costs cannot be avoided, and hence are irrelevant. The decision should be analyzed as follows.

If the housewares line is dropped, then the company will lose $20,000 per month in contribution margin, but by dropping the line it may be possible to avoid some fixed costs such as salaries or advertising costs. If dropping the housewares line enables the company to avoid more in fixed costs than it loses in contribution margin, then its overall net operating income will improve by eliminating the product line. On the other hand, if the company is not able to avoid as much in fixed costs as it loses in contribution margin, then the housewares line should be kept. In short, the manager should ask, "What costs can I avoid if I drop this product line?"

As we have seen from our earlier discussion, not all costs are avoidable. For example, some of the costs associated with a product line may be sunk costs. Other costs may be allocated fixed costs that will not differ in total regardless of whether the product line is dropped or retained.

EXHIBIT 10–2

Discount Drug Company Product Lines

| | | Product Line | | |
|---|---|---|---|---|
| | Total | Drugs | Cosmetics | Housewares |
| Sales | $250,000 | $125,000 | $75,000 | $50,000 |
| Variable expenses | 105,000 | 50,000 | 25,000 | 30,000 |
| Contribution margin | 145,000 | 75,000 | 50,000 | 20,000 |
| Fixed expenses: | | | | |
| Salaries | 50,000 | 29,500 | 12,500 | 8,000 |
| Advertising | 15,000 | 1,000 | 7,500 | 6,500 |
| Utilities | 2,000 | 500 | 500 | 1,000 |
| Depreciation—fixtures | 5,000 | 1,000 | 2,000 | 2,000 |
| Rent | 20,000 | 10,000 | 6,000 | 4,000 |
| Insurance | 3,000 | 2,000 | 500 | 500 |
| General administrative | 30,000 | 15,000 | 9,000 | 6,000 |
| Total fixed expenses | 125,000 | 59,000 | 38,000 | 28,000 |
| Net operating income (loss) | $ 20,000 | $ 16,000 | $12,000 | $ (8,000) |

To show how to proceed in a product-line analysis, suppose that Discount Drug Company has analyzed the fixed costs being charged to the three product lines and determined the following:

1. The salaries expense represents salaries paid to employees working directly on the product. All of the employees working in housewares would be discharged if the product line is dropped.
2. The advertising expense represents advertisements that are specific to each product line and are avoidable if the line is dropped.
3. The utilities expense represents utilities costs for the entire company. The amount charged to each product line is an allocation based on space occupied and is not avoidable if the product line is dropped.
4. The depreciation expense represents depreciation on fixtures used to display the various product lines. Although the fixtures are nearly new, they are custom-built and will have no resale value if the housewares line is dropped.
5. The rent expense represents rent on the entire building housing the company; it is allocated to the product lines on the basis of sales dollars. The monthly rent of $20,000 is fixed under a long-term lease agreement.
6. The insurance expense is for insurance carried on inventories within each of the three product lines. If housewares is dropped, the related inventories will be liquidated and the insurance premiums will decrease proportionately.
7. The general administrative expense represents the costs of accounting, purchasing, and general management, which are allocated to the product lines on the basis of sales dollars. These costs will not change if the housewares line is dropped.

With this information, management can determine that $15,000 of the fixed expenses associated with the housewares product line are avoidable and $13,000 are not:

| Fixed Expenses | Total Cost Assigned to Housewares | Not Avoidable* | Avoidable |
|---|---|---|---|
| Salaries | $ 8,000 | | $ 8,000 |
| Advertising | 6,500 | | 6,500 |
| Utilities | 1,000 | $ 1,000 | |
| Depreciation—fixtures | 2,000 | 2,000 | |
| Rent | 4,000 | 4,000 | |
| Insurance | 500 | | 500 |
| General administrative | 6,000 | 6,000 | |
| Total | $28,000 | $13,000 | $15,000 |

*These fixed costs represent either sunk costs or future costs that will not change whether the housewares line is retained or discontinued.

As stated earlier, if the housewares product line were dropped, the company would lose the product's contribution margin of $20,000, but would save its associated avoidable fixed expenses. We now know that those avoidable fixed expenses total $15,000. Therefore, dropping the housewares product line would result in a $5,000 *reduction* in net operating income as shown below:

| | |
|---|---|
| Contribution margin lost if the housewares line is discontinued (see Exhibit 10–2) | $(20,000) |
| Less fixed costs that can be avoided if the housewares line is discontinued (see above) | 15,000 |
| Decrease in overall company net operating income | $ (5,000) |

In this case, the fixed costs that can be avoided by dropping the housewares product line ($15,000) are less than the contribution margin that will be lost ($20,000). Therefore, based on the data given, the housewares line should not be discontinued unless a more profitable use can be found for the floor and counter space that it is occupying.

**HELPFUL HINT**

Use the following three steps to quantify the financial impact of discontinuing a business segment:

Step 1: Calculate the contribution margin that would disappear if the segment is dropped. Put this number in parentheses to denote it as a negative number.

Step 2: Calculate the fixed costs that would be avoided if the segment is dropped. Do not put this number in parentheses.

Step 3: Add the amounts from steps 1 and 2. If the result is a negative number, then do not drop the segment. If it is a positive number, then choose to drop the segment.

While you may need to add additional steps when solving complex problems, these three steps will help organize your analysis.

## A Comparative Format

This decision can also be approached by preparing comparative income statements showing the effects of either keeping or dropping the product line. Exhibit 10–3 contains such an analysis for the Discount Drug Company. As shown in the last column of the exhibit, if the housewares line is dropped, then overall company net operating income will decrease by $5,000 each period. This is the same answer, of course, as we obtained when we focused just on the lost contribution margin and avoidable fixed costs.

**EXHIBIT 10–3**
A Comparative Format for Product-Line Analysis

| | Keep Housewares | Drop Housewares | Difference: Net Operating Income Increase (or Decrease) |
|---|---|---|---|
| Sales | $50,000 | $ 0 | $(50,000) |
| Variable expenses | 30,000 | 0 | 30,000 |
| Contribution margin | 20,000 | 0 | (20,000) |
| Fixed expenses: | | | |
| Salaries | 8,000 | 0 | 8,000 |
| Advertising | 6,500 | 0 | 6,500 |
| Utilities | 1,000 | 1,000 | 0 |
| Depreciation—fixtures | 2,000 | 2,000 | 0 |
| Rent | 4,000 | 4,000 | 0 |
| Insurance | 500 | 0 | 500 |
| General administrative | 6,000 | 6,000 | 0 |
| Total fixed expenses | 28,000 | 13,000 | 15,000 |
| Net operating loss | $ (8,000) | $(13,000) | $ (5,000) |

## Beware of Allocated Fixed Costs

Go back to Exhibit 10–2. Does this exhibit suggest that the housewares product line should be kept—as we have just concluded? No, it does not. Exhibit 10–2 suggests that the housewares product line is losing money. Why keep a product line that is showing a loss? The explanation for this apparent inconsistency lies in part with the common fixed costs that are being allocated to the product lines. One of the great dangers in allocating common fixed costs is that such allocations can make a product line (or other business segment) look less profitable than it really is. In this instance, allocating the common fixed costs among all product lines makes the housewares product line appear to be unprofitable. However, as we have just shown, dropping the product line would result in a decrease in the company's overall net operating income. This point can be seen clearly if we redo Exhibit 10–2 by eliminating the allocation of the common fixed costs. Exhibit 10–4 uses the segmented approach from Chapter 6 to estimate the profitability of the product lines.

Exhibit 10–4 gives us a much different perspective of the housewares line than does Exhibit 10–2. As shown in Exhibit 10–4, the housewares line is covering all of its own traceable fixed costs and generating a $3,000 segment margin toward covering the common fixed costs of the company. Unless another product line can be found that will generate a segment margin greater than $3,000, the company would be better off keeping the housewares line. By keeping the product line, the company's overall net operating income will be higher than if the product line were dropped.

Additionally, managers may choose to retain an unprofitable product line if the line helps sell other products, or if it serves as a "magnet" to attract customers. Bread, for example, may not be an especially profitable line in some food stores, but customers expect it to be available, and many of them would undoubtedly shift their buying elsewhere if a particular store decided to stop carrying it.

**EXHIBIT 10–4**
Discount Drug Company Product Lines—Recast in Contribution Format (from Exhibit 10–2)

| | | Product Line | | |
|---|---|---|---|---|
| | Total | Drugs | Cosmetics | Housewares |
| Sales | $250,000 | $125,000 | $75,000 | $50,000 |
| Variable expenses | 105,000 | 50,000 | 25,000 | 30,000 |
| Contribution margin | 145,000 | 75,000 | 50,000 | 20,000 |
| Traceable fixed expenses: | | | | |
| Salaries | 50,000 | 29,500 | 12,500 | 8,000 |
| Advertising | 15,000 | 1,000 | 7,500 | 6,500 |
| Depreciation—fixtures | 5,000 | 1,000 | 2,000 | 2,000 |
| Insurance | 3,000 | 2,000 | 500 | 500 |
| Total traceable fixed expenses | 73,000 | 33,500 | 22,500 | 17,000 |
| Product-line segment margin | 72,000 | $ 41,500 | $27,500 | $ 3,000* |
| Common fixed expenses: | | | | |
| Utilities | 2,000 | | | |
| Rent | 20,000 | | | |
| General administrative | 30,000 | | | |
| Total common fixed expenses | 52,000 | | | |
| Net operating income | $ 20,000 | | | |

*If the housewares line is dropped, the company will lose the $3,000 segment margin generated by this product line. In addition, we have seen that the $2,000 depreciation on the fixtures is a sunk cost that cannot be avoided. The sum of these two figures ($3,000 + $2,000 = $5,000) would be the decrease in the company's overall profits if the housewares line were discontinued. Of course, the company may later choose to drop the product if circumstances change—such as a pending decision to replace the fixtures.

## Poor Economy Leads to Segment Discontinuations

IN BUSINESS

When the economy declines, many companies must decide whether to retain or discontinue struggling products and services. For example, **Condé Nast Publications** reacted to a steep drop in advertising revenues by cutting 180 jobs and discontinuing four magazines—*Gourmet, Modern Bride, Elegant Bride,* and *Cookie.* It also cut the budgets of its remaining magazines by 20–25%. **Pioneer Corp.**'s annual plasma television sales dropped from 460,000 units to 290,000 units. The company responded to its shrinking customer demand by cutting thousands of jobs and withdrawing from the plasma television business.

Sources: Russell Adams, "Ax Falls on Four Condé Nast Titles," *The Wall Street Journal,* October 6, 2009, p. B1; and Daisuke Wakabayashi, "Pioneer Unplugs Its TV Business," *The Wall Street Journal,* February 13, 2009, p. B1.

# THE MAKE OR BUY DECISION

**LEARNING OBJECTIVE 3**

Prepare a make or buy analysis.

Providing a product or service to a customer involves many steps. For example, consider all of the steps that are necessary to develop and sell a product such as tax preparation software in retail stores. First the software must be developed, which involves highly skilled software engineers and a great deal of project management effort. Then the product must be put into a form that can be delivered to customers. This involves burning the application onto a blank CD or DVD, applying a label, and packaging the result in an attractive box. Then the product must be distributed to retail stores. Then the product must be sold. And finally, help lines and other forms of after-sale service may have to be provided. And we should not forget that the blank CD or DVD, the label, and the box must of course be made by someone before any of this can happen. All of these activities, from development, to production, to after-sales service are called a *value chain*.

Separate companies may carry out each of the activities in the value chain or a single company may carry out several. When a company is involved in more than one activity in the entire value chain, it is **vertically integrated.** Some companies control all of the activities in the value chain from producing basic raw materials right up to the final distribution of finished goods and provision of after-sales service. Other companies are content to integrate on a smaller scale by purchasing many of the parts and materials that go into their finished products. A decision to carry out one of the activities in the value chain internally, rather than to buy externally from a supplier, is called a **make or buy decision.** Quite often these decisions involve whether to buy a particular part or to make it internally. Make or buy decisions also involve decisions concerning whether to outsource development tasks, after-sales service, or other activities.

## Cessna Outsources Airplane Construction to China

IN BUSINESS

**Cessna Aircraft Company** hired China's state-owned **Shenyang Aircraft Corporation** to produce its new 162 SkyCatcher aircraft. While **Boeing** and **Airbus** have used Chinese manufacturers for component parts, Cessna is the first company to turn over the complete production of an airplane to a Chinese company. Cessna hopes that buying the planes from a Chinese partner will provide cost savings that enable it to sell the plane for $71,000 less than if the plane were made at its plant in Wichita, Kansas. Cessna expects to sell the first 1,000 SkyCatchers for $109,500, whereas the company's least expensive model manufactured in Wichita sells for $219,500. What are some of the risks that accompany Cessna's decision to outsource production to China?

Source: J. Lynn Lunsford, "Cessna's New Plane to Be Built in China," *The Wall Street Journal,* November 28, 2007, p. A14.

## An Example of Make or Buy

To provide an illustration of a make or buy decision, consider Mountain Goat Cycles. The company is now producing the heavy-duty gear shifters used in its most popular line of mountain bikes. The company's Accounting Department reports the following costs of producing 8,000 units of the shifter internally each year:

| | Per Unit | 8,000 Units |
|---|---|---|
| Direct materials | $ 6 | $ 48,000 |
| Direct labor | 4 | 32,000 |
| Variable overhead | 1 | 8,000 |
| Supervisor's salary | 3 | 24,000 |
| Depreciation of special equipment | 2 | 16,000 |
| Allocated general overhead | 5 | 40,000 |
| Total cost | $21 | $168,000 |

An outside supplier has offered to sell 8,000 shifters a year to Mountain Goat Cycles for a price of $19 each, or a total of $152,000 (= 8,000 shifters × $19 each). Should the company stop producing the shifters internally and buy them from the outside supplier? As always, the focus should be on the relevant costs—those that differ between the alternatives. And the costs that differ between the alternatives consist of the costs that could be avoided by purchasing the shifters from the outside supplier. If the costs that can be avoided by purchasing the shifters from the outside supplier total less than $152,000, then the company should continue to manufacture its own shifters and reject the outside supplier's offer. On the other hand, if the costs that can be avoided by purchasing the shifters from the outside supplier total more than $152,000, the outside supplier's offer should be accepted.

Note that depreciation of special equipment is listed as one of the costs of producing the shifters internally. Because the equipment has already been purchased, this depreciation is a sunk cost and is therefore irrelevant. If the equipment could be sold, its salvage value would be relevant. Or if the machine could be used to make other products, this could be relevant as well. However, we will assume that the equipment has no salvage value and that it has no other use except making the heavy-duty gear shifters.

Also note that the company is allocating a portion of its general overhead costs to the shifters. Any portion of this general overhead cost that would actually be eliminated if the gear shifters were purchased rather than made would be relevant in the analysis. However, it is likely that the general overhead costs allocated to the gear shifters are in fact common to all items produced in the factory and would continue unchanged even if the shifters were purchased from the outside. Such allocated common costs are not relevant costs (because they do not differ between the make or buy alternatives) and should be eliminated from the analysis along with the sunk costs.

The variable costs of producing the shifters can be avoided by buying the shifters from the outside supplier so they are relevant costs. We will assume in this case that the variable costs include direct materials, direct labor, and variable overhead. The supervisor's salary is also relevant if it could be avoided by buying the shifters. Exhibit 10–5 contains the relevant cost analysis of the make or buy decision assuming that the supervisor's salary can indeed be avoided.

Because the avoidable costs related to making the shifters is $40,000 less than the total amount that would be paid to buy them from the outside supplier, Mountain Goat Cycles should reject the outside supplier's offer. However, the company may wish to consider one additional factor before coming to a final decision—the opportunity cost of the space now being used to produce the shifters.

**EXHIBIT 10–5**
Mountain Goat Cycles Make or Buy Analysis

| | Total Relevant Costs—8,000 units | |
|---|---|---|
| | **Make** | **Buy** |
| Direct materials (8,000 units × $6 per unit) | $ 48,000 | |
| Direct labor (8,000 units × $4 per unit) | 32,000 | |
| Variable overhead (8,000 units × $1 per unit) | 8,000 | |
| Supervisor's salary | 24,000 | |
| Depreciation of special equipment (not relevant) | | |
| Allocated general overhead (not relevant) | | |
| Outside purchase price | | $152,000 |
| Total cost | $112,000 | $152,000 |
| Difference in favor of continuing to make | $40,000 | |

## HELPFUL HINT

Use the following three steps to quantify the financial impact of make or buy decisions:

Step 1: Calculate the total amount that would be paid to the supplier if the buy option is chosen.

Step 2: Calculate the total differential manufacturing costs. These are the variable manufacturing costs and traceable fixed manufacturing costs that will be incurred if the company chooses to make, but avoided if the company chooses to buy.

Step 3: Calculate the difference between the amounts from steps 1 and 2. If the amount from step 1 exceeds the amount from step 2, then choose the make option. If the amount from step 1 is less than the amount from step 2, then choose the buy option.

While you may need to add additional steps when solving complex problems, these three steps will help organize your analysis.

## Outsourcing Tasks Rather Than Jobs

IN BUSINESS

**Pfizer** saved 4,000 of its managers 66,500 hours of work by enabling them to outsource their tedious, time-consuming tasks to companies in India. With the click of a mouse the managers go to a website called PfizerWorks to prepare online work orders for services such as Powerpoint slide preparation, spreadsheet preparation, or basic market research. The requests are sent overseas and completed by a services-outsourcing firm. This outsourcing enables Pfizer's managers to spend their time on higher value work such as motivating teams, creating new products, and strategy formulation.

Source: Jena McGregor, "The Chore Goes Offshore," *BusinessWeek*, March 23 & 30, 2009, p. 50–51.

## OPPORTUNITY COST

If the space now being used to produce the shifters *would otherwise be idle*, then Mountain Goat Cycles should continue to produce its own shifters and the supplier's offer should be rejected, as stated above. Idle space that has no alternative use has an opportunity cost of zero.

But what if the space now being used to produce shifters could be used for some other purpose? In that case, the space would have an opportunity cost equal to the segment margin that could be derived from the best alternative use of the space.

To illustrate, assume that the space now being used to produce shifters could be used to produce a new cross-country bike that would generate a segment margin of $60,000 per year. Under these conditions, Mountain Goat Cycles should accept the supplier's offer and use the available space to produce the new product line:

| | Make | Buy |
|---|---|---|
| Total annual cost (see Exhibit 10–5) | $112,000 | $152,000 |
| Opportunity cost—segment margin forgone on a potential new product line | 60,000 | |
| Total cost | $172,000 | $152,000 |
| Difference in favor of purchasing from the outside supplier | $20,000 | |

Opportunity costs are not recorded in the organization's general ledger because they do not represent actual dollar outlays. Rather, they represent economic benefits that are *forgone* as a result of pursuing some course of action. The opportunity cost for Mountain Goat Cycles is sufficiently large in this case to change the decision.

DECISION POINT

**Vice President of Production**

You are faced with a make or buy decision. The company currently makes a component for one of its products but is considering whether it should instead purchase the component. If the offer from an outside supplier were accepted, the company would no longer need to rent the machinery currently being used to manufacture the component. You realize that the annual rental cost is a fixed cost, but recall some sort of warning about fixed costs. Is the annual rental cost relevant to this make or buy decision?

## SPECIAL ORDERS

LEARNING OBJECTIVE 4

Prepare an analysis showing whether a special order should be accepted.

Managers must often evaluate whether a *special order* should be accepted, and if the order is accepted, the price that should be charged. A **special order** is a one-time order that is not considered part of the company's normal ongoing business. To illustrate, Mountain Goat Cycles has just received a request from the Seattle Police Department to produce 100 specially modified mountain bikes at a price of $558 each. The bikes would be used to patrol some of the more densely populated residential sections of the city. Mountain Goat Cycles can easily modify its City Cruiser model to fit the specifications of the Seattle Police. The normal selling price of the City Cruiser bike is $698, and its unit product cost is $564 as shown below:

| | |
|---|---|
| Direct materials | $372 |
| Direct labor | 90 |
| Manufacturing overhead | 102 |
| Unit product cost | $564 |

The variable portion of the above manufacturing overhead is $12 per unit. The order would have no effect on the company's total fixed manufacturing overhead costs.

The modifications requested by the Seattle Police Department consist of welded brackets to hold radios, nightsticks, and other gear. These modifications would require $34 in incremental variable costs. In addition, the company would have to pay a graphics design studio $2,400 to design and cut stencils that would be used for spray painting the Seattle Police Department's logo and other identifying marks on the bikes.

This order should have no effect on the company's other sales. The production manager says that she can handle the special order without disrupting any of the company's regular scheduled production.

What effect would accepting this order have on the company's net operating income?

Only the incremental costs and benefits are relevant. Because the existing fixed manufacturing overhead costs would not be affected by the order, they are not relevant. The incremental net operating income can be computed as follows:

| | Per Unit | Total 100 Bikes |
|---|---|---|
| Incremental revenue | $558 | $55,800 |
| Less incremental costs: | | |
| Variable costs: | | |
| Direct materials | 372 | 37,200 |
| Direct labor | 90 | 9,000 |
| Variable manufacturing overhead | 12 | 1,200 |
| Special modifications | 34 | 3,400 |
| Total variable cost | $508 | 50,800 |
| Fixed cost: | | |
| Purchase of stencils | | 2,400 |
| Total incremental cost | | 53,200 |
| Incremental net operating income | | $ 2,600 |

Therefore, even though the $558 price on the special order is below the normal $564 unit product cost and the order would require additional costs, the order would increase net operating income. In general, a special order is profitable if the incremental revenue from the special order exceeds the incremental costs of the order. However, it is important to make sure that there is indeed idle capacity and that the special order does not cut into normal unit sales or undercut prices on normal sales. For example, if the company was operating at capacity, opportunity costs would have to be taken into account, as well as the incremental costs that have already been detailed above.

### HELPFUL HINT

Use the following three steps to quantify the financial impact of accepting a special order:

Step 1: Calculate the total revenue generated by the special order.

Step 2: Calculate the total incremental costs that will be incurred to produce the special order.

Step 3: Take the amount in step 1 and subtract from it the amount in step 2. If the result is a positive number, then accept the special order. If it is a negative number, then reject the special order.

While you may need to add additional steps when solving complex problems, these three steps will help organize your analysis.

## UTILIZATION OF A CONSTRAINED RESOURCE

**LEARNING OBJECTIVE 5**

Determine the most profitable use of a constrained resource.

Managers routinely face the problem of deciding how constrained resources are going to be used. A department store, for example, has a limited amount of floor space and therefore cannot stock every product that may be available. A manufacturer has a limited number of machine-hours and a limited number of direct labor-hours at its disposal. When a limited resource of some type restricts the company's ability to satisfy demand, the company has a **constraint.** Because the company cannot fully satisfy demand, managers must decide which products or services should be cut back. In other words, managers must decide which products or services make the best use of the constrained resource. Fixed costs are usually unaffected by such choices, so the course of action that will maximize the company's total contribution margin should ordinarily be selected.

## Contribution Margin per Unit of the Constrained Resource

If some products must be cut back because of a constraint, the key to maximizing the total contribution margin may seem obvious—favor the products with the highest unit contribution margins. Unfortunately, that is not quite correct. Rather, the correct solution is to favor the products that provide the highest *contribution margin per unit of the constrained resource.* To illustrate, in addition to its other products, Mountain Goat Cycles makes saddlebags for bicycles called *panniers.* These panniers come in two models—a touring model and a mountain model. Cost and revenue data for the two models of panniers follow:

| | Mountain Pannier | Touring Pannier |
|---|---|---|
| Selling price per unit | $25 | $30 |
| Variable cost per unit | 10 | 18 |
| Contribution margin per unit | $15 | $12 |
| Contribution margin (CM) ratio | 60% | 40% |

The mountain pannier appears to be much more profitable than the touring pannier. It has a $15 per unit contribution margin as compared to only $12 per unit for the touring model, and it has a 60% CM ratio as compared to only 40% for the touring model.

But now let us add one more piece of information—the plant that makes the panniers is operating at capacity. This does not mean that every machine and every person in the plant is working at the maximum possible rate. Because machines have different capacities, some machines will be operating at less than 100% of capacity. However, if the plant as a whole cannot produce any more units, some machine or process must be operating at capacity. The machine or process that is limiting overall output is called the **bottleneck**—it is the constraint.

At Mountain Goat Cycles, the bottleneck (i.e., constraint) is a stitching machine. The mountain pannier requires two minutes of stitching time per unit, and the touring pannier requires one minute of stitching time per unit. The stitching machine is available for 12,000 minutes per month, and the company can sell up to 4,000 mountain panniers and 7,000 touring panniers per month. Producing up to this demand for both products would require 15,000 minutes, as shown below:

| | Mountain Pannier | Touring Pannier | Total |
|---|---|---|---|
| Monthly demand (a) | 4,000 units | 7,000 units | |
| Stitching machine time required to produce one unit (b) | 2 minutes | 1 minute | |
| Total stitching time required (a) × (b) | 8,000 minutes | 7,000 minutes | 15,000 minutes |

Producing up to demand would require 15,000 minutes, but only 12,000 minutes are available. This simply confirms that the stitching machine is the bottleneck. By definition, because the stitching machine is a bottleneck, the stitching machine does not have enough capacity to satisfy the existing demand for mountain panniers and touring panniers Therefore, some orders for the products will have to be turned down. Naturally, managers will want to know which product is less profitable. To answer this question, they should focus on the contribution margin per unit of the constrained resource. This figure is computed by dividing a product's contribution margin per unit by the amount of the constrained resource required to make a unit of that product. These calculations are carried out below for the mountain and touring panniers:

| | Mountain Pannier | Touring Pannier |
|---|---|---|
| Contribution margin per unit (a) | $15.00 | $12.00 |
| Stitching machine time required to produce one unit (b) | 2 minutes | 1 minute |
| Contribution margin per unit of the constrained resource, (a) ÷ (b) | $7.50 per minute | $12.00 per minute |

It is now easy to decide which product is less profitable and should be deemphasized. Each minute on the stitching machine that is devoted to the touring pannier results in an increase of $12.00 in contribution margin and profits. The comparable figure for the mountain pannier is only $7.50 per minute. Therefore, the touring model should be emphasized. Even though the mountain model has the larger contribution margin per unit and the larger CM ratio, the touring model provides the larger contribution margin in relation to the constrained resource.

To verify that the touring model is indeed the more profitable product, suppose an hour of additional stitching time is available and that unfilled orders exist for both products. The additional hour on the stitching machine could be used to make either 30 mountain panniers (60 minutes ÷ 2 minutes per mountain pannier) or 60 touring panniers (60 minutes ÷ 1 minute per touring pannier), with the following profit implications:

| | Mountain Pannier | Touring Pannier |
|---|---|---|
| Contribution margin per unit | $ 15 | $ 12 |
| Additional units that can be processed in one hour | × 30 | × 60 |
| Additional contribution margin | $450 | $720 |

Because the additional contribution margin would be $720 for the touring panniers and only $450 for the mountain panniers, the touring panniers make the most profitable use of the company's constrained resource—the stitching machine.

The stitching machine is available for 12,000 minutes per month, and producing the touring panniers is the most profitable use of the stitching machine. Therefore, to maximize profits, the company should produce all of the touring panniers the market will demand (7,000 units) and use any remaining capacity to produce mountain panniers. The computations to determine how many mountain panniers can be produced are as follows:

| | |
|---|---|
| Monthly demand for touring panniers (a) | 7,000 units |
| Stitching machine time required to produce one touring pannier (b) | 1 minute |
| Total stitching time required to produce touring panniers (a) × (b) | 7,000 minutes |
| Remaining stitching time available (12,000 minutes − 7,000 minutes) (c) | 5,000 minutes |
| Stitching machine time required to produce one mountain pannier (d) | 2 minutes |
| Production of mountain panniers (c) ÷ (d) | 2,500 units |

Therefore, profit would be maximized by producing 7,000 touring panniers and then using the remaining capacity to produce 2,500 mountain panniers.

This example clearly shows that looking at unit contribution margins alone is not enough; the contribution margin must be viewed in relation to the amount of the constrained resource each product requires.

**HELPFUL HINT**

Use the following four steps to help determine the most profitable use of a constrained resource:

Step 1: Calculate each product's contribution margin per unit.

Step 2: Identify the constraining resource and the quantity of that resource that is consumed to make one unit of each product.

Step 3: Calculate each product's contribution margin per unit of the constraining resource.

Step 4: Rank the products from the highest contribution margin per unit of the constraining resource to the lowest.

If you start by completing these four steps, it will help you compute the most profitable use of a constrained resource.

## Managing Constraints

**LEARNING OBJECTIVE 6**

Determine the value of obtaining more of the constrained resource.

Effectively managing an organization's constraints is a key to increased profits. As discussed above, when a constraint exists in the production process, managers can increase profits by producing the products with the highest contribution margin per unit of the constrained resource. However, they can also increase profits by increasing the capacity of the bottleneck operation.

When a manager increases the capacity of the bottleneck, it is called **relaxing** (or **elevating) the constraint.** In the case of Mountain Goat Cycles, the company is currently working one eight-hour shift. To relax the constraint, the stitching machine operator could be asked to work overtime. No one else would have to work overtime. Because all of the other operations involved in producing panniers have excess capacity, up to a point, the additional panniers processed through the stitching machine during overtime could be finished during normal working hours in the other operations.

The benefits from relaxing the constraint are often enormous and can be easily quantified—the key is the contribution margin per unit of the constrained resource that we have already computed. This number, which was originally stated in terms of minutes in the Mountain Goat Cycles example, is restated on the next page in terms of hours for easier interpretation:

| | Mountain Pannier | Touring Pannier |
|---|---|---|
| Contribution margin per unit of the constrained resource (in minutes)........ | \$7.50 per minute<br>× 60 minutes per hour | \$12.00 per minute<br>× 60 minutes per hour |
| Contribution margin per unit of the constrained resource (in hours)........ | = \$450 per hour | = \$720 per hour |

So what is the value of relaxing the constraint—the time on the stitching machine? The manager should first ask, "What would I do with additional capacity at the bottleneck if it were available?" If the time were to be used to make additional mountain panniers, it would be worth \$450 per hour. If the time were to be used to make additional touring panniers, it would be worth \$720 per hour. In this latter case, the company should be willing to pay an overtime *premium* to the stitching machine operator of up to \$720 per hour! Suppose, for example, that the stitching machine operator is paid \$20 per hour during normal working hours and time-and-a-half, or \$30 per hour, for overtime. In this case, the premium for overtime is only \$10 per hour, whereas in principle, the company should be willing to pay a premium of up to \$720 per hour. The difference between what the company should be willing to pay as a premium, \$720 per hour, and what it would actually have to pay, \$10 per hour, is pure profit of \$710 per hour.

To reinforce this concept, suppose that there are only unfilled orders for the mountain pannier. How much would it be worth to the company to run the stitching machine overtime in this situation? Because the additional capacity would be used to make the mountain pannier, the value of that additional capacity would drop to \$7.50 per minute or \$450 per hour. Nevertheless, the value of relaxing the constraint would still be quite high and the company should be willing to pay an overtime premium of up to \$450 per hour.

These calculations indicate that managers should pay great attention to the bottleneck operation. If a bottleneck machine breaks down or is ineffectively utilized, the losses to the company can be quite large. In our example, for every minute the stitching machine is down due to breakdowns or setups, the company loses between \$7.50 and \$12.00.[2] The losses on an hourly basis are between \$450 and \$720! In contrast, there is no such loss of contribution margin if time is lost on a machine that is not a bottleneck—such machines have excess capacity anyway.

The implications are clear. Managers should focus much of their attention on managing the bottleneck. As we have discussed, managers should emphasize products that most profitably utilize the constrained resource. They should also make sure that products are processed smoothly through the bottleneck, with minimal lost time due to breakdowns and setups. And they should try to find ways to increase the capacity at the bottleneck.

The capacity of a bottleneck can be effectively increased in a number of ways, including:

- Working overtime on the bottleneck.
- Subcontracting some of the processing that would be done at the bottleneck.
- Investing in additional machines at the bottleneck.
- Shifting workers from processes that are not bottlenecks to the process that is the bottleneck.
- Focusing business process improvement efforts on the bottleneck.

[2]Setups are required when production switches from one product to another. For example, consider a company that makes automobile side panels. The panels are painted before shipping them to an automobile manufacturer for final assembly. The customer might require 100 blue panels, 50 black panels, and 20 yellow panels. Each time the color is changed, the painting equipment must be purged of the old paint color, cleaned with solvents, and refilled with the new paint color. This takes time. In fact, some equipment may require such lengthy and frequent setups that it is unavailable for actual production more often than not.

- Reducing defective units. Each defective unit that is processed through the bottleneck and subsequently scrapped takes the place of a good unit that could have been sold.

The last three methods of increasing the capacity of the bottleneck are particularly attractive because they are essentially free and may even yield additional cost savings.

The methods and ideas discussed in this section are all part of the Theory of Constraints, which was introduced in the Prologue. A number of organizations have successfully used the Theory of Constraints to improve their performance, including **Avery Dennison**, **Bethlehem Steel**, **Binney & Smith**, **Boeing**, **Champion International**, **Ford Motor Company**, **General Motors**, **ITT**, **Monster Cable**, **National Semiconductor**, **Pratt and Whitney Canada**, **Pretoria Academic Hospital**, **Procter and Gamble**, **Texas Instruments**, **United Airlines**, **United Electrical Controls**, the **United States Air Force Logistics Command**, and the **United States Navy Transportation Corps**.

## CONCEPT CHECK

4. A company has received a special order from a customer to make 5,000 units of a customized product. The direct materials cost per unit of the customized product is \$15, the direct labor cost per unit is \$5, and the manufacturing overhead per unit is \$18, including \$6 of variable manufacturing overhead. If the company has sufficient available manufacturing capacity, what is the minimum price that can be accepted for the special order?
   a. \$24 c. \$32
   b. \$26 d. \$38
5. Refer to the facts from question 4; however, in answering this question assume that the company is operating at 100% of its capacity without the special order. If the company normally manufactures only one product that has a contribution margin of \$20 per unit and that consumes 2 minutes of the constrained resource per unit, what is the opportunity cost (stated in terms of forgone contribution margin) of taking the special order? Assume the special order would require 1.5 minutes of the constrained resource per unit.
   a. \$25,000 c. \$75,000
   b. \$50,000 d. \$100,000

## IN BUSINESS

### Boeing Is Constrained by a Supplier

**Boeing Co.** had to delay delivery of its model 777 airplanes to **Emirates** airline because the German supplier **Sell GmbH** could not provide the equipment for cooking galleys to Boeing on time. The production bottleneck forced Emirates to repeatedly postpone its planned expansion into the U.S. west coast. It also forced Boeing to accept payment delays for airplanes that sell for more than \$200 million apiece. In response, Sell GmbH hired 250 more employees and invested millions of euros in new machine tools and factory space to expand its production capacity.

Source: Daniel Michaels and J. Lynn Lunsford, "Lack of Seats, Galleys Stalls Boeing, Airbus," *The Wall Street Journal*, August 8, 2008, pp. B1 and B4.

## JOINT PRODUCT COSTS AND THE CONTRIBUTION APPROACH

**LEARNING OBJECTIVE 7**

Prepare an analysis showing whether joint products should be sold at the split-off point or processed further.

In some industries, a number of end products are produced from a single raw material input. For example, in the petroleum refining industry a large number of products are extracted from crude oil, including gasoline, jet fuel, home heating oil, lubricants, asphalt, and various organic chemicals. Another example is provided by the Santa Maria Wool Cooperative of New Mexico. The company buys raw wool from local sheepherders, separates the wool into three grades—coarse, fine, and superfine—and then dyes the wool using traditional methods that rely on pigments from local materials. Exhibit 10–6 contains a diagram of the production process.

At Santa Maria Wool Cooperative, coarse wool, fine wool, and superfine wool are produced from one input—raw wool. Two or more products that are produced from a common input are known as **joint products.** The **split-off point** is the point in the manufacturing process at which the joint products can be recognized as separate products. This

**EXHIBIT 10–6** Santa Maria Wool Cooperative

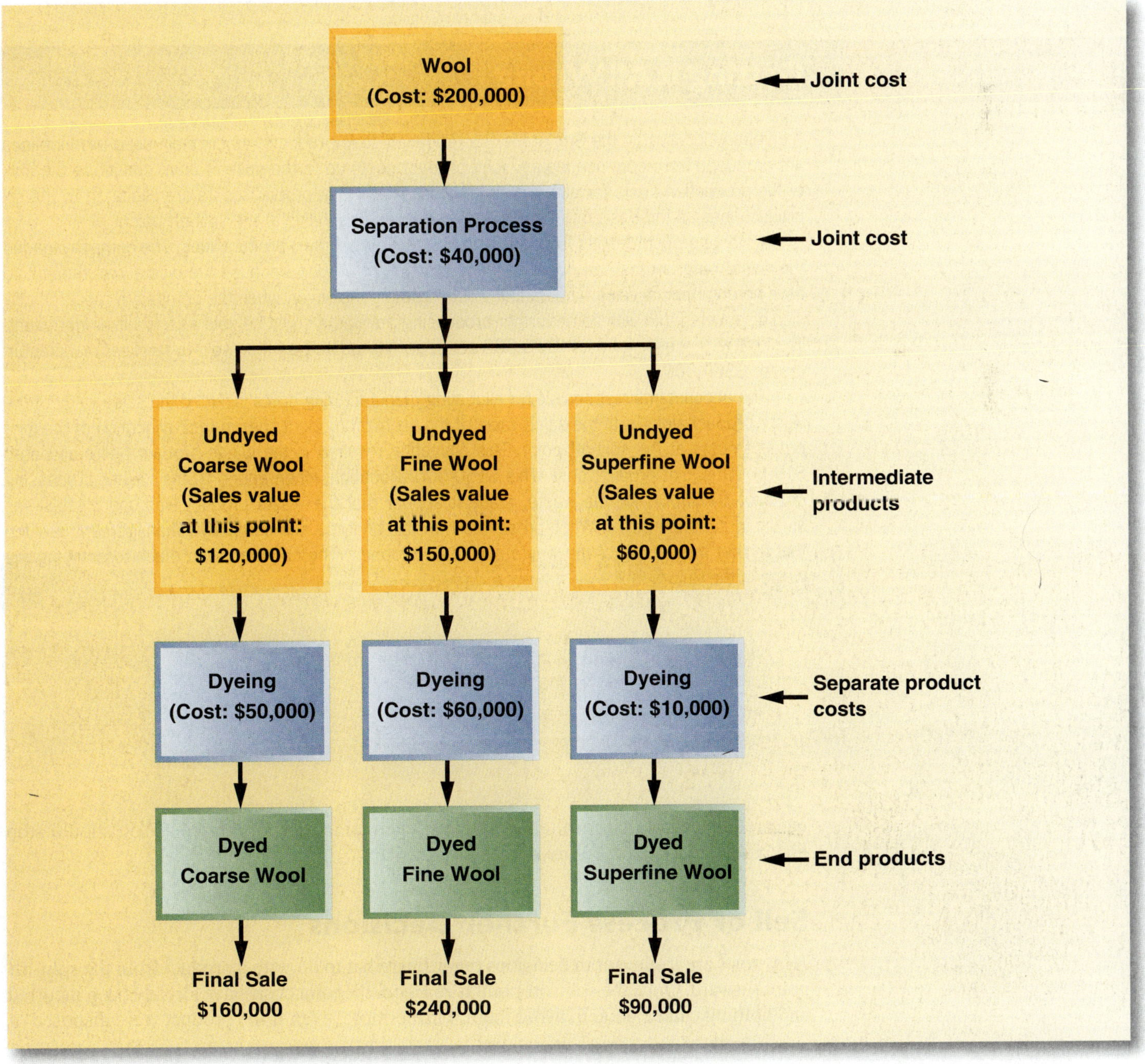

does not occur at Santa Maria Wool Cooperative until the raw wool has gone through the separating process. The term **joint cost** is used to describe the costs incurred up to the split-off point. At Santa Maria Wool Cooperative, the joint costs are the $200,000 cost of the raw wool and the $40,000 cost of separating the wool. The undyed wool is called an *intermediate product* because it is not finished at this point. Nevertheless, a market does exist for undyed wool—although at a significantly lower price than finished, dyed wool.

## The Pitfalls of Allocation

Joint costs are common costs that are incurred to simultaneously produce a variety of end products. These joint costs are traditionally allocated among the different products at the split-off point. A typical approach is to allocate the joint costs according to the relative sales value of the end products.

Although allocation of joint product costs is needed for some purposes, such as balance sheet inventory valuation, allocations of this kind are extremely misleading for decision making. The In Business box "Getting It All Wrong" (see below) illustrates an

### IN BUSINESS — Getting It All Wrong

A company located on the Gulf of Mexico produces soap products. Its six main soap product lines are produced from common inputs. Joint product costs up to the split-off point constitute the bulk of the production costs for all six product lines. These joint product costs are allocated to the six product lines on the basis of the relative sales value of each line at the split-off point.

A waste product results from the production of the six main product lines. The company loaded the waste onto barges and dumped it into the Gulf of Mexico because the waste was thought to have no commercial value. The dumping was stopped, however, when the company's research division discovered that with some further processing the waste could be sold as a fertilizer ingredient. The further processing costs $175,000 per year. The waste was then sold to fertilizer manufacturers for $300,000.

The accountants responsible for allocating manufacturing costs included the sales value of the waste product along with the sales value of the six main product lines in their allocation of the joint product costs at the split-off point. This allocation resulted in the waste product being allocated $150,000 in joint product cost. This $150,000 allocation, when added to the further processing costs of $175,000 for the waste, made it appear that the waste product was unprofitable—as shown in the table below. When presented with this analysis, the company's management decided that further processing of the waste should be stopped. The company went back to dumping the waste in the Gulf.

| | |
|---|---|
| Sales value of the waste product after further processing ............... | $300,000 |
| Less costs assigned to the waste product ...................................... | 325,000 |
| Net loss ........................................................................................ | $ (25,000) |

incorrect decision that resulted from using such an allocated joint cost. You should stop now and read that box before proceeding further.

## Sell or Process Further Decisions

Joint costs are irrelevant in decisions regarding what to do with a product from the split-off point forward. Once the split-off point is reached, the joint costs have already been incurred and nothing can be done to avoid them. Furthermore, even if the product were disposed of in a landfill without any further processing, all of the joint costs must be incurred to obtain the other products that come out of the joint process. None of the joint costs are avoidable by disposing of any one of the products that emerge from the split-off point. Therefore, none of the joint costs are economically attributable to any one of the intermediate or end products. The joint costs are a common cost of all of the intermediate and end products and should not be allocated to them for purposes of making decisions about the individual products. In the case of the soap company in the accompanying In Business box "Getting It All Wrong," the $150,000 in allocated joint costs should not have influenced what was done with the waste product from the split-off point forward. Even ignoring the negative environmental impact of dumping the waste in the Gulf of Mexico, a correct analysis would have shown that the company was making money by further processing the waste into a fertilizer ingredient. The analysis should have been done as follows:

| | Dump in Gulf | Process Further |
|---|---|---|
| Sales value of fertilizer ingredient | 0 | $300,000 |
| Additional processing costs | 0 | 175,000 |
| Contribution margin | 0 | $125,000 |
| Advantage of processing further | $125,000 | |

Decisions of this type are known as **sell or process further decisions.** It is profitable to continue processing a joint product after the split-off point *so long as the incremental revenue from such processing exceeds the incremental processing cost incurred after the split-off point.* Joint costs that have already been incurred up to the split-off point are always irrelevant in decisions concerning what to do from the split-off point forward.

To provide a detailed example of the sell or process further decision, return to the data for Santa Maria Wool Cooperative in Exhibit 10–6. We can answer several important questions using this data. First, is the company making money if it runs the entire process from beginning to end? Assuming there are no costs other than those displayed in Exhibit 10–6, the company is indeed making money as follows:

| | | |
|---|---|---|
| **Analysis of the profitability of the overall operation:** | | |
| Combined final sales value ($160,000 + $240,000 + $90,000) | | $490,000 |
| Less costs of producing the end products: | | |
| Cost of wool | $200,000 | |
| Cost of separating wool | 40,000 | |
| Combined costs of dyeing ($50,000 + $60,000 + $10,000) | 120,000 | 360,000 |
| Profit | | $130,000 |

Note that the joint costs of buying the wool and separating the wool *are* relevant when considering the profitability of the entire operation. This is because these joint costs *could* be avoided if the entire operation were shut down. However, these joint costs are *not* relevant when considering the profitability of any one product. As long as the process is being run to make the other products, no additional joint costs are incurred to make the specific product in question.

Even though the company is making money overall, it may be losing money on one or more of the products. If the company buys wool and runs the separation process, it will get all three intermediate products. Nothing can be done about that. However, each of these products can be sold *as is* without further processing. It may be that the company would be better off selling one or more of the products prior to dyeing to avoid the dyeing costs. The appropriate way to make this choice is to compare the incremental revenues to the incremental costs from further processing as follows:

| Analysis of sell or process further: | Coarse Wool | Fine Wool | Superfine Wool |
|---|---|---|---|
| Final sales value after further processing | $160,000 | $240,000 | $90,000 |
| Less sales value at the split-off point | 120,000 | 150,000 | 60,000 |
| Incremental revenue from further processing | 40,000 | 90,000 | 30,000 |
| Less cost of further processing (dyeing) | 50,000 | 60,000 | 10,000 |
| Profit (loss) from further processing | $ (10,000) | $ 30,000 | $20,000 |

As this analysis shows, the company would be better off selling the undyed coarse wool as is rather than processing it further. The other two products should be processed further and dyed before selling them.

Note that the joint costs of the wool ($200,000) and of the wool separation process ($40,000) play no role in the decision to sell or further process the intermediate products. These joint costs are relevant in a decision of whether to buy wool and to run the wool separation process, but they are not relevant in decisions about what to do with the intermediate products once they have been separated.

## HELPFUL HINT

For each end product, use the following three steps to make sell or process further decisions:

Step 1: Calculate the sales value if processed further minus the sales value at the split-off point.

Step 2: Determine the cost of further processing beyond the split-off point.

Step 3: Take the amount in step 1 and subtract from it the amount in step 2. If the result is a positive number, then choose to process further. If it is a negative number, then choose to sell at the split-off point.

While you may need to add additional steps when solving complex problems, these three steps will help organize your analysis.

## SUMMARY

**LO1 Identify relevant and irrelevant costs and benefits in a decision.**

Every decision involves a choice from among at least two alternatives. Only those costs and benefits that differ in total between the alternatives are relevant; costs and benefits that are the same for all alternatives are not affected by the decision and can be ignored. Only future costs that differ between alternatives are relevant. Sunk costs are always irrelevant.

**LO2 Prepare an analysis showing whether a product line or other business segment should be added or dropped.**

A decision of whether a product line or other segment should be dropped should focus on the differences in the costs and benefits between dropping or retaining the product line or segment. Caution should be exercised when using reports in which common fixed costs have been allocated among segments. If these common fixed costs are unaffected by the decision of whether to add or drop the segment, they are irrelevant and should be removed before determining the real profitability of a segment.

**LO3 Prepare a make or buy analysis.**

When deciding whether to make or buy a component, focus on the costs and benefits that differ between those two alternatives. As in other decisions, sunk costs—such as the depreciation on old equipment—should be ignored. Future costs that do not differ between alternatives—such as allocations of common fixed costs like general overhead—should be ignored.

**LO4 Prepare an analysis showing whether a special order should be accepted.**
When deciding whether to accept or reject a special order, focus on the benefits and costs that differ between those two alternatives. Specifically, a special order should be accepted when the incremental revenue from the sale exceeds the incremental cost. As always, sunk costs and future costs that do not differ between the alternatives are irrelevant.

**LO5 Determine the most profitable use of a constrained resource.**
When demand for a company's products and services exceeds its ability to supply them, the company has a bottleneck. The bottleneck, whether it is a particular material, skilled labor, or a specific machine, is a constrained resource. Since the company is unable to make everything it could sell, managers must decide what the company will make and what the company will not make. In this situation, the profitability of a product is best measured by its contribution margin per unit of the constrained resource. The products with the highest contribution margin per unit of the constrained resource should be favored.

**LO6 Determine the value of obtaining more of the constrained resource.**
Managers should focus their attention on effectively managing the constraint. This involves making the most profitable use of the constrained resource and increasing the amount of the constrained resource that is available. The value of relaxing the constraint is determined by the contribution margin per unit of the constrained resource for the work that would be done if more of the resource were available.

**LO7 Prepare an analysis showing whether joint products should be sold at the split-off point or processed further.**
Managers should recommend further processing of an intermediate product so long as the incremental revenue from such processing exceeds the incremental processing cost incurred after the split-off point. Joint costs are irrelevant in decisions regarding what to do with a product from the split-off point forward. Once the split-off point is reached, the joint costs have already been incurred and nothing can be done to avoid them.

## GUIDANCE ANSWER TO DECISION POINT

**Vice President of Production (p. 454)**
The annual rental cost for the machinery is an *avoidable* fixed cost. An avoidable fixed cost is a cost that can be eliminated in whole or in part by choosing one alternative over another. Because the annual rental cost of the machinery can be avoided if the company purchases the components from an outside supplier, it is relevant to this decision.

## GUIDANCE ANSWERS TO CONCEPT CHECKS

1. **Choices a and d.** Sunk costs are always irrelevant. Fixed costs can be relevant costs.
2. **Choice a.** The cost of the airline ticket to Telluride is a sunk cost; it has already been incurred and the ticket is nonrefundable.
3. **Choice b.** The cost of going to Stowe would be \$1,000 [\$400 + (\$150 per night × 4 nights)] whereas the incremental cost of going to Telluride would be \$1,020 [\$300 + (\$180 per night × 4 nights)]. Note that the \$450 cost of flying to Telluride is irrelevant at this point because it is a sunk cost. The analysis favors Stowe by \$20.
4. **Choice b.** The minimum price would be \$15 direct materials + \$5 direct labor + \$6 variable manufacturing overhead = \$26.
5. **Choice c.** The special order requires 7,500 minutes (5,000 units × 1.5 minutes per unit). Taking the special order would require sacrificing 3,750 units (7,500 minutes ÷ 2 minutes per unit) of the regular product. The forgone contribution margin would be 3,750 units × \$20 per unit = \$75,000.

## REVIEW PROBLEM: DIFFERENTIAL ANALYSIS

Charter Sports Equipment manufactures round, rectangular, and octagonal trampolines. Sales and expense data for the past month follow:

| | | Trampoline | | |
|---|---|---|---|---|
| | Total | Round | Rectangular | Octagonal |
| Sales | $1,000,000 | $140,000 | $500,000 | $360,000 |
| Variable expenses | 410,000 | 60,000 | 200,000 | 150,000 |
| Contribution margin | 590,000 | 80,000 | 300,000 | 210,000 |
| Fixed expenses: | | | | |
| Advertising—traceable | 216,000 | 41,000 | 110,000 | 65,000 |
| Depreciation of special equipment | 95,000 | 20,000 | 40,000 | 35,000 |
| Line supervisors' salaries | 19,000 | 6,000 | 7,000 | 6,000 |
| General factory overhead* | 200,000 | 28,000 | 100,000 | 72,000 |
| Total fixed expenses | 530,000 | 95,000 | 257,000 | 178,000 |
| Net operating income (loss) | $ 60,000 | $ (15,000) | $ 43,000 | $ 32,000 |

*A common fixed cost that is allocated on the basis of sales dollars.

Management is concerned about the continued losses shown by the round trampolines and wants a recommendation as to whether or not the line should be discontinued. The special equipment used to produce the trampolines has no resale value. If the round trampoline model is dropped, the two line supervisors assigned to the model would be discharged.

***Required:***

1. Should production and sale of the round trampolines be discontinued? The company has no other use for the capacity now being used to produce the round trampolines. Show computations to support your answer.
2. Recast the above data in a format that would be more useful to management in assessing the profitability of the various product lines.

**Solution to Review Problem**

1. No, production and sale of the round trampolines should not be discontinued. Computations to support this answer follow:

| | | |
|---|---|---|
| Contribution margin lost if the round trampolines are discontinued | | $(80,000) |
| Less fixed costs that can be avoided: | | |
| Advertising—traceable | $41,000 | |
| Line supervisors' salaries | 6,000 | 47,000 |
| Decrease in net operating income for the company as a whole | | $(33,000) |

The depreciation of the special equipment is a sunk cost, and therefore it is not relevant to the decision. The general factory overhead is allocated and will presumably continue regardless of whether or not the round trampolines are discontinued; thus, it is not relevant.

2. If management wants a clearer picture of the profitability of the segments, the general factory overhead should not be allocated. It is a common cost and therefore should be deducted from the total product-line segment margin. A more useful income statement format would be as follows:

| | | Trampoline | | |
|---|---|---|---|---|
| | Total | Round | Rectangular | Octagonal |
| Sales | $1,000,000 | $140,000 | $500,000 | $360,000 |
| Variable expenses | 410,000 | 60,000 | 200,000 | 150,000 |
| Contribution margin | 590,000 | 80,000 | 300,000 | 210,000 |
| Traceable fixed expenses: | | | | |
| Advertising—traceable | 216,000 | 41,000 | 110,000 | 65,000 |
| Depreciation of special equipment | 95,000 | 20,000 | 40,000 | 35,000 |
| Line supervisors' salaries | 19,000 | 6,000 | 7,000 | 6,000 |
| Total traceable fixed expenses | 330,000 | 67,000 | 157,000 | 106,000 |
| Product-line segment margin | 260,000 | $ 13,000 | $143,000 | $104,000 |
| Common fixed expenses | 200,000 | | | |
| Net operating income | $ 60,000 | | | |

## GLOSSARY

**Avoidable cost** A cost that can be eliminated by choosing one alternative over another in a decision. This term is synonymous with *relevant cost.* (p. 440)

**Bottleneck** A machine or some other part of a process that limits the total output of the entire system. (p. 456)

**Constraint** A limitation under which a company must operate, such as limited available machine time or raw materials, that restricts the company's ability to satisfy demand. (p. 456)

**Joint costs** Costs that are incurred up to the split-off point in a process that produces joint products. (p. 462)

**Joint products** Two or more products that are produced from a common input. (p. 461)

**Make or buy decision** A decision concerning whether an item should be produced internally or purchased from an outside supplier. (p. 451)

**Relaxing** (or **elevating) the constraint** An action that increases the amount of a constrained resource. Equivalently, an action that increases the capacity of the bottleneck. (p. 458)

**Relevant benefit** A benefit that differs between alternatives in a decision. Synonyms are *differential benefit* and *incremental benefit.* (p. 440)

**Relevant cost** A cost that differs between alternatives in a decision. Synonyms are *avoidable cost, differential cost,* and *incremental cost.* (p. 440)

**Sell or process further decision** A decision as to whether a joint product should be sold at the split-off point or sold after further processing. (p. 463)

**Special order** A one time order that is not considered part of the company's normal ongoing business. (p. 454)

**Split-off point** That point in the manufacturing process where some or all of the joint products can be recognized as individual products. (p. 461)

**Sunk cost** Any cost that has already been incurred and that cannot be changed by any decision made now or in the future. (p. 440)

**Vertical integration** The involvement by a company in more than one of the activities in the entire value chain from development through production, distribution, sales, and after-sales service. (p. 451)

## QUESTIONS

**10–1** What is a *relevant cost?*

**10–2** Define the following terms: *incremental cost, opportunity cost,* and *sunk cost.*

**10–3** Are variable costs always relevant costs? Explain.

**10–4** "Sunk costs are easy to spot—they're the fixed costs associated with a decision." Do you agree? Explain.

**10–5** "Variable costs and differential costs mean the same thing." Do you agree? Explain.

**10–6** "All future costs are relevant in decision making." Do you agree? Why?

**10–7** Prentice Company is considering dropping one of its product lines. What costs of the product line would be relevant to this decision? What costs would be irrelevant?

**10–8** "If a product is generating a loss, then it should be discontinued." Do you agree? Explain.

**10–9** What is the danger in allocating common fixed costs among products or other segments of an organization?

**10–10** How does opportunity cost enter into a make or buy decision?

**10–11** Give at least four examples of possible constraints.

**10–12** How will relating product contribution margins to the amount of the constrained resource they consume help a company maximize its profits?

**10–13** Define the following terms: *joint products, joint costs,* and *split-off point.*

**10–14** From a decision-making point of view, should joint costs be allocated among joint products?

**10–15** What guideline should be used in determining whether a joint product should be sold at the split-off point or processed further?

**10–16** Airlines sometimes offer reduced rates during certain times of the week to members of a businessperson's family if they accompany him or her on trips. How does the concept of relevant costs enter into the decision by the airline to offer reduced rates of this type?

**Multiple-choice questions are provided on the text website at www.mhhe.com/brewer6e.**

## APPLYING EXCEL

Connect ACCOUNTING

LO7

**Available with McGraw-Hill's *Connect® Accounting.***

The Excel worksheet form that appears below is to be used to recreate the example in the text on pages 461–464. Download the workbook containing this form from the Online Learning Center at www.mhhe.com/brewer6e. *On the website you will also receive instructions about how to use this worksheet form.*

| | A | B | C | D | E |
|---|---|---|---|---|---|
| 1 | Chapter 10: Applying Excel | | | | |
| 2 | | | | | |
| 3 | **Data** | | | | |
| 4 | **Exhibit 10-6 Santa Maria Wool Cooperative** | | | | |
| 5 | Cost of wool | $200,000 | | | |
| 6 | Cost of separation process | $40,000 | | | |
| 7 | Sales value of intermediate products at split-off point: | | | | |
| 8 | Undyed coarse wool | $120,000 | | | |
| 9 | Undyed fine wool | $150,000 | | | |
| 10 | Undyed superfine wool | $60,000 | | | |
| 11 | Costs of further processing (dyeing) intermediate products: | | | | |
| 12 | Undyed coarse wool | $50,000 | | | |
| 13 | Undyed fine wool | $60,000 | | | |
| 14 | Undyed superfine wool | $10,000 | | | |
| 15 | Sales value of end products: | | | | |
| 16 | Dyed coarse wool | $160,000 | | | |
| 17 | Dyed fine wool | $240,000 | | | |
| 18 | Dyed superfine wool | $90,000 | | | |
| 19 | | | | | |
| 20 | *Enter a formula into each of the cells marked with a ? below* | | | | |
| 21 | **Example: Joint Product Costs and the Contribution Approach** | | | | |
| 22 | | | | | |
| 23 | ***Analysis of the profitability of the overall operation:*** | | | | |
| 24 | Combined final sales value | | ? | | |
| 25 | Less costs of producing the end products: | | | | |
| 26 | Cost of wool | ? | | | |
| 27 | Cost of separation process | ? | | | |
| 28 | Combined costs of dyeing | ? | ? | | |
| 29 | Profit | | ? | | |
| 30 | | | | | |
| 31 | ***Analysis of sell or process further:*** | | | | |
| 32 | | *Coarse* | *Fine* | *Superfine* | |
| 33 | | *Wool* | *Wool* | *Wool* | |
| 34 | Final sales value after further processing | ? | ? | ? | |
| 35 | Less sales value at the split-off point | ? | ? | ? | |
| 36 | Incremental revenue from further processing | ? | ? | ? | |
| 37 | Less cost of further processing (dyeing) | ? | ? | ? | |
| 38 | Profit (loss) from further processing | ? | ? | ? | |
| 39 | | | | | |

Chapter 10 Form | Filled in Chapter 10 Form | Chapter

You should proceed to the requirements below only after completing your worksheet.

***Required:***

1. Check your worksheet by changing the cost of further processing undyed coarse wool in cell B12 to $30,000. The overall profit from processing all intermediate products into final products should now be $150,000 and the profit from further processing coarse wool should now be $10,000. If you do not get these answers, find the errors in your worksheet and correct them.

   How should operations change in response to this change in cost?
2. In industries that process joint products, the costs of the raw materials inputs and the sales values of intermediate and final products are often volatile. Change the data area of your worksheet to match the following:

| Data<br>Exhibit 10–6 Santa Maria Wool Cooperative | |
|---|---|
| Cost of wool | $290,000 |
| Cost of separation process | $40,000 |
| Sales value of intermediate products at split-off point: | |
| Undyed coarse wool | $100,000 |
| Undyed fine wool | $110,000 |
| Undyed superfine wool | $90,000 |
| Costs of further processing (dyeing) intermediate products: | |
| Undyed coarse wool | $50,000 |
| Undyed fine wool | $60,000 |
| Undyed superfine wool | $10,000 |
| Sales value of end products: | |
| Dyed coarse wool | $180,000 |
| Dyed fine wool | $210,000 |
| Dyed superfine wool | $90,000 |

a. What is the overall profit if all intermediate products are processed into final products?
b. What is the profit from further processing each of the intermediate products?
c. With these new costs and selling prices, what recommendations would you make concerning the company's operations? If your recommendation is followed, what should be the overall profit of the company?

connect ACCOUNTING

## THE FOUNDATIONAL 15

### Available with McGraw-Hill's *Connect®* *Accounting.*

LO2, LO3, LO4, LO5, LO6

Cane Company manufactures two products called Alpha and Beta that sell for $120 and $80, respectively. Each product uses only one type of raw material that costs $6 per pound. The company has the capacity to annually produce 100,000 units of each product. Its unit costs for each product at this level of activity are given below:

| | Alpha | Beta |
|---|---|---|
| Direct materials | $ 30 | $12 |
| Direct labor | 20 | 15 |
| Variable manufacturing overhead | 7 | 5 |
| Traceable fixed manufacturing overhead | 16 | 18 |
| Variable selling expenses | 12 | 8 |
| Common fixed expenses | 15 | 10 |
| Total cost per unit | $100 | $68 |

The company considers its traceable fixed manufacturing overhead to be avoidable, whereas its common fixed expenses are deemed unavoidable and have been allocated to products based on sales dollars.

***Required:***

(Answer each question independently unless instructed otherwise.)

1. What is the total amount of traceable fixed manufacturing overhead for the Alpha product line and for the Beta product line?

2. What is the company's total amount of common fixed expenses?
3. Assume that Cane expects to produce and sell 80,000 Alphas during the current year. One of Cane's sales representatives has found a new customer that is willing to buy 10,000 additional Alphas for a price of $80 per unit. If Cane accepts the customer's offer, how much will its profits increase or decrease?
4. Assume that Cane expects to produce and sell 90,000 Betas during the current year. One of Cane's sales representatives has found a new customer that is willing to buy 5,000 additional Betas for a price of $39 per unit. If Cane accepts the customer's offer, how much will its profits increase or decrease?
5. Assume that Cane expects to produce and sell 95,000 Alphas during the current year. One of Cane's sales representatives has found a new customer that is willing to buy 10,000 additional Alphas for a price of $80 per unit. If Cane accepts the customer's offer, it will decrease Alpha sales to regular customers by 5,000 units. Should Cane accept this special order?
6. Assume that Cane normally produces and sells 90,000 Betas per year. If Cane discontinues the Beta product line, how much will profits increase or decrease?
7. Assume that Cane normally produces and sells 40,000 Betas per year. If Cane discontinues the Beta product line, how much will profits increase or decrease?
8. Assume that Cane normally produces and sells 60,000 Betas and 80,000 Alphas per year. If Cane discontinues the Beta product line, its sales representatives could increase sales of Alpha by 15,000 units. If Cane discontinues the Beta product line, how much would profits increase or decrease?
9. Assume that Cane expects to produce and sell 80,000 Alphas during the current year. A supplier has offered to manufacture and deliver 80,000 Alphas to Cane for a price of $80 per unit. If Cane buys 80,000 units from the supplier instead of making those units, how much will profits increase or decrease?
10. Assume that Cane expects to produce and sell 50,000 Alphas during the current year. A supplier has offered to manufacture and deliver 50,000 Alphas to Cane for a price of $80 per unit. If Cane buys 50,000 units from the supplier instead of making those units, how much will profits increase or decrease?
11. How many pounds of raw material are needed to make one unit of Alpha and one unit of Beta?
12. What contribution margin per pound of raw material is earned by Alpha and Beta?
13. Assume that Cane's customers would buy a maximum of 80,000 units of Alpha and 60,000 units of Beta. Also assume that the company's raw material available for production is limited to 160,000 pounds. How many units of each product should Cane produce to maximize its profits?
14. If Cane follows your recommendation in requirement 13, what total contribution margin will it earn?
15. If Cane uses its 160,000 pounds of raw materials as you recommended in requirement 13, up to how much should it be willing to pay per pound for additional raw materials?

## EXERCISES

connect ACCOUNTING

**All applicable exercises are available with McGraw-Hill's *Connect®* *Accounting*.**

### EXERCISE 10–1 Identifying Relevant Costs [LO1]

A number of costs are listed below that may be relevant in decisions faced by the management of Poulsen & Sonner A/S, a Danish furniture manufacturer:

| | Case 1 | | Case 2 | |
|---|---|---|---|---|
| Item | Relevant | Not Relevant | Relevant | Not Relevant |
| a. Sales revenue | | | | |
| b. Direct materials | | | | |
| c. Direct labor | | | | |
| d. Variable manufacturing overhead | | | | |
| e. Book value—Model A3000 machine | | | | |
| f. Disposal value—Model A3000 machine | | | | |
| g. Depreciation—Model A3000 machine | | | | |
| h. Market value—Model B3800 machine (cost) | | | | |
| i. Fixed manufacturing overhead (general) | | | | |
| j. Variable selling expense | | | | |
| k. Fixed selling expense | | | | |
| l. General administrative overhead | | | | |

***Required:***

Copy the information from the previous page onto your answer sheet and place an X in the appropriate column to indicate whether each item is relevant or not relevant in the following situations. Requirement 1 relates to Case 1, and requirement 2 relates to Case 2. Consider the two cases independently.

1. The company chronically runs at capacity and the old Model A3000 machine is the company's constraint. Management is considering the purchase of a new Model B3800 machine to use in addition to the company's present Model A3000 machine. The old Model A3000 machine will continue to be used to capacity as before, with the new Model B3800 being used to expand production. The increase in volume will be large enough to require increases in fixed selling expenses and in general administrative overhead, but not in the general fixed manufacturing overhead.
2. The old Model A3000 machine is not the company's constraint, but management is considering replacing it with a new Model B3800 machine because of the potential savings in direct materials cost with the new machine. The Model A3000 machine would be sold. This change will have no effect on production or sales, other than some savings in direct materials costs due to less waste.

**EXERCISE 10–2 Dropping or Retaining a Segment [LO2]**

Jackson County Senior Services is a nonprofit organization devoted to providing essential services to seniors who live in their own homes within the Jackson County area. Three services are provided for seniors—home nursing, Meals On Wheels, and housekeeping. Data on revenue and expenses for the past year follow:

| | Total | Home Nursing | Meals On Wheels | House-keeping |
|---|---|---|---|---|
| Revenues | $900,000 | $260,000 | $400,000 | $240,000 |
| Variable expenses | 490,000 | 120,000 | 210,000 | 160,000 |
| Contribution margin | 410,000 | 140,000 | 190,000 | 80,000 |
| Fixed expenses: | | | | |
| Depreciation | 68,000 | 8,000 | 40,000 | 20,000 |
| Liability insurance | 42,000 | 20,000 | 7,000 | 15,000 |
| Program administrators' salaries | 115,000 | 40,000 | 38,000 | 37,000 |
| General administrative overhead* | 180,000 | 52,000 | 80,000 | 48,000 |
| Total fixed expenses | 405,000 | 120,000 | 165,000 | 120,000 |
| Net operating income (loss) | $ 5,000 | $ 20,000 | $ 25,000 | $ (40,000) |

*Allocated on the basis of program revenues.

The head administrator of Jackson County Senior Services, Judith Miyama, is concerned about the organization's finances and considers the net operating income of $5,000 last year to be too small. (Last year's results were very similar to the results for previous years and are representative of what would be expected in the future.) Therefore, she has asked for more information about the financial advisability of discontinuing the housekeeping program.

The depreciation in housekeeping is for a van that transports housekeepers and their equipment from job to job. If the program were discontinued, the van would be donated to a charitable organization. Depreciation charges assume zero salvage value. None of the general administrative overhead would be avoided if the housekeeping program were dropped, but the liability insurance and the salary of the program administrator would be avoided.

***Required:***

1. Should the housekeeping program be discontinued? Explain. Show computations to support your answer.
2. Recast the above data in a format that would be more useful to management in assessing the long-run financial viability of the various services.

**EXERCISE 10–3 Make or Buy a Component [LO3]**

Climate-Control, Inc., manufactures a variety of heating and air-conditioning units. The company is currently manufacturing all of its own component parts. An outside supplier has offered to sell a thermostat to Climate-Control for $20 per unit. To evaluate this offer, Climate-Control, Inc., has gathered the following information relating to its own cost of producing the thermostat internally:

| | Per Unit | 15,000 Units per Year |
|---|---|---|
| Direct materials | $ 6 | $ 90,000 |
| Direct labor | 8 | 120,000 |
| Variable manufacturing overhead | 1 | 15,000 |
| Fixed manufacturing overhead, traceable | 5* | 75,000 |
| Fixed manufacturing overhead, common, but allocated | 10 | 150,000 |
| Total cost | $30 | $450,000 |

*40% supervisory salaries; 60% depreciation of special equipment (no resale value).

***Required:***

1. Assuming that the company has no alternative use for the facilities now being used to produce the thermostat, should the outside supplier's offer be accepted? Show all computations.
2. Suppose that if the thermostats were purchased, Climate-Control, Inc., could use the freed capacity to launch a new product. The segment margin of the new product would be $65,000 per year. Should Climate-Control, Inc., accept the offer to buy the thermostats from the outside supplier for $20 each? Show computations.

TAKE TWO

Special price = $288.50

**EXERCISE 10–4 Evaluating a Special Order [LO4]**

Miyamoto Jewelers is considering a special order for 10 handcrafted gold bracelets to be given as gifts to members of a wedding party. The normal selling price of a gold bracelet is $389.95 and its unit product cost is $264.00 as shown below:

| | |
|---|---|
| Direct materials | $143.00 |
| Direct labor | 86.00 |
| Manufacturing overhead | 35.00 |
| Unit product cost | $264.00 |

Most of the manufacturing overhead is fixed and unaffected by variations in how much jewelry is produced in any given period. However, $7 of the overhead is variable with respect to the number of bracelets produced. The customer who is interested in the special bracelet order would like special filigree applied to the bracelets. This filigree would require additional materials costing $6 per bracelet and would also require acquisition of a special tool costing $465 that would have no other use once the special order is completed. This order would have no effect on the company's regular sales and the order could be fulfilled using the company's existing capacity without affecting any other order.

***Required:***

What effect would accepting this order have on the company's net operating income if a special price of $349.95 is offered per bracelet for this order? Should the special order be accepted at this price?

**EXERCISE 10–5 Utilizing a Constrained Resource [LO5]**

Sport Luggage Inc. makes high-end hard-sided luggage for sports equipment. Data concerning three of the company's most popular models appear below.

TAKE TWO

Selling price of Golf Caddy = $330

| | Ski Vault | Golf Caddy | Fishing Quiver |
|---|---|---|---|
| Selling price per unit | $220 | $300 | $175 |
| Variable cost per unit | $60 | $120 | $55 |
| Plastic injection molding machine processing time required to produce one unit | 4 minutes | 5 minutes | 2 minutes |
| Pounds of plastic pellets per unit | 5 pounds | 6 pounds | 5 pounds |

***Required:***

1. The total time available on the plastic injection molding machine is the constraint in the production process. Which product would be the most profitable use of this constraint? Which product would be the least profitable use of this constraint?

2. A severe shortage of plastic pellets has required the company to cut back its production so much that the plastic injection molding machine is no longer the bottleneck. Instead, the constraint is the total available pounds of plastic pellets. Which product would be the most profitable use of this constraint? Which product would be the least profitable use of this constraint?
3. Which product has the largest unit contribution margin? Why wouldn't this product always be the most profitable use of the constrained resource?

**EXERCISE 10–6 Managing a Constrained Resource [LO6]**

Georgian Ambience Ltd. makes fine colonial reproduction furniture. Upholstered furniture is one of its major product lines and the bottleneck on this production line is time in the upholstery shop. Upholstering is a craft that takes years of experience to master and the demand for upholstered furniture far exceeds the company's capacity in the upholstering shop. Information concerning three of the company's upholstered chairs appears below:

| | Gainsborough Armchair | Leather Library Chair | Chippendale Fabric Armchair |
|---|---|---|---|
| Selling price per unit | $1,300 | $1,800 | $1,400 |
| Variable cost per unit | $800 | $1,200 | $1,000 |
| Upholstery shop time required to produce one unit | 8 hours | 12 hours | 5 hours |

***Required:***

1. More time could be made available in the upholstery shop by asking the employees who work in this shop to work overtime. Assuming that this extra time would be used to produce Leather Library Chairs, up to how much should the company be willing to pay per hour to keep the upholstery shop open after normal working hours?
2. A small nearby upholstering company has offered to upholster furniture for Georgian Ambience at a fixed charge of $45 per hour. The management of Georgian Ambience is confident that this upholstering company's work is high quality and their craftsmen should be able to work about as quickly as Georgian Ambience's own craftsmen on the simpler upholstering jobs such as the Chippendale Fabric Armchair. Should management accept this offer? Explain.

**EXERCISE 10–7 Sell or Process Further [LO7]**

TAKE TWO

Solex Company manufactures three products from a common input in a joint processing operation. Joint processing costs up to the split-off point total $100,000 per year. The company allocates these costs to the joint products on the basis of their total sales value at the split-off point. These sales values are as follows: product X, $50,000; product Y, $90,000; and product Z, $60,000.

Each product may be sold at the split-off point or processed further. Additional processing requires no special facilities. The additional processing costs and the sales value after further processing for each product (on an annual basis) are shown below:

Additional processing costs for X = $25,000 and Z = $16,000

| Product | Additional Processing Costs | Sales Value after Further Processing |
|---|---|---|
| X | $35,000 | $80,000 |
| Y | $40,000 | $150,000 |
| Z | $12,000 | $75,000 |

***Required:***

Which product or products should be sold at the split-off point, and which product or products should be processed further? Show computations.

**EXERCISE 10–8 Sell or Process Further [LO7]**

TAKE TWO

Morrell Company produces several products from processing krypton, a rare mineral. Joint processing costs total $30,000 per ton, one-third of which is allocated to the product merifulon. The merifulon produced from a ton of krypton can either be sold at the split-off point for $40,000, or processed further at a cost of $13,000 and then sold for $60,000.

Cost of further processing = $21,000

***Required:***

Should merifulon be processed further or sold at the split-off point?

TAKE TWO

**EXERCISE 10–9 Utilization of a Constrained Resource [LO5]**

Shelby Company produces three products: product X, product Y, and product Z. Data concerning the three products follow (per unit):

Product X direct material cost per unit = $15

| | Product X | Product Y | Product Z |
|---|---|---|---|
| Selling price | $80 | $56 | $70 |
| Variable expenses: | | | |
| Direct materials | 24 | 15 | 9 |
| Labor and overhead | 24 | 27 | 40 |
| Total variable expenses | 48 | 42 | 49 |
| Contribution margin | $32 | $14 | $21 |
| Contribution margin ratio | 40% | 25% | 30% |

Demand for the company's products is very strong, with far more orders each month than the company can produce with the available raw materials. The same material is used in each product. The material costs $3 per pound, with a maximum of 5,000 pounds available each month.

***Required:***

Which orders would you advise the company to accept first, those for product X, for product Y, or for product Z? Which orders second? Third?

TAKE TWO

**EXERCISE 10–10 Dropping or Retaining a Segment [LO2]**

Dexter Products, Inc., manufactures and sells a number of items, including an overnight case. The company has been experiencing losses on the overnight case for some time, as shown on the following contribution format income statement:

Sales = $325,000; Variable expenses are unchanged

**Dexter Products, Inc.**
**Income Statement—Overnight Cases**
**For the Quarter Ended June 30**

| | | |
|---|---|---|
| Sales | | $450,000 |
| Variable expenses: | | |
| Variable manufacturing expenses | $130,000 | |
| Sales commissions | 48,000 | |
| Shipping | 12,000 | |
| Total variable expenses | | 190,000 |
| Contribution margin | | 260,000 |
| Fixed expenses: | | |
| Salary of product-line manager | 21,000 | |
| General factory overhead | 104,000* | |
| Depreciation of equipment (no resale value) | 36,000 | |
| Advertising—traceable | 110,000 | |
| Insurance on inventories | 9,000 | |
| Purchasing department | 50,000† | |
| Total fixed expenses | | 330,000 |
| Net operating loss | | $ (70,000) |

*Allocated on the basis of machine-hours.
†Allocated on the basis of sales dollars.

Discontinuing the overnight cases would not affect the company's sales of its other product lines, its total general factory overhead, or its total purchasing department expenses.

***Required:***

Would you recommend that the company discontinue the manufacture and sale of overnight cases? Support your answer with appropriate computations.

**EXERCISE 10–11 Identification of Relevant Costs [LO1]**

Samantha Ringer purchased a used automobile for $10,000 at the beginning of last year and incurred the following operating costs:

| | |
|---|---|
| Depreciation ($10,000 ÷ 5 years)..... | $2,000 |
| Insurance.......... | $960 |
| Garage rent.......... | $480 |
| Automobile tax and license.......... | $60 |
| Variable operating cost.......... | 8¢ per mile |

TAKE TWO

Purchase price of used automobile = $12,000

The variable operating costs consist of gasoline, oil, tires, maintenance, and repairs. Samantha estimates that at her current rate of usage the car will have zero resale value in five years, so the annual straight-line depreciation is $2,000. The car is kept in a garage for a monthly fee.

***Required:***

1. Samantha drove the car 10,000 miles last year. Compute the average cost per mile of owning and operating the car.
2. Samantha is unsure about whether she should use her own car or rent a car to go on an extended cross-country trip for two weeks during spring break. What costs above are relevant in this decision? Explain.
3. Samantha is thinking about buying an expensive sports car to replace the car she bought last year. She would drive the same number of miles regardless of which car she owns and would rent the same parking space. The sports car's variable operating costs would be roughly the same as the variable operating costs of her old car. However, her insurance and automobile tax and license costs would go up. What costs are relevant in estimating the incremental cost of owning the more expensive car? Explain.

**EXERCISE 10–12 Make or Buy a Component [LO3]**

Royal Company manufactures 20,000 units of part R-3 each year for use on its production line. At this level of activity, the cost per unit for part R-3 is:

TAKE TWO

Annual rental = $80,000

| | |
|---|---|
| Direct materials.......... | $ 4.80 |
| Direct labor.......... | 7.00 |
| Variable manufacturing overhead.......... | 3.20 |
| Fixed manufacturing overhead.......... | 10.00 |
| Total cost per part.......... | $25.00 |

An outside supplier has offered to sell 20,000 units of part R-3 each year to Royal Company for $23.50 per part. If Royal Company accepts this offer, the facilities now being used to manufacture part R-3 could be rented to another company at an annual rental of $150,000. However, Royal Company has determined that $6 of the fixed manufacturing overhead being applied to part R-3 would continue even if part R-3 were purchased from the outside supplier.

***Required:***

Prepare computations showing how much profits will increase or decrease if the outside supplier's offer is accepted.

**EXERCISE 10–13 Utilization of a Constrained Resource [LO5, LO6]**

Banner Company produces three products: A, B, and C. The selling price, variable costs, and contribution margin for one unit of each product follow:

TAKE TWO

Direct labor cost per unit for product C = $12

| | Product | | |
|---|---|---|---|
| | A | B | C |
| Selling price.......... | $60 | $90 | $80 |
| Variable costs: | | | |
| Direct materials.......... | 27 | 14 | 40 |
| Direct labor.......... | 12 | 32 | 16 |
| Variable manufacturing overhead.......... | 3 | 8 | 4 |
| Total variable cost.......... | 42 | 54 | 60 |
| Contribution margin.......... | $18 | $36 | $20 |
| Contribution margin ratio.......... | 30% | 40% | 25% |

Due to a strike in the plant of one of its competitors, demand for the company's products far exceeds its capacity to produce. Management is trying to determine which product(s) to concentrate on next week in filling its backlog of orders. The direct labor rate is $8 per hour, and only 3,000 hours of labor time are available each week.

***Required:***

1. Compute the amount of contribution margin that will be obtained per hour of labor time spent on each product.
2. Which orders would you recommend that the company work on next week—the orders for product A, product B, or product C? Show computations.
3. By paying overtime wages, more than 3,000 hours of direct labor time can be made available next week. Up to how much should the company be willing to pay per hour in overtime wages as long as there is unfilled demand for the three products? Explain.

**EXERCISE 10–14 Special Order [LO4]**

Glade Company produces a single product. The costs of producing and selling a single unit of this product at the company's current activity level of 8,000 units per month are:

| | |
|---|---|
| Direct materials | $2.50 |
| Direct labor | $3.00 |
| Variable manufacturing overhead | $0.50 |
| Fixed manufacturing overhead | $4.25 |
| Variable selling and administrative expenses | $1.50 |
| Fixed selling and administrative expenses | $2.00 |

The normal selling price is $15 per unit. The company's capacity is 10,000 units per month. An order has been received from a potential customer overseas for 2,000 units at a price of $12.00 per unit. This order would not affect regular sales.

***Required:***

1. If the order is accepted, by how much will monthly profits increase or decrease? (The order would not change the company's total fixed costs.)
2. Assume the company has 500 units of this product left over from last year that are inferior to the current model. The units must be sold through regular channels at reduced prices. What unit cost is relevant for establishing a minimum selling price for these units? Explain.

**EXERCISE 10–15 Dropping or Retaining a Segment [LO2]**

Boyle's Home Center, a retailing company, has two departments, Bath and Kitchen. The company's most recent monthly contribution format income statement follows:

| | | Department | |
|---|---|---|---|
| | Total | Bath | Kitchen |
| Sales | $5,000,000 | $1,000,000 | $4,000,000 |
| Variable expenses | 1,900,000 | 300,000 | 1,600,000 |
| Contribution margin | 3,100,000 | 700,000 | 2,400,000 |
| Fixed expenses | 2,700,000 | 900,000 | 1,800,000 |
| Net operating income (loss) | $ 400,000 | $ (200,000) | $ 600,000 |

A study indicates that $370,000 of the fixed expenses being charged to the Bath Department are sunk costs or allocated costs that will continue even if the Bath Department is dropped. In addition, the elimination of the Bath Department would result in a 10% decrease in the sales of the Kitchen Department.

***Required:***

If the Bath Department is dropped, what will be the effect on the net operating income of the company as a whole?

### EXERCISE 10–16 Make or Buy a Component [LO3]

Supplier's price = $8.00

For many years, Diehl Company has produced a small electrical part that it uses in the production of its standard line of diesel tractors. The company's unit product cost for the part, based on a production level of 60,000 parts per year, is as follows:

| | Per Part | Total |
|---|---|---|
| Direct materials | $ 4.00 | |
| Direct labor | 2.75 | |
| Variable manufacturing overhead | 0.50 | |
| Fixed manufacturing overhead, traceable | 3.00 | $180,000 |
| Fixed manufacturing overhead, common (allocated on the basis of labor-hours) | 2.25 | $135,000 |
| Unit product cost | $12.50 | |

An outside supplier has offered to supply the electrical parts to the Diehl Company for only $10.00 per part. One-third of the traceable fixed manufacturing cost is supervisory salaries and other costs that can be eliminated if the parts are purchased. The other two-thirds of the traceable fixed manufacturing costs consist of depreciation of special equipment that has no resale value. Economic depreciation on this equipment is due to obsolescence rather than wear and tear. The decision to buy the parts from the outside supplier would have no effect on the common fixed costs of the company, and the space being used to produce the parts would otherwise be idle.

***Required:***

Prepare computations showing how much profits would increase or decrease as a result of purchasing the parts from the outside supplier rather than making them inside the company.

### EXERCISE 10–17 Identification of Relevant Costs [LO1]

Steve has just returned from salmon fishing. He was lucky on this trip and brought home two salmon. Steve's wife, Wendy, disapproves of fishing, and to discourage Steve from further fishing trips, she has presented him with the following cost data. The cost per fishing trip is based on an average of 10 fishing trips per year.

| | |
|---|---|
| Cost per fishing trip: | |
| Depreciation on fishing boat* (annual depreciation of $1,500 ÷ 10 trips) | $150 |
| Boat storage fees (annual rental of $1,200 ÷ 10 trips) | 120 |
| Expenditures on fishing gear, except for snagged lures (annual expenditures of $200 ÷ 10 trips) | 20 |
| Snagged fishing lures | 7 |
| Fishing license (yearly license of $40 ÷ 10 trips) | 4 |
| Fuel and upkeep on boat per trip | 25 |
| Junk food consumed during trip | 8 |
| Total cost per fishing trip | $334 |
| Cost per salmon ($334 ÷ 2 salmon) | $167 |

*The original cost of the boat was $15,000. It has an estimated useful life of 10 years, after which it will have no resale value. The boat does not wear out through use, but it does become less desirable for resale as it becomes older.

***Required:***

1. Assuming that the salmon fishing trip Steve has just completed is typical, what costs are relevant to a decision as to whether he should go on another trip this year?
2. Suppose that on Steve's next fishing trip he gets lucky and catches three salmon in the amount of time it took him to catch two salmon on his last trip. How much would the third salmon have cost him to catch? Explain.
3. Discuss the costs that are relevant in a decision of whether Steve should give up fishing.

## PROBLEMS

Alternate problem set is available on the text website and in *Connect® Accounting.*

**All applicable problems are available with McGraw-Hill's *Connect® Accounting*.**

### PROBLEM 10–18A Dropping or Retaining a Tour [LO2]

Blueline Tours, Inc., operates tours throughout the United States. A study has indicated that some of the tours are not profitable, and consideration is being given to dropping these tours to improve the company's overall operating performance.

One such tour is a two-day Historic Mansions bus tour conducted in the southern states. An income statement from a typical Historic Mansions tour is given below:

CHECK FIGURE
(1) Decrease in profits: $450

| | | |
|---|---|---|
| Ticket revenue (100 seat capacity × 40% occupancy × $75 ticket price per person) | $3,000 | 100% |
| Variable expenses ($22.50 per person) | 900 | 30 |
| Contribution margin | 2,100 | 70% |
| Tour expenses: | | |
| Tour promotion | $600 | |
| Salary of bus driver | 350 | |
| Fee, tour guide | 700 | |
| Fuel for bus | 125 | |
| Depreciation of bus | 450 | |
| Liability insurance, bus | 200 | |
| Overnight parking fee, bus | 50 | |
| Room and meals, bus driver and tour guide | 175 | |
| Bus maintenance and preparation | 300 | |
| Total tour expenses | 2,950 | |
| Net operating loss | $ (850) | |

The following additional information is available about the tour:

a. Bus drivers are paid fixed annual salaries; tour guides are paid for each tour conducted.
b. The "Bus maintenance and preparation" cost is an allocation of the salaries of mechanics and other service personnel who are responsible for keeping the company's fleet of buses in good operating condition.
c. Depreciation of buses is due to obsolescence. Depreciation due to wear and tear is negligible.
d. Liability insurance premiums are based on the number of buses in the company's fleet.
e. Dropping the Historic Mansions bus tour would not allow Blueline Tours to reduce the number of buses in its fleet, the number of bus drivers on the payroll, or the size of the maintenance and preparation staff.

***Required:***

1. Prepare an analysis showing what the impact will be on the company's profits if this tour is discontinued.
2. The company's tour director has been criticized because only about 50% of the seats on Blueline's tours are being filled as compared to an industry average of 60%. The tour director has explained that Blueline's average seat occupancy could be improved considerably by eliminating about 10% of its tours, but that doing so would reduce profits. Explain how this could happen.

### PROBLEM 10–19A Sell or Process Further [LO7]

(Prepared from a situation suggested by Professor John W. Hardy.) Abilene Meat Processing Corporation is a major processor of beef and other meat products. The company has a large amount of T-bone steak on hand, and it is trying to decide whether to sell the T-bone steaks as is or to process them further into filet mignon and New York cut steaks.

Management believes that a 1-pound T-bone steak would yield the following profit:

CHECK FIGURE
(1) $0.35 per pound profit from further processing

| | |
|---|---|
| Wholesale selling price ($2.25 per pound) | $2.25 |
| Less joint costs incurred up to the split-off point where T-bone steak can be identified as a separate product | 1.70 |
| Profit per pound | $0.55 |

As previously mentioned, instead of being sold as is, the T-bone steaks could be further processed into filet mignon and New York cut steaks. Cutting one side of a T-bone steak provides the filet mignon, and cutting the other side provides the New York cut. One 16-ounce T-bone steak cut in this way will yield one 6-ounce filet mignon and one 8-ounce New York cut; the remaining ounces are waste. The cost of processing the T-bone steaks into these cuts is $0.20 per pound. The filet mignon can be sold for $3.60 per pound, and the New York cut can be sold wholesale for $2.90 per pound.

***Required:***

1. Determine the profit per pound from processing the T-bone steaks further into filet mignon and New York cut steaks.
2. Would you recommend that the T-bone steaks be sold as is or processed further? Why?

**PROBLEM 10–20A Shutting Down or Continuing to Operate a Plant [LO2]**

(Note: This type of decision is similar to dropping a product line.)

Hallas Company manufactures a fast-bonding glue in its Northwest plant. The company normally produces and sells 40,000 gallons of the glue each month. This glue, which is known as MJ-7, is used in the wood industry to manufacture plywood. The selling price of MJ-7 is $35 per gallon, variable costs are $21 per gallon, fixed manufacturing overhead costs in the plant total $230,000 per month, and the fixed selling costs total $310,000 per month.

CHECK FIGURE
(1) $140,000 disadvantage to close

Strikes in the mills that purchase the bulk of the MJ-7 glue have caused Hallas Company's sales to temporarily drop to only 11,000 gallons per month. Hallas Company's management estimates that the strikes will last for two months, after which sales of MJ-7 should return to normal. Due to the current low level of sales, Hallas Company's management is thinking about closing down the Northwest plant during the strike.

If Hallas Company does close down the Northwest plant, fixed manufacturing overhead costs can be reduced by $60,000 per month and fixed selling costs can be reduced by 10%. Start-up costs at the end of the shutdown period would total $14,000. Because Hallas Company uses Lean Production methods, no inventories are on hand.

***Required:***

1. Assuming that the strikes continue for two months, would you recommend that Hallas Company close the Northwest plant? Explain. Show computations to support your answer.
2. At what level of sales (in gallons) for the two-month period should Hallas Company be indifferent between closing the plant or keeping it open? Show computations. (Hint: This is a type of break-even analysis, except that the fixed cost portion of your break-even computation should include only those fixed costs that are relevant [i.e., avoidable] over the two-month period.)

**PROBLEM 10–21A Accept or Reject a Special Order [LO4]**

Pietarsaari Oy, a Finnish company, produces cross-country ski poles that it sells for €32 a pair. (The Finnish unit of currency, the euro, is denoted by €.) Operating at capacity, the company can produce 50,000 pairs of ski poles a year. Costs associated with this level of production and sales are given below:

CHECK FIGURE
(1) Increased net operating income: €90,000

| | Per Pair | Total |
|---|---|---|
| Direct materials | €12 | € 600,000 |
| Direct labor | 3 | 150,000 |
| Variable manufacturing overhead | 1 | 50,000 |
| Fixed manufacturing overhead | 5 | 250,000 |
| Variable selling expenses | 2 | 100,000 |
| Fixed selling expenses | 4 | 200,000 |
| Total cost | €27 | €1,350,000 |

***Required:***

1. The Finnish army would like to make a one-time-only purchase of 10,000 pairs of ski poles for its mountain troops. The army would pay a fixed fee of €4 per pair, and in addition it would reimburse the Pietarsaari Oy company for its unit manufacturing costs (both fixed and variable). Due to a recession, the company would otherwise produce and sell only 40,000 pairs of ski poles this year. (Total fixed manufacturing overhead cost would be the same whether 40,000 pairs or 50,000 pairs of ski poles were produced.) The company would not incur its usual variable selling expenses with this special order.

    If the Pietarsaari Oy company accepts the army's offer, by how much would net operating income increase or decrease from what it would be if only 40,000 pairs of ski poles were produced and sold during the year?
2. Assume the same situation as described in (1) above, except that the company is already operating at capacity and could sell 50,000 pairs of ski poles through regular channels. Thus, accepting the army's offer would require giving up sales of 10,000 pairs at the normal price of €32 a pair. If the army's offer is accepted, by how much will net operating income increase or decrease from what it would be if the 10,000 pairs were sold through regular channels?

**PROBLEM 10–22A Make or Buy Decision [LO3]**

Bronson Company manufactures a variety of ballpoint pens. The company has just received an offer from an outside supplier to provide the ink cartridge for the company's Zippo pen line, at a price of $0.48 per dozen cartridges. The company is interested in this offer because its own production of cartridges is at capacity.

CHECK FIGURE
(2) Maximum price: $0.43 per box

Bronson Company estimates that if the supplier's offer were accepted, the direct labor and variable manufacturing overhead costs of the Zippo pen line would be reduced by 10% and the direct materials cost would be reduced by 20%.

Under present operations, Bronson Company manufactures all of its own pens from start to finish. The Zippo pens are sold through wholesalers at $4 per box. Each box contains one dozen pens. Fixed manufacturing overhead costs charged to the Zippo pen line total $50,000 each year. (The same equipment and facilities are used to produce several pen lines.) The present cost of producing one dozen Zippo pens (one box) is given below:

| | |
|---|---|
| Direct materials | $ 1.50 |
| Direct labor | 1.00 |
| Manufacturing overhead | 0.80* |
| Total cost | $ 3.30 |

*Includes both variable and fixed manufacturing overhead, based on production of 100,000 boxes of pens each year.

***Required:***

1. Should Bronson Company accept the outside supplier's offer? Show computations.
2. What is the maximum price that Bronson Company should be willing to pay the outside supplier per dozen cartridges? Explain.
3. Due to the bankruptcy of a competitor, Bronson Company expects to sell 150,000 boxes of Zippo pens next year. As previously stated, the company presently has enough capacity to produce the cartridges for only 100,000 boxes of Zippo pens annually. By incurring $30,000 in added fixed cost each year, the company could expand its production of cartridges to satisfy the anticipated demand for Zippo pens. The variable cost per unit to produce the additional cartridges would be the same as at present. Under these circumstances, how many boxes of cartridges should be purchased from the outside supplier and how many should be made by Bronson? Show computations to support your answer.
4. What qualitative factors should Bronson Company consider in determining whether it should make or buy the ink cartridges?

(CMA, adapted)

**PROBLEM 10–23A Close or Retain a Store [LO2]**

Thrifty Markets, Inc., operates three stores in a large metropolitan area. The company's segmented absorption costing income statement for the last quarter follows:

CHECK FIGURE
(1) Decrease in net operating income if the downtown store is closed: $9,800

**Thrifty Markets, Inc.**
**Income Statement**
**For the Quarter Ended March 31**

| | Total | Uptown Store | Downtown Store | Westpark Store |
|---|---|---|---|---|
| Sales | $2,500,000 | $900,000 | $600,000 | $1,000,000 |
| Cost of goods sold | 1,450,000 | 513,000 | 372,000 | 565,000 |
| Gross margin | 1,050,000 | 387,000 | 228,000 | 435,000 |
| Selling and administrative expenses: | | | | |
| Selling expenses: | | | | |
| Direct advertising | 118,500 | 40,000 | 36,000 | 42,500 |
| General advertising* | 20,000 | 7,200 | 4,800 | 8,000 |
| Sales salaries | 157,000 | 52,000 | 45,000 | 60,000 |
| Delivery salaries | 30,000 | 10,000 | 10,000 | 10,000 |
| Store rent | 215,000 | 70,000 | 65,000 | 80,000 |
| Depreciation of store fixtures | 46,950 | 18,300 | 8,800 | 19,850 |
| Depreciation of delivery equipment | 27,000 | 9,000 | 9,000 | 9,000 |
| Total selling expenses | 614,450 | 206,500 | 178,600 | 229,350 |
| Administrative expenses: | | | | |
| Store management salaries | 63,000 | 20,000 | 18,000 | 25,000 |
| General office salaries* | 50,000 | 18,000 | 12,000 | 20,000 |
| Utilities | 89,800 | 31,000 | 27,200 | 31,600 |
| Insurance on fixtures and inventory | 25,500 | 8,000 | 9,000 | 8,500 |
| Employment taxes | 36,000 | 12,000 | 10,200 | 13,800 |
| General office expenses—other* | 25,000 | 9,000 | 6,000 | 10,000 |
| Total administrative expenses | 289,300 | 98,000 | 82,400 | 108,900 |
| Total operating expenses | 903,750 | 304,500 | 261,000 | 338,250 |
| Net operating income (loss) | $ 146,250 | $ 82,500 | $ (33,000) | $ 96,750 |

*Allocated on the basis of sales dollars.

Management is very concerned about the Downtown Store's inability to show a profit, and consideration is being given to closing the store. The company has asked you to make a recommendation as to what course of action should be taken. The following additional information is available about the store:

a. The manager of the store has been with the company for many years; he would be retained and transferred to another position in the company if the store were closed. His salary is $6,000 per month, or $18,000 per quarter. If the store were not closed, a new employee would be hired to fill the other position at a salary of $5,000 per month.
b. The lease on the building housing the Downtown Store can be broken with no penalty.
c. The fixtures being used in the Downtown Store would be transferred to the other two stores if the Downtown Store were closed.
d. The company's employment taxes are 12% of salaries.
e. A single delivery crew serves all three stores. One delivery person could be discharged if the Downtown Store were closed; this person's salary amounts to $7,000 per quarter. The delivery equipment would be distributed to the other stores. The equipment does not wear out through use, but it does eventually become obsolete.
f. One-third of the Downtown Store's insurance relates to its fixtures.
g. The general office salaries and other expenses relate to the general management of Thrifty Markets, Inc. The employee in the general office who is responsible for the Downtown Store would be discharged if the store were closed. This employee's compensation is $8,000 per quarter.

***Required:***

1. Prepare a schedule showing the change in revenues and expenses and the impact on the overall company net operating income that would result if the Downtown Store were closed.
2. Based on your computations in (1) above, what recommendation would you make to the management of Thrifty Markets, Inc.?
3. Assume that if the Downtown Store were closed, sales in the Uptown Store would increase by $200,000 per quarter due to loyal customers shifting their buying to the Uptown Store. The Uptown Store has ample capacity to handle the increased sales, and its gross margin is 43% of sales. What effect would these factors have on your recommendation concerning the Downtown Store? Show computations.

**PROBLEM 10–24A Relevant Cost Analysis in a Variety of Situations [LO2, LO3, LO4]**

Barker Company has a single product called a Zet. The company normally produces and sells 80,000 Zets each year at a selling price of $40 per unit. The company's unit costs at this level of activity are given below:

CHECK FIGURE
(2) Break-even price: $24.50

| | | |
|---|---|---|
| Direct materials | $ 9.50 | |
| Direct labor | 10.00 | |
| Variable manufacturing overhead | 2.80 | |
| Fixed manufacturing overhead | 5.00 | ($400,000 total) |
| Variable selling expenses | 1.70 | |
| Fixed selling expenses | 4.50 | ($360,000 total) |
| Total cost per unit | $33.50 | |

A number of questions relating to the production and sale of Zets are given below. Each question is independent.

***Required:***

1. Assume that Barker Company has sufficient capacity to produce 100,000 Zets each year without any increase in fixed manufacturing overhead costs. The company could increase sales by 25% above the present 80,000 units each year if it were willing to increase the fixed selling expenses by $150,000. Would the increased fixed selling expenses be justified?
2. Assume again that Barker Company has sufficient capacity to produce 100,000 Zets each year. The company has an opportunity to sell 20,000 units in an overseas market. Import duties, foreign permits, and other special costs associated with the order would total $14,000. The only selling costs that would be associated with the order would be $1.50 per unit shipping cost. Compute the per unit break-even price on this order.
3. One of the materials used in the production of Zets is obtained from a foreign supplier. Civil unrest in the supplier's country has caused a cutoff in material shipments that is expected to last for three months. Barker Company has enough material on hand to operate at 25% of normal levels for the three-month period. As an alternative, the company could close the plant down entirely for the three months. Closing the plant would reduce fixed manufacturing overhead costs by 40% during the three-month period and the fixed selling expenses would continue at two-thirds of their normal level. What would be the impact on profits of closing the plant for the three-month period?
4. The company has 500 Zets on hand that were produced last month and have small blemishes. Due to the blemishes, it will be impossible to sell these units at the normal price. If the company wishes to sell them through regular distribution channels, what unit cost figure is relevant for setting a minimum selling price? Explain.
5. An outside manufacturer has offered to produce Zets and ship them directly to Barker's customers. If Barker Company accepts this offer, the facilities that it uses to produce Zets would be idle; however, fixed manufacturing overhead costs would continue at 30%. Because the outside manufacturer would pay for all shipping costs, the variable selling expenses would be reduced by 60%. Compute the unit cost that is relevant for comparison to the price quoted by the outside manufacturer.

**PROBLEM 10–25A Make or Buy Analysis [LO3]**

"That old equipment for producing subassemblies is worn out," said Paul Taylor, president of Timkin Company. "We need to make a decision quickly." The company is trying to decide whether it should rent new equipment and continue to make its subassemblies internally, or whether it should discontinue production of its subassemblies and purchase them from an outside supplier. The alternatives are as follows:

CHECK FIGURE
(1) $18,000 advantage to buy

*Alternative 1:* Rent new equipment for producing the subassemblies for $60,000 per year.
*Alternative 2:* Purchase subassemblies from an outside supplier for $8 each.

Timkin Company's current costs per unit of producing the subassemblies internally (with the old equipment) are given below. These costs are based on a current activity level of 40,000 subassemblies per year:

| | |
|---|---|
| Direct materials | $ 2.75 |
| Direct labor | 4.00 |
| Variable overhead | 0.60 |
| Fixed overhead ($0.75 supervision, $0.90 depreciation, and $2 general company overhead) | 3.65 |
| Total cost per unit | $11.00 |

The new equipment would be more efficient and, according to the manufacturer, would reduce direct labor costs and variable overhead costs by 25%. Supervision cost ($30,000 per year) and direct materials cost per unit would not be affected by the new equipment. The new equipment's capacity would be 60,000 subassemblies per year.

The total general company overhead would be unaffected by this decision.

***Required:***

1. The president is unsure what the company should do and would like an analysis showing the unit costs and total costs for each of the two alternatives given above. Assume that 40,000 subassemblies are needed each year. Which course of action would you recommend to the president?
2. Would your recommendation in (1) above be the same if the company's needs were (*a*) 50,000 subassemblies per year, or (*b*) 60,000 subassemblies per year?
3. What other factors would you recommend that the company consider before making a decision?

**PROBLEM 10–26A Dropping or Retaining a Product [LO2]**

Tracey Douglas is the owner and managing director of Heritage Garden Furniture, Ltd., a South African company that makes museum-quality reproductions of antique outdoor furniture. Ms. Douglas would like advice concerning the financial implications of eliminating the model C3 lawnchair. These lawnchairs have been among the company's best-selling products, but they seem to be unprofitable.

A condensed absorption costing income statement for the company and for the model C3 lawnchair for the quarter ended June 30 follows:

CHECK FIGURE
(1) Total avoidable cost: R252,000

| | All Products | Model C3 Lawnchair |
|---|---|---|
| Sales | R2,900,000 | R300,000 |
| Cost of goods sold: | | |
| Direct materials | 759,000 | 122,000 |
| Direct labor | 680,000 | 72,000 |
| Fringe benefits (20% of direct labor) | 136,000 | 14,400 |
| Variable manufacturing overhead | 28,000 | 3,600 |
| Building rent and maintenance | 30,000 | 4,000 |
| Depreciation | 75,000 | 19,100 |
| Total cost of goods sold | 1,708,000 | 235,100 |
| Gross margin | 1,192,000 | 64,900 |
| Selling and administrative expenses: | | |
| Product managers' salaries | 75,000 | 10,000 |
| Sales commissions (5% of sales) | 145,000 | 15,000 |
| Fringe benefits (20% of salaries and commissions) | 44,000 | 5,000 |
| Shipping | 120,000 | 10,000 |
| General administrative expenses | 464,000 | 48,000 |
| Total selling and administrative expenses | 848,000 | 88,000 |
| Net operating income (loss) | R 344,000 | R (23,100) |

The currency in South Africa is the rand, denoted here by R.

The following additional data have been supplied by the company:

a. Direct labor is a variable cost.
b. All of the company's products are manufactured in the same facility and use the same equipment. Building rent and maintenance and depreciation are allocated to products using various bases. The equipment does not wear out through use; it eventually becomes obsolete.
c. There is ample capacity to fill all orders.
d. Dropping the model C3 lawnchair would have no effect on sales of other product lines.
e. Work in process and finished goods inventories are insignificant.
f. Shipping costs are traced directly to products.
g. General administrative expenses are allocated to products on the basis of sales. There would be no effect on the total general administrative expenses if the model C3 lawnchair were dropped.
h. If the model C3 lawnchair were dropped, the product manager would be laid off.

***Required:***

Given the current level of sales, would you recommend that the model C3 lawnchair be dropped? Prepare appropriate computations to support your answer.

**PROBLEM 10–27A Utilization of a Constrained Resource [LO5, LO6]**

The Brandilyn Toy Company manufactures a line of dolls and a doll dress sewing kit. Demand for the dolls is increasing, and management requests assistance from you in determining the best sales and production mix for the coming year. The company has provided the following data:

CHECK FIGURE
(2) Hours required: 161,900 DLHs

| Product | Demand Next Year (units) | Selling Price per Unit | Direct Materials | Direct Labor |
|---|---|---|---|---|
| Marcy ........... | 26,000 | $35.00 | $3.50 | $4.80 |
| Tina .............. | 42,000 | $24.00 | $2.30 | $3.00 |
| Cari................ | 40,000 | $22.00 | $4.50 | $8.40 |
| Lenny ........... | 46,000 | $18.00 | $3.10 | $6.00 |
| Sewing kit...... | 450,000 | $14.00 | $1.50 | $2.40 |

The following additional information is available:

a. The company's plant has a capacity of 150,000 direct labor-hours per year on a single-shift basis. The company's present employees and equipment can produce all five products.
b. The direct labor rate of $12.00 per hour is expected to remain unchanged during the coming year.
c. Fixed costs total $356,000 per year. Variable overhead costs are $4.00 per direct labor-hour.
d. All of the company's nonmanufacturing costs are fixed.
e. The company's finished goods inventory is negligible and can be ignored.

***Required:***

1. Determine the contribution margin per direct labor-hour expended on each product.
2. Prepare a schedule showing the total direct labor-hours that will be required to produce the units estimated to be sold during the coming year.
3. Examine the data you have computed in (1) and (2) above. How would you allocate the 150,000 direct labor-hours of capacity to Brandilyn Toy Company's various products?
4. What is the highest price, in terms of a rate per hour, that Brandilyn Toy Company should be willing to pay for additional capacity (that is, for added direct labor time)?
5. Identify ways in which the company might be able to obtain additional output so that it would not have to leave some demand for its products unsatisfied.

(CMA, adapted)

**PROBLEM 10–28A Sell or Process Further [LO7]**

The Heather Honey Company purchases honeycombs from beekeepers for $2.00 a pound. The company produces two main products from the honeycombs—honey and beeswax. Honey is drained from the honeycombs, and then the honeycombs are melted down to form cubes of beeswax. The beeswax is sold for $1.50 a pound.

The honey can be sold in raw form for $3.00 a pound. However, some of the raw honey is used by the company to make honey drop candies. The candies are packed in a decorative container and are sold in gift and specialty shops. A container of honey drop candies sells for $4.40.

Each container of honey drop candies contains three quarters of a pound of honey. The other variable costs associated with making the candies are as follows:

CHECK FIGURE
(1) Incremental contribution margin: $0.98 per container

| | |
|---|---|
| Decorative container | $0.40 |
| Other ingredients | 0.25 |
| Direct labor | 0.20 |
| Variable manufacturing overhead | 0.10 |
| Total variable manufacturing cost | $0.95 |

The monthly fixed manufacturing overhead costs associated with making the candies follow:

| | |
|---|---|
| Master candy maker's salary | $3,880 |
| Depreciation of candy making equipment | 400 |
| Total fixed manufacturing cost | $4,280 |

The master candy maker has no duties other than to oversee production of the honey drop candies. The candy making equipment is special-purpose equipment that was constructed specifically to make this particular candy. The equipment has no resale value and does not wear out through use.

A salesperson is paid $2,000 per month plus a commission of 5% of sales to market the honey drop candies.

The company had enjoyed robust sales of the candies for several years, but the recent entrance of a competing product into the marketplace has depressed sales of the candies. The management of the company is now wondering whether it would be more profitable to sell all of the honey rather than converting some of it into candies.

***Required:***

1. What is the incremental contribution margin per container from further processing the honey into candies?
2. What is the minimum number of containers of candy that must be sold each month to justify the continued processing of honey into candies? Explain. Show all computations.

(CMA, adapted)

# BUILDING YOUR SKILLS

## CASE [LO1, LO3, LO5]

Storage Systems, Inc., sells a wide range of drums, bins, boxes, and other containers that are used in the chemical industry. One of the company's products is a heavy-duty corrosion-resistant metal drum, called the XSX drum, used to store toxic wastes. Production is constrained by the capacity of an automated welding machine that is used to make precision welds. A total of 2,000 hours of welding time are available annually on the machine. Because each drum requires 0.8 hours of welding time, annual production is limited to 2,500 drums. At present, the welding machine is used exclusively to make the XSX drums. The accounting department has provided the following financial data concerning the XSX drums:

| | XSX Drums | |
|---|---|---|
| Selling price per drum | | $154.00 |
| Cost per drum: | | |
| Direct materials | $44.50 | |
| Direct labor ($18 per hour) | 4.50 | |
| Manufacturing overhead | 3.15 | |
| Selling and administrative expense | 15.40 | 67.55 |
| Margin per drum | | $ 86.45 |

Management believes 3,000 XSX drums could be sold each year if the company had sufficient manufacturing capacity. As an alternative to adding another welding machine, management has looked into the possibility of buying additional drums from an outside supplier. Metal Products, Inc., a supplier of quality products, would be able to provide up to 1,800 XSX-type drums per year at a price of $120 per drum, which Storage Systems would resell to its customers at its normal selling price after appropriate relabeling.

Jasmine Morita, Storage Systems' production manager, has suggested that the company could make better use of the welding machine by manufacturing premium mountain bike frames, which would require only 0.2 hours of welding time per frame. Jasmine believes that Storage Systems could sell up to 3,500 mountain bike frames per year to mountain bike manufacturers at a price of $65 per frame. The accounting department has provided the following data concerning the proposed new product:

| Mountain Bike Frames | | |
|---|---|---|
| Selling price per frame | | $65.00 |
| Cost per frame: | | |
| Direct materials | $17.50 | |
| Direct labor ($18 per hour) | 22.50 | |
| Manufacturing overhead | 15.75 | |
| Selling and administrative expense | 6.50 | 62.25 |
| Margin per frame | | $ 2.75 |

The mountain bike frames could be produced with existing equipment and personnel. Manufacturing overhead is allocated to products on the basis of direct labor-hours. Most of the manufacturing overhead consists of fixed common costs such as rent on the factory building, but some of it is variable. The variable manufacturing overhead has been estimated at $1.05 per XSX drum and $0.60 per mountain bike frame. The variable manufacturing overhead cost would not be incurred on drums acquired from the outside supplier.

Selling and administrative expenses are allocated to products on the basis of revenues. Almost all of the selling and administrative expenses are fixed common costs, but it has been estimated that variable selling and administrative expenses amount to $0.85 per XSX drum and would be $0.40 per mountain bike frame. The variable selling and administrative expenses of $0.85 per drum would be incurred when drums acquired from the outside supplier are sold to the company's customers.

All of the company's employees—direct and indirect—are paid for full 40-hour workweeks and the company has a policy of laying off workers only in major recessions.

***Required:***

1. Given the margins of the two products as indicated in the reports submitted by the accounting department, does it make any sense to even consider producing the mountain bike frames? Explain.
2. Compute the contribution margin per unit for:
   *a.* Purchased XSX drums.
   *b.* Manufactured XSX drums.
   *c.* Manufactured mountain bike frames.
3. Determine the number of XSX drums (if any) that should be purchased and the number of XSX drums and/or mountain bike frames (if any) that should be manufactured. What is the improvement in net income that would result from this plan over current operations?

As soon as your analysis was shown to the top management team at Storage Systems, several managers got into an argument concerning how direct labor costs should be treated when making this decision. One manager argued that direct labor is always treated as a variable cost in textbooks and in practice and has always been considered a variable cost at Storage Systems. After all, "direct" means you can directly trace the cost to products. If direct labor is not a variable cost, what is? Another manager argued just as strenuously that direct labor should be considered a fixed cost at Storage Systems. No one had been laid off in over a decade, and for all practical purposes, everyone at the plant is on a monthly salary. Everyone classified as direct labor works a regular 40-hour workweek and overtime has not been necessary since the company adopted Lean Production techniques. Whether the welding machine is used to make drums or frames, the total payroll would be exactly the same. There is enough slack, in the form of idle time, to accommodate any increase in total direct labor time that the mountain bike frames would require.

4. Redo requirements (2) and (3) above, making the opposite assumption about direct labor from the one you originally made. In other words, if you treated direct labor as a variable cost, redo the analysis

treating it as a fixed cost. If you treated direct labor as a fixed cost, redo the analysis treating it as a variable cost.

5. What do you think is the correct way to treat direct labor in this situation—as a variable cost or as a fixed cost? Explain.

## ETHICS CHALLENGE [LO2]

Marvin Braun had just been appointed vice president of the Great Basin Region of the Financial Services Corporation (FSC). The company provides check processing services for small banks. The banks send checks presented for deposit or payment to FSC, which then records the data on each check in a computerized database. FSC sends the data electronically to the nearest Federal Reserve Bank check-clearing center where the appropriate transfers of funds are made between banks. The Great Basin Region consists of three check processing centers in Eastern Idaho—Pocatello, Idaho Falls, and Ashton. Prior to his promotion to vice president, Mr. Braun had been manager of a check processing center in Indiana.

Immediately upon assuming his new position, Mr. Braun requested a complete financial report for the just-ended fiscal year from the region's controller, Lance Whiting. Mr. Braun specified that the financial report should follow the standardized format required by corporate headquarters for all regional performance reports. That report appears below:

**Financial Performance**
**Great Basin Region**

| | | Check Processing Centers | | |
|---|---|---|---|---|
| | **Total** | **Pocatello** | **Idaho Falls** | **Ashton** |
| Revenues | $20,000,000 | $7,000,000 | $8,000,000 | $5,000,000 |
| Operating expenses: | | | | |
| Direct labor | 12,200,000 | 4,400,000 | 4,700,000 | 3,100,000 |
| Variable overhead | 400,000 | 150,000 | 160,000 | 90,000 |
| Equipment depreciation | 2,100,000 | 700,000 | 800,000 | 600,000 |
| Facility expenses | 2,000,000 | 600,000 | 500,000 | 900,000 |
| Local administrative expenses* | 450,000 | 150,000 | 180,000 | 120,000 |
| Regional administrative expenses† | 400,000 | 140,000 | 160,000 | 100,000 |
| Corporate administrative expenses‡ | 1,600,000 | 560,000 | 640,000 | 400,000 |
| Total operating expense | 19,150,000 | 6,700,000 | 7,140,000 | 5,310,000 |
| Net operating income (loss) | $ 850,000 | $ 300,000 | $ 860,000 | $ (310,000) |

*Local administrative expenses are the administrative expenses incurred at the check processing centers.
†Regional administrative expenses are allocated to the check processing centers based on revenues.
‡Corporate administrative expenses represent a standard 8% charge against revenues.

Upon seeing this report, Mr. Braun summoned Lance Whiting for an explanation.

***Braun:*** What's the story on Ashton? It didn't have a loss the previous year, did it?

***Whiting:*** No, the Ashton facility has had a nice profit every year since it was opened six years ago, but Ashton lost a big contract this year.

***Braun:*** Why?

***Whiting:*** One of our national competitors entered the local market and bid very aggressively on the contract. We couldn't afford to meet the bid. Ashton's costs—particularly their facility expenses—are just too high. When Ashton lost the contract, we had to lay off a lot of employees, but we could not reduce the fixed costs of the Ashton facility.

***Braun:*** Why is Ashton's facility expense so high? It's a smaller facility than either Pocatello or Idaho Falls and yet its facility expense is higher.

***Whiting:*** The problem is that we are able to rent suitable facilities very cheaply at Pocatello and Idaho Falls. No such facilities were available at Ashton, so we had them built. Unfortunately, there were big cost overruns. The contractor we hired was inexperienced at this kind of work and in fact went bankrupt before the project was completed. After hiring another contractor to finish the work, we were way over budget. The large depreciation charges on the facility didn't matter at first because we didn't have much competition at the time and could charge premium prices.

***Braun:*** Well, we can't do that anymore. The Ashton facility will obviously have to be shut down. Its business can be shifted to the other two check processing centers in the region.

***Whiting:*** I would advise against that. The $900,000 in depreciation charges at the Ashton facility are misleading. That facility should last indefinitely with proper maintenance. And it has no resale value; there is no other commercial activity around Ashton.

***Braun:*** What about the other costs at Ashton?

***Whiting:*** If we shifted Ashton's business over to the other two processing centers in the region, we wouldn't save anything on direct labor or variable overhead costs. We might save $60,000 or so in local administrative expenses, but we would not save any regional administrative expense. And corporate headquarters would still charge us 8% of our revenues as corporate administrative expenses.

In addition, we would have to rent more space in Pocatello and Idaho Falls to handle the work transferred from Ashton; that would probably cost us at least $400,000 a year. And don't forget that it will cost us something to move the equipment from Ashton to Pocatello and Idaho Falls. And the move will disrupt service to customers.

***Braun:*** I understand all of that, but a money-losing processing center on my performance report is completely unacceptable.

***Whiting:*** And if you do shut down Ashton, you are going to throw some loyal employees out of work.

***Braun:*** That's unfortunate, but we have to face hard business realities.

***Whiting:*** And you would have to write off the investment in the facilities at Ashton.

***Braun:*** I can explain a write-off to corporate headquarters; hiring an inexperienced contractor to build the Ashton facility was my predecessor's mistake. But they'll have my head at headquarters if I show operating losses every year at one of my processing centers. Ashton has to go. At the next corporate board meeting, I am going to recommend that the Ashton facility be closed.

***Required:***

1. From the standpoint of the company as a whole, should the Ashton processing center be shut down and its work redistributed to the other processing centers in the region? Explain.
2. Do you think Marvin Braun's decision to shut down the Ashton facility is ethical? Explain.
3. What influence should the depreciation on the facilities at Ashton have on prices charged by Ashton for its services?

## ANALYTICAL THINKING [LO7]

Midwest Mills has a plant that can mill wheat grain into a cracked wheat cereal and then further mill the cracked wheat into flour. The company can sell all the cracked wheat cereal that it can produce at a selling price of $490 per ton. In the past, the company has sold only part of its cracked wheat as cereal and has retained the rest for further milling into flour. The flour has been selling for $700 per ton, but recently the price has become unstable and has dropped to $625 per ton. The costs and revenues associated with a ton of flour follow:

CHECK FIGURE
(2) Selling price of flour should at least be $670

| | | Per Ton of Flour |
|---|---|---|
| Selling price | | $625 |
| Cost to manufacture: | | |
| Raw materials: | | |
| Enrichment materials | $ 80 | |
| Cracked wheat | 470 | |
| Total raw materials | 550 | |
| Direct labor | 20 | |
| Manufacturing overhead | 60 | 630 |
| Manufacturing profit (loss) | | $ (5) |

Because of the weak price for flour, the sales manager believes that the company should discontinue milling flour and use its entire milling capacity to produce cracked wheat to sell as cereal.

The same milling equipment is used for both products. Milling one ton of cracked wheat into one ton of flour requires the same capacity as milling one ton of wheat grain into one ton of cracked wheat. Hence, the choice is between one ton of flour and two tons of cracked wheat. Current cost and revenue data on the cracked wheat cereal follow:

| | | Per Ton of Cracked Wheat |
|---|---|---|
| Selling price | | $490 |
| Cost to manufacture: | | |
| Wheat grain | $390 | |
| Direct labor | 20 | |
| Manufacturing overhead | 60 | 470 |
| Manufacturing profit | | $ 20 |

The sales manager argues that because the present $625 per ton price for the flour results in a $5 per ton loss, the milling of flour should not be resumed until the price per ton rises above $630.

The company assigns manufacturing overhead cost to the two products on the basis of milling hours. The same amount of time is required to mill either a ton of cracked wheat or a ton of flour. Virtually all manufacturing overhead costs are fixed. Materials and labor costs are variable.

The company can sell all of the cracked wheat and flour it can produce at the current market prices.

***Required:***

1. Do you agree with the sales manager that the company should discontinue milling flour and use the entire milling capacity to mill cracked wheat if the price of flour remains at $625 per ton? Support your answer with computations and explanations.
2. What is the lowest price that the company should accept for a ton of flour? Again support your answer with computations and explanations.

## A LOOK BACK

Chapter 10 used the basic decision-making framework, which focuses on differential costs and benefits, to analyze a wide variety of situations.

## A LOOK AT THIS CHAPTER

Chapter 11 expands coverage of decision making by focusing on decisions about investments in long-term projects. It illustrates a variety of techniques used by managers faced with these decisions.

## A LOOK AHEAD

Chapter 12 covers the statement of cash flows. It addresses how to classify various types of cash inflows and outflows along with the interpretation of information reported on that financial statement.

# 11 Capital Budgeting Decisions

## CHAPTER OUTLINE

DECISION FEATURE

# Capital Investments: A Key to Profitable Growth

**Cintas Corporation**, headquartered in Cincinnati, Ohio, provides highly specialized services to over 900,000 businesses of all types throughout North America, Europe, Latin America, and Asia. The backbone of its success is providing corporate identity uniform programs to more than five million North American workers. Cintas has 419 uniform rental facilities, six manufacturing plants, and eight distribution centers across North America and has expanded its service offerings in the past decade to include document management, first aid and safety, fire protection, entrance mats, restroom cleaning and supplies, carpet and tile cleaning, promotional products and cleanroom resources. Cintas operates approximately 430 facilities companywide, including six manufacturing plants and nine distribution centers. The challenge for Cintas is choosing among competing capital expansion opportunities.

At Cintas, each capital investment proposal must be accompanied by a financial analysis that estimates the project's cash inflows and outflows. The job of the Controller of Cintas' Rental Division, is to challenge the validity of the assumptions underlying the financial estimates. Is the cost to build the new facility underestimated? Are future revenue growth rates overly optimistic? Is it necessary to build a new facility, or could an existing facility be refurbished or expanded? Asking these types of constructive questions helps Cintas channel its limited investment funds to the most profitable opportunities.

Source: Author's conversation with Paul Carmichael, Senior Controller, Cintas Corporation.

## LEARNING OBJECTIVES

*After studying Chapter 11, you should be able to:*

**LO1** Evaluate the acceptability of an investment project using the net present value method.

**LO2** Rank investment projects in order of preference.

**LO3** Determine the payback period for an investment.

**LO4** Compute the simple rate of return for an investment.

**LO5** (Appendix 11A) Understand present value concepts and the use of present value tables.

**Managers often consider decisions** that involve an investment today in the hope of realizing future profits. For example, Tri-Con Global Restaurants, Inc., makes an investment when it opens a new Pizza Hut restaurant. L. L. Bean makes an investment when it installs a new computer to handle customer billing. Chrysler makes an investment when it redesigns a product such as the Jeep Grand Cherokee. Merck & Co. invests in medical research. Amazon.com makes an investment when it redesigns its website. All of these investments require spending now with the expectation of additional future net cash flows.

The term **capital budgeting** is used to describe how managers plan significant investments in projects that have long-term implications such as the purchase of new equipment or the introduction of new products. Most companies have many more potential projects than can actually be funded. Hence, managers must carefully select those projects that promise the greatest future return. How well managers make these capital budgeting decisions is a critical factor in the long-run financial health of the organization.

# CAPITAL BUDGETING—PLANNING INVESTMENTS

## Typical Capital Budgeting Decisions

Any decision that involves an outlay now in order to obtain a future return is a capital budgeting decision. Typical capital budgeting decisions include:

1. Cost reduction decisions. Should new equipment be purchased to reduce costs?
2. Expansion decisions. Should a new plant, warehouse, or other facility be acquired to increase capacity and sales?
3. Equipment selection decisions. Which of several available machines should be purchased?
4. Lease or buy decisions. Should new equipment be leased or purchased?
5. Equipment replacement decisions. Should old equipment be replaced now or later?

Capital budgeting decisions fall into two broad categories—*screening decisions* and *preference decisions.* **Screening decisions** relate to whether a proposed project is acceptable—whether it passes a preset hurdle. For example, a company may have a policy of accepting projects only if they provide a return of at least 20% on the investment. The required rate of return is the minimum rate of return a project must yield to be acceptable. **Preference decisions,** by contrast, relate to selecting from among several acceptable alternatives. To illustrate, a company may be considering several different machines to replace an existing machine on the assembly line. The choice of which machine to purchase is a preference decision. In this chapter, we first discuss screening decisions and then move on to preference decisions toward the end of the chapter.

## The Time Value of Money

Capital investments usually earn returns that extend over fairly long periods of time. Consequently, it is important to recognize *the time value of money* when evaluating investment proposals. A dollar today is worth more than a dollar a year from now if for no other reason than you could put a dollar in a bank today and have more than a dollar a year from now. Therefore, projects that promise earlier returns are preferable to those that promise later returns.

Capital budgeting techniques that recognize the time value of money involve *discounting cash flows.* We will spend most of this chapter showing how to use discounted cash flow analysis in making capital budgeting decisions. If you are not already familiar with discounting and the use of present value tables, you should read Appendix 11A: The Concept of Present Value, at the end of this chapter, before proceeding any further.

**HELPFUL HINT**

There are two types of cash flows that you'll need to discount in this chapter. The first type is a single sum of money that is received (or paid) at a single point in the future. For example, if a company expects to sell a piece of equipment five years from today for $10,000, this amount represents a single sum of money that we assume the company will receive on the last day of the fifth year from now. Exhibit 11B–1 is used to discount a single sum of money that will be received or paid in the future to its value as of today, also known as its present value.

The second type of cash flow that you'll need to discount is an annuity. An annuity refers to a series of identical sums of money that will be received or paid in consecutive future periods. For example, if a company expects to annually receive $20,000 from customers for each of the next five years, this amount represents an annuity that we assume the company will receive on the last day of five consecutive years. Exhibit 11B–2 is used to discount an annuity that will be received or paid in consecutive future periods to its lump sum value as of today.

## THE NET PRESENT VALUE METHOD

**LEARNING OBJECTIVE 1**

Evaluate the acceptability of an investment project using the net present value method.

Under the net present value method, the present value of a project's cash inflows is compared to the present value of the project's cash outflows. The difference between the present value of these cash flows, called the **net present value,** determines whether or not the project is an acceptable investment. To illustrate, consider the following data:

> **Example A:** Harper Company is contemplating the purchase of a machine capable of performing some operations that are now performed manually. The machine will cost $50,000, and it will last for five years. At the end of the five-year period, the machine will have a zero scrap value. Use of the machine will reduce labor costs by $18,000 per year. Harper Company requires a minimum pretax return of 20% on all investment projects.[1]

Should the machine be purchased? Harper Company must determine whether a cash investment now of $50,000 can be justified if it will result in an $18,000 reduction in cost in each of the next five years. It may appear that the answer is obvious because the total cost savings is $90,000 ($18,000 per year × 5 years). However, the company can earn a 20% return by investing its money elsewhere. It is not enough that the cost reductions cover just the original cost of the machine; they must also yield a return of at least 20% or the company would be better off investing the money elsewhere.

To determine whether the investment is desirable, the stream of annual $18,000 cost savings should be discounted to its present value and then compared to the cost of the new machine. Harper Company's minimum required return of 20% is used as the *discount rate* in the discounting process. Exhibit 11–1 illustrates the computation of the net present value of this proposed project. The annual cost savings of $18,000 is multiplied by 2.991, the present value factor of a five-year annuity at the discount rate of 20%, to obtain $53,838.[2] This is the present value of the annual cost savings. The present value of the initial investment is computed by multiplying the investment amount of $50,000 by 1.000, the present value factor for any cash flow that occurs immediately.

According to the analysis, Harper Company should purchase the new machine. The present value of the cost savings is $53,838, whereas the present value of the required investment (cost of the machine) is only $50,000. Deducting the present value of the required investment from the present value of the cost savings yields the *net present value*

[1]For simplicity, we ignore inflation and taxes.

[2]Unless otherwise stated, for the sake of simplicity we will assume in this chapter that all cash flows other than the initial investment occur at the ends of years.

**EXHIBIT 11–1**
Net Present Value Analysis of a Proposed Project

| | |
|---|---|
| Initial cost | $50,000 |
| Life of the project | 5 years |
| Annual cost savings | $18,000 |
| Salvage value | $0 |
| Required rate of return | 20% |

| Item | Year(s) | Amount of Cash Flow | 20% Factor | Present Value of Cash Flows |
|---|---|---|---|---|
| Annual cost savings | 1–5 | $18,000 | 2.991* | $53,838 |
| Initial investment | Now | $(50,000) | 1.000 | (50,000) |
| Net present value | | | | $ 3,838 |

*From Exhibit 11B–2 in Appendix 11B at the end of this chapter.

of $3,838. Whenever the net present value is zero or greater, as in our example, an investment project is acceptable. Whenever the net present value is negative (the present value of the cash outflows exceeds the present value of the cash inflows), an investment project is not acceptable. In sum:

| If the Net Present Value Is .... | Then the Project Is ..... |
|---|---|
| Positive | Acceptable because its return is greater than the required rate of return. |
| Zero | Acceptable because its return is equal to the required rate of return. |
| Negative | Not acceptable because its return is less than the required rate of return. |

There is another way to interpret the net present value. Harper Company could spend up to $53,838 for the new machine and still obtain the minimum required 20% rate of return. The net present value of $3,838, therefore, shows the amount of "cushion" or "margin of error." One way to look at this is that the company could underestimate the cost of the new machine by up to $3,838, or overestimate the net present value of the future cash savings by up to $3,838, and the project would still be financially attractive.

## Emphasis on Cash Flows

Accounting net income is based on accruals that ignore when cash flows occur. However, in capital budgeting, the timing of cash flows is critical. The present value of a cash flow depends on when it occurs. For that reason, cash flow rather than accounting net income is the focus in capital budgeting.[3] Examples of cash outflows and cash inflows that are often relevant to capital investment decisions are described below.

**Typical Cash Outflows** Most projects have at least three types of cash outflows. First, they often require an immediate cash outflow in the form of an initial investment in equipment, other assets, and installation costs. Any salvage value realized from the sale of old equipment can be recognized as a reduction in the initial investment or as a cash inflow. Second, some projects require a company to expand its working capital. **Working capital** is current assets (e.g., cash, accounts receivable, and inventory) less

[3]Under certain conditions, capital budgeting decisions can be correctly made by discounting appropriately defined accounting net income. However, this approach requires advanced techniques that are beyond the scope of this book.

current liabilities. When a company takes on a new project, the balances in the current asset accounts often increase. For example, opening a new Nordstrom's department store requires additional cash in sales registers and more inventory. These additional working capital needs are treated as part of the initial investment in a project. Third, many projects require periodic outlays for repairs and maintenance and additional operating costs.

**Typical Cash Inflows** Most projects also have at least three types of cash inflows. First, a project will normally increase revenues or reduce costs. Either way, the amount involved should be treated as a cash inflow for capital budgeting purposes. Notice that from a cash flow standpoint, a reduction in costs is equivalent to an increase in revenues. Second, cash inflows are also frequently realized from selling equipment for its salvage value when a project ends, although the company may actually have to pay to dispose of some low-value or hazardous items. Third, any working capital that was tied up in the project can be released for use elsewhere at the end of the project and should be treated as a cash inflow at that time. Working capital is released, for example, when a company sells off its inventory or collects its accounts receivable.

In summary, the following types of cash flows are common in business investment projects:

Cash outflows:
- Initial investment (including installation costs).
- Increased working capital needs.
- Repairs and maintenance.
- Incremental operating costs.

Cash inflows:
- Incremental revenues.
- Reduction in costs.
- Salvage value.
- Release of working capital.

## Simplifying Assumptions

Two simplifying assumptions are usually made in net present value analysis.

The first assumption is that all cash flows other than the initial investment occur at the end of periods. This is somewhat unrealistic in that cash flows typically occur *throughout* a period rather than just at its end. The purpose of this assumption is to simplify computations.

The second assumption is that all cash flows generated by an investment project are immediately reinvested at a rate of return equal to the discount rate. Unless these conditions are met, the net present value computed for the project will not be accurate.

## Choosing a Discount Rate

A positive net present value indicates that the project's return exceeds the discount rate. A negative net present value indicates that the project's return is less than the discount rate. Therefore, if the company's minimum required rate of return is used as the discount rate, a project with a positive net present value has a return that exceeds the minimum required rate of return and is acceptable. Contrarily, a project with a negative net present value has a return that is less than the minimum required rate of return and is unacceptable.

What is a company's minimum required rate of return? The company's *cost of capital* is usually regarded as the minimum required rate of return. The **cost of capital** is the average rate of return the company must pay to its long-term creditors and its shareholders for the use of their funds. If a project's rate of return is less than the cost of capital, the company does not earn enough to compensate its creditors and shareholders. Therefore, any project with a rate of return less than the cost of capital should be rejected.

The cost of capital serves as a *screening device.* When the cost of capital is used as the discount rate in net present value analysis, any project with a negative net present value does not cover the company's cost of capital and should be discarded as unacceptable.

## IN BUSINESS — Buck Knives Packs Its Bags

**Buck Knives** was losing money at its plant in San Diego, California. The company responded by loading its entire factory into a caravan of tractor-trailers and moving to Post Falls, Idaho. The relocation cost $6.5 million, but Buck Knives justified the move based on the annual cost savings summarized below.

| | San Diego | Post Falls |
|---|---|---|
| Electricity (cost per kilowatt hour) | $0.118 | $0.031 |
| Workers' compensation (cost per employee per year) | $2,095 | $210 |
| Median hourly wage | $15.15 | $12.40 |
| State business tax | 8.84% | 7.6% |
| Health insurance (per family per year) | $9,091 | $8,563 |
| Office space (cost per square foot) | $34.20 | $1.50 |
| Sales tax | 7.75% | 5% |

How would you analyze the financial viability of this decision? The first step would be to convert the data in the above table into annual lump sum savings. Then, net present value analysis could be used to compare the discounted value of the annual cost savings to the initial cash outlay associated with the relocation.

Source: Chris Lydgate, "The Buck Stopped Here," *Inc.* magazine, May 2006, pp. 86–95.

## An Extended Example of the Net Present Value Method

Example B provides an extended example of how the net present value method is used to analyze a proposed project. This example helps tie together and reinforce many of the ideas discussed thus far.

**Example B:** Under a special licensing arrangement, Swinyard Corporation has an opportunity to market a new product for a five-year period. The product would be purchased from the manufacturer, with Swinyard responsible for promotion and distribution costs. The licensing arrangement could be renewed at the end of the five-year period. After careful study, Swinyard estimated the following costs and revenues for the new product:

| | |
|---|---|
| Cost of equipment needed | $60,000 |
| Working capital needed | $100,000 |
| Overhaul of the equipment in four years | $5,000 |
| Salvage value of the equipment in five years | $10,000 |
| Annual revenues and costs: | |
| Sales revenues | $200,000 |
| Cost of goods sold | $125,000 |
| Out-of-pocket operating costs (for salaries, advertising, and other direct costs) | $35,000 |

**EXHIBIT 11–2** The Net Present Value Method—An Extended Example

| | |
|---|---|
| Sales revenues | $200,000 |
| Less cost of goods sold | 125,000 |
| Less out-of-pocket costs for salaries, advertising, etc. | 35,000 |
| Annual net cash inflows | $ 40,000 |

| Item | Year(s) | Amount of Cash Flow | 14% Factor | Present Value of Cash Flows |
|---|---|---|---|---|
| Purchase of equipment | Now | $(60,000) | 1.000 | $ (60,000) |
| Working capital needed | Now | $(100,000) | 1.000 | (100,000) |
| Overhaul of equipment | 4 | $(5,000) | 0.592* | (2,960) |
| Annual net cash inflows from sales of the product line | 1–5 | $40,000 | 3.433† | 137,320 |
| Salvage value of the equipment | 5 | $10,000 | 0.519* | 5,190 |
| Working capital released | 5 | $100,000 | 0.519* | 51,900 |
| Net present value | | | | $ 31,450 |

*From Exhibit 11B–1 in Appendix 11B.
†From Exhibit 11B–2 in Appendix 11B.

At the end of the five-year period, if Swinyard decides not to renew the licensing arrangement the working capital would be released for investment elsewhere. Swinyard uses a 14% discount rate. Would you recommend that the new product be introduced?

This example involves a variety of cash inflows and cash outflows. The solution is given in Exhibit 11–2.

Notice how the working capital is handled in this exhibit. It is counted as a cash outflow at the beginning of the project and as a cash inflow when it is released at the end of the project. Also notice how the sales revenues, cost of goods sold, and out-of-pocket costs are handled. **Out-of-pocket costs** are actual cash outlays for salaries, advertising, and other operating expenses.

Because the net present value of the proposal is positive, the new product is acceptable.

## HELPFUL HINT

Microsoft Excel is often used to perform net present value analysis. For example, the solution depicted in Exhibit 11–2 might be depicted in Microsoft Excel as follows:

| | A | B | C | D | E | F | G |
|---|---|---|---|---|---|---|---|
| 1 | Item | Now | Year 1 | Year 2 | Year 3 | Year 4 | Year 5 |
| 2 | Purchase of equipment | $ (60,000) | | | | | |
| 3 | Working capital needed | $ (100,000) | | | | | |
| 4 | Overhaul of equipment | | | | | $ (5,000) | |
| 5 | Annual net cash inflows | | $ 40,000 | $ 40,000 | $ 40,000 | $ 40,000 | $ 40,000 |
| 6 | Salvage value of equipment | | | | | | $ 10,000 |
| 7 | Working capital released | | | | | | $100,000 |
| 8 | Annual net cash flows (a) | $ (160,000) | $ 40,000 | $ 40,000 | $ 40,000 | $ 35,000 | $150,000 |
| 9 | Discount rate (b) | 1.000 | 0.877 | 0.769 | 0.675 | 0.592 | 0.519 |
| 10 | Present value of cash flows (a) × (b) | $ (160,000) | $ 35,080 | $ 30,760 | $ 27,000 | $ 20,720 | $ 77,850 |
| 11 | Net present value | $ 31,410 | | | | | |
| 12 | | | | | | | |

Sheet1 Sheet2 Sheet3

This approach creates one column in the spreadsheet for "Now" and for each of years one through five. All cash flows are inserted into the column of the spreadsheet that corresponds to when they occur. For example, the $60,000 purchase of equipment appears in the "Now" column because the cash outflow takes place immediately. In addition, all cash flows, including annuities, are discounted

## HELPFUL HINT

(continued)

using the factors from Exhibit 11B–1. For example, although the $40,000 annual net cash inflows that are shown above represent an annuity, each of these five $40,000 amounts is discounted using factors from Exhibit 11B–1.

The net present value of $31,410 that is shown in cell B11 is computed by adding together cells B10 through G10. This amount is $40 lower than the net present value shown in Exhibit 11–2; however, this difference exists solely because the discount factors in Exhibits 11B–1 and 11B–2 have been rounded to three decimal places. The computations shown within this Helpful Hint and those in Exhibit 11–2 are equivalent.

## IN BUSINESS

### Economic Woes Shrink Capital Budgets

When the health of the economy is uncertain, capital spending declines. **Rite Aid** CEO Mary Sammons cut her company's capital budget by $50 million due to uncertain economic conditions. **PetroHawk Energy** responded to a weak economy by slashing its $1.5 billion capital budget by one-third. **Estee Lauder** tightened its belt by challenging managers to defend what they must have and define what they can give up. **YUM! Brands** (owner of **Pizza Hut**, **KFC**, and **Taco Bell**) navigated the difficult economy by abandoning projects that "might come true" in favor of a "must have" capital budgeting mentality.

Source: Matthew Boyle, "The Budget Knives Come Out," *BusinessWeek*, October 13, 2008, p. 30.

# EXPANDING THE NET PRESENT VALUE METHOD

So far, all of our examples have involved an evaluation of a single investment project. In the following section we expand the discussion of the net present value method to include evaluation of two alternative projects. In addition, we integrate relevant cost concepts into the discounted cash flow analysis. We use two approaches to compare competing investment projects—the *total-cost approach* and the *incremental-cost approach.* Each approach is illustrated in the next few pages.

## The Total-Cost Approach

The total-cost approach is the most flexible method for comparing competing projects. To illustrate the mechanics of the approach, consider the following data:

**Example C:** Harper Ferry Company operates a high-speed passenger ferry service across the Mississippi River. One of its ferryboats is in poor condition. This ferry can be renovated at an immediate cost of $200,000. Further repairs and an overhaul of the motor will be needed five years from now at a cost of $80,000. In all, the ferry will be usable for 10 years if this work is done. At the end of 10 years, the ferry will have to be scrapped at a salvage value of $60,000. The scrap value of the ferry right now is $70,000. It will cost $300,000 each year to operate the ferry, and revenues will total $400,000 annually.

As an alternative, Harper Ferry Company can purchase a new ferryboat at a cost of $360,000. The new ferry will have a life of 10 years, but it will require some repairs costing $30,000 at the end of 5 years. At the end of 10 years, the ferry will have a scrap value of $60,000. It will cost $210,000 each year to operate the ferry, and revenues will total $400,000 annually.

Harper Ferry Company requires a return of at least 14% on all investment projects.

**EXHIBIT 11–3** The Total-Cost Approach to Project Selection

| | New Ferry | Old Ferry |
|---|---|---|
| Annual revenues | $400,000 | $400,000 |
| Annual cash operating costs | 210,000 | 300,000 |
| Annual net cash inflows | $190,000 | $100,000 |

| Item | Year(s) | Amount of Cash Flows | 14% Factor* | Present Value of Cash Flows |
|---|---|---|---|---|
| Buy the new ferry: | | | | |
| Initial investment | Now | $(360,000) | 1.000 | $(360,000) |
| Salvage value of the old ferry | Now | $70,000 | 1.000 | 70,000 |
| Repairs in five years | 5 | $(30,000) | 0.519 | (15,570) |
| Annual net cash inflows | 1–10 | $190,000 | 5.216 | 991,040 |
| Salvage value of the new ferry | 10 | $60,000 | 0.270 | 16,200 |
| Net present value | | | | 701,670 |
| Keep the old ferry: | | | | |
| Renovation | Now | $(200,000) | 1.000 | (200,000) |
| Repairs in five years | 5 | $(80,000) | 0.519 | (41,520) |
| Annual net cash inflows | 1–10 | $100,000 | 5.216 | 521,600 |
| Salvage value of the old ferry | 10 | $60,000 | 0.270 | 16,200 |
| Net present value | | | | 296,280 |
| Net present value in favor of buying the new ferry | | | | $ 405,390 |

*All present value factors are from Exhibits 11B–1 and 11B–2 in Appendix 11B.

Should the company purchase the new ferry or renovate the old ferry? Exhibit 11–3 shows the solution using the total-cost approach.

Two points should be noted from the exhibit. First, *all* cash inflows and *all* cash outflows are included in the solution under each alternative. No effort has been made to isolate those cash flows that are relevant to the decision and those that are not relevant. The inclusion of all cash flows associated with each alternative gives the approach its name—the *total-cost* approach.

Second, notice that a net present value is computed for each alternative. This is a distinct advantage of the total-cost approach because an unlimited number of alternatives can be compared side by side to determine the best option. For example, another alternative for Harper Ferry Company would be to get out of the ferry business entirely. If management desired, the net present value of this alternative could be computed to compare with the alternatives shown in Exhibit 11–3. Still other alternatives might be available to the company. In the case at hand, given only two alternatives, the data indicate that the most profitable choice is to purchase the new ferry.[4]

## The Incremental-Cost Approach

When only two alternatives are being considered, the incremental-cost approach offers a simpler and more direct route to a decision. In the incremental-cost approach, only those costs and revenues that *differ* between the two alternatives are included in the analysis. To

[4]The alternative with the highest net present value is not always the best choice, although it is the best choice in this case. For further discussion, see the section Preference Decisions—The Ranking of Investment Projects.

**EXHIBIT 11–4** The Incremental-Cost Approach to Project Selection

| Item | Year(s) | Amount of Cash Flows | 14% Factor* | Present Value of Cash Flows |
|---|---|---|---|---|
| Incremental investment to buy the new ferry | Now | $(160,000) | 1.000 | $(160,000) |
| Salvage value of the old ferry now | Now | $70,000 | 1.000 | 70,000 |
| Difference in repair costs in five years | 5 | $50,000 | 0.519 | 25,950 |
| Increase in annual net cash inflows | 1–10 | $90,000 | 5.216 | 469,440 |
| Difference in salvage value in 10 years | 10 | $0 | 0.270 | 0 |
| Net present value in favor of buying the new ferry | | | | $ 405,390 |

*All present value factors are from Exhibits 11B–1 and 11B–2 in Appendix 11B.

illustrate, refer again to the data in Example C relating to Harper Ferry Company. The solution using only differential costs is presented in Exhibit 11–4.[5]

Two things should be noted from the data in this exhibit. First, the net present value in favor of buying the new ferry of $405,390 shown in Exhibit 11–4 agrees with the net present value shown under the total-cost approach in Exhibit 11–3. The two approaches are equivalent.

Second, the costs used in Exhibit 11–4 are just the differences between the costs shown for the two alternatives in the prior exhibit. For example, the $160,000 incremental investment required to purchase the new ferry in Exhibit 11–4 is the difference between the $360,000 cost of the new ferry and the $200,000 cost required to renovate the old ferry from Exhibit 11–3. The other numbers in Exhibit 11–4 have been computed in the same way.

## Least-Cost Decisions

Some decisions do not involve any revenues. For example, a company may be trying to decide whether to buy or lease an executive jet. The choice would be made on the basis of which alternative—buying or leasing—would be least costly. In situations such as these, where no revenues are involved, the most desirable alternative is the one with the *least total cost* from a present value perspective. Hence, these are known as least-cost decisions. To illustrate a least-cost decision, consider the following data:

**Example D:** Val-Tek Company is considering replacing an old threading machine with a new threading machine that would substantially reduce annual operating costs. Selected data relating to the old and new machines are presented below:

| | Old Machine | New Machine |
|---|---|---|
| Purchase cost when new | $200,000 | $250,000 |
| Salvage value now | $30,000 | — |
| Annual cash operating costs | $150,000 | $90,000 |
| Overhaul needed immediately | $40,000 | — |
| Salvage value in six years | $0 | $50,000 |
| Remaining life | 6 years | 6 years |

Val-Tek Company uses a 10% discount rate.

Exhibit 11–5 analyzes the alternatives using the total-cost approach. Because this is a least-cost decision, the present values are negative for both alternatives. However, the present value of the alternative of buying the new machine is $109,500 higher than the other alternative. Therefore, buying the new machine is the less costly alternative.

[5]Technically, the incremental-cost approach is misnamed because it focuses on differential costs (that is, on both cost increases and decreases) rather than just on incremental costs. As used here, the term *incremental costs* should be interpreted broadly to include both cost increases and cost decreases.

**EXHIBIT 11–5** The Total-Cost Approach (Least-Cost Decision)

| Item | Year(s) | Amount of Cash Flows | 10% Factor* | Present Value of Cash Flows |
|---|---|---|---|---|
| Buy the new machine: | | | | |
| Initial investment | Now | $(250,000) | 1.000 | $(250,000)† |
| Salvage value of the old machine | Now | $30,000 | 1.000 | 30,000 † |
| Annual cash operating costs | 1–6 | $(90,000) | 4.355 | (391,950) |
| Salvage value of the new machine | 6 | $50,000 | 0.564 | 28,200 |
| Present value of net cash outflows | | | | (583,750) |
| Keep the old machine: | | | | |
| Overhaul needed now | Now | $(40,000) | 1.000 | $ (40,000) |
| Annual cash operating costs | 1–6 | $(150,000) | 4.355 | (653,250) |
| Present value of net cash outflows | | | | (693,250) |
| Net present value in favor of buying the new machine | | | | $ 109,500 |

*All factors are from Exhibits 11B–1 and 11B–2 in Appendix 11B.

†These two items could be netted into a single $220,000 incremental-cost figure ($250,000 − $30,000 = $220,000).

**EXHIBIT 11–6** The Incremental-Cost Approach (Least-Cost Decision)

| Item | Year(s) | Amount of Cash Flows | 10% Factor* | Present Value of Cash Flows |
|---|---|---|---|---|
| Incremental investment required to purchase the new machine | Now | $(210,000) | 1.000 | $(210,000)† |
| Salvage value of the old machine | Now | $30,000 | 1.000 | 30,000† |
| Savings in annual cash operating costs | 1–6 | $60,000 | 4.355 | 261,300 |
| Difference in salvage value in six years | 6 | $50,000 | 0.564 | 28,200 |
| Net present value in favor of buying the new machine | | | | $ 109,500 |

*All factors are from Exhibits 11B–1 and 11B–2 in Appendix 11B.

†These two items could be netted into a single $180,000 incremental-cost figure ($210,000 − $30,000 = $180,000).

Exhibit 11–6 presents an analysis of the same alternatives using the incremental-cost approach. Once again, when done correctly, the total-cost and incremental-cost approaches arrive at the same answer.

## Home Construction Goes Green—Or Does It?

IN BUSINESS

Many homebuyers like the idea of building environmentally friendly homes until they get the bill. **Specpan**, an Indianapolis research firm, estimates a "green" home costs 10%–19% more than a comparable conventional home. For example, installing solar-electric glass-faced tiles on a roof costs $15,000 per 100 square feet compared to $1,200 per 100 square feet for standard fiber-cement tiles. Environmentally friendly interior paint costs $35–$42 per gallon compared to $20–$32 per gallon for standard latex paint. To further complicate this least-cost decision, the average homeowner lives in a house only seven years before moving. Within this time frame, many green investments appear to be financially unattractive. Nonetheless, the American Institute of Architects reports that 63% of their clients expressed an interest in renewable flooring materials such as cork and bamboo, up from 53% a year earlier.

Source: June Fletcher, "The Price of Going Green," *The Wall Street Journal*, February 29, 2008, p. W8.

**CONCEPT CHECK**

1. Which of the following statements is false? (You may select more than one answer.)
   a. The total-cost and incremental-cost approaches to net present value analysis can occasionally lead to conflicting results.
   b. The cost of capital is a screening mechanism for net present value analysis.
   c. The present value of a dollar increases as the time of receipt extends further into the future.
   d. The higher the cost of capital, the lower the present value of a dollar received in the future.

**DECISION POINT**

## Financing the Sports Car

Assume you would like to buy a new sports car that can be purchased for $21,495 in cash or acquired from the dealer via a leasing arrangement. Under the terms of the lease, you would have to make a payment of $2,078 when the lease is signed and then monthly payments of $300 for 24 months. At the end of the 24-month lease, you can choose to buy the car you have leased for an additional payment of $13,776. If you do not make that final payment, the car reverts to the dealer.

You have enough cash to make the initial payment on the lease, but not enough to buy the car for cash. However, you could borrow the additional cash from a credit union for 1% per month. Do you think you should borrow money from a credit union to purchase the car or should you sign a lease with the dealer?

Hints: The net present value of the cash purchase option, including any payments to the credit union, is $21,495 using 1% per month as the discount rate. (Accept this statement as true; don't try to do the computations to verify it.) Determine the net present value of the lease, using 1% per month as the discount rate. The present value of an annuity of $1 for 24 periods at 1% per period is 21.243 and the present value of a single payment of $1 at the end of 24 periods at 1% per period is 0.788.

# PREFERENCE DECISIONS—THE RANKING OF INVESTMENT PROJECTS

**LEARNING OBJECTIVE 2**

Rank investment projects in order of preference.

Recall that when considering investment opportunities, managers must make two types of decisions—screening decisions and preference decisions. Screening decisions, which come first, pertain to whether or not a proposed investment is acceptable. Preference decisions come *after* screening decisions and attempt to answer the following question: "How do the remaining investment proposals, all of which have been screened and provide an acceptable rate of return, rank in terms of preference? That is, which one(s) would be *best* for the company to accept?"

Sometimes preference decisions are called rationing decisions, or ranking decisions. Limited investment funds must be rationed among many competing alternatives. Hence, the alternatives must be ranked.

The net present value of one project cannot be directly compared to the net present value of another project unless the initial investments are equal. For example, assume that a company is considering two competing investments, as shown below:

| | Investment A | Investment B |
|---|---|---|
| Investment required | $(10,000) | $(5,000) |
| Present value of cash inflows | 11,000 | 6,000 |
| Net present value | $ 1,000 | $ 1,000 |

Although each project has a net present value of $1,000, the projects are not equally desirable if the funds available for investment are limited. The project requiring an investment of only $5,000 is much more desirable than the project requiring an investment of $10,000. This fact can be highlighted by dividing the net present value of the project by the investment required. The result, shown below in equation form, is called the **project profitability index.**

$$\text{Project profitability index} = \frac{\text{Net present value of the project}}{\text{Investment required}} \qquad (1)$$

The project profitability indexes for the two investments on the previous page would be computed as follows:

| | Investment | |
|---|---|---|
| | A | B |
| Net present value (a) | $1,000 | $1,000 |
| Investment required (b) | $10,000 | $5,000 |
| Project profitability index, (a) ÷ (b) | 0.10 | 0.20 |

When using the project profitability index to rank competing investments projects, the preference rule is: *The higher the project profitability index, the more desirable the project.*[6] Applying this rule to the two investments above, investment B should be chosen over investment A.

The project profitability index is an application of the techniques for utilizing constrained resources discussed in an earlier chapter. In this case, the constrained resource is the limited funds available for investment, and the project profitability index is similar to the contribution margin per unit of the constrained resource.

A few details should be clarified with respect to the computation of the project profitability index. The "Investment required" refers to any cash outflows that occur at the beginning of the project, reduced by any salvage value recovered from the sale of old equipment. The "Investment required" also includes any investment in working capital that the project may need.

## Fedex Goes Green—Well, Not Exactly!

IN BUSINESS

In 2003, **FedEx** announced a 10-year plan to replace 3,000 delivery trucks per year with environmentally friendly hybrid vehicles, thereby eliminating 250,000 tons of greenhouse gases per year. The hybrid vehicles cost 75% more than conventional trucks, but over 10 years they generate fuel savings that offset the higher cost. By 2007, FedEx had purchased less than 100 hybrid vehicles because management decided that the eco-friendly investment was not the most profitable use of the company's resources. FedEx's environmental director justified the company's actions by saying "we do have a fiduciary responsibility to our shareholders ... we can't subsidize the development of this technology for our competitors."

This example illustrates the challenges that companies face when attempting to satisfy the expectations of various stakeholders. Perhaps FedEx shareholders would applaud the company's decision to retreat from its 10-year plan, whereas environmentally conscious customers may criticize the company's actions. What do you think?

Source: Ben Elgin, "Little Green Lies," *BusinessWeek,* October 29, 2007, pp. 45–52.

[6]Because of the "lumpiness" of projects, the project profitability index ranking may not be perfect. Nevertheless, it is a good starting point. Furthermore, these complexities are beyond the scope of this book.

## THE INTERNAL RATE OF RETURN METHOD

The *internal rate of return* method is a popular alternative to the net present value method. The **internal rate of return** is the rate of return promised by an investment over its useful life. It is computed by finding the discount rate at which the net present value of the investment is zero. The internal rate of return can be used either to screen projects or to rank them. Any project whose internal rate of return is less than the cost of capital is rejected and, in general, the higher a project's rate of return, the more desirable it is.

For technical reasons that are discussed in more advanced texts, the net present value method is generally considered to be more reliable than the internal rate of return method for both screening and ranking projects.

## THE NET PRESENT VALUE METHOD AND INCOME TAXES

Our discussion of the net present value method has assumed that there are no income taxes. In most countries—including the United States—income taxes, both on individual income and on business income, are a fact of life.

Income taxes affect net present value analysis in two ways. First, income taxes affect the cost of capital in that the cost of capital should reflect the *after-tax* cost of long-term debt and of equity. Second, net present value analysis should focus on *after-tax cash flows.* The effects of income taxes on both revenues and expenses should be fully reflected in the analysis. This includes taking into account the tax deductibility of depreciation. Whereas depreciation is not itself a cash flow, it reduces taxable income and therefore income taxes, which *are* a cash flow. The techniques for adjusting the cost of capital and cash flows for income taxes are beyond the scope of this book and are covered in more advanced texts.

## OTHER APPROACHES TO CAPITAL BUDGETING DECISIONS

**LEARNING OBJECTIVE 3**

Determine the payback period for an investment.

The net present value and internal rate of return methods are widely used as decision-making tools. However, some managers also use the payback method and simple rate of return method to make capital budgeting decisions. Each of these methods will be discussed in turn.

### The Payback Method

The payback method focuses on the *payback period.* The **payback period** is the length of time that it takes for a project to recover its initial cost from the net cash inflows that it generates. This period is sometimes referred to as "the time that it takes for an investment to pay for itself." The basic premise of the payback method is that the more quickly the cost of an investment can be recovered, the more desirable is the investment.

The payback period is expressed in years. *When the annual net cash inflow is the same every year,* the following formula can be used to compute the payback period:

$$\text{Payback period} = \frac{\text{Investment required}}{\text{Annual net cash inflow}} \qquad (2)$$

To illustrate the payback method, consider the following data:

**Example E:** York Company needs a new milling machine. The company is considering two machines: machine A and machine B. Machine A costs $15,000, has a useful life of ten years, and will reduce operating costs by $5,000 per year. Machine B costs only $12,000, will also reduce operating costs by $5,000 per year, but has a useful life of only five years.

**Required:**
Which machine should be purchased according to the payback method?

$$\text{Machine A payback period} = \frac{\$15{,}000}{\$5{,}000} = 3.0 \text{ years}$$

$$\text{Machine B payback period} = \frac{\$12{,}000}{\$5{,}000} = 2.4 \text{ years}$$

According to the payback calculations, York Company should purchase machine B because it has a shorter payback period than machine A.

## Evaluation of the Payback Method

The payback method is not a true measure of the profitability of an investment. Rather, it simply tells a manager how many years are required to recover the original investment. Unfortunately, a shorter payback period does not always mean that one investment is more desirable than another.

To illustrate, refer back to Example E. Machine B has a shorter payback period than machine A, but it has a useful life of only 5 years rather than 10 years for machine A. Machine B would have to be purchased twice—once immediately and then again after the fifth year—to provide the same service as just one machine A. Under these circumstances, machine A would probably be a better investment than machine B, even though machine B has a shorter payback period. Unfortunately, the payback method ignores all cash flows that occur after the payback period.

A further criticism of the payback method is that it does not consider the time value of money. A cash inflow to be received several years in the future is weighed the same as a cash inflow received right now. To illustrate, assume that for an investment of $8,000 you can purchase either of the two following streams of cash inflows:

| Year............ | 0 | 1 | 2 | 3 | 4 | 5 | 6 | 7 | 8 |
|---|---|---|---|---|---|---|---|---|---|
| Stream 1...... | | | | | $8,000 | $2,000 | $2,000 | $2,000 | $2,000 |
| Stream 2...... | | $2,000 | $2,000 | $2,000 | $2,000 | $8,000 | | | |

Which stream of cash inflows would you prefer to receive in return for your $8,000 investment? Each stream has a payback period of 4.0 years. Therefore, if payback alone is used to make the decision, the streams would be considered equally desirable. However, from a time value of money perspective, stream 2 is much more desirable than stream 1.

On the other hand, under certain conditions the payback method can be very useful. For one thing, it can help identify which investment proposals are in the "ballpark." That is, it can be used as a screening tool to help answer the question, "Should I consider this proposal further?" If a proposal doesn't provide a payback within some specified period, then there may be no need to consider it further. In addition, the payback period is often important to new companies that are "cash poor." When a company is cash poor, a project with a short payback period but a low rate of return might be preferred over another project with a high rate of return but a long payback period. The reason is that the company may simply need a faster return of its cash investment. And finally, the payback method is sometimes used in industries where products become obsolete very rapidly—such as consumer electronics. Because products may last only a year or two, the payback period on investments must be very short.

## An Extended Example of Payback

As shown by formula (2) on page 504, the payback period is computed by dividing the investment in a project by the project's annual net cash inflows. If new equipment is replacing old equipment, then any salvage value to be received when disposing of the old equipment should be deducted from the cost of the new equipment, and only the *incremental* investment should be used in the payback computation. In addition, any depreciation deducted in arriving at the project's net operating income must be added back to obtain the project's expected annual net cash inflow. To illustrate, consider the following data:

**Example F:** Goodtime Fun Centers, Inc., operates amusement parks. Some of the vending machines in one of its parks provide very little revenue, so the company is considering removing the machines and installing equipment to dispense soft ice cream. The equipment would cost $80,000 and have an eight-year useful life with no salvage value. Incremental annual revenues and costs associated with the sale of ice cream would be as follows:

| | |
|---|---|
| Sales | $150,000 |
| Variable expenses | 90,000 |
| Contribution margin | 60,000 |
| Fixed expenses: | |
| Salaries | 27,000 |
| Maintenance | 3,000 |
| Depreciation | 10,000 |
| Total fixed expenses | 40,000 |
| Net operating income | $ 20,000 |

The vending machines can be sold for a $5,000 scrap value. The company will not purchase equipment unless it has a payback period of three years or less. Does the ice cream dispenser pass this hurdle?

Exhibit 11–7 computes the payback period for the ice cream dispenser. Several things should be noted. First, depreciation is added back to net operating income to obtain the annual net cash inflow from the new equipment. Depreciation is not a cash outlay; thus, it must be added back to adjust net operating income to a cash basis. Second, the payback computation deducts the salvage value of the old machines from the cost of the new equipment so that only the incremental investment is used in computing the payback period.

Because the proposed equipment has a payback period of less than three years, the company's payback requirement has been met.

## Payback and Uneven Cash Flows

When the cash flows associated with an investment project change from year to year, the simple payback formula that we outlined earlier cannot be used. Consider the following data:

| Year | Investment | Cash Inflow |
|---|---|---|
| 1 | $4,000 | $1,000 |
| 2 | | $0 |
| 3 | | $2,000 |
| 4 | $2,000 | $1,000 |
| 5 | | $500 |
| 6 | | $3,000 |
| 7 | | $2,000 |

**EXHIBIT 11–7**
Computation of the Payback Period

Step 1: *Compute the annual net cash inflow.* Because the annual net cash inflow is not given, it must be computed before the payback period can be determined:

| | |
|---|---|
| Net operating income | $20,000 |
| Add: Noncash deduction for depreciation | 10,000 |
| Annual net cash inflow | $30,000 |

Step 2: *Compute the payback period.* Using the annual net cash inflow from above, the payback period can be determined as follows:

| | |
|---|---|
| Cost of the new equipment | $80,000 |
| Less salvage value of old equipment | 5,000 |
| Investment required | $75,000 |

$$\text{Payback period} = \frac{\text{Investment required}}{\text{Annual net cash inflow}}$$

$$= \frac{\$75{,}000}{\$30{,}000} = 2.5 \text{ years}$$

What is the payback period on this investment? The answer is 5.5 years, but to obtain this figure it is necessary to track the unrecovered investment year by year. The steps involved in this process are shown in Exhibit 11–8. By the middle of the sixth year, sufficient cash inflows will have been realized to recover the entire investment of $6,000 ($4,000 + $2,000).

## The Economics of Hybrid Vehicles

IN BUSINESS

The table below shows the price premiums (after tax credits) that customers must pay to buy four types of hybrid vehicles. It also depicts the annual gas savings that customers realize by driving a hybrid version of the vehicle instead of a standard model of the same vehicle (assuming the vehicles are driven 15,000 miles per year and gas costs $2.79 a gallon). Dividing the price premium by the annual gas savings yields the payback period when purchasing the hybrid version of the vehicle.

| Make and Model | Price Premium | Annual Gas Savings | Payback Period |
|---|---|---|---|
| Ford Escape | $1,364 | $438 | 3.1 |
| Honda Civic | $1,482 | $317 | 4.7 |
| Toyota Camry | $3,763 | $310 | 12.1 |
| Toyota Highlander | $4,372 | $388 | 11.3 |

The above payback figures highlight the dilemma faced by customers who want to make environmentally friendly purchases, but are constrained by limited financial resources.

Source: Mike Spector, "The Economics of Hybrids," *The Wall Street Journal,* October 29, 2007, pp. R5–R6.

**EXHIBIT 11–8**
Payback and Uneven Cash Flows

| Year | Investment | Cash Inflow | Unrecovered Investment* |
|---|---|---|---|
| 1 ................ | $4,000 | $1,000 | $3,000 |
| 2 ................ | | $0 | $3,000 |
| 3 ................ | | $2,000 | $1,000 |
| 4 ................ | $2,000 | $1,000 | $2,000 |
| 5 ................ | | $500 | $1,500 |
| 6 ................ | | $3,000 | $0 |
| 7 ................ | | $2,000 | $0 |

*Year X unrecovered investment = Year X-1 unrecovered investment + Year X investment − Year X cash inflow.

**LEARNING OBJECTIVE 4**

Compute the simple rate of return for an investment.

## The Simple Rate of Return Method

The **simple rate of return** method is another capital budgeting technique that does not involve discounting cash flows. The simple rate of return is also known as the accounting rate of return or the unadjusted rate of return.

Unlike the other capital budgeting methods that we have discussed, the simple rate of return method focuses on accounting net operating income rather than cash flows. To obtain the simple rate of return, the annual incremental net operating income generated by a project is divided by the initial investment in the project, as shown below.

$$\text{Simple rate of return} = \frac{\text{Annual incremental net operating income}}{\text{Initial investment}} \qquad (3)$$

Two additional points should be made. First, depreciation charges that result from making the investment should be deducted when determining the annual incremental net operating income. Second, the initial investment should be reduced by any salvage value realized from the sale of old equipment.

**Example G:** Brigham Tea, Inc., is a processor of low-acid tea. The company is contemplating purchasing equipment for an additional processing line that would increase revenues by $90,000 per year. Incremental cash operating expenses would be $40,000 per year. The equipment would cost $180,000 and have a nine-year life with no salvage value.

To apply the formula for the simple rate of return, we must first determine the annual incremental net operating income from the project:

| | | |
|---|---|---|
| Annual incremental revenues ........................................ | | $90,000 |
| Annual incremental cash operating expenses .................. | $40,000 | |
| Annual depreciation ($180,000 − $0)/9 ............................ | 20,000 | |
| Annual incremental expenses ........................................ | | 60,000 |
| Annual incremental net operating income ........................ | | $30,000 |

Given that the annual incremental net operating income from the project is $30,000 and the initial investment is $180,000, the simple rate of return is 16.7% as shown below:

$$\text{Simple rate of return} = \frac{\text{Annual incremental net operating income}}{\text{Initial investment}}$$

$$= \frac{\$30{,}000}{\$180{,}000}$$

$$= 16.7\%$$

**Example H:** Midwest Farms, Inc., hires people on a part-time basis to sort eggs. The cost of hand sorting is $30,000 per year. The company is investigating an egg-sorting machine that would cost $90,000 and have a 15-year useful life. The machine would have negligible salvage value, and it would cost $10,000 per year to operate and maintain. The egg-sorting equipment currently being used could be sold now for a scrap value of $2,500.

This project is slightly different from the preceding project because it involves cost reductions with no additional revenues. Nevertheless, the annual incremental net operating income can be computed by treating the annual cost savings as if it were incremental revenues as follows:

| | | |
|---|---|---|
| Annual incremental cost savings | | $30,000 |
| Annual incremental cash operating expenses | $10,000 | |
| Annual depreciation ($90,000 − $0)/15 | 6,000 | |
| Annual incremental expenses | | 16,000 |
| Annual incremental net operating income | | $14,000 |

Thus, even though the new equipment would not generate any additional revenues, it would reduce costs by $14,000 a year. This would have the effect of increasing net operating income by $14,000 a year.

Finally, the salvage value of the old equipment offsets the initial cost of the new equipment as follows:

| | |
|---|---|
| Cost of the new equipment | $90,000 |
| Less salvage value of the old equipment | 2,500 |
| Initial investment | $87,500 |

Given the annual incremental net operating income of $14,000 and the initial investment of $87,500, the simple rate of return is 16.0% computed as follows:

$$\text{Simple rate of return} = \frac{\text{Annual incremental net operating income}}{\text{Initial investment}}$$

$$= \frac{\$14,000}{\$87,500}$$

$$= 16.0\%$$

## Criticisms of the Simple Rate of Return

The simple rate of return method ignores the time value of money. It considers a dollar received 10 years from now to be as valuable as a dollar received today. Thus, the simple rate of return method can be misleading if the alternatives have different cash flow patterns. Additionally, many projects do not have constant incremental revenues and expenses over their useful lives. As a result, the simple rate of return will fluctuate from year to year, with the possibility that a project may appear to be desirable in some years and undesirable in others. In contrast, the net present value method provides a single number that summarizes all of the cash flows over the entire useful life of the project.

**CONCEPT CHECK**

2. If a $300,000 investment has a project profitability index of 0.25, what is the net present value of the project?
   a. $75,000
   b. $225,000
   c. $25,000
   d. $275,000
3. Which of the following statements is false? (You may select more than one answer.)
   a. The payback period increases as the cost of capital decreases.
   b. The simple rate of return will be the same for two alternatives that have identical cash flow patterns even if the pattern of accounting net operating income differs between the alternatives.
   c. The internal rate of return will be higher than the cost of capital for projects that have positive net present values.
   d. If two alternatives have the same present value of cash inflows, the alternative that requires the higher investment will have the higher project profitability index.

**HELPFUL HINT**

The simple rate of return has two important limitations when used to make capital budgeting decisions—it does not focus on cash flows and it does not recognize the time value of money. However, the simple rate of return is important because it can influence how managers perceive investment opportunities. For example, assume that you are the manager of a division within a company that pays or withholds your annual bonus based on whether your division exceeds its historical return on investment (ROI) of 20%. Now assume that your division has an investment opportunity that provides a net present value of $100,000 and a simple rate of return of 16%. Would you make the investment? The company would want you to make the investment because of its positive net present value; however, from your division's standpoint the investment is undesirable because its simple rate of return is less than the division's historical ROI.

## POSTAUDIT OF INVESTMENT PROJECTS

After an investment project has been approved and implemented, a *postaudit* should be conducted. A **postaudit** involves checking whether or not expected results are actually realized. This is a key part of the capital budgeting process because it helps keep managers honest in their investment proposals. Any tendency to inflate the benefits or downplay the costs in a proposal should become evident after a few postaudits have been conducted. The postaudit also provides an opportunity to reinforce and possibly expand successful projects and to cut losses on floundering projects.

The same capital budgeting method should be used in the postaudit as was used in the original approval process. That is, if a project was approved on the basis of a net present value analysis, then the same procedure should be used in performing the postaudit. However, the data used in the postaudit analysis should be *actual observed data* rather than estimated data. This gives management an opportunity to make a side-by-side comparison to see how well the project has succeeded. It also helps assure that estimated data received on future proposals will be carefully prepared because the persons submitting the data knows that their estimates will be compared to actual results in the postaudit process. Actual results that are far out of line with original estimates should be carefully reviewed.

## Royal Caribbean Cruises Launches *Oasis of the Seas*

IN BUSINESS

**Royal Caribbean Cruises** invested $1.4 billion to build the *Oasis of the Seas*, a cruise ship that carries 5,400 passengers and stands 20 stories above the sea. The vessel is a third larger than any other cruise ship and contains 21 pools, 24 restaurants, 13 retail shops, and 300-foot water slides. The company hopes the ship's extraordinary amenities will attract large numbers of customers willing to pay premium prices. However, the economic downturn has caused many customers to refrain from spending on lavish vacations.

Source: Mike Esterl, "Huge Cruise Ships Prepare for Launch but Face Uncertain Waters," *The Wall Street Journal*, December 4, 2009, pp. B1–B2.

## SUMMARY

**LO1 Evaluate the acceptability of an investment project using the net present value method.**

Investment decisions should take into account the time value of money because a dollar today is more valuable than a dollar received in the future. In the net present value method, future cash flows are discounted to their present value so that they can be compared with current cash outlays. The difference between the present value of the cash inflows and the present value of the cash outflows is called the project's net present value. If the net present value of the project is negative, the project is rejected. The company's cost of capital is often used as the discount rate in the net present value method.

**LO2 Rank investment projects in order of preference.**

After screening out projects whose net present values are negative, the company may still have more projects than can be supported with available funds. The remaining projects can be ranked using the project profitability index, which is computed by dividing the net present value of the project by the required initial investment.

**LO3 Determine the payback period for an investment.**

The payback period is the number of periods that are required to recover the investment in a project from the project's net cash inflows. The payback period is most useful for projects whose useful lives are short and uncertain. Generally speaking it is not a reliable method for evaluating investment opportunities because it ignores the time value of money and all cash flows that occur after the investment has been recovered.

**LO4 Compute the simple rate of return for an investment.**

The simple rate of return is determined by dividing a project's accounting net operating income by the initial investment in the project. The simple rate of return is not a reliable guide for evaluating potential projects because it ignores the time value of money.

## GUIDANCE ANSWER TO DECISION POINT

**Financing the Sports Car (p. 502)**
The formal analysis, using the least-cost approach, appears below:

| Item | Month(s) | Amount of Cash Flows | 1% Factor | Present Value of Cash Flows |
|---|---|---|---|---|
| Pay cash for the car: | | | | |
| Cash payment | Now | $(21,495) | 1.000 | $(21,495) |
| Net present value | | | | $(21,495) |
| Lease the car: | | | | |
| Cash payment on lease signing | Now | $(2,078) | 1.000 | $ (2,078) |
| Monthly lease payment | 1–24 | $(300) | 21.243 | (6,373) |
| Final payment | 24 | $(13,776) | 0.788 | (10,855) |
| Net present value | | | | $(19,306) |
| Net present value in favor of leasing | | | | $ 2,189 |

The leasing alternative is $2,189 less costly, in terms of net present value, than the cash purchase alternative. In addition, the leasing alternative has the advantage that you can choose to not make the final payment of $13,776 at the end of 24 months if for some reason you decide you do not want to keep the car. For example, if the resale value of the car at that point is far less than $13,776, you may choose to return the car to the dealer and save the $13,776. If, however, you had purchased the car outright, you would not have this option—you could only realize the resale value. Because of this "real option," the leasing alternative is even more valuable than the net present value calculations indicate. Therefore, you should lease the car rather than pay cash (and borrow from the credit union).

## GUIDANCE ANSWERS TO CONCEPT CHECKS

1. **Choices a and c.** The total-cost and incremental-cost approaches always provide identical results. The present value of a dollar decreases as the time of receipt extends further into the future.
2. **Choice a.** The net present value of the project is $300,000 × 0.25 = $75,000.
3. **Choices a, b, and d.** The payback period does not consider the time value of money; the cost of capital is ignored. The simple rate of return is based on accounting net operating income, not cash flows. If two alternatives have the same present value of cash inflows, the alternative that requires the lower investment, as opposed to the higher investment, will have the higher project profitability index.

## REVIEW PROBLEM: COMPARISON OF CAPITAL BUDGETING METHODS

Lamar Company is considering a project that would have an eight-year life and require a $2,400,000 investment in equipment. At the end of eight years, the project would terminate and the equipment would have no salvage value. The project would provide net operating income each year as follows:

| | | |
|---|---|---|
| Sales | | $3,000,000 |
| Variable expenses | | 1,800,000 |
| Contribution margin | | 1,200,000 |
| Fixed expenses: | | |
| Advertising, salaries, and other fixed out-of-pocket costs | $700,000 | |
| Depreciation | 300,000 | |
| Total fixed expenses | | 1,000,000 |
| Net operating income | | $ 200,000 |

The company's discount rate is 12%.

***Required:***

1. Compute the annual net cash inflow from the project.
2. Compute the project's net present value. Is the project acceptable?
3. Compute the project's payback period.
4. Compute the project's simple rate of return.

**Solution to Review Problem**

1. The annual net cash inflow can be computed by deducting the cash expenses from sales:

| | |
|---|---|
| Sales | $3,000,000 |
| Variable expenses | 1,800,000 |
| Contribution margin | 1,200,000 |
| Advertising, salaries, and other fixed out-of-pocket costs | 700,000 |
| Annual net cash inflow | $ 500,000 |

Or the annual net cash inflow can be computed by adding depreciation back to net operating income:

| | |
|---|---|
| Net operating income | $200,000 |
| Add: Noncash deduction for depreciation | 300,000 |
| Annual net cash inflow | $500,000 |

2. The net present value is computed as follows:

| Item | Year(s) | Amount of Cash Flows | 12% Factor | Present Value of Cash Flows |
|---|---|---|---|---|
| Cost of new equipment | Now | $(2,400,000) | 1.000 | $(2,400,000) |
| Annual net cash inflow | 1–8 | $500,000 | 4.968 | 2,484,000 |
| Net present value | | | | $ 84,000 |

Yes, the project is acceptable because it has a positive net present value.

3. The formula for the payback period is:

$$\text{Payback period} = \frac{\text{Investment required}}{\text{Annual net cash flow}}$$

$$= \frac{\$2,400,000}{\$500,000}$$

$$= 4.8 \text{ years}$$

4. The formula for the simple rate of return is:

$$\text{Simple rate of return} = \frac{\text{Annual incremental net operating income}}{\text{Initial investment}}$$

$$= \frac{\$200{,}000}{\$2{,}400{,}000}$$

$$= 8.3\%$$

## GLOSSARY

**Capital budgeting** The process of planning significant investments in projects that have long-term implications such as the purchase of new equipment or the introduction of a new product. (p. 492)

**Cost of capital** The average rate of return a company must pay to its long-term creditors and shareholders for the use of their funds. (p. 495)

**Internal rate of return** The discount rate at which the net present value of an investment project is zero; the rate of return of a project over its useful life. (p. 504)

**Net present value** The difference between the present value of an investment project's cash inflows and the present value of its cash outflows. (p. 493)

**Out-of-pocket costs** Actual cash outlays for salaries, advertising, repairs, and similar costs. (p. 497)

**Payback period** The length of time that it takes for a project to fully recover its initial cost out of the net cash inflows that it generates. (p. 504)

**Postaudit** The follow-up after a project has been approved and implemented to determine whether expected results were actually realized. (p. 510)

**Preference decision** A decision in which the alternatives must be ranked. (p. 492)

**Project profitability index** The ratio of the net present value of a project's cash flows to the investment required. (p. 503)

**Screening decision** A decision as to whether a proposed investment project is acceptable. (p. 492)

**Simple rate of return** The rate of return computed by dividing a project's annual incremental accounting net operating income by the initial investment required. (p. 508)

**Working capital** Current assets less current liabilities. (p. 494)

## QUESTIONS

**11–1** What is the difference between capital budgeting screening decisions and capital budgeting preference decisions?

**11–2** What is meant by the term *time value of money?*

**11–3** What is meant by the term *discounting?*

**11–4** Why isn't accounting net income used in the net present value method of making capital budgeting decisions?

**11–5** Why are discounted cash flow methods of making capital budgeting decisions superior to other methods?

**11–6** What is net present value? Can it ever be negative? Explain.

**11–7** Identify two simplifying assumptions associated with discounted cash flow methods of making capital budgeting decisions.

**11–8** If a company has to pay interest of 14% on long-term debt, then its cost of capital is 14%. Do you agree? Explain.

**11–9** Explain how the cost of capital serves as a screening tool when using (*a*) the net present value method and (*b*) the internal rate of return method.

**11–10** As the discount rate increases, the present value of a given future cash flow also increases. Do you agree? Explain.

**11–11** Refer to Exhibit 11–4. Is the return on this investment proposal exactly 14%, more than 14%, or less than 14%? Explain.

**11–12** How is the project profitability index computed, and what does it measure?

**11–13** What is meant by the term *payback period?* How is the payback period determined? How can the payback method be useful?

**11–14** What is the major criticism of the payback and simple rate of return methods of making capital budgeting decisions?

**Multiple-choice questions are provided on the text website at www.mhhe.com/brewer6e.**

connect ACCOUNTING

## APPLYING EXCEL

### Available with McGraw-Hill's *Connect® Accounting.*

LO1, LO3

The Excel worksheet form that appears below is to be used to recreate Example B and Exhibit 11–2 on pages 496–497. Download the workbook containing this form from the Online Learning Center at www.mhhe.com/brewer6e. *On the website you will also receive instructions about how to use this worksheet form.*

| | A | B | C | D | E | F | G |
|---|---|---|---|---|---|---|---|
| 1 | Chapter 11: Applying Excel | | | | | | |
| 2 | | | | | | | |
| 3 | **Data** | | | | | | |
| 4 | **Example** B | | | | | | |
| 5 | Cost of equipment needed | | | $60,000 | | | |
| 6 | Working capital needed | | | $100,000 | | | |
| 7 | Overhaul of equipment in | 4 | years | $5,000 | | | |
| 8 | Salvage value of the equipment in | 5 | years | $10,000 | | | |
| 9 | Annual revenues and costs: | | | | | | |
| 10 | Sales revenues | | | $200,000 | | | |
| 11 | Cost of goods sold | | | $125,000 | | | |
| 12 | Out-of-pocket operating costs | | | $35,000 | | | |
| 13 | Discount rate | | | 14% | | | |
| 14 | | | | | | | |
| 15 | *Enter a formula into each of the cells marked with a ? below* | | | | | | |
| 16 | **Exhibit** 11-2 | | | | | | |
| 17 | | | | | | | |
| 18 | Sales revenues | | | ? | | | |
| 19 | Less cost of goods sold | | | ? | | | |
| 20 | Less out-of-pocket costs | | | ? | | | |
| 21 | Annual net cash inflows | | | ? | | | |
| 22 | | | | | | | |
| 23 | | | | *Amount of* | ? | *Present Value* | |
| 24 | | | *Year(s)* | *Cash Flow* | *Factor** | *of Cash Flows* | |
| 25 | Purchase of equipment | | Now | ? | 1.000 | ? | |
| 26 | Working capital needed | | Now | ? | 1.000 | ? | |
| 27 | Overhaul of equipment | | ? | ? | ? | ? | |
| 28 | Annual net cash inflows from sales of the product line | 1- | ? | ? | ? | ? | |
| 29 | Salvage value of equipment | | ? | ? | ? | ? | |
| 30 | Working capital released | | ? | ? | ? | ? | |
| 31 | Net present value | | | | | ? | |
| 32 | | | | | | | |
| 33 | *Use the formulas from Appendix 11B: | | | | | | |
| 34 | Present value of $1 = 1/(1+r)^n | | | | | | |
| 35 | Present value of an annuity of $1 = (1/r)*(1-(1/(1+r)^n)) | | | | | | |
| 36 | where n is the number of years and r is the discount rate | | | | | | |
| 37 | | | | | | | |

Chapter 11 Form / Filled in Chapter 11 Form / Chapter 11 Form

You should proceed to the requirements below only after completing your worksheet.

***Required:***

1. Check your worksheet by changing the discount rate to 10%. The net present value should now be between $56,518 and $56,535—depending on the precision of the calculations. If you do not get an answer in this range, find the errors in your worksheet and correct them.

   Explain why the net present value has fallen as a result of reducing the discount rate from 14% to 10%.

2. The company is considering another project involving the purchase of new equipment. Change the data area of your worksheet to match the following:

| Data | | |
|---|---|---|
| Example B | | |
| Cost of equipment needed | | $120,000 |
| Working capital needed | | $80,000 |
| Overhaul of equipment in | 5 years | $40,000 |
| Salvage of the equipment in | 10 years | $20,000 |
| Annual revenues and costs: | | |
| Sales revenues | | $245,000 |
| Cost of goods sold | | $160,000 |
| Out-of-pocket operating costs | | $50,000 |
| Discount rate | | 14% |

a. What is the net present value of the project?
b. Experiment with changing the discount rate in one percent increments (e.g., 13%, 12%, 15%, etc.). At what interest rate does the net present value turn from negative to positive?

## THE FOUNDATIONAL 15

connect ACCOUNTING

**Available with McGraw-Hill's *Connect® Accounting.***

LO1, LO2, LO3, LO4

Cardinal Company is considering a project that would require a $2,975,000 investment in equipment with a useful life of five years. At the end of five years, the project would terminate and the equipment would be sold for its salvage value of $300,000. The company's discount rate is 14%. The project would provide net operating income each year as follows:

| | | |
|---|---|---|
| Sales | | $2,735,000 |
| Variable expenses | | 1,000,000 |
| Contribution margin | | 1,735,000 |
| Fixed expenses: | | |
| Advertising, salaries, and other fixed out-of-pocket costs | $735,000 | |
| Depreciation | 535,000 | |
| Total fixed expenses | | 1,270,000 |
| Net operating income | | $ 465,000 |

***Required:***

1. Which item(s) in the income statement shown above will not affect cash flows?
2. What are the project's annual net cash inflows?
3. What is the present value of the project's annual net cash inflows?
4. What is the present value of the equipment's salvage value at the end of five years?
5. What is the project's net present value?
6. What is the project profitability index for this project? (Round your answer to the nearest whole percent.)
7. What is the project's payback period?
8. What is the project's simple rate of return for each of the five years?
9. If the company's discount rate was 16% instead of 14%, would you expect the project's net present value to be higher than, lower than, or the same as your answer to question 4? No computations are necessary
10. If the equipment's salvage value was $500,000 instead of $300,000, would you expect the project's payback period to be higher than, lower than, or the same as your answer to question 7? No computations are necessary.
11. If the equipment's salvage value was $500,000 instead of $300,000, would you expect the project's net present value to be higher than, lower than, or the same as your answer to question 4? No computations are necessary.

12. If the equipment's salvage value was $500,000 instead of $300,000, what would be the project's simple rate of return?
13. Assume a postaudit showed that all estimates (including total sales) were exactly correct except for the variable expense ratio, which actually turned out to be 45%. What was the project's actual net present value?
14. Assume a postaudit showed that all estimates (including total sales) were exactly correct except for the variable expense ratio, which actually turned out to be 45%. What was the project's actual payback period?
15. Assume a postaudit showed that all estimates (including total sales) were exactly correct except for the variable expense ratio, which actually turned out to be 45%. What was the project's actual simple rate of return?

## EXERCISES

**All applicable exercises are available with McGraw-Hill's *Connect® Accounting.***

### EXERCISE 11–1 Net Present Value Method [LO1]

The management of Opry Company, a wholesale distributor of suntan products, is considering the purchase of a $25,000 machine that would reduce operating costs in its warehouse by $4,000 per year. At the end of the machine's 10-year useful life, it will have no scrap value. The company's required rate of return is 12%.

Required rate of return = 9%

***Required:***
(Ignore income taxes.)
1. Determine the net present value of the investment in the machine.
2. What is the difference between the total, undiscounted cash inflows and cash outflows over the entire life of the machine?

### EXERCISE 11–2 Preference Ranking [LO2]

Information on four investment proposals is given below:

| | Investment Proposal | | | |
|---|---|---|---|---|
| | A | B | C | D |
| Investment required | $(85,000) | $(200,000) | $(90,000) | $(170,000) |
| Present value of cash inflows | 119,000 | 250,000 | 135,000 | 221,000 |
| Net present value | $ 34,000 | $ 50,000 | $ 45,000 | $ 51,000 |
| Life of the project | 5 years | 7 years | 6 years | 6 years |

***Required:***
1. Compute the project profitability index for each investment proposal.
2. Rank the proposals in terms of preference.

### EXERCISE 11–3 Payback Method [LO3]

The management of Weimar, Inc., a civil engineering design company, is considering an investment in a high-quality blueprint printer with the following cash flows:

Investment in year 1 = $29,000

| Year | Investment | Cash Inflow |
|---|---|---|
| 1 | $38,000 | $2,000 |
| 2 | $6,000 | $4,000 |
| 3 | | $8,000 |
| 4 | | $9,000 |
| 5 | | $12,000 |
| 6 | | $10,000 |
| 7 | | $8,000 |
| 8 | | $6,000 |
| 9 | | $5,000 |
| 10 | | $5,000 |

***Required:***

1. Determine the payback period of the investment.
2. Would the payback period be affected if the cash inflow in the last year were several times larger?

**EXERCISE 11–4 Simple Rate of Return Method [LO4]**

*Useful life of new machine = 8 years*

The management of Wallingford MicroBrew is considering the purchase of an automated bottling machine for $80,000. The machine would replace an old piece of equipment that costs $33,000 per year to operate. The new machine would cost $10,000 per year to operate. The old machine currently in use could be sold now for a scrap value of $5,000. The new machine would have a useful life of 10 years with no salvage value.

***Required:***

Compute the simple rate of return on the new automated bottling machine.

**EXERCISE 11–5 Payback Period and Simple Rate of Return [LO3, LO4]**

The Heritage Amusement Park would like to construct a new ride called the Sonic Boom, which the park management feels would be very popular. The ride would cost $450,000 to construct, and it would have a 10% salvage value at the end of its 15-year useful life. The company estimates that the following annual costs and revenues would be associated with the ride:

*Ticket revenues = $235,000*

| | | |
|---|---|---|
| Ticket revenues ............................ | | $250,000 |
| Less operating expenses: | | |
| Maintenance ............................ | $40,000 | |
| Salaries.................................... | 90,000 | |
| Depreciation ............................ | 27,000 | |
| Insurance.................................. | 30,000 | |
| Total operating expenses ............. | | 187,000 |
| Net operating income.................... | | $ 63,000 |

***Required:***

(Ignore income taxes.)

1. Assume that the Heritage Amusement Park will not construct a new ride unless the ride provides a payback period of six years or less. Does the Sonic Boom ride satisfy this requirement?
2. Compute the simple rate of return promised by the new ride. If Heritage Amusement Park requires a simple rate of return of at least 12%, does the Sonic Boom ride meet this criterion?

**EXERCISE 11–6 Comparison of Projects Using Net Present Value [LO1]**

Sharp Company has $15,000 to invest. The company is trying to decide between two alternative uses of the funds as follows:

*Discount rate = 8%*

| | Invest in Project A | Invest in Project B |
|---|---|---|
| Investment required.................................. | $15,000 | $15,000 |
| Annual cash inflows.................................. | $4,000 | $0 |
| Single cash inflow at the end of 10 years.... | | $60,000 |
| Life of the project...................................... | 10 years | 10 years |

Sharp Company uses a 16% discount rate.

***Required:***

(Ignore income taxes.) Which investment would you recommend that the company accept? Show all computations using net present value. Prepare separate computations for each investment.

**EXERCISE 11–7 Basic Payback Period and Simple Rate of Return Computations [LO3, LO4]**

Martin Company is considering the purchase of a new piece of equipment. Relevant information concerning the equipment follows:

| | |
|---|---|
| Purchase cost | $180,000 |
| Annual cost savings that will be provided by the equipment | $37,500 |
| Life of the equipment | 12 years |

TAKE TWO

Life of the equipment = 15 years

***Required:***

(Ignore income taxes.)

1. Compute the payback period for the equipment. If the company rejects all proposals with a payback period of more than four years, would the equipment be purchased?
2. Compute the simple rate of return on the equipment. Use straight-line depreciation based on the equipment's useful life. Would the equipment be purchased if the company's required rate of return is 14%?

**EXERCISE 11–8 Net Present Value Analysis of Two Alternatives [LO1]**

Wriston Company has $300,000 to invest. The company is trying to decide between two alternative uses of the funds. The alternatives are as follows:

| | A | B |
|---|---|---|
| Cost of equipment required | $300,000 | $0 |
| Working capital investment required | $0 | $300,000 |
| Annual cash inflows | $80,000 | $60,000 |
| Salvage value of equipment in seven years | $20,000 | $0 |
| Life of the project | 7 years | 7 years |

TAKE TWO

Alternative A: salvage value = $50,000

The working capital needed for project B will be released for investment elsewhere at the end of seven years. Wriston Company uses a 20% discount rate.

***Required:***

(Ignore income taxes.) Which investment alternative (if either) would you recommend that the company accept? Show all computations using the net present value format. Prepare separate computations for each project.

**EXERCISE 11–9 Basic Net Present Value Analysis [LO1]**

On January 2, Fred Critchfield paid $18,000 for 900 shares of the common stock of Acme Company. Mr. Critchfield received an $0.80 per share dividend on the stock at the end of each year for four years. At the end of four years, he sold the stock for $22,500. Mr. Critchfield has a goal of earning a minimum return of 12% on all of his investments.

***Required:***

(Ignore income taxes.) Did Mr. Critchfield earn a 12% return on the stock? Use the net present value method and the general format shown in Exhibit 11–2. Round all computations to the nearest whole dollar.

TAKE TWO

Dividend = $1.50 per share

## PROBLEMS

connect ACCOUNTING Alternate problem set is available on the text website and in Connect® Accounting.

**All applicable problems are available with McGraw-Hill's *Connect® Accounting*.**

CHECK FIGURE
NPV: $(45,210)

**PROBLEM 11–10A Basic Net Present Value Analysis [LO1]**

Renfree Mines, Inc., owns the mining rights to a large tract of land in a mountainous area. The tract contains a mineral deposit that the company believes might be commercially attractive to mine and sell. An engineering and cost analysis has been made, and it is expected that the following cash flows would be associated with opening and operating a mine in the area:

| | |
|---|---|
| Cost of equipment required | $850,000 |
| Annual net cash receipts | $230,000* |
| Working capital required | $100,000 |
| Cost of road repairs in three years | $60,000 |
| Salvage value of equipment in five years | $200,000 |

*Receipts from sales of ore, less out-of-pocket costs for salaries, utilities, insurance, and so forth.

The mineral deposit would be exhausted after five years of mining. At that point, the working capital would be released for reinvestment elsewhere. The company's required rate of return is 14%.

***Required:***

(Ignore income taxes.) Determine the net present value of the proposed mining project. Should the project be accepted? Explain.

CHECK FIGURE
(1) Project profitability index for project 1: 0.182

**PROBLEM 11–11A Preference Ranking of Investment Projects [LO2]**

Austin Company is investigating four different investment opportunities. Information on the four projects under study is given below:

| | Project Number | | | |
|---|---|---|---|---|
| | 1 | 2 | 3 | 4 |
| Investment required | $(480,000) | $(360,000) | $(270,000) | $(450,000) |
| Present value of cash inflows at a 10% discount rate | 567,270 | 433,400 | 336,140 | 522,970 |
| Net present value | $ 87,270 | $ 73,400 | $ 66,140 | $ 72,970 |
| Life of the project | 6 years | 12 years | 6 years | 3 years |
| Internal rate of return | 16% | 14% | 18% | 19% |

Because the company's required rate of return is 10%, a 10% discount rate has been used in the above present value computations. Limited funds are available for investment, so the company can't accept all of the available projects.

***Required:***

1. Compute the project profitability index for each investment project.
2. Rank the four projects according to preference, in terms of:
   a. Net present value.
   b. Project profitability index.
   c. Internal rate of return.
3. Which ranking do you prefer? Why?

**PROBLEM 11–12A Preference Ranking of Investment Projects [LO2]**

CHECK FIGURE
(1) Project profitability index for Project A: 0.28

Yancey Company has limited funds available for investment and must ration the funds among four competing projects. Selected information on the four projects follows:

| Project | Investment Required | Net Present Value | Life of the Project (years) | Internal Rate of Return |
|---|---|---|---|---|
| A.................... | $800,000 | $221,615 | 7 | 18% |
| B.................... | $675,000 | $210,000 | 12 | 16% |
| C.................... | $500,000 | $175,175 | 7 | 20% |
| D.................... | $700,000 | $152,544 | 3 | 22% |

The net present values above have been computed using a 10% discount rate. The company wants your assistance in determining which project to accept first, which to accept second, and so forth. The company's investment funds are limited.

***Required:***

1. Compute the project profitability index for each project.
2. In order of preference, rank the four projects in terms of:
   a. Net present value.
   b. Project profitability index.
   c. Internal rate of return.
3. Which ranking do you prefer? Why?

**PROBLEM 11–13A Simple Rate of Return; Payback [LO3, LO4]**

CHECK FIGURE
(2) 14% simple rate of return

Lugano's Pizza Parlor is considering the purchase of a large oven and related equipment for mixing and baking "crazy bread." The oven and equipment would cost $120,000 delivered and installed. It would be usable for about 15 years, after which it would have a 10% scrap value. The following additional information is available:

a. Mr. Lugano estimates that purchase of the oven and equipment would allow the pizza parlor to bake and sell 72,000 loaves of crazy bread each year. The bread sells for $1.25 per loaf.
b. The cost of the ingredients in a loaf of bread is 40% of the selling price. Mr. Lugano estimates that other costs each year associated with the bread would be as follows: salaries, $18,000; utilities, $9,000; and insurance, $3,000.
c. The pizza parlor uses straight-line depreciation on all assets, deducting salvage value from original cost.

***Required:***

(Ignore income taxes.)

1. Prepare a contribution format income statement showing the net operating income each year from production and sale of the crazy bread.
2. Compute the simple rate of return for the new oven and equipment. If a simple rate of return above 12% is acceptable to Mr. Lugano, will he purchase the oven and equipment?
3. Compute the payback period on the oven and equipment. If Mr. Lugano purchases any equipment with less than a six-year payback, will he purchase this equipment?

**PROBLEM 11–14A Basic Net Present Value Analysis [LO1]**

eXcel

CHECK FIGURE
(2) NPV: $12,516

Doughboy Bakery would like to buy a new machine for putting icing and other toppings on pastries. These are now put on by hand. The machine that the bakery is considering costs $90,000 new. It would last the bakery for eight years but would require a $7,500 overhaul at the end of the fifth year. After eight years, the machine could be sold for $6,000.

The bakery estimates that it will cost $14,000 per year to operate the new machine. The present manual method of putting toppings on the pastries costs $35,000 per year. In addition to reducing operating costs, the new machine will allow the bakery to increase its production of pastries by 5,000 packages per year. The bakery realizes a contribution margin of $0.60 per package. The bakery requires a 16% return on all investments in equipment.

***Required:***

(Ignore income taxes.)

1. What are the annual net cash inflows that will be provided by the new machine?
2. Compute the new machine's net present value. Use the incremental cost approach, and round all dollar amounts to the nearest whole dollar.

CHECK FIGURE
(1) NPV in favor of leasing: $52,340

**PROBLEM 11–15A Net Present Value Analysis of a Lease or Buy Decision [LO1]**

Blinko Products wants an airplane for use by its corporate staff. The airplane that the company wishes to acquire, a Zephyr II, can be either purchased or leased from the manufacturer. The company has made the following evaluation of the two alternatives:

*Purchase alternative.* If the Zephyr II is purchased, then the costs incurred by the company would be as follows:

| | |
|---|---|
| Purchase cost of the plane | $850,000 |
| Annual cost of servicing, licenses, and taxes | $9,000 |
| Repairs: | |
| First three years, per year | $3,000 |
| Fourth year | $5,000 |
| Fifth year | $10,000 |

The plane would be sold after five years. Based on current resale values, the company would be able to sell it for about one-half of its original cost at the end of the five-year period.

*Lease alternative.* If the Zephyr II is leased, then the company would have to make an immediate deposit of $50,000 to cover any damage during use. The lease would run for five years, at the end of which time the deposit would be refunded. The lease would require an annual rental payment of $200,000 (the first payment is due at the end of Year 1). As part of this lease cost, the manufacturer would provide all servicing and repairs, license the plane, and pay all taxes. At the end of the five-year period, the plane would revert to the manufacturer, as owner.

Blinko Products' required rate of return is 18%.

***Required:***

(Ignore income taxes.)

1. Use the total-cost approach to determine the present value of the cash flows associated with each alternative.
2. Which alternative would you recommend that the company accept? Why?

CHECK FIGURE
(1b) 9.2% simple rate of return

**PROBLEM 11–16A Simple Rate of Return and Payback Analysis of Two Machines [LO3, LO4]**

Blue Ridge Furniture is considering the purchase of two different items of equipment, as described below:

**Machine A.** A machine has just come onto the market that compresses sawdust into various shelving products. Currently, the sawdust is disposed of as a waste product. The following information is available about the machine:

a. The machine would cost $780,000 and would have a 25% salvage value at the end of its 10-year useful life. The company uses straight-line depreciation and considers salvage value in computing depreciation deductions.
b. The shelving products produced by the machine would generate revenues of $350,000 per year. Variable manufacturing costs would be 20% of sales.
c. Fixed annual expenses associated with the new shelving products would be: advertising, $42,000; salaries, $86,000; utilities, $9,000; and insurance, $13,000.

**Machine B.** A second machine has come onto the market that would automate a sanding process that is now done largely by hand. The following information is available about this machine:

a. The new sanding machine would cost $220,000 and would have no salvage value at the end of its 10-year useful life. The company would use straight-line depreciation.
b. Several old pieces of sanding equipment that are fully depreciated would be disposed of at a scrap value of $7,200.
c. The new sanding machine would provide substantial annual savings in cash operating costs. It would require an operator at an annual salary of $26,000 and $3,000 in annual maintenance costs. The current, hand-operated sanding procedure costs the company $85,000 per year.

Blue Ridge Furniture requires a simple rate of return of 16% on all equipment purchases. Also, the company will not purchase equipment unless the equipment has a payback period of four years or less.

***Required:***

(Ignore income taxes.)

1. For machine A:
   a. Prepare a contribution format income statement showing the expected net operating income each year from the new shelving products.

b. Compute the simple rate of return.
c. Compute the payback period.

2. For machine B:
   a. Compute the simple rate of return.
   b. Compute the payback period.
3. According to the company's criteria, which machine, if either, should the company purchase?

**PROBLEM 11–17A Simple Rate of Return; Payback [LO3, LO4]**

CHECK FIGURE
(3) Payback: 2.5 years

Nagoya Amusements Corporation places electronic games and other amusement devices in supermarkets and similar outlets throughout Japan. Nagoya Amusements is investigating the purchase of a new electronic game called Mystic Invaders. The manufacturer will sell 20 games to Nagoya Amusements for a total price of ¥180,000. (The Japanese currency is the yen, which is denoted by the symbol ¥.) Nagoya Amusements has determined the following additional information about the game:

a. The game would have a five-year useful life and a negligible salvage value. The company uses straight-line depreciation.
b. The game would replace other games that are unpopular and generating little revenue. These other games would be sold for a total of ¥30,000.
c. Nagoya Amusements estimates that Mystic Invaders would generate annual incremental revenues of ¥200,000 (total for all 20 games). Annual incremental out-of-pocket costs would be (in total): maintenance, ¥50,000; and insurance, ¥10,000. In addition, Nagoya Amusements would have to pay a commission of 40% of total revenues to the supermarkets and other outlets in which the games were placed.

***Required:***

(Ignore income taxes.)

1. Prepare a contribution format income statement showing the net operating income each year from Mystic Invaders.
2. Compute the simple rate of return on Mystic Invaders. Will the game be purchased if Nagoya Amusements accepts any project with a simple rate of return greater than 14%?
3. Compute the payback period on Mystic Invaders. If the company accepts any investment with a payback period of less than three years, will the game be purchased?

**PROBLEM: 11–18A Net Present Value; Total and Incremental Approaches [LO1]**

CHECK FIGURE
(1) NPV in favor of the new generator: $14,635

Eastbay Hospital has an auxiliary generator that is used when power failures occur. The generator is worn out and must be either overhauled or replaced with a new generator. The hospital has assembled the following information:

| | Present Generator | New Generator |
|---|---|---|
| Purchase cost new | $16,000 | $20,000 |
| Remaining book value | $9,000 | — |
| Overhaul needed now | $8,000 | — |
| Annual cash operating costs | $12,500 | $7,500 |
| Salvage value-now | $4,000 | — |
| Salvage value-eight years from now | $3,000 | $6,000 |

If the company keeps and overhauls its present generator, then the generator will be usable for eight more years. If a new generator is purchased, it will be used for eight years, after which it will be replaced. The new generator would be diesel-powered, resulting in a substantial reduction in annual operating costs, as shown above.

The hospital computes depreciation on a straight-line basis. All equipment purchases are evaluated using a 16% discount rate.

***Required:***

(Ignore income taxes.)

1. Should Eastbay Hospital keep the old generator or purchase the new one? Use the total-cost approach to net present value in making your decision.
2. Redo (1) above, this time using the incremental-cost approach.

eXcel

CHECK FIGURE
(1) Year 3 net cash flow: $30,000

**PROBLEM 11–19A Net Present Value Analysis of a New Product [LO1]**

Atwood Company has an opportunity to produce and sell a revolutionary new smoke detector for homes. To determine whether this would be a profitable venture, the company has gathered the following data on probable costs and market potential:

a. New equipment would have to be acquired to produce the smoke detector. The equipment would cost $100,000 and be usable for 12 years. After 12 years, it would have a salvage value equal to 10% of the original cost.
b. Production and sales of the smoke detector would require a working capital investment of $40,000 to finance accounts receivable, inventories, and day-to-day cash needs. This working capital would be released for use elsewhere after 12 years.
c. An extensive marketing study projects sales in units over the next 12 years as follows:

| Year | Sales in Units |
|---|---|
| 1 .......................... | 4,000 |
| 2 .......................... | 7,000 |
| 3 .......................... | 10,000 |
| 4–12 ...................... | 12,000 |

d. The smoke detectors would sell for $45 each; variable costs for production, administration, and sales would be $25 per unit.
e. To gain entry into the market, the company would have to advertise heavily in the early years of sales. The advertising program follows:

| Year | Amount of Yearly Advertising |
|---|---|
| 1–2 ................... | $70,000 |
| 3 ..................... | $50,000 |
| 4–12 .................. | $40,000 |

f. Other fixed costs for salaries, insurance, maintenance, and straight-line depreciation on equipment would total $127,500 per year. (Depreciation is based on cost less salvage value.)
g. The company's required rate of return is 20%.

***Required:***

(Ignore income taxes.)

1. Compute the net cash inflow (cash receipts less yearly cash operating expenses) anticipated from sale of the smoke detectors for each year over the next 12 years.
2. Using the data computed in (1) above and other data provided in the problem, determine the net present value of the proposed investment. Would you recommend that Atwood Company accept the smoke detector as a new product?

eXcel

CHECK FIGURE
(1) Net annual cash receipts: $63,900

**PROBLEM 11–20A Net Present Value Analysis [LO1]**

Frank White will retire in six years. He wants to open some type of small business operation that can be managed in the free time he has available from his regular occupation, but that can be closed easily when he retires. He is considering several investment alternatives, one of which is to open a laundromat. After careful study, Mr. White has determined the following:

a. Washers, dryers, and other equipment needed to open the laundromat would cost $194,000. In addition, $6,000 in working capital would be required to purchase an inventory of soap, bleaches, and related items and to provide change for change machines. (The soap, bleaches, and related items would be sold to customers at cost.) After six years, the working capital would be released for investment elsewhere.
b. The laundromat would charge $1.50 per use for the washers and $0.75 per use for the dryers. Mr. White expects the laundromat to gross $1,800 each week from the washers and $1,125 each week from the dryers.
c. The only variable costs in the laundromat would be 7½ cents per use for water and electricity for the washers and 9 cents per use for gas and electricity for the dryers.

d. Fixed costs would be $3,000 per month for rent, $1,500 per month for cleaning, and $1,875 per month for maintenance, insurance, and other items.
e. The equipment would have a 10% disposal value in six years.

Mr. White will not open the laundromat unless it provides at least a 12% return.

***Required:***

(Ignore income taxes.)

1. Assuming that the laundromat would be open 52 weeks a year, compute the expected annual net cash receipts from its operation (gross cash receipts less cash disbursements). (Do not include the cost of the equipment, the working capital, or the salvage values in these computations.)
2. Would you advise Mr. White to open the laundromat? Show computations using the net present value method of investment analysis. Round all dollar amounts to the nearest whole dollar.

**PROBLEM 11–21A Net Present Value Analysis of Securities [LO1]**

CHECK FIGURE
(1) $6,760 NPV of common stock

Anita Vasquez received $160,000 from her mother's estate. She placed the funds into the hands of a broker, who purchased the following securities on Anita's behalf:

a. Common stock was purchased at a cost of $80,000. The stock paid no dividends, but it was sold for $180,000 at the end of four years.
b. Preferred stock was purchased at its par value of $30,000. The stock paid a 6% dividend (based on par value) each year for four years. At the end of four years, the stock was sold for $24,000.
c. Bonds were purchased at a cost of $50,000. The bonds paid $3,000 in interest every six months. After four years, the bonds were sold for $58,500. (Note: In discounting a cash flow that occurs semiannually, the procedure is to halve the discount rate and double the number of periods. Use the same procedure in discounting the proceeds from the sale.)

The securities were all sold at the end of four years so that Anita would have funds available to start a new business venture. The broker stated that the investments had earned more than a 20% return, and he gave Anita the following computation to support his statement:

| | |
|---|---|
| Common stock: | |
| Gain on sale ($180,000 − $80,000) | $100,000 |
| Preferred stock: | |
| Dividends paid (6% × $30,000 × 4 years) | 7,200 |
| Loss on sale ($24,000 − $30,000) | (6,000) |
| Bonds: | |
| Interest paid ($3,000 × 8 periods) | 24,000 |
| Gain on sale ($58,500 − $50,000) | 8,500 |
| Net gain on all investments | $133,700 |

$$\frac{\$133{,}700 \div 4 \text{ years}}{\$160{,}000} = 20.9\%$$

***Required:***

(Ignore income taxes.)

1. Using a 20% discount rate, compute the net present value of each of the three investments. On which investment(s) did Anita earn a 20% rate of return? (Round computations to the nearest whole dollar.)
2. Considering all three investments together, did Anita earn a 20% rate of return? Explain.
3. Anita wants to use the $262,500 proceeds ($180,000 + $24,000 + $58,500 = $262,500) from sale of the securities to open a fast-food franchise under a 10-year contract. What net annual cash inflow must the store generate for Anita to earn a 16% return over the 10-year period? Anita will not receive back her original investment at the end of the contract. (Round computations to the nearest whole dollar.)

**PROBLEM 11–22A Keep or Sell Property [LO1]**

Ben Ryatt, professor of languages at a southern university, owns a small office building adjacent to the university campus. He acquired the property 12 years ago at a total cost of $560,000—$52,000 for the land and $508,000 for the building. He has just received an offer from a realty company that wants to purchase the property; however, the property has been a good source of income over the years, so Professor Ryatt is unsure whether he should keep it or sell it. His alternatives are:

CHECK FIGURE
PV of cash flows for the alternative of keeping the property: $251,543

**Keep the property.** Professor Ryatt's accountant has kept careful records of the income realized from the property over the past 10 years. These records indicate the following annual revenues and expenses:

| | | |
|---|---|---|
| Rental receipts | | $150,000 |
| Less building expenses: | | |
| Utilities | $28,600 | |
| Depreciation of building | 17,800 | |
| Property taxes and insurance | 19,500 | |
| Repairs and maintenance | 10,500 | |
| Custodial help and supplies | 43,500 | 119,900 |
| Net operating income | | $ 30,100 |

Professor Ryatt makes a $12,600 mortgage payment each year on the property. The mortgage will be paid off in 10 more years. He has been depreciating the building by the straight-line method, assuming a salvage value of $9,600 for the building, which he still thinks is an appropriate figure. He feels sure that the building can be rented for another 16 years. He also feels sure that 16 years from now the land will be worth 2.5 times what he paid for it.

**Sell the property.** A realty company has offered to purchase the property by paying $150,000 immediately and $23,000 per year for the next 16 years. Control of the property would go to the realty company immediately. To sell the property, Professor Ryatt would need to pay the mortgage off, which could be done by making a lump-sum payment of $71,000.

***Required:***

(Ignore income taxes.) Professor Ryatt requires a 14% rate of return. Would you recommend he keep or sell the property? Show computations using the total-cost approach to net present value.

## BUILDING YOUR SKILLS

### ETHICS CHALLENGE

After five years with a national CPA firm with mostly large manufacturing clients, Amy Kimbell joined Hi-Quality Productions Inc. (Hi-Q) as manager of Manufacturing Accounting. Amy has both CPA and CMA credentials.

Hi-Q is a publicly held company producing automotive components. One operation in the Alpha Division requires a highly automated process. Hi-Q's top management and board of directors had outsourced this particular high-tech operation to another company to avoid making a large investment in technology they viewed as constantly changing.

Each operating division of Hi-Q has a budget committee. Two years ago, the Alpha Division budget committee presented to the board its proposal to bring the high-tech operation in house. This would require a capital investment of approximately $4 million but would lead to more than enough cost savings to justify this expenditure. The board approved the proposal, and the investment was made. Later the same year, Amy Kimbell was promoted to assistant corporate controller. In this position, she sits on the budget committee of all divisions.

A little more than a year after the high-tech process was put into operation, the board requested a postaudit review of the actual cost savings. When the board requests such a review, the data are supplied by the management of the affected division and are reviewed by the division's budget committee. When the data were sent to the budget committee for review, Amy Kimbell noted that several of the projections in the original proposal were very aggressive. These included a very high salvage value for the equipment as well as a very long useful life over which cost savings were projected to occur. If more realistic projections had been used, Amy doubted that the board would have agreed to make the investment.

Also in the postaudit review, Amy noted that substantial amounts of incremental service department operating costs directly caused by the new investment were not being attributed to the high-tech operation. Instead, these costs were being allocated as general overhead to all departments. In addition, she noted that the estimated rate for spoiled and defective work contained in the proposal was being used in the review rather than the actual rate, which was considerably higher.

When Amy Kimbell brought these points to the attention of the division's budget committee, she was told that as a new member of the committee she would not be held responsible for decisions, such as the investment in the high-tech operation, that were made prior to her arrival. Accordingly, she should let the seasoned members of the committee handle this particular review. When Amy continued to express her concerns, she was firmly informed that it had been the unanimous decision of the committee to approve the original proposal because it was thought to be in the best long-run interest of the company. And given this consensus, it was felt that certain "adjustments and exceptions" to the postaudit review were justified to ensure the overall long-run well-being of the company.

**Required:**

1. What should Amy do? (Refer to the IMA's Statement of Ethical Professional Practice for guidance.)
2. Do you have any suggestions for revising the way in which postaudits are conducted at Hi-Q? (Adapted from Roland L. Madison and Curtis C. Verschoor, "New Position Brings Ethical Dilemma," *Strategic Finance,* December 2000, pp. 22, 24. Used with permission from the IMA, Montvale, NJ, USA, www.imanet.org.)

## ANALYTICAL THINKING [LO1]

CHECK FIGURE
(1) NPV in favor of leasing: $3,949,950

Wyndham Stores operates a regional chain of upscale department stores. The company is going to open another store soon in a prosperous and growing suburban area. In discussing how the company can acquire the desired building and other facilities needed to open the new store, Harry Wilson, the company's marketing vice president, stated, "I know most of our competitors are starting to lease facilities, rather than buy, but I just can't see the economics of it. Our development people tell me that we can buy the building site, put a building on it, and get all the store fixtures we need for $14 million. They also say that property taxes, insurance, maintenance, and repairs would run $200,000 a year. When you figure that we plan to keep a site for 20 years, that's a total cost of $18 million. But then when you realize that the building and property will be worth at least $5 million in 20 years, that's a net cost to us of only $13 million. Leasing costs a lot more than that."

"I'm not so sure," replied Erin Reilley, the company's executive vice president. "Guardian Insurance Company is willing to purchase the building site, construct a building and install fixtures to our specifications, and then lease the facility to us for 20 years for an annual lease payment of only $1 million."

"That's just my point," said Harry. "At $1 million a year, it would cost us $20 million over the 20 years instead of just $13 million. And what would we have left at the end? Nothing! The building would belong to the insurance company! I'll bet they would even want the first lease payment in advance."

"That's right," replied Erin. "We would have to make the first payment immediately and then one payment at the beginning of each of the following 19 years. However, you're overlooking a few things. For one thing, we would have to tie up a lot of our funds for 20 years under the purchase alternative. We would have to put $6 million down immediately if we buy the property, and then we would have to pay the other $8 million off over four years at $2 million a year."

"But that cost is nothing compared to $20 million for leasing," said Harry. "Also, if we lease, I understand we would have to put up a $400,000 security deposit that we wouldn't get back until the end. And besides that, we would still have to pay all the repair and maintenance costs just like we owned the property. No wonder those insurance companies are so rich if they can swing deals like this."

"Well, I'll admit that I don't have all the figures sorted out yet," replied Erin. "But I do have the operating cost breakdown for the building, which includes $90,000 annually for property taxes, $60,000 for insurance, and $50,000 for repairs and maintenance. If we lease, Guardian will handle its own insurance costs and will pay the property taxes, but we'll have to pay for the repairs and maintenance. I need to put all this together and see if leasing makes any sense with our 12% before-tax required rate of return. The president wants a presentation and recommendation in the executive committee meeting tomorrow."

**Required:**

(Ignore income taxes.)

1. Using the net present value approach, determine whether Wyndham Stores should lease or buy the new store. Assume that you will be making your presentation before the company's executive committee.
2. How will you reply in the meeting if Harry Wilson brings up the issue of the building's future sales value?

## CASE [LO1]

CHECK FIGURE
(1) NPV in favor of alternative 2: $24,640

Woolrich Company's market research division has projected a substantial increase in demand over the next several years for one of the company's products. To meet this demand, the company will need to produce units as follows:

| Year | Production in Units |
|---|---|
| 1 | 20,000 |
| 2 | 30,000 |
| 3 | 40,000 |
| 4–10 | 45,000 |

At present, the company is using a single model 2600 machine to manufacture this product. To increase its productive capacity, the company is considering two alternatives:

*Alternative 1.* The company could purchase another model 2600 machine that would operate along with the one it now owns. The following information is available on this alternative:

a. The model 2600 machine now in use was purchased for $165,000 four years ago. Its present book value is $99,000, and its present market value is $90,000.
b. A new model 2600 machine costs $180,000 now. The old model 2600 machine will have to be replaced in six years at a cost of $200,000. The replacement machine will have a market value of about $100,000 when it is four years old.
c. The variable cost required to produce one unit of product using the model 2600 machine is given under the "general information" below.
d. Repairs and maintenance costs each year on a single model 2600 machine total $3,000.

*Alternative 2.* The company could purchase a model 5200 machine and use the old model 2600 machine as standby equipment. The model 5200 machine is a high-speed unit with double the capacity of the model 2600 machine. The following information is available on this alternative:

a. The cost of a new model 5200 machine is $250,000.
b. The variable cost required to produce one unit of product using the model 5200 machine is given under the "general information" below.
c. The model 5200 machine is more costly to maintain than the model 2600 machine. Repairs and maintenance on a model 5200 machine and on a model 2600 machine used as a standby would total $4,600 per year.

The following general information is available on the two alternatives:

a. Both the model 2600 machine and the model 5200 machine have a 10-year life from the time they are first used in production. The scrap value of both machines is negligible and can be ignored. Straight-line depreciation is used by the company.
b. The two machine models are not equally efficient. Comparative variable costs per unit of product are as follows:

| | Model 2600 | Model 5200 |
|---|---|---|
| Direct materials per unit | $0.36 | $0.40 |
| Direct labor per unit | 0.50 | 0.22 |
| Supplies and lubricants per unit | 0.04 | 0.08 |
| Total variable cost per unit | $0.90 | $0.70 |

c. No other factory costs would change as a result of the decision between the two machines.
d. Woolrich Company uses an 18% discount rate.

***Required:***

(Ignore income taxes.)

1. Which alternative should the company choose? Use the net present value approach. (Round to the nearest whole dollar.)
2. Suppose that the cost of direct materials increases by 50%. Would this make the model 5200 machine more or less desirable? Explain. No computations are needed.
3. Suppose that the cost of direct labor increases by 25%. Would this make the model 5200 machine more or less desirable? Explain. No computations are needed.

# APPENDIX 11A: THE CONCEPT OF PRESENT VALUE

**LEARNING OBJECTIVE 5**

Understand present value concepts and the use of present value tables.

A dollar received today is more valuable than a dollar received a year from now for the simple reason that if you have a dollar today, you can put it in the bank and have more than a dollar a year from now. Because dollars today are worth more than dollars in the future, cash flows that are received at different times must be valued differently.

## The Mathematics of Interest

If a bank pays 5% interest, then a deposit of $100 today will be worth $105 one year from now. This can be expressed as follows:

$$F_1 = P(1 + r) \quad (1)$$

where $F_1$ = the balance at the end of one period, $P$ = the amount invested now, and $r$ = the rate of interest per period.

In the case where $100 is deposited in a savings account that earns 5% interest, $P$ = $100 and $r = 0.05$. Under these conditions, $F_1$ = $105.

The $100 present outlay is called the **present value** of the $105 amount to be received in one year. It is also known as the *discounted value* of the future $105 receipt. The $100 represents the value in present terms of $105 to be received a year from now when the interest rate is 5%.

**Compound Interest** What if the $105 is left in the bank for a second year? In that case, by the end of the second year the original $100 deposit will have grown to $110.25:

| | |
|---|---|
| Original deposit | $100.00 |
| Interest for the first year: | |
| $100 × 0.05 | 5.00 |
| Balance at the end of the first year | 105.00 |
| Interest for the second year: | |
| $105 × 0.05 | 5.25 |
| Balance at the end of the second year | $110.25 |

Notice that the interest for the second year is $5.25, as compared to only $5.00 for the first year. This difference arises because interest is being paid on interest during the second year. That is, the $5.00 interest earned during the first year has been left in the account and has been added to the original $100 deposit when computing interest for the second year. This is known as **compound interest.** In this case, the compounding is annual. Interest can be compounded on a semiannual, quarterly, monthly, or even more frequent basis. The more frequently compounding is done, the more rapidly the balance will grow.

We can determine the balance in an account after $n$ periods of compounding using the following equation:

$$F_n = P(1 + r)^n \quad (2)$$

where $n$ = the number of periods of compounding.

If $n$ = 2 years and the interest rate is 5% per year, then the balance in two years will be computed as follows:

$$F_2 = \$100(1 + 0.05)^2$$

$$F_2 = \$110.25$$

**Present Value and Future Value** Exhibit 11A–1 shows the relationship between present value and future value. As shown in the exhibit, if $100 is deposited in a bank at 5% interest compounded annually, it will grow to $127.63 by the end of five years.

## Computation of Present Value

An investment can be viewed in two ways—either in terms of its future value or in terms of its present value. We have seen from our computations above that if we know the present value of a sum (such as our $100 deposit), the future value in $n$ years can be computed

**EXHIBIT 11A–1**
The Relationship between Present Value and Future Value

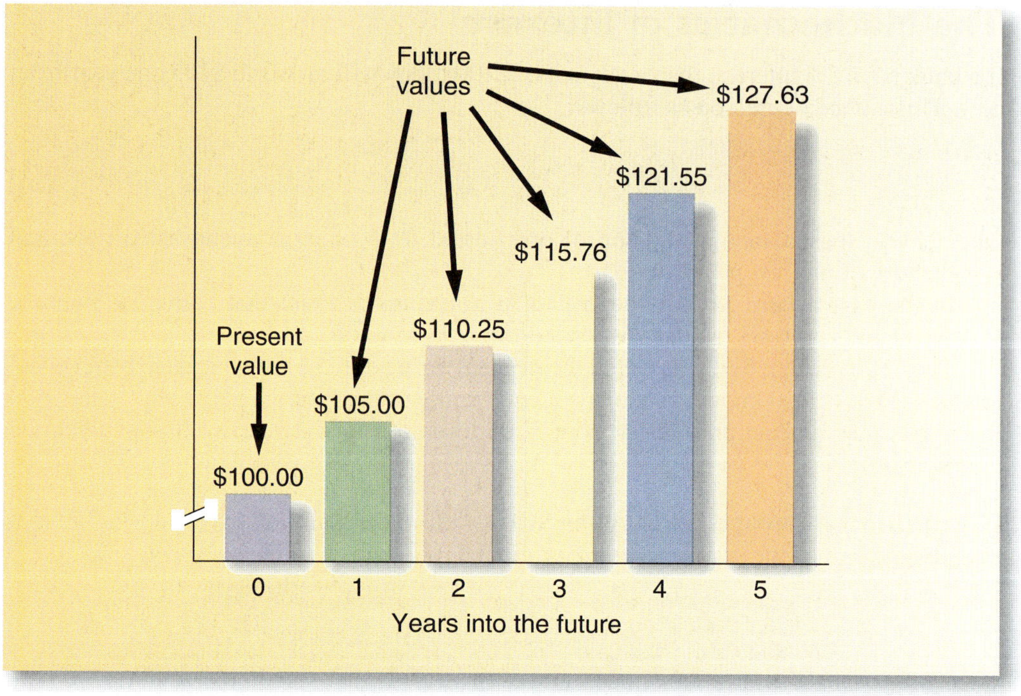


by using equation (2). But what if the situation is reversed and we know the *future* value of some amount but we do not know its present value?

For example, assume that you are to receive \$200 two years from now. You know that the future value of this sum is \$200 because this is the amount that you will be receiving in two years. But what is the sum's present value—what is it worth *right now?* The present value of any sum to be received in the future can be computed by turning equation (2) around and solving for $P$:

$$P = \frac{F_n}{(1 + r)^n} \qquad (3)$$

In our example, $Fn = \$200$ (the amount to be received in the future), $r = 0.05$ (the annual rate of interest), and $n = 2$ (the number of years in the future that the amount will be received).

$$P = \frac{\$200}{(1 + 0.05)^2}$$

$$P = \frac{\$200}{1.1025}$$

$$P = \$181.40$$

As shown by the computation above, the present value of a \$200 amount to be received two years from now is \$181.40 if the interest rate is 5%. In effect, \$181.40 received *right now* is equivalent to \$200 received two years from now.

The process of finding the present value of a future cash flow, which we have just completed, is called **discounting.** We have *discounted* the \$200 to its present value of \$181.40. The 5% interest that we have used to find this present value is called the **discount rate.** Discounting future sums to their present value is a common practice in business, particularly in capital budgeting decisions.

If you have a power key ($y^x$) on your calculator, the above calculations are fairly easy. However, some of the present value formulas we will be using are more complex. Fortunately, tables are available in which many of the calculations have already been done. For example, Exhibit 11B–1 in Appendix 11B shows the discounted present value of $1 to be received at various periods in the future at various interest rates. The table indicates that the present value of $1 to be received two periods from now at 5% is 0.907. Because in our example we want to know the present value of $200 rather than just $1, we need to multiply the factor in the table by $200:

$$\$200 \times 0.907 = \$181.40$$

This answer is the same as we obtained earlier using the formula in equation (3).

## Present Value of a Series of Cash Flows

Although some investments involve a single sum to be received (or paid) at a single point in the future, other investments involve a *series* of cash flows. A series of identical cash flows is known as an **annuity.** To provide an example, assume that a company has just purchased some government bonds. The bonds will yield interest of $15,000 each year and will be held for five years. What is the present value of the stream of interest receipts from the bonds? As shown in Exhibit 11A–2, if the discount rate is 12%, the present value of this stream is $54,075. The discount factors used in this exhibit were taken from Exhibit 11B–1 in Appendix 11B.

**EXHIBIT 11A–2**
Present Value of a Series of Cash Receipts

| Year | Factor at 12% (Exhibit 11B–1) | Interest Received | Present Value |
|---|---|---|---|
| 1 .................... | 0.893 | $15,000 | $13,395 |
| 2 .................... | 0.797 | $15,000 | 11,955 |
| 3 .................... | 0.712 | $15,000 | 10,680 |
| 4 .................... | 0.636 | $15,000 | 9,540 |
| 5 .................... | 0.567 | $15,000 | 8,505 |
| | | | $54,075 |

Exhibit 11A–2 illustrates two important points. First, the present value of the $15,000 interest declines the further it is into the future. The present value of $15,000 received a year from now is $13,395, as compared to only $8,505 if received five years from now. This point underscores the time value of money.

The second point is that the computations used in Exhibit 11A–2 involved unnecessary work. The same present value of $54,075 could have been obtained more easily by referring to Exhibit 11B–2 in Appendix 11B. Exhibit 11B–2 contains the present value of $1 to be received each year over a *series* of years at various interest rates. Exhibit 11B–2 has been derived by simply adding together the factors from Exhibit 11B–1, as follows:

| Year | Factors at 12% (from Exhibit 11B–1) |
|---|---|
| 1 ................ | 0.893 |
| 2 ................ | 0.797 |
| 3 ................ | 0.712 |
| 4 ................ | 0.636 |
| 5 ................ | 0.567 |
| | 3.605 |

The sum of these five factors is 3.605. Notice from Exhibit 11B–2 that the factor for $1 to be received each year for five years at 12% is also 3.605. If we use this factor and multiply it by the $15,000 annual cash inflow, then we get the same $54,075 present value that we obtained earlier in Exhibit 11A–2.

$$\$15{,}000 \times 3.605 = \$54{,}075$$

Therefore, when computing the present value of a series of equal cash flows that begins at the end of period 1, Exhibit 11B–2 should be used.

To summarize, the present value tables in Appendix 11B should be used as follows:

Exhibit 11B–1: This table should be used to find the present value of a single cash flow (such as a single payment or receipt) occurring in the future.

Exhibit 11B–2: This table should be used to find the present value of a series of identical cash flows beginning at the end of the current period and continuing into the future.

The use of both of these tables is illustrated in various exhibits in the main body of the chapter. *When a present value factor appears in an exhibit, you should take the time to trace it back into either Exhibit 11B–1 or Exhibit 11B–2 to get acquainted with the tables and how they work.*

## REVIEW PROBLEM: BASIC PRESENT VALUE COMPUTATIONS

Each of the following situations is independent. Work out your own solution to each situation, and then check it against the solution provided.

1. John plans to retire in 12 years. Upon retiring, he would like to take an extended vacation, which he expects will cost at least $40,000. What lump-sum amount must he invest now to have $40,000 at the end of 12 years if the rate of return is:
   a. Eight percent?
   b. Twelve percent?
2. The Morgans would like to send their daughter to a music camp at the end of each of the next five years. The camp costs $1,000 a year. What lump-sum amount would have to be invested now to have $1,000 at the end of each year if the rate of return is:
   a. Eight percent?
   b. Twelve percent?
3. You have just received an inheritance from a relative. You can either receive a $200,000 lump-sum amount at the end of 10 years or receive $14,000 at the end of each year for the next 10 years. If your discount rate is 12%, which alternative would you prefer?

**Solution to Review Problem**

1. a. The amount that must be invested now would be the present value of the $40,000, using a discount rate of 8%. From Exhibit 11B–1 in Appendix 11B, the factor for a discount rate of 8% for 12 periods is 0.397. Multiplying this discount factor by the $40,000 needed in 12 years will give the amount of the present investment required: $40,000 × 0.397 = $15,880.
   b. We will proceed as we did in (*a*) above, but this time we will use a discount rate of 12%. From Exhibit 11B–1 in Appendix 11B, the factor for a discount rate of 12% for 12 periods is 0.257. Multiplying this discount factor by the $40,000 needed in 12 years will give the amount of the present investment required: $40,000 × 0.257 = $10,280.
   Notice that as the discount rate (desired rate of return) increases, the present value decreases.
2. This part differs from (1) above in that we are now dealing with an annuity rather than with a single future sum. The amount that must be invested now is the present value of the $1,000 needed at the end of each year for five years. Because we are dealing with an annuity, or a series of annual cash flows, we must refer to Exhibit 11B–2 in Appendix 11B for the appropriate discount factor.
   a. From Exhibit 11B–2 in Appendix 11B, the discount factor for 8% for five periods is 3.993. Therefore, the amount that must be invested now to have $1,000 available at the end of each year for five years is $1,000 × 3.993 = $3,993.
   b. From Exhibit 11B–2 in Appendix 11B, the discount factor for 12% for five periods is 3.605. Therefore, the amount that must be invested now to have $1,000 available at the end of each year for five years is $1,000 × 3.605 = $3,605.

Again, notice that as the discount rate increases, the present value decreases. When the rate of return increases, less must be invested today to yield a given amount in the future.

3. For this part we will need to refer to both Exhibits 11B–1 and 11B–2 in Appendix 11B. From Exhibit 11B–1, we will need to find the discount factor for 12% for 10 periods, then apply it to the $200,000 lump sum to be received in 10 years. From Exhibit 11B–2, we will need to find the discount factor for 12% for 10 periods, then apply it to the series of $14,000 payments to be received over the 10-year period. Whichever alternative has the higher present value is the one that should be selected.

$$\$200{,}000 \times 0.322 = \$64{,}400$$
$$\$14{,}000 \times 5.650 = \$79{,}100$$

Thus, you should prefer to receive the $14,000 per year for 10 years rather than the $200,000 lump sum. This means that you could invest the $14,000 received at the end of each year at 12% and have *more* than $200,000 at the end of 10 years.

## APPENDIX 11A GLOSSARY

**Annuity** A series of identical cash flows. (p. 531)
**Compound interest** The process of paying interest on interest in an investment. (p. 529)
**Discount rate** The rate of return that is used to find the present value of a future cash flow. (p. 530)
**Discounting** The process of finding the present value of a future cash flow. (p. 530)
**Present value** The value now of an amount that will be received in some future period. (p. 529)

## APPENDIX 11A EXERCISES

**All applicable exercises are available with McGraw-Hill's *Connect® Accounting.***

**EXERCISE 11A–1 Basic Present Value Concepts [LO5]**

Largo Freightlines plans to build a new garage in three years to have more space for repairing its trucks. The garage will cost $400,000.

***Required:***

What lump-sum amount should the company invest now to have the $400,000 available at the end of the three-year period? Assume that the company can invest money at:

a. Eight percent.
b. Twelve percent.

**EXERCISE 11A–2 Basic Present Value Concepts [LO5]**

You have just learned that you are a beneficiary in the will of your late Aunt Susan. The executrix of her estate has given you three options as to how you may receive your inheritance:

a. You may receive $50,000 immediately.
b. You may receive $75,000 at the end of six years.
c. You may receive $12,000 at the end of each year for six years (a total of $72,000).

***Required:***

If you can invest money at a 12% return, which option would you prefer?

**EXERCISE 11A–3 Basic Present Value Concepts [LO5]**

At the end of three years, when you graduate from college, your father has promised to give you a used car that will cost $12,000.

***Required:***

What lump sum must he invest now to have the $12,000 at the end of three years if he can invest money at:

a. Six percent?
b. Ten percent?

**EXERCISE 11A–4 Basic Present Value Concepts [LO5]**
Sally has just won the million-dollar Big Slam jackpot at a gambling casino. The casino will pay her $50,000 per year for 20 years as the payoff.

***Required:***
If Sally can invest money at a 10% rate of return, what is the present value of her winnings? Did she really win a million dollars? Explain.

**EXERCISE 11A–5 Basic Present Value Concepts [LO5]**
Annual cash inflows from two competing investment opportunities are given below. Each investment opportunity will require the same initial investment.

| | Investment X | Investment Y |
|---|---|---|
| Year 1 | $ 1,000 | $ 4,000 |
| Year 2 | 2,000 | 3,000 |
| Year 3 | 3,000 | 2,000 |
| Year 4 | 4,000 | 1,000 |
| Total | $10,000 | $10,000 |

***Required:***
Compute the present value of the cash inflows for each investment using a 20% discount rate.

**EXERCISE 11A–6 Basic Present Value Concepts [LO5]**
Martell Products Inc. can purchase a new copier that will save $5,000 per year in copying costs. The copier will last for six years and have no salvage value.

***Required:***
What is the maximum purchase price that Martell Products should be willing to pay for the copier if the company's required rate of return is:

a. Ten percent?
b. Sixteen percent?

# APPENDIX 11B: PRESENT VALUE TABLES

**EXHIBIT 11B–1** Present Value of \$1; $\frac{1}{(1+r)^n}$

| Periods | 4% | 5% | 6% | 7% | 8% | 9% | 10% | 11% | 12% | 13% | 14% | 15% | 16% | 17% | 18% | 19% | 20% | 21% | 22% | 23% | 24% | 25% |
|---|---|---|---|---|---|---|---|---|---|---|---|---|---|---|---|---|---|---|---|---|---|---|
| 1 | 0.962 | 0.952 | 0.943 | 0.935 | 0.926 | 0.917 | 0.909 | 0.901 | 0.893 | 0.885 | 0.877 | 0.870 | 0.862 | 0.855 | 0.847 | 0.840 | 0.833 | 0.826 | 0.820 | 0.813 | 0.806 | 0.800 |
| 2 | 0.925 | 0.907 | 0.890 | 0.873 | 0.857 | 0.842 | 0.826 | 0.812 | 0.797 | 0.783 | 0.769 | 0.756 | 0.743 | 0.731 | 0.718 | 0.706 | 0.694 | 0.683 | 0.672 | 0.661 | 0.650 | 0.640 |
| 3 | 0.889 | 0.864 | 0.840 | 0.816 | 0.794 | 0.772 | 0.751 | 0.731 | 0.712 | 0.693 | 0.675 | 0.658 | 0.641 | 0.624 | 0.609 | 0.593 | 0.579 | 0.564 | 0.551 | 0.537 | 0.524 | 0.512 |
| 4 | 0.855 | 0.823 | 0.792 | 0.763 | 0.735 | 0.708 | 0.683 | 0.659 | 0.636 | 0.613 | 0.592 | 0.572 | 0.552 | 0.534 | 0.516 | 0.499 | 0.482 | 0.467 | 0.451 | 0.437 | 0.423 | 0.410 |
| 5 | 0.822 | 0.784 | 0.747 | 0.713 | 0.681 | 0.650 | 0.621 | 0.593 | 0.567 | 0.543 | 0.519 | 0.497 | 0.476 | 0.456 | 0.437 | 0.419 | 0.402 | 0.386 | 0.370 | 0.355 | 0.341 | 0.328 |
| 6 | 0.790 | 0.746 | 0.705 | 0.666 | 0.630 | 0.596 | 0.564 | 0.535 | 0.507 | 0.480 | 0.456 | 0.432 | 0.410 | 0.390 | 0.370 | 0.352 | 0.335 | 0.319 | 0.303 | 0.289 | 0.275 | 0.262 |
| 7 | 0.760 | 0.711 | 0.665 | 0.623 | 0.583 | 0.547 | 0.513 | 0.482 | 0.452 | 0.425 | 0.400 | 0.376 | 0.354 | 0.333 | 0.314 | 0.296 | 0.279 | 0.263 | 0.249 | 0.235 | 0.222 | 0.210 |
| 8 | 0.731 | 0.677 | 0.627 | 0.582 | 0.540 | 0.502 | 0.467 | 0.434 | 0.404 | 0.376 | 0.351 | 0.327 | 0.305 | 0.285 | 0.266 | 0.249 | 0.233 | 0.218 | 0.204 | 0.191 | 0.179 | 0.168 |
| 9 | 0.703 | 0.645 | 0.592 | 0.544 | 0.500 | 0.460 | 0.424 | 0.391 | 0.361 | 0.333 | 0.308 | 0.284 | 0.263 | 0.243 | 0.225 | 0.209 | 0.194 | 0.180 | 0.167 | 0.155 | 0.144 | 0.134 |
| 10 | 0.676 | 0.614 | 0.558 | 0.508 | 0.463 | 0.422 | 0.386 | 0.352 | 0.322 | 0.295 | 0.270 | 0.247 | 0.227 | 0.208 | 0.191 | 0.176 | 0.162 | 0.149 | 0.137 | 0.126 | 0.116 | 0.107 |
| 11 | 0.650 | 0.585 | 0.527 | 0.475 | 0.429 | 0.388 | 0.350 | 0.317 | 0.287 | 0.261 | 0.237 | 0.215 | 0.195 | 0.178 | 0.162 | 0.148 | 0.135 | 0.123 | 0.112 | 0.103 | 0.094 | 0.086 |
| 12 | 0.625 | 0.557 | 0.497 | 0.444 | 0.397 | 0.356 | 0.319 | 0.286 | 0.257 | 0.231 | 0.208 | 0.187 | 0.168 | 0.152 | 0.137 | 0.124 | 0.112 | 0.102 | 0.092 | 0.083 | 0.076 | 0.069 |
| 13 | 0.601 | 0.530 | 0.469 | 0.415 | 0.368 | 0.326 | 0.290 | 0.258 | 0.229 | 0.204 | 0.182 | 0.163 | 0.145 | 0.130 | 0.116 | 0.104 | 0.093 | 0.084 | 0.075 | 0.068 | 0.061 | 0.055 |
| 14 | 0.577 | 0.505 | 0.442 | 0.388 | 0.340 | 0.299 | 0.263 | 0.232 | 0.205 | 0.181 | 0.160 | 0.141 | 0.125 | 0.111 | 0.099 | 0.088 | 0.078 | 0.069 | 0.062 | 0.055 | 0.049 | 0.044 |
| 15 | 0.555 | 0.481 | 0.417 | 0.362 | 0.315 | 0.275 | 0.239 | 0.209 | 0.183 | 0.160 | 0.140 | 0.123 | 0.108 | 0.095 | 0.084 | 0.074 | 0.065 | 0.057 | 0.051 | 0.045 | 0.040 | 0.035 |
| 16 | 0.534 | 0.458 | 0.394 | 0.339 | 0.292 | 0.252 | 0.218 | 0.188 | 0.163 | 0.141 | 0.123 | 0.107 | 0.093 | 0.081 | 0.071 | 0.062 | 0.054 | 0.047 | 0.042 | 0.036 | 0.032 | 0.028 |
| 17 | 0.513 | 0.436 | 0.371 | 0.317 | 0.270 | 0.231 | 0.198 | 0.170 | 0.146 | 0.125 | 0.108 | 0.093 | 0.080 | 0.069 | 0.060 | 0.052 | 0.045 | 0.039 | 0.034 | 0.030 | 0.026 | 0.023 |
| 18 | 0.494 | 0.416 | 0.350 | 0.296 | 0.250 | 0.212 | 0.180 | 0.153 | 0.130 | 0.111 | 0.095 | 0.081 | 0.069 | 0.059 | 0.051 | 0.044 | 0.038 | 0.032 | 0.028 | 0.024 | 0.021 | 0.018 |
| 19 | 0.475 | 0.396 | 0.331 | 0.277 | 0.232 | 0.194 | 0.164 | 0.138 | 0.116 | 0.098 | 0.083 | 0.070 | 0.060 | 0.051 | 0.043 | 0.037 | 0.031 | 0.027 | 0.023 | 0.020 | 0.017 | 0.014 |
| 20 | 0.456 | 0.377 | 0.312 | 0.258 | 0.215 | 0.178 | 0.149 | 0.124 | 0.104 | 0.087 | 0.073 | 0.061 | 0.051 | 0.043 | 0.037 | 0.031 | 0.026 | 0.022 | 0.019 | 0.016 | 0.014 | 0.012 |
| 21 | 0.439 | 0.359 | 0.294 | 0.242 | 0.199 | 0.164 | 0.135 | 0.112 | 0.093 | 0.077 | 0.064 | 0.053 | 0.044 | 0.037 | 0.031 | 0.026 | 0.022 | 0.018 | 0.015 | 0.013 | 0.011 | 0.009 |
| 22 | 0.422 | 0.342 | 0.278 | 0.226 | 0.184 | 0.150 | 0.123 | 0.101 | 0.083 | 0.068 | 0.056 | 0.046 | 0.038 | 0.032 | 0.026 | 0.022 | 0.018 | 0.015 | 0.013 | 0.011 | 0.009 | 0.007 |
| 23 | 0.406 | 0.326 | 0.262 | 0.211 | 0.170 | 0.138 | 0.112 | 0.091 | 0.074 | 0.060 | 0.049 | 0.040 | 0.033 | 0.027 | 0.022 | 0.018 | 0.015 | 0.012 | 0.010 | 0.009 | 0.007 | 0.006 |
| 24 | 0.390 | 0.310 | 0.247 | 0.197 | 0.158 | 0.126 | 0.102 | 0.082 | 0.066 | 0.053 | 0.043 | 0.035 | 0.028 | 0.023 | 0.019 | 0.015 | 0.013 | 0.010 | 0.008 | 0.007 | 0.006 | 0.005 |
| 25 | 0.375 | 0.295 | 0.233 | 0.184 | 0.146 | 0.116 | 0.092 | 0.074 | 0.059 | 0.047 | 0.038 | 0.030 | 0.024 | 0.020 | 0.016 | 0.013 | 0.010 | 0.009 | 0.007 | 0.006 | 0.005 | 0.004 |
| 26 | 0.361 | 0.281 | 0.220 | 0.172 | 0.135 | 0.106 | 0.084 | 0.066 | 0.053 | 0.042 | 0.033 | 0.026 | 0.021 | 0.017 | 0.014 | 0.011 | 0.009 | 0.007 | 0.006 | 0.005 | 0.004 | 0.003 |
| 27 | 0.347 | 0.268 | 0.207 | 0.161 | 0.125 | 0.098 | 0.076 | 0.060 | 0.047 | 0.037 | 0.029 | 0.023 | 0.018 | 0.014 | 0.011 | 0.009 | 0.007 | 0.006 | 0.005 | 0.004 | 0.003 | 0.002 |
| 28 | 0.333 | 0.255 | 0.196 | 0.150 | 0.116 | 0.090 | 0.069 | 0.054 | 0.042 | 0.033 | 0.026 | 0.020 | 0.016 | 0.012 | 0.010 | 0.008 | 0.006 | 0.005 | 0.004 | 0.003 | 0.002 | 0.002 |
| 29 | 0.321 | 0.243 | 0.185 | 0.141 | 0.107 | 0.082 | 0.063 | 0.048 | 0.037 | 0.029 | 0.022 | 0.017 | 0.014 | 0.011 | 0.008 | 0.006 | 0.005 | 0.004 | 0.003 | 0.002 | 0.002 | 0.002 |
| 30 | 0.308 | 0.231 | 0.174 | 0.131 | 0.099 | 0.075 | 0.057 | 0.044 | 0.033 | 0.026 | 0.020 | 0.015 | 0.012 | 0.009 | 0.007 | 0.005 | 0.004 | 0.003 | 0.003 | 0.002 | 0.002 | 0.001 |
| 40 | 0.208 | 0.142 | 0.097 | 0.067 | 0.046 | 0.032 | 0.022 | 0.015 | 0.011 | 0.008 | 0.005 | 0.004 | 0.003 | 0.002 | 0.001 | 0.001 | 0.001 | 0.000 | 0.000 | 0.000 | 0.000 | 0.000 |

**EXHIBIT 11B–2** Present Value of an Annuity of $1 in Arrears; $\frac{1}{r}\left[1 - \frac{1}{(1+r)^n}\right]$

| Periods | 4% | 5% | 6% | 7% | 8% | 9% | 10% | 11% | 12% | 13% | 14% | 15% | 16% | 17% | 18% | 19% | 20% | 21% | 22% | 23% | 24% | 25% |
|---|---|---|---|---|---|---|---|---|---|---|---|---|---|---|---|---|---|---|---|---|---|---|
| 1 | 0.962 | 0.952 | 0.943 | 0.935 | 0.926 | 0.917 | 0.909 | 0.901 | 0.893 | 0.885 | 0.877 | 0.870 | 0.862 | 0.855 | 0.847 | 0.840 | 0.833 | 0.826 | 0.820 | 0.813 | 0.806 | 0.800 |
| 2 | 1.886 | 1.859 | 1.833 | 1.808 | 1.783 | 1.759 | 1.736 | 1.713 | 1.690 | 1.668 | 1.647 | 1.626 | 1.605 | 1.585 | 1.566 | 1.547 | 1.528 | 1.509 | 1.492 | 1.474 | 1.457 | 1.440 |
| 3 | 2.775 | 2.723 | 2.673 | 2.624 | 2.577 | 2.531 | 2.487 | 2.444 | 2.402 | 2.361 | 2.322 | 2.283 | 2.246 | 2.210 | 2.174 | 2.140 | 2.106 | 2.074 | 2.042 | 2.011 | 1.981 | 1.952 |
| 4 | 3.630 | 3.546 | 3.465 | 3.387 | 3.312 | 3.240 | 3.170 | 3.102 | 3.037 | 2.974 | 2.914 | 2.855 | 2.798 | 2.743 | 2.690 | 2.639 | 2.589 | 2.540 | 2.494 | 2.448 | 2.404 | 2.362 |
| 5 | 4.452 | 4.329 | 4.212 | 4.100 | 3.993 | 3.890 | 3.791 | 3.696 | 3.605 | 3.517 | 3.433 | 3.352 | 3.274 | 3.199 | 3.127 | 3.058 | 2.991 | 2.926 | 2.864 | 2.803 | 2.745 | 2.689 |
| 6 | 5.242 | 5.076 | 4.917 | 4.767 | 4.623 | 4.486 | 4.355 | 4.231 | 4.111 | 3.998 | 3.889 | 3.784 | 3.685 | 3.589 | 3.498 | 3.410 | 3.326 | 3.245 | 3.167 | 3.092 | 3.020 | 2.951 |
| 7 | 6.002 | 5.786 | 5.582 | 5.389 | 5.206 | 5.033 | 4.868 | 4.712 | 4.564 | 4.423 | 4.288 | 4.160 | 4.039 | 3.922 | 3.812 | 3.706 | 3.605 | 3.508 | 3.416 | 3.327 | 3.242 | 3.161 |
| 8 | 6.733 | 6.463 | 6.210 | 5.971 | 5.747 | 5.535 | 5.335 | 5.146 | 4.968 | 4.799 | 4.639 | 4.487 | 4.344 | 4.207 | 4.078 | 3.954 | 3.837 | 3.726 | 3.619 | 3.518 | 3.421 | 3.329 |
| 9 | 7.435 | 7.108 | 6.802 | 6.515 | 6.247 | 5.995 | 5.759 | 5.537 | 5.328 | 5.132 | 4.946 | 4.772 | 4.607 | 4.451 | 4.303 | 4.163 | 4.031 | 3.905 | 3.786 | 3.673 | 3.566 | 3.463 |
| 10 | 8.111 | 7.722 | 7.360 | 7.024 | 6.710 | 6.418 | 6.145 | 5.889 | 5.650 | 5.426 | 5.216 | 5.019 | 4.833 | 4.659 | 4.494 | 4.339 | 4.192 | 4.054 | 3.923 | 3.799 | 3.682 | 3.571 |
| 11 | 8.760 | 8.306 | 7.887 | 7.499 | 7.139 | 6.805 | 6.495 | 6.207 | 5.938 | 5.687 | 5.453 | 5.234 | 5.029 | 4.836 | 4.656 | 4.486 | 4.327 | 4.177 | 4.035 | 3.902 | 3.776 | 3.656 |
| 12 | 9.385 | 8.863 | 8.384 | 7.943 | 7.536 | 7.161 | 6.814 | 6.492 | 6.194 | 5.918 | 5.660 | 5.421 | 5.197 | 4.988 | 4.793 | 4.611 | 4.439 | 4.278 | 4.127 | 3.985 | 3.851 | 3.725 |
| 13 | 9.986 | 9.394 | 8.853 | 8.358 | 7.904 | 7.487 | 7.103 | 6.750 | 6.424 | 6.122 | 5.842 | 5.583 | 5.342 | 5.118 | 4.910 | 4.715 | 4.533 | 4.362 | 4.203 | 4.053 | 3.912 | 3.780 |
| 14 | 10.563 | 9.899 | 9.295 | 8.745 | 8.244 | 7.786 | 7.367 | 6.982 | 6.628 | 6.302 | 6.002 | 5.724 | 5.468 | 5.229 | 5.008 | 4.802 | 4.611 | 4.432 | 4.265 | 4.108 | 3.962 | 3.824 |
| 15 | 11.118 | 10.380 | 9.712 | 9.108 | 8.559 | 8.061 | 7.606 | 7.191 | 6.811 | 6.462 | 6.142 | 5.847 | 5.575 | 5.324 | 5.092 | 4.876 | 4.675 | 4.489 | 4.315 | 4.153 | 4.001 | 3.859 |
| 16 | 11.652 | 10.838 | 10.106 | 9.447 | 8.851 | 8.313 | 7.824 | 7.379 | 6.974 | 6.604 | 6.265 | 5.954 | 5.668 | 5.405 | 5.162 | 4.938 | 4.730 | 4.536 | 4.357 | 4.189 | 4.033 | 3.887 |
| 17 | 12.166 | 11.274 | 10.477 | 9.763 | 9.122 | 8.544 | 8.022 | 7.549 | 7.120 | 6.729 | 6.373 | 6.047 | 5.749 | 5.475 | 5.222 | 4.990 | 4.775 | 4.576 | 4.391 | 4.219 | 4.059 | 3.910 |
| 18 | 12.659 | 11.690 | 10.828 | 10.059 | 9.372 | 8.756 | 8.201 | 7.702 | 7.250 | 6.840 | 6.467 | 6.128 | 5.818 | 5.534 | 5.273 | 5.033 | 4.812 | 4.608 | 4.419 | 4.243 | 4.080 | 3.928 |
| 19 | 13.134 | 12.085 | 11.158 | 10.336 | 9.604 | 8.950 | 8.365 | 7.839 | 7.366 | 6.938 | 6.550 | 6.198 | 5.877 | 5.584 | 5.316 | 5.070 | 4.843 | 4.635 | 4.442 | 4.263 | 4.097 | 3.942 |
| 20 | 13.590 | 12.462 | 11.470 | 10.594 | 9.818 | 9.129 | 8.514 | 7.963 | 7.469 | 7.025 | 6.623 | 6.259 | 5.929 | 5.628 | 5.353 | 5.101 | 4.870 | 4.657 | 4.460 | 4.279 | 4.110 | 3.954 |
| 21 | 14.029 | 12.821 | 11.764 | 10.836 | 10.017 | 9.292 | 8.649 | 8.075 | 7.562 | 7.102 | 6.687 | 6.312 | 5.973 | 5.665 | 5.384 | 5.127 | 4.891 | 4.675 | 4.476 | 4.292 | 4.121 | 3.963 |
| 22 | 14.451 | 13.163 | 12.042 | 11.061 | 10.201 | 9.442 | 8.772 | 8.176 | 7.645 | 7.170 | 6.743 | 6.359 | 6.011 | 5.696 | 5.410 | 5.149 | 4.909 | 4.690 | 4.488 | 4.302 | 4.130 | 3.970 |
| 23 | 14.857 | 13.489 | 12.303 | 11.272 | 10.371 | 9.580 | 8.883 | 8.266 | 7.718 | 7.230 | 6.792 | 6.399 | 6.044 | 5.723 | 5.432 | 5.167 | 4.925 | 4.703 | 4.499 | 4.311 | 4.137 | 3.976 |
| 24 | 15.247 | 13.799 | 12.550 | 11.469 | 10.529 | 9.707 | 8.985 | 8.348 | 7.784 | 7.283 | 6.835 | 6.434 | 6.073 | 5.746 | 5.451 | 5.182 | 4.937 | 4.713 | 4.507 | 4.318 | 4.143 | 3.981 |
| 25 | 15.622 | 14.094 | 12.783 | 11.654 | 10.675 | 9.823 | 9.077 | 8.422 | 7.843 | 7.330 | 6.873 | 6.464 | 6.097 | 5.766 | 5.467 | 5.195 | 4.948 | 4.721 | 4.514 | 4.323 | 4.147 | 3.985 |
| 26 | 15.983 | 14.375 | 13.003 | 11.826 | 10.810 | 9.929 | 9.161 | 8.488 | 7.896 | 7.372 | 6.906 | 6.491 | 6.118 | 5.783 | 5.480 | 5.206 | 4.956 | 4.728 | 4.520 | 4.328 | 4.151 | 3.988 |
| 27 | 16.330 | 14.643 | 13.211 | 11.987 | 10.935 | 10.027 | 9.237 | 8.548 | 7.943 | 7.409 | 6.935 | 6.514 | 6.136 | 5.798 | 5.492 | 5.215 | 4.964 | 4.734 | 4.524 | 4.332 | 4.154 | 3.990 |
| 28 | 16.663 | 14.898 | 13.406 | 12.137 | 11.051 | 10.116 | 9.307 | 8.602 | 7.984 | 7.441 | 6.961 | 6.534 | 6.152 | 5.810 | 5.502 | 5.223 | 4.970 | 4.739 | 4.528 | 4.335 | 4.157 | 3.992 |
| 29 | 16.984 | 15.141 | 13.591 | 12.278 | 11.158 | 10.198 | 9.370 | 8.650 | 8.022 | 7.470 | 6.983 | 6.551 | 6.166 | 5.820 | 5.510 | 5.229 | 4.975 | 4.743 | 4.531 | 4.337 | 4.159 | 3.994 |
| 30 | 17.292 | 15.372 | 13.765 | 12.409 | 11.258 | 10.274 | 9.427 | 8.694 | 8.055 | 7.496 | 7.003 | 6.566 | 6.177 | 5.829 | 5.517 | 5.235 | 4.979 | 4.746 | 4.534 | 4.339 | 4.160 | 3.995 |
| 40 | 19.793 | 17.159 | 15.046 | 13.332 | 11.925 | 10.757 | 9.779 | 8.951 | 8.244 | 7.634 | 7.105 | 6.642 | 6.233 | 5.871 | 5.548 | 5.258 | 4.997 | 4.760 | 4.544 | 4.347 | 4.166 | 3.999 |

### A LOOK BACK

Capital budgeting decisions involve significant investments in long-term projects. Chapter 11 covered various techniques used for capital budgeting decisions.

### A LOOK AT THIS CHAPTER

The statement of cash flows provides invaluable information. After addressing the classification of various types of cash inflows and outflows, we discuss how to prepare the statement of cash flows and how to interpret it.

### A LOOK AHEAD

Chapter 13 explains how to use financial statements to assess the financial health of a company. It describes how to prepare comparative and common-size form financial statements and how to compute and interpret financial ratios.

# 12 Statement of Cash Flows

## CHAPTER OUTLINE

**The Statement of Cash Flows: Key Concepts**

- Organizing the Statement of Cash Flows
- Operating Activities: Direct or Indirect Method?
- The Indirect Method: A Three-Step Process
- Investing and Financing Activities: Gross Cash Flows
- Summary of Key Concepts

**An Example of a Statement of Cash Flows**

- Operating Activities
- Investing Activities
- Financing Activities
- Seeing the Big Picture

**Interpreting the Statement of Cash Flows**

- Consider a Company's Specific Circumstances
- Consider the Relationships among Numbers

**Appendix 12A: The Direct Method of Determining the Net Cash Provided by Operating Activities**

- Similarities and Differences in the Handling of Data
- Specific Rules—Direct and Indirect Methods

## DECISION FEATURE

# Understanding Cash Flows

In 2009, **The Kroger Company**, the largest food and drug retailer in the United States, reported net income of $57 million. During the same year the company spent $2.3 billion for plant and equipment, paid dividends totaling $238 million, paid off $432 million of long-term debt, and spent $218 million to purchase shares of its own common stock. At first glance, these figures may seem confusing because Kroger is spending amounts of money that far exceed its net income. In this chapter you'll learn about the statement of cash flows that explains the relationship between a company's net income and its cash inflows and outflows.

Source: The Kroger Company, 2009 Form 10-K Annual Report, www.sec.gov/edgar/searchedgar/companysearch.html.

## LEARNING OBJECTIVES

*After studying Chapter 12, you should be able to:*

**LO1** Classify cash inflows and outflows as relating to operating, investing, or financing activities.

**LO2** Prepare a statement of cash flows using the indirect method to determine the net cash provided by operating activities.

**LO3** Compute free cash flow.

**LO4** (Appendix 12A) Use the direct method to determine the net cash provided by operating activities.

**Three major financial statements** are required for external reports—an income statement, a balance sheet, and a statement of cash flows. The **statement of cash flows** highlights the major activities that impact cash flows and, hence, affect the overall cash balance. Managers focus on cash for a very good reason—without sufficient cash at the right times, a company may miss golden investment opportunities or may even go bankrupt.

The statement of cash flows answers questions that cannot be easily answered by looking at the income statement and balance sheet. For example, where did **Delta Airlines** get the cash to pay a dividend of nearly $140 million in a year in which, according to its income statement, it lost more than $1 billion? How was **The Walt Disney Company** able to invest nearly $800 million to expand and renovate its theme parks despite a loss of more than $500 million on its investment in EuroDisney? Where did **The Kroger Company** get $2.3 billion to invest in plant and equipment in a year when its net income was only $57 million? The answers to such questions can be found on the statement of cash flows.

The statement of cash flows is a valuable analytical tool for managers as well as for investors and creditors, although managers tend to be more concerned with forecasted statements of cash flows that are prepared as part of the budgeting process. The statement of cash flows can be used to answer crucial questions such as:

1. Is the company generating sufficient positive cash flows from its ongoing operations to remain viable?
2. Will the company be able to repay its debts?
3. Will the company be able to pay its usual dividend?
4. Why do net income and net cash flow differ?
5. To what extent will the company have to borrow money in order to make needed investments?

Managers prepare the statement of cash flows by applying a fundamental principle of double-entry bookkeeping—the change in the cash balance must equal the changes in all other balance sheet accounts besides cash.[1] This principle ensures that properly analyzing the changes in all noncash balance sheet accounts always quantifies the cash inflows and outflows that explain the change in the cash balance. Our goal in this chapter is to translate this fairly complex principle into a small number of concepts and steps that simplify the process of preparing and interpreting a statement of cash flows.

Before delving into the specifics of how to prepare the statement of cash flows, we need to review two basic equations that apply to all asset, contra-asset, liability, and stockholders' equity accounts:

*Basic Equation for Asset Accounts*
Beginning balance + Debits − Credits = Ending balance

*Basic Equation for Contra-Asset, Liability, and Stockholders' Equity Accounts*
Beginning balance − Debits + Credits = Ending balance

These equations will help you compute various cash inflows and outflows that are reported in the statement of cash flows and they'll be referred to throughout the chapter.

[1]The statement of cash flows is based on the following fundamental balance sheet and income statement equations:
(1) Change in cash + Changes in noncash assets = Changes in liabilities + Changes in stockholders' equity
(2) Net cash flow = Change in cash
(3) Changes in stockholders' equity = Net income − Dividends + Changes in capital stock
These three equations can be used to derive the following equation:
(4) Net cash flow = Net income − Changes in noncash assets + Changes in liabilities − Dividends + Changes in capital stock.
Essentially, the statement of cash flows, which explains net cash flow, is constructed by starting with net income and then adjusting it for changes in noncash balance sheet accounts.

# THE STATEMENT OF CASH FLOWS: KEY CONCEPTS

The statement of cash flows summarizes all of a company's cash inflows and outflows during a period, thereby explaining the change in its cash balance. In a statement of cash flows, cash is broadly defined to include both cash and cash equivalents. **Cash equivalents** consist of short-term, highly liquid investments such as Treasury bills, commercial paper, and money market funds that are made solely for the purpose of generating a return on temporarily idle funds. Most companies invest their excess cash reserves in these types of interest-bearing assets that can be easily converted into cash. Because such assets are equivalent to cash, they are included with cash in a statement of cash flows.

The remainder of this section discusses four key concepts that you'll need to understand to prepare a statement of cash flows. These four concepts include organizing the statement of cash flows, distinguishing between the direct and indirect methods of preparing a portion of the statement of cash flows, completing the three-step process underlying the indirect method, and recording gross cash flows where appropriate within a statement of cash flows.[2]

## Apple's Cash Stash

IN BUSINESS

**Apple Inc.** accumulated $20.8 billion in cash and short-term investments. Its investors had a variety of opinions about how the company should use this money. Some investors wanted Apple to explore acquisition targets in the music industry. Others believed Apple should invest in start-up companies that are developing emerging technologies, such as improved batteries for the iPhone. Still others felt the company should stockpile raw materials in the face of looming price hikes.

This example illustrates the never-ending cycle of managing a business. Once a company succeeds in generating positive cash flows, it immediately raises another question in the minds of investors—what are you planning to do for me now?

Source: Peter Burrows, "Apple's Cash Conundrum," *BusinessWeek*, August 11, 2008, p. 32.

## Organizing the Statement of Cash Flows

**LEARNING OBJECTIVE 1**

Classify cash inflows and outflows as relating to operating, investing, or financing activities.

To make it easier to compare data from different companies, U.S. generally accepted accounting principles (GAAP) and International Financial Reporting Standards (IFRS) require companies to follow prescribed rules when preparing the statement of cash flows. One of these rules requires organizing the statement into three sections that report cash flows resulting from *operating activities, investing activities,* and *financing activities.* **Operating activities** generate cash inflows and outflows related to revenue and expense transactions that affect net income. **Investing activities** generate cash inflows and outflows related to acquiring or disposing of noncurrent assets such as property, plant, and

[2]Another concept that relates to the statement of cash flows is direct exchange transactions, which refer to transactions where noncurrent balance sheet items are swapped. For example, a company might issue common stock in a direct exchange for property. Direct exchange transactions are not reported on the statement of cash flows; however, they are disclosed in a separate schedule that accompanies the statement. More advanced accounting courses cover this topic in greater detail. We will not include direct exchange transactions in this chapter.

**EXHIBIT 12–1**
Cash Inflows and Outflows Resulting from Operating, Investing, and Financing Activities

| | Cash Inflow | Cash Outflow |
|---|---|---|
| **Operating activities** | | |
| Collecting cash from customers | √ | |
| Paying suppliers for inventory purchases | | √ |
| Paying bills to insurers, utility providers, etc | | √ |
| Paying wages and salaries to employees | | √ |
| Paying taxes to governmental bodies | | √ |
| Paying interest to lenders | | √ |
| **Investing activities** | | |
| Buying property, plant, and equipment | | √ |
| Selling property, plant, and equipment | √ | |
| Buying stocks and bonds as a long-term investment | | √ |
| Selling stocks and bonds held for long-term investment | √ | |
| Lending money to another entity | | √ |
| Collecting the principal on a loan to another entity | √ | |
| **Financing activities** | | |
| Borrowing money from a creditor | √ | |
| Repaying the principal amount of a debt | | √ |
| Collecting cash from the sale of common stock | √ | |
| Paying cash to repurchase your own common stock | | √ |
| Paying a dividend to stockholders | | √ |

equipment, long-term investments, and loans to another entity. **Financing activities** generate cash inflows and outflows related to borrowing from and repaying principal to creditors and completing transactions with the company's owners, such as selling or repurchasing shares of common stock and paying dividends. The most common types of cash inflows and outflows resulting from these three activities are summarized in Exhibit 12–1.[3]

## Operating Activities: Direct or Indirect Method?

U.S. GAAP and IFRS allow companies to compute the net amount of cash inflows and outflows resulting from operating activities, which is known formally as the **net cash provided by operating activities,** using either the *direct* or *indirect* method. Both of these methods have the same purpose, which is to translate accrual-based net income to a cash basis. However, they approach this task in two different ways.

Under the **direct method,** the income statement is reconstructed on a cash basis from top to bottom. For example, cash collected from customers is listed instead of revenue, and payments to suppliers is listed instead of cost of goods sold. In essence, cash receipts are counted as revenues and cash disbursements pertaining to operating activities are counted as expenses. The difference between the cash receipts and cash disbursements is the net cash provided by operating activities.

Under the **indirect method,** net income is adjusted to a cash basis. That is, rather than directly computing cash sales, cash expenses, and so forth, these amounts are derived *indirectly* by removing from net income any items that do not affect cash flows. The indirect method has an advantage over the direct method because it shows the reasons for any differences between net income and net cash provided by operating activities.

Although both methods result in the same amount of net cash provided by operating activities, only about 1% of companies use the direct method and the remaining 99% use

[3]Operating cash inflows can also include interest income and dividend income; however, in this chapter we will limit our scope to cash receipts from sales to customers.

the indirect method.[4] If a company uses the direct method to prepare its statement of cash flows, then it must also provide a supplementary report that uses the indirect method. However, if a company chooses to use the indirect method, there is no requirement that it also report results using the direct method. Because the direct method requires more work, very few companies choose this approach. Therefore, we will explain the direct method in Appendix 12A, and we will cover the indirect method in the main body of the chapter.

## The Indirect Method: A Three-Step Process

The indirect method adjusts net income to net cash provided by operating activities using a three-step process.

**Step 1** The first step is to *add depreciation charges* to net income. Depreciation charges are the credits to the Accumulated Depreciation account during the period—the sum total of the entries that have increased Accumulated Depreciation. Why do we do this? Because Accumulated Depreciation is a noncash balance sheet account and we must adjust net income for all of the changes in the noncash balance sheet accounts that have occurred during the period.

To compute the credits to the Accumulated Depreciation account we use the equation for contra-assets that was mentioned earlier:

*Basic Equation for Contra-Asset Accounts*
Beginning balance − Debits + Credits = Ending balance

For example, assume the Accumulated Depreciation account had beginning and ending balances of $300 and $500, respectively. Also, assume that the company sold equipment with accumulated depreciation of $70 during the period. Given that we use debits to the Accumulated Depreciation account to record accumulated depreciation on assets that have been sold or retired, the depreciation that needs to be added to net income is computed as follows:

Beginning balance − Debits + Credits = Ending balance
$300 − $70 + Credits = $500
Credits = $500 − $300 + $70
Credits = $270

The same logic can be depicted using an Accumulated Depreciation T-account. Given that we know the account's beginning and ending balances and the amount of the debit that would have been recorded for the sale of equipment, the credit side of the T-account must equal $270.

**Accumulated Depreciation**

| | | | |
|---|---|---|---|
| | | Beg. Bal. | $300 |
| Sale of equipment | 70 | | 270 |
| | | End. Bal. | $500 |

For service and merchandising companies, the credits to the Accumulated Depreciation T-account equal the debits to the Depreciation Expense account. For these companies, the adjustment in step one consists of adding depreciation expense to net income. However, for manufacturing companies, some of the credits to the Accumulated

[4]American Institute of Certified Public Accountants, *Accounting Trends and Techniques: 2007* (Jersey City, NJ, 2007), p. 503.

Depreciation T-account relate to depreciation on production assets that are debited to work in process inventories rather than depreciation expense. For these companies, the depreciation charges do not simply equal depreciation expense.

Because depreciation is added back to net income on the statement of cash flows, some people erroneously conclude that a company can increase its cash flow by simply increasing its depreciation expense. This is false; a company cannot increase its net cash provided by operating activities by increasing its depreciation expense. If it increases its depreciation expense by X dollars, then net income will decline by X dollars and the amount of the adjustment in step one of this process will increase by X dollars. The decline in net income and the increase in the amount of the adjustment in step one exactly offset each other, resulting in zero impact on the net cash provided by operating activities.

## HELPFUL HINT

When completing step one in the indirect method, do not assume that the change in the balance of the Accumulated Depreciation account equals the amount of the required adjustment. Instead, you must check to see if any depreciable assets were sold during the period. If so, the amount of accumulated depreciation on the asset that was sold needs to be included in the basic equation for contra-asset accounts or included on the debit side of the Accumulated Depreciation T-account when determining the amount of the adjustment.

Step 2 The second step is to *analyze net changes in noncash balance sheet accounts* that impact net income. Exhibit 12–2 provides general guidelines for how to analyze current asset and current liability accounts.[5] For each account shown in the exhibit, you'll begin by referring to the balance sheet to compute the change in the account balance from the beginning to the end of the period. Then, you will either add each of these amounts to net income or subtract them from net income as shown in Exhibit 12–2. Notice that changes in all current asset accounts (Accounts Receivable, Inventory, and Prepaid Expenses) result in the same type of adjustment to net income. If an asset account balance increases during the period, then the amount of the increase is subtracted from net income. If an asset account balance decreases during the period, then the amount of the decrease is added to net income. The current liability accounts (Accounts Payable, Accrued Liabilities, and Income Taxes Payable) are handled in the opposite fashion. If a liability account balance increases, then the amount of the increase is added to net income. If a liability account balance decreases, then the amount of the decrease is subtracted from net income.

Keep in mind that the purpose of these adjustments is to translate net income to a cash basis. For example, the change in the accounts receivable balance measures the difference between credit sales and cash collections from customers who purchased on account.

**EXHIBIT 12–2**
General Guidelines for Analyzing How Changes in Noncash Balance Sheet Accounts Affect Net Income on the Statement of Cash Flows

| | Increase in Account Balance | Decrease in Account Balance |
|---|---|---|
| **Current Assets** | | |
| Accounts receivable | Subtract | Add |
| Inventory | Subtract | Add |
| Prepaid expenses | Subtract | Add |
| **Current Liabilities** | | |
| Accounts payable | Add | Subtract |
| Accrued liabilities | Add | Subtract |
| Income taxes payable | Add | Subtract |

[5]Other accounts such as Interest Payable can impact these computations. However, for simplicity, in this chapter we will focus on the accounts shown in Exhibit 12–2.

When the accounts receivable balance increases it means that the amount of credit sales exceeds the amount of cash collected from customers. In this case, the change in the accounts receivable balance is subtracted from net income because it reflects the amount by which credit sales exceeds cash collections from customers. When the accounts receivable balance decreases it means that cash collected from customers exceeds credit sales. In this case, the change in the accounts receivable balance is added to net income because it reflects the amount by which cash collections from customers exceeds credit sales.

The other accounts shown in Exhibit 12–2 have a similar underlying logic. The inventory and accounts payable adjustments translate cost of goods sold to cash paid for inventory purchases. The prepaid expenses and accrued liabilities adjustments help translate selling and administrative expenses to a cash basis. The income taxes payable adjustment translates income tax expense to a cash basis.

### HELPFUL HINT

Beyond memorizing the adjustments shown in Exhibit 12–2, you should understand the reasons for them. The adjustment pertaining to accounts receivable quantifies the difference between sales, as reported on the income statement, and cash collections from customers. The adjustments related to inventory and accounts payable quantify the difference between cost of goods sold and cash paid to suppliers. The adjustments related to prepaid expenses and accrued liabilities help quantify the difference between selling and administrative expenses and cash paid for those expenses. Finally, the adjustment pertaining to income taxes payable quantifies the difference between income tax expense and income tax payments.

**Step 3** The third step in computing the net cash provided by operating activities is to *adjust for gains/losses* included in the income statement. Under U.S. GAAP and IFRS rules, the cash proceeds from the sale of noncurrent assets must be included in the investing activities section of the statement of cash flows. To comply with these rules, the gains and losses pertaining to the sale of noncurrent assets must be removed from net income as reported in the operating activities section of the statement of cash flows. To make this adjustment, subtract gains from net income and add losses to net income in the operating activities section.

### CONCEPT CHECK

1. Which of the following statements is false? (You may select more than one answer.)
   a. Depreciation charges are subtracted from net income.
   b. An increase in inventory is subtracted from net income.
   c. A loss on the sale of an asset is subtracted from net income.
   d. A decrease in accrued liabilities is subtracted from net income.
2. Assume that a company's beginning and ending balances in its Accumulated Depreciation account are $2,000 and $2,900, respectively. Also assume that the company sold a piece of equipment that had an original cost of $400 and accumulated depreciation of $350 for cash proceeds of $75. How much depreciation would the company add to net income in the operating activities section of its statement of cash flows?
   a. $550
   b. $500
   c. $1,300
   d. $1,250
3. Refer to the data in question 2 above. Which of the following choices is true?
   a. The company should subtract a gain of $25 from net income.
   b. The company should add a gain of $25 to net income.
   c. The company should subtract a loss of $25 from net income.
   d. The company should add a loss of $25 to net income.

## Investing and Financing Activities: Gross Cash Flows

U.S. GAAP and IFRS require that the investing and financing sections of the statement of cash flows disclose gross cash flows. To illustrate, suppose Macy's Department Stores purchases $50 million in property during the year and sells other property for $30 million. Instead of showing the net change of $20 million, the company must show the gross amounts of both the purchases and sales. The $50 million purchase would be disclosed as a cash outflow and the $30 million sale would be reported as a cash inflow in the investing section of the statement of cash flows. Similarly, if Alcoa receives $80 million from selling long-term bonds and then pays out $30 million to retire other bonds, the two transactions must be reported separately in the financing section of the statement of cash flows rather than being netted against each other.

The gross method of reporting cash flows is not used in the operating activities section of the statement of cash flows, where debits and credits are netted against each other. For example, if Sears adds $600 million to its accounts receivable as a result of sales during the year and $520 million of accounts receivable are collected, only the net increase of $80 million is reported on the statement of cash flows.

To compute gross cash flows for the investing and financing activities sections of the statement of cash flows, you'll begin by calculating the changes in the balance of each applicable balance sheet account. As with the current assets, when a noncurrent asset account balance (including Property, Plant, and Equipment; Long-Term Investments; and Loans to Other Entities) increases, it signals the need to subtract cash outflows in the investing activities section of the statement of cash flows. If the balance in a noncurrent asset account decreases during the period, then it signals the need to add cash inflows. The liability and equity accounts (Bonds Payable and Common Stock) are handled in the opposite fashion. If a liability or equity account balance increases, then it signals a need to add cash inflows to the financing activities section of the statement of cash flows. If a liability or equity account balance decreases, then it signals a need to subtract cash outflows. Exhibit 12–3 summarizes these general guidelines.

While these guidelines provide a helpful starting point, to properly calculate each account's *gross* cash inflows and outflows you'll need to analyze the transactions that occurred within that account during the period. We will illustrate how to do this using Property, Plant, and Equipment and Retained Earnings.

**Property, Plant, and Equipment** When a company purchases property, plant, or equipment it debits the Property, Plant, and Equipment account for the amount of the purchase. When it sells or disposes of these kinds of assets, it credits the Property, Plant, and

**EXHIBIT 12–3**
General Guidelines for Analyzing How Changes in Noncash Balance Sheet Accounts Affect the Investing and Financing Sections of the Statement of Cash Flows

| | Increase in Account Balance | Decrease in Account Balance |
|---|---|---|
| **Noncurrent Assets (Investing activities)** | | |
| Property, plant, and equipment | Subtract | Add |
| Long-term investments | Subtract | Add |
| Loans to other entities | Subtract | Add |
| **Liabilities and Stockholders' Equity (Financing activities)** | | |
| Bonds payable | Add | Subtract |
| Common stock | Add | Subtract |
| Retained earnings | * | * |

*Requires further analysis to quantify cash dividends paid.

Equipment account for the original cost of the asset. To compute the cash outflows related to Property, Plant, and Equipment we use the basic equation for assets mentioned earlier:

*Basic Equation for Asset Accounts*
Beginning balance + Debits − Credits = Ending balance

For example, assume that a company's beginning and ending balances in its Property, Plant, and Equipment account are $1,000 and $1,800, respectively. In addition, during the period the company sold a piece of equipment for $40 cash that originally cost $100 and had accumulated depreciation of $70. The company recorded a gain on the sale of $10, which had been included in net income.

We start by calculating the $800 increase in the Property, Plant, and Equipment account. This increase signals the need to subtract cash outflows in the investing activities section of the statement of cash flows. In fact, it may be tempting to conclude that the proper way to analyze Property, Plant, and Equipment in this instance is to record an $800 cash outflow corresponding with the $800 increase in the account balance. However, that would only be correct if the company did not sell any property, plant, and equipment during the year. Because the company did sell equipment, we must use the basic equation for asset accounts to compute the cash outflows as follows:

Beginning balance + Debits − Credits = Ending balance
$1,000 + Debits − $100 = $1,800
Debits = $1,800 − $1,000 + $100
Debits = $900

The same logic can be depicted using a Property, Plant, and Equipment T-account. Given that we know the account's beginning and ending balances and the amount of the credit that would have been recorded to write off the *original cost* of the equipment that was sold, the additions to the account, as summarized on the debit side of the T-account, must equal $900.

**Property, Plant, and Equipment**

| | | | |
|---|---|---|---|
| Beg. Bal. | $1,000 | | |
| Additions | 900 | Sale of equipment | 100 |
| End. Bal. | $1,800 | | |

So, instead of reporting an $800 cash outflow pertaining to Property, Plant, and Equipment in the investing activities section of the statement of cash flows, the proper accounting requires subtracting the $10 gain on the sale of equipment from net income in the operating activities section of the statement. It also requires disclosing a $40 cash inflow from the sale of equipment and a $900 cash outflow for additions to Property, Plant and Equipment in the investing activities section of the statement.

**CONCEPT CHECK**

4. Assume that a company's beginning and ending balances in its Property, Plant, and Equipment account are $5,000 and $6,000, respectively. Also assume that the company sold a piece of equipment that originally cost $700 and had accumulated depreciation of $450 for cash proceeds of $500. Based solely on the available information, what is the company's net cash provided by (used in) investing activities?
   a. $1,200
   b. $1,500
   c. $(1,200)
   d. $(1,500)

**Retained Earnings** When a company earns net income it credits the Retained Earnings account and when it pays a dividend it debits the Retained Earnings account. To compute the amount of a cash dividend payment we use the basic equation for stockholders' equity accounts mentioned earlier:

*Basic Equation for Stockholders' Equity Accounts*

Beginning balance − Debits + Credits = Ending balance

For example, assume that a company's beginning and ending balances in its Retained Earnings account are $2,000 and 3,000, respectively. In addition, the company reported net income of $1,200 and paid a cash dividend, but we don't know how much. We start by calculating the $1,000 increase in the Retained Earnings account. However, this amount reflects the net income earned during the period as well as the amount of the dividend payment. Therefore, we must use the equation above to calculate the amount of the dividend payment as follows:

Beginning balance − Debits + Credits = Ending balance

$2,000 − Debits + $1,200 = $3,000

$3,200 = $3,000 + Debits

Debits = $200

The same logic can be depicted using a Retained Earnings T-account. Given that we know the account's beginning and ending balances and the net income that would have been recorded on the credit side of the T-account, the dividend, as reported on the debit side of the T-account, must equal $200.

**Retained Earnings**

| | | | |
|---|---|---|---|
| | | Beg. Bal. | $2,000 |
| Dividend | 200 | Net income | 1,200 |
| | | End. Bal. | $3,000 |

So, instead of erroneously reporting a $1,000 cash flow pertaining to the overall change in Retained Earnings, the proper accounting requires disclosing net income of $1,200 within the operating activities section of the statement of cash flows and a $200 cash dividend in the financing activities section of the statement.

## HELPFUL HINT

Net income is the first number recorded on a statement of cash flows prepared using the indirect method. However, how would you determine net income if it was not explicitly disclosed within an exercise or problem? The secret is to use the basic equation for stockholders' equity accounts to determine the credit to the Retained Earnings account. Input into this equation the beginning and ending balances in Retained Earnings as well as the debit pertaining to cash dividends and then solve for the credit to the account—which corresponds to net income.

## IN BUSINESS

## Delta Petroleum Sells Stock to Fund Expansion

**Delta Petroleum Corporation** wanted to increase its drilling for natural gas and oil in Colorado and Utah. However, the company's capital budget for 2008 exceeded its cash flow. To make up the difference, Delta sold 36 million new shares of its common stock to **Tracinda Corporation** for $684 million. Delta is confident that the cash inflow from this transaction will increase its reserve of natural resources and ultimately drive up its stock price; however, the transaction gave Tracinda a 35% ownership stake in Delta and allows Tracinda to appoint one-third of Delta's board of directors.

**IN BUSINESS**

(continued)

When companies cannot finance their expansion plans with internally generated cash, they usually pursue one of two options for gaining access to cash. They can either borrow money from lenders or sell common stock to buyers who take an ownership stake in their company.

Source: Russell Gold, "Delta Petroleum's Stake Sale Eases Need for Cash," *The Wall Street Journal*, January 2, 2008, p. A3.

## Summary of Key Concepts

Exhibit 12–4 summarizes the four key concepts just discussed. The first key concept is that the statement of cash flows is divided into three sections: operating activities, investing activities, and financing activities. The net cash used or provided by these three types of activities is combined to derive the net increase/decrease in cash and cash equivalents,

**EXHIBIT 12–4** Summary of Key Concepts Needed to Prepare a Statement of Cash Flows

**Key Concept #1**

The statement of cash flows is divided into three sections:

| | |
|---|---|
| **Operating activities** | |
| Net cash provided by (used in) operating activities | $xx |
| **Investing activities** | |
| Net cash provided by (used in) investing activities | xx |
| **Financing activities** | |
| Net cash provided by (used in) financing activities | xx |
| Net increase/decrease in cash and cash equivalents | xx |
| Cash and cash equivalents, beginning balance | xx |
| Cash and cash equivalents, ending balance | $xx |

**Key Concept #2**

U.S. GAAP and IFRS allow two methods for preparing the operating activities section of the statement of cash flows:

| | |
|---|---|
| **Direct Method (Appendix 12A)** | |
| Cash receipts from customers | $ xx |
| Cash paid for inventory purchases | (xx) |
| Cash paid for selling and administrative expenses | (xx) |
| Cash paid for income taxes | (xx) |
| Net cash provided by (used in) operating activities | $ xx |
| **Indirect Method** | |
| Net income | $ xx |
| Various adjustments (+/−) | xx |
| Net cash provided by (used in) operating activities | $ xx |

**Key Concept #3**

Computing the net cash provided by operating activities using the indirect method is a three step process:

| | | |
|---|---|---|
| | **Operating Activities** | |
| | Net income | $xx |
| | Adjustments to convert net income to a cash basis: | |
| Step 1 | Add: Depreciation | xx |
| Step 2 | Analyze net changes in noncash balance sheet accounts: | |
| | Increase in current asset accounts | (xx) |
| | Decrease in current asset accounts | xx |
| | Increase in current liability accounts | xx |
| | Decrease in current liability accounts | (xx) |
| Step 3 | Adjust for gains/losses: | |
| | Gain on sale | (xx) |
| | Loss on sale | xx |
| | Net cash provided by (used in) operating activities | $xx |

**Key Concept #4**

The investing and financing sections of the statement of cash flows must report gross cash flows:

| | |
|---|---|
| Net cash provided by (used in) operating activities | $ xx |
| **Investing Activities** | |
| Purchase of property, plant, and equipment | (xx) |
| Sale of property, plant, and equipment | xx |
| Purchase of long-term investments | (xx) |
| Sale of long-term investments | xx |
| Net cash provided by (used in) investing activities | (xx) |
| **Financing Activities** | |
| Issuance of bonds payable | xx |
| Repaying principal on bonds payable | (xx) |
| Issuance of common stock | xx |
| Purchase own shares of common stock | (xx) |
| Paying a dividend | (xx) |
| Net cash provided by (used in) financing activities | xx |
| Net increase/decrease in cash and cash equivalents | xx |
| Cash and cash equivalents, beginning balance | xx |
| Cash and cash equivalents, ending balance | $ xx |

which explains the change in the cash balance. The second key concept is that the operating activities section of the statement of cash flows can be prepared using the direct or indirect method. The direct method translates sales, cost of goods sold, selling and administrative expenses, and income tax expense to a cash basis. The indirect method begins with accrual-based net income and adjusts it to a cash basis. The third key concept is that the indirect method requires three steps to compute net cash provided by operating activities. The first step is to add back depreciation to net income. The second step is to analyze net changes in noncash balance sheet accounts that impact net income. The third step is to adjust for gains or losses included in the income statement. The fourth key concept is to record gross cash inflows and outflows in the investing and financing activities sections of the statement of cash flows.

## AN EXAMPLE OF A STATEMENT OF CASH FLOWS

**LEARNING OBJECTIVE 2**

Prepare a statement of cash flows using the indirect method to determine the net cash provided by operating activities.

To illustrate the ideas introduced in the preceding section, we will now construct a statement of cash flows for a merchandising company called Apparel, Inc. The company's income statement and balance sheet are shown in Exhibits 12–5 and 12–6.

Let's also assume the following facts with respect to Apparel, Inc.:

1. The company sold a store that had an original cost of $15 million and accumulated depreciation of $10 million. The cash proceeds from the sale were $8 million. The gain on the sale was $3 million.
2. The company did not issue any new bonds during the year.
3. The company did not repurchase any of its own common stock during the year.
4. The company paid a cash dividend during the year.

Notice that the balance sheet in Exhibit 12–6 includes the amount of the change in each balance sheet account. For example, the beginning and ending balances in Cash and Cash Equivalents are $29 million and $91 million, respectively. This is a $62 million increase in the account balance. A similar computation is performed for all other balance sheet accounts. Study the changes in these account balances because we will be referring to them in the forthcoming pages. For example, keep in mind that the purpose of Apparel's statement of cash flows is to disclose the operating, investing, and financing cash flows underlying the $62 million increase in Cash and Cash Equivalents shown in Exhibit 12–6. *Also, please be advised that although the changes in account balances are computed for you in Exhibit 12–6, you'll ordinarily need to compute these amounts yourself before attempting to construct the statement of cash flows.*

**EXHIBIT 12–5**
Apparel, Inc., Income Statement

**Apparel, Inc.**
**Income Statement**
**(dollars in millions)**

| | |
|---|---|
| Sales | $3,638 |
| Cost of goods sold | 2,469 |
| Gross margin | 1,169 |
| Selling and administrative expenses | 941 |
| Net operating income | 228 |
| Nonoperating items: Gain on sale of store | 3 |
| Income before taxes | 231 |
| Income taxes | 91 |
| Net income | $ 140 |

**EXHIBIT 12–6**
Apparel, Inc., Balance Sheet

| Apparel, Inc. Comparative Balance Sheet (dollars in millions) | Ending Balance | Beginning Balance | Change |
|---|---|---|---|
| **Assets** | | | |
| Current assets: | | | |
| Cash and cash equivalents | $ 91 | $ 29 | +62 |
| Accounts receivable | 637 | 654 | −17 |
| Inventory | 586 | 537 | +49 |
| Total current assets | 1,314 | 1,220 | |
| Property, plant, and equipment | 1,517 | 1,394 | +123 |
| Less accumulated depreciation | 654 | 561 | +93 |
| Net property, plant, and equipment | 863 | 833 | |
| Total assets | $2,177 | $2,053 | |
| **Liabilities and Stockholders' Equity** | | | |
| Current liabilities: | | | |
| Accounts payable | $ 264 | $ 220 | +44 |
| Accrued liabilities | 193 | 190 | +3 |
| Income taxes payable | 75 | 71 | +4 |
| Total current liabilities | 532 | 481 | |
| Bonds payable | 479 | 520 | −41 |
| Total liabilities | 1,011 | 1,001 | |
| Stockholders' equity: | | | |
| Common stock | 157 | 155 | +2 |
| Retained earnings | 1,009 | 897 | +112 |
| Total stockholders' equity | 1,166 | 1,052 | |
| Total liabilities and stockholders' equity | $2,177 | $2,053 | |

## Operating Activities

This section uses the three-step process explained earlier to construct Apparel's operating activities section of the statement of cash flows.

**Step 1** The first step in computing Apparel's net cash provided by operating activities is to *add depreciation* to net income. The balance sheet in Exhibit 12–6 shows Apparel's Accumulated Depreciation account had beginning and ending balances of $561 million and $654 million, respectively. We also know from the assumptions listed on the previous page that Apparel sold a store during the year that had $10 million of accumulated depreciation. Given these facts, we can use the basic equation for contra-assets (introduced on page 540) to determine that Apparel needs to add $103 million of depreciation to its net income:

$$\text{Beginning balance} - \text{Debits} + \text{Credits} = \text{Ending balance}$$

$$\$561 \text{ million} - \$10 \text{ million} + \text{Credits} = \$654 \text{ million}$$

$$\text{Credits} = \$654 \text{ million} - \$561 \text{ million} + \$10 \text{ million}$$

$$\text{Credits} = \$103 \text{ million}$$

**Step 2** The second step in computing net cash provided by operating activities is to *analyze net changes in noncash balance sheet accounts* that impact net income. Exhibit 12–7 explains the five adjustments Apparel needs to make to complete this step. For your ease of reference, the top half of Exhibit 12–7 reproduces an excerpt of the

**EXHIBIT 12–7**
Apparel, Inc.: Analyzing How Net Changes in Noncash Balance Sheet Accounts Affect Net Income on the Statement of Cash Flows

| | Increase in Account Balance | Decrease in Account Balance |
|---|---|---|
| **General Guidelines from Exhibit 12–2** | | |
| *Current Assets* | | |
| Accounts receivable | Subtract | Add |
| Inventory | Subtract | Add |
| *Current Liabilities* | | |
| Accounts payable | Add | Subtract |
| Accrued liabilities | Add | Subtract |
| Income taxes payable | Add | Subtract |

| | Increase in Account Balance | Decrease in Account Balance |
|---|---|---|
| **Apparel's Account Analysis** | | |
| *Current Assets* | | |
| Accounts receivable | | +17 |
| Inventory | −49 | |
| *Current Liabilities* | | |
| Accounts payable | +44 | |
| Accrued liabilities | +3 | |
| Income taxes payable | +4 | |

general guidelines for completing this step that were previously summarized in Exhibit 12–2. The bottom half of Exhibit 12–7 applies the general guidelines from the top half of the exhibit to Apparel's balance sheet. For example, Exhibit 12–6 shows that Apparel's Accounts Receivable balance decreased by $17 million. The top half of Exhibit 12–7 says that decreases in accounts receivable are added to net income. This explains why the bottom half of Exhibit 12–7 includes a plus sign in front of Apparel's $17 million decrease in Accounts Receivable. Similarly, Exhibit 12–6 shows that Apparel's Inventory balance increased by $49 million. When inventory increases, the amount of the increase is subtracted from net income. This explains why the bottom half of Exhibit 12–7 includes a minus sign in front of Apparel's $49 million increase in Inventory. Similar logic can be used to explain why the increases from Exhibit 12–6 in Accounts Payable (+44), Accrued Liabilities (+3), and Income Taxes Payable (+4) all result in the additions to Apparel's net income that are shown in the bottom half of Exhibit 12–7.

**Step 3** The third step in computing the net cash provided by operating activities is to *adjust for gains/losses* included in the income statement. Apparel reported a $3 million gain on its income statement in Exhibit 12–5; therefore, this amount needs to be subtracted from net income. Subtracting the gain on sale removes the gain from the operating activities section of the statement of cash flows. The entire amount of the cash proceeds related to this sale will be recorded in the investing activities section of the statement.

Exhibit 12–8 shows the operating activities section of Apparel's statement of cash flows. Take a moment to trace each of the numbers that we just computed to this exhibit. The total amount of the adjustments to net income is $119 million, which results in net cash provided by operating activities of $259 million.

**EXHIBIT 12–8** Apparel, Inc. Operating Activities Section of the Statement of Cash Flows

| Apparel, Inc. (dollars in millions) | | | |
|---|---|---|---|
| | **Operating Activities** | | |
| | Net income | | $140 |
| | Adjustments to convert net income to a cash basis: | | |
| Step 1 → | Depreciation | 103 | |
| Step 2 → | Decrease in accounts receivable | 17 | |
| | Increase in inventory | (49) | |
| | Increase in accounts payable | 44 | |
| | Increase in accrued liabilities | 3 | |
| | Increase in income taxes payable | 4 | |
| Step 3 → | Gain on sale of store | (3) | 119 |
| | Net cash provided by operating activities | | $259 |

## Investing Activities

Apparel's investing cash flows pertain to its Property, Plant, and Equipment account, which according to Exhibit 12–6 had beginning and ending balances of $1,394 million and $1,517 million, respectively, for an increase of $123 million. This increase suggests that Apparel purchased equipment; however, it does not capture the gross cash flows that need to be reported in the statement of cash flows.

The assumptions on page 550 say that Apparel sold a store that had an original cost of $15 million for $8 million in cash. The cash inflow from this sale needs to be recorded in the investing activities section of the statement of cash flows. To compute the cash outflows related to purchases of property, plant, and equipment we use the basic equation for assets that was mentioned in the beginning of the chapter:

$$\text{Beginning balance} + \text{Debits} - \text{Credits} = \text{Ending balance}$$
$$\$1{,}394 \text{ million} + \text{Debits} - \$15 \text{ million} = \$1{,}517 \text{ million}$$
$$\text{Debits} = \$1{,}517 \text{ million} - \$1{,}394 \text{ million} + \$15 \text{ million}$$
$$\text{Debits} = \$138 \text{ million}$$

Notice the credits in the equation above include the original cost of the store that was sold. When the cash outflows of $138 million are combined with the $8 million of cash proceeds from the sale of the store, Apparel's net cash used in investing activities is $130 million.

## Financing Activities

Exhibit 12–9 explains how to compute Apparel's financing cash flows related to its Bonds Payable and Common Stock balance sheet accounts. The top half of the exhibit reproduces an excerpt of the general guidelines for analyzing financing cash flows that was previously summarized in Exhibit 12–3. The bottom half of Exhibit 12–9 applies the general guidelines from the top half of the exhibit to these two accounts from Apparel's balance sheet. We will analyze each account in turn.

Exhibit 12–6 shows that Apparel's Bonds Payable balance decreased by $41 million. Because, as stated on page 550, Apparel did not issue any bonds during the year, we can conclude that the $41 million decrease in the account is due solely to retiring bonds payable. The top half of Exhibit 12–9 says that a decrease in Bonds Payable signals the need to subtract cash outflows in the investing activities section of the statement of cash flows. This explains why the bottom half of the exhibit includes a minus sign in front of Apparel's $41 million decrease in Bonds Payable. Similarly, Exhibit 12–6 shows that Apparel's Common Stock balance increased by $2 million. Because, as stated on page 550, Apparel did not repurchase any of its own stock during the year, we can conclude that the $2 million increase in the account is due solely to issuing common stock. The top half of Exhibit 12–9 says that increases in common stock signal the need to add cash inflows in the investing activities section of the statement of cash flows. This explains

**EXHIBIT 12–9**
Apparel, Inc.: Analyzing How Changes in Noncash Balance Sheet Accounts Affect Financing Cash Flows on the Statement of Cash Flows

| | Increase in Account Balance | Decrease in Account Balance |
|---|---|---|
| **General Guidelines from Exhibit 12–3** | | |
| *Liabilities and Stockholders' Equity* | | |
| Bonds payable | Add | Subtract |
| Common stock | Add | Subtract |
| | **Increase in Account Balance** | **Decrease in Account Balance** |
| **Apparel's Account Analysis** | | |
| *Liabilities and Stockholders' Equity* | | |
| Bonds payable | | −41 |
| Common stock | +2 | |

why the bottom half of the exhibit includes a plus sign in front of Apparel's $2 million increase in Common Stock.

The final financing cash outflow for Apparel is its dividend payment to common stockholders. The dividend payment can be computed using the basic equation for stockholders' equity accounts mentioned at the beginning of the chapter:

$$\text{Beginning balance} - \text{Debits} + \text{Credits} = \text{Ending balance}$$
$$\$897 \text{ million} - \text{Debits} + \$140 \text{ million} = \$1{,}009 \text{ million}$$
$$\$1{,}037 \text{ million} = \$1{,}009 \text{ million} + \text{Debits}$$
$$\text{Debits} = \$28 \text{ million}$$

When the cash outflows of $69 million (= $41 million + $28 million) are combined with the cash inflows of $2 million, Apparel's net cash used in financing activities is $67 million.

**EXHIBIT 12–10**
Apparel, Inc. Statement of Cash Flows

**Apparel, Inc.**
**Statement of Cash Flows—Indirect Method**
**(dollars in millions)**

| | | |
|---|---|---|
| **Operating Activities** | | |
| Net income | | $140 |
| Adjustments to convert net income to a cash basis: | | |
| Depreciation | 103 | |
| Decrease in accounts receivable | 17 | |
| Increase in inventory | (49) | |
| Increase in accounts payable | 44 | |
| Increase in accrued liabilities | 3 | |
| Increase in income taxes payable | 4 | |
| Gain on sale of store | (3) | 119 |
| Net cash provided by operating activities | | 259 |
| **Investing Activities** | | |
| Additions to property, plant, and equipment | (138) | |
| Proceeds from sale of store | 8 | |
| Net cash used in investing activities | | (130) |
| **Financing Activities** | | |
| Retirement of bonds payable | (41) | |
| Issuance of common stock | 2 | |
| Cash dividends paid | (28) | |
| Net cash used in financing activities | | (67) |
| Net increase in cash and cash equivalents | | 62 |
| Cash and cash equivalents, beginning balance | | 29 |
| Cash and cash equivalents, ending balance | | $ 91 |

Exhibit 12–10 on page 554 shows Apparel's statement of cash flows. The operating activities section of this statement is carried over from Exhibit 12–8. Take a moment to trace the investing and financing cash flows just discussed to Exhibit 12–10. Notice, the net increase in cash and cash equivalents is $62 million (= $259 million − $130 million − $67 million), which agrees with the change in the Cash and Cash Equivalents account shown on the balance sheet in Exhibit 12–6.

## Seeing the Big Picture

In the beginning of the chapter, we mentioned that a statement of cash flows is prepared by analyzing the changes in noncash balance sheet accounts. We then presented a method of preparing a statement of cash flows. This method simplified the process of creating the statement of cash flows, and now we will show that it is equivalent to analyzing the changes in noncash balance sheet accounts.

Exhibit 12–11 uses T-accounts to summarize how the changes in Apparel Inc.'s noncash balance sheet accounts quantify the cash inflows and outflows that explain the change in its cash balance. The top portion of the exhibit is Apparel's Cash T-account and the bottom portion provides T-accounts for the company's remaining balance sheet

**EXHIBIT 12–11** T-Accounts after Posting of Account Changes—Apparel, Inc. (in millions)

**Cash**

| | | | | | |
|---|---|---|---|---|---|
| Net income | (1) | 140 | 49 | (4) | Increase in inventory |
| Depreciation | (2) | 103 | 3 | (12) | Gain on sale of store |
| Decrease in accounts receivable | (3) | 17 | | | |
| Increase in accounts payable | (5) | 44 | | | |
| Increase in accrued liabilities | (6) | 3 | | | |
| Increase in income taxes payable | (7) | 4 | | | |
| Net cash provided by operating activities | | 259 | | | |
| Proceeds from sale of store | (12) | 8 | 138 | (8) | Additions to property, plant, and equipment |
| Increase in common stock | (11) | 2 | 41 | (9) | Decrease in bonds payable |
| | | | 28 | (10) | Cash dividends paid |
| Net increase in cash and cash equivalents | | 62 | | | |

**Accounts Receivable**

| | | | |
|---|---|---|---|
| Bal. | 654 | | |
| | | 17 | (3) |
| Bal. | 637 | | |

**Inventory**

| | | | |
|---|---|---|---|
| Bal. | 537 | | |
| (4) | 49 | | |
| Bal. | 586 | | |

**Property, Plant, and Equipment**

| | | | |
|---|---|---|---|
| Bal. | 1,394 | | |
| (8) | 138 | 15 | (12) |
| Bal. | 1,517 | | |

**Accumulated Depreciation**

| | | | |
|---|---|---|---|
| | | 561 | Bal. |
| (12) | 10 | 103 | (2) |
| | | 654 | Bal. |

**Accounts Payable**

| | | | |
|---|---|---|---|
| | | 220 | Bal. |
| | | 44 | (5) |
| | | 264 | Bal. |

**Accrued Liabilities**

| | | | |
|---|---|---|---|
| | | 190 | Bal. |
| | | 3 | (6) |
| | | 193 | Bal. |

**Income Taxes Payable**

| | | | |
|---|---|---|---|
| | | 71 | Bal. |
| | | 4 | (7) |
| | | 75 | Bal. |

**Bonds Payable**

| | | | |
|---|---|---|---|
| | | 520 | Bal. |
| (9) | 41 | | |
| | | 479 | Bal. |

**Common Stock**

| | | | |
|---|---|---|---|
| | | 155 | Bal. |
| | | 2 | (11) |
| | | 157 | Bal. |

**Retained Earnings**

| | | | |
|---|---|---|---|
| | | 897 | Bal. |
| (10) | 28 | 140 | (1) |
| | | 1,009 | Bal. |

accounts. Notice that the net cash provided by operating activities ($259 million) and the net increase in cash and cash equivalents ($62) shown in the Cash T-account agree with the corresponding figures in the statement of cash flows shown in Exhibit 12–10.

We will explain Exhibit 12–11 in five steps. Entry (1) records Apparel's net income ($140 million) in the credit side of the Retained Earnings account and the debit side of the Cash account. The net income of $140 million shown in the Cash T-account will be adjusted until it reflects the $62 million net increase in cash and cash equivalents. Entry (2) adds the depreciation of $103 million to net income. Entries (3) through (7) adjust net income for the changes in the current asset and current liability accounts. Entries (8) through (11) summarize the cash outflows and inflows related to the additions to property, plant, and equipment, the retirement of bonds payable, the payment of the cash dividend, and the issuance of common stock. Entry (12) records the sale of the store. Notice that the gain on the sale ($3 million) is recorded in the credit side of the Cash T-account. This is equivalent to subtracting the gain from net income so that the entire amount of the cash proceeds from the sale ($8 million) can be recorded in the investing activities section of the statement of cash flows.

## INTERPRETING THE STATEMENT OF CASH FLOWS

Managers can derive many useful insights by studying the statement of cash flows. In this section, we will discuss two guidelines managers should use when interpreting the statement of cash flows.

### Consider a Company's Specific Circumstances

A statement of cash flows should be evaluated in the context of a company's specific circumstances. To illustrate this point, let's consider two examples related to start-up companies and companies with growing versus declining sales. Start-up companies are usually unable to generate positive cash flows from operations; therefore, they rely on issuing stock and taking out loans to fund investing activities. This means that start-up companies often have negative net cash provided by operating activities and large spikes in net cash used for investing activities and net cash provided by financing activities. However, as a start-up company matures, it should begin generating enough cash to sustain day-to-day operations and maintain its plant and equipment without issuing additional stock or borrowing money. This means the net cash provided by operating activities should swing from a negative to a positive number. The net cash used for investing activities should decline somewhat and stabilize and the net cash provided by financing activities should decrease.

A company with growing sales would understandably have an increase in its accounts receivable, inventory, and accounts payable balances. On the other hand, if a company with declining sales has increases in these account balances, it could signal trouble. Perhaps accounts receivable is increasing because the company is attempting to boost sales by selling to customers who can't pay their bills. Perhaps the increase in inventory suggests the company is stuck with large amounts of obsolete inventory. Accounts payable may be increasing because the company is deferring payments to suppliers in an effort to inflate its net cash provided by operating activities. Notice that the plausible interpretations of these changes in account balances depend on the company's circumstances.

**DECISION POINT** **Owner**

You are the owner of a small manufacturing company. The company started selling its products internationally this year, which has resulted in a very significant increase in sales revenue and net income during the last two months of the year. The operating activities section of the company's statement of cash flows shows a negative number (that is, cash was *used* rather than *provided* by operations). Would you be concerned?

## Consider the Relationships among Numbers

While each number in a statement of cash flows provides useful information, managers derive the most meaningful insights by examining the relationships among numbers.

For example, some managers study their company's trends in cash flow margins by comparing the net cash provided by operating activities to sales. The goal is to continuously increase the operating cash flows earned per sales dollar. If we refer back to Apparel's income statement in Exhibit 12–5 and its statement of cash flows in Exhibit 12–10, we can determine that its cash flow margin is about $0.07 per dollar of sales (= $259 ÷ $3,638). Managers also compare the net cash provided by operating activities to the ending balance of current liabilities. If the net cash provided by operating activities is greater than (less than) the current liabilities, it indicates the company did (did not) generate enough operating cash flow to pay its bills at the end of the period. Apparel's net cash provided by operating activities of $259 million (see Exhibit 12–10) was not enough to pay its year-end current liabilities of $481 million (see Exhibit 12–6).

As a third example, managers compare the additions to property, plant, and equipment in the investing activities section of the statement of cash flows to the depreciation included in the operating activities section of the statement. If the additions to property, plant, and equipment are consistently less than depreciation, it suggests the company is not investing enough money to maintain its noncurrent assets. If we refer back to Apparel's statement of cash flows in Exhibit 12–10, its additions to property, plant, and equipment ($138 million) are greater than its depreciation ($103 million). This suggests that Apparel is investing more than enough money to maintain its noncurrent assets.

**LEARNING OBJECTIVE 3**

Compute free cash flow.

**Free Cash Flow** *Free cash flow* is a measure used by managers to look at the relationship among three numbers from the statement of cash flows—net cash provided by operating activities, additions to property, plant, and equipment (also called capital expenditures), and dividends. **Free cash flow** measures a company's ability to fund its capital expenditures for property, plant, and equipment and its dividends from its net cash provided by operating activities.[6] The equation for computing free cash flow is as follows:

$$\text{Free cash flow} = \text{Net cash provided by operating activities} - \text{Capital expenditures} - \text{Dividends}$$

Using this equation and the statement of cash flows shown in Exhibit 12–10, we can compute Apparel's free cash flow (in millions) as follows:

$$\text{Free cash flow} = \$259 - \$138 - \$28$$
$$\text{Free cash flow} = \$93$$

The interpretation of free cash flow is straightforward. A positive number indicates that the company generated enough cash flow from its operating activities to fund its capital expenditures and dividend payments. A negative number suggests that the company needed to obtain cash from other sources, such as borrowing money from lenders or issuing shares of common stock, to fund its investments in property, plant, and equipment and its dividend payments. Negative free cash flow does not automatically signal poor performance. As previously discussed, a new company with enormous growth

[6]For a summary of alternative definitions of free cash flow, see John Mills, Lynn Bible, and Richard Mason, "Defining Free Cash Flow," *CPA Journal,* January 2002, pp. 36–42.

prospects would be expected to have negative free cash flow during its start-up phase. However, even new companies will eventually need to generate positive free cash flow to survive.

**Earnings Quality** Managers and investors often look at the relationship between net income and net cash provided by operating activities to help assess the extent to which a company's earnings truly reflects operational performance. Managers generally perceive that earnings are of higher quality, or more indicative of operational performance, when the earnings (1) are not unduly influenced by inflation, (2) are computed using conservative accounting principles and estimates, and (3) are correlated with net cash provided by operating activities. When a company's net income and net cash provided by operating activities move in tandem with one another (in other words, are correlated with one another), it suggests that earnings result from changes in sales and operating expenses. Conversely, if a company's net income is steadily increasing and its net cash provided by operating activities is declining, it suggests that net income is being influenced by factors unrelated to operational performance, such as nonrecurring transactions or aggressive accounting principles and estimates.

IN BUSINESS

## Slow Payments Squeeze Small Businesses

When the California real estate market crashed, Artisan Shutter Company encountered severe cash flow problems. Half of the company's customers started making late payments. Eventually, the company had to lay off 15% of its employees due to insufficient cash inflows. This problem would be evident from the statement of cash flows, which would show that the late payments increased Artisan's accounts receivable balance and, hence, decreased its net cash provided by operating activities. The company's owners had to raid their retirement accounts and rack up huge credit card debts just to pay their bills and avoid bankruptcy.

Take a moment to contrast this In Business box with the box titled "Amazon.com Boosts Cash Flows" that is shown below. What are your thoughts?

Source: Kelly K. Spors and Simona Covel, "Slow Payments Squeeze Small-Business Owners," *The Wall Street Journal*, October 31, 2008, pp. B1 and B6.

IN BUSINESS

## Amazon.com Boosts Cash Flows

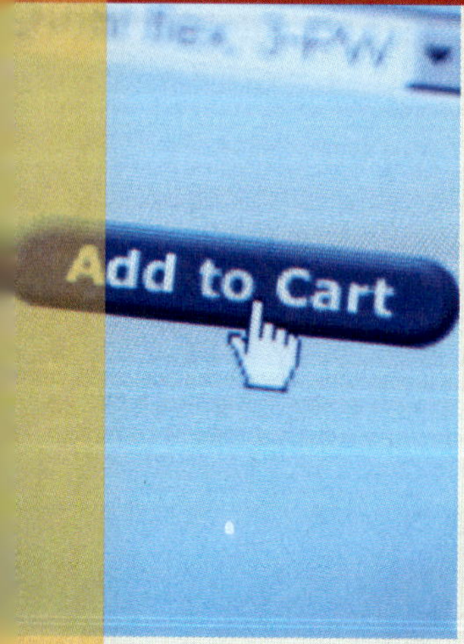


**Amazon.com** immediately receives cash from its customers when sales occur on its website. When the company stretched the number of days taken to pay its suppliers from 63 to 72 days, this created a huge jump in the company's accounts payable balance, which helped increase free cash flow from $346 million to $1.36 billion. In one quarter, Amazon.com's sales increased 28%, but its accounts payable nearly doubled, causing a 116% increase in free cash flow. Do you think managers should increase cash flows by delaying payments to suppliers? Would it promote a cooperative relationship with suppliers?

Source: Martin Peers, "Amazon's Astute Timing," *The Wall Street Journal*, October 30, 2009, p. C10.

## SUMMARY


**LO1 Classify cash inflows and outflows as relating to operating, investing, or financing activities.**
The statement of cash flows is organized into three sections: operating activities, investing activities, and financing activities. Operating activities generate cash inflows and outflows related to revenue and expense transactions that affect net income. Investing activities generate cash inflows and outflows related to acquiring or disposing of noncurrent assets. Financing activities generate cash inflows and outflows related to borrowing from and repaying principal to creditors and completing transactions with the company's owners.

**LO2 Prepare a statement of cash flows using the indirect method to determine the net cash provided by operating activities.**
The net cash provided by operating activities can be depicted using either the direct or indirect method. Under the direct method, the income statement is reconstructed on a cash basis from top to bottom. For example, cash collected from customers is listed instead of revenue, and payments to suppliers is listed instead of cost of goods sold. Under the indirect method, net income is adjusted to a cash basis. That is, rather than directly computing cash sales, cash expenses, and so forth, these amounts are derived indirectly by removing from net income any items that do not affect cash flows.

The indirect method adjusts net income to net cash provided by operating activities using a three-step process. The first step is to add depreciation charges to net income. The second step is to analyze net changes in noncash balance sheet accounts that impact net income. The third step is to adjust for gains/losses included in the income statement.

The investing and financing sections of the statement of cash flows record gross cash flows rather than net cash flows. The net increase in cash and cash equivalents shown on the statement of cash flows agrees with the change in the Cash account shown on the balance sheet.

**LO3 Compute free cash flow.**
Free cash flow is the net cash provided by operating activities less capital expenditures and dividends.


## GUIDANCE ANSWER TO DECISION POINT

**Owner (p. 556)**
Even though the company reported net income, the net effect of the company's operations was to *consume* rather than *generate* cash during the year. Cash disbursements relating to the company's operations exceeded the amount of cash receipts from operations. If the company generated a significant amount of sales just before the end of the year, it is quite possible that cash has not yet been received from the customers. In fact, given that the additional sales were international, a longer collection period would be expected. Nevertheless, as owner, you probably would want to ensure that the company's credit-granting policies and procedures were adhered to when these sales were made, and you should also monitor the length of time it takes to collect accounts receivable.

## GUIDANCE ANSWERS TO CONCEPT CHECKS

1. **Choices a and c.** Depreciation charges are added to net income. A loss on the sale of an asset should be added to net income.
2. **Choice d.** Using the basic equation for contra-assets, \$2,000 − \$350 + Credits = \$2,900. The credits = \$1,250.
3. **Choice a.** The cash proceeds from the sale of the asset were \$75 and the book value of the asset that was sold is \$50 (= \$400 − \$350). The \$25 difference between these two amounts is the gain on the sale of the asset and it should be subtracted from net income in the operating activities section of the statement of cash flows.
4. **Choice c.** Using the basic equation for assets, \$5,000 + Debits − \$700 = \$6,000. The debits equal \$1,700 and this amount relates to purchases of noncurrent assets. Since the company sold an asset for \$500 and it purchased noncurrent assets for \$1,700, its net cash provided by (used in) investing activities is \$(1,200).

## REVIEW PROBLEM

Rockford Company's comparative balance sheet for 2012 and the company's income statement for the year follow:

**Rockford Company**
**Comparative Balance Sheet**
**(dollars in millions)**

| | 2012 | 2011 |
|---|---|---|
| **Assets** | | |
| Current assets: | | |
| Cash and cash equivalents | $ 26 | $ 10 |
| Accounts receivable | 180 | 270 |
| Inventory | 205 | 160 |
| Prepaid expenses | 17 | 20 |
| Total current assets | 428 | 460 |
| Property, plant, and equipment | 430 | 309 |
| Less accumulated depreciation | 218 | 194 |
| Net property, plant, and equipment | 212 | 115 |
| Long-term investments | 60 | 75 |
| Total assets | $700 | $650 |
| **Liabilities and Stockholders' Equity** | | |
| Current liabilities: | | |
| Accounts payable | $230 | $310 |
| Accrued liabilities | 70 | 60 |
| Income taxes payable | 15 | 8 |
| Total current liabilities | 315 | 378 |
| Bonds payable | 135 | 40 |
| Total liabilities | 450 | 418 |
| Stockholders' equity: | | |
| Common stock | 140 | 140 |
| Retained earnings | 110 | 92 |
| Total stockholders' equity | 250 | 232 |
| Total liabilities and stockholders' equity | $700 | $650 |

**Rockford Company**
**Income Statement**
**For the Year Ended December 31, 2012**
**(dollars in millions)**

| | |
|---|---|
| Sales | $1,000 |
| Cost of goods sold | 530 |
| Gross margin | 470 |
| Selling and administrative expenses | 352 |
| Net operating income | 118 |
| Nonoperating items: | |
| Loss on sale of equipment | 4 |
| Income before taxes | 114 |
| Income taxes | 48 |
| Net income | $ 66 |

Additional data:

1. Rockford paid a cash dividend in 2012.
2. The $4 million loss on sale of equipment reflects a transaction in which equipment with an original cost of $12 million and accumulated depreciation of $5 million was sold for $3 million in cash.
3. Rockford did not purchase any long-term investments during the year. There was no gain or loss on the sale of long-term investments.
4. Rockford did not retire any bonds payable during 2012, or issue or repurchase any common stock.

***Required:***

1. Using the indirect method, determine the net cash provided by operating activities for 2012.
2. Construct a statement of cash flows for 2012.

**Solution to Review Problem**

The first task you should complete before turning your attention to the problem's specific requirements is to compute the changes in each balance sheet account as shown below (all amounts are in millions):

**Rockford Company**
**Comparative Balance Sheet**
**(dollars in millions)**

| | 2012 | 2011 | Change |
|---|---|---|---|
| **Assets** | | | |
| Current assets: | | | |
| Cash and cash equivalents | $ 26 | $ 10 | −16 |
| Accounts receivable | 180 | 270 | −90 |
| Inventory | 205 | 160 | +45 |
| Prepaid expenses | 17 | 20 | −3 |
| Total current assets | 428 | 460 | |
| Property, plant, and equipment | 430 | 309 | +121 |
| Less accumulated depreciation | 218 | 194 | +24 |
| Net property, plant, and equipment | 212 | 115 | |
| Long-term investments | 60 | 75 | −15 |
| Total assets | $700 | $650 | |
| **Liabilities and Stockholders' Equity** | | | |
| Current liabilities: | | | |
| Accounts payable | $230 | $310 | −80 |
| Accrued liabilities | 70 | 60 | +10 |
| Income taxes payable | 15 | 8 | +7 |
| Total current liabilities | 315 | 378 | |
| Bonds payable | 135 | 40 | +95 |
| Total liabilities | 450 | 418 | |
| Stockholders' equity: | | | |
| Common stock | 140 | 140 | +0 |
| Retained earnings | 110 | 92 | +18 |
| Total stockholders' equity | 250 | 232 | |
| Total liabilities and stockholders' equity | $700 | $650 | |

***Requirement 1:***

You should perform three steps to compute the net cash provided by operating activities.

Step 1: Add depreciation to net income.

To complete this step, apply the equation on page 543 as follows:

Beginning balance − Debits + Credits = Ending balance

$194 million − $5 million + Credits = $218 million

Credits = $218 million − $194 million + $5 million

Credits = $29 million

Step 2: Analyze net changes in noncash balance sheet accounts that affect net income. To complete this step, apply the logic from Exhibit 12–2 as follows:

| | Increase in Account Balance | Decrease in Account Balance |
|---|---|---|
| *Current Assets* | | |
| Accounts receivable.................... | | +90 |
| Inventory.................................... | −45 | |
| Prepaid expenses......................... | | +3 |
| *Current Liabilities* | | |
| Accounts payable......................... | | −80 |
| Accrued liabilities......................... | +10 | |
| Income taxes payable.................. | +7 | |

Step 3: Adjust for gains/losses included in the income statement. Rockford's $4 million loss on the sale of equipment must be added to net income.

Having completed these three steps, the operating activities section of the statement of cash flows would appear as follows:

| Rockford Company<br>Statement of Cash Flows—Indirect Method<br>For the Year Ended December 31, 2012<br>(dollars in millions) | | |
|---|---|---|
| **Operating Activities** | | |
| Net income ................................................................ | | $66 |
| Adjustments to convert net income to a cash basis: | | |
| Depreciation................................................................ | $29 | |
| Decrease in accounts receivable................................ | 90 | |
| Increase in inventory................................................ | (45) | |
| Decrease in prepaid expenses.................................... | 3 | |
| Decrease in accounts payable.................................... | (80) | |
| Increase in accrued liabilities.................................... | 10 | |
| Increase in income taxes payable............................... | 7 | |
| Loss on sale of equipment......................................... | 4 | 18 |
| Net cash provided by operating activities........................ | | $84 |

***Requirement 2:***

To finalize the statement of cash flows, we must complete the investing and financing sections of the statement. This requires analyzing the Property, Plant, and Equipment; Long-Term Investments; Bonds Payable; Common Stock; and Retained Earnings accounts. The table below is based on Exhibit 12–3 and it captures the changes in four account balances for Rockford.

| | Increase in Account Balance | Decrease in Account Balance |
|---|---|---|
| **Noncurrent Assets (Investing activities)** | | |
| Property, plant, and equipment................................ | −121 | |
| Long-term investments............................................ | | +15 |
| **Liabilities and Stockholders' Equity (Financing activities)** | | |
| Bonds payable.......................................................... | +95 | |
| Common stock.......................................................... | No change | No change |
| Retained earnings.................................................... | * | * |

*Requires further analysis to quantify cash dividends paid.

The data at the beginning of the problem state that Rockford did not purchase any long-term investments during the year and that there was no gain or loss on the sale of long-term investments. This means that the $15 million decrease in Long-Term Investments corresponds with a $15 million cash inflow from the sale of long-term investments that is recorded in the investing section of the statement of cash flows. The data also state that Rockford did not retire any bonds payable during the year; therefore, the $95 million increase in Bonds Payable must be due to issuing bonds payable. This cash inflow is recorded in the financing section of the statement of cash flows.

The Common Stock account had no activity during the period, so it does not impact the statement of cash flows. This leaves two accounts that require further analysis—Property, Plant, and Equipment and Retained Earnings.

The company sold equipment that had an original cost of $12 million for $3 million in cash. The cash proceeds from the sale need to be recorded in the investing activities section of the statement of cash flows. The cash outflows related to Rockford's investing activities can be computed using the basic equation for assets mentioned on page 540:

$$\text{Beginning balance} + \text{Debits} - \text{Credits} = \text{Ending balance}$$
$$\$309\text{ million} + \text{Debits} - \$12\text{ million} = \$430\text{ million}$$
$$\text{Debits} = \$430\text{ million} - \$309\text{ million} + \$12\text{ million}$$
$$\text{Debits} = \$133\text{ million}$$

Rockford's Retained Earnings account and the basic equation for stockholders' equity (introduced on page 540) can be used to compute the company's dividend payment as follows:

$$\text{Beginning balance} - \text{Debits} + \text{Credits} = \text{Ending balance}$$
$$\$92\text{ million} - \text{Debits} + \$66\text{ million} = \$110\text{ million}$$
$$\$158\text{ million} = \$110\text{ million} + \text{Debits}$$
$$\text{Debits} = \$48\text{ million}$$

The company's complete statement of cash flows is shown below. Notice that the net increase in cash and cash equivalents ($16 million) equals the change in the Cash and Cash Equivalents account balance.

**Rockford Company**
**Statement of Cash Flows—Indirect Method**
**For the Year Ended December 31, 2012**
**(dollars in millions)**

| | | |
|---|---|---|
| **Operating Activities:** | | |
| Net income | | $ 66 |
| Adjustments to convert net income to a cash basis: | | |
| Depreciation | $ 29 | |
| Decrease in accounts receivable | 90 | |
| Increase in inventory | (45) | |
| Decrease in prepaid expenses | 3 | |
| Decrease in accounts payable | (80) | |
| Increase in accrued liabilities | 10 | |
| Increase in income taxes payable | 7 | |
| Loss on sale of equipment | 4 | 18 |
| Net cash provided by operating activities | | 84 |
| **Investing Activities:** | | |
| Additions to property, plant, and equipment | (133) | |
| Decrease in long-term investments | 15 | |
| Proceeds from sale of equipment | 3 | |
| Net cash used in investing activities | | (115) |
| **Financing Activities:** | | |
| Increase in bonds payable | 95 | |
| Cash dividends paid | (48) | |
| Net cash provided by financing activities | | 47 |
| Net increase in cash and cash equivalents | | 16 |
| Cash and cash equivalents at beginning of year | | 10 |
| Cash and cash equivalents at end of year | | $ 26 |

## GLOSSARY

**Cash equivalents** Short-term, highly liquid investments such as Treasury bills, commercial paper, and money market funds, that are made solely for the purpose of generating a return on temporarily idle funds. (p. 541)

**Direct method** A method of computing the net cash provided by operating activities in which the income statement is reconstructed on a cash basis from top to bottom. (p. 542)

**Financing activities** These activities generate cash inflows and outflows related to borrowing from and repaying principal to creditors and completing transactions with the company's owners, such as selling or repurchasing shares of common stock and paying dividends. (p. 542)

**Free cash flow** A measure that assesses a company's ability to fund its capital expenditures and dividends from its net cash provided by operating activities. (p. 557)

**Indirect method** A method of computing the net cash provided by operating activities that starts with net income and adjusts it to a cash basis. (p. 542)

**Investing activities** These activities generate cash inflows and outflows related to acquiring or disposing of noncurrent assets such as property, plant, and equipment, long-term investments, and loans to another entity. (p. 541)

**Net cash provided by operating activities** The net result of the cash inflows and outflows arising from day-to-day operations. (p. 542)

**Operating activities** These activities generate cash inflows and outflows related to revenue and expense transactions that affect net income. (p. 541)

**Statement of cash flows** A financial statement that highlights the major activities that impact cash flows and, hence, affect the overall cash balance. (p. 540)

## QUESTIONS

**12–1** What is the purpose of a statement of cash flows?

**12–2** What are *cash equivalents,* and why are they included with cash on a statement of cash flows?

**12–3** What are the three major sections on a statement of cash flows, and what type of cash inflows and outflows should be included in each section?

**12–4** What general guidelines can you provide for interpreting the statement of cash flows?

**12–5** If an asset is sold at a gain, why is the gain subtracted from net income when computing the net cash provided by operating activities under the indirect method?

**12–6** Why aren't transactions involving accounts payable considered to be financing activities?

**12–7** Assume that a company repays a $300,000 loan from its bank and then later in the same year borrows $500,000. What amount(s) would appear on the statement of cash flows?

**12–8** How do the direct and the indirect methods differ in their approach to computing the net cash provided by operating activities?

**12–9** A business executive once stated, "Depreciation is one of our biggest operating cash inflows." Do you agree? Explain.

**12–10** If the Accounts Receivable balance increases during a period, how will this increase be recognized using the indirect method of computing the net cash provided by operating activities?

**12–11** Would a sale of equipment for cash be considered a financing activity or an investing activity? Why?

**12–12** What is the difference between net cash provided by operating activities and free cash flow?

**Multiple-choice questions are provided on the text website at www.mhhe.com/brewer6e.**

## THE FOUNDATIONAL 15

LO1, LO2

**Available with McGraw-Hill's *Connect® Accounting*.**

Ravenna Company is a merchandiser that uses the indirect method to prepare the operating activities section of its statement of cash flows. Its balance sheet for this year is as follows:

| | Ending Balance | Beginning Balance |
|---|---|---|
| Cash | $ 48,000 | $ 57,000 |
| Accounts receivable | 41,000 | 44,000 |
| Inventory | 55,000 | 50,000 |
| Property, plant, and equipment | 150,000 | 140,000 |
| Less accumulated depreciation | (50,000) | (35,000) |
| Total assets | $244,000 | $256,000 |
| Accounts payable | $ 32,000 | $ 57,000 |
| Income taxes payable | 25,000 | 28,000 |
| Bonds payable | 60,000 | 50,000 |
| Common stock | 70,000 | 60,000 |
| Retained earnings | 57,000 | 61,000 |
| Total liabilities and stockholders' equity | $244,000 | $256,000 |

During the year Ravenna paid a $6,000 cash dividend and it sold a piece of equipment for $3,000 that had originally cost $6,000 and had accumulated depreciation of $4,000. The company did not retire any bonds or repurchase any of its own common stock during the year.

***Required:***

1. What is the amount of the net increase or decrease in cash and cash equivalents that would be shown on the company's statement of cash flows?
2. What net income would the company include on its statement of cash flows?
3. How much depreciation would the company add to net income on its statement of cash flows?
4. (To help answer this question, create an Accounts Receivable T-account and insert the beginning and ending balances.) If the company credited sales and debited accounts receivable for $600,000 during the year, what is the total amount of credits recorded in accounts receivable during the year? What does the amount of these credits represent?
5. What is the amount and direction (+ or −) of the accounts receivable adjustment to net income in the operating activities section of the statement of cash flows? What does this adjustment represent?
6. (To help answer this question, create T-accounts for Inventory and Accounts Payable and insert their beginning and ending balances.) If the company debited cost of goods sold and credited inventory for $400,000 during the year, what is the total amount of inventory purchases recorded on the debit side of the Inventory T-account and the credit side of the Accounts Payable T-account? What is the total amount of the debits recorded in the Accounts Payable T-account during the year? What does the amount of these debits represent?
7. What is the combined amount and direction (+ or −) of the inventory and accounts payable adjustments to net income in the operating activities section of the statement of cash flows? What does this amount represent?
8. (To help answer this question, create an Income Taxes Payable T-account and insert the beginning and ending balances.) If the company debited income tax expense and credited income taxes payable $25,000 during the year, what is the total amount of the debits recorded in the Income Taxes Payable account? What does the amount of these debits represent?
9. What is the amount and direction (+ or −) of the income taxes payable adjustment to net income in the operating activities section of the statement of cash flows? What does this adjustment represent?
10. Would the operating activities section of the company's statement of cash flows contain an adjustment for a gain or a loss? What would be the amount and direction (+ or −) of the adjustment?
11. What is the amount of net cash provided by operating activities in the company's statement of cash flows?
12. What is the amount of gross cash outflows reported in the investing section of the company's statement of cash flows?
13. What is the company's net cash provided by (used in) investing activities?
14. What is the amount of gross cash inflows reported in the financing section of the company's statement of cash flows?
15. What is the company's net cash provided by (used in) financing activities?

# EXERCISES

connect ACCOUNTING

**All applicable exercises are available with McGraw-Hill's *Connect® Accounting.***

### EXERCISE 12–1 Classifying Transactions [LO1]

Below are certain events that took place at Hazzard, Inc., last year:

a. Paid bills to insurers and utility providers.
b. Purchased equipment with cash.
c. Paid wages and salaries to employees.
d. Paid taxes to the government.
e. Loaned money to another entity.
f. Sold common stock.
g. Paid a cash dividend to stockholders.
h. Paid interest to lenders.
i. Repaid the principal amount of a debt.
j. Paid suppliers for inventory purchases.
k. Borrowed money from a creditor.
l. Paid cash to repurchase its own stock.
m. Collected cash from customers.

***Required:***

Prepare an answer sheet with the following headings:

| | Activity | | |
|---|---|---|---|
| **Transaction** | **Operating** | **Investing** | **Financing** |
| a. | | | |
| b. | | | |
| Etc. | | | |

Enter the cash inflows and outflows above on your answer sheet and indicate how each of them would be classified on a statement of cash flows. Place an X in the Operating, Investing, or Financing column as appropriate.

### EXERCISE 12–2 Net Cash Provided by Operating Activities [LO2]

For the just completed year, Strident Company had net income of $84,000. Balances in the company's current asset and current liability accounts at the beginning and end of the year were as follows:

| | December 31 | |
|---|---|---|
| | **End of Year** | **Beginning of Year** |
| Current assets: | | |
| Cash | $60,000 | $80,000 |
| Accounts receivable | $165,000 | $190,000 |
| Inventory | $437,000 | $360,000 |
| Prepaid expenses | $12,000 | $14,000 |
| Current liabilities: | | |
| Accounts payable | $370,000 | $390,000 |
| Accrued liabilities | $8,000 | $12,000 |
| Income taxes payable | $36,000 | $30,000 |

The Accumulated Depreciation account had total credits of $50,000 during the year.

***Required:***

Using the indirect method, determine the net cash provided by operating activities for the year.

**EXERCISE 12–3 Calculating Free Cash Flow [LO3]**

Paisley Company prepared the following statement of cash flows for the current year:

| Paisley Company<br>Statement of Cash Flows—Indirect Method | | |
|---|---|---|
| **Operating activities:** | | |
| Net income | | $ 40,000 |
| Adjustments to convert net income to cash basis: | | |
| Depreciation | $ 22,000 | |
| Increase in accounts receivable | (50,000) | |
| Increase in inventory | (35,000) | |
| Decrease in prepaid expenses | 6,000 | |
| Increase in accounts payable | 60,000 | |
| Decrease in accrued liabilities | (12,000) | |
| Increase in income taxes payable | 5,000 | (4,000) |
| Net cash provided by operating activities | | 36,000 |
| **Investing activities:** | | |
| Proceeds from the sale of equipment | 24,000 | |
| Loan to Allen Company | (30,000) | |
| Additions to plant and equipment | (120,000) | |
| Net cash used for investing activities | | (126,000) |
| **Financing activities:** | | |
| Increase in bonds payable | 80,000 | |
| Increase in common stock | 50,000 | |
| Cash dividends | (20,000) | |
| Net cash provided by financing activities | | 110,000 |
| Net increase in cash | | 20,000 |
| Cash balance, beginning of year | | 27,000 |
| Cash balance, end of year | | $ 47,000 |

***Required:***

Compute Paisley Company's free cash flow for the current year.

**EXERCISE 12–4 Prepare a Statement of Cash Flows; Free Cash Flow [LO1, LO2, LO3]**

Comparative financial statement data for Holly Company are given below:

| | December 31 | |
|---|---|---|
| | This Year | Last Year |
| **Assets** | | |
| Cash | $ 4 | $ 7 |
| Accounts receivable | 36 | 29 |
| Inventory | 75 | 61 |
| Total current assets | 115 | 97 |
| Property, plant, and equipment | 210 | 180 |
| Less accumulated depreciation | 40 | 30 |
| Net property, plant, and equipment | 170 | 150 |
| Total assets | $285 | $247 |
| **Liabilities and Stockholders' Equity** | | |
| Accounts payable | $ 45 | $ 39 |
| Common stock | 90 | 70 |
| Retained earnings | 150 | 138 |
| Total liabilities and stockholders' equity | $285 | $247 |

For this year, the company reported net income as follows:

| | |
|---|---|
| Sales | $500 |
| Cost of goods sold | 300 |
| Gross margin | 200 |
| Selling and administrative expenses | 180 |
| Net income | $ 20 |

This year Holly declared and paid a cash dividend. There were no sales of plant and equipment during this year. The company did not repurchase any of its own stock this year.

***Required:***

1. Using the indirect method, prepare a statement of cash flows for this year.
2. Compute Holly's free cash flow for this year.

**EXERCISE 12–5 Prepare a Statement of Cash Flows [LO1, LO2]**

The following changes took place last year in Herald Company's balance sheet accounts:

| Asset and Contra-Asset Accounts | | Liabilities and Equity Accounts | |
|---|---|---|---|
| Cash | $20 I | Accounts payable | $20 I |
| Accounts receivable | $10 D | Accrued liabilities | $10 D |
| Inventory | $30 I | Income taxes payable | $15 I |
| Prepaid expenses | $5 D | Bonds payable | $20 D |
| Long-term investments | $30 D | Common stock | $40 I |
| Property, plant, and equipment | $120 I | Retained earnings | $40 I |
| Accumulated depreciation | $40 I | | |

D = Decrease; I = Increase.

Long-term investments that had cost the company $50 were sold during the year for $45, and land that had cost $30 was sold for $70. In addition, the company declared and paid $35 in cash dividends during the year. Besides the sale of land, no other sales or retirements of plant and equipment took place during the year. Herald did not issue any bonds during the year or repurchase any of its own stock.

The company's income statement for the year follows:

| | | |
|---|---|---|
| Sales | | $600 |
| Cost of goods sold | | 250 |
| Gross margin | | 350 |
| Selling and administrative expenses | | 280 |
| Net operating income | | 70 |
| Nonoperating items: | | |
| Loss on sale of investments | $(5) | |
| Gain on sale of land | 40 | 35 |
| Income before taxes | | 105 |
| Income taxes | | 30 |
| Net income | | $ 75 |

The company's beginning cash balance was $100 and its ending balance was $120.

***Required:***

1. Use the indirect method to determine the net cash provided by operating activities for the year.
2. Prepare a statement of cash flows for the year.

**EXERCISE 12–6 Net Cash Provided by Operating Activities [LO2]**

Changes in various accounts and gains and losses on the sale of assets during the year for Weston Company are given at the top of the next page.

| Item | Amount |
|---|---|
| Accounts receivable | $70,000 decrease |
| Inventory | $110,000 increase |
| Prepaid expenses | $3,000 decrease |
| Accounts payable | $40,000 decrease |
| Accrued liabilities | $9,000 increase |
| Income taxes payable | $15,000 increase |
| Sale of equipment | $8,000 gain |
| Sale of long-term investments | $12,000 loss |

***Required:***
For each item, place an X in the Add or Subtract column to indicate whether the dollar amount should be added to or subtracted from net income under the indirect method when computing the net cash provided by operating activities for the year. Use the following column headings in preparing your answers:

| Item | Amount | Add | Subtract |
|---|---|---|---|

Alternate problem set is available on the text website and in *Connect® Accounting.*

connect ACCOUNTING

## PROBLEMS

**All applicable problems are available with McGraw-Hill's *Connect® Accounting*.**

**PROBLEM 12–7A Understanding a Statement of Cash Flows [LO1, LO2]**

Logan Company is a merchandiser that prepared a statement of cash flows and income statement as follows:

**Logan Company**
**Statement of Cash Flows—Indirect Method**

| | | |
|---|---|---|
| **Operating Activities** | | |
| Net income | | $175 |
| Adjustments to convert net income to cash basis: | | |
| Depreciation | $108 | |
| Decrease in accounts receivable | 21 | |
| Decrease in inventory | 39 | |
| Decrease in accounts payable | (50) | |
| Decrease in accrued liabilities | (6) | |
| Increase in income taxes payable | 5 | |
| Loss on sale of equipment | 3 | 120 |
| Net cash provided by operating activities | | 295 |
| **Investing Activities** | | |
| Additions to property, plant, and equipment | (110) | |
| Proceeds from sale of equipment | 9 | |
| Net cash used in investing activities | | (101) |
| **Financing Activities** | | |
| Retirement of bonds payable | (31) | |
| Issuance of common stock | 4 | |
| Cash dividends paid | (35) | |
| Net cash used in financing activities | | (62) |
| Net increase in cash and cash equivalents | | 132 |
| Cash and cash equivalents, beginning balance | | 70 |
| Cash and cash equivalents, ending balance | | $202 |

| Logan Company<br>Income Statement | |
|---|---|
| Sales | $4,120 |
| Cost of goods sold | 2,890 |
| Gross margin | 1,230 |
| Selling and administrative expenses | 835 |
| Net operating income | 395 |
| Nonoperating items: Loss on sale of equipment | (3) |
| Income before taxes | 392 |
| Income taxes | 217 |
| Net income | $ 175 |

***Required:***

Assume that you have been asked to teach a workshop to the employees within Logan Company's Marketing Department. The purpose of your workshop is to explain how the statement of cash flows differs from the income statement. Your audience is expecting you to explain the logic underlying each number included in the statement of cash flows. Prepare a memo that explains the format of the statement of cash flows and the rationale for each number included in Logan's statement of cash flows.

CHECK FIGURE
(1) Net cash provided by operating activities: $104

excel

**PROBLEM 12–8A Prepare a Statement of Cash Flows [LO1, LO2]**

A comparative balance sheet and income statement for Eaton Company follow:

| Eaton Company<br>Comparative Balance Sheet<br>December 31, 2011 and 2010 | 2011 | 2010 |
|---|---|---|
| **Assets** | | |
| Cash | $ 4 | $ 11 |
| Accounts receivable | 310 | 230 |
| Inventory | 160 | 195 |
| Prepaid expenses | 8 | 6 |
| Total current assets | 482 | 442 |
| Property, plant, and equipment | 500 | 420 |
| Less accumulated depreciation | 85 | 70 |
| Net property, plant, and equipment | 415 | 350 |
| Long-term investments | 31 | 38 |
| Total assets | $928 | $830 |
| **Liabilities and Stockholders' Equity** | | |
| Accounts payable | $300 | $225 |
| Accrued liabilities | 70 | 80 |
| Income taxes payable | 71 | 63 |
| Total current liabilities | 441 | 368 |
| Bonds payable | 195 | 170 |
| Total liabilities | 636 | 538 |
| Common stock | 160 | 200 |
| Retained earnings | 132 | 92 |
| Total stockholders' equity | 292 | 292 |
| Total liabilities and stockholders' equity | $928 | $830 |

**Eaton Company**
**Income Statement**
**For the Year Ended December 31, 2011**

| | | |
|---|---|---|
| Sales | | $750 |
| Cost of goods sold | | 450 |
| Gross margin | | 300 |
| Selling and administrative expenses | | 223 |
| Net operating income | | 77 |
| Nonoperating items: | | |
| Gain on sale of investments | $5 | |
| Loss on sale of equipment | (2) | 3 |
| Income before taxes | | 80 |
| Income taxes | | 24 |
| Net income | | $ 56 |

During 2011, Eaton sold some equipment for $18 that had cost $30 and on which there was accumulated depreciation of $10. In addition, the company sold long-term investments for $12 that had cost $7 when purchased several years ago. A cash dividend was paid during 2011 and the company, repurchased $40 of its own stock. Eaton did not retire any bonds during 2011.

***Required:***

1. Using the indirect method, determine the net cash provided by operating activities for 2011.
2. Using the information in (1) above, along with an analysis of the remaining balance sheet accounts, prepare a statement of cash flows for 2011.

**PROBLEM 12–9A Prepare a Statement of Cash Flows; Free Cash Flow [LO1, LO2, LO3]**

Foxboro Company's income statement for Year 2 follows:

CHECK FIGURE
(2) Net cash used in investing activities: $164,000

| | |
|---|---|
| Sales | $700,000 |
| Cost of goods sold | 400,000 |
| Gross margin | 300,000 |
| Selling and administrative expenses | 216,000 |
| Net operating income | 84,000 |
| Gain on sale of equipment | 6,000 |
| Income before taxes | 90,000 |
| Income taxes | 27,000 |
| Net income | $ 63,000 |

Its balance sheet amounts at the end of Years 1 and 2 are as follows:

| | Year 2 | Year 1 |
|---|---|---|
| **Assets** | | |
| Cash | $ 11,000 | $ 19,000 |
| Accounts receivable | 250,000 | 180,000 |
| Inventory | 318,000 | 270,000 |
| Prepaid expenses | 7,000 | 16,000 |
| Total current assets | 586,000 | 485,000 |
| Plant and equipment | 620,000 | 500,000 |
| Accumulated depreciation | 165,000 | 130,000 |
| Net plant and equipment | 455,000 | 370,000 |
| Loan to Harker Company | 40,000 | — |
| Total assets | $1,081,000 | $855,000 |

(continued on next page)

| (concluded) | Year 2 | Year 1 |
|---|---|---|
| **Liabilities and Stockholders' Equity** | | |
| Accounts payable | $ 310,000 | $260,000 |
| Accrued liabilities | 42,000 | 50,000 |
| Income taxes payable | 84,000 | 80,000 |
| Total current liabilities | 436,000 | 390,000 |
| Bonds payable | 190,000 | 100,000 |
| Total liabilities | 626,000 | 490,000 |
| Common stock | 335,000 | 275,000 |
| Retained earnings | 120,000 | 90,000 |
| Total stockholders' equity | 455,000 | 365,000 |
| Total liabilities and stockholders' equity | $1,081,000 | $855,000 |

Equipment that had cost $30,000 and on which there was accumulated depreciation of $10,000 was sold during Year 2 for $26,000. The company declared and paid a cash dividend during Year 2. It did not retire any bonds or repurchase any of its own stock.

***Required:***

1. Using the indirect method, compute the net cash provided by operating activities for Year 2.
2. Prepare a statement of cash flows for Year 2.
3. Compute the free cash flow for Year 2.
4. Briefly explain why cash declined so sharply during the year.

**PROBLEM 12–10A Classification of Transactions [LO1]**

Below are several transactions that took place in Mohawk Company last year:

a. Bonds were retired by paying the principal amount due.
b. Interest was paid to a lender.
c. Income taxes were paid to the government.
d. A long-term loan was made to a supplier.
e. Cash dividends were declared and paid.
f. Common stock was sold for cash to investors.
g. Equipment was sold for cash.
h. Paid wages to employees.
i. Collected cash from customers.
j. Paid cash to repurchase its own stock.
k. Bought equipment for cash.
l. Paid suppliers for inventory purchases.

***Required:***

Prepare an answer sheet with the following headings:

| | Activity | | | Cash | Cash |
|---|---|---|---|---|---|
| Transaction | Operating | Investing | Financing | Inflow | Outflow |
| a. | | | | | |
| b. | | | | | |
| Etc. | | | | | |

Enter the transactions above on your answer sheet and indicate how each of them would be classified on a statement of cash flows. As appropriate, place an X in the Operating, Investing, or Financing column. Also, place on X in the Cash Inflow or Cash Outflow column.

**PROBLEM 12–11A Prepare a Statement of Cash Flows [LO1, LO2]**

A comparative balance sheet and an income statement for Blankley Company are presented below:

CHECK FIGURE
Net cash provided by operating activities: $317

**Blankley Company**
**Comparative Balance Sheet**
**(dollars in millions)**

| | Ending Balance | Beginning Balance |
|---|---|---|
| **Assets** | | |
| Current assets: | | |
| Cash and cash equivalents | $ 39 | $ 81 |
| Accounts receivable | 640 | 588 |
| Inventory | 650 | 610 |
| Total current assets | 1,329 | 1,279 |
| Property, plant, and equipment | 1,505 | 1,484 |
| Less accumulated depreciation | 770 | 651 |
| Net property, plant, and equipment | 735 | 833 |
| Total assets | $2,064 | $2,112 |
| **Liabilities and Stockholders' Equity** | | |
| Current liabilities: | | |
| Accounts payable | $ 260 | $ 160 |
| Accrued liabilities | 180 | 170 |
| Income taxes payable | 77 | 72 |
| Total current liabilities | 517 | 402 |
| Bonds payable | 415 | 600 |
| Total liabilities | 932 | 1,002 |
| Stockholders' equity: | | |
| Common stock | 145 | 145 |
| Retained earnings | 987 | 965 |
| Total stockholders' equity | 1,132 | 1,110 |
| Total liabilities and stockholders' equity | $2,064 | $2,112 |

**Blankley Company**
**Income Statement**
**(dollars in millions)**

| | |
|---|---|
| Sales | $3,700 |
| Cost of goods sold | 2,540 |
| Gross margin | 1,160 |
| Selling and administrative expenses | 880 |
| Net operating income | 280 |
| Nonoperating items: Gain on sale of equipment | 2 |
| Income before taxes | 282 |
| Income taxes | 112 |
| Net income | $ 170 |

Blankley also provided the following information:

1. The company sold equipment that had an original cost of $12 million and accumulated depreciation of $7 million. The cash proceeds from the sale were $7 million. The gain on the sale was $2 million.
2. The company did not issue any new bonds during the year.
3. The company paid a cash dividend during the year.
4. The company did not complete any common stock transactions during the year.

***Required:***
1. Using the indirect method, prepare a statement of cash flows for the year.
2. Assume that Blankley had sales of $3,900, net income of $190, and net cash provided by operating activities of $160 in the prior year (all numbers are stated in millions). Prepare a memo that summarizes your interpretations of Blankley's financial performance.

CHECK FIGURE
Net cash provided by financing activities: $310,000

**PROBLEM 12–12A Missing Data; Statement of Cash Flows [LO1, LO2]**
Estes Company listed the *net changes* in its balance sheet accounts for the past year as follows:

| | Debits > Credits by: | Credits > Debits by: |
|---|---|---|
| Cash | $ 51,000 | |
| Accounts receivable | 170,000 | |
| Inventory | | $ 63,000 |
| Prepaid expenses | 4,000 | |
| Long-term loans to subsidiaries | | 80,000 |
| Long-term investments | 90,000 | |
| Plant and equipment | 340,000 | |
| Accumulated depreciation | | 65,000 |
| Accounts payable | | 48,000 |
| Accrued liabilities | 5,000 | |
| Income taxes payable | | 9,000 |
| Bonds payable | | 200,000 |
| Common stock | | 120,000 |
| Retained earnings | | 75,000 |
| | $660,000 | $660,000 |

The following additional information is available about last year's activities:

a. Net income for the year was $ ? .
b. The company sold equipment during the year for $35,000. The equipment originally cost the company $160,000, and it had $145,000 in accumulated depreciation at the time of sale.
c. The company declared and paid $10,000 in cash dividends during the year.
d. The beginning and ending balances in the Plant and Equipment and Accumulated Depreciation accounts are given below:

| | Beginning | Ending |
|---|---|---|
| Plant and equipment | $2,850,000 | $3,190,000 |
| Accumulated depreciation | $975,000 | $1,040,000 |

e. The balance in the Cash account at the beginning of the year was $109,000; the balance at the end of the year was $ ? .
f. If data are not given explaining the change in an account, make the most reasonable assumption as to the cause of the change.

***Required:***
Using the indirect method, prepare a statement of cash flows for the year.

**PROBLEM 12–13A Prepare and Interpret a Statement of Cash Flows [LO1, LO2]**
A comparative balance sheet for Alcorn Company containing data for the last two years is as follows:

CHECK FIGURE
(2) Net cash used in investing activities: $570,000

| Alcorn Company<br>Comparative Balance Sheet | This Year | Last Year |
|---|---|---|
| **Assets** | | |
| Current assets: | | |
| Cash and cash equivalents | $ 71,000 | $ 50,000 |
| Accounts receivable | 590,000 | 610,000 |
| Inventory | 608,000 | 420,000 |
| Prepaid expenses | 10,000 | 5,000 |
| Total current assets | 1,279,000 | 1,085,000 |
| Property, plant, and equipment | 2,370,000 | 1,800,000 |
| Less accumulated depreciation | 615,000 | 560,000 |
| Net property, plant, and equipment | 1,755,000 | 1,240,000 |
| Long-term investments | 80,000 | 130,000 |
| Loans to subsidiaries | 120,000 | 70,000 |
| Total assets | $3,234,000 | $2,525,000 |
| **Liabilities and Stockholders' Equity** | | |
| Current liabilities: | | |
| Accounts payable | $ 870,000 | $ 570,000 |
| Accrued liabilities | 25,000 | 42,000 |
| Income taxes payable | 133,000 | 118,000 |
| Total current liabilities | 1,028,000 | 730,000 |
| Bonds payable | 620,000 | 400,000 |
| Total liabilities | 1,648,000 | 1,130,000 |
| Stockholders' equity: | | |
| Common stock | 1,090,000 | 1,000,000 |
| Retained earnings | 496,000 | 395,000 |
| Total stockholders' equity | 1,586,000 | 1,395,000 |
| Total liabilities and stockholders' equity | $3,234,000 | $2,525,000 |

The following additional information is available about the company's activities during this year:

a. The company declared and paid a cash dividend this year.
b. Bonds with a principal balance of $380,000 were repaid during this year.
c. Equipment was sold during this year for $70,000. The equipment had cost $130,000 and had $40,000 in accumulated depreciation on the date of sale.
d. Long-term investments were sold during the year for $110,000. These investments had cost $50,000 when purchased several years ago.
e. The subsidiaries did not repay any outstanding loans during the year.
f. Alcorn did not repurchase any of its own stock during the year.

The company reported net income this year as follows:

| | | |
|---|---|---|
| Sales | | $3,000,000 |
| Cost of goods sold | | 1,860,000 |
| Gross margin | | 1,140,000 |
| Selling and administrative expenses | | 930,000 |
| Net operating income | | 210,000 |
| Nonoperating items: | | |
| Gain on sale of investments | $60,000 | |
| Loss on sale of equipment | 20,000 | 40,000 |
| Income before taxes | | 250,000 |
| Income taxes | | 80,000 |
| Net income | | $ 170,000 |

***Required:***

1. Using the indirect method, prepare a statement of cash flows for this year.
2. What problems relating to the company's activities are revealed by the statement of cash flows that you have prepared?

**PROBLEM 12–14A Prepare and Interpret a Statement of Cash Flows; Free Cash Flow [LO1, LO2, LO3]**

Sharon Feldman, president of Allied Company, considers $20,000 to be a minimum cash balance for operating purposes. As can be seen from the following statements, only $15,000 in cash was available at the end of 2011. Because the company reported a large net income for the year, and also issued bonds and sold some long-term investments, the sharp decline in cash is puzzling to Ms. Feldman.

CHECK FIGURE
(2) Net cash provided by financing activities: $67,000

**Allied Company**
**Comparative Balance Sheet**
**December 31, 2011, and 2010**

| | 2011 | 2010 |
|---|---|---|
| **Assets** | | |
| Current assets: | | |
| Cash | $ 15,000 | $ 33,000 |
| Accounts receivable | 200,000 | 210,000 |
| Inventory | 250,000 | 196,000 |
| Prepaid expenses | 7,000 | 15,000 |
| Total current assets | 472,000 | 454,000 |
| Long-term investments | 90,000 | 120,000 |
| Plant and equipment | 860,000 | 750,000 |
| Less accumulated depreciation | 210,000 | 190,000 |
| Net plant and equipment | 650,000 | 560,000 |
| Total assets | $1,212,000 | $1,134,000 |
| **Liabilities and Stockholders' Equity** | | |
| Current liabilities: | | |
| Accounts payable | $ 175,000 | $ 230,000 |
| Accrued liabilities | 8,000 | 15,000 |
| Income taxes payable | 42,000 | 39,000 |
| Total current liabilities | 225,000 | 284,000 |
| Bonds payable | 200,000 | 100,000 |
| Total liabilities | 425,000 | 384,000 |
| Stockholders' equity: | | |
| Common stock | 595,000 | 600,000 |
| Retained earnings | 192,000 | 150,000 |
| Total stockholders' equity | 787,000 | 750,000 |
| Total liabilities and stockholders' equity | $1,212,000 | $1,134,000 |

**Allied Company**
**Income Statement**
**For the Year Ended December 31, 2011**

| | | |
|---|---|---|
| Sales | | $800,000 |
| Cost of goods sold | | 500,000 |
| Gross margin | | 300,000 |
| Selling and administrative expenses | | 214,000 |
| Net operating income | | 86,000 |
| Nonoperating items: | | |
| Gain on sale of investments | $20,000 | |
| Loss on sale of equipment | (6,000) | 14,000 |
| Income before taxes | | 100,000 |
| Income taxes | | 30,000 |
| Net income | | $ 70,000 |

The following additional information is available for the year 2011:

a. The company sold long-term investments with an original cost of $30,000 for $50,000 during the year.
b. Equipment that had cost $90,000 and on which there was $40,000 in accumulated depreciation was sold during the year for $44,000.
c. The company declared and paid a cash dividend during the year.
d. The stock of a dissident stockholder was repurchased for cash and retired during the year. No issues of stock were made.
e. The company did not retire any bonds during the year.

***Required:***

1. Using the indirect method, compute the net cash provided by operating activities for 2011.
2. Prepare a statement of cash flows for 2011.
3. Compute free cash flow for 2011.
4. Explain the major reasons for the decline in the company's cash balance.

# BUILDING YOUR SKILLS

### COMMUNICATING IN PRACTICE [LO2, LO3]

Use an online yellow pages directory to find a company in your area that has a website on which it has an annual report, including a statement of cash flows. Make an appointment with the controller or chief financial officer of the company. Before your meeting, find out as much as you can about the organization's operations from its website.

***Required***

After asking the following questions, write a brief memorandum to your instructor that summarizes the information obtained from the company's website and addresses what you found out during your interview.

1. Does the company use the direct method or the indirect method to determine the net cash provided by operating activities when preparing its statement of cash flows? Why?
2. How is the information reported on the statement of cash flows used for decision-making purposes?

# APPENDIX 12A: THE DIRECT METHOD OF DETERMINING THE NET CASH PROVIDED BY OPERATING ACTIVITIES

**LEARNING OBJECTIVE 4**

Use the direct method to determine the net cash provided by operating activities.

To compute the net cash provided by operating activities under the direct method, we must reconstruct the income statement on a cash basis from top to bottom. Exhibit 12A–1 shows the adjustments that must be made to adjust sales, expenses, and so forth, to a cash basis. To illustrate, we have included in the exhibit the Apparel, Inc., data from the chapter.

Note that the net cash provided by operating activities of $259 million agrees with the amount computed in the chapter using the indirect method. The two amounts agree because the direct and indirect methods are just different roads to the same destination. The investing and financing activities sections of the statement will be exactly the same as shown for the indirect method in Exhibit 12–10. The only difference between the indirect and direct methods is in the operating activities section.

## Similarities and Differences in the Handling of Data

Although we arrive at the same destination under either the direct or indirect method, not all data are handled the same way in the two adjustment processes. Stop for a moment, flip back to the bottom half of Exhibit 12–7 on page 552 and compare the adjustments described in that exhibit to the adjustments made for the direct method in Exhibit 12A–1. The adjustments for accounts that affect revenue (which includes only accounts receivable

**EXHIBIT 12A–1**
General Model: Direct Method of Determining the Net Cash Provided by Operating Activities

| Revenue or Expense Item | Add (+) or Deduct (–) to Adjust to a Cash Basis | Illustration—Apparel, Inc. (in millions) | |
|---|---|---|---|
| Sales (as reported) | | $3,638 | |
| Adjustments to a cash basis: | | | |
| Increase in accounts receivable | – | | |
| Decrease in accounts receivable | + | + 17 | $3,655 |
| Cost of goods sold (as reported) | | 2,469 | |
| Adjustments to a cash basis: | | | |
| Increase in inventory | + | + 49 | |
| Decrease in inventory | – | | |
| Increase in accounts payable | – | – 44 | |
| Decrease in accounts payable | + | | 2,474 |
| Selling and administrative expenses (as reported) | | 941 | |
| Adjustments to a cash basis: | | | |
| Increase in prepaid expenses | + | | |
| Decrease in prepaid expenses | – | | |
| Increase in accrued liabilities | – | – 3 | |
| Decrease in accrued liabilities | + | | |
| Depreciation | – | – 103 | 835 |
| Income tax expense (as reported) | | 91 | |
| Adjustments to a cash basis: | | | |
| Increase in income taxes payable | – | – 4 | |
| Decrease in income taxes payable | + | | 87 |
| Net cash provided by operating activities | | | $ 259 |

in our example) are handled the same way in the two methods. In either case, increases in the accounts are subtracted and decreases are added. However, the adjustments for accounts that affect expenses (which include all remaining accounts in Exhibit 12–7) are handled in opposite ways in the indirect and direct methods. This is because under the indirect method the adjustments are made to *net income,* whereas under the direct method the adjustments are made to the *expense accounts* themselves.

To illustrate this difference, note the handling of inventory and depreciation in the indirect and direct methods. Under the indirect method (Exhibit 12–7 on page 552), an increase in the Inventory account ($49) is *subtracted* from net income in computing the amount of net cash provided by operating activities. Under the direct method (Exhibit 12A–1), an increase in inventory is *added* to cost of goods sold. The reason for the difference can be explained as follows: An increase in inventory means that the period's inventory purchases exceeded the cost of goods sold included in the income statement. Therefore, to adjust net income to a cash basis, we must either subtract this increase from net income (indirect method) or we must add this increase to cost of goods sold (direct method). Either way, we will end up with the same figure for net cash provided by operating activities. Similarly, depreciation is added to net income under the indirect method to cancel out its effect (Exhibit 12–8), whereas it is subtracted from selling and administrative expenses under the direct method to cancel out its effect (Exhibit 12A–1). These differences in the handling of data are true for all other expense items in the two methods.

In the matter of gains and losses on sale of assets, no adjustments are needed under the direct method. These gains and losses are simply ignored because they are not part of sales, cost of goods sold, selling and administrative expenses, or income taxes. Observe that in Exhibit 12A–1, Apparel's $3 million gain on the sale of the store is not listed as an adjustment in the operating activities section.

### Special Rules—Direct and Indirect Methods

As stated earlier, when the direct method is used, U.S. GAAP and IFRS require a reconciliation between net income and the net cash provided by operating activities, as determined by the indirect method. Thus, *when a company elects to use the direct method, it must also present the indirect method* in a separate schedule accompanying the statement of cash flows.

On the other hand, if a company elects to use the indirect method to compute the net cash provided by operating activities, then it must also provide a special breakdown of data. The company must provide a separate disclosure of the amount of interest and the amount of income taxes paid during the year. This separate disclosure is required so that users can take the data provided by the indirect method and make estimates of what the amounts for sales, income taxes, and so forth, would have been if the direct method had been used instead.

## APPENDIX 12A EXERCISES AND PROBLEMS

**All applicable exercises and problems are available with McGraw-Hill's *Connect*® *Accounting*.**

**EXERCISE 12A–1 Net Cash Provided by Operating Activities [LO4]**

Refer to the data for Strident Company in Exercise 12–2. The company's income statement for the most recent year was:

| | |
|---|---|
| Sales | $1,000,000 |
| Cost of goods sold | 580,000 |
| Gross margin | 420,000 |
| Selling and administrative expenses | 300,000 |
| Income before taxes | 120,000 |
| Income taxes | 36,000 |
| Net Income | $ 84,000 |

***Required:***

Using the direct method (and the data from Exercise 12–2), convert the company's income statement to a cash basis.

**EXERCISE 12A–2 Net Cash Provided by Operating Activities [LO4]**

Refer to the data for Holly Company in Exercise 12–4.

***Required:***

Using the direct method, convert the company's income statement to a cash basis.

**EXERCISE 12A–3 Adjust Net Income to a Cash Basis [LO4]**

Refer to the data for Herald Company in Exercise 12–5.

***Required:***

Use the direct method to convert the company's income statement to a cash basis.

**EXERCISE 12A–4 Net Cash Provided by Operating Activities [LO4]**

Jones Company is a merchandiser whose income statement for Year 2 follows:

| | |
|---|---|
| Sales | $2,000 |
| Cost of goods sold | 1,200 |
| Gross margin | 800 |
| Selling and administrative expenses | 500 |
| Income before taxes | 300 |
| Income taxes | 120 |
| Net income | $ 180 |

The company's selling and administrative expense for Year 2 includes $80 of depreciation expense. Selected balance sheet accounts for Jones at the end of Years 1 and 2 are as shown below:

| | Year 2 | Year 1 |
|---|---|---|
| **Current Assets** | | |
| Accounts receivable | $200 | $230 |
| Inventory | $160 | $180 |
| Prepaid expenses | $40 | $36 |
| **Current Liabilities** | | |
| Accounts payable | $100 | $80 |
| Accrued liabilities | $15 | $20 |
| Income taxes payable | $90 | $70 |

***Required:***

1. Using the direct method, convert the company's income statement to a cash basis.
2. Assume that during Year 2 Jones has a $7,000 gain on the sale of investments and a $2,000 loss on the sale of equipment. Explain how these two transactions would affect your computations in (1) above.

**PROBLEM 12A–5A Prepare a Statement of Cash Flows [LO1, LO4]**

Refer to the financial statement data for Eaton Company in Problem 12–8.

CHECK FIGURE
(1) Net cash provided by operating activities: $104

***Required:***

1. Using the direct method, adjust the company's income statement for 2011 to a cash basis.
2. Using the information obtained in (1) above, along with an analysis of the remaining balance sheet accounts, prepare a statement of cash flows for 2011.

**PROBLEM 12A–6A Prepare and Interpret a Statement of Cash Flows [LO1, LO4]**

Refer to the financial statement data for Foxboro Company in Problem 12–9. Mike Perry, president of the company, considers $15,000 to be the minimum cash balance for operating purposes. As can be seen from the balance sheet data, only $11,000 in cash was available at the end of the current year. The sharp decline is puzzling to Mr. Perry, particularly because sales and profits are at a record high.

CHECK FIGURE
(1) Net cash provided by operating activities: $39,000

***Required:***

1. Using the direct method, adjust the company's income statement to a cash basis for Year 2.
2. Using the data from (1) above and other data from the problem as needed, prepare a statement of cash flows for Year 2.
3. Explain why cash declined so sharply during the year.

**PROBLEM 12A–7A Prepare and Interpret a Statement of Cash Flows [LO1, LO4]**

Refer to the financial statements for Allied Company in Problem 12–14. Because the Cash account decreased substantially during 2011, the company's executive committee is anxious to see how the income statement would appear on a cash basis.

CHECK FIGURE
(1) Net cash provided by operating activities: $21,000

***Required:***

1. Using the direct method, adjust the company's income statement for 2011 to a cash basis.
2. Using the data from (1) above and other data from the problem as needed, prepare a statement of cash flows for 2011.

## A LOOK BACK

In Chapter 12 we showed how to construct the statement of cash flows and discussed how to interpret it.

## A LOOK AT THIS CHAPTER

In Chapter 13 we focus on the analysis of financial statements to help forecast the financial health of a company. We discuss the use of trend data, comparisons with other organizations, and financial ratios.

# 13 Financial Statement Analysis

## CHAPTER OUTLINE

## DECISION FEATURE

# Keeping an Eye on Dividends

When the economy sours, investors look closely at a company's ability to pay dividends. In 2008, 36 of the Standard & Poor's 500 companies suspended $33.3 billion of dividend payments. Citigroup sliced its dividend 41%, Washington Mutual (now part of **JPMorgan Chase**) reduced its quarterly dividend per share from 15 cents to a penny, and **CIT Group** slashed its dividend by 60%. Some companies increase their market appeal during difficult economic times by remaining committed to generous dividend payments. For example, in 2008 Adrian Darley, of **Ignis Asset Management**, recommended investing in **Vivendi**, **France Telecom**, and **Deutsche Telekom** because these companies committed to making scheduled dividend payments that ranged from 4.9% to 7.2% of their respective stock prices.

Sources: Andrea Tryphonides, "Dividends Replace P/Es as Stock Guides," *The Wall Street Journal,* November 24, 2008, p. C2; Tom Lauricella, "Keeping the Cash: Slowdown Triggers Stingy Dividends," *The Wall Street Journal,* April 21, 2008, p. C1; and Annelena Lobb, "Investors Lick Wounds from Dividend Cuts," *The Wall Street Journal,* November 7, 2008, p. C1.

## LEARNING OBJECTIVES

*After studying Chapter 13, you should be able to:*

**LO1** Prepare and interpret financial statements in comparative and common-size form.

**LO2** Compute and interpret financial ratios that would be useful to a common stockholder.

**LO3** Compute and interpret financial ratios that would be useful to a short-term creditor.

**LO4** Compute and interpret financial ratios that would be useful to a long-term creditor.

**All financial statements are** historical documents. They summarize what *has happened* during a particular period. However, most users of financial statements are concerned with what *will happen* in the future. For example, stockholders are concerned with future earnings and dividends and creditors are concerned with the company's future ability to repay its debts. While financial statements are historical in nature, they can still provide users with valuable insights. These users rely on *financial statement analysis*, which involves examining trends in key financial data, comparing financial data across companies, and analyzing financial ratios to assess the financial health and future prospects of a company. In this chapter, we focus our attention on the most important ratios and other analytical tools that financial analysts use.

In addition to stockholders and creditors, managers are also vitally concerned with the financial ratios discussed in this chapter. First, the ratios provide indicators of how well the company and its business units are performing. Some of these ratios might be used in a balanced scorecard approach as discussed in an earlier chapter. The specific ratios selected depend on the company's strategy. For example, a company that wants to emphasize responsiveness to customers may closely monitor the inventory turnover ratio discussed later in this chapter. Second, because managers must report to stockholders and may want to raise funds from external sources, managers must pay attention to the financial ratios used by external investors.

## LIMITATIONS OF FINANCIAL STATEMENT ANALYSIS

This section discusses two limitations of financial statement analysis related to comparing financial data across companies and looking beyond ratios when formulating conclusions.

### Comparing Financial Data across Companies

Comparisons of one company with another can provide valuable clues about the financial health of an organization. Unfortunately, differences in accounting methods between companies sometimes make it difficult to compare their financial data. For example, if one company values its inventories by the LIFO method and another company by the average cost method, then direct comparisons of their financial data such as inventory valuations and cost of goods sold may be misleading. Sometimes enough data are presented in footnotes to the financial statements to restate data to a comparable basis. Otherwise, the analyst should keep in mind any lack of comparability. Even with this limitation in mind, comparisons of key ratios with other companies and with industry averages often suggest avenues for further investigation.

### Looking beyond Ratios

Ratios should not be viewed as an end, but rather as a *starting point.* They raise many questions and point to opportunities for further analysis, but they rarely answer any questions by themselves. In addition to ratios, analysts should evaluate industry trends, technological changes, changes in consumer tastes, changes in broad economic factors, and changes within the company itself.

## STATEMENTS IN COMPARATIVE AND COMMON-SIZE FORM

**LEARNING OBJECTIVE 1**

Prepare and interpret financial statements in comparative and common-size form.

An item on a balance sheet or income statement has little meaning by itself. Suppose a company's sales for a year were $250 million. In isolation, that is not particularly useful information. How does that stack up against last year's sales? How do the sales relate to the cost of goods sold? In making these kinds of comparisons, three analytical techniques are widely used:

1. Dollar and percentage changes on statements (*horizontal analysis*).
2. Common-size statements (*vertical analysis*).
3. Ratios.

The first and second techniques are discussed in this section; the third technique is discussed in the remainder of the chapter. Throughout the chapter, we will illustrate these analytical techniques using the financial statements of Brickey Electronics, a producer of specialized electronic components.

## Dollar and Percentage Changes on Statements

**Horizontal analysis** (also known as **trend analysis**) involves analyzing financial data over time, such as computing year-to-year dollar and percentage changes within a set of financial statements. Exhibits 13–1 and 13–2 show Brickey Electronics' financial

EXHIBIT 13–1

**Brickey Electronics**
**Comparative Balance Sheet**
**(dollars in thousands)**

| | This Year | Last Year | Increase (Decrease) Amount | Increase (Decrease) Percent |
|---|---|---|---|---|
| **Assets** | | | | |
| Current assets: | | | | |
| Cash | $ 1,200 | $ 2,350 | $(1,150) | (48.9)%* |
| Accounts receivable, net | 6,000 | 4,000 | 2,000 | 50.0% |
| Inventory | 8,000 | 10,000 | (2,000) | (20.0)% |
| Prepaid expenses | 300 | 120 | 180 | 150.0% |
| Total current assets | 15,500 | 16,470 | (970) | (5.9)% |
| Property and equipment: | | | | |
| Land | 4,000 | 4,000 | 0 | 0.0% |
| Buildings and equipment, net | 12,000 | 8,500 | 3,500 | 41.2% |
| Total property and equipment | 16,000 | 12,500 | 3,500 | 28.0% |
| Total assets | $31,500 | $28,970 | $ 2,530 | 8.7% |
| **Liabilities and Stockholders' Equity** | | | | |
| Current liabilities: | | | | |
| Accounts payable | $ 5,800 | $ 4,000 | $ 1,800 | 45.0% |
| Accrued payables | 900 | 400 | 500 | 125.0% |
| Notes payable, short term | 300 | 600 | (300) | (50.0)% |
| Total current liabilities | 7,000 | 5,000 | 2,000 | 40.0% |
| Long-term liabilities: | | | | |
| Bonds payable, 8% | 7,500 | 8,000 | (500) | (6.3)% |
| Total liabilities | 14,500 | 13,000 | 1,500 | 11.5% |
| Stockholders' equity: | | | | |
| Preferred stock, $100 par, 6% | 2,000 | 2,000 | 0 | 0.0% |
| Common stock, $12 par | 6,000 | 6,000 | 0 | 0.0% |
| Additional paid-in capital | 1,000 | 1,000 | 0 | 0.0% |
| Total paid-in capital | 9,000 | 9,000 | 0 | 0.0% |
| Retained earnings | 8,000 | 6,970 | 1,030 | 14.8% |
| Total stockholders' equity | 17,000 | 15,970 | 1,030 | 6.4% |
| Total liabilities and stockholders' equity | $31,500 | $28,970 | $ 2,530 | 8.7% |

*The changes between this year and last year are expressed as a percentage of the dollar amount for last year. For example, Cash decreased by $1,150 between this year and last year. This decrease expressed in percentage form is computed as follows: $1,150 ÷ $2,350 = 48.9%. Other percentage figures in this exhibit and Exhibit 13–2 are computed in the same way.

**EXHIBIT 13–2**

**Brickey Electronics**
**Comparative Income Statement and Reconciliation of Retained Earnings**
**(dollars in thousands)**

| | This Year | Last Year | Increase (Decrease) Amount | Increase (Decrease) Percent |
|---|---|---|---|---|
| Sales | $52,000 | $48,000 | $4,000 | 8.3% |
| Cost of goods sold | 36,000 | 31,500 | 4,500 | 14.3% |
| Gross margin | 16,000 | 16,500 | (500) | (3.0)% |
| Selling and administrative expenses: | | | | |
| Selling expenses | 7,000 | 6,500 | 500 | 7.7% |
| Administrative expenses | 5,860 | 6,100 | (240) | (3.9)% |
| Total selling and administrative expenses | 12,860 | 12,600 | 260 | 2.1% |
| Net operating income | 3,140 | 3,900 | (760) | (19.5)% |
| Interest expense | 640 | 700 | (60) | (8.6)% |
| Net income before taxes | 2,500 | 3,200 | (700) | (21.9)% |
| Income taxes (30%) | 750 | 960 | (210) | (21.9)% |
| Net income | 1,750 | 2,240 | $ (490) | (21.9)% |
| Dividends to preferred stockholders, $6 per share (see Exhibit 13–1) | 120 | 120 | | |
| Net income remaining for common stockholders | 1,630 | 2,120 | | |
| Dividends to common stockholders, $1.20 per share | 600 | 600 | | |
| Net income added to retained earnings | 1,030 | 1,520 | | |
| Retained earnings, beginning of year | 6,970 | 5,450 | | |
| Retained earnings, end of year | $ 8,000 | $ 6,970 | | |

statements in this *comparative form.* The dollar changes highlight the changes that are the most important economically; the percentage changes highlight the changes that are the most unusual.

Horizontal analysis can be even more useful when data from a number of years are used to compute *trend percentages.* To compute **trend percentages,** a base year is selected and the data for all years are stated as a percentage of that base year. To illustrate, consider the sales and net income of **McDonald's Corporation**, the world's largest food service retailer, with more than 31,000 restaurants worldwide:

| | 2008 | 2007 | 2006 | 2005 | 2004 | 2003 | 2002 | 2001 | 2000 | 1999 |
|---|---|---|---|---|---|---|---|---|---|---|
| Sales (millions) | $23,522 | $22,787 | $20,895 | $19,117 | $17,889 | $16,154 | $14,527 | $14,074 | $13,794 | $13,251 |
| Net income (millions) | $4,313 | $2,395 | $3,544 | $2,602 | $2,279 | $1,471 | $893 | $1,637 | $1,977 | $1,948 |

Be careful to note that the above data have been arranged with the most recent year on the left. This may be the opposite of what you are used to, but it is the way financial data are commonly displayed in annual reports and other sources. By simply looking at these data, you can see that sales increased every year, but the net income has not. However, recasting these data into trend percentages aids interpretation:

| | 2008 | 2007 | 2006 | 2005 | 2004 | 2003 | 2002 | 2001 | 2000 | 1999 |
|---|---|---|---|---|---|---|---|---|---|---|
| Sales................. | 178% | 172% | 158% | 144% | 135% | 122% | 110% | 106% | 104% | 100% |
| Net income ....... | 221% | 123% | 182% | 134% | 117% | 76% | 46% | 84% | 101% | 100% |

In the above table, both sales and net income have been restated as a percentage of the 1999 sales and net income. For example, the 2008 sales of $23,522 are 178% of the 1999 sales of $13,251. This trend analysis is particularly striking when the data are plotted as in Exhibit 13–3. McDonald's sales growth was impressive throughout the 10-year period, but net income was far more erratic. Notice that net income plummeted in 2001 and 2002, fully recovered by 2004, and then plummeted again in 2007. In 2008, McDonald's earned record sales and profits.

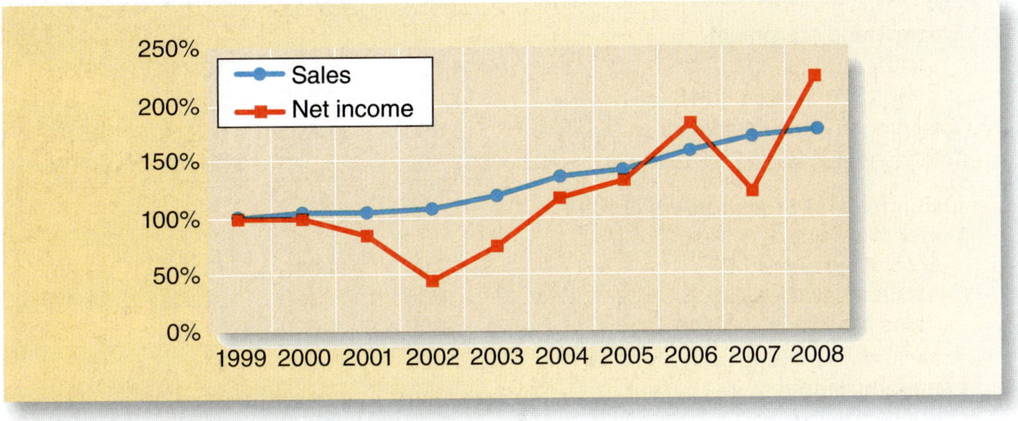


**EXHIBIT 13–3**
McDonald's Corporation: Trend Analysis of Sales and Net Income

## Common-Size Statements

Horizontal analysis, which was discussed in the previous section, examines changes in financial statement accounts over time. **Vertical analysis** focuses on the relations among financial statement accounts at a given point in time. A **common-size financial statement** is a vertical analysis in which each financial statement account is expressed as a percentage. In income statements, all items are usually expressed as a percentage of sales. In balance sheets, all items are usually expressed as a percentage of total assets. Exhibit 13–4 contains Brickey Electronics' common-size balance sheet and Exhibit 13–5 contains its common-size income statement.

Notice from Exhibit 13–4 that placing all assets in common-size form clearly shows the relative importance of the current assets as compared to the noncurrent assets. It also shows that significant changes have taken place in the composition of the current assets over the last year. For example, accounts receivable have increased in relative importance and both cash and inventory have declined in relative importance. Judging from the sharp increase in accounts receivable, the deterioration in the cash balance may be a result of an inability to collect from customers.

Shifting now to the income statement, in Exhibit 13–5 the cost of goods sold as a percentage of sales increased from 65.6% last year to 69.2% this year. Or looking at this from a different viewpoint, the *gross margin percentage* declined from 34.4% last year to 30.8% this year. Managers and investment analysts often pay close attention to this measure of profitability. The **gross margin percentage** is computed as follows:

$$\text{Gross margin percentage} = \frac{\text{Gross margin}}{\text{Sales}}$$

**EXHIBIT 13–4**

**Brickey Electronics**
**Common-Size Comparative Balance Sheet**
**(dollars in thousands)**

| | This Year | Last Year | Common-Size Percentages This Year | Common-Size Percentages Last Year |
|---|---|---|---|---|
| **Assets** | | | | |
| Current assets: | | | | |
| Cash | $ 1,200 | $ 2,350 | 3.8%* | 8.1% |
| Accounts receivable, net | 6,000 | 4,000 | 19.0% | 13.8% |
| Inventory | 8,000 | 10,000 | 25.4% | 34.5% |
| Prepaid expenses | 300 | 120 | 1.0% | 0.4% |
| Total current assets | 15,500 | 16,470 | 49.2% | 56.9% |
| Property and equipment: | | | | |
| Land | 4,000 | 4,000 | 12.7% | 13.8% |
| Buildings and equipment, net | 12,000 | 8,500 | 38.1% | 29.3% |
| Total property and equipment | 16,000 | 12,500 | 50.8% | 43.1% |
| Total assets | $31,500 | $28,970 | 100.0% | 100.0% |
| **Liabilities and Stockholders' Equity** | | | | |
| Current liabilities: | | | | |
| Accounts payable | $ 5,800 | $ 4,000 | 18.4% | 13.8% |
| Accrued payables | 900 | 400 | 2.9% | 1.4% |
| Notes payable, short term | 300 | 600 | 1.0% | 2.1% |
| Total current liabilities | 7,000 | 5,000 | 22.2% | 17.3% |
| Long-term liabilities: | | | | |
| Bonds payable, 8% | 7,500 | 8,000 | 23.8% | 27.6% |
| Total liabilities | 14,500 | 13,000 | 46.0% | 44.9% |
| Stockholders' equity: | | | | |
| Preferred stock, $100, 6% | 2,000 | 2,000 | 6.3% | 6.9% |
| Common stock, $12 par | 6,000 | 6,000 | 19.0% | 20.7% |
| Additional paid-in capital | 1,000 | 1,000 | 3.2% | 3.5% |
| Total paid-in capital | 9,000 | 9,000 | 28.6% | 31.1% |
| Retained earnings | 8,000 | 6,970 | 25.4% | 24.0% |
| Total stockholders' equity | 17,000 | 15,970 | 54.0% | 55.1% |
| Total liabilities and stockholders' equity | $31,500 | $28,970 | 100.0% | 100.0% |

*Each asset account on a common-size statement is expressed as a percentage of total assets, and each liability and equity account is expressed as a percentage of total liabilities and stockholders' equity. For example, the percentage figure above for this year's Cash balance is computed as follows: $1,200 ÷ $31,500 = 3.8%.

The gross margin percentage should be more stable for retailing companies than for other companies because the cost of goods sold in retailing excludes fixed costs. When fixed costs are included in the cost of goods sold, the gross margin percentage should increase and decrease with sales volume. With increases in sales volume, fixed costs are spread across more units and the gross margin percentage should improve.

Common-size statements are particularly useful when comparing the performance of different companies. For example, in 2008 Burger King's net income was $190 million and McDonald's was $4,313 million. It would be naïve to look at these two numbers and conclude that McDonald's outperformed Burger King. McDonald's is much larger than Burger King, so its higher net income may be due solely to its larger size rather than its

EXHIBIT 13–5

**Brickey Electronics**
**Common-Size Comparative Income Statement**
**(dollars in thousands)**

| | | | Common-Size Percentages* | |
|---|---|---|---|---|
| | This Year | Last Year | This Year | Last Year |
| Sales | $52,000 | $48,000 | 100.0% | 100.0% |
| Cost of goods sold | 36,000 | 31,500 | 69.2% | 65.6% |
| Gross margin | 16,000 | 16,500 | 30.8% | 34.4% |
| Selling and administrative expenses: | | | | |
| Selling expenses | 7,000 | 6,500 | 13.5% | 13.5% |
| Administrative expenses | 5,860 | 6,100 | 11.3% | 12.7% |
| Total selling and administrative expenses | 12,860 | 12,600 | 24.7% | 26.3% |
| Net operating income | 3,140 | 3,900 | 6.0% | 8.1% |
| Interest expense | 640 | 700 | 1.2% | 1.5% |
| Net income before taxes | 2,500 | 3,200 | 4.8% | 6.7% |
| Income taxes (30%) | 750 | 960 | 1.4% | 2.0% |
| Net income | $ 1,750 | $ 2,240 | 3.4% | 4.7% |

*Note that the percentage figures for each year are expressed as a percentage of total sales for the year. For example, the percentage figure for this year's cost of goods sold is computed as follows: $36,000 ÷ $52,000 = 69.2%

managerial performance. To control for their different sizes, each company's net income can be expressed as a percentage of its sales revenues. Given that Burger King's sales revenues were $2,455 million and McDonald's were $23,522 million, Burger King's net income as a percentage of sales was 7.7% and McDonald's was 18.3%. These common-size percentages support the more informed conclusion that McDonald's performance compares favorably with Burger King's performance.

**HELPFUL HINT**

Common-size balance sheets express each balance sheet account as a percentage of total assets. Common-size income statements express each income statement account as a percentage of sales.

## RATIO ANALYSIS—THE COMMON STOCKHOLDER

**LEARNING OBJECTIVE 2**

Compute and interpret financial ratios that would be useful to a common stockholder.

Common stockholders use financial ratios related to net income, dividends, and stockholders' equity to assess a company's financial performance. This section describes seven of those ratios. *All calculations will be performed for this year.*

### Earnings per Share

An investor buys a stock in the hope of realizing a return in the form of either dividends or future increases in the value of the stock. Because earnings form the basis for dividend payments and future increases in the value of shares, investors are interested in a company's *earnings per share.*

**Earnings per share** is computed by dividing net income available for common stockholders by the average number of common shares outstanding during the year. "Net income available for common stockholders" is net income minus dividends paid to preferred stockholders.

$$\text{Earnings per share} = \frac{\text{Net income} - \text{Preferred dividends}}{\text{Average number of common shares outstanding}}$$

Using the data in Exhibits 13–1 and 13–2, Brickey Electronics' earnings per share would be computed as follows:

$$\text{Earnings per share} = \frac{\$1{,}750{,}000 - \$120{,}000}{(500{,}000 \text{ shares}^* + 500{,}000 \text{ shares})/2} = \$3.26 \text{ per share}$$

*$6,000,000 total par value ÷ $12 par value per share = 500,000 shares.

**HELPFUL HINT**

The number of common shares outstanding is calculated by taking the dollar amount of common stock shown in the balance sheet and dividing it by the common stock's par value per share.

**IN BUSINESS**

### Do Analysts Bias their Earnings Forecasts?

Research from Penn State University suggests that Wall Street analysts' earnings per share (EPS) forecasts are intentionally overstated. The study examined analysts' long-term (three to five years) and short-term (one year) EPS forecasts from 1984 through 2006. Over this 22-year period, the analysts' average estimated long-term EPS growth rate was 14.7% compared to an actual average long-term growth rate of 9.1%. The analysts' average short-term EPS projection was 13.8% compared with an actual annual EPS growth rate of 9.8%. The professors who conducted the study claim that "analysts are rewarded for biased forecasts by their employers, who want them to hype stocks so that the brokerage house can garner trading commissions and win underwriting deals."

Source: Andrew Edwards, "Study Suggests Bias in Analysts' Rosy Forecasts," *The Wall Street Journal*, March 21, 2008, p. C6.

## Price-Earnings Ratio

The **price-earnings ratio** expresses the relationship between a stock's market price per share and its earnings per share. If we assume that Brickey Electronics' stock has a market price of $40 per share at the end of this year, then its price-earnings ratio would be computed as follows:

$$\text{Price-earnings ratio} = \frac{\text{Market price per share}}{\text{Earnings per share}}$$

$$= \frac{\$40 \text{ per share}}{\$3.26 \text{ per share}} = 12.3$$

The price-earnings ratio is 12.3; that is, the stock is selling for about 12.3 times its current earnings per share.

A high price-earnings ratio means that investors are willing to pay a premium for the company's stock—presumably because the company is expected to have higher than average future earnings growth. Conversely, if investors believe a company's future earnings growth prospects are limited, the company's price-earnings ratio would be relatively low. In the late 1990s, the stock prices of some dot.com companies—particularly those with little or no earnings—were selling at levels that resulted in huge and nearly unprecedented price-earnings ratios. Many commentators cautioned that these price-earnings ratios were unsustainable in the long run—and they were right. The stock prices of almost all dot.com companies subsequently crashed.

## Dividend Payout and Yield Ratios

Investors in a company's stock make money in two ways—increases in the market value of the stock and dividends. In general, earnings should be retained in a company and not paid out in dividends as long as the rate of return on funds invested inside the company exceeds the rate of return that stockholders could earn on alternative investments outside the company. Therefore, companies with excellent prospects of profitable growth often pay little or no dividend. Companies with little opportunity for profitable growth, but with steady, dependable earnings, tend to pay out a higher percentage of their cash flow from operations as dividends.

**The Dividend Payout Ratio** The **dividend payout ratio** quantifies the percentage of current earnings being paid out in dividends. This ratio is computed by dividing the dividends per share by the earnings per share for common stock:

$$\text{Dividend payout ratio} = \frac{\text{Dividends per share}}{\text{Earnings per share}}$$

For Brickey Electronics, the dividend payout ratio is computed as follows:

$$\text{Dividend payout ratio} = \frac{\$1.20 \text{ per share (see Exhibit 13–2)}}{\$3.26 \text{ per share}} = 36.8\%$$

There is no such thing as a "right" dividend payout ratio, although the ratio tends to be similar for companies within the same industry. As noted above, companies with ample growth opportunities at high rates of return tend to have low payout ratios, whereas companies with limited reinvestment opportunities tend to have higher payout ratios.

**The Dividend Yield Ratio** The **dividend yield ratio** is computed by dividing the current dividends per share by the current market price per share:

$$\text{Dividend yield ratio} = \frac{\text{Dividends per share}}{\text{Market price per share}}$$

Because the market price for Brickey Electronics' stock is $40 per share, the dividend yield is computed as follows:

$$\text{Dividend yield ratio} = \frac{\$1.20 \text{ per share}}{\$40 \text{ per share}} = 3.0\%$$

The dividend yield ratio measures the rate of return (in the form of cash dividends only) that would be earned by an investor who buys common stock at the current market price. A low dividend yield ratio is neither bad nor good by itself.

IN BUSINESS

## IBM Raises Its Dividend by 25%

In the early 1990s, **IBM** nearly collapsed and was forced to slash its dividend payout. However, since then the company has rebounded nicely. In 2008, IBM raised its quarterly dividend per share by 25%, thereby increasing the company's annual payout to about $2.5 billion. The 25% increase marked the 13th straight year that IBM has increased its dividend per share. The company also plans to spend $12 billion to buy back shares of its own stock. This transaction will reduce the number of shares of stock outstanding and increase the company's earnings per share.

Source: William M. Bulkeley, "IBM, Flush with Cash, Raises Dividend 25%," *The Wall Street Journal*, April 30, 2008, p. B7.

## Return on Total Assets

The **return on total assets** is a measure of operating performance that is defined as follows:

$$\text{Return on total assets} = \frac{\text{Net income} + [\text{Interest expense} \times (1 - \text{Tax rate})]}{\text{Average total assets}}$$

Interest expense is added back to net income to show what earnings would have been if the company had no debt. With this adjustment, the return on total assets can be compared for companies with differing amounts of debt, or for a single company that has changed its mix of debt and equity over time. Notice that the interest expense is placed on an after-tax basis by multiplying it by the factor (1 − Tax rate).

The return on total assets for Brickey Electronics is computed as follows (from Exhibits 13–1 and 13–2):

$$\text{Return on total assets} = \frac{\$1{,}750{,}000 + [\$640{,}000 \times (1 - 0.30)]}{(\$31{,}500{,}000 + \$28{,}970{,}000)/2} = 7.3\%$$

Brickey Electronics has earned a return of 7.3% on average total assets employed over the last year.

## Return on Common Stockholders' Equity

The **return on common stockholders' equity** is based on the book value of common stockholders' equity. It is computed as follows:

$$\begin{array}{c}\text{Return on common}\\ \text{stockholders' equity}\end{array} = \frac{\text{Net income} - \text{Preferred dividends}}{\text{Average common stockholders' equity}}$$

where

$$\begin{array}{c}\text{Average common}\\ \text{stockholders' equity}\end{array} = \begin{array}{c}\text{Average total stockholders' equity}\\ - \text{Average preferred stock}\end{array}$$

For Brickey Electronics, the return on common stockholders' equity is computed as follows:

$$\text{Average total stockholders' equity} = \frac{(\$17{,}000{,}000 + \$15{,}970{,}000)}{2} = \$16{,}485{,}000$$

$$\text{Average preferred stock} = \frac{(\$2{,}000{,}000 + \$2{,}000{,}000)}{2} = \$2{,}000{,}000$$

$$\text{Average common stockholders' equity} = \$16{,}485{,}000 - \$2{,}000{,}000 = \$14{,}485{,}000$$

$$\text{Return on common stockholders' equity} = \frac{\$1{,}750{,}000 - \$120{,}000}{\$14{,}485{,}000} = 11.3\%$$

Compare the return on common stockholders' equity above (11.3%) with the return on total assets computed in the preceding section (7.3%). Why is the return on common stockholders' equity so much higher? The answer lies in *financial leverage.*

**HELPFUL HINT**

When the numerator of a financial ratio contains an amount from the income statement and the denominator contains an amount derived from the balance sheet, the denominator must be expressed as an average. This averaging process is done because the income statement summarizes performance for a period of time, whereas the balance sheet reflects a company's financial position at a point in time. The average for a balance sheet account is typically computed by taking the account's beginning balance plus its ending balance and dividing this sum by two.

## Financial Leverage

**Financial leverage** results from the difference between the rate of return the company earns on investments in its own assets and the rate of return that the company must pay its creditors. If the company's rate of return on total assets exceeds the rate of return the company pays its creditors, *financial leverage is positive.* If the rate of return on total assets is less than the rate of return the company pays its creditors, *financial leverage is negative.*

We can see financial leverage in operation in the case of Brickey Electronics. Notice from Exhibit 13–1 that the company pays 8% interest on its bonds payable. The after-tax interest cost of these bonds is only 5.6% [8% interest rate × (1 − 0.30) = 5.6%]. As shown earlier, the company's after-tax return on total assets is 7.3%. Because the return on total assets of 7.3% is greater than the 5.6% after-tax interest cost of the bonds, leverage is positive, and the difference goes to the common stockholders. This explains in part why the return on common stockholders' equity of 11.3% is greater than the return on total assets of 7.3%. If financial leverage is positive, having some debt in the capital structure can substantially benefit common stockholders. For this reason, companies often try to maintain a level of debt that is considered to be normal within their industry.

Unfortunately, leverage is a two-edged sword. If assets do not earn a high enough return to cover the interest costs of debt and preferred stock dividends, then the common stockholder suffers. In that case, financial leverage is negative.

## Book Value per Share

**Book value per share** measures the amount that would be distributed to holders of each share of common stock if all assets were sold at their balance sheet carrying amounts (i.e., book values) and if all creditors were paid off. Book value per share is based entirely on historical costs. The formula for computing it is:

$$\text{Book value per share} = \frac{\text{Total stockholders' equity} - \text{Preferred stock}}{\text{Number of common shares outstanding}}$$

The book value per share of Brickey Electronics' common stock is computed as follows:

$$\text{Book value per share} = \frac{\$17{,}000{,}000 - \$2{,}000{,}000}{500{,}000\text{ shares}} = \$30\text{ per share}$$

If this book value is compared with the $40 market value of Brickey Electronics' stock, then the stock may appear to be overpriced. However, as we discussed earlier, market prices reflect expectations about future earnings and dividends, whereas book value largely reflects the results of events that have occurred in the past. Ordinarily, the market value of a stock exceeds its book value. For example, in one year, **Microsoft**'s common stock often traded at over 4 times its book value, and **Coca-Cola**'s market value was over 17 times its book value.

## RATIO ANALYSIS—THE SHORT-TERM CREDITOR

**LEARNING OBJECTIVE 3**

Compute and interpret financial ratios that would be useful to a short-term creditor.

Short-term creditors, such as suppliers, want to be paid on time. Therefore, they focus on the company's cash flows and on its *working capital* because these are the company's short-term primary sources of cash. *All calculations in this section will be performed for this year.*

### Working Capital

The excess of current assets over current liabilities is known as **working capital**.

$$\text{Working capital} = \text{Current assets} - \text{Current liabilities}$$

The working capital for Brickey Electronics is computed as follows:

$$\text{Working capital} = \$15{,}500{,}000 - \$7{,}000{,}000 = \$8{,}500{,}000$$

Ample working capital provides some assurance to short-term creditors that they will be paid by the company. However, maintaining large amounts of working capital isn't free. Working capital must be financed with long-term debt and equity—both of which are expensive. Therefore, managers often want to minimize working capital.

A large and growing working capital balance may not be a good sign. For example, it could be the result of unwarranted growth in inventories. To put working capital into proper perspective, it should be supplemented with the following four ratios—the current ratio, the acid-test ratio, the accounts receivable turnover, and the inventory turnover—each of which will be discussed in turn.

### Current Ratio

A company's working capital is frequently expressed in ratio form. A company's current assets divided by its current liabilities is known as the **current ratio**:

$$\text{Current ratio} = \frac{\text{Current assets}}{\text{Current liabilities}}$$

For Brickey Electronics, the current ratio is computed as follows:

$$\text{Current ratio} = \frac{\$15{,}500{,}000}{\$7{,}000{,}000} = 2.21$$

Although widely regarded as a measure of short-term debt-paying ability, the current ratio must be interpreted with great care. A *declining* ratio might be a sign of a deteriorating financial condition, or it might be the result of eliminating obsolete inventories or other stagnant current assets. An *improving* ratio might be the result of stockpiling inventory, or it might indicate an improving financial situation. In short, the current ratio is useful, but tricky to interpret.

The general rule of thumb calls for a current ratio of at least 2. However, many companies successfully operate with a current ratio below 2. The adequacy of a current ratio depends heavily on the *composition* of the assets. For example, as we see in the table below, both Worthington Corporation and Greystone, Inc., have current ratios of 2. However, they are not in comparable financial condition. Greystone is more likely to have difficulty meeting its current financial obligations because almost all of its current assets consist of inventory rather than more liquid assets such as cash and accounts receivable.

| | Worthington Corporation | Greystone, Inc. |
|---|---|---|
| Current assets: | | |
| Cash | $ 25,000 | $ 2,000 |
| Accounts receivable, net | 60,000 | 8,000 |
| Inventory | 85,000 | 160,000 |
| Prepaid expenses | 5,000 | 5,000 |
| Total current assets (a) | $175,000 | $175,000 |
| Current liabilities (b) | $ 87,500 | $ 87,500 |
| Current ratio, (a) ÷ (b) | 2 | 2 |

## Acid-Test (Quick) Ratio

The **acid-test (quick) ratio** is a more rigorous test of a company's ability to meet its short-term debts than the current ratio. Inventories and prepaid expenses are excluded from total current assets, leaving only the more liquid (or "quick") assets to be divided by current liabilities.

$$\text{Acid-test ratio} = \frac{\text{Cash} + \text{Marketable securities} + \text{Accounts receivable} + \text{Short-term notes receivable}}{\text{Current liabilities}}$$

The acid-test ratio measures how well a company can meet its obligations without having to liquidate or depend too heavily on its inventory. Ideally, each dollar of liabilities should be backed by at least $1 of quick assets. However, acid-test ratios as low as 0.3 are common.

The acid-test ratio for Brickey Electronics is computed below:

$$\text{Acid-test ratio} = \frac{\$1{,}200{,}000 + \$0 + \$6{,}000{,}000 + \$0}{\$7{,}000{,}000} = 1.03$$

Although Brickey Electronics' acid-test ratio is within the acceptable range, an analyst might be concerned about several trends revealed in the company's balance sheet. Notice in Exhibit 13–1 that short-term debts are rising, while the cash balance is declining. Perhaps the lower cash balance is a result of the substantial increase in accounts receivable. In short, as with the current ratio, the acid-test ratio should be interpreted with one eye on its basic components.

## Accounts Receivable Turnover

The *accounts receivable turnover* and *average collection period* ratios measure how quickly credit sales are converted into cash. The **accounts receivable turnover** is computed by dividing sales on account (i.e., credit sales) by the average accounts receivable balance for the year:

$$\text{Accounts receivable turnover} = \frac{\text{Sales on account}}{\text{Average accounts receivable balance}}$$

Assuming that all of Brickey Electronics' sales were on account, its accounts receivable turnover is computed as follows:

$$\text{Accounts receivable turnover} = \frac{\$52{,}000{,}000}{(\$6{,}000{,}000 + \$4{,}000{,}000)/2} = 10.4$$

The accounts receivable turnover can then be divided into 365 days to determine the average number of days required to collect an account (known as the **average collection period**).

$$\text{Average collection period} = \frac{365 \text{ days}}{\text{Accounts receivable turnover}}$$

The average collection period for Brickey Electronics is computed as follows:

$$\text{Average collection period} = \frac{365 \text{ days}}{10.4} = 35 \text{ days}$$

This means that on average it takes 35 days to collect a credit sale. Whether this is good or bad depends on the credit terms Brickey Electronics is offering its customers. Many customers will tend to withhold payment for as long as the credit terms allow. If the credit terms are 30 days, then a 35-day average collection period would usually be viewed as very good. On the other hand, if the company's credit terms are 10 days, then a 35-day average collection period is worrisome. A long collection period may result from having too many old uncollectible accounts, failing to bill promptly or follow up on late accounts, lax credit checks, and so on. In practice, average collection periods ranging all the way from 10 days to 180 days are common, depending on the industry.

## Inventory Turnover

The **inventory turnover ratio** measures how many times a company's inventory has been sold and replaced during the year. It is computed by dividing the cost of goods sold by the average level of inventory [(Beginning inventory balance + Ending inventory balance) ÷ 2]:

$$\text{Inventory turnover} = \frac{\text{Cost of goods sold}}{\text{Average inventory balance}}$$

Brickey's inventory turnover is computed as follows:

$$\text{Inventory turnover} = \frac{\$36{,}000{,}000}{(\$8{,}000{,}000 + \$10{,}000{,}000)/2} = 4.0$$

The number of days needed on average to sell the entire inventory (called the **average sale period**) can be computed by dividing 365 by the inventory turnover:

$$\text{Average sale period} = \frac{365 \text{ days}}{\text{Inventory turnover}}$$

$$= \frac{365 \text{ days}}{4 \text{ times}} = 91\tfrac{1}{4} \text{ days}$$

The average sale period varies from industry to industry. Grocery stores, with significant perishable stocks, tend to turn over their inventory quickly. On the other hand, jewelry stores tend to turn over their inventory slowly. In practice, average sales periods of 10 days to 90 days are common, depending on the industry.

A company whose inventory turnover ratio is much slower than the average for its industry may have too much inventory or the wrong sorts of inventory. Some managers argue that they must buy in large quantities to take advantage of quantity discounts. But these discounts must be compared to the added costs of insurance, taxes, financing, and risks of obsolescence and deterioration that result from carrying added inventories.

Inventory turnover should increase in companies that adopt Lean Production. If properly implemented, Lean Production should result in both a decrease in inventories and an increase in sales due to better customer service.

**CONCEPT CHECK**

1. Total sales at a store are $1,000,000 and 80% of those sales are on credit. The beginning and ending accounts receivable balances are $100,000 and $140,000, respectively. What is the accounts receivable turnover?
   a. 3.33
   b. 6.67
   c. 8.33
   d. 10.67
2. A retailer's total sales are $1,000,000 and the gross margin percentage is 60%. The beginning and ending inventory balances are $240,000 and $260,000, respectively. What is the inventory turnover?
   a. 1.60
   b. 2.40
   c. 3.40
   d. 3.60

**DECISION POINT**

### Portfolio Manager

Assume that you work for a mutual fund and have the responsibility of selecting stocks to include in its investment portfolio. You have been analyzing the financial statements of a chain of retail clothing stores and noticed that the company's current ratio has increased, but its acid-test (quick) ratio has decreased. In addition, the company's accounts receivable turnover has decreased and its inventory turnover ratio has decreased. Finally, the company's price-earnings ratio is at an all-time high. Would you recommend buying stock in this company?

## RATIO ANALYSIS—THE LONG-TERM CREDITOR

**LEARNING OBJECTIVE 4**

Compute and interpret financial ratios that would be useful to a long-term creditor.

Long-term creditors are concerned with a company's ability to repay its loans over the long run. For example, if a company paid out all of its available cash in the form of dividends, then nothing would be left to pay back creditors. Consequently, creditors often seek protection by requiring that borrowers agree to various restrictive covenants, or rules. These restrictive covenants typically include restrictions on dividend payments as well as rules stating that the company must maintain certain financial ratios at specified levels. Although restrictive covenants are widely used, they do not ensure that creditors will be paid when loans come due. The company still must generate sufficient earnings to cover payments.

## Times Interest Earned Ratio

The most common measure of a company's ability to provide protection to its long-term creditors is the **times interest earned ratio.** It is computed by dividing earnings before interest expense and income taxes (i.e., net operating income) by interest expense:

$$\text{Times interest earned} = \frac{\text{Earnings before interest expense and income taxes}}{\text{Interest expense}}$$

For Brickey Electronics, the times interest earned ratio for this year is computed as follows:

$$\text{Times interest earned} = \frac{\$3{,}140{,}000}{\$640{,}000} = 4.9$$

The times interest earned ratio is based on earnings before interest expense and income taxes because that is the amount of earnings that is available for making interest payments. Interest expenses are deducted *before* income taxes are determined; creditors have first claim on the earnings before taxes are paid.

A times interest earned ratio of less than 1 is inadequate because interest expense exceeds the earnings that are available for paying that interest. In contrast, a times interest earned ratio of 2 or more may be considered sufficient to protect long-term creditors.

IN BUSINESS

### Home Builders Face a Liquidity Crisis

The economic downturn took a toll on the home building industry. Many builders, who borrowed large amounts of money to buy land during the earlier housing boom, slashed home prices in an attempt to generate cash to make their interest payments. The share prices of home builders **Tousa**, **Standard Pacific**, and **WCI Communities, Inc.**, dropped 98%, 88%, and 82%, respectively. WCI, a high-rise condominium builder in coastal Florida, failed to maintain the minimum times interest earned ratio required in its loan agreement. The uncertainty surrounding the Florida condo market made it unclear if WCI would be able to pay its $120 million of interest expense in the coming year.

Source: Michael Corkery, "Beware of Liquidity Traps in Builders," *The Wall Street Journal,* November 29, 2007, pp. C1–C2.

## Debt-to-Equity Ratio

Long-term creditors are also concerned with a company's ability to keep a reasonable balance between its debt and equity. This balance is measured by the **debt-to-equity ratio:**

$$\text{Debt-to-equity ratio} = \frac{\text{Total liabilities}}{\text{Stockholders' equity}}$$

Brickey's debt-to-equity ratio for this year is computed as follows:

$$\text{Debt-to-equity ratio} = \frac{\$14{,}500{,}000}{\$17{,}000{,}000} = 0.85$$

The debt-to-equity ratio indicates the relative proportions of debt and equity on the company's balance sheet. At the end of this year, Brickey Electronics' creditors were providing 85 cents for each $1 being provided by stockholders.

Creditors and stockholders have different views about the optimal debt-to-equity ratio. Ordinarily, stockholders would like a lot of debt to take advantage of positive financial leverage. On the other hand, because equity represents the excess of total assets over total liabilities, and hence a buffer of protection for the creditors, creditors would like to see less debt and more equity.

In practice, debt-to-equity ratios from 0.0 (no debt) to 3.0 are common. Generally speaking, in industries with little financial risk, creditors tolerate high debt-to-equity ratios. In industries with more financial risk, creditors demand lower debt-to-equity ratios.

**CONCEPT CHECK**

3. Total assets are $1,500,000 and stockholders' equity is $900,000. What is the debt-to-equity ratio?
   a. 0.33
   b. 0.50
   c. 0.60
   d. 0.67

## Small Business Struggles to Manage Its Debt

IN BUSINESS

Chuck Bidwell and Jennifer Guarino bought **J.W. Hulme Company** to expand the business into luxury briefcases, backpacks, and handbags. The co-owners planned to grow the company's catalog mailing list tenfold to 10,000 households while doubling its product assortment to 250 items. To finance this growth strategy, the company borrowed more than $2 million, causing its debt-to-equity ratio to jump from 2.94 to 5.53. When the company subsequently sought $250,000 in additional loans to finance its next round of catalogs, lenders were apprehensive. The company's most recent annual sales of $1.5 million fell $500,000 short of the owners' projections. Furthermore, inventory levels had ballooned to $1 million signaling declining demand for the company's products.

Source: Julie Jargon, "On Front Lines of Debt Crisis, Luggage Maker Fights for Life," *The Wall Street Journal*, January 9, 2009, pp. A1 and A8.

## SUMMARY OF RATIOS AND SOURCES OF COMPARATIVE RATIO DATA

Exhibit 13–6 contains a summary of the ratios discussed in this chapter. The formula for each ratio and a summary comment on each ratio's significance are included in the exhibit.

Exhibit 13–7 (page 601) contains a listing of public sources that provide comparative ratio data organized by industry. These sources are used extensively by managers, investors, and analysts. The **EDGAR** database listed in Exhibit 13–7 is a particularly rich source of data. It contains copies of all reports filed by companies with the SEC since about 1995—including annual reports filed as Form 10-K.

**EXHIBIT 13–6** Summary of Ratios

| Ratio | Formula | Significance |
|---|---|---|
| Gross margin percentage | Gross margin ÷ Sales | A broad measure of profitability |
| Earnings per share (of common stock) | (Net income − Preferred dividends) ÷ Average number of common shares outstanding | Affects the market price per share, as reflected in the price-earnings ratio |
| Price-earnings ratio | Market price per share ÷ Earnings per share | An index of whether a stock is relatively cheap or relatively expensive in relation to current earnings |
| Dividend payout ratio | Dividends per share ÷ Earnings per share | An index showing whether a company pays out most of its earnings in dividends or reinvests the earnings internally |
| Dividend yield ratio | Dividends per share ÷ Market price per share | Shows the return in terms of cash dividends being provided by a stock |
| Return on total assets | {Net income + [Interest expense × (1 − Tax rate)]} ÷ Average total assets | Measures how well assets have been employed by management |
| Return on common stockholders' equity | (Net income − Preferred dividends) ÷ (Average total stockholders' equity − Average preferred stock) | When compared to the return on total assets, measures the extent to which financial leverage is working for or against common stockholders |
| Book value per share | (Total stockholders' equity − Preferred stock) ÷ Number of common shares outstanding | Measures the amount that would be distributed to common stockholders if all assets were sold at their balance sheet carrying amounts and if all creditors were paid off |
| Working capital | Current assets − Current liabilities | Measures the company's ability to repay current liabilities using only current assets |
| Current ratio | Current assets ÷ Current liabilities | Test of short-term debt-paying ability |
| Acid-test ratio | (Cash + Marketable securities + Accounts receivable + Short-term notes receivable) ÷ Current liabilities | Test of short-term debt-paying ability without having to rely on inventory |
| Accounts receivable turnover | Sales on account ÷ Average accounts receivable balance | Measures how many times a company's accounts receivable have been turned into cash during the year |
| Average collection period | 365 days ÷ Accounts receivable turnover | Measures the average number of days taken to collect an account receivable |
| Inventory turnover | Cost of goods sold ÷ Average inventory balance | Measures how many times a company's inventory has been sold during the year |
| Average sale period | 365 days ÷ Inventory turnover | Measures the average number of days taken to sell the inventory one time |
| Times interest earned | Earnings before interest expense and income taxes ÷ Interest expense | Measures the company's ability to make interest payments |
| Debt-to-equity ratio | Total liabilities ÷ Stockholders' equity | Measures the amount of assets being provided by creditors for each dollar of assets being provided by the stockholders |

**EXHIBIT 13–7** Sources of Financial Ratios

| Source | Content |
|---|---|
| *Almanac of Business and Industrial Financial Ratios,* Aspen Publishers; published annually | An exhaustive source that contains common-size income statements and financial ratios by industry and by the size of companies within each industry. |
| *AMA Annual Statement Studies,* Risk Management Association; published annually. | A widely used publication that contains common-size statements and financial ratios on individual companies; the companies are arranged by industry. |
| *EDGAR,* Securities and Exchange Commission; website that is continually updated; www.sec.gov | An exhaustive Internet database that contains reports filed by companies with the SEC; these reports can be downloaded. |
| *FreeEdgar,* EDGAR Online, Inc.; website that is continually updated; www.freeedgar.com | A site that allows you to search SEC filings; financial information can be downloaded directly into Excel worksheets. |
| *Hoover's Online,* Hoovers, Inc.; website that is continually updated; www.hoovers.com | A site that provides capsule profiles for 10,000 U.S. companies with links to company websites, annual reports, stock charts, news articles, and industry information. |
| *Industry Norms & Key Business Ratios,* Dun & Bradstreet; published annually | Fourteen commonly used financial ratios are computed for over 800 major industry groupings. |
| *Mergent Industrial Manual and Mergent Bank and Finance Manual;* published annually | An exhaustive source that contains financial ratios on all companies listed on the New York Stock Exchange, the American Stock Exchange, and regional American exchanges. |
| *Standard & Poor's Industry Survey,* Standard & Poor's; published annually | Various statistics, including some financial ratios, are given by industry and for leading companies within each industry grouping. |

## XBRL: The Next Generation of Financial Reporting

IN BUSINESS

The **Securities and Exchange Commission (SEC)** encourages companies to submit financial reports using a computer code known as Extensible Business Reporting Language, or XBRL for short. XBRL is a "financial reporting derivation of Extensible Markup Language, or XML—a framework that establishes individual 'tags' for elements in structured documents, allowing specific elements to be immediately accessed and aggregated."

XBRL dramatically improves the financial reporting process in two ways. First, data are tagged in accordance with a generally accepted framework. This simplifies the process of making apples-to-apples comparisons of financial results across companies. For example, "many of the components of a 'property, plant, and equipment' listing on a balance sheet . . . may be described differently by different companies, but when tagged in XBRL, a straight comparison becomes much simpler."

Second, XBRL simplifies the exchange of financial data. Without XBRL, a company's financial data are typically stored in a format that is unique to that company's specific financial software application and that cannot be easily read by other financial software. This problem is overcome with XBRL because the tagged data become "independent of the originating application and can readily be shared with any application that recognizes XBRL. This feature of XBRL makes the markup language very attractive for government regulators and financial analysts."

Sources: Glenn Cheney, "U.S. gets its XBRL in gear: SEC, FDIC OK tagged data," *Accounting Today,* March 14–April 3, 2005, pp. 26–27; Neal Hannon, "XBRL Fundamentals," *Strategic Finance,* April 2005, pp. 57–58; and Ghostwriter, "From Tags to Riches," *CFO-IT,* Spring 2005, pp. 13–14.

## SUMMARY

**LO1 Prepare and interpret financial statements in comparative and common-size form.**

Raw data from financial statements should be standardized so that the data can be compared over time and across companies. For example, all of the financial data for a company can be expressed as a percentage of the data in some base year. This makes it easier to spot trends over time. To make it easier to compare companies, common-size financial statements are often used in which income statement data are expressed as a percentage of sales and balance sheet data are expressed as a percentage of total assets.

**LO2 Compute and interpret financial ratios that would be useful to a common stockholder.**

Common stockholders are concerned with the company's earnings per share, price-earnings ratio, dividend payout and yield ratios, return on total assets, book value per share, and return on common stockholders' equity. Generally speaking, the higher these ratios, the better it is for common stockholders.

**LO3 Compute and interpret financial ratios that would be useful to a short-term creditor.**

Short-term creditors are concerned with the company's ability to repay its debt in the near future. Consequently, these investors focus on the relation between current assets and current liabilities and the company's ability to generate cash. Specifically, short-term creditors monitor working capital, the current ratio, the acid-test (quick) ratio, accounts receivable turnover, and inventory turnover.

**LO4 Compute and interpret financial ratios that would be useful to a long-term creditor.**

Long-term creditors have many of the same concerns as short-term creditors, but also monitor the times interest earned ratio and the debt-to-equity ratio. These ratios indicate the company's ability to pay interest out of operations and how heavily the company is financially leveraged.

## GUIDANCE ANSWERS TO DECISION POINT

**Portfolio Manager (p. 597)**

All of the ratios—current ratio, acid-test (quick) ratio, accounts receivable turnover, and inventory turnover ratio—indicate deteriorating operations. And yet the company's price-earnings ratio is at an all-time high, suggesting that the stock market is optimistic about the company's future and its stock price. It would be risky to invest in this company without digging deeper and finding out what has caused the deteriorating operating ratios.

## GUIDANCE ANSWERS TO CONCEPT CHECKS

1. **Choice b.** The accounts receivable turnover is \$800,000 of credit sales ÷ \$120,000 average accounts receivable balance = 6.67.
2. **Choice a.** First, calculate the cost of goods sold as follows: \$1,000,000 × (1 − 0.60) = \$400,000. Next, the inventory turnover is calculated as follows: \$400,000 of cost of goods sold ÷ \$250,000 average inventory = 1.60.
3. **Choice d.** Total assets of \$1,500,000 − \$900,000 of stockholders' equity = \$600,000 of total liabilities. The debt-to-equity ratio is \$600,000 ÷ \$900,000 = 0.67.

## REVIEW PROBLEM: SELECTED RATIOS AND FINANCIAL LEVERAGE

Starbucks Corporation is the leading retailer and roaster of specialty coffee in North America selling freshly brewed coffee, pastries, and coffee beans. Data (slightly modified) from the company's financial statements are as follows:

**Starbucks Corporation**
**Comparative Balance Sheet**
**(dollars in millions)**

| | This Year | Last Year |
|---|---|---|
| **Assets** | | |
| Current assets: | | |
| Cash | $ 281 | $ 313 |
| Marketable securities | 157 | 141 |
| Accounts receivable | 288 | 224 |
| Inventories | 692 | 636 |
| Other current assets | 278 | 216 |
| Total current assets | 1,696 | 1,530 |
| Property and equipment, net | 2,890 | 2,288 |
| Other assets | 758 | 611 |
| Total assets | $5,344 | $4,429 |
| **Liabilities and Stockholders' Equity** | | |
| Current liabilities: | | |
| Accounts payable | $ 391 | $ 341 |
| Short-term bank loans | 710 | 700 |
| Accrued payables | 757 | 662 |
| Other current liabilities | 298 | 233 |
| Total current liabilities | 2,156 | 1,936 |
| Long-term liabilities | 904 | 265 |
| Total liabilities | 3,060 | 2,201 |
| Stockholders' equity: | | |
| Preferred stock | 0 | 0 |
| Common stock and additional paid-in capital | 40 | 40 |
| Retained earnings | 2,244 | 2,188 |
| Total stockholders' equity | 2,284 | 2,228 |
| Total liabilities and stockholders' equity | $5,344 | $4,429 |

**Starbucks Corporation**
**Income Statement**
**(dollars in millions)**

| | This Year |
|---|---|
| Sales | $9,411 |
| Cost of goods sold | 3,999 |
| Gross margin | 5,412 |
| Selling and administrative expenses: | |
| Store operating expenses | 3,216 |
| Other operating expenses | 294 |
| Depreciation and amortization | 467 |
| General and administrative expenses | 489 |
| Total selling and administrative expenses | 4,466 |
| Net operating income | 946 |
| Plus interest and other income | 110 |
| Interest expense | 0 |
| Net income before taxes | 1,056 |
| Income taxes (about 36%) | 384 |
| Net income | $ 672 |

***Required:***
1. Compute the return on total assets.
2. Compute the return on common stockholders' equity.
3. Is Starbucks' financial leverage positive or negative? Explain.
4. Compute the current ratio.
5. Compute the acid-test ratio.
6. Compute the inventory turnover.
7. Compute the average sale period.
8. Compute the debt-to-equity ratio.

**Solution to Review Problem**

1. Return on total assets:

$$\text{Return on total assets} = \frac{\text{Net income} + [\text{Interest expense} \times (1 - \text{Tax rate})]}{\text{Average total assets}}$$

$$= \frac{\$672 + [\$0 \times (1 - 0.36)]}{(\$5{,}344 + \$4{,}429)/2} = 13.8\% \text{ (rounded)}$$

2. Return on common stockholders' equity:

$$\text{Return on common stockholders' equity} = \frac{\text{Net income} - \text{Preferred dividends}}{\text{Average common stockholders' equity}}$$

$$= \frac{\$672 - \$0}{(\$2{,}284 + \$2{,}228)/2} = 29.8\% \text{ (rounded)}$$

3. The company has positive financial leverage because the return on common stockholders' equity of 29.8% is greater than the return on total assets of 13.8%. The positive financial leverage was obtained from current and long-term liabilities.
4. Current ratio:

$$\text{Current ratio} = \frac{\text{Current assets}}{\text{Current liabilities}}$$

$$= \frac{\$1{,}696}{\$2{,}156} = 0.79 \text{ (rounded)}$$

5. Acid-test ratio:

$$\text{Acid-test ratio} = \frac{\text{Cash} + \text{Marketable securities} + \text{Accounts receivable} + \text{Short-term notes receivable}}{\text{Current liabilities}}$$

$$= \frac{\$281 + \$157 + \$288 + \$0}{\$2{,}156} = 0.34 \text{ (rounded)}$$

6. Inventory turnover:

$$\text{Inventory turnover} = \frac{\text{Cost of goods sold}}{\text{Average inventory balance}}$$

$$= \frac{\$3{,}999}{(\$692 + \$636)/2} = 6.02 \text{ (rounded)}$$

7. Average sale period:

$$\text{Average sale period} = \frac{365 \text{ days}}{\text{Inventory turnover}}$$

$$= \frac{365 \text{ days}}{6.02} = 61 \text{ days (rounded)}$$

8. Debt-to-equity ratio:

$$\text{Debt-to-equity ratio} = \frac{\text{Total liabilities}}{\text{Stockholders' equity}}$$

$$= \frac{\$2{,}156 + \$904}{\$2{,}284} = 1.34 \text{ (rounded)}$$

## GLOSSARY

(Note: Definitions and formulas for all financial ratios are shown in Exhibit 13–6. These definitions and formulas are not repeated here.)

**Common-size financial statements** A statement that shows the items appearing on it in percentage form as well as in dollar form. On the income statement, the percentages are based on total sales revenue; on the balance sheet, the percentages are based on total assets. (p. 587)

**Financial leverage** A difference between the rate of return on assets and the rate paid to creditors. (p. 593)

**Horizontal analysis** A side-by-side comparison of two or more years' financial statements. (p. 585)

**Trend analysis** See *Horizontal analysis.* (p. 585)

**Trend percentages** Several years of financial data expressed as a percentage of performance in a base year. (p. 586)

**Vertical analysis** The presentation of a company's financial statements in common-size form. (p. 587)

## QUESTIONS

**13–1** Distinguish between horizontal and vertical analysis of financial statement data.

**13–2** What is the basic purpose for examining trends in a company's financial ratios and other data? What other kinds of comparisons might an analyst make?

**13–3** Assume that two companies in the same industry have equal earnings. Why might these companies have different price-earnings ratios? If a company has a price-earnings ratio of 20 and reports earnings per share for the current year of $4, at what price would you expect to find the stock selling on the market?

**13–4** Would you expect a company in a rapidly growing technological industry to have a high or low dividend payout ratio?

**13–5** What is meant by the dividend yield on a common stock investment?

**13–6** What is meant by the term financial leverage?

**13–7** The president of a plastics company was quoted in a business journal as stating, "We haven't had a dollar of interest-paying debt in over 10 years. Not many companies can say that." As a stockholder in this company, how would you feel about its policy of not taking on debt?

**13–8** If a stock's market value exceeds its book value, then the stock is overpriced. Do you agree? Explain.

**13–9** A company seeking a line of credit at a bank was turned down. Among other things, the bank stated that the company's 2 to 1 current ratio was not adequate. Give reasons why a 2 to 1 current ratio might not be adequate.

**Multiple-choice questions are provided on the text website at www.mhhe.com/brewer6e.**

## THE FOUNDATIONAL 15

**Available with McGraw-Hill's *Connect® Accounting.***

LO2, LO3, LO4

Markus Company's common stock sold for $2.75 per share at the end of this year. The company paid preferred stock dividends totaling $4,400 and a common stock dividend of $0.55 per share this year. It also provided the following *data excerpts* from this year's financial statements:

| | Ending Balance | Beginning Balance |
|---|---|---|
| Cash | $35,000 | $30,000 |
| Accounts receivable | $60,000 | $50,000 |
| Inventory | $55,000 | $60,000 |
| Current assets | $150,000 | $140,000 |
| Total assets | $450,000 | $460,000 |
| Current liabilities | $60,000 | $40,000 |
| Total liabilities | $130,000 | $120,000 |
| Preferred stock | $40,000 | $40,000 |
| Common stock, $1 par value | $80,000 | $80,000 |
| Total stockholders' equity | $320,000 | $340,000 |
| Total liabilities and stockholders' equity | $450,000 | $460,000 |

| | This Year |
|---|---|
| Sales (all on account) | $700,000 |
| Cost of goods sold | $400,000 |
| Gross margin | $300,000 |
| Net operating income | $140,000 |
| Interest expense | $8,000 |
| Net income | $92,400 |

***Required:***

1. What is the earnings per share?
2. What is the price-earnings ratio?
3. What is the dividend payout ratio?
4. What is the dividend yield ratio?
5. What is the return on total assets (assuming a 30% tax rate)?
6. What is the return on common stockholders' equity?
7. What is the book value per share at the end of this year?
8. What is the amount of working capital and the current ratio at the end of this year?
9. What is the acid-test ratio at the end of this year?
10. What is the accounts receivable turnover?
11. What is the average collection period?
12. What is the inventory turnover?
13. What is the average sale period?
14. What is the time interest earned ratio?
15. What is the debt-to-equity ratio at the end of this year?

## EXERCISES

connect ACCOUNTING

**All applicable exercises are available with McGraw-Hill's *Connect*® *Accounting.***

**EXERCISE 13–1 Common-Size Income Statement [LO1]**

A comparative income statement is given below for Ryder Company:

**Ryder Company**
**Comparative Income Statement**

| | This Year | Last Year |
|---|---|---|
| Sales | $5,000,000 | $4,000,000 |
| Cost of goods sold | 3,160,000 | 2,400,000 |
| Gross margin | 1,840,000 | 1,600,000 |
| Selling and administrative expenses: | | |
| Selling expenses | 900,000 | 700,000 |
| Administrative expenses | 680,000 | 584,000 |
| Total selling and administrative expenses | 1,580,000 | 1,284,000 |
| Net operating income | 260,000 | 316,000 |
| Interest expense | 70,000 | 40,000 |
| Net income before taxes | $ 190,000 | $ 276,000 |

The president is concerned that net income is down even though sales have increased during the year. The president is also concerned that administrative expenses have increased because the company made a concerted effort to cut waste out of the organization.

***Required:***

1. Express each year's income statement in common-size percentages. Carry computations to one decimal place.
2. Comment briefly on the changes between the two years.

**EXERCISE 13–2 Financial Ratios for Common Stockholders [LO2]**

Comparative financial statements for Heritage Antiquing Services for the fiscal year ending December 31 appear below and on the following page. The company did not issue any new common or preferred stock during the year. A total of 600 thousand shares of common stock were outstanding. The interest rate on the bond payable was 14%, the income tax rate was 40%, and the dividend per share of common stock was $0.75. The market value of the company's common stock at the end of the year was $26. All of the company's sales are on account.

**Heritage Antiquing Services**
**Comparative Balance Sheet**
**(dollars in thousands)**

| | This Year | Last Year |
|---|---|---|
| **Assets** | | |
| Current assets: | | |
| Cash | $ 1,080 | $ 1,210 |
| Accounts receivable, net | 9,000 | 6,500 |
| Inventory | 12,000 | 10,600 |
| Prepaid expenses | 600 | 500 |
| Total current assets | 22,680 | 18,810 |
| Property and equipment: | | |
| Land | 9,000 | 9,000 |
| Buildings and equipment, net | 36,800 | 38,000 |
| Total property and equipment | 45,800 | 47,000 |
| Total assets | $68,480 | $65,810 |
| **Liabilities and Stockholders' Equity** | | |
| Current liabilities: | | |
| Accounts payable | $18,500 | $17,400 |
| Accrued payables | 900 | 700 |
| Notes payable, short term | — | 100 |
| Total current liabilities | 19,400 | 18,200 |
| Long-term liabilities: | | |
| Bonds payable | 8,000 | 8,000 |
| Total liabilities | 27,400 | 26,200 |
| Stockholders' equity: | | |
| Preferred stock | 1,000 | 1,000 |
| Common stock | 2,000 | 2,000 |
| Additional paid-in capital | 4,000 | 4,000 |
| Total paid-in capital | 7,000 | 7,000 |
| Retained earnings | 34,080 | 32,610 |
| Total stockholders' equity | 41,080 | 39,610 |
| Total liabilities and stockholders' equity | $68,480 | $65,810 |

| Heritage Antiquing Services<br>Comparative Income Statement and Reconciliation<br>(dollars in thousands) | This Year | Last Year |
|---|---|---|
| Sales | $66,000 | $64,000 |
| Cost of goods sold | 43,000 | 42,000 |
| Gross margin | 23,000 | 22,000 |
| Selling and administrative expenses: | | |
| Selling expenses | 11,500 | 11,000 |
| Administrative expenses | 7,400 | 7,000 |
| Total selling and administrative expenses | 18,900 | 18,000 |
| Net operating income | 4,100 | 4,000 |
| Interest expense | 800 | 800 |
| Net income before taxes | 3,300 | 3,200 |
| Income taxes | 1,320 | 1,280 |
| Net income | 1,980 | 1,920 |
| Dividends to preferred stockholders | 60 | 400 |
| Net income remaining for common stockholders | 1,920 | 1,520 |
| Dividends to common stockholders | 450 | 450 |
| Net income added to retained earnings | 1,470 | 1,070 |
| Retained earnings, beginning of year | 32,610 | 31,540 |
| Retained earnings, end of year | $34,080 | $32,610 |

***Required:***

Compute the following financial ratios for common stockholders for this year:

1. Gross margin percentage.
2. Earnings per share of common stock.
3. Price-earnings ratio.
4. Dividend payout ratio.
5. Dividend yield ratio.
6. Return on total assets.
7. Return on common stockholders' equity.
8. Book value per share.

**EXERCISE 13–3 Financial Ratios for Short-Term Creditors [LO3]**

Refer to the data in Exercise 13–2 for Heritage Antiquing Services.

***Required:***

Compute the following financial data for short-term creditors for this year:

1. Working capital.
2. Current ratio.
3. Acid-test ratio.
4. Accounts receivable turnover.
5. Average collection period.
6. Inventory turnover.
7. Average sale period.

**EXERCISE 13–4 Financial Ratios for Long-Term Creditors [LO4]**

Refer to the data in Exercise 13–2 for Heritage Antiquing Services.

***Required:***

Compute the following financial ratios for long-term creditors for this year:

1. Times interest earned ratio.
2. Debt-to-equity ratio.

**EXERCISE 13–5 Selected Financial Measures for Short-Term Creditors [LO3]**

Rightway Products had a current ratio of 2.5 on June 30 of the current year. On that date, the company's assets were as follows:

| | |
|---|---|
| Cash | $ 80,000 |
| Accounts receivable, net | 460,000 |
| Inventory | 750,000 |
| Prepaid expenses | 10,000 |
| Plant and equipment, net | 1,900,000 |
| Total assets | $3,200,000 |

***Required:***

1. What was the company's working capital on June 30?
2. What was the company's acid-test ratio on June 30?
3. The company paid an account payable of $100,000 immediately after June 30.
   a. What effect did this transaction have on working capital? Show computations.
   b. What effect did this transaction have on the current ratio? Show computations.

**EXERCISE 13–6 Selected Financial Ratios [LO3, LO4]**

Recent financial statements for Madison Company follow:

**Madison Company**
**Balance Sheet**
**June 30**

| | | |
|---|---|---|
| **Assets** | | |
| Current assets: | | |
| Cash | | $ 21,000 |
| Accounts receivable, net | | 160,000 |
| Merchandise inventory | | 300,000 |
| Prepaid expenses | | 9,000 |
| Total current assets | | 490,000 |
| Plant and equipment, net | | 810,000 |
| Total assets | | $1,300,000 |
| **Liabilities and Stockholders' Equity** | | |
| Liabilities: | | |
| Current liabilities | | $ 200,000 |
| Bonds payable, 10% | | 300,000 |
| Total liabilities | | 500,000 |
| Stockholders' equity: | | |
| Common stock, $5 par value | $100,000 | |
| Retained earnings | 700,000 | |
| Total stockholders' equity | | 800,000 |
| Total liabilities and stockholders' equity | | $1,300,000 |

**Madison Company**
**Income Statement**
**For the Year Ended June 30**

| | |
|---|---|
| Sales | $2,100,000 |
| Cost of goods sold | 1,260,000 |
| Gross margin | 840,000 |
| Selling and administrative expenses | 660,000 |
| Net operating income | 180,000 |
| Interest expense | 30,000 |
| Net income before taxes | 150,000 |
| Income taxes | 45,000 |
| Net income | $ 105,000 |

Account balances at the beginning of the company's fiscal year were: accounts receivable, $140,000; and inventory, $260,000. All sales were on account.

***Required:***

Compute financial ratios as follows:

1. Gross margin percentage.
2. Current ratio.
3. Acid-test ratio.
4. Average collection period.
5. Average sale period.
6. Debt-to-equity ratio.
7. Times interest earned.
8. Book value per share.

**EXERCISE 13–7 Selected Financial Ratios for Common Stockholders [LO2]**

Refer to the financial statements for Madison Company in Exercise 13–6. In addition to the data in these statements, assume that Madison Company paid dividends of $3.15 per share during the year. Also assume that the company's common stock had a market price of $63 per share on June 30 and that there was no change in the number of outstanding shares of common stock during the fiscal year.

***Required:***

Compute the following:

1. Earnings per share.
2. Dividend payout ratio.
3. Dividend yield ratio.
4. Price-earnings ratio.

**EXERCISE 13–8 Selected Financial Ratios for Common Stockholders [LO2]**

Refer to the financial statements for Madison Company in Exercise 13–6. Assets at the beginning of the year totaled $1,100,000, and the stockholders' equity totaled $725,000.

***Required:***

Compute the following:

1. Return on total assets.
2. Return on common stockholders' equity.
3. Was financial leverage positive or negative for the year? Explain.

**EXERCISE 13–9 Selected Financial Ratios for Common Stockholders [LO2]**

Selected financial data from the September 30 year-end statements of Kosanka Company are given below:

| | |
|---|---|
| Total assets | $5,000,000 |
| Long-term debt (12% interest rate) | $750,000 |
| Preferred stock, $100 par, 7% | $800,000 |
| Total stockholders' equity | $3,100,000 |
| Interest paid on long-term debt | $90,000 |
| Net income | $470,000 |

Total assets at the beginning of the year were $4,800,000; total stockholders' equity was $2,900,000. There has been no change in preferred stock during the year. The company's tax rate is 30%.

***Required:***

1. Compute the return on total assets.
2. Compute the return on common stockholders' equity.
3. Is the company's financial leverage positive or negative? Explain.

**EXERCISE 13–10 Trend Percentages [LO1]**

Starkey Company's sales, current assets, and current liabilities (all in thousands of dollars) have been reported as follows over the last five years (Year 5 is the most recent year):

| | Year 5 | Year 4 | Year 3 | Year 2 | Year 1 |
|---|---|---|---|---|---|
| Sales | $5,625 | $5,400 | $4,950 | $4,725 | $4,500 |
| Current assets: | | | | | |
| Cash | $ 64 | $ 72 | $ 84 | $ 88 | $ 80 |
| Accounts receivable | 560 | 496 | 432 | 416 | 400 |
| Inventory | 896 | 880 | 816 | 864 | 800 |
| Total current assets | $1,520 | $1,448 | $1,332 | $1,368 | $1,280 |
| Current liabilities | $390 | $318 | $324 | $330 | $300 |

***Required:***

1. Express all of the asset, liability, and sales data in trend percentages. (Show percentages for each item.) Use Year 1 as the base year, and carry computations to one decimal place.
2. Comment on the results of your analysis.

**Alternate problem set is available on the text website and in *Connect® Accounting*.**

connect ACCOUNTING

## PROBLEMS

**All applicable problems are available with McGraw-Hill's *Connect® Accounting*.**

**PROBLEM 13–11A Common-Size Statements and Financial Ratios for Creditors [LO1, LO3, LO4]**

excel

CHECK FIGURE
(1d) Average collection period this year: 27.4 days; (1g) Times interest earned this year: 7.0 times

Modern Building Supply sells various building materials to retail outlets. The company has just approached Linden State Bank requesting a $300,000 loan to strengthen the Cash account and to pay certain pressing short-term obligations. The company's financial statements for the most recent two years follow:

**Modern Building Supply**
**Comparative Balance Sheet**

| | This Year | Last Year |
|---|---|---|
| **Assets** | | |
| Current assets: | | |
| Cash | $ 90,000 | $ 200,000 |
| Marketable securities | 0 | 50,000 |
| Accounts receivable, net | 650,000 | 400,000 |
| Inventory | 1,300,000 | 800,000 |
| Prepaid expenses | 20,000 | 20,000 |
| Total current assets | 2,060,000 | 1,470,000 |
| Plant and equipment, net | 1,940,000 | 1,830,000 |
| Total assets | $4,000,000 | $3,300,000 |
| **Liabilities and Stockholders' Equity** | | |
| Liabilities: | | |
| Current liabilities | $1,100,000 | $ 600,000 |
| Bonds payable, 12% | 750,000 | 750,000 |
| Total liabilities | 1,850,000 | 1,350,000 |
| Stockholders' equity: | | |
| Preferred stock, $50 par, 8% | 200,000 | 200,000 |
| Common stock, $10 par | 500,000 | 500,000 |
| Retained earnings | 1,450,000 | 1,250,000 |
| Total stockholders' equity | 2,150,000 | 1,950,000 |
| Total liabilities and stockholder's equity | $4,000,000 | $3,300,000 |

**Modern Building Supply**
**Comparative Income Statement and Reconciliation**

| | This Year | Last Year |
|---|---|---|
| Sales | $7,000,000 | $6,000,000 |
| Cost of goods sold | 5,400,000 | 4,800,000 |
| Gross margin | 1,600,000 | 1,200,000 |
| Selling and administrative expenses | 970,000 | 710,000 |
| Net operating income | 630,000 | 490,000 |
| Interest expense | 90,000 | 90,000 |
| Net income before taxes | 540,000 | 400,000 |
| Income taxes (40%) | 216,000 | 160,000 |
| Net income | 324,000 | 240,000 |
| Dividends paid: | | |
| Preferred dividends | 16,000 | 16,000 |
| Common dividends | 108,000 | 60,000 |
| Total dividends paid | 124,000 | 76,000 |
| Net income retained | 200,000 | 164,000 |
| Retained earnings, beginning of year | 1,250,000 | 1,086,000 |
| Retained earnings, end of year | $1,450,000 | $1,250,000 |

During the past year, the company has expanded the number of lines that it carries in order to stimulate sales and increase profits. It has also moved aggressively to acquire new customers. Sales terms are 2/10, n/30. All sales are on account.

Assume that the following ratios are typical of companies in the building supply industry:

| | |
|---|---|
| Current ratio | 2.5 |
| Acid-test ratio | 1.2 |
| Average collection period | 18 days |
| Average sale period | 50 days |
| Debt-to-equity ratio | 0.75 |
| Times interest earned | 6.0 |
| Return on total assets | 10% |
| Price-earnings ratio | 9 |

***Required:***

1. Linden State Bank is uncertain whether the loan should be made. To assist it in making a decision, you have been asked to compute the following amounts and ratios for both this year and last year:
   a. Working capital.
   b. Current ratio.
   c. Acid-test ratio.
   d. Average collection period. (The accounts receivable at the beginning of last year totaled $350,000.)
   e. Average sale period. (The inventory at the beginning of last year totaled $720,000.)
   f. Debt-to-equity ratio.
   g. Times interest earned.
2. For both this year and last year (carry computations to one decimal place):
   a. Present the balance sheet in common-size form.
   b. Present the income statement in common-size form down through net income.
3. From your analysis in (1) and (2) above, what problems or strengths do you see for Modern Building Supply? Make a recommendation as to whether the loan should be approved.

**PROBLEM 13–12A Financial Ratios for Common Stockholders [LO2]**

Refer to the financial statements and other data in Problem 13–11A. Assume that you have just inherited several hundred shares of Modern Building Supply stock. Not being acquainted with the company, you decide to do some analytical work before making a decision about whether to retain or sell the stock you have inherited.

CHECK FIGURE
(1a) Earnings per share this year: $6.16;
(1d) Price-earnings ratio this year: 7.3

***Required:***

1. You decide first to assess the well-being of the common stockholders. For both this year and last year, compute the following:
   a. The earnings per share.
   b. The dividend yield ratio for common stock. The company's common stock is currently selling for $45 per share; last year it sold for $36 per share.
   c. The dividend payout ratio for common stock.
   d. The price-earnings ratio. How do investors regard Modern Building Supply as compared to other companies in the industry? Explain.
   e. The book value per share of common stock. Does the difference between market value and book value suggest that the stock at its current price is too high? Explain.
2. You decide next to assess the company's rate of return. Compute the following for both this year and last year:
   a. The return on total assets. (Total assets at the beginning of last year were $2,700,000.)
   b. The return on common stockholders' equity. (Stockholders' equity at the beginning of last year was $1,786,000.)
   c. Is the company's financial leverage positive or negative? Explain.
3. Based on your analytical work (and assuming that you have no immediate need for cash), would you retain or sell the stock you have inherited? Explain.

**PROBLEM 13–13A Interpretation of Financial Ratios [LO2, LO3]**

Being a prudent investor, Sally Perkins always investigates a company thoroughly before purchasing shares of its stock for investment. Ms. Perkins is interested in the common stock of Plunge Enterprises. The following data are available for the company:

| | Year 3 | Year 2 | Year 1 |
|---|---|---|---|
| Current ratio | 2.8 | 2.5 | 2.0 |
| Acid-test ratio | 0.7 | 0.9 | 1.2 |
| Accounts receivable turnover | 8.6 | 9.5 | 10.4 |
| Inventory turnover | 5.0 | 5.7 | 6.8 |
| Sales trend | 130.0 | 118.0 | 100.0 |
| Dividends paid per share* | $2.50 | $2.50 | $2.50 |
| Dividend yield ratio | 5% | 4% | 3% |
| Dividend payout ratio | 40% | 50% | 60% |
| Return on total assets | 13.0% | 11.8% | 10.4% |
| Return on common stockholders' equity | 16.2% | 14.5% | 9.0% |

*There were no changes in common stock outstanding over the three-year period.

Ms. Perkins would like answers to a number of questions about the trend of events over the last three years in Plunge Enterprises. Her questions are as follows:

a. Is the market price of the company's stock going up or down?
b. Is the earnings per share increasing or decreasing?
c. Is the price-earnings ratio going up or down?
d. Is the company employing financial leverage to the advantage of its common stockholders?
e. Is it becoming easier for the company to pay its bills as they come due?
f. Are customers paying their bills at least as fast now as they did in Year 1?
g. Is the total of the accounts receivable increasing, decreasing, or remaining constant?
h. Is the level of inventory increasing, decreasing, or remaining constant?

***Required:***

Answer each of Ms. Perkins's questions and explain how you arrived at your answer.

CHECK FIGURE
(1b) Current ratio: 2.5

**PROBLEM 13–14A Effects of Transactions on Various Ratios [LO3]**

Selected amounts from Reingold Company's balance sheet from the beginning of the year follow:

| | |
|---|---|
| Cash | $70,000 |
| Marketable Securities | $12,000 |
| Accounts receivable, net | $350,000 |
| Inventory | $460,000 |
| Prepaid expenses | $8,000 |
| Plant and equipment, net | $950,000 |
| Accounts payable | $200,000 |
| Accrued liabilities | $60,000 |
| Notes due within one year | $100,000 |
| Bonds payable in five years | $140,000 |

During the year, the company completed the following transactions:

x. Purchased inventory on account, $50,000.
a. Declared a cash dividend, $30,000.
b. Paid accounts payable, $100,000.
c. Collected cash on accounts receivable, $80,000.
d. Purchased equipment for cash, $75,000.
e. Paid a cash dividend previously declared, $30,000.
f. Borrowed cash on a short-term note with the bank, $60,000.
g. Sold inventory costing $70,000 for $100,000, on account.
h. Wrote off uncollectible accounts in the amount of $10,000 reducing the accounts receivable balance accordingly.
i. Sold marketable securities costing $12,000 for cash, $9,000.
j. Issued additional shares of common stock for cash, $200,000.
k. Paid off all short-term notes due, $160,000.

***Required:***

1. Compute the following amounts and ratios as of the beginning of the year:
   a. Working capital.
   b. Current ratio.
   c. Acid-test ratio.
2. Indicate the effect of each of the transactions given above on working capital, the current ratio, and the acid-test ratio. Give the effect in terms of increase, decrease, or none. Item (x) is given as an example of the format to use:

| | The Effect on | | |
|---|---|---|---|
| Transaction | Working Capital | Current Ratio | Acid-Test Ratio |
| (x) Purchased inventory on account | None | Decrease | Decrease |

**PROBLEM 13–15A Effects of Transactions on Various Financial Ratios [LO2, LO3, LO4]**

In the right-hand column below, certain financial ratios are listed. To the left of each ratio is a business transaction or event relating to the operating activities of Graham Company.

| Business Transaction or Event | Ratio |
|---|---|
| 1. Inventory was sold for cash at a profit. | Debt-to-equity ratio |
| 2. Land was purchased for cash. | Earnings per share |
| 3. Inventory was sold on account at cost. | Acid-test ratio |
| 4. Some accounts payable were paid off. | Working capital |
| 5. A customer paid an overdue bill. | Average collection period |
| 6. A cash dividend was declared, but not yet paid. | Current ratio |
| 7. A previously declared cash dividend was paid. | Current ratio |
| 8. The company's common stock price increased. | Book value per share |
| 9. The company's common stock price increased and earnings per share remained unchanged. | Dividend yield ratio |
| 10. Property was sold for a profit. | Return on total assets |
| 11. Obsolete inventory was written off as a loss. | Inventory turnover ratio |
| 12. Bonds were sold with an interest rate less than the company's return on assets. | Return on common stockholders' equity |
| 13. The company's common stock price decreased and the dividend paid per share remained the same. | Dividend payout ratio |
| 14. The company's net income decreased, but long-term debt remained unchanged. | Times interest earned |
| 15. An uncollectible account was written off against the Allowance for Bad Debts. | Current ratio |
| 16. Inventory was purchased on credit. | Acid-test ratio |
| 17. The company's common stock price increased and earnings per share remained unchanged. | Price-earnings ratio |
| 18. The company paid off some accounts payable. | Debt-to-equity ratio |

***Required:***

Indicate the effect that each transaction or event would have on the ratio listed opposite to it. State the effect in terms of increase, decrease, or no effect on the ratio involved, and give the reason for your choice. In all cases, assume that the current assets exceed current liabilities both before and after the event or transaction. Use the following format for your answers:

| | Effect on Ratio | Reason for Increase, Decrease, or No Effect |
|---|---|---|
| 1. | | |
| 2. | | |
| Etc. | | |

**PROBLEM 13–16A Comprehensive Ratio Analysis [LO2, LO3, LO4]**

You have just been hired as a loan officer at Fairfield State Bank. Your supervisor has given you a file containing a request from Hedrick Company, a manufacturer of auto components, for a $1,000,000 five-year loan. Financial statement data on the company for the last two years are given below:

eXcel

CHECK FIGURE
(1a) Return on total assets this year: 6.8%; (2e) Book value per share this year: $52

**Hedrick Company**
**Comparative Balance Sheet**

| | This Year | Last Year |
|---|---|---|
| **Assets** | | |
| Current assets: | | |
| Cash | $ 320,000 | $ 420,000 |
| Marketable securities | 0 | 100,000 |
| Accounts receivable, net | 900,000 | 600,000 |
| Inventory | 1,300,000 | 800,000 |
| Prepaid expenses | 80,000 | 60,000 |
| Total current assets | 2,600,000 | 1,980,000 |
| Plant and equipment, net | 3,100,000 | 2,980,000 |
| Total assets | $5,700,000 | $4,960,000 |
| **Liabilities and Stockholders' Equity** | | |
| Liabilities: | | |
| Current liabilities | $1,300,000 | $ 920,000 |
| Bonds payable, 10% | 1,200,000 | 1,000,000 |
| Total liabilities | 2,500,000 | 1,920,000 |
| Stockholders' equity: | | |
| Preferred stock, 8%, $30 par value | 600,000 | 600,000 |
| Common stock, $40 par value | 2,000,000 | 2,000,000 |
| Retained earnings | 600,000 | 440,000 |
| Total stockholders' equity | 3,200,000 | 3,040,000 |
| Total liabilities and stockholders' equity | $5,700,000 | $4,960,000 |

**Hedrick Company**
**Comparative Income Statement and Reconciliation**

| | This Year | Last Year |
|---|---|---|
| Sales (all on account) | $5,250,000 | $4,160,000 |
| Cost of goods sold | 4,200,000 | 3,300,000 |
| Gross margin | 1,050,000 | 860,000 |
| Selling and administrative expenses | 530,000 | 520,000 |
| Net operating income | 520,000 | 340,000 |
| Interest expense | 120,000 | 100,000 |
| Net income before taxes | 400,000 | 240,000 |
| Income taxes (30%) | 120,000 | 72,000 |
| Net income | 280,000 | 168,000 |
| Dividends paid: | | |
| Preferred stock | 48,000 | 48,000 |
| Common stock | 72,000 | 36,000 |
| Total dividends paid | 120,000 | 84,000 |
| Net income retained | 160,000 | 84,000 |
| Retained earnings, beginning of year | 440,000 | 356,000 |
| Retained earnings, end of year | $ 600,000 | $ 440,000 |

Marva Rossen, who just two years ago was appointed president of Hedrick Company, admits that the company has been "inconsistent" in its performance over the past several years. But Rossen argues that the company has its costs under control and is now experiencing strong sales growth, as evidenced by the more than 25% increase in sales over the last year. Rossen also argues that investors have recognized the improving situation at Hedrick Company, as shown by the jump in the price of its common stock from $20 per share last year to $36 per share this year. Rossen believes that with strong leadership and with the modernized equipment that the $1,000,000 loan will enable the company to buy, profits will be even stronger in the future.

Anxious to impress your supervisor, you decide to generate all the information you can about the company. You determine that the following ratios are typical of companies in Hedrick's industry:

| | |
|---|---|
| Current ratio | 2.3 |
| Acid-test ratio | 1.2 |
| Average collection period | 31 days |
| Average sale period | 60 days |
| Return on assets | 9.5% |
| Debt-to-equity ratio | 0.65 |
| Times interest earned | 5.7 |
| Price-earnings ratio | 10 |

***Required:***

1. You decide first to assess the rate of return that the company is generating. Compute the following for both this year and last year:
   a. The return on total assets. (Total assets at the beginning of last year were $4,320,000.)
   b. The return on common stockholders' equity. (Stockholders' equity at the beginning of last year totaled $3,016,000. There has been no change in preferred or common stock over the last two years.)
   c. Is the company's financial leverage positive or negative? Explain.
2. You decide next to assess the well-being of the common stockholders. For both this year and last year, compute:
   a. The earnings per share.
   b. The dividend yield ratio for common stock.
   c. The dividend payout ratio for common stock.
   d. The price-earnings ratio. How do investors regard Hedrick Company as compared to other companies in the industry? Explain.
   e. The book value per share of common stock. Does the difference between market value per share and book value per share suggest that the stock at its current price is a bargain? Explain.
   f. The gross margin percentage.
3. You decide, finally, to assess creditor ratios to determine both short-term and long-term debt paying ability. For both this year and last year, compute:
   a. Working capital.
   b. The current ratio.
   c. The acid-test ratio.
   d. The average collection period. (The accounts receivable at the beginning of last year totaled $520,000.)
   e. The average sale period. (The inventory at the beginning of last year totaled $640,000.)
   f. The debt-to-equity ratio.
   g. The times interest earned.
4. Make a recommendation to your supervisor as to whether the loan should be approved.

**PROBLEM 13–17A Common-Size Financial Statements [LO1]**

Refer to the financial statement data for Hedrick Company given in Problem 13–16A.

***Required:***

For both this year and last year:

1. Present the balance sheet in common-size format.
2. Present the income statement in common-size format down through net income.
3. Comment on the results of your analysis.

# BUILDING YOUR SKILLS

## ETHICS CHALLENGE [LO3]

Mountain Aerosport was founded by Jurgen Prinz to produce a ski he had designed for doing aerial tricks. Up to this point, Jurgen has financed the company with his own savings and with cash generated by his business. However, Jurgen now faces a cash crisis. In the year just ended, an acute shortage of a vital tungsten steel alloy arose just as the company was beginning production for the Christmas season. Jurgen had been assured by his suppliers that the steel would be delivered in time to make Christmas shipments, but the suppliers had been unable to fully deliver on this promise. As a consequence, Mountain Aerosport had large stocks of unfinished skis at the end of the year and had been unable to fill all of the orders that had come in from retailers for the Christmas season. Consequently, sales were below expectations for the year, and Jurgen does not have enough cash to pay his creditors.

Well before the accounts payable were due, Jurgen visited a local bank and inquired about obtaining a loan. The loan officer at the bank assured Jurgen that there should not be any problem getting a loan to pay off his accounts payable—providing that on his most recent financial statements the current ratio was above 2.0, the acid-test ratio was above 1.0, and net operating income was at least four times the interest on the proposed loan. Jurgen promised to return later with a copy of his financial statements.

Jurgen would like to apply for a $120 thousand six-month loan bearing an interest rate of 10% per year. The unaudited financial reports of the company are as follows:

**Mountain Aerosport**
**Comparative Balance Sheet**
**As of December 31, This Year and Last Year**
**(in thousands of dollars)**

| | This Year | Last Year |
|---|---|---|
| **Assets** | | |
| Current assets: | | |
| Cash | $105 | $225 |
| Accounts receivable, net | 75 | 60 |
| Inventory | 240 | 150 |
| Prepaid expenses | 15 | 18 |
| Total current assets | 435 | 453 |
| Property and equipment | 405 | 270 |
| Total assets | $840 | $723 |
| **Liabilities and Stockholders' Equity** | | |
| Current liabilities: | | |
| Accounts payable | $231 | $135 |
| Accrued payables | 15 | 15 |
| Total current liabilities | 246 | 150 |
| Long-term liabilities | 0 | 0 |
| Total liabilities | 246 | 150 |
| Stockholders' equity: | | |
| Common stock and additional paid-in capital | 150 | 150 |
| Retained earnings | 444 | 423 |
| Total stockholders' equity | 594 | 573 |
| Total liabilities and stockholders' equity | $840 | $723 |

| Mountain Aerosport<br>Income Statement<br>For the Year Ended December 31, This Year<br>(in thousands of dollars) | |
|---|---|
| Sales (all on account) | $630 |
| Cost of goods sold | 435 |
| Gross margin | 195 |
| Selling and administrative expenses: | |
| Selling expenses | 63 |
| Administrative expenses | 102 |
| Total selling and administrative expenses | 165 |
| Net operating income | 30 |
| Interest expense | 0 |
| Net income before taxes | 30 |
| Income taxes (30%) | 9 |
| Net income | $ 21 |

***Required:***

1. Based on the above unaudited financial statements and the statement made by the loan officer, would the company qualify for the loan?
2. Last year Jurgen purchased and installed new, more efficient equipment to replace an older heat-treating furnace. Jurgen had originally planned to sell the old equipment, but found that it is still needed whenever the heat-treating process is a bottleneck. When Jurgen discussed his cash flow problems with his brother-in-law, he suggested to Jurgen that the old equipment be sold or at least reclassified as inventory on the balance sheet because it could be readily sold. At present, the equipment is carried in the Property and Equipment account and could be sold for its net book value of $68,000. The bank does not require audited financial statements. What advice would you give to Jurgen concerning the machine?

**ANALYTICAL THINKING [LO2, LO3, LO4]**

Incomplete financial statements for Tanner Company follow:

eXcel

CHECK FIGURE
Total assets: $1,500,000;
Net income: $162,000

| Tanner Company<br>Income Statement<br>For the Year Ended December 31 | |
|---|---|
| Sales | $2,700,000 |
| Cost of goods sold | ? |
| Gross margin | ? |
| Selling and administrative expenses | ? |
| Net operating income | ? |
| Interest expense | 45,000 |
| Net income before taxes | ? |
| Income taxes (40%) | ? |
| Net income | $ ? |

**Tanner Company**
**Balance Sheet**
**December 31**

| | |
|---|---|
| Current assets: | |
| Cash | $ ? |
| Accounts receivable, net | ? |
| Inventory | ? |
| Total current assets | ? |
| Plant and equipment, net | ? |
| Total assets | $ ? |
| Current liabilities | $250,000 |
| Bonds payable, 10% | ? |
| Total liabilities | ? |
| Stockholders' equity: | |
| Common stock, $2.50 par value | ? |
| Retained earnings | ? |
| Total stockholders' equity | ? |
| Total liabilities and stockholders' equity | $ ? |

The following additional information is available about the company:

a. Selected financial ratios computed from Tanner's financial statements are given below:

| | |
|---|---|
| Current ratio | 2.40 |
| Acid-test ratio | 1.12 |
| Accounts receivable turnover | 15.0 |
| Inventory turnover | 6.0 |
| Debt-to-equity ratio | 0.875 |
| Times interest earned | 7.0 |
| Earnings per share | $4.05 |
| Return on total assets | 14% |

b. All sales during the year were on account.

c. The interest expense on the income statement relates to the bonds payable; the amount of bonds outstanding did not change throughout the year.

d. There were no changes in the number of shares of common stock outstanding during the year.

e. Selected balances at the *beginning* of the current year (January 1) were as follows:

| | |
|---|---|
| Accounts receivable | $160,000 |
| Inventory | $280,000 |
| Total assets | $1,200,000 |

***Required:***

Compute the missing amounts on the company's financial statements. (Hint: You may find it helpful to think about the difference between the current ratio and the acid-test ratio.)

### TEAMWORK IN ACTION [LO1, LO2, LO3, LO4]

Obtain the most recent annual report or SEC filing 10-K of a publicly traded company that interests you. It may be a local company or it may be a company in an industry that you would like to know more about. Using the annual report, compute as many of the financial ratios covered in this chapter as you can for at least the past two years. This may pose some difficulties—particularly because companies often use different terms for many income statement and balance sheet items than were shown in the chapter. Nevertheless, do the best that you can. After you have computed the financial ratios, summarize the company's performance for the current year. Has it improved, gotten worse, or remained about the same? Do the ratios indicate any potential problems or any areas that have shown significant improvement? What recommendations, if any, would you make to a bank about extending short-term credit to this company? What recommendations, if any, would you make to an insurance company about extending long-term credit to this company? What recommendations, if any, would you make to an investor about buying or selling this company's stock?

# PHOTO CREDITS

## Prologue

**9** Imagestate Media (John Foxx); **16** Punchstock

## Chapter 1

**21** Mark Graham/The New York Times/Redux; **24** Moodboard/Corbis; **28** Sandee Noreen; **30** © 2008 Majestic Ocean Kayaking; **37** Getty Images

## Chapter 2

**65** Courtesy of University Tees, Inc.; **67** Sandee Noreen; **74** Keith Brofsky/Getty Images

## Chapter 3

**117** Ali Goldstein/NBCU Photo Bank via AP Images; **122-123** Sandee Noreen; **129** Stock Connection Blue/Alamy

## Chapter 4

**157** Dejan Krsmanovic/Alamy; **160** AP Photo/Yves Logghe; **162** Mark Ralston/AFP/Getty Images

## Chapter 5

**187** Comstock Images; **201** Yellow Dog Productions/ Getty Images; **204** Bloomberg via Getty Images; **209** CORBIS

## Chapter 6

**237** Tetra Images/Jupiterimages; **246** Photodisc Collection/ Getty Images; **250** TRBfoto/Getty Images; **257** Duncan Smith/Getty Images

## Chapter 7

**283** Sandee Noreen; **298** Ryan McVay/Getty Images; **301** Eric Noreen; **305** AP Photo/Stew Milne

## Chapter 8

**335** Bloomberg via Getty Images; **350** CORBIS; **352** Ariel Skelley/Blend Images/Corbis

## Chapter 9

**399** Junko Kimura/Getty Images; **406** AP Photo/Marcio Jose Sanchez; **415** TongRo Image Stock/Alamy; **418** Ryan McVay/Getty Images

## Chapter 10

**439** Braddock Park/Alamy; **453** Getty Images/PictureIndia; **460** The McGraw-Hill Companies, Inc./Andy Resek, photographer

## Chapter 11

**491** Courtesy of Cintas Corporation; **501** Ingram Publishing/SuperStock; **503** The McGraw-Hill Companies, Inc./ Jill Braaten, photographer; **511** © PRNewsFoto/Royal Caribbean International

## Chapter 12

**539** DAVID KOHL/AP/Corbis; **541** The McGraw-Hill Companies, Inc./Jill Braaten, photographer; **558** (a)Steve Mason/Getty Images, (b)Randy Allbritton/Getty Images

## Chapter 13

**583** AP Photo/Mary Altaffer; **590** Doug Menuez/Getty Images; **599** Jack Hollingsworth/Getty Images

# INDEX

Page numbers followed by n refer to footnotes.

## A



## B

# C

## D

## G



## H



## I

## J



## K



## L



## M

## N

# O



# P

# Q



# R

## S

# T



# U

## V



## W



## Y



## Z